Compton Mackenzie, Collection novels

In this book:
The Early Life and
Adventures of Sylvia, 1918
The Vanity Girl, 1920
Rich Relatives, 1921
Poor Relations, 1919
The Altar Steps, 1922

Sir Compton Mackenzie, (1883–1972) was a prolific writer of fiction, biography, histories, and memoir, as well as a cultural commentator, raconteur, and lifelong Scottish nationalist. It is described by Dr. John MacInnes (formerly of the School of Scottish Studies) as "one of the greatest works of English literature produced in the twentieth century."

In this book:

The Early Life and Adventures of Sylvia Scarlett

Prelude

AT six o'clock on the morning of Ash Wednesday in the year 1847, the Honorable Charles Cunningham sat sipping his coffee in the restaurant of the Vendanges de Bourgogne. He was somewhat fatigued by the exertions that as "lion" of the moment he had felt bound to make, exertions that had included a display of English eccentricity and had culminated in a cotillion at a noble house in the Faubourg St.-Germain, the daughter of which had been assigned to him by Parisian gossip as his future wife. Marriage, however, did not present itself to his contemplation as an urgent duty; and he sipped his coffee, reassured by the example of his brother Saxby, who, with the responsibility of a family succession, remained a bachelor. In any case, the notion of marrying a French girl was preposterous; he was not to be flattered into an unsuitable alliance by compliments upon his French. Certainly he spoke French uncommonly well, devilishly well for an Englishman, he told himself; and he stroked his whiskers in complacent meditation.

Charles Cunningham had arrived at the Vendanges de Bourgogne to watch that rowdy climax of Carnival, the *descente de la Courtille*. And now through the raw air they were coming down from Belleville, all sorts of revelers in masks and motley and rags. The noise of tin trumpets and toy drums, of catcalls and cocoricots, of laughter and cheers and whistling, came nearer. Presently the road outside was thronged for the aristocrats of the Faubourg St.-Germain to alight from their carriages and mix with the mob. This was the traditional climax of Carnival for Parisian society: every year they drove here on Ash Wednesday morning to get themselves banged on the head by bladders, to be spurted with cheap scent and pelted with sugar-plums, and to retaliate by flinging down hot louis for the painful enrichment of the masses. The noise was for a time deafening; but gradually the cold light of morning and the melancholy Lenten bells cast a gloom upon the crowd, which passed on toward the boulevards, diminishing in sound and size at every street corner.

The tall, fair Englishman let himself be carried along by the exodus, thinking idly what excitable folk foreigners were, but conscious, nevertheless, of a warmth of intimacy that was not at all disagreeable, the kind of intimacy that is bestowed on a man by taking a pack of friendly dogs for a country walk. Suddenly he was aware of a small hand upon his sleeve, a small hand that lay there like a white butterfly; and, looking down, he saw a poke-bonnet garlanded with yellow rosebuds. The poke-bonnet was all he could see, for the wearer kept her gaze steadily on the road, while with little feet she mimicked his long strides. The ineffable lightness of the arm laid on his own, the joyous mockery of her footsteps, the sense of an exquisite smile beneath the poke-bonnet, and the airy tremor of invitation that fluttered from the golden shawl of Siamese crêpe about her shoulders tempted him to withdraw from the crowd at the first opportunity. Soon they were in a by-street, whence the clamor of Carnival slowly died away, leaving no sound upon the morning air but their footfalls and the faint whisper of her petticoats where she tripped along beside him.

Presently the poke-bonnet was raised; Charles Cunningham beheld his companion's face, a perfect oval, set with eyes of deepest brown, demurely passionate, eyes that in this empty street were all for him. He had never considered himself a romantic young man; when this encounter had faded to a mere flush upon the dreamy sky of the past, he was always a little scornful of his first remark, and apt to wonder how the deuce he ever came to make it.

"By Jove! *vous savez, vous êtes tout à fait comme un oiseau!*"

"*Eh, alors?*" she murmured, in a tone that was neither defiance nor archness nor indifference nor invitation, but something that was compounded of all four and expressed exactly herself. "*Eh, alors?*"

"*Votre nid est loin d'ici?*" he asked.

Nor did he blush for the guise of his speech at the time: afterward it struck him as most indecorously poetic.

"*Viens donc,*" she whispered.

"*Comment appelez-vous?*"

"*Moi, je suis Adèle.*"

"*Adèle quoi?*" he pressed.

"*Mais Adèle alors, tout simplement ça.*"

"*C'est un peu—vous savez—un peu.*" He made a sweep with his unoccupied arm to indicate the vagueness of it all.

"I love you," she trilled; deep down in her ivory throat emotion caught the trill and made of it a melody that set his heart beating.

"*Vraiment?*" he asked, very solemnly; then laying syllable upon syllable in a kind of amazed deliberation, as a child builds a tower of bricks, he began to talk to her in French.

"*Mais, comme tu parles bien,*" she told him.

"*Tu m'inspires,*" he murmured, hoarsely.

Afterward, when he looked back at the adventure, he awarded this remark the prize for folly.

The adventure did not have a long life; a week later Charles Cunningham was called back to England by the news of his brother's illness. Before Lent was out he had become the Earl of Saxby, who really had to think seriously of marriage and treat it with more respect than the Parisian gossip over which Charles Cunningham had idly mused at six o'clock of Ash Wednesday morning in the year 1847. As for Adèle, she met in May the owner of a traveling-booth, a widower called Bassompierre with a small son, who had enough of the gipsy to attract the irresponsible Adèle and enough of the bourgeois to induce her to marry him for the sake of a secure and solid future. She need not have troubled about her future, the deep-voiced Adèle; for just when November darkens to December she died in giving birth to Juliette. The gipsy in Albert Bassompierre accepted as his own daughter Juliette; the bourgeois in him erected a cross in the cemetery and put a wreath of immortelles in a glass case to lie on Adèle's tomb. Then he locked away the few pieces of jewelry that life had brought her, hung another daguerreotype beside the one of his first wife, and wrapped Juliette in a golden shawl of Siamese crêpe. Lightly the two daguerreotypes swung to and fro; and lightly rocked the cradle where the baby Juliette lay sleeping, while the caravan jolted southward along the straight French roads where the poplars seemed to be commenting to one another in the wind.

For eighteen years the caravan jolted along these roads, until young Edouard Bassompierre was old enough to play leading man throughout the repertory and thereby most abruptly plunge his predecessor into old age. At the same time Juliette was allowed to act the soubrettes; her father was too much afraid of the leading lady to play any tricks of suddenly imposed senility with her. It was, on the whole, a jolly life, this vagrancy from fair to fair of all the towns of France. It was jolly, when the performance was done, to gather in the tent behind the stage and eat chipped potatoes and drink red wine with all the queer people whose voices were hoarse with crying their wares all the day long.

Then came, one springtime, the fair at Compiègne. Business was splendid, for the Emperor was there to hunt the wild boar in the forest. Never had old Albert Bassompierre beaten his big drum so confidently at the entrance of his booth; never had Edouard captured so many young women's hearts; both of them were too much occupied with their own triumphs to notice the young officer who came every night to the play. The Emperor left Compiègne in April; when he departed, the young officer departed also, accompanied by Juliette.

"*Ah, la vache,*" cried old Bassompierre; "it's perhaps as well her mother didn't live, for she might have done the same."

"You should have let her play the lead," said Edouard.

"She can play lead in real life," replied old Bassompierre. "If she can," he added, fiercely.

But when Juliette wrote to him from Paris and told him how happy she was with her lover, the gipsy in Bassompierre drove out the bourgeois, and he sent his daughter her mother's jewelry and the golden shawl; but he kept the daguerreotype, for, after all, Juliette was not really his daughter and Adèle had really been his wife.

Three years passed. Juliette lived in a little house at Belleville with two baby girls called Elène and Henriette. When in after years she looked back to this time it seemed to her smothered in roses, the roses of an operatic scene. Everything, indeed, in retrospect was like that—the arrival of her lover in his gay uniform, the embowered kisses, the lights of Paris far below, the suppers on the veranda, the warm Sunday mornings, the two babies asleep on the lawn and their father watching them, herself before a glass and her lover's face seen over her shoulder, the sudden sharp embrace; all were heavy with the intolerable sense of a curtain that must fall. Then came the war; there was a hurried move down to stuffy apartments in Paris; ready money hastily got together by the young officer, who spoke confidently of the large sum it was, since, after all, the war would be over in a month and the Prussians have had their lesson; and at last a breathless kiss. The crowds surged cheering through the streets, the two babies screamed disapproval of their new surroundings, and

Juliette's lover was killed in the first battle; he had only time to scribble a few trembling lines:

Mon adorée, je t'ai flanqué un mauvais coup. Pardonnez-moi. Mes dernières pensées sont pour toi. Adieu. Deux gros bécots aux bébés. J'ai parlé pour toi à mon père. Cherche argent—je t'embrasse follement follem——

Yet when she received this letter, some impulse kept her from going to her lover's father. She could not bear the possibility of being made to realize that those debonair years of love were regarded by him as an intrigue to be solved by money. If André's mother had been alive, she might have felt differently; now she would not trouble a stricken family that might regard her tears as false; she would not even try to return to her own father. No doubt he would welcome her; but pride, all the strange and terrible pride that was henceforth to haunt Juliette's soul, forbade her.

It was impossible, however, to remain in Paris; and without any reason for her choice she took her babies to Lyon and settled down in rooms overlooking the Rhône, to await the end of the war. When she had paid the cost of the journey and bought herself the necessary mourning, she found she had nearly eleven thousand francs left; with care this could surely be made to last three years at least; in three years much might happen. As a matter of fact, much happened almost at once; for the beauty of Juliette, a lustrous and imperial beauty, caught the fancy of Gustave Lataille, who was conductor of the orchestra at one of the smaller theaters in Lyon. To snare his fancy might not have been enough; but when with her dowry she captured also his imagination, he married her. Juliette did not consider it wrong to marry this somber, withered, and uncommunicative man of forty, for whom she had neither passion nor affection. He struck her as essentially like most of the husbands she had observed hitherto; and she esteemed herself lucky not to have met such a one before she had been granted the boon of love. She must have inherited from that unknown father her domestic qualities; she certainly acquired none from Adèle. From him, too, may have come that pride which, however it may have found its chief expression in ideals of bourgeois respectability, was nevertheless a fine fiery virtue and supported her spirit to the very last.

Juliette and Lataille lived together without anything to color a drab existence. Notwithstanding his connection with the theater, Lataille had no bohemian tastes; once when his wife suggested, after a visit from her father, that there seemed no reason why she should not apply for an engagement to act, he unhesitatingly refused his permission; when she attempted to argue, he reminded her that he had given his name to Elène and Henriette, and she was silent. Henceforth she devoted herself to sewing, and brought into the world four girls in successive years—Françoise, Marie, Marguerite, and Valentine. The last was born in 1875, soon after the Latailles had moved to Lille, where Gustave had

4

secured the post of conductor at the principal theater. Juliette welcomed the change, for it gave her the small house of her own which she had long wanted; moreover, nobody in Lille knew at first hand of the circumstances in which Gustave had married her, so that Elène and Henrietta could go to school without being teased about their mother's early lapse from the standards of conduct which she fervently desired they would adopt.

Unfortunately, the conductor had only enjoyed his advancement a year when he was struck down by a paralytic stroke. With six small children and a palsied husband upon her hands, Juliette had to find work. Partly from compassion for her ill-fortune, but chiefly because by now she was a most capable seamstress, the management of the theater engaged her as wardrobe mistress; and for five years Juliette sustained her husband, her children, and her house. They were years that would have rubbed the bloom from most women; but Juliette's beauty seemed to grow rather than diminish. Her personality became proverbial in the town of Lille, and though as wardroom mistress she was denied the public triumph of the footlights, she had nevertheless a fame of her own that was considered unique in the history of her profession. Her pride flourished on the deference that was shown her even by the management; between her beauty and her sharp tongue she achieved an authority that reached its height in the way she brought up her children. Their snowy pinafores, their trim stockings, their manners, and their looks were the admiration of the *quartier*; and when in the year 1881 Gustave Lataille died, the neatness of their new black dresses surprised even the most confirmed admirers of Madame Lataille's industry and taste. At no time could Juliette have seemed so beautiful as when, after the funeral, she raised her widow's veil and showed the attendant sympathizers a countenance unmarked by one tear of respectable emotion. She was far too proud to weep for a husband whom she had never loved and whose death was a relief; when the neighbors expressed astonishment at the absence of any outward sorrow, she flung out a challenge to fate:

"I have not reached the age of thirty-four, and brought up six children, and never once been late with so much as a ribbon, to cry for any man now. He'll be a wonderful man that will ever make me cry. Henriette, don't tug at your garter."

And as she stood there, with great brown eyes burning beneath a weight of lustrous black hair, she seemed of marble without and within.

Nevertheless, before six months had passed, Madame Lataille fell impetuously in love with a young English clerk of twenty-one, called Henry Snow; what is more, she married him. Nobody in Lille was able to offer a credible explanation of her behavior. People were willing to admit that his conduct was comprehensible, notwithstanding the fourteen years of her seniority; and it says much for the way Juliette had impressed her personality upon a dull provincial world that Henry Snow's action should have been so immediately understood. Before the problem of her conduct, however, the world remained in perplexity. Financial considerations could not have supplied a motive; from all accounts the Englishman was unlikely to help; indeed, gossip said that even in his obscure position he had already had opportunities of showing that, such as it was, the position was better than he deserved and unlikely to be bettered in the future. Nor could his good looks have attracted her, for he was insignificant; and since Englishmen in the experience of Lille were, whatever their faults, never insignificant, the insignificance of Henry Snow acquired an active quality which contradicted its characterization and made him seem not merely unattractive, but positively displeasing. Nor could she have required some one to help in managing her six children; altogether the affair was a mystery, which gathered volume when the world began to realize the depth of the feeling that Henry Snow had roused in Juliette. All the world loves a lover, but only when it is allowed to obtrude itself upon the love. Juliette, absorbed by her emotion and the eternal jealousy of the woman who marries a man much younger than herself, refused to admit any spectators to marvel at the development of the mystery. She carried on her work as usual; but instead of maintaining her position as a figure she became an object of curiosity, and presently, because that curiosity was never gratified, an object of suspicion. The lover-loving world began to shake its head and calumny whispered everywhere its commentary; she could never have been a *femme propre*; this marriage must have been forced upon the young Englishman as the price of a five-year-old intrigue. When some defender of Juliette pointed out that the clerk had only been in Lille three years, that his name had never been connected with hers, and that in any case he was only twenty-one now, calumny retorted with a long line of Henry Snows; presently the story of Juliette's life with André Duchesnil was dragged to light, and by an infinite multiplication of whispers her career from earliest youth was established as licentious, mercenary, and cruel.

For a while Juliette was so much wrapped up in her own joy that she did not observe the steady withdrawal of popular esteem. Having made it clear to everybody that she wished to be left alone with her husband, she supposed she had been successful and congratulated herself accordingly, until one day a persistent friend, proof against Juliette's icy discouragement, drove into her that the *quartier* was pitying Henry Snow, that things were being said against her, and that the only way to put a stop to unkind gossip was to move about among the neighbors in more friendly fashion.

Gradually it dawned upon Juliette that her friend was the emissary of a universally accepted calumny, the voice of the *quartier*, the first to brave her, and only now rash enough to do so because she had public opinion at her back. This did not prevent Juliette from showing her counselor the door to the street, nor from slamming it so abruptly that a meter of stuff was torn from her skirt; yet when she went back to her room and picked up her needlework there came upon her with a shock the realization of what effect all this might have on Henry. If the world were pitying him now, it would presently be laughing; if he were laughed at, he would grow to hate her. Hitherto she had been so happy in her love that she had never stopped to consider anything or anybody. She remembered now Henry's amazement when, in the first tumultuous wave of passion dammed for so many years, she had refused to let herself be swept away; she recalled his faint hesitation when first she spoke of marriage and gave him to understand that without marriage she would not be his. Even then he must have foreseen the possibility of ridicule, and he had only married her because she had been able to seem so desirable. And she was still desirable; he was still enthralled; he was still vain of her love; yet how was the flattery of one woman to mitigate for a man the contempt of the crowd? Mercifully, he was an Englishman in a French town, therefore it would take longer for the popular feeling to touch him; but soon or late it would strike home to his vanity. Something must be devised to transfix him with the dignity of marriage. They must have a child; no father could do anything but resent and despise laughter that would be directed against his fatherhood. Juliette's wish was granted very shortly afterward; and when she told her husband of their expectation she held him close and looked deep into his eyes for the triumph she sought. Perhaps the fire in her own was reflected in his, for she released him from her embrace with a sigh of content.

Through the months of waiting Juliette longed for a boy. It seemed to her somehow essential for the retention of Henry's love that she should give him a boy; she could scarcely bear another girl, she who had brought into the world six girls. Much of Juliette's pride during those months was softened by her longing; she began once more to frequent the company of her neighbors in her zest for the least scrap of information that would help the fulfilment of it. There was no fantastic concoction she would not drink, nor any omen she would not propitiate. Half the saints in the calendar were introduced to her by ladies that knew them and vouched for the interest they would take in her pregnancy. Juliette never confided to anybody her reason for wanting a boy; and nobody suspected it, since half a dozen girls were enough to explain any woman's desire for a change. One adviser discovered in a tattered volume of obstetrical theory that when the woman was older than the man the odds were on a male child. Juliette's researches to gather confirmation of this remark led her into discussions about unequal marriages; and as the time of her confinement drew near she became gentler and almost anxious to discuss her love for Henry Snow, so much gentler and less reserved that those who had formerly whispered loudest and most falsely to one another now whispered sympathetically to her.

On the day before Juliette's confinement her husband came in from work very irritable.

"Here, when's this baby going to be born? I'm getting a bit annoyed. The men at the office are betting on its being a boy. It makes me look a fool, you know, that sort of thing."

She clutched his arm. "Which do you want, Henri? Tell me, *mon amour, mon homme.*"

"I don't care which it is, as long as you're quick about it and this betting stops."

That night she was delivered of a girl, and because it was his she choked down the wild disappointment and loved Sylvia the best of all her seven girls.

Sylvia Scarlett

CHAPTER I

THE first complete memory of her father that Sylvia possessed was of following her mother out into the street on a clear moonlight night after rain and of seeing him seated in a puddle outside the house, singing an unintelligible song which he conducted with his umbrella. She remembered her mother's calling to him sharply, and how at last after numerous shakings and many reproaches he had walked into the house on all fours, carrying the umbrella in his mouth like a dog. She remembered that the umbrella was somehow wrong at the end, different from any other umbrella she had ever seen, so that when it was put into the hall-stand it looked like a fat old market woman instead of the trim young lady it should have resembled. She remembered how she had called her mother's attention to the loss of its feet and how her mother, having apparently realized for the first time her presence at the scene, had promptly hustled her up-stairs to bed with so much roughness that she had cried.

When Sylvia was older and had become in a way her mother's confidante, sitting opposite to her in the window to sew until it was no longer possible to save oil for the lamp, she ventured to recall this scene. Her mother had laughed at the remembrance of it and had begun to hum the song her father had sung:

La donna è mobile
La da-di la-di-da.

"Shall I ever forget him?" Madame Snow had cried. "It was the day your sister Elène was married, and he had been down to the railway-station to see them off to Bruxelles."

Sylvia had asked what the words of the song meant, and had been told that they meant women were always running around.

"Where?" she had pressed.

"Some of them after men and others running away from them," her mother had replied.

"Shall I do that when I'm big?" Sylvia had continued. "Which shall I do?"

But it had been time to fetch the lamp and the question had remained unanswered.

Sylvia was five when her sister Elène was married; soon afterward Henriette married, too. She remembered that very well, because Marie went to join Françoise in the other bedroom, and with only Marguerite and Valentine left, they no longer slept three in a bed. This association had often been very uncomfortable because Marguerite would eat biscuits, the crumbs of which used to scratch her legs; and worse than the crumbs was the invariable quarrel between Marguerite and Valentine that always ended in their pinching each other across Sylvia, so that she often got pinched by mistake.

For several years Sylvia suffered from being the youngest of many sisters, and her mother's favorite. When she went to school, she asked other girls if it were not nicer to have brothers, but the stories she heard about the behavior of boys made her glad there were only girls in her house. She had practical experience of the ways of boys when at the age of eight she first took part in the annual *féerie* at the Lille theater. On her first appearance she played a monster; though all the masks were very ugly, she, being the smallest performer, always got the ugliest, and with the progress of the season the one that was most knocked about. In after years these performances seemed like a nightmare of hot cardboard-scented breath, of being hustled down the stone stairs from the dressing-room, of noisy rough boys shouting and scrambling for the best masks, of her legs being pinched, while she was waiting in the wings, by invisible boys, and once of somebody's twisting her mask rightround as they made the famous entrance of the monsters, so that, being able to see nothing, she fell down and made all the audience laugh. Such were boys!

In contrast with scenes of discomfort and misery like these were the hours when she sat sewing with her mother in the quiet house. There would be long silences only broken by the sound of her mother's hand searching for new thread or needle in the work-basket, of clocks, of kettle on the hob, or of distant street cries. Then her mother would suddenly laugh to herself and begin a tale so interesting that Sylvia's own needlework would lie idly on her knee, until she was reproved for laziness, and silence again inclosed the room. Sometimes the sunset would glow through the window-panes upon her mother's work, and Sylvia would stare entranced at the great silken roses that slowly opened their petals for those swift fingers. Sometimes it would be a piece of lace that lay on her mother's lap, lace that in the falling dusk became light and mysterious as a cloud. Yet even these tranquil hours had storms, as on the occasion when her mother had been working all day at a lace cap which had been promised without fail to somebody at the theater who required it that night. At six o'clock she had risen with a sigh and given the cap to Sylvia to hold while she put on her things to take it down to the theater. Sylvia had stood by the fire, dreaming over the beauty of the lace; and then without any warning the cap had fallen into the fire and in a moment was ashes. Sylvia wished she could have followed the cap when she saw her mother's face of despair on realizing what had happened. It was then that for the first time she learned how much depended upon her mother's work; for during all that week, whenever she was sent out on an errand, she was told to buy only the half of everything, half the usual butter, half the usual sugar, and what was stranger still to go to shops outside the *quartier* at which Madame Snow never dealt. When she inquired the reason of this her mother asked her if she wanted all the *quartier* to know that they were poor and could only afford to buy half the usual amount that week.

Sylvia, when the first shame of her carelessness had died away, rather enjoyed these excursions to streets more remote, where amusing adventures were always possible. One Saturday afternoon in April Sylvia set out with a more than usually keen sense of the discoveries and adventures that might befall her. The first discovery was a boy on a step-ladder, polishing a shop window; and the second discovery was that she could stand on the curbstone and never once fail to spit home upon the newly polished glass. She did this about a dozen times, watching the saliva dribble down the pane and speculating with herself which driblet would make the longest journey. Regretfully she saw that the boy was preparing to descend and admire his handiwork, because two driblets were still progressing slowly downward, one of which had been her original fancy for the prize of endurance. As she turned to flee, she saw on the pavement at her feet a golden ten-franc piece; she picked it up and grasping it tightly in her hot little hand ran off, not forgetting, even in the excitement of her sudden wealth, to turn round at a safe distance and put out her tongue at the boy to mark her contempt for him, for the rest of his class, and for all their handiwork, especially that newly polished window-pane. Then she examined the gold piece and marveled at it, thinking how it obliterated the memory of that mother-o'-pearl button which only the other day she had found on the dust-heap and lost a few hours afterward.

It was a wonderful afternoon, an afternoon of unbridled acquisition, which began with six very rich cakes and ended with a case of needles for her mother that used up her last sou. Coming out of the needle-shop, her arms full of packages, she met a regiment of soldiers marching and singing. The soldiers expressed her triumphant mood, and Sylvia marched with them, joining in their songs. She had a few cakes left and, being grateful to the soldiers, she handed them round among them, which earned her much applause from passers-by. When the regiment had arrived at the barracks and her particular friends had all kissed her farewell and there were no more bystanders to smile their approbation, Sylvia thought it would be wise to do the shopping for her mother. She had marched farther than she realized with the soldiers; it was nearly dusk when she reached the grocer's where she was to buy the small quantity of sugar that was all that could be afforded this week. She made her purchase, and put her hand into the pocket of her pinafore for the money: the pocket was empty. Everything in the grocer's shop seemed to be tumbling about her in a great and universal catastrophe. She searched feverishly again; there was a small hole; of course her mother had given her a ten-franc piece, telling her to be very careful indeed of the change, which was wanted badly for the rent. She could not explain to the man what had happened and, leaving the packet on the counter, she rushed from the shop into the cruel twilight, choked by tearless sobs and tremors of apprehension. At first she thought of trying to find the shops where she had made her own purchases that she might recover such of the money as had not been eaten; but her nervous fears refused to let her mind work properly, and everything that had happened on this luckless afternoon seemed to have happened in a dream. It was already dark; all she could do was to run home, clutching the miserable toys to her heart and wondering if the needle-case could possibly allay a little, a very little, of her mother's anger.

Madame Snow began as soon as Sylvia entered the house by demanding what she had been doing to be so late in coming home. Sylvia stammered and was silent; stammered again and let fall all her parcels; then she burst into a flood of tears that voiced a despair more profound than she had ever known. When her mother at last extracted from Sylvia what had happened she, too, wept; and the pair of them sat filling the room with their sobs, until Henry Snow appeared upon the scene and asked if they had both gone mad.

His wife and daughter sobbed a violent negative. Henry stared at the floor littered with Sylvia's numerous purchases, but found there no answer to the riddle. He moved across to Juliette and shook her, urging her not to become hysterical.

"The last bit of money I had and the rent due on Monday!" she wailed.

"Don't you worry about money," said Henry, importantly. "I've had a bit of luck at cards," and he offered his wife a note. Moreover, when he heard the reason for all this commotion of grief, he laughed, said it might have happened to any one, congratulated Sylvia upon her choice of goods, declared it was time she began to study English seriously and vowed that he was the one to be her teacher, yes, by gad, he was, and that to-morrow morning being Sunday they would make a start. Then he began to fondle his wife, which embarrassed Sylvia, but nevertheless because these caresses so plainly delighted her mother, they consoled her for the disaster. So she withdrew to a darker corner of the room and played with the doll she had bought, listening to the conversation between her parents.

"Do you love me, Henri?"

"Of course I love you."

"You know that I would sacrifice the world for you? I've given you everything. If you love me still, then you must love me for myself—myself alone, *mon homme*."

"Of course I do."

"But I'm growing old," protested Juliette. "There are others younger than I. *Ah, Henri, amour de ma vie*, I'm jealous even of the girls. I want them all out of the house. I hate them now, except ours—ours, *ma poupée*."

Sylvia regarding her own doll could not help feeling that this was a most inappropriate name for her father; she wondered why her mother called him that and decided finally that it must be because he was shorter than she was. The evening begun so disastrously ended most cheerfully; when Françoise and Marie arrived back at midnight, they escaped even the mildest rebuke from their mother.

Sylvia's father kept his promise about teaching her English, and she was granted the great pleasure of being admitted to his room every evening when he returned from work. This room until now had always been a Bluebeard's chamber, not merely for Sylvia, but for every one else in the house. To be sure Sylvia had sometimes, when supper was growing cold, peeped in to warn her father of fleeting time, but it had always been impressed upon her that in no circumstances was she to enter the room; though she had never seen in these quick glimpses anything more exciting than her father sitting in his shirt-sleeves and reading in a tumble-down arm-chair, there had always been the sense of a secret. Now that she was made free of this apartment she perceived nothing behind the door but a bookcase fairly full of books, nothing indeed anywhere that seemed to merit concealment, unless it were some pictures of undressed ladies looking at themselves in a glass. Once she had an opportunity of opening one of the books and she was astonished, when her father came in and caught her, that he said nothing, for she felt sure that her mother would have been very angry if she had seen her reading such a book. She had blushed when her father found her; when he had said nothing and even laughed in a queer unpleasant sort of a way, she had blushed still more deeply. Yet whenever she had a chance she read these books afterward and henceforth regarded her father with an affectionate contempt which was often expressed too frankly to please her mother, who finally became so much irritated by it that she sent her away to Bruxelles to stay with Elène, her eldest married sister. Sylvia did not enjoy this visit very much, because her brother-in-law was always making remarks about her personal appearance, comparing it most unfavorably with his wife's. It seemed that Elène had recently won a prize for beauty at the Exposition, and though Sylvia would have been suitably proud of this family achievement in ordinary circumstances, this continual harping upon it to her own disadvantage made her wish that Elène had been ignobly defeated.

"Strange her face should be so round and yours such a perfect oval," Elène's husband would say. "And her lips are so thin and her eyes so much lighter than yours. She's short, too, for her age. I don't think she'll ever be as tall as you. But of course every one can't be beautiful."

"Of course they can't," Sylvia snapped. "If they could, Elène might not have won the prize so easily."

"She's not a great beauty, but she has a tongue. And she's smart," her brother-in-law concluded.

Sylvia used to wonder why every one alluded to her tongue. Her mother had told her just before she was sent to Bruxelles that the priest had put too much salt on it when she was christened. She resolved to be silent in future; but this resolve reacted upon her nerves to such an extent that she wrote home to Lille and begged to be allowed to come back. There had been diplomacy in the way she had written to her father in English rather than to her mother in French. Such a step led her mother to suppose that she repented of criticizing her father; it also prevented her sister Elène from understanding the letter and perhaps writing home to suggest keeping her in Bruxelles. Sylvia was overjoyed at receiving an early reply from her mother bidding her come home, and sending stamps for her to buy a picture post-card album, which would be much cheaper in Belgium; she was enjoined to buy one picture post-card and put it in the album, so that the customs officials should not charge duty.

Sylvia had heard a great deal of smuggling and was thrilled by the illegal transaction, which seemed to her the most exciting enterprise of her life. She said good-by to Bruxelles without regret; clasping her album close, she waited anxiously for the train to start, thinking to herself that Elène only kept on putting her head into the carriage window to make stupid remarks because the compartment was crowded and she hoped some one would recognize her as the winner of the beauty competition at the Bruxelles Exposition.

At last the train started, and Sylvia settled down to the prospect of crossing the frontier with contraband. She looked at all the people in the carriage, thinking to herself what dangers she would presently encounter. It was almost impossible not to tell them, as they sat there in the stuffy compartment scattering crumbs everywhere with their lunches. Soon a pleasant woman in black engaged Sylvia in conversation by offering her an orange from a string-bag. It was very difficult to eat the orange and keep a tight hold of the album; in the end it fell on the floor, whereupon a fat old gentleman sitting opposite stooped over and picked it up for her. He had grunted so in making the effort that Sylvia felt she must reward him with more than thanks; she decided to divulge her secret and explain to him and the pleasant woman with the string-bag the history of the album. Sylvia was glad when all her other fellow-travelers paid attention to the tale, and she could point out that an album like this cost two francs fifty centimes in Lille, whereas in Bruxelles she had been able to buy it for two francs. Then, because everybody smiled so encouragingly, she unwrapped the album and showed the single picture post-card, discoursing upon the ruse. Everybody congratulated her, and everybody told one another anecdotes about smuggling, until finally a tired and anxious-looking woman informed the company that she was at that very moment smuggling lace to the value of more than two thousand francs. Everybody warned her to be very careful, so strict were the customs officials; but the anxious-looking woman explained that it was wrapped round her and that in any case she must take the risk, so much depended upon her ability to sell this lace at a handsome profit in France.

When the frontier was reached Sylvia alighted with the rest of the travelers to pass through the customs, and with quickening heart she presented herself at the barrier, her album clutched tightly to her side. No, she had nothing to declare, and with a sigh of relief at escape from danger she saw her little valise safely chalked. When she passed through to take her seat in the train again, she saw a man whom she recognized as a traveler from her own compartment that had told several anecdotes about contraband. He was talking earnestly now to one of the officials at the barrier and pointing out the anxious woman, who was still waiting to pass through.

"I tell you she had two thousand francs' worth of lace wrapped round her. She admitted it in the train."

Sylvia felt her legs give way beneath her when she heard this piece of treachery. She longed to cry out to the woman with the lace that she had been betrayed, but already she had turned deathly pale at the approach of the officials. They were beckoning her to follow them to a kind of cabin, and she was moving toward it hopelessly. It was dreadful to see a poor woman so treated, and Sylvia looked round to find the man who had been the cause of it, but he had vanished.

Half an hour afterward the woman of the lace wearily climbed into the compartment and took her seat with the rest; her eyes were red and she was still weeping bitterly. The others asked what had happened.

"They found it on me," she moaned. "And now what shall I do? It was all we had in the world to pay the mortgage on our house. My poor husband is ill, very ill, and it was the only way to save him. I should have sold that lace for four thousand francs, and now they have confiscated it and we shall be fined one thousand francs. We haven't any money. It was everything—everything. We shall lose our house and our furniture, and my husband will die. Oh, *mon Dieu! mon Dieu!*"

She rocked backward and forward in her grief; nothing that any one could say comforted her. Sylvia told how she had been betrayed; everybody execrated the spy and said how careful one should be to whom one spoke when traveling; but that did not help the poor woman, who sobbed more and more despairingly.

At last the train came to its first stop in France, and the man that had denounced the poor woman suddenly jumped in, as they were starting again, and took his old seat. The fat gentleman next to Sylvia swelled with indignation; his veins stood out, and he shouted angrily at the man what a rascal he was. Everybody in the carriage joined in abusing him; and the poor woman herself wailed out her sad story and reproached him for the ruin he had brought upon her. As for Sylvia, she could not contain herself, but jumped up and with all her might kicked him on the shins, an action which made the fat gentleman shout: *"Bravo! Vas-y! Encore, la gosse! Bravo! Bis! Bis!"*

When the noise had subsided the man began to speak.

"I regret infinitely, madame, the inconvenience to which I was unfortunately compelled to put you, but the fact is that I myself was carrying diamonds upon me to the value of more than two hundred thousand francs."

He suddenly took out a wallet from his pocket and emptied the stones into his hand, where they lay sparkling in the dusty sunshine of the compartment. Everybody was silent with surprise for a moment; when they began to abuse him again, he trickled the diamonds back into the wallet and begged for attention.

"How much have you lost, madame?" he inquired, very politely.

The woman of the lace poured forth her woes for the twentieth time.

"Permit me to offer you these notes to the value of six thousand francs," he said. "I hope the extra thousand will recompense you for the temporary inconvenience to which I was unfortunately compelled to put you. Pray accept my deepest apologies, but at the same time let me suggest greater discretion in future. Yet we are all human, are we not, monsieur?" he added, turning to the fat gentleman next to Sylvia. "Will you be very much surprised when I tell you that I have never traveled from Amsterdam but I have found some indiscreet fellow-traveler that has been of permanent service to me at temporary inconvenience to himself. This time I thought I was going to be unlucky, for this was the last compartment left; fortunately that young lady set a bad example."

He smiled at Sylvia.

This story, when she told it at home, seemed to make a great impression upon her father, who maintained that the stranger was a fool ever to return to the carriage.

"Some people seem to think money's made to throw into the gutter," he grumbled.

Sylvia was sorry about his point of view, but when she argued with him he told her to shut up; later on that same evening he had a dispute with his wife about going out.

"I want to win it back," he protested. "I've had a run of bad luck lately. I feel to-night it's going to change. Did I tell you I saw the new moon over my right shoulder, as I came in?"

"So did I," said his wife. "But I don't rush off and gamble away other people's money for the sake of the moon."

"You saw it, too, did you?" said Henry, eagerly. "Well, there you are!"

The funny thing was that Henry was right; he did have a run of good luck, and the house became more cheerful again. Sylvia went on with her English studies; but nowadays even during lessons her father never stopped playing cards. She asked him once if he were telling his fortune, and he replied that he was trying to make it. "See if you can pick out the queen," he would say. And Sylvia never could, which made her father chuckle to himself with pleasure.

About this time, too, he developed a habit of playing with a ten-centime piece. Whenever he or any one else was talking, he used to fidget with this coin; in the middle of something important or interesting it used to jingle down on the floor, and everybody had to go on hands and knees to search for it. This habit became so much the intrinsic Henry Snow that Sylvia could never think of him without that ten-centime piece sliding over his long mobile hands, in and out of his prehensile fingers: and though with the progress of time he ceased to drop the coin very often, the restless motion always irritated her. When Sylvia was eleven her uncle Edouard came to Lille with his caravan and brought the news of the death of her grandfather. She was not much impressed by this, but the caravan and the booth delighted her; and when her uncle asked if he might not take her away with him on a long tour through the south of France, she begged to be allowed to go. Her mother had so often held her spellbound by tales of her own wandering life that, when she seemed inclined to withhold her permission, Sylvia blamed her as the real origin of this longing to taste the joys of vagrancy, pleading so earnestly that at last her mother gave way and let her go.

Uncle Edouard and Aunt Elise, who sat in the box outside the booth and took the money, were both very kind to Sylvia, and since they had no children of their own, she was much spoilt. Indeed, there was not a dull moment throughout the tour; for even when she went to bed, which was always delightfully late, bed was really a pleasure in a caravan.

In old Albert Bassompierre's days the players had confined themselves to the legitimate drama; Edouard had found it more profitable to tour a variety show interspersed with one-act farces and melodrama. Sylvia's favorites in the company were Madame Perron, the wife of the *chanteur grivois*, and Blanche, a tall, fair, noisy girl who called herself a *diseuse*, but who usually sang indecent ballads in a powerful contralto. Madame Perron was Sylvia's first attraction, because she had a large collection of dolls with which she really enjoyed playing. She was a *femme très-propre*, and never went farther with any of her admirers in the audience than to exact from him the gift of a doll.

"*Voilà ses amours manqués*," her husband used to say with a laugh.

In the end Sylvia found her rather dull, and preferred to go tearing about the country with Blanche, who, though she had been a scullery-maid in a Boulogne hotel only a year ago, had managed during her short career on the stage to collect more lovers than Madame Perron had collected dolls. She had a passion for driving. Sylvia could always be sure that on the morning after their opening performance in any town a wagonette or dog-cart would be waiting to take them to some neighboring village, where a jolly party would make a tremendous noise, scandalize the inhabitants, and depart, leaving a legacy of unpopularity in the district for whichever of Blanche's lovers had paid for the entertainment with his purse and his reputation. Once they arrived at a village where a charity bazaar was being held under the direction of the *curé*. Blanche was presented to him as a distinguished actress from Paris who was seeking peace and recreation in the depths of the country. The *curé* asked if it would be presuming too far on her good nature to give them a taste of her art in the cause of holy charity, a speech perhaps from Corneill or Racine. Blanche assented immediately and recited a piece stuffed so full of spicy argot that the rustic gentility understood very little of it, though enough to make them blush—all except the priest, that is, who was very deaf and asked Blanche, when she had finished, if it were not a speech from Phèdre she had declaimed, thanking her very earnestly for the pleasure she had given his simple parish folk, a pleasure, alas, which he regretted he had not been able to enjoy as much as he should have enjoyed it before he became deaf.

On another occasion they drove to see the ruins of an ancient castle in Brittany, and afterward went down into the village to drink wine in the garden of the inn, where an English family was sitting at afternoon tea. Sylvia stared curiously at the two little girls who obeyed their governess so promptly and ate their cakes so mincingly. They were the first English girls she had ever seen, and she would very much have liked to tell them that her father was English, for they seemed to want cheering up, so solemn were their light-blue eyes and so high their boots. Sylvia whispered to Blanche that they were English, who replied that so much was very obvious, and urged Sylvia to address them in their native tongue; it would give them much pleasure, she thought. Sylvia, however, was too shy, so Blanche in her loudest voice suddenly shouted:

"Oh yes! T'ank you! I love you! All right! You sleep with me? Goddambleudi!"

The English family looked very much shocked, but the governess came to their rescue by asking in a thin throaty voice for the "attition," and presently they all walked out of the garden. Blanche judged the English to be a dull race, and, mounting on a table, began a rowdy dance. It happened that, just when the table cracked, the English governess came back for an umbrella she had left behind, and that Blanche, leaping wildly to save herself from falling, leaped on the governess and brought her to the ground in a general ruin of chairs and tables. Blanche picked up the victim and said that it was all very *rigolo*, which left miss as wise as she was before, her French not extending beyond the tea-table and the chaster portions of a bedroom. Blanche told Sylvia to explain to miss that she had displayed nothing more in her fall than had given much pleasure to all the world. Sylvia, who really felt the poor governess required such practical consolation, translated accordingly, whereat miss became very red and, snatching her umbrella, walked away muttering, "Impertinent little gipsy." When Blanche was told the substance of her last remark, she exclaimed, indignantly:

"*Elles sont des vrais types, vous savez, ces gonzesses. Mince, alors! Pourquoi s'emballer comme ça? Elle portait un pantalon fermé! Quelle race infecte, ces Anglais! Moi, je ne peux pas les suffrir.*"

Sylvia, listening to Blanche's tirade, wondered if all the English were like that. She thought of her father's books, and decided that life in France must have changed him somehow. Then she called to mind with a shiver the solemn light-blue eyes of the little girls. England must be a cold sort of a place where nobody ever laughed; perhaps that was why her father had come away. Sylvia decided to remain in France, always in a caravan if possible, where no English miss could poke about with bony fingers in one's bread and butter.

Sylvia acquired a good deal of worldly wisdom from being so continuously in the society of Blanche, and for a child of eleven she was growing up somewhat rapidly. Yet it would have been hard to say that the influence of her noisy friend was hurtful, for it never roused in Sylvia a single morbid thought. Life in those days presented itself to her mostly as an amusing game, a game that sometimes caused tears, but tears that were easily dried, because, after all, it was only a game. Such was the situation created on one occasion by the unexpected arrival of Blanche's *fiancé* from his regiment, the 717th of the line.

The company was playing at St.-Nazaire at the time, and Louis Moreau telegraphed from Nantes that he had been granted a *congé* of forty-eight hours.

"*Mince, alors!*" cried Blanche to Sylvia. "And, you know, I don't want to give him up, because he has thirty thousand francs and he loves me *à la folie*. We are only waiting till he has finished his military service to get married. But I don't want him here. First of all, I have a very *chic* lover, who has a *poignon fou* and doesn't care how much he spends, and then the lover of my heart is here."

Sylvia protested that she had heard the last claim too often.

"No, but this is something much greater than a *béguin*. It is real love. *Il est très trr-ès-beau garçon, tu sais*. And, *chose très-drôle*, he also is doing his military service here. *Tout ça ne se dessine pas du tout bien, tu sais, mais pas du tout, tu comprends! Moi, je ne suis pas veineuse. Ah, non, alors, c'est le comble!*"

Blanche had been sufficiently agile to extract the usual wagonette and pair of horses from the chic lover to whom she had introduced her real lover, a tall cuirassier with fierce mustaches, as her brother; but the imminent arrival of Louis was going to spoil all this, because Louis knew well that she did not possess a relative in the world, in fact, as Blanche emphasized, her solitary position had been one of her charms.

"You'll have to get rid of Monsieur Beaujour." This was the rich lover.

"And lose my horses? *Ah, non, alors!*"

"Well, then you'll have to tell Marcel he mustn't come near you until Louis has gone."

"And see him go off with that Jeanne at the Clair de la Lune Concert!"

"Couldn't Louis pay for the horses?" suggested Sylvia.

"I'm not going to let him waste his money like that; besides, he'll only be here two nights. *C'est assommant, tu sais*," Blanche sighed.

In the middle of the discussion Louis arrived, a very short little *sous-officier* with kind watery eyes and a mustache that could only be seen properly out of doors. Louis had not had more than five minutes with his *fiancée* before M. Beaujour drove up with the wagonette and pair. He was the son of a rich shipping agent in St.-Nazaire, with a stiff manner that he mistook for evidence of aristocratic descent, and bad teeth that prevented him from smiling more than he could help.

"I shall tell him you're my brother," said Blanche, quickly. Louis began to protest.

"*Pas de boniment*," Blanche went on. "I must be pleasant to strangers in front. Madame Bassompierre insists on that, and you know I've never given you any cause to be really jealous."

M. Beaujour looked very much surprised when Blanche presented Louis to him as her brother; Sylvia, remembering the tall cuirassier with the fierce mustaches that had also been introduced as Blanche's brother, appreciated his sensations. However, he accepted the relationship and invited Louis to accompany them on the drive, putting him with Sylvia and seating himself next Blanche on the box; Louis, who found Sylvia sympathetic, talked all the time about the wonderful qualities of Blanche, continually turning round to adore her shapely back.

M. Beaujour invited Louis to a supper he was giving that evening in honor of Blanche, and supposed, perhaps a little maliciously, that Monsieur would be glad to meet his brother again, who was also to be of the party. Louis looked at Blanche in perplexity; she frowned at him and said nothing.

That supper, to which M. and Mme. Perron with several other members of the company were invited, was a very restless meal. First, Blanche would go out with the host while Marcel and Louis glared alternately at each other and the door; then she would withdraw with Louis, while M. Beaujour and Marcel glared and fidgeted; finally she would disappear with Marcel, once for such a long time that Sylvia grew nervous and went outside to find her. Blanche was in tears; Marcel was stalking up and down the passage, twisting his fierce mustaches and muttering his annoyance. Sylvia was involved in a bitter discussion about the various degrees of Blanche's love, and in the end Blanche cried that her whole life had been shattered, and rushed back to the supper-room. Sylvia took this opportunity of representing Blanche's point of view to Marcel, and so successful was she with her tale of the emotional stress caused by the conflict of love with prudence that finally Marcel burst into tears, called down benedictions upon Sylvia's youthful head, and rejoined the supper-party, where he drank a great quantity of red wine and squeezed Blanche's hand under the table for the rest of the evening.

Sylvia, having been successful once, now invited Louis to accompany her outside. To him she explained that Marcel loved Blanche madly, that she, the owner, as Louis knew, of a melting heart, had been much upset by her inability to return his love, and that Louis must not be jealous, because Blanche loved only him. Louis's eyes became more watery than ever, and he took his seat at table again, a happy man until he drank too much wine and had to retire permanently from the feast. Finally Sylvia tackled M. Beaujour, and, recognizing that he was probably tired of lies, told him the truth of the situation, leaving it to him as an *homme supérieur* to realize that he could only be an episode in Blanche's life and begging him not to force his position that night. M. Beaujour could not help being flattered by this child's perception of his superiority, and for the rest of the entertainment played the host in a manner that was, as Madame Perron said, *très très-correcte.*

However, amusing evenings like this came to an end for Sylvia when once more the caravan returned to Lille. Her uncle and aunt had so much enjoyed her company that they proposed to Madame Snow to adopt Sylvia as their own daughter. Sylvia, much as she loved her mother, would have been very glad to leave the house at Lille, for it seemed, when she saw it again, poverty-stricken and pinched. There was only Valentine now left of her sisters, and her mother looked very care-worn. Her father, however, declined most positively to listen to the Bassompierres' proposal, and was indeed almost insulting about it. Madame Snow wearily bade Sylvia say no more, and the caravan went on its way again. Sylvia wondered whether life in Lille had always been as dull in reality as this, or if it were dull merely in contrast with the gay life of vagrancy. Everybody in Lille seemed to be quarreling. Her mother was always reproaching Valentine for being late, and her father for losing money, and herself for idleness in the house. She tried to make friends with her sister, but Valentine was suspicious of her former intimacy with their mother, and repelled her advances. The months dragged on, months of eternal sewing, eternal saving, eternal nagging, eternal sameness. Then one evening, when her mother was standing in the kitchen, giving a last glance at everything before she went down to the theater, she suddenly threw up her arms, cried in a choking voice, "Henri!" and collapsed upon the floor. There was nobody in the house except Sylvia, who, though she felt very much frightened, tried for a long time, without success, to restore her mother to consciousness. At last her father came in and bent over his wife.

"Good God, she's dead!" he exclaimed, and Sylvia broke into a sweat of horror to think that she had been alone in the twilight with something dead. Her father struggled to lift the body on the sofa, calling to Sylvia to come and help him. She began to whimper, and he swore at her for cowardice. A clock struck and Sylvia shrieked. Her father began to drag the body toward the sofa; playing-cards fell from his sleeves on the dead woman's face.

"Didn't she say anything before she died?" he asked. Sylvia shook her head.

"She was only forty-six, you know," he said; in and out of his fingers, round and round his hand, slipped the ten-centime piece.

For some time after his wife's death Henry Snow was inconsolable, and his loudly expressed grief had the effect of making Sylvia seem hard, for she grew impatient with him, especially when every week he used to sell some cherished piece of furniture. She never attempted to explain her sentiments when he accused her of caring more for furniture than for her dead mother; she felt it would be useless to explain them to him, and suffered in silence. What Sylvia found most inexplicable was the way in which her father throve on sorrow and every day seemed to grow younger. This fact struck her so sharply that one day she penetrated the hostility that had been gathering daily between her and Valentine and asked her sister if she had observed this queer change. Valentine got very angry; demanded what Sylvia meant; flung out some cruel sneers; and involved her in a scene with her father, who charged her with malice and underhanded behavior. Sylvia was completely puzzled by the effect of her harmless observation, and supposed that Valentine, who had always been jealous of her, had seized the opportunity to make further mischief. She could never understand why Valentine was jealous of her, because Valentine was really beautiful, and very much like her mother, enviable from any point of view, and even now obviously dearer to her stepfather than his own daughter. She would have liked to know where the caravan was now; she was sure that her father would no longer wish to forbid her adoption by Uncle Edouard and Aunt Elise.

The house grew emptier and emptier of furniture; Sylvia found it so hard to obtain any money from her father for current expenses that she was often hungry. She did not like to write to any of her older sisters, because she was afraid that Valentine would make it appear that she was in the wrong and trying to stir up trouble. Summer passed into autumn, and with the lengthening darkness the house became unbearably still; neither her father nor her sister was ever at home; even the clocks had now all disappeared. Sylvia could not bear to remain indoors; for in her nervous, hungry state old childish terrors were revived, and the great empty loft at the top of the house was once again inhabited by that one-legged man with whose clutches her mother used to frighten her when naughty long ago. There recurred, too, a story told by her mother on just such a gusty evening as these, of how, when she first came to Lille, she had found an armed burglar under her bed, and of how the man had been caught and imprisoned. Even her mother, who was not a nervous woman, had been frightened by his threats of revenge when he should be free again, and once when she and her mother were sewing together close to the dusky window her mother had fancied she had seen him pass the house, a large pale man in a dark suit. Supposing he should come back now for his revenge? And above all these other terrors was the dread of her mother's ghost.

Sylvia took to going out alone every evening, whether it rained or blew, to seek in the streets relief from the silence of the desolate house. Loneliness came to seem to her the worst suffering imaginable, and the fear of it which was bred during these months haunted her for years to come.

In November, about half past eight of a windy night, Sylvia came back from one of her solitary walks and found her father sitting with a bottle of brandy in the kitchen. His face was haggard; his collar was loose; from time to time he mopped his forehead with a big blue handkerchief and stared at himself in a small cracked shaving-glass that he must have brought down from his bedroom. She asked if he were ill, and he told her not to worry him, but to go out and borrow a railway time-table.

When Sylvia returned she heard Valentine's angry voice in the kitchen, and waited in the passage to know the cause of the dispute.

"No, I won't come with you," Valentine was saying. "You must be mad! If you're in danger of going to prison, so much the worse for you. I've got plenty of people who'll look after me."

12

"But I'm your stepfather."

Valentine's laugh made Sylvia turn pale.

"Stepfather! Fine stepfather! Why, I hate you! Do you hear? I hate you! My man is waiting for me now, and he'll laugh when he hears that a convict wants his step-daughter to go away with him. My mother may have loved you, but I'd like her to see you now. *L'amour de sa vie. Son homme! Sa poupée, sa poupée! Ah, mais non alors! Sa poupée!*"

Sylvia could not bear any longer this mockery of her mother's love, and, bursting into the kitchen, she began to abuse Valentine with all the vulgar words she had learned from Blanche.

Valentine caught her sister by the shoulders and shook her violently:

"Tu seras bien avec ton père, sale gosse!"

Then she smacked her cheek several times and left the house.

Sylvia flung her arms round her father.

"Take me with you," she cried. "You hate her, don't you? Take me, father."

Henry rose and, in rising, upset the bottle of brandy.

"Thank God," he said, fervently. "My own daughter still loves me."

Sylvia perceived nothing ludicrous in the tone of her father's speech, and happy tears rose to her eyes.

"See! here is the time-table. Must we go to-night? Sha'n't we go to-night?"

She helped her father to pack; at midnight they were in the train going north.

CHAPTER II

THE amount of brandy that Henry Snow had drunk to support what he called his misfortune made him loquacious for the first part of the journey. While he and Sylvia waited during the night at a railway junction, he held forth at length not merely upon the event that was driving him out of France, but generally upon the whole course of his life. Sylvia was glad that her father treated her as if she were grown up, because having conceived for him a kind of maternal solicitude, not so much from pity or affection as from the inspiration to quit Lille forever which she gratefully owed to his lapse, she had no intention of letting him re-establish any authority over herself. His life's history, poured forth while they paced the dark platform or huddled before the stove in the dim waiting-room, confirmed her resolve.

"Of course, when I first got that job in Lille it seemed just what I was looking for. I'd had a very scrappy education, because my father, who was cashier in a bank, died, and my mother, who you're a bit like—I used to have a photograph of her, but I suppose it's lost, like everything else—my mother got run over and killed coming back from the funeral. There's something funny about that, you know. I remember your mother laughed very much when I told her about it once. But I didn't laugh at the time, I can tell you, because it meant two aunts playing battledore and shuttlecock. Don't interrupt, there's a good girl. It's a sort of game. I can't remember what it is in French. I dare say it doesn't exist in France. You'll have to stick to English now. Good old England, it's not a bad place. Well, these two aunts of mine grudged every penny they spent on me, but one of them got married to a man who knew the firm I worked for in Lille. That's how I came to France. Where are my aunts now? Dead, I hope. Don't you fret, Sylvia, we sha'n't trouble any of our relations for a long time to come. Then after I'd been in France about four years I married your mother. If you ask me why, I can't tell you. I loved her; but the thing was wrong somehow. It put me in a false position. Well, look at me! I'm only thirty-four now. Who'd think you were my daughter?

"And while we're talking on serious subjects, let me give you a bit of advice. Keep off jealousy. Jealousy is hell; and your mother was jealous. Well—Frenchwomen are more jealous than Englishwomen. You can't get over that fact. The scenes I've had with her. It was no good my pointing out that she was fourteen years older than me. Not a bit of good. It made her worse. That's why I took to reading. I had to get away from her sometimes and shut myself up. That's why I took to cards. And that's where your mother was wrong. She'd rather I gambled away her money, because it's no use to pretend that it wasn't her money, than go and sit at a café and perhaps observe—mind you, simply observe—another woman. I used to drink a bit too much when we were first married, but it caused such rows that I gave that up. I remember I broke an umbrella once, and you'd really have thought there wasn't another umbrella in the whole world. Why, that little drop of brandy I drank to-night has made me feel quite funny. I'm not used to it. But there was some excuse for drinking to-night. I've had runs of bad luck before, but anything like these last two months I've never had in my life. The consequence was I borrowed some of my salary in advance without consulting anybody. That's where the manager had me this afternoon. He couldn't see that it was merely borrowing. As a matter of fact, the sum wasn't worth an argument; but he wasn't content with that; he actually told me he was going to examine—well—you wouldn't understand if I tried to explain to you. It would take a commercial training to understand what I've been doing. Anyway, I made up my mind to make a bolt for it. Now don't run away with the notion that the police will be after me, because I very much hope they won't. In fact, I don't think they'll do anything. But the whole affair gave me a shock and Valentine's behavior upset me. You see, when your mother was alive if I'd had a bad week she used to help me out; but Valentine actually asked me for money. She accused me of all sorts of things which, luckily, you're too young to understand; and I really didn't like to refuse her when I'd got the money.

"Well, it's been a lesson to me and I tell you I've missed your mother these last months. She was jealous; she was close; she had a tongue; but a finer woman never lived, and I'm proud of her. She used to wish you were a boy. Well, I don't blame her. After all, she'd had six girls, and what use are they to anybody? None at all. They might as well not exist. Women go off and get married and take somebody else's name, and it's finished. There's not one of your sisters that's really stayed in the family. A selfish crowd, and the worst of the lot was Valentine. Yes, you ought to have been a boy. I'll tell you what, it wouldn't be a bad idea if you *were* a boy for a bit. You see, in case the French police make inquiries, it would be just as well to throw them off the scent; and, another thing, it would be much easier for me till I find my feet again in London. Would you like to be a boy, Sylvia? There's no reason against it that I can see, and plenty of reasons for it. Of course it means cutting off your hair, but they say that's a very good thing for the hair once in a way. You'll be more free, too, as a boy, and less of a responsibility. There's no doubt a girl would be a big responsibility in London."

"But could I be a boy?" Sylvia asked. "I'd like to be a boy if I could. And what should I be called?"

"Of course you could be a boy," her father affirmed, enthusiastically. "You were always a bit of a *garçon manqué*, as the French say. I'll buy you a Norfolk suit."

Sylvia was not yet sufficiently unsexed not to want to know more about her proposed costume. Her father pledged his word that it would please her; his description of it recalled the dress that people in Lille put on to go shooting sparrows on Sunday.

"*Un sporting?*" Sylvia queried.

"That's about it," her father agreed. "If you had any scissors with you, I'd start right in now and cut your hair."

Sylvia said she had scissors in her bag; and presently she and her father retired to the outer gloom of the junction, where, undisturbed by a single curious glance, Sylvia's curls were swept away by the wind.

"I've not done it quite so neatly as I might," said her father, examining the effect under a wavering gas-jet. "I'll have you properly cropped to-morrow at a hairdresser's."

Sylvia felt cold and bare round the neck, but she welcomed the sensation as one of freedom. How remote Lille seemed already—utterly, gloriously far away! Now arose the problem of her name.

"The only boy's name I can think of that's anything like Sylvia is Silas, and that's more Si than Sil. Wait a bit. What about Silvius? I've seen that name somewhere. Only, we'll call you Sil for short."

"Why was I ever called Sylvia?" she asked.

"It was a fancy of your mother's. It comes in a song called '*Plaisir d'amour*.' And your mother liked the English way of saying it. I've got it. Sylvester! Sylvester Snow! What do you want better than that?"

When the train approached Boulogne, Henry Snow gave up talking and began to juggle with the ten-centime piece; while they were walking along to the boat he looked about him furtively. Nobody stopped them, however; and with the kind of relief she had felt when she had brought her album safely over the frontier Sylvia saw the coast of France recede. There were many English people on the boat, and Sylvia watched them with such concentration that several elderly ladies at whom she stared in turn thought she was waiting for them to be sick, and irritably waved her away. The main impression of her fellow-travelers was their resemblance to the blind beggars that one saw sitting outside churches. She was tempted to drop a sou in one of the basins, but forbore, not feeling quite sure how such humor would appeal to the English. Presently she managed to engage in conversation an English girl of her own age, but she had not got far with the many questions she wanted to ask when her companion was whisked away and she heard a voice reproving her for talking to strange little girls. Sylvia decided that the strangeness of her appearance must be due to her short hair, and she longed for the complete transformation. Soon it began to rain; the shores of that mysterious land to which she actually belonged swam toward her. Her father came up from below, where, as he explained, he had been trying to sleep off the effects of a bad night. Indeed, he did not recover his usual jauntiness until they were in the train, traveling through country that seemed to Sylvia not very different from the country of France. Would London, after all, prove to be very different from Lille? Then slowly the compartment grew dark, and from time to time the train stopped.

"A fog," said her father, and he explained to her the meaning of a London fog.

It grew darker and darker, with a yellowish-brown darkness that was unlike any obscurity she had ever known.

"Bit of luck," said her father. "We sha'n't be noticed in this. Phew! It is thick. We'd better go to some hotel close by for to-night. No good setting out to look for rooms in this."

In the kitchen at Lille there had been a picture called "The Impenitent Sinner," in which demons were seen dragging a dead man from his bed into flames and darkness; Sylvia pointed out its likeness to the present scene at Charing Cross. Outside the station it was even worse. There was a thunderous din; horses came suddenly out of the darkness; everybody seemed to be shouting; boys were running along with torches; it was impossible to breathe.

"Why did they build a city here?" she inquired.

At last they came to a house in a quieter street, where they walked up high, narrow stairs to their bedrooms.

The next morning her father took Sylvia's measurements and told her not to get up before he came back. When she walked out beside him in a Norfolk suit nobody seemed to stare at her; when her hair had been properly cut by a barber and she could look at herself in a long glass, she plunged her hands into her trousers pockets and felt securely a boy.

While they were walking to a mysterious place called the Underground, her father asked if she had caught bronchitis, and he would scarcely accept her word that she was trying to practise whistling.

"Well, don't do it when I'm inquiring about rooms or the people in the house may think it's something infectious," he advised. "And don't forget your name's Sylvester. Which reminds me it wouldn't be a bad notion if I was to change my own name. There's no sense in running one's head into a noose, and if inquiries *were* made by the police it would be foolish to ram my name right down their throats. Henry Snow. What about Henry White? Better keep to the same initials. I've got it. Henry Scarlett. You couldn't find anything more opposite to Snow than that."

Thus Sylvia Snow became Sylvester Scarlett.

After a long search they took rooms with Mrs. Threadgould, a widow who with her two boys, Willie and Ernie, lived at 45 Pomona Terrace, Shepherd's Bush. There were no other lodgers, for the house was small; and Henry Scarlett

14

decided it was just the place in which to stay quietly for a while until the small sum of money he had brought with him from Lille was finished, when it would be necessary to look for work. Meanwhile he announced that he should study very carefully the advertisements in the daily papers, leaving everybody with the impression that reading advertisements was a most erudite business, a kind of scientific training that when the moment arrived would produce practical results.

Sylvia meanwhile was enjoined to amuse herself in the company of Mrs. Threadgould's two boys, who were about her own age. It happened that at this time Willie Threadgould, the elder, was obsessed by secret societies, to which his brother Ernie and many other boys in the neighborhood had recently been initiated. Sylvia was regarded with suspicion by Willie until she was able to thrill him with the story of various criminal associations in France and so became his lieutenant in all enterprises. Most of the secret societies that had been rapidly formed by Willie and as rapidly dissolved had possessed a merely academic value; now with Sylvia's advent they were given a practical intention. Secrecy for secrecy's sake went out of fashion. Muffling the face in dusters, giving the sign and countersign, lurking at the corner of the road to meet another conspirator, were excellent decorations, but Sylvia pointed out that they led nowhere and produced nothing; to illustrate her theory she proposed a secret society for ringing other people's bells. She put this forward as a kind of elementary exercise; but she urged that, when the neighborhood had realized the bell-ringing as something to which they were more continuously exposed than other neighborhoods, the moment would be ripe to form another secret society that should inflict a more serious nuisance. From the secret society that existed to be a nuisance would grow another secret society that existed to be a threat; and finally there seemed no reason why Willie Threadgould (Sylvia was still feminine enough to let Willie think it was Willie) should control Shepherd's Bush and emulate the most remarkable brigands of history. In the end Sylvia's imagination banished her from the ultimate power at which she aimed. The Secret Society for Ringing Other People's Bells did its work so well that extra policemen were put on duty to cope with the nuisance and an inspector made a house-to-house visitation, which gave her father such a shock that he left Pomona Terrace the next day and took a room in Lillie Road, Fulham.

"We have been betrayed," Sylvia assured Willie. "Do not forget to avenge my capture."

Willie vowed he would let nothing interfere with his vengeance, not even if the traitor turned out to be his own brother Ernie.

Sylvia asked if he would kill him, and reminded Willie that it was a serious thing to betray a secret society when that society was doing something more than dressing up. Willie doubted if it would be possible to kill the culprit, but swore that he should prefer death to what should happen to him.

Sylvia was so much gratified by Willie's severity that she led him into a corner, where, having exacted his silence with the most solemn oaths, she betrayed herself and the secret of her sex; then they embraced. When they parted forever next day, Sylvia felt that she had left behind her in Willie's heart a romantic memory that would never fade.

Mrs. Meares, who kept the house in Lillie Road, was an Irishwoman whose husband had grown tired of her gentility and left her. She did not herself sum up her past so tersely as this, but Sylvia was sure that Mr. Meares had left her because he could no longer endure the stories about her royal descent. Perhaps he might have been able to endure his wife's royal descent, because, after all, he had married into the family and might have extracted some pride out of that fact; but all her friends apparently came from kings and queens, too. Ireland, if Mrs. Meares was to be believed, consisted of one large poverty-stricken royal family, which must have cheapened the alliance for Mr. Meares. It was lucky that he was still alive, for otherwise Sylvia was sure that her father would have married their new landlady, such admiration did he always express for the manner in which she struggled against misfortune without losing her dignity. This, from what Sylvia could see, consisted of wearing silk skirts that trailed in the dust of her ill-kept house and of her fanning herself in an arm-chair however cold the weather. The only thing that stirred her to action was the necessity of averting an ill-omen. Thus, she would turn back on a flight of stairs rather than pass anybody descending; although ordinarily when she went up-stairs she used to sigh and hold her heart at every step. Sylvia remembered her mother's scrupulous care of her house, even in the poorest days; she could not help contrasting her dignity with this Irish dignity that was content to see indefinite fried eggs on her table, cockroaches in the bedrooms, and her own placket always agape. Mrs. Meares used to say that she would never let any of her rooms to ladies, because ladies always fussed.

"Gentlemen are so much more considerate," said Mrs. Meares.

Their willingness to be imposed upon made Sylvia contemptuous of the sex she had adopted, and she tried to spur her father to protest when his bed was still unmade at four o'clock in the afternoon.

"Why don't you make it?" he suggested. "I don't like to worry poor Mrs. Meares."

Sylvia, however contemptuous of manhood, had no intention of relinquishing its privileges; she firmly declined to have anything to do with the making of beds.

The breakfast-room was placed below the level of the street. Here, in an atmosphere of cat-haunted upholstery and broken springs, of overcooked vegetables and dingy fires, yet withal of a kind of frowsy comfort, Sylvia sometimes met the other lodgers. One of them was Baron von Statten, a queer German, whom Sylvia could not make out at all, for he spoke English as if he had been taught by a maid-of-all-work with a bad cold, powdered his pink face, and wore three rings, yet was so poor that sometimes he stayed in bed for a week at a stretch, pending negotiations with his laundress. The last piece of information Sylvia obtained from Clara, the servant, who professed a great contempt for the baron. Mrs. Meares, on the other hand, derived much pride from his position in her house, which she pointed out was really that of an honored guest, since he owed now nearly seven weeks' rent; she never failed to refer to him by his title with warm affection. Another lodger was a Welsh pianist called Morgan, who played the piano all day long and billiards for as much of the night as he could. He was a bad-tempered young man with long black hair and a great antipathy to the baron, whom he was always trying to insult; indeed, once at breakfast he actually poured a cup of coffee over him.

"Mr. Morgan!" Mrs. Meares had cried. "No Irishman would have done that."

"No Irishman would ever do anything," the pianist snapped, "if he could get somebody else to do it for him."

Sylvia welcomed the assault, because the scalding coffee drove the baron to unbutton his waistcoat in a frenzy of discomfort and thereby confirmed Clara's legend about the scarcity of his linen.

The third lodger was Mr. James Monkley, about whom Sylvia was undecided; sometimes she liked him very much, at other times she disliked him equally. He had curly red hair, finely cut red lips, a clear complexion, and an authoritative, determined manner, but his eyes, instead of being the pleasant blue they ought to have been in such a face, were of a shade of muddy green and never changed their expression. Sylvia once mentioned about Mr. Monkley's eyes to Clara, who said they were like a fish.

"But Monkley's not like a fish," Sylvia argued.

"I don't know what he's like, I'm sure," said Clara. "All I know is he gives any one the creeps something shocking whenever he stares, which he's forever doing. Well, fine feathers don't make a summer and he looks best who looks last, as they say."

One reason for disliking Mr. Monkley was his intimacy with her father. Sylvia would not have objected to this if it had not meant long confabulations during which she was banished from the room and, what was worse, thrown into the society of Mrs. Meares, who always seemed to catch her when she was trying to make her way down-stairs to Clara.

"Come in and talk to me," Mrs. Meares would say. "I'm just tidying up my bedroom. Ah, Sil, if God had not willed otherwise I should have had a boy just your age now. Poor little innocent!"

Sylvia knew too well this counterpart of hers and hated him as much in his baby's grave as she might have done were he still her competitor in life.

"Ah, it's a terrible thing to be left as I've been left, to be married and not married, to have been a mother and to have lost my child. And I was never intended for this life. My father kept horses. We had a carriage. But they say, 'trust an Irishwoman to turn her hand to anything.' And it's true. There's many people would wonder how I do it with only one maid. How's your dear father? He seems comfortable. Ah, it's a privilege to look after a gentleman like him. He seems to have led a most adventurous life. Most of his time spent abroad, he tells me. Well, travel gives an air to a man. Ah, now if one of the cats hasn't been naughty just when I'd got my room really tidy! Will you tell Clara, if you are going down-stairs, to bring up a dustpan? I don't mind asking you, for at your age I think you would be glad to wait on the ladies like a little gentleman. Sure, as your father said the other day, it's a very good thing you're in a lady's house. That's why the dear baron's so content; and the poor man has much to try him, for his relations in Berlin have treated him abominably."

Such speeches inflicted upon her because Monkley wanted to talk secrets with her father made her disapprove of Monkley. Nevertheless, she admired him in a way; he was the only person in the house who was not limp, except Mr. Morgan, the pianist; but he used to glare at her, when they occasionally met, and seemed to regard her as an unpleasant result of being late for breakfast, like a spot on the table-cloth made by a predecessor's egg.

Monkley used to ask Sylvia sometimes about what she was going to do. Naturally he treated her future as a boy's future, which took most of the interest out of the conversation; for Sylvia did not suppose that she would be able to remain a boy very much longer. The mortifying fact, too, was that she was not getting anything out of her transformation: for all the fun she was having, she might as well have stayed a girl. There had been a brief vista of liberty at Pomona Terrace; here, beyond going out to buy a paper or tobacco for her father, she spent most of her time in gossiping with Clara, which she could probably have done more profitably in petticoats.

Winter drew out to spring; to the confabulations between Jimmy Monkley and Henry Scarlett were now added absences from the house that lasted for a day or two at a time. These expeditions always began with the friends' dressing up in pearl-buttoned overcoats very much cut in at the waist. Sylvia felt that such careful attention to externals augured the great secrecy and importance of the enterprise; remembering the effect of Willie Threadgould's duster-shrouded countenance upon his fellow-conspirators, she postulated to herself that with the human race, particularly the male portion, dress was always the prelude to action. One morning after breakfast, when Monkley and her father had hurried off to catch a train, the baron said in his mincing voice:

"Off ra-c-cing again! They do enjoy themselves-s-s."

She asked what racing meant, and the baron replied:

"Hors-s-se-ra-c-cing, of cour-se."

Sylvia, being determined to arrive at the truth of this business, put the baron through a long interrogation, from which she managed to learn that the jockeys wore colored silk jackets and that in his prosperous days the baron had found the sport too exciting for his heart. After breakfast Sylvia took the subject with her into the kitchen, and tried to obtain fuller information from Clara, who, with the prospect of a long morning's work, was disinclined to be communicative.

"What a boy you are for asking questions! Why don't you ask your dad when he comes home, or that Monkley? As if I'd got time to talk about racing. I've got enough racing of my own to think about; but if it goes on much longer I shall race off out of it one of these days, and that's a fact. You may take a pitcher to the well, but you can't make it drink, as they say."

Sylvia withdrew for a while, but later in the afternoon she approached Clara again.

"God bless the boy! He's got racing on the brain," the maid exclaimed. "I had a young man like that once, but I soon gave him the go-by. He was that stuffed up with halfpenny papers he couldn't cuddle any one without crackling like an egg-shell. 'Don't carry on so, Clara,' he said to me. 'I had a winner to-day in the three-thirty.' 'Did you?' I answered, very cool. 'Well, you've got a loser now,' and with that I walked off very dignified and left him. It's the last straw, they say, that gives the camel the hump. And he properly gave me the hump. But I reckon, I do, that it's mugs like him as keeps your dad and that Monkley so smart-looking. I reckon most of the racing they do is racing to see which can get some silly josser to give them his money first."

Sylvia informed Clara that her father used to play cards for money in France.

"There you are. What did I tell you?" Clara went on. "Nap, they call it, but I reckon that there Monkley keeps wide enough awake. Oh, he's an artful one, he is! Birds and feathers keep together, they say, and I reckon your dad's cleverer than what he makes out to be."

Sylvia produced in support of this idea her father's habit of juggling with a penny.

"What did I tell you?" Clara exclaimed, triumphantly. "Take it from me, Sil, the two of them has a rare old time with this racing. I've got a friend, Maudie Tilt, who's in service, and her brother started off to be a jockey, only he never got very far, because he got kicked on the head by a horse when he was sweeping out the stable, which was very aggravating for his relations, because he had a sister who died in a galloping consumption the same week. I reckon horses was very unlucky for them, I do."

"My grandmother got run over coming back from my grandfather's funeral," Sylvia proclaimed.

"By the hearse?" Clara asked, awestruck.

Sylvia felt it would be well to make the most of her story, and replied without hesitation in the affirmative.

"Well, they say to meet an empty hearse means a pleasant surprise," said Clara. "But I reckon your grandma didn't think so. Here, I'll tell you what, my next afternoon off I'll take you round to see Maudie Tilt. She lives not far from where the Cedars 'bus stops."

About a week after this conversation Clara, wearing balloon sleeves of last year's fashion and with her hair banked up to support a monstrous hat, descended into the basement, whence she and Sylvia emerged into a fine April afternoon and hailed an omnibus.

"Mind you don't get blown off the top, miss," said the conductor, with a glance at Clara's sleeves.

"No fear of that. I've grown a bit heavier since I saw your face," Clara replied, climbing serenely to the top of the omnibus. "Two, as far as you go," she said, handing twopence to the conductor when he came up for the fares.

"I could go a long way with you, miss," he said, punching the tickets with a satisfied twinkle. "What a lovely hat!"

"Is it? Well, don't start in trying to eat it because you've been used to green food all your life."

"Your sister answers very sharp, doesn't she, Tommy?" said the conductor to Sylvia.

After this display of raillery Sylvia felt it would be weak merely to point out that Clara was not a sister, so she remained silent.

The top of the omnibus was empty except for Clara and Sylvia; the conductor, whistling a cheerful tune, descended again.

"Saucy things," Clara commented. "But there, you can't blame them. It makes any one feel cheerful to be out in the open air like this."

Maudie's house in Castleford Road was soon reached after they left the omnibus. When they rang the area bell, Maudie herself opened the door.

"Oh, you did give me a turn!" she exclaimed. "I thought it was early for the milkman. You couldn't have come at a better time, because they've both gone away. She's been ill, and they'll be away for a month. Cook's gone for a holiday, and I'm all alone."

Sylvia was presented formally to the hostess; and when, at Clara's prompting, she had told the story of her grandmother's death, conversation became easy. Maudie Tilt took them all over the house, and, though Clara said she should die of nervousness, insisted upon their having tea in the drawing-room.

"Supposing they come back," Clara whispered. "Oh, lor'! Whatever's that?"

Maudie told her not to be silly, and went on to boast that she did not care if they did come back, because she had made up her mind to give up domestic service and go on the stage.

"Fancy!" said Clara. "Whoever put that idea into your head?"

"Well, I started learning some of the songs they sing in the halls, and some friends of mine gave a party last January and I made quite a hit. I'll sing you a song now, if you like."

And Maudie, sitting down at the piano, accompanied herself with much effect in one of Miss Vesta Victoria's songs.

"For goodness' sake keep quiet, Maudie," Clara begged. "You'll have the neighbors coming 'round to see whatever's the matter. You have got a cheek."

Sylvia thoroughly enjoyed Maudie's performance and thought she would have a great success. She liked Maudie's smallness and neatness and glittering, dark eyes. Altogether it was a delightful afternoon, and she was sorry to go away.

"Come again," cried Maudie, "before they come back, and we'll have some more."

"Oh, I did feel frightened!" Clara said, when she and Sylvia were hurrying to catch the omnibus back to Lillie Road. "I couldn't enjoy it, not a bit. I felt as if I was in the bath and the door not bolted, though they do say stolen fruit is the sweetest."

When she got home, Sylvia found that her father had returned also, and she held forth on the joys of Maudie Tilt's house.

"Wants to go on the stage, does she?" said Monkley, who was in the room. "Well, you'd better introduce us and we'll see what we can do. Eh, Harry?"

17

Sylvia approved of this suggestion and eagerly vouched for Maudie's willingness.

"We'll have a little supper-party," said Monkley. "Sil can go round and tell her we're coming."

Sylvia blessed the persistency with which she had worried Clara on the subject of racing; otherwise, bisexual and solitary, she might have been moping in Lillie Road. She hoped that Maudie Tilt would not offer any objections to the proposed party, and determined to point out most persuasively the benefit of Monkley's patronage, if she really meant to go on the stage. However, Maudie was not at all difficult to convince and showed herself as eager for the party as Sylvia herself. She was greatly impressed by her visitor's experience of the stage, but reckoned that no boys should have pinched her legs or given her the broken masks.

"You ought to have punched into them," she said. "Still, I dare say it wasn't so easy for you, not being a girl. Boys are very nasty to one another, when they'd be as nice as anything to a girl."

Sylvia was conscious of a faint feeling of contempt for Maudie's judgment, and she wondered from what her illusions were derived.

Clara, when she heard of the proposed party, was dubious. She had no confidence in Monkley, and said so frankly.

"No one wants to go chasing after a servant-girl for nothing," she declared. "Every cloud's got a silver lining."

"But what could he want to do wrong?" Sylvia asked.

"Ah, now you're asking. But if I was Maudie Tilt I'd keep myself to myself."

Clara snapped out the last remark and would say nothing more on the subject.

A few days later, under Sylvia's guidance, James Monkley and Henry Scarlett sought Castleford Road. Maudie had put on a black silk dress, and with her hair done in what she called the French fashion she achieved a kind of Japanese piquancy.

"*N'est-ce pas qu'elle a un chic?*" Sylvia whispered to her father.

They had supper in the dining-room and made a good deal of noise over it, for Monkley had brought two bottles of champagne, and Maudie could not resist producing a bottle of cognac from her master's cellar. When Monkley asked if everything were not kept under lock and key, Maudie told him that if they couldn't trust her they could lump it; she could jolly soon find another place; and, any way, she intended to get on the stage somehow. After supper they went up-stairs to the drawing-room; and Maudie was going to sit down at the piano, when Monkley told her that he would accompany her, because he wanted to see how she danced. Maudie gave a most spirited performance, kicking up her legs and stamping until the ornaments on the mantelpiece rattled. Then Monkley showed Maudie where she could make improvements in her renderings, which surprised Sylvia very much, because she had never connected Monkley with anything like this.

"Quite an artist is Jimmy," Henry Scarlett declared. Then he added in an undertone to Sylvia: "He's a wonderful chap, you know. I've taken a rare fancy to him. Do anything. Sharp as a needle. I may as well say right out that he's made all the difference to my life in London."

Presently Monkley suggested that Maudie should show them over the house, and they went farther up-stairs to the principal bedroom, where the two men soused their heads with the various hair-washes left behind by the master of the house. Henry expressed a desire to have a bath, and retired with an enormous sponge and a box of bath-salts. Monkley began to flirt with Maudie; Sylvia, feeling that the evening was becoming rather dull, went down-stairs again to the drawing-room and tried to pass the time away with a stereoscope.

After that evening Monkley and Scarlett went often to see Maudie, but, much to Sylvia's resentment, they never took her with them. When she grumbled about this to Clara, Clara told her that she was well out of it.

"Too many cooks drink up the soup, which means you're one too many, my lad, and a rolling stone doesn't let the grass grow under its feet, which means as that Monkley's got some game on."

Sylvia did not agree with Clara's point of view; she still felt aggrieved by being left out of everything. Luckily, when life in Lillie Road was becoming utterly dull again, a baboon escaped from Earl's Court Exhibition, climbed up the drain-pipe outside the house, and walked into Mrs. Meares's bedroom; so that for some time after this she had palpitations whenever a bell rang. Mr. Morgan was very unkind about her adventure, for he declared that the baboon looked so much like an Irishman that she must have thought it was her husband come back; Mr. Morgan had been practising the Waldstein Sonata at the time, and had been irritated by the interruption of a wandering ape.

A fortnight after this there was a scene in the house that touched Sylvia more sharply, for Maudie Tilt arrived one morning and begged to speak with Mr. Monkley, who, being in the Scarletts' room at the moment, looked suddenly at Sylvia's father with a question in his eyes.

"I told you not to take them all," Henry said.

"I'll soon calm her down," Monkley promised. "If you hadn't insisted on taking those bottles of hair-wash she'd never have thought of looking to see if the other things were still there."

Henry indicated his daughter with a gesture.

"Rot! The kid's got to stand in on this," Monkley said, with a laugh. "After all, it was he who introduced us. I'll bring her up here to talk it out," he added.

Presently he returned with Maudie, who had very red eyes and a frightened expression.

"Oh, Jimmy!" she burst out. "Whatever did you want to take that jewelry for? I only found out last night, and they'll be home to-morrow. Whatever am I going to say?"

"Jewelry?" repeated Monkley, in a puzzled voice. "Harry took some hair-wash, if that's what you mean."

"Jewelry?" Henry murmured, taking the cue from his friend. "Was there any jewelry?"

18

"Oh, don't pretend you don't know nothing about it," Maudie cried, dissolving into tears. "For the love of God give it to me, so as I can put it back. If you're hard up, Jimmy, you can take what I saved for the stage; but give us back that jewelry."

"If you act like that you'll make your fortune as a professional," Monkley sneered.

Maudie turned to Sylvia in desperation. "Sil," she cried, "make them give it back. It'll be the ruin of me. Why, it's burglary! Oh, whatever shall I do?"

Maudie flung herself down on the bed and wept convulsively. Sylvia felt her heart beating fast, but she strung herself up to the encounter and faced Monkley.

"What's the good of saying you haven't got the jewelry," she cried, "when you know you have? Give it to her or I'll—I'll go out into the middle of the road and shout at the top of my voice that there's a snake in the house, and people will have to come in and look for it, because when they didn't believe about the baboon in Mrs. Meares's room the baboon was there all the time."

She stopped and challenged Monkley with flashing eyes, head thrown back, and agitated breast.

"You oughtn't to talk to a grown-up person like that, you know," said her father.

Something unspeakably soft in his attitude infuriated Sylvia, and spinning round she flashed out at him:

"If you don't make Monkley give back the things you stole I'll tell everybody about *you*. I mean it. I'll tell everybody." She stamped her feet.

"That's a daughter," said Henry. "That's the way they're bringing them up nowadays—to turn round on their fathers."

"A daughter?" Monkley echoed, with an odd look at his friend.

"I mean son," said Henry, weakly. "Anyway, it's all the same."

Monkley seemed to pay no more attention to the slip, but went over to Maudie and began to coax her.

"Come on, Maudie, don't turn away from a good pal. What if we did take a few things? They shouldn't have left them behind. People deserve to lose things if they're so careless."

"That's quite true," Henry agreed, virtuously. "It'll be a lesson to them."

"Go back and pack up your things, my dear, and get out of the house. I'll see you through. You shall take another name and go on the stage right away. What's the good of crying over a few rings and bangles?"

But Maudie refused to be comforted. "Give them back to me. Give them back to me," she moaned.

"Oh, all right," Monkley said, suddenly. "But you're no sport, Maudie. You've got the chance of your life and you're turning it down. Well, don't blame me if you find yourself still a slavey five years hence."

Monkley went down-stairs and came back again in a minute or two with a parcel wrapped up in tissue-paper.

"You haven't kept anything back?" Maudie asked, anxiously.

"My dear girl, you ought to know how many there were. Count them."

"Would you like me to give you back the hair-wash?" Henry asked, indignantly.

Maudie rose to go away.

"You're not angry with me, Jim?" she asked, pleadingly.

"Oh, get out!" he snapped.

Maudie turned pale and rushed from the room.

"Silly b——h," Monkley said. "Well, it's been a very instructive morning," he added, fixing Sylvia with his green eyes and making her feel uncomfortable.

"Some people make a fuss about the least little thing," Henry said. "There was just the same trouble when I pawned my wife's jewelry. Coming round the corner to have one?" he inquired, looking at Monkley, who said he would join him presently and followed him out of the room.

When she was alone, Sylvia tried to put her emotions in order, without success. She had wished for excitement, but, now that it had arrived, she wished it had kept away from her. She was not so much shocked by the revelation of what her father and Monkley had done (though she resented their cowardly treatment of Maudie), as frightened by what might ultimately happen to her in their company. They might at any moment find themselves in prison, and if she were to be let out before the others, what would she do? She would be utterly alone and would starve; or, what seemed more likely, they would be arrested and she would remain in Lillie Road, waiting for news and perhaps compelled to earn her living by working for Mrs. Meares. At all costs she must be kept informed of what was going on. If her father tried to shut her out of his confidence, she would appeal to Monkley. Her meditation was interrupted by Monkley himself.

"So you're a little girl," he said, suddenly. "Fancy that."

"What if I am?" challenged Sylvia, who saw no hope of successfully denying the accusation.

"Oh, I don't know," Monkley murmured. "It's more fun, that's all. But, look here, girl or boy, don't let me ever have any more heroics from you. D'ye hear? Or, by God! I'll—"

Sylvia felt that the only way of dealing with Monkley was to stand up to him from the first.

"Oh, shut up!" she broke in. "You can't frighten me. Next time, perhaps you'll tell me beforehand what you're going to do, and then I'll see if I'll let you do it."

He began to laugh. "You've got some pluck."

"Why?"

"Why, to cheek me like that."

"I'm not Maudie, you see," Sylvia pointed out.

Presently a spasm of self-consciousness made her long to be once more in petticoats, and, grabbing wildly at her flying boyhood, she said how much she wanted to have adventures. Monkley promised she should have as many as she liked, and bade her farewell, saying that he was going to join her father in a saloon bar round the corner. Sylvia volunteered to accompany him, and after a momentary hesitation he agreed to take her. On the stairs they overtook the baron, very much dressed up, who, in answer to an inquiry from Monkley, informed them that he was going to lunch with the Emperor of Byzantium.

"Give my love to the Empress," Monkley laughed.

"It's-s nothing to laugh at," the baron said, severely. "He lives in West Kensington."

"Next door to the Pope, I suppose," Monkley went on.

"You never will be serious, but I'll take you there one afternoon, if you don't believe me."

The baron continued on his way down-stairs with a kind of mincing dignity, and Mrs. Meares came out of her bedroom.

"Isn't it nice for the dear baron?" she purred. "He's received some of his money from Berlin, and at last he can go and look up his old friends. He's lunching with the Emperor to-day."

"I hope he won't drop his crown in the soup," Monkley said.

"Ah, give over laughing, Mr. Monkley, for I like to think of the poor baron in the society to which he belongs. And he doesn't forget his old friends. But there, after all, why would he, for, though I'm living in Lillie Road, I've got the real spirit of the past in my blood, and the idea of meeting the Emperor doesn't elate me at all. It seems somehow as if I were used to meeting emperors."

On the way to the public house Monkley held forth to Sylvia on the prevalence of human folly, and vowed that he would hold the baron to his promise and visit the Emperor himself.

"And take me with you?" Sylvia asked.

"You seem very keen on the new partnership," he observed.

"I don't want to be left out of things," she explained. "Not out of anything. It makes me look stupid. Father treats me like a little girl; but it's he who's stupid, really."

They had reached the public house, and Henry was taken aback by Sylvia's arrival. She, for her part, was rather disappointed in the saloon bar. The words had conjured something much more sumptuous than this place that reminded her of a chemist's shop.

"I don't want the boy to start learning to drink," Henry protested.

Monkley told him to give up the fiction of Sylvia's boyhood with him, to which Henry replied that, though, as far as he knew, he had only been sitting here ten minutes, Jimmy and Sylvia seemed to have settled the whole world between them in that time.

"What's more, if she's going to remain a boy any longer, she's got to have some new clothes," Monkley announced.

Sylvia flushed with pleasure, recognizing that cooperative action of which preliminary dressing-up was the pledge.

"You see, I've promised to take her round with me to the Emperor of Byzantium."

"I don't know that pub," said Henry. "Is it Walham Green way?"

Monkley told him about meeting the baron, and put forward his theory that people who were willing to be duped by the Emperor of Byzantium would be equally willing to be duped by other people, with much profit to the other people.

"Meaning you and me?" said Henry.

"Well, in this case I propose to leave you out of the first act," Monkley said. "I'm going to have a look at the scene myself. There's no one like you with the cards, Harry, but when it comes to the patter I think you'll give me first."

Presently, Sylvia was wearing Etons, at Monkley's suggestion, and waiting in a dream of anticipation; the baron proclaimed that the Emperor would hold a reception on the first Thursday in June. When Monkley said he wanted young Sylvester to go with them, the baron looked doubtful; but Monkley remarked that he had seen the baron coming out of a certain house in Earl's Court Road the other day, which seemed to agitate him and make him anxious for Sylvia to attend the reception.

Outside the very commonplace house in Stanmore Crescent, where the Emperor of Byzantium lived, Monkley told the baron that he did not wish anything said about Sylvester's father. Did the baron understand? He wished a certain mystery to surround Sylvester. The baron after his adventure in Earl's Court Road would appreciate the importance of secrecy.

"You are a regular devil, Monkley," said von Statten, in his most mincing voice. Remembering the saloon bar, Sylvia had made up her mind not to be disappointed if the Emperor's reception failed to be very exciting; yet on the whole she was rather impressed. To be sure, the entrance hall of 14 Stanmore Crescent was not very imperial; but a footman took their silk hats, and, though Monkley whispered that he was carrying them like flower-pots and was evidently the jobbing gardener from round the corner, Sylvia was agreeably awed, especially when they were invited to proceed to the antechamber.

"In other words, the dining-room," said Monkley to the baron.

"Hush! Don't you see the throne-room beyond?" the baron whispered.

Sure enough, opening out of the antechamber was a smaller room in which was a dais covered with purple cloth. On a high Venetian chair sat the Emperor, a young man with dark, bristling hair, in evening dress. Sylvia stood on tiptoe to get a better look at him; but there was such a crush in the entrance to the throne-room that she had to be content for the present with staring at the numerous courtiers and listening to Monkley's whispered jokes, which the baron tried in vain to stop.

"I suppose where the young man with a head like a door-mat and a face like a scraper is sitting is where the Imperial family congregates after dinner. I'd like to see what's under that purple cloth. Packing-cases, I'll bet a quid."

"Hush! hush! not so loud," the baron implored. "Here's Captain Grayrigg, the Emperor's father."

He pointed to a very small man with pouched eyes and a close-cropped pointed beard.

"Do you mean to tell me the Emperor hasn't made his father a field-marshal? He ought to be ashamed of himself."

"My dear man, Captain Grayrigg married the late Empress. He is nothing himself."

"I suppose he has to knock the packing-cases together and pay for the ices."

But the baron had pressed forward to meet Captain Grayrigg and did not answer. Presently he came back very officiously and beckoned to Monkley, whom he introduced.

"From New York City, Colonel," said Monkley, with a quick glance at the baron.

Sylvia nearly laughed, because Jimmy was talking through his nose in the most extraordinary way.

"Ah! an American," said Captain Grayrigg. "Then I expect this sort of thing strikes you as quite ridiculous."

"Why, no, Colonel. Between ourselves I may as well tell you I'm over here myself on a job not unconnected with royalty."

Monkley indicated Sylvia with a significant look.

"This little French boy who is called Master Sylvestre at present may be heard of later."

Jimmy had accentuated her nationality. Sylvia, quick enough to see what he wanted her to do, replied in French.

A tall young man with an olive complexion and priestly gestures, standing close by, pricked up his ears at Monkley's remark. When Captain Grayrigg had retired he came forward and introduced himself as the Prince de Condé.

Monkley seemed to be sizing up the prince; then abruptly with an air of great cordiality he took his arm.

"Say, Prince, let's go and find an ice. I guess you're the man I've been looking for ever since I landed in England."

They moved off together to find refreshment. Sylvia was left in the antechamber, which was filled with a most extraordinary crowd of people. There were young men with very pink cheeks who all wore white roses or white carnations in their buttonholes; there was a battered-looking woman with a wreath of laurel in her hair who suddenly began to declaim in a wailful voice. Everybody said, "Hush," and tried to avoid catching his neighbor's eye. At first, Sylvia decided that the lady must be a lunatic whom people had to humor, because her remarks had nothing to do with the reception and were not even intelligible; then she decided that she was a ventriloquist who was imitating a cat. An old gentleman in kilts was standing near her, and Sylvia remembered that once in France she had seen somebody dressed like that, who had danced in a tent; this lent color to the theory of their both being entertainers. The old gentleman asked the baron if he had the Gaelic, and the baron said he had not; whereupon the old gentleman sniffed very loudly, which made Sylvia feel rather uncomfortable, because, though she had not eaten garlic, she had eaten onions for lunch. Presently the old gentleman moved away and she asked the baron when he was going to begin his dance; the baron told her that he was the chief of a great Scottish clan and that he always dressed like that. A clergyman with two black-and-white dogs under his arms was walking about and protesting in a high voice that he couldn't shake hands; and a lady in a Grecian tunic, standing near Sylvia, tried to explain to her in French that the dogs were descended from King Charles I. Sylvia wanted to tell her she spoke English, because she was sure something had gone wrong with the explanation, owing to the lady's French; but she did not like to do so after Jimmy's deliberate insistence upon her nationality.

Presently a very fussy woman with a long, stringy neck, bulging eyes, and arched fingers came into the antechamber and wanted to know who had not yet been presented to the Emperor. Sylvia looked round for Jimmy, but he was nowhere to be seen, and, being determined not to go away without entering the throne-room, she said loudly:

"Moi, je n'ai pas encore vu l'empereur."

"Oh, the little darling!" trilled the fussy woman. *"Venez avec moi, je vous présenterai moi-même."*

"How beautifully Miss Widgett speaks French!" somebody murmured, when Sylvia was being led into the throne-room. "It's such a gift."

Sylvia was very much impressed by a large orange flag nailed to the wall above the Emperor's throne.

"Le drapeau impériale de Byzance," Miss Widgett said. *"Voyez-vous l'aigle avec deux têtes. Il était fait pour sa majesté impériale par le Société du roi Charles I de West London."*

"King Charles again," Sylvia thought.

"Il faut baiser la main," Miss Widgett prompted. Sylvia followed out the suggestion; and the Emperor, to whom Miss Widgett had whispered a few words, said:

"Ah, vous êtes français," and to Miss Widgett, "Who did you say he was?"

"I really don't know. He came with Baron von Statten. *Comment vous appelez-vous?"* Miss Widgett asked, turning to Sylvia.

Sylvia answered that she was called Monsieur Sylvestre, and just then a most unusual squealing was heard in the antechamber.

"Mon dieu! qu'est-ce que c'est que ça?" Sylvia cried.

"C'est le—comment dit-on bagpipes *en Français? C'est le 'baagpeep' vous savez,"* which left Sylvia as wise as she was before. However, as there was no general panic, she ceased to be frightened. Soon she saw Jimmy beckoning to her from the antechamber, and shortly afterward they left the reception, which had interested Sylvia very much, though she regretted that nobody had offered her an ice.

Monkley congratulated Sylvia upon her quickness in grasping that he had wanted her to pretend she was French, and by his praise roused in her the sense of ambition, which, though at present it was nothing more than a desire to please him personally, marked, nevertheless, a step forward in the development of her character; certainly from this moment the old fear of having no one to look after her began to diminish, and though she still viewed with pleasure the prospect of being alone, she began to have a faint conception of making herself indispensable, perceiving dimly the independence that would naturally follow. Meanwhile, however gratifying Monkley's compliment, it could not compensate her for the ice she had not been given, and Sylvia made this so plain to him that he invited her into a confectioner's shop on the way home and gave her a larger ice than any she had seen at the Emperor's.

Ever since Sylvia had made friends with Jimmy Monkley, her father had adopted the attitude of being left out in the cold, which made him the worst kind of audience for an enthusiastic account of the reception. Mrs. Meares, though obviously condescending, was a more satisfactory listener, and she was able to explain to Sylvia some of the things that had puzzled her, among others the old gentleman's remark about Gaelic.

"This keeping up of old customs and ceremonies in our degenerate days is most commendable," said Mrs. Meares. "I wish I could be doing more in that line here, but Lillie Road does not lend itself to the antique and picturesque; Mr. Morgan, too, gets so impatient even if Clara only hums at her work that I don't like to ask that Scotchman to come and play his bagpipes here, though I dare say he should be only too glad to do so for a shilling. No, my dear boy, I don't mean the gentleman you met at the Emperor's. There is a poor man who plays in the street round here from time to time and dances a sword dance. But the English have no idea of beauty or freedom. I remember last time I saw him the poor man was being moved on for obstructing the traffic."

Clara put forward a theory that the reception had been a church treat. There had been a similar affair in her own parish once, in which the leading scholars of the Sunday-school classes had portrayed the kings and queens of England. She herself had been one of the little princes who were smothered in the Tower, and had worn a pair of her mother's stockings. There had been trouble, she remembered, because the other little prince had been laced up so tightly that he was sick over the pillow that was wanted to stuff out the boy who was representing Henry VIII and could not be used at the last moment.

Sylvia assured her that nothing like this had taken place at the Emperor's, but Clara remained unconvinced.

A week or two passed. The reception was almost forgotten, when one day Sylvia found the dark-complexioned young man with whom Monkley had made friends talking earnestly to him and her father.

"You understand," he was saying. "I wouldn't do this if I didn't require money for my work. You must not look upon me as a pretender. I really am the only surviving descendant in the direct line of the famous Prince de Condé."

"Of course," Monkley answered. "I know you're genuine enough. All you've got to do is to back—Well, here he is," he added, turning round and pointing to Sylvia.

"I don't think Sil looks much like a king," Henry said, pensively. "Though I'm bound to say the only one I ever saw in real life was Leopold of Belgium."

Sylvia began to think that Clara had been right, after all.

"What about the present King of Spain, then?" Monkley asked. "He isn't much more than nine years old, if he's as much. You don't suppose he looks like a king, do you? On the Spanish stamps he looks more like an advertisement for Mellin's food than anything else."

"Naturally the *de jure* King of Spain, who until the present has been considered to be Don Carlos, is also the *de jure* King of France," said the Prince de Condé.

"Don't you start any of your games with kings of France," Henry advised. "I know the French well and they won't stand it. What does he want to be king of two places for? I should have thought Spain was enough for anybody."

"The divine right of monarchs is something greater than mere geography," the Prince answered, scornfully.

"All right. Have it your own way. You're the authority here on kings. But don't overdo it. That's all I advise," Henry said, finally. "I know everybody thinks I'm wrong nowadays," he added, with a glance at Monkley and Sylvia. "But what about Condy's Fluid?"

"What about it?" Monkley asked. "What do you want Condy's for?"

"I don't want it," said Henry. "I simply passed the remark. Our friend here is the Prince de Condé. Well, I merely remark 'What about Condy's Fluid?' I don't want to start an argument, because, as I said, I'm always wrong nowadays, but I think if he wanted to be a prince he ought to have chosen a more *recherché* title, not gone routing about among patent medicines."

The Prince de Condé looked inquiringly at Monkley.

"Don't you bother about him, old chap. He's gone off at the deep end."

"I knew it," Henry said. "I knew I should be wrong. That's right, laugh away," he added, bitterly, to Sylvia.

There followed a long explanation by the prince of Sylvia's royal descent, which she could not understand at all. Monkley, however, seemed to be understanding it very well, so well that her father gave up being offended and loudly expressed his admiration for Jimmy's grip of the subject.

"Now," said Monkley, "the question is who are we going to touch?"

The prince asked if he had noticed at the reception a young man, a rather good-looking, fair young man with a white rose in his buttonhole. Monkley said that most of the young men he had seen in Stanmore Crescent would answer to that description, and the prince gave up trying to describe him except as the only son of a wealthy and distinguished painter—Sir Francis Hurndale. It seemed that young Godfrey Hurndale could always command the paternal purse; and the prince suggested that a letter should be sent to his father from the secretary of the *de jure* King of Spain and France, offering him the post of court painter on his accession. Monkley objected that a man who had made money out of painting would not be taken in by so transparent a fraud as that; and the prince explained that Sir Francis would only be amused, but that he would certainly pass the letter on to his son, who was an enthusiastic Legitimist; that the son would consult him, the Prince de Condé; and that afterward it lay with Monkley to make the most of the situation, bearing in mind that he, the prince, required a fair share of the profits in order to advance his great propaganda for a universal Platonic system of government.

"At present," the prince proclaimed, becoming more and more sacerdotal as he spoke of his scheme—"at present I am a lay member of the Society of Jesus, which represents the Platonic tendency in modern thought. I am vowed to exterminate republicanism, anarchy, socialism, and to maintain the conservative instincts of humanity against—"

"Well, nobody's going to quarrel with you about spending your own money," Monkley interrupted.

"He can give it to the Salvation Army if he likes," Henry agreed.

The discussion of the more practical aspects of the plan went on for several days. Ultimately it was decided to leave Lillie Road as a first step and take a small house in a suburb; to Sylvia's great delight, for she was tired of the mustiness of Lillie Road, they moved to Rosemary Avenue, Streatham. It was a newly built house and it was all their own, with the Common at one end of the road, and, better still, a back garden. Sylvia had never lived where she had been able to walk out of her own door to her own patch of green; moreover she thoroughly enjoyed the game of being an exiled king that might be kidnapped by his foes at any moment. To be sure, there were disadvantages; for instance, she was not allowed to cultivate an acquaintanceship with the two freckled girls next door on their right, nor with the boy who had an air-gun on their left; but generally the game was amusing, especially when her father became the faithful old French servant, who had guarded her all these years, until Mr. James Monkley, the enthusiastic American amateur of genealogy, had discovered the little king hidden away in the old servant's cottage. Henry objected to being ordered about by his own daughter, but his objections were overruled by Jimmy, and Sylvia gave him no rest.

"That damned Condé says he's a lay Jesuit," Henry grumbled. "But what am I? A lay figure. I suppose you wouldn't like me to sleep in a kennel in the back yard?" he asked. "Another thing I can't understand is why on earth you had to be an American, Jimmy."

Monkley told Henry of his sudden impulse to be an American at the Emperor's reception.

"Never give way to impulse," Henry said. "You're not a bit like an American. You'll get a nasty growth in your nose or strain it or something. Americans may talk through the nose a bit; but you make a noise like a cat that's had its tail shut in a door. It's like living in a Punch and Judy show. It may not damage your nose, but it's very bad for my ears, old man. It's all very fine for me to be a French servant. I can speak French; though I don't look like the servant part of it. But you can't speak American, and if you go on trying much harder you very soon won't be able to speak any language at all. I noticed to-day, when you started talking to the furniture fellow, he looked very uneasy. I think he thought he was sitting on a concertina."

"Anyway, he cleared off without getting this month's instalment," Monkley said.

"Oh, it's a very good voice to have when there are duns kicking around," Henry said. "Or in a crowded railway carriage. But as a voice to live with, it's rotten. However, don't listen to me. My advice doesn't count nowadays. Only," and Henry paused impressively, "when people advise you to try linseed oil for your boots as soon as you start talking to them, then don't say I didn't warn you."

Notwithstanding Henry's pessimism, Monkley continued to practise his American; day by day the task of imposing Sylvia on the world as the King of Spain and France was being carefully prepared, too carefully, it seemed to Sylvia, for so much talk beforehand was becoming tiresome. The long delay was chiefly due to Henry's inability to keep in his head the numerous genealogical facts that were crammed down his throat by the Prince de Condé.

"I never was any good at history even when I was a boy," Henry protested. "Never. And I was never good at working out cousins and aunts. I know I had two aunts, and hated them both."

At last Henry's facts were considered firmly enough implanted to justify a move; and in September the prince and Monkley sat down to compose their preliminary letter to Sir Francis Hurndale. Sylvia by now was so much accustomed to the behavior of her companions that she never thought seriously about the fantastic side of the affair. Her own masquerade as a boy had been passed off so successfully even upon such an acute observer as Jimmy, until her father had let out the secret by a slip of the tongue, that she had no qualms about being accepted as a king. She realized that money was to be made out of it; but the absence of money had already come to seem a temporary discomfort, to relieve which people in a position like her own and her father's had no reason to be scrupulous. Not that she really ever bothered her head with the morality of financial ways and means. When she spent the ten-franc piece that she thought she had found, the wrong had lain in unwittingly depriving her mother whom she loved; if she had not loved her mother she might have still had scruples about stealing from her; but stealing from people who had plenty of money and with whom there was no binding link of affection would have been quite incomprehensible to her. Therefore the sight of Jimmy Monkley and her father and the Prince de Condé sitting round a spindle-legged tea-table in this new house that smelled pleasantly of varnish was merely something in a day's work of the life they were leading, like a game of cards. It was a much jollier life than any she had yet known; her alliance with Jimmy had been a very good move; her father was treated as he ought to be treated by being kept under; she was shortly going to have some more clothes.

Sylvia sat watching the trio, thinking how much more vividly present Jimmy seemed to be than either of the other two—the prince with his greenish complexion never really well shaved, and his turn-down collars that made his black suit more melancholy, or her father with his light, plaintive eyes and big ears. She was glad that she was not going to resemble her father except perhaps in being short and in the shape of her wide nose; yet she was not really very short; it was only that her mother had been so tall; perhaps, too, when her hair grew long again her nose would not seem so wide.

23

The letter was finished and Jimmy was reading it aloud:

SIR,—I have the honor to ask if, in the probable event of a great dynastic change taking place in one of the chief countries of Europe, you would welcome the post of court painter, naturally at a suitable remuneration. If you read the daily papers, as no doubt you do, you will certainly have come to the conclusion that neither the present ruling house nor what is known as the Carlist party had any real hold upon the affections of the Spanish people. Verb. sap. Interesting changes may be foreshadowed, of which I am not yet at liberty to write more fully. Should you entertain the proposal I shall be happy to wait upon you with further particulars.

I have the honor to be, sir,
Your obedient servant,
JOSEPHE-ERNESTE,
PRINCE DE CONDÉ.

"Do you know what it sounds like?" said Henry. "Mind I'm not saying this because I didn't write the letter myself. It sounds to me like a cross between a prophecy in Old Moore's Almanack and somebody trying to sell a patent knife-cleaner."

"There's a good deal in what you say," Monkley agreed, in rather a dissatisfied tone.

Henry was so much flattered by the reception of his criticism that he became compassionate to the faults of the letter and tried hard to point out some of its merits.

"After all," said Jimmy, "the great thing is that the prince has signed it. If his name doesn't draw Master Godfrey, no letters are going to. We'll send it off as it is."

So the letter was sent. Two days afterward the prince arrived with the news that Godfrey Hurndale had called upon him and that he had been inexpressibly happy at the prospect of meeting the *de jure* King of France and Spain.

"Bring him round to-morrow afternoon about tea-time," said Monkley. "You haven't forgotten the family history, Henry?"

Henry said that he had not forgotten a single relation, and that he damned them severally each morning in all their titles while he was dressing.

The next afternoon Sylvia sat in an arm-chair in the presence-room, which Henry supposed was so called because none of the furniture had been paid for, and waited for Godfrey Hurndale's coming. Her father put on the rusty black evening-dress of the family retainer, and Jimmy wore a most conspicuous check suit and talked so loudly and nasally that Henry was driven to a final protest:

"Look here, Jimmy, I've dressed up to help this show in a suit that's as old as one of those infernal ancestors of Sil's, but if you don't get less American it'll fall to pieces. Every time you guess I can hear a seam give."

"Remember to talk nothing but French," Monkley warned Sylvia, when the bell rang. "Go on, Harry. You've got to open the door. And don't forget that *you* can only speak French."

Monkley followed him out of the room, and his voice could be heard clanking about the hall as he invited young Hurndale into the dining-room first. Henry came back and took up his position behind Sylvia's chair; she felt very solemn and excited, and asked her father rather irritably why he was muttering. The reason, however, remained a mystery, for the dining-room door opened again and, heralded by Monkley's twanging invitation, Mr. Hurndale stood shyly in the entrance to the presence-room.

"Go right in, Mr. Hurndale," Monkley said. "I guess his Majesty's just about ready to meet you."

Sylvia, when she saw the young man bowing before her, really felt a kind of royal exaltation and held out her hand to be kissed.

Hurndale reverently bent over it and touched it with his lips; so did the prince, an action for which Sylvia was unprepared and which she rather resented, thinking to herself that he really did not shave and that it had not only been his grubby appearance. Then Hurndale offered her a large bunch of white carnations and she became kingly again.

"*François,*" she commanded her father, "*mets ces œillets dans ma chambre.*"

And when her father passed out with a bow Sylvia was indeed a king. The audience did not last long. There were practical matters to discuss, for which his Majesty was begged to excuse their withdrawal. Sylvia would have liked a longer ceremony. When the visitor had gone they all sat down to a big tea in the presence-room, and she was told that the young man had been so completely conquered by her gracious reception of him that he had promised to raise five hundred pounds for her cause. His reward in addition to royal favors was to be a high class of the Order of Isabella the Catholic. Everybody, even Henry, was in high good humor. The prince did not come to Streatham again; but a week later Monkley got a letter from him with the Paris postmark.

DEAR MR. MONKLEY,—Our young friend handed me a check for £200 the day before yesterday. As he seemed uncertain about the remainder of the sum promised, I took the liberty of drawing my share at once. My great work requires immediate assistance, and I am now busily occupied in Paris. My next address will be a castle in Spain, where perhaps we shall meet when you are looking for your next site.

Most truly yours,
JOSEPHE-ERNESTE,
PRINCE DE CONDÉ.

Jimmy and Henry stared at each other.

"I knew it," said Henry. "I'm always wrong; but I knew it. Still, if I could catch him, it would take more than Condy's Fluid to disinfect that pea-green welsher after I'd done with him."

Monkley sat biting his lips in silence; and Sylvia, recognizing the expression in his eyes that she dreaded formerly, notwithstanding that he was now her best friend, felt sharply her old repugnance for him. Henry was still abusing the defaulter when Monkley cut him short.

"Shut up. I rather admire him."

"Admire him?" Henry gasped. "I suppose you'd admire the hangman and shake hands with him on the scaffold. It's all very fine for you. You didn't have to learn how Ferdinand the Fifty-eighth married Isabella the Innocent, daughter of Alphonso the Eighth, commonly called Alphonso the Anxious. Condy's Fluid! I swallowed enough of it, I can tell you."

Monkley told him gruffly to keep quiet; then he sat down and began to write, still with that expression in his eyes. Presently he tore up the letter and paced the room.

"Damn that swine," he suddenly shouted, kicking the spindle-legged table into the fireplace. "We wanted the money, you know. We wanted the money badly."

Shortly before dawn the three of them abandoned the new house in Streatham and occupied rooms in the Kennington Park Road. Monkley and Sylvia's father resumed the racing that had temporarily been interrupted by ambition. Sylvia wandered about the streets in a suit of Etons that was rapidly showing signs of wear.

One day early in the new year Sylvia was leaning over the parapet of Waterloo Bridge and munching hot chestnuts. The warmth of them in her pockets was grateful. Her pastime of dropping the shells into the river did not lack interest; she was vaguely conscious in the frosty sunshine of life's bounty, and she offered to the future a welcome from the depths of her being; meanwhile there still remained forty chestnuts to be eaten.

Her meditation was interrupted by a voice from a passerby who had detached himself from the stream of traffic that she had been disregarding in her pensive greed; she looked up and met the glance of a pleasant middle-aged gentleman in a dark-gray coat with collar and cuffs of chinchilla, who was evidently anxious to begin a conversation.

"You're out of school early," he observed.

Sylvia replied that she did not go to school.

"Private tutor?" he asked; and, partly to save further questions about her education, partly because she was not quite sure what a private tutor was, she answered in the affirmative.

The stranger looked along the parapet inquisitively.

"I'm out alone this afternoon," Sylvia said, quickly.

The stranger asked her what amused her most, museums or theaters or listening to bands, and whether she preferred games or country walks. Sylvia would have liked to tell him that she preferred eating chestnuts to anything else on earth at that moment; but, being unwilling to create an impression of trying to snub such a benevolent person, she replied vaguely that she did not know what she liked best. Then because such an answer seemed to imply a lack of intelligence that she did not wish to impute to herself, she informed him that she liked looking at people, which was strictly true, for if she had not been eating chestnuts she would certainly have still been contemplating the traffic across the bridge.

"I'll show you some interesting people, if you care to come with me," the stranger proposed. "Have you anything to do this afternoon?"

Sylvia admitted that her time was unoccupied.

"Come along, then," said the middle-aged gentleman, a little fussily, she thought, and forthwith he hailed a passing hansom. Sylvia had for a long time been ambitious to travel in a hansom. She had already eaten thirty-five chestnuts, only seven of which had been bad; she decided to accept the stranger's invitation. He asked her where she lived and promised to send her home by cab when the entertainment was over.

Sylvia asked if it was a reception to which he was taking her. The middle-aged gentleman laughed, squeezed her hand, and said that it might be called a reception, adding, with a chuckle, "a very warm reception, in fact." Sylvia did not understand the joke, but laughed out of politeness.

There followed an exchange of names, and Sylvia learnt that her new acquaintance was called Corydon.

"You'll excuse me from offering you one of my cards," he said. "I haven't one with me this afternoon."

They drove along for some time, during which the conversation of Mr. Corydon always pursued the subject of her likes and dislikes. They drew clear of the press of traffic and bowled westward toward Sloane Street; Sylvia, recognizing one of the blue West Kensington omnibuses, began to wonder if the cab would take her past Lillie Road where Jimmy had specially forbidden her to go, because both he and her father owed several weeks' rent to Mrs. Meares and he did not want to remind her of their existence. When they drew nearer and nearer to Sylvia's former lodging she began to feel rather uneasy and wish that the cab would turn down a side-street. The landmarks were becoming more and more familiar, and Sylvia was asking herself if Mrs. Meares had employed the stranger to kidnap her as a hostage for the unpaid rent, when the cab turned off into Redcliffe Gardens and soon afterward pulled up at a house.

"Here we are," said Mr. Corydon. "You'll enjoy yourself most tremendously, Sylvester."

The door was opened by a servant, who was apparently dressed as a brigand, which puzzled Sylvia so much that she asked the reason in a whisper. Mr. Corydon laughed.

"He's a Venetian. That's the costume of a gondolier, my dear boy. My friend who is giving the reception dresses all his servants like gondoliers. So much more picturesque than a horrible housemaid."

Sylvia regarded this exotic Clara with considerable interest; the only other Venetian product of which she had hitherto been aware was blinds.

25

The house, which smelt strongly of incense and watered flowers, awed Sylvia with its luxury, and she began to regret having put foot in a place where it was so difficult to know on what she was intended to tread. However, since Mr. Corydon seemed to walk everywhere without regard for the softness of the carpets, Sylvia made up her mind to brave the silent criticism of the gondolier and follow up-stairs in his footsteps. Mr. Corydon took her arm and introduced her to a large room where a fume of cigarette smoke and incense blurred the outlines of the numerous guests that sat about in listening groups, while some one played the grand piano. There were many low divans round the room, to one of which Mr. Corydon guided Sylvia, and while the music continued she had an opportunity of studying her fellow-guests. They were mostly young men of about eighteen, rather like the young men at the Emperor's reception; but there were also several middle-aged men of the same type as Mr. Corydon, one of whom came across and shook hands with them both when the music stopped.

"So glad you've come to see me," he said in a voice that sounded as if each word were being delicately fried upon his tongue. "Aren't you going to smoke a cigarette? These are Russian. Aren't they beautiful to look at?"

He proffered a green cigarette-case. Sylvia, who felt that she must take advantage of this opportunity to learn something about a sphere of life which was new to her, asked him what it was made of.

"Jade, my dear. I brought such heaps of beautiful jade back with me from China. I've even got a jade toilet-set. My dear, it was dreadfully expensive."

He giggled. Sylvia, blowing clouds of smoke from her cigarette, thought dreamily what funny things her father would have said about him.

"Raymond's going to dance for us," he said, turning to Corydon. "Isn't it too sweet of him?"

At that moment somebody leaped into the middle of the room with a wild scream and began to throw himself into all sorts of extraordinary attitudes.

"Oh, Raymond, you're too wonderful!" the host ejaculated. "You make me feel quite Bacchic."

Sylvia was not surprised that anybody should feel "backache" (she had thus understood her host) in the presence of such contortions. The screaming Raymond was followed into the arena by another lightly clad and equally shrill youth called Sydney, and both of them flung themselves into a choric frenzy, chasing each other round and round, sawing the air with their legs, and tearing roses from their hair to fling at the guests, who flung them back at the dancers. Suddenly Raymond collapsed upon the carpet and began to moan.

"What's the matter, my dear?" cried the host, rushing forward and kneeling to support the apparently agonized youth in his arms.

"Oh, my foot!" Raymond wailed. "I've trodden on something."

"He's trodden on a thorn. He's trodden on a thorn," everybody said at once.

Raymond was borne tenderly to a divan, and was so much petted that Sydney became jealous and began to dance again, this time on the top of the piano. Presently everybody else began to dance, and Mr. Corydon would have liked to dance with Sylvia; but she declined. Gondoliers entered with trays of liqueurs, and Sylvia, tasting crème de menthe for the first time, found it so good that she drank four glasses, which made her feel rather drowsy. New guests were continually arriving, to whom she did not pay much attention until suddenly she recognized the baron with Godfrey Hurndale, who at the same moment recognized her. The baron rushed forward and seized Sylvia's arm. She thought he was going to drag her back by force to Mrs. Meares to answer for the missing rent, but he began to arch his unoccupied arm like an excited swan, and call out in his high, mincing voice:

"Blackmailers-s-s! blackmailers-s-s!"

"They blackmailed me out of four hundred pounds," said Hurndale.

"Who brought him here?" the baron cried. "It's-s-s true. Godfrey has been persecuted by these horrid people. Blackmailers-s-s!"

All the other guests gathered round Sylvia and behaved like angry women trying to mount an omnibus. Mr. Corydon had turned very pale and was counting his visiting-cards. Sylvia could not understand the reason for all this noise; but vaguely through a green mist of crème de menthe she understood that she was being attacked on all sides and began to get annoyed. Somebody pinched her arm, and without waiting to see who it was she hit the nearest person within reach, who happened to be Mr. Corydon. His visiting-cards fell on the floor, and he groveled on the carpet trying to sweep them together. Sylvia followed her attack on Mr. Corydon by treading hard on Sydney's bare toes, who thereupon slapped her face; presently everybody was pushing her and pinching her and hustling her, until she got in such a rage and kicked so furiously that her enemies retired.

"Who brought him here?" Godfrey Hurndale was demanding. "I tell you he belongs to a gang of blackmailers."

"Most dreadful people," the baron echoed.

"Antonio! Domenico!" the host cried.

Two gondoliers entered the room, and at a word from their master they seized Sylvia and pushed her out into the street, flinging her coat and cap after her. By this time she was in a blind fury, and, snatching the bag of chestnuts from her pocket, she flung it with all her force at the nearest window and knew the divine relief of starring the pane.

An old lady that was passing stopped and held up her hands.

"You wicked young rascal, I shall tell the policeman of you," she gasped, and began to belabor Sylvia with her umbrella.

Such unwarrantable interference was not to be tolerated; Sylvia pushed the old lady so hard that she sat down heavily in the gutter. Nobody else was in sight, and she ran as fast as she could until she found an omnibus, in which she traveled to Waterloo Bridge. There she bought fifty more chestnuts and walked slowly back to Kennington Park Road, vainly trying to find an explanation of the afternoon's adventure.

Her father and Monkley were not back when Sylvia reached home, and she sat by the fire in the twilight, munching her chestnuts and pondering the whole extraordinary business. When the others came in she told her story, and Jimmy looked meaningly at her father.

"Shows how careful you ought to be," he said. Then turning to Sylvia, he asked her what on earth she thought she was doing when she broke the window.

"Suppose you'd been collared by the police, you little fool. We should have got into a nice mess, thanks to you. Look here, in future you're not to speak to people in the street. Do you hear?"

Sylvia had no chestnuts left to throw at Jimmy, so in her rage she took an ornament from the mantelpiece and smashed it on the fender.

"You've got the breaking mania," said Henry. "You'd better spend the next money you've got on cocoanuts instead of chestnuts."

"*Oh, ta gueule!* I'm not going to be a boy any longer."

CHAPTER III

WHILE her hair was growing long again Sylvia developed a taste for reading. She had nothing else to do, for it was not to be supposed that with her head cropped close she could show herself to the world in petticoats. Her refusal any longer to wear male attire gave Monkley and her father an excuse to make one of their hurried moves from Kennington Park Road, where by this time they owed enough money to justify the trouble of evading payment. Henry had for some time expressed a desire to be more central; and a partially furnished top floor was found in Fitzroy Street, or, as the landlord preferred to call it, a self-contained and well-appointed flat. The top floor had certainly been separated from the rest of the house by a wooden partition and a door of its own, which possibly justified the first half of the description, but the good appointments were limited to a bath that looked like an old palette, and a geyser that was not always safe according to Mrs. Bullwinkle, a decrepit charwoman, left behind by the last tenants, together with some under-linen and two jars containing a morbid growth that may formerly have been pickles.

"How d'ye mean, not safe?" Henry asked. "Is it liable to blow up?"

"It went off with a big bang last April and hasn't been lit since," the charwoman said. "But perhaps it 'll be all right now. The worst of it is I never can remember which tap you put the match to."

"You leave it alone, old lady," Henry advised. "Nobody's likely to do much bathing in here; from what I can see of it that bath gives more than it gets. What did the last people use it for—growing watercress or keeping chickens?"

"It was a very nice bath once," the charwoman said.

"Do you mean to say you've ever tried it? Go on! You're mixing it up with the font in which you were baptized. There's never been any water in this bath since the flood."

Nevertheless, however inadequately appointed, the new abode had one great advantage over any other they had known, which was a large raftered garret with windows at either end that ran the whole depth of the house. The windows at the back opened on a limitless expanse of roofs and chimneys, those in front looked across to a dancing-academy on the top floor but one of the house opposite, a view that gave perpetual pleasure to Sylvia during the long period of her seclusion.

Now that Sylvia had become herself again, her father and Monkley insisted upon her doing the housework, which, as Henry reminded her, she was perfectly able to do on account of the excellent training she had received in that respect from her mother. Sylvia perceived the logic of this and made no attempt to contest it; though she stipulated that Mrs. Bullwinkle should not be considered to be helping her.

"We don't want her," Henry protested, indignantly.

"Well, tell her not to come any more," Sylvia said.

"I've shoved her away once or twice," said Henry. "But I expect the people here before us used to give her a saucer of milk sometimes. The best way would be to go out one afternoon and tell her to light the geyser. Then perhaps when we came back she'd be gone for good."

Nevertheless, Mrs. Bullwinkle was of some service to Sylvia, for one day, when she was sadly washing down the main staircase of the house, she looked up from her handiwork and asked Sylvia, who was passing at the moment, if she would like some books to read, inviting her down-stairs to take her choice.

"Mr. Bullwinkle used to be a big reader," the charwoman said. "A very big reader. A very big reader indeed he used to be, did Mr. Bullwinkle. In those days he was caretaker at a Congregational chapel in Gospel Oak, and he used to say that reading took his mind off of religion a bit. Otherwise he'd have gone mad before he did, which was shortly after he left the chapel through an argument he had with Pastor Phillips, who wrote his name in the dust on the reading-desk, which upset my old man, because he thought it wasn't all a straightforward way of telling him that his services wasn't considered satisfactory. Yes," said Mrs. Bullwinkle, with a stertorous sniff, "he died in Bedlam, did my old man. He had a very queer mania; he thought he was inside out, and it preyed on his mind. He wouldn't never have been shut up at all if he hadn't of always been undressing himself in the street and putting on his trousers inside out to suit his complaint. They had to feed him with a chube in the end, because he would have it his mouth couldn't be got at through him being inside out. Queer fancies some people has, don't they? Oh, well, if we was all the same, it would be a dull world I suppose."

Sylvia sat up in the big garret and read through one after another of the late Mr. Bullwinkle's tattered and heterogeneous collection. She did not understand all she read; but there were few books that did not give her on one page a vivid impression, which she used to elaborate with her imagination into something that was really a more substantial experience than the book itself. The days grew longer and more sunny, and Sylvia dreamed them away, reading and thinking and watching from her window the little girls pirouette in the shadowy room opposite. Her hair was quite long now, a warm brown with many glinting strands.

In the summer Jimmy and Henry made a good deal of money by selling a number of tickets for a non-existent stand in one of the best positions on the route of the Diamond Jubilee procession; indeed they felt prosperous enough to buy for themselves and Sylvia seats in a genuine stand. Sylvia enjoyed the pageant, which seemed more like something out of a book than anything in real life. She took advantage of the temporary prosperity to ask for money to buy herself new clothes.

"Can't you see other people dressed up without wanting to go and do the same yourself?" Henry asked. "What's the matter with the frock you've got on?"

However, she talked to Monkley about it and had her own way. When she had new clothes, she used to walk about the streets again, but, though she was often accosted, she would never talk to anybody. Yet it was a dull life, really, and once she brought up the subject of getting work.

"Work!" her father exclaimed, in horror. "Good heavens! what will you think of next? First it's clothes. Now it's work. Ah, my dear girl, you ought to have had to slave for your living as I had; you wouldn't talk about work."

"Well, can I have a piano and learn to play?" Sylvia asked.

"Perhaps you'd like the band of the Grenadier Guards to come and serenade you in your bedroom while you're dressing?" Henry suggested.

"Why shouldn't she have a piano?" Monkley asked. "I'll teach her to play. Besides, I'd like a piano myself."

So the piano was obtained. Sylvia learned to play, and even to sing a little with her deep voice; and another regular caller for money was added to the already long list.

In the autumn Sylvia's father fell in love, and brought a woman to live in what was henceforth always called the flat, even by Henry, who had hitherto generally referred to it as The Hammam.

In Sylvia's opinion the advent of Mabel Bannerman had a most vitiating effect upon life in Fitzroy Street. Her father began to deteriorate immediately. His return to England and the unsurveyed life he had been leading for nearly two years had produced an expansion of his personality in every direction. He had lost the shiftless insignificance that had been his chief characteristic in France, and though he was still weak and lacking in any kind of initiative, he had acquired a quaintness of outlook and faculty for expressing it which disguised his radical futility under a veil of humor. He was always dominated by Monkley in practical matters where subordination was reasonable and beneficial, but he had been allowed to preserve his own point of view, that with the progress of time had even come to be regarded as important. When Sylvia was much younger she had always criticized her father's behavior; but, like everybody else, she had accepted her mother's leadership of the house and family as natural and inevitable, and had regarded her father as a kind of spoiled elder brother whose character was fundamentally worthless and whose relation to her mother was the only one imaginable. Now that Sylvia was older, she did not merely despise her father's weakness; she resented the shameful position which he occupied in relation to this intruder. Mabel Bannerman belonged to that full-blown intensely feminine type that by sheer excess of femininity imposes itself upon a weak man, smothering him, as it were, with her emotions and her lace, and destroying by sensuality every trait of manhood that does not directly contribute to the justification of herself. Within a week or two Henry stood for no more in the Fitzroy Street house than a dog that is alternately patted and scolded, that licks the hand of its mistress more abjectly for each new brutality, and that asks as its supreme reward permission to fawn upon her lap. Sylvia hated Mabel Bannerman; she hated her peroxide hair, she hated her full, moist lips, she hated her rounded back and her shining finger-nails spotted with white, she hated with a hatred so deep as to be forever incommunicable each blowsy charm that went to make up what was called "a fine woman"; she hated her inability ever to speak the truth; she hated the way she looked at Monkley, who should have been nothing to her; she hated the sight of her drinking tea in the morning; she hated the smell of her wardrobe and the pink ribbons which she tied to every projection in her bedroom; she hated her affectation of babyishness; she hated the way she would make Henry give money to beggars for the gratification of an impulsive and merely sensual generosity of her own; she hated her embedded garters and smooth legs.

"O God," Sylvia cried aloud to herself once, when she was leaning out of the window and looking down into Fitzroy Street, "O God, if I could only throw her into the street and see her eaten by dogs."

Monkley hated her too; that was some consolation. Now often, when he was ready for an expedition, Henry would be unable to accompany him, because Mabel was rather seedy that morning; or because Mabel wanted him to go out with her; or because Mabel complained of being left alone so much. Monkley used to look at him with a savage contempt; and Sylvia used to pray sometimes that he would get angry enough to rush into Mabel's room and pound her, where she lay so softly in her soft bed.

Mabel used to bring her friends to the flat to cheer her up, as she used to say, and when she had filled the room she had chosen as her sitting-room (the garret was not cozy enough for Mabel) with a scented mob of chattering women, she would fix upon one of them as the object of her jealousy, accusing Henry of having looked at her all the evening. There would sometimes be a scene at the moment when half the mob would cluster around Mabel to console her outraged feelings and the rest of it would hover about her rival to assure her she was guiltless. Sylvia, standing sullenly apart, would ponder the result of throwing a lighted lamp into the middle of the sickly sobbing pandemonium. The quarrel was not so bad as the inevitable reconciliation afterward, with its profuse kissing and interminable explanations that seemed like an orchestra from which Mabel emerged with a plaintive solo that was the signal for the whole scene to be lived over again in maddeningly reiterated accounts from all the women talking at once. Worse even than such evenings were those when Mabel restrained, or rather luxuriously hoarded up, her jealousy until the last visitor had departed; for then through half the night Sylvia must listen to her pouring over Henry a stream of reproaches which he would weakly try to divert by arguments or more weakly try to dam with caresses. Such methods of treatment usually ended in Mabel's dressing herself and rushing from the bedroom to leave the flat forever. Unfortunately she never carried out her threat.

"Why don't you go?" Sylvia once asked, when Mabel was standing by the door, fully dressed, with heaving breast, making no effort to turn the handle.

"These shoes hurt me," said Mabel. "He knows I can't go out in these shoes. The heartless brute!"

"If you knew those shoes hurt, why did you put them on?" Sylvia asked, scornfully.

"I was too much upset by Harry's treatment of me. Oh, whatever shall I do? I'm so miserable."

Whereupon Mabel collapsed upon the mat and wept black tears, until Henry came and tried to lift her up, begging her not to stay where she might catch cold.

"You know when a jelly won't set?" Sylvia said, when she was recounting the scene to Monkley afterward. "Well, she was just like a jelly and father simply couldn't make her stand up on the plate."

Jimmy laughed sardonically.

These continued altercations between Mabel and Henry led to altercations with their neighbors underneath, who complained of being kept awake at night. The landlord, a fiery little Jew, told them that what between the arrears of rent and the nuisance they were causing to his other tenants he would have to give them notice. Sylvia could never get any money for the purposes of housekeeping except from Jimmy, and when she wanted clothes it was always Jimmy whom she must ask.

"Let's go away," she said to him one day. "Let's leave them here together."

Monkley looked at her in surprise.

"Do you mean that?"

"Of course I mean it."

"But if we left Harry with her he'd starve and she'd leave him in a week."

"Let him starve," Sylvia cried. "He deserves to starve."

"You hard-hearted little devil," Monkley said. "After all, he is your father."

"That's what makes me hate him," Sylvia declared. "He's no right to be my father. He's no right to make me think like that of him. He must be wrong to make me feel as I do about him."

Monkley came close and took her hand. "Do you mean what you said about leaving them and going away with me?"

Sylvia looked at him, and, meeting his eyes, she shook her head. "No, of course I don't really mean it, but why can't you think of some way to stop all this? Why should we put up with it any longer? Make him turn her out into the street."

Monkley laughed. "You *are* very young, aren't you? Though I've thought once or twice lately that you seemed to be growing up."

Again Sylvia caught his eyes and felt a little afraid, not really afraid, she said to herself, but uneasy, as if somebody she could not see had suddenly opened a door behind her.

"Don't let's talk about me, anyway," she said. "Think of something to change things here."

"I'd thought of a concert-party this summer. Pierrots, you know. How d'ye think your father would do as a pierrot? He might be very funny if she'd let him be funny."

Sylvia clapped her hands. "Oh, Jimmy, it would be such fun!"

"You wouldn't mind if she came too?"

"I'd rather she didn't," Sylvia said. "But it would be different, somehow. We shouldn't be shut up with her as we are here. I'll be able to sing, won't I?"

"That was my idea."

Before Henry met Mabel he would have had a great deal to say about this concert-party; now he accepted Monkley's announcement with a dull equanimity that settled Sylvia. He received the news that he would become a pierrot just as he had received the news that, his nightgown not having been sent back that week by the laundress, he would have to continue with the one he was wearing.

Early summer passed away quickly enough in constant rehearsals. Sylvia was pleased to find that she had been right in supposing that the state of domestic affairs would be improved by Jimmy's plan. Mabel turned out to be a good singer for the kind of performance they were going to give, and the amount of emotion she put into her songs left her with less to work off on Henry, who recovered some of his old self and was often really funny, especially in his duologues with Monkley. Sylvia picked out for herself and learned a few songs, most of which were condemned as unsuitable by Jimmy. The one that she liked best and in her own opinion sang best was the "Raggle Taggle Gipsies," though the others all prophesied for it certain failure. Monkley himself played all the accompaniments and by his personality kept the whole show together; he also sang a few songs, which, although he had practically no voice, were given with such point that Sylvia felt convinced that his share in the performance would be the most popular of the lot. Shortly before they were to start on tour, which was fixed for the beginning of July, Monkley decided that they wanted another man who could really sing, and a young tenor known as Claude Raglan was invited to join the party. He was a good-looking youth, much in earnest, and with a tendency toward consumption, of which he was very proud.

"Though what there is to be proud of in losing one of your lungs I don't know. I might as well be proud because I lost a glove the other day."

Henry was severe upon Claude Raglan from the beginning. Perhaps he suspected him of admiring Mabel. There was often much tension at rehearsals on account of Henry's attitude; once, for instance, when Claude Raglan had sung "Little Dolly Daydreams" with his usual romantic fervor, Henry took a new song from his pocket and, having planted it down with a defiant snap on the music-stand, proceeded to sing:

"I'll give him Dolly Daydreams
Down where the poppies grow;
I'll give him Dolly Daydreams,
The pride of Idaho.
And if I catch him kissing her
There's sure to be some strife,
Because if he's got anything he wants to give away,
Let him come and give it to his wife."

The tenor declared that Henry's song, which was in the nature of a derogatory comment upon his own, could only have the effect of spoiling the more serious contribution.

"What of it?" Henry asked, truculently.

"It seems to me perfectly obvious," Claude said, with an effort to restrain his annoyance.

"I consider that it won't hurt your song at all," Henry declared. "In fact, I think it will improve it. In my opinion it will have a much greater success than yours. In fact, I may as well say straight out that if it weren't for my song I don't believe the audience would let you sing yours more than once. ''Cos no one's gwine ter kiss dat gal but me!'" he went on, mimicking the indignant Claude. "No wonder you've got consumption coming on! And the audience will notice there's something wrong with you, and start clearing out to avoid infection. That's where my song will come in. My song will be a tonic. Now don't start breathing at me, or you'll puncture the other lung. Let's try that last verse over again, Jimmy."

In the end, after a long discussion, during which Mabel introduced the most irrelevant arguments, Monkley decided that both songs should be sung, but with a long enough interval between them to secure Claude against the least impression that he was being laughed at.

At last the company, which called itself The Pink Pierrots, was ready to start for the South Coast. It took Monkley all his ingenuity to get out of London without paying for the dresses or the properties, but it was managed somehow; and at the beginning of July they pitched a small tent on the beach at Hastings. There were many rival companies, some of which possessed the most elaborate equipment, almost a small theater with railed-off seats and a large piano; but Sylvia envied none of these its grandeur. She thought that none was so tastefully dressed as themselves, that there was no leader so sure of keeping the attention of an audience as Jimmy was, that no tenor could bring tears to the eyes of the young women on the Marina as Claude could, that no voice could be heard farther off than Mabel's, and that no comedian could so quickly gain the sympathy of that large but unprofitable portion of an audience—the small boys—as her father could.

Sylvia enjoyed every moment of the day from the time they left their lodgings, pushing before them the portable piano in the morning sunshine, to the journey home after the last performance, which was given in a circle of rosy lantern-light within sound of the sea. They worked so hard that there was no time for quarreling except with competitors upon whose preserves they had trespassed. Mabel was so bent upon fascinating the various patrons, and Henry was so obviously a success only with the unsentimental small boys, that she never once accused him of making eyes even at a nursemaid. Sylvia was given a duet with Claude Raglan, and, whether it was that she was conscious of being envied by many of the girls in the audience or whether the sentimental tune influenced her imagination, she was certainly aware of a faint thrill of pleasure—a hardly perceptible quickening of the heart—every time that Claude took her in his arms to sing the last verse. After they had sung together for a week, Jimmy said the number was a failure and abolished it, which Sylvia thought was very unfair, because it had always been well applauded.

She grumbled to Claude about their deprivation, while they were toiling home to dinner (they were at Bournemouth now, and the weather was extremely hot), and he declared in a tragical voice that people were always jealous of him.

"It's the curse of being an artist," he announced. "Everywhere I go I meet with nothing but jealousy. I can't help having a good voice. I'm not conceited about it. I can't help the girls sending me chocolates and asking me to sign the post-cards of me which they buy. I'm not conceited about that, either. There's something about my personality that appeals to women. Perhaps it's my delicate look. I don't suppose I shall live very long, and I think that makes women sorry for me. They're quicker to see these things than men. I know Harry thinks I'm as healthy as a beefsteak. I'm positive I coughed up some blood this morning, and when I told Harry he asked me with a sneer if I'd cleaned my teeth. You're not a bit like your dad, Sylvia. There's something awfully sympathetic about you, little girl. I'm sorry Jimmy's cut out our number. He's a jolly good manager and all that, but he does not like anybody else to make a hit. Have you noticed that lately he's taken to gagging during my songs? Luckily I'm not at all easy to dry up."

Sylvia wondered why anybody like Jimmy should bother to be jealous of Claude. He was pleasant enough, of course, and he had a pretty, girlish mouth and looked very slim and attractive in his pierrot's dress; but nobody could take him seriously except the stupid girls who bought his photograph and sighed over it, when they brushed their hair in the morning.

The weather grew hotter and the hard work made them all irritable; when they got home for dinner at midday it was impossible to eat, and they used to loll about in the stuffy sitting-room, which the five of them shared in common, while the flies buzzed everywhere. It was never worth while to remove the make-up; so all their faces used to get mottled with pale streaks of perspiration, the rouge on their lips would cake, and their ruffles hung limp and wet, stained round the neck with dirty carmine. Sylvia lost all enjoyment in the tour, and used to lie on the horsehair sofa that pricked her cheeks, watching distastefully the cold mutton, the dull knives, and the spotted cloth, and the stewed fruit over which lay a faint silvery film of staleness. Round the room her fellow-mountebanks were still seated on the chairs into which they had first collapsed when they reached the lodgings, motionless, like great painted dolls.

The weather grew hotter. The men, particularly Henry, took to drinking brandy at every opportunity; toward the end of their stay in Bournemouth the quarrels between him and Mabel broke out again, but with a difference, because now it was Henry who was the aggressor. He had never objected to Mabel's admirers hitherto, had, indeed, been rather proud of their existence in a fatuous way and derived from their numbers a showman's satisfaction. When it was her turn to take round the hat, he used to smirk over the quantity of post-cards she sold of herself and call everybody's attention to her capricious autography that was so successful with the callow following. Then suddenly one day he made an angry protest against the admiration which an older man began to accord her, a pretentious sort of man with a diamond ring and yellow cummerbund, who used to stand with his straw hat atilt and wink at Mabel, tugging at his big drooping mustache and jingling the money in his pockets.

Everybody told Henry not to be foolish; he only sulked and began to drink more brandy than ever. The day after Henry's outbreak, the Pink Pierrots moved to Swanage, where their only rivals were a troupe of niggers, upon whom Henry was able to loose some of his spleen in a dispute that took place over the new-comers' right to plant their pink tent where they did.

"This isn't Africa, you know," Henry said. "This is Swanage. It's no good your waving your banjo at me. I know it's a banjo, all right, though I may forget, next time I hear you play it."

"We've been here every year for the last ten years," the chief nigger shouted.

"I thought so by your songs," Henry retorted. "If you told me you got wrecked here with Christopher Columbus I shouldn't have contradicted you."

"This part of the beach belongs to us," the niggers proclaimed.

"I suppose you bought it off Noah, didn't you, when he let you out of the ark?" said Henry.

In the end, however, the two companies adjusted their differences and removed themselves out of each other's hearing. Mabel's voice defeated even the tambourines and bones of the niggers. Swanage seemed likely to be an improvement upon Bournemouth, until one day Mabel's prosperous admirer appeared on the promenade and Henry's jealousy rose to fury.

"Don't you tell me you didn't tell him to follow you here," he said, "because I don't believe you. I saw you smile at him."

Monkley remonstrated with Mabel, when Henry had gone off in a fever of rage to his room, but she seemed to be getting a certain amount of pleasure from the situation.

"You must cut it out," Monkley said. "I don't want the party broken up on account of you and Henry. I tell you he really is upset. What the deuce do you want to drag in all this confounded love business now for? Leave that to Claude. It'll burst up the show, and it's making Harry drink, which his head can't stand."

Mabel looked at herself in the glass over the fireplace and patted her hair complacently. "I'm rather glad to see Harry can get jealous. After all, it's always a pleasure to think some one's really fond of you."

Sylvia watched Mabel very carefully and perceived that she actually was carrying on a flirtation with the man who had followed her from Bournemouth. She hoped that it would continue and that her father would get angry enough with Mabel to get rid of her when the tour came to an end.

One Saturday afternoon, when Mabel was collecting, Sylvia distinctly saw her admirer drop a note into the hat, which she took with her into the tent to read and tore up; during her next song Sylvia noticed that the man with the yellow cummerbund was watching her with raised eyebrows, and that, when Mabel smiled and nodded, he gently clapped his hands and went away.

Sylvia debated with herself the advisability of telling her father at once what she had seen, thus bringing things to an immediate climax and getting rid of Mabel forever, even if by doing so the show were spoilt. But when she saw his glazed eyes and realized how drunk he was, she thought she would wait. The next afternoon, when Henry was taking his Sunday rest, Mabel dressed herself and went out. Sylvia followed her and, after ascertaining that she had taken the path toward the cliffs to the east of the town, came back to the lodgings and again debated with herself a course of action. She decided in the end to wait a little longer before she denounced Mabel. Later on, when her father had wakened and was demanding Mabel's company for a stroll in the moonlight, a letter was brought to the lodgings by a railway porter from Mabel herself to say that she had left the company and had gone away with her new friend by train. Sylvia thought how near she had been to spoiling the elopement and hugged herself with pleasure; but she could not resist telling her father now that she had seen the intrigue in progress and of her following Mabel that afternoon and seeing her take the path toward the cliffs. Henry seemed quite shattered by his loss, and could do nothing but drink brandy, while Monkley swore at Mabel for wrecking a good show and wondered where he was going to find another girl, even going so far as to suggest telegraphing on the off chance to Maudie Tilt.

31

It was very hot on Monday, and after the morning performance Henry announced that he did not intend to walk all the way back to the lodgings for dinner. He should go to the hotel and have a snack. What did it matter about his being in his pierrot's rig? Swanage was a small place, and if the people were not used to his costume by now, they never would be. It was no good any one arguing; he intended to stay behind this morning. The others left him talking in his usual style of melancholy humor to the small boy who for the sum of twopence kept an eye on the portable piano and the book of songs during the hot midday hours. When they looked round he was juggling with one of the pennies, to the admiration of the owner. They never saw him alive again. He was brought back dead that evening on a stretcher, his pink costume splashed with blood. The odd thing was that the hotel carving-knife was in his pocket, though it was proved conclusively at the inquest that death was due to falling over the cliffs on the east side of the town.

Sylvia wondered if she ought to blame herself for her father's death, and she confided in Jimmy what she had told him about Mabel's behavior. Jimmy asked her why she could not have let things alone, and made her very miserable by his strictures upon her youthful tactlessness; so miserable, indeed, that he was fain to console her and assure her that it had all been an accident due to Henry's fondness for brandy—that and the sun must have turned his head.

"You don't think he took the knife to kill himself?" she asked.

"More likely he took it with some idea of killing them, and, being drunk, fell over the cliff. Poor old Harry! I shall miss him, and now you're all alone in the world."

That was true, and the sudden realization of this fact drove out of Sylvia's mind the remorse for her father's death by confronting her with the instancy of the great problem that had for so long haunted her mind. She turned to Jimmy almost fearfully.

"I shall have you to look after me?"

Jimmy took her hand and gazed into her eyes.

"You want to stay with me, then?" he asked, earnestly.

"Of course I do. Who else could I stay with?"

"You wouldn't prefer to be with Claude, for example?" he went on.

"Claude?" she repeated, in a puzzled voice. And then she grasped in all its force the great new truth that for the rest of her life the choice of her companions lay with herself alone. She had become at this moment grown up and was free, like Mabel, to choose even a man with a yellow cummerbund.

CHAPTER IV

SYLVIA begged Monkley not to go back and live in Fitzroy Street. She felt the flat would be haunted by memories of her father and Mabel. It was as well that she did not want to return there, for Jimmy assured her that nothing would induce him to go near Fitzroy Street. A great deal of money was owing, and he wished the landlord luck in his dispute with the furnishing people when he tried to seize the furniture for arrears of rent. It would be necessary to choose for their next abode a quarter of London to which he was a stranger, because he disliked having to make détours to avoid streets where he owed money. Finsbury Park was melancholy; Highgate was inaccessible; Hampstead was expensive and almost equally inaccessible; but they must go somewhere in the North of London, for there did not remain a suburb in the West or South the tradesmen and house-owners of which he had not swindled at one time or another. On second thoughts, there was a part of Hampstead that was neither so expensive nor so inaccessible, which was reached from Haverstock Hill; they would look for rooms there. They settled down finally in one of a row of old houses facing the southerly extremity of the Heath, the rural aspect of which was heightened by long gardens in front that now in late summer were filled with sunflowers and hollyhocks. The old-fashioned house, which resembled a large cottage both without and within, belonged to a decayed florist and nursery gardener called Samuel Gustard, whose trade was now confined to the sale of penny packets of seeds, though a weather-beaten sign-board facing the road maintained a legend of greater glories. Mr. Gustard himself made no effort to live up to his sign-board; indeed, he would not even stir himself to produce a packet of seeds, for if his wife were about he would indicate to her with the stem of his pipe which packet was wanted, and if she were not about, he would tell the customer that the variety was no longer in stock. A greenhouse kept from collapse by the sturdy vine it was supposed to protect ran along the fence on one side of the garden; the rest was a jungle of coarse herbaceous flowers, presumably the survivors of Mr. Gustard's last horticultural effort, about ten years ago.

The money made by the tour of the Pink Pierrots did not last very long, and Jimmy was soon forced back to industry. Sylvia nowadays heard more about his successes and failures than when her father was alive, and she begged very hard to be allowed to help on some of his expeditions.

"You're no good to me yet," Monkley told her. "You're too old to be really innocent and not old enough to pretend to be. Besides, people don't take school-girls to race meetings. Later on, when you've learned a bit more about life, we'll start a gambling club in the West End and work on a swell scale what I do now in a small way in railway-carriages."

This scheme of Jimmy's became a favorite topic; and Sylvia began to regard a flash gambling-hell as the crown of human ambition. Jimmy's imagination used to run riot amid the splendor of it all, as he discoursed of the footmen with plush breeches; of the shaded lamps; of the sideboard loaded with hams and jellies and fruit at which the guests would always be able to refresh themselves, for it would never do to let them go away because they were hungry, and people were always hungry at three in the morning; of the smart page-boy in the entrance of the flats who would know how to reckon up a visitor and give the tip up-stairs by ringing a bell; and of the rigid exclusion of all women except Sylvia herself.

"I can see it all before me," Jimmy used to sigh. "I can smell the cigars and whisky. I'm flinging back the curtains when every one has gone and feeling the morning air. And here we are stuck in this old cucumber-frame at Hampstead! But we'll get it, we'll get it. I shall have a scoop one of these days and be able to start saving, and when I've saved a couple of hundred I'll bluff the rest."

In October Jimmy came home from Newmarket and told Sylvia he had run against an old friend, who had proposed a money-making scheme which would take him away from London for a couple of months. He could not explain the details to Sylvia, but he might say that it was a confidence trick on the grand scale and that it meant his residing in a northern city. He had told his friend he would give him an answer to-morrow, and wanted to know what Sylvia thought about it.

She was surprised by Jimmy's consulting her in this way. She had always taken it for granted that from time to time she would be left alone. Jimmy's action made her realize more clearly than ever that to a great extent she already possessed that liberty of choice the prospect of which had dawned upon her at Swanage.

She assured Jimmy of her readiness to be left alone in Hampstead. When he expatiated on his consideration for her welfare she was bored and longed for him to be gone; his solicitude gave her a feeling of restraint; she became impatient of his continually wanting to know if she should miss him and of his commendation of her to the care of Mr. and Mrs. Gustard, from whom she desired no interference, being quite content with the prospect of sitting in her window with a book and a green view.

The next morning Monkley left Hampstead; and Sylvia inhaled freedom with the autumn air. She had been given what seemed a very large sum of money to sustain herself until Jimmy's return. She had bought a new hat; a black kitten had adopted her; it was pearly October weather. Sylvia surveyed life with a sense of pleasure that was nevertheless most unreasonably marred by a faint breath of restlessness, an almost imperceptible discontent. Life had always offered itself to her contemplation, whether of the past or of the future, as a set of vivid impressions that formed a crudely colored panorama of action without any emotional light and shade, the intervals between which, like the intervals of a theatrical performance, were only tolerable with plenty of chocolates to eat. At the present moment she had plenty of chocolates to eat, more, in fact, than she had ever had before, but the interval was seeming most exasperatingly long.

"You ought to take a walk on the Heath," Mr. Gustard advised. "It isn't good to sit about all day doing nothing."

"You don't take walks," Sylvia pointed out. "And you sit about all day doing nothing. I do read a book, anyway."

"I'm different," Mr. Gustard pronounced, very solemnly. "I've lived my life. If I was to take a walk round Hampstead I couldn't hardly peep into a garden without seeing a tree as I'd planted myself. And when I'm gone, the trees 'll still be there. That's something to *think* about, that is. There was a clergyman came nosing round here the other day to ask me why I didn't go to church. I told him I'd done without church as a lad, and I couldn't see why I shouldn't do without it now. 'But you're growing old, Mr. Gustard,' he says to me. 'That's just it,' I says to him. 'I'm getting very near the time when, if all they say is true, I shall be in the heavenly choir for ever and ever, amen, and the less singing I hear for the rest of my time on earth the better.' 'That's a very blasphemous remark,' he says to me. 'Is it?' says I to him. 'Well, here's another. Perhaps all this talk by parsons,' I says, 'about this life on earth being just a choir practice for heaven won't bear looking into. Perhaps we shall all die and go to sleep and never wake up and never dream and never do nothing at all, never. And if that's true,' I says, 'I reckon I shall bust my coffin with laughing when I think of my trees growing and growing and growing and you preaching to a lot of old women and children about something you don't know nothing about and they don't know nothing about and nobody don't know nothing about.' With that I offered him a pear, and he walked off very offended with his head in the air. You get out and about, my dear. Bustle around and enjoy yourself. That's my motto for the young."

Sylvia felt that there was much to be said for Mr. Gustard's attitude, and she took his advice so far as to go for a long walk on the Heath that very afternoon. Yet there was something lacking. When she got home again she found that the book of adventure which she had been reading was no longer capable of keeping her thoughts fixed. The stupid part of it was that her thoughts wandered nowhere in particular and without attaching themselves to a definite object. She would try to concentrate them upon Jimmy and speculate what he was doing, but Jimmy would turn into Claude Raglan; and when she began to speculate what Claude was doing, Claude would turn back again into Jimmy. Her own innermost restlessness made her so fidgety that she went to the window and stared at the road along the dusky Heath. The garden gate of next door swung to with a click, and Sylvia saw a young man coming toward the house. She was usually without the least interest in young men, but on this afternoon of indefinable and errant thoughts she welcomed the least excuse for bringing herself back to a material object; and this young man, though it was twilight and his face was not clearly visible, managed to interest her somehow, so that at tea she found herself asking Mr. Gustard who he might be and most unaccountably blushing at the question.

"That 'ud be young Artie, wouldn't it?" he suggested to his wife. She nodded over the squat teapot that she so much resembled:

"That must be him come back from his uncle's. Mrs. Madden was only saying to me this morning, when we was waiting for the grocer's man, that she was expecting him this evening. She spoils him something shocking. If you please, his highness has been down into Hampshire to see if he would like to be a gentleman farmer. Whoever heard, I should like to know? Why he can't be long turned seventeen. It's a pity his father isn't alive to keep him from idling his time away."

"There's no harm in giving a bit of liberty to the young," Mr. Gustard answered, preparing to be as eloquent as the large piece of bread and butter in his mouth would let him. "I'm not in favor of pushing a young man too far."

"No, you was never in favor of pushing anything, neither yourself nor your business," said Mrs. Gustard, sharply. "But I think it's a sin to let a boy like that moon away all his time with a book. Books were only intended for the gentry and people as have grown too old for anything else, and even then they're bad for their eyes."

Sylvia wondered whether Mrs. Gustard intended to criticize unfavorably her own manner of life, but she left the defense of books to Mr. Gustard, who was so impatient to begin that he nearly choked:

"Because I don't read," he said, "that's no reason for me to try and stop others from reading. What I say is 'liberty for all.' If young Artie Madden wants to read, let him read. If Sylvia here wants to read, let her read. Books give employment to a lot of people—binders, printers, paper-makers, booksellers. It's a regular trade. If people didn't like to smell flowers and sit about under trees, there wouldn't be no gardeners, would there? Very well, then; and if there wasn't people who wanted to read, there wouldn't be no printers."

"What about the people who write all the rubbish?" Mrs. Gustard demanded, fiercely. "Nice, idle lot of good-for-nothings they are, I'm sure."

"That's because the only writing fellow we ever knew got that servant-girl of ours into trouble."

"Samuel," Mrs. Gustard interrupted, "that'll do!"

"I don't suppose every writing fellow's like him," Mr. Gustard went on. "And, anyway, the girl was a saucy hussy."

"Samuel! That will do, I said."

"Well, so she was," Mr. Gustard continued, defiantly. "Didn't she used to powder her face with your Borwick's?"

"I'll trouble you not to spit crumbs all over my clean cloth," said Mrs. Gustard, "making the whole place look like a bird-cage!"

Mr. Gustard winked at Sylvia and was silent. She for her part had already begun to weave round Arthur Madden a veil of romance, when the practical side of her suddenly roused itself to a sense of what was going on and admonished her to leave off dreaming and attend to her cat.

Up-stairs in her bedroom, she opened her window and looked out at the faint drizzle of rain which was just enough to mellow the leafy autumnal scents and diffuse the golden beams of the lamps along the Heath. There was the sound of another window's being opened on a line with hers; presently a head and shoulders scarcely definable in the darkness leaned out, whistling an old French air that was familiar to her from earliest childhood, the words of which had long ago been forgotten. She could not help whistling the air in unison; and after a moment's silence a voice from the head and shoulders asked who it was.

"A girl," Sylvia said.

"Anybody could tell that," the voice commented, a little scornfully. "Because the noise is all woolly."

"It's not," Sylvia contradicted, indignantly. "Perhaps you'll say I'm out of tune? I know quite well who you are. You're Arthur Madden, the boy next door."

"But who are you?"

"I'm Sylvia Scarlett."

"Are you a niece of Mrs. Gustard?" the voice inquired.

"Of course not," Sylvia scoffed. "I'm just staying here."

"Who with?"

"By myself."

"By yourself?" the voice echoed, incredulously.

"Why not? I'm nearly sixteen."

This was too much for Arthur Madden, who struck a match to illuminate the features of the strange unknown. Although he did not succeed in discerning Sylvia, he lit up his own face, which she liked well enough to suggest they should go for a walk, making the proposal a kind of test for herself of Arthur Madden's character, and deciding that if he showed the least hesitation in accepting she would never speak to him again. The boy, however, was immediately willing; the two pairs of shoulders vanished; Sylvia put on her coat and went down-stairs.

"Going out for a blow?" Mr. Gustard asked.

Sylvia nodded. "With the boy next door," she answered.

"You haven't been long," said Mr. Gustard, approvingly. "That's the way I like to see it. When I courted Mrs. Gustard, which was forty years ago come next November, it was in the time of toolip-planting, and I hove a toolip bulb at her and caught her in the chignon. 'Whatever are you doing of?' she says to me. 'It's a proposal of marriage,' I says, and when she started giggling I was that pleased I planted half the toolips upside down. But that's forty years ago, that is. Mrs. Gustard's grown more particular since, and so as she's washing up the tea-things in the scullery, I should just slip out, and I'll tell her you've gone out to get a paper to see if it's true what somebody said about Buckingham Palace being burned to a cinder."

Sylvia was not at all sure that she ought to recognize Mrs. Gustard's opinion even so far as by slipping out and thereby giving her an idea that she did not possess perfect liberty of action. However, she decided that the point was too trifling to worry about, and, with a wave of her hand, she left her landlord to tell what story he chose to his wife.

Arthur Madden was waiting for her by his gate when she reached the end of the garden; while they wandered along by the Heath, indifferent to the drizzle, Sylvia felt an extraordinary release from the faint discontent of these past days, an extraordinary delight in finding herself with a companion who was young like herself and who, like herself, seemed full of speculation upon the world which he was setting out to explore, regarding it as an adventure and ready to exchange hopes and fears and fancies with her in a way that no one had ever done hitherto; moreover, he was ready to be most flatteringly impressed by her experiences, even if he still maintained she could not whistle properly. The friendship between Sylvia and Arthur begun upon that night grew daily closer. Mrs. Gustard used to say that they wasted each other's time, but she was in the minority; she used to say also that Arthur was being more spoiled than ever by his mother; but it was this very capacity for being spoiled that endeared him to Sylvia, who had spent a completely free existence for so long now that unless Arthur had been allowed his freedom she would soon have tired of the friendship. She liked Mrs. Madden, a beautiful and unpractical woman, who unceasingly played long sonatas on a cracked piano; at least she would have played them unceasingly had she not continually been jumping up to wait on Arthur, hovering round him like a dark and iridescent butterfly.

In the course of many talks together Arthur told Sylvia the family history. It seemed that his mother had been the daughter of a gentleman, not an ordinary kind of top-hatted gentleman, but a squire with horses and hounds and a park; his father had been a groom and she had eloped with him, but Sylvia was not to suppose that his father had been an ordinary kind of groom; he too came from good stock, though he had been rather wild. His father's father had been a farmer in Sussex, and he had just come back from staying at the farm, where his uncle had offered to give him a start in life, but he had found he did not care much for farm-work. His mother's family would have nothing to do with her beyond allowing her enough to live upon without disturbing them.

"What are you going to do?" Sylvia asked.

Arthur replied that he did not know, but that he had thoughts of being a soldier.

"A soldier?" said Sylvia, doubtfully. Her experience of soldiers was confined to Blanche's lovers, and the universal connotation in France of soldiery with a vile servitude that could hardly be avoided.

"But of course the worst of it is," Arthur explained, "there aren't any wars nowadays."

They were walking over the Heath on a fine November day about Martinmas; presently, when they sat down under some pines and looked at London spread beneath them in a sparkling haze, Arthur took Sylvia's hand and told her that he loved her.

She nearly snatched her hand away and would have told him not to be silly, but suddenly the beauty of the tranquil city below and the wind through the pines conquered her spirit; she sat closer to him, letting her head droop upon his shoulder; when his clasp tightened round her unresisting hand she burst into tears, unable to tell him that her sorrow was nothing but joy, that he had nothing to do with it nor with her, and yet that he had everything to do with it, because with no one else could she have borne this incommunicable display of life. Then she dried her tears and told Arthur she thought he had better become a highwayman.

"Highwaymen don't exist any longer," Arthur objected. "All the jolly things have disappeared from the world—war and highwaymen and pirates and troubadours and crusaders and maypoles and the Inquisition. Everything."

Gradually Sylvia learned from Arthur how much of what she had been reading was mere invention, and in the first bitterness of disillusionment she wished to renounce books forever; but Arthur dissuaded her from doing that, and they used to read simultaneously the same books so as to be able to discuss them during their long walks. They became two romantics born out of due season, two romantics that should have lived a century ago and that now bewailed the inability of the modern world to supply what their adventurous souls demanded.

Arthur was inclined to think that Sylvia had much less cause to repine than he; the more tales she told him of her life, the more tributes of envy he paid to her good fortune. He pointed out that Monkley scarcely differed from the highwayman of romance; nor did he doubt but that if all his enterprises could be known he would rival Dick Turpin himself. Sylvia agreed with all he said, but she urged the inequality of her own share in the achievement. What she wanted was something more than to sit at home and enjoy fruits in the stealing of which she had played no part. She wanted none of Arthur's love unless he were prepared to face the problem of living life at its fullest in company with her. She would let him kiss her sometimes, because, unhappily, it seemed that even very young men were infected with this malady, and that if deprived of this odious habit they were liable to lose determination and sink into incomprehensible despondency. At the same time Sylvia made Arthur clearly understand that she was yielding to his weakness, not to her own, and that, if he wished to retain her compassion, he must prove that the devotion of which he boasted was vital to his being.

"You mustn't just kiss me," Sylvia warned him, "because it's easy. It's very difficult, really, because it's very difficult for me to let you do it. I have to wind myself up beforehand just as if I were going to pull out a loose tooth."

Arthur gazed at her with wide-open, liquid eyes; his mouth trembled. "You say such cruel things," he murmured.

Sylvia punched him as hard as she could. "I won't be stared at like that. You look like a cow when you stare at me like that. Buck up and think what we're going to do."

"I'm ready to do anything," Arthur declared, "as long as you're decent to me. But you're such an extraordinary girl. One moment you burst into tears and put your head on my shoulder, and the next moment you're punching me."

"And I shall punch you again," Sylvia said, fiercely, "if you dare to remind me that I ever cried in front of you. You weren't there when I cried."

"But I was," he protested.

"No, you weren't. You were only there like a tree or a cloud."

"Or a cow," said Arthur, gloomily.

"I think that if we did go away together," Sylvia said, meditatively, "I should leave you almost at once, because you will keep returning to things I said. My father used to be like that."

"But if we go away," Arthur asked, "how are we going to live? I shouldn't be any use on racecourses. I'm the sort of person that gets taken in by the three-card trick."

35

"You make me so angry when you talk like that," Sylvia said. "Of course if you think you'll always be a fool, you always will be a fool. Being in love with me must make you think that you're not a fool. Perhaps we never shall go away together; but if we do, you'll have to begin by stealing bicycles. Jimmy Monkley and my father did that for a time. You hire a bicycle and sell it or pawn it a long way off from the shop it came from. It's quite easy. Only, of course, it's best to disguise yourself. Father used to paint out his teeth, wear blue glasses, and powder his mustache gray. But once he made himself so old in a place called Lewisham that the man in the bicycle-shop thought he was too old to ride and wouldn't let him have a machine."

Sylvia was strengthened in her resolve to launch Arthur upon the stormy seas of an independent existence by the placid harbor in which his mother loved to see him safely at anchor. Sylvia could not understand how a woman like Mrs. Madden, who had once been willing to elope with a groom, could bear to let her son spend his time so ineffectively. Not that she wished Mrs. Madden to exert her authority by driving him into a clerkship, or indeed into any profession for which he had no inclination, but she deplored the soft slavery which a fond woman can impose, the slavery of being waited upon that is more deadening than the slavery of waiting upon other people. She used to make a point of impressing upon Mrs. Madden the extent to which she and Arthur went shares in everything, lest she might suppose that Sylvia imitated her complaisance, and when Mrs. Madden used to smile in her tired way and make some remark about boy and girl lovers, Sylvia used to get angry and try to demonstrate the unimportance of that side of life.

"You funny child," Mrs. Madden said. "When you're older, how you'll laugh at what you think now. Of course, you don't know anything about love yet, mercifully for you. I wish I were richer; I should so like to adopt you."

"Oh, but I wouldn't be adopted," Sylvia quickly interposed. "I can't tell you how glad I am that I belong to nobody. And please don't think I'm so innocent, because I'm not. I've seen a great deal of love, you must remember, and I've thought a lot about it, and made up my mind that I'll never be a slave to that sort of thing. Arthur may be stupidly in love with me, but I'm very strict with him and it doesn't do him any harm."

"Come and sing your favorite song," Mrs. Madden laughed. "I'll play your accompaniment."

All the discussions between them ended in music; Sylvia would sing that she was off with the raggle-taggle gipsies—or, stamping with her foot upon the floor of the old house until it shook and crossing her arms with such resolution that Arthur's eyes would grow larger than ever, as if he half expected to see her act upon the words and fling herself out into the December night, regardless of all but a mad demonstration of liberty.

Sylvia would sometimes sing about the gipsies to herself while she was undressing, which generally called forth a protest from Mrs. Gustard, who likened the effect to that of a young volcano let loose.

Another person that was pained by Sylvia's exuberance was Maria, her black cat, so called on account of his color before he was definitely established as a gentleman. He had no ear for music and he disapproved of dancing; nor did he have the least sympathy with the aspirations of the lawless song she sang. Mrs. Gustard considered that he was more artful than what any one would think, but she repudiated as "heathenish" Sylvia's contention that she outwardly resembled Maria.

"Still I do think I'm like a cat," Sylvia argued. "Perhaps not very like a black cat, more like a tabby. One day you'll come up to my room and find me purring on the bed."

Mrs. Gustard exclaimed against such an unnatural event.

Sylvia received one or two letters from Jimmy Monkley during the winter, in which he wrote with considerable optimism of the success of his venture and thought he might be back in Hampstead by February. He came back unexpectedly, however, in the middle of January, and Sylvia was only rather glad to see him; she had grown fond of her life alone and dreaded Jimmy's habit of arranging matters over her head. He was not so amiable as formerly, because the scheme had only been partially successful and he had failed to make enough money to bring the flash gambling-hell perceptibly nearer. Sylvia had almost forgotten that project; it seemed to her now a dull project, neither worthy of herself nor of him. She did not attempt, on Jimmy's return, to change her own way of spending the time, and she persisted in taking the long walks with Arthur as usual.

"What the devil you see to admire in that long-legged, saucer-eyed, curly-headed mother's pet I don't know," Jimmy grumbled.

"I don't admire him," Sylvia said. "I don't admire anybody except Joan of Arc. But I like him."

Jimmy scowled; and later on that day Mr. Gustard warned Sylvia that her uncle (as such was Jimmy known in the lodgings) had carried on alarmingly about her friendship with young Artie.

"It's nothing to do with him," Sylvia affirmed, with out-thrust chin.

"Nothing whatever," Mr. Gustard agreed. "But if I was you I wouldn't throw young Artie in his face. I've never had a niece myself, but from what I can make out an uncle feels something like a father; and a father gets very worried about his rights."

"But you've never had any children, and so you can't know any more about the feelings of a father," Sylvia objected.

"Ah, but I've got my own father to look back upon," Mr. Gustard said. "He mostly took a spade to me, I remember, though he wasn't against jabbing me in the ribs with a trowel if there wasn't a spade handy. I reckon it was him as first put the notion of liberty for all into my head. I never set much store by uncles, though. The only uncle I ever had died of croup when he was two years old."

"My father didn't like his aunts," Sylvia added to the condemnation. "He was brought up by two aunts."

"Aunts in general is sour bodies, 'specially when they're in charge and get all the fuss of having children with none of the fun."

"Mr. Monkley isn't really my uncle," Sylvia abruptly proclaimed.

36

"Go on! you don't mean it?" said Mr. Gustard. "I suppose he's your guardian?"

"He's nothing at all," Sylvia answered.

"He must be something."

"He's absolutely nothing," she insisted. "He used to live with my father, and when my father died he just went on living with me. If I don't want to live with him I needn't."

"But you must live with somebody," said Mr. Gustard. "There's a law about having visible means of support. You couldn't have a lot of kids living on their own."

"Why not?" Sylvia asked, in contemptuous amazement.

"Why not?" Mr. Gustard repeated. "Why because every one would get pestered to death. It's the same with stray dogs. Stray dogs have got to have a home. If they haven't a home of their own, they're taken to the Dogs' Home at Battersea and cremated, which is a painless and mercenary death."

"I don't call that much of a home," Sylvia scoffed. "A place where you're killed."

"That's because we're speaking of dogs. Of course, if the police started in cremating children, there'd be a regular outcry. So the law insists on children having homes."

Sylvia tried hard to convince Mr. Gustard that she was different from other children, and in any case no longer a child; but though the discussion lasted a long time he would not admit the logic of Sylvia's arguments; in the end she decided he did not know what he was talking about.

Monkley so much disliked Sylvia's intimacy with Arthur that he began to talk of moving from Hampstead, whereupon she warned him that if he tried to go away without paying the rent she would make a point of letting Mr. Gustard know where they had gone.

"It strikes me," Monkley said, and when he spoke, Sylvia was reminded of the tone he used when she had protested against his treatment of Maudie Tilt—"it strikes me that since I've been away you've taken things a bit too much into your own hands. That's a trick you'd better drop with me, or we shall quarrel."

Sylvia braced herself to withstand him as she had withstood him before; but she could not help feeling a little apprehensive, so cold were his green eyes, so thin his mouth.

"I don't care if we quarrel or not," she declared. "Because if we quarreled it would mean that I couldn't bear you near me any longer and that I was glad to quarrel. If you make me hate you, Jimmy, you may be sorry, but I shall never be sorry. If you make me hate you, Jimmy, you can't think how dreadfully much I shall hate you."

"Don't try to come the little actress over me," Monkley said. "I've known too many women in my life to be bounced by a kid like you. But that's enough. I can't think why I pay so much attention to you."

"No," Sylvia said. "All the women you've known don't seem to have been able to teach you how to manage a little girl like me. What a pity!"

She laughed and left him alone.

There was a halcyon week that February, and Sylvia spent every day and all day on the Heath with Arthur. People used to turn and stare after them as they walked arm-in-arm over the vivid green grass.

"I think it's you they stare at," Sylvia said. "You look interesting with your high color and dark curly hair. You look rather foreign. Perhaps people think you're a poet. I read the other day about a poet called Keats who lived in Hampstead and loved a girl called Fanny Brawne. I wish I knew what she looked like. It's not a very pretty name. Now I've got rather a pretty name, I think; though I'm not pretty myself."

"You're not exactly pretty," Arthur agreed. "But I think if I saw you I should turn round to look at you. You're like a person in a picture. You seem to stand out and to be the most important figure. In paintings that's because the chief figure is usually so much larger than the others. Well, that's the impression you give me."

Speculation upon Sylvia's personality ceased when they got home; Monkley threatened Arthur in a very abusive way, even going as far as to pick up a stone and fling it through one of the few panes of glass left in the tumble-down greenhouse in order to illustrate the violent methods he proposed to adopt.

The next day, when Sylvia went to fetch Arthur for their usual walk, he made some excuse and was obviously frightened to accompany her.

"What can he do to you?" Sylvia demanded, in scornful displeasure. "The worst he can do is to kill you, and then you'd have died because you wouldn't surrender. Haven't you read about martyrs?"

"Of course I've read about martyrs," said Arthur, rather querulously. "But reading about martyrs is very different from being a martyr yourself. You seem to think everybody can be anything you happen to read about. You wouldn't care to be a martyr, Sylvia."

"That's just where you're wrong," she loftily declared. "I'd much sooner be a martyr than a coward."

Arthur winced at her plain speaking. "You don't care what you say," was his reproach.

"No, and I don't care what I do," Sylvia agreed. "Are you coming out with me? Because if you're not, you shall never be my friend again."

Arthur pulled himself together and braved Monkley's threats. On a quiet green summit he demanded her impatient kisses for a recompense; she, conscious of his weakness and against her will made fonder of him by this very weakness, kissed him less impatiently than was her wont, so that Arthur, under the inspiration of that rare caress, vowed he cared for nobody and for nothing, if she would but always treat him thus kindly.

Sylvia, who was determined to make Jimmy pay for his bad behavior, invited herself to tea with Mrs. Madden; afterward, though it was cloudy and ominous, Arthur and she walked out on the Heath once more, until it rained so hard that they were driven home. It was about seven o'clock when Sylvia reached her room, her hair all tangled with moisture, her eyes and cheeks on fire with the exhilaration of that scurry through the rain. She had not stood a moment to regard herself in the glass when Monkley, following close upon her heels, shut the door behind him and turned the key in the lock. Sylvia looked round in astonishment; by a trick of candle-light his eyes gleamed for an instant, so that she felt a tremor of fear.

"You've come back at last, have you?" he began in a slow voice, so deliberate and gentle in its utterance that Sylvia might not have grasped the extent of his agitation, had not one of his legs, affected by a nervous twitch, drummed upon the floor a sinister accompaniment. "You shameless little b——h, I thought I forbade you to go out with him again. You've been careering over the Heath. You've been encouraging him to make love to you. Look at your hair—it's in a regular tangle! and your cheeks—they're like fire. Well, if you can let that nancified milksop mess you about, you can put up with me. I've wanted to long enough, God knows; and this is the reward I get for leaving you alone. You give yourself to the first b——y boy that comes along."

Before Sylvia had time to reply, Monkley had leaped across the room and crushed her to him.

"Kiss me, damn you, kiss me! Put your arms round me."

Sylvia would not scream, because she could not have endured that anybody should behold her in such an ignominious plight. Therefore she only kicked and fought, and whispered all the while, with savage intensity! "You frog! you frog! You look like a frog! Leave me alone!"

Monkley held her more closely and forced her mouth against his own, but Sylvia bit through his under lip till her teeth met. The pain caused him to start back and tread on Maria, who, searching in a panic for better cover than the bed afforded, had run between his legs. The cat, uttering one of those unimaginable wails with which only cats have power so horribly to surprise, retired to a corner, where he hissed and growled. In another corner Sylvia spat forth the unclean blood and wiped from her lips the soilure of the kisses.

Monkley had had enough for the present. The pain and sudden noise had shaken his nerves. When the blood ran down his chin, bedabbling his tie, he unlocked the door and retired, crying out almost in a whimper for something to stop a bad razor cut. Mrs. Gustard went to the wood-shed for cobwebs; but Monkley soon shouted down that he had found some cotton wool, and Sylvia heard a cork being drawn. She made up her mind to kill him that night, but she was perplexed by the absence of a suitable weapon, and gradually it was borne in upon her mind that if she killed Monkley she would have to pay the penalty, which did not seem to her a satisfactory kind of revenge. She gave up the notion of killing him and decided to run away with Arthur instead.

For a long time Sylvia sat in her bedroom, thinking over her plan; then she went next door and asked Arthur to come out and talk to her about something important. They stood whispering in the wet garden, while she bewitched him into offering to share her future. He was dazed by the rapidity with which she disposed of every objection he brought forward. She knew how to get enough money for them to start with. She knew how to escape from the house, and because the creeper beneath Arthur's window was not strong enough to bear his weight, he must tie his sheets together. He must not bring much luggage; she would only bring a small valise, and Maria could travel in her work-basket.

"Maria?" echoed Arthur, in dismay.

"Of course! it was Maria who saved me," said Sylvia. "I shall wait till Monkley is asleep. I expect he'll be asleep early, because he's drinking brandy hard now; then I shall whistle the last line of the raggle-taggle gipsies and slither down from my window by the ivy."

She stuffed Arthur's reeling brain with further details, and, catching him to her heart, she kissed him with as much enthusiasm as might have been mistaken for passion. In the end, between coaxing and frightening, threatening and inspiring, Sylvia made Arthur agree to everything, and danced back indoors.

"Anybody would think you were glad because your guardian angel's gone and sliced a rasher off of his mouth," Mr. Gustard observed.

By ten o'clock all was quiet in the house. Sylvia chose with the greatest care her equipment for the adventure. She had recently bought a tartan frock, which, not having yet been worn, she felt would excellently become the occasion; this she put on, and plaited her tangled hair in a long pigtail. The result was unsatisfactory, for it made her look too prim for a heroine; she therefore undid the pigtail and tied her hair loosely back with a nut-brown bow. It was still impossibly early for an escape, so Sylvia sat down on the edge of her bed and composed herself to read the escape of Fabrizio from the Sforza tower in Parma. The book in which she read this was not one that she had been able to read through without a great deal of skipping; but this escape which she had only come across a day or two before seemed a divine omen to approve her decision. Sylvia regretted the absence of the armed men at the foot of the tower, but said to herself that, after all, she was escaping with her lover, whereas Fabrizio had been compelled to leave Clelia Conti behind. The night wore away; at half past eleven Sylvia dropped her valise from the window and whistled that she was off with the raggle-taggle gipsies—oh. Then she waited until a ghostly snake was uncoiled from Arthur's window.

"My dearest boy, you're an angel," she trilled, in an ecstasy, when she saw him slide safely down into the garden.

"Catch Maria," she whispered. "I'm coming myself in a moment."

Arthur caught her work-basket, and a faint protesting mew floated away on the darkness. Sylvia wrapped herself up, and then very cautiously, candle in hand, walked across to the door of Monkley's room and listened. He was snoring loudly. She pushed open the door and beheld him fast asleep, a red-and-white beard of cotton wool upon his chin. Then risking all in an impulse to be quick, though she was almost stifled by fear, she hurried across the room to his trunk. He kept all his money in a tin box. How she hoped there was enough to make him rue her flight. Monkley never stirred; the box was safe in her muff. She stole back to her room, blew out the candle, flung the muff down to Arthur, held her breath when the coins rattled, put one leg over the sill, and scrambled down by the ivy.

"I wish it had been higher," she whispered, when Arthur clasped her with affectionate solicitude where she stood in the sodden vegetation.

"I'm jolly glad it wasn't," he said. "Now what are we going to do?"

"Why, find a 'bus, of course!" Sylvia said. "And get as far from Hampstead as possible."

"But it's after twelve o'clock," Arthur objected. "There won't be any 'buses now. I don't know what we're going to do. We can't look for rooms at this time of night."

"We must just walk as far as we can away from Hampstead," said Sylvia, cheerfully.

"And carry our luggage? Supposing a policeman asks us where we're going?"

"Oh, bother policemen! Come along. You don't seem to be enjoying yourself nearly as much as I am. I care for nobody. I'm off with the raggle-taggle gipsies—oh," she lightly sang.

Maria mewed at the sound of his mistress's voice.

"You're as bad as Maria," she went on, reproachfully. "Look how nice the lamp-posts look. One, two, three, four, five, six, seven, I can see. Let's bet how many lamp-posts we pass before we're safe in our own house."

They set out for London by the road along the Heath. At first trees overhung the path, and they passed pool after pool of checkered lamplight that quivered in the wet road. Followed a space of open country where they heard the last whispers of a slight and desultory wind. Soon they were inclosed by mute and unillumined houses on either side, until they found themselves on the top of Haverstock Hill, faced by the tawny glow of the London sky, and stretching before them a double row of lamp-posts innumerable and pale that converged to a dim point in the heart of the city below.

"I think I'm rather frightened," Sylvia said. "Or perhaps I'm a little tired."

"Shall we go back?" Arthur suggested.

"No, no. We'll just rest a moment or two, and I'll be all right." They sat down on their bags, and she stroked Maria pensively.

Sylvia was relieved when the silence was interrupted by a policeman. She felt the need of opposition to drive away the doubts that took advantage of that first fatigue to shake her purpose.

"Now then, what are you doing?" he demanded, gruffly.

"We're sitting down," Sylvia informed him.

"Loitering isn't allowed here," the policeman said.

"Where is it allowed, please?" she asked, sweetly.

"Loitering isn't allowed nowhere," the policeman declared.

"Well, why did you say it wasn't allowed here?" she continued. "I thought you were going to tell us of a place where it was allowed."

Arthur jogged Sylvia's elbow and whispered to her not to annoy the policeman.

"Come along, now, move on," the policeman commanded. In order to emphasize his authority he flashed his bull's-eye in Sylvia's face. "Where do you live?" he asked, after the scrutiny.

"Lillie Road, Fulham. We missed the last train from Hampstead, and we're walking home. I never heard of any rule against sitting on one's own luggage in the middle of the night. I think you'd better take us to the police station. We must rest somewhere."

The policeman looked puzzled.

"What did you want to miss your train for?" he asked.

"We didn't want to miss it," Sylvia gently explained. "We were very angry when we missed it. Come on, Arthur, I don't feel tired any longer."

She got up and started off down Haverstock Hill, followed by Arthur.

"I'm sorry you can't recommend any proper loitering-places on the road," said Sylvia, turning round, "because we shall probably have to loiter about thirty-six times before we get to Lillie Road. Good night. If we meet any burglars we'll give them your love and say there's a nice policeman living on Haverstock Hill who'd like a chat."

"Suppose he had run us in?" Arthur said, when they had left the policeman behind them.

"I wanted him to at first," Sylvia replied. "But afterward I thought it might be awkward on account of Monkley's cash-box. I wish we could open it now and see how much there is inside, but perhaps it would look funny at this time of night."

They had nearly reached the bottom of Haverstock Hill, and there were signs of life in the squalid streets they were approaching.

"I don't think we ought to hang about here," Arthur said. "These are slums. We ought to be careful; I think we ought to have waited till the morning."

"You wouldn't have come, if we'd waited," Sylvia maintained. "You'd have been too worried about leaving your mother."

"I'm still worried about that," said Arthur, gloomily.

"Why? You can send a post-card to say that you're all right. Knowing where you are won't make up for your being away. In any case, you'd have had to go away soon. You couldn't have spent your whole life in that house at Hampstead."

"Well, I think this running away will bring us bad luck."

Sylvia made a dramatic pause and dropped her valise on the pavement.

"Go home, then. Go home and leave me alone. If you can't enjoy yourself, I'd rather you went home. I can't bear to be with somebody who is not enjoying himself as much as I am."

"You can't be enjoying this waking about all night with two bags and a cat," Arthur insisted. "But I'm not going home without you. If you want to go on, I shall go on, too. I'm feeling rather tired. I expect I shall enjoy myself more to-morrow."

Sylvia picked up her valise again. "I hope you will, I'm sure," she said. "You're spoiling the fun by grumbling all the time like this. What is there to grumble at? Just a small bag which makes your arm ache. You ought to be glad you haven't got mine to carry as well as your own."

After another quarter of an hour among the ill-favored streets Sylvia called a rest; this time they withdrew from the pavement into the area of an unoccupied house, where they leaned against the damp brick wall, quite exhausted, and heard without interest the footsteps of the people who went past above. Maria began to mew and Sylvia let her out of the basket. A lean and amorous tom-cat in pursuit of love considered that Maria had prejudiced his chance of success, and their recriminations ended in a noisy scuffle during which the lid of a dust-bin in the next area was upset with a loud clatter; somebody, throwing open a window, emptied a utensil partly over Arthur.

"Don't make such a noise. It was only a jug," Sylvia whispered. "You'll wake up all the houses."

"It's your damned cat making the noise," Arthur said. "Come here, you brute."

Maria was at last secured and replaced in his basket, and Arthur asked Sylvia if she was sure it was only a jug.

"It's simply beastly in this area," he added. "Anything's better than sitting here."

After making sure that nobody was in sight, they went on their way, though by now their legs were so weary that from time to time the bags scraped along the pavement.

"The worst of it is," Sylvia sighed, "we've come so far now that it would be just as tiring to go back to Hampstead as to go on."

"Oh, *you're* thinking now of going back!" Arthur jeered. "It's a pity you didn't think of that when we were on Haverstock Hill."

"I'm not thinking at all of going back," Sylvia snapped. "I'm not tired."

"Oh no," said Arthur, sarcastically. "And I'm not at all wet, really."

They got more and more irritable with each other. The bow in Sylvia's hair dropped off, and with all the fretful obstinacy of fatigue she would go wandering back on their tracks to see if she could find it; but the bow was lost. At last they saw a hansom coming toward them at a walking pace, and Sylvia announced that they would ride.

"But where shall we drive to?" Arthur asked. "We can't just get in and drive anywhere."

"We'll tell him to go to Waterloo," said Sylvia. "Stations are always open; we can wait there till the morning and then look for a house."

She hailed the cab; with sighs of relief they sank back upon the seat, exhausted. Presently an odd noise like a fishmonger's smacking a cod could be heard beside the cab, and, leaning out over the apron to see what was the cause of it, Arthur was spattered with mud by a piece of the tire which was flogging the road with each revolution of the wheel. The driver pulled up and descended from the box to restrain it.

"I've been tying it up all day, but it will do it," he complained. "There's nothing to worry over, but it fidgets one, don't it, flapping like that? I've tied it up with string and I've tied it up with wire, and last time I used my handkerchief. Now I suppose it's got to be my bootlace. Well, here goes," he said, and with many grunts he stooped over to undo his lace.

Neither Sylvia nor Arthur could ever say what occurred to irritate a horse that with equanimity had tolerated the flapping all day, but suddenly it leaped forward at a canter, while the loose piece of tire slapped the road with increasing rapidity and noise. The reins slipped down; and Sylvia, who had often been allowed to drive with Blanche, managed to gather them up and keep the horse more or less in the middle of the road. After the cab had traveled about a mile the tire that all day had been seeking freedom achieved its purpose and, lancing itself before the vehicle in a swift parabola, looped itself round the ancient ragman who was shuffling along the gutter in pursuit of wealth. The horse chose that moment to stop abruptly and an unpleasant encounter with the ragman seemed inevitable. Already he was approaching the cab, waving in angry fashion his spiked stick and swearing in a bronchial voice; he stopped his abuse, however, on perceiving the absence of the driver, and muttering to himself: "A lucky night, so help me! A lovely long strip of india-rubber! Gor! what a find!" he turned round and walked away as fast as he could, stuffing the tire into his basket as he went.

"I wonder whether I could drive the cab properly if I climbed up on the box," said Sylvia, thoughtfully.

"Oh no! For goodness' sake, don't do anything of the kind!" Arthur begged. "Let's get down while the beast is quiet. Come along. We shall never be able to explain why we're in this cab. It's like a dream."

Sylvia gave way so far as not to mount the box, but she declined to alight, and insisted they ought to stay where they were and rest as long as they could; there were still a number of dark hours before them.

"But my dear girl, this beast of a horse may start off again," Arthur protested.

"Well, what if it does?" Sylvia said. "We can't be any more lost than we are now. I don't know in the least what part of London we've got to."

"I'm sure there's something the matter with this cab," Arthur woefully exclaimed.

"There is," she agreed. "You've just set fire to it with that match."

"I'm so nervous," said Arthur. "I don't know what I'm doing. Phew! what a stink of burnt hair. Do let's get out."

He stamped on the smoldering mat.

"Shut up," Sylvia commanded. "I'm going to try and have a sleep. Wake me up if the horse tries to walk into a shop or anything."

40

But this was more than Arthur could stand, and he shook her in desperation. "You sha'n't go to sleep. You don't seem to mind what happens to us."

"Not a bit," Sylvia agreed. Then suddenly she sang at the top of her voice, "for I'm off with the raggle-taggle gipsies—oh!"

The horse at once trotted forward, and Arthur was in despair.

"Oh, damn!" he moaned. "Now you've started that horrible brute off again. Whatever made me come away with you?"

"You can go home whenever you like," said Sylvia, coldly.

"What's the good of telling me that when we're tearing along in a cab without a driver?" Arthur bewailed.

"We're not tearing along," Sylvia contradicted. "And I'm driving. I expect the horse will go back to its stable if we don't interfere with him too much."

"Who wants to interfere with the brute? Oh, listen to that wheel. I'm sure it's coming off."

"Here's a cab shelter," Sylvia said, encouragingly. "I'm going to try and pull up."

Luckily the horse was ready enough to stop, and both of them got out. Sylvia walked without hesitation into the shelter, followed by Arthur with the bags. There were three or four cabmen inside, eating voluptuously in an atmosphere of tobacco smoke, steam, and burnt grease. She explained to them about the cab's running away, was much gratified by the attention her story secured, and learned that it was three o'clock and that she was in Somers Town.

"Where are you going, missie?" one of the cabmen asked.

"We were going to Waterloo, but we don't mind staying here," Sylvia said. "My brother is rather tired and my cat would like some milk."

"What did the driver look like, missie?" one of the men asked.

Sylvia described him vaguely as rather fat, a description which would have equally suited any of the present company, with the exception of the attendant tout, who was exceptionally lean.

"I wonder if it 'ud be Bill?" said one of the cabmen.

"I shouldn't be surprised."

"Wasn't Bill grumbling about his tire this morning?"

"I don't know if it was his tire; he was grumbling about something."

"I reckon it's Bill. Did you notice if the gentleman as drove you had a swelling behind his ear?" asked the man who had first propounded the theory of the missing driver's being Bill.

"I didn't notice," said Sylvia.

"About the size of a largish potato?" the theorist pressed, encouragingly.

"I'm afraid I didn't notice," said Sylvia.

"It must be Bill," the theorist decided. "Any one wouldn't notice that swelling in the dark, 'specially if Bill had his collar turned up."

"He did have his collar turned up," Arthur put in.

"There you are," said the theorist. "What did I tell you? Of course it's Bill. No one wouldn't see his swelling with his coat turned up. Poor old Bill, he won't half swear when he has to walk home to-night. Here, Joe," he went on, addressing the attending tout. "Give Bill's horse a bit of a feed."

Sylvia and Arthur were given large slices of bread and butter and large cups of coffee; Maria had a saucer of milk. Life was looking much more cheerful. Presently a burly cabman appeared in the entrance of the shelter and was greeted with shouts of merriment.

"What ho, Bill, old cock! Lost your ruddy cab, old sporty? Lor! we haven't half laughed to think of you having to use your bacon and eggs to get here. I reckon you didn't half swear."

"Who are you getting at, you blinking set of mugs? Who's lost his ruddy cab?" demanded Bill.

"That's not the driver," Sylvia said.

"I thought it couldn't be Bill," said the theorist quickly. "As soon as I heard she never noticed that lump behind his ear, I thought it wasn't Bill."

"Here, less of it, you and your lumps behind the ear," said Bill, aggressively. "You'll have a blurry lump behin' your own blurry ear, Fred Organ, before you knows where you are."

Sylvia could not refrain from observing the famous lump with a good deal of curiosity, and she wondered how any one could ever have supposed it might be unnoticed. She would have described it as more like a beet root than a potato, she thought.

A long discussion about the future of the driverless cab ensued; finally it was decided that Joe the tout should lead it to the police station if it were not claimed by daylight. The company then turned to the discussion of the future of the abandoned fares. Sylvia had by this time evolved an elaborate tale of running away from a stepfather whose conduct to Arthur, herself, and Maria had been extremely brutal.

"Knocked the cat about, did he?" said the theorist, whose name was Fred Organ. "I never could abide people as ill-treated dumb animals."

Sylvia went on to explain that they had intended to throw themselves on the mercy of an aunt who lived at Dover, and with that intention had been bound for Waterloo when they lost their driver. When she was told that they were going to the wrong station for Dover, she began to express fears of the reception her aunt might accord them. Did any one present know where they could find lodgings, for which, of course, they would pay, because their mother had provided them with the necessary money.

"That's a mother all over," said Fred Organ, with enthusiastic sentiment. "Ain't it, boys? Ah, I wish I hadn't lost my poor old mother."

Various suggestions about rooms were made, but finally Fred Organ was so much moved by the emotional details with which Sylvia continually supplemented her tale that he offered to give them lodgings in his own house near Finsbury Park. Sylvia would have preferred a suburb that was barred to Monkley, but she accepted the offer because, with Arthur turning out so inept at adventure, it seemed foolish to take any more risks that night.

Fred Organ had succeeded to the paternal house and hansom about two years before. He was now twenty-six, but his corpulence made him appear older; for the chubby smoothness of youth had vanished with continual exposure to the weather, leaving behind many folds and furrows in his large face. Mr. Organ, senior, had bought No. 53 Colonial Terrace by instalments, the punctual payment of which had worried him so much as probably to shorten his life, the last one having been paid just before his death. He had only a week or two for the enjoyment of possession, which was as well; for the house that had cost its owner so much effort to obtain was nearly as ripe for dissolution as himself, and the maintenance of it in repair seemed likely to cause Fred Organ as much financial stress in the future as the original purchase had caused his father in the past.

So much of his history did Fred Organ give them while he was stabling his horse, before he could introduce them to his inheritance. It was five o'clock of a chill February morning, and the relief of finding herself safely under a roof after such a tiring and insecure night compensated Sylvia for the impression of unutterable dreariness that Colonial Terrace first made upon her mind, a dreariness quite out of accord with the romantic beginning to the life of independence of which she had dreamed. They could not go to bed when they reached the house, because Fred Organ, master though he was, doubted if it would be wise to wake up his sister to accommodate the guests.

"Not that she'd have any call to make a fuss," he observed, "because if I says a thing in No. 53, no one hasn't got the right to object. Still, I'd rather you got a nice first impression of my sister Edith. Well, make yourselves at home. I'll rout round and get the kitchen fire going."

Fred routed round with such effect that he woke his sister, who began to scream from the landing above:

"Hube! Get up, you great coward! There's somebody breaking in at the back. Get up, Hube, and fetch a policeman before we're both murdered."

"It's only me, Ede," Fred called out. "Keep your hair on."

When Sylvia saw Edith Organ's curl-papers she thought the last injunction was rather funny. Explanations were soon given and Edith was so happy to find her alarm unnecessary that she was as pleasant as possible and even invited Sylvia to come and share her bed and sleep late into the morning; whereupon Fred Organ invited Arthur to share his bed, which Arthur firmly declined to do, notwithstanding Sylvia's frown.

"Well, you can't go to bed with the girls," said Fred.

"Oh, Fred, you are a.... Oh, he is a.... Oh, isn't he? Oh, I never. Fancy! What a thing to say! There! Well! Who ever did? I'm sure. What a remark to pass!" Edith exclaimed, quite incoherent from embarrassment, pleasure, and sleep.

"Where's Hube?" Fred asked.

"Oh, Hube!" snapped Edith. "He's well underneath the bedclothes. Trust Hube for that. Nothing'd get him out of bed except an earthquake."

"Wouldn't it, then?" said a sleek voice, and Hube himself, an extremely fat young man in a trailing nightgown, appeared in the doorway.

"You wouldn't think he was only nineteen, would you?" said Fred, proudly.

"Nice noise to kick up in the middle of the night," Hubert grumbled. "I dreamt the house was falling down on top of me."

"And it will, too," Fred prophesied, "if I can't soon scrape together some money for repairs. There's a crack as wide as the strand down the back."

Sylvia wondered how so rickety a house was able to withstand the wear and tear of such a fat family when they all, with the exception of Arthur, who lay down on the kitchen table, went creaking up-stairs to bed.

The examination of Monkley's cash-box produced £35; Sylvia felt ineffably rich, so rich that she offered to lend Fred Organ the money he wanted to repair his property. He accepted the offer in the spirit in which it was made, as he said, and Sylvia, whom contact with Monkley had left curiously uncynical, felt that she had endeared herself to Fred Organ for a long time to come. She was given a room of her own at No. 53, for which she was glad, because sleeping with Edith had been rather like eating scented cornflour pudding, a combination of the flabby with the stuffy that had never appeared to her taste. Arthur was given the choice of sleeping with Hubert or in the bath, and he chose the latter without a moment's hesitation.

Relations between Arthur and Hubert had been strained ever since. Hubert offered Arthur a bite from an apple he was munching, which was refused with a too obvious disgust.

"Go on, what do you take me for? Eve?" asked Hubert, indignantly. "It won't poison you."

The strain was not relaxed by Hubert's obvious fondness for Sylvia.

"I thought when I came away with you," Arthur said, "that we were going to live by ourselves and earn our own living; instead of which you let that fat brute hang around you all day."

"I can't be always rude to him," Sylvia explained. "He's very good-natured."

"Do you call it good-natured to turn the tap on me when I'm lying in bed?" Arthur demanded.

"I expect he only did it for fun."

"Fun!" said Arthur, darkly. "I shall hit him one of these days."

Arthur did hit him; but Hubert, with all his fat, hit harder than he, and Arthur never tried again. Sylvia found herself growing very tired of him; the universal censure upon his namby-pambyness was beginning to react upon her. The poetical youth of Hampstead Heath seemed no longer so poetical in Colonial Terrace. Yet she did not want to quarrel with him finally, for in a curious way he represented to her a link with what she still paradoxically spoke of as home. Sylvia had really had a great affection for Monkley, which made her hate him more for what he had tried to do. Yet, though she hated him and though the notion of being with him again made her shudder, she could not forget that he had known her father, who was bound up with the memory of her mother and of all the past that, being so irreparably over, was now strangely cherished. Sylvia felt that, were Arthur to go, she would indeed find herself alone, in that state which first she had dreaded, then desired, and now once again dreaded, notwithstanding her bold conceptions of independence and belief in her own ability to determine the manner of life she wished. There were times when she felt what almost amounted to a passionate hatred of Colonial Terrace, which had brought her freedom, indeed, but the freedom of a world too gray to make freedom worth possessing. She was fond of Fred Organ, and she fancied that he would have liked formally to adopt her; yet the idea of being adopted by him somehow repelled her. She was fond of Edith Organ too, but no fonder than she had been of Clara; Edith seemed to have less to tell her about life than Clara, perhaps because she was older now and had read so many books. As for Hubert, who claimed to be in love with her, he existed about the house like a large over-fed dog; that was all, that and his capacity for teasing Arthur, which amused her.

Everything about this escapade was so different from what she had planned. Always in her dreams there had been a room with a green view over trees or a silver view over water, and herself encouraging some one (she supposed it must have been Arthur, though she could hardly believe this when she looked at him now) to perform the kind of fantastic deeds that people performed in books. Surely some books were true. Looking back on her old fancies, Sylvia came to the conclusion that she had always pictured herself married to Arthur; yet how ridiculous such an idea now seemed. He had always talked with regret of the adventures that were no longer possible in dull modern days; but when the very small adventure of being in a runaway cab had happened, how miserably Arthur had failed to rise to the occasion, and now here he was loafing in Colonial Terrace. Hubert had secured a position in a bookshop near Finsbury Park railway station, which he had forfeited very soon afterward, but only because he had made a habit of borrowing for Sylvia's perusal the books which customers had bought, and of sending them on to their owners two or three days later. To be sure, they had nearly all been very dull books of a religious bent, but in such a district as Finsbury Park what else could be expected? At least Hubert had sacrificed something for her. Arthur had done nothing; even when Fred Organ, to please Sylvia, had offered to teach him to drive a hansom, he had refused to learn.

One day Edith Organ announced that there was to be a supper-party at a public house in Harringay where one of the barmaids was a friend of hers. It seemed that Mrs. Hartle, the proprietress, had recently had cause to rejoice over a victory, but whether it was domestic, political, or professional Edith was unable to remember; at any rate, a jolly evening could be counted upon.

"You must wear that new white dress, Syl; it suits you a treat," Edith advised. "I was told only to bring one gentleman, and I think it's Artie's turn."

"Why?" Hubert demanded, fiercely.

"Oh, Hube, you know you don't like parties. You always want to go home early, and I'm out to enjoy myself and I don't care who knows it."

Sylvia suspected that Edith's real reason for wishing Arthur to be the guest was his greater presentableness; she had often heard her praise Arthur's appearance while deprecating his namby-pamby manner; however, for a party like this, of which Edith was proclaiming the extreme selectness, that might be considered an advantage. Mrs. Hartle was reputed to be a woman to whom the least vulgarity was disgusting.

"She's highly particular, they tell me, not to say stand-offish. You know, doesn't like to make herself cheap. Well, I don't blame her. She's thought a lot of round here. She had some trouble with her husband—her second husband that is—and everybody speaks very highly of the dignified way in which she made him sling his hook out of it."

"I don't think so much of her," Hubert grunted. "I went into the saloon-bar once, and she said, 'Here, my man, the public bar is the hother side.' 'Oh, his it?' I said. 'Well, I can't round the corner for the crowd,' I said, 'listening to your old man singing "At Trinity Church I met my doom" on the pavement outside.' She didn't half color up, I can tell you. So he was singing, too, fit to give any one the earache to listen to him. I don't want to go to her supper-party."

"Well, if you're not going, you needn't be so nasty about it, Hube. I'd take you if I could."

"I wouldn't come," Hubert declared. "Not if Mrs. Hartle was to go down on her knees and ask me to come. So shut your mouth."

The chief event of the party for Sylvia was her meeting with Danny Lewis, who paid her a good deal of attention at supper and danced with her all the time afterward. Sylvia was grateful to him for his patience with her bad dancing at first, and she learned so quickly under his direction that when it was time to go she really danced rather well. Sylvia's new friend saw them back to Colonial Terrace and invited himself to tea the following afternoon. Edith, who could never bear the suggestion of impoliteness, assured him that he would be most welcome, though she confided in Sylvia, as they went up to bed, that she could not feel quite sure about him. Sylvia insisted he was everything he should be, and praised his manners so highly that Edith humbly promised to believe in his perfection. Arthur went up-stairs and slammed his door without saying good night.

The next morning, a morning of east wind, Arthur attacked Sylvia on the subject of her behavior the night before.

"Look here," he opened, very grandly, "if you prefer to spend the evenings waltzing with dirty little Jews, I won't stand it."

Sylvia regarded him disdainfully.

"Do you hear?" repeated Arthur. "I won't stand it. It's bad enough with that great hulking lout here, but when it comes to a greasy Jew I've had enough."

"So have I," Sylvia said. "You'd better go back to Hampstead."

"I'm going to-day," Arthur declared, and waited pathetically for Sylvia to protest. She was silent. Then he tried to be affectionate, and vowed he had not meant a word he said, but she brushed away his tentative caress and meek apology.

"I don't want to talk to you any more," she said. "There are lots of things I could tell you; but you'll always be unhappy anyway, because you're soft and silly, so I won't. You'll be home for dinner," she added.

When Arthur was ready to start he looked so forlorn that Sylvia was sorry for him.

"Here, take Maria," she said, impulsively. "He'll remind you of me."

"I don't want anything to remind me of you," said Arthur in a hollow voice, "but I'll take Maria."

That afternoon Danny Lewis, wearing a bright orange tie and a flashing ring, came to visit Sylvia. She had already told him a good deal about herself the night before, and when now she told him how she had dismissed Arthur he suggested that Monkley would probably find out where she was and come to take her back. Sylvia turned pale; the possibility of Arthur's betrayal of her address had never struck her. She cried in a panic that she must leave Finsbury Park at once. Danny offered to find her a room.

"I've got no money. I spent all I had left on new frocks," she bewailed.

"That's all right, kid; bring the frocks along with you. I've got plenty of money."

Sylvia packed in a frenzy of haste, expecting every moment to hear the bell ring and see Monkley waiting grimly outside; his cold eyes, when her imagination recalled them, made her shiver with fear. When they got down-stairs Hubert, who was in the passage, asked where she was going, and she told him that she was going away.

"Not with that—" said Hubert, barring the way to the front door.

Danny did not hesitate; his arm shot out, and Hubert went over, bringing down the hat-stand with a crash.

"Quick, quick!" cried Sylvia, in exultation at being with some one who could act. "Edie's gone round to the baker's to fetch some crumpets for tea. Let's go before she gets back."

They hurried out. The wind had fallen. Colonial Terrace looked very gray, very quiet, very long in the bitter March air. Danny Lewis with his orange tie promised a richer, warmer life beyond these ridiculous little houses that imitated one another.

CHAPTER V

DANNY LEWIS took Sylvia to an eating-house in Euston Road kept by a married couple called Gonner. Here everything—the meat, the pies, the butter, the streaky slabs of marble, the fly-blown face of the weary clock, the sawdust sprinkled on the floor, the cane-seated chairs—combined to create an effect of greasy pallor that extended even to Mr. and Mrs. Gonner themselves, who seemed to have acquired the nature of their environment. Sylvia shrank from their whitish arms bare to the elbow and glistering with fats, and from their faces, which seemed to her like bladders of lard, especially Mrs. Gonner's, who wore on the top of her head a knob of dank etiolated hair. In such an atmosphere Danny Lewis with his brilliant tie and green beaver hat acquired a richness of personality that quite overpowered Sylvia's judgment and preserved the condition of abnormal excitement set up by the rapidity and completeness with which this time she had abandoned herself to independence.

There was a brief conversation between Danny and the Gonners, after which Mr. Gonner returned to his task of cutting some very fat bacon into rashers and Mrs. Gonner held up the flap of the counter for Sylvia and Danny to pass up-stairs through the back of the shop. For one moment Sylvia hesitated when the flap dropped back into its place, for it seemed to make dangerously irrevocable her admittance to the unknown house above; Danny saw her hesitation and with a word or two of encouragement checked her impulse to go no farther. Mrs. Gonner led the way up-stairs and showed them into a bedroom prematurely darkened by coarse lace curtains that shut out the fading daylight. Sylvia had a vague impression of too much furniture, which was confirmed when Mrs. Gonner lit a gas-jet over the mantelpiece; she looked round distastefully at the double-bed pushed against the wall, at the crimson vases painted with butterflies, at the faded oleograph of two children on the edge of a precipice with a guardian angel behind them, whose face had at some time been eaten away by mice. There was a short silence, only broken by Mrs. Gonner's whispering breath.

"We shall be all right here, kid, eh?" exclaimed Danny, in a tone that was at once suave and boisterous.

"What's your room like?" Sylvia asked.

He looked at her a moment, seemed about to speak, thought better of it, and turned to Mrs. Gonner, who told Danny that he could have the front room as well if he wanted it; they moved along the passage to inspect this room, which was much larger and better lighted than the other and was pleasantly filled with the noise of traffic. Sylvia immediately declared that she preferred to be here.

"So I'm to have the rabbit-hutch," said Danny, laughing easily. "Trust a woman to have her own way! That's right, isn't it, Mrs. Gonner?"

Mrs. Gonner stared at Sylvia a moment, and murmured that she had long ago forgotten what she wanted, but that, anyway, for her one thing was the same as another, which Sylvia was very ready to believe.

When Mrs. Gonner had left the room, Danny told Sylvia that he must go and get a few things together from his flat in Shaftsbury Avenue, and asked if she would wait till he came back.

"Of course I'll wait," she told him. "Do you think I want to run away twice in one day?"

Danny still hesitated, and she wondered why he should expect her, who was so much used to being left alone, to mind waiting for him an hour or two.

"We might go to the Mo to-night," he suggested.

She looked blank.

"The Middlesex," he explained. "It's a music-hall. Be a good girl while I'm out. I'll bring you back some chocolates."

He seemed anxious to retain her with the hint of pleasures that were in his power to confer; it made Sylvia impatient that he should rely on them rather than upon her capacity for knowing her own mind.

"I may be young," she said, "but I do know what I want. I'm not like that woman down-stairs."

"And you know how to make other people want, eh?" Danny muttered. He took a step forward, and Sylvia hoped he was not going to try to kiss her—she felt disinclined at this moment for a long explanation—but he went off, whistling.

For a long time Sylvia stood by the window, looking down at the traffic and the lights coming out one by one in the windows opposite. She hoped that Danny would not end like Monkley, and she determined to be prompt in checking the first signs of his doing so. Standing here in this room, that was now dark except for the faint transitory shadows upon the walls and ceiling of lighted vehicles below, Sylvia's thoughts went back to the time she had spent with Blanche. It seemed to her that then she had been wiser than she was now, for all the books she had read since; or was it that she was growing up and becoming an actress in scenes that formerly she had regarded with the secure aloofness of a child?

"I'm not innocent," she said to herself. "I know everything that can be known. But yet when Monkley tried to do that I was horrified. I felt sick and frightened and angry, oh, dreadfully angry! Yet when Blanche behaved as she did I did not mind at all; I used to encourage her. Oh, why am I not a boy? If I were a boy, I would show people that making love isn't really a bit necessary. Yet sometimes I liked Arthur to make love to me. I can't make myself out. I think I must be what people call an exceptional person. I hope Danny won't make love to me. But I feel he will; and if he does I shall kill myself; I can't go on living like this with everybody making love to me. I'm not like Blanche or Mabel; I don't like it. How I used to hate Mabel! Shall I ever get like her? Oh, I wish, I wish, I wish I were a boy. I don't believe Danny will be any better than Jimmy was. Yet he doesn't frighten me so much. He doesn't seem so much there as Jimmy was. But if he does make love to me, it will be more dangerous. How shall I ever escape from here? I'm sure Mrs. Gonner will never lift the flap."

Sylvia began to be obsessed by that flap, and the notion of it wrought upon her fancy to such an extent that she was impelled to go down-stairs and see if the way out was open or shut, excusing her abrupt appearance by asking for a box of matches. There were two or three people eating at the white tables, who eyed her curiously; she wondered what they would have done if she had suddenly begged their help. She was vexed with herself for giving way to her nerves like this, and she went up-stairs again with a grand resolve to be very brave. She even challenged her terrors by going into that bedroom behind and contending with its oppressiveness. So successful was she in calming her overwrought nerves that, when Danny suddenly came back and found her in his bedroom, she was no longer afraid; she looked at him there in the doorway, wearing now a large tie of pale-blue silk, as she would have looked at any brigand in an opera. When he presented her with a large box of chocolates she laughed. He wondered why; she said it was she who ought to give him chocolates, which left him blank. She tried to explain her impression of him as a brigand, and he asked her if she meant that he looked like an actor.

"Yes, that's what I mean," she said, impatiently, though she meant nothing of the kind.

Danny seemed gratified as by a compliment and said that he was often mistaken for an actor; he supposed it was his hair.

They dined at a restaurant in Soho, where Sylvia was conscious of arousing a good deal of attention; afterward they went to the Middlesex music-hall, but she felt very tired, and did not enjoy it so much as she expected. Moreover, Danny irritated her by sucking his teeth with an air of importance all through the evening.

For a fortnight Danny treated Sylvia with what was almost a luxurious consideration. She was never really taken in by it, but she submitted so willingly to being spoiled that, as she told herself, she could hardly blame Danny for thinking he was fast making himself indispensable to her happiness. He was very anxious for her to lead a lazy existence, encouraged her to lie in bed the whole morning, fed her with chocolates, and tried to cultivate in her a habit of supposing that it was impossible to go anywhere without driving in a hansom; he also used to buy her brightly colored blouses and scarves, which she used to wear out of politeness, for they gave her very little pleasure. He flattered her consistently, praising her cleverness and comparing her sense of humor with that of other women always to their disadvantage. He told stories very well, particularly those against his own race; and though Sylvia was a little scornful of this truckling self-mockery, she could not help laughing at the stories. Sylvia realized by the contempt with which Danny referred to women that his victories had usually been gained very easily, and she was much on her guard. Encouraged, however, by the way in which Sylvia seemed to enjoy the superficial pleasures he provided for her, Danny soon attempted to bestow his favors as he bestowed his chocolates. Sylvia, who never feared Danny personally as she had feared Monkley, repulsed him, yet not so firmly as she would have done had not her first impression of the house still affected her imagination. Danny, who divined her malaise, but mistook it for the terror he was used to inspiring, began to play the bully. It was twilight, one of those sapphire twilights of early spring; the gas had not been lighted and the fire had died away to a glow. Sylvia had thrown off his caressing arm three times, when Danny suddenly jumped up, pulled out a clasp-knife, and, standing over Sylvia, threatened her with death if she would not immediately consent to be his. Sylvia's heart beat a little faster at such a threat delivered with all the additional force vile language could give to it, but she saw two things quite clearly: first, that, if Danny were really to kill her, death would be far preferable to surrender; secondly, that the surest way of avoiding either would be by assuming he would turn out a coward in the face of the unexpected. She rose from the arm-chair; Danny rushed to the door, flourishing his knife and forbidding her to think of escape.

"Who wants to escape?" she asked, in so cool a tone that Danny, who had naturally anticipated a more feminine reception of his violence, failed to sustain his part by letting her see that he was puzzled. She strolled across the room to the wash-stand; then she strolled up to the brigand.

"Put that knife away," she said. "I want to tell you something, darling Danny."

In the gloom she could see that he threw a suspicious glance at her for the endearing epithet, but he put away the knife.

"What do you want to say?" he growled.

"Only this." She brought her arm swiftly round and emptied the water-bottle over him. "Though I ought to smash it on your greasy head. I read in a book once that the Jews were a subject race. You'd better light the gas."

He spluttered that he was all wet, and she turned away from him, horribly scared that in a moment his fingers would be tightening round her neck; but he had taken off his coat and was shaking it.

Sylvia poked the fire and sat down again in the arm-chair. "Listen," she began.

He came across the room in his shirt-sleeves, his tie hanging in a cascade of amber silk over his waistcoat.

"No, don't pull down the blinds," she added. "I want to be quite sure you really have cooled down and aren't going to play with that knife again. Listen. It's no good your trying to make love to me. I don't want to be made love to by anybody, least of all by you."

Danny looked more cheerful when she assured him of her indifference to other men.

"It's no use your killing me, because you'll only be hanged. It's no use your stabbing me, because you'll go to prison. If you hit me, I shall hit you back. You thought I was afraid of you. I wasn't. I'm more afraid of a bug than I am of you. I saw a bug to-day; so I'm going to leave this house. The weather's getting warmer. You and the bugs have come out together. Come along, Danny, dry your coat and tell me a story that will make me laugh. Tell me the story of the Jew who died of grief because he bought his wife a new hat and found his best friend had bought her one that day and he might have saved his money. Do make me laugh, Danny."

They went to the Middlesex music-hall that evening, and Danny did not suck his teeth once. The next morning he told Sylvia that he had been to visit a friend who wished very much to meet her, and that he proposed to introduce him that afternoon, if she agreed. He was a fellow in a good way of business, the son of a bootmaker in Drury Lane, quite a superior sort of fellow and one by whom she could not fail to be impressed; his name was Jay Cohen. The friend arrived toward four o'clock, and Danny on some excuse left him with Sylvia. He had big teeth and round, prominent eyes; his boots were very glossy and sharply pointed at the toes, with uppers of what looked like leopard-skin. Observing Sylvia's glances directed to his boots, he asked with a smile if she admired the latest thing. She confessed they were rather too late for her taste, and Mr. Cohen excused them as a pair sent back to his father by a well-known music-hall comedian, who complained of their pinching him. Sylvia said it was lucky they only pinched him; she should not have been astonished if they had bitten him.

"You're a Miss Smartie, aren't you?" said Jay Cohen.

The conversation languished for a while, but presently he asked Sylvia why she was so unkind to his friend Danny.

"What do you mean, 'unkind'?" she repeated. "Unkind what about?"

Mr. Cohen smiled in a deprecating way. "He's a good boy, is Danny. Real good. He is, really. All the girls are mad about Danny. You know, smart girls, girls that get around. He's very free, too. Money's nothing to Danny when he's out to spend. His father's got a tobacconist's shop in the Caledonian Road. A good business—a very good business. Danny told me what the turn-over was once, and I was surprised. I remember I thought what a rare good business it was. Well, Danny's feeling a bit upset to-day, and he came round to see me early this morning. He must have been very upset, because it was very early, and he said to me that he was mad over a girl and would I speak for him? He reckoned he'd made a big mistake and he wanted to put it right, but he was afraid of being laughed at, because the young lady in question was a bit high-handed. He wants to marry you. There it is right out. He'd like to marry you at once, but he's afraid of his father, and he thought...."

Mr. Cohen broke off suddenly in his proposal and listened: "What's that?"

"It sounds like some one shouting down-stairs," Sylvia said. "But you often hear rows going on down there. There was a row yesterday because a woman bit on a stone in a pie and broke her tooth."

"That's Jubie's voice," said Mr. Cohen, blinking his eyes and running his hands nervously through his sleek hair.

"Who's Jubie?"

Before he could explain there was a sound of impassioned footsteps on the stairs. In a moment the door was flung open, and a handsome Jewess with flashing eyes and ear-rings slammed it behind her.

"Where's Danny?" she demanded.

"Is that you, Jubie?" said Mr. Cohen. "Danny's gone over to see his dad. He won't be here to-day."

"You liar, he's here this moment. I followed him into the shop and he ran up-stairs. So you're the kid he's been trailing around with him," she said, eying Sylvia. "The dirty rotter!"

Sylvia resented the notion of being trailed by such a one as Danny Lewis, but, feeling undecided how to appease this tropical creature, she took the insult without reply.

"He thinks to double cross Jubie Myers! Wait till my brother Sam knows where he is."

Mr. Cohen had retired to the window and was studying the traffic of Euston Road; one of his large ears was twitching nervously toward the threats of the outraged Miss Myers, who after much breathless abuse of Sylvia at last retired to fetch her brother Sam. When she was gone, Mr. Cohen said he thought he would go too, because he did not feel inclined to meet Sam Myers, who was a pugilist with many victories to his credit at Wonderland; just as he reached the door, Danny entered and with a snarl accused him of trying to round on him.

"You know you fetched Jubie here on purpose, so as you could do me in with the kid," said Danny. "I know you, Jay Cohen."

They wrangled for some time over this, until suddenly Danny landed his friend a blow between the eyes. Sylvia, recognizing the Danny who had so neatly knocked out Hubert Organ in Colonial Terrace, became pleasantly enthusiastic on his behalf, and cried "Bravo!"

The encouragement put a fine spirit into Danny's blows; he hammered the unfortunate Cohen round and round the room, upsetting tables and chairs and wash-stand until with a stinging blow he knocked him backward into the slop-pail, in which he sat so heavily that when he tried to rise the slop-pail stuck and gave him the appearance of a large baboon crawling with elevated rump on all-fours. Danny kicked off the slop-pail, and invited Cohen to stand up to him; but when he did get on his feet he ran to the door and reached the stairs just as Mrs. Gonner was wearily ascending to find out what was happening. He tried to stop himself by clutching the knob of the baluster, which broke; the result was that he dragged Mrs. Gonner with him in a glissade which ended behind the counter. The confusion in the shop became general: Mr. Gonner cut his thumb, and the sight of the blood caused a woman who was eating a sausage to choke; another customer took advantage of the row to snatch a side of bacon and try to escape, but another customer with a finer moral sense prevented him; a dog, who was sniffing in the entrance, saw the bacon on the floor and tried to seize it, but, getting his tail trodden upon by somebody, it took fright and bit a small boy who was waiting to change a shilling into coppers. Meanwhile Sylvia, who expected every moment that Jubie and her pugilistic brother would return and increase the confusion with possibly unpleasant consequences for herself, took advantage of Danny's being occupied in an argument with Cohen and the two Gonners to put on her hat and coat and escape from the shop. She jumped on the first omnibus and congratulated herself when she looked round and saw a policeman entering the eating-house.

Presently the conductor came up for her fare; she found she had fivepence in the world. She asked him where the omnibus went, and was told to the Cedars Hotel, West Kensington.

"Past Lillie Road?"

He nodded, and she paid away her last penny. After all, even if Monkley and her father did owe Mrs. Meares a good deal of money, Sylvia did not believe she would have her arrested. She would surely be too much interested to find that she was a girl and not a boy. Sylvia laughed when she thought of Jay Cohen in the slop-pail, for she remembered the baboon in Lillie Road, and she wondered if Clara was still there. What a lot she would have to tell Mrs. Meares, and if the baron had not left she would ask him why he had attacked her in that extraordinary way when she went to the party in Redcliffe Gardens. That was more than two years ago now. Sylvia wished she had gone to Lillie Road with Arthur Madden when she had some money and could have paid Mrs. Meares what was owing to her. Now she had not a penny in the world; she had not even any clothes. The omnibus jogged on, and Sylvia's thoughts jogged with it.

"I wonder if I shall always have adventures," she said to herself, "but I wish I could sometimes have adventures that have nothing to do with love. It's such a nuisance to be always running away for the same reason. It's such a stupid reason. But it's rather jolly to run away. It's more fun than being like that girl in front." She contemplated a girl of about her own age, to whom an elderly woman was pointing out the St. James's Hall with a kind of suppressed excitement, a fever of unsatisfied pleasure.

"You've never been to the Moore and Burgess minstrels, have you, dear?" she was saying. "We *must* get your father to take us some afternoon. Look at the people coming out."

The girl looked dutifully, but Sylvia thought it was more amusing to look at the people struggling to mount omnibuses already full. She wondered what that girl would have done with somebody like Danny Lewis, and she felt sorry for the prim and dutiful young creature who could never see Jay Cohen sitting in a slop-pail. Sylvia burst into a loud laugh, and a stout woman who was occupying three-quarters of her seat edged away from her a little.

"We shall be late for tea," said the elderly woman in an ecstasy of dissipation, when she saw the clock at Hyde Park Corner. "We sha'n't be home till after six. We ought to have had tea at King's Cross."

The elderly woman was still talking about tea when they stopped at Sloane Street, and Sylvia's counterpart was still returning polite answers to her speculation; when they got down at South Kensington Station the last thing Sylvia heard was a suggestion that perhaps it might be possible to arrange for dinner to be a quarter of an hour earlier.

It was dark when Sylvia reached the house in Lillie Road and she hoped very much that Clara would open the door; but another servant came, and when she asked for Mrs. Meares a sudden alarm caught her that Mrs. Meares might no longer be here and that she would be left alone in the night without a penny in the world. But Mrs. Meares was in.

"Have you come about the place?" whispered the new servant. "Because if you have you'll take my advice and have nothing to do with it."

Sylvia asked why.

"Why, it's nothing but a common lodging-house in my opinion. The woman who keeps it—lady *she* calls herself—tries to kid you as they're all paying guests. And the cats! You may like cats. I don't. Besides I've been used to company where I've been in service, and the only company you get here is beetles. If any one goes down into the kitchen at night it's like walking on nutshells, they're so thick."

"I haven't come about the place," Sylvia explained. "I want to see Mrs. Meares herself."

"Oh, a friend of hers. I'm sorry, I'm shaw," said the servant, "but I haven't said nothing but what is gospel truth, and I told her the same. You'd better come up to the droring-room—well, droring-room! You'll have to excuse the laundry, which is all over the chairs because we had the sweep in this morning. A nice hullabaloo there was yesterday! Fire-engines and all. Mrs. Meares was very upset. She's up in her bedroom, I expect."

The servant lit the gas in the drawing-room and, leaving Sylvia among the outspread linen, went up-stairs to fetch Mrs. Meares, who shortly afterward descended in a condition of dignified bewilderment and entered the room with one arm arched like a note of interrogation in cautious welcome.

"Miss Scarlett? The name is familiar, but—?"

Sylvia poured out her story, and at the end of it Mrs. Meares dreamily smoothed her brow.

"I don't quite understand. Were you a girl dressed as a boy then or are you a boy dressed as a girl now?"

Sylvia explained, and while she was giving the explanation she became aware of a profound change in Mrs. Meares's attitude toward her, an alteration of standpoint much more radical than could have been caused by any resentment at the behavior of Monkley and her father. Suddenly Sylvia regarded Mrs. Meares with the eyes of Clara, or of that new servant who had whispered to her in the hall. She was no longer the bland and futile Irishwoman of regal blood; the good-natured and feckless creature with open placket and draperies trailing in the dust of her ill-swept house; the soft-voiced, soft-hearted Hibernian with a gentle smile for man's failings and foibles, and a tear ever welling from that moist gray eye in memory of her husband's defection and the death of her infant son. Sylvia felt that now she was being sized up by some one who would never be indulgent again, who would exact from her the uttermost her girlhood could give, who would never forget the advantage she had gained in learning how desperate was the state of Sylvia Scarlett, and who would profit by it accordingly.

"It seems so peculiar to resort to me," Mrs. Meares was saying, "after the way your father treated me, but I'm not the woman to bear a grudge. Thank God, I can meet the blows of fortune with nobility and forgive an injury with any one in the world. It's lucky indeed that I can show my true character and offer you assistance. The servant is leaving to-morrow, and though I will not take advantage of your position to ask you to do anything in the nature of menial labor, though to be sure it's myself knows too well the word—to put it shortly, I can offer you board and lodging in return for any little help you may give me until I will get a new servant. And it's not easy to get servants these days. Such grand ideas have they."

Sylvia felt that she ought to accept this offer; she was destitute and she wished to avoid charity, having grasped that, though it was a great thing to make oneself indispensable, it was equally important not to put oneself under an obligation; finally it would be a satisfaction to pay back what her father owed. Not that she fancied his ghost would be disturbed by the recollection of any earthly debts; it would be purely a personal satisfaction, and she told Mrs. Meares that she was willing to help under the proposed terms.

Somewhere about nine o'clock Sylvia sat down with Mrs. Meares in the breakfast-room to supper, which was served by Amelia as if she had been unwillingly dragged into a game of cards and was showing her displeasure in the way she dealt the hand. The incandescent gas jigged up and down, and Mrs. Meares swept her plate every time she languorously flung morsels to the numerous cats, some of which they did not like and left to be trodden into the threadbare carpet by Amelia. Sylvia made inquiries about Mr. Morgan and the baron, but they had both left; the guests at present were a young actor who hoped to walk on in the new production at the St. James's, a Nonconformist minister who had been persecuted by his congregation into resigning, and an elderly clerk threatened with locomotor ataxia, who had a theory, contrary to the advice of his doctor, that it was beneficial to walk to the city every morning. His symptoms were described with many details, but, owing to Mrs. Meares's diving under the table to show the cats where a morsel of meat had escaped their notice, it was difficult to distinguish between the symptoms of the disease, the topography of the meat, and the names of the cats.

Next day Sylvia watched Amelia put on the plumage of departure and leave with her yellow tin trunk; then she set to work to help Mrs. Meares make the beds of Mr. Leslie Warburton, the actor; Mr. Croasdale, the minister; and Mr. Witherwick, the clerk. Her companion's share was entirely verbal and she disliked the task immensely. When the beds were finished, she made an attempt with Mrs. Meares to put away the clean linen, but Mrs. Meares went off in the middle to find the words of a poem she could not remember, leaving behind her towels to mark her passage as boys in paper-chases strew paper on Hampstead Heath. She did not find the words of the poem, or, if she did, she had forgotten them when Sylvia discovered her; but she had decided to alter the arrangement of the drawing-room curtains, so that to the unassorted unburied linen were added long strips of faded green silk which hung about the house for some days. Mrs. Meares asked Sylvia if she would like to try her hand at an omelette; the result was a failure, whether on account of the butter or the eggs was not quite certain; the cat to which it was given was sick.

The three lodgers made no impression on Sylvia. Each of them in turn tried to kiss her when she first went into his room; each of them afterward complained bitterly of the way the eggs were poached at breakfast and asked Mrs. Meares why she had got rid of Amelia. Gradually Sylvia found that she was working as hard as Clara used to work, that slowly and gently she was being smothered by Mrs. Meares, and that the process was regarded by Mrs. Meares as an act of holy charity, to which she frequently alluded in a very superior way.

Early one afternoon at the end of April Sylvia went out shopping for Mrs. Meares, which was not such a simple matter, because a good deal of persuasiveness had to be used nowadays with the tradesmen on account of unpaid books. As she passed the entrance to the Earl's Court Exhibition she saw Mabel Bannerman coming out; though she had hated Mabel and had always blamed her for her father's death, past enmity fled away in the pleasure of seeing somebody who belonged to a life that only a month of Mrs. Meares had wonderfully enchanted. She called after her; Mabel, only slightly more flaccid nowadays, welcomed her without hesitation.

"Why, if it isn't Sylvia! Well, I declare! You are a stranger."

They talked for a while on the pavement, until Mabel, who disliked such publicity except in a love-affair, and who was frankly eager for a full account of what had happened after she left Swanage, invited Sylvia to "have one" at the public house to which her father in the old days used to invite Jimmy, and where once he had been surprised by Sylvia's arrival with his friend.

Mabel was shocked to think that Henry had perhaps died on her account, but she assured Sylvia that for any wrong she had done him she had paid ten times over in the life she had led with the other man.

"Oh, he was a brute. Your dad was an angel beside him, dear. Oh, I was a stupid girl! But there, it's no good crying over spilt milk. What's done can't be undone, and I've paid. My voice is quite gone. I can't sing a note. What do you think I'm doing now? Working at the Exhibition. It opens next week, you know."

"Acting?" Sylvia asked.

"Acting? No! I'm in Open Sesame, the Hall of a Thousand and One Marvels. Well, I suppose it is acting in a way, because I'm supposed to be a Turkish woman. You know, sequins and trousers and a what d'ye call it—round my face. You know. Oh dear, whatever is it called? A hookah!"

"But a hookah's a pipe," Sylvia objected. "You mean a yashmak."

"That's it. Well, I sell Turkish Delight, but some of the girls sell coffee, and for an extra threepence you can see the Sultan's harem. It ought to go well. There's a couple of real Turks and a black eunuch who gives me the creeps. The manager's very hopeful. Which reminds me. He's looking out for some more girls. Why don't you apply? It isn't like you, Sylvia, to be doing what's nothing better than a servant's job. I'm so afraid I shall get a varicose vein through standing about so much, and an elastic stocking makes one look so old. Oh dear, don't let's talk about age. Drink up and have another."

Sylvia explained to Mabel about her lack of money and clothes, and it was curious to discover how pleasant and sympathetic Mabel was now—another instance of the degrading effect of love, for Sylvia could hardly believe that this was the hysterical creature who used to keep her awake in Fitzroy Street.

"I'd lend you the money," said Mabel, "but really, dear, until we open I haven't got very much. In fact," she added, looking at the empty glasses, "when I've paid for these two I shall be quite stony. Still, I live quite close. Finborough Road. Why don't you come and stay with me? I'll take you round to the manager to-morrow morning. He's sure to engage you. Of course, the salary is small. I don't suppose he'll offer more than fifteen shillings. Still, there's tips, and anything would be better than slaving for that woman. I live at three hundred and twenty. I've got a nice room with a view over Brompton Cemetery. One might be in the country. It's beautifully quiet except for the cats, and you hardly notice the trains."

Sylvia promised that she would think it over and let her know that evening.

"That's right, dear. The landlady's name is Gowndry."

They parted with much cordiality and good wishes, and Sylvia went back to Lillie Road. Mrs. Meares was deeply injured when she was informed that her lady-help proposed to desert her.

"But surely you shall wait till I've got a servant," she said. "And what will poor Mr. Witherwick do? He's so fond of you, Sylvia. I'm sure your poor father would be most distressed to think of you at Earl's Court. Such temptations for a young girl. I look upon myself as your guardian, you know. I would feel a big responsibility if anything came to you."

Sylvia, however, declined to stay.

"And I wanted to give you a little kitten. Mavourneen will be having kittens next month, and May cats are so lucky. When you told me about your black cat, Maria, I said to myself that I would be giving you one. And dear Parnell is the father, and if it's not Parnell, it's my darling Brian Boru. You beauty! Was you the father of some sweet little kitties? Clever man!"

When Mrs. Meares turned away to congratulate Brian Boru upon his imminent if ambiguous paternity, Sylvia went up-stairs to get her only possession—a coat with a fur-trimmed collar and cuffs, which she had worn alternately with underclothing for a month; this week the underclothing was, luckily, not at the wash. Sylvia shook off Mrs. Meares's last remonstrances and departed into the balmy April afternoon. The weather was so fine that she pawned her overcoat and bought a hat; then she pawned her fur cap, bought a pair of stockings (the pair in the wash belonged to Mrs. Meares), and went to Finborough Road.

Mrs. Gowndry asked if she was the young lady who was going to share Miss Bannerman's room; when Sylvia said she was, Mrs. Gowndry argued that the bed would not hold two and that she had not bargained for the sofa's being used for anything but sitting on.

"That sofa's never been slept on in its life," she protested. "And if I start in letting people sleep anywhere, I might as well turn my house into a public convenience and have done with it; but, there, it's no good grumbling. Such is life. It's the back room. Second floor up. The last lodger burnt his name on the door with a poker, so you can't make no mistake."

Mrs. Gowndry dived abruptly into the basement and left Sylvia to find her way up to Mabel's room alone. Her hostess was in a kimono, Oriental even away from the Hall of a Thousand and One Marvels; she had tied pink bows to every projection and there was a strong smell of cheap scent. Sylvia welcomed the prettiness and sweetness after Lillie

Road; her former dislike of Mabel's domestic habits existed no longer; she told her of the meeting with Mrs. Gowndry and was afraid that the plan of living here might not be allowed.

"Oh, she's always like that," Mabel explained. "She's a silly old crow, but she's very nice, really. Her husband's a lavatory attendant, and, being shut up all day underground, he grumbles a lot when he comes home, and of course his wife has to suffer for it. Where's your luggage?"

"I told you I hadn't got any."

"You really are a caution, Sylvia. Fancy! Never mind. I expect I'll be able to fit you out."

"I sha'n't want much," Sylvia said, "with the warm weather coming."

"But you'll have to change when you go to the Exhibition, and you don't want the other girls to stare."

They spent the evening in cutting down some of Mabel's underclothes, and Sylvia wondered more than ever how she could have once found her so objectionable. In an excess of affection she hugged Mabel and thanked her warmly for her kindness.

"Go on," said Mabel. "There's nothing to thank me for. You'd do the same for me."

"But I used to be so beastly to you."

"Oh, well, you were only a kid. You didn't understand about love. Besides, I was very nervous in those days. I expect there were faults on both sides. I spoke to the manager about you, and I'm sure it'll be all right."

The following morning Sylvia accompanied Mabel to the Exhibition and, after being presented to Mr. Woolfe, the manager, she was engaged to sell cigarettes and serve coffee in the Hall of a Thousand and One Marvels from eleven in the morning till eleven at night on a salary of fourteen shillings a week, all extras to be shared with seven other young ladies similarly engaged.

"You'll be Amethyst," said Mr. Woolfe. "You'd better go and try on your dress. The idea is that there are eight beautiful odalisques dressed like precious stones. Pretty fancy, isn't it? Now don't grumble and say you'd rather be Diamond or Turquoys, because all the other jools are taken."

Sylvia passed through an arched doorway hung with a heavy curtain into the dressing-room of the eight odalisques, which lacked in Eastern splendor, and was very draughty. Seven girls, mostly older than herself, were wrestling with veils and brocades.

"He said we was to cover up our faces with this. It is chiffong or tool, dear?"

"Oh, Daisy, you are silly to let him make you Rewby. Why don't you ask him to let you be Saffer? You don't mind, do you, kiddie? You're dark. You take Daisy's Rewby, and let her be Saffer."

"Aren't we going to wear anything over these drawers? Oh, girls, I shall feel shy."

Sylvia did not think that any of them would feel half as shy as she felt at the present moment in being plunged into the company of girls of whose thoughts and habits and sensations and manners she was utterly ignorant. She felt more at ease when she had put on her mauve dress and had veiled her face. When they were all ready, they paraded before Mr. Woolfe.

"Very good. Very good," he said. "Quite a lot of atmosphere. Here you, my dear, Emruld, put your yashmak up a bit higher. You look as if you'd got mumps like that. Now then, here's the henna to paint your finger-nails, and the kohl for your eyes."

"Coal for our eyes," echoed all the girls. "Why can't we use liquid black the same as we always do? Coal! What a liberty! Whatever next?"

"That shows you don't know anything about the East. K-O-H-L, not C-O-A-L, you silly girls. And don't you get hennering your hair. It's only to be used for the nails."

When the Exhibition opened on the 1st of May the Hall of a Thousand and One Marvels was the only sideshow that was in full working order. The negro eunuch stood outside and somewhat inappropriately bellowed his invitation to the passing crowds to visit Sesame, where all the glamour of the East was to be had for sixpence, including a cup of delicious Turkish coffee specially made by the Sultan's own coffee-maker. Once inside, visitors could for a further sum of threepence view an exact reproduction of a Turkish harem, where real Turkish ladies in all the abandonment of languorous poses offered a spectacle of luxury that could only be surpassed by paying another threepence to see a faithless wife tied up in a sack and flung into the Bosphorus once every hour. Other threepennies secured admission to Aladdin's Cave, where the Genie of the Lamp told fortunes, or to the Cave of the Forty Thieves, where a lucky ticket entitled the owner to draw a souvenir from Ali Baba's sack of treasure, and see Morgiana dance a voluptuous *pas seul* once every hour. Visitors to the Hall could also buy attar of roses, cigarettes, seraglio pastilles, and Turkish Delight. It was very Oriental—even Mr. Woolfe wore a fez.

Either because Sylvia moved in a way that seemed to Mr. Woolfe more Oriental than the others or because she got on very well with him personally, she was soon promoted to a small inner room more richly draped and lighted by a jeweled lamp hanging from the ceiling of gilded arabesques. Here Mr. Woolfe as a mark of his esteem introduced regular customers who could appreciate the softer carpet and deeper divans. At one end was a lattice, beyond which might be seen two favorites of the harem, who, slowly fanning themselves, reclined eternally amid perfumed airs—that is, except during the intervals for dinner and tea, which lasted half an hour and exposed them to the unrest of European civilization. One of these favorites was Mabel, whom Mr. Woolfe had been heard to describe as his beau ideel of a sultana, and whom he had taken from the sale of Turkish Delight to illustrate his conception. Mabel was paid a higher salary in consequence, because, inclosed in the harem, she was no longer able to profit by the male admirers who had bought Turkish Delight at her plump hands. The life was well suited to her natural laziness; though she dreaded getting fat, she was glad to be relieved of the menace from her varicose vein. Sylvia was the only odalisque that waited in this inner room, but her salary was not raised, since she now had the sole right to all the extras; she certainly preferred this darkened chamber to the other, and when there were no intruders from the world outside she could gossip through the lattice with the two favorites.

Mrs. Gowndry had let Sylvia a small room at the very top of the house; notwithstanding Mabel's good nature, she might have grown tired of being always at close quarters with her. Sylvia's imagination was captured by the life she led at Earl's Court; she made up her mind that one day she would somehow visit the real East. When Mr. Woolfe found out her deep interest in the part she was playing and her fondness for reading, he lent her various books that had inspired his creation at Earl's Court; she had long ago read the *Arabian Nights*, but there were several volumes of travels which fed her ambition to leave this dull Western world. On Sunday mornings she used to lean out of her window and fancy the innumerable tombs of Brompton Cemetery were the minarets of an Eastern town; and later on, when June made every hour in the open air desirable after being shut up so long at Earl's Court, Sylvia used to spend her Sunday afternoons in wandering about the cemetery, in reading upon the tombs the exalted claims they put forward for poor mortality, and in puzzling over the broken columns, the urns and anchors and weeping angels that commemorated the wealthy dead. Every one buried here had lived on earth a life of perfect virtue, it seemed; every one buried here had been confident of another life after the grave. Long ago at Lille she had been taught something about the future these dead people seemed to have counted upon; but there had been so much to do on Sunday mornings, and she could not remember that she had ever gone to church after she was nine. Perhaps she had made a mistake in abandoning so early the chance of finding out more about religion; it was difficult not to be impressed by the universal testimony of these countless tombs. Religion had evidently a great influence upon humanity, though in her reading she had never been struck by the importance of it. People in books attended church just as they wore fine clothes, or fought duels, or went to dinner-parties; the habit belonged to the observances of polite society and if she ever found herself in such society she would doubtless behave like her peers. She had not belonged to a society with leisure for church-going. Yet in none of the books that she had read had religion seemed anything like so important as love or money. She herself thought that the pleasures of both these were much exaggerated, though in her own actual experience their power of seriously disturbing some people was undeniable. But who was ever disturbed by religion? Probably all these tombs were a luxury of the rich, rather like visiting-cards, which, as every one knew, must be properly inscribed and follow a certain pattern. She remembered that old Mr. Gustard, who was not rich, had been very doubtful of another life, and she was consoled by this reflection, for she had been rendered faintly anxious by the pious repetitions of faith in a future life, practical comfort in which could apparently only be secured by the strictest behavior on earth. She had the fancy to invent her own epitaph: "Here lies Sylvia Scarlett, who was always running away. If she has to live all over again and be the same girl, she accepts no responsibility for anything that may occur." She printed this on a piece of paper, fastened it to a twig, and stuck it into the earth to judge the effect. Sylvia was so deeply engrossed in her task that she did not see that somebody was watching her until she had stepped back to admire her handiwork.

"You extraordinary girl!" said a pleasant voice.

Looking round, Sylvia saw a thin clean-shaven man of about thirty, who was leaning on a cane with an ivory crook and looking at her epitaph through gold-rimmed glasses. She blushed, to her annoyance, and snatched up the twig.

"What are you always running away from?" the stranger asked. "Or is that an indiscreet question?"

Sylvia could have shaken herself for not giving a ready answer, but this new-comer seemed entitled to something better than rudeness, and her ready answers were usually rude.

"Now don't go away," the stranger begged. "It's so refreshing to meet something alive in this wilderness of death. I've been inspecting a grave for a friend who is abroad, and I'm feeling thoroughly depressed. One can't avoid reading epitaphs in a cemetery, can one? Or writing them?" he added, with a pleasant laugh. "I like yours much the best of any I've read so far. What a charming name. Sylvia Scarlett. Balzac said the best epitaphs were single names. If I saw Sylvia Scarlett on a tomb with nothing else, my appetite for romance would be perfectly satisfied."

"Have you read many books of Balzac?" Sylvia asked.

The stranger's conversation had detained her; she could ask the question quite simply.

"I've read most of them, I think."

"I've read some," Sylvia said. "But he's not my favorite writer. I like Scott better. But now I only read books about the Orient."

She was rather proud of the last word and hoped the stranger would notice it.

"What part attracts you most?"

"I think Japan," Sylvia said. "But I like Turkey rather. Only I wouldn't ever let myself be shut up in a harem."

"I suppose you'd run away?" said the stranger, with a smile. "Which reminds me that you haven't answered my first question. Please do, if it's not impertinent."

They wandered along the paths shaded by yews and willows, and Sylvia told him many things about her life; he was the easiest person to talk to that she had ever met.

"And so this passion for the East has been inspired by the Hall of a Thousand and One Marvels. Dear me, what an unexpected consequence. And this Hall of a Thousand and One Marbles," he indicated the cemetery with a sweep of his cane, "this inspires you to write an epitaph? Well, my dear, such an early essay in mortuary literature may end in a famous elegy. You evidently possess the poetic temperament."

"I don't like poetry," Sylvia interrupted. "I don't believe it ever. Nobody really talks like that when they're in love."

"Quite true," said the stranger. "Poets have often ere this been charged with exaggeration. Perhaps I wrong you in attributing to you the poetic temperament. Yes, on second thoughts, I'm sure I do. You are an eminently practical young lady. I won't say prosaic, because the word has been debased. I suspect by the poets who are always uttering base currency of thoughts and words and emotions. Dear me, this is a most delightful adventure."

"Adventure?" repeated Sylvia.

"Our meeting," the stranger explained.

"Do you call that an adventure?" said Sylvia, contemptuously. "Why, I've had adventures much more exciting than this."

"I told you that your temperament was anti-poetic," said the stranger. "How severe you are with my poor gossamers. You are like the Red Queen. You've seen adventures compared with which this is really an ordinary afternoon walk."

"I don't understand half you're saying," said Sylvia. "Who's the Red Queen? Why was she red?"

"Why was Sylvia Scarlett?" the stranger laughed.

"I don't think that's a very good joke," said Sylvia, solemnly.

"It wasn't, and to make my penitence, if you'll let me, I'll visit you at Earl's Court and present you with copies of *Alice's Adventures in Wonderland and through The Looking-glass*."

"Books," said Sylvia, in a satisfied tone. "All right. When will you come? To-morrow?"

The stranger nodded.

"What are you?" Sylvia asked, abruptly.

"My name is Iredale—Philip Iredale. No profession."

"Are you what's called a gentleman?" Sylvia went on.

"I hope most people would so describe me," said Mr. Iredale.

"I asked you that," Sylvia said, "because I never met a gentleman before. I don't think Jimmy Monkley was a gentleman, and Arthur Madden was too young. Perhaps the Emperor of Byzantium was a gentleman."

"I hope so indeed," said Mr. Iredale. "The Palaeologos family is an old one. Did you meet the Emperor in the course of your Oriental studies? Shall I meet him in the Hall of a Thousand and One Marvels?"

Sylvia told him the story of the Emperor's reception, which seemed to amuse him very much.

"Where do you live?" Sylvia asked.

"Well, I live in Hampshire generally, but I have rooms in the Temple."

"The Temple of who?" Sylvia asked, grandly.

"Mammon is probably the dedication, but by a legal fiction the titular god is suppressed."

"Do you believe in God?" Sylvia asked.

"My dear Miss Scarlett, I protest that such a question so abruptly put in a cemetery is most unfair."

"Don't call me Miss Scarlett. It makes me feel like a girl in a shop. Call me Sylvia. That's my name."

"Dear me, how very refreshing you are," said Mr. Iredale. "Do you know I'm positively longing for to-morrow. But meanwhile, dear child, dear girl, we have to-day. What shall we do with the rest of it? Let's get on top of a 'bus and ride to Kensington Gardens. Hallowed as this spot is both by the mighty dead and the dear living, I'm tired of tombs."

"I can't go on the top of a 'bus," Sylvia said. "Because I've not got any petticoats underneath my frock. I haven't saved up enough money to buy petticoats yet. I had to begin with chemises."

"Then we must find a hansom," said Mr. Iredale, gravely.

They drove to Kensington Gardens and walked under the trees to Hyde Park Corner; there they took another hansom and drove to a restaurant with very comfortable chairs and delicious things to eat. Mr. Iredale and Sylvia talked hard all the time; after dinner he drove her back to Finborough Road and lifted his hat when she waved good-by to him from the steps.

Mabel was furiously interested by Sylvia's account of her day, and gave her much advice.

"Now don't let everything be too easy," she said. "Remember he's rich and can afford to spend a little money. Don't encourage him to make love to you at the very commencement, or he'll get tired and then you'll be sorry."

"Oh, who's thinking about making love?" Sylvia exclaimed. "That's just why I've enjoyed myself to-day. There wasn't a sign of love-making. He told me I was the most interesting person he'd ever met."

"There you are," Mabel said. "There's only one way a girl can interest a man, is there?"

Sylvia burst into tears and stamped her foot on the floor.

"I won't believe you," she cried. "I don't want to believe you."

"Well, there's no need to cry about it," Mabel said. "Only he'd be a funny sort of man if he didn't want to make love to you."

"Well, he is a funny sort of man," Sylvia declared. "And I hope he's going on being funny. He's coming to the Exhibition to-morrow and you'll see for yourself how funny he is."

Mabel was so deeply stirred by the prospect of Mr. Iredale's visit that she practised a more than usually voluptuous pose, which was frustrated by her fellow-favorite, who accused her of pushing her great legs all over the place and invited her to keep to her own cushions. Mabel got very angry and managed to drop a burning pastille on her companion's trousers, which caused a scene in the harem and necessitated the intervention of Mr. Woolfe.

"She did it for the purpose, the spiteful thing," the outraged favorite declared. "Behaves more like a performing seal than a Turkish lady, and then burns my costume. No, it's no good trying to 'my dear' me. I've stood it long enough and I'm not going to stand it no longer."

Mabel expressed an opinion that the rival favorite was a vulgar person; luckily, before Mr. Iredale arrived the quarrel had been adjusted, and when he sat down on the divan and received a cup of coffee from Sylvia, whose brown eyes twinkled merry recognition above her yashmak, the two favorites were languorously fanning the perfumed airs of their seclusion, once again in drowsy accord.

Mr. Iredale came often to the Hall of a Thousand and One Marvels; he never failed to bring with him books for Sylvia and he was always eager to discuss with her what she had last read. On Sundays he used to take her out to Richmond or Kew, but he never invited her to visit him at his rooms.

"He's awfully gone on you," said Mabel. "Well, I wish you the best of luck, I'm sure, for he's a very nice fellow."

Mr. Iredale was not quite so enthusiastic over Mabel; he often questioned Sylvia about her friend's conduct and seemed much disturbed by the materialism and looseness of her attitude toward life.

"It seems dreadful," he used to say to her, "that you can't find a worthier friend than that blond enormity. I hope she never introduces you to any of her men."

Sylvia assured him that Mabel was much too jealous to do anything of the sort.

"Jealous!" he ejaculated. "How monstrous that a child like you should already be established in competition with that. Ugh!"

June passed away to July. Mr. Iredale told Sylvia that he ought to be in the country by now and that he could not understand himself. One day he asked her if she would like to live in the country, and became lost in meditation when she said she might. Sylvia delighted in his company and had a deep affection for this man who had so wonderfully entered into her life without once shocking her sensibility or her pride. She understood, however, that it was easy for him to behave himself, because he had all he wanted; nevertheless the companionship of a man of leisure had for herself such charm that she did not feel attracted to any deeper reflection upon moral causes; he was lucky to be what he was, but she was equally lucky to have found him for a friend.

Sometimes when he inveighed against her past associates and what he called her unhappy bringing up, she felt impelled to defend them.

"You see, you have all you want, Philip."

Sylvia had learned with considerable difficulty to call him Philip; she could never get rid of the idea that he was much older than herself and that people who heard her call him by his Christian name would laugh. Even now she could only call him Philip when the importance of the remark was enough to hide what still seemed an unpardonable kind of pertness.

"You think I have all I want, do you?" he answered, a little bitterly. "My dear child, I'm in the most humiliating position in which a man can find himself. There is only one thing I want, but I'm afraid to make the effort to secure it: I'm afraid of being laughed at. Sylvia dear, you were wiser than you knew when you objected to calling me Philip for that very reason. I wish I could spread my canvas to a soldier's wind like you and sail into life, but I can't. I've been taught to tack, and I've never learned how to reach harbor. I suppose some people, in spite of our system of education, succeed in learning," he sighed.

"I don't understand a bit what you're talking about," she said.

"Don't you? It doesn't matter. I was really talking to myself, which is very rude. Impose a penalty."

"Admit you have everything you want," Sylvia insisted. "And don't be always running down poor Jimmy and my father and every one I've ever known."

"From their point of view I confess I have everything I want," he agreed.

On another occasion Sylvia asked him if he did not think she ought to consider religion more than she had done. Being so much in Philip's company was giving her a desire to experiment with the habits of well-regulated people, and she was perplexed to find that he paid no attention to church-going.

"Ah, there you can congratulate yourself," he said, emphatically. "Whatever was deplorable in your bringing up, at least you escaped that damnable imposition, that fraudulent attempt to flatter man beyond his deserts."

"Oh, don't use so many long words all at once," Sylvia begged. "I like a long word now and then, because I'm collecting long words, but I can't collect them and understand what you're talking about at the same time. Do you think I ought to go to church?"

"No, no, a thousand times no," Philip replied. "You've luckily escaped from religion as a social observance. Do you feel the need for it? Have you ineffable longings?"

"I know that word," Sylvia said. "It means something that can't be said in words, doesn't it? Well, I've often had longings like that, especially in Hampstead, but no longings that had anything to do with going to church. How could they have, if they were ineffable?"

"Quite true," Philip agreed. "And therefore be grateful that you're a pagan. If ever a confounded priest gets hold of you and tries to bewitch you with his mumbo-jumbo, send for me and I'll settle him. No, no, going to church of one's own free will is either a drug (sometimes a stimulant, sometimes a narcotic) or it's mere snobbery. In either case it is a futile waste of time, because there are so many problems in this world—you're one of the most urgent—that it's criminal to avoid their solution by speculating upon the problem of the next world, which is insoluble."

"But is there another world?" she asked.

"I don't think so."

"And all those announcements in the cemetery meant nothing?"

"Nothing but human vanity—the vanity of the dead and the vanity of the living."

"Thanks," Sylvia said. "I thought that was probably the explanation."

Mabel, who had long ago admitted that Philip was just as funny as Sylvia had described him, often used to ask her what they found to talk about.

"He can't be interested in Earl's Court, and you're such a kid. I can't understand it."

"Well, we talked about religion to-day," Sylvia told her.

"Oh, that's it, is it?" Mabel said, very knowingly. "He's one of those fellows who ought to have been a clergyman, is he? I knew he reminded me of some one. He's the walking image of the clergyman where we used to live in Clapham. But you be careful, Sylvia. It's an old trick, that."

"You're quite wrong. He hates clergymen."

"Oh," Mabel exclaimed, taken aback for a moment, but quickly recovering herself. "Oh, well, people always pretend to hate what they can't get. And I dare say he wanted to be a clergyman. But don't let him try to convert you. It's an old trick to get something for nothing. And I know, my dear."

July passed away into August, and Sylvia, buried for so many hours in the airless Hall of a Thousand and One Marvels, was flagging visibly. Philip used to spend nearly every afternoon and evening in the inner room where she worked—so many, indeed, that Mr. Woolfe protested and told her he would really have to put her back into the outer hall, because good customers were being annoyed by her admirer's glaring at them through his glasses.

Philip was very much worried by Sylvia's wan looks, and urged her more insistently to leave her job, and let him provide for her. But having vowed to herself that never again would she put herself under an obligation to anybody, she would not hear of leaving the Exhibition.

One Sunday in the middle of August Philip took Sylvia to Oxford, of which he had often talked to her. She enjoyed the day very much and delighted him by the interest she took in all the colleges they visited; but he was very much worried, so he said, by the approach of age.

"You aren't so very old," Sylvia reassured him. "Old, but not very old."

"Fifteen years older than you," he sighed.

"Still, you're not old enough to be my father," she added, encouragingly.

In the afternoon they went to St. Mary's Walks and sat upon a bench by the Cherwell. Close at hand a Sabbath bell chimed a golden monotone; Philip took Sylvia's hand and looked right into her face, as he always did when he was not wearing his glasses:

"Little delightful thing, if you won't let me take you away from that inferno of Earl's Court, will you marry me? Not at once, because it wouldn't be fair to you and it wouldn't be fair to myself. I'm going to make a suggestion that will make you laugh, but it is quite a serious suggestion. I want you to go to school."

Sylvia drew back and stared at him over her shoulder.

"To school?" she echoed. "But I'm sixteen."

"Lots of girls—most girls in the position I want you to take—are still at school then. Only a year, dear child, and then if you will have me, we'll get married. I don't think you'd be bored down in Hampshire. I have thousands of books and you shall read them all. Don't get into your head that I'm asking you to marry me because I'm sorry for you—"

"There's nothing to be sorry for," Sylvia interrupted, sharply.

"I know there's not, and I want you terribly. You fascinate me to an extent I never could have thought possible for any woman. I really haven't cared much about women; they always seemed in the way. I do believe you would be happy with me. We'll travel to the East together. You shall visit Japan and Turkey. I love you so much, Sylvia. Tell me, don't you love me a little?"

"I like you very much indeed," she answered, gently. "Oh, very, very, very much. Perhaps I love you. I don't think I love you, because if I loved you I think my heart would beat much faster when you asked me to marry you, and it isn't beating at all. Feel."

She put his hand upon her heart.

"It certainly doesn't seem to be unusually rapid," he agreed.

Sylvia looked at him in perplexity. His thin face was flushed, and the golden light of the afternoon gave it a warmer glow; his very blue eyes without their glasses had such a wide-open pleading expression; she was touched by his kindness.

"If you think I ought to go to school," she offered, "I will go to school."

He looked at her with a question in his eyes. She saw that he wanted to kiss her, and she pretended she thought he was dissatisfied with her answer about school.

"I won't promise to marry you," she said. "Because I like to keep promises and I can't say now what I shall be like in a year, can I? I'm changing all the time. Only I do like you very, very, very much. Don't forget that."

He took her hand and kissed it with the courtesy that for her was almost his greatest charm; manners seemed to Sylvia the chief difference between Philip and all the other people she had known. Once he had told her she had very bad manners, and she had lain awake half the night in her chagrin. She divined that the real reason of his wanting her to go to school was his wish to correct her manners. How little she knew about him, and yet she had been asked to marry him. His father and mother were dead, but he had a sister whom she would have to meet.

"Have you told your sister about me?" Sylvia asked.

"Not yet," he confessed. "I think I won't tell anybody about you except the lady to whose care I am going to intrust you."

Sylvia asked him how long he had made up his mind to ask her to marry him, and he told her he had been thinking about it for a long time, but that he had always been afraid at the last moment.

"Afraid I should disgrace you, I suppose?" Sylvia said.

He put on his glasses and coughed, a sure sign he was embarrassed. She laughed.

"And of course there's no doubt that I *should* disgrace you. I probably shall now as a matter of fact. Mabel will be rather sorry," she went on, pensively. "She likes me to be there at night in case she gets frightened. She told me once that the only reason she ever went wrong was because she was frightened to sleep alone. She was married to a commercial traveler, who, of course, was just the worst person she could have married, because he was always leaving her alone. Poor Mabel!"

Philip took her hand again and said in a tone of voice which she resented as adumbrating already, however faintly, a hint of ownership:

"Sylvia dear, you won't talk so freely as that in the school, will you? Promise me you won't."

"But it used to amuse you when I talked like that," she said. "You mustn't think now that you've got the right to lecture me."

"My dear child, it doesn't matter what you say to me; I understand. But some people might not."

"Well, don't say I didn't warn you," she almost sighed.

CHAPTER VI

MISS ASHLEY'S school for young ladies, situated in its own grounds on Campden Hill, was considered one of the best in England; a day or two after they got back from Oxford, Philip announced to Sylvia that he was glad to say Miss Ashley would take her as a pupil. She was a friend of his family; but he had sworn her to secrecy, and it had been decided between them that Sylvia should be supposed to be an orphan educated until now in France.

"Mayn't I tell the other girls that I've been an odalisque?" Sylvia asked.

"Good heavens! no!" said Philip, earnestly.

"But I was looking forward to telling them," she explained. "Because I'm sure it would amuse them."

Philip smiled indulgently and thought she would find lots of other ways of amusing them. He had told Miss Ashley, who, by the way, was an enthusiastic rationalist, that he did not want her to attend the outward shows of religion, and Miss Ashley had assented, though as a schoolmistress she was bound to see that her other pupils went to church at least once every Sunday. He had reassured her about the bad example Sylvia would set by promising to come himself and take her out every Sunday in his capacity as guardian.

"You'll be glad of that, won't you?" he asked, anxiously.

"I expect so," Sylvia said. "But of course I may find being at school such fun that I sha'n't want to leave it."

Again Philip smiled indulgently and hoped she would. Of course, it was now holiday-time, but Miss Ashley had quite agreed with him in the desirableness of Sylvia's going to Hornton House before the term began. She would be able to help her to equip herself with all the things a school-girl required. He knew, for instance, that she was short of various articles of clothing. Sylvia could take Miss Ashley completely into her confidence, but even with her he advised a certain reticence with regard to some of her adventures. She was of course a woman of infinite experience and extremely broad-minded, but many years as a schoolmistress might have made her consider some things were better left unsaid; there were some people, particularly English people, who were much upset by details. Perhaps Sylvia would spare her the details?

"You see, my dear child, you've had an extraordinary number of odd adventures for your age, and they've made you what you are, you dear. But now is the chance of setting them in their right relation to your future life. You know, I'm tremendously keen about this one year's formal education. You're just the material that can be perfected by academic methods, which with ordinary material end in mere barren decoration."

"I don't understand. I don't understand," Sylvia interrupted.

"Sorry! My hobby-horse has bolted with me and left you behind. But I won't try to explain or even to advise. I leave everything to you. After all, you are you; and I'm the last person to wish you to be any one else."

Philip was humming excitedly when they drove up to Hornton House, and Sylvia was certainly much impressed by its Palladian grandeur and the garden that seemed to spread illimitably behind it. She felt rather shy of Miss Ashley herself, who was apparently still in her dressing-gown, a green-linen dressing-gown worked in front with what Sylvia considered were very bad reproductions of flowers in brownish silk. She was astonished at seeing a woman of Miss Ashley's dignity still in her dressing-gown at three o'clock in the afternoon, but she was still more astonished to see her in a rather battered straw hat, apparently ready to go shopping in Kensington High Street without changing her attire. She looked at Philip, who, however, seemed unaware of anything unusual. A carriage was waiting for them when they went out, and Philip left her with Miss Ashley, promising to dine at Hornton House that night.

The afternoon passed away rapidly in making all sorts of purchases, even of trunks; it seemed to Sylvia that thousands of pounds must have been spent upon her outfit, and she felt a thrill of pride. Everybody behind the various counters treated Miss Ashley with great deference; Sylvia was bound to admit that, however careless she might be of her own appearance, she was splendidly able to help other people to choose jolly things. They drove back to Hornton House in a carriage that seemed full of parcels, though they only took with them what Miss Ashley considered immediately important. Tea was waiting in the garden under a great cedar-tree; and by the time tea was finished Sylvia was sure that she should like Miss Ashley and that she should not run away that night, which she had made up her mind to do unless she was absolutely contented with the prospect of her new existence. She liked her bedroom very much, and the noise that the sparrows made in the creeper outside her window. The starched maid-servant who came to help her dress for dinner rather frightened her, but she decided to be very French in order to take away the least excuse for ridicule.

Sylvia thought at dinner that the prospect of marriage had made Philip seem even older, or perhaps it was his assumption of guardianship which gave him this added seriousness.

"Of course, French she already knows," he was saying, "though it might be as well to revise her grammar a little. History she has a queer, disjointed knowledge of—it would be as well to fill in the gaps. I should like her to learn a little Latin. Then there are mathematics and what is called science. Of course, one would like her to have a general acquaintance with both, but I don't want to waste time with too much elementary stuff. It would be almost better for her to be completely ignorant of either."

"I think you will have to leave the decision to me, Philip," said Miss Ashley, in that almost too deliberately tranquil voice, which Sylvia felt might so easily become in certain circumstances exasperating. "I think you may rely on my judgment where girls are concerned."

Philip hastened to assure Miss Ashley that he was not presuming to dictate to her greater experience of education; he only wished to lay stress on the subjects that he considered would be most valuable for the life Sylvia was likely to lead.

"I have a class," said Miss Ashley, "which is composed of older girls and of which the routine is sufficiently elastic to fit any individual case. I take that class myself."

Sylvia half expected that Miss Ashley would suggest including Philip in it, if he went on talking any longer. Perhaps Philip himself suspected as much, for he said no more about Sylvia's education and talked instead about the gravity of the situation in South Africa.

Sylvia was vividly aware of the comfort of her bedroom and of the extraordinary freshness of it in comparison with all the other rooms she had so far inhabited. Miss Ashley faintly reminded her of her mother, not that there was the least outward resemblance except in height, for Miss Ashley's hair was gray, whereas her mother's until the day of her death had kept all its lustrous darkness. Yet both wore their hair in similar fashion, combed up high from the forehead so as to give them a majestic appearance. Her mother's eyes had been of a deep and glowing brown set in that pale face; Miss Ashley's eyes were small and gray, and her complexion had the hard rosiness of an apple. The likeness between the two women lay rather in the possession of a natural authority which warned one that disobedience would be an undertaking and defiance an impossibility. Sylvia rejoiced in the idea of being under control; it was invigorating, like the delicious torment of a cold bath. Of course she had no intention of being controlled in big things, but she was determined to submit over little things for the sheer pleasure of submitting to Miss Ashley, who was, moreover, likely to be always right. In the morning, when she came down in one of her new frocks, her hair tied back with a big brown bow, and found Miss Ashley sitting in the sunny green window of the dining-room, reading the *Morning Post*, she congratulated herself upon the positive pleasure that such a getting up was able to give her and upon this new sense of spaciousness that such a beginning of the day was able to provide.

"You're looking at my dress," said Miss Ashley, pleasantly. "When you're my age you'll abandon fashion and adopt what is comfortable and becoming."

"I thought it was a dressing-gown yesterday," Sylvia admitted.

"Rather an elaborate dressing-gown." Miss Ashley laughed. "I'm not so vain as all that."

Sylvia wondered what she would have said to some of Mabel's dressing-gowns. Now that she was growing used to Miss Ashley's attire, she began to think she rather liked it. This gown of peacock-blue linen was certainly attractive, and the flowers embroidered upon its front were clearly recognizable as daisies.

During the fortnight before school reopened Sylvia gave Miss Ashley a good deal of her confidence, and found her much less shocked by her experiences than Philip had been. She told her that she felt rather ungrateful in so abruptly cutting herself off from Mabel, who had been very kind to her; but on this point Miss Ashley was firm in her agreement with Philip, and would not hear of Sylvia's making any attempt to see Mabel again.

"You are lucky, my dear, in having only one person whose friendship you are forced to give up, as it seems to you, a little harshly. Great changes are rarely made with so slight an effort of separation. I am not in favor personally of violent uprootings and replantings, and it was only because you were in such a solitary position that I consented to do what Philip asked. Your friend Mabel was, I am sure, exceedingly kind to you; but you are much too young to repay her kindness. It is the privilege of the very young to be heartless. From what you have told me, you have often been heartless about other people, so I don't think you need worry about Mabel. Besides, let me assure you that Mabel herself would be far from enjoying any association with you that included Hornton House."

Sylvia had no arguments to bring forward against Miss Ashley; nevertheless, she felt guilty of treating Mabel shabbily, and wished that she could have explained to her that it was not really her fault.

Miss Ashley took her once or twice to the play, which Sylvia enjoyed more than music-halls. In the library at Hornton House she found plenty of books to read, and Miss Ashley was willing to talk about them in a very interesting way. Philip came often to see her and told her how much Miss Ashley liked her and how pleased they both were to see her settling down so easily and quickly.

The night before term began the four assistant mistresses arrived; their names were Miss Pinck, Miss Primer, Miss Hossack, and Miss Lee. Sylvia was by this time sufficiently at home in Hornton House to survive the ordeal of introduction without undue embarrassment, though, to Miss Ashley's amusement, she strengthened her French accent. Miss Pinck, the senior assistant mistress, was a very small woman with a sharp chin and knotted fingers, two features which contrasted noticeably with her general plumpness. She taught History and English Literature and had an odd habit, when she was speaking, of suddenly putting her hands behind her back, shooting her chin forward, and screwing up her eyes so fiercely that the person addressed involuntarily drew back in alarm. Sylvia, to whom this gesture became very familiar, used to wonder if in the days of her vanity Miss Pinck had cultivated it to avoid displaying her fingers, so that from long practice her chin had learned to replace the forefinger in impressing a fact.

The date was 1689, Miss Pinck would say, and one almost expected to see a pencil screwed into her chin which would actually write the figures upon somebody's notebook.

Miss Primer was a thin, melancholy, and sandy-haired woman, who must have been very pretty before her face was netted with innumerable small lines that made her look as if birds had been scratching on it when she was asleep. Miss Primer took an extremely gloomy view of everything, and with the prospect of war in South Africa she arrived in a condition of exalted, almost ecstatic depression; she taught Art, which at Hornton House was no cure for pessimism. Miss Hossack, the Mathematical and Scientific mistress, did not have much to do with Sylvia; she was a robust woman with a loud voice who liked to be asked questions. Finally there was Miss Lee, who taught music and was the particular adoration of every girl in the school, including Sylvia. She was usually described as "ethereal," "angelic," or "divine." One girl with a taste for painting discovered that she was her ideal conception of St. Cecilia; this naturally roused the jealousy of rival adorers that would not be "copy-cats," until one of them discovered that Miss Lee, whose first name was Mary, had Annabel for a second name, the very mixture of the poetic and the intimate that was required. Sylvia belonged neither to the Cecilias nor to the Annabels, but she loved dear Miss Lee none the less deeply and passed exquisite moments in trying to play the Clementi her mistress wanted her to learn.

"What a strange girl you are, Sylvia!" Miss Lee used to say. "Anybody would think you had been taught music by an accompanist. You don't seem to have any notion of a piece, but you really play accompaniments wonderfully. It's not mere vamping."

Sylvia wondered what Miss Lee would have thought of Jimmy Monkley and the Pink Pierrots.

The afternoon that the girls arrived at Hornton House Sylvia was sure that nothing could keep her from running away that night; the prospect of facing the chattering, giggling mob that thronged the hitherto quiet hall was overwhelming. From the landing above she leaned over to watch them, unable to imagine what she would talk about to them or what they would talk about to her. It was Miss Lee who saved the situation by inviting Sylvia to meet four of the girls at tea in her room and cleverly choosing, as Sylvia realized afterward, the four leaders of the four chief sets. Who would not adore Miss Lee?

"Oh, Miss Lee, *did* you notice Gladys and Enid Worstley?" Muriel ejaculated, accentuating some of her words like the notes of an unevenly blown harmonium, and explaining to Sylvia in a sustained tremolo that these twins, whose real name was Worsley, were always called Worstley because it was impossible to decide which was more wicked. "Oh, Miss Lee, they've got the most *lovely* dresses," she went on, releasing every stop in a diapason of envy. "Simply *gorgeously* beautiful. I do think it's a shame to dress them up like that. I do, *really*."

Sylvia made a mental note to cultivate this pair not for their dresses, but for their behavior. Muriel was all very well, but those eyebrows eternally arched and those eyes eternally staring out of her head would sooner or later have most irresistibly to be given real cause for amazement.

"Their mother likes them to be prettily dressed," said Miss Lee.

"Of course she does," Gwendyr put in, primly. "She was an actress."

To hell with Gwendyr, thought Sylvia. Why shouldn't their mother have been an actress?

"Oh, but they're so conceited!" said Dorothy. "Enid Worsley *never* can pass a glass, and their frocks are most frightfully short. *Don't* you remember when they danced at last breaking-up?"

"This is getting unbearable," Sylvia thought.

"I think they're rather dears," Phyllis drawled. "They're jolly pretty, anyway."

Sylvia looked at Phyllis and decided that she was jolly pretty, too, with her golden hair and smocked linen frock of old rose; she would like to be friends with Phyllis. The moment had come, however, when she must venture all her future on a single throw. She must either shock Miss Lee and the four girls irretrievably or she must be henceforth accepted at Hornton House as herself; there must be none of these critical sessions about Sylvia Scarlett. She pondered for a minute or two the various episodes of her past. Then suddenly she told them how she had run away from school in France, arrived in England without a penny, and earned her living as an odalisque at the Exhibition. Which would she be, she asked, when she saw the girls staring at her open-mouthed now with real amazement, villain or heroine? She became a heroine, especially to Gladys and Enid, with whom she made friends that night, and who showed her in strictest secrecy two powder-puffs and a tin of Turkish cigarettes.

There were moments when Sylvia was sad, especially when war broke out and so many of the girls had photographs of brothers and cousins and friends in uniform, not to mention various generals whose ability was as yet unquestioned. She did not consider the photograph of Philip a worthy competitor of these and begged him to enlist, which hurt his feelings. Nevertheless, her adventures as an odalisque were proof in the eyes of the girls against martial relations; their only regret was that the Exhibition closed before they had time to devise a plot to visit the Hall of a Thousand and One Marvels and be introduced by Sylvia to the favorites of the harem.

Miss Ashley was rather cross with Sylvia for her revelations and urged her as a personal favor to herself not to make any more. Sylvia explained the circumstances quite frankly and promised that she would not offend again; but she pointed out that the girls were all very inquisitive about Philip and asked how she was to account for his taking her out every Sunday.

"He's your guardian, my dear. What could be more natural?"

"Then you must tell him not to blush and drop his glasses when the girls tell him I'm nearly ready. They *all* think he's in love with me."

"Well, it doesn't matter," said Miss Ashley, impatiently.

"But it does matter," Sylvia contradicted. "Because even if he is going to marry me he's not the sort of lover one wants to put in a frame, now is he? That's why I bought that photograph of George Alexander which Miss Pinck made such a fuss about. I *must* have a secret sorrow. All the girls have secret sorrows this term."

Miss Ashley shook her head gravely, but Sylvia was sure she was laughing like herself.

Sylvia's chief friend was Phyllis Markham—the twins were only fourteen—and the two of them headed a society for toleration, which was designed to contend with stupid and ill-natured criticism. The society became so influential and so tolerant that the tone of the school was considered in danger, especially by Miss Primer, who lamented it much, together with the reverses in South Africa; and when after the Christmas holidays (which Sylvia spent with Miss Ashley at Bournemouth) a grave defeat coincided with the discovery that the Worsleys were signaling from their window to some boys in a house opposite, Miss Primer in a transport of woe took up the matter with the head-mistress. Miss Ashley called a conference of the most influential girls, at which Sylvia was present, and with the support of Phyllis maintained that the behavior of the twins had been much exaggerated.

"But in their nightgowns," Miss Primer wailed. "The policeman at the corner must have seen them. At such a time, too, with these deadful Boers winning everywhere. And their hair streaming over their shoulders."

"It always is," said Sylvia.

Miss Ashley rebuked her rather sharply for interrupting.

"A bull's-eye lantern. The room reeked of hot metal. I could not read the code. I took it upon myself to punish them with an extra hour's freehand to-day. But the punishment is most inadequate. I detect a disturbing influence right through the school."

Miss Ashley made a short speech in which she pointed out the responsibilities of the older girls in such matters and emphasized the vulgarity of the twins' conduct. No one wished to impute nasty motives to them, but it must be clearly understood that the girls of Hornton House could not and should not be allowed to behave like servants. She relied upon Muriel Battersby, Dorothy Hearne, Gwendyr Jones, Phyllis Markham, Georgina Roe, Helen Macdonald, and Sylvia Scarlett to prevent in future such unfortunate incidents as this that had been brought to her notice by Miss Primer, she was sure much against Miss Primer's will.

Miss Primer at these words threw up her eyes to indicate the misery she had suffered before she had been able to bring herself to the point of reporting the twins. Phyllis whispered to Sylvia that Miss Primer looked like a dying duck in a thunder-storm, a phrase which she now heard for the first time and at which she laughed aloud.

Miss Ashley paused in her discourse and fixed Sylvia with her gray eyes in pained interrogation; Miss Pinck's chin shot out; Miss Lee bit her under lip and tenderly shook her head; the other girls stared at their laps and tried to look at one another without moving their heads. Phyllis quickly explained that it was she who had made Sylvia laugh.

"I'm awfully sorry, Miss Ashley," she drawled.

"I'm glad to hear that you are *very* sorry," said Miss Ashley, "but Sylvia must realize when it is permissible and when it is not permissible to laugh. I'm afraid I must ask her to leave the room."

"I ought to go, too," Phyllis declared. "I made her laugh."

"I'm sure, Phyllis, that to yourself your wit seems irresistible. Pray let us have an opportunity of judging."

"Well, I said that Miss Primer looked like a dying duck in a thunder-storm."

The horrified amazement of everybody in the room expressed itself in a gasp that sounded like a ghostly, an infinitely attenuated scream of dismay. Sylvia, partly from nervousness, partly because the simile even on repetition appealed to her sense of the ridiculous, laughed aloud for a second time—laughed, indeed, with a kind of guffaw the sacrilegious echoes of which were stifled in an appalled silence.

"Sylvia Scarlett and Phyllis Markham will both leave the room immediately," said Miss Ashley. "I will speak to them later."

Outside the study of the head-mistress, Sylvia and Phyllis looked at each other like people who have jointly managed to break a mirror.

"What will she do?"

"Sylvia, I simply couldn't help it. I simply couldn't bear them all any longer."

"My dear, I know. Oh, I think it was wonderful of you."

Sylvia laughed heartily for the third time, and just at this moment the twins, who were the original cause of all the commotion, came sidling up to know what everybody had said.

"You little beasts with your bull's-eye lamps and your naughtiness," Phyllis cried. "I expect we shall all be expelled. What fun! I shall get some hunting. Oh, three cheers, I say!"

"Of course you know why Miss Primer was really in such a wax?" Gladys asked, with the eyes of an angel and the laugh of a fairy.

"No, let me tell, Gladys," Enid burst in. "You know I won the toss. We tossed up which should tell and I won. You *are* a chiseler. You see, when Miss Primer came tearing up into our room we turned the lamps onto her, and she was simply furious because she thought everybody in the street could see her in that blue-flannel wrapper."

"Which, of course, they could," Sylvia observed.

"Of course!" the twins shrieked together. "And the boys opposite clapped, and she heard them and tried to pull down the blind, and her wrapper came open and she was wearing a chest-protector!"

The interview with Miss Ashley was rather distressing, because she took from the start the altogether unexpected line of blaming Phyllis and Sylvia not for the breach of discipline, but for the wound they had inflicted upon Miss Primer.

All that had seemed fine and honest and brave and noble collapsed immediately; it was impossible after Miss Ashley's words not to feel ashamed, and both the girls offered to beg Miss Primer's pardon. Miss Ashley said no more about the incident after this, though she took rather an unfair advantage of their chastened spirits by exacting a promise that they would in common with the rest of the school leaders set their faces against the encouragement of such behavior as that of the twins last night.

The news from South Africa was so bad that Miss Primer's luxury of grief could scarcely have been heightened by Phyllis's and Sylvia's rudeness; however, she wept a few tears, patted their hands, and forgave them. A few days afterward she was granted the boon of another woe, which she shared with the whole school, in the news of Miss Lee's approaching marriage. Any wedding would have upset Miss Primer, but in this case the sorrow was rendered three times as poignant by the fact that Miss Lee was going to marry a soldier under orders for the front. This romantic accessory could not fail to thrill the girls, though it was not enough to compensate for the loss of their beloved Miss Lee. Rivalries between the Cecilias and Annabels were forever finished; several girls had been learning Beethoven's Pathetic Sonata and the amount of expression put into it would, they hoped, show Miss Lee the depth of their emotion when for the last time these frail fingers so lightly corrected their touch, when for the last time that delicate pencil inscribed her directions upon their music.

"Of course the school will *never* be the same without her," said Muriel.

"I shall write home and ask if I can't take up Italian instead of music," said Dorothy.

"Fancy playing duets with any one but Miss Lee," said Gwendyr. "The very idea makes me shudder."

"Perhaps we shall have a music-master now," said Gladys.

Whereupon everybody told her she was a heartless thing. Poor Gladys, who really loved Miss Lee as much as anybody, retired to her room and cried for the rest of the evening, until she was consoled by Enid, who pointed out that now she *must* use her powder-puff.

For Sylvia the idea of Miss Lee's departure and marriage was desolating; it was an abrupt rending of half the ties that bound her to Hornton House. Phyllis, Miss Ashley, and the twins were all that really remained, and Phyllis was always threatening to persuade her people to take her away when the weather was tolerably warm, so deeply did she resent the loss of hunting. It was curious how much more Phyllis meant to her than Philip, so much, indeed, that she had never confided in her that she was going to marry Philip. How absurd that two names so nearly alike could be in the one case so beautiful, in the other so ugly. Yet she was still very fond of Philip and she still enjoyed going out with him on Sundays, even though it meant being deprived of pleasant times with Phyllis. She had warned Philip that she might get too fond of school, and he had smiled in that superior way of his. Ought she to marry him at all? He had been so kind to her that if she refused to marry him she would have to run away, for she could not continue under an obligation. Why did people want to marry? Why must she marry? Worst of all, why must Miss Lee marry? But these were questions that not even Miss Hossack would be able to answer. Ah, if it had only been Miss Hossack who had been going to marry. Sylvia began to make up a rhyme about Miss Hossack marrying a Cossack and going for her honeymoon to the Trossachs, where Helen Macdonald lived.

All the girls had subscribed to buy Miss Lee a dressing-case, which they presented to her one evening after tea with a kind of dismal beneficence, as if they were laying a wreath upon her tomb. Next morning she went away by an early train to the north of England, and after lunch every girl retired with the secret sorrow that now had more than fashion to commend it. Sylvia's sorrow was an aching regret that she had not told Miss Lee more about herself and her life and Philip; now it was too late. She met the twins wandering disconsolately enlaced along the corridor outside her room.

"Oh, Sylvia, dearest Sylvia!" they moaned. "We've lost our duet with Miss Lee's fingering."

"I'll help you to look for it."

"Oh, but we lost it on purpose, because we didn't like it, and the next day Miss Lee said she was going to be married."

Sylvia asked where they lost it.

"Oh, we put it in an envelope and posted it to the Bishop of London."

Sylvia suggested they should write to the Bishop and explain the circumstances in which the duet was sent to him; he would no doubt return it.

"Oh no," said the twins, mournfully. "We never put a stamp on and we wrote inside, 'A token of esteem and regard from two sinners who you confirmed.' How can we ask for it back?"

Sylvia embraced the twins, and the three of them wandered in the sad and wintry garden until it was time for afternoon school.

The next day happened to be Sunday, and Philip came as usual to take Sylvia out. He had sent her the evening before an overcoat trimmed with gray squirrel, which, if it had not arrived after Miss Lee's departure, would have been so much more joyfully welcomed. Philip asked her why she was so sad and if the coat did not please her. She told him about its coming after Miss Lee had gone, and, as usual, he had a lot to say:

"You strange child, how quickly you have adopted the outlook and manners of the English school-girl. One would say that you had never been anything else. How absurd I was to be afraid that you were a wild bird whom I had caught too late. I'm quite positive now that you'll be happy with me down in Hampshire. I'm sorry you've lost Miss Lee. A charming woman, I thought, and very cultivated. Miss Ashley will miss her greatly, but she herself will be glad to get away from music-teaching. It must be an atrocious existence."

Here was a new point of view altogether. Could it really be possible that those delicious hours with Miss Lee were a penance to the mistress? Sylvia looked at Philip angrily, for she found it unforgivable in him to destroy her illusions like this. He did not observe her expression and continued his monologue:

"Really atrocious. Exercises! Scales! Other people's chilblains! A creaking piano-stool! What a purgatory! And all to teach a number of young women to inflict an objectionable noise upon their friends and relations."

"Thanks," Sylvia broke in. "You won't catch me playing again."

"I'm not talking about you," Philip said. "You have temperament. You're different from the ordinary school-girl." He took her arm affectionately. "You're you, dear Sylvia."

"And yours," she added, sullenly. "I thought you said just now that I was just like any other English school-girl and that you were so happy about it."

"I said you'd wonderfully adopted the outlook," Philip corrected. "Not quite the same thing."

"Oh, well, take your horrible coat, because I don't want it," Sylvia exclaimed, and, rapidly unbuttoning her new overcoat, she flung it on the pavement at his feet.

Nobody was in sight at the moment, so Philip did not get angry.

"Now don't tell me it's illogical to throw away only the coat and not undress myself completely. I know quite well that everything I've got on is yours."

"Oh no, it's not," Philip said, gently. "It's yours."

"But you paid for everything."

"No, you paid yourself," he insisted.

"How?"

"By being Sylvia. Come along, don't trample on your poor coat. There's a most detestable wind blowing."

He picked up the offending overcoat and helped her into it again with so much sympathy half humorous, half grave in his demeanor that she could not help being sorry for her outburst.

Nevertheless, the fact of her complete dependence upon Philip for everything, even before marriage, was always an oppression to Sylvia's mind, which was increased by the continual reminders of her loneliness that intercourse with other girls forced upon her. They, when they should marry, should be married from a background; the lovers, when they came for them, would have to fight for their love by breaking down the barriers of old associations, old friendships, and old affections; in a word, they would have to win the brides. What was her own background? Nothing but a panorama of streets which offered no opposition to Philip's choice except in so far as it was an ugly background for a possession of his own and therefore fit to be destroyed. It was all very well for Philip to tell her that she was herself and that he loved her accordingly. If that were true, why was he taking so much trouble to turn her into something different? Other girls at Hornton House, when they married, would not begin with ugly backgrounds to be obliterated; their pasts would merge beautifully with the pasts of their husbands; they were not being transformed by Miss Pinck and Miss Primer; they were merely being supplied by them with value for their parents' money. It was a visit to Phyllis Markham's home in Leicestershire during the Easter holidays that had branded with the iron of jealousy these facts upon her meditation. Phyllis used to lament that she had no brothers; and Sylvia used to wonder what she would have said if she had been like herself, without mother, without father, without brothers, without sisters, without relations, without friends, without letters, without photographs, with nothing in the whole world between herself and the shifting panorama from which she had been snatched but the love of a timid man inspired by an unusual encounter in Brompton Cemetery. This visit to Phyllis Markham was the doom upon their friendship; however sweet, however sympathetic, however loyal Phyllis might be, she must ultimately despise her friend's past; every word Sylvia listened to during those Easter holidays seemed to cry out the certain fulfilment of this conjecture.

"I expect I'm too sensitive," Sylvia said to herself. "I expect I really am common, because apparently common people are always looking out for slights. I don't look out for them now, but if I were to tell Phyllis all about myself, I'm sure I should begin to look out for them. No, I'll just be friends with her up to a point, for so long as I stay at Hornton House; then we'll separate forever. I'm really an absolute fraud. I'm just as much of a fraud now as when I was dressed up as a boy. I'm not real in this life. I haven't been real since I came down to breakfast with Miss Ashley that first morning. I'm simply a very good impostor. I must inherit the talent from father. Another reason against telling Phyllis about myself is that, if I do, I shall become her property. Miss Ashley knows all about me, but I'm not her property, because it's part of her profession to be told secrets. Phyllis would love me more than ever, so long as she was the only person that owned the secret, but if anybody else ever knew, even if it were only Philip, she would be jealous and she would have to make a secret of it with some one else. Then she would be ashamed of herself and would begin to hate and despise me in self-defense. No, I must never tell any of the girls."

Apart from these morbid fits, which were not very frequent, Sylvia enjoyed her stay at Markham Grange. In a way it encouraged the idea of marrying Philip; for the country life appealed to her not as to a cockney by the strangeness of its inhabitants and the mere quantity of grass in sight, but more deeply with those old ineffable longings of Hampstead.

At the end of the summer term the twins invited Sylvia to stay with them in Hertfordshire. She refused at first, because she felt that she could not bear the idea of being jealously disturbed by a second home. The twins were inconsolable at her refusal and sent a telegram to their mother, who had already written one charming letter of invitation, and who now wrote another in which she told Sylvia of her children's bitter disappointment and begged her to come. Miss Ashley, also, was anxious that Sylvia should go, and told her frankly that it seemed an excellent chance to think over seriously her marriage with Philip in the autumn. Philip, now that the date of her final decision was drawing near, wished her to remain with Miss Ashley in London. His opposition was enough to make Sylvia insist upon going; so, when at the end of July the school was swept by a tornado of relations and friends, Sylvia was swept away with the twins to Hertfordshire, and Philip was left to wait till the end of September to know whether she would marry him or not in October.

The Worsleys' home at Arbour End made an altogether different impression upon Sylvia from Markham Grange. She divined in some way that the background here was not immemorial, but that the Worsleys had created it themselves. And a perfect background it was—a very comfortable red brick house with a garden full of flowers, an orchard loaded with fruit, fields promenaded by neat cows, pigsties inhabited by clean pigs, a shining dog-cart and a shining horse, all put together with the satisfying completeness of a picture-puzzle. Mr. Worsley was a handsome man, tall and fair with a boyish face and a quantity of clothes; Mrs. Worsley was slim and fair, with a rose-leaf complexion and as many clothes as her husband. The twins were even naughtier and more charming than they were at Hornton House; there was a small brother called Hercules, aged six, who was as charming as his sisters and surpassed them in wickedness. The maids were trim and tolerant; the gardener was never grumpy; Hercules's governess disapproved of holiday tasks; the dogs wagged their tails at the least sound.

"I love these people," Sylvia said to herself, when she was undressing on the first night of her stay. "I love them, I love them. I feel at home—at home—at home!" She leaped into bed and hugged the pillow in a triumph of good-fellowship.

At Arbour End Sylvia banished the future and gave herself to the present. One seemed to have nothing to do but to amuse oneself then, and it was so easy to amuse oneself that one never grew tired of doing so. As the twins pointed out, their father was so much nicer than any other father, because whatever was suggested he always enjoyed. If it was a question of learning golf, Mr. Worsley took the keenest interest in teaching it. When Gladys drove a ball through the drawing-room window, no one was more delighted than Mr. Worsley himself; he infected everybody with his pleasure, so that the gardener beamed at the notion of going to fetch the glazier from the village, and the glazier beamed when he mended the window, and the maids beamed while they watched him at work, and the dogs sat down in a loose semicircle, thumping the lawn with appreciative tails. The next day, when Hercules, who, standing solemnly apart from the rest, had observed all that happened, threw a large stone through the mended window, there was the same scene of pleasure slightly intensified.

Mrs. Worsley flitted through the house, making every room she entered more beautiful and more gay for her presence. She had only one regret, which was that the twins were getting so big, and this not as with other mothers because it made her feel old, but because she would no more see their black legs and their tumbled hair. Sylvia once asked her how she could bear to let them go to school, and Mrs. Worsley's eyes filled with tears.

"I had to send them to school," she whispered, sadly. "Because they *would* fall in love with the village boys and they were getting Hertfordshire accents. Perhaps you've noticed that I myself speak with a slight cockney accent. Do you understand, dear?"

The August days fled past and in the last week came a letter from Miss Ashley.

MURREN, *August 26, 1900.*

MY DEAR SYLVIA,—I shall be back from Switzerland by September 3d, and I shall be delighted to see you at Hornton House again. Philip nearly followed me here in order to talk about you, but I declined his company. I want you to think very seriously about your future, as no doubt you have been doing all this month. If you have the least hesitation about marrying Philip, let me advise you not to do it. I shall be glad to offer you a place at Hornton House, not as a schoolmistress, but as a kind of director of the girls' leisure time. I have grown very fond of you during this year and have admired the way in which you settled down here more than I can express. We will talk this over more fully when we meet, but I want you to know that, if you feel you ought not to marry, you have a certain amount of security for the future while you are deciding what you will ultimately do. Give my love to the twins. I shall be glad to see you again.

Your affectionate
CAROLINE ASHLEY.

The effect of Miss Ashley's letter was the exact contrary of what she had probably intended; it made Sylvia feel that she was not bound to marry Philip, and, from the moment she was not bound, that she was willing, even anxious, to marry him. The aspects of his character which she had criticized to herself vanished and left only the first impression of him, when she was absolutely free and was finding his company such a relief from the Exhibition. Another result of the letter was that by removing the shame of dependence and by providing an alternative it opened a way to discussion, for which Sylvia fixed upon Mrs. Worsley, divining that she certainly would look at her case unprejudiced by anything but her own experience.

Sylvia never pretended to herself that she would be at all influenced by advice. Listening to advice from Mrs. Worsley would be like looking into a shop-window with money in one's pocket, but with no intention of entering the shop to make a purchase; listening to her advice before Miss Ashley's offer would have been like looking at a shop-window without a penny in the world, a luxury of fancy to which Sylvia had never given way. So at the first opportunity Sylvia talked to Mrs. Worsley about Philip, going back for her opinion of him and feeling toward him to those first days together, and thereby giving her listener an impression that she liked him a very great deal, which was true, as Sylvia assured herself, yet not without some misgivings about her presentation of the state of affairs.

"He sounds most fascinating," said Mrs. Worsley. "Of course Lennie was never at all clever. I don't think he ever read a book in his life. When I met him first I was acting in burlesque, and I had to make up my mind between him and my profession; I'm so glad I chose him. But at first I was rather miserable. His parents were still alive, and though they were very kind to me, I was always an intruder, and of course Lennie was dependent on them, for he was much too stupid an old darling to earn his own living. He really has nothing but his niceness. Then his parents died and, being an only son, Lennie had all the money. We lived for a time in his father's house, but it became impossible. We had my poor old mother down to stay with us, and the neighbors called, as if she were a curiosity. When she didn't appear at tea, you could feel they were staying on, hoping against hope to get a glimpse of her. I expect I was sensitive and rather silly, but I was miserable. And then Lennie, who is not clever, but so nice that it always leads him to do exactly the right thing, went away suddenly and bought this house, where life has been one long dream of happiness. You've seen how utterly self-contained we are. Nobody comes to visit us very much, because when we first came here we used to hide when people called. And then the twins have always been such a joy—oh, dear, I wish they would never grow up; but there's still Hercules, and you never know, there might be another baby. Oh, my dear Sylvia, I'm sure you ought to get married. And you say his parents are dead?"

"But he has a sister."

"Oh, a sister doesn't matter. And it doesn't matter his being clever and fond of books, because you're fond of books yourself. The twins tell me you've read everything in the world and that there's nothing you don't know. I'm sure you'd soon get tired of Hornton House—oh, yes, I strongly advise you to get married."

When Sylvia got back to London the memory of Arbour End rested in her thoughts like a pleasant dream of the night that one ponders in a summer dawn. She assured Miss Ashley that she was longing to marry Philip; and when she seemed to express in her reception of the announcement a kind of puzzled approval, Sylvia spoke with real enthusiasm of her marriage. Miss Ashley never knew that the real inspiration of such enthusiasm was Arbour End and not at all Philip himself. As for Sylvia, because she would by no means admit even to herself that she had taken Mrs. Worsley's advice, she passed over the advice and remarked only the signs of happiness at Arbour End.

Sylvia and Philip were married at a registry-office early in October. The honeymoon was spent in the Italian lakes, where Philip denounced the theatrical scenery, but crowned Sylvia with vine-leaves and wrote Latin poetry to her, which he translated aloud in the evenings as well as the mosquitoes would let him.

CHAPTER VII

GREEN LANES lay midway between the market town of Galton and the large village of Newton Candover. It is a small, tumble-down hamlet remote from any highroad, the confluence of four deserted by-ways leading to other hamlets upon the wooded downland of which Green Lanes was the highest point. Hare Hall, the family mansion of the Iredales, was quite two miles away in the direction of Newton Candover and was let for a long term of years to a rich stockbroker. Philip himself lived at The Old Farm, an Elizabethan farm-house which he had filled with books. The only other "gentleman" in Green Lanes was the vicar, Mr. Dorward, with whom Philip had quarreled. The squire as lay rector drew a yearly revenue of £300, but he refused to allow the living more than £90 until the vicar gave up his ritualistic fads, to which, though he never went inside the church, he strongly objected.

Sylvia's first quarrel with Philip was over the vicar, whom she met through her puppy's wandering into his cottage while he was at tea and refusing to come out. She might never have visited him again if Philip had not objected, for he was very shy and eccentric; but after two more visits to annoy Philip, she began to like Mr. Dorward, and her friendship with him became a standing source of irritation to her husband and a pleasure to herself which she declined to give up. Her second quarrel with Philip was over his sister Gertrude, who came down for a visit soon after they got back from Como. Gertrude, having until her brother's marriage always lived at The Old Farm, could not refrain from making Sylvia very much aware of this; her conversation was one long, supercilious narrative of what she used to do at Green Lanes, with which were mingled fears for what might be done there in the future. Philip was quite ready to admit that his sister could be very irritating, but he thought Sylvia's demand for her complete exclusion from The Old Farm for at least a year was unreasonable.

"Well, if she comes, I shall go," Sylvia said, sullenly.

"My dear child, do remember that you're married and that you can't go and come as you like," Philip answered. "However, I quite see your point of view about poor Gertrude and I quite agree with you that for a time it will be wiser to keep ourselves rather strictly to ourselves."

Why could he not have said that at first, Sylvia thought. She would have been so quickly generous if he had, but the preface about her being married had spoiled his concession. He was a curious creature, this husband of hers. When they were alone he would encourage her to be as she used to be; he would laugh with her, show the keenest interest in what she was reading, search for a morning to find some book that would please her, listen with delight to her stories of Jimmy Monkley or of her father or of Blanche, and be always, in fact, the sympathetic friend, never obtruding himself, as lover or monitor, two aspects of him equally repugnant to Sylvia. Yet when there was the least likelihood not alone of a third person's presence, but even of a third person's hearing any roundabout gossip of her real self, Philip would shrivel her up with interminable corrections, and what was far worse, try to sweeten the process by what she considered fatuous demonstrations of affection. For a time there was no great tension between them, because Sylvia's adventurous spirit was occupied by her passion for knowledge; she felt vaguely that at any time the moment might arrive when mere knowledge without experience would not be enough; at present the freedom of Philip's library was adventure enough. He was most eager to assist her progress, and almost reckless in the way he spurred her into every liberty of thought, maintaining the stupidity of all conventional beliefs—moral, religious, or political. He warned her that the expression of such opinions, or, still worse, action under the influence of them, would be for her or for any one else in the present state of society quite impossible; Sylvia used to think at the time that it was only herself as his wife whom he wished to keep in check, and resented his reasons accordingly; afterward looking back to this period she came to the conclusion that Philip was literally a theorist, and that his fierce denunciations of all conventional opinions could never in any circumstances have gone further than quarreling with the vicar and getting married in a registry-office. Once when she attacked him for his cowardice he retorted by citing his marriage with her, and immediately afterward apologized for what he characterized as "caddishness."

"If you had married me and been content to let me remain myself," Sylvia said, "you might have used that argument. But you showed you were frightened of what you'd done when you sent me to Hornton House."

"My dear child, I wanted you to go there for your own comfort, not for mine. After all, it was only like reading a book; it gave you a certain amount of academic theory that you could prove or disprove by experience."

"A devil of a lot of experience I get here," Sylvia exclaimed.

"You're still only seventeen," Philip answered. "The time will come."

"It will come," Sylvia murmured, darkly.

"You're not threatening to run away from me already?" Philip asked, with a smile.

"I might do anything," she owned. "I might poison you."

Philip laughed heartily at this; just then Mr. Dorward passed over the village green, which gave him an opportunity to rail at his cassock.

"It's ridiculous for a man to go about dressed up like that. Of course, nobody attends his church. I can't think why my father gave him the living. He's a ritualist, and his manners are abominable."

"But he looks like a Roman Emperor," said Sylvia.

Philip spluttered with indignation. "Oh, he's Roman enough, my dear child; but an Emperor! Which Emperor?"

"I'm not sure which it is, but I think it's Nero."

"Yes, I see what you mean," Philip assented, after a pause. "You're amazingly observant. Yes, there is that kind of mixture of sensual strength and fineness about his face. But it's not surprising. The line between degeneracy and the 'twopence colored' type of religion is not very clearly drawn."

It was after this conversation that, in searching for a picture of Nero's head to compare with Mr. Dorward's, Sylvia came across the Satyricon of Petronius in a French translation. She read it through without skipping a word, applied it to the test of recognition, and decided that she found more satisfactorily than in any book she had yet read a distorting mirror of her life from the time she left France until she met Philip, a mirror, however, that never distorted so wildly as to preclude recognition. Having made this discovery, she announced it to him, who applauded her sense of humor and of literature, but begged her to keep it to herself; people might get a wrong idea of her; he knew what she meant and appreciated the reflection, but it was a book that, generally speaking, no woman would read, still less talk about, and least of all claim kinship with. It was of course an immortal work of art, humorous, witty, fantastic.

"And true," Sylvia added.

"And no doubt true to its period and its place, which was southern Italy in the time of Nero."

"And true to southern England in the time of Victoria," Sylvia insisted. "I don't mean that it's exactly the same," she went on, striving almost painfully to express her thoughts. "The same, though. I *feel* it's true. I don't *know* it's true. Oh, can't you understand?"

"I fancy you're trying to voice your esthetic consciousness of great art that, however time may change its accessories, remains inherently changeless. Realism in fact as opposed to what is wrongly called realism. Lots of critics, Sylvia, have tried to define what is worrying you, and lots of long words have been enlisted on their behalf. A better and more ancient word for realism was 'poetry'; but the word has been debased by the versifiers who call themselves poets just as painters call themselves artists—both are titles that only posterity can award. Great art is something that is made and that lives in itself; like that stuff, radium, which was discovered the year before last, it eternally gives out energy without consuming itself. Radium, however, does not solve the riddle of life, and until we solve that, great art will remain undefinable. Which reminds me of a mistake that so-called believers make. I've often heard Christians maintain the truth of Christianity, because it is still alive. What nonsense! The words of Christ are still alive, because Christ Himself was a great poet, and therefore expressed humanity as perhaps no one else ever expressed humanity before. But the lying romantic, the bad poet, in fact, who tickles the vain and credulous mob with miracles and theogonies, expresses nothing. It is a proof of nothing but the vitality of great art that the words of Christ can exist and can continue to affect humanity notwithstanding the mountebank behavior attributed to Him, out of which priests have manufactured a religion. It is equally surprising that Cervantes could hold his own against the romances of chivalry he tried to kill. He may have killed one mode of expression, but he did not prevent *East Lynne* from being written; he yet endures because Don Quixote, whom he made, has life. By the way, you never got on with Don Quixote, did you?"

Sylvia shook her head.

"I think it's a failure on your part, dear Sylvia."

"He is so stupid," she said.

"But he realized how stupid he was before he died."

She shrugged her shoulders. "I can't help my bad taste, as you call it. He annoys me."

"You think the Yanguesian carriers dealt with him in the proper way?"

"I don't remember them."

"They beat him."

"I think I could beat a person who annoyed me very much," Sylvia said. "I don't mean with sticks, of course, but with my behavior."

63

"Is that another warning?" Philip asked.

"Perhaps."

"Anyway, you think Petronius is good?"

She nodded her head emphatically.

"Come, you shall give a judgment on Aristophanes. I commend him to you in the same series of French translations."

"I think Lysistrata is simply splendid," Sylvia said, a week or so later. "And I like the Thesmos-something and the Eck-something."

"I thought you might," Philip laughed. "But don't quote from them when my millionaire tenant comes to tea."

"Don't be always harping upon the dangers of my conversation," she exhorted.

"Mayn't I even tease you?" Philip asked, in mock humility.

"I don't mind being teased, but it isn't teasing. It's serious."

"Your sense of humor plays you tricks sometimes," he said.

"Oh, don't talk about my sense of humor like that. My sense of humor isn't a watch that you can take out and tap and regulate and wind up and shake your head over. I hate people who talk about a sense of humor as you do. Are you so sure you have one yourself?"

"Perhaps I haven't," Philip agreed, but by the way in which he spoke Sylvia knew that he would maintain he had a sense of humor, and that the rest of humanity had none if it combined to contradict him. "I always distrust people who are too confidently the possessors of one," he added.

"You don't understand in the least what I mean," Sylvia cried out, in exasperation. "You couldn't distrust anybody else's sense of humor if you had one yourself."

"That's what I said," Philip pointed out, in an aggrieved voice.

"Don't go on; you'll make me scream," she adjured him. "I won't talk about a sense of humor, because if there is such a thing it obviously can't be talked about."

Lest Philip should pursue the argument, she left him and went for a long muddy walk by herself half-way to Galton. She had never before walked beyond the village of Medworth, but she was still in such a state of nervous exasperation that she continued down the hill beyond it without noticing how far it was taking her. The country on either side of the road ascended in uncultivated fields toward dense oak woods. In many of these fields were habitations with grandiose names, mostly built of corrugated iron. Sylvia thought at first that she was approaching the outskirts of Galton and pressed on to explore the town, the name of which was familiar from the rickety tradesmen's carts that jogged through Green Lanes. There was no sign of a town, however, and after walking about two miles through a landscape that recalled the pictures she had seen of primitive settlements in the Far West, she began to feel tired and turned round upon her tracks, wishing she had not come quite so far. Suddenly a rustic gate that was almost buried in the unclipped hazel hedge on one side of the road was flung open, and an elderly lady with a hooked nose and fierce bright eyes, dressed in what looked at a first glance like a pair of soiled lace window-curtains, asked Sylvia with some abruptness if she had met a turkey going in her direction. Sylvia shook her head, and the elderly lady (Sylvia would have called her an old lady from her wrinkled countenance, had she not been so astonishingly vivacious in her movements) called in a high harsh voice:

"Emmie! There's a girl here coming from Galton way, and *she* hasn't seen Major Kettlewell."

In the distance a female voice answered, shrilly, "Perhaps he's crossed over to the Pluepotts'!"

Sylvia explained that she had misunderstood the first inquiry, but that nobody had passed her since she turned back five minutes ago.

"We call the turkey Major Kettlewell because he looks like Major Kettlewell, but Major Kettlewell himself lives over there."

The elderly lady indicated the other side of the road with a vague gesture, and went on:

"Where can that dratted bird have got to? Major! Major! Major! Chuch—chick—chilly—chilly—chuck—chuck," she called.

Sylvia hoped that the real major lived far enough away to be out of hearing.

"Never keep a turkey," the elderly lady went on, addressing Sylvia. "We didn't kill it for Christmas, because we'd grown fond of it, even though he is like that old ruffian of a major. And ever since he's gone on the wander. It's the springtime coming, I suppose."

The elderly lady's companion had by this time reached the gate, and Sylvia saw that she was considerably younger, but with the same hall-mark of old-maidishness.

"Don't worry any more about the bird, Adelaide," said the new-comer. "It's tea-time. Depend upon it, he's crossed over to the Pluepotts'. This time I really will wring his neck."

Sylvia prepared to move along, but the first lady asked her where she was going, and, when she heard Green Lanes, exclaimed:

"Gemini! That's beyond Medworth, isn't it? You'd better come in and have a cup of tea with us. I'm Miss Horne, and my friend here is Miss Hobart."

Sunny Bank, as this particular tin house was named, not altogether inappropriately, although it happened to be on the less sunny side of the road, was built half-way up a steepish slope of very rough ground from which enough flints had been extracted to pave a zigzag of ascending paths, and to vary the contour of the slope with a miniature mountain range of unused material without apparently smoothing the areas of proposed cultivation.

"These paths are something dreadful, Emmie," said Miss Horne, as the three of them scrambled up through the garden. "Never mind, we'll get the roller out of the hedge when Mr. Pluepott comes in on Wednesday. Miss Hobart nearly got carried away by the roller yesterday," she explained to Sylvia.

A trellised porch outside the bungalow—such apparently was the correct name for these habitations—afforded a view of the opposite slope, which was sprinkled with bungalows surrounded like Sunny Bank by heaps of stones; there were also one or two more pretentious buildings of red brick and one or two stony gardens without a dwelling-place as yet.

"I suppose you're wondering why the name over the door isn't the same as the one on the gate? Mr. Pluepott is always going to take it out, but he never remembers to bring the paint. It's the name the man from whom we bought it gave the bungalow," said Miss Hobart, crossly. Sylvia read in gothic characters over the door Floral Nook, and agreed with the two ladies that Sunny Bank was much more suitable.

"For whatever else it may be, it certainly isn't damp," Miss Horne declared. "But, dear me, talking of names, you haven't told us yours."

Sylvia felt shy. It was actually the first time she had been called upon to announce herself since she was married. The two ladies exclaimed on hearing she was Mrs. Iredale, and Sylvia felt that there was a kind of impropriety in her being married, when Miss Horne and Miss Hobart, who were so very much older than she, were still spinsters.

The four small rooms of which the bungalow consisted were lined with varnished match-boarding; everything was tied up with brightly colored bows of silk, and most of the pictures were draped with small curtains; the bungalow was full of knickknacks and shivery furniture, but not full enough to satisfy the owners' passion for prettiness, so that wherever there was a little space on the walls silk bows had been nailed about like political favors. Sylvia thought it would have been simpler to tie a wide sash of pink silk round the house and call it The Chocolate Box. Tea, though even the spoons were tied up with silk, was a varied and satisfying meal. The conversation of the two ladies was remarkably entertaining when it touched upon their neighbors, and when twilight warned Sylvia that she must hurry away she was sorry to leave them. While she was making her farewells there was a loud tap at the door, followed immediately by the entrance of a small bullet-headed man with quick black eyes.

"I've brought back your turkey, Miss Horne."

"Oh, thank you, Mr. Pluepott. There you are, Emmie. You were right."

At this moment the bird began to flap its wings as violently as its position head downward would allow; nor, not being a horse, did it pay any attention to Mr. Pluepott's repeated shouts of "Woa! Woa back, will you!"

"I think you'd better let him flap outside, Mr. Pluepott," Miss Hobart advised.

Sylvia thought so too when she looked at the floor.

"Shall I wring its neck now or would you rather I waited till I come in on Wednesday?"

"Oh, I think we'll wait, thank you, Mr. Pluepott," Miss Horne said. "Perhaps you wouldn't mind shutting him up in the coop. He does wander so. Are you going into Galton?"

Mr. Pluepott replied, as he confined Major Kettlewell to his barracks, that, on the contrary, he was driving up to Medworth to see about some beehives for sale there, whereupon Miss Horne and Miss Hobart asked if he would mind taking Mrs. Iredale that far upon her way.

A few minutes later Sylvia, on a very splintery seat, was jolting along beside Mr. Pluepott toward Medworth.

"Rum lot of people hereabouts," he said, by way of opening the conversation, "Some of the rummest people it's ever been my luck to meet. I came here because my wife had to leave the Midlands. Chest was bad. I used to be a cobbler at Bedford. Since I've been here I've become everything—carpenter, painter, decorator, gardener, mason, bee expert, poultry-keeper, blacksmith, livery-stables, furniture-remover, house agent, common carrier, bricklayer, dairyman, horse-breaker. The only thing I don't do now is make boots. Funny thing, and you won't believe it, but last week I had to buy myself the first pair of boots I ever bought since I was a lad of fifteen. Oh, well, I like the latest better than the last, as I jokingly told my missus the other night. It made her laugh," said Mr. Pluepott, looking at Sylvia rather anxiously; she managed to laugh too, and he seemed relieved.

"I often make jokes for my missus. She's apt to get very melancholy with her chest. But, as I was saying, the folk round here they beat the band. It just shows what advertisement will do."

Sylvia asked why.

"Well, when I first came here, and I was one of the three first, I came because I read an advertisement in the paper: 'Land for the Million in lots from a quarter of an acre.' Some fellow had bought an old farm that was no use to nobody and had the idea of splitting it up into lots. Originally this was the Oak Farm Estate and belonged to St. Mary's College, Oxford. Now we call it Oaktown—the residents, that is—but when we applied the other day to the Galton Rural District Council, so as we could have the name properly recognized, went in we did with the major, half a dozen of us, as smart as a funeral, one of the wise men of Gotham, which is what I jokingly calls Galton nowadays, said he thought Tintown would be a better name. The major got rare and angry, but his teeth slipped just as he was giving it 'em hot and strong, which is a trick they have. He nearly swallowed 'em last November, when he was taking the chair at a Conservative meeting, in an argument with a Radical about the war. They had to lead him outside and pat his back. It's a pity the old ladies can't get on with him. They fell out over blackberrying in his copse last Michaelmas. Well, the fact is the major's a bit close, and I think he meant to sell the blackberries. He's put up a notice now 'Beware of Dangerous Explosives,' though there's nothing more dangerous than a broken air-gun in the whole house. Miss Horne was very bitter about it; oh, very bitter she was. Said she always knew the major was a guy, and he only wanted to stuff himself with gunpowder to give the boys a rare set out on the Fifth."

65

"How did Miss Horne and Miss Hobart come here?" Sylvia asked.

"Advertisement. They lived somewhere near London, I believe; came into a bit of money, I've heard, and thought they'd settle in the country. I give them a morning a week on Wednesdays. The man they bought it off had been a tax-collector somewhere in the West Indies. He swindled them properly, but they were sorry for him because he had a floating kidney—floating in alcohol, I should think, by the amount he drank. But they won't hear a word against him even now. He's living in Galton and they send him cabbages every week, which he gives to his rabbits when he's sober and throws at his housekeeper when he's drunk. Sunny Bank! I'm glad it's not my Bank. As I jokingly said to my missus, I should soon be stony-broke. Ah, well, there's all sorts here and that's a fact," Mr. Pluepott continued, with a pensive flick at his pony. "That man over there, for instance." He pointed with his whip through the gathering darkness to a particularly small tin cottage. "He used to play the trombone in a theater till he played his inside out; now he thinks he's going to make a fortune growing early tomatoes for Covent Garden market. You get him with a pencil in his hand of an evening and you'd think about borrowing money from him next year; but when you see him next morning trying to cover a five-by-four packing-case with a broken sash-light, you'd be more afraid of his trying to borrow from you."

With such conversation did Mr. Pluepott beguile the way to Medworth; and when he heard that Sylvia intended to walk in the dusk to Green Lanes he insisted on driving her the extra two miles.

"The hives won't fly away," he said, cheerfully, "and I like to make a good job of a thing. Well, now you've found your way to Oaktown, I hope you'll visit us again. Mrs. Pluepott will be very glad to see you drop in for a cup of tea any day, and if you've got any comical reading-matter, she'd be glad to borrow from you; for her chest does make her very melancholy, and, being accustomed to having me always about the house when I was cobbling, she doesn't seem to get used to being alone. Only the other day she said if she'd known I was going to turn into a Buffalo Bill she'd rather have stayed in Bedford. 'Land for the Millions!' she said, 'I reckon you'd call it Land for the Million, if you had to sweep the house clean of the mud you bring into it.' Well, good night to you. Very glad I was able to oblige, I'm sure."

Philip was relieved when Sylvia got back. She had never been out for so long before, and she teased him about the running away, that he had evidently imagined. She felt in a good humor after her expedition, and was glad to be back in this dignified and ancient house with its books and lamplight and not a silken bow anywhere to be seen.

"So you've been down to that abomination of tin houses? It's an absolute blot on the countryside. I don't recommend too close an acquaintanceship. I'm told it's inhabited by an appalling set of rascals. Poor Melville, who owns the land all 'round, says he can't keep a hare."

Sylvia said the people seemed rather amusing, and was not at all inclined to accept Philip's condemnation of them; he surely did not suggest that Miss Horne and Miss Hobart, for instance, were poachers?

"My dear child, people who come and live in a place like the Oak Farm Estate—Oaktown, as they have the impudence to call it—are there for no good. They've either done something discreditable in town or they hope to do something discreditable in the country. Oh yes, I've heard all about our neighbors. There's a ridiculous fellow who calls himself a major—I believe he used to be in the volunteers—and can't understand why he's not made a magistrate. I'm told he's the little tin god of Tintown. No, no, I prefer even your friendship with our vicar. Don't be cross with me, Sylvia, for laughing at your new friends, but you mustn't take them too seriously. I shall have finished the text I'm writing this month, and we'll go up to London for a bit. Shall we? I'm afraid you're getting dull down here."

The spring wore away, but the text showed no signs of being finished. Sylvia suggested that she should invite Gladys and Enid Worsley to stay with her, but Philip begged her to postpone the invitation while he was working, and thought in any case it would be better to have them down in summer. Sylvia went to Oaktown once or twice, but said nothing about it to Philip, because from a sort of charitableness she did not want him to diminish himself further in her eyes by airing his prejudices with the complacency that seemed to increase all the time they stayed in the country.

One day at the end of April Miss Horne and Miss Hobart announced they had bought a governess-car and a pony, built a stable, and intended to celebrate their first drive by calling on Sylvia at Green Lanes. Mr. Pluepott had promised, even if it should not be on a Wednesday, to superintend the first expedition and gave his opinion of the boy whom it was proposed to employ as coachman. The boy in question, whom Mr. Pluepott called Jehuselah, whether from an attempt to combine a satirical expression of his driving and his age, or too slight acquaintance with Biblical personalities, was uncertain, was known as Ernie to Miss Horne and Miss Hobart when he was quick and good, but as Ernest when he was slow and bad; his real name all the time was Herbert.

"Good heavens!" Philip ejaculated, when he beheld the governess-car from his window. "Who on earth is this?"

"Friends of mine," said Sylvia. "Miss Horne and Miss Hobart. I told you about them."

"But they're getting out," Philip gasped, in horror. "They're coming here."

"I know," Sylvia said. "I hope there's plenty for tea. They always give me the most enormous teas." And without waiting for any more of Philip's protests she hurried down-stairs and out into the road to welcome the two ladies. They were both of them dressed in pigeon's-throat silk under more lace even than usual, and arrived in a state of enthusiasm over Ernie's driving and thankfulness for the company of Mr. Pluepott, who was also extremely pleased with the whole turn-out.

"A baby in arms couldn't have handled that pony more carefully," he declared, looking at Ernie with as much pride as if he had begotten him.

"We're so looking forward to meeting Mr. Iredale," said Miss Horne.

"We hear he's a great scholar," said Miss Hobart.

Sylvia took them into the dining-room, where she was glad to see that a gigantic tea had been prepared—a match even for the most profuse of Sunny Bank's.

Then she went up-stairs to fetch Philip, who flatly refused to come down.

"You must come," Sylvia urged. "I'll never forgive you if you don't."

"My dearest Sylvia, I really cannot entertain the eccentricities of Tintown here. You invited them. You must look after them. I'm busy."

"Are you coming?" Sylvia asked, biting her lips.

"No, I really can't. It's absurd. I don't want this kind of people here. Besides, I must work."

"You sha'n't work," Sylvia cried, in a fury, and she swept all his books and papers on the floor.

"I certainly sha'n't come now," he said, in the prim voice that was so maddening.

"Did you mean to come before I upset your books?"

"Yes, I probably should have come," he answered.

"All right. I'm so sorry. I'll pick everything up," and she plunged down on the floor. "There you are," she said when everything was put back in its place. "Now will you come?"

"No, my dear. I told you I wouldn't after you upset my things."

"Philip," she cried, her eyes bright with rage, "you're making me begin to hate you sometimes."

Then she left him and went back to her guests, to whom she explained that her husband had a headache and was lying down. The ladies were disappointed, but consoled themselves by recommending a number of remedies which Miss Horne insisted that Sylvia should write down. When tea was finished, Miss Hobart said that their first visit to Green Lanes had been most enjoyable and that there was only one thing they would like to do before going home, which would be to visit the church. Sylvia jumped at an excuse for not showing them over the house, and they set out immediately through the garden to walk to the little church that stood in a graveyard grass-grown like the green lanes of the hamlet whose dead were buried there. The sun was westering, and in the golden air they lowered their voices for a thrush that was singing his vespers upon a moldering wooden cross.

"Nobody ever comes here," Sylvia said. "Hardly anybody comes to church ever. The people don't like Mr. Dorward's services. They say he can't be heard."

Suddenly the vicar himself appeared, and seemed greatly pleased to see Sylvia and her visitors; she felt a little guilty, because, though she was great friends with Mr. Dorward, she had never been inside the church, nor had he ever hinted he would like her to come. It would seem so unkind for her to come like this for the first time with strangers, as if the church which she knew he deeply loved was nothing but a tea-time entertainment. There was no trace of reproachfulness in his manner, as he showed Miss Horne and Miss Hobart the vestments and a little image of the Virgin in peach-blow glaze that he moved caressingly into the sunlight, as a child might fondle reverently a favorite doll. He spoke of his plans for restoration and unrolled the design of a famous architect, adding with a smile for Sylvia that the lay rector disapproved of it thoroughly. They left him arranging the candlesticks on the altar, a half-pathetic, half-humorous figure that seemed to be playing a solitary game.

"And you say nobody goes to his church!" Miss Horne exclaimed. "But he's most polite and charming."

"Scarcely anybody goes," Sylvia said.

"Emmie," said Miss Horne, standing upright and flashing forth an eagle's glance. "*We* will attend his service."

"That is a very good idea of yours, Adelaide," Miss Hobart replied.

Then they got into the governess-car with much determination, and with friendly waves of the hand to Sylvia set out back to Oaktown.

When Miss Horne and Miss Hobart had left, Sylvia went up-stairs to have it out with Philip. At this rate there would very soon be a crisis in their married life. She was a little disconcerted by his getting up the moment she entered his room and coming to meet her with an apology.

"Dearest Sylvia, you can call me what you will; I shall deserve the worst. I can't understand my behavior this afternoon. I think I must have been working so hard that my nerves are hopelessly jangled. I very nearly followed you into the churchyard to make myself most humbly pleasant, but I saw Dorward go 'round almost immediately afterward, and I could not have met him in the mood I was in without being unpardonably rude."

He waited for her with an arm stretched out in reconciliation, but Sylvia hesitated.

"It's all very well to hurt my feelings like that because you happened to be feeling in a bad temper," she said, "and then think you've only got to make a pleasant little speech to put everything right again. Besides, it isn't only to-day; it's day after day since we've been married. I feel like Gulliver when he was being tied up by the Lilliputians. I can't find any one big rope that's destroying my freedom, but somehow or other my freedom is being destroyed. Did you marry me casually, as people buy birds, to put me in a cage?"

"My dear, I married you because I loved you. You know I fought against the idea of marrying you for a long time, but I loved you too much."

"Are you afraid of my loyalty?" she demanded. "Do you think I go to Oaktown to be made love to?"

"Sylvia!" he protested.

"I go there because I'm bored, bored, endlessly, hopelessly, paralyzingly bored. It's my own fault. I never ought to have married you. I can't think why I did, but at least it wasn't for any mercenary reason. You're not to believe that. Philip, I do like you, but why will you always upset me?"

He thought for a moment and asked her presently what greater freedom she wanted, what kind of freedom.

"That's it," she went on. "I told you I couldn't find any one big rope that bound me. There isn't a single thread I can't snap with perfect ease, but it's the multitude of insignificant little threads that almost choke me."

"You told me you thought you would like to live in the country," he reminded her.

"I do, but, Philip, do remember that I really am still a child. I've got a deep voice and I can talk like a professor, but I'm still a hopeless kid. I oughtn't to have to tell you this. You ought to see it for yourself if you love me."

"Dearest Sylvia, I'm always telling you how young you are, and there's nothing that annoys you more," he said.

"Oh, Philip, Philip, you really are pathetic! When did you ever meet a young person who liked to have her youth called attention to? You're so remote from beginning to understand how to manage me, and I'm still manageable. Very soon I sha'n't be, though; and there'll be such a dismal smash-up."

"If you'd only explain exactly," he began; but she interrupted him at once.

"My dear man, if I explain and you take notes and consult them for your future behavior to me, do you think that's going to please me? It can all be said in two words. I'm human. For the love of God be human yourself."

"Look here, let's go away for a spell," said Philip, brightly.

"The cat's miaowing. Let's open the door. No, seriously, I think I should like to go away from here for a while."

"By yourself?" he asked, in a frightened voice.

"Oh no, not by myself. I'm perfectly content with you. Only don't suggest the Italian lakes and try to revive the early sweets of our eight months of married life. Don't let's have a sentimental rebuilding. It will be so much more practical to build up something quite new."

Philip really seemed to have been shaken by this conversation. Sylvia knew he had not finished his text, but he put everything aside in order not to keep her waiting; and before May was half-way through they had reached the island of Sirene. Here they stayed two months in a crumbling pension upon the cliff's edge until Sylvia was sun-dried without and within; she was enthralled by the evidences of imperial Rome, and her only regret was that she did not meet an eccentric Englishman who was reputed to have found, when digging a cistern, at least one of the lost books of Elephantis, which he read in olive-groves by the light of the moon. However, she met several other eccentrics of different nationalities and was pleased to find that Philip's humanism was, with Sirene as a background, strong enough to lend him an appearance of humanity. They planned, like all other visitors to Sirene, to build a big villa there; they listened like all other visitors to the Italian and foreign inhabitants' depreciation of every villa but the one in which they lived, either because they liked it or because they wanted to let it or because they wished new-comers to fall into snares laid for themselves when they were new-comers.

At last they tore themselves from Sirenean dreams and schemes, chiefly because Sylvia had accepted an invitation to stay at Arbour End. They lingered for a while at Naples on the way home, where Sylvia looked about her with Petronian eyes, so much so, indeed, that a guide mistook what was merely academic curiosity for something more practical. It cost Philip fifty liras and nearly all the Italian he knew to get rid of the pertinacious and ingenious fellow.

Arbour End had not changed at all in a year. Sylvia, when she thought of Green Lanes, laughed a little bitterly at herself (but not so bitterly as she would have laughed before the benevolent sunshine of Sirene) for ever supposing that she and Philip could create anything like it. Gladys and Enid, though they were now fifteen, had not yet lengthened their frocks; their mother could not yet bring herself to contemplate the disappearance of those slim black legs.

"But we shall have to next term," Gladys said, "because Miss Ashley's written home about them."

"And that stuck-up thing Gwendyr Jones said they were positively disgusting," Enid went on.

"Yes," added Gladys, "and I told her they weren't half as disgusting as her ankles. And they aren't, are they, Sylvia?"

"Some of the girls call her marrow-bones," said Enid.

Sylvia would have preferred to avoid any intimate talks with Mrs. Worsley, but it was scarcely to be expected that she would succeed, and one night, looking ridiculously young with her fair hair hanging down her back, she came to Sylvia's bedroom, and sitting down at the end of her bed, began:

"Well, are you glad you got married?"

At any rate, Sylvia thought, she had the tact not to ask if she was glad she had taken her advice.

"I'm not so sorry as I was," Sylvia told her.

"Ah, didn't I warn you against the first year? You'll see that I was right."

"But I was not sorry in the way you prophesied. I've never had any bothers with the country. Philip's sister was rather a bore, always wondering about his clothes for the year after next; but we made a treaty, and she's been excluded from The Old Farm—wait a bit, only till next October. By Jove! I say, the treaty'll have to be renewed. I don't believe even memories of Sirene would enable me to deal with Gertrude this winter. No, what worries me most in marriage is not other people, but our two selves. I hate writing Sylvia Iredale instead of Sylvia Scarlett. Quite unreasonable of me, but most worries are unreasonable. I don't want to be owned. I'm a book to Philip; he bought me for my binding and never intended to read me, even if he could. I don't mean to say I was beautiful, but I was what an American girl at Hornton House used to call cunning; the pattern was unusual, and he couldn't resist it. But now that he's bought me, he expects me to stay quite happily on a shelf in a glass case; one day he may perhaps try to read me, but at present, so long as I'm taken out and dusted—our holiday at Sirene was a dusting—he thinks that's enough. But the worm that flies in the heart of the storm has got in, Victoria, and is making a much more unusual pattern across my inside—I say, I think it's about time to drop this metaphor, don't you?"

"I don't think I quite understand all you're saying," said Victoria Worsley.

Sylvia brought her hand from beneath the bedclothes and took her friend's.

"Does it matter?"

"Oh, but I like to understand what people are saying," Mrs. Worsley insisted. "That's why we never go abroad for our holidays. But, Sylvia, about being owned, which is where I stopped understanding. Lennie doesn't own me."

"No, you own *him*, but I don't own Philip."

"I expect you will, my dear, after you've been married a little longer."

"You think I shall acquire him in monthly instalments. I should find at the end the cost too much in repairs, like Fred Organ."

"Who's he?"

"Hube's brother, the cabman. Don't you remember?"

"Oh, of course, how silly of me! I thought it might be an Italian you met at Sirene. You've made me feel quite sad, Sylvia. I always want everybody to be happy," she sighed. "I am happy—perfectly happy—in spite of being married."

"Nobody's happy because of being married," Sylvia enunciated, rather sententiously.

"What nonsense you talk, and you're only just eighteen!"

"That's why I talk nonsense," Sylvia said, "but all the same it's very true nonsense. You and Lennie couldn't have ever been anything but happy."

"Darling Lennie, I think it must be because he's so stupid. I wonder if he's smoking in bed. He always does if I leave him to go and talk to anybody. Good night, dear."

Sylvia returned to her book, wondering more than ever how she could have supposed a year ago that she could follow Victoria Worsley along the pathway of her simple and happy life.

The whole family from Arbour End came to London for the ten days before term began, and Sylvia stayed with them at a hotel. Gladys and Enid had to get their new frocks, and certain gaps in Hercules's education had to be filled up, such as visiting the Zoo and the Tower of London and the Great Wheel at Earl's Court. Sylvia and the twins searched in vain for the Hall of a Thousand and One Marvels, but they found Mabel selling Turkish Delight by herself at a small stall in another part of the Exhibition. Sylvia thought the best way of showing her penitence for the heartless way she had treated her was to buy as much Turkish Delight as could possibly be carried away, since she probably received a percentage on the takings. Mabel seemed to bear no resentment, but she was rather shy, because she mistook the twins for Sylvia's sisters-in-law and therefore avoided the only topic upon which she could talk freely, which was men. They left the florid and accommodating creature with a callow youth who was leaning familiarly across the counter and smacking with a cane his banana-colored boots; then they ate as much Turkish Delight as they could and divided the rest among some ducks and the Kaffirs in the kraal.

Sylvia also visited Hornton House and explained to Miss Ashley why she had demanded the banishment of Gertrude from Green Lanes.

"Poor Gertrude, she was very much upset," Miss Ashley said.

Sylvia, softened by the memories of a so happy year that her old school evoked, made up her mind not to carry on the war against Gertrude. She felt, too, a greater charity toward Philip, who, after all, had been the cause of her being given that so happy year, and she went back to Hampshire with the firm intention of encouraging this new mood that the last four months had created in her. Philip was waiting on the platform and was so glad to see her again that he drove even more absent-mindedly than usual, until she took the reins from him and whipped up the horse with a quite positive anticipation of home.

Sylvia learned from Philip that the visit of Miss Horne and Miss Hobart had influenced other lives than their own, for it seemed that Miss Horne's announcement of their attendance in future at Mr. Dorward's empty church had been fully carried out. Not a Sunday passed but that they drove up in the governess-car to Mass, so Philip said with a wry face for the word; what was more, they stayed to lunch with the vicar, presided at the Sunday-school, and attended the evening service, which had been put forward half an hour to suit their supper.

"They absolutely rule Green Lanes ecclesiastically," Philip said. "And some of the mercenary bumpkins and boobies 'round here have taken to going to church for what they can get out of the two old ladies. I'm glad to say, however, that the farmers and their families haven't come 'round yet."

Sylvia said she was glad for Mr. Dorward's sake, and she wondered why Philip made such a fuss about the form of a service in the reality of which, whatever way it was presented, he had no belief.

"I suppose you're right," he agreed. "Perhaps what I'm really afraid of is that our fanatical vicar will really convert the parish to his childish religion. Upon my soul, I believe Miss Horne has her eye upon me. I know she's been holding forth upon my iniquitous position as lay rector, and these confounded Radicals will snatch hold of anything to create prejudice against landowners."

"Why don't you make friends with Mr. Dorward?" Sylvia suggested. "You could surely put aside your religious differences and talk about the classics."

"I dare say I'm bigoted in my own way," Philip answered. "But I can't stand a priest, just as some people can't stand cats or snakes. It's a positively physical repulsion that I can't get over. No, I'm afraid I must leave Dorward to you, Sylvia. I don't think there's much danger of your falling a victim to man-millinery. It'll take all your strength of mind, however, to resist the malice of these two old witches, and I wager you'll be excommunicated from the society of Tintown in next to no time."

Sylvia found that Philip had by no means magnified the activities of Miss Horne and Miss Hobart, and for the first time on a Sunday morning at Green Lanes a thin black stream of worshipers flowed past the windows of The Old Farm after service. It was more than curiosity could bear; without saying a word to anybody Sylvia attended the evening service herself. The church was very small, and her entrance would have attracted much more attention than it did if

Ernie, who was holding the thurible for Mr. Dorward to put in the incense, had not given at that moment a mighty sneeze, scattering incense and charcoal upon the altar steps and frightening the woman at the harmonium into a violent discord, from which the choir was rescued by Miss Horne's unmoved and harsh soprano that positively twisted back the craning necks of the congregation into their accustomed apathy. Sylvia wondered whether fear, conversion, or extra wages had induced Ernie to put on that romantic costume which gave him the appearance of a rustic table covered with a tea-cloth, as he waited while the priest tried to evoke a few threads of smoke from the ruin caused by his sneeze. Sylvia was so much occupied in watching Ernie that she did not notice the rest of the congregation had sat down. Mr. Dorward must have seen her, for he had thrown off the heavy vestment he was wearing and was advancing apparently to say how d'ye do. No, he seemed to think better of it, and had turned aside to read from a large book, but what he read neither Sylvia nor the congregation had any idea. She decided that all this standing up and kneeling and sitting down again was too confusing for a novice, and during the rest of the service she remained seated, which was at once the most comfortable and the least conspicuous attitude. Sylvia had intended to slip out before the service was over, as she did not want Miss Horne and Miss Hobart to exult over her imaginary conversion, but the finale came sooner than she expected in a fierce hymnal outburst during which Mr. Dorward hurriedly divested himself and reached the vestianel. Miss Horne had scarcely thumped the last beat on the choir-boy's head in front of her, the echoes of the last amen had scarcely died away, before the female sexton, an old woman called Cassandra Batt, was turning out the oil-lamps and the little congregation had gathered 'round the vicar in the west door to hear Miss Horne's estimate of its behavior. There was no chance for Sylvia to escape.

"Ernest," said Miss Horne, "what did you sneeze for during the Magnificat? Father Dorward never got through with censing the altar, you bad boy."

"The stoff got all up me nose," said Ernie. "Oi couldn't help meself."

"Next time you want to sneeze," said Miss Hobart, kindly, "press your top lip below the nose, and you'll keep it back."

"I got too much to do," Ernie muttered, "and too much to think on."

"Jane Frost," said Miss Horne, quickly turning the direction of her attack, "you must practise all this week. Suppose Father Dorward gets a new organ? You wouldn't like not to be allowed to play on it. Some of your notes to-night weren't like a musical instrument at all. The Nunc Dimittis was more like water running out of a bath. 'Lord, now lettest thou thy servant depart in peace,' are the words, not in pieces, which was what it sounded like the way you played it."

Miss Jane Frost, a daughter of the woman who kept the Green Lanes shop, blushed as deeply as her anemia would let her, and promised she would do better next week.

"That's right, Jane," said Miss Hobart, whose part seemed to be the consolation of Miss Horne's victims. "I dare say the pedal is a bit obstinate."

"Oh, it's turble obstinate," said Cassandra, the sexton, who, having extinguished all the lamps, now elbowed her way through the clustered congregation, a lighted taper in her hand. "I jumped on un once or twice this morning to make um a bit easier like, but a groaned at me like a wicked old toad. It's ile that a wants."

The congregation, on which a good deal of grease was being scattered by Cassandra's taper in her excitement, hastened to support her diagnosis.

"Oh yass, yass, 'tis ile that a wants."

"I will bring a bottle of oil up during the week," Miss Horne proclaimed. "Good night, everybody, and remember to be punctual next Sunday."

The congregation murmured its good night, and Sylvia, to whom it probably owed such a speedy dismissal, was warmly greeted by Miss Horne.

"So glad you've come, Mrs. Iredale, though I wish you'd brought the lay rector. Lay rector, indeed! Sakes alive, what will they invent next?"

"Yes, we're so glad you've come, dear," Miss Hobart added. Mr. Dorward came up in his funny quick way. When they were all walking across the churchyard, he whispered to Sylvia, in his funny quick voice:

"Church fowls, church fowls, you know! Mustn't discourage them. Pious fowls! Godly fowls! An example for the parish. Better attendance lately."

Then he caught up the two ladies and helped them into the vehicle, wishing them a pleasant drive and promising a nearly full moon shortly, after Medworth, very much as if the moon was really made of cheese and would be eaten for supper by Miss Horne and Miss Hobart.

When Sylvia got back to The Old Farm she amused Philip so much with her account of the service that he forgot to be angry with her for doing what at first he maintained put him in a false position.

All that autumn and winter Miss Horne and Miss Hobart wrestled with Satan for the souls of the hamlet; incidentally they wrestled with him for Sylvia's soul, but she scratched the event by ceasing to appear at all in church, and intercourse between them became less frequent; the friends of Miss Horne and Miss Hobart had to be all or nothing, and not the least divergence of belief or opinion, manners or policy, was tolerated by these two bigoted old ladies. The congregation, notwithstanding their efforts, remained stationary, much to Philip's satisfaction.

"The truth is," he said, "that the measure of their power is the pocket. Every scamp in the parish who thinks it will pay him to go to church is going to church. The others don't go at all or walk over to Medworth."

Her contemplation of the progress of religion in Green Lanes, which, however much she affected to laugh at it, could not help interesting Sylvia on account of her eccentric friend the vicar, was temporarily interrupted by a visit from

70

Gertrude Iredale. Remembering what Miss Ashley had told her, Sylvia had insisted upon Philip's asking his sister to stay, and he had obviously been touched by her suggestion. Gertrude perhaps had also taken some advice from Miss Ashley, for she was certainly less inclined to wonder what her brother would do about his clothes the year after next. She could not, however, altogether keep to herself her criticism of the housewifery at The Old Farm, a simple business in Sylvia's eyes, which consisted of letting the cook do exactly as she liked, with what she decided were very satisfactory results.

"But it's so extravagant," Gertrude objected.

"Well, Philip doesn't grumble. We can afford to pay a little extra every week to have the house comfortably run."

"But the principle is so bad," Gertrude insisted.

"Oh, principle," said Sylvia in an airy way, which must have been galling to her sister-in-law. "I don't believe in principles. Principles are only excuses for what we want to think or what we want to do."

"Don't you believe in abstract morality?" Gertrude asked, taking off her glasses and gazing with weak and earnest eyes at Sylvia.

"I don't believe in anything abstract," Sylvia replied.

"How strange!" the other murmured. "Goodness me! if I didn't believe in abstract morality I don't know where I should be—or what I should do."

Sylvia regarded the potential sinner with amused curiosity.

"Do tell me what you might do," she begged. "Would you live with a man without marrying him?"

"Please don't be coarse," said Gertrude. "I don't like it."

"I could put it much more coarsely," Sylvia said, with a laugh. "Would you—"

"Sylvia!" Gertrude whistled through her teeth in an agony of apprehensive modesty. "I entreat you not to continue."

"There you are," said Sylvia. "That shows what rubbish all your scruples are. You're shocked at what you thought I was going to say. Therefore you ought to be shocked at yourself. As a matter of fact, I was going to ask if you would marry a man without loving him."

"If I were to marry," Gertrude said, primly, "I should certainly want to love my husband."

"Yes, but what do you understand by love? Do you mean by love the emotion that makes people go mad to possess—"

Gertrude rose from her chair. "Sylvia, the whole conversation is becoming extremely unpleasant. I must ask you either to stop or let me go out of the room."

"You needn't be afraid of any personal revelations," Sylvia assured her. "I've never been in love that way. I only wanted to find out if you had been and ask you about it."

"Never," said Gertrude, decidedly. "I've certainly never been in love like that, and I hope I never shall."

"I think you're quite safe. And I'm beginning to think I'm quite safe, too," Sylvia added. "However, if you won't discuss abstract morality in an abstract way, you mustn't expect me to do so, and the problem of housekeeping returns to the domain of practical morality, where principles don't count."

Sylvia decided after this conversation to accept Gertrude as a joke, and she ceased to be irritated by her any longer, though her sister-in-law stayed from Christmas till the end of February. In one way her presence was of positive utility, because Philip, who was very much on the lookout for criticism of his married life, was careful not to find fault with Sylvia while she remained at Green Lanes; it also acted as a stimulus to Sylvia herself, who used her like a grindstone on which to sharpen her wits. Another advantage from Gertrude's visit was that Philip was able to finish his text, thanks to her industrious docketing and indexing and generally fussing about in his study. Therefore, when Sylvia proposed that the twins should spend their Easter holidays at The Old Farm, he had no objection to offer.

The prospect of the twins' visit kept Sylvia at the peak of pleasurable expectation throughout the month of March, and when at last, on a budding morn in early April, she drove through sky-enchanted puddles to meet them, she sang for the first time in months the raggle-taggle gipsies, and reached the railway station fully half an hour before the train was due. Nobody got out but the twins; yet they laughed and talked so much, the three of them, in the first triumph of meeting, that several passengers thought the wayside station must be more important than it was, and asked anxiously if this was Galton.

Gladys and Enid had grown a good deal in six months, and now with their lengthened frocks and tied-back hair they looked perhaps older than sixteen. Their faces, however, had not grown longer with their frocks; they were as full of spirits as ever, and Sylvia found that while they still charmed her as of old with that quality of demanding to be loved for the sheer grace of their youth, they were now capable of giving her the intimate friendship she so greatly desired.

"You darlings," she cried. "You're like champagne-cup in two beautiful crystal glasses with rose-leaves floating about on top."

The twins, who with all that zest in their own beauty which is the prerogative of a youth unhampered by parental jealousy, frankly loved to be admired; Sylvia's admiration never made them self-conscious, because it seemed a natural expression of affection. Their attitude toward Philip was entirely free from any conventional respect; as Sylvia's husband he was candidate for all the love they had for her, but when they found that Philip treated them as Sylvia's toys they withheld the honor of election and began to criticize him. When he seemed shocked at their criticism they began to tease him, explaining to Sylvia that he had obviously never been teased in his life. Philip, for his part, found them precocious and vain, which annoyed Sylvia and led to her seeking diversions and entertainment for the twins' holidays outside The Old Farm. As a matter of fact, she had no need to search far, because they both took a great fancy to Mr.

Dorward, who turned out to have an altogether unusual gift for drawing nonsensical pictures, which were almost as funny as his own behavior, that behavior which irritated so many more people than it amused.

The twins teased Mr. Dorward a good deal about his love-affair with Miss Horne and Miss Hobart, and though this teasing may only have coincided with Mr. Dorward's previous conviction that the two ladies were managing him and his parish rather too much for his dignity and certainly too much for his independence, there was no doubt that the quarrel between them was prepared during the time that Gladys and Enid were staying at Green Lanes; indeed, Sylvia thought she could name the actual afternoon.

Sylvia's intercourse with Miss Horne and Miss Hobart was still friendly enough to necessitate an early visit to Sunny Bank to present the twins. The two ladies were very fond of what they called "young people," and at first they were enraptured by Gladys and Enid, particularly when they played some absurd school-girl's trick upon Major Kettlewell. Sylvia, too, had by her tales of the island of Sirene inspired them with a longing to go there; they liked nothing better than to make her describe the various houses and villas that were for sale or to let, in every one of which in turn Miss Horne and Miss Hobart saw themselves installed.

On the particular afternoon from which Sylvia dated the preparation of the quarrel, they were all at tea with Mr. Dorward in his cottage. The conversation came round to Sirene, and Sylvia told how she had always thought that the vicar resembled a Roman Emperor. Was it Nero? He was perhaps flattered by the comparison, notwithstanding the ladies' loud exclamations of dissent, and was anxious to test the likeness from a volume of engraved heads which he produced. With Gladys sitting on one arm of his chair and Enid on the other, the pages were turned over slowly to allow time for a careful examination of each head, which involved a good deal of attention to Mr. Dorward's own. In the end Nero was ruled out and a more obscure Emperor was hailed as his prototype, after which the twins rushed out into the garden and gathered strands of ivy to encircle his imperial brow; Miss Horne and Miss Hobart, who had taken no part in the discussion, left immediately after the coronation, and though it was a perfectly fine evening, they announced, as they got into their vehicle, that it looked very much like rain.

Next Sunday the ladies came to church as usual, but Mr. Dorward kept them waiting half an hour for lunch while he showed the twins his ornaments and vestments, which they looked at solemnly as a penance for having spent most of the service with their handkerchiefs in their mouths. What Miss Horne and Miss Hobart said at lunch Sylvia never found out, but they drove away before Sunday-school and never came back to Green Lanes, either on that Sunday or on any Sunday afterward.

All that Mr. Dorward would say about the incident was:

"Church fowls! Chaste fowls! Chaste and holy, but tiresome. The vicar mustn't be managed. Doesn't like it. Gets frightened. Felt remote at lunch. That was all. Would keep on talking. Got bored and more remote. Vicar got so remote that he had to finish his lunch under the table."

"Oh no, you didn't really?" cried the twins, in an ecstasy of pleasure. "You didn't really get under the table, Mr. Dorward?"

"Of course, of course, of course. Vicar always speaks the truth. Delicious lunch."

Sylvia had to tell Philip about this absurd incident, but he would only say that the man was evidently a buffoon in private as well as in public.

"But, Philip, don't you think it's a glorious picture? We laughed till we were tired."

"Gladys and Enid laugh very easily," he answered. "Personally I see nothing funny in a man, especially a clergyman, behaving like a clown."

"Oh, Philip, you're impossible!" Sylvia cried.

"Thanks," he said, dryly. "I've noticed that ever since the arrival of our young guests you've found more to complain of in my personality even than formerly."

"Young guests!" Sylvia echoed, scornfully. "Who would think, to hear you talk now, that you married a child? Really you're incomprehensible."

"Impossible! Incomprehensible! In fact thoroughly negative," Philip said.

Sylvia shrugged her shoulders and left him.

The twins went back to school at the beginning of May, and Sylvia, who missed them very much, had to fall back on Mr. Dorward to remind her of their jolly company. Their intercourse, which the twins had established upon a certain plane, continued now upon the same plane. Life had to be regarded as Alice saw it in Wonderland or through the looking-glass. Sylvia remembered with irony that it was Philip who first introduced her to those two books; she decided he had only liked them because it was correct to like them. Mr. Dorward, however, actually was somebody in that fantastic world, not like anybody Alice met there, but another inhabitant whom she just happened to miss.

To whom else but Mr. Dorward could have occurred that ludicrous adventure when he was staying with a brother priest in a remote part of Devonshire?

"I always heard he was a little odd. However, we had dinner together in the kitchen. He only dined in the drawing-room on Thursdays."

"When did he dine in the dining-room?" Sylvia asked.

"Never. There wasn't a dining-room. There were a lot of rooms that were going to be the dining-room, but it was never decided which. And that cast a gloom over the whole house. My host behaved in the most evangelical way at dinner and only once threw the salad at the cook. After dinner we sat comfortably before the kitchen fire and discussed the Mozarabic rite and why yellow was no longer a liturgical color for confessors. At half past eleven my host suggested it was time to go to bed. He showed me up-stairs to a very nice bedroom and said good night, advising me to lock the door. I locked the door, undressed, said my prayers, and got into bed. I was just dozing off when I heard a loud tap at the door. I felt rather frightened. Rather frightened I felt. But I went to the door and opened it. Outside in the passage was my host in his nightgown with a candlestick.

"'Past twelve o'clock,' he shouted. 'Time to change beds!' and before I knew where I was he had rushed past me and shut me out into the passage."

"Did you change beds?"

"There wasn't another bed in the house. I had to sleep in one of the rooms that might one day be a dining-room, and the next morning a rural dean arrived, which drove me away."

Gradually from underneath what Philip called "a mass of affectation," but what Sylvia divined as an armor assumed against the unsympathetic majority by a shy, sensitive, and lovable spirit, there emerged for her the reality of Mr. Dorward. She began to comprehend his faith, which was as simple as a little child's; she began to realize also that he was impelled to guard what he held to be most holy against the jeers of unbelievers by diverting toward his own eccentricity the world's mockery. He was a man of the deepest humility who considered himself incapable of proselytizing. Sylvia used to put before him sometimes the point of view of the outside world and try to show how he could avoid criticism and gain adherents. He used always to reply that if God had intended him to be a missionary he would not have been placed in this lowly parish, that here he was unable to do much harm, and that any who found faith in his church must find it through the grace of God, since it was impossible to suppose they would ever find it through his own ministrations. He insisted that people who stayed away from church because he read the service badly or burned too many candles or wore vestments were only ostentatious worshipers who looked upon the church as wax-works must regard Madame Tussaud's. He explained that he had been driven to discourage the work of Miss Horne and Miss Hobart because he had detected in himself a tendency toward spiritual pride in the growth of a congregation that did not belong either to him or to God; if he had tolerated Miss Horne's methods for a time it was because he feared to oppose the Divine intention. However, as soon as he found that he was thinking complacently of a congregation of twenty-four, nearly every one of which was a pensioner of Miss Horne, he realized that they were instruments of the devil, particularly when at lunch they began to suggest....

"What?" Sylvia asked, when he paused.

"The only thing to do was to finish my lunch under the table," he snapped; nor would he be persuaded to discuss the quarrel further.

Sylvia, who felt that the poor ladies had, after all, been treated in rather a cavalier fashion and was reproaching herself for having deserted them, went down to Oaktown shortly after this to call at Sunny Bank. They received her with freezing coldness, particularly Miss Hobart, whose eyes under lowering eyelids were sullen with hate. She said much less than Miss Horne, who walked in and out of the shivery furniture, fanning herself in her agitation and declaiming against Mr. Dorward at the top of her voice.

"And your little friends?" Miss Hobart put in with a smile that was not a smile. "We thought them just a little badly brought up."

"You liked them very much at first," Sylvia said.

"Yes, one often likes people at first."

And as Sylvia looked at her she realized that Miss Hobart was not nearly so old as she had thought her, perhaps not yet fifty. Still, at fifty one had no right to be jealous.

"In fact," said Sylvia, brutally, "you liked them very much till you thought Mr. Dorward liked them too."

Miss Hobart's eyelids almost closed over her eyes and her thin lips disappeared. Miss Horne stopped in her restless parade and, pointing with her fan to the door, bade Sylvia be gone and never come to Sunny Bank again.

"The old witch," thought Sylvia, when she was toiling up the hill to Medworth in the midsummer heat. "I believe he's right and that she is the devil."

She did not tell Philip about her quarrel, because she knew that he would have reminded her one by one of every occasion he had taken to warn Sylvia against being friendly with any inhabitant of Tintown. A week or two later, Philip announced with an air of satisfaction that a van of Treacherites had arrived in Newton Candover and might be expected at Green Lanes next Sunday.

Sylvia asked what on earth Treacherites were, and he explained that they were the followers of a certain Mr. John Treacher, who regarded himself as chosen by God to purify the Church of England of popish abuses.

"A dreadful little cad, I believe," he added. "But it will be fun to see what they make of Dorward. It's a pity the old ladies have been kept away by the heat, or we might have a free fight."

Sylvia warned Mr. Dorward of the Treacherites' advent, and he seemed rather worried by the news; she had a notion he was afraid of them, which made her impatient, as she frankly told him.

"Not many of us. Not many of us," said Mr. Dorward. "Hope they won't try to break up the church."

The Treacherites arrived on Saturday evening and addressed a meeting by The Old Farm, which fetched Philip out into the road with threats of having them put in jail for creating a disturbance.

"If you want to annoy people, go to church to-morrow and annoy the vicar," he said, grimly.

Sylvia, who had heard Philip's last remark, turned on him in a rage: "What a mean and cowardly thing to say when you know Mr. Dorward can't defend himself as you can. Let them come to church to-morrow and annoy the vicar. You see what they'll get."

"Come, come, Sylvia," Philip said, with an attempt at pacification and evidently ashamed of himself. "Let these Christians fight it out among themselves. It's nothing to do with us, as long as they don't...."

"Thank you, it's everything to do with me," she said. He looked at her in surprise.

Next morning Sylvia took up her position in the front of the church and threatened with her eye the larger congregation that had gathered in the hope of a row as fiercely as Miss Horne and Miss Hobart might have done. The Treacherites were two young men with pimply faces who swaggered into church and talked to one another loudly before the service began, commenting upon the ornaments with cockney facetiousness. Cassandra Batt came over to Sylvia and whispered hoarsely in her ear that she was afraid there would be trouble, because some of the village lads had looked in for a bit of fun. The service was carried through with constant interruptions, and Sylvia felt her heart beating faster and faster with suppressed rage. When it was over, the congregation dispersed into the churchyard, where the yokels hung about waiting for the vicar to come out. As he appeared in the west door a loud booing was set up, and one of the Treacherites shouted:

"Follow me, loyal members of the Protestant Established Church, and destroy the idols of the Pope." Whereupon the iconoclast tried to push past Mr. Dorward, who was fumbling in his vague way with the lock of the door. He turned white with rage and, seizing the Treacherite by the scruff of his neck, he flung him head over heels across two mounds. At this the yokels began to boo more vehemently, but Mr. Dorward managed to shut the door and lock it, after which he walked across to the discomfited Treacherite and, holding out his hand, apologized for his violence. The yokels, who mistook generosity for weakness, began to throw stones at the vicar, one of which cut his face. Sylvia, who had been standing motionless in a trance of fury, was roused by the blood to action. With a bound she sprang at the first Treacherite and pushed him into a half-dug grave; then turning swiftly, she advanced against his companion with upraised stick.

The youth just had time to gasp a notification to the surrounding witnesses that Sylvia assaulted him first, before he ran; but the yokels, seeing that the squire's wife was on the side of the parson, and fearing for the renewal of their leases and the repairs to their cottages, turned round upon the Treacherites and dragged them off toward the village pond.

"Come on, Cassandra," Sylvia cried. "Let's go and break up the van."

Cassandra seized her pickax and followed Sylvia, who with hair streaming over her shoulders and elation in her aspect charged past The Old Farm just when Philip was coming out of the gate.

"Come on, Philip!" she cried. "Come on and help me break up their damned van."

By this time the attack had brought most of the village out of doors. Dogs were barking; geese and ducks were flapping in all directions; Sylvia kept turning round to urge the sexton, whose progress was hampered by a petticoat's slipping down, not to bother about her clothes, but to come on. A grandnephew of the old woman picked up the crimson garment and, as he pursued his grandaunt to restore it to her, waved it in the air like a standard. The yokels, who saw the squire watching from his gate, assumed his complete approval of what was passing (as a matter of fact he was petrified with dismay), and paid no attention to the vicar's efforts to rescue the Treacherites from their doom in the fast-nearing pond. The van of the iconoclasts was named Ridley: "By God's grace we have to-day lit such a candle as will never be put out" was printed on one side. On the other was inscribed, "John Treacher's Poor Preachers. Supported by Voluntary Contributions." By the time Sylvia, Cassandra, and the rest had finished with the van it was neither legible without nor habitable within.

Naturally there was a violent quarrel between Sylvia and Philip over her behavior, a quarrel that was not mended by her being summoned later on by the outraged Treacherites, together with Mr. Dorward and several yokels.

"You've made a fool of me from one end of the county to the other," Philip told her. "Understand once and for all that I don't intend to put up with this sort of thing."

"It was your fault," she replied. "You began it by egging on these brutes to attack Mr. Dorward. You could easily have averted any trouble if you'd wanted to. It serves you jolly well right."

"There's no excuse for your conduct," Philip insisted. "A stranger passing through the village would have thought a lunatic asylum had broken loose."

"Oh, well, it's a jolly good thing to break loose sometimes—even for lunatics," Sylvia retorted. "If you could break loose yourself sometimes you'd be much easier to live with."

"The next time you feel repressed," he said, "all I ask is that you'll choose a place where we're not quite so well known in which to give vent to your feelings."

The argument went on endlessly, for neither Sylvia nor Philip would yield an inch; it became, indeed, one of the eternal disputes that reassert themselves at the least excuse. If Philip's egg were not cooked long enough, the cause would finally be referred back to that Sunday morning; if Sylvia were late for lunch, her unpunctuality would ultimately be dated from the arrival of the Treacherites.

Luckily the vicar, with whom the events of that Sunday had grown into a comic myth that was continually being added to, was able to give Sylvia relief from Philip's exaggerated disapproval. Moreover, the Treacherites had done him a service by advertising his church and bringing a certain number of strangers there every Sunday out of curiosity; these pilgrims inflated the natives of Green Lanes with a sense of their own importance, and they now filled the church, taking pride and pleasure in the ownership of an attraction and boasting to the natives of the villages round about the size of the offertory. Mr. Dorward's popery and ritualism were admired now as commercial smartness, and if he had chosen to ride into church on Palm Sunday or any other Sunday on a donkey (a legendary ceremony invariably attributed to High Church vicars), there was not a man, woman, or child in the parish of Green Lanes that would not have given a prod of encouragement to the sacred animal.

One hot September afternoon Sylvia was walking back from Medworth when she was overtaken by Mr. Pluepott in his cart. They stopped to exchange the usual country greetings, at which by now Sylvia was an adept. When presently

Mr. Pluepott invited her to take advantage of a lift home she climbed up beside him. For a while they jogged along in silence; suddenly Mr. Pluepott delivered himself of what was evidently much upon his mind:

"Mrs. Iredale," he began, "you and me has known each other the best part of two years, and your coming and having a cup of tea with Mrs. Pluepott once or twice and Mrs. Pluepott having a big opinion of you makes me so bold."

He paused and reined in his pony to a walk that would suit the gravity of his communication.

"I'd like to give you a bit of a warning as from a friend and, with all due respect, an admirer. Being a married man myself and you a young lady, you won't go for to mistake my meaning when I says to you right out that women is worse than the devil. Miss Horne! As I jokingly said to Mrs. Pluepott, though, being a sacred subject, she wouldn't laugh, 'Miss Horne!' I said. 'Miss Horns! That's what she ought to be called.' Mrs. Iredale," he went on, pulling up the pony to a dead, stop and turning round with a very serious countenance to Sylvia—"Mrs. Iredale, you've got a wicked, bad enemy in that old woman."

"I know," she agreed. "We quarreled over something."

"If you quarreled, and whether it was your fault or whether it was hers, isn't nothing to do with me, but the lies she's spreading around about you and the Reverend Dorward beat the band. I'm not speaking gossip. I'm not going by hearsay. I've heard her myself, and Miss Hobart's as bad, if not worse. There, now I've told you and I hope you'll pardon the liberty, but I couldn't help it."

With which Mr. Pluepott whipped up his pony to a frantic gallop, and very soon they reached the outskirts of Green Lanes, where Sylvia got down.

"Thanks," she said, offering her hand. "I don't think I need bother about Miss Horne, but it was very kind of you to tell me. Thanks very much," and with a wave of her stick Sylvia walked pensively along into the village. As she passed Mr. Dorward's cottage she rattled her stick on his gate till he looked out from a window in the thatch, like a bird disturbed on its nest.

"Hullo, old owl!" Sylvia cried. "Come down a minute. I want to say something to you."

The vicar presently came blinking out into the sunlight of the garden.

"Look here," she said, "do you know that those two old villains in Oaktown are spreading it about that you and I are having a love-affair? Haven't you got a prescription for that sort of thing in your church business? Can't you curse them with bell, book, and candle, or something? I'll supply the bell, if you'll supply the rest of the paraphernalia."

Dorward shook his head. "Can't be done. Cursing is the prerogative of bishops. Not on the best terms with my bishop, I'm afraid. Last time he sent for me I had to spend the night and I left a rosary under my pillow. He was much pained, my spies at the Palace tell me."

"Well, if *you* don't mind, I don't mind," she said. "All right. So long."

Three days later, an anonymous post-card was sent to Sylvia, a vulgar Temptation of St. Anthony; and a week afterward Philip suddenly flung a letter down before her which he told her to read. It was an ill-spelled ungrammatical screed, which purported to warn Philip of his wife's behavior, enumerated the hours she had spent alone with Dorward either in his cottage or in the church, and wound up with the old proverb of there being none so blind as those who won't see. Sylvia blushed while she read it, not for what it said about herself, but for the vile impulse that launched this smudged and scrabbled impurity.

"That's a jolly thing to get at breakfast," Philip said.

"Beastly," she agreed. "And your showing it to me puts you on a level with the sender."

"I thought it would be a good lesson for you," he said.

"A lesson?" she repeated.

"Yes, a lesson that one can't behave exactly as one likes, particularly in the country among a lot of uneducated peasants."

"But I don't understand," Sylvia went on. "Did you show me this filthy piece of paper with the idea of asking me to change my manner of life?"

"I showed it to you in order to impress upon you that people talk, and that you owe it to me to keep their tongues quiet."

"What do you want me to do?"

"Something perfectly simple," Philip said. "I want you to give up visiting Dorward in his cottage and, as you have no religious inclinations, I should like you to avoid his church."

"And that's why you showed me this anonymous letter?"

He nodded.

"In fact you're going to give it your serious attention?" she continued.

"Not at all," he contradicted. "For a long time I've objected to your friendship with Dorward, but, knowing you were too headstrong to listen to my advice, I said nothing. This letter makes it impossible to keep silent any longer about my wishes."

"But you don't really believe that Dorward and I are having an affair?" she gasped.

Philip made an impatient gesture.

"What a foolish question! Do you suppose that if I had for one moment thought such a thing I shouldn't have spoken before? No, no, my dear, it's all very unpleasant, but you must see that as soon as I am made aware, however crude the method of bringing it to my knowledge, that people are talking about you and my vicar, I have no alternative but to forbid you to do anything that will make these tongues go on wagging."

"To forbid me?" she repeated.

Philip bowed ironically, Sylvia thought; the gesture, infinitely slight and unimportant as it was, cut the last knot.

"I shall have to tell Mr. Dorward about this letter and explain to him," she said.

Philip hesitated for a moment. "Yes, I think that would be the best thing to do," he agreed.

Sylvia regarded him curiously.

"You don't mind his knowing that you showed it to me?" she asked.

"Not at all," said Philip.

She laughed, and he took alarm at the tone.

"I thought you were going to be sensible," he began, but she cut him short.

"Oh, I am, my dear man. Don't worry."

Now that the unpleasant scene was over, he seemed anxious for her sympathy.

"I'm sorry this miserable business has occurred, but you understand, don't you, that it's been just as bad for me as for you?"

"Do you want me to apologize?" Sylvia demanded, in her brutal way.

"No, of course not. Only I thought perhaps you might have shown a little more appreciation of my feelings."

"Ah, Philip, if you want that, you'll have to let me really go wrong with Dorward."

"Personally I consider that last remark of yours in very bad taste; but I know we have different standards of humor."

Sylvia found Dorward in the church, engaged in an argument with Cassandra about the arrangement of the chrysanthemums for Michaelmas.

"I will not have them like this," he was saying.

"But we always putts them fan-shaped like that."

"Take them away," he shouted, and, since Cassandra still hesitated, he flung the flowers all over the church.

The short conversation that followed always remained associated in Sylvia's mind with Cassandra's grunts and her large base elevated above the pews, while she browsed hither and thither, bending over to pick up the scattered chrysanthemums.

"Mr. Dorward, I want to ask you something very serious."

He looked at her sharply, almost suspiciously.

"Does it make you very much happier to have faith?"

"Yes, yes, yes, yes, yes," he said, brushing petals from his cassock.

"But would it make me?"

"I expect so—I expect so," he said, still brushing and trying with that shy curtness to avoid the contact of reality.

"Well, how can I get faith?"

"You must pray, dear lady, you must pray."

"You'll have to pray for me," Sylvia said.

"Always do. Always pray for you. Never less than three prayers every day. Mass once a week."

Sylvia felt a lump in her throat; it seemed to her that this friend, accounted mad by the world, had paid her the tenderest and most exquisite courtesy she had ever known.

"Come along now, Cassandra," cried the vicar, clapping his hands impatiently to cover his embarrassment. "Where are the flowers? Where are the flowers, you miserable old woman?"

Cassandra came up to him, breathing heavily with exertion. "You know, Mr. Dorward, you're enough to try the patience of an angel on a tomb; you are indeed."

Sylvia left them arguing all over again about the chrysanthemums. That afternoon she went away from Green Lanes to London.

Three months later, she obtained an engagement in a musical comedy company on tour and sent back to Philip the last shred of clothing that she had had through him, with a letter and ten pounds in bank-notes:

You *must* divorce me now. I've not been able to earn enough to pay you back more than this for your bad bargain. I don't think I've given any more pleasure to the men who have paid less for me than you did, if that's any consolation.

SYLVIA SCARLETT.

CHAPTER VIII

SYLVIA stood before the looking-glass in the Birmingham lodgings and made a speech to herself:

"Humph! You look older, my dear. You look more than nineteen and a half. You're rather glad, though, aren't you, to have finished with the last three months? You feel degraded, don't you? What's that you say? You don't feel degraded any more by what you've done now than by what you did when you were married? You consider the net result of the last three months has simply been to prove what you'd suspected for a long time—the wrong you did yourself in marrying Philip Iredale? Wait a minute; don't go so fast; there's something wrong with your moral sense. You know perfectly well your contention is impossible; or do you accuse every woman who marries to have a position and a home of being a prostitute? Ah, but you didn't marry Philip for either of those reasons, you say? Yes, you did—you married him to make something like Arbour End."

Tears welled up in Sylvia's eyes. She thought she had driven Arbour End from her mind forever.

"Come, come, we don't want any tears. What are you crying for? You knew when you left Green Lanes that everything which had come into your life through Philip Iredale must be given up. You were rather proud of your ruthlessness. Don't spoil it now. That's right, no more tears. You're feeling a bit *abrutie*, aren't you? My advice to you is to obliterate the last three months from your imagination. I quite understand that you suffered a good deal, but novices must be prepared to suffer. In my opinion you can congratulate yourself on having come through so easily. Here you are, a jolly little *cabotine* with a complete contempt for men. You're not yet twenty; you're not likely to fall in love, for you must admit that after those three months the word sounds more than usually idiotic. From what I've seen of you I should say that for the future you'll be very well able to look after yourself; you might even become a famous actress. Ah, that makes you smile, eh?"

Sylvia dabbed her face with the powder-puff and went down-stairs to dinner. Her two companions had not yet begun; for this was the first meal at which they would all sit down together, and an atmosphere of politeness hung over life at present. Lily Haden and Dorothy Lonsdale had joined the "Miss Elsie of Chelsea" company at the same time as Sylvia, and were making their first appearance on any stage, having known each other in the dullness of West Kensington. For a fortnight they had clung together, but, having been given an address for rooms in Birmingham that required a third person's contribution, they had invited Sylvia to join them. Lily was a tall, slim girl with very fair, golden hair, who had an air of romantic mystery that was due to indolence of mind and body. Dorothy also was fair, with a mass of light-brown hair, a perfect complexion, profile, and figure, and, what finally gave her a really distinguished beauty in such a setting, brown eyes instead of blue. Lily's languorous grace of manner and body was so remarkable that in a room it was difficult to choose between her and Dorothy, but behind the footlights there was no comparison; there Dorothy had everybody's glances, and Lily's less definite features went for nothing.

Each girl was prompt to take Sylvia into her confidence about the other. Thus from Lily she learned that Dorothy's real name was Norah Caffyn; that she was the eldest of a very large family; that Lily had known her at school; that she had been engaged to a journalist who was disapproved of by her family; that she had offered to break with Wilfred Curlew, if she were allowed to go on the stage; and that she had taken the name of Lonsdale from the road where she lived, and Dorothy from the sister next to her.

"I suppose in the same way as she used to take her dolls?" Sylvia suggested.

Lily looked embarrassed. She was evidently not sure whether a joke was intended, and when Sylvia encouraged her to suppose it was, she laughed a little timidly, being rather doubtful if it were not a pun.

"Her sister was awfully annoyed about it, because she hasn't got a second name. She's the only one in the family who hasn't."

Lily also told Sylvia something about herself, how her mother had lately died and how she could not get on with her sister, who had married an actor and was called Doris. Her mother had been a reciter, and there had always been lots of theatrical people at their house, so it had been easy for her to get an introduction to Mr. Walter Keal, who had the touring rights of all John Richards's great Vanity Theater productions.

From Dorothy Sylvia learned that she had known Lily at school, but not for long, as Mrs. Haden never paid her daughters' fees; that Mr. Haden had always been supposed to live in Burmah, but that people who knew Mrs. Haden declared he had never existed; and finally that Lily had been "awfully nice" to herself and helped her to get an introduction to Mr. Walter Keal.

The association of Sylvia with the two girls begun at Birmingham was not interrupted until the end of the tour. Lily and Dorothy depended upon it, Lily because Sylvia saved her the trouble of thinking for herself, Dorothy because she found in Sylvia some one who could deflect all the difficulties of life on tour and leave her free to occupy herself with her own prosperity and her own comforts. Dorothy possessed a selfishness that almost attained to the dignity of ambition, though never quite, as her conceit would not allow her to state an object in her career, for fear of failure; her method was invariably to seize the best of any situation that came along, whether it was a bed, a chair, a potato, or a man; this method with ordinary good luck would insure success through life. Lily was too lazy to minister to Dorothy's selfishness; moreover, she often managed in taking the nearest and easiest to rob Dorothy of the best.

Sylvia was perfectly aware of their respective characters, but she was always willing to give herself any amount of trouble to preserve beauty around her; Lily and Dorothy were not really more troublesome than two cats would have been; in fact, rather less, because at any rate they could carry themselves, if not their bags.

Life on tour went its course with the world divided into three categories—the members of the company, the public expressing its personality in different audiences, and for the actors saloon-bars and the drinks they were stood, for the actresses admirers and the presents they were worth. Sometimes when the saloon-bars and the admirers were alike unprofitable, the members of the company mixed among themselves whether in a walk round a new town or at tea in rooms where a landlady possessed hospitable virtues. Sylvia had a special gift for getting the best out of landladies, and the men of the company came more often to tea with herself and her friends than with the other ladies. They came, indeed, too often to please Dorothy, who disapproved of Lily's easy-going acceptance of the sort of love that is made because at the moment there is nothing else to do. She spoke to Sylvia about this, who agreed with her, but thought that with Lily it was inevitable.

"But not with boys in the company," Dorothy urged, disdainfully. "It makes us all so cheap. I don't want to put on side, but, after all, we are a little different from the other girls."

Sylvia found this belief universal in the chorus. She could not think of any girl who had not at one time or another taken her aside and claimed for herself, and by the politeness owed to present company for Sylvia, this "little difference."

"Personally," Sylvia said, "I think we're all much the same. Some of us drop our aitches, others our p's and q's; some of us sing flat, the rest sing sharp; and we all look just alike when we're waiting for the train on Sunday morning."

Nevertheless, with all her prevision of a fate upon Lily's conduct, Sylvia did speak to her about the way in which she tolerated the familiarity of the men in the company.

"I suppose you're thinking of Tom," Lily said.

"Tom, Dick, and Harry," Sylvia put in.

"Well. I don't like to seem stuck up," Lily explained. "Tom's always very nice about carrying my bag and getting me tea when we're traveling."

"If I promise to look after the bag," Sylvia asked, "will you promise to discourage Tom?"

"But, my dear, why should you carry my bag when I can get Tom to do it?"

"It bores me to see you and him together," Sylvia explained. "These boys in the company are all very well, but they aren't really men at all."

"I know," Lily said, eagerly. "That's what I feel. They don't seem real to me. Of course, I shouldn't let anybody make love to me seriously."

"What do you call serious love-making?"

"Oh, Sylvia, how you do go on asking questions. You know perfectly well what I mean. You only ask questions to make me feel uncomfortable."

"Just as I might disarrange the cushions of your chair?"

"I know quite well who's been at you to worry me," Lily went on. "I know it's Dorothy. She's always been used to being the eldest and finding fault with everybody else. She doesn't really mind Tom's kissing me—she's perfectly ready to make use of him herself—but she's always thinking about other people and she's so afraid that some of the men she goes out with will laugh at his waistcoat. I'm used to actors; she isn't. I never bother about her. I don't complain about her practising her singing or talking for hours and hours about whether I think she looks better with a teardrop or without. Why can't she let me alone? Nobody ever lets me alone. It's all I've ever asked all my life."

The feeling between Lily and Dorothy was reaching the point of tension. Sylvia commented on it one evening to Fay Onslow, the oldest member of the chorus, a fat woman, wise and genial, universally known as Onzie except by her best boy of the moment, who had to call her Fay. However, she cost him very little else, and was generally considered to throw herself away, though, of course, as her friends never failed to add, she was getting on and could no longer afford to be too particular.

"Well, between you and I, Sylvia, I've often wondered you've kept your little family together for so long. I've been on the stage now for twenty-five years. I'm not far off forty, dear. I used to be in burlesque at the old Frivolity."

"Do you remember Victoria Deane?" Sylvia asked.

"Of course I do. She made a big hit and then got married and left the stage. A sweetly pretty little thing, she was. But, as I was saying, dear, in all my experience I never knew two fair girls get through a tour together without falling out, two girls naturally fair, that is, and you mark my words, Lily Haden and Dolly Lonsdale will have a row."

Sylvia was anxious to avert this, because she would have found it hard to choose between their rival claims upon her. She was fonder of Lily, but she was very fond of Dorothy, and she believed that Dorothy might attain real success in her profession. It seemed more worth while to take trouble over Dorothy; yet something warned her that an expense of devotion in that direction would ultimately be, from a selfish point of view, wasted. Dorothy would never consider affection where advancement was concerned; yet was it not just this quality in her that she admired? There would certainly be an unusual exhilaration in standing behind Dorothy and helping her to rise and rise, whereas with Lily the best that could be expected was to prevent her falling infinitely low.

"How I've changed since I left Philip," she said to herself. "I seem to have lost myself somehow and to have transferred all my interest in life to other people. I suppose it won't last. God forbid I should become a problem to myself like a woman in a damned novel. Down with introspection, though, Heaven knows, observation in 'Miss Elsie of Chelsea' is not a profitable pastime."

Sylvia bought an eye-glass next day, and though all agreed with one another in private that it was an affectation, everybody assured her that she was a girl who could wear an eye-glass with advantage. Lily thought the cord must be rather a bore.

"It's symbolic," Sylvia declared to the dressing-room.

"I think I'll have my eyes looked at in Sheffield," said Onzie. "There's a doctor there who's very good to pros. I often feel my eyes are getting a bit funny. It may be the same as Sylvia's got."

The tour was coming to an end; the last three nights would be played at Oxford, to which everybody looked forward. All the girls who had been to Oxford before told wonderful tales of the pleasures that might be anticipated. Even some of the men were heard to speculate if such or such a friend were still there, which annoyed those who could not even boast of having had a friend there two years ago. The jealous ones revenged themselves by criticizing the theatrical manners of the undergraduate, especially upon the last night of a musical comedy. One heard a great deal of talk, they said, about a college career, but personally and without offense to anybody present who had friends at college, they considered that a college career in nine cases out of ten meant rowdiness and a habit of thinking oneself better than other people.

Sylvia, Lily, and Dorothy had rooms in Eden Square, which was the recognized domain of theatrical companies playing in Oxford. Numerous invitations to lunch and tea were received, and Sylvia, who had formed a preconceived idea of Oxford based upon Philip, was astonished how little the undergraduates she met resembled him. Dorothy managed with her usual instinct for the best to secure as an admirer Lord Clarehaven, or, as the other girls preferred to call him with a nicer formality, the Earl of Clarehaven. He invited her with a friend to lunch at Christ Church on the last day. Dorothy naturally chose Sylvia, and, as Lily was already engaged elsewhere, Sylvia accepted. Later in the afternoon Dorothy proposed that the young men should come back and have tea in Eden Square, and Sylvia divined

Dorothy's intention of proving to these young men that the actress in her own home would be as capable of maintaining propriety as she had been at lunch.

"We'll buy the cakes on the way," said Dorothy, which was another example of her infallible instinct for the best and the most economical.

Loaded with éclairs, meringues, and chocolates, Dorothy, Sylvia, and their four guests reached Eden Square.

"You'll have to excuse the general untidiness," Dorothy said, with an affected little laugh, flinging open the door of the sitting-room. She would probably have chosen another word for the picture of Lily sitting on Tom's knee in the worn leather-backed arm-chair if she had entered first: unfortunately, Lord Clarehaven was accorded that privilege, and the damage was done. Sylvia quickly introduced everybody, and nobody could have complained of the way in which the undergraduates sailed over an awkward situation, nor could much have been urged against Tom, for he left immediately. As for Lily, she was a great success with the young men and seemed quite undisturbed by the turn of events.

As soon as the three girls were alone together, Dorothy broke out:

"I hope you don't think I'll ever live with you again after that disgusting exhibition. I suppose you think just because you gave me an introduction that you can do what you like. I don't know what Sylvia thinks of you, but I can tell you what I think. You make me feel absolutely sick. That beastly chorus-boy! The idea of letting anybody like that even look at you. Thank Heaven, the tour's over. I'm going down to the theater. I can't stay in this room. It makes me blush to think of it. I'll take jolly good care who I live with in future."

Then suddenly, to Sylvia's immense astonishment, Dorothy slapped Lily's face. What torments of mortification must be raging in that small soul to provoke such an unlady-like outburst!

"I should hit her back if I were you, my lass," Sylvia advised, putting up her eye-glass for the fray; but Lily began to cry and Dorothy flounced out of the room.

Sylvia bent over her in consolation, though her sense of justice made her partly excuse Dorothy's rage.

"How did I know she would bring her beastly men back to tea? She only did it to brag about having a lord to our digs. After all, they're just as much mine as hers. I was sorry for Tom. He doesn't know anybody in Oxford, and he felt out of it with all the other boys going out. He asked me if I was going to turn him down because I'd got such fine friends. I was sorry for him, Sylvia, and so I asked him to tea. I don't see why Dorothy should turn round and say nasty things to me. I've always been decent to her. Oh, Sylvia, you don't know how lonely I feel sometimes."

This appeal was too much for Sylvia, who clasped Lily to her and let her sob forth her griefs upon her shoulder.

"Sylvia, I've got nobody. I hate my sister Doris. Mother's dead. Everybody ran her down, but she had a terrible life. Father used to take drugs, and then he stole and was put in prison. People used to say mother wasn't married, but she was. Only the truth was so terrible, she could never explain. You don't know how she worked. She brought up Doris and me entirely. She used to recite, and she used to be always hard up. She died of heart failure, and that comes from worry. Nobody understands me. I don't know what will become of me."

"My dear," Sylvia said, "you know I'm your pal."

"Oh, Sylvia, you're a darling! I'd do anything for you."

"Even carry your own bag at the station to-morrow?"

"No, don't tease me," Lily begged. "If you won't tease me, I'll do anything."

That evening Mr. Keal, with the mighty Mr. Richards himself, came up from London to see the show. The members of the chorus were much agitated. It could only mean that girls were to be chosen for the Vanity production in the autumn. Every one of them put on rather more make-up than usual, acted hard all the time she was on the stage, and tried to study Mr. Richards's face from the wings.

"You and I are one of the 'also rans,'" Sylvia told Lily. "The great man eyed me with positive dislike."

In the end it was Dorothy Lonsdale who was engaged for the Vanity: she was so much elated that she was reconciled with Lily and told everybody in the dressing-room that she had met a cousin at Oxford, Arthur Lonsdale, Lord Cleveden's son.

"Which side of the road are you related to him?" Sylvia asked. Dorothy blushed, but she pretended not to understand what Sylvia meant, and said quite calmly that it was on her mother's side. She parted with Sylvia and Lily very cordially at Paddington, but she did not invite either of them to come and see her at Lonsdale Road.

Sylvia and Lily stayed together at Mrs. Gowndry's in Finborough Road, for it happened that the final negotiations for Sylvia's divorce from Philip were being concluded and she took pleasure in addressing her communications from the house where she had been living when he first met her. Philip was very anxious to make her an allowance, but she declined it; her case was undefended. Lily and she managed to get an engagement in another touring company, which opened in August somewhere on the south coast. About this time Sylvia read in a paper that Jimmy Monkley had been sentenced to three years' penal servitude for fraud, and by an odd coincidence in the same paper she read of the decree nisi made absolute that set Philip and herself free. Old associations seemed to be getting wound up. Unfortunately, the new ones were not promising; no duller collection of people had surely ever been gathered together than the company in which she was working at present. Not only was the company tiresome, but Sylvia and Lily failed to meet anywhere on the tour one amusing person. To be sure, Lily thought that Sylvia was too critical, and therefore so alarming that several "nice boys" were discouraged too early in their acquaintanceship for a final judgment to be passed upon them.

"The trouble is," said Sylvia, "that at this rate we shall never make our fortunes. I stipulate that, if we adopt a gay life, it really will be a gay life. I don't want to have soul-spasms and internal wrestles merely for the sake of being bored."

Sylvia tried to produce Lily as a dancer; for a week or two they worked hard at imitations of the classical school, but very soon they both grew tired of it.

"The nearest we shall ever get to jingling our money at this game," Sylvia said, "is jingling our landlady's ornaments on the mantelpiece. Lily, I think we're not meant for the stage. And yet, if I could only find my line, I believe.... I believe.... Oh, well, I can't, and so there's an end of it. But look here, winter's coming on. We've got nothing to wear. We haven't saved a penny. Ruin stares us in the face. Say something, Lily; do say something, or I shall scream."

"I don't think we ought to have eaten those plums at dinner. They weren't really ripe," Lily said.

"Well, anyhow, that solves the problem of the moment. Put your things on. You'd better come out and walk them off."

They were playing in Eastbourne that week, where a sudden hot spell had prolonged the season farther into September than usual; a new company of entertainers known as "The Highwaymen" was attracting audiences almost as large as in the prime of summer. Sylvia and Lily paused to watch them from the tamarisks below the Marina.

Suddenly Sylvia gave an exclamation.

"I do believe that's Claude Raglan who's singing now. Do you remember, Lily, I told you about the Pink Pierrots? I'm sure it is."

Presently the singer came round with the bag and a packet of his picture post-cards. Sylvia asked if he had a photograph of Claude Raglan. When he produced one she dug him in the ribs, and cried:

"Claudie, you consumptive ass, don't you recognize me? Sylvia."

He was delighted to see her again, and willingly accepted an invitation to supper after the show, if he might bring a friend with him.

"Jack Airdale—an awfully decent fellow. Quite a good voice, too, though I think from the point of view of the show it's a mistake to have a high barytone when they've already got a tenor. However, he does a good deal of accompanying. In fact, he's a much better accompanist than he is singer."

"I suppose you've got more girls than ever in love with you, now you wear a mask?" said Sylvia.

Claude seemed doubtful whether to take this remark as a compliment to his voice or as an insult to his face. Finally he took it as a joke and laughed.

"Just the same, I see," he said. "Always chaffing a fellow."

Claude Raglan and Jack Airdale came to supper in due course. Sylvia liked Jack; he was a round-faced young man in the early twenties, with longish light hair that flopped all over his face when he became excited. Sylvia and he were good friends immediately and made a great deal of noise over supper, while Claude and Lily looked at each other.

"How's the consumption, Claudie?" Sylvia asked.

Claude sighed with a soulful glance at Lily's delicate form.

"Don't imagine she's sympathizing with you," Sylvia cried. "She's only thinking about plums."

"He's grown out of it," Airdale said. "Look at the length of his neck."

"I have to wear these high collars. My throat...." Claude began.

"Oh, shut up with your ailments," Sylvia interrupted.

"Hear, hear," Airdale shouted. "Down with ailments," and he threw a cushion at Claude.

"I wish you wouldn't behave like a clown," said Claude, smoothing his ruffled hair and looking to see if Lily was joining in the laugh against him.

Presently the conversation turned upon the prospects of the two girls for next winter, about which Sylvia was very pessimistic.

"Why don't we join together and run a street show—Pierrot, Pierrette, Harlequin, and Columbine?" Airdale suggested. "I'll swear there's money in it."

"About enough to pay for our coffins," said Claude. "Sing out of doors in the winter? My dear Jack, you're mad."

Sylvia thought the idea was splendid, and had sketched out Lily's Columbine dress before Lily herself had realized that the conversation had taken a twist.

"Light-blue crêpe de Chine with bunches of cornflowers for Columbine. Pierrette in dark blue with bunches of forget-me-nots, Pierrot in light blue. Silver and dark-blue lozenges for Harlequin."

"Paregoric lozenges would suit Claude better," said Airdale. "O Pagliacci! Can't you hear him? No, joking apart, I think it would be a great effort. We sha'n't have to sing much outside. We shall get invited into people's houses."

"Shall we?" Claude muttered.

"And if the show goes," Airdale went on, "we might vary our costumes. For instance, we might be Bacchanals in pink fleshings and vine leaves."

"Vine leaves," Claude ejaculated. "Vine Street more likely."

"Don't laugh, old boy, with that lung of yours," said Airdale, earnestly.

In the end, before the company left Eastbourne, it was decided, notwithstanding Claude's lugubrious prophecies, to launch the enterprise; when the tour broke up in December Sylvia had made dresses both for Lily and for herself as she had first planned them with an eye only for what became Lily. Claude's hypochondria was appeased by letting him wear a big patchwork cloak over his harlequin's dress in which white lozenges had been substituted for silver ones, owing to lack of money. They hired a small piano very much like the one that belonged to the Pink Pierrots, and on Christmas Eve they set out from Finborough Road, where Claude and Jack had rooms near Mrs. Gowndry's. They came into collision with a party of carol-singers who seemed to resent their profane competition, and, much to Jack

Airdale's disappointment, they were not invited into a single house; the money taken after three hours of wandering music was one shilling and fivepence in coppers.

"Never mind," said Jack. "We aren't known yet. It's a pity we didn't start singing last Christmas Eve. We should have had more engagements than we should have known what to do with this year."

"We must build up the show for next year," Sylvia agreed, enthusiastically.

"I shall sing the 'Lost Chord' next year," Claude answered. "They may let me in, if I worry them outside heaven's gates, to hear that last Amen."

Jack and Sylvia were justified in their optimism, for gradually the Carnival Quartet, as they called themselves, became known in South Kensington, and they began to get engagements to appear in other parts of London. Jack taught Sylvia to vamp well enough on the guitar to accompany herself in duets with him; Claude looked handsome in his harlequin's dress, which prosperity had at last endowed with silver lozenges; Lily danced actively enough for the drawing-rooms in which they performed; Sylvia, inspired by the romantic exterior of herself and her companions, invented a mime to the music of Schumann's "Carnival" which Jack Airdale played, or, as Claude said, maltreated.

The Quartet showed signs of increasing vitality with the approach of spring, and there was no need to think any more of touring in musical comedy, which was a relief to Sylvia. When summer came, they agreed to keep together and work the South Coast.

However, all these plans came suddenly to nothing, because one misty night early in March Harlequin and Columbine lost Pierrot and Pierrette on the way home from a party in Chelsea; a brief note from Harlequin to Pierrot, which he found when he got home, indicated that the loss should be considered permanent.

This treachery was a shock to Sylvia, and she was horrified at herself for feeling it so deeply. Ever since that day in Oxford when Lily had sobbed out her griefs, Sylvia had concentrated upon her all the capacity for affection which had begun to blossom during the time she was with Philip and which had been cut off ruthlessly with everything else that belonged to life with him. She knew that she should have foreseen the possibility, nay the probability, of this happening, but she had charmed herself with the romantic setting of their musical adventure and let all else go.

"I'm awfully sorry, Sylvia," said Jack; "I ought to have kept a better lookout on Claude."

"It's not your fault, old son. But, O God! why can't four people stay friends without muddling everything up with this accursed love?"

Jack was sympathetic, but it was useless to confide in him her feeling for Lily; he would never understand. She would seem to him so little worth while; for him the behavior of such a one meant less than the breaking of a porcelain figure.

"It did seem worth while," Sylvia said to herself, that night, "to keep that frail and lovely thing from this. It was my fault, of course, for I knew both Lily and Claude through and through. Yet what does it matter? What a fool I am. It was absurd of me to imagine we could go on forever as we were. I don't really mind about Lily; I'm angry because my conceit has been wounded. It serves me right. But that dirty little actor won't appreciate her. He's probably sick of her easiness already. Oh, why the hell am I not a man?"

Presently, however, Sylvia's mood of indignation burned itself out; she began to attribute the elopement of Claude and Lily to the characters they had assumed of Harlequin and Columbine, and to regard the whole affair as a scene from a play which must not be taken more deeply to heart than with the pensive melancholy that succeeds the fall of the curtain on mimic emotions. After all, what had Lily been to her more than a puppet whose actions she had always controlled for her pleasure until she was stolen from her? Without Lily she was once more at a loose end; there was the whole history of her sorrow.

"I can't think what they wanted to run away for," said Jack. Sylvia fancied the flight was the compliment both Harlequin and Columbine had paid to her authority.

"I don't find you so alarming," he said.

"No, old son, because you and I have always regarded the Quartet from a strictly professional point of view, and consequently each other. Meanwhile the poor old Quartet is done in. We two can't sustain a program alone."

Airdale gloomily assented, but thought it would be well to continue for a week or so, in case Claude and Lily came back.

"I notice you take it for granted that I'll be willing to continue busking with them," Sylvia said.

That evening Airdale and she went out as usual; but the loss of the other two seemed somehow to have robbed the entertainment of its romantic distinction, and Sylvia was dismayed to find with what a shameful timidity she now took herself and her guitar into saloon-bars; she felt like a beggar and was humiliated by Jack's apologetic manner, and still more by her own instinctive support of such cringing to the benevolence of potmen and barmaids.

One evening, after about a week of these distasteful peregrinations, the two mountebanks came out of a public house in Fulham Road where they had been forced to endure a more than usually intolerable patronage. Sylvia vowed she would not perform again under such conditions, and they turned up Tinderbox Lane to wander home. This thoroughfare, only used by pedestrians, was very still, and trees planted down the middle of the pavement gave to the mild March evening an effluence of spring. Sylvia began to strum upon her guitar the tune that Arthur Madden and she sang together from the windows at Hampstead on the night she met him first; her companion soon caught hold of the air, and they strolled slowly along, dreaming, she looking downward of the past, he of the future with his eyes fixed on the chimneys of the high flats that encircled the little houses and long gardens of Tinderbox Lane. They were passing a wall on their right in which numbered doors were set at intervals. From one of these a tall figure emerged and stopped a moment to say good-by to somebody standing in the entrance. The two musicians with a simultaneous instinct for an audience that might appreciate them stopped and addressed their song to the parting pair, a tall old gentleman with drooping gray whiskers, very much muffled up, and an exceedingly stout woman of ripe middle age.

"Bravo!" said the old gentleman, in a tremulous voice, as he tapped his cane on the pavement. "Polly, this is devilish appropriate. By gad! it makes me feel inclined to dance again, Polly," and the old gentleman forthwith postured with his thin legs like a cardboard antic at the end of a string. The fat woman standing in the doorway came out into the lamplight, and clasping her hands in alarm, begged him not to take cold, but the old gentleman would not stop until Polly had made a pretense of dancing a few steps with him, after which he again piped, "Bravo," vowed he must have a whisky, and invited Sylvia and Jack to come inside and join them.

"Dashwood is my name, Major-General Dashwood, and this is Mrs. Gainsborough."

"Come along," said Mrs. Gainsborough. "The captain—"

"She will call me Captain," said the general, with a chuckle. "Obstinate gal! Knew me first when I was a captain, thirty-six years ago, and has never called me anything since. What a woman, though!"

"He's very gay to-night. We've been celebrating our anniversary," Mrs. Gainsborough explained, while the four of them walked along a gravel path toward a small square creeper-covered house at the end of a very long garden.

"We met first at the Argyll Rooms in March, 1867, and in September, 1869, Mulberry Cottage was finished. I planted those mulberry-trees myself, and they'll outlive us both," said the general.

"Now don't let's have any more dismals," Mrs. Gainsborough begged. "We've had quite enough to-night, talking over old times."

Mulberry Cottage was very comfortable inside, full of mid-Victorian furniture and ornaments that suited its owner, who, Sylvia now perceived by the orange lamplight, was even fatter than she had seemed at first. Her hair, worn in a chignon, was black, her face was rosy and large, almost monumental, with a plinth of chins.

The general so much enjoyed having a fresh audience for his tales, and sat so long over the whisky, that Mrs. Gainsborough became worried.

"Bob, you ought to go. You know I don't like to argue before strangers, but your sister will be getting anxious. Miss Dashwood's quite alone," she explained to her guests. "I wonder if you'd mind walking back with him?" she whispered to Sylvia. "He lives in Redcliffe Gardens. That's close to you, isn't it?"

"If we can have music all the way, by gad! of course," said the general, standing up so straight that Sylvia was afraid he would bump his head on the ceiling.

"Now, Bob dear, don't get too excited and do keep your muffler well wrapped round your throat."

The general insisted on having one more glass for the sake of old times, and there was a short delay in the garden, because he stuck his cane fast in the ground to show the size of the mulberry-trees when he planted them, but ultimately they said good night to Mrs. Gainsborough, upon whom Sylvia promised to call next day, and set out for Redcliffe Gardens to the sound of guitars.

General Dashwood turned round from time to time to shake his cane at passers-by that presumed to stare at the unusual sight of an old gentleman, respectable in his dress and demeanor, escorted down Fulham Road by two musicians.

"Do you see anything so damned odd in our appearance?" he asked Sylvia.

"Nothing at all," she assured him.

"Sensible gal! I've a very good mind to knock down the next scoundrel who stares at us."

Presently the general, on whom the fresh air was having an effect, took Sylvia's arm and grew confidential.

"Go on playing," he commanded Jack Airdale. "I'm only talking business. The fact is," he said to Sylvia, "I'm worried about Polly. Hope I shall live another twenty years, but fact is, my dear, I've never really got over that wound of mine at Balaclava. Damme! I've never been the same man since."

Sylvia wondered what he could have been before.

"Naturally she's well provided for. Bob Dashwood always knew how to treat a woman. No wife, no children, you understand me? But it's the loneliness. She ought to have somebody with her. She's a wonderful woman, and she was a handsome gal. Damme! she's still handsome—what? Fifty-five you know. By gad, yes. And I'm seventy. But it's the loneliness. Ah, dear, if the gods had been kind; but then she'd have probably been married by now."

The general blew his nose, sighed, and shook his head. Sylvia asked tenderly how long the daughter had lived.

"Never lived at all," said the general, stopping dead and opening his eyes very wide, as he looked at Sylvia. "Never was born. Never was going to be born. Hale and hearty, but too late now, damme! I've taken a fancy to you. Sensible gal! Damned sensible. Why don't you go and live with Polly?"

In order to give Sylvia time to reflect upon her answer, the general skipped along for a moment to the tune that Jack was playing.

"Nothing between you and him?" he asked, presently, indicating Jack with his cane.

Sylvia shook her head.

"Thought not. Very well, then, why don't you go and live with Polly? Give you time to look round a bit. Understand what you feel about playing for your bread and butter like this. Finest thing in the world music, if you haven't got to do it. Go and see Polly to-morrow. I spoke to her about it to-night. She'll be delighted. So shall I. Here we are in Redcliffe Gardens. Damned big house and only myself and my sister to live in it. Live there like two needles in a haystack. Won't ask you in. Damned inhospitable, but no good because I shall have to go to bed at once. Perhaps you wouldn't mind pressing the bell? Left my latch-key in me sister's work-basket."

The door opened, and the general, after bidding Sylvia and Jack a courteous good night, marched up his front-door steps with as much martial rigidity as he could command.

On the way back to Finborough Road, Sylvia, who had been attracted to the general's suggestion, postponed raising the question with Jack by telling him about her adventure in Redcliffe Gardens when she threw the bag of chestnuts through the window. She did not think it fair, however, to make any other arrangement without letting him know, and before she went to see Mrs. Gainsborough the next day she announced her idea and asked him if he would be much hurt by her backing out of the busking.

"My dear girl, of course not," said Jack. "As a matter of fact, I've had rather a decent offer to tour in a show through the East. I should rather like to see India and all that. I didn't say anything about it, because I didn't want to let you down. However, if you're all right, I'm all right."

Mrs. Gainsborough by daylight appealed to Sylvia as much as ever. She told her what the general had said, and Mrs. Gainsborough begged her to come that very afternoon.

"The only thing is," Sylvia objected, "I've got a friend, a girl, who's away at present, and she might want to go on living with me."

"Let her come too," Mrs. Gainsborough cried. "The more the merrier. Good Land! What a set-out we shall have. The captain won't know himself. He's very fond of me, you know. But it would be more jolly for him to have some youngsters about. He's that young. Upon my word, you'd think he was a boy. And he's always the same. Oh, dearie me! the times we've had, you'd hardly believe. Life with him was a regular circus."

So it was arranged that Sylvia should come at once to live with Mrs. Gainsborough in Tinderbox Lane, and Jack went off to the East.

The general used to visit them nearly every afternoon, but never in the evening.

"Depend upon it, Sylvia," Mrs. Gainsborough said, "he got into rare hot water with his sister the other night. Of course it was an exception, being our anniversary, and I dare say next March, if we're all spared, he'll be allowed another evening. It's a great pity, though, that we didn't meet first in June. So much more seasonable for jollifications. But there, he was young and never looked forward to being old."

The general was not spared for another anniversary. Scarcely a month after Sylvia had gone to live with Mrs. Gainsborough, he died very quietly in the night. His sister came herself to break the news, a frail old lady who seemed very near to joining her brother upon the longest journey.

"She'll never be able to keep away from him," Mrs. Gainsborough sobbed. "She'll worry and fret herself for fear he might catch cold in his coffin. And look at me! As healthy and rosy as a great radish!"

The etiquette of the funeral caused Mrs. Gainsborough considerable perplexity.

"Now tell me, Sylvia, ought I or ought I not to wear a widow's veil? Miss Dashwood inviting me in that friendly way, I do want to show that I appreciate her kindness. I know that strictly we weren't married. I dare say nowadays it would be different, but people was much more old-fashioned about marrying ballet-girls when I was young. Still, it doesn't seem hardly decent for me to go gallivanting to his funeral in me black watered silk, the same as if I were going to the upper boxes of a theater with Mrs. Marsham or Mrs. Beardmore."

Sylvia told Mrs. Gainsborough that in her opinion a widow's cap at the general's funeral would be like the dash of mauve at the wedding in the story. She suggested the proper thing to do would be to buy a new black dress unprofaned by visits to the upper boxes.

"If I can get such an out size in the time," Mrs. Gainsborough sighed, "which is highly doubtful."

However, the new dress was obtained, and Mrs. Gainsborough went off to the funeral at Brompton.

"On, it was a beautiful ceremony," she sobbed, when she got home. "And really Miss Dashwood, well, she couldn't have been nicer. Oh, my poor dear captain, if only all the clergyman said was true. And yet I should feel more comfortable somehow if it wasn't. Though I suppose if it was true there'd be no objection to our meeting in heaven as friends only. Dear me, it all sounded so real when I heard the clergyman talking about it. Just as if he was going up in a lift, as you might say. So natural it sounded. 'A gallant soldier,' he said, 'a veteran of the Crimea.' So he was gallant, the dear captain. You should have seen him lay out two roughs who tried to snatch me watch and chain once at the Epsom Derby. He was a gentleman, too. I'm sure nobody ever treated any woman kinder than he treated me. Seventy years old he was. Captain Bob Dashwood of the Seventeenth Hussars. I can see him now as he used to be. He liked to come stamping up the garden. Oh, he was a stamper, and 'Polly,' he hollered out, 'get on your frills. Here's Dick Avon—the Markiss of Avon *that* was' (oh, he was a wild thing) 'and Jenny Ward' (you know, she threw herself off Westminster Bridge and caused such a stir in Jubilee year). People talked a lot about it at the time. I remember we drove to the Star and Garter at Richmond that day—a lovely June day it was—and caused quite a sensation, because we all looked so smart. Oh, my Bob, my Bob, it only seems yesterday."

Sylvia consoled Mrs. Gainsborough and rejoiced in her assurance that she did not know what she should have done.

"Fancy him thinking about me being so lonely and wanting you to come and live with me. Depend upon it he knew he was going to die all of a sudden," said Mrs. Gainsborough. "Oh, there's no doubt he was clever enough to have been a doctor. Only of course with his family he had to be a soldier."

Sylvia mostly spent these spring days in the garden with Mrs. Gainsborough, listening to her tales about the past and helping her to overlook the labors of the jobbing gardener who came in twice a week. Her landlady or hostess (for the exact relation was not yet determined) was very strict in this regard, because her father had been a nursery gardener and she insisted upon a peculiar knowledge of the various ways in which horticultural obligations could be avoided. When Sylvia raised the question of her status at Mulberry Cottage, Mrs. Gainsborough always begged her not to be in a hurry to settle anything; later on, when Sylvia was able to earn some money, she should pay for her board, but payment for her lodging, so long as Mrs. Gainsborough was alive and the house was not burned to the ground, was never to be mentioned. That was certainly the captain's intention and it must be respected.

Sylvia often went to see Mrs. Gowndry in Finborough Road in case there should be news of Lily. Her old landlady was always good enough to say that she missed her, and in her broken-up existence the affection even of Mrs. Gowndry was very grateful.

"I've told me old man to keep a good lookout for her," said Mrs. Gowndry.

"He's hardly likely to meet her at his work," Sylvia said.

"Certainly not. No. But he often goes up to get a breath of air—well—it isn't to be expected that he wouldn't. I often say to him when he comes home a bit grumblified that his profession is as bad as a miner's, and *they* only does eight hours, whereas in his lavatory they does twelve. Too long, too long, and it must be fidgety work, with people bobbing in and out all the time and always in a hurry, as you might say. Of course now and again you get a lodger who makes himself unpleasant, but, year in year out, looking after lodgers is a more peaceful sort of a life than looking after a lavatory. Don't you be afraid, Miss Scarlett. If ever a letter comes for you our Tommy shall bring it straight round, and he's a boy as can be trusted not to lose anything he's given. You wouldn't lose the pretty lady's letter, would you, Tommy? You never lose nothing, do you?"

"I lost a acid-drop once."

"There, fancy him remembering. That's a hit for his ma, that is. He'd only half sucked this here acid-drop and laid it aside to finish sucking it when he went up to bed, and I must have swept it up, not thinking what it was. Fancy him remembering. He don't talk much, but he's a artful one."

Tommy had a bagful of acid-drops soon after this, for he brought a letter to Sylvia from Lily:

DEAR SYLVIA,—I suppose you're awfully angry with me, but Claude went on tour a month ago, and I hate being alone. I wonder if this will find you. I'm staying in rotten rooms in Camden Town. 14 Winchester Terrace. Send me a card if you're in London.

Loving, LILY.

Sylvia immediately went over to Camden Town and brought Lily away from the rooms, which were indeed "rotten." When she had installed her at Mulberry Cottage she worked herself up to having a clear understanding with Lily, but when it came to the point she felt it was useless to scold her except in fun, as a child scolds her doll. She did, however, treat her henceforth in what Mrs. Gainsborough called a "highly dictatorial way." Sylvia thought she could give Lily the appearance of moral or immoral energy, however impossible it might be to give her the reality. With this end in view she made Lily's will entirely subordinate to her own, which was not difficult. The affection that Sylvia now had for her was not so much tender as careful, the affection one might feel for a bicycle rather than for a horse. She was always brutally frank with herself about their relation to each other, and because she never congratulated herself upon her kindness she was able to sustain her affection.

"There is nothing so fickle as a virtuous impulse," Sylvia declared to herself. "It's a kind of moral usury which is always looking for a return on the investment. The moment the object fails to pay an exorbitant interest in gratitude, the impulse to speculate withers up. The lowest circle in hell should be reserved for people who try to help others and cannot understand why their kindness is not appreciated. Really that was Philip's trouble. He never got over being hurt that I didn't perpetually remind him of his splendid behavior toward me. I suppose I'm damned inhuman. Well, well, I couldn't have stood those three months after I left him if I hadn't been."

The affair between Lily and Claude Raglan was not much discussed. He had, it seemed, only left her because his career was at stake; he had received a good offer and she had not wished to detain him.

"But is it over between you?" Sylvia demanded.

"Yes, of course, it's over—at any rate, for a long time to come," Lily answered. "He cried when he left me. He really was a nice boy. If he lives, he thinks he will be a success—a real success. He introduced me to a lot of nice boys."

"That was rash of him," Sylvia laughed. "Were they as nice as the lodgings he introduced you to?"

"No, don't laugh at him. He couldn't afford anything else."

"But why in Heaven's name, if you wanted to play around together, had you got to leave Finborough Road?"

Lily blushed faintly. "You won't be angry if I tell you?"

Sylvia shook her head.

"Claude said he couldn't bear the idea that you were looking at us. He said it spoiled everything."

"What did he think I was going to do?" Sylvia snapped. "Put pepper on the hymeneal pillow?"

"You said you wouldn't be angry."

"I'm not."

"Well, don't use long words, because it makes me think you are."

Soon after Lily came to Tinderbox Lane, Sylvia met Dorothy Lonsdale with a very lovely dark girl called Olive Fanshawe, a fellow-member of the Vanity chorus. Dorothy was glad to see her, principally, Sylvia thought, because she was able to talk about lunch at Romano's and supper at the Savoy.

"Look here," Sylvia said. "A little less of the Queen of Sheba, if you don't mind. Don't forget I'm one of the blokes as is glad to smell the gratings outside a baker's."

Miss Fanshawe laughed, and Sylvia looked at her quickly, wondering if she were worth while.

Dorothy was concerned to hear she was still with Lily. "That dreadful girl," she simpered.

"Oh, go to hell," said Sylvia, sharply, and walked off.

Next day a note came from Dorothy to invite her and Lily to tea at the flat she shared with Olive.

"Wonderful how attractive rudeness is," Sylvia commented.

"Oh, do let's go. Look, she lives in Half Moon Street," Lily said.

"And a damned good address for the demi-monde," Sylvia added.

However, the tea-party was definitely a success, and for the rest of the summer Sylvia and Lily spent a lot of time on the river with what Sylvia called the semicircle of intimate friends they had brought away from Half Moon Street. She grew very fond of Olive Fanshawe and warned her against her romantic adoration of Dorothy.

"But you're just as romantic over Lily," Olive argued.

"Not a single illusion left, my dear," Sylvia assured her. "Besides, I should never compare Lily with Dorothy. Dorothy is more beautiful, more ambitious, more mercenary. She'll probably marry a lord. She's acquired the art of getting a lot for nothing to a perfection that could only be matched by a politician or a girl with the same brown eyes in the same glory of light-brown hair. And when it suits her she'll go back on her word just as gracefully, and sell her best friend as readily as a politician will sell his country."

"You're very down on politicians. I think there's something so romantic about them," Olive declared. "Young politicians, of course."

"My dear, you'd think a Bradshaw romantic."

"It is sometimes," said Olive.

"Well, I know two young politicians," Sylvia continued. "A Liberal and a Conservative. They both spend their whole time in hoping I sha'n't suggest walking down Bond Street with them, the Liberal because I may see a frock and the Conservative because he may meet a friend. They both make love to me as if they were addressing their future constituents, with a mixture of flattery, condescension, and best clothes; but they reserve all their affection for the constituency. As I tell them, if they'd fondle the constituency and nurse me, I should endure their company more easily. Unhappily, they both think I'm intelligent, and a man who admires a woman's intelligence is like a woman who admires her friend's looking-glass—each one is granting an audience to himself."

"At any rate," said Olive, "you've managed to make yourself quite a mystery. All the men we know are puzzled by you."

"Tell them, my dear, I'm quite simple. I represent the original conception of the Hetæra, a companion. I don't want to be made love to, and every man who makes love to me I dislike. If I ever do fall in love, I'll be a man's slave. Of that I'm sure. So don't utter dark warnings, for I've warned myself already. I do want a certain number of things—nice dresses, because I owe them to myself, good books, and—well, really, I think that's all. In return for the dresses and the books—I suppose one ought to add an occasional fiver just to show there's no ill feeling about preferring to sleep in my own room—in return for very little. I'm ready to talk, walk, laugh, sing, dance, tell incomparably bawdy stories, and, what is after all the most valuable return of all, I'm ready to sit perfectly still and let myself be bored to death while giving him an idea that I'm listening intelligently. Of course, sometimes I do listen intelligently without being bored. In that case I let him off with books only."

"You really are an extraordinary girl," said Olive.

"You, on the other hand, my dear," Sylvia went on, "always give every man the hope that if he's wise and tender, and of course lavish—ultimately all men believe in the pocket—he will be able to cry Open Sesame to the mysterious treasure of romantic love that he discerns in your dark eyes, in your caressing voice, and in your fervid aspirations. In the end you'll give it all to a curly-headed actor and live happily ever afterward at Ravenscourt Park. Farewell to Coriolanus in his smart waistcoat; farewell to Julius Cæsar and his amber cigarette-holder; farewell to every nincompoop with a top-hat as bright as a halo; farewell incidentally to Dolly Lonsdale, who'll discover that Ravenscourt Park is too difficult for the chauffeur to find."

"Oh, Sylvia, shut up!" Olive said. "I believe you drank too much champagne at lunch."

"I'm glad you reminded me," Sylvia cried. "By Jove! I'd forgotten the fizz. That's where we all meet on common ground—or rather, I should say in common liquid. It sounds like mixed bathing. It is a kind of mixed bathing, after all. You're quite right, Olive, whatever our different tastes in men, clothes, and behavior, we all must have champagne. Champagne is a bloody sight thicker than water, as the prodigal said when his father uncorked a magnum to wash down the fatted calf."

Gradually Sylvia did succeed in sorting out from the various men a few who were content to accept the terms of friendship she offered. She had to admit that most of them fell soon or late, and with each new man she gave less and took more. As regards Lily, she tried to keep her as unapproachable as herself, but it was not always possible. Sometimes with a shrug of the shoulders she let Lily go her own way, though she was always hard as steel with the fortunate suitor. Once a rich young financier called Hausberg, who had found Lily somewhat expensive, started a theory that Sylvia was living on her friend; she heard of the slander and dealt with it very directly. The young man in question was anxious to set Lily up in a flat of her own. Sylvia let Lily appear to view the plan with favor. The flat was taken and furnished; a date was fixed for Lily's entrance; the young man was given the latch-key and told to come at midnight. When he arrived, there was nobody in the flat but a chimpanzee that Sylvia had bought at Jamrack's. She and Lily were at Brighton with Arthur Lonsdale and Tony Clarehaven, whom they had recently met again at a Covent Garden ball.

They were both just down from Oxford, and Lonsdale had taken a great fancy to Lily. He was a jolly youth, whose father, Lord Cleveden, had consented after a struggle to let him go into partnership with a distinguished professional motorist. It was with him that Dorothy Lonsdale claimed distant kinship. Clarehaven's admiration for

Dorothy had not diminished; somebody had told him that the best way to get hold of her would be to make her jealous. This was his object in inviting Sylvia to Brighton. Sylvia agreed to go, partly to tease Dorothy, partly to disappoint Clarehaven. Lonsdale had helped her to get the chimpanzee into the flat, and all the way down to Brighton they laughed.

"My word, you know!" Lonsdale chuckled, "the jolly old chimpanzee will probably eat the wall-paper. What do you think Hausberg will say when he opens the door?"

"I expect he'll say, 'Are you there, Lily?'" Sylvia suggested.

"What do you think the jolly old chimpanzee will do? Probably bite his ear off—what? Topping. Good engine this. We're doing fifty-nine or an unripe sixty. Why does a chicken cross the road? No answer, thank you, this time. Must slow down a bit. There's a trap somewhere here. I say, you know, I've got a sister called Sylvia. Hullo! hullo! Mind your hoop, Tommy! Too late. Funeral on Friday. Colonial papers please copy. I wonder how they'll get the chimpanzee out again. I told the hall porter, when he cast a cold and glassy eye on the crate, it was a marble Venus that Mr. Hausberg was going to use as a hat-stand. My word! I expect the jolly old flat looks like the last days of Pompeii by now. When I undid the door of the crate the brute was making a noise like a discontented cistern. I rapidly scattered Brazil nuts and bananas on the floor to occupy his mind and melted away like a strawberry ice on a grill. Hullo! We're getting into Brighton."

Clarehaven did not enjoy his week-end, for it consisted entirely of a lecture by Sylvia on his behavior. This caused him to drink many more whisky-and-sodas than usual, and he came back to London on Monday with a bad headache, which he attributed to Sylvia's talking.

"My dear man, *I* haven't got a mouth. You have," she said.

This week-end caused a quarrel between Sylvia and Dorothy, for which she was not sorry. She had recently met a young painter, Ronald Walker, who wanted Lily to sit for him; he had taken them once or twice to the Café Royal, which Sylvia had found a pleasant change from the society of Half Moon Street. Soon after this Lonsdale began a liaison with Queenie Molyneux, of the Frivolity Theater. The only member of the Half Moon Street set with whom Sylvia kept up a friendship was Olive Fanshawe.

CHAPTER IX

DURING her second year at Mulberry Cottage Sylvia achieved an existence that, save for the absence of any one great motive like art or love, was complete. She had also one real friend in Jack Airdale, who had returned from his tour. Apart from the pleasant security of knowing that he would always be content with good-fellowship only, he encouraged her to suppose that somewhere, could she but find the first step, a career lay before her. Sylvia did not in her heart believe in this career, but in moments of depression Jack's confidence was of the greatest comfort, and she was always ready to play with the notion, particularly as it seemed to provide a background for her present existence and to cover the futility of its perfection. Jack was anxious that she should try to get on the proper stage, but Sylvia feared to destroy by premature failure a part of the illusion of ultimate success she continued to allow herself by finally ruling out the theater as one of the possible channels to that career. In the summer Lily became friendly with one or two men whom Sylvia could not endure, but a lassitude had descended upon her and she lacked any energy to stop the association. As a matter of fact she was sickening for diphtheria at the time, and while she was in the hospital Lily took to frequenting the Orient promenade with these new friends. As soon as Sylvia came out they were banished; but each time that she intervened on Lily's behalf it seemed to her a little less worth while. Nevertheless, finding that Lily was bored by her own habit of staying in at night, she used much against her will to accompany her very often to various places of amusement without a definite invitation from a man to escort them.

One day at the end of December Mrs. Gainsborough came home from shopping with two tickets for a fancy-dress dance at the Redcliffe Hall in Fulham Road. When the evening arrived Sylvia did not want to go, for the weather was raw and foggy; but Mrs. Gainsborough was so much disappointed at her tickets not being used that to please her Sylvia agreed to go. It seemed unlikely to be an amusing affair, so she and Lily went in the most ordinary of their fancy dresses as masked Pierrettes. The company, as they had anticipated, was quite exceptionally dull.

"My dear, it's like a skating-rink on Saturday afternoon," Sylvia said. "We'll have one more dance together and then go home."

They were standing at the far end of the hall near the orchestra, and Sylvia was making disdainful comments upon the various couples that were passing out to refresh themselves or flirt in the draughty corridors.

Suddenly Sylvia saw a man in evening dress pushing his way in their direction, regardless of what ribbons he tore or toes he outraged in his transit. He was a young man of about twenty-three or twenty-four, with a countenance in which eagerness was curiously mixed with impassivity. Sylvia saw him as one sees a picture on first entering a gallery, which one postpones visiting with a scarcely conscious and yet perfectly deliberate anticipation of pleasure later on. She continued talking to Lily, who had her back to the new-comer; while she talked she was aware that all her own attention was fixed upon this new-comer and that she was asking herself the cause of the contradictions in his face and deciding that it was due to the finely carved immobile mouth beneath such eager eyes. Were they brown or blue? The young man had reached them, and from that immobile mouth came in accents that were almost like despair a salutation to Lily. Sylvia felt for a moment as if she had been wounded; she saw that Lily was looking at her with that expression she always put on when she thought Sylvia was angry with her; then after what seemed an age turned round slowly to the young man and, lifting her mask, engaged in conversation with him. Sylvia felt that she was trespassing upon the borders of great emotion and withdrew out of hearing, until Lily beckoned her forward to introduce the young man as Mr. Michael Fane. Sylvia did not raise her mask, and after nodding to him again retired from the conversation.

"But this is absurd," she said to herself, after a while; and abruptly raising her mask she broke in upon the duologue. The music had begun. He was asking Lily to dance, and she, waiting for Sylvia's leave in a way that made Sylvia want to slap her, was hesitating.

"What rot, Lily!" she exclaimed, impatiently. "Of course you may dance."

The young man turned toward Sylvia and smiled. A moment later he and Lily had waltzed away.

"Good God!" said Sylvia to herself. "Am I going mad? A youth smiles at me and I feel inclined to cry. What is this waltz they're playing?"

She looked at one of the sheets of music, but the name was nowhere legible, and she nearly snatched it away from the player in exasperation. Nothing seemed to matter in the world except that she should know the name of this waltz. Without thinking what she was doing she thumped the clarinet-player on the shoulder, who stopped indignantly and asked if she was trying to knock his teeth out.

"What waltz are you playing? What waltz are you playing?"

"'Waltz Amarousse.' Perhaps you'll punch one of the strings next time, miss?"

"Happy New-Year," Sylvia laughed, and the clarinet-player with a disgusted glance turned round to his music again.

By the time the dance was over and the other two had rejoined her, Sylvia was laughing at herself; but they thought she was laughing at them. Fane and Lily danced several more dances together, and gradually Sylvia made up her mind that she disapproved of this new intimacy, this sudden invasion of Lily's life from the past from which she should have cut herself off as completely as Sylvia had done from her own. What right had Lily to complicate their existence in this fashion? How unutterably dull this masquerade was! She whispered to Lily in the next interval that she was tired and wanted to go home.

The fog outside was very dense. Fane took their arms to cross the road, and Sylvia, though he caught her arm close to him, felt drearily how mechanical its gesture was toward her, how vital toward Lily. Neither of her companions spoke to each other, and she asked them questions about their former friendship, which Lily did not answer because she was evidently afraid of her annoyance, and which he did not answer because he did not hear. Sylvia had made up her mind that Fane should not enter Mulberry Cottage, when Lily whispered to her that she should ask him, but at the last moment she remembered his smile and invited him to supper. A strange shyness took possession of her, which she tried to cover by exaggeration, almost, she thought, hysterical fooling with Mrs. Gainsborough that lasted until two o'clock in the morning of New-Year's day, when Michael Fane went home after exacting a promise from the two girls to lunch with him at Kettner's that afternoon. Lily was so sleepy that she did not rise to see him out. Sylvia was glad of the indifference.

Next morning Sylvia found out that Michael was a "nice boy" whom Lily had known in West Kensington when she was seventeen. He had been awfully in love with her, and her mother had been annoyed because he wanted to marry her. He had only been seventeen himself, and like many other school-boy loves of those days this one had just ended somehow, but exactly how Lily could not recall. She wished that Sylvia would not go on asking so many questions; she really could not remember anything more about it. They had gone once for a long drive in a cab, and there had been a row about that at home.

"Are you in love with him now?" Sylvia demanded.

"No, of course not. How could I be?"

Sylvia was determined that she never should be, either: there should be no more Claude Raglans to interfere with their well-devised existence.

During the next fortnight Sylvia took care that Lily and Michael should never be alone together, and she tried very often, after she discovered that Michael was sensitive, to shock him by references to their life, and with an odd perverseness to try particularly to shock him about herself by making brutally coarse remarks in front of Lily, taking pleasure in his embarrassment. Yet there was in the end little pleasure in shocking him, for he had no conventional niceness; yet there was a pleasure in hurting him, a fierce pleasure.

"Though why on earth I bother about his feelings, I can't imagine," Sylvia said to herself. "All I know is that he's an awful bore and makes us break all sorts of engagements with other people. You liar! You know he's not a bore, and you know that you don't care a damn how many engagements you break. Don't pose to yourself. You're jealous of him because you think that Lily may get really fond of him. You don't want her to get fond of him, because you don't think she's good enough for him. You don't want him to get fond of *her*."

The boldness of this thought, the way in which it had attacked the secret recesses of her being, startled Sylvia. It was almost a sensation of turning pale at herself, of fearing to understand herself, that made her positively stifle the mood and flee from these thoughts, which might violate her personality.

Down-stairs, there was a telegram from Olive Fanshawe at Brighton, begging Sylvia to come at once; she was terribly unhappy; Sylvia could scarcely tear herself away from Mulberry Cottage at such a moment even for Olive, but, knowing that if she did not go she would be sorry, she went.

Sylvia found Olive in a state of collapse. Dorothy Lonsdale and she had been staying in Brighton for a week's holiday, and yesterday Dorothy had married Clarehaven. Sylvia laughed.

"Oh, Sylvia, don't laugh!" Olive begged. "It was perfectly dreadful. Of course it was a great shock to me, but I did not show it. I told her she could count on me as a pal to help her in every way. And what do you think she said? Sylvia, you'll never guess. It was too cruel. She said to me in a voice of ice, dear—really, a voice of ice—she said the best way

I could help her was by not seeing her any more. She did not intend to go near the stage door of a theater again. She did not want to know any of her stage friends any more. She didn't even say she was sorry; she was quite calm. She was like ice, Sylvia dear. Clarehaven came in and she asked if he'd telegraphed to his mother, and when he said he had she got up as if she'd been calling on me quite formally and shook hands, and said: 'Good-by, Olive. We're going down to Clare Court to-morrow, and I don't expect we shall see each other again for a long time.' Clarehaven said what rot and that I must come down to Devonshire and stay with them, and Dolly froze him, my dear; she froze him with a look. I never slept all night, and the book I was reading began to repeat itself, and I thought I was going mad; but this morning I found the printers had made some mistake and put sixteen pages twice over. But I really thought I was going mad, so I wired for you. Oh, Sylvia, Sylvia, say something to console me! She was like ice, dear, really like a block of ice."

"If she'd only waited till you had found the curly-headed actor it wouldn't have mattered so much," Sylvia said.

Poor Olive really was on the verge of a nervous collapse, and Sylvia stayed with her three days, though it was agony to leave Lily in London with Michael Fane. Nor could she talk of her own case to Olive. It would seem like a competitive sorrow, a vulgar bit of egotistic assumption to suit the occasion.

When Sylvia got back to Mulberry Cottage she found an invitation from Jack Airdale to dine at Richmond and go to a dance with him afterward. Conscious from something in Michael's watchful demeanor of a development in the situation, she was pleased to be able to disquiet him by insisting that Lily should go with her.

On the way, Sylvia extracted from Lily that Michael had asked her to marry him. It took all Jack Airdale's good nature not to be angry with Sylvia that night—as she tore the world to shreds. At the moment when Lily had told her she had felt with a despair that was not communicable, as Olive's despair had been, how urgent it was to stop Michael from marrying Lily. She was not good enough for him. The knowledge rang in her brain like a discordant clangor of bells, and Sylvia knew in that moment that the real reason of her thinking this was jealousy of Lily. The admission tortured her pride, and after a terrible night in which the memory of Olive's grief interminably dwelt upon and absorbed helped her to substitute the pretense, so passionately invoked that it almost ceased to be a pretense, that she was opposing the marriage partly because Michael would never keep Lily faithful, partly because she could not bear the idea of losing her friend.

When, the next day, Sylvia faced Michael for the discussion of the marriage, she was quite sure not merely that he had never attracted her, but even that she hated him and, what was more deadly, despised him. She taunted him with wishing to marry Lily for purely sentimental reasons, for the gratification of a morbid desire to save her. She remembered Philip, and all the hatred she had felt for Philip's superiority was transferred to Michael. She called him a prig and made him wince by speaking of Lily and herself as "tarts," exacting from the word the uttermost tribute of its vulgarity. She dwelt on Lily's character and evolved a theory of woman's ownership by man that drove her into such illogical arguments and exaggerated pretensions that Michael had some excuse for calling her hysterical. The dispute left Lily on one side for a time and became personal to herself and him. He told her she was jealous. In an access of outraged pride she forgot that he was referring to her jealousy about Lily, and to any one less obsessed by an idea than he was she would have revealed her secret. Suddenly he seemed to give way. When he was going he told her that she hated him because he loved Lily and hated him twice as much because his love was returned.

Sylvia felt she would go mad when Michael said that he loved Lily; but he was thinking it was because Lily loved him that she was biting her nails and glaring at him. Then he asked her what college at Oxford her husband had been at. She had spoken of Philip during their quarrel. This abrupt linking of himself with Philip restored her balance, and coolly she began to arrange in her mind for Lily's withdrawal from London for a while. Of passion and fury there was nothing left except a calm determination to disappoint Master Michael. She remembered Olive Fanshawe's, "Like ice, dear, she was like a block of ice." She, too, was like a block of ice as she watched him walking away down the long garden.

When Michael had gone Sylvia told Lily that marriage with him was impossible.

"Why do you want to be married?" she demanded. "Was your mother so happy in her marriage? I tell you, child, that marriage is almost inconceivably dull. What have you got in common with him? Nothing, absolutely nothing."

"I'm not a bit anxious to be married," Lily protested. "But when somebody goes on and on asking, it's so difficult to refuse. I liked Claude better than I like Michael. But Claude had to think about his future."

"And what about your future?" Sylvia exclaimed.

"Oh, I expect it'll be all right. Michael has money."

"I say you shall not marry him," Sylvia almost shouted.

"Oh, don't keep on so," Lily fretfully implored. "It gives me a headache. I won't marry him if it's going to upset you so much. But you mustn't leave me alone with him again, because he worries me just as much as you do."

"We'll go away to-morrow," Sylvia announced, abruptly. It flashed upon her that she would like to go to Sirene with Lily, but, alas! there was not enough money for such a long journey, and Bournemouth or Brighton must be the colorless substitute.

Lily cheered up at the idea of going away, and Sylvia was half resentful that she could accept parting from Michael so easily. Lily's frocks were not ready the next day, and in the morning Michael's ring was heard.

"Oh, now I suppose we shall have more scenes," Lily complained.

Sylvia ran after Mrs. Gainsborough, who was waddling down the garden path to open the door.

"Come back, come back at once!" she cried. "You're not to open the door."

"Well, there's a nice thing. But it may be the butcher."

"We don't want any meat. It's not the butcher. It's Fane. You're not to open the door. We've all gone away."

"Well, don't snap my head off," said Mrs. Gainsborough, turning back unwillingly to the house.

All day long at intervals the bell rang.

"The neighbors 'll think the house is on fire," Mrs. Gainsborough bewailed.

"Nobody hears it except ourselves, you silly old thing," Sylvia said.

"And what 'll the passers-by think?" Mrs. Gainsborough asked. "It looks so funny to see any one standing outside a door, ringing all day long like a chimney-sweep who's come on Monday instead of Tuesday. Let me go out and tell him you've gone away. I'll hold the door on the jar, the same as if I was arguing with a hawker. Now be sensible, Sylvia. I'll just pop out, pop my head round the door, and pop back in again."

"You're not to go. Sit down."

"You do order any one about so. I might be a serviette, the way you crumple me up. Sylvia, don't keep prodding into me. I may be fat, but I have got some feelings left. You're a regular young spiteful. A porter wouldn't treat luggage so rough. Give over, Sylvia."

"What a fuss you make about nothing!" Sylvia said.

"Well, that ping-ping-pinging gets on my nerves. I feel as if I were coming out in black spots like a domino. Why don't the young fellow give over? It's a wonder his fingers aren't worn out."

The ringing continued until nearly midnight in bursts of half an hour at a stretch. Next morning Sylvia received a note from Fane in which he invited her to be sporting and let him see Lily.

"How I hate that kind of gentlemanly attitude!" she scoffed to herself.

Sylvia wrote as unpleasant a letter as she could invent, which she left with Mrs. Gainsborough to be given to Michael when he should call in answer to an invitation she had posted for the following day at twelve o'clock. Then Lily and she left for Brighton. All the way down in the train she kept wondering why she had ended her letter to Michael by calling him "my little Vandyck." Suddenly she flew into a rage with herself, because she knew that she was making such speculation an excuse to conjure his image to her mind.

Toward the end of February Sylvia and Lily came back to Mulberry Cottage. Sylvia had awakened one morning with the conviction that it was beneath her dignity to interfere further between Lily and Michael. She determined to leave everything to fate. She would go and stay with Olive for a while, and if Lily went away with Michael, so much the better. To hell with both of them. This resolution once taken, Sylvia, who had been rather charming to Lily all the time at Brighton, began now to treat her with a contempt that was really an expression of the contempt she felt for Michael. A week after their return to London she spent the whole of one day in ridiculing him so cruelly that even Mrs. Gainsborough protested. Then she was seized with an access of penitence, and, clasping Lily to her, she almost entreated her to vow that she loved her better than any one else in the world. Lily, however, was by this time thoroughly sulky and would have nothing to do with Sylvia's tardy sweetness. The petulant way in which she shook herself free from the embrace at last brought Sylvia up to the point of leaving Lily to herself. She should go and stay with Olive Fanshawe, and if, when she came back, Lily were still at Mulberry Cottage, she would atone for the way she had treated her lately; if she were gone, it would be only one more person ruthlessly cut out of her life. It was curious to think of everybody—Monkley, Philip, the Organs, Mabel, the twins, Miss Ashley, Dorward, all going on with their lives at this moment regardless of her.

"I might just as well be dead," she told herself. "What a fuss people make about death!"

Sylvia was shocked to find how much Olive had suffered from Dorothy's treatment of her. For the first time in her life she was unable to dispose of emotion as mere romantic or sentimental rubbish; there was indeed something deeper than the luxury of grief that could thus ennoble even a Vanity girl.

"I do try, Sylvia, not to mope all the time. I keep on telling myself that, if I really loved Dorothy, I should be glad for her to be Countess of Clarehaven, with everything that she wants. She was always a good girl. I lived with her more than two years and she was *frightfully* strict about men. She deserved to be a countess. And I'm sure she's quite right in wanting to cut herself off altogether from the theater. I think, you know, she may have meant to be kind in telling me at once like that, instead of gradually dropping me, which would have been worse, wouldn't it? Only I do miss her so. She was such a lovely thing to look at."

"So are you," Sylvia said.

"Ah, but I'm dark, dear, and a dark girl never has that almost unearthly beauty that Dolly had."

"Dark girls have often something better than unearthly and seraphic beauty," Sylvia said. "They often have a gloriously earthly and human faithfulness."

"Ah, you need to tease me about being romantic, but I think it's you that's being romantic now. You were quite right, dear; I used to be stupidly romantic over foolish little things without any importance, and now it all seems such a waste of time. That's really what I feel most of all, now that I've lost my friend. It seems to me that every time I patted a dog I was wasting time."

Sylvia had a fleeting thought that perhaps Gladys and Enid Worsley might have felt like that about her, but in a moment she quenched the fire it kindled in her heart. She was not going to bask in the warmth of self-pity like a spoiled little girl that hopes she may die to punish her brother for teasing her.

"I think, you know," Olive went on, "that girls like us aren't prepared to stand sorrow. We've absolutely nothing to fall back upon. I've been thinking all these days what an utterly unsatisfactory thing lunch at Romano's really is. The only thing in my life that I can look back to for comfort is summer at the convent in Belgium. Of course we giggled all the time; but all the noise of talking has died away, and I can only see a most extraordinary peacefulness. I wonder if the nuns would have me as a boarder for a little while this summer. I feel I absolutely must go there. It isn't being sentimental, because I never knew Dorothy in those days."

Perhaps Olive's regret for her lost friend affected Sylvia. When she went back to Mulberry Cottage and found that Lily had gone away, notwithstanding her own deliberate provocation of the elopement, she was dismayed. There was nothing left of Lily but two old frocks in the wardrobe, two old frocks the color of dead leaves; and this poignant reminder of a physical loss drove out all the other emotions. She told herself that it was ridiculous to be moved like this and she jeered at herself for imitating Olive's grief. But it was no use; those two frocks affrighted her courage with their deadness. No kind of communion after marriage would compensate for the loss of Lily's presence; it was like the fading of a flower in the completeness of its death. Even if she had been able to achieve the selflessness of Olive and take delight in Lily's good fortune, how impossible it was to believe in the triumph of this marriage. Lily would either be bored or she would become actively miserable—Sylvia snorted at the adverb—and run away or rather slowly melt to damnation. It would not even be necessary for her to be miserable; any unscrupulous friend of her husband's would have his way with her. For an instant Sylvia had a tremor of compassion for Michael, but it died in the thought of how such a disillusion would serve him right. He had built up this passion out of sentimentality; he was like Don Quixote; he was stupid. No doubt he had managed by now to fall in love with Lily, but it had never been an inevitable passion, and no pity should be shown to lovers that did not love wildly at first sight. They alone could plead fate's decrees.

Jack Airdale came to see Sylvia, and he took advantage of her despair to press his desire for her to go upon the stage. He was positive that she had in her the makings of a great actress. He did not want to talk about himself, but he must tell Sylvia that there was a wonderful joy in getting on. He would never, of course, do anything very great, but he was understudy to some one or other at some theater or other, and there was always a chance of really showing what he could do one night or at any rate one afternoon. Even Claude was getting on; he had met him the other day in a tail coat and a top-hat. Since there had been such an outcry against tubercular infection, he had been definitely cured of his tendency toward consumption; he had nothing but neurasthenia to contend with now.

But Sylvia would not let Jack "speak about her" to the managers he knew. She had no intention of continuing as she was at present, but she should wait till she was twenty-three before she took any step that would involve anything more energetic than turning over the pages of a book; she intended to dream away the three months that were left to twenty-two. Jack Airdale went away discouraged.

Sylvia met Ronald Walker, who had painted Lily. From him she learned that Fane had taken a house for her somewhere near Regent's Park. By a curious coincidence, a great friend of his who was also a friend of Fane's had helped to acquire the house. Ronald understood that there was considerable feeling against the marriage among Fane's friends. What was Fane like? He knew several men who knew him, and he seemed to be one of those people about whose affairs everybody talked.

"Thank Heaven, nobody bothers about me," said Ronald. "This man Fane seems to have money to throw about. I wish he'd buy my picture of Lily. You're looking rather down, Sylvia. I suppose you miss her? By Jove! what an amazing sitter! She wasn't really beautiful, you know—I mean to say with the kind of beauty that lives outside its setting. I don't quite mean that, but in my picture of her, which most people consider the best thing I've done, she never gave me what I ought to have had from such a model. I felt cheated, somehow, as if I'd cut a bough from a tree and in doing so destroyed all its grace. It was her gracefulness really; and dancing's the only art for that. I can't think why I didn't paint you."

"You're not going to begin now," Sylvia assured him.

"Well, of course, now you challenge me," he laughed. "The fact is, Sylvia, I've never really seen you in repose till this moment. You were always tearing around and talking. Look here, I do want to paint you. I say, let me paint you in this room with Mrs. Gainsborough. By Jove! I see exactly what I want."

"It sounds as if you wanted an illustration for the Old and New Year," Sylvia said.

In the end, however, she gave way; and really, it passed the time, sitting for Ronald Walker with Mrs. Gainsborough in that room where nothing of Lily remained.

"Well," Mrs. Gainsborough declared, when the painter had finished. "I knew I was fat, but really it's enough to make any one get out of breath just to look at any one so fat as you've made me. He hasn't been stingy with his paint, I'll say that. But really, you know, it looks like a picture of the fat woman in a fair. Now Sylvia's very good. Just the way she looks at you with her chin stuck out like a step-ladder. Your eyes are very good, too. He's just got that nasty glitter you get into them sometimes."

One day in early June, without any warning, Michael Fane revisited Mulberry Cottage. Sylvia had often declaimed against him to Mrs. Gainsborough, and now while they walked up the garden she could see that Mrs. Gainsborough was nervous, and by the way that Michael walked either that he was nervous or that something had happened. Sylvia came down the steps from the balcony to meet them, and, reading in his countenance that he had come to ask her help, she was aware of an immense relief, which she hid under an attitude of cold hostility. They sat on the garden seat under the budding mulberry-tree, and without any preliminaries of conversation Michael told her that he and Lily had parted. Sylvia resented an implication in his tone that she would somehow be awed by this announcement; she felt bitterly anxious to disappoint and humiliate him by her indifference, hoping that he would beg her to get Lily back for him. Instead of this he spoke of putting her out of his life, and Sylvia perceived that it was not at all to get Lily back that he had come to her. She was angry at missing her opportunity and she jeered at the stately way in which he confessed his failure and his loss; nor would he wince when she mocked his romantic manner of speech. At last she was almost driven into the brutality of picturing in unforgivable words the details of Lily's infidelity, but from this he flinched, stopping her with a gesture. He went on to give Sylvia full credit for her victory, to grant that she had been right from the first, and gradually by dwelling on the one aspect of Lily that was common to both of them, her beauty, he asked her very gently to take Lily back to live with her again. Sylvia could not refrain from sneers, and he was stung into another allusion to her jealousy, which Sylvia set out to disprove almost mathematically, though all the time she was afraid of what clear perception he might not have attained through sorrow. But he was still obsessed by the salvation of Lily; and Sylvia, because she could forgive him for his indifference to her own future except so far as it might help Lily, began to mock at herself, to accuse herself for those three months after she left Philip, to rake up that corpse from its burial-place so that this youth who troubled her very soul might turn his face from her in irremediable disgust and set her free from the spell he was unaware of casting.

When she had worn herself out with the force of her denunciation both of herself and of mankind, he came back to his original request; Sylvia, incapable of struggling further, yielded to his perseverance, but with a final flicker of self-assertion she begged him not to suppose that she was agreeing to take Lily back for any other reason than because she wanted to please herself.

Michael began to ask her about Lily's relation to certain men with whom he had heard her name linked—with Ronald Walker, and with Lonsdale, whom he had known at Oxford. Sylvia told him the facts quite simply; and then because she could not bear this kind of self-torture he was inflicting on himself, she tried to put out of its agony his last sentimental regret for Lily by denying to her and by implication to herself also the justification even of a free choice.

"Money is necessary sometimes, you know," she said.

Sylvia expected he would recoil from this, but he accepted it as the statement of a natural fact, agreed with its truth, and begged that in the future if ever money should be necessary he should be given the privilege of helping. So long as it was apparently only Lily whom he desired to help thus, Michael had put forward his claims easily enough. Then in a flash Sylvia felt that now he was transferring half his interest in Lily to her. He was stumbling hopelessly over that; he was speaking in a shy way of sending her books that she would enjoy; then abruptly he had turned from her and the garden door had slammed behind him. It was with a positive exultation that Sylvia realized that he had forgotten to give her Lily's address and that it was the dread of seeming to intrude upon her which had driven him away like that. She ran after him and called him back. He gave her a visiting-card on which his name was printed above the address; it was like a little tombstone of his dead love. He was talking now about selling the furniture and sending the money to Lily. Sylvia all the time was wondering why the first man that had ever appealed to her in the least should be like the famous hero of literature that had always bored her. With an impulse to avenge Michael she asked the name of the man for whom Lily had betrayed him. But he had never known; he had only seen his hat.

Sylvia pulled Michael to her and kissed him with the first kiss she had given to any man that was not contemptuous either of him or of herself.

"How many women have kissed you suddenly like that?" she asked.

"One—well, perhaps two!" he answered.

Even this kiss of hers was not hers alone, but because she might never see him again Sylvia broke the barrier of jealousy and in a sudden longing to be prodigal of herself for once she gave him all she could, her pride, by letting him know that she for her part had never kissed any man like that before.

Sylvia went back to the seat under the mulberry-tree and made up her mind that the time was ripe for activity again. She had allowed herself to become the prey of emotion by leading this indeterminate life in which sensation was cultivated at the expense of incident. It was a pity that Michael had intrusted her with Lily, for at this moment she would have liked to be away out of it at once; any adventure embarked upon with Lily would always be bounded by her ability to pack in time. Sylvia could imagine how those two dresses she had left behind must have been the most insuperable difficulty of the elopement. Another objection to Lily's company now was the way in which it would repeatedly remind her of Michael.

"Of course it won't remind me sentimentally," Sylvia assured herself. "I'm not such a fool as to suppose that I'm going to suffer from a sense of personal loss. On the other hand, I sha'n't ever be able to forget what an exaggerated impression I gave him. It's really perfectly damnable to divine one's sympathy with a person, to know that one could laugh together through life, and by circumstances to have been placed in an utterly abnormal relation to him. It really is damnable. He'll think of me, if he ever thinks of me at all, as one of the great multitude of wronged women. I shall think of him—though as a matter of fact I shall avoid thinking of him—either as what might have been, a false concept, for of course what might have been is fundamentally inconceivable, or as what he was, a sentimental fool. However, the mere fact that I'm sitting here bothering my head about what either of us thinks shows that I need a change of air."

That afternoon a parcel of books arrived for Sylvia from Michael Fane; among them was Skelton's Don Quixote and Adlington's *Apuleius*, on the fly-leaf of which he had written:

I've eaten rose leaves and I am no longer a golden ass.

"No, damn his eyes!" said Sylvia, "I'm the ass now. And how odd that he should send me *Don Quixote*."

At twilight Sylvia went to see Lily at Ararat House. She found her in a strange rococo room that opened on a garden bordered by the Regent's Canal; here amid candles and mirrors she was sitting in conversation with her housekeeper. Each of them existed from every point of view and infinitely reduplicated in the mirrors, which was not favorable to toleration of the housekeeper's figure, that was like an hour-glass. Sylvia waited coldly for her withdrawal before she acknowledged Lily's greeting. At last the objectionable creature rose and, accompanied by a crowd of reflections, left the room.

"Don't lecture me," Lily begged. "I had the most awful time yesterday."

"But Michael said he had not seen you."

"Oh, not with Michael," Lily exclaimed. "With Claude."

"With Claude?" Sylvia echoed.

"Yes, he came to see me and left his hat in the hall and Michael took it away with him in his rage. It was the only top-hat he'd got, and he had an engagement for an 'at home,' and he couldn't go out in the sun, and, oh dear, you never heard such a fuss, and when Mabel—"

"Mabel?"

"—Miss Harper, my housekeeper, offered to go out and buy him another, he was livid with fury. He asked if I thought he was made of money and could buy top-hats like matches. I'm glad you've come. Michael has broken off the engagement, and I expected you rather. A friend of his—rather a nice boy called Maurice Avery—is coming round this evening to arrange about selling everything. I shall have quite a lot of money. Let's go away and be quiet after all this bother and fuss."

"Look here," Sylvia said. "Before we go any further I want to know one thing. Is Claude going to drop in and out of your life at critical moments for the rest of time?"

"Oh no! We've quarreled now. He'll never forgive me over the hat. Besides, he puts some stuff on his hair now that I don't like. Sylvia, do come and look at my frocks. I've got some really lovely frocks."

Maurice Avery, to whom Sylvia took an instant dislike, came in presently. He seemed to attribute the ruin of his friend's hopes entirely to a failure to take his advice:

"Of course this was the wrong house to start with. I advised him to take one at Hampstead, but he wouldn't listen to me. The fact is Michael doesn't understand women."

"Do you?" Sylvia snapped.

Avery looked at her a moment, and said he understood them better than Michael.

"Of course nobody can ever really understand a woman," he added, with an instinct of self-protection. "But I advised him not to leave Lily alone. I told him it wasn't fair to her or to himself."

"Did you give him any advice about disposing of the furniture?" Sylvia asked.

"Well, I'm arranging about that now."

"Sorry," said Sylvia. "I thought you were paving Michael's past with your own good intentions."

"You mustn't take any notice of her," Lily told Avery, who was looking rather mortified. "She's rude to everybody."

"Well, shall I tell you my scheme for clearing up here?" he asked.

"If it will bring us any nearer to business," Sylvia answered, "we'll manage to support the preliminary speech."

A week or two later Avery handed Lily £270, which she immediately transferred to Sylvia's keeping.

"I kept the Venetian mirror for myself," Avery said. "You know the one with the jolly little cupids in pink and blue glass. I shall always think of you and Ararat House when I look at myself in it."

"I suppose all your friends wear their hearts on your sleeve," Sylvia said. "That must add a spice to vanity."

Mrs. Gainsborough was very much upset at the prospect of the girls' going away.

"That comes of having me picture painted. I felt it was unlucky when he was doing it. Oh, dearie me! whatever shall I do?"

"Come with us," Sylvia suggested. "We're going to France. Lock up your house, give the key to the copper on the beat, put on your gingham gown, and come with us, you old sea-elephant."

"Come with you?" Mrs. Gainsborough gasped. "But there, why shouldn't I?"

"No reason at all."

"Why, then I will. I believe the captain would have liked me to get a bit of a blow."

"Anything to declare?" the customs official asked at Boulogne.

"I declare I'm enjoying myself," said Mrs. Gainsborough, looking round her and beaming at France.

CHAPTER X

WHEN she once more landed on French soil, Sylvia, actuated by a classic piety, desired to visit her mother's grave. She would have preferred to go to Lille by herself, for she lacked the showman's instinct; but her companions were so horrified at the notion of being left to themselves in Paris until she rejoined them, that in the end she had to take them with her.

The sight of the old house and the faces of some of the older women in the *quartier* conjured up the past so vividly for Sylvia that she could not bring herself to make any inquiries about the rest of her family. It seemed as if she must once more look at Lille from her mother's point of view and maintain the sanctity of private life against the curiosity or criticism of neighbors. She did not wish to hear the details of her father's misdoing or perhaps be condoled with over Valentine. The simplest procedure would have been to lay a wreath upon the grave and depart again. This she might have done if Mrs. Gainsborough's genial inquisitiveness about her relatives had not roused in herself a wish to learn something about them. She decided to visit her eldest sister in Brussels, leaving it to chance if she still lived where Sylvia had visited her twelve years ago.

"Brussels," said Mrs. Gainsborough. "Well, that sounds familiar, anyway. Though I suppose the sprout-gardens are all built over nowadays. Ah dear!"

The building over of her father's nursery-garden and of many other green spots she had known in London always drew a tear from Mrs. Gainsborough, who was inclined to attribute most of human sorrow to the utilitarian schemes of builders.

"Yes, they found the Belgian hares ate up all the sprouts," Sylvia said. "And talking of hair," she went on, "what's the matter with yours?"

"Ah, well, there! Now I meant to say nothing about it. But I've left me mahogany wash at home. There's a calamity!"

"You'd better come out with me and buy another bottle," Sylvia advised.

"You'll never get one here," said Mrs. Gainsborough. "This is a wash, not a dye, you must remember. It doesn't tint the hair; it just brings up the color and gives it a nice gloss."

"If that's all it does, I'll lend you my shoe-polish. Go along, you wicked old fraud, and don't talk to me about washes. I can see the white hairs coming out like stars."

Sylvia found Elène in Brussels, and was amazed to see how much she resembled her mother nowadays. M. Durand, her husband, had prospered and he now owned a large confectioner's shop in the heart of the city, above which Madame Durand had started a pension for economical tourists. Mrs. Gainsborough could not get over the fact that her hostess did not speak English; it struck her as unnatural that Sylvia should have a sister who could only speak French. The little Durands were a more difficult problem. She did not so much mind feeling awkward with grown-up people through having to sit dumb, but children stared at her so, if she said nothing; and if she talked, they stared at her still more; she kept feeling that she ought to stroke them or pat them, which might offend their mother. She found ultimately that they were best amused by her taking out two false teeth she had, one of which once was lost, because the eldest boy would play dice with them.

Elène gave Sylvia news of the rest of the family, though, since all the four married sisters were in different towns in France and she had seen none of them for ten years, it was not very fresh news. Valentine, in whose career Sylvia was most interested, was being very well *entretenue* by a *marseillais* who had bought her an apartment that included a porcelain-tiled bath-room; she might be considered lucky, for the man with whom she had left Lille had been a rascal. It happened that her news of Valentine was fresh and authentic, because a *lilleoise* who lived in Bruxelles had recently been obliged to go to Marseilles over some legal dispute and, meeting Valentine, had been invited to see her apartment. It was a pity that she was not married, but her position was the next best thing to marriage. Of the Bassompierres Elène had heard nothing for years, but what would interest Sylvia were some family papers and photographs that Sylvia's father had sent to her as the eldest daughter when their mother died, together with an old-fashioned photograph of their grandmother. From these papers it seemed that an English *milord* and not Bassompierre had really been their grandfather. Sylvia being half English already, it might not interest her so much, but for herself to know she had English blood *l'avait beaucoup impressioné*, so many English tourists came to her pension.

Sylvia looked at the daguerreotype of her grandmother, a glass faintly bloomed, the likeness of a ghost indeed. She then had loved an Englishman; her mother, too; herself.... Sylvia packed the daguerreotype out of sight and turned to look at a golden shawl of a material rather like crêpe de Chine, which had been used to wrap up their mother when she was a baby. Would Sylvia like it? It was no use to Elène, too old and frail and faded. Sylvia stayed in Brussels for a week and left with many promises to return soon. She was glad she had paid the visit; for it had given back to her the sense of continuity which in the shifting panorama of her life she had lost, so that she had come to regard herself as an unreal person, an exception in humanity, an emotional freak; this separation from the rest of the world had been irksome to Sylvia since she had discovered the possibility of her falling in love, because it was seeming the cause of her not being loved. Henceforth she would meet man otherwise than with defiance or accusation in her eyes; she, too, perhaps would meet a lover thus.

Sylvia folded up the golden shawl to put it at the bottom of her trunk; figuratively, she wrapped up in it her memories, tender, gay, sorrowful, vile all together.

"Soon be in Paris, shall we?" said Mrs. Gainsborough, when the train reached the eastern suburbs. "It makes one feel quite naughty, doesn't it? The captain was always going to take me, but we never went, somehow. What's that? There's the Eiffel Tower? So it is, upon my word, and just what it looks like in pictures. Not a bit different. I hope it won't fall down while we're still in Paris. Nice set-out that would be. I've always been afraid of sky accidents since a friend of mine, a Mrs. Ewings, got stuck in the Great Wheel at Earl's Court with a man who started undressing himself. It was all right, as it happened, because he only wanted to wave his shirt to his wife, who was waiting for him down below, so as she shouldn't get anxious, but it gave Mrs. Ewings a nasty turn. Two hours she was stuck with nothing in her bag but a box of little liver pills, which made her mouth water, she said, she was that hungry. She *thinks* she'd have eaten them if she'd have been alone; but the man, who was an undertaker from Wandsworth, told her a lot of interesting stories about corpses, and that kept her mind occupied till the wheel started going round again, and the Exhibition gave her soup and ten shillings compensation, which made a lot of people go up in it on the chance of being stuck."

It was strange, Sylvia thought, that she should be as ignorant of Paris as Mrs. Gainsborough, but somehow the three of them would manage to enjoy themselves. Lily was more nearly vivacious than she had ever known her.

"Quite saucy," Mrs. Gainsborough vowed. "But there, we're all young, and you soon get used to the funny people you see in France. After all, they're foreigners. We ought to feel sorry for them."

"I say steady, Mrs. Gainsborough," Lily murmured, with a frown. "Some of these people in the carriage may speak English."

"Speak English?" Mrs. Gainsborough repeated. "You don't mean to tell me they'd go on jabbering to one another in French if they could speak English! What an idea!"

A young man who had got into the compartment at Chantilly had been casting glances of admiration at Lily ever since, and it was on account of him that she had warned Mrs. Gainsborough. He was a slim, dark young man dressed by an English tailor, very diffident for a Frenchman, but when Sylvia began to speculate upon the choice of a hotel he could no longer keep silence and asked in English if he could be of any help. When Sylvia replied to him in French, he was much surprised:

"*Mais vous êtes française!*"

"*Je suis du pays de la lune,*" Sylvia said.

"Now don't encourage the young fellow to gabble in French," Mrs. Gainsborough protested. "It gives me the pins and needles to hear you. You ought to encourage people to speak English, if they want to, I'm sure."

The young Frenchman smiled at this and offered his card to Sylvia, whom he evidently accepted as the head of the party. She read, "Hector Ozanne," and smiled for the heroic first name; somehow he did not look like Hector and because he was so modest she presented him to Lily to make him happy.

"I am enchanted to meet a type of English beauty," he said. "You must forgive my sincerity, which arises only from admiration. Madame," he went on, turning to Mrs. Gainsborough, "I am honored to meet you."

Mrs. Gainsborough, who was not quite sure how to deal with such politeness, became flustered and dropped her bag. Ozanne and she both plunged for it simultaneously and bumped their heads; upon this painful salute a general friendliness was established.

"I am a bachelor," said Ozanne. "I have nothing to occupy myself, and if I might be permitted to assist you in a research for an apartment I shall be very elated."

Sylvia decided in favor of rooms on the *rive gauche*. She felt it was a conventional taste, but held to her opinion against Ozanne's objections.

"But I have an apartment in the Rue Montpensier, with a view of the Palais Royal. I do not live there now myself. I beseech you to make me the pleasure to occupy it. It is so very good, the view of the garden. And if you like an ancient house, it is very ancient. Do you concur?"

"And where will you go?" Sylvia asked.

"I live always in my club. For me it would be a big advantage, I assure you."

"We should have to pay rent," said Sylvia, quickly.

"The rent will be one thousand a year."

"God have mercy upon us!" Mrs. Gainsborough gasped. "A thousand a year? Why, the man must think that we're the royal family broken out from Windsor Castle on the randan."

"Shut up, you silly old thing," said Sylvia. "He's asking nothing at all. Francs, not pounds. *Vous êtes trop gentil pour nous, Monsieur.*"

"*Alors, c'est entendu?*"

"*Mais oui.*"

"*Bon! Nous y irons ensemble tout de suite, n'est-ce pas?*"

The apartment was really charming. From the windows one could see the priests with their breviaries muttering up and down the old garden of the Palais Royal; and, as in all gardens in the heart of a great city, many sorts of men and women were resting there in the sunlight. Ozanne invited them to dine with him that night and left them to unpack.

"Well, I'm bound to say we seem to have fallen on our feet right off," Mrs. Gainsborough said. "I shall quite enjoy myself here; I can see that already."

The acquaintance with Hector Ozanne ripened into friendship, and from friendship his passion for Lily became obvious, not that really it had ever been anything else, Sylvia thought; the question was whether it should be allowed to continue. Sylvia asked Ozanne his intentions. He declared his desperate affection, exclaimed against the iniquity of not being able to marry on account of a mother from whom he derived his entire income, stammered, and was silent.

"I suppose you'd like me and Mrs. Gainsborough to clear out of this?" Sylvia suggested.

No, he would like nothing of the kind; he greatly preferred that they should all stay where they were as they were, save only that of course they must pay no rent in future and that he must be allowed to maintain entirely the upkeep of the apartment. He wished it to be essentially their own and he had no intention of intruding there except as a guest. From time to time no doubt Lily would like to see something of the French countryside and of the *plages*, and no doubt equally Sylvia would not be lonely in Paris with Mrs. Gainsborough. He believed that Lily loved him. She was, of course, like all English girls, cold, but for his part he admired such coldness, in fact he admired everything English. He knew that his happiness depended upon Sylvia, and he begged her to be kind.

Hector Ozanne was the only son of a rich manufacturer who had died about five years ago. The business had for some time been a limited company of which Madame Ozanne held the greater number of shares. Hector himself was now twenty-five and would within a year be found a wife by his mother; until then he would be allowed to choose a mistress by himself. He was kind-hearted, simple, and immensely devoted to Lily. She liked lunching and dining with him, and would like still better dressing herself at his expense; she certainly cared for him as much now as his future wife would care for him on the wedding-day. There seemed no reason to oppose the intimacy. If it should happen that Hector should fail to treat Lily properly, Sylvia would know how to deal with him, or rather with his mother. Amen.

July was burning fiercely and Hector was unwilling to lose delightful days with Lily; they drove away together one morning in a big motor-car, which Mrs. Gainsborough blessed with as much fervor as she would have blessed a hired brougham at a suburban wedding. She and Sylvia were left together either to visit some *plage* or amuse themselves in Paris.

"Paris I think, you uncommendable mammoth, you phosphor-eyed hippopotamus, Paris I *think*."

"Well, I should like to see a bit of life, I must say. We've led a very quiet existence so far. I don't want to go back to England and tell my friend Mrs. Marsham that I've seen nothing. She's a most enterprising woman herself. I don't think you ever saw her, did you? Before she was going to have her youngest she had a regular passion to ride on a camel. She used to dream of camels all night long, and at last, being as I said a very enterprising woman and being afraid when her youngest was born he might be a humpback through her dreaming of camels all the time, she couldn't stand it no longer and one Monday morning, which is a sixpenny day, she went off to the Zoo by herself, being seven months gone at the time, and took six rides on the camel right off the reel, as they say."

"That must have been the last straw," Sylvia said.

"Have I told you this story before, then?"

Sylvia shook her head.

"Well, that's a queer thing. I was just about to say that when she'd finished her rides she went to look at the giraffes, and one of them got hold of her straw hat in his mouth and nearly tore it off her head. She hollered out, and the keeper asked her if she couldn't read the notice that visitors was requested not to feed these animals. This annoyed Mrs. Marsham very much, and she told the keeper he wasn't fit to manage performing fleas, let alone giraffes, which annoyed *him* very much. It's a pity you never met her. I sent her a post-card the other day, as vulgar a one as I could find, but you can buy them just as vulgar in London."

Sylvia did so far gratify Mrs. Gainsborough's desire to impress Mrs. Marsham as to take her to one or two Montmartre ballrooms; but she declared they did not come up to her expectations, and decided that she should have to fall back on her own imagination to thrill Mrs. Marsham.

"As most travelers do," Sylvia added.

They also went together to several plays, at which Sylvia laughed very heartily, much to Mrs. Gainsborough's chagrin.

"I'm bothered if I know what you're laughing at," she said, finally. "I can't understand a word of what they're saying."

"Just as well you can't," Sylvia told her.

"Now there's a tantalizing hussy for you. But I can guess, you great tomboy."

Whereupon Mrs. Gainsborough laughed as heartily as anybody in the audience at her own particular thoughts. She attracted a good deal of attention by this, because she often laughed at them without reference to what was happening on the stage. When Sylvia dug her in the ribs to make her keep quiet, she protested that, if she could only tell the audience what she was thinking, they would not bother any more about the stage.

"A penny for your thoughts, they say. I reckon mine are worth the price of a seat in the circle, anyway."

It was after this performance that Sylvia and Mrs. Gainsborough went to the Café de la Chouette, which was frequented mostly by the performers, poets, and composers of the music-hall world. The place was crowded, and they were forced to sit at a table already occupied by one of those figures that only in Paris seem to have the right to live on an equality with the rest of mankind, merely on account of their eccentric appearance. He was probably not more than forty years old, but his gauntness made him look older. He wore blue-and-white checked trousers, a tail coat from which he or somebody else had clipped off the tails, a red velvet waistcoat, and a yachting-cap. His eyes were cavernous, his cheeks were rouged rather than flushed with fever. He carried a leather bag slung round his middle filled with waste paper, from which he occasionally took out a piece and wrote upon it a few words. He was drinking an unrecognizable liqueur.

Mrs. Gainsborough was rather nervous of sitting down beside so strange a creature, but Sylvia insisted. The man made no gesture at their approach, but turned his eyes upon them with the impassivity of a cat.

"Look here, Sylvia, in two twos he's going to give me an attack of the horrors," Mrs. Gainsborough whispered. "He's staring at me and twitching his nose like a hungry child at a jam roll. It's no good you telling me to give over. I can't help it. Look at his eyes. More like coal-cellars than eyes. I've never been able to abide being stared at since I sat down beside a wax-work at Louis Tussaud's and asked it where the ladies' cloak-room was."

"He amuses me," Sylvia said. "What are you going to have?"

"Well, I *was* going to have a grenadier, but really if that skelington opposite is going to look at me all night, I think I'll take something stronger."

"Try a cuirassier," Sylvia suggested.

"Whatever's that?"

"It's the same relation to a curaçao that a grenadier is to a grenadine."

"What I should really like is a nice little drop of whisky with a little tiddley bit of lemon; but there, I've noticed if you ask for whisky in Paris it causes a regular commotion. The waiter holds the bottle as if it was going to bite him, and the proprietor winks at him he's pouring out too much, and I can't abide those blue siphons. Sells they call them, and sells they are."

"I shall order you a bock in a moment," Sylvia threatened.

"Now don't be unkind just because I made a slight complaint about being stared at. Perhaps they won't make such a bother if I *do* have a little whisky. But there, I can't resist it. It's got a regular taste of London, whisky has."

The man at the table leaned over suddenly and asked, in a tense voice:

"Scotch or Irish?"

"Oh, good land! what a turn you gave me! I couldn't have jumped more," Mrs. Gainsborough exclaimed, "not if one of the lions in Trafalgar Square had said pip-ip as I passed!"

"You didn't think I was English, did you?" said the stranger. "I forget it myself sometimes. I'm a terrible warning to the world. I'm a pose that's become a reality."

"Pose?" Mrs. Gainsborough echoed. "Oh, I didn't understand you for the moment. You mean you're an artist's model?"

The stranger turned his eyes upon Sylvia, and, whether from sympathy or curiosity, she made friends with him, so that when they were ready to go home the eccentric Englishman, whom every one called Milord and who did not offer any alternative name to his new friends, said he would walk with them a bit of the way, much to Mrs. Gainsborough's embarrassment.

"I'm the first of the English decadents," he proclaimed to Sylvia. "Twenty years ago I came to Paris to study art. I hadn't a penny to spend on drugs. I hadn't enough money to lead a life of sin. There's a tragedy! For five years I starved myself instead. I thought I should make myself interesting. I did. I became a figure. I learned the raptures of hunger. Nothing surpasses them—opium, morphine, ether, cocaine, hemp. What are they beside hunger? Have you got any coco with you? Just a little pinch? No? Never mind. I don't really like it. Not really. Some people like it, though. Who's the old woman with you? A procuress? Last night I had a dream in which I proved the non-existence of God by the least common multiple. I can't exactly remember how I did it now. That's why I was so worried this evening; I can't remember if the figures were two, four, sixteen, and thirty-eight. I worked it out last night in my dream. I obtained a view of the universe as a geometrical abstraction. It's perfectly simple, but I cannot get it right now. There's a crack in my ceiling which indicates the way. Unless I can walk along that crack I can't reach the center of the universe, and of course it's hopeless to try to obtain a view of the universe as a geometrical abstraction if one can't reach the center. I take it you agree with me on that point. That point! Wait a minute. I'm almost there. That point. Don't let me forget. That point. That is the point. Ah!"

The abstraction eluded him and he groaned aloud.

"The more I listen to him," said Mrs. Gainsborough, "the more certain sure I am he ought to see a doctor."

"I must say good night," the stranger murmured, sadly. "I see that I must start again at the beginning of that crack in my ceiling. I was lucky to find the room that had such a crack, though in a way it's rather a nuisance. It branches off so, and I very often lose the direction. There's one particular branch that always leads away from the point. I'm afraid to do anything about it in the morning. Of course, I might put up a notice to say, *this is the wrong way*; but supposing it were really the right way? It's a great responsibility to own such a crack. Sometimes I almost go mad with the burden of responsibility. Why, by playing about with that ceiling when my brain isn't perfectly clear I might upset the whole universe! We'll meet again one night at the Chouette. I think I'll cross the boulevard now. There's no traffic, and I have to take a certain course not to confuse my line of thought."

The eccentric stranger left them and, crossing the road in a series of diagonal tacks, disappeared.

"Coco," said Sylvia.

"Cocoa?" echoed Mrs. Gainsborough. "Brandy, more like."

"Or hashish."

"Ashes? Well, I had a fox-terrier once that died in convulsions from eating coke, so perhaps it is ashes."

"We must meet him again," said Sylvia. "These queer people outside ordinary life interest me."

"Well, it's interesting to visit a hospital," Mrs. Gainsborough agreed. "But that doesn't say you want to go twice. Once is enough for that fellow, to my thinking. He's interesting, but uncomfortable, like the top of a 'bus."

Sylvia, however, was determined to pursue her acquaintance with the outcast Englishman. She soon discovered that for years he had been taking drugs and that nothing but drugs had brought him to his present state of abject buffoonery. Shortly before he became friends with Sylvia he had been taken up as a week's amusement by some young men who were under the impression that they were seeing Parisian life in his company. They had been generous to him, and latterly he had been able to drug himself as much as he wanted. The result had been to hasten his supreme collapse. Even in his last illness he would not talk to Sylvia about his youth before he came to Paris, and in the end she was inclined to accept him at his own estimate, a pose that was become a reality.

One evening he seemed more haggard than usual and talked much less; by the twitching of his nostrils, he had been dosing himself hard with cocaine. Suddenly, he stretched his thin hand across the marble table and seized hers feverishly:

"Tell me," he asked. "Are you sorry for me?"

"I think it's an impertinence to be sorry for anybody," she answered. "But if you mean do I wish you well, why, yes, old son, I wish you very well."

"What I told you once about my coming to Paris to work at art was all lies. I came here because I had to leave nothing else behind, not even a name. You said, one evening when we were arguing about ambition, that if you could only find your line you might do something on the stage. Why don't you recite my poems? Read them through. One or two are in English, but most of them are in French. They are really more sighs than poems. They require no acting. They want just a voice."

He undid the leather strap that supported his satchel and handed it to Sylvia.

"To-morrow," he said, "if I'm still alive, I'll come here and find out what you think of them. But you've no idea how threatening that 'if' is. It gets longer and longer. I can't see the end if it anywhere. It was very long last night. The dot of the 'i' was already out of sight. It's the longest 'if' that was ever imagined."

He rose hurriedly and left the café; Sylvia never saw him again.

The poems of this strange and unhappy creature formed a record of many years' slow debasement. Many of them seemed to her too personal and too poignant to be repeated aloud, almost even to be read to oneself. There was nothing, indeed, to do but burn them, that no one else might comprehend a man's degradation. Some of the poems, however, were objective, and in their complete absence of any effort to impress or rend or horrify they seemed not so much poems as actual glimpses into human hearts. Nor was that a satisfactory definition, for there was no attempt to explain any of the people described in these poems; they were ordinary people of the streets that lived in a few lines. This could only be said of the poems written in French; those in English seemed to her not very remarkable. She wondered if perhaps the less familiar tongue had exacted from him an achievement that was largely fortuitous.

"I've got an idea for a show," Sylvia said to Mrs. Gainsborough. "One or two old folk-songs, and then one of these poems half sung, half recited to an improvised accompaniment. Not more than one each evening."

Sylvia was convinced of her ability to make a success, and spent a couple of weeks in searching for the folk-songs she required.

Lily and Hector came back in the middle of this new idea, and Hector was sure that Sylvia would be successful. She felt that he was too well pleased with himself at the moment not to be uncritically content with the rest of the world, but he was useful to Sylvia in securing an *audition* for her. The agent was convinced of the inevitable failure of Sylvia's performance with the public, and said he thought it was a pity to waste such real talent on antique rubbish like the songs she had chosen. As for the poems, they were no doubt all very well in their way; he was not going to say he had not been able to listen to them, but the public did not expect that kind of thing. He did not wish to discourage a friend of M. Ozanne; he had by him the rights for what would be three of the most popular songs in Europe, if they were well sung. Sylvia read them through and then sang them. The agent was delighted. She knew he was really pleased because he gave up referring to her as a friend of M. Ozanne and addressed her directly. Hector advised her to begin with the ordinary stuff, and when she was well known enough to experiment upon the public with her own ideas. Sylvia, who was feeling the need to do something at once, decided to risk an audition at one of the outlying music-halls. She herself declared that the songs were so good in their own way that she could not help making a hit, but the others insisted that the triumph belonged to her.

"*Vous avez vraiment de l'espièglerie,*" said Hector.

"You really were awfully jolly," said Lily.

"I didn't understand a word, of course," said Mrs. Gainsborough. "But you looked that wicked—well, really—I thoroughly enjoyed myself."

During the autumn Sylvia had secured engagements in music-halls of the *quartier*, but the agent advised her to take a tour before she ventured to attack the real Paris. It seemed to her a good way of passing the winter. Lily and Hector were very much together, and though Hector was always anxious for Sylvia to make a third, she found that the kind of amusement that appealed to him was much the same as that which had appealed to the young men who frequented Half Moon Street. It was a life of going to races, at which Hector would pass ladies without saluting or being saluted, who, he informed Sylvia and Lily afterward, were his aunts or his cousins, and actually on one occasion his mother. Sylvia began to feel the strain of being in the demi-monde but not of it; it was an existence that suited Lily perfectly, who could not understand why Sylvia should rail at their seclusion from the world. Mrs. Gainsborough began to grow restless for the peace of Mulberry Cottage and the safety of her furniture.

"You never know what will happen. I had a friend once—a Mrs. Beardmore. She was housekeeper to two maiden ladies in Portman Square—well, housekeeper, she was more of a companion because one of them was stone deaf. One summer they went away to Scarborough, and when they came back some burglars had brought a furniture-van three days running and emptied the whole house, all but the bell-pulls. Drove back, they did, from King's Cross in a four-wheeler, and the first thing they saw was a large board up—TO BE LET OR SOLD. A fine how-de-do there was in Portman Square, I can tell you; and the sister that was deaf had left her ear-trumpet in the train and nobody couldn't explain to her what had happened."

So Mrs. Gainsborough, whose fears had been heightened by the repetition of this tale, went back to London with what she described as a collection of vulgarities for Mrs. Marsham. Sylvia went away on tour.

Sylvia found the life of a music-hall singer on tour very solitary. Her fellow-vagabonds were so much more essentially mountebanks than in England, and so far away from normal existence, that even when she traveled in company because her next town coincided with the next town of other players, she was never able to identify herself with them, as in England she had managed to identify herself with the other members of the chorus. She found that it paid her best to be English, and to affect in her songs an almost excessive English accent. She rather resented the exploitation of her nationality, because it seemed to her the same kind of appeal that would have been made by a double-headed woman or a performing seal. Nobody wanted her songs to be well rendered so much as unusually rendered; everybody wanted to be surprised by her ability to sing at all in French. But if the audiences wished her to be English, she found that being English off the stage was a disadvantage among these continental mountebanks. Sylvia discovered the existence of a universal prejudice against English actresses, partly on account of their alleged personal uncleanliness, partly on account of their alleged insincerity. On several occasions astonishment was expressed at the trouble she took with her hair and at her capacity for being a good *copaine*; when, later on, it would transpire that she was half French, everybody would find almost with relief an explanation of her apparent unconformity to rule.

Sylvia grew very weary of the monotonous life in which everybody's interest was bounded by the psychology of an audience. Interest in the individual never extended beyond the question of whether she would or would not, if she were a woman; of whether he desired or did not desire, if he were a man. When either of these questions was answered the interest reverted to the audience. It seemed maddeningly unimportant to Sylvia that the audience on Monday night should have failed to appreciate a point which the audience of Tuesday night would probably hail with enthusiasm; yet often she had to admit to herself that it was just her own inability or unwillingness to treat an audience as an individual that prevented her from gaining real success. She decided that every interpretative artist must pander his emotion, his humor, his wit, his movements nightly, and that somehow he must charm each audience into the complacency with which a sophisticated libertine seeks an admission of enduring love from the woman he has paid to satisfy a momentary desire. Assuredly the most successful performers in the grand style were those who could conceal even from the most intelligent audiences their professional relation to them. A performer of acknowledged reputation would not play to the gallery with battered wiles and manifest allurements, but it was unquestionable that the foundation of success was playing to the gallery, and that the third-rate performer who flattered these provincial audiences with the personal relation could gain louder applause than Sylvia, who wanted no audience but herself. It was significant how a word of *argot* that meant a fraud of apparent brilliancy executed by an artist upon the public had extended itself into daily use. Everything was *chic*. It was *chic* to wear a hat of the latest fashion; it was *chic* to impress one's lover by a jealous outburst; it was *chic* to refuse a man one's favors. Everything was chic: it was impossible to think or act or speak in this world of vagabonds without *chic*.

The individualistic life that Sylvia had always led both in private and in public seemed to her, notwithstanding the various disasters of her career, infinitely worthier than this dependency upon the herd that found its most obvious expression in the theater. It was revolting to witness human nature's lust for the unexceptional or its cruel pleasure in the exception. Yet now, looking back at her past, she could see that it had always been her unwillingness to conform that had kept her apart from so much human enjoyment and human gain, though equally she might claim apart from human sorrow and human loss.

"The struggle, of course, would be terrible for a long while," Sylvia said to herself, "if everybody renounced entirely any kind of co-operation or interference with or imitation of or help from anybody else, but out of that struggle might arise the true immortals. A cat with a complete personality is surely higher than a man with an incomplete personality. Anyway, it's quite certain that this *cabotinage* is for me impossible. I believe that if I pricked a vein sawdust would trickle out of me now."

In such a mood of cheated hope did Sylvia return to Paris in the early spring; she was about to comment on Lily's usual state of molluscry, by yielding to which in abandoning the will she had lost the power to develop, when Lily herself proceeded to surprise her.

The affection between Hector and Lily had apparently made a steady growth and had floated in an undisturbed and equable depth of water for so long that Lily, like an ambitious water-lily, began to be ambitious of becoming a terrestrial plant. While for nearly a year she had been blossoming apparently without regard for anything but the beauty of the moment, she had all the time been sending out long roots beneath the water, long roots that were growing more and more deeply into the warm and respectable mud.

"You mean you'd like to marry Hector?" Sylvia asked.

"Why, yes, I think I should, rather. I'm getting tired of never being settled."

"But does he want to marry you?"

"We've talked about it often. He hates the idea of not marrying me."

"He'd like to go away with you and live on the top of a mountain remote from mankind, or upon a coral island in the Pacific with nothing but the sound of the surf and the cocoanuts dropping idly one by one, wouldn't he?"

"Well, he did say he wished we could go away somewhere all alone. How did you guess? How clever you are, Sylvia!" Lily exclaimed, opening wide her deep-blue eyes.

"My dear girl, when a man knows that it's impossible to be married either because he's married already or for any other reason, he always hymns a solitude for two. You never heard any man with serious intentions propose to live with his bride-elect in an Alpine hut or under a lonely palm. The man with serious intentions tries to reconcile his purse, not his person, with poetic aspirations. He's in a quandary between Hampstead and Kensington, not between mountain-tops and lagoons. I suppose he has also talked of a dream-child—a fairy miniature of his Lily?" Sylvia went on.

"We have talked about a baby," Lily admitted.

"The man with serious intentions talks about the aspect of the nursery and makes reluctant plans to yield, if compelled to, the room he had chosen for his study."

"You make fun of everything," Lily murmured, rather sulkily.

"But, my dear," Sylvia argued, "for me to be able to reproduce Hector's dream so accurately proves that I'm building to the type. I'll speculate further. I'm sure he has regretted the irregular union and vowed that, had he but known at first what an angel of purity you were, he would have died rather than propose it."

Lily sat silent, frowning. Presently she jumped up, and the sudden activity of movement brought home to Sylvia more than anything else the change in her.

"If you promise not to laugh, here are his letters," Lily said, flinging into Sylvia's lap a bundle tied up with ribbon.

"Letters!" Sylvia snapped. "Who cares about letters? The love-letters of a successful lover have no value. When he has something to write that he cannot say to your face, then I'll read his letter. All public blandishments shock me."

Hector was called away from Paris to go and stay with his mother at Aix-les-Bains; for a fortnight two letters arrived every day.

"The snow in Savoy will melt early this year," Sylvia mocked. "It's lucky he's not staying at St.-Moritz. Winter sports could never survive such a furnace."

Then followed a week's silence.

"The Alpine Club must have protested," Sylvia mocked. "Avalanches are not expected in March."

"He's probably motoring with his mother," Lily explained.

98

The next day a letter arrived from Hector.

HOTEL SUPERBE,
AIX-LES-BAINS.

MY DEAR LILY,—I do not know how to express myself. You have known always the great difficulties of my position opposite to my mother. She has found that I owe to marry myself, and I have demanded the hand of Mademoiselle Arpenteur-Legage. I dare not ask your pardon, but I have written to make an arrangement for you, and from now please use the apartment which has for me memories the most sacred. It is useless to fight against circumstances.

HECTOR.

"I think he might have used mourning paper," Sylvia said. "They always have plenty at health resorts."

"Don't be so unkind, Sylvia," Lily cried. "How can you be so unkind, when you see that my heart is broken?" She burst into tears.

In a moment Sylvia was on her knees beside her.

"Lily, my dearest Lily, you did not really love him? Oh no, my dear, not really. If you really loved him, I'll go now to Aix myself and arrange matters over the head of his stuffy old mother. But you didn't really love him. You're simply upset at the breaking of a habit. Oh, my dear, you couldn't really have loved him!"

"He sha'n't marry this girl," Lily declared, standing up in a rage. "I'll go to Aix-les-Bains myself and I'll see this Mademoiselle." She snatched the letter from the floor to read the odious name of her rival. "I'll send her all his letters. You mightn't want to read them, but she'll want to read them. She'll read every word. She'll read how, when he was thinking of proposing to her, he was calling me his angel, his life, his soul, how he was—Oh, she'll read every word, and I'll send them to her by registered post, and then I'll know she gets them. How dare a Frenchman treat an English girl like that? How dare he? How dare he? French people think English girls have no passion. They think we're cold. Are we cold? We may not like being kissed all the time like French girls, but we're not cold. Oh, I feel I could kill him!"

Sylvia interrupted her rage.

"My dear, if all this fire and fury is because you're disappointed at not being married, twist him for fifty thousand francs, buy a silver casket, put his letters inside, and send them to him for a wedding-present with your good wishes. But if you love him, darling Lily, let me go and tell him the truth; if I think he's not worth it, then come away with me and be lonely with me somewhere. My beautiful thing, I can't promise you a coral island, but you shall have all my heart if you will."

"Love him?" echoed Lily. "I hate him. I despise him after this, but why should he marry her?"

"If you feel like that about him, I should have thought the best way to punish him would be to let the marriage proceed; to punish him further you've only to refuse yourself to him when he's married, for I'm quite sure that within six months he'll be writing to say what a mistake he made, how cold his wife is, and how much he longs to come back to you, *la jolie maîtresse de sa jeunesse, le souvenir du bon temps jadis*, and so on with the sentimental eternities of reconstructed passion."

"Live with him after he's married?" Lily exclaimed. "Why, I've never even kissed a married man! I should never forgive myself."

"You don't love him at all, do you?" Sylvia asked, pressing her hands down on Lily's shoulders and forcing her to look straight at her. "Laugh, my dear, laugh! Hurrah! you can't pretend you care a bit about him. Fifty thousand francs and freedom! And just when I was getting bored with Paris."

"It's all very well for you, Sylvia," Lily said, resentfully, as she tried to shake off Sylvia's exuberance. "You don't want to be married. I do. I really looked forward to marrying Michael."

Sylvia's face hardened.

"Oh, I know you blame me entirely for that," she continued. "But it wasn't my fault, really. It was bad luck. It's no good pretending I wasn't fond of Claude. I was, and when I met him—"

"Look here, don't let's live that episode over again in discussion," Sylvia said. "It belongs to the past, and I've always had a great objection to body-snatching."

"What I was going to explain," Lily went on, "was that Michael put the idea of marriage into my head. Then being always with Hector, I got used to being with somebody. I was always treated like a married woman when we went to the seaside or on motoring tours. You always think that because I sit still and say nothing my mind's an absolute blank, but it isn't. I've been thinking for a long time about marriage. After all, there must be something in marriage, or so many people wouldn't get married. You married the wrong man, but I don't believe you'll ever find the right man. You're much, much, much too critical. I *will* get married."

"And now," Sylvia said, with a laugh, "to all the other riddles that torment my poor brain I must add you."

Hector Ozanne tried to stanch Lily's wounded ideals with a generous compress of notes; he succeeded.

"After all," she admitted, twanging the elastic round the bundle. "I'm not so badly off."

"We must buy that silver casket for the letters," Sylvia said. "His wedding-day draws near. I think I shall dress up like the Ancient Mariner and give them to him myself."

"How much will a silver casket cost?" Lily asked.

Sylvia roughly estimated.

"It seems a good deal," said Lily, thoughtfully. "I think I shall just send them to him in a cardboard box. I finished those chocolates after dinner. Yes, that will do quite well. After all, he treated me very badly and to get his letters back safely will be quite a good-enough present. What could he do with a silver casket? He'd probably use it for visiting-cards."

That evening Sylvia, greatly content to have Lily to herself, again took her to the Café de la Chouette.

Her agent, who was drinking in a corner, came across to speak to her.

"Brazil?" she repeated, doubtfully.

"Thirty francs for three songs and you can go home at twelve. It isn't as if you had to sit drinking champagne and dancing all night."

Sylvia looked at Lily.

"Would you like a voyage?"

"We might as well go."

The contract was arranged.

CHAPTER XI

ONE of the habits that Sylvia had acquired on tour in France was card-playing; perhaps she inherited her skill from Henry, for she was a very good player. The game on the voyage was poker. Before they were through the Straits of Gibraltar Sylvia had lost five hundred francs; she borrowed five hundred francs from Lily and set herself to win them back. The sea became very rough in the Atlantic; all the passengers were seasick. The other four poker-players, who were theatrical folk, wanted to stop, but Sylvia would not hear of it; she was much too anxious about her five hundred francs to feel seasick. She lost Lily's first five hundred francs and borrowed five hundred more. Lily began to feel less seasick now, and she watched the struggle with a personal interest. The other players, with the hope that Sylvia's bad luck would hold, were so deeply concentrated upon maintaining their advantage that they too forgot to be seasick. The ship rolled, but the poker-players only left the card-room for meals in the deserted saloon. Sylvia began to win again. Blue skies and calmer weather appeared; the other poker-players had no excuse for not continuing, especially now that it was possible to play on deck. Sylvia had won back all she had lost and two hundred francs besides when the ship entered the harbor of Rio de Janeiro.

"I think I should like gambling," Lily said, "if only one didn't have to shuffle and cut all the time."

The place where Sylvia was engaged to sing was one of those centers of aggregated amusement that exist all over the world without any particular characteristic to distinguish one from another, like the dinners in what are known as first-class hotels on the Continent. Everything here was more expensive than in Europe; even the roulette-boards had zero and double zero to help the bank. The tradition of Brazil for supplying gold and diamonds to the world had bred a familiarity with the external signs of wealth that expressed itself in overjeweled men and women, whose display one forgave more easily on account of the natural splendor of the scene with which they had to compete.

Lily, with the unerring bad taste that nearly always is to be found in sensuous and indolent women, to whom the obvious makes the quickest and easiest appeal, admired the flashing stones and stars and fireflies with an energy that astonished Sylvia, notwithstanding the novel glimpse she had been given of Lily's character in the affair with Hector Ozanne. The climate was hot, but a sea breeze freshened the city after sunset; the enforced day-long inactivity, with the luxurious cool baths and competent negresses who attended upon her lightest movement, satisfied Lily's conception of existence, and when they drove along the margin of the bay before dinner her only complaint was that she could not coruscate like other women in the carriages they passed.

With the money they had in hand Sylvia felt justified in avoiding a *pension d'artistes*, and they had taken a flat together. This meant that when Sylvia went to work at the cabaret, Lily, unless she came with her, was left alone, which did not at all suit her. Sylvia therefore suggested that she should accept an engagement to dance at midnight, with the stipulation that she should not be compelled to stay until 3 A.M. unless she wanted to, and that by foregoing any salary she should not be expected to drink gooseberry wine at 8,000 reis a bottle, on which she would receive a commission of 1,000 reis. The management knew what a charm the tall, fair English girl would exercise over the swart Brazilians, and was glad enough to engage her at her own terms. Sylvia had not counted upon Lily's enjoying the cabaret life so much. The heat was affecting her much more than Lily, and she began to complain of the long hours of what for her was a so false gaiety. Nothing, however, would persuade Lily to go home before three o'clock at the earliest, and Sylvia, on whom a great lassitude and indifference had settled, used to wait for her, sitting alone while Lily danced the *machiche*.

One night, when Sylvia had sung two of her songs with such a sense of hopeless depression weighing her down that the applause which followed each of them seemed to her a mockery, she had a sudden vertigo from which she pulled herself together with a conviction that nothing would induce her to sing the third song. She went on the scene, seated herself at the piano, and to the astonishment and discomfort of the audience and her fellow-players, half chanted, half recited one of the eccentric Englishman's poems about a body in the morgue. Such a performance in such a place created consternation, but in the silence that followed Sylvia fainted. When she came to herself she was back in her own bedroom, with a Brazilian doctor jabbering and mouthing over her symptoms. Presently she was taken to a clinic and, when she was well enough to know what had happened, she learned that she had yellow fever, but that the crisis had passed. At first Lily came to see her every day, but when convalescence was further advanced she gave up coming, which worried Sylvia intensely and hampered her progress. She insisted that something terrible had happened to Lily and worked herself up into such a state that the doctor feared a relapse. She was too weak to walk; realizing at last that the only way of escaping from the clinic would be to get well, she fought against her apprehensions for Lily's safety and after a fortnight of repressed torments was allowed out. When Sylvia reached the flat she was met by the grinning negresses, who told her that Lily had gone to live elsewhere and let her understand that it was with a man.

Sylvia was not nearly well enough to reappear at the cabaret, but she went down that evening and was told by the other girls that Lily was at the tables. They were duly shocked at Sylvia's altered appearance, congratulated her upon having been lucky enough to escape the necessity of shaving her head, and expressed their regrets at not knowing in which clinic she had been staying so that they might have brought her the news of their world. Sylvia lacked the energy to resent their hypocrisy and went to look for Lily, whom she found blazing with jewels at one of the roulette-tables.

There was something so fantastic in Lily's appearance, thus bedecked, that Sylvia thought for a moment it was a feverish vision such as had haunted her brain at the beginning of the illness. Lily wore suspended from a fine chain round her neck a large diamond, one of those so-called blue diamonds of Brazil that in the moonlight seem like sapphires; her fingers flashed fire; a large brooch of rubies in the likeness of a butterfly winked somberly from her black corsage.

Sylvia made her way through the press of gamblers and touched Lily's arm. So intent was she upon the tables that she brushed away the hand as if it had been a mosquito.

"Lily! Lily!" Sylvia called, sharply. "Where have you been? Where have you gone?"

At that moment the wheel stopped, and the croupier cried the number and the color in all their combinations. Sylvia was sure that he exchanged glances with Lily and that the gold piece upon the 33 on which he was paying had not been there before the wheel had stopped.

"Lily! Lily! Where have you been?" Sylvia called, again. Lily gathered in her winnings and turned round. It was curious how changed her eyes were; they seemed now merely like two more rich jewels that she was wearing.

"I'm sorry I've not been to see you," she said. "My dear, I've won nearly four thousand pounds."

"You have, have you?" Sylvia said. "Then the sooner you leave Brazil the better."

Lily threw a swift glance of alarm toward the croupier, a man of almost unnatural thinness, who, while he intoned the invitation to place the stakes, fixed his eyes upon her.

"I can't leave Brazil," she said, in a whisper. "I'm living with him."

"Living with a croupier?" Sylvia gasped.

"Hush! He belongs to quite a good family. He ruined himself. His name is Manuel Camacho. Don't talk to me any more, Sylvia. Go away. He's madly jealous. He wants to marry me."

"Like Hector, I suppose," Sylvia scoffed.

"Not a bit like Hector. He brings a priest every morning and says he'll kill me and himself and the priest, too, if I don't marry him. But I want to make more money, and then I will marry him. I must. I'm afraid of what he'll do if I refuse. Go away from me, Sylvia, go away. There'll be a fearful scene to-night if you will go on talking to me. Last night a man threw a flower into our carriage when we were driving home, and Manuel jumped out and beat him insensible with his cane. Go away."

Sylvia demanded where she was living, but Lily would not tell her, because she was afraid of what her lover might do.

"He doesn't even let me look out of the window. If I look out of the window he tears his clothes with rage and digs his finger-nails into the palms of his hands. He's very violent. Sometimes he shoots at the chandelier."

Sylvia began to laugh. There was something ridiculous in the notion of Lily's leading this kind of lion-tamer's existence. Suddenly the croupier with an angry movement swept a pile of money from the table.

"Go away, Sylvia, go away. I know he'll break out in a moment. That was meant for a warning."

Sylvia understood that it was hopeless to persist for the moment, and she made her way back to the cabaret. The girls were eager to know what she thought of Lily's protector.

"Elle a de la veine, tu sais, la petite Lili. Elle l'a pris comme ça, et il l'aime à la folie. Et elle gagne! mon Dieu, comme elle gagne! Tout va pour elle. Tu sais, elle a des brillants merveilleux. Ça fait riche, tu sais. Y'a pas de chic, mais il est jaloux! Il se porte comme un fou. Ça me raserait, tu sais, être collée avec un homme pareil. Pourtant, elle est busin?use, la petite Lili! Elle ne lui donne pas un rond. Y'a pas de dos vert. Ah, non, elle est la vraie anglaise sans blague. Et le mec, dis, n'est-ce pas qu'il est maigre comme tout? On dirait un squelette."

With all their depreciation of the croupier, it seemed to Sylvia that most of the girls would have been well pleased to change places with Lily. But how was she herself to regard the affair? During those long days of illness, when she had lain hour after hour with her thoughts, to what a failure her life had seemed to be turning, and what a haphazard, harborless course hers had seemed to be. Now she must perhaps jettison the little cargo she carried, or would it be fairer to say that she must decide whether she should disembark it? It was absurd to pretend that Michael would have viewed with anything but dismay the surrender of Lily to such a one as that croupier, and if she made that surrender, she would be violating his trust that counted for so much in her aimless career. Yet was she not attributing to Michael the sentiment he felt before Lily's betrayal of him? He had only demanded of Sylvia that she should prevent Lily from drifting downward along the dull road of undistinguished ruin. If this fantastic Brazilian wished to marry her, why should he not do so? Then she herself should be alone indeed and, unless a miracle happened, should be lost in the eternal whirl of vagabonds to and fro across the face of the earth.

"They say one must expect to be depressed after yellow fever," Sylvia reassured herself. "Perhaps this mood won't last, but, oh, the endlessness of it all! How even one's brush and comb seem weighed down by an interminable melancholy. As I look round me I can see nothing that doesn't strike me as hopelessly, drearily, appallingly superfluous. The very soap in its china dish looks wistful. How pathetic the life of a piece of soap is, when one stops to contemplate it. A slow and steady diminution. Oh, I must do something to shake off this intolerable heaviness!"

The simplest and most direct path to energy and action seemed to be an attempt to interview Camacho, and the following evening Sylvia tried to make Lily divulge her address; but she begged not to be disturbed, and Sylvia, seeing that she was utterly absorbed by the play, had to leave her.

"Either I am getting flaccid beyond belief," she said to herself, "or Lily has acquired an equally incredible determination. I think it's the latter. It just shows what passion will do even for a Lily. All her life she has remained unmoved, until roulette reveals itself to her and she finds out what she was intended for. Of course I must leave her to her fierce skeleton; he represents the corollary to the passion. Queer thing, the way she always wins. I'm sure they're cheating, somehow, the two of them. There's the final link. They'll go away presently to Europe, and Lily will enjoy the sweetest respectability that exists—the one that is founded on early indiscretion and dishonesty—a paradise preceded by the fall."

Sylvia waited by the entrance to the roulette-room on the next night until play was finished, watched Lily come out with Camacho, and saw them get into a carriage and drive away immediately. None of the attendants or the other croupiers knew where Camacho lived, or, if they knew, they refused to tell Sylvia. On the fourth evening, therefore, she waited in a carriage by the entrance and ordered her driver to follow the one in which Lily was. She found that Camacho's apartments were not so far from her own; the next morning she waited at the corner of the street until she saw him come out; then she rang the bell. The negress who opened the door shook her head at the notion of letting Sylvia enter, but the waiting in the sun had irritated her and she pushed past and ran up-stairs. The negress had left the upper door open, and Sylvia was able to enter the flat. Lily was in bed, playing with her jewels as if they were toys.

"Sylvia!" she cried, in alarm. "He'll kill you if he finds you here. He's gone to fetch the priest. They'll be back in a moment. Go away."

Sylvia said she insisted on speaking to Camacho; she had some good advice to give him.

"But he's particularly jealous of you. The first evening you spoke to me ... look!" Lily pointed to the ceiling, which was marked like a die with five holes. "He did that when he came home to show what he would do to you."

"Rubbish!" said Sylvia. "He'll be like a lamb when we meet. If he hadn't fired at the ceiling I should have felt much more alarmed for the safety of my head."

"But, Sylvia," Lily entreated. "You don't know what he's like. Once, when he thought a man nudged me, he came home and tore all the towels to pieces with his teeth. The servant nearly cried when she saw the room in the morning. It was simply covered with bits of towel, and he swallowed one piece and nearly choked. You don't know what he's like. I can manage him, but nobody else could."

Here was a new Lily indeed, who dared to claim that she could manage somebody of whom Sylvia must be afraid. She challenged Lily to say when she had ever known her to flinch from an encounter with a man.

"But, my dear, Manuel isn't English. When he's in one of those rages he's not like a human being at all. You can't soothe him by arguing with him. You have to calm him without talking."

"What do you use? A red-hot poker?"

Lily became agitated at Sylvia's obstinacy, and, regardless of her jewels, which tinkled down into a heap on the floor, she jumped out of bed and implored her not to stay.

"I want to know one or two things before I go," Sylvia said, and was conscious of taking advantage of Lily's alarm to make her speak the truth, owing to the lack of time for the invention of lies.

"Do you love this man?"

"Yes, in a way I do."

"You could be happy married to him?"

"Yes, when I've won five thousand pounds."

"He cheats for you?"

Lily hesitated.

"Never mind," Sylvia went on. "I know he does."

"Oh, my dear," Lily murmured, biting her lip. "Then other people might notice. Never mind. I ought to finish to-night. The boat sails the day after to-morrow."

"And what about me?" Sylvia asked.

Lily looked shamefaced for a moment, but the natural optimism of the gambler quickly reasserted itself.

"I thought you wouldn't like to break your contract."

"My contract," Sylvia repeated, bitterly. "What about—— Oh, but how foolish I am. You dear unimaginative creature!"

"I'm not at all unimaginative," Lily interposed, quickly. "One of the reasons why I want to leave Brazil is because the black people here make me nervous. That's why I left our flat. I didn't know what to do. I was so frightened. I think I'm very imaginative. You got ill. What was I to do?"

She asked this like an accusation, and Sylvia knew that it would be impossible to make her see any other point of view.

"Besides, it was your fault I started to gamble. I watched you on the boat."

"But you were going away without a word to me?" Sylvia could not refrain from tormenting herself with this question.

"Oh no, I was coming to say good-by, but you don't understand how closely he watches me."

The thought of Camacho's jealous antics recurred to Lily with the imminence of his return; she begged Sylvia, now that all her questions were answered, to escape. It was too late; there was a sound of footsteps upon the stairs and the noise of angry voices above deep gobbles of protested innocence from the black servant.

The entrance reminded Sylvia of "Il Barbiere di Siviglia," for when Camacho came leaping into the room, as thin and active as a grasshopper, the priest was holding his coattails with one hand and with the other making the most operatic gestures of despair, like Don Basilio. In the doorway the black servant continued to gobble at everybody in turn, including the Almighty, to witness the clarity of her conscience.

"What language do you speak?" Sylvia asked, sharply, while Camacho was struggling to free himself from the restraint of the priest.

"I speak English! Gaddam! Hell! Five hundred hells!" the croupier shouted. "And I have sweared a swore that you will not interrupt between me myself and my Lili."

Camacho raised his arm to shake his fist, and the priest caught hold of it, which made Camacho turn round and open on him with Portuguese expletives.

"When you've quite done cracking Brazil nuts with your teeth, perhaps you'll listen to me," Sylvia began.

"No, you hear me, no, no, no, no, no, no!" Camacho shouted. "And I will not hear you. I have heard you enough. You shall not take her away. *Putain!*"

"If you want to be polite in French," Sylvia said. "Come along!

"Ce marloupatte pâle et mince
Se nommait simplement Navet,
Mais il vivait ainsi qu'un prince,
Il aimait les femmes qu'on rince.

Tu comprends? Mais moi, je ne suis pas une femme qu'on rince."

It was certainly improbable, Sylvia thought, that the croupier had understood much of Richepin's verse, but the effect of the little recitation was excellent because it made him choke. Lily now intervened, and when Sylvia beheld her soothing the inarticulate Camacho by stroking his head, she abandoned the last faint inclination to break off this match and called upon the priest to marry them at once. No doubt the priest would have been willing to begin the ceremony if he had been able to understand a word of what Sylvia said, but he evidently thought she was appealing to him against Camacho's violence, and with a view to affording the ultimate assistance of which he was capable he crossed himself and turned up his eyes to heaven.

"What an awful noise there is!" Sylvia cried, and, looking round her with a sudden realization of its volume, she perceived that the negress in the doorway had been reinforced by what was presumably the cook—another negress who was joining in her fellow-servant's protestations. At the same time the priest was talking incessantly in rapid Portuguese; Camacho was probably swearing in the same language; and Lily was making a noise that was exactly half-way between a dove cooing and an ostler grooming a horse.

"Look here, Mr. Camacho," Sylvia began.

"Oh, don't speak to him, Sylvia," Lily implored. "He can't be spoken to when he's like this. It's a kind of illness, really."

Sylvia paid no attention to her, but continued to address the croupier.

"If you'll listen to me, Mr. Camacho, instead of behaving like an exasperated toy terrier, you'll find that we both want the same thing."

"You shall not have her," the croupier chattered. "I will shoot everybody before you shall have her."

"I don't want her," Sylvia screamed. "I've come here to be a bridesmaid or a godmother or any other human accessory to a wedding you like to mention. Take her, my dear man, she's yours."

At last Sylvia was able to persuade him that she was not to be regarded as an enemy of his matrimonial intentions, and after a final burst of rage directed against the negresses, whom he ejected from the room, as a housemaid turns a mattress, he made a speech:

"I am to marry Lily. We go to Portugal, where I am not to be a croupier, but a gentleman. I excuse my furage. You grant excusals, yes? It is a decomprehence."

"He's apologizing," Lily explained in the kind of way one might call attention to the tricks of an intelligent puppy.

"She's actually proud of him," Sylvia thought. "But, of course, to her he represents gold and diamonds."

The priest, who had grasped that the strain was being relaxed, began to exude smiles and to rub his hands; he sniffed the prospect of a fee so richly that one seemed to hear the notes crackle like pork. Camacho produced the wedding-ring that was even more outshone than wedding-rings usually are by the diamonds of betrothal.

"But I can't be married in my dressing-gown," Lily protested.

Sylvia felt inclined to say it was the most suitable garment, except a nightgown, that she could have chosen, but in the end, after another discussion, it was decided that the ecclesiastical ceremony should be performed to-morrow in church and that to-day should be devoted to the civil rite. Sylvia promised not to say a word about the departure to Europe.

Three days later Sylvia went on board the steamer to make her farewells. She gave Lily a delicate little pistol for a wedding-present; from Lily, in memory of her marriage, she received a box of chocolates.

It was impossible not to feel lonely, when Lily had gone: in three and a half years they had been much together. For a while Sylvia tried to content herself with the company of the girls in the *pension d'artistes*, to which she had been forced to go because the flat was too expensive for her to live in now. Her illness had swallowed up any money she had saved, and the manager took advantage of it to lower her salary. When she protested the manager told her he would be willing to pay the original salary, if she would go to São Paulo. Though Sylvia understood that the management was trying to get the best of a bargain, she was too listless to care much and she agreed to go. The voyage there was like a nightmare. The boat was full of gaudy negroes who sang endlessly their mysterious songs; the smell was vile; the food was worse; cockroaches swarmed. São Paulo was a squalid reproduction of Rio de Janeiro, and the women who sang in the cabaret were all seamed with ten years' longer vagabondage than those at Rio. The men of São Paulo treated them with the insolence of the half-breeds they all seemed. On the third night a big man with teeth like an ancient fence and a diamond in his shirt-front like a crystal stopper leaned over from a box and shouted to Sylvia to come up and join him when she had finished her songs; he said other things that made her shake with anger. When she left the scene, the grand pimp, who was politely known as the manager, congratulated Sylvia upon her luck: she had caught the fancy of the richest patron.

"You don't suppose I'm going to see that *goujat* in his box?" she growled.

The grand pimp was in despair. Did she wish to drive away their richest patron? He would probably open a dozen bottles of champagne. He might ... the grand pimp waved his arms to express mental inability to express all the splendors within her grasp. Presently the impatient suitor came behind the scene to know the reason of Sylvia's delay. He grasped her by the wrist and tried to drag her up to his box. She seized the only weapon in reach—a hand-glass—and smashed it against his face. The suitor roared; the grand pimp squealed; Sylvia escaped to the stage, which was almost flush with the main dancing-hall. She forced her way through the orchestra, kicking the instruments right and left, and fell into the arms of a man more resplendent than the rest, but a *rastaquouère* of more Parisian cut, who in a dago-American accent promised to plug the first guy that tried to touch her.

Sylvia felt like Carmen on the arm of the Toreador when she and her protector walked out of the cabaret. He was a youngish man, wearing a blue serge suit and high-heeled shoes half buckskin, half patent-leather, tied with white silk laces, so excessively American in shape that one looked twice to be sure he was not wearing them on the wrong feet. His trousers, after exhausting the ordinary number of buttons in front, prolonged themselves into a kind of corselet that drew attention to the slimness of his waist. He wore a frilled white shirt sown with blue hearts and a white silk tie with a large diamond pin. The back of his neck was shaved, which gave his curly black hair the look of a wig. He was the Latin dandy after being operated upon in an American barber shop, and his name was Carlos Morera.

Sylvia noted his appearance in such detail, because the appearance of anybody after that monster in the box would have come as a relief and a diversion. Morera had led her to a bar that opened out of the cabaret, and after placing two automatic pistols on the counter he ordered champagne cocktails for them both.

"He won't come after you in here. Dat stiff don't feel he would like to meet Carlos Morera. Say, do you know why? Why, because Carlos Morera's ready to plug any stiff dat don't happen to suit his fancy right away. Dat's me, Carlos Morera. I'm pretty rich, I am. I'm a gentleman, I am. But dat ain't going to stop me using those"; he indicated the pistols. "Drink up and let's have another. Don't you want to drink? See here, then." He poured Sylvia's cocktail on the floor. "Nothing won't stop Carlos Morera if he wants to call another round of drinks. Two more champagne cocktails!"

"Is this going to be my Manuel?" Sylvia asked herself. She felt at the moment inclined to let him be anything rather than go back to the concert and face that man in the box.

"You're looking some white," Morera commented. "I believe he scared you. I believe I ought to have shot him. Say, you sit here and drink up. I t'ink I'll go back and shoot him now. I sha'n't be gone long."

"Sit still, you fire-eater," cried Sylvia, catching hold of his arm.

"Say, dat's good. Fire-eater! Yes, I believe I'd eat fire if it came to it. I believe you could make me laugh. I'm going to Buenos Aires to-morrow. Why don't you come along of me? This São Paulo is a bum Brazilian town. You want to see the Argentine. I'll show you lots of life."

"Look here," said Sylvia. "I don't mind coming with you to make you laugh and to laugh myself, but that's all. Understand?"

"Dat's all right," Carlos agreed. "I'm a funny kind of a fellow, I am. As soon as I found I could buy any girl I wanted, I didn't seem to want them no more. 'Sides, I've got seven already. You come along of me. I'm good company, I am. Everybody dat goes along of me laughs and has good fun. Hear that?"

He jingled the money in his pocket with a joyful reverence, as if he were ringing a sanctus-bell. "Now, you come back with me into the cabaret."

Sylvia hesitated.

"Don't you worry. Nobody won't dare to look at you when you're with me."

Morera put her arm in his, and back they walked into the cabaret again, more than ever like Carmen with her Toreador. The grand pimp, seeing that Sylvia was safely protected, came forward with obeisances and apologies.

"See here. Bring two bottles of champagne," Morera commanded.

The grand pimp beckoned authoritatively to a waiter, but Morera stood up in a fury.

"I didn't tell you to bring a waiter. I told you to bring two bottles of champagne. Bring them yourself."

The grand pimp returned very meekly with the bottles.

"Dat's more like. Draw the cork of one."

The grand pimp asked if he should put the other on ice.

"Don't you worry about the other," said Morera. "The other's only there so I can break it on your damned head in case I get tired of looking at you. See what I mean?"

The grand pimp professed the most perfect comprehension.

"Well, this is a bum place," Morera declared, after they had sat for a while. "I believe we sha'n't get no fun here. Let's quit."

He drove her back to the pension, and the next day they took ship to La Plata for Buenos Aires.

Morera insisted on Sylvia's staying at an expensive hotel and was very anxious for her to buy plenty of new evening frocks.

"I've got a fancy," he explained, "to show you a bit of life. You hadn't seen life before you came to Argentina."

The change of air had made Sylvia feel much better, and when she had fitted herself out with new clothes, to which Morera added a variety of expensive and gaudy jewels, she felt quite ready to examine life under his guidance.

He took her to one or two theaters, to the opera, and to the casinos; then one evening he decided upon a special entertainment of which he made a secret.

"I want you to dress yourself up fine to-night," he said. "We're going to some smart ball. Put on all your jewelry. I'm going to dress up smart, too."

Sylvia had found that overdressing was the best way of returning his hospitality; this evening she determined to surpass all previous efforts.

"Heavens!" she ejaculated, when she made the final survey of herself in the looking-glass. "Do I look more like a Christmas tree or a chemist's shop?"

When she joined Morera in the lounge, she saw that he was in evening dress, with diamonds wherever it was possible to put them.

"You're fine," he said, contentedly. "Dat's the way I like to see a goil look. I guess we're going to have lots of fun to-night."

They drank a good deal of champagne at dinner, and about eleven o'clock went out to their carriage. When the coachman was given the address of the ballroom, he looked round in surprise and was sworn at for his insolence, so with a shrug of the shoulders he drove off. They left the ordinary centers of amusement behind them and entered a meaner quarter where half-breeds and negroes predominated; at last after a very long drive they pulled up before what looked like a third-rate saloon. Sylvia hesitated before she got out; it did not seem at all a suitable environment for their conspicuous attire.

"We shall have lots of fun," Morera promised. "This is the toughest dancing-saloon in Buenos Aires."

"It looks it," Sylvia agreed.

They entered a vestibule that smelt of sawdust, niggers, and raw spirits, and went up-stairs to a crowded hall that was thick with tobacco smoke and dust. A negro band was playing ragtime in a corner; all along one side of the hall ran a bar. The dancers were a queer medley. The men were mostly of the Parisian apache type, though naturally more swarthy; the women were mostly in black dresses, with shawls of brilliantly colored silk and tawdry combs in their black hair. There were one or two women dancing in coat and skirt and hat, whose lifted petticoats and pale, dissolute faces shocked even Sylvia's masculine tolerance; there was something positively evil in their commonplace attire and abandoned motion; they were like anemic shop-girls possessed with unclean spirits.

"I believe we shall make these folks mad," said Morera, with a happy chuckle. Before Sylvia could refuse he had taken her in his arms and was dancing round the room at double time. The cracked mirrors caught their reflections as they swept round, and Sylvia realized with a shock the amount of diamonds they were wearing between them and the effect they must be having in this thieves' kitchen.

"Some of these guys are looking mad already," Morera proclaimed, enthusiastically.

The dance came to an end, and they leaned back against the wall exhausted. Several men walked provocatively past, looking Sylvia and her partner slowly up and down.

"Come along of me," Morera said. "We'll promenade right around the hall."

He put her arm in his and swaggered up and down. The other dancers were gathering in knots and eyeing them menacingly. At last an enormous American slouched across the empty floor and stood in their path.

"Say, who the hell are you, anyway?" he asked.

"Say, what the hell's dat to you?" demanded Morera.

"Quit!" bellowed the American.

Morera fired without taking his hand from his pocket, and the American dropped.

"Hands up! *Manos arriba!*" cried Morera, pulling out his two pistols and covering the dancers while he backed with Sylvia toward the entrance. When they were up-stairs in the vestibule he told her to look if the carriage were at the door; when he heard that it was not he gave a loud whoop of exultation.

"I said I believed we was going to have lots of fun. We got to run now and see if any of those guys can catch us."

He seized Sylvia's arm, and they darted down the steps and out into the street. Morera looked rapidly right and left along the narrow thoroughfare. They could hear the noise of angry voices gathering in the vestibule of the saloon.

"This way and round the turning," he cried, pulling Sylvia to the left. There was only one window alight in the narrow alley up which they had turned, a dim orange stain in the darkness. Morera hammered on the door as their pursuers came running round the corner. Two or three shots were fired, but before they were within easy range the door had opened and they were inside. The old hag who had opened it protested when she saw Sylvia, but Morera commanded her in Spanish to bolt it, and she seemed afraid to disobey. Somewhere in a distant part of the house there was a sound of women's crooning; outside they could hear the shuffling of their pursuers' feet.

"Say, this is fun," Morera chuckled. "We've arrived into a *burdel*."

It was impossible for Sylvia to be angry with him, so frank was he in his enjoyment of the situation. The old woman, however, was very angry indeed, for the pursuers were banging upon her door and she feared a visit from the police. Her clamor was silenced with a handful of notes.

"Champagne for the girls," Morera cried.

For Sylvia the evening had already taken on the nature of a dream, and she accepted the immediate experience as only one of an inconsequent procession of events. Having attained this state of mind, she saw nothing unusual in sitting down with half a dozen women who clung to their sofas as sea-anemones to the rocks of an aquarium. She had a fleeting astonishment that they should have names, that beings so utterly indistinguishable should be called Juanilla or Belita or Tula or Lola or Maruca, but the faint shock of realizing a common humanity passed off almost at once, and she found herself enjoying a conversation with Belita, who spoke a few words of broken French. With the circulation of the champagne the women achieved a kind of liveliness and examined Sylvia's jewels with murmurs of admiration. The ancient bawd who owned them proposed a dance, to which Morera loudly agreed. The women whispered and giggled among themselves, looking bashfully over their shoulders at Sylvia in a way that made the crone thump her stick on the floor with rage. She explained in Spanish the cause of their hesitation.

"They don't want to take off their clothes in front of you," Morera translated to Sylvia, with apologies for such modesty from women who no longer had the right to possess even their own emotions; nevertheless, he suggested that they might be excused to avoid spoiling a jolly evening.

"Good heavens! I should think so!" Sylvia agreed.

Morera gave a magnanimous wave of his arm, in which he seemed to confer upon the women the right to keep on their clothes. They clapped their hands and laughed like children. Soon to the sound of castanets they wriggled their bodies in a way that was not so much suggestive of dancing as of flea-bites. A lamp with a tin reflector jarred fretfully upon a shelf, and the floor creaked.

Suddenly Morera held up his hand for silence. The knocking on the street door was getting louder. He asked the old woman if there was any way of getting out at the back.

"Dat's all right, kid," he told Sylvia. "We can crawl over the dooryards at the back. Dat door in front ain't going to hold not more than five minutes."

He tore the elastic from a bundle of notes and scattered them in the air like leaves; the women pounced upon the largesse and were fighting with one another on the floor when Sylvia and Morera followed the old woman to the back door and out into a squalid yard.

How they ever surmounted the various walls and crossed the various yards they encountered Sylvia could never understand. All she remembered was being lifted on packing-cases and dust-bins, of slipping once and crashing into a hen-coop, of tearing her dress on some broken glass, of riding astride walls and pricking her face against plants, and of repeating to herself all the time, "When lilacs last in the dooryard bloomed." When at last they extricated themselves from the maze of dooryards they wandered for a long time through a maze of narrow streets. Sylvia had managed to stuff all her jewelry out of sight into her corsage, where it scratched her most uncomfortably, but any discomfort was preferable to the covetous eyes of the half-breeds that watched her from the shadows.

"I guess you enjoyed yourself," said Morera, in a satisfied voice, when at last they found a carriage and leaned back to breathe the gentle night air.

"I enjoyed myself thoroughly," said Sylvia.

"Dat's the way to see a bit of life," he declared. "What's the good of sitting in a bum theater all the night? Dat don't amuse me any. I plugged him in the leg," he added, in a tone of almost tender reminiscence.

Sylvia expressed surprise at his knowing where he had hit him, and Morera was very indignant at the idea of her supposing that he should shoot a man without knowing exactly at what part of him he was aiming and where he should hit him.

"Why, I might have killed him dead," he added. "I didn't want to kill a man dead just for a bit of fun. I started them guys off, see. They thought they'd got a slob. Dat's where I was laughing. I guess I'll sleep good to-night."

Sylvia spent a month seeing life with Carlos Morera; though she never had another experience so exciting as the first, she passed a good deal of her time upon the verge of melodramatic adventure. She grew fond of this child-like creature with his spendthrift ostentation and bravado. He never showed the least sign of wanting to make love to her, and demanded nothing from Sylvia but overdressing and admiration of his exploits. At the end of the month he told Sylvia that business called him to New York and invited her to come with him. He let her understand, however, that now he wanted her as his mistress. Even if she could have tolerated the idea, Sylvia was sure that from the moment she accepted such a position he would begin to despise her. She had heard too many of his contemptuous references to the women he had bought. She refused to accompany him, on the plea of wanting to go back to Europe. Morera looked sullen, and she had a feeling that he was regretting the amount he had spent upon her. Her pride found such a sensation insupportable and she made haste to return him all his jewels.

"Say, what sort of a guy do you think I am?" He threw the jewels at her feet and left her like a spoiled child.

An hour or two later he came back with a necklace that must have cost five thousand dollars.

"Dat's the sort of guy I am," he said, and would take no refusal from her to accept it.

"You can't go on spending money for nothing like this," Sylvia protested.

"I got plenty, ha'n't I?" he asked.

She nodded.

"And I believe it's my money, ain't it?" he continued.

She nodded again.

"Well, dat finishes dat argument right away. Now I got another proposition. You listening? I got a proposition dat we get married. I believe I 'ain't met no girl like you. I know you've been a cabaret girl. Dat don't matter a cent to me. You're British. Well, I've always had a kind of notion I'd like to marry a British girl. Don't you tink I'm always the daffy guy you've bummed around with in Buenos Aires. You saw me in dat dancing-saloon? Well, I guess you know what I can do. Dat's what I am in business. Say, Sylvia, will you marry me?"

She shook her head.

"My dear old son, it wouldn't work for you or for me."

"I don't see how you figure dat out."

"I've figured it out to seventy times seven. It wouldn't do. Not for another mad month even. Come, let's say good-by. I want to go to Europe. I'm going to have a good time. It'll be you that's going to give it to me. My dear old Carlos, you may have spent your money badly from your point of view, but you haven't really. You never spent any money better in all your life."

Morera did not bother her any more. With all his exterior foolishness he had a very deep perception of individual humanity. There was a boat sailing for Marseilles in a day or two, and he bought a ticket for Sylvia.

"It's a return ticket," he told her. "It's good for a year."

She assured him that even if she came back it could never be to marry him, but he insisted upon her keeping it, and to please him she yielded.

Sylvia left the Argentine worth nearly as much as Lily when she went away from Brazil, and as if her luck was bent upon an even longer run, she gained heavily at poker all the way back across the Atlantic.

When she reached Marseilles, Sylvia conceived a longing to meet Valentine again, and she telegraphed to Elène at Brussels for her address. It was with a quite exceptional anticipation that Sylvia asked the *concierge* if Madame Lataille was in. While she walked up-stairs to her sister's apartment she remembered how she had yearned to be friends with Valentine nearly thirteen years ago, forgetting all about the disappointment of her hope in a sudden desire to fill up a small corner of her present loneliness.

Valentine had always lingered in Sylvia's imagination as a rather wild figure, headstrong to such a pitch where passion was concerned that she herself had always felt colorless and insignificant in comparison. There was something splendidly tropical about Valentine as she appeared to Sylvia's fancy; in all the years after she quitted France she had cherished a memory of Valentine's fiery anger on the night of her departure as something nobly independent.

Like other childish memories, Sylvia found Valentine much less impressive when she met her again—much less impressive, for instance, than Elène, who, though she had married a shopkeeper and had settled down to a most uncompromising and ordinary respectability, retained a ripening outward beauty that made up for any pinching of the spirit. Here was Valentine, scarcely even pretty, who achieved by neatness any effect of personality that she did. She had fine eyes—it seemed impossible for any of her mother's children to avoid them, however dull and inexpressive might have been the father's. Sylvia was thinking of Henry's eyes, but what she had heard of M. Lataille in childhood had never led her to picture him as more remarkable outwardly than her own father.

"Twelve years since we met," Valentine was murmuring, and Sylvia was agreeing and thinking to herself all the time how very much compressed Valentine was, not uncomfortably or displeasingly, but like a new dress before it has blossomed to the individuality of the wearer. There recurred to Sylvia out of the past a likeness between Valentine and Maudie Tilt when Maudie had dressed up for the supper-party with Jimmy Monkley.

When the first reckonings of lapsed years were over there did not seem much to talk about, but presently Sylvia described with much detail the voyage from La Plata to Marseilles, just as, when one takes up a long-interrupted correspondence, great attention is often devoted to the weather at the moment.

"*Alors, vous êtes chanteuse?*" Valentine asked.

"*Oui, je suis chanteuse,*" Sylvia replied.

Neither of the sisters used the second person singular: the conversation, which was desultory, like the conversation of travelers in a railway carriage, ended abruptly as if the train had entered a tunnel.

"*Vous êtes très-bien ici,*" said Sylvia, looking round. The train had emerged and was running through a dull cutting.

"*Oui, je suis très-bien ici,*" Valentine replied.

There was no hostility between the sisters; there was merely a blank, a sundering stretch of twelve years, that dismayed both of them with its tracklessness. Presently Sylvia noticed a photograph upon the wall so conspicuously framed as to justify a supposition that it represented the man who was responsible for Valentine's well-being.

"*Oui, c'est mon amant,*" said Valentine, in reply to the unspoken question.

Sylvia was faced by the problem of commenting satisfactorily upon a photograph. To begin with, it was one of those photographs that preserve the individual hairs of the mustache but eradicate every line from the face. It was impossible to comment on it, and it would have been equally impossible to comment on the original in person. The only fact emerging from the photograph was that in addition to a mustache the subject of it owned a pearl tie-pin; but even of the genuineness of the pearl it was unable to give any assurance.

"Photographs tell one nothing, do they?" Sylvia said, at last. "They're like somebody else's dreams."

Valentine knitted her brows in perplexity.

"Or somebody else's baby," Sylvia went on, desperately.

"I don't like babies," said Valentine.

"*Vraiment on est très-bien ici,*" said Sylvia.

She felt that by flinging an accentuated compliment to the room Valentine might feel her lover was included in the approbation.

"And it's mine," said Valentine, complacently. "He bought it for me. *C'est pour la vie.*"

Passion might be quenched in the slough of habitude; love's pinions might molt like any farm-yard hen's. What was that, when the apartment was hers for life?

"How many rooms have you?" Sylvia asked.

"Besides this one I have a bedroom, a dining-room, a kitchen, and a bath-room. Would you like to see the bath-room?"

When Valentine asked the last question she was transformed; a latent exultation flamed out from her immobility.

"I should love to see the bath-room," said Sylvia. "I think bath-rooms are often the most interesting part of a house."

"But this is an exceptional bath-room. It cost two thousand francs to install."

Valentine led the way to the admired chamber, to which a complicated arrangement of shining pipes gave an orchestral appearance. Valentine flitted from tap to tap. Aretino himself could scarcely have imagined more methods of sprinkling water upon the human body.

"And these pipes are for warming the towels," she explained. It was a relief to find pipes that led a comparatively passive existence amid such a convolution of fountainous activity.

"I thought while I was about it that I would have the tiles laid right up to the ceiling," Valentine went on, pensively. "And you see, the ceiling is made of looking-glass. When the water is very hot, *ça fait drôle, tu sais, on ne se voit plus.*"

It was the first time she had used the second person singular; the bath-room had created in Valentine something that almost resembled humanity.

"Yes," Sylvia agreed. "I suppose that is the best way of making the ceiling useful."

"*C'est pour la vie,*" Valentine contentedly sighed.

"But if he were to marry?" Sylvia ventured.

"It would make no difference," Valentine answered. "I have saved money and with a bath-room like this one can always get a good rent. Everything in the apartment is mine, and the apartment is mine, too."

"*Alors, tu es contente?*" said Sylvia.

"*Oui, je suis contente,*" said Valentine.

"*Elle est jolie, ta salle de bain.*"

"*Oui, elle est jolie comme un amour,*" Valentine assented, with a sweet maternal smile.

They talked of the bath-room for a while when they came back to the boudoir; Sylvia was conscious of displaying the politeness with which one descends from the nursery at an afternoon call.

"*Enfin,*" said Sylvia, "*Je file.*"

"*Tu pars tout de suite de Marseilles?*"

"*Oui, je pars ce soir.*"

She had not really intended to leave Marseilles that evening, but there seemed no reason to stay.

"*C'est dommage que tu n'as pas vu Louis.*"

"*Il s'appelle Louis?*"

"*Oui, il s'appelle Louis. Il est à Lyon pour ses affaires.*"

"*Alors, au revoir, Valentine.*"

"*Au revoir, Sylvie.*"

They hesitated, both of them, to see which would offer her cheek first; in the end they managed to be simultaneous.

"Even the farewell was a stalemate," Sylvia said to herself on the way down-stairs.

She wondered, while she was walking back to her hotel, what was going to be the passion of her own life. One always started out with a dim conception of perfect love, however one might scoff at it openly in self-protection, but evidently it by no means followed that love for a man, let alone perfect love, would ever arrive. Lily had succeeded in inspiring at least one man with love for her, but she had found her own passion in roulette with Camacho tacked to it, inherited like a husband's servant, familiar with any caprice, but jealous and irritable. Valentine had found her grand passion in a bath-room that satisfied even her profoundest maternal instincts. Dorothy had loved a coronet with such fervor that she had been able to abandon everything that could smirch it. Sylvia's own mother had certainly found at thirty-four her grand passion, but Sylvia felt that it would be preferable to fall in love with a bath-room now than wait ten years for a Henry.

Sylvia reached the hotel, packed up her things, and set out to Paris without any definite plans in her head for the future, and just because she had no definite plans and nothing to keep her from sleeping, she could not sleep and tossed about on the *wagon-lit* half the night.

"It's not as if I hadn't got money. I'm amazingly lucky. It's really fantastic luck to find somebody like poor old Carlos to set me up for five years of luxurious independence. I suppose if I were wise I should buy a house in London—and yet I don't want to go back to London. The trouble with me is that, though I like to be independent, I don't like to be alone. Yet with Michael.... But what's the use of thinking about him? Do I actually miss him? No, certainly not. He's nothing more to me than something I might have had, but failed to secure. I'm regretting a missed experience. If one loses somebody like that, it leaves a sense of incompletion. How often does one feel a quite poignant regret because one has forgotten to finish a cup of coffee; but the regret is always for the incomplete moment; it doesn't endure. Michael in a year will have changed; I've changed, also. There is nothing to suggest that if we met again now, we should meet in the same relation, with the same possibility in the background of our intercourse. Then why won't I go back to Mulberry Cottage? Obviously because I have out-lived Mulberry Cottage. I don't want to stop my course by running into a backwater that's already been explored. I want to go on and on until ... yes, until what? I can travel now, if I want to. Well, why shouldn't I travel? If I visit my agent in Paris—and I certainly shall visit him in order to tell him what I think of the management of that damned Casino at Rio—he'll offer me another contract to sing in some outlandish corner of the globe, and if I weren't temporarily independent, I should have to accept it with all its humiliations. Merely to travel would be a mistake I think. I've got myself into the swirl of mountebanks, and somehow I must continue with them. It's a poor little loyalty, but even that is better than nothing. Really, if one isn't tied down by poverty, one can have a very good time, traveling the world as a singer. Or I could live in Paris for a while. I should soon meet amusing people. Oh, I don't know what I want. I should rather like to get hold of Olive again. She may be married by now. She probably is married. She's bound to be married. A superfluity of romantic affection was rapidly accumulating that must have been deposited somewhere by now. I might get Gainsborough out from England to come with me. Come with me, where? It seems a shame to uproot the poor old thing again. She's nearly sixty. But I must have somebody."

When Sylvia reached Paris she visited two trunks that were in a repository. Among other things she took out the volume of Adlington's *Apuleius*.

"Yes, there's no doubt I'm still an ass," she said. "And since the Argentine really a golden ass; but oh, when, when, when shall I eat the rose-leaves and turn into Sylvia again? One might make a joke about that, as the White Knight said, something about Golden and Silver and Argentine."

Thinking of jokes reminded Sylvia of Mr. Pluepott, and thinking of Alice through the looking-glass brought back the Vicar. What a long way off they seemed.

"I can't let go of everybody," she cried. So she telegraphed and wrote urgently to Mrs. Gainsborough, begging her to join her in Paris. While she was waiting for a reply, she discussed projects for the future with her agent, who, when he found that she had some money, was anxious for her to invest a certain amount in the necessary *réclame* and appear at the Folies Bergères.

"But I don't want to make a success by singing French songs with an English accent," Sylvia protested. "I'd as soon make a success by singing without a roof to my mouth. You discouraged me from doing something I really wanted to do. All I want now is an excuse for roaming."

"What about a tour in Spain?" the agent suggested. "I can't get you more than ten francs a night, though, if you only want to sing. Still, Spain's much cheaper than America."

"*Mon cher ami, j'ai besoin du travail pour me distraire.* Ten francs is the wage of a slave, but pocket-money, if one is not a slave."

"*Vous avez de la veine, vous.*"

"*Vraiment?*"

"*Mais oui.*"

"*Peut-être quelqu'un m'a plaqué.*"

He tried to look grave and sympathetic.

"*Salaud,*" she mocked. "*Crois-tu que je t'en dirais. Bigre! je creverais plutôt.*"

She had dropped into familiarity of speech with him, but he, still hopeful of persuading her to intrust a profitable *réclame* to him, continued to treat her formally. Sylvia realized the *arrière pensée* and laughed at him.

"*Je ne suis pas encore en grande vedette, tu sais.*"

He assured her that such a triumph would ultimately come to her, and she scoffed.

"*Mon vieux, si je n'avais pas de la galette, je pourrais crever de faim devant ta porte. Ce que tu me dis, c'est du chic.*"

"Well, will you go to Spain?"

The contract was signed.

A day or two later, when she was beginning to give up hope of getting an answer from Mrs. Gainsborough, the old lady herself turned up at the hotel, looking not a minute older.

"You darling and daring old plesiosaurus," cried Sylvia, seizing her by the hand and twirling her round the vestibule.

"Yes, I am pleased to see you and no mistake," said Mrs. Gainsborough. "But what a tyrant! Well, really, I was in me bed when your telegram came and that boy he knocked like a tiger. Knock—knock! all the time I was trying to slip on me petticoat, which through me being in a regular fluster I put on wrong way up and got me feet all wound up with the strings. Knock—knock! 'Whatever do you think you're doing?' I said when at last I was fairly decent and went to open the door. 'Telegram,' he says, as saucy as brass. 'Telegram?' I said. 'I thought by the row you was making that you was building St. Paul's Cathedral.' 'Wait for the answer?' he said. 'Answer?' I said. 'Certainly not.' Well, there was I with your telegram in one hand and me petticoat slipping down in the other. Then on the top of that came your letter, and I couldn't resist a sight of you, my dearie. Fancy that Lily waltzing off like that. And with a Portuguese. She'll get Portuguese before he's finished with her. Portuguese is what she'll be. And the journey! Well, really, I don't know how I managed. I kept on saying, 'France,' the same as if I was asking a policeman the way to Oxford Circus, and they bundled me about like ... well, really, everybody was most kind. Still when I got to France, it wasn't much use going on shouting 'France' to everybody. However, I met a nice young fellow in the train, and he very thoughtfully assisted me into a cab and ... well, I am glad to see you."

"Now you're coming with me to Spain," Sylvia announced.

"Good land alive! Where?"

"Spain."

"Are you going chasing after Lily again?"

"No, we're going off on our own."

"Well, I may have started on the gad late in life, but I've certainly started now," said Mrs. Gainsborough. "Spain? That's where the Spanish flies come from, isn't it? Well, they ought to be lively enough, so I suppose we shall enjoy ourselves. And how do we get there?"

"By train!"

"Dear land! it's wonderful what they can do nowadays. What relation then is Spain to Portugal exactly? You must excuse my ignorance, Sylvia, but really I'm still all of a fluster. Fancy being bounced out of me bed into Spain. You really are a demon. Fancy you getting yellow fever. You haven't changed color much. Spain! Upon my word I never heard anything like it. We'd better take plenty with us to eat. I knew it reminded me of something. The Spanish Armada! I once heard a clergyman recite the Spanish Armada, though what it was all about I've completely forgotten. There was some fighting in it though. I went with the captain. Well, if he could see me now. You may be sure he's laughing, wherever he is. The idea of me going to Spain."

The idea materialized; that night they drove to the Gare d'Orléans.

CHAPTER XII

THE journey to Madrid was for Mrs. Gainsborough a long revelation of human eccentricity.

"Not even Mrs. Ewings would believe it," she assured Sylvia. "It's got to be seen to be believed. I opened my mouth a bit wide when I first came to France, but France is Peckham Rye if you put it alongside of Spain. When that guard or whatever he calls himself opened our door and bobbed in out of the runnel with the train going full speed and asked for our tickets, you could have knocked me down with a feather. Showing off, that's what I call it. And carrying wine inside of goats! Disgusting I should say. Nice set-out there'd be in England if the brewers started sending round beer inside of sheep. Why, it would cause a regular outcry; but these Spanish seem to put up with everything. I'm not surprised they come round selling water at every station. The cheek of it though, when you come to think about it. Putting wine inside of goats so as to make people buy water. If I'd have been an enterprising woman like Mrs. Marsham, I should have got out at the last station and complained to the police about it. But really the stations aren't fit for a decent person to walk about in. I'm not considered very particular, but when a station consists of nothing but a signal-box and a lavatory and no platform, I don't call it a station. And what a childish way of starting a train—blowing a toy horn like that. More like a school treat than a railway journey. And the turkeys! Now I ask you, Sylvia, would you believe it? Four turkeys under the seat and three on the rack over me head. A regular Harlequinade! And every time anybody takes out a cigarette or a bit of bread they offer it all around the compartment. Fortunately I don't look hungry, or they might have been offended. No wonder England's full of aliens. I shall explain the reason of it when I get home."

The place of entertainment where Sylvia worked was called the Teatro Japonés, for what reason it would have been difficult to say. The girls were, as usual, mostly French, but there were one or two Spanish dancers that, as Mrs. Gainsborough put it, kept one "rum-tum-tumming in one's seat all the time it was going on." Sylvia found Madrid a dull city entirely without romance of aspect, nor did the pictures in the Prado make up for the bull-ring's wintry desolation. Mrs. Gainsborough considered the most remarkable evidence of Spanish eccentricity was the way in which flocks of turkeys, after traveling in passenger-trains, actually wandered about the chief thoroughfares.

"Suppose if I was to go shooing across Piccadilly with a herd of chickens, let alone turkeys, well, it would be a circus, and that's a fact."

When they first arrived they stayed at a large hotel in the Puerta del Sol, but Mrs. Gainsborough got into trouble with the baths, partly because they cost five pesetas each and partly because she said it went to her heart to see a perfectly clean sheet floating about in the water. After that they tried a smaller hotel, where they were fairly comfortable, though Mrs. Gainsborough took a long time to get used to being brought chocolate in the morning.

"I miss my morning tea, Sylvia, and it's no use me pretending I don't. I don't feel like chocolate in the morning. I'd just as lieve have a slice of plum-pudding in a cup. Why, if you try to put a lump of sugar in, it won't sink; it keeps bobbing up like a kitten. And another thing I can't seem to get used to is having the fish after the meat. Every time it comes in like that it seems a kind of carelessness. What fish it is, too, when it does come. Well, they say a donkey can eat thistles, but it would take him all his time to get through one of those fish. No wonder they serve them after the meat. I should think they were afraid of the amount of meat any one might eat, trying to get the bones out of one's throat. I've felt like a pincushion ever since I got to Madrid, and how you can sing beats me. Your throat must be like a zither by now."

It really did not seem worth while to remain any longer in Madrid, and Sylvia asked to be released from her contract. The manager, who had been wondering to all the other girls why Sylvia had ever been sent to him, discovered that she was his chief attraction when she wanted to break the contract. However, a hundred pesetas in his own pocket removed all objections, and she was free to leave Spain.

"Well, do you want to go home?" she asked Mrs. Gainsborough. "Or would you come to Seville?"

"Now we've come so far, we may as well go on a bit farther," Mrs. Gainsborough thought.

Seville was very different from Madrid.

"Really, when you see oranges growing in the streets," Mrs. Gainsborough said, "you begin to understand why people ever goes abroad. Why, the flowers are really grand, Sylvia. Carnations as common as daisies. Well, I declare, I wrote home a post-card to Mrs. Beardmore and told her Seville was like being in a conservatory. She's living near Kew now, so she'll understand my meaning."

They both much enjoyed the dancing in the cafés, when solemn men hurled their sombreros on the dancers' platform to mark their appreciation of the superb creatures who flaunted themselves there so gracefully.

"But they're bold hussies with it all, aren't they?" Mrs. Gainsborough observed. "Upon me word, I wouldn't care to climb up there and swing my hips about like that."

From Seville, after an idle month of exquisite weather, often so warm that Sylvia could sit in the garden of the Alcazar and read in the shade of the lemon-trees, they went to Granada.

"So they've got an Alhambra here, have they?" said Mrs. Gainsborough. "But from what I've seen of the performances in Spain it won't come up to good old Leicester Square."

On Sylvia the Alhambra cast an enchantment more powerful than any famous edifice she had yet seen. Her admiration of cathedrals had always been tempered by a sense of missing most of what they stood for. They were still exercising their functions in a modern world and thereby overshadowed her personal emotions in a way that she found most discouraging to the imagination. The Alhambra, which once belonged to kings, now belonged to individual dreams. Those shaded courts where even at midday the ice lay thick upon the fountains; that sudden escape from a frozen chastity of brown stone out on the terraces rich with sunlight; that vision of the Sierra Nevada leaping against the blue sky with all its snowy peaks; this incredible meeting of East and South and North—to know all these was to stand in the center of the universe, oneself a king.

"What's it remind you of, Sylvia?" Mrs. Gainsborough asked.

"Everything," Sylvia cried. She felt that it would take but the least effort of will to light in one swoop upon the Sierra Nevada and from those bastions storm ... what?

"It reminds me just a tiddly-bit of Earl's Court," said Mrs. Gainsborough, putting her head on one side like a meditative hen. "If you shut one eye against those mountains, you'll see what I mean."

Sylvia came often by herself to the Alhambra; she had no scruples in leaving Mrs. Gainsborough, who had made friends at the pension with a lonely American widower.

"He knows everything," said Mrs. Gainsborough. "I've learned more in a fortnight with him than I ever learned in my whole life. What that man doesn't know! Well, I'm sure it's not worth knowing. He's been in trade and never been able to travel till now, but he's got the world off by heart, as you might say. I sent a p. c. to Mrs. Ewings to say I'd found a masher at last. The only thing against him is the noises he makes with his throat. I gave him some lozenges at first, but he made more noise than ever sucking them, and I had to desist."

Soon after Mrs. Gainsborough met her American, Sylvia made the acquaintance of a youthful guide of thirteen or fourteen years, who for a very small wage adopted her and gave her much entertainment. Somehow or other Rodrigo had managed to pick up a good deal of English and French, which, as he pointed out, enabled him to compete with the older guides who resented his intrusion. Rodrigo did not consider that the career of a guide was worthy of real ambition. For the future he hesitated between being a gentleman's servant and a tobacconist in Gibraltar. He was a slim child with the perfect grace of the young South in movements and in manners alike.

Rodrigo was rather distressed at the beginning by Sylvia's want of appetite for mere sight-seeing; he reproved her indeed very gravely for wasting valuable time in repeating her visits to favorite spots while so many others remained unvisited. He was obsessed by the rapidity with which most tourists passed through Granada, but when he discovered that Sylvia had no intention of hurrying or being hurried, his native indolence blossomed to her sympathy and he adapted himself to her pleasure in sitting idle and dreaming in the sun.

Warmer weather came in February, and Rodrigo suggested that the Alhambra should be visited by moonlight. He did not make this suggestion because it was the custom of other English people to desire this experience; he realized that the Señorita was not influenced by what other people did; at the same time the Alhambra by moonlight could scarcely fail to please the Señorita's passion for beauty. He himself had a passion for beauty, and he pledged his word she would not regret following his advice; moreover, he would bring his guitar.

On a February night, when the moon was still high, Sylvia and Rodrigo walked up the avenue that led to the Alhambra. There was nobody on the summit but themselves. Far down lights flitted in the gipsy quarter, and there came up a faint noise of singing and music.

It was Carnival, Rodrigo explained, and the Señorita would have enjoyed it; but, alas! there were many rascals about on such nights, and though he was armed, he did not recommend a visit. He brought out his guitar; from beneath her Spanish cloak Sylvia also brought out a guitar.

"The Señorita plays? *Maravilloso!*" Rodrigo exclaimed. "But why the Señorita did not inform me to carry her guitar? The hill was long. The Señorita will be tired."

Sylvia opened with one of her old French songs, after which Rodrigo, who had paid her a courteous and critical attention, declared that she had a musician's soul like himself, and forthwith, in a treble that was limpid as the moon, light, unpassionate as the snow, remote as the mountains, he too sang.

"Exquisite," Sylvia sighed.

The Señorita was too kind, and as if to disclaim the compliment he went off into a mad gipsy tune. Suddenly he broke off.

"Hark! Does the Señorita hear a noise of weeping?"

There was indeed a sound of some one's crying, a sound that came nearer every moment.

111

"It is most unusual to hear a sound of weeping in the Alhambra *au clair de la lune*," said Rodrigo. "If the Señorita will permit me, I shall find out the cause."

Soon he came back with a girl whose cheeks glistened with tears.

"She is a dancer," Rodrigo explained. "She says she is Italian, but—" With a shrug of the shoulders he gave Sylvia to understand that he accepted no responsibility for her statement. It was Carnival.

Sylvia asked the new-comer in French what was the matter, but for some time she could only sob without saying a word. Rodrigo, who was regarding her with a mixture of disapproval and compassion, considered that she had reached the stage—he spoke with all possible respect for the Señorita, who must not suppose herself included in his generalization—the stage of incoherence that is so much more frequent with women than with men whose feelings have been upset. If he might suggest a remedy to the Señorita, it would be to leave her alone for a few minutes and continue the interrupted music. They had come here to enjoy the Alhambra by moonlight; it seemed a pity to allow the grief of an unknown dancer to spoil the beauty of the scene, grief that probably had nothing to do with the Alhambra, but was an echo of the world below. It might be a lovers' quarrel due to the discovery of a masked flirtation, a thing of no importance compared with the Alhambra by moonlight.

"I'm not such a philosopher as you, Rodrigo. I am a poor, inquisitive woman."

Certainly inquisitiveness might be laid to the charge of the feminine sex, he agreed, but not to all. There must be exceptions, and with a gesture expressive of tolerance for the weaknesses of womankind he managed to convey his intention of excepting Sylvia from Eve's heritage. Human nature was not all woven to the same pattern. Many of his friends, for instance, would fail to appreciate the Alhambra on such a night, and would prefer to blow horns in the streets.

By this time the grief of the stranger was less noisy, and Sylvia again asked her who she was and why she was weeping. She spoke in English this time; the fair, slim child, for when one looked at her she was scarcely more than fifteen, brightened.

"I don't know where I was," she said.

Rodrigo clicked his tongue and shook his head; he was shocked by this avowal much more deeply than in his sense of locality. Sylvia was puzzled by her accent. The 'w's' were nearly 'v's,' but the intonation was Italian.

"And you're a dancer?" she asked.

"Yes, I was dancing at the Estrella."

Rodrigo explained that this was a cabaret, the kind of place with which the Señorita would not be familiar.

"And you're Italian?"

The girl nodded, and Sylvia, seeing that it would be impossible to extract anything about her story in her present overwrought state, decided to take her back to the pension.

"And I will carry the Señorita's guitar," said Rodrigo. "To-morrow morning at eleven o'clock?" he asked by the gate of Sylvia's pension. "Or would the Señorita prefer that I waited to conduct the *señorita extraviada?*"

Sylvia bade him come in the morning; with a deep bow to her and to the stranger he departed, twanging his guitar. Mrs. Gainsborough, who by this time had reached the point of thinking that her American widower existed only to be oracular, wished to ask his advice about the stranger, and was quite offended with Sylvia for telling her rather sharply that she did not want all the inmates of the pension buzzing round the frightened child.

"Chocolate would be more useful than advice," Sylvia said.

"I know you're very down on poor Mr. Linthicum, but he's a mass of information. Only this morning he was explaining how you can keep eggs fresh for a year by putting them in a glass of water. Now I like a bit of advice. I'm not like you, you great harum-scarum thing."

Mrs. Gainsborough was unable to remain very long in a state of injured dignity; she soon came up to Sylvia's bedroom with cups of chocolate.

"And though you laugh at poor Mr. Linthicum," she said, "it's thanks to him you've got this chocolate so quick, for he talked to the servant himself."

With this Mrs. Gainsborough left the room in high good humor at the successful rehabilitation of the informative widower.

The girl, whose name was Concetta, had long ceased to lament, but she was still very shy, and Sylvia found it extremely difficult at first to reach any clear comprehension of her present trouble. Gradually, however, by letting her talk in her own breathless way, and in an odd mixture of English, French, German, and Italian, she was able to put together the facts into a kind of consecutiveness.

Her father had been an Italian, who for some reason that was not at all clear had lived at Aix-la-Chapelle. Her mother, to whom he had apparently never been married, had been a Fleming. This mother had died when Concetta was about four, and her father had married a German woman who had beaten her, particularly after her father had either died or abandoned his child to the stepmother—it was not clear which. At this point an elder brother appeared in the tale, who at the age of eleven had managed to steal some money and run away. Of this brother Concetta had made an ideal hero. She dreamed of him even now and never came to any town but that she expected to meet him there. Sylvia had asked her how she expected to recognize somebody who had disappeared from her life when she was only six years old, but Concetta insisted that she should know him again. When she said this, she looked round her with an expression of fear and asked if anybody could overhear them. Sylvia assured her that they were quite alone, and Concetta said in a whisper:

"Once in Milano I saw Francesco. Hush! he passed in the street, and I said, 'Francesco,' and he said, 'Concettina,' but we could not speak together more longer."

Sylvia would not contest this assertion, though she made up her mind that it must have been a dream.

"It was a pity you could not speak," she said.

"Yes, nothing but Francesco and Concettina before he was gone. *Peccato! Peccato!*"

Francesco's example had illuminated his sister's life with the hope of escaping from the stepmother, and she had hoarded pennies month after month for three years. She would not speak in detail of the cruelty of her stepmother; the memory of it even at this distance of time was too much charged with horror. It was evident to Sylvia that she had suffered exceptional things and that this was no case of ordinary unkindness. There was still in Concetta's eyes the look of an animal in a trap, and Sylvia felt a rage at human cruelty hammering upon her brain. One read of these things with an idle shudder, but, oh, to behold before one a child whose very soul was scarred. There was more for the imagination to feed upon, because Concetta said that not only was her stepmother cruel, but also her school-teachers and schoolmates.

"Everybody was liking to beat me. I don't know why, but they was liking to beat me; no, really, they was liking it."

At last, and here Concetta was very vague, as if she were seeking to recapture the outlines of a dream that fades in the light of morning, somehow or other she ran away and arrived at a big place with trees in a large city.

"Where, at Aix-la-Chapelle?"

"No, I got into a train and came somewhere to a big place with trees in the middle of a city."

"Was it a park in Brussels?"

She shrugged her shoulders and came back to her tale. In this park she had met some little girls who had played with her; they had played a game of joining hands and dancing round in a circle until they all fell down in the grass. A gentleman had laughed to see them amusing themselves so much, and the little girls had asked her to come with them and the gentleman; they had danced round him and pulled his coat to make him take Concetta. He had asked her whence she came and whither she was going; he was a schoolmaster and he was going far away with all these other little girls. Concetta had cried when they were leaving her, and the gentleman, when he found that she was really alone in this big city, had finally been persuaded to take her with him. They went far away in the train to Dantzic, where he had a school to learn dancing. She had been happy there; the master was very kind. When she was thirteen she had gone with the other girls from the school to dance in the ballet at La Scala in Milan, but before that she had danced at Dresden and Munich. Then about six months ago a juggler called Zozo had wanted her and another girl to join his act. He was a young man; she had liked him and she had left Milan with him. They had performed in Rome and Naples and Bari and Palermo. At Palermo the other girl had gone back to her home in Italy, and Concetta had traveled to Spain with Zozo through Tunis and Algiers and Oran. Zozo had treated her kindly until they came here to the Estrella Concert; but here he had changed and, when she did not like him to make love to her, he had beaten her. To-night before they went to the cabaret he had told her that unless she would let him love her he would throw the daggers at her heart. In their act she was tied up and he threw daggers all round her. She had been frightened, and when he went to dress she had run away; but the streets were full of people in masks, and she had lost herself.

Sylvia looked at this child with her fair hair, who but for the agony and fear in her blue eyes would have been like one of those rapturous angels in old Flemish pictures. Here she sat, as ten years ago Sylvia had sat in the cab-shelter talking to Fred Organ. Her story and Concetta's met at this point in man's vileness.

"My poor little thing, you must come and live with me," cried Sylvia, clasping Concetta in her arms. "I too am all alone, and I should love to feel that somebody was dependent on me. You shall come with me to England. You're just what I've been looking for. Now I'm going to put you to bed, for you're worn out."

"But he'll come to find me," Concetta gasped, in sudden affright. "He was so clever. On the program you can read. ZOZO: *el mejor prestigitador del mundo*. He knows everything."

"We must introduce him to Mrs. Gainsborough. She likes encyclopedias with pockets."

"Please?"

"I was talking to myself. My dear, you'll be perfectly safe here with me from the greatest magician in the world."

In the end she was able to calm Concetta's fears; in sleep, when those frightened eyes were closed, she seemed younger than ever, and Sylvia brooded over her by candle-light as if she were indeed her child.

Mrs. Gainsborough, on being told next morning Concetta's story and Sylvia's resolve to adopt her, gave her blessing to the plan.

"Mulberry Cottage'll be nice for her to play about in. She'll be able to dig in the garden. We'll buy a bucket and spade. Fancy, what wicked people there are in this world. But I blame her stepmother more than I do this Shoushou."

Mrs. Gainsborough persisted in treating Concetta as if she were about nine years old and was continually thinking of toys that might amuse her. When at last she was brought to realize that she was fifteen, she was greatly disappointed on behalf of Mr. Linthicum, to whom she had presented Concetta as an infant prodigy.

"He commented so much on the languages she could speak, and he told her of a quick way to practise elemental American, which I always thought was the same as English, but apparently it's not. It's a much older language, really, and came over with Christopher Columbus in the *Mayflower*."

Rodrigo was informed by Sylvia that henceforth the Señorita Concetta would live with her. He expressed no surprise and accepted with a charming courtliness the new situation at the birth of which he had presided. Sylvia thought it might be prudent to take Rodrigo so far into her confidence as to give him a hint about a possible attempt by the juggler to get Concetta back into his power. Rodrigo looked very serious at the notion, and advised the Señorita to leave

Granada quickly. It was against his interest to give this counsel, for he should lose his Señorita, the possession of whom had exposed him to a good deal of envy from the other guides. Besides, he had grown fond of the Señorita and he should miss her. He had intended to practise much on his guitar this spring, and he had looked forward to hearing the nightingales with her; they would be singing next month in the lemon-groves. Many people were deaf to the song of birds, but personally he could not listen to them without ... a shrug of the shoulders expressed the incommunicable emotion.

"You shall come with us, Rodrigo."

"To Gibraltar?" he asked, quickly, with flashing eyes.

"Why not?" said Sylvia.

He seized her hand and kissed it.

"*El destino,*" he murmured. "I shall certainly see there the tobacco-shop that one day I shall have."

For two or three days Rodrigo guarded the pension against the conjuror and his spies. By this time between Concetta's apprehensions and Mrs. Gainsborough's exaggeration of them, Zozo had acquired a demoniac menace, lurking in the background of enjoyment like a child's fear.

The train for Algeciras would leave in the morning at four o'clock. It was advisable, Rodrigo thought, to be at the railway station by two o'clock at the latest; he should come with a carriage to meet them. Would the Señorita excuse him this evening, because his mother—he gave one of his inimitable shrugs to express the need of sometimes yielding to maternal fondness—wished him to spend his last evening with her.

At two o'clock next morning Rodrigo had not arrived, but at three a carriage drove up and the coachman handed Sylvia a note. It was in Spanish to say that Rodrigo had met with an accident and that he was very ill. He kissed the Señorita's hand. He believed that he was going to die, which was his only consolation for not being able to go with her to Gibraltar; it was *el destino*; he had brought the accident on himself.

Sylvia drove with Mrs. Gainsborough and Concetta to the railway station. When she arrived and found that the train would not leave till five, she kept the coachman and, after seeing her companions safely into their compartment, drove to where Rodrigo lived.

He was lying in a hovel in the poorest part of the city. His mother, a ragged old woman, was lamenting in a corner; one or two neighbors were trying to quiet her. On Sylvia's arrival they all broke out in a loud wail of apology for the misfortune that had made Rodrigo break his engagement. Sylvia paid no attention to them, but went quickly across to the bed of the sick boy. He opened his eyes and with an effort put out a slim brown arm and caught hold of her hand to kiss it. She leaned over and kissed his pale lips. In a very faint voice, hiding his head in the pillow for shame, he explained that he had brought the accident on himself by his boasting. He had boasted so much about the tobacco-shop and the favor of the Señorita that an older boy, another guide, a—he tried to shrug his shoulders in contemptuous expression of this older boy's inferior quality, but his body contracted in a spasm of pain and he had to set criticism on one side. This older boy had hit him out of jealousy, and, alas! Rodrigo had lost his temper and drawn a knife, but the other boy had stabbed first. It was *el destino* most unhappily precipitated by his own vainglory.

Sylvia turned to the women to ask what could be done. Their weeping redoubled. The doctor had declared it was only a matter of hours; the priest had given unction. Suddenly Rodrigo with a violent effort clutched at Sylvia's hand:

"Señorita, the train!"

He fell back dead.

Sylvia left money for the funeral; there was nothing more to be done. In the morning twilight she went down the foul stairs and back to the carriage that seemed now to smell of death.

When she arrived at the station a great commotion was taking place on the platform, and Mrs. Gainsborough appeared, surrounded by a gesticulating crowd of porters, officials, and passengers.

"Sylvia! Well, I'm glad you've got here at last. She's gone. He's whisked her away. And can I explain what I want to these Spanish idiots? No. I've shouted as hard as I could, and they *won't* understand. They *won't* understand me. They don't want to understand, that's my opinion."

With which Mrs. Gainsborough sailed off again along the platform, followed by the crowd, which, in addition to arguing with her occasionally, detached from itself small groups to argue furiously with one another about her incomprehensible desire. Sylvia extricated their luggage from the compartment, for the train to go to Algeciras without them; then she extricated Mrs. Gainsborough from the general noise and confusion that was now being added to by loud whistles from the impatient train.

"I was sitting in one corner and Concertina was sitting in the other," Mrs. Gainsborough explained to Sylvia. "I'd just bobbed down to pick up me glasses when I saw that Shoushou beckoning to her, though for the moment I thought it was the porter. Concertina went as white as paper. 'Here,' I hollered, 'what are you doing?' and with that I got up from me place and tripped over *your* luggage and came down bump on the foot-warmer. When I got up she was gone. Depend upon it, he'd been watching out for her at the station. As soon as I could get out of the carriage I started hollering, and every one in the station came running round to see what was the matter. I tried to tell them about Shoushou, and they pretended—for don't you tell me I can't make myself understood if people want to understand— they pretended they thought I was asking whether I was in the right train. When I hollered 'Shoushou,' they all started to holler 'Shoushou' as well and nod their heads and point to the train. I got that aggravated, I could have killed them. And then what do you think they did? Insulting I call it. Why, they all began to laugh and beckon to me, and I, thinking that at last they'd found out me meaning, went and followed them like a silly juggins, and where do you think they took me? To the moojeries! what *we* call the ladies' cloak-room. Well, that did make me annoyed, and I started in to tell them what I thought of such behavior. 'I don't want themoojeries,' I shouted. Then I tried to explain by illustrating my meaning. I took hold of some young fellow and said 'Shoushou,' and then I caught hold of a hussy that was laughing, intending to make her Concertina, but the silly little bitch—really it's enough to make any one a bit unrefined—*she* thought I was going to hit her and started in to scream the station-roof down. After that you came along, but of course it was too late."

Sylvia was very much upset by the death of Rodrigo and the loss of Concetta, but she could not help laughing over Mrs. Gainsborough's woes.

"It's all very well for you to sit there and laugh, you great tomboy, but it's your own fault. If you'd have let me bring Mr. Linthicum, this wouldn't have happened. What could I do? I felt like a missionary among a lot of cannibals."

In the end Sylvia was glad to avail herself of the widower's help, but after two days even he had to admit himself beaten.

"And if he says they can't be found," said Mrs. Gainsborough, "depend upon it they can't be found—not by anybody. That man's as persistent as a beggar. When he came up to me this morning and cleared his throat and shook his head, well, then I knew we might as well give up hope."

Sylvia stayed on for a while in Granada because she did not like to admit defeat, but the sadness of Rodrigo's death and the disappointment over Concetta had spoiled the place for her. Here was another of these incomplete achievements that made life so bitter. She had thought for a brief space that the solitary and frightened child would provide the aim that she had so ardently desired. Concetta had responded so sweetly to her protection, had chattered with such delight of going to England and of becoming English; now she had been dragged back. El destino! Rodrigo's death did not affect her so much as the loss of that fair, slim child. His short life had been complete; he was spared forever from disillusionment, and by existing in her memory eternally young and joyous and wise he had spared his Señorita also the pain of disillusionment, just as when he was alive he had always assumed the little bothers upon his shoulders, the little bothers of every-day existence. His was a perfect episode, but Concetta disturbed her with vain regrets and speculations. Yet in a way Concetta had helped her, for she knew now that she held in her heart an inviolate treasure of love. Never again could anything happen like those three months after she left Philip; never again could she treat any one with the scorn she had treated Michael; never again could she take such a cynical attitude toward any one as that she had taken toward Lily. All these disappointments added a little gold tried by fire to the treasure in her heart, and firmly she must believe that it was being stored to some purpose soon to be showered prodigally, ah, how prodigally, upon somebody.

That evening Sylvia had made up her mind to return to England at once, but after she had gone to bed she was awakened by Mrs. Gainsborough's coming into her room and in a choked voice asking for help. When the light was turned on, Sylvia saw that she was enmeshed in a mosquito-net and looking in her nightgown like a large turbot.

"I knew it would happen," Mrs. Gainsborough panted. "Every night I've said to myself, 'It's bound to happen,' and it has. I was dreaming how that Shoushou was chasing me with a butterfly-net, and look at me! Don't tell me dreams don't sometimes come true. Now don't stand there in fits of laughter. I can't get out of it, you unfeeling thing. I've swallowed about a pint of Keating's. I hope I sha'n't come out in spots. Come and help me out. I daren't move a finger, or I shall start off sneezing again. And every time I sneeze I get deeper in. It's something chronic."

"Didn't Linthicum ever inform you how to get out of a mosquito-net that collapses in the middle of the night?" Sylvia asked, when she had extricated the old lady.

"No, the conversation never happened to take a turn that way. But depend upon it, I shall ask him to-morrow. I won't be caught twice."

Sylvia suddenly felt that it would be impossible to return to England yet.

"We must go on," she told Mrs. Gainsborough. "You must have more opportunities for practising what Linthicum has been preaching to you."

"What you'd like is for me to make a poppy-show of myself all over the world and drag me round the Continent like a performing bear."

"We'll go to Morocco," Sylvia cried.

"Don't shout like that. You'll set me off on the sneeze again. You're here, there, and everywhere like a demon king, I do declare. Morocco? That's where the leather comes from, isn't it? Do they have mosquito-nets there too?"

Sylvia nodded.

"Well, the first thing I shall do to-morrow is to ask Mr. Linthicum what's the best way of fastening up a mosquito-net in Morocco. And now I suppose I shall wake up in the morning with a nose like a tomato. Ah, well, such is life."

Mrs. Gainsborough went back to bed, and Sylvia lay awake thinking of Morocco.

Mr. Linthicum came to see them off on their second attempt to leave Granada. He cleared his throat rather more loudly than usual to compete with the noise of the railway, invited them to look him up if they ever came to Schenectady, pressed a book called *Five Hundred Facts for the Waistcoat Pocket* into Mrs. Gainsborough's hands, and waved them out of sight with a large bandana handkerchief.

"Well, I shall miss that man," said Mrs. Gainsborough, settling down to the journey. "He must have been a regular education for his customers, and I shall never forget his recipe for avoiding bunions when mountaineering."

"How's that done?"

"Oh, I don't remember the details. I didn't pay any attention to them, because it's not to be supposed that I'm going to career up Mont Blong at my time of life. No, I was making a reference to the tone of his voice. They may be descended from Indians, but I dare say Adam wasn't much better than a red Indian, if it comes to that."

They traveled to Cadiz for the boat to Tangier. Mrs. Gainsborough got very worried on the long spit of land over which the train passed, and insisted on piling up all the luggage at one end of the compartment in case they fell into the sea, though she was unable to explain her motive for doing this. The result was that, when they stopped at a station before Cadiz and the door of the compartment was opened suddenly, all the luggage fell out on top of three priests that were preparing to climb in, one of whom was knocked flat. Apart from the argument that ensued the journey was uneventful.

The boat from Tangier left in the dark. At dawn Cadiz glimmered like a rosy pearl upon the horizon.

"We're in Trafalgar Bay now," said Sylvia.

But Mrs. Gainsborough, who was feeling the effects of getting up so early, said she wished it was Trafalgar Square and begged to be left in peace. After an hour's doze in the sunlight she roused herself slightly:

"Where's this Trafalgar Bay you were making such a fuss about?"

"We've passed it now," Sylvia said.

"Oh, well, I dare say it wasn't anything to look at. I'm bound to say the chocolate we had this morning does not seem to go with the sea air. They're arguing the point inside me something dreadful. I suppose this boat is safe? It seems to be jigging a good deal. Mr. Linthicum said it was a good plan to put the head between the knees when you felt a bit— well, I wouldn't say seasick—but you know.... I'm bound to say I think he was wrong for once. I feel more like putting my knees up over my head. Can't you speak to the captain and tell him to go a bit more quietly? It's no good racing along like he's doing. Of course the boat jigs. I shall get aggravated in two twos. It's to be hoped Morocco will be worth it. I never got up so early to go anywhere. Was that sailor laughing at me when he walked past? It's no good my getting up to tell him what I think of him, because every time I try to get up the boat gets up with me. It keeps butting into me behind like a great billy-goat."

Presently Mrs. Gainsborough was unable even to protest against the motion, and could only murmur faintly to Sylvia a request to remove her veil.

"Here we are," cried Sylvia, three or four hours later. "And it's glorious!"

Mrs. Gainsborough sat up and looked at the rowboats filled with Moors, negroes, and Jews.

"But they're nearly all of them black," she gasped.

"Of course they are. What color did you expect them to be? Green like yourself?"

"But do you mean to say you've brought me to a place inhabited by blacks? Well, I never did. It's to be hoped we sha'n't be eaten alive. Mrs. Marsham! Mrs. Ewings! Mrs. Beardmore! Well, I don't say they haven't told me some good stories now and again, but—"

Mrs. Gainsborough shook her head to express the depths of insignificance to which henceforth the best stories of her friends would have to sink when she should tell about herself in Morocco.

"Ali Baba and the Forty Thieves," said Mrs. Gainsborough, when they stood upon the quay. "I feel like the widow Twankay myself."

Sylvia remembered her ambition to visit the East, when she herself wore a yashmak in Open Sesame: here it was fulfilling perfectly her most daring hopes.

Mrs. Gainsborough was relieved to find a comparatively European hotel, and next morning after a long sleep she was ready for any adventure.

"Sylvia!" she suddenly screamed when they were being jostled in the crowded bazaar. "Look, there's a camel coming toward us! Did you ever hear such a hollering and jabbering in all your life? I'm sure I never did. Mrs. Marsham and her camel at the Zoo. Tut-tut-tut! Do you suppose Mrs. Marsham ever saw a camel coming toward her in the street like a cab-horse might? Certainly not. Why, after this there's nothing *in* her story. It's a mere anecdote."

They wandered up to the outskirts of the prison, and saw a fat Jewess being pushed along under arrest for giving false weight. She made some resistance in the narrow entrance, and the guard planted his foot in the small of her back, so that she seemed suddenly to crumple up and fall inside.

"Well, I've often said lightly 'what a heathen' or 'there's a young heathen,' but that brings it home to one," said Mrs. Gainsborough, gravely.

Sylvia paid no attention to her companion's outraged sympathy. She was in the East where elderly obese Jewesses who gave false weight were well treated thus. She was living with every moment of rapturous reality the dreams of wonder that the *Arabian Nights* had brought her in youth. Yet Tangier was only a gateway to enchantments a hundredfold more powerful. She turned suddenly to Mrs. Gainsborough and asked her if she could stay here while she rode into the interior.

"Stay here alone?" Mrs. Gainsborough exclaimed. "Not if I know it."

This plan of Sylvia's to explore the interior of Morocco was narrowed down ultimately into riding to Tetuan, which was apparently just feasible for Mrs. Gainsborough, though likely to be rather fatiguing.

A dragoman was found, a certain Don Alfonso reported to be comparatively honest. He was an undersized man rather like the stump of a tallow candle into which the wick has been pressed down by the snuffer, for he was bald and cream-colored, with a thin, uneven black mustache and two nodules on his forehead. His clothes, too, were crinkled like a candlestick. He spoke French well, but preferred to speak English, of which he only knew two words, "all right"; this often made his advice unduly optimistic. In addition to Don Alfonso they were accompanied by a Moorish trooper and a native called Mohammed.

"A soldier, is he?" said Mrs. Gainsborough, regarding the grave bearded man to whose care they were intrusted. "He looks more like the outside of an ironmonger's shop. Swords, pistols, guns, spears. It's to be hoped he won't get aggravated with us on the way. I should look very funny lying in the road with a pistol through my heart."

They rode out of Tangier before a single star had paled in the east, and when dawn broke they were in a wide valley fertile and bright with flowers; green hills rose to right and left of them and faded far away into blue mountains.

"I wish you'd tell that Mahomet not to irritate my poor mule by egging it on all the time," Mrs. Gainsborough said to Don Alfonso, who, realizing by her gestures that she wanted something done to her mount, and supposing by her smile that the elation of adventure had seized her, replied "All right," and said something in Moorish to Mohammed. He at once caught the mule a terrific whack on the crupper, causing the animal to leap forward and leave Mrs. Gainsborough and the saddle in the path.

"Now there's a nice game to play!" said Mrs. Gainsborough, indignantly. "'All right,' he says, and 'boomph'! What's he think I'm made of? Well, of course here we shall have to sit now until some one comes along with a step-ladder. If you'd have let me ride on a camel," she added, reproachfully, to Sylvia, "this wouldn't have occurred. I'm not sitting on myself any more; I'm sitting on bumps like eggs. I feel like a hen. It's all very fine for Mr. Alfonso to go on gabbling, 'All right,' but it's all wrong, and if you'll have the goodness to tell him so in his own unnatural language I'll be highly obliged."

The Moorish soldier sat regarding the scene from his horse with immutable gravity.

"I reckon he'd like nothing better than to get a good jab at me now," said Mrs. Gainsborough. "Yes, I dare say I look very inviting sitting here on the ground. Well, it's to be hoped they'll have the 'Forty Thieves' or 'Aladdin' for the next pantomime at Drury Lane. I shall certainly invite Mrs. Marsham and Mrs. Beardmore to come with me into the upper boxes so as I can explain what it's all about. Mrs. Ewings doesn't like panto, or I'd have taken her too. She likes a good cry when she goes to the theater."

Mrs. Gainsborough was settling down to spend the rest of the morning in amiable reminiscence and planning, but she was at last persuaded to get up and mount her mule again after the strictest assurances had been given to her of Mohammed's good behavior for the rest of the journey.

"He's not to bellow in the poor animal's ear," she stipulated.

Sylvia promised.

"And he's not to go screeching, 'Arrassy,' or whatever it is, behind, so as the poor animal thinks it's a lion galloping after him."

Mrs. Gainsborough was transferring all consideration for herself to the mule.

"And he's to throw away that stick."

This clause was only accepted by the other side with a good deal of protestation.

"And he's to keep his hands and feet to himself, and not to throw stones or nothing at the poor beast, who's got quite enough to do to carry me."

"And Ali Baba's to ride in front." She indicated the trooper. "It gets me on the blink when he's behind me, as if I was in a shooting-gallery. If he's going to be any use to us, *which* I doubt, he'll be more useful in front than hiding behind me."

"All right," said Don Alfonso, who was anxious to get on, because they had a long way to go.

"And that's enough of 'all right' from him," said Mrs. Gainsborough. "I don't want to hear any more 'all rights.'"

At midday they reached a khan, where they ate lunch and rested for two hours in the shade.

Soon after they had started again, they met a small caravan with veiled women and mules loaded with oranges.

"Quite pleasant-looking people," Mrs. Gainsborough beamed. "I should have waved my hand if I could have been sure of not falling off again. Funny trick, wearing that stuff round their faces. I suppose they're ashamed of being so black."

Mrs. Gainsborough's progress, which grew more and more leisurely as the afternoon advanced, became a source of real anxiety to Don Alfonso; he confided to Sylvia that he was afraid the gates of Tetuan would be shut. When Mrs. Gainsborough was told of his alarm she was extremely scornful.

"He's having you on, Sylvia, so as to give Mohamet the chance of sloshing my poor mule again. Whoever heard of a town having gates? He'll tell us next that we've got to pay sixpence at the turnstile to pass in."

They came to a high place where a white stone by the path recorded a battle between Spaniards and Moors. Far below were the domes and rose-dyed minarets of Tetuan and a shining river winding to the sea. They heard the sound of a distant gun.

"Sunset," cried Don Alfonso, much perturbed. "In half an hour the gates will be shut."

He told tales of brigands and of Riffs, of travelers found with their throats cut outside the city walls, and suddenly, as if to give point to his fears, a figure leaning on a long musket appeared in silhouette upon the edge of the hill above them. It really seemed advisable to hurry, and, notwithstanding Mrs. Gainsborough's expostulations, the speed of the party was doubled down a rocky descent to a dried-up watercourse with high banks. Twilight came on rapidly and the soldier prepared one of his numerous weapons for immediate use in an emergency. Mrs. Gainsborough was much too nervous about falling off to bother about brigands, and at last without any mishap they reached the great castellated gate of Tetuan. It was shut.

"Well, I never saw the like," said Mrs. Gainsborough. "It's true, then. We must ring the bell, that's all."

The soldier, Mohammed, and Don Alfonso raised their voices in a loud hail, but nobody paid any attention, and the twilight deepened. Mrs. Gainsborough alighted from her mule and thumped at the iron-studded door. Silence answered her.

"Do you mean to tell me seriously that they're going to keep us outside here all night? Why, it's laughable!" Suddenly she lifted her voice and cried, "Milk-ho!" Whether the unusual sound aroused the curiosity or the alarm of the porter within was uncertain, but he leaned his head out of a small window above the gate and shouted something at the belated party below. Immediately the dispute for which Mohammed and Don Alfonso had been waiting like terriers on a leash was begun; it lasted for ten minutes without any of the three participants drawing breath.

In the end Don Alfonso announced that the porter declined to open for less than two francs, although he had offered him as much as one franc fifty. With a determination not to be beaten that was renewed by the pause for breath, Don Alfonso flung himself into the argument again, splendidly assisted by Mohammed, who seemed to be tearing out his hair in baffled fury.

"I wish I knew what they were calling each other," said Sylvia.

"Something highly insulting, I should think," Mrs. Gainsborough answered. "Wonderful the way they use their hands. He doesn't seem to be worrying himself so very much. I suppose he'll start in shooting in the end."

She pointed to the soldier, who was regarding the dispute with contemptuous gravity. Another window in a tower on the other side of the gate was opened, and the first porter was reinforced. Perspiration was dripping from Don Alfonso's forehead; he looked more like a candle stump than ever, when presently he stood aside from the argument to say that he had been forced to offer one franc seventy-five to enter Tetuan.

"Tetuan," said Mrs. Gainsborough. "Tetuarn't, I should say."

Sylvia asked Don Alfonso what he was calling the porter, and it appeared, though he minimized the insult by a gesture, that he had just invited forty-three dogs to devour the corpse of the porter's grandmother. This, however, he hastened to add, had not annoyed him so much as his withdrawal from one franc fifty to one franc twenty-five.

In the end the porter agreed to open the gate for one franc seventy-five.

"Which is just as well," said Mrs. Gainsborough, "for I'm sure Mohamet would have thrown a fit soon. He's got to banging his forehead with his fists, and that's a very bad sign."

They rode through the darkness between double walls, disturbing every now and then a beggar who whined for alms or cursed them if the mule trod upon his outspread legs. They found an inn called the Hôtel Splendide, a bug-ridden tumble-down place kept by Spanish Jews as voracious as the bugs. Yet out on the roof, looking at the domes and minarets glimmering under Venus setting in the west from a sky full of stars, listening to the howling of distant dogs, breathing the perfume of the East, Sylvia felt like a conqueror.

Next morning Mrs. Gainsborough, finding that the bugs had retreated with the light, decided to spend the morning in sleeping off some of her bruises. Sylvia wandered through the bazaars with Don Alfonso, and sat for a while in the garden of a French convent, where a fountain whispered in the shade of pomegranates. Suddenly, walking along the path toward her she saw Maurice Avery.

Sylvia had disliked Avery very much when she met him in London nearly two years ago; but the worst enemy, the most flagitious bore, is transformed when encountered alone in a distant country, and now Sylvia felt well disposed toward him and eager to share with any one who could appreciate her pleasure the marvel of being in Tetuan. He too, by the way his face lighted up, was glad to see her, and they shook hands with a cordiality that was quite out of proportion to their earlier acquaintance.

"I say, what a queer place to meet!" he exclaimed. "Are you alone, then?"

"I've got Mrs. Gainsborough with me, that's all. I'm not married ... or anything."

It was absurd how eager she felt to assure Avery of this; and then in a moment the topic had been started.

"No, have you really got Mrs. Gainsborough?" he exclaimed. "Of course I've heard about her from Michael. Poor old Michael!"

"Why, what's the matter?" Sylvia asked, sharply.

"Oh, he's perfectly all right, but he's lost to his friends. At least I suppose he is—buried in a monastery. He's not actually a monk. I believe he's what's called an oblate, pursuing the Fata Morgana of faith—a sort of dream...."

"Yes, yes," Sylvia interrupted. "I understand the allusion. You needn't talk down to me."

Avery blushed. The color in his cheeks made him seem very young.

"Sorry. I was thinking of somebody else for the moment. That sounds very discourteous also. I must apologize again. What's happened to Lily Haden?"

Sylvia told him briefly the circumstances of Lily's marriage at Rio. "Does Michael ever talk about her?" she asked.

"Oh no, never!" said Avery. "He's engaged in saving his own soul now. That sounds malicious, but seriously I don't think she was ever more to him than an intellectual landmark. To understand Michael's point of view in all that business you've got to know that he was illegitimate. His father, Lord Saxby, had a romantic passion for the daughter of a country parson—a queer, cross-grained old scholar. You remember Arthur Lonsdale? Well, his father, Lord Cleveden, knew the whole history of the affair. Lady Saxby wouldn't divorce him; so they were never married. I suppose Michael brooded over this and magnified his early devotion to Lily in some way or other up to a vow of reparation. I'm quite sure it was a kind of indirect compliment to his own mother. Of course it was all very youthful and foolish—and yet I don't know...." he broke off with a sigh.

"You think one can't afford to bury the past?"

Avery looked at her quickly. "What made you ask me that?"

"I thought you seemed to admire Michael's youthful foolishness."

"I do really. I admire any one that's steadfast even to a mistaken idea. It's strange to meet an Englishwoman here," he said, looking intently at Sylvia. "One's guard drops. I'm longing to make a confidante of you, but you might be bored. I'm rather frightened of you, really. I always was."

"I sha'n't exchange confidences," Sylvia said, "if that's what you're afraid of."

"No, of course not," Avery said, quickly. "Last spring I was in love with a girl...."

Sylvia raised her eyebrows.

"Oh yes, it's a very commonplace beginning and rather a commonplace end, I'm afraid. She was a ballet-girl—the incarnation of May and London. That sounds exaggerated, for I know that lots of other Jenny Pearls have been the same to somebody, but I do believe most people agreed with me. I wanted her to live with me. She wouldn't. She had sentimental, or what I thought were sentimental, ideas about her mother and family. I was called away to Spain. When my business was finished I begged her to come out to me there. That was last April. She refused, and I was piqued, I suppose, at first, and did not go back to England. Then, as one does, I made up my mind to the easiest thing at the moment by letting myself be enchanted by my surroundings into thinking that I was happier as it was. For a while I was happier; in a way our love had been a great strain upon us both. I came to Morocco, and gradually ever since I've been realizing that I left something unfinished. It's become a kind of obsession. Do you know what I mean?"

"Indeed I do, very well indeed," Sylvia said.

"Thanks," he said with a grateful look. "Now comes the problem. If I go back to England this month, if I arrive in England on the first of May exactly a year later, there's only one thing I can do to atone for my behavior—I must ask her to marry me. You see that, don't you? This little thing is proud, oh, but tremendously proud. I doubt very much if she'll forgive me, even if I show the sincerity of my regret by asking her to marry me now; but it's my only chance. And yet—oh, I expect this will sound damnable to you, but it's the way we've all been molded in England—she's common. Common! What an outrageous word to use. But then it is used by everybody. She's the most frankly cockney thing you ever saw. Can I stand her being snubbed and patronized? Can I stand my wife's being snubbed and patronized? Can love survive the sort of ambushed criticism that I shall perceive all round us? For I wouldn't try to change her. No, no, no! She must be herself. I'll have no throaty 'aws' masquerading as 'o's.' She must keep her own clear 'aou's.' There must not be any 'naceness' or patched-up shop-walker's English. I love her more at this moment than I ever loved her, but can I stand it? And I'm not asking this egotistically: I'm asking it for both of us. That's why you meet me in Tetuan, for I dare not go back to England lest the first cockney voice I hear may kill my determination, and I really am longing to marry her. Yet I wait here, staking what I know in my heart is all my future happiness on chance, assuring myself that presently impulse and reason will be reconciled and will send me back to her, but still I wait."

He paused. The fountain whispered in the shade of the pomegranates. A nun was gathering flowers for the chapel. Outside, the turmoil of the East sounded like the distant chattering of innumerable monkeys.

"You've so nearly reached the point at which a man has the right to approach a woman," Sylvia said, "that if you're asking my advice, I advise you to wait until you do actually reach that point. Of course you may lose her by waiting. She may marry somebody else."

"Oh, I know; I've thought of that. In a way that would be a solution."

"So long as you regard her marriage with somebody else as a solution, you're still some way from the point. It's curious she should be a ballet-girl, because Mrs. Gainsborough, you know, was a ballet-girl. In 1869, when she took her emotional plunge, she was able to exchange the wings of Covent Garden for the wings of love easily enough. In 1869 ballet-girls never thought of marrying what were and are called 'gentlemen.' I think Mrs. Gainsborough would consider her life a success; she was not too much married to spoil love, and the captain was certainly more devoted to her than most husbands would have been. The proof that her life was a success is that she has remained young. Yet if I introduce you to her you'll see at once your own Jenny at sixty like her—that won't be at all a hard feat of imagination. But you'll still be seeing yourself at twenty-five or whatever you are; you'll never be able to see yourself at sixty; therefore I sha'n't introduce you. I'm too much of a woman not to hope with all my heart that you'll go home to England, marry your Jenny, and live happily ever afterward, and I think you'd better not meet Mrs. Gainsborough, in case she prejudices your resolve. Thanks for giving me your confidence."

"Oh no! Thank *you* for listening," said Avery.

"I'm glad you're not going to develop her. I once suffered from that kind of vivisection myself, though I never had a cockney accent. Some souls can't stand straight lacing, just as some bodies revolt from stays. And so Michael is in a monastery? I suppose that means all his soul spasms are finally allayed?"

"O Lord! No!" said Avery. "He's in the very middle of them."

"What I really meant to say was heart palpitations."

"I don't think, really," said Avery, "that Michael ever had them."

"What was Lily, then?"

"Oh, essentially a soul spasm," he declared.

"Yes, I suppose it was," Sylvia agreed, pensively.

"I think, you know, I must meet Mrs. Gainsborough," said Avery. "Fate answers for you. Here she comes."

Don Alfonso, with the pain that every dog and dragoman feels in the separation of his charges, had taken advantage of Sylvia's talk with Avery to bring Mrs. Gainsborough triumphantly back to the fold.

"Here we are again," said Mrs. Gainsborough, limping down the path. "And my behind looks like a magic lantern. Oh, I beg your pardon! I didn't see you'd met a friend. So that's what Alfonso was trying to tell me. He's been going like an alarm-clock all the way here. Pleased to meet you, I'm sure. How do you like Morocco? We got shut out last night."

"This is a friend of Michael Fane's," said Sylvia.

"Did you know *him*? He *was* a nice young fellow. Very nice he was. But he wouldn't know me now. Very stay-at-home I was when he used to come to Mulberry Cottage. Why, he tried to make me ride in a hansom once, and I was actually too nervous. You know, I'd got into a regular rut. But now, well, upon me word, I don't believe now I should say 'no' if any one was to invite me to ride inside of a whale. It's her doing, the tartar."

Avery had learned a certain amount of Arabic during his stay in Morocco and he made the bazaars of Tetuan much more interesting than Don Alfonso could have done. He also had many tales to tell of the remote cities like Fez and Mequinez and Marakeesh. Sylvia almost wished that she could pack Mrs. Gainsborough off to England and accompany him into the real interior. Some of her satisfaction in Tetuan had been rather spoiled that morning by finding a visitor's book in the hotel with the names of traveling clergymen and their daughters patronizingly inscribed therein. However, Avery decided to ride away almost at once, and said that he intended to banish the twentieth century for two or three months.

They stayed a few days at Tetuan, but the bugs were too many for Mrs. Gainsborough, who began to sigh for a tranquil bed. Avery and Sylvia had a short conversation together before they left. He thanked her for her sympathy, held to his intention of spending the summer in Morocco, but was nearly sure he should return to England in the autumn, with a mind serenely fixed.

"I wish, if you go back to London, you'd look Jenny up," he said.

Sylvia shook her head very decidedly. "I can't imagine anything that would annoy her more, if she's the girl I suppose her to be."

"But I'd like her to have a friend like you," he urged.

Sylvia looked at him severely. "Are you quite sure that you don't want to change her?" she asked.

"Of course. Why?"

"Choosing friends for somebody else is not very wise; it sounds uncommonly like a roundabout way of developing her. No, no, I won't meet your Jenny."

"I see what you mean," Avery assented. "I'll write to Michael and tell him I've met you. Shall I tell him about Lily? Where is she now?"

"I don't know. I've never had even a post-card. My fault, really. Yes, you can tell Michael that she's probably quite happy and—no, I don't think there's any other message. Oh yes, you might say I've eaten one or two rose-leaves but not enough yet."

Avery looked puzzled.

"Apuleius," she added.

"Strange girl. I *wish* you would go and see Jenny."

"Oh no! She's eaten all the rose-leaves she wants, and I'm sure she's not the least interested in Apuleius."

Next day Sylvia and Mrs. Gainsborough set out on the return journey to Tangier, which, apart from a disastrous attempt by Mrs. Gainsborough to eat a prickly pear, lacked incident.

"Let sleeping pears lie," said Sylvia.

"Well, you don't expect a fruit to be so savage," retorted Mrs. Gainsborough. "I thought I must have aggravated a wasp. Talk about nettles. They're chammyleather beside them. Prickly pears! I suppose the next thing I try to eat will be stabbing apples."

They went home by Gibraltar, where Mrs. Gainsborough was delighted to see English soldiers.

"It's nice to know we've got our eyes open even in Spain. I reckon I'll get a good cup of tea here."

They reached England at the end of April, and Sylvia decided to stay for a while at Mulberry Cottage. Reading through *The Stage*, she found that Jack Airdale was resting at Richmond in his old rooms, and went down to see him. He was looking somewhat thin and worried.

"Had rather a rotten winter," he told her. "I got ill with a quinsey and had to throw up a decent shop, and somehow or other I haven't managed to get another one yet."

"Look here, old son," Sylvia said, "I don't want any damned pride from you. I've got plenty of money at present. You've got to borrow fifty pounds. You want feeding up and fitting out. Don't be a cad now, and refuse a 'lidy.' Shut up! Shut up! Shut up! You know me by this time. Who's going to be more angry, you at being lent money or me at being refused by one of the few, the very few, mark you, good pals I've got? Don't be a beast, Jack. You've got to take it."

He surrendered, from habit. Sylvia gave him all her news, but the item that interested him most was her having half taken up the stage.

"I knew you'd make a hit," he declared.

"But I didn't."

"My dear girl, you don't give yourself a chance. You can't play hide and seek with the public, though, by Jove!" he added, ruefully, "I have been lately."

"For the present I can afford to wait."

"Yes, you're damned lucky in one way, and yet I'm not sure that you aren't really very unlucky. If you hadn't found some money you'd have been forced to go on."

"My dear lad, lack of money wouldn't make me an artist."

"What would, then?"

"Oh, I don't know. Being fed up with everything. That's what drove me into self-expression, as I should call it if I were a temperamental miss with a light-boiled ego swimming in a saucepan of emotion for the public to swallow or myself to crack. But conceive my disgust! There was I yearning unattainable 'isms' from a soul nurtured on tragic disillusionment, and I was applauded for singing French songs with an English accent. No, seriously, I shall try again, old Jack, when I receive another buffet. At present I'm just dimly uncomfortable. I shall blossom late like a chrysanthemum. I ain't no daffodil, I ain't. Or perhaps it would be truer to say that I was forced when young—don't giggle, you ribald ass, not that way—and I've got to give myself a rest before I bloom, *en plein air*."

"But you really have got plenty of money?" Airdale inquired, anxiously.

"Masses! Cataracts! And all come by perfectly honest. No, seriously, I've got about four thousand pounds."

"Well, I really do think you're rather lucky, you know."

"Of course. But it's all written in the book of Fate. Listen. I've got a mulberry mark on my arm; I live at Mulberry Cottage; and Morera, that's the name of my fairy godfather, is Spanish for mulberry-tree. Can you beat it?"

"I hope you've invested this money," said Airdale.

"It's in a bank."

He begged her to be careful of her riches, and she rallied him on his inconsistency, because a moment back he had been telling her that their possession was hindering her progress in art.

"My dear Sylvia, I haven't known you for five years not to have discovered that I might as well advise a schoolmaster as you, but what *are* you going to do?"

"Plans for this summer? A little gentle reading. A little browsing among the classics. A little theater-going. A little lunching at Verrey's with Mr. John Airdale. Resting address, six Rosetree Terrace, Richmond, Surrey. A little bumming around town, as Señor Morera would say. Plans for the autumn? A visit to the island of Sirene, if I can find a nice lady-like young woman to accompany me. Mrs. Gainsborough has decided that she will travel no more. Her brain is bursting with unrelated adventure."

"But you can't go on from month to month like that."

"Well, if you'll tell me how to skip over December, January, and August I'll be grateful," Sylvia laughed.

"No, don't rag about. I mean for the future in general," he explained. "Are you going to get married? You can't go on forever like this."

"Why not?"

"Well, you're young now. But what's more gloomy than a restless old maid?"

"My dear man, don't you fret about my withering. I've got a little crystal flask of the finest undiluted strychnine. I believe strychnine quickens the action of the heart. Verdict. Death from attempted galvanization of the cardiac muscles. No flowers by request. Boomph! as Mrs. Gainsborough would say. Ring off. The last time I wrote myself an epitaph it led me into matrimony. *Absit omen*."

Airdale was distressed by Sylvia's joking about her death, and begged her to stop.

"Then don't ask me any more about the future in general. And now let's go and be Epicurean at Verrey's."

After Jack Airdale the only other old friend that Sylvia took any trouble to find was Olive Fanshawe. She was away on tour when Sylvia returned to England, but she came back to London in June, was still unmarried, and had been promised a small part in the Vanity production that autumn. Sylvia found that Olive had recaptured her romantic ideals and was delighted with her proposal that they should live together at Mulberry Cottage. Olive took very seriously her small part at the Vanity, of which the most distinguished line was: "Girls, have you seen the Duke of Mayfair? He's awfully handsome." Sylvia was not very encouraging to Olive's opportunities of being able to give an original reading of such a line, but she listened patiently to her variations in which each word was overaccentuated in turn. Luckily there was also a melodious quintet consisting of the juvenile lead and four beauties of whom Olive was to be one; this, it seemed, promised to be a hit, and indeed it was.

The most interesting event for the Vanity world that autumn, apart from the individual successes and failures in the new production, was the return of Lord and Lady Clarehaven to London, and not merely their return, but their re-entry into the Bohemian society from which Lady Clarehaven had so completely severed herself.

"I know it's perfectly ridiculous of me," said Olive, "but, Sylvia, do you know, I'm quite nervous at the idea of meeting her again."

A most cordial note had arrived from Dorothy inviting Olive to lunch with her in Curzon Street.

"Write back and tell her you're living with me," Sylvia advised. "That'll choke off some of the friendliness."

But to Sylvia's boundless surprise a messenger-boy arrived with an urgent invitation for her to come too.

"Curiouser and curiouser," she murmured. "What does it mean? She surely can't be tired of being a countess already. I'm completely stumped. However, of course we'll put on our clean bibs and go. Don't look so frightened. Olive, if conversation hangs fire at lunch, we'll tickle the footmen."

"I really feel quite faint," said Olive. "My heart's going pitter-pat. Isn't it silly of me?"

Lunch, to which Arthur Lonsdale had also been invited, did nothing to enlighten Sylvia about the Clarehavens' change of attitude. Dorothy, more beautiful than ever and pleasant enough superficially, seemed withal faintly resentful; Clarehaven was in exuberant spirits and evidently enjoying London tremendously. The only sign of tension, well not exactly tension, but slight disaccord, and that was too strong a word, was once when Clarehaven, having been exceptionally rowdy, glanced at Dorothy a swift look of defiance for checking him.

"She's grown as prim as a parlor-maid," said Lonsdale to Sylvia when, after lunch, they had a chance of talking together. "You ought to have seen her on the ancestral acres. My mother, who presides over our place like a Queen Turnip, is without importance beside Dolly, absolutely without importance. It got on Tony's nerves, that's about the truth of it. He never could stand the land. It has the same effect on him as the sea has on some people. Black vomit, coma, and death—what?"

"Dorothy, of course, played the countess in real life as seriously as she would have played her on the stage. She was the star," Sylvia said.

"Star! My dear girl, she was a comet. And the dowager loved her. They used to drive round in a barouche and administer gruel to the village without anesthetics."

"I suppose they kept them for Clarehaven," Sylvia laughed.

"That's it. Of course, I shouted when I saw the state of affairs, having first of all been called in to recover old Lady Clarehaven's reason when she heard that her only child was going to wed a Vanity girl. But they loved her. Every frump in the county adored her. It's Tony who insisted on this move to London. He stood it in Devonshire for two and a half years, but the lights of the wicked city—soft music, please—called him, and they've come back. Dolly's fed up to the wide about it. I say, we are a pair of gossips. What's your news?"

"I met Maurice Avery, in Morocco."

"What, Mossy Avery! Not really? Disguised as a slipper, I suppose. Rum bird. He got awfully keen on a little girl at the Orient and tootled her all over town for a while, but I haven't seen him for months. I used to know him rather well at the 'Varsity: he was one of the esthetic push. I say, what's become of Lily?"

"Married to a croupier? Not, really. By Jove! what a time I had over her with Michael Fane's people. His sister, an awfully good sort, put me through a fearful catechism."

"His sister?" repeated Sylvia.

"You know what Michael's doing now? Greatest scream on earth. He's a monk. Some special kind of a monk that sounds like omelette, but isn't. Nothing to be done about it. I buzzed down to see him last year, and he was awfully fed up. I asked him if he couldn't stop monking for a bit and come out for a spin on my new forty-five Shooting Star. He wasn't in uniform, so there's no reason why he shouldn't have come."

"He's in England, now, then?" Sylvia asked.

"No, he got fed up with everybody buzzing down to see what he looked like as a monk, and he's gone off to Chartreuse or Benedictine or somewhere—I know it's the name of a liqueur—somewhere abroad. I wanted him to become a partner in our business, and promised we'd put a jolly little runabout on the market called The Jovial Monk, but he wouldn't. Look here, we'd better join the others. Dolly's got her eye on me. I say," he chuckled, in a whisper, "I suppose you know she's a connection of mine?"

"Yes, by carriage."

Lonsdale asked what she meant, and Sylvia told him the origin of Dorothy's name.

"Oh, I say, that's topping. What's her real name?"

"No, no," Sylvia said. "I've been sufficiently spiteful."

"Probably Buggins, really. I say, Cousin Dorothy," he went on, in a louder voice. "What about bridge to-morrow night after the Empire?"

Lady Clarehaven flashed a look at Sylvia, who could not resist shaking her head and earning thereby another sharper flash. When Sylvia talked over the Clarehavens with Olive, she found that Olive had been quite oblivious of anything unusual in the sudden move to town.

"Of course, Dorothy and I can never be what we were to each other; but I thought they seemed so happy together. I'm so glad it's been such a success."

"Well, has it?" said Sylvia, doubtfully.

"Oh yes, my dear! How can you imagine anything else?"

With the deepening of winter Olive fell ill and the doctors prescribed the Mediterranean for her. The malady was nothing to worry about; it was nothing more than fatigue; and if she were to rest now and if possible not work before the following autumn, there was every reason to expect that she would be perfectly cured.

Sylvia jumped at an excuse to go abroad again and suggested a visit to Sirene. The doctor, on being assured that Sirene was in the Mediterranean, decided that it was exactly the place best suited to Olive's state of health. Like most English doctors, he regarded the Mediterranean as a little larger than the Serpentine, with a characteristic climate throughout. Olive, however, was much opposed to leaving London, and when Sylvia began to get annoyed with her obstinacy, she confessed that the real reason for wishing to stay was Jack.

"Naturally, I wanted to tell you at once, my dear. But Jack wouldn't let me, until he could see his way clear to our being married. He was quite odd about you, for you know how fond he is of you—he thinks there's nobody like you—but he particularly asked me not to tell you just yet."

"Of course I know the reason," Sylvia proclaimed, instantly. "The silly, scrupulous, proud ass. I'll have it out with him to-morrow at lunch. Dearest Olive, I'm so happy that I like your curly-headed actor."

"Oh, but, darling Sylvia, his hair's quite straight!"

"Yes, but it's very long and gets into his eyes. It's odd hair, anyway. And when did the flaming arrow pin your two hearts together?"

"It was that evening you played baccarat at Curzon Street—about ten days ago. You didn't think we'd known long, did you? Oh, my dear, I couldn't have kept the secret any longer."

Next day Sylvia lunched with Jack Airdale and came to the point at once.

"Look here, you detestably true-to-type, impossibly sensitive ass, because I to please me lent you fifty pounds, is that any excuse for you to keep me out in the cold over you and Olive? Seriously, Jack, I do think it was mean of you."

Jack was abashed and mumbled many excuses. He had been afraid Sylvia would despise him for talking about marriage when he owed her money. He felt, anyway, that he wasn't good enough for Olive. Before Olive had known anything about it, he had been rather ashamed of himself for being in love with her; he felt he was taking advantage of Sylvia's friendship.

"All which excuses are utterly feeble," Sylvia pronounced. "Now listen. Olive's ill. She ought to go abroad. I very selfishly want a companion. You've got to insist on her going. The fifty pounds I lent you will pay her expenses, so that debt's wiped out, and you're standing her a holiday in the Mediterranean."

Jack thought for a moment with a puzzled air.

"Don't be absurd, Sylvia. Really for the moment you took me in with your confounded arithmetic. Why, you're doubling the obligation."

"Obligation! Obligation! Don't you dare to talk about obligations to me. I don't believe in obligations. Am I to understand that for the sake of your unworthy—well, it can't be dignified with the word—pride, Olive is to be kept in London throughout the spring?"

Jack protested he had been talking about the loan to himself. Olive's obligation would be a different one.

"Jack, have you ever seen a respectable woman throw a sole Morny across a restaurant? Because you will in one moment. Amen to the whole discussion. Please! The only thing you've got to do is to insist on Olive's coming with me. Then while she's away you must be a good little actor and act away as hard as you know how, so that you can be married next June as a present to me on my twenty-sixth birthday."

"You're the greatest dear," said Jack, fervently.

"Of course I am. But I'm waiting."

"What for?"

"Why, for an exhortation to matrimony. Haven't you noticed that people who are going to get married always try to persuade everybody else to come in with them? I'm sure human co-operation began with paleolithic bathers."

So Olive and Sylvia left England for Sirene.

"I'd like to be coming with you," said Mrs. Gainsborough at Charing Cross. "But I'm just beginning to feel a tiddley-bit stiff, and well, there, after Morocco, I shouldn't be satisfied with anything less than a cannibal island, and it's too late for me to start in being a Robinson Crusoe, which reminds me that when I took Mrs. Beardmore to the Fulham pantomime last night it was Dick Whittington. And upon my soul, if he didn't go to Morocco with his cat. 'Well,' I said to Mrs. Beardmore, 'it's not a bit like it.' I told her that if Dick Whittington went there now he wouldn't take his cat with him. He'd take a box of Keating's. Somebody behind said, 'Hush.' And I said, 'Hush yourself. Perhaps *you've* been to Morocco?' Which made him look very silly, for I don't suppose he's ever been further East than Aldgate in his life. We had no more 'hushes' from him, I can tell you; and Mrs. Beardmore looked round at him in a very lady-like way which she's got from being a housekeeper, and said, 'My friend *has* been to Morocco.' After that we la-la'd the chorus in peace and quiet. Good-by, duckies, and don't gallivant about too much."

Sylvia had brought a bagful of books about the Roman emperors, and Olive had brought a number of anthologies that made up by the taste of the binder for the lack of it in the compiler. They were mostly about love. To satisfy Sylvia's historical passion a week was spent in Rome and another week in Naples. She told Olive of her visit to Italy with Philip over seven years ago, and, much to her annoyance, Olive poured out a good deal of emotion over that hapless marriage.

"Don't you feel any kind of sentimental regret?" she asked while they were watching from Posilipo the vapors of Vesuvius rose-plumed in the wintry sunset. "Surely you feel softened toward it all now. Why, I think I should regret anything that had once happened in this divinely beautiful place."

"The thing I remember most distinctly is Philip's having read somewhere that the best way to get rid of an importunate guide was to use the local negative and throw the head back instead of shaking it. The result was that Philip used to walk about as if he were gargling. To annoy him I used to wink behind his back at the guides, and naturally with such encouragement his local negative was absolutely useless."

"I think you must have been rather trying, Sylvia dear."

"Oh, I was—infernally trying, but one doesn't marry a child of seventeen as a sedative."

"I think it's all awfully sad," Olive sighed.

Sylvia had rather a shock, a few days after they had reached Sirene, when she saw Miss Horne and Miss Hobart drive past on the road up to Anasirene, the green rival of Sirene among the clouds to the west of the island. She made inquiries at the pension and was informed that two sisters Miss Hobart-Horne, English millionaires many times over, had lived at Sirene these five years. Sylvia decided that it would be quite easy to avoid meeting them, and warned Olive against making friends with any of the residents, on the plea that she did not wish to meet people whom she had met here seven years ago with her husband. In the earlier part of the spring they stayed at a pension, but Sylvia found that it was difficult to escape from people there, and they moved up to Anasirene, where they took a *villino* that was cut off from all dressed-up humanity by a sea of olives. Here it was possible to roam by paths that were not frequented save by peasants whose personalities so long attuned to earth had lost the power of detaching themselves from the landscape and did not affect the onlooker more than the movement of trees or the rustle of small beasts. Life was made up of these essentially undisturbing personalities set in a few pictures that escaped from the swift southern spring: anemones splashed out like wine upon the green corn; some girl with slanting eyes that regarded coldly a dead bird in her thin brown hand; red-beaded cherry-trees that threw shadows on the tawny wheat below; wind over the olives and the sea, wind that shook the tresses of the broom and ruffled the scarlet poppies; then suddenly the first cicala and eternal noon.

It would have been hard to say how they spent these four months, Sylvia thought.

"Can you bear to leave your beloved trees, your namesakes?" she asked.

"Jack is getting impatient," said Olive.

"Then we must fade out of Anasirene just as one by one the flowers have all faded."

"I don't think I've faded much," Olive laughed. "I never felt so well in my life, thanks to you."

Jack and Olive were married at the end of June. It was necessary to go down to a small Warwickshire town and meet all sorts of country people that reminded Sylvia of Green Lanes. Olive's father, who was a solicitor, was very anxious for Sylvia to stay when the wedding was over. He was cheating the gods out of half their pleasure in making him a solicitor by writing a history of Warwickshire worthies. Sylvia had so much impressed him as an intelligent observer that he would have liked to retain her at his elbow for a while. She would not stay, however. The particular song that the sirens had sung to her during her sojourn in their territory was about writing a book. They called her back now and flattered her with a promise of inspiration. Sylvia was not much more ready to believe in sirens than in mortals, and she resisted the impulse to return. Nevertheless, with half an idea of scoring off them by writing the book somewhere else, she settled down in Mulberry Cottage to try: the form should be essays, and she drew up a list of subjects:—

1. *Obligations.*
Judiac like the rest of our moral system; post obits on human gratitude.

2. *Friendship.*
A flowery thing. Objectionable habit of keeping pressed flowers.

3. *Marriage.*
Judiac. Include this with obligations; nothing wrong with the idea of marriage. The marriage of convenience probably more honest than the English marriage of so-called affection. Levi the same as Lewis.

4. *Gambling.*
A moral occupation that brings out the worst side of everybody.

5. *Development.*
Exploiting human personality. Judiac, of course.

6. *Acting.*
A low art form; oh yes, very low; being paid for what the rest of the world does for nothing.

7. *Prostitution.*
Selling one's body to keep one's soul. This is the meaning of the sins that were forgiven to the woman because she loved much. One might say of most marriages that they were selling one's soul to keep one's body.

Sylvia found that when she started to write on these and other subjects she knew nothing about them; the consequence was that summer passed into autumn and autumn into winter while she went on reading history and philosophy. For pastime she played baccarat at Curzon Street and lost six hundred pounds. In February she decided that, so much having been written on the subjects she had chosen, it was useless to write any more. She went to stay with Jack and Olive, who were now living in West Kensington. Olive was expecting a baby in April.

"If it's a boy, we're going to call him Sylvius. But if it's a girl, Jack says we can't call her Sylvia, because for us there can never be more than one Sylvia."

"Call her Argentina."

"No, we're going to call her Sylvia Rose."

"Well, I hope it'll be a boy," said Sylvia. "Anyway, I hope it'll be a boy, because there are too many girls."

Olive announced that she had taken a cottage in the country close to where her people lived, and that Sylvius or Sylvia Rose was to be born there; she thought it was right.

"I don't know why childbirth should be more moral in the country," Sylvia said.

"Oh, it's nothing to do with morals; it's on account of baby's health. You will come and stay with me, won't you?"

In March, therefore, Sylvia went down to Warwickshire with Olive, much to the gratification of Mr. Fanshawe. It was a close race whether he would be a grandfather or an author first, but in the end Mr. Fanshawe had the pleasure of placing a copy of his work on Warwickshire worthies in the hands of the monthly nurse before she could place in his arms a grandchild. Three days later Olive brought into the world a little girl and a little boy. Jack was acting in Dundee. The problem of nomenclature was most complicated. Olive had to think it all out over again from the beginning. Jack had to be consulted by telegram about every change, and on occasions where accuracy was all-important, the post-office clerks were usually most careless. For instance, Mr. Fanshawe thought it would be charming to celebrate the forest of Arden by calling the children Orlando and Rosalind; Jack thereupon replied:

Do not like Rosebud. What will boy be called. Suggest Palestine. First name arrived Ostend. If Oswald no.

"Palestine!" exclaimed Olive.

"Obviously Valentine," said Sylvia. "But look here, why not Sylvius for the boy and Rose for the girl? 'Rose Airdale, all were thine!'"

When several more telegrams had been exchanged to enable Olive, in Warwickshire, to be quite sure that Jack, by this time in Aberdeen, had got the names right, Sylvius and Rose were decided upon, though Mr. Fanshawe advocated Audrey for the girl with such pertinacity that he even went as far as to argue with his daughter on the steps of the font.

Indeed, as Sylvia said afterward, if the clergyman had not been so deaf, Rose would probably be Audrey at this moment.

On the afternoon of the christening Sylvia received a telegram.

"Too late," she said, with a laugh, as she tore it open. "He can't change his mind now."

But the telegram was signed "Beardmore" and asked Sylvia to come at once to London because Mrs. Gainsborough was very ill.

When she arrived at Mulberry Cottage, on a fine morning in early June, Mrs. Beardmore, whom Sylvia had never seen, was gravely accompanying two other elderly women to the garden door.

"She's not dead?" Sylvia cried.

The three friends shook their heads and sighed.

"Not yet, poor soul," said the thinnest, bursting into tears.

This must be Mrs. Ewings.

"I'm just going to send another doctor," said the most majestic, which must be Mrs. Marsham.

Mrs. Beardmore said nothing, but she sniffed and led the way toward the house. Mrs. Marsham and Mrs. Ewings went off together.

Inside the darkened room, but not so dark in the June sunshine as to obscure entirely the picture of Captain Dashwood in whiskers that hung upon the wall by her bed, Mrs. Gainsborough lay breathing heavily. The nurse made a gesture of silence and came out tiptoe from the room. Down-stairs in the parlor Sylvia listened to Mrs. Beardmore's story of the illness.

"I heard nothing till three days ago, when the woman who comes in of a morning ascertained from Mrs. Gainsborough the wish she had for me to visit her. The Misses Hargreaves, with who I reside, was exceptionally kind and insisted upon me taking the tram from Kew that very moment. I communicated with Mrs. Marsham and Mrs. Ewings, but they, both having lodgers, was unable to evacuate their business, and Mrs. Gainsborough was excessively anxious as you should be communicated with on the telegraph, which I did accordingly. We have two nurses night and day, and the doctor is all that can be desired, all that can be desired, notwithstanding whatever Mrs. Marsham may say to the contrary; Mrs. Marsham, who I've known for some years, has that habit of contradicting everybody else something outrageous. Mrs. Ewings and me was both entirely satisfied with Doctor Barker. I'm very glad you've come, Miss Scarlett, and Mrs. Gainsborough will be very glad you've come. If you'll permit the liberty of the observation, Mrs. Gainsborough is very fond of you. As soon as she wakes up I shall have to get back to Kew, not wishing to trespass too much on the kindness of the two Misses Hargreaves to who I act as housekeeper. It's her heart that's the trouble. Double pneumonia through pottering in the garden. That's what the doctor diag—yes, that's what the doctor says, and though Mrs. Marsham contradicted him, taking the words out of his mouth and throwing them back in his face, and saying it was nothing of the kind but going to the King's funeral, I believe he's right."

Mrs. Beardmore went back to Kew. Mrs. Gainsborough, who had been in a comatose state all the afternoon, began to wander in her mind about an hour before sunset.

"It's very dark. High time the curtain went up. The house will be getting impatient in a minute. It's not to be supposed they'll wait all night. Certainly not."

Sylvia drew the curtains back, and the room was flooded with gold.

"That's better. Much better. The country smells beautiful, don't it, this morning? The glory die-johns are a treat this year, but the captain he always likes a camellia or a gardenia. Well, if they start in building over your nursery, pa.... Certainly not, certainly not. They'll build over everything. Now don't talk about dying, Bob. Don't let's be dismal on our anniversary. Certainly not."

She suddenly recognized Sylvia and her mind cleared.

"Oh, I *am* glad you've come. Really, you know, I hate to make a fuss, but I'm not feeling at all meself. I'm just a tiddley-bit ill, it's my belief. Sylvia, give me your hand. Sylvia, I'm joking. I really am remarkably ill. Oh, there's no doubt I'm going to die. What a beautiful evening! Yes, it's not to be supposed I'm going to live forever, and there, after all, I'm not sorry. As soon as I began to get that stiffness I thought it meant I was not meself. And what's the good of hanging about if you're not yourself?"

The nurse came forward and begged her not to talk too much.

"You can't stop me talking. There was a clergyman came through Mrs. Ewings's getting in a state about me, and he talked till I was sick and tired of the sound of his voice. Talked away, he did, about the death of Our Lord and being nailed to the cross. It made me very dismal. 'Here, when did all this occur?' I asked. 'Nineteen hundred and ten years ago,' he said. 'Oh well,' I said, 'it all occurred such a long time ago and it's all so sad, let's hope it never occurred at all.'"

The nurse said firmly that if Mrs. Gainsborough would not stop talking she should have to make Sylvia go out of the room.

"There's a tyrant," said Mrs. Gainsborough. "Well, just sit by me quietly and hold my hand."

The sun set behind the housetops. Mrs. Gainsborough's hand was cold when twilight came.

Sylvia felt that it was out of the question to stay longer at Mulberry Cottage, though Miss Dashwood, to whom the little property reverted, was very anxious for her to do so. After the funeral Sylvia joined Olive and Jack in Warwickshire.

They realized that she was feeling very deeply the death of Mrs. Gainsborough, and were anxious that she should arrange to live with them in West Kensington.

Sylvia, however, said that she wished to remain friends with them, and declined the proposal.

"Do you remember what I told you once," she said to Jack, "about going back to the stage in some form or another when I was tired of things?"

Jack, who had not yet renounced his ambition for Sylvia's theatrical career, jumped at the opportunity of finding her an engagement, and when they all went back to London with the babies he rushed about the Strand to see what was going. Sylvia moved all her things from Mulberry Cottage to the Airdales' house, refusing once more Miss Dashwood's almost tearful offer to make over the cottage to her. She was sorry to withstand the old lady, who was very frail by now, but she knew that if she accepted, it would mean more dreaming about writing books and gambling at Curzon Street, and ultimately doing nothing until it was too late.

"I'm reaching the boring idle thirties. I'm twenty-seven," she told Jack and Olive. "I must sow a few more wild oats before my face is plowed with wrinkles to receive the respectable seeds of a flourishing old age. By the way, as demon-godmother I've placed one thousand pounds to the credit of Rose and Sylvius."

The parents protested, but Sylvia would take no denial.

"I've kept lots for myself," she assured them. As a matter of fact, she had nearly another £1,000 in the bank.

At the end of July Jack came in radiant to say that a piece with an English company was being sent over to New York the following month. There was a small part for which the author required somebody whose personality seemed to recall Sylvia's. Would she read it? Sylvia said she would.

"The author was pleased, eh?" Jack asked, enthusiastically, when Sylvia came back from the trial.

"I don't really know. Whenever he tried to speak, the manager said, 'One moment, please'; it was like a boxing-match. However, as the important thing seemed to be that I should speak English with a French accent, I was engaged."

Sylvia could not help being amused at herself when she found that her first essay with legitimate drama was to be the exact converse of her first essay with the variety stage, dependent, as before, upon a kind of infirmity. Really, the only time she had been able to express herself naturally in public had been when she sang "The Raggle-taggle Gipsies" with the Pink Pierrots, and that had been a failure. However, a tour in the States would give her a new glimpse of life, which at twenty-seven was the important consideration; and perhaps New York, more generous than other capitals, would give her life itself, or one of the only two things in life that mattered, success and love.

CHAPTER XIII

THE play in which Sylvia was to appear in New York was called "A Honeymoon in Europe," and if it might be judged from the first few rehearsals, at which the performers had read their parts like half-witted board-school children, it was thin stuff. Still, it was not fair to pass a final opinion without the two American stars who were awaiting the English company in their native land.

The author, Mr. Marchmont Hearne, was a timid little man who between the business manager and producer looked and behaved very much like the Dormouse at the Mad Tea-party. The manager did not resemble the Hatter except in the broad brim of his top-hat, which in mid-Atlantic he reluctantly exchanged for a cloth cap. The company declared he was famous for his tact; certainly he managed to suppress the Dormouse at every point by shouting, "One minute, Mr. Stern, *please*," or, "Please, Mr. Burns, one minute," and apologizing at once so effusively for not calling him by his right name that the poor little Dormouse had no courage to contest the real point at issue, which had nothing to do with his name. When the manager had to exercise a finer tactfulness, as with obdurate actresses, he was wont to soften his remarks by adding that nothing "derogatory" had been intended; this seemed to mollify everybody, probably, Sylvia thought, because it was such a long word. The Hatter's name was Charles Fitzherbert. The producer, Mr. Wade Fortescue, by the length of his ears, by the way in which his electrical hair propelled itself into a peak on either side of his head, and by his wild, artistic eye, was really rather like the March Hare outwardly; his behavior was not less like. Mr. Fortescue's attitude toward "A Honeymoon in Europe" was one that Beethoven might have taken up on being invited to orchestrate "Ta-ra-ra-boom-de-ay." The author did not go so far as to resent this attitude, but on many occasions he was evidently pained by it, notwithstanding Mr. Fitzherbert's assurances that Mr. Fortescue had intended nothing "derogatory."

Sylvia's part was that of a French chambermaid. The author had drawn it faithfully to his experience of Paris in the course of several week-ends. As his conception coincided with that of the general public in supposing a French chambermaid to be a cross between a street-walker and a tight-rope walker, it seemed probable that the part would be a success; although Mr. Fortescue wanted to mix the strain still further by introducing the blood of a comic ventriloquist.

"You must roll your 'r's' more, Miss Scarlett," he assured her. "That line will go for nothing as you said it."

"I said it as a French chambermaid would say it," Sylvia insisted.

"If I might venture—" the Dormouse began.

"One minute, please, Mr. Treherne," interrupted the Mad Hatter. "What Mr. Fortescue wants, Miss Scarlett, is exaggeration—a leetle exaggeration. I believe that is what you want, Mr. Fortescue?"

"I don't want a caricature," snapped the March Hare. "The play is farcical enough as it is. What I want to impart is realism. I want Miss Scarlett to say the line as a French girl would say it."

"Precisely," said the Hatter. "That's precisely what I was trying to explain to Miss Scarlett. You're a bit hasty, old chap, you know, and I think you frightened her a little. That's all right, Miss Scarlett, there's nothing to be frightened about. Mr. Fortescue intended nothing derogatory."

"I'm not in the least frightened," said Sylvia, indignantly.

"If I might make a suggestion, I think that—" the Dormouse began.

"One minute please, please, Mr. Burns, one minute—Ah, dear me, Mr. Hearne, I was confusing you with the poet. Nothing derogatory in that, eh?" he laughed jovially.

"May I ask a question?" said Sylvia, and asked it before Mr. Fitzherbert could interrupt again. "Why do all English authors draw all Frenchwomen as cocottes and all French authors draw all English women as governesses? The answer's obvious."

The Mad Hatter and the March Hare were so much taken aback by this attack from Alice that the Dormouse was able to emit an entire sentence.

"I should like to say that Miss Scarlett's rendering of the accent gives me great satisfaction. I have no fault to find. I shall be much obliged, Miss Scarlett, if you will correct my French whenever necessary. I am fully sensible of its deficiencies."

Mr. Marchmont Hearne blinked after this challenge and breathed rather heavily.

"I've had a good deal of experience," said Mr. Fortescue, grimly, "but I never yet found that it improved a play to allow the performers of minor rôles, essentially minor rôles, to write their parts in at rehearsal."

Mr. Fitzherbert was in a quandary for a moment whether he should smoothe the rufflings of the author or of the actress or of the producer, but deciding that the author could be more profitable to his career in the end, he took him up-stage and tried to whisper away Mr. Fortescue's bad temper. In the end Sylvia was allowed to roll her "r's" at her own pace.

"I'm glad you stood up to him, dear," said an elderly actress like a pink cabbage rose fading at the tips of the petals, who had been sitting throughout the rehearsal so nearly on the scene that she was continually being addressed in mistake by people who really were "on." The author, who had once or twice smiled at her pleasantly, was evidently under the delusion that she was interested in his play.

"Yes, I was delighted with the way you stood up to them," continued Miss Nancy Tremayne. "My part's wretched, dear. All feeding! Still, if I'm allowed to slam the door when I go off in the third act, I may get a hand. Have you ever been to New York before? I like it myself, and you can live quite cheaply if you know the ropes. Of course, I'm drawing a very good salary, because they wanted me. I said I couldn't come for a penny under one hundred dollars, and I really didn't want to come at all. However, he *would* have me, and between you and me, I'm really rather glad to have the chance of saving a little money. The managers are getting very stingy in England. Don't tell anybody what I'm getting, will you, dear? One doesn't like to create jealousy at the commencement of a tour. It seems to be quite a nice crowd, though the girls look a little old, don't you think? Amy Melhuish, who's playing the ingénue, must be at least thirty. It's wonderful how some women have the nerve to go on. I gave up playing ingénues as soon as I was over twenty-eight, and that's four years ago now, or very nearly. Oh dear, how time flies!"

Sylvia thought that, if Miss Tremayne was only twenty-eight four years ago, time must have crawled.

"They're sending us out in the *Minneworra*. The usual economy, but really in a way it's nicer, because it's all one class. Yes, I'm glad you stood up to them, dear. Fortescue's been impossible ever since he produced one of those filthy Strindberg plays last summer for the Unknown Plays Committee. I hate this continental muck. Degenerate, I say it is. In my opinion Ibsen has spoiled the drama in England. What do you think of Charlie Fitzherbert? He's such a nice man. Always ready to smooth over any little difficulties. When Mr. Vernon said to me that Charlie would be coming with us, I felt quite safe."

"Morally?" Sylvia asked.

"Oh, go on! You know what I mean. Comfortable, and not likely to be stranded. Well, I'm always a little doubtful about American productions. I suppose I'm conservative. I like old-fashioned ways."

Which was not surprising, Sylvia thought.

"Miss Tremayne, I can't hear myself speak. Are you on in this scene?" demanded the producer.

"I really don't know. My next cue is—"

"I don't think Miss Tremayne comes on till Act Three," said the author.

"We sha'n't get there for another two hours," the producer growled.

Miss Tremayne moved her chair back three feet, and turned to finish her conversation with Sylvia.

"What I was going to say when I was interrupted, dear, was that, if you're a bad sailor, you ought to make a point of making friends with the purser. Unfortunately I don't know the purser on the *Minneworra*, but the purser on the *Minnetoota* was quite a friend of mine, and gave me a beautiful deck-cabin. The other girls were very jealous."

"Damn it, Miss Tremayne, didn't I ask you not to go on talking?" the producer shouted.

"Nice gentlemanly way of asking anybody not to whisper a few words of advice, isn't it?" said Miss Tremayne, with a scathing glance at Mr. Fortescue as she moved her chair quite six feet farther away from the scene.

"Now, of course, we're in a draught," she grumbled to Sylvia. "But I always say that producers never have any consideration for anybody but themselves."

By the time the S.S. *Minneworra* reached New York Sylvia had come to the conclusion that the representatives of the legitimate drama differed only from the chorus of a musical comedy in taking their temperaments and exits more seriously. Sylvia's earlier experience had led her to suppose that the quantity of make-up and proximity to the footlights were the most important things in art.

Whatever hopes of individual ability to shine the company might have cherished before it reached New York were quickly dispelled by the two American stars, up to whom and not with whom they were expected to twinkle. Mr. Diomed Olver and Miss Marcia Neville regarded the rest of the company as Jupiter and Venus might regard the Milky Way. Miss Tremayne's exit upon a slammed door was forbidden the first time she tried it, because it would distract the attention of the audience from Miss Neville, who at that moment would be sustaining a dimple, which she called holding a situation. This dimple, which was famous from Boston to San Francisco, from Buffalo to New Orleans, had, when Miss Neville first swam into the ken of a manager's telescope, been easy enough to sustain. Of late years a slight tendency toward stoutness had made it necessary to assist the dimple with the forefinger and internal suction; the slamming of a door might disturb so nice an operation, and an appeal, which came oddly from Miss Neville, was made to Miss Tremayne's sense of natural acting.

Mr. Olver did not bother to conceal his intention of never moving from the center of the stage, where he maintained himself with the noisy skill of a gyroscope.

"See here," he explained to members of the company who tried to compete with his stellar supremacy. "The public pays to see Diomed Olver and Marcia Neville; they don't care a damned cent for anything else in creation. Got me? That's good. Now we'll go along together fine."

Mr. Charles Fitzherbert assisted no more at rehearsals, but occupied himself entirely with the box-office. Mr. Wade Fortescue was very fierce about 2 A.M. in the bar of his hotel, but very mild at rehearsals. Mr. Marchmont Hearne hibernated during this period, and when he appeared very shyly at the opening performance in Brooklyn the company greeted him with the surprised cordiality that is displayed to some one who has broken his leg and emerges weeks later from hospital without a limp.

New York made a deep and instant impression on Sylvia. No city that she had seen was so uncompromising; so sure of its flamboyant personality; so completely an ingenious, spoiled, and precocious child; so lovable for its extravagance and mischief. To her the impression was of some Gargantuan boy in his nursery building up tall towers to knock them down, running his clockwork-engines for fun through the streets of his toy city, scattering in corners quantities of toy bricks in readiness for a new fit of destructive construction, scooping up his tin inhabitants at the end of a day's play to put them helter-skelter into their box, eking out the most novel electrical toys of that Christmas with the battered old trams of the Christmas before, cherishing old houses with a child's queer conservatism, devoting a large stretch of bright carpet to a park, and robbing his grandmother's mantelpiece of her treasures to put inside his more permanent structures. After seeing New York she sympathized very much with the remark she had heard made by a young New-Yorker on board the *Minneworra*, which at the time she had thought a mere callow piece of rudeness.

A grave doctor from Toledo, Ohio, almost as grave as if he were from the original Toledo, had expressed a hope to Sylvia that she would not accept New York as representative of the United States. She must travel to the West. New York had no family life. If Miss Scarlett wished to see family life, he should be glad to show it to her in Toledo. For confirmation of his criticism he had appealed to a young man standing at his elbow.

"Well," the young man had replied, "I've never been fifty miles west of New York in my life, and I hope I never shall. When I want to travel I cross over to Europe for a month."

The Toledo doctor had afterward spoken severely to Sylvia on the subject of this young New-Yorker, citing him as a dangerous element in the national welfare. Now, after seeing the Gargantuan boy's nursery, she understood the spirit that wanted to enjoy his nursery and not be bothered to go for polite walks with maiden aunts in the country; equally, no doubt, in Toledo she should appreciate the point of view of the doctor and recognize the need for the bone that would support the vast bulk of the growing child.

Sylvia had noticed that as she grew older impressions became less vivid; her later and wider experience of London was already dim beside those first years with her father and Monkley. It had been the same during her travels. Already even the Alhambra was no longer quite clearly imprinted upon her mind, and each year it had been growing less and less easy to be astonished. But this arrival in New York had been like an arrival in childhood, as surprising, as exciting, as terrifying, as stimulating. New York was like a rejuvenating potion in the magic influence of which the memories of past years dissolved. Partly, no doubt, this effect might be ascribed to the invigorating air, and partly, Sylvia thought, to the anxiously receptive condition of herself now within sight of thirty; but neither of these explanations was wide enough to include all that New York gave of regenerative emotion, of willingness to be alive and unwillingness to go to bed, and of zest in being amused. Sylvia had supposed that she had long ago outgrown the pleasure of wandering about streets for no other reason than to be wandering about streets, of staring into shops, of staring after people, of staring at advertisements, of staring in company with a crowd of starers as well entertained as herself at a bat that was flying about in daylight outside the Plaza Hotel; but here in New York all that old youthful attitude of assuming that the world existed for one's diversion, mixed with a sharp, though always essentially contemptuous, curiosity about the method it was taking to amuse one, was hers again. Sylvia had always regarded England as the frivolous nation that thought of nothing but amusement, England that took its pleasure so earnestly and its business so lightly. In New York there was no question of qualifying adverbs; everything was a game. It was a game, and apparently, by the enthusiasm with which it was played, a novel game, to control the traffic in Fifth Avenue—a rather dangerous game like American football, in which at first the casualties to the policemen who played it were considerable. Street-mending was another game, rather an elementary game that contained a large admixture of practical joking. Getting a carriage after the theater was a game played with counters. Eating, even, could be made into a game either mechanical like the automatic dime lunch, or intellectual like the free lunch, or imaginative like the quick lunch.

Sylvia had already made acquaintance with the crude material of America in Carlos Morera. New York was Carlos Morera much more refined and more matured, sweetened by its own civilization, which, having severed itself from other civilizations like the Anglo-Saxon or Latin, was already most convincingly a civilization of its own, bearing the veritable stamp of greatness. Sometimes Sylvia would be faced even in New York by a childishness that scarcely differed from the childishness of Carlos Morera. One evening, for instance, two of the men in the company who knew her tastes invited her to come with them to Murden's all-night saloon off Sixth Avenue. They had been told it was a sight worth seeing. Sylvia, with visions of something like the dancing-saloon in Buenos Aires, was anxious to make the experiment. It sounded exciting when she heard that the place was kept going by "graft." After the performance she and her companions went to Jack's for supper; thence they walked along Sixth Avenue to Murden's. It was only about two o'clock when they entered by a side door into a room exactly like the bar parlor of an English public house, where they sat rather drearily drinking some inferior beer, until one of Sylvia's companions suggested that they had arrived too near the hours of legal closing. They left Murden's and visited a Chinese restaurant in Broadway with a cabaret attached. The prices, the entertainment, the food, and the company were in a descending scale; the prices were much the highest. Two hours later they went back to Murden's; the parlor was not less dreary; the beer was still abominable. However, just as they had decided that this could not be the right place, an enormous man slightly drunk entered under the escort of two ladies of the town. Perceiving that Sylvia and her companions had risen, the new-comer waved them back into their chairs and called for drinks all round.

"British?" he asked.

They nodded.

"Yes, I thought you were Britishers. I'm Under-Sheriff McMorris." With this he seated himself, hugging the two nymphs on either side of him like a Dionysius in his chariot.

"Actor folk?" he asked.

They nodded.

"Yes, I thought you were actor folk. Ever read Shakespeare? Some boy, eh? Gee! I used to be able to spout Parsha without taking breath."

Forthwith he delivered the speech about the quality of mercy.

"Wal?" he demanded at the end.

The English actors congratulated him and called for another round. Mr. McMorris turned to one of the nymphs:

"Wal, honey?"

"Cut it out, you fat old slob; you're tanked!" said honey.

Mr. McMorris recited several other speeches, including the vision of the dagger from "Macbeth." From Shakespeare he passed to Longfellow, and from Longfellow to Byron. After an hour of recitations he was persuaded by the bartender to give some of his reminiscences of criminals in New York, which he did so vividly that Sylvia began to suppose that at one time or another he really had been connected with the law. Finally about six o'clock he became pathetic and wept away most of what he had drunk.

"I'm feeling bad this morning. I gart to go and arrest a man for whom I have a considerable admiration. I gart to go down-town to Washington Square and arrest a prominent citizen at eight o'clock sharp. I guess they're waiting right now for me to come along and make that arrest. Where's my black-jack?"

He fumbled in his pocket for a leather-covered life-preserver, which he flourished truculently. Leaning upon the shoulders of the nymphs, he waved a farewell and staggered out.

Sylvia asked the bartender what he really was.

"He's Under-Sheriff McMorris. At eight o'clock he's going to arrest a prominent New York citizen for misappropriation of some fund."

That evening in the papers Sylvia read that Under-Sheriff McMorris had burst into tears when ex-Governor Somebody or other had walked down the steps of his house in Washington Square and offered himself to the custody of the law.

"I don't like to have to do this, Mr. Governor," Under-Sheriff McMorris had protested.

"You must do your duty, Mr. Under-Sheriff."

The crowd had thereupon cheered loudly, and the wife of the ex-Governor, dissolved in tears, had waved the Stars and Stripes from an upper window.

"Jug for the ex-Governor and a jag for the under-sheriff," said Sylvia. "If only the same spirit could be applied to minor arrests. That may come. It's wonderful, really, how in this mighty republic they manage to preserve any vestige of personality, but they do."

The play ran through the autumn and went on tour in January. Sylvia did not add much to her appreciation of America in the course of it, because, as was inevitable in the short visits they paid to various towns, she had to depend for intercourse upon the members of the company. She reached New York again shortly before her twenty-eighth birthday. When nearly all her fellow-players returned to England, she decided to stay behind. The first impression she had received of entering upon a new phase of life when she landed in New York had not yet deserted her, and having received an offer from the owner of what sounded, from his description, like a kind of hydropathic establishment to entertain the visitors there during the late summer and fall, she accepted. In August, therefore, she left New York and went to Sulphurville, Indiana.

Sylvia had had glimpses of rural America in Vermont and New Hampshire during the tour; in such a cursory view it had not seemed to differ much from rural England. Now she was going to see rustic America, if a distinction between the two adjectives might be made. At Indianapolis she changed from the great express into a smaller train that deposited her at a railway station consisting of a tumble-down shed. Nobody came out to welcome the train, but the colored porter insisted that this was the junction from which she would ultimately reach Sulphurville and denied firmly Sylvia's suggestion that the engine-driver had stopped here for breath. She was the only passenger who alighted, and she saw the train continue on its way with something near despair. The sun was blazing down. All around was a grasshopper-haunted wilderness of Indian corn. It was the hottest, greenest, flattest, most God-forsaken spot she had ever seen. The heat was so tremendous that she ventured inside the hut for shade. The only sign of life was a bug proceeding slowly across a greasy table. Sylvia went out and wandered round to the other side. Here, fast asleep, was a man dressed in a pair of blue trousers, a neckerchief, and an enormous straw hat. As the trousers reached to his armpits, he was really fully dressed, and Sylvia was able to recognize him as a human being from an illustrated edition she possessed of *Huckleberry Finn*; at the same time, she thought it wiser to let him sleep and returned to the front of the shed. To her surprise, for it seemed scarcely possible that anybody could inhabit the second floor, she perceived a woman with curl-papers, in a spotted green-and-yellow bed-wrapper, looking out of what until now she had supposed to be a gap in the roof caused by decay. Sylvia asked the woman if this was the junction for Sulphurville. She nodded, but vanished from the window before there was time to ask her when the train would arrive.

Sylvia waited for an hour in the heat, and had almost given up hope of ever reaching Sulphurville when suddenly a train arrived, even smaller than the one into which she had changed at Indianapolis, but still considerably larger than any European train. The hot afternoon wore away while this new train puffed slowly deeper and deeper into rustic America until it reached Bagdad. Hitherto Sylvia had traveled in what was called a parlor-car, but at Bagdad she had to enter a fourth train that did not possess a parlor-car and that really resembled a local train in England, with oil-lamps and semi-detached compartments. At every station between Bagdad and Sulphurville crowds of country folk got in, all of whom were wearing flags and flowers in their buttonholes and were in a state of perspiring festivity. At the last station before Sulphurville the train was invaded by the members of a local band, whose instruments fought for a place as hard as their masters. Sylvia was nearly elbowed out of her seat by an aggressive ophicleide, but an old gentleman opposite with a saxhorn behind him and a euphonium on his knees told her by way of encouragement that the soldiers didn't pass through Indiana every day.

"The last time I saw soldiers like that was during the war," he said, "and I don't allow any of us here will ever see so many soldiers again." He looked round the company defiantly, but nobody seemed inclined to contradict him, and he grunted with disappointment. It seemed hard that the old gentleman's day should end so tamely, but fortunately a young man in the far corner proclaimed it not merely as his opinion, but supported it from inside information, that the regiment was being marched through Indiana like this in order to get it nearer to the Mexican border.

"Shucks!" said the old gentleman, and blew his nose so violently that every one looked involuntarily at one of the brass instruments. "Shucks!" he repeated. Then he smiled at Sylvia, who, sympathizing with the happy close of his day, smiled back just as the train entered the station of Sulphurville.

The Plutonian Hotel, Sulphurville, had presumably been built to appease the same kind of human credulity that created the pump-rooms at Bath or Wiesbaden or Aix-les-Bains. Sylvia had observed that one of the great elemental beliefs of the human race, a belief lost in primeval fog, was that if water with an odd taste bubbled out of the earth, it must necessarily possess curative qualities; if it bubbled forth without a nasty enough taste to justify the foundation of a spa, it was analyzed by prominent chemists, bottled, and sold as a panacea to the great encouragement of lonely dyspeptics with nothing else to read at dinner. In the Middle Ages, and possibly in the classic times of Æsculapius, these natural springs had fortified the spiritual side of man; in late days they served to dilute his spirits. The natural springs at Sulphurville fully justified the erection of the Plutonian Hotel and the lowest depths of mortal credulity, for they had a revolting smell, an exceptionally unpleasant taste, and a high temperature. Everything that balneal ingenuity could suggest had been done, and in case the internal cure was not nasty enough as it was, the first glass of water was prescribed for six o'clock in the morning. Though it was necessary to test human faith by the most arduous and vexatious ordinances for human conduct, lest it might grow contemptuous of the cure, it was equally necessary to prevent boredom, if not of the devotees themselves, at any rate of their families. Accordingly, there was an annex of the ascetic hotel where everybody was driven to bed at eleven by the uncomfortable behavior of the servants, and where breakfast was served not later than seven; this annex possessed a concert-hall, a small theater, a gaming-saloon with not merely roulette, but many apparently childish games of chance that nevertheless richly rewarded the management. Sylvia wondered if there was any moral intention on the part of the proprietors in the way they encouraged gambling, if they wished to accentuate the chances and changes of human life and thereby secure for their clients a religious attitude toward their bodily safety. Certainly at the Plutonian Hotel it was impossible to obtain anything except meals without gambling. In order to buy a cigar or a box of chocolates it was necessary to play dice with the young woman who sold them, with more or less profit to the hotel, according to one's luck. Every morning some new object was on view in the lobby to be raffled that evening. Thus on the fourth night of her stay Sylvia became the owner of a large trunk, the emptiness of which was continuous temptation.

The Plutonian was not merely a resort for gouty Easterners; it catered equally for the uric acid of the West. Sylvia liked the families from the West, particularly the girls with their flowing hair and big felt hats who rode on Kentucky ponies to see smugglers' caves in the hills, conforming invariably to the traditional aspect of the Western belle in the cinema. The boys were not so picturesque; in fact, they scarcely differed from European boys of the same age. The East supplied the exotic note among the children; candy-fed, shrill, and precocious with a queer gnomelike charm, they resembled expensive toys. These visitors to Sulphurville were much more affable with one another than their fellows in Europe would have been in similar circumstances. Sylvia had already noticed that in America stomachic subjects could inspire the dullest conversation; here at the Plutonian the stomach had taken the place of the soul, and it was scarcely an exaggeration to say that in the lounges people rose up to testify in public about their insides.

The morning after Sylvia's arrival the guests were much excited by the visit of the soldiers, who were to camp for a week on the hotel grounds and perform various maneuvers. Sylvia observed that everybody talked as if a troupe of acrobats was going to visit the hotel; nobody seemed to have any idea that the American army served any purpose but the entertainment of the public with gymnastic displays. That afternoon the regiment marched past the hotel to its camping-ground; the band played the "Star-spangled Banner"; all the visitors grouped upon the steps in front clapped their hands; the colonel took off his hat, waved it at the audience, and bowed like a successful author. At first Sylvia considered his behavior undignified and absurd; afterward she rather approved of its friendliness, its absence of pomp and arrogance, its essentially democratic inspiration—in a word, its familiarity.

The proprietor of the Plutonian, a leading political "boss," was so much moved by the strains of the music, the martial bearing of the men, and the opportunity of self-advertisement, that he invited the officers of the regiment to mess free in the hotel during their visit. Everybody praised Mr. O'Halloran's generosity and patriotism, the more warmly because it gave everybody an occasion to commiserate with the officers upon their absurdly small pay. Such commiseration gratified the individual's sense of superiority and made it easy for him to brag about his own success in life. Sylvia resented the business man's point of view about his national army; it was almost as patronizing as an Englishman's attitude to an artist or a German's to a woman or a Frenchman's to anybody but a Frenchman. Snobbishness was only tolerable about the past. Perhaps that was the reason why the Italians were the only really democratic nation she had met so far. The Italians were aristocrats trying to become tradesmen; the rest of mankind were tradesmen striving to appear aristocrats.

Sylvia had sung her songs and was watching the roulette, when a young lieutenant who had been playing with great seriousness turned to her and asked if she was not British.

"We got to know some British officers out in China," he told her. "We couldn't seem to understand them at first, but afterward we found out they were good boys, really. Only the trouble was we were never properly introduced at first, and that worried them some. Say, there's a fellow-countryman of yours sick in Sulphurville. I kind of found out by accident this morning, because I went into a drug-store and the storekeeper was handing out some medicine to a colored girl who was arguing with him whether she should pay for it. Seems this young Britisher's expecting his remittance. That's a God-awful place to be stranded, Sulphurville."

They chatted for a while together. Sylvia liked the simple good-fellowship of the young American, his inquisitiveness about her reasons for coming to sing at the Plutonian Hotel, and his frank anticipation of any curiosity on her side by telling her all about himself and his career since he left West Point. He was amused by her account of the excitement over the passage of the troops through the villages, and seized the occasion to moralize on the vastness of a country through one state of which a regiment could march and surprise half the inhabitants with their first view of an American soldier.

"Seems kind of queer," he said.

"But very Arcadian," Sylvia added.

When Sylvia went to bed her mind reverted to the young Englishman; at the time she had scarcely taken in the significance of what the officer had told her. Now suddenly the sense of his loneliness and suffering overwhelmed her fancy. She thought of the desolation of that railway junction where she had waited for the train to Sulphurville, of the heat and the grasshoppers and the flat, endless greenery. Even that brief experience of being alone in the heart of America had frightened her. She had not taken heed of the vastness of it while she was traveling with the company, and here at the hotel definitely placed as an entertainer she had a certain security. But to be alone and penniless in Sulphurville, to be ill, moreover, and dependent on the charity of foreigners, so much the more foreign because, though they spoke the same language, they spoke it with strange differences like the people in a dream. The words were the same, but they expressed foreign ideas. Sylvia began to speculate upon the causes that had led to this young Englishman's being stranded in Sulphurville. There seemed no explanation, unless he were perhaps an actor who had been abandoned because he was too ill to travel with the company. At this idea she almost got out of bed to walk through the warm frog-haunted night to his rescue. She became sentimental about him in the dark. It seemed to her that nothing in the world was so pitiable as a sick artist; always the servant of the public's curiosity, he was now the helpless prey of it. He would be treated with the contempt that is accorded to sick animals whose utility is at an end. She visualized him in the care of a woman like the one who had leaned out of that railway shed in a spotted green-and-yellow wrapper. Yet, after all, he might not be a mountebank; there was really no reason to suppose he was anything but poor and lonely, though that was enough indeed.

"I must be getting very old," Sylvia said to herself. "Only approaching senility could excuse this prodigal effusion of what is really almost maternal lust. I've grown out of any inclination to ask myself why I think things or why I do things. I've nothing now but an immense desire to do—do—do. I was beginning to think this desperate determination to be impressed, like a child whose father is hiding conspicuously behind the door, was due to America. It's nothing to do with America; it's myself. It's a kind of moral and mental drunkenness. I know what I'm doing. I'm entirely responsible for my actions. That's the way a drunken man argues. Nobody is so utterly convinced of his rightness and reasonableness and judgment as a drunken man. I might argue with myself till morning that it's ridiculous to excite myself over the prospect of helping an Englishman stranded in Sulphurville, but when, worn out with self-conviction, I fall asleep, I shall wake on tiptoe, as it were. I shall be quite violently awake at once. The fact is I'm absolutely tired of observing human nature. I just want to tumble right into the middle of its confusion and forget how to criticize anybody or anything. What's the good of meeting a drunken man with generalizations about human conduct or direction or progression? He won't listen to generalizations, because drunkenness is the apotheosis of the individual. That's why drunken people are always so earnestly persuasive, so anxious to convince the unintoxicated observer that it is better to walk on all-fours than upright. Eccentricity becomes a moral passion; every drunken man is a missionary of the peculiar. At the present moment I'm in the mental state that, did I possess an honest taste for liquor, would make me get up and uncork the brandy-bottle. It's a kind of defiant self-expression. Oh, that poor young Englishman lying alone in Sulphurville! To-morrow, to-morrow! Who knows? Perhaps I really shall find that I am necessary to somebody. Even as a child I conceived the notion of being indispensable. I want somebody to say to me: 'You! You! What should I have done without you?' I suppose every woman feels that; I suppose that is the maternal instinct. But I don't believe many women can feel it so sharply as I do, because very few women have ever been compelled by circumstances to develop their personalities so early and so fully, and then find that nobody wants that personality. I could cry just at the mere notion of being wanted, and surely this young Englishman, whoever he is, will want me. Oh, Sylvia, Sylvia, you're deliberately working yourself up to an adventure! And who has a better right? Tell me that. That's exactly why I praised the drunkard; he knows how to dodge self-consciousness. Why shouldn't you set out to have an adventure? You shall, my dear. And if you're disappointed? You've been disappointed before. Damn those tree-frogs! Like all croakers, they disturb oblivion. I wonder if he'd like my new trunk. And I wonder how old he is. I'm assuming that he's young, but he may be a matted old tramp."

Sylvia woke next morning, as she had prefigured herself, on tiptoe; at breakfast she was sorry for all the noisy people round her, so important to her was life seeming. She set out immediately afterward to walk along the hot, dusty road to the town, elated by the notion of leaving behind her the restlessness and stark cleanliness of the big hotel. The main street of Sulphurville smelled of straw and dry grain; and if it had not been for the flies she would have found the air sweet enough after the damp exhalations of brimstone that permeated the atmosphere of the Plutonian and its surroundings. The flies, however, tainted everything; not even the drug-store was free from them. Sylvia inquired for the address of the Englishman, and the druggist looked at her sharply. She wondered if he was hoping for the settlement of his account.

"Madden's the name, ain't it?" the druggist asked.

"Madden," she repeated, mechanically. A wave of emotion flooded her mind, receded, and left it strewn with the jetsam of the past. The druggist and the drug-store faded out of her consciousness; she was in Colonial Terrace again, insisting upon Arthur's immediate departure.

"What a little beast I was!" she thought, and a desire came over her to atone for former heartlessness by her present behavior. Then abruptly she realized that the Madden of Sulphurville was not necessarily, or even probably, the Arthur Madden of Hampstead. Yet behind this half-disappointment lay the conviction that it was he. "Which accounts for my unusual excitement," Sylvia murmured. She heard herself calmly asking the storekeeper for his address.

"The Auburn Hotel," she repeated. "Thank you."

The storekeeper seemed inclined to question her further; no doubt he wished to be able to count upon his bill's being paid; but Sylvia hurried from the shop before he could speak.

The Auburn Hotel, Sulphurville, was perhaps not worse than a hotel of the same class would have been in England, but the colored servant added just enough to the prevailing squalor to make it seem worse. When Sylvia asked to see Mr. Madden the colored servant stared at her, wiped her mouth with her apron, and called:

"Mrs. Lebus!"

"Oh, Julie, is that you? What is it you want?" twanged a voice from within that sounded like a cat caught in a guitar.

"You're wanted right now, Mrs. Lebus," the servant called back.

The duet was like a parody of a 'coon song, and Sylvia found herself humming to ragtime:

"Oh, Mrs. Lebus, you're wanted,
Oh yes, you're wanted, sure you're wanted, Mrs. Lebus,
You're wanted, you're wanted,
You're wanted—right now."

Mrs. Lebus was one of those women whose tongues are always hunting, like eager terriers. With evident reluctance she postponed the chase of an artful morsel that had taken refuge in some difficult country at the back of her mouth, and faced the problem of admitting Sylvia to the sick man's room.

"You a relative?" she asked.

Sylvia shook her head.

"Perhaps you've come about his remittance. He told me he was expecting a hundred dollars any time. You staying in Sulphurville?"

Sylvia understood that the apparent disinclination to admit her was only due to unsatisfied curiosity and that there was not necessarily any suspicion of her motives. At this moment something particularly delicious ran across the path of Mrs. Lebus's tongue, and Sylvia took advantage of the brief pause during which it was devoured, to penetrate into the lobby, where a melancholy citizen in a frock-coat and a straw hat was testing the point of a nib upon his thumb, whether with the intention of offering it to Mrs. Lebus to pick her teeth or of writing a letter was uncertain.

"Oh, Scipio!" said Mrs. Lebus. She pronounced it "Skipio."

"Wal?"

"She wants to see Mr. Madden."

"Sure."

The landlady turned to Sylvia.

"Mr. Lebus don't have no objections. Julie, take Miss—What did you say your name was?"

Sylvia saw no reason against falling into what Mrs. Lebus evidently considered was a skilfully laid trap, and told her.

"Scarlett," Mr. Lebus repeated. "We don't possess that name in Sulphurville. Yes, ma'am, that name's noo to Sulphurville."

"Sakes alive, Scipio, are you going to keep Miss Scarlett hanging around all day whiles you gossip about Sulphurville?" his wife asked. Aware of her husband's enthusiasm for his native place, she may have foreseen a dissertation upon its wonders unless she were ruthless.

"Julie'll take you up to his apartment. And don't you forget to knock before you open the door, Julie."

On the way up-stairs in the wake of the servant, Sylvia wondered how she should explain her intrusion to a stranger, even though he were an Englishman. She had so firmly decided to herself it was Arthur that she could not make any plans for meeting anybody else. Julie was quite ready to open the door of the bedroom and let Sylvia enter unannounced; she was surprised by being requested to go in first and ask the gentleman if he could receive Miss Scarlett. However, she yielded to foreign eccentricity, and a moment later ushered Sylvia in.

It was Arthur Madden; and Sylvia, from a mixture of penitence for the way she treated him at Colonial Terrace, of self-congratulation for being so sure beforehand that it was he, and from swift compassion for his illness and loneliness, ran across the room and greeted him with a kiss.

"How on earth did you get into this horrible hole?" Arthur asked.

"My dear, I knew it was you when I heard your name." Breathlessly she poured out the story of how she had found him.

"But you'd made up your mind to play the Good Samaritan to whoever it was—you never guessed for a moment at first that it was me."

She forgave him the faint petulance because he was ill, and also because it brought back to her with a new vividness long bygone jealousies, restoring a little more of herself as she once was, nearly thirteen years ago. How little he had changed outwardly, and much of what change there was might be put down to his illness.

"Arthur, do you remember Maria?" she asked.

He smiled. "He died only about two years ago. He lived with my mother after I went on the stage."

Sylvia wondered to him why they had never met all these years. She had known so many people on the stage, but then, of course, she had been a good deal out of England. What had made Arthur go on the stage first? He had never talked of it in the old days.

"I used always to be keen on music."

Sylvia whistled the melody that introduced them to each other, and he smiled again.

"My mother still plays that sometimes, and I've often thought of you when she does. She lives at Dulwich now."

They talked for a while of Hampstead and laughed over the escape.

"You were a most extraordinary kid," he told her. "Because, after all, I was seventeen at the time—older than you. Good Lord! I'm thirty now, and you must be twenty-eight!"

To Sylvia it was much more incredible that he should be thirty; he seemed so much younger than she, lying here in this frowsy room, or was it that she felt so much older than he?

"But how on earth *did* you get stranded in this place?" she asked.

"I was touring with a concert party. The last few years I've practically given up the stage proper. I don't know why, really, for I was doing quite decently, but concert-work was more amusing, somehow. One wasn't so much at the beck and call of managers."

Sylvia knew, by the careful way in which he was giving his reasons for abandoning the stage, that he had not yet produced the real reason. It might have been baffled ambition or it might have been a woman.

"Well, we came to Sulphurville," said Arthur. He hesitated for a moment. Obviously there had been a woman. "We came to Sulphurville," he went on, "and played at the hotel you're playing at now—a rotten hole," he added, with retrospective bitterness. "I don't know how it was, but I suppose I got keen on the gambling—anyway, I had a row with the other people in the show, and when they left I refused to go with them. I stayed behind and got keen on the gambling."

"It was after the row that you took to roulette?" Sylvia asked.

"Well, as a matter if fact, I had a row with a girl. She treated me rather badly, and I stayed on. I lost a good deal of money. Well, it wasn't a very large sum, as a matter of fact, but it was all I had, and then I fell ill. I caught cold and I was worried over things. I cabled to my mother for some money, but there's been no reply. I'm afraid she's had difficulty in raising it. She quarreled with my father's people when I went on the stage. Damned narrow-minded set of yokels. Furious because I wouldn't take up farming. How I hate narrow-minded people!" And with an invalid's fretful intolerance he went on grumbling at the ineradicable characteristics of an English family four thousand miles away.

"Of course something may have happened to my mother," he added. "You may be sure that if anything had those beasts would never take the trouble to write and tell me. It would be a pleasure to them if they could annoy me in any way."

A swift criticism of Arthur's attitude toward the possibility of his mother's death rose to Sylvia's mind, but she repressed it, pleading with herself to excuse him because he was ill and overstrained. She was positively determined to see henceforth nothing but good in people, and in her anxiety to confirm herself in this resolve she was ready not merely to exaggerate everything in Arthur's favor, but even to twist any failure on his side into actual merit. Thus when she hastened to put her own resources at his disposal, and found him quite ready to accept without protest her help, she choked back the comparison with Jack Airdale's attitude in similar circumstances, and was quite angry with herself, saying how much more naturally Arthur had received her good-will and how splendid it was to find such simplicity and sincerity.

"I'll nurse you till you're quite well, and then why shouldn't we take an engagement together somewhere?"

Arthur became enthusiastic over this suggestion.

"You've not heard me sing yet. My throat's still too weak, but you'll be surprised, Sylvia."

"I haven't got anything but a very deep voice," she told him. "But I can usually make an impression."

"Can you? Of course, where I've always been held back is by lack of money. I've never been able to afford to buy good songs."

Arthur began to sketch out for himself a most radiant future, and as he talked Sylvia thought again how incredible it was that he should be older than herself. Yet was not this youthful enthusiasm exactly what she required? It was just the capacity of Arthur's for thinking he had a future that was going to make life tremendously worth while for her, tremendously interesting—oh, it was impossible not to believe in the decrees of fate, when at the very moment of her greatest longing to be needed by somebody she had met Arthur again. She could be everything to him, tend him through his illness, provide him with money to rid himself of the charity of Mrs. Lebus and the druggist, help him in his career, and watch over his fidelity to his ambition. She remembered how, years ago at Hampstead, his mother had watched over him; she could recall every detail of the room and see Mrs. Madden interrupt one of her long sonatas to be sure Arthur was not sitting in a draught. And it had been she who had heedlessly lured him away from that tender mother. There was poetic justice in this opportunity of reparation now accorded to her. To be sure, it had been nothing but a childish escapade—reparation was too strong a word; but there was something so neat about this encounter years afterward in a place like Sulphurville. How pale he was, which, nevertheless, made him more romantic to look at; how thin and white his hands were! She took one of them in her own boy's hands, as so many people had called them, and clasped it with the affection that one gives to small helpless things, to children and kittens, an affection that is half gratitude because one feels good-will rising like a sweet fountain from the depth of one's being, the freshness of which playing upon the spirit is so dear, that no words are enough to bless the wand that made the stream gush forth.

"I shall come and see you all day," said Sylvia. "But I think I ought not to break my contract at the Plutonian."

"Oh, you'll come and live here," Arthur begged. "You've no idea how horrible it is. There was a cockroach in the soup last night, and of course there are bugs. For goodness' sake, Sylvia, don't give me hope and then dash it away from me. I tell you I've had a hell of a time in this cursed hole. Listen to the bed; it sounds as if it would collapse at any moment. And the bugs have got on my nerves to such a pitch that I spend the whole time looking at spots on the ceiling and fancying they've moved. It's so hot, too; everything's rotted with heat. You mustn't desert me. You must come and stay here with me."

"Why shouldn't you move up to the Plutonian?" Sylvia suggested. "I'll tell you what I'll do. I'll get one of the doctors to come and look at you, and if he thinks it's possible you shall move up there at once. Poor boy, it really is too ghastly here."

Arthur was nearly weeping with self-pity.

"But, my dear girl, it's much worse than you think. You know those horrible birds' bath-tubs in which they bring your food at third-rate American hotels, loathsome saucers with squash and bits of grit in watery milk that they call cereals, and bony bits of chicken, well, imagine being fed like that when you're ill; imagine your bed covered with those infernal saucers. One of them always used to get left behind when Julie cleared away, and it always used to fall with a crash on the floor, and I used to wonder if the mess would tempt the cockroaches into my room. And then Lebus used to come up and make noises in his throat and brag about Sulphurville, and I used to know by his wandering eye that he was looking for what he called the cuspidor, which I'd put out of sight. And Mrs. Lebus used to come up and suck her teeth at me until I felt inclined to strangle her."

"The sooner you're moved away the better," Sylvia said, decidedly.

"Oh yes, if you think it can be managed. But if not, Sylvia, for God's sake don't leave me alone."

"Are you really glad to see me?" she asked.

"Oh, my dear, it was like heaven opening before one's eyes!"

"Tell me about the girl you were fond of," she said, abruptly.

"What do you want to talk about her for? There's nothing to tell you, really. She had red hair."

Sylvia was glad that Arthur spoke of her with so little interest; it certainly was definitely comforting to feel the utter dispossession of that red-haired girl.

"Look here," said Sylvia. "I'm going to let these people suppose that I'm your long-lost relative. I shall pay their bill and bring the doctor down to see you. Arthur, I'm glad I've found you. Do you remember the cab-horse? Oh, and do you remember the cats in the area and the jug of water that splashed you? You were so unhappy, almost as unhappy as you were when I found you here. Have you always been treated unkindly?"

"I have had a pretty hard time," Arthur said.

"Oh, but you mustn't be sorry for yourself," she laughed.

"No, seriously, Sylvia, I've always had a lot of people against me."

"Yes, but that's such fun. You simply must be amused by life when you're with me. I'm not hard-hearted a bit, really, but you mustn't be offended with me when I tell you that really there's something a tiny bit funny in your being stranded in the Auburn Hotel, Sulphurville."

"I'm glad you think so," said Arthur, in rather a hurt tone of voice.

"Don't be cross, you foolish creature."

134

"I'm not a bit cross. Only I *would* like you to understand that my illness isn't a joke. You don't suppose I should let you pay my bills and do all this for me unless it were really something serious."

Sylvia put her hand on his mouth. "I forgive you," she murmured, "because you really are ill. Oh, Arthur, *do* you remember Hube? What fun everything is!"

Sylvia left him and went down-stairs to arrange matters with Mrs. Lebus.

"It was a relation, after all," she told her. "The Maddens have been related to us for hundreds of years."

"My! My! Now ain't that real queer? Oh, Scipio!"

Mr. Lebus came into view cleaning his nails with the same pen, and was duly impressed with the coincidence.

"Darned if I don't tell Pastor Gollick after next Sunday meeting. He's got a kind of hankering after the ways of Providence. Gee! Why, it's a sermonizing cinch."

There was general satisfaction in the Auburn Hotel over the payment of Arthur's bill.

"Not that I wouldn't have trusted him for another month and more," Mrs. Lebus affirmed. "But it's a satisfaction to be able to turn round and say to the neighbors, 'What did I tell you?' Folks in Sulphurville was quite sure I'd never be paid back a cent. This'll learn them!"

Mr. Lebus, in whose throat the doubts of the neighbors had gathered to offend his faith, cleared them out forever in one sonorous rauque.

The druggist's account was settled, and though, when Sylvia first heard him, he had been doubtful if his medicine was doing the patient any good, he was now most anxious that he should continue with the prescription. That afternoon one of the doctors in residence at the Plutonian visited Arthur and at once advised his removal thither.

Arthur made rapid progress when he was once out of the hospitable squalor of the Auburn Hotel, and the story of Sylvia's discovery of her unfortunate cousin became a romantic episode for all the guests of the Plutonian, a never-failing aid to conversation between wives waiting for their husbands to emerge from their daily torture at the hands of the masseurs, who lived like imps in the sulphurous glooms of the bath below; maybe it even provided the victims themselves with a sufficiently absorbing topic to mitigate the penalties of their cure.

Arthur himself expanded wonderfully as the subject of so much discussion. It gave Sylvia the greatest pleasure to see the way in which his complexion was recovering its old ruddiness and his steps their former vigor; but she did not approve of the way in which the story kept pace with Arthur's expansion. She confided to him how very personally the news of the sick Englishman had affected her and how she had made up her mind from the beginning that it was a stranded actor, and afterward, when she heard in the drug-store the name Madden, that it actually was Arthur himself. He, however, was unable to stay content with such an incomplete telepathy; indulging human nature's preference for what is not true, both in his own capacity as a liar and in his listeners' avid and wanton credulity, he transferred a woman's intimate hopes into a quack's tale.

"Then you didn't see your cousin's spirit go up in the elevator when you were standing in the lobby? Now isn't that perfectly discouraging?" complained a lady with an astral reputation in Illinois.

"I'm afraid the story's been added to a good deal," Sylvia said. "I'm sorry to disappoint the faithful."

"She's shy about giving us her experiences," said another lady from Iowa. "I know I was just thrilled when I heard it. It seemed to me the most wonderful story I'd ever imagined. I guess you felt kind of queer when you saw him lying on a bed in your room."

"He was in his own room," Sylvia corrected, "and I didn't feel at all queer. It was he who felt queer."

"Isn't she secretive?" exclaimed the lady from Illinois. "Why, I was going to ask you to write it up in our society's magazine, *The Flash*. We don't print any stories that aren't established as true. Well, your experience has given me real courage, Miss Scarlett. Thank you."

The astral enthusiast clasped Sylvia's hand and gazed at her as earnestly as if she had noticed a smut on her nose.

"Yes, I'm sure we ought to be grateful," said the lady from Iowa. "My! Our footsteps are treading in the unseen every day of our lives! You certainly are privileged," she added, wrapping Sylvia in a damp mist of benign fatuity.

"I wish you wouldn't elaborate everything so," Sylvia begged of Arthur when she had escaped from the deification of the two psychical ladies. "It makes me feel so dreadfully old to see myself assuming a legendary shape before my own eyes. It's as painful as being stuffed alive—stuffed alive with nonsense," she added, with a laugh.

Arthur's expansion, however, was not merely grafted on Sylvia's presentiment of his discovery in Sulphurville; he blossomed upon his own stock, a little exotically, perhaps, like the clumps of fiery cannas in the grounds of the hotel, but with a quite conspicuous effectiveness. Like the cannas, he required protection from frost, for there was a very real sensitiveness beneath all that flamboyance, and it was the knowledge of this that kept Sylvia from criticizing him at all severely. Besides, even if he did bask a little too complacently in expressions of interest and sympathy, it was a very natural reaction from his wretched solitude at the Auburn Hotel, for which he could scarcely be held culpable, least of all by herself. Moreover, was not this so visible recovery the best tribute he could have paid to her care? If he appeared to strut—for, indeed, there was a hint of strutting in his demeanor—he only did so from a sense of well-being. Finally, if any further defense was necessary, he was an Englishman among a crowd of Americans; the conditions demanded a good deal of competitive self-assertion.

Meanwhile summer was gone; the trees glowed with every shade of crimson. Sylvia could not help feeling that there was something characteristic in the demonstrative richness of the American fall; though she was far from wishing to underrate its beauty, the display was oppressive. She sighed for the melancholy of the European autumn, a conventional emotion, no doubt, but so closely bound up with old associations that she could not wish to lose it. This cremation of summer, these leafy pyrotechnics, this holocaust of color, seemed a too barbaric celebration of the year's death. It was significant that autumn with its long-drawn-out suggestion of decline should here have failed to displace fall; for there was something essentially catastrophic in this ruthless bonfire of foliage. It was not surprising that the aboriginal inhabitants should have been redskins, nor that the gorgeousness of nature should have demanded from the humanity it overwhelmed a readjustment of decorative values which superficial observers were apt to mistake for gaudy ostentation. Sylvia could readily imagine that if she had been accustomed from childhood to these crimson woods, these beefy robins, and these saucer-eyed daisies, she might have found her own more familiar landscapes merely tame and pretty; but as it was she felt dazzled and ill at ease. It's a little more and how much it is, she told herself, pondering the tantalizing similarity that was really as profoundly different as an Amazonian forest from Kensington Gardens.

Arthur's first flamboyance was much toned down by all that natural splendor; in fact, it no longer existed, and Sylvia found a freshening charm in his company amid these crimson trees and unfamiliar birds, and in this staring white hotel with its sulphurous exhalations. His complete restoration to health, moreover, was a pleasure and a pride that nothing could mar, and she found herself planning his happiness and prosperity as if she had already transferred to him all she herself hoped from life.

At the end of September the long-expected remittance arrived from Mrs. Madden, and Sylvia gathered from the letter that the poor lady had been much puzzled to send the money.

"We must cable it back to her at once," Sylvia said.

"Oh, well, now it's come, is that wise?" Arthur objected. "She may have had some difficulty in getting it, but that's over now."

"No, no. It must be cabled back to her. I've got plenty of money to carry us on till we begin to work together."

"But I can't go on accepting charity like this," Arthur protested. "It's undignified, really. I've never done such a thing before."

"You accepted it from your mother."

"Oh, but my mother's different."

"Only because she's less able to afford it than I am," Sylvia pointed out. "Look, she's sent you fifty pounds. Think how jolly it would be for her suddenly to receive fifty pounds for herself."

Arthur warmed to the idea; he could not resist the picture of his mother's pleasure, nor the kind of inverted generosity with which it seemed to endow himself. He talked away about the arrival of the money in England till it almost seemed as if he were sending his mother the accumulation of hard-earned savings to buy herself a new piano; that was the final purpose to which, in Arthur's expanding fancy, the fifty pounds was to be put. Sylvia found his attitude rather boyish and charming, and they had an argument, on the way to cable the money back, whether it would be better for Mrs. Madden to buy a Bechstein or a Blüthner.

Sylvia's contract with the Plutonian expired with the first fortnight of October, and they decided to see what likelihood there was of work in New York before they thought of returning to Europe. They left Sulphurville with everybody's good wishes, because everybody owed to their romantic meeting an opportunity of telling a really good ghost story at first hand, with the liberty of individual elaboration.

New York was very welcome after Sulphurville. They passed the wooded heights of the Hudson at dusk in a glow of somber magnificence softened by the vapors of the river. It seemed to Sylvia that scarcely ever had she contemplated a landscape of such restrained splendor, and she thought of that young New-Yorker who had preferred not to travel more than fifty miles west of his native city, though the motive of his loyalty had most improbably been the beauty of the Hudson. She wondered if Arthur appreciated New York, but he responded to her enthusiasm with the superficial complaints of the Englishman, complaints that when tested resolved themselves into conventional formulas of disapproval.

"I suppose trite opinions are a comfortable possession," Sylvia said. "But a good player does not like a piano that is too easy. You complain of the morning papers' appearing shortly after midnight, but confess that in your heart you prefer reading *them* in bed to reading a London evening paper, limp from being carried about in the pocket and with whatever is important in it illegible."

"But the flaring head-lines," Arthur protested. "You surely don't like them?"

"Oh, but I do!" she avowed. "They're as much more amusing than the dreary column beneath as tinned tongue is nicer than the dry undulation for which you pay twice as much. Head-lines are the poetry of journalism, and, after all, what would the Parthenon be without its frieze?"

"Of course you'd argue black was white," Arthur said.

"Well, that's a better standpoint than accepting everything as gray."

"Most things are gray."

"Oh no, they're not! Some things are. Old men's beards and dirty linen and Tschaikowsky's music and oysters and Wesleyans."

"There you go," he jeered.

"Where do I go?"

"Right off the point," said Arthur, triumphantly. "No woman can argue."

"Oh, but I'm not a woman," Sylvia contradicted. "I'm a mythical female monster, don't you know—one of those queer beasts with claws like hay-rakes and breasts like peg-tops and a tail like a fish."

"Do you mean a Sphinx?" Arthur asked, in his literal way. He was always rather hostile toward her extravagant fancies, because he thought it dangerous to encourage a woman in much the same way as he would have objected to encouraging a beggar.

"No, I really meant a grinx, which is rather like a Sphinx, but the father was a griffin—the mother in both cases was a minx, of course."

"What was the father of the Sphinx?" he asked, rather ungraciously.

Sylvia clapped her hands.

"I knew you wouldn't be able to resist the question. A sphere—a woman's sphere, of course, which is nearly as objectionable a beast as a lady's man."

"You do talk rot sometimes," said Arthur.

"Don't you ever have fancies?" she demanded, mockingly.

"Yes, of course, but practical fancies."

"Practical fancies," Sylvia echoed. "Oh, my dear, it sounds like a fairy in Jaeger combinations! You don't know what fun it is talking rot to you, Arthur. It's like hoaxing a chicken with marbles. You walk away from my conversation with just the same disgusted dignity."

"You haven't changed a bit," Arthur proclaimed. "You're just the same as you were at fifteen."

Sylvia, who had been teasing him with a breath of malice, was penitent at once; after all, he had once run away with her, and it would be difficult for any woman of twenty-eight not to rejoice a little at the implication of thirteen undestructive years.

"That last remark was like a cocoanut thrown by a monkey from the top of the cocoanut-palm," she said. "You meant it to be crushing, but it was crushed instead, and quite deliciously sweet inside."

All the time that Sylvia had been talking so lightly, while the train was getting nearer and nearer to New York, there had lain at the back of her mind the insistent problem of her relationship to Arthur. The impossibility of their going on together as friends and nothing more had been firmly fixed upon her consciousness for a long time now, and the reason of this was to be sought for less in Arthur than in herself. So far they had preserved all the outward semblances of friendship, but she knew that one look from her eyes deep into his would transform him into her lover. She gave Arthur credit for telling himself quite sincerely that it would be "caddish" to make love to her while he remained under what he would consider a grave obligation; and because with his temperament it would be as much in the ordinary routine of the day to make love to a woman as to dress himself in the morning. She praised his decorum and was really half grateful to him for managing to keep his balance on the very small pedestal that she had provided. She might fairly presume, too, that if she let Arthur fall in love with her he would wish to marry her. Why should she not marry him? It was impossible to answer without accusing herself of a cynicism that she was far from feeling, yet without which she could not explain even to herself her quite definite repulsion from the idea of marrying him. The future, really, now, the very immediate future, must be flung to chance; it was hopeless to arrogate to her forethought the determination of it; besides, here was New York already.

"We'd better go to my old hotel," Sylvia suggested. Was it the reflection of her own perplexity, or did she detect in Arthur's accents a note of relief, as if he too had been watching the Palisades of the Hudson and speculating upon the far horizon they concealed?

They dined at Rector's, and after dinner they walked down Broadway into Madison Square, where upon this mild October night the Metropolitan Tower, that best of all the Gargantuan baby's toys, seemed to challenge the indifferent moon. They wandered up Madison Avenue, which was dark after the winking sky-signs of Broadway and with its not very tall houses held a thought of London in the darkness. But when Sylvia turned to look back it was no longer London, for she could see the great, illuminated hands and numerals of the clock in the Metropolitan flashing from white to red for the hour. This clock without a dial-plate was the quietest of the Gargantuan baby's toys, for it did not strike; one was conscious of the almost pathetic protest against all those other damnably noisy toys: one felt he might become so enamoured of its pretty silence that to provide himself with a new diversion he might take to doubling the hours to keep pace with the rapidity of the life with which he played.

"It's almost as if we were walking up Haverstock Hill again," said Arthur.

"And we're grown up now," Sylvia murmured. "Oh, dreadfully grown up, really!"

They walked on for a while in silence. It was impossible to keep back the temptation to cheat time by leaping over the gulf of years and being what they were when last they walked along together like this. Sylvia kept looking over her shoulder at the bland clock hanging in the sky behind them; at this distance the fabric of the tower had melted into the night and was no longer visible, which gave to the clock a strange significance and made it a simulacrum of time itself.

"You haven't changed a bit," she said.

"Do you remember when you told me I looked like a cow? It was after"—he breathed perceptibly faster—"after I kissed you."

She would not ascribe his remembering what she had called him to an imperfectly healed scar of vanity, but with kindlier thoughts turned it to a memento of his affection for her. After all, she had loved him then; it had been a girl's love, but did there ever come with age a better love than that first flushed gathering of youth's opening flowers?

"Sylvia, I've thought about you ever since. When you drove me away from Colonial Terrace I felt like killing myself. Surely we haven't met again for nothing."

"Is it nothing unless I love you?" she asked, fiercely, striving to turn the words into weapons to pierce the recesses of his thoughts and blunt themselves against a true heart.

"Ah no, I won't say that," he cried. "Besides, I haven't the right to talk about love. You've been—Sylvia, I can't tell you what you've been to me since I met you again."

"If I could only believe—oh, but believe with all of me that was and is and ever will be—that I could have been so much."

"You have, you have."

"Don't take my love as a light thing," she warned him. "It's not that I'm wanting so very much for myself, but I want to be so much to you."

"Sylvia, won't you marry me? I couldn't ever take your love lightly. Indeed. Really."

"Ah, it's not asking me to marry you that means you're serious. I'm not asking you what your intentions are. I'm asking if you want me."

"Sylvia, I want you dreadfully."

"Now, now?" she pressed.

"Now and always."

They had stopped without being aware of it. A trolley-car jangled by, casting transitory lights that wavered across Arthur's face, and Sylvia could see how his eyes were shining. She dreaded lest by adding a few conventional words he should spoil what he had said so well, but he waited for her, as in the old days he had always waited.

"You're not cultivating this love, like a convalescent patient does for his nurse?" Sylvia demanded.

She stopped herself abruptly, conscious that every question she put to him was ultimately being put to herself.

"Did I ever not love you?" he asked. "It was you that grew tired of me. It was you that sent me away."

"Don't pretend that all these years you've been waiting for me to come back," she scoffed.

"Of course not. What I'm trying to explain is that we can start now where we left off; that is, if you will."

He held out his hand half timidly.

"And if I won't?"

The hand dropped again to his side, and there was so much wounded sensitiveness in the slight gesture that Sylvia caught him to her as if he were a child who had fallen and needed comforting.

"When I first put my head on your shoulder," she murmured. "Oh, how well I can remember the day—such a sparkling day, with London spread out like life at our feet. Now we're in the middle of New York, but it seems just as far away from us two as London was that day—and life," she added, with a sigh.

CHAPTER XIV

CIRCUMSTANCES seemed to applaud almost immediately the step that Sylvia had taken. There was no long delay caused by looking for work in New York, which might have destroyed romance by its interposition of fretful hopes and disappointments. A variety company was going to leave in November for a tour in eastern Canada. At least two months would be spent in the French provinces, and Sylvia's bilingual accomplishment was exactly what the manager wanted.

"I'm getting on," she laughed. "I began by singing French songs with an English accent; I advanced from that to acting English words with a French accent; now I'm going to be employed in doing both. But what does it matter? The great thing is that we should be together."

That was where Arthur made the difference to her life; he was securing her against the loneliness that at twenty-eight was beginning once more to haunt her imagination. What did art matter? It had never been anything but a refuge.

Arthur himself was engaged to sing, and though he had not such a good voice as Claude Raglan, he sang with much better taste and was really musical. Sylvia was annoyed to find herself making comparisons between Claude and Arthur. It happened at the moment that Arthur was fussing about his number on the program, and she could not help being reminded of Claude's attitude toward his own artistic importance. She consoled herself by thinking that it should always be one of her aims to prevent the likeness growing any closer; then she laughed at herself for this resolve, which savored of developing Arthur, that process she had always so much condemned.

They opened at Toronto, and after playing a week Arthur caught a chill and was out of the program for a fortnight; this gave Sylvia a fresh opportunity of looking after him; and Toronto in wet, raw weather was so dreary that, to come back to the invalid after the performance, notwithstanding the ineffable discomfort of the hotel, was to come back home. During this time Sylvia gave Arthur a history of the years that had gone by since they parted, and it puzzled her that he should be so jealous of the past. She wondered why she could not feel the same jealousy about his past, and she found herself trying to regret that red-haired girl and many others on account of the obvious pleasure such regrets afforded Arthur. She used to wonder, too, why she always left out certain incidents and obscured certain aspects of her own past, whether, for instance, she did not tell him about Michael Fane on her own account or because she was afraid that Arthur would perceive a superficial resemblance between himself and Claude and a very real one between herself and Lily, or because she would have resented from Arthur the least expression, not so much of contempt as even of mild surprise, at Michael's behavior. Another subject she could never discuss with Arthur was her mother's love for her father, notwithstanding that his own mother's elopement with a groom must have prevented the least criticism on his side. Here again she wondered if her reserve was due to loyalty or to a vague sense of temperamental repetition that was condemning her to stand in the same relation to Arthur as her mother to her father. She positively had to run away from the idea that Arthur had his prototype; she was shutting him up in a box and scarcely even looking at him, which was as good as losing him altogether, really. Even when she did look at him she handled him with such exaggerated carefulness, for fear of his getting broken, that all the pleasure of possession was lost. Perhaps she should have had an equal anxiety to preserve intact anybody else with whom she might have thrown in her lot; but when she thought over this attitude it was dismaying enough and seemed to imply an incapacity on her part to enjoy fully anything in life.

"I've grown out of being destructive; at least I think I have. I wonder if the normal process from Jacobinism to the intense conservatism of age is due to wisdom, jealousy, or fear.

"Arthur, what are your politics?" she asked, aloud.

He looked up from the game of patience he was playing, a game in which he was apt to attribute the pettiest personal motives to the court-cards whenever he failed to get out.

"Politics?" he echoed, vaguely. "I don't think I ever had any. I suppose I'm a Conservative. Oh yes, certainly I'm a Conservative. That infernal knave of hearts is covered now!" he added, in an aggrieved voice.

"Well, I didn't cover it," said Sylvia.

"No, dear, of course you didn't. But it really is a most extraordinary thing that I always get done by the knaves."

"You share your misfortune with the rest of humanity, if that's any consolation."

The conversation was interrupted by the entrance of Orlone. He was a huge Neapolitan with the countenance of a gigantic and swarthy Punch, who had been trying to get back to Naples for twenty years, but had been prevented at first by his passion for gambling and afterward by an unwilling wife and a numerous family. Orlone made even Toronto cheerful, and before he had come two paces into a room Sylvia always began to laugh. He never said anything deliberately funny except on the stage, but laughter emanated from him infectiously, as yawning might. Though he had spent twenty years in America, he still spoke the most imperfect English; and when he and Sylvia had done laughing at each other they used to laugh all over again, she at his English, he at her Italian. When they had finished laughing at that Orlone used to swear marvelously for Sylvia's benefit whenever she should again visit Sirene; and she would teach him equally tremendous oaths in case he should ever come to London. When they had finished laughing at this, Orlone would look over Arthur's shoulder and, after making the most ridiculous gestures of caution, would finally burst out into an absolute roar of laughter right in Arthur's ear.

"*Pazienza,*" Sylvia would say, pointing to the outspread cards.

"*Brava signora! Come parla bene!*"

And of course this was obviously so absurd a statement that it would set them off laughing again.

"You are a pair of lunatics," Arthur would protest; he would have liked to be annoyed at his game's being interrupted, but he was powerless to repulse Orlone's good humor.

When they returned to New York in the spring and Sylvia looked back at the tour, she divined how much of her pleasure in it had been owed to Orlone's all-pervading mirth. He had really provided the robust and full-blooded contrast to Arthur that had been necessary. It was not exactly that without him their existence together would have been insipid—oh no, there was nothing insipid about Arthur, but one appreciated his delicacy after that rude and massive personality. When they had traveled over leagues of snow-covered country, Orlone had always lightened the journey with gay Neapolitan songs, and sometimes with tender ones like "Torno di Surriento." It was then that, gazing out over the white waste, she had been able to take Arthur's hand and sigh to be sitting with him on some Sirenian cliff, to smell again the rosemary and crumble with her fingers the sunburnt earth. But this capacity of Orlone's for conjuring up the long Parthenopean shore was nothing more than might have been achieved by any terra-cotta Silenus in a provincial museum. After Silenus, what nymph would not turn to Hylas somewhat gratefully? It had been the greatest fun in the world to drive in tinkling sledges through Montreal, with Orlone to tease the driver until he was as sore as the head of the bear that in his fur coat he resembled; it had been fun to laugh with Orlone in Quebec and Ottawa and everywhere else; but after so much laughter it had always been particularly delightful to be alone again with Arthur, and to feel that he too was particularly enjoying being alone with her.

"I really do think we get on well together," she said to him.

"Of course we do."

And was there in the way he agreed with her just the least suggestion that he should have been surprised if she had not enjoyed his company, an almost imperceptible hint of complacency, or was it condescension?

"I really must get out of this habit of poking my nose into other people's motives," Sylvia told herself. "I'm like a horrid little boy with a new penknife. Arthur could fairly say to me that I forced myself upon him. I did really. I went steaming into the Auburn Hotel like a salvage-tug. There's the infernal side of obligations—I can't really quite free myself from the notion that Arthur ought to be grateful to me. He's in a false position through no fault of his own, and he's behaving beautifully. It's my own cheap cynicism that's to blame. I wish I could discover some mental bitter aloes that would cure me of biting my mind, as I cured myself of biting my nails."

Sylvia was very glad that Arthur succeeded in getting an engagement that spring to act, and that she did not; she was really anxious to let him feel that she should be dependent on him for a while. The result would have been entirely satisfactory but for one flaw—the increase in Arthur's sense of his own artistic importance. Sylvia would not have minded this so much if he had possessed enough of it to make him oblivious of the world's opinion, but it was always more of a vanity than a pride, chiefly concerned with the personal impression he made. It gave him much more real pleasure to be recognized by two shop-girls on their afternoon out than to be praised by a leading critic. Sylvia would have liked him to be equally contemptuous of either form of flattery, but that he should revel in both, and actually esteem more valuable the recognition accorded him by a shop-girl's backward glance and a nudge from her companion seemed to be lamentable.

"I don't see why you should despise me for being pleased," Arthur said. "I'm only pleased because it's a proof that I'm getting known."

"But they'd pay the same compliment to a man with a wen on his nose."

"No doubt, but also to any famous man," Arthur added.

Sylvia could have screamed with irritation at his lack of any sense of proportion. Why could he not be like Jack Airdale, who had never suffered from any illusion that what he was doing, so far as art was concerned, was not essentially insignificant? Yet, after all, was she not being unreasonable in paying so much attention to a childish piece of vanity that was inseparable from the true histrionic temperament?

"I'm sorry, Arthur. I think I'm being unfair to you. I only criticize you because I want you to be always the best of you. I see your point of view, but I was irritated by the giggles."

"I wasn't paying the least attention to the girls."

"Oh, I wasn't jealous," she said, quickly. "Oh no, darling Arthur, even with the great affection that I have for you, I shall never be able to be jealous of your making eyes at shop-girls."

When Arthur's engagement seemed likely to come to an end in the summer, they discussed plans and decided to take a holiday in the country, somewhere in Maine or Vermont. Arthur, as usual, set the scene beforehand, but as he set it quite in accord with Sylvia's taste she did not mind. Indeed, their holiday in Vermont on the borders of Lake Champlain was as near as she ever got to being perfectly happy with Arthur—happy, that is, to the point of feeling like a chill the prospect of separation. Sylvia was inclined to say that all Arthur's faults were due to the theater, and that when one had him like this in simple surroundings the best side of him was uppermost and visible, like a spun coin that shows a simple head when it falls.

Sylvia found that she had brought with her by chance the manuscript of the poems given to her by the outcast Englishman in Paris, and Arthur was very anxious that she should come back to her idea of rendering these. He had already composed a certain number of unimportant songs in his career, but now the Muses smiled upon him (or perhaps it might be truer to speak of her own smiles, Sylvia thought) with such favor that he set a dozen poems to the very accompaniment they wanted, the kind of music, moreover, that suited Sylvia's voice.

"We must get these done in New York," he said; but that week a letter came from Olive Airdale, and Sylvia had a sudden longing for England. She did not think she would make an effort to do anything in America. The truth was that she had supplemented the Englishman's poems with an idea of her own to give impressions gathered from her own life. It was strange how abruptly the longing to express herself had arrived, but it had arrived, with a force and fierceness that were undeniable. It had come, too, with that authentic fever of secrecy that she divined a woman must feel in the first moment of knowing that she has conceived. She could not have imparted her sense of creation to any one else; such an intimacy of revelation was too shocking to be contemplated. Somehow she was sure that this strange shamefulness was right and that she was entitled to hug within herself the conception that would soon enough be turned to the travail of birth.

"By, Jove! Sylvia, this holiday *has* done you good!" Arthur exclaimed.

She kissed him because, ignorant though he was of the true reason, she owed him thanks for her looks.

"Sylvia, if we go back to England, do let's be married first."

"Why?"

"Why, because it's not fair on me."

"On you?"

"Yes, on me. People will always blame me, of course."

"What has it got to do with anybody else except me?"

"My mother—"

"My dear Arthur," Sylvia interrupted, sharply, "if your mother ran away with a groom, she'll be the first person to sympathize with my point of view."

"I suppose you're trying to be cruel," said Arthur.

"And succeeding, to judge by your dolorous mouth. No, my dear, let the suggestion of marriage come from me. I sha'n't be hurt if you refuse."

"Well, are we to pretend we're married?" Arthur asked, hopelessly.

"Certainly not, if by that you mean that I'm to put 'Mrs. Arthur Madden' on a visiting-card. Don't look so frightened. I'm not proposing to march into drawing-rooms with a big drum to proclaim my emancipation from the social decencies. Don't worry me, Arthur. It's all much too complicated to explain, but I'll tell you one thing, I'm not going to marry you merely to remove the world's censure of your conduct, and as long as you feel about marrying me as you might feel about letting me carry a heavy bag, I'll never marry you."

"I don't feel a bit like that about it," he protested. "If I could leave you, I'd leave you now. But the very thought of losing you makes my heart stop beating. It's like suddenly coming to the edge of a precipice. I know perfectly well that you despise me at heart. You think I'm a wretched actor with no feelings off the stage. You think I don't know my own mind, if you even admit that I've got a mind at all. But I'm thirty-one. I'm not a boy. I've had a good many women in love with me. Now don't begin to laugh. I'm determined to say what I ought to have said long ago, and should have said if I hadn't been afraid the whole time of losing you. If I lose you now it can't be helped. I'd sooner lose you than go on being treated like a child. What I want to say is that, though I know you think it wasn't worth while being loved by the women who've loved me, I do think it was. I'm not in the least ashamed of them. Most of them, at any rate, were beautiful, though I admit that all of them put together wouldn't have made up for missing you. You're a thousand times cleverer than I. You've got much more personality. You've every right to consider you've thrown yourself away on me. But the fact remains that you've done it. We've been together now a year. That proves that there *is* something in me. I'm prouder of this year with you than of all the rest of my life. You've developed me in the most extraordinary way."

"I have?" Sylvia burst in.

"Of course you have. But I'm not going to be treated like a mantis."

"Like a what?"

"A mantis. You can read about it in that French book on insects. The female eats the male. Well, I'm damned well not going to be eaten. I'm not going back to England with you unless you marry me."

"Well, I'm not going to marry you," Sylvia declared.

"Very well, then I shall try to get an engagement on tour and we'll separate."

"So much the better," she said. "I've got a good deal to occupy myself at present."

"Of course you can have the music I wrote for those poems," said Arthur.

"Damn your music," she replied.

Sylvia was so much obsessed with the conviction of having at last found a medium for expressing herself in art that, though she was vaguely aware of having a higher regard for Arthur at this moment than she had ever had, she could only behold him as a troublesome visitor that was preventing her from sitting down to work.

Arthur went off on tour. Sylvia took an apartment in New York far away up-town and settled down to test her inspiration. In six months she lived her whole life over again, and of every personality that had touched her own and left its mark she made a separate presentation. Her great anxiety was to give to each sketch the air of an improvisation, and in the course of it to make her people reveal their permanent characters rather than their transient emotions. It was really based on the art of the impersonator who comes on with a cocked hat, sticks out his neck, puts his hands behind his back, and his legs apart, leans over to the audience, and whispers Napoleon. Sylvia thought she could extend the pleasures of recognition beyond the mere mimicry of externals to a finer mimicry of essentials. She wanted an audience to clap not because she could bark sufficiently like a real dog to avoid being mistaken for a kangaroo, but because she could be sufficiently Mrs. Gainsborough not to be recognized as Mrs. Beardmore—yet without relying upon their respective sizes in corsets to mark the difference. She did not intend to use even make-up; the entertainment was always to be an improvisation. It was also to be undramatic; that is to say, it was not to obtain its effect by working to a climax, so that, however well hidden the mechanism might have been during the course of the presentation, the machinery would reveal itself at the end. Sylvia wanted to make each member of the audience feel that he had dreamed her improvisation, or rather she hoped that he would gain from it that elusive sensation of having lived it before, and that the effect upon each person listening to her should be ultimately incommunicable, like a dream. She was sure now that she could achieve this effect with the poems, not, as she had originally supposed, through their objective truthfulness, but through their subjective truth. That outcast Englishman should be one of her improvisations, and of course the original idea of letting the poems be accompanied by music would be ruinous; one might as well illustrate them with a magic lantern. As to her own inventions, she must avoid giving them a set form, because, whatever actors might urge to the contrary, a play could never really be performed twice by the same caste. She would have a scene painted like those futurist Italian pictures; they were trying to do with color what she was trying to do with acting; they were striving to escape from the representation of mere externals, and often succeeding almost too well, she added, with a smile. She would get hold of Ronald Walker in London, who doubtless by now would be too prosperous to serve her purpose himself, but who would probably know of some newly fledged painter anxious to flap his wings.

At the end of six months Sylvia had evolved enough improvisations to make a start. She went to bed tired out with the last night's work, and woke up in the morning with a sense of blankness at the realization of there being nothing to do that day. All the time she had been working she had been content to be alone; she had even looked forward to amusing herself in New York when her work was finished. Now the happy moment had come and she could feel nothing but this empty boredom. She wondered what Arthur was doing, and she reproached herself for the way in which she had discarded him. She had been so thrilled by the notion that she was necessary to somebody; it had seemed to her the consummation of so many heedless years. Yet no sooner had she successfully imposed herself upon Arthur than she was eager to think of nothing but herself without caring a bit about his point of view. Now that she could do nothing more with her work until the test of public performance was applied to it, she was bored; in fact, she missed Arthur. The truth was that half the pleasure of being necessary to somebody else had been that he should be necessary to her. But marriage with Arthur? Marriage with a curly-headed actor? Marriage with anybody? No, that must wait, at any rate until she had given the fruit of these six months to the world. She could not be hampered by belonging to anybody before that.

"I do think I'm justified in taking myself a little seriously for a while," said Sylvia, "and in shutting my eyes to my own absurdity. Self-mockery is dangerous beyond a certain point. I really will give this idea of mine a fair chance. If I'm a failure, Arthur will love me all the more through vanity, and if I'm a success—I suppose really he'll be vain of that, too."

Sylvia telegraphed to Arthur, and heard that he expected to be back in New York at the end of the month. He was in Buffalo this week. Nothing could keep her a moment longer in New York alone, and she went up to join him. She had a sudden fear when she arrived that she might find him occupied with a girl; in fact, really, when she came to think of the manner in which she had left him, it was most improbable that she should not. She nearly turned round and went back to New York; but her real anxiety to see Arthur and talk to him about her work made her decide to take the risk of what might be the deepest humiliation of her life. It was strange how much she wanted to talk about what she had done; the desire to do so now was as overmastering an emotion as had been in the first moment of conception the urgency of silence.

Sylvia was spared the shock of finding Arthur wrapped up in some one else.

"Sylvia, how wonderful! What a relief to see you again!" he exclaimed. "I've been longing for you to see me in the part I'm playing now. It's certainly the most successful thing I've done. I'm so glad you kept me from wasting myself any longer on that concert work. I really believe I've made a big hit at last."

Sylvia was almost as much taken aback to find Arthur radiant with the prospect of success as she would have been to find him head over ears in love. She derived very little satisfaction from the way in which he attributed his success to her; she was not at all in the mood for being a godmother, now that she had a baby of her own.

"I'm so glad, old son. That's splendid. Now I want to talk about the work I've been doing all these six months."

Forthwith she plunged into the details of the scheme, to which Arthur listened attentively enough, though he only became really enthusiastic when she could introduce analogies with his own successful performance.

"You will go in front to-night?" he begged. "I'm awfully keen to hear what you think of my show. Half my pleasure in the hit has been spoiled by your not having seen it. Besides, I think you'll be interested in noticing that once or twice I try to get the same effect as you're trying for in these impersonations."

"Damn your eyes, Arthur, they're not impersonations; they're improvisations."

"Did I say impersonations? I'm sorry," said Arthur, looking rather frightened.

"Yes, you'd better placate me," she threatened. "Or I'll spend my whole time looking at Niagara and never go near your show."

However, Sylvia did go to see the play that night and found that Arthur really was excellent in his part, which was that of the usual young man in musical comedy who wanders about in a well-cut flannel suit, followed by six young women with parasols ready to smother him with affection, melody, and lace. But how, even in the intoxication of success, he had managed to establish a single analogy with what she proposed to do was beyond comprehension.

Arthur came out of the stage door, wreathed in questions.

"You were in such a hurry to get out," said Sylvia, "that you didn't take off your make-up properly. You'll get arrested if you walk about like that. I hear the sumptuary laws in Buffalo are very strict."

"No, don't rag. Did you like the hydrangea song? Do you remember the one I mean?"

He hummed the tune.

"I warn you, Arthur, there's recently been a moral up-lift in Buffalo. You will be sewn up in a barrel and flung into Niagara if you don't take care. No, seriously. I think your show was capital. Which brings me to the point. We sail for Europe at the end of April."

"Oh, but do you think it's wise for me to leave America now that I've really got my foot in?"

"Do you still want to marry me?"

"More than ever," he assured her.

"Very well, then. Your only chance of marrying me is to leave New York without a murmur. I've thought it all out. As soon as I get back I shall spend my last shilling on fitting out my show. When I've produced it and when I've found out that I've not been making a fool of myself for the last six months, perhaps I'll marry you. Until then—as friends we met, as anything more than friends we part. Got me, Steve?"

"But, Sylvia—"

"But me no buts, or you'll get my goat. Understand my meaning, Mr. Stevenson?"

"Yes, only—"

"The discussion's closed."

"Are we engaged?"

"I don't know. We'll have to see our agents about that."

"Oh, don't rag. Marriage is not a joke. You are a most extraordinary girl."

"Thanks for the discount. I shall be thirty in three months, don't forget. Talking of the advantages of rouge, you might get rid of some of yours before supper, if you don't mind."

"Are we engaged?" Arthur repeated, firmly.

"No, the engagement ring and the marriage-bells will be pealed simultaneously. You're as free as Boccaccio, old son."

"You're in one of those moods when it's impossible to argue with you."

"So much the better. We shall enjoy our supper all the more. I'm so excited at the idea of going back to England. After all, I shall have been away nearly three years. I shall find godchildren who can talk. Think of that. Arthur, don't you want to go back?"

"Yes, if I can get a shop. I think it's madness for me to leave New York, but I daren't let you go alone."

The anticipation of being in England again and of putting to the test her achievement could not charm away all Sylvia's regret at leaving America, most of all New York. She owed to New York this new stability that she discovered in her life. She owed to some action of New York upon herself the delight of inspiration, the sweet purgatory of effort, the hope of a successful end to her dreams. It was the only city of which she had ever taken a formal farewell, such as she took from the top of the Metropolitan Tower upon a lucid morning in April. The city lay beneath, with no magic of smoke to lend a meretricious romance to its checkered severity; a city encircled with silver waters and pavilioned by huge skies, expressing modern humanity, as the great monuments of ancient architecture express the mighty dead.

"We too can create our Parthenons," thought Sylvia, as she sank to earth in the florid elevator.

They crossed the Atlantic on one of the smaller Cunard liners. The voyage was uneventful. Nearly all the passengers in turn told Sylvia why they were not traveling by one of the large ships, but nobody suggested as a reason that the smaller ships were cheaper.

142

When they reached England Arthur went to stay with his mother at Dulwich. Sylvia went to the Airdales; she wanted to set her scheme in motion, but she promised to come and stay at Dulwich later on.

"At last you've come back," Olive said, on the verge of tears. "I've missed you dreadfully."

"Great Scott! Look at Sylvius and Rose!" Sylvia exclaimed. "They're like two pigs made of pink sugar. Pity we never thought of it at the time, or they could have been christened Scarlet and Crimson."

"Darlings, isn't godmamma horrid to you?" said Olive.

"Here! Here! What are you teaching them to call me?"

"Dat's godmamma," said Sylvius, in a thick voice.

"Dat's godmamma," Rose echoed.

"Not on your life, cullies," their godmother announced, "unless you want a thick ear each."

"Give me one," said Sylvius, stolidly.

"Give me one," Rose echoed.

"How can you tease the poor darlings so?" Olive exclaimed.

"Sylvius will have one," he announced, in the same thick monotone.

"Rose will have one," echoed his sister.

Sylvia handed her godson a large painted ball.

"Here's your thick ear, Pork."

Sylvius laughed fatly; the ball and the new name both pleased him.

"And here's yours," she said, offering another to Rose, who waited to see what her brother did with his and then proceeded to do the same with the same fat laugh. Suddenly, however, her lips puckered.

"What is it, darling?" her mother asked, anxiously.

"Rose wants to be said Pork."

"You didn't call her Pork," Olive translated, reproachfully, to Sylvia.

"Give me back the ball," said Sylvia. "Now then, here's your thick ear, Porka."

Rose laughed ecstatically. After two ornaments had been broken Jack came in, and the children retired with their nurse.

Sylvia found that family life had not spoiled Jack's interest in that career of hers; indeed, he was so much excited by her news that he suggested omitting for once the ceremony of seeing the twins being given their bath in order not to lose any of the short time available before he should have to go down to the theater. Sylvia, however, would not hear of any change in the domestic order, and reminded Jack that she was proposing to quarter herself on them for some time.

"I know, it's terrific," he said.

The excitement of the bath was always considerable, but this evening, with Sylvia's assistance, it became acute. Sylvius hit his nurse in the eye with the soap, and Rose, wrought up to a fever of emulation, managed to hurl the sponge into the grate.

Jack was enthusiastic about Sylvia's scheme. She was not quite sure that he understood exactly at what she was aiming, but he wished her so well that in any case his criticism would have had slight value; he gave instead his devoted attention, and that seemed a pledge of success. Success! Success! it sounded like a cataract in her ears, drowning every other sound. She wondered if the passion of her life was to be success. On no thoughts urged so irresistibly had she ever sailed to sleep, nor had she ever wakened in such a buoyancy, greeting the day as a swimmer greets the sea.

"Now what about the backing?" Jack asked.

"Backing? I'll back myself. You'll be my manager. I've enough to hire the Pierian Hall for a day and a night. I've enough to pay for one scene. Which reminds me I must get hold of Ronald Walker. You'll sing, Jack, two songs? Oh, and there's Arthur Madden. He'll sing, too."

"Who's he?" Olive asked.

"Oh, didn't I tell you about him?" said Sylvia, almost too nonchalantly, she feared. "He's rather good. Quite good, really. I'll tell you about him sometime. By the way, I've talked so much about myself and my plans that I've never asked about other people. How's the countess?"

Olive looked grave. "We don't ever see them, but everybody says that Clarehaven is going the pace tremendously."

"Have they retreated to Devonshire?"

"Oh no! Didn't you hear? I thought I'd told you in one of my letters. He had to sell the family place. Do you remember a man called Leopold Hausberg?"

"Do I not?" Sylvia exclaimed. "He took a flat once for a chimpanzee instead of Lily."

"Well, he's become Lionel Houston this year, and he's talked about with Dorothy a good deal. Of course he's very rich, but I do hope there's nothing in what people say. Poor Dorothy!"

"She'll survive even the divorce court," Sylvia said. "I wish I knew what had become of Lily. She might have danced in my show. I suppose it's too late now, though. Poor Lily! I say, we're getting very compassionate, you and I, Olive. Are you and Jack going to have any more kids?"

"Sylvia darling," Olive exclaimed, with a blush.

Sylvia had intended to stay a week or two with the Airdales, and, after having set in motion the preliminaries of her undertaking, to go down to Dulwich and visit Mrs. Madden, but she thought she would get hold of Ronnie Walker first, and with this object went to the Café Royal, where she should be certain of finding either him or a friend who would know where he was.

Sylvia had scarcely time to look round her in the swirl of gilt and smoke and chatter before Ronald Walker himself, wearing now a long pale beard, greeted her.

"My dear Ronald, what's the matter? Are you tired of women? You look more like a grate than a great man," Sylvia exclaimed. "Cut it off and give it to your landlady to stuff her fireplace this summer."

"What shall we drink?" he asked, imperturbably.

"I've been absinthe for so long that really—"

"It's a vermouth point," added Ronald.

"Ronnie, you devil, I can't go on, it's too whisky. Well, of course after that we ought both to drink port and brandy. Don't you find it difficult to clean your beard?"

"I'm not a messy feeder," said Ronnie.

"You don't paint with it, then?"

"Only Cubist pictures."

Sylvia launched out into an account of her work, and demanded his help for the painting of the scene.

"I want the back-cloth to be a city, not to represent a city, mark you, but to be a city."

She told him about New York as beheld from the Metropolitan Tower, and exacted from the chosen painter the ability to make the audience think that.

"I'm too old-fashioned for you, my dear," said Ronald.

"Oh, you, my dear man, of course. If I asked you for a city, you'd give me a view from a Pierrot's window of a Harlequin who'd stolen the first five numbers of the Yellow Book from a Pantaloon who kept a second-hand bookshop in a street-scene by Steinlen, and whose daughter, Columbine, having died of grief at being deserted by the New English Art Club, had been turned into a book-plate. No, I want some fierce young genius of to-day."

Over their drinks they discussed possible candidates; finally Ronald said he would invite a certain number of the most representative and least representational modern painters to his studio, from whom Sylvia might make her choice. Accordingly, two or three days later Sylvia visited Ronald in Grosvenor Road. For the moment, when she entered, she thought that he had been playing a practical joke upon her, for it seemed impossible that these extraordinary people could be real. The northerly light of the studio, severe and virginal, was less kind than the feverish exhalation of the Café Royal.

"They are real?" she whispered to her host.

"Oh yes, they're quite real, and in deadly earnest. Each of them represents a school and each of them thinks I've been converted to his point of view. I'll introduce Morphew."

He beckoned to a tall young man in black, who looked like a rolled-up umbrella with a jade handle.

"Morphew, this is Miss Scarlett. She's nearly as advanced as you are. Sylvia, this is Morphew, the Azurist."

Walker maliciously withdrew when he had made the introduction.

"Ought I to know what an Azurist is?" Sylvia asked. She felt that it was an unhappy opening for the conversation, but she did not want to hurt his religious feelings if Azurism was a religion, and if it was a trade she might be excused for not knowing what it was, such a rare trade must it be.

Mr. Morphew smiled in a superior way. "I think most people have heard about me by now."

"Ah, but I've been abroad."

"Several of my affirmations have been translated and published in France, Germany, Russia, Spain, Italy, Sweden, Hungary, and Holland," said Mr. Morphew, in a tone that seemed to imply that if Sylvia had not grasped who he was by now she never would, in which case it was scarcely worth his while to go on talking to her.

"Oh dear! What a pity!" she exclaimed. "I was in Montenegro all last year, so I must have missed them. I don't *think* you're known in Montenegro yet. It's such a small country, I should have been sure to hear about anything like that.

"Like what?" thought Sylvia, turning up her mind's eyes to heaven.

Mr. Morphew was evidently not sure what sort of language was spoken in Montenegro, and thought it wiser to instruct Sylvia than to expose his own ignorance.

"What color is that?" he suddenly demanded, pointing to the orange coverlet of a settee.

"Orange," said Sylvia. "Perhaps it's inclining to some shade of brown."

"Orange! Brown!" Mr. Morphew scoffed. "It's blue."

"Oh, but it's not!" she contradicted. "There's nothing blue about it."

"Blue," repeated Mr. Morphew. "All is blue. The Azurists deny that there is anything but blue. Blue," he continued in a rapt voice. "Blue! I was a Blanchist at first; but when we quarreled most of the Blanchists followed me. I shall publish the nineteenth affirmation of the Azurists next week. If you give me your address I'll send you a copy. We're going to give the Ovists hell in a new magazine that we're bringing out. We find that affirmations are not enough."

"Will it be an ordinary magazine?" Sylvia asked. "Will you have stories, for instance?"

"We don't admit that stories exist. Life-rays exist. There will be life-rays in our magazine."

"I suppose they'll be pretty blue," said Sylvia.

"All life-rays are blue."

"I suppose you don't mind wet weather?" she suggested. "Because it must be rather difficult to know when it's going to clear up."

"There are degrees of blue," Mr. Morphew explained.

"I see. Life isn't just one vast, reckless blue. Well, thank you very much for being so patient with my old-fashioned optical ideas. I do hope you'll go to America and tell them that their leaves turn blue in autumn. Anyway, you'll feel quite at home crossing the ocean, though some people won't even admit that's blue."

Sylvia left the Azurist and rejoined Ronald.

"Well," he laughed. "You look quite frightened."

"My dear, I've just done a bolt from the blue. You are a beast to rag my enthusiasms. Isn't there anybody here whose serious view of himself I can indorse?"

"Well, there's Pattison, the Ovist. He maintains that everything resolves itself into ovals."

"I think I should almost prefer Azurism," said Sylvia. "What about the Blanchists?"

"Oh, you wouldn't like them! They maintain that there's no such thing as color; their pictures depend on the angle at which they're hung."

"But if there's no such thing as color, how can they paint?"

"They don't. Their canvases are blank. Then there are the Combinationists. They don't repudiate color, but they repudiate paint. The most famous Combinationist picture exhibited so far consisted of half a match-box, a piece of orange-peel, and some sealing-wax, all stuck upon a slip of sugar-paper. The other Combinationists wanted to commit suicide because they despaired of surpassing it. Roger Cadbury wrote a superb introduction, pointing out that it must be either liked or disliked, but that it was impossible to do both or neither. It was that picture which inspired Hezekiah Penny to write what is considered one of his finest poems. You know it, perhaps?

"Why do I sing?
There is no reason why I should continue:
This image of the essential bin is better
Than the irritated uvulas of modern poets.

That caused almost as great sensation as the picture, because some of his fellow-poets maintained that he had no right to speak for anybody but himself."

"Who is Hezekiah Penny?" Sylvia asked.

"Hezekiah Penny is a provincial poet who began by writing Provençal verse."

"But this is madness," Sylvia exclaimed, looking round her at the studio, where the representatives of modernity eyed one another with surprise and distaste like unusual fish in the tank of an aquarium. "Behind all this rubbish surely something truly progressive exists. You've deliberately invited all the charlatans and impostors to meet me. I tell you, Ronnie, I saw lots of pictures in New York that were eccentric, but they were striving to rediscover life in painting. You're prejudiced because you belong to the decade before all this, and you've taken a delight in showing me all the extravagant side of it. You should emulate Tithonus."

"Who was he?"

"Now don't pretend you can't follow a simple allusion. The gentleman who fell in love with Aurora."

"Didn't he get rather tired of living forever?"

"Oh, well, that was because he grew a beard like you. Don't nail my allusions to the counter; they're not lies."

"I'll take pity on you," said Ronnie. "There is quite a clever youth whom I intended for you from the beginning. He's coming in later, when the rest have gone."

When she and Ronnie were alone again and before Lucian Hope, the young painter, arrived, Sylvia, looking through one of his sketch-books, came across a series of studies of a girl in the practice-dress of dancing; he told her it was Jenny Pearl.

"Maurice Avery's Jenny," she murmured. "What happened to her?"

"Didn't you hear about it? She was killed by her husband. It was a horrible business. Maurice went down to see her where she lived in the country, and this brute shot her. It was last summer. The papers were full of it."

"And what happened to Maurice?"

"Oh, he nearly went off his head. He's wandering about in Morocco probably."

"Where I met him," said Sylvia.

"But didn't he tell you?"

"Oh, it was before. More than three years ago. We talked about her."

Sylvia shuddered. One of her improvisations had been Maurice Avery; she must burn it.

Lucian Hope arrived before Sylvia could ask any more questions about the horrible event; she was glad to escape from the curiosity that would have turned it into a tale of the police-court. The new-comer was not more than twenty-two, perhaps less—too young, at any rate, to have escaped from the unconventionality of artistic attire that stifles all personality. But he had squirrel's eyes, and was not really like an undertaker. He was shy, too, so shy that Sylvia wondered how he could tolerate being stared at in the street on account of his odd appearance. She would have liked to ask him what pleasure he derived from such mimicry of a sterile and professional distinction, but she feared to hurt his young vanity; moreover, she was disarmed by those squirrel's eyes, so sharp and bright even in the falling dusk. The three of them talked restlessly for a while, and Sylvia, seeing that Ronald was preparing to broach the subject for which they were met, anticipated him with a call for attention, and began one of her improvisations. It was of Concetta lost in a greater city than Granada. By the silence that followed she knew that her companions had cared for it, and she changed to Mrs. Gainsborough. Then she finished up with three of the poems.

"Could you paint me a scene for that?" she asked, quickly, to avoid any comment.

"Oh, rather!" replied the young man, very eagerly; though it was nearly dark now, she could see his eyes flashing real assurance.

They all three dined together that evening, and Lucian Hope, ever since Sylvia had let him know that she stood beside him to conquer the world, lost his early shyness and talked volubly of what she wanted and what he wanted to do. Ronald Walker presided in the background of the ardent conversation, and as they came out of the restaurant he took Sylvia's arm for a moment.

"All right?"

"Quite all right, thanks."

"So's your show going to be. Not so entirely modern as you gave me to suppose. But that's not a great fault."

Sylvia and Lucian Hope spent a good deal of time together, so much was there to talk about in connection with the great enterprise. She brought him to the Airdales' that he might meet Jack, who was supposed to have charge of the financial arrangements. The sight of the long-haired young man made Sylvius cry, and, as a matter of course, Rose, also, which embarrassed Lucian Hope a good deal, especially when he had to listen to an explanation of himself by Olive for the children's consolation.

"He's a gollywog," Sylvius howled.

"He's a gollywog," Rose echoed.

"He's tum to gobble us," Sylvius bellowed.

"To gobble us, to gobble us," Rose wailed.

"He's not a gollywog, darlings," their mother declared. "He makes pretty pictures, oh, such pretty pictures of—"

"He *is* a gollywog," choked Sylvius, in an ecstasy of rage and fear.

"A gollywog, a gollywog," Rose insisted.

Their mother changed her tactics. "But he's a kind gollywog. Oh, such a kind gollywog, the kindest, nicest gollywog that was ever thought of."

"He *is*—ent," both children proclaimed. "He's bad!"

"Don't you think I'd better go?" asked the painter. "I think it must be my hair that's upsetting them."

He started toward the door, but, unfortunately, he was on the wrong side of the children, who, seeing him make a move in their direction, set up such an appalling yell that the poor young man drew back in despair. In the middle of this the maid entered, announcing Mr. Arthur Madden, who followed close upon her heels. Sylvius and Rose were by this time obsessed with the idea of an invasion by an army of gollywogs, and Arthur's pleasant face took on for them the dreaded lineaments of the foe. Both children clung shrieking to their mother's skirts. Sylvia and Jack were leaning back, incapable through laughter. Arthur and Lucian Hope surveyed miserably the scene they had created. At last the nurse arrived to rescue the twins, and they were carried away without being persuaded to change their minds about the inhuman nature of the two visitors.

Arthur apologized for worrying Sylvia, but his mother was so anxious to know when she was coming down to Dulwich, and as he had been up in town seeing about an engagement, he had not been able to resist coming to visit her.

Sylvia felt penitent for having abandoned Arthur so completely since they had arrived in England, and she told him she would go back with him that very afternoon.

"Oh, but Miss Scarlett," protested Lucian, "don't you remember? We arranged to explore Limehouse to-morrow."

Arthur looked at the painter very much as if he were indeed the gollywog for which he had just been taken.

"I don't want to interfere with previous arrangements," he said, with such a pathetic haughtiness that Sylvia had not the heart to wound his dignity, and told Lucian Hope that the expedition to Limehouse must be postponed. The young painter looked disconsolate and Arthur blossomed from his fading. However, Lucian had the satisfaction of saying, in a mysterious voice, to Sylvia before he went:

"Well, then, while you're away I'll get on with it."

It was not until they were half-way to Dulwich in the train that Arthur asked Sylvia what he was going to get on with.

"My scene," she said.

"What scene?"

"Arthur, don't be stupid. The set for my show."

"You're not going to let a youth like that paint a set for you? You're mad. What experience has he had?"

"None. That's exactly why I chose him. I'm providing the experience."

"Have you known him long?" Arthur demanded. "You can't have known him very long. He must have been at school when you left England."

"Don't be jealous," said Sylvia.

"Jealous? Of him? Huh!"

Mrs. Madden had changed more than Sylvia expected. Arthur had seemed so little altered that she was surprised to see his mother with white hair, for she could scarcely be fifty-five yet. The drawing-room of the little house in Dulwich recalled vividly the drawing-room of the house in Hampstead; nor had Mrs. Madden bought herself a new piano with the fifty pounds that was cabled back to her from Sulphurville. It suddenly occurred to Sylvia that this was the first time she had seen her since she ran away with Arthur, fifteen years ago, and she felt that she ought to apologize for that behavior now; but, after all, Mrs. Madden had run away herself once upon a time with her father's groom and could scarcely have been greatly astonished at Arthur's elopement.

"You have forgiven me for carrying him off from Hampstead?" she asked, with a smile.

Mrs. Madden laughed gently. "Yes, I was frightened at the time. But in the end it did Arthur good, I think. It's been such a pleasure to me to hear how successful he's been lately." She looked at Sylvia with an expression of marked sympathy.

After supper Mrs. Madden came up to Sylvia's room and, taking her hand, said, in her soft voice, "Arthur has told me all about you two."

Sylvia flushed and pulled her hand away. "He's no business to tell you anything about me," she said, hotly.

"You mustn't be angry, Sylvia. He made it quite clear that you hadn't quite made up your mind yet. Poor boy," she added, with a sigh.

Sylvia, when she understood that Arthur had not said anything about their past, had a strong desire to tell Mrs. Madden that she had lived with him for a year. She resented the way she had said "poor boy." She checked the impulse and assured her that if Arthur had spoken of their marriage he had had no right to do so. It really was most improbable that she should marry him; oh, but most improbable.

"You always spoke very severely about love when you were a little girl. Do you remember? You must forgive a mother, but I must tell you that I believe Arthur's happiness depends upon your marrying him. He talks of nothing else and makes such plans for the future."

"He makes too many plans," Sylvia said, severely.

"Ah, there soon comes a time when one ceases to make plans," Mrs. Madden sighed. "One is reduced to expedients. But now that you're a woman, and I can easily believe that you're the clever woman Arthur says you are, for you gave every sign of it when you were young—now that you're a woman, I do hope you'll be a merciful woman. It's such a temptation—you must forgive my plain speaking—it's such a temptation to keep a man like Arthur hanging on. You must have noticed how young he is still—to all intents and purposes quite a boy; and believe me he has the same romantic adoration for you and your wonderfulness as he had when he was seventeen. Don't, I beg of you, treat such devotion too lightly."

Sylvia could not keep silent under this unjustified imputation of heartlessness, and broke out:

"I'm sure you'll admit that Arthur has given quite a wrong idea of me when I tell you that we lived together for a year; and you must remember that I've been married already and know what it means. Arthur has no right to complain of me."

"Oh, Sylvia, I'm sorry!" Mrs. Madden almost whispered. "Oh dear! how could Arthur do such a thing?"

"Because I made him, of course. Now you must forgive *me* if I say something that hurts your feelings, but I must say it. When you ran away with your husband, you must have made him do it. You *must* have done."

"Good gracious me!" Mrs. Madden exclaimed. "I suppose I did. I never looked at it in that light before. You've made me feel quite ashamed of my behavior. Quite embarrassed. And I suppose everybody has always blamed me entirely; but because my husband was one of my father's servants I always used to be defending him. I never thought of defending myself."

Sylvia was sorry for stirring up in Mrs. Madden's placid mind old storms. It was painful to see this faded gentlewoman in the little suburban bedroom, blushing nervously at the unlady-like behavior of long ago. Presently Mrs. Madden pulled herself up and said, with a certain decision:

"Yes, but I did marry him."

"Yes, but you hadn't been married already. You hadn't knocked round half the globe for twenty-eight years. It's no good my pretending to be shocked at myself. I don't care a bit what anybody thinks about me, and, anyway, it's done now."

"Surely you'd be happier if you married Arthur after—after that," Mrs. Madden suggested.

"But I'm not in the least unhappy. I can't say whether I shall marry Arthur until I've given my performance. I can't say what effect either success or failure will have on me. My whole mind is concentrated in the Pierian Hall next October."

"I'm afraid I cant understand this modern way of looking at things."

"But there's nothing modern about my point of view, Mrs. Madden. There's nothing modern about the egotism of an artist. Arthur is as free as I am. He has his own career to think about. He does think about it a great deal. He's radically much more interested in that than in marrying me. The main point is that he's free at present. From the moment I promise to marry him and he accepts that promise he won't be free. Nor shall I. It wouldn't be fair on either of us to make that promise now, because I must know what October is going to bring forth."

"Well, I call it very modern. When I was young we looked at marriage as the most important event in a girl's life."

"But you didn't, dear Mrs. Madden. You, or rather your contemporaries, regarded marriage as a path to freedom—social freedom, that is. Your case was exceptional. You fell passionately in love with a man beneath you, as the world counts it. You married him, and what was the result? You were cut off by your relations as utterly as if you had become the concubine of a Hottentot."

"Oh, Sylvia dear, what an uncomfortable comparison!"

"Marriage to your contemporaries was a social observance. I'm not religious, but I regard marriage as so sacred that, because I've been divorced and because, so far as I know, my husband is still alive, I have something like religious qualms about marrying again. It takes a cynic to be an idealist; the sentimentalist gets left at the first fence. It's just because I'm fond of Arthur in a perfectly normal way when I'm not immersed in my ambition that I even contemplate the *notion* of marrying him. I've got a perfectly normal wish to have children and a funny little house of my own. So far as I know at present, I should like Arthur to be the father of my children. But it's got to be an equal business. Personally

147

I think that the Turks are wiser about women than we are; I think the majority of women are only fit for the harem and I'm not sure that the majority wouldn't be much happier under such conditions. The incurable vanity of man, however, has removed us from our seclusion to admire his antics, and it's too late to start shutting us up in a box now. Woman never thought of equality with man until he put the notion into her head."

"I think perhaps supper may be ready," Mrs. Madden said. "It all sounds very convincing as you speak, but I can't help feeling that you'd be happier if you wouldn't take everything to pieces to look at the works. Things hardly ever go so well again afterward. Oh dear, I wish you hadn't lived together first."

"It breaks the ice of the wedding-cake, doesn't it?" said Sylvia.

"And I wish you wouldn't make such bitter remarks. You don't really mean what you say. I'm sure supper must be ready."

"Oh, but I do," Sylvia insisted, as they passed out into the narrow little passage and down the narrow stairs into the little dining-room. Nevertheless, in Sylvia's mind there was a kindliness toward this little house, almost a tenderness, and far away at the back of her imagination was the vision of herself established in just such another little house.

"But even the Albert Memorial would look all right from the wrong end of a telescope," she said to herself.

One thing was brought home very vividly during her stay in Dulwich, which was the difference between what she had deceived herself into thinking was that first maternal affection she had felt for Arthur and the true maternal love of his mother. Whenever she had helped Arthur in any way, she had always been aware of enjoying the sensation of her indispensableness; it had been an emotion altogether different from this natural selfishness of the mother; it was really one that had always reflected a kind of self-conscious credit upon herself. Here in Dulwich, with this aspect of her affection for Arthur completely overshadowed, Sylvia was able to ask herself more directly if she loved him in the immemorial way of love; and though she could not arrive at a finally positive conclusion, she was strengthened in her resolve not to let him go. Arthur himself was more in love with her than he had ever been, and she thought that perhaps this was due to that sudden and disquieting withdrawal of herself; in the midst of possession he had been dispossessed, and until he could pierce her secret reasons he would inevitably remain deeply in love, even to the point of being jealous of a boy like Lucian Hope. Sylvia understood Arthur's having refused an engagement to tour as juvenile lead in a successful musical piece and his unwillingness to leave her alone in town; he was rewarded, too, for his action, because shortly afterward he obtained a good engagement in London to take the place of a singer who had retired from the cast of the Frivolity Theater. At that rate he would soon find himself at the Vanity Theater itself.

In June Sylvia went back to the Airdales', and soon afterward took rooms near them in West Kensington. It was impossible to continue indefinitely to pretend that Arthur and herself were mere theatrical acquaintances, and one day Olive asked Sylvia if she intended to marry him.

"What do you advise?" Sylvia asked. "There's a triumph, dearest Olive. Have I ever asked your advice before?"

"I like him; Jack likes him, too, and says that he ought to get on fast now; but I don't know. Well, he's not the sort of man I expected you to marry."

"You've had an ideal for me all the time," Sylvia exclaimed. "And you've never told me."

"Oh no, I've never had anybody definite in my mind, but I think I should be able to say at once if the man you had chosen was the right one. Don't ask me to describe him, because I couldn't do it. You used to tease me about marrying a curly-headed actor, but Arthur Madden seems to me much more of a curly-headed actor than Jack is."

"In fact, you thoroughly disapprove of poor Arthur?" Sylvia pressed.

"Oh dear, no! Oh, not at all! Please don't think that. I'm only anxious that you shouldn't throw yourself away."

"Remnants always go cheap," said Sylvia. "However, don't worry. I'll be quite sure of myself before I marry anybody again."

The summer passed away quickly in a complexity of arrangements for the opening performance at the Pierian Hall. Sylvia stayed three or four times at Dulwich and grew very fond of Mrs. Madden, who never referred again to the subject of marriage. She also went up to Warwickshire with Olive and the children, much to the pleasure of Mr. Fanshawe, who was now writing a supplementary volume called *More Warwickshire Worthies*. In London she scarcely met any old friends; indeed, she went out of her way to avoid people like the Clarehavens, because they would not have been interested in what she was doing. By this time Sylvia had reached the point of considering everybody either for the interest and belief he evinced in her success or by the use he could be to her in securing it. The first rapturous egoism of Arthur's own success in London had worn off with time, and he was able to devote himself entirely to running about for Sylvia, which gradually made her regard him more and more as a fixture. As for Lucian Hope, he thought of nothing but the great occasion, and would have fought anybody who had ventured to cast a breath of doubt upon the triumph at hand. The set that he had painted was exactly what Sylvia required, and though both Arthur and Jack thought it would distract the audience's attention by puzzling them, they neither of them on Sylvia's account criticized it at all harshly.

At last in mid-October the very morning of the day arrived, so long anticipated with every kind of discussion that its superficial resemblance to other mornings seemed heartless and unnatural. It was absurd that a milkman's note should be the same as yesterday, that servants should shake mats on front-door steps as usual, and that the maid who knocked at Sylvia's door should not break down beneath the weightiness of her summons. Nor, when Sylvia looked out of the window, were Jack and Arthur and Ronald and Lucian pacing with agitated steps the pavement below, an absence of enthusiasm, at any rate on the part of Arthur and Lucian, that hurt her feelings, until she thought for a moment how foolishly unreasonable she was being.

As soon as Sylvia was dressed she went round to the Airdales'; everybody she met on the way inspired her with a longing to confide in him the portentousness of the day, and she found herself speculating whether several business men, who were hurrying to catch the nine-o'clock train, had possibly an intention of visiting the Pierian Hall that afternoon. She was extremely annoyed to find, when she reached the Airdales' house, that neither Jack nor Olive was up.

"Do they know the time?" she demanded of the maid, in a scandalized voice. "Their clock must have stopped."

"Oh no, miss, I don't think so. Breakfast is at ten, as usual. There's Mr. Airdale's dressing-room bell going now, miss. That 'll be for his shaving-water. Shall I say you're waiting to see him?"

What a ridiculous time to begin shaving, Sylvia thought.

"Yes, please," she added, aloud. "Or no, don't bother him; I'll come back at ten o'clock."

Sylvia saw more of the streets of West Kensington in that hour than she had ever seen of them before, and decided that the neighborhood was impossible. Nothing so intolerably monotonous as these rows of stupid and meaningless houses had ever been designed. One after another of them blinked at her in the autumnal sunshine with a fatuous complacency that made her long to ring all the bells in the street. Presently she found herself by the play-fields of St. James's School, where the last boys were hurrying across the grass like belated ants. She looked at the golden clock in the school-buildings—half past nine. In five hours and a half she would be waiting for the curtain to go up; in seven hours and a half the audience would be wondering if it should have tea in Bond Street or cross Piccadilly and walk down St. James's Street to Rumpelmayer's. This problem of the audience began to worry Sylvia. She examined the alternatives with a really anxious gravity. If it went to Rumpelmayer's it would have to walk back to the Dover Street Tube, which would mean recrossing Piccadilly; on the other hand, it would be on the right side for the omnibuses. On the other hand, it would find Rumpelmayer's full, because other audiences would have arrived before it, invading the tea-shop from Pall Mall. Sylvia grew angry at the thought of these other audiences robbing her audience of its tea—her audience, some members of which would have read in the paper this morning:

PIERIAN HALL.

This afternoon at 3 p. m.

SYLVIA SCARLETT

IN

IMPROVISATIONS

and would actually have paid, some of them, as much as seven shillings and sixpence to see Sylvia Scarlett. Seven hours and a half: seven shillings and sixpence: 7½ plus 7½ made fifteen. When she was fifteen she had met Arthur. Sylvia's mind rambled among the omens of numbers, and left her audience still undecided between Bond Street and Rumpelmayer's, left it upon the steps of the Pierian Hall, the sport of passing traffic, hungry, thirsty, homesick. In seven and a half hours she would know the answer to that breathless question asked a year ago in Vermont. To think that the exact spot on which she had stood when she asked was existing at this moment in Vermont! In seven and a half hours, no, in seven hours and twenty-five minutes; the hands were moving on. It was really terrible how little people regarded the flight of time; the very world might come to an end in seven hours and twenty-five minutes.

"Have you seen Sylvia Scarlett yet?"

"No, we intended to go yesterday, but there were no seats left. They say she's wonderful."

"Oh, my dear, she's perfectly amazing! Of course it's something quite new. You really must go."

"Who is she like?"

"Oh, she's not like anybody else. I'm told she's half French."

"Oh, really! How interesting."

"Good morning! Have you used Pear's soap?"

"V-vi-vin-vino-vinol-vinoli-vinolia."

Sylvia pealed the Airdales' bell, and found Jack in the queer mixed costume which a person wears on the morning of an afternoon that will be celebrated by his best tail-coat.

"My dear girl, you really mustn't get so excited," he protested, when he saw Sylvia's manner.

"Oh, Jack, do you think I shall be a success?"

"Of course you will. Now, do, for goodness' sake, drink a cup of coffee or something."

Sylvia found that she was hungry enough to eat even an egg, which created a domestic crisis, because Sylvius and Rose quarreled over which of them was to have the top. Finally it was adjusted by awarding the top to Sylvius, but by allowing Rose to turn the empty egg upside down for the exquisite pleasure of watching Sylvia tap it with ostentatious greed, only to find that there was nothing inside, after all, an operation that Sylvius watched with critical jealousy and Rose saluted with ecstatic joy. Sylvia's disappointment was so beautifully violent that Sylvius regretted the material choice he had made, and wanted Sylvia to eat another egg, of which Rose might eat the top and he offer the empty shell; but it was too late, and Sylvius learned that often the shadow is better than the substance.

It had been decided in the end that Jack should confine himself to the cares of general management, and Arthur was left without a rival. Sylvia had insisted that he should only sing old English folk-songs, a decision which he had challenged at first on the ground that he required the advertisement of more modern songs, and that Sylvia's choice was not going to help him.

"You're not singing to help yourself," she had told him. "You're singing to help me."

In addition to Arthur there was a girl whom Lucian Hope had discovered, a delicate creature with red hair, whose chief claim to employment was that she was starving, though incidentally she had a very sweet and pure soprano voice. Finally there was an Irish pianist whose technique and good humor were alike unassailable.

Before the curtain went up, Sylvia could think of nothing but the improvisations that she ought to have invented instead of the ones that she had. It was a strain upon her common sense to prevent her from canceling the whole performance and returning its money to the audience. The more she contemplated what she was going to do the more she viewed the undertaking as a fraud upon the public. There had never been any *chicane* like the *chicane* she was presently going to commit. What was that noise? Who had given the signal to O'Hea? What in hell's name did he think he was doing at the piano? The sound of the music was like water running into one's bath while one was lying in bed—nothing could stop it from overflowing presently. Nothing could stop the curtain from rising. At what a pace he was playing that Debussy! He was showing off, the fool! A ridiculous joke came into her mind that she kept on repeating while the music flowed: "Many a minim makes a maxim. Many a minim makes a maxim." How cold it was in the dressing-room, and the music was getting quicker and quicker. There was a knock at the door. It was Arthur. How nice he looked with that red carnation in his buttonhole.

"How nice you look, Arthur, in that buttonhole."

The flower became tremendously important; it seemed to Sylvia that, if she could go on flattering the flower, O'Hea would somehow be kept at the piano.

"Well, don't pull it to pieces," said Arthur, ruthfully. But it was too late; the petals were scattered on the floor like drops of blood.

"Oh, I'm sorry! Come along back to my dressing-room. I'll give you another flower."

"No, no; there isn't time now. Wait till you come off after your first set."

Now it was seeming the most urgent thing in the world to find another flower for Arthur's buttonhole. At all cost the rise of that curtain must be delayed. But Arthur had brought her on the stage and the notes were racing toward the death of the piece. It was absurd of O'Hea to have chosen Debussy; the atmosphere required a ballade of Chopin, or, better still, Schumann's Noveletten. He could have played all the Noveletten. Oh dear, what a pity she had not thought of making that suggestion. The piano would have been scarcely half-way through by now.

Suddenly there was silence. Then there followed the languid applause of an afternoon audience for an unimportant part of the program.

"He's stopped," Sylvia exclaimed, in horror. "What *has* happened?"

She turned to Arthur in despair, but he had hurried off the stage. Lucian Hope's painted city seemed to press forward and stifle her; she moved down-stage to escape it. The curtain went up and she recoiled as from a chasm at her feet. Why on earth was O'Hea sitting in that idiotic attitude, as if he were going to listen to a sermon, looking down like that, with his right arm supporting his left elbow and his left hand propping up his chin? How hot the footlights were! She hoped nothing had happened, and looked round in alarm; but the fireman was standing quite calmly in the wings. Just as Sylvia was deciding that her voice could not possibly escape from her throat, which had closed upon it like a pair of pincers, the voice tore itself free and went traveling out toward that darkness in front, that nebulous darkness scattered with hands and faces and programs. Like Concetta in a great city, Sylvia was lost in that darkness; she *was* Concetta. It seemed to her that the applause at the end was not so much approval of Concetta as a welcome to Mrs. Gainsborough; when isolated laughs and volleys of laughter came out of the darkness and were followed sometimes by the darkness itself laughing everywhere, so that O'Hea looked up very personally and winked at her, then Sylvia fell in love with her audience. The laughter increased, and suddenly she recognized at the end of each volley that Sylvius and Rose were supplementing its echoes with rapturous echoes of their own. She could not see them, but their gurgles in the darkness were like a song of nightingales to Sylvia. She ceased to be Mrs. Gainsborough, and began to say three or four of the poems. Then the curtain fell, and came up again, and fell, and came up again, and fell, and came up again.

Jack was standing beside her and saying:

"Splendid, splendid, splendid, splendid!"

"Delighted, delighted, delighted, delighted!"

"Very good audience! Splendid audience! Delighted audience! Success! Success! Success!"

Really, how wonderfully O'Hea was playing, Sylvia thought, and how good that Debussy was!

The rest of the performance was as much of a success as the beginning. Perhaps the audience liked best Mrs. Gowndry and the woman who smuggled lace from Belgium into France. Sylvius and Rose laughed so much at the audience's laughter at Mrs. Gowndry that Sylvius announced in the ensuing lull that he wanted to go somewhere, a desire which was naturally indorsed by Rose. The audience was much amused, because it supposed that Sylvius's wish was a tribute to the profession of Mrs. Gowndry's husband, and whatever faint doubts existed about the propriety of alluding in the Pierian Hall to a lavatory-attendant were dispersed.

Sylvia forgot altogether about the audience's tea when the curtain fell finally. It was difficult to think about anything with so many smiling people pressing round her on the stage. Several old friends came and reminded her of their existence, but there was no one who had quite such a radiant smile as Arthur Lonsdale.

"Lonnie! How nice of you to come!"

"I say, topping, I mean. What? I say, that's a most extraordinary back-cloth you've got. What on earth is it supposed to be? It reminds me of what you feel like when you're driving a car through a strange town after meeting a man you haven't seen for some time and who's just found out a good brand of fizz at the hotel where he's staying. I was afraid you'd get bitten in the back before you'd finished. I say, Mrs. Gowndry was devilish good. Some of the other lads and lasses were a bit beyond me."

"And how's business?"

"Oh, very good. We've just put the neatest little ninety h. p. torpedo-body two-seater on the market. I'll tootle you down to Brighton in it one Sunday morning. Upon my word, you'll scarcely have time to wrap yourself up before you'll have to unwrap yourself to shake hands with dear old Harry Burnly coming out to welcome you from the Britannia."

"Not married yet, Lonnie?"

"No, not yet. Braced myself up to do it the other day, dived in, and was seized with cramp at the deep end. She offered to be a sister to me and I sank like a stone. My mother's making rather a nuisance of herself about it. She keeps producing girls out of her muff like a conjurer, whenever she comes to see me. And what girls! Heather mixture most of them, like Guggenheim's Twelfth of August. I shall come to it at last, I suppose. Mr. Arthur Lonsdale and his bride leaving St. Margaret's, Westminster, under an arch of spanners formed by grateful chauffeurs whom the brilliant and handsome young bride-groom has recommended to many titled readers of this paper. Well, so long, Sylvia; there's a delirious crowd of admirers waiting for you. Send me a line where you're living and we'll have a little dinner somewhere—"

Sylvia's success was not quite so huge as in the first intoxication of her friends' enthusiasm she had begun to fancy. However, it was unmistakably a success, and she was able to give two recitals a week through the autumn, with certainly the prospect of a good music-hall engagement for the following spring, if she cared to accept it. Most of the critics discovered that she was not as good as Yvette Guilbert. In view of Yvette Guilbert's genius, of which they were much more firmly convinced now than they would have been when Yvette Guilbert first appeared, this struck them as a fairly safe comparison; moreover, it gave their readers an impression that they understood French, which enhanced the literary value of their criticism. To strengthen this belief most of them were inclined to think that the French poems were the best part of Miss Sylvia Scarlett's performance. One or two of the latter definitely recalled some of Yvette Guilbert's early work, no doubt by the number of words they had not understood, because somebody had crackled a program or had shuffled his feet or had coughed. As for the English character studies, or, as some of them carried away by reminiscences of Yvette Guilbert into oblivion of their own language preferred to call them, *études*, they had a certain distinction, and in many cases betrayed signs of an almost meticulous observation, though at the same time, like everybody else doing anything at the present moment except in France, they did not have as much distinction or meticulousness as the work of forerunners in England or contemporaries abroad. Still, that was not to say that the work of Miss Sylvia Scarlett was not highly promising and of the greatest possible interest. The *timbre* of her voice was specially worthy of notice and justified the italics in which it was printed. Finally, two critics, who were probably sitting next to each other, found a misprint in the program, no doubt in searching for a translation of the poems.

If Sylvia fancied a lack of appreciation in the critics, all her friends were positive that they were wonderful notices for a beginner.

"Why, I think that's a splendid notice in the *Telegraph*," said Olive. "I found it almost at once. Why, one often has to read right through the paper before one can find the notice."

"Do you mean to tell me that the most self-inebriated egotist on earth ever read right through the *Daily Telegraph*? I don't believe it. He'd have been drowned like Narcissus."

Arthur pressed for a decision about their marriage, now that Sylvia knew what she had so long wanted to know; but she was wrapped up in ideas for improving her performance and forbade Arthur to mention the subject until she raised it herself; for the present she was on with a new love twice a week. Indeed, they were fascinating to Sylvia, these audiences each with a definite personality of its own. She remembered how she had scoffed in old days at the slavish flattery of them by her fellow-actors and actresses; equally in the old days she had scoffed at love. She wished that she could feel toward Arthur as she felt now toward her audiences, which were as absorbing as children with their little clevernesses and precocities. The difference between what she was doing now and what she had done formerly when she sang French songs with an English accent was the difference between the realism of an old knotted towel that is a baby and an expensive doll that may be a baby but never ceases to be a doll. Formerly she had been a mechanical thing and had never given herself because she had possessed neither art nor truth, but merely craft and accuracy. She had thought that the personality was degraded by depending on the favor of an audience. All that old self-consciousness and false shame were gone. She and her audience communed through art as spirits may commune after death. In the absorption of studying the audience as a separate entity, Sylvia forgot that it was made up of men and women. When she knew that any friends of hers were in front, they always remained entirely separate in her mind from the audience. Gradually, however, as the autumn advanced, several people from long ago re-entered her life and she began to lose that feeling of seclusion from the world and to realize the gradual setting up of barriers to her complete liberty of action. The first of these visitants was Miss Ashley, who in her peacock-blue gown looked much as she had looked when Sylvia last saw her.

"I could not resist coming round to tell you how greatly I enjoyed your performance," she said. "I've been so sorry that you never came to see me all these years."

Sylvia felt embarrassed, because she dreaded presently an allusion to her marriage with Philip, but Miss Ashley was too wise.

"How's Hornton House!" asked Sylvia, rather timidly. It was like inquiring after the near relation of an old friend who might have died.

"Just the same. Miss Primer is still with me. Miss Hossack now has a school of her own. Miss Pinck became very ill with gouty rheumatism and had to retire. I won't ask you about yourself; you told me so much from the stage. Now that we've been able to meet again, won't you come and visit your old school sometime?"

Sylvia hesitated.

"Please," Miss Ashley insisted. "I'm not inviting you out of politeness. It would really give me pleasure. I have never ceased to think about you all these years. Well, I won't keep you, for I'm sure you must be tired. Do come. Tell me, Sylvia. I should so like to bring the girls one afternoon. What would be a good afternoon to come?"

"You mean, when will there be nothing in the program that—"

"We poor schoolmistresses," said Miss Ashley, with a whimsical look of deprecation.

"Come on Saturday fortnight, and afterward I'll go back with you all to Hornton House. I'd love that."

So it was arranged.

On Wednesday of the following week it happened that there was a particularly appreciative audience, and Sylvia became so much enamoured of the laughter that she excelled herself. It was an afternoon of perfect accord, and she traced the source of it to a group somewhere in the middle of the stalls, too far back for her to recognize its composition. After the performance a pack of visiting-cards was brought to the door of her dressing-room. She read: "Mrs. Ian Campbell, Mrs. Ralph Dennison." Who on earth were they? "Mr. Leonard Worsley"—

Sylvia flung open the door, and there they all were, Mr. and Mrs. Worsley, Gladys and Enid, two good-looking men in the background, two children in the foreground.

"Gladys! Enid!"

"Sylvia!"

"Oh, Sylvia, you were priceless! Oh, we enjoyed ourselves no end! You don't know my husband. Ian, come and bow nicely to the pretty lady," cried Gladys.

"Sylvia, it was simply ripping. We laughed and laughed. Ralph, come and be introduced, and this is Stumpy, my boy," Enid cried, simultaneously.

"Fancy, he's a grandfather," the daughters exclaimed, dragging Mr. Worsley forward. He looked younger than ever.

"Hercules is at Oxford, or of course he'd have come, too. This is Proodles," said Gladys, pointing to the little girl.

"Sylvia, why did you desert us like that?" Mrs. Worsley reproachfully asked. "When are you coming down to stay with us at Arbor End? Of course the children are married...." She broke off with half a sigh.

"Oh, but we can all squash in," Gladys shouted.

"Oh, rather," Enid agreed. "The kids can sleep in the coal-scuttles. We sha'n't notice any difference."

"Dears, it's so wonderful to see you," Sylvia gasped. "But do tell me who you all are over again. I'm so muddled."

"I'm Mrs. Ian Campbell," Gladys explained. "And this is Ian. And this is Proodles, and at home there's Groggles, who's too small for anything except pantomimes. And that's Mrs. Ralph Dennison, and that's Ralph, and that's Stumpy, and at home Enid's got a girlie called Barbara. Mother hates being a grandmother four times over, so she's called Aunt Victoria, and of course father's still one of the children. We've both been married seven years."

Nothing had so much brought home to Sylvia the flight of time as this meeting with Gladys and Enid, who when she last saw them were only sixteen. It was incredible. And they had not forgotten her; in what seemed now a century they had not forgotten her! Sylvia told them about Miss Ashley's visit and suggested that they should come and join the party of girls from Hornton House. It would be fun, would it not? Miss Primer was still at the school.

Gladys and Enid were delighted with the plan, and on the day fixed about twenty girls invaded Sylvia's dressing-room, shepherded by Miss Primer, who was still melting with tears for Rodrigo's death in the scene. Miss Ashley had brought the carriage to drive Sylvia back, but she insisted upon going in a motor-'bus with the others and was well rewarded by Miss Primer's ecstasies of apprehension. Sylvia wandered with Gladys and Enid down well-remembered corridors, in and out of bedrooms and class-rooms; she listened to resolutions to send Prudence and Barbara to Hornton House in a few years. For Sylvia it was almost too poignant, the thought of these families growing up all round her, while she, after so many years, was still really as much alone as she had always been. The company of all these girls with their slim black legs, their pigtails and fluffy hair tied back with big bows, the absurdly exaggerated speech and the enlaced loves of girlhood—the accumulation of it all was scarcely to be borne.

When Sylvia visited Arbor End and talked once again to Mrs. Worsley, sitting at the foot of her bed, about the wonderful lives of that so closely self-contained family, the desolation of the future came visibly nearer; it seemed imperative at whatever cost to drive it back.

Shortly before Christmas a card was brought round to Sylvia—"Mrs. Prescott-Merivale, Hardingham Hall, Hunts."

"Who is it?" she asked her maid.

"It's a lady, miss."

"Well of course I didn't suppose a cassowary had sent up his card. What's she like?"

The maid strove to think of some phrase that would describe the visitor, but she fell back hopelessly upon her original statement.

"She's a lady, miss." Then, with a sudden radiancy lighting her eyes, she added, "And there's a little boy with her."

"My entertainment seems to be turning into a children's treat," Sylvia muttered to herself. "*Sic itur ad astra.*"

"I beg your pardon, miss, did you say to show her in?"

Sylvia nodded.

Presently a tall young woman in the late twenties, with large and brilliant gray eyes, rose-flushed and deep in furs, came in, accompanied by an extraordinarily handsome boy of seven or eight.

"How awfully good of you to let me waste a few minutes of your time," she said, and as she spoke, Sylvia had a fleeting illusion that it was herself who was speaking, a sensation infinitely rapid, but yet sufficiently clear to make her ask herself the meaning of it, and to find in the stranger's hair the exact replica of her own. The swift illusion and the equally swift comparison were fled before she had finished inviting her visitor to sit down.

"I must explain who I am. I've heard about you, oh, of course, publicly, but also from my brother."

"Your brother?" repeated Sylvia.

"Yes, Michael Fane."

"He's not with you?"

"No. I wish he had been. Alas! he's gone off to look for a friend who, by the way, I expect you know also. Maurice Avery? All sorts of horrid rumors about what had happened to him in Morocco were being brought back to us, so Michael went off last spring, and has been with him ever since."

"But I thought he was a monk," Sylvia said.

Mrs. Merivale laughed with what seemed rather like relief. "No, he's neither priest nor monk, thank goodness, though the prospect still hangs over us."

"After all these years?" Sylvia asked, in astonishment.

"Oh, my dear Miss Scarlett, don't forget the narrow way is also long. But I didn't come to talk to you about Michael. I simply most shamelessly availed myself of his having met you a long time ago to give myself an excuse for talking to you about your performance. Of course it's absolutely great. How lucky you are!"

"Lucky?" Sylvia could not help glancing at the handsome boy beside her.

"He's rather a lamb, isn't he?" Mrs. Merivale agreed. "But you started all sorts of old, forgotten, hidden-away, burned-out fancies of mine this afternoon, and—you see, I intended to be a professional pianist once, but I got married instead. Much better, really, because, unless—Oh, I don't know. Yes, I *am* jealous of you. You've picked me up and put me down again where I was once. Now the conversation's backed into me, and I really do want to talk about you. Your performance is the kind about which one wonders why nobody ever did it before. That's the greatest compliment one can pay an artist, I think. All great art is the great expression of a great commonplace; that's why it always looks so easy. I do hope you're having the practical success you deserve."

"Yes, I think I shall be all right," Sylvia said. "Only, I expect that after the New-Year I shall have to cut my show considerably and take a music-hall engagement. I'm not making a fortune at the Pierian."

"How horrid for you! How I should love to play with you! Oh dear! It's heartrending to say it, but it's much too late. Well, I mustn't keep you. You've given me such tremendous pleasure and just as much pain with it as makes the pleasure all the sharper.... I'll write and tell Michael about you."

"I expect he's forgotten my name by now," Sylvia said.

"Oh no, he never forgets anybody, even in the throes of theological speculation. Good-by. I see that this is your last performance for the present. I shall come and hear you again when you reopen. How odious about music-halls. You ought to have called yourself Silvia Scarletti, told your press agent that you were the direct descendant of the composer, vowed that when you came to England six months ago you could speak nothing but Polish, and you could have filled the Pierian night and day for a year. We're queer people, we English. I think, you know, it's a kind of shyness, the way we treat native artists. You get the same thing in families. It's not really that the prophet has no honor, etc.; it really is, I believe, a fear of boasting, which would be such bad form, wouldn't it? Of course we've ruined ourselves as a nation by our good manners and our sense of humor. Why, we've even insisted that what native artists we do support shall be gentlemen first and artists second. In what other country could an actor be knighted for his trousers or an author for his wife's dowry? Good-by. I do wish you great, great success."

"Anyway, I can't be knighted," Sylvia laughed.

"Oh, don't be too sure. A nation that has managed to turn its artists into gentlemen will soon insist on turning its women into gentlemen, too, or at any rate on securing their good manners in some way."

"Women will never really have good manners," Sylvia said.

"No, thank God. There you're right. Well, good-by. It's been so jolly to talk to you, and again I've loved every moment of this afternoon. Charles," she added to the handsome boy, "after bragging about your country's good manners, let's see you make a decent bow."

He inclined his head with a grave courtesy, opened the door for his mother, and followed her out.

The visit of Michael's sister, notwithstanding that she had envied Sylvia's luck, left her with very little opinion of it herself. What was her success, after all? A temporary elation dependent upon good health and the public taste, financially uncertain, emotionally wearing, radically unsatisfying and insecure, for, however good her performance was, it was always mummery, really, as near as mummery could get to creative work, perhaps, but mortal like its maker.

"Sad to think this is the last performance here," said her maid.

Sylvia agreed with her. It was a relief to find a peg on which to hang the unreasonable depression that was weighing her down. She passed out of her dressing-room. As the stage door swung to behind her a figure stepped into the lamplight of the narrow court; it was Jimmy Monkley. The spruceness had left him; all the color, too, had gone from his face, which was now sickly white—an evil face with its sandy mustache streaked with gray and its lusterless green eyes. Sylvia was afraid that from the way she started back from him he would think that she scorned him for having been in prison, and with an effort she tried to be cordial.

"You've done damned well for yourself," he said, paying no attention to what she was saying. She found this meeting overwhelmingly repulsive and moved toward her taxi. It was seeming to her that Monkley had the power to snatch her away and plunge her back into that life of theirs. She would really rather have met Philip than him.

"Damned well for yourself," he repeated.

"I'm sorry I can't stay. I'm in a hurry. I'm in a hurry."

She reached the taxi and slammed the door in his face.

This unexpected meeting convinced Sylvia of the necessity of attaching herself finally to a life that would make the resurrection of a Monkley nothing more influential than a nightmare. She knew that she was giving way to purely nervous fears in being thus affected by what, had she stopped to think, was the natural result of her name's becoming known. But the liability to nervous fears was in itself an argument that something was wrong. When had she ever been a prey to such hysteria before? When had she allowed herself to be haunted by a face, as now she was being haunted by Monkley's face? Suppose he had seated himself behind the taxi and that when she reached the Airdales' house he should once more be standing on the pavement in the lamplight?

In Brompton Road Sylvia told the driver to stop. She wanted to do some Christmas shopping. After an hour or more spent among toys she came out with a porter loaded with packages, and looked round her quickly; but of course he was not upon the pavement. How absurd she had been! In any case, what could Monkley do? She would forget all about him. To-morrow was Christmas Eve. There was going to be such a jolly party at the Airdales'. The taxi hummed toward West Kensington. Sylvia leaned back, huddled up with her thoughts, until they reached Lillie Road. She had passed Mrs. Meares's house so many times without giving it a second look. Now she found herself peering out into the thickening fog in case Monkley should be standing upon the door-step. She was glad when she reached the Airdales' house, warm and bright, festooned with holly and mistletoe. There were pleasant little household noises everywhere, comfortable little noises, and a rosy glow from the silken shades of the lamps; the carpet was so quiet and the parlor-maid in a clean cap and apron so efficient, so quick to get in all the parcels and shut out the foggy night.

Olive was already in the drawing-room, and because this was to be a specially unceremonious evening in preparation for the party to-morrow, Olive was in a pink tea-gown that blended with the prettiness of her cozy house and made her more essentially a part of it all. How bleak was her own background in comparison with this, Sylvia thought. Jack was dining out most unwillingly and had left a great many pleas to be forgiven by Sylvia on the first night of her Christmas visit. After dinner they sat in the drawing-room, and Sylvia told Olive about her meeting with Monkley. She said nothing about Michael Fane's sister; that meeting did not seem to have any bearing upon the subject she wanted to discuss.

"Can you understand," Sylvia asked, "being almost frightened into marriage?"

"Yes, I think so," Olive replied, as judicially as the comfort of her surroundings would allow. It was impossible to preserve a critical attitude in this room; in such a suave and genial atmosphere one accepted anything.

"Well, do you still object to my marrying Arthur?" Sylvia demanded.

"But, my dear, I never objected to your marrying him. I may have suggested, when I first saw him, that he seemed rather too much the type of the ordinary actor for you, but that was only because you yourself had always scoffed at actors so haughtily. Since I've known him I've grown to like him. Please don't think I ever objected to your marrying him. I never felt more sure about anybody's knowing her own mind than I do about you."

"Well, I am going to marry him," Sylvia said.

"Darling Sylvia, why do you say it so defiantly? Everybody will be delighted. Jack was talking only the other day about his perpetual dread that you'd never give yourself a chance of establishing your position finally, because you were so restless."

Sylvia contemplated an admission to Olive of having lived with Arthur for a year in America, but in this room the fact had an ugly look and seemed to belong rather to that evil face of the past that had confronted her with such ill omen this evening, rather than to anything so homely as marriage.

"Arthur may not be anything more than an actor," she went on. "But in my profession what else do I want? He has loved me for a long time; I'm very fond of him. It's essential that I should have a background so that I shall never be shaken out of my self-possession by anything like this evening's encounter. I've lived a life of feverish energy, and it's only since the improvisations that I can begin to believe it wasn't all wasted. I made a great mistake when I was seventeen, and when I was nineteen I tried to repair it with a still greater mistake. Then came Lily; she was a mistake. Oh, when I look back at it all, it's nothing but mistake after mistake. I long for such funny ordinary little pleasures. Olive darling, I've tried, I've tried to think I can do without love, without children, without family, without friends. I can't."

The tears were running swiftly, and all the time more swiftly, down Sylvia's cheeks while she was speaking. Olive jumped up from her soft and quilted chair and knelt beside her friend.

"My darling Sylvia, you have friends, you have, indeed you have."

"I know," Sylvia went on. "It's ungrateful of me. Why, if it hadn't been for you and Jack I should have gone mad. But just because you're so happy together, and because you have Sylvius and Rose, and because I flit about on the outskirts of it all like a timid, friendly, solitary ghost, I must have some one to love me. I've really treated Arthur very badly. I've kept him waiting now for a year. I wasn't brave enough to let him go, and I wasn't brave enough to marry him. I've never been undecided in my life. It must be that the gipsy in me has gone forever, I think. This success of mine has been leading all the time to settling down properly. Most of the people who came back to me out of the past were the nice people, like my old mistress and the grown-up twins, and I want to be like them. Oh, Olive, I'm so tired of being different, of people thinking that I'm hard and brutal and cynical. I'm not. Indeed I'm not. I couldn't have felt that truly appalling horror of Monkley this evening if I were really bad."

"Sylvia dear, you're working yourself up needlessly. How can you say that you're bad? How can you say such things about yourself? You're not religious, perhaps."

"Listen, Olive, if I marry Arthur I swear I'll make it a success. You know that I have a strong will. I'm not going to criticize him. I'm simply determined to make him and myself happy. It's very easy to love him, really. He's like a boy—very weak, you know—but with all sorts of charming qualities, and his mother would be so glad if it were all settled. Olive, I meant to tell you a whole heap of things about myself, about what I've done, but I won't. I'm going to forget it all and be happy. I'm glad it's Christmas-time. I've bought such ripping things for the kids. When I was buying them to-night there came into my head almost my first adventure when I was a very little girl and thought I'd found a ten-franc piece which was really the money I'd been given for the marketing. I had just such an orgy of buying to-night. Did you know that a giraffe could make a noise? Well, it can, or at any rate the giraffe I bought for Sylvius can. You twist its neck and it protests like a bronchial calf."

The party on Christmas Eve was a great success. Lucian Hope burnt a hole in the table-cloth with what was called a drawing-room firework. Jack split his coat trying to hide inside his bureau. Arthur, sitting on a bottle with his legs crossed, lit a candle, twice running. The little red-haired singer found the ring in the pudding. Sylvia found the sixpence. Nobody found the button, so it must have been swallowed. It was a splendid party. Sylvius and Rose did not begin to cry steadily until after ten o'clock.

When the guests were getting ready to leave, about two o'clock on Christmas morning, and while Lucian Hope was telling everybody in turn that somebody must have swallowed the button inadvertently, to prove that he was quite able to pronounce "inadvertently," Sylvia took Arthur down the front-door steps and walked with him a little way along the foggy street.

"Arthur, I'll marry you when you like," she said, laying a hand upon his arm.

"Sylvia, what a wonderful Christmas present!"

"To us both," she whispered.

Then on an impulse she dragged him back to the house and proclaimed their engagement, which meant the opening of new bottles of champagne and the drinking of so many healths that it was three o'clock before the party broke up. Nor was there any likelihood of anybody's being able to say "inadvertently" by the time he had reached the corner of the street.

Arthur had begged Sylvia to come down to Dulwich on Christmas day, and Mrs. Madden rejoiced over the decision they had reached at last. There were one or two things to be considered, the most important of which was the question of money. Sylvia had spent the last penny of what was left of Morera's money in launching herself, and she owed nearly two hundred pounds besides. Arthur had saved nothing. Both of them, however, had been offered good engagements for the spring, Arthur to tour as lead in one of the Vanity productions, which might mean an engagement at the Vanity itself in the autumn; Sylvia to play a twenty minutes' turn at all the music-halls of a big circuit. It seemed unsatisfactory to marry and immediately afterward to separate, and they decided each to take the work that had been offered, to save all the money possible, and to aim at both playing in London next autumn, but in any case to be married in early June when the tours would end. They should then have a couple of months to themselves. Mrs. Madden wanted them to be married at once; but the other way seemed more prudent, and Sylvia, having once made up her mind, was determined to be practical and not to run the risk of spoiling by financial worries the beginning of their real life together. Her marriage in its orderliness and forethought and simplicity of intention was to compensate for everything that had gone before. Mrs. Madden thought they were both of them being too deliberate, but then she had run away once with her father's groom and must have had a fundamentally impulsive, even a reckless temperament.

The engagement was announced with an eye to the most advantageous publicity that is the privilege of being servants of the public. One was able to read everywhere of a theatrical romance or more coldly of a forthcoming theatrical marriage; nearly all the illustrated weeklies had two little oval photographs underneath which ran the legend:

INTERESTING ENGAGEMENT

We learn that Miss Sylvia Scarlett, who recently registered such an emphatic success in her original entertainment at the Pierian Hall, will shortly wed Mr. Arthur Madden, whom many of our readers will remember for his rendering of "Somebody is sitting in the sunset" at the Frivolity Theater.

In one particularly intimate paper was a short interview headed:

ACTRESS'S DELIGHTFUL CANDOR

"No," said Miss Scarlett to our representative who had called upon the clever and original young performer to ascertain when her marriage with Mr. Arthur Madden of "Somebody is sitting in the sunset" fame would take place. "No, Arthur and I have decided to wait till June. Frankly, we can't afford to be married yet...."

and so on, with what was described as a portrait of Miss Sylvia Scarlet inset, but which without the avowal would probably have been taken for the thumbprint of a paperboy.

"This is all terribly vulgar," Sylvia bewailed, but Jack, Arthur, and Olive were all firm in the need for thorough advertisement, and she acquiesced woefully. In January she and Arthur parted for their respective tours. Jack, before she went away, begged Sylvia for the fiftieth time to take back the money she had settled on her godchildren. He argued with her until she got angry.

"Jack, if you mention that again I'll never come to your house any more. One of the most exquisite joys in all my life was when I was able to do that, and when you and Olive were sweet enough to let me, for you really were sweet and simple in those days and not purse-proud *bourgeois*, as you are now. Please, Jack!" She had tears in her eyes. "Don't be unkind."

"But supposing you have children of your own?" he urged.

"Jack, don't go on. It really upsets me. I cannot bear the idea of that money's belonging to anybody but the twins."

"Did you tell Arthur?"

"It's nothing to do with Arthur. It's only to do with me. It was my present. It was made before Arthur came on the scene."

With great unwillingness Jack obeyed her command not to say anything more on the subject.

Sylvia earned a good enough salary to pay off nearly all her debts by May, when her tour brought her to the suburban music-halls and she was able to amuse herself by house-hunting for herself and Arthur. All her friends, and not the least old ones like Gladys and Enid, took a profound interest in her approaching marriage. Wedding-presents even began to arrive. The most remarkable omen of the gods' pleasure was a communication she received in mid-May from Miss Dashwood's solicitors to say that Miss Dashwood had died and had left to Sylvia in her will the freehold of Mulberry Cottage with all it contained. Olive was enraptured with her good fortune, and wanted to telegraph to Arthur, who was in Leeds that week; but Sylvia said she would rather write:

DEAREST ARTHUR,—You remember my telling you about Mulberry Cottage? Well, the most wonderful thing has happened. That old darling, Miss Dashwood, the sister of Mrs. Gainsborough's captain, has left it to me with everything in it. It has of course for me all sorts of memories, and I want to tell you very seriously that I regard it as a sign, yes, really a sign of my wanderings and restlessness being forever finished. It seems to me somehow to consecrate our marriage. Don't think I'm turning religious: I shall never do that. Oh no, never! But I can't help being moved by what to you may seem only a coincidence. Arthur, you must forgive me for the way in which I've often treated you. You mustn't think that because I've always bullied you in the past I'm always going to in the future. If you want me now, I'm yours *really*, much more than I ever was in America, much, much more. You *shall* be happy with me. Oh, it's such a dear house with a big garden, for London a very big garden, and it held once two such true hearts. Do you see the foolish tears smudging the ink? They're my tears for so much. I'm going to-morrow morning to dust our house. Think of me when you get this letter as really at last

Your SYLVIA.

The next morning arrived a letter from Leeds, which had crossed hers:

MY DEAR SYLVIA,—I don't know how to tell you what I must tell. I was married this morning to Maimie Vernon. I don't know how I let myself fall in love with her. I never looked at her when she sang at the Pierian with you. But she got an engagement in this company and—well, you know the way things happen on tour. The only thing that makes me feel not an absolutely hopeless cad is that I've a feeling somehow that you were going to marry me more out of kindness and pity than out of love.

Forgive me. ARTHUR.

"That funny little red-haired girl!" Sylvia gasped. Then like a surging wave the affront to her pride overwhelmed her. With an effort she looked at her other letters. One was from Michael Fane's sister:

HARDINGHAM HALL,
HUNTS,
May, 1914.

DEAR MISS SCARLETT,—My brother is back in England and so anxious to meet you again. I know you're playing near town at present. Couldn't you possibly come down next Sunday morning and stay till Monday? It would give us the greatest pleasure.

Yours sincerely,
STELLA PRESCOTT-MERIVALE.

"Never," Sylvia cried, tearing the letter into small pieces. "Ah no! That, never, never!"

She left her rooms, and went to Mulberry Cottage. The caretaker fluttered round her to show her sense of Sylvia's importance as her new mistress. Was there nothing that she could do? Was there nothing that she could get?

Sylvia sat on the seat under the mulberry-tree in the still morning sunlight of May. It was impossible to think, impossible to plan, impossible, impossible. The ideas in her brain went slowly round and round. Nothing would stop them. Round and round they went, getting every moment more mixed up with one another. But gradually from the confusion one idea emerged, sharp, strong, insistent—she must leave England. The moment this idea had stated itself, Sylvia could think of nothing but the swiftness and secrecy of her departure. She felt that if one person should ever fling a glance of sympathy or condolence or pity or even of mild affection, she should kill herself to set free her outraged soul. She made no plans for the future. She had no reproaches for Arthur. She had nothing but the urgency of flight as from the Furies themselves. Quickly she went back to her rooms and packed. All her big luggage she took to Mulberry Cottage and placed with the caretaker. She sent a sum of money to the solicitors and asked them to pay the woman until she came back.

At the last moment, in searching through her trunks, she found the yellow shawl that was wrapped round her few treasures of ancestry. She was going to leave it behind, but on second thought she packed it in the only trunk she took with her. She was going back perhaps to the life of which these treasures were the only solid pledge.

"This time, yes, I'm off with the raggle-taggle gipsies in deadly earnest. Charing Cross," she told the taxi-driver.

THE END

The Altar Steps
CHAPTER I
THE BISHOP'S SHADOW

Frightened by some alarm of sleep that was forgotten in the moment of waking, a little boy threw back the bedclothes and with quick heart and breath sat listening to the torrents of darkness that went rolling by. He dared not open his mouth to scream lest he should be suffocated; he dared not put out his arm to search for the bell-rope lest he should be seized; he dared not hide beneath the blankets lest he should be kept there; he could do nothing except sit up trembling in a vain effort to orientate himself. Had the room really turned upside down? On an impulse of terror he jumped back from the engorging night and bumped his forehead on one of the brass knobs of the bedstead. With horror he apprehended that what he had so often feared had finally come to pass. An earthquake had swallowed up London in spite of everybody's assurance that London could not be swallowed up by earthquakes. He was going down down to smoke and fire . . . or was it the end of the world? The quick and the dead . . . skeletons . . . thousands and thousands of skeletons. . . .

"Guardian Angel!" he shrieked.

Now surely that Guardian Angel so often conjured must appear. A shaft of golden candlelight flickered through the half open door. The little boy prepared an attitude to greet his Angel that was a compound of the suspicion and courtesy with which he would have welcomed a new governess and the admiring fellowship with which he would have thrown a piece of bread to a swan.

"Are you awake, Mark?" he heard his mother whisper outside.

He answered with a cry of exultation and relief.

"Oh, Mother," he sighed, clinging to the soft sleeves of her dressing-gown. "I thought it was being the end of the world."

"What made you think that, my precious?"

"I don't know. I just woke up, and the room was upside down. And first I thought it was an earthquake, and then I thought it was the Day of Judgment." He suddenly began to chuckle to himself. "How silly of me, Mother. Of course it couldn't be the Day of Judgment, because it's night, isn't it? It couldn't ever be the Day of Judgment in the night, could it?" he continued hopefully.

Mrs. Lidderdale did not hesitate to reassure her small son on this point. She had no wish to add another to that long list of nightly fears and fantasies which began with mad dogs and culminated in the Prince of Darkness himself.

"The room looks quite safe now, doesn't it?" Mark theorized.

"It is quite safe, darling."

"Do you think I could have the gas lighted when you really *must* go?"

"Just a little bit for once."

"Only a little bit?" he echoed doubtfully. A very small illumination was in its eerie effect almost worse than absolute darkness.

"It isn't healthy to sleep with a great deal of light," said his mother.

"Well, how much could I have? Just for once not a crocus, but a tulip. And of course not a violet."

Mark always thought of the gas-jets as flowers. The dimmest of all was the violet; followed by the crocus, the tulip, and the water-lily; the last a brilliant affair with wavy edges, and sparkling motes dancing about in the blue water on which it swam.

"No, no, dearest boy. You really can't have as much as that. And now snuggle down and go to sleep again. I wonder what made you wake up?"

Mark seized upon this splendid excuse to detain his mother for awhile.

"Well, it wasn't ergzackly a dream," he began to improvise. "Because I was awake. And I heard a terrible plump and I said 'what can that be?' and then I was frightened and. . . ."

"Yes, well, my sweetheart, you must tell Mother in the morning."

Mark perceived that he had been too slow in working up to his crisis and desperately he sought for something to arrest the attention of his beloved audience.

"Perhaps my Guardian Angel was beside me all the time, because, look! here's a feather."

He eyed his mother, hoping against hope that she would pretend to accept his suggestion; but alas, she was severely unimaginative.

"Now, darling, don't talk foolishly. You know perfectly that is only a feather which has worked its way out of your pillow."

"Why?"

The monosyllable had served Mark well in its time; but even as he fell back upon this stale resource he knew it had failed at last.

"I can't stay to explain 'why' now; but if you try to think you'll understand why."

"Mother, if I don't have any gas at all, will you sit with me in the dark for a little while, a tiny little while, and stroke my forehead where I bumped it on the knob of the bed? I really did bump it quite hard—I forgot to tell you that. I forgot to tell you because when it was you I was so excited that I forgot."

"Now listen, Mark. Mother wants you to be a very good boy and turn over and go to sleep. Father is very worried and very tired, and the Bishop is coming tomorrow."

"Will he wear a hat like the Bishop who came last Easter? Why is he coming?"

"No darling, he's not that kind of bishop. I can't explain to you why he's coming, because you wouldn't understand; but we're all very anxious, and you must be good and brave and unselfish. Now kiss me and turn over."

Mark flung his arms round his mother's neck, and thrilled by a sudden desire to sacrifice himself murmured that he would go to sleep in the dark.

"In the quite dark," he offered, dipping down under the clothes so as to be safe by the time the protecting candle-light wavered out along the passage and the soft closing of his mother's door assured him that come what might there was only a wall between him and her.

"And perhaps she won't go to sleep before I go to sleep," he hoped.

At first Mark meditated upon bishops. The perversity of night thoughts would not allow him to meditate upon the pictures of some child-loving bishop like St. Nicolas, but must needs fix his contemplation upon a certain Bishop of Bingen who was eaten by rats. Mark could not remember why he was eaten by rats, but he could with dreadful distinctness remember that the prelate escaped to a castle on an island in the middle of the Rhine, and that the rats swam after him and swarmed in by every window until his castle was—ugh!—Mark tried to banish from his mind the picture of the wicked Bishop Hatto and the rats, millions of them, just going to eat him up. Suppose a lot of rats came swarming up Notting Hill and unanimously turned to the right into Notting Dale and ate him? An earthquake would be better than that. Mark began to feel thoroughly frightened again; he wondered if he dared call out to his mother and put forward the theory that there actually was a rat in his room. But he had promised her to be brave and unselfish, and . . . there was always the evening hymn to fall back upon.

Now the day is over,Night is drawing nigh,Shadows of the eveningSteal across the sky.

Mark thought of a beautiful evening in the country as beheld in a Summer Number, more of an afternoon really than an evening, with trees making shadows right across a golden field, and spotted cows in the foreground. It was a blissful and completely soothing picture while it lasted; but it soon died away, and he was back in the midway of a London night with icy stretches of sheet to right and left of him instead of golden fields.

Now the darkness gathers,Stars begin to peep,Birds and beasts and flowersSoon will be asleep.

But rats did not sleep; they were at their worst and wake-fullest in the night time.

Jesu, give the wearyCalm and sweet repose,With thy tenderest blessingMay mine eyelids close.

Mark waited a full five seconds in the hope that he need not finish the hymn; but when he found that he was not asleep after five seconds he resumed:

Grant to little childrenVisions bright of Thee;Guard the sailors tossingOn the deep blue sea.

Mark envied the sailors.

Comfort every suffererWatching late in pain.

This was a most encouraging couplet. Mark did not suppose that in the event of a great emergency—he thanked Mrs. Ewing for that long and descriptive word—the sufferers would be able to do much for him; but the consciousness that all round him in the great city they were lying awake at this moment was most helpful. At this point he once more waited five seconds for sleep to arrive. The next couplet was less encouraging, and he would have been glad to miss it out.

Those who plan some evilFrom their sin restrain.

Yes, but prayers were not always answered immediately. For instance he was still awake. He hurried on to murmur aloud in fervour:

Through the long night watchesMay Thine Angels spreadTheir white wings above me,Watching round my bed.

A delicious idea, and even more delicious was the picture contained in the next verse.

When the morning wakens,Then may I arisePure, and fresh, and sinlessIn Thy Holy Eyes.
Glory to the Father,Glory to the Son,And to thee, blest Spirit,Whilst all ages run. Amen.

Mark murmured the last verse with special reverence in the hope that by doing so he should obtain a speedy granting of the various requests in the earlier part of the hymn.

In the morning his mother put out Sunday clothes for him.

"The Bishop is coming to-day," she explained.

"But it isn't going to be like Sunday?" Mark inquired anxiously. An extra Sunday on top of such a night would have been hard to bear.

"No, but I want you to look nice."

"I can play with my soldiers?"

"Oh, yes, you can play with your soldiers."

"I won't bang, I'll only have them marching."

"No, dearest, don't bang. And when the Bishop comes to lunch I want you not to ask questions. Will you promise me that?"

"Don't bishops like to be asked questions?"

"No, darling. They don't."

Mark registered this episcopal distaste in his memory beside other facts such as that cats object to having their tails pulled.

CHAPTER II

THE LIMA STREET MISSION

In the year 1875, when the strife of ecclesiastical parties was bitter and continuous, the Reverend James Lidderdale came as curate to the large parish of St. Simon's, Notting Hill, which at that period was looked upon as one of the chief expositions of what Disraeli called "man-millinery." Inasmuch as the coiner of the phrase was a Jew, the priests and people of St. Simon's paid no attention to it, and were proud to consider themselves an outpost of the Catholic Movement in the Church of England. James Lidderdale was given the charge of the Lima Street Mission, a tabernacle of corrugated iron dedicated to St. Wilfred; and Thurston, the Vicar of St. Simon's, who was a wise, generous and single-hearted priest, was quick to recognize that his missioner was capable of being left to convert the Notting Dale slum in his own way.

"If St. Simon's is an outpost of the Movement, Lidderdale must be one of the vedettes," he used to declare with a grin.

The Missioner was a tall hatchet-faced hollow-eyed ascetic, harsh and bigoted in the company of his equals whether clerical or lay, but with his flock tender and comprehending and patient. The only indulgence he accorded to his senses was in the forms and ceremonies of his ritual, the vestments and furniture of his church. His vicar was able to give him a free hand in the obscure squalor of Lima Street; the ecclesiastical battles he himself had to fight with bishops who were pained or with retired military men who were disgusted by his own conduct of the services at St. Simon's were not waged within the hearing of Lima Street. There, year in, year out for six years, James Lidderdale denied himself nothing in religion, in life everything. He used to preach in the parish church during the penitential seasons, and with such effect upon the pockets of his congregation that the Lima Street Mission was rich for a long while afterward. Yet few of the worshippers in the parish church visited the object of their charity, and those that did venture seldom came twice. Lidderdale did not consider that it was part of the Lima Street religion to be polite to well-dressed explorers of the slum; in fact he rather encouraged Lima Street to suppose the contrary.

"I don't like these dressed up women in my church," he used to tell his vicar. "They distract my people's attention from the altar."

"Oh, I quite see your point," Thurston would agree.

"And I don't like these churchy young fools who come simpering down in top-hats, with rosaries hanging out of their pockets. Lima Street doesn't like them either. Lima Street is provoked to obscene comment, and that just before Mass. It's no good, Vicar. My people are savages, and I like them to remain savages so long as they go to their duties, which Almighty God be thanked they do."

On one occasion the Archdeacon, who had been paying an official visit to St. Simon's, expressed a desire to see the Lima Street Mission.

"Of which I have heard great things, great things, Mr. Thurston," he boomed condescendingly.

The Vicar was doubtful of the impression that the Archdeacon's gaiters would make on Lima Street, and he was also doubtful of the impression that the images and prickets of St. Wilfred's would make on the Archdeacon. The Vicar need not have worried. Long before Lima Street was reached, indeed, halfway down Strugwell Terrace, which was the main road out of respectable Notting Hill into the Mission area, the comments upon the Archdeacon's appearance became so embarrassing that the dignitary looked at his watch and remarked that after all he feared he should not be able to spare the time that afternoon.

"But I am surprised," he observed when his guide had brought him safely back into Notting Hill. "I am surprised that the people are still so uncouth. I had always understood that a great work of purification had been effected, that in fact—er—they were quite—er—cleaned up."

"In body or soul?" Thurston inquired.

"The whole district," said the Archdeacon vaguely. "I was referring to the general tone, Mr. Thurston. One might be pardoned for supposing that they had never seen a clergyman before. Of course one is loath—very loath indeed—to criticize sincere effort of any kind, but I think that perhaps almost the chief value of the missions we have established in these poverty-stricken areas lies in their capacity for civilizing the poor people who inhabit them. One is so anxious to bring into their drab lives a little light, a little air. I am a great believer in education. Oh, yes, Mr. Thurston, I have great hopes of popular education. However, as I say, I should not dream of criticizing your work at St. Wilfred's."

"It is not my work. It is the work of one of my curates. And," said the Vicar to Lidderdale, when he was giving him an account of the projected visitation, "I believe the pompous ass thought I was ashamed of it."

Thurston died soon after this, and, his death occurring at a moment when party strife in the Church was fiercer than ever, it was considered expedient by the Lord Chancellor, in whose gift the living was, to appoint a more moderate man than the late vicar. Majendie, the new man, when he was sure of his audience, claimed to be just as advanced as Thurston; but he was ambitious of preferment, or as he himself put it, he felt that, when a member of the Catholic party had with the exercise of prudence and tact an opportunity of enhancing the prestige of his party in a higher ecclesiastical sphere, he should be wrong to neglect it. Majendie's aim therefore was to avoid controversy with his ecclesiastical superiors, and at a time when, as he told Lidderdale, he was stepping back in order to jump farther, he was anxious that his missioner should step back with him.

"I'm not suggesting, my dear fellow, that you should bring St. Wilfred's actually into line with the parish church. But the Asperges, you know. I can't countenance that. And the Adoration of the Cross on Good Friday. I really think that kind of thing creates unnecessary friction."

Lidderdale's impulse was to resign at once, for he was a man who found restraint galling where so much passion went to his belief in the truth of his teaching. When, however, he pondered how little he had done and how much he had vowed to do, he gave way and agreed to step back with his vicar. He was never convinced that he had taken the right course at this crisis, and he spent hours in praying for an answer by God to a question already answered by himself. The added strain of these hours of prayer, which were not robbed from his work in the Mission, but from the already short enough time he allowed himself for sleep, told upon his health, and he was ordered by the doctor to take a holiday to avoid a complete breakdown of health. He stayed for two months in Cornwall, and came back with a wife, the daughter of a Cornish parson called Trehawke. Lidderdale had been a fierce upholder of celibacy, and the news of his marriage astonished all who knew him.

Grace Lidderdale with her slanting sombre eyes and full upcurving lips made the pink and white Madonnas of the little mission church look insipid, and her husband was horrified when he found himself criticizing the images whose ability to lure the people of Lima Street to worship in the way he believed to be best for their souls he had never doubted. Yet, for all her air of having *trafficked for strange webs with Eastern merchants*, Mrs. Lidderdale was only outwardly Phoenician or Iberian or whatever other dimly imagined race is chosen for the strange types that in Cornwall more than elsewhere so often occur. Actually she was a simple and devout soul, loving husband and child and the poor people with whom they lived. Doubtless she had looked more appropriate to her surroundings in the tangled garden of her father's vicarage than in the bleak Mission House of Lima Street; but inasmuch as she never thought about her appearance it would have been a waste of time for anybody to try to romanticize her. The civilizing effect of her presence in the slum was quickly felt; and though Lidderdale continued to scoff at the advantages of civilization, he finally learnt to give a grudging welcome to her various schemes for making the bodies of the flock as comfortable as her husband tried to make their souls.

When Mark was born, his father became once more the prey of gloomy doubt. The guardianship of a soul which he was responsible for bringing into the world was a ceaseless care, and in his anxiety to dedicate his son to God he became a harsh and unsympathetic parent. Out of that desire to justify himself for having been so inconsistent as to take a wife and beget a son Lidderdale redoubled his efforts to put the Lima Street Mission on a permanent basis. The civilization of the slum, which was attributed by pious visitors to regular attendance at Mass rather than to Mrs. Lidderdale's gentleness and charm, made it much easier for outsiders to explore St. Simon's parish as far as Lima Street. Money for the great church he designed to build on a site adjoining the old tabernacle began to flow in; and five years after his marriage Lidderdale had enough money subscribed to begin to build. The rubbish-strewn waste-ground overlooked by the back-windows of the Mission House was thronged with workmen; day by day the walls of the new St. Wilfred's rose higher. Fifteen years after Lidderdale took charge of the Lima Street Mission, it was decided to ask for St. Wilfred's, Notting Dale, to be created a separate parish. The Reverend Aylmer Majendie had become a canon residentiary of Chichester and had been succeeded as vicar by the Reverend L. M. Astill, a man more of the type of Thurston and only too anxious to help his senior curate to become a vicar, and what is more cut £200 a year off his own net income in doing so.

But when the question arose of consecrating the new St. Wilfred's in order to the creation of a new parish, the Bishop asked many questions that were never asked about the Lima Street Mission. There were Stations of the Cross reported to be of an unusually idolatrous nature. There was a second chapel apparently for the express purpose of worshipping the Virgin Mary.

"He writes to me as if he suspected me of trying to carry on an intrigue with the Mother of God," cried Lidderdale passionately to his vicar.

"Steady, steady, dear man," said Astill. "You'll ruin your case by such ill-considered exaggeration."

"But, Vicar, these cursed bishops of the Establishment who would rather a whole parish went to Hell than give up one jot or one tittle of their prejudice!" Lidderdale ejaculated in wrath.

Furthermore, the Bishop wanted to know if the report that on Good Friday was held a Roman Catholic Service called the Mass of the Pre-Sanctified followed by the ceremony of Creeping to the Cross was true. When Majendie departed, the Lima Street Missioner jumped a long way forward in one leap. There were many other practices which he (the Bishop) could only characterize as highly objectionable and quite contrary to the spirit of the Church of England, and would Mr. Lidderdale pay him a visit at Fulham Palace as soon as possible. Lidderdale went, and he argued with the Bishop until the Chaplain thought his Lordship had heard enough, after which the argument was resumed by letter. Then Lidderdale was invited to lunch at Fulham Palace and to argue the whole question over again in person. In the end the Bishop was sufficiently impressed by the Missioner's sincerity and zeal to agree to withhold his decision until the Lord Bishop Suffragan of Devizes had paid a visit to the proposed new parish. This was the visit that was expected on the day after Mark Lidderdale woke from a nightmare and dreamed that London was being swallowed up by an earthquake.

CHAPTER III
RELIGIOUS EDUCATION

When Mark was grown up and looked back at his early childhood—he was seven years old in the year in which his father was able to see the new St. Wilfred's an edifice complete except for consecration—it seemed to him that his education had centered in the prevention of his acquiring a Cockney accent. This was his mother's dread and for this reason he was not allowed to play more than Christian equality demanded with the boys of Lima Street. Had his mother had her way, he would never have been allowed to play with them at all; but his father would sometimes break out into fierce tirades against snobbery and hustle him out of the house to amuse himself with half-a-dozen little girls looking after a dozen babies in dilapidated perambulators, and countless smaller boys and girls ragged and grubby and mischievous.

"You leave that kebbidge-stalk be, Elfie!"

"Ethel! Jew hear your ma calling you, you naughty girl?"

"Stanlee! will you give over fishing in that puddle, this sminute. I'll give you such a slepping, you see if I don't."

"Come here, Maybel, and let me blow your nose. Daisy Hawkins, lend us your henkerchif, there's a love! Our Maybel wants to blow her nose. Oo, she is a sight! Come here, Maybel, do, and leave off sucking that orange peel. There's the Father's little boy looking at you. Hold your head up, do."

Mark would stand gravely to attention while Mabel Williams' toilet was adjusted, and as gravely follow the shrill raucous procession to watch pavement games like Hop Scotch or to help in gathering together enough sickly greenery from the site of the new church to make the summer grotto, which in Lima Street was a labour of love, since few of the passers by in that neighbourhood could afford to remember St. James' grotto with a careless penny.

The fact that all the other little boys and girls called the Missioner Father made it hard for Mark to understand his own more particular relationship to him, and Lidderdale was so much afraid of showing any more affection to one child of his flock than to another that he was less genial with his own son than with any of the other children. It was natural that in these circumstances Mark should be even more dependent than most solitary children upon his mother, and no doubt it was through his passion to gratify her that he managed to avoid that Cockney accent. His father wanted his first religious instruction to be of the communal kind that he provided in the Sunday School. One might have thought that he distrusted his wife's orthodoxy, so strongly did he disapprove of her teaching Mark by himself in the nursery.

"It's the curse of the day," he used to assert, "this pampering of children with an individual religion. They get into the habit of thinking God is their special property and when they get older and find he isn't, as often as not they give up religion altogether, because it doesn't happen to fit in with the spoilt notions they got hold of as infants."

Mark's bringing up was the only thing in which Mrs. Lidderdale did not give way to her husband. She was determined that he should not have a Cockney accent, and without irritating her husband any more than was inevitable she was determined that he should not gobble down his religion as a solid indigestible whole. On this point she even went so far as directly to contradict the boy's father and argue that an intelligent boy like Mark was likely to vomit up such an indigestible whole later on, although she did not make use of such a coarse expression.

"All mothers think their sons are the cleverest in the world."

"But, James, he *is* an exceptionally clever little boy. Most observant, with a splendid memory and plenty of imagination."

"Too much imagination. His nights are one long circus."

"But, James, you yourself have insisted so often on the personal Devil; you can't expect a little boy of Mark's sensitiveness not to be impressed by your picture."

"He has nothing to fear from the Devil, if he behaves himself. Haven't I made that clear?"

Mrs. Lidderdale sighed.

"But, James dear, a child's mind is so literal, and though I know you insist just as much on the reality of the Saints and Angels, a child's mind is always most impressed by the things that have power to frighten it."

"I want him to be frightened by Evil," declared James. "But go your own way. Soften down everything in our Holy Religion that is ugly and difficult. Sentimentalize the whole business. That's our modern method in everything."

This was one of many arguments between husband and wife about the religious education of their son.

Luckily for Mark his father had too many children, real children and grown up children, in the Mission to be able to spend much time with his son; and the teaching of Sunday morning, the clear-cut uncompromising statement of hard religious facts in which the Missioner delighted, was considerably toned down by his wife's gentle commentary.

Mark's mother taught him that the desire of a bad boy to be a good boy is a better thing than the goodness of a Jack Horner. She taught him that God was not merely a crotchety old gentleman reclining in a blue dressing-gown on a mattress of cumulus, but that He was an Eye, an all-seeing Eye, an Eye capable indeed of flashing with rage, yet so rarely that whenever her little boy should imagine that Eye he might behold it wet with tears.

"But can God cry?" asked Mark incredulously.

"Oh, darling. God can do everything."

"But fancy crying! If I could do everything I shouldn't cry."

Mrs. Lidderdale perceived that her picture of the wise and compassionate Eye would require elaboration.

"But do you only cry, Mark dear, when you can't do what you want? Those are not nice tears. Don't you ever cry because you're sorry you've been disobedient?"

"I don't think so, Mother," Mark decided after a pause. "No, I don't think I cry because I'm sorry except when you're sorry, and that sometimes makes me cry. Not always, though. Sometimes I'm glad you're sorry. I feel so angry that I like to see you sad."

"But you don't often feel like that?"

"No, not often," he admitted.

"But suppose you saw somebody being ill-treated, some poor dog or cat being teased, wouldn't you feel inclined to cry?"

"Oh, no," Mark declared. "I get quite red inside of me, and I want to kick the people who is doing it."

"Well, now you can understand why God sometimes gets angry. But even if He gets angry," Mrs. Lidderdale went on, for she was rather afraid of her son's capacity for logic, "God never lets His anger get the better of Him. He is not only sorry for the poor dog, but He is also sorry for the poor person who is ill-treating the dog. He knows that the poor person has perhaps never been taught better, and then the Eye fills with tears again."

"I think I like Jesus better than God," said Mark, going off at a tangent. He felt that there were too many points of resemblance between his own father and God to make it prudent to persevere with the discussion. On the subject of his father he always found his mother strangely uncomprehending, and the only times she was really angry with him was when he refused out of his basic honesty to admit that he loved his father.

"But Our Lord *is* God," Mrs. Lidderdale protested.

Mark wrinkled his face in an effort to confront once more this eternal puzzle.

"Don't you remember, darling, three Persons and one God?"

Mark sighed.

"You haven't forgotten that clover-leaf we picked one day in Kensington Gardens?"

"When we fed the ducks on the Round Pond?"

"Yes, darling, but don't think about ducks just now. I want you to think about the Holy Trinity."

"But I can't understand the Holy Trinity, Mother," he protested.

"Nobody can understand the Holy Trinity. It is a great mystery."

"Mystery," echoed Mark, taking pleasure in the word. It always thrilled him, that word, ever since he first heard it used by Dora the servant when she could not find her rolling-pin.

"Well, where that rolling-pin's got to is a mystery," she had declared.

Then he had seen the word in print. The Coram Street Mystery. All about a dead body. He had pronounced it "micetery" at first, until he had been corrected and was able to identify the word as the one used by Dora about her rolling-pin. History stood for the hard dull fact, and mystery stood for all that history was not. There were no dates in "mystery:" Mark even at seven years, such was the fate of intelligent precocity, had already had to grapple with a few conspicuous dates in the immense tale of humanity. He knew for instance that William the Conqueror landed in 1066, and that St. Augustine landed in 596, and that Julius Cæsar landed, but he could never remember exactly when. The last time he was asked that date, he had countered with a request to know when Noah had landed.

"The Holy Trinity is a mystery."

It belonged to the category of vanished rolling-pins and dead bodies huddled up in dustbins: it had no date.

But what Mark liked better than speculations upon the nature of God were the tales that were told like fairy tales without its seeming to matter whether you remembered them or not, and which just because it did not matter you were able to remember so much more easily. He could have listened for ever to the story of the lupinseeds that rattled in their pods when the donkey was trotting with the boy Christ and His mother and St. Joseph far away from cruel Herod into Egypt and how the noise of the rattling seeds nearly betrayed their flight and how the plant was cursed for evermore and made as hungry as a wolf. And the story of how the robin tried to loosen one of the cruel nails so that the blood from the poor Saviour drenched his breast and stained it red for evermore, and of that other bird, the crossbill, who pecked at the nails until his beak became crossed. He could listen for ever to the tale of St. Cuthbert who was fed by ravens, of St. Martin who cut off his cloak and gave it to a beggar, of St. Anthony who preached to the fishes, of St. Raymond who put up his cowl and floated from Spain to Africa like a nautilus, of St. Nicolas who raised three boys from the dead after they had been killed and cut up and salted in a tub by a cruel man that wanted to eat them, and of that strange insect called a Praying Mantis which alighted upon St. Francis' sleeve and sang the *Nunc Dimittis* before it flew away.

These were all stories that made bedtime sweet, stories to remember and brood upon gratefully in the darkness of the night when he lay awake and when, alas, other stories less pleasant to recall would obtrude themselves.

Mark was not brought up luxuriously in the Lima Street Mission House, and the scarcity of toys stimulated his imagination. All his toys were old and broken, because he was only allowed to have the toys left over at the annual Christmas Tree in the Mission Hall; and since even the best of toys on that tree were the cast-offs of rich little children whose parents performed a vicarious act of charity in presenting them to the poor, it may be understood that Mark's share of these was not calculated to spoil him. His most conspicuous toy was a box of mutilated grenadiers, whose stands had been melted by their former owner in the first rapture of discovering that lead melts in fire and who in consequence were only able to stand up uncertainly when stuck into sliced corks.

Luckily Mark had better armies of his own in the coloured lines that crossed the blankets of his bed. There marched the crimson army of St. George, the blue army of St. Andrew, the green army of St. Patrick, the yellow army of St. David, the rich sunset-hued army of St. Denis, the striped armies of St. Anthony and St. James. When he lay awake in the golden light of the morning, as golden in Lima Street as anywhere else, he felt ineffably protected by the Seven Champions of Christendom; and sometimes even at night he was able to think that with their bright battalions they were still marching past. He used to lie awake, listening to the sparrows and wondering what the country was like and most of all the sea. His father would not let him go into the country until he was considered old enough to go with one of the annual school treats. His mother told him that the country in Cornwall was infinitely more beautiful than Kensington Gardens, and that compared with the sea the Serpentine was nothing at all. The sea! He had heard it once in a prickly shell, and it had sounded beautiful. As for the country he had read a story by Mrs. Ewing called *Our Field*, and if the country was the tiniest part as wonderful as that, well . . . meanwhile Dora brought him back from the greengrocer's a pot of musk, which Mark used to sniff so enthusiastically that Dora said he would sniff it right away if he wasn't careful. Later on when Lima Street was fetid in the August sun he gave this pot of musk to a little girl with a broken leg, and when she died in September her mother put it on her grave.

CHAPTER IV
HUSBAND AND WIFE

Mark was impressed by the appearance of the Bishop of Devizes; a portly courtly man, he brought to the dingy little Mission House in Lima Street that very sense of richness and grandeur which Mark had anticipated. The Bishop's pink plump hands of which he made such use contrasted with the lean, scratched, and grimy hands of his father; the Bishop's hair white and glossy made his father's bristly, badly cut hair look more bristly and worse cut than ever, and the Bishop's voice ripe and unctuous grew more and more mellow as his father's became harsher and more assertive. Mark found himself thinking of some lines in *The Jackdaw of Rheims* about a cake of soap worthy of washing the hands of the Pope. The Pope would have hands like the Bishop's, and Mark who had heard a great deal about the Pope looked at the Bishop of Devizes with added interest.

"While we are at lunch, Mr. Lidderdale, you will I am sure pardon me for referring again to our conversation of this morning from another point of view—the point of view, if I may use so crude an expression, the point of view of—er—expediency. Is it wise?"

"I'm not a wise man, my lord."

"Pardon me, my dear Mr. Lidderdale, but I have not completed my question. Is it right? Is it right when you have an opportunity to consolidate your great work . . . I use the adjective advisedly and with no intention to flatter you, for when I had the privilege this morning of accompanying you round the beautiful edifice that has been by your efforts, by your self-sacrifice, by your eloquence, and by your devotion erected to the glory of God . . . I repeat, Mr. Lidderdale, is it right to fling all this away for the sake of a few—you will not misunderstand me—if I call them a few excrescences?"

The Bishop helped himself to the cauliflower and paused to give his rhetoric time to work.

"What you regard, my lord, as excrescences I regard as fundamentals of our Holy Religion."

"Come, come, Mr. Lidderdale," the Bishop protested. "I do not think that you expect to convince me that a ceremony like the—er—Asperges is a fundamental of Christianity."

"I have taught my people that it is," said the Missioner. "In these days when Bishops are found who will explain away the Incarnation, the Atonement, the Resurrection of the Body, I hope you'll forgive a humble parish priest who will explain away nothing and who would rather resign, as I told you this morning, than surrender a single one of these excrescences."

"I do not admit your indictment, your almost wholesale indictment of the Anglican episcopate; but even were I to admit at lunch that some of my brethren have been in their anxiety to keep the Man in the Street from straying too far from the Church, have been as I was saying a little too ready to tolerate a certain latitude of belief, even as I said just now were that so, I do not think that you have any cause to suspect me of what I should repudiate as gross infidelity. It was precisely because the Bishop of London supposed that I should be more sympathetic with your ideals that he asked me to represent him in this perfectly informal—er—"

"Inquest," the Missioner supplied with a fierce smile.

The Bishop encouraged by the first sign of humour he had observed in the bigoted priest hastened to smile back.

"Well, let us call it an inquest, but not, I hope, I sincerely and devoutly hope, Mr. Lidderdale, not an inquest upon a dead body." Then hurriedly he went on. "I may smile with the lips, but believe me, my dear fellow labourer in the vineyard of Our Lord Jesus Christ, believe me that my heart is sore at the prospect of your resignation. And the Bishop of London, if I have to go back to him with such news, will be pained, bitterly grievously pained. He admires your work, Mr. Lidderdale, as much as I do, and I have no doubt that if it were not for the unhappy controversies that are tearing asunder our National Church, I say I do not doubt that he would give you a free hand. But how can he give you a free hand when his own hands are tied by the necessities of the situation? May I venture to observe that some of you working priests are too ready to criticize men like myself who from no desire of our own have been called by God to occupy a loftier seat in the eyes of the world than many men infinitely more worthy. But to return to the question immediately before us, let me, my dear Mr. Lidderdale, do let me make to you a personal appeal for moderation. If you will only consent to abandon one or two—I will not say excrescences since you object to the word—but if you will only abandon one or two purely ceremonial additions that cannot possibly be defended by any rubric in the Book of Common Prayer, if you will only consent to do this the Bishop of London will, I can guarantee, permit you a discretionary latitude that he would scarcely be prepared to allow to any other priest in his diocese. When I was called to be Bishop Suffragan of Devizes, Mr. Lidderdale, do you suppose that I did not give up something? Do you suppose that I was anxious to abandon some of the riches to which by my reading of the Ornaments Rubric we are entitled? But I felt that I could do something to help the position of my fellow priests struggling against the prejudice of ignorance and the prey of political moves. In twenty years from now, Mr. Lidderdale, you will be glad you took my advice. Ceremonies that to-day are the privilege of the few will then be the privilege of the many. Do not forget that by what I might almost describe as the exorbitance of your demands you have gained more freedom than any other priest in England. Be moderate. Do not resign. You will be inhibited in every diocese; you will have the millstone of an unpaid debt round your neck; you are a married man."

"That has nothing . . ." Lidderdale interrupted angrily.

"Pray let me finish. You are a married man, and if you should seek consolation, where several of your fellow priests have lately sought it, in the Church of Rome, you will have to seek it as a layman. I do not pretend to know your private affairs, and I should consider it impertinent if I tried to pry into them at such a moment. But I do know your worth as a priest, and I have no hesitation in begging you once more with a heart almost too full for words to pause, Mr. Lidderdale, to pause and reflect before you take the irreparable step that you are contemplating. I have already talked too much, and I see that your good wife is looking anxiously at my plate. No more cauliflower, thank you, Mrs. Lidderdale, no more of anything, thank you. Ah, there is a pudding on the way? Dear me, that sounds very tempting, I'm afraid."

The Bishop now turned his attention entirely to Mrs. Lidderdale at the other end of the table; the Missioner sat biting his nails; and Mark wondered what all this conversation was about.

While the Bishop was waiting for his cab, which, he explained to his hosts, was not so much a luxury as a necessity owing to his having to address at three o'clock precisely a committee of ladies who were meeting in Portman Square to discuss the dreadful condition of the London streets, he laid a fatherly arm on the Missioner's threadbare cassock.

"Take two or three days to decide, my dear Mr. Lidderdale. The Bishop of London, who is always consideration personified, insisted that you were to take two or three days to decide. Once more, for I hear my cab-wheels, once more let me beg you to yield on the following points. Let me just refer to my notes to be sure that I have not omitted anything of importance. Oh, yes, the following points: no Asperges, no unusual Good Friday services, except of course the Three Hours. *Is* not that enough?"

"The Three Hours I *would* give up. It's a modern invention of the Jesuits. The Adoration of the Cross goes back. . . ."

"Please, please, Mr. Lidderdale, my cab is at the door. We must not embark on controversy. No celebrations without communicants. No direct invocation of the Blessed Virgin Mary or the Saints. Oh, yes, and on this the Bishop is particularly firm: no juggling with the *Gloria in Excelsis*. Good-bye, Mr. Lidderdale, good-bye, Mrs. Lidderdale. Many thanks for your delicious luncheon. Good-bye, young man. I had a little boy like you once, but he is grown up now, and I am glad to say a soldier."

The Bishop waved his umbrella, which looked much like a pastoral staff, and lightly mounted the step of his cab.

"Was the Bishop cross with Father?" Mark inquired afterward; he could find no other theory that would explain so much talking to his father, so little talking by his father.

"Dearest, I'd rather you didn't ask questions about the Bishop," his mother replied, and discerning that she was on the verge of one of those headaches that while they lasted obliterated the world for Mark, he was silent. Later in the afternoon Mr. Astill, the Vicar, came round to see the Missioner and they had a long talk together, the murmur of which now softer now louder was audible in Mark's nursery where he was playing by himself with the cork-bottomed grenadiers. His instinct was to play a quiet game, partly on account of his mother's onrushing headache, which had already driven her to her room, partly because he knew that when his father was closeted like this it was essential not to make the least noise. So he tiptoed about the room and disposed the cork-bottomed grenadiers as sentinels before the coal-scuttle, the washstand, and other similar strongholds. Then he took his gun, the barrel of which, broken before it was given to him, had been replaced by a thin bamboo curtain-rod, and his finger on the trigger (a wooden match) he waited for an invader. After ten minutes of statuesque silence Mark began to think that this was a dull game, and he wished that his mother had not gone to her room with a headache, because if she had been with him she could have undoubtedly invented, so clever was she, a method of invading the nursery without either the attackers or the defenders making any noise about it. In her gentle voice she would have whispered of the hordes that were stealthily creeping up the mountain side until Mark and his vigilant cork-bottomed grenadiers would have been in a state of suppressed exultation ready to die in defence of the nursery, to die stolidly and silently at their posts with nobody else in the house aware of their heroism.

"Rorke's Drift," said Mark to himself, trying to fancy that he heard in the distance a Zulu *impi* and whispering to his cork-bottomed grenadiers to keep a good look-out. One of them who was guarding the play-cupboard fell over on his face, and in the stillness the noise sounded so loud that Mark did not dare cross the room to put him up again, but had to assume that he had been shot where he stood. It was no use. The game was a failure; Mark decided to look at *Battles of the British Army*. He knew the pictures in every detail, and he could have recited without a mistake the few lines of explanation at the bottom of each page; but the book still possessed a capacity to thrill, and he turned over the pages not pausing over Crecy or Poitiers or Blenheim or Dettingen; but enjoying the storming of Badajoz with soldiers impaled on *chevaux de frise* and lingering over the rich uniforms and plumed helmets in the picture of Joseph Bonaparte's flight at Vittoria. There was too a grim picture of the Guards at Inkerman fighting in their greatcoats with clubbed muskets against thousands of sinister dark green Russians looming in the snow; and there was an attractive picture of a regiment crossing the Alma and eating the grapes as they clambered up the banks where they grew. Finally there was the Redan, a mysterious wall, apparently of wickerwork, with bombs bursting and broken scaling-ladders and dead English soldiers in the open space before it.

Mark did not feel that he wanted to look through the book again, and he put it away, wondering how long that murmur of voices rising and falling from his father's study below would continue. He wondered whether Dora would be annoyed if he went down to the kitchen. She had been discouraging on the last two or three occasions he had visited her, but that had been because he could not keep his fingers out of the currants. Fancy having a large red jar crammed full of currants on the floor of the larder and never wanting to eat one! The thought of those currants produced in Mark's mouth a craving for something sweet, and as quietly as possible he stole off downstairs to quench this craving somehow or other if it were only with a lump of sugar. But when he reached the kitchen he found Dora in earnest talk with two women in bonnets, who were nodding away and clicking their tongues with pleasure.

"Now whatever do you want down here?" Dora demanded ungraciously.

"I wanted," Mark paused. He longed to say "some currants," but he had failed before, and he substituted "a lump of sugar." The two women in bonnets looked at him and nodded their heads and clicked their tongues.

"Did you ever?" said one.

"Fancy! A lump of sugar! Goodness gracious!"

"What a sweet tooth!" commented the first.

The sugar happened to be close to Dora's hand on the kitchen-table, and she gave him two lumps with the command to "sugar off back upstairs as fast as you like." The craving for sweetness was allayed; but when Mark had crunched up the two lumps on the dark kitchen-stairs, he was as lonely as he had been before he left the nursery. He wished now that he had not eaten up the sugar so fast, that he had taken it back with him to the nursery and eked it out to wile away this endless afternoon. The prospect of going back to the nursery depressed him; and he turned aside to linger in the dining-room whence there was a view of Lima Street, down which a dirty frayed man was wheeling a barrow and shouting for housewives to bring out their old rags and bottles and bones. Mark felt the thrill of trade and traffick, and he longed to be big enough to open the window and call out that he had several rags and bottles and bones to sell; but instead he had to be content with watching two self-important little girls chaffer on behalf of their mothers, and go off counting their pennies. The voice of the rag-and-bone man, grew fainter and fainter round corners out of sight; Lima Street became as empty and uninteresting as the nursery. Mark wished that a knife-grinder would come along and that he would stop under the dining-room window so that he could watch the sparks flying from the grindstone. Or that a gipsy would sit down on the steps and begin to mend the seat of a chair. Whenever he had seen those gipsy chair-menders at work, he had been out of doors and afraid to linger watching them in case he should be stolen and his face stained with walnut juice and all his clothes taken away from him. But from the security of the dining-room of the Mission House he should enjoy watching them. However, no gipsy came, nor anybody else except women with men's caps pinned to their skimpy hair and little girls with wrinkled stockings carrying jugs to and from the public houses that stood at every corner.

Mark turned away from the window and tried to think of some game that could be played in the dining-room. But it was not a room that fostered the imagination. The carpet was so much worn that the pattern was now scarcely visible and, looked one at it never so long and intently, it was impossible to give it an inner life of its own that gradually revealed itself to the fanciful observer. The sideboard had nothing on it except a dirty cloth, a bottle of harvest burgundy, and half a dozen forks and spoons. The cupboards on either side contained nothing edible except salt, pepper, mustard, vinegar, and oil. There was a plain deal table without a drawer and without any interesting screws and levers to make it grow smaller or larger at the will of the creature who sat beneath it. The eight chairs were just chairs; the wallpaper was like the inside of the bath, but alas, without the water; of the two pictures, the one over the mantelpiece was a steel-engraving of the Good Shepherd and the one over the sideboard was an oleograph of the Sacred Heart. Mark knew every fly speck on their glasses, every discoloration of their margins. While he was sighing over the sterility of the room, he heard the door of his father's study open, and his father and Mr. Astill do down the passage, both of them still talking unceasingly. Presently the front door slammed, and Mark watched them walk away in the direction of the new church. Here was an opportunity to go into his father's study and look at some of the books. Mark never went in when his father was there, because once his mother had said to his father:

"Why don't you have Mark to sit with you?"

And his father had answered doubtfully:

"Mark? Oh yes, he can come. But I hope he'll keep quiet, because I shall be rather busy."

Mark had felt a kind of hostility in his father's manner which had chilled him; and after that, whenever his mother used to suggest his going to sit quietly in the study, he had always made some excuse not to go. But if his father was out he used to like going in, because there were always books lying about that were interesting to look at, and the smell of tobacco smoke and leather bindings was grateful to the senses. The room smelt even more strongly than usual of tobacco smoke this afternoon, and Mark inhaled the air with relish while he debated which of the many volumes he should pore over. There was a large Bible with pictures of palm-trees and camels and long-bearded patriarchs surrounded by flocks of sheep, pictures of women with handkerchiefs over their mouths drawing water from wells, of Daniel in the den of lions and of Shadrach, Meshach and Abednego in the fiery furnace. The frontispiece was a coloured picture of Adam and Eve in the Garden of Eden surrounded by amiable lions, benevolent tigers, ingratiating bears and leopards and wolves. But more interesting than the pictures were some pages at the beginning on which, in oval spaces framed in leaves and flowers, were written the names of his grandfather and grandmother, of his father and of his father's brother and sister, with the dates on which they were born and baptized and confirmed. What a long time ago his father was born! 1840. He asked his mother once about this Uncle Henry and Aunt Helen; but she told him they had quarrelled with his father, and she had said nothing more about them. Mark had been struck by the notion that grown-up people could quarrel: he had supposed quarrelling to be peculiar to childhood. Further, he noticed that Henry Lidderdale had married somebody called Ada Prewbody who had died the same year; but nothing was said in the oval that enshrined his father about his having married anyone. He asked his mother the reason of this, and she explained to him that the Bible had belonged to his grandfather who had kept the entries up to date until he died, when the Bible came to his eldest son who was Mark's father.

"Does it worry you, darling, that I'm not entered?" his mother had asked with a smile.

"Well, it does rather," Mark had replied, and then to his great delight she took a pen and wrote that James Lidderdale had married Grace Alethea Trehawke on June 28th, 1880, at St. Tugdual's Church, Nancepean, Cornwall, and to his even greater delight that on April 25th, 1881, Mark Lidderdale had been born at 142 Lima Street, Notting Dale, London, W., and baptized on May 21st, 1881, at St. Wilfred's Mission Church, Lima Street.

"Happy now?" she had asked.

Mark had nodded, and from that moment, if he went into his father's study, he always opened the Family Bible and examined solemnly his own short history wreathed in forget-me-nots and lilies of the valley.

This afternoon, after looking as usual at the entry of his birth and baptism written in his mother's pretty pointed handwriting, he searched for Dante's *Inferno* illustrated by Gustave Doré, a large copy of which had recently been presented to his father by the Servers and Choir of St. Wilfred's. The last time he had been looking at this volume he had caught a glimpse of a lot of people buried in the ground with only their heads sticking out, a most attractive picture which he had only just discovered when he had heard his father's footsteps and had closed the book in a hurry.

Mark tried to find this picture, but the volume was large and the pictures on the way of such fascination that it was long before he found it. When he did, he thought it even more satisfying at a second glance, although he wished he knew what they were all doing buried in the ground like that. Mark was not satisfied with horrors even after he had gone right through the Dante; in fact, his appetite was only whetted, and he turned with relish to a large folio of Chinese tortures, in the coloured prints of which a feature was made of blood profusely outpoured and richly tinted. One picture of a Chinaman apparently impervious to the pain of being slowly sawn in two held him entranced for five minutes. It was growing dusk by now, and as it needed the light of the window to bring out the full quality of the blood, Mark carried over the big volume, propped it up in a chair behind the curtains, and knelt down to gloat over these remote oriental barbarities without pausing to remember that his father might come back at any moment, and that although he had never actually been forbidden to look at this book, the thrill of something unlawful always brooded over it. Suddenly the door of the study opened and Mark sat transfixed by terror as completely as the Chinaman on the page before him was transfixed by a sharpened bamboo; then he heard his mother's voice, and before he could discover himself a conversation between her and his father had begun of which Mark understood enough to know that both of them would be equally angry if they knew that he was listening. Mark was not old enough to escape tactfully from such a difficult situation, and the only thing he could think of doing was to stay absolutely still in the hope that they would presently go out of the room and never know that he had been behind the curtain while they were talking.

"I didn't mean you to dress yourself and come downstairs," his father was saying ungraciously.

"My dear, I should have come down to tea in any case, and I was anxious to hear the result of your conversation with Mr. Astill."

"You can guess, can't you?" said the husband.

Mark had heard his father speak angrily before; but he had never heard his voice sound like a growl. He shrank farther back in affright behind the curtains.

"You're going to give way to the Bishop?" the wife asked gently.

"Ah, you've guessed, have you? You've guessed by my manner? You've realized, I hope, what this resolution has cost me and what it's going to cost me in the future. I'm a coward. I'm a traitor. *Before the cock crow twice, thou shalt deny me thrice.* A coward and a traitor."

"Neither, James—at any rate to me."

"To you," the husband scoffed. "I should hope not to you, considering that it is on your account I am surrendering. Do you suppose that if I were free, as to serve God I ought to be free, do you suppose then that I should give up my principles like this? Never! But because I'm a married priest, because I've a wife and family to support, my hands are tied. Oh, yes, Astill was very tactful. He kept insisting on my duty to the parish; but did he once fail to rub in the position in which I should find myself if I did resign? No bishop would license me; I should be inhibited in every diocese—in other words I should starve. The beliefs I hold most dear, the beliefs I've fought for all these years surrendered for bread and butter! *Woman, what have I to do with thee?* Our Blessed Lord could speak thus even to His Blessed Mother. But I! *He that loveth son or daughter more than me is not worthy of me. And he that taketh not his cross, and followeth after me, is not worthy of me.*"

The Missioner threw himself into his worn armchair and stared into the unlighted grate. His wife came behind him and laid a white hand upon his forehead; but her touch seemed to madden him, and he sprang away from her.

"No more of that," he cried. "If I was weak when I married you I will never be weak again. You have your child. Let that be enough for your tenderness. I want none of it myself. Do you hear? I wish to devote myself henceforth to my parish. My parish! The parish of a coward and a traitor."

Mark heard his mother now speaking in a voice that was strange to him, in a voice that did not belong to her, but that seemed to come from far away, as if she were lost in a snowstorm and calling for help.

"James, if you feel this hatred for me and for poor little Mark, it is better that we leave you. We can go to my father in Cornwall, and you will not feel hampered by the responsibility of having to provide for us. After what you have said to me, after the way you have looked at me, I could never live with you as your wife again."

"That sounds a splendid scheme," said the Missioner bitterly. "But do you think I have so little logic that I should be able to escape from my responsibilities by planting them on the shoulders of another? No, I sinned when I married you. I did not believe and I do not believe that a priest ought to marry; but having done so I must face the situation and do my duty to my family, so that I may also do my duty to God."

"Do you think that God will accept duty offered in that spirit? If he does, he is not the God in Whom I believe. He is a devil that can be propitiated with burnt offerings," exclaimed the woman passionately.

"Do not blaspheme," the priest commanded.

"Blaspheme!" she echoed. "It is you, James, who have blasphemed nature this afternoon. You have committed the sin against the Holy Ghost, and may you be forgiven by your God. I can never forgive you."

"You're becoming hysterical."

"How dare you say that? How dare you? I have loved you, James, with all the love that I could give you. I have suffered in silence when I saw how you regarded family life, how unkind you were to Mark, how utterly wrapped up in the outward forms of religion. You are a Pharisee, James, you should have lived before Our Lord came down to earth. But I will not suffer any longer. You need not worry about the evasion of your responsibilities. You cannot make me stay with you. You will not dare keep Mark. Save your own soul in your own way; but Mark's soul is as much mine as yours to save."

During this storm of words Mark had been thinking how wicked it was of his father to upset his mother like that when she had a headache. He had thought also how terrible it was that he should apparently be the cause of this frightening quarrel. Often in Lima Street he had heard tales of wives who were beaten by their husbands and now he supposed that his own mother was going to be beaten. Suddenly he heard her crying. This was too much for him; he sprang from his hiding place and ran to put his arms round her in protection.

"Mother, mother, don't cry. You are bad, you are bad," he told his father. "You are wicked and bad to make her cry."

"Have you been in the room all this time?" his father asked.

Mark did not even bother to nod his head, so intent was he upon consoling his mother. She checked her emotion when her son put his arms round her neck, and whispered to him not to speak. It was almost dark in the study now, and what little light was still filtering in at the window from the grey nightfall was obscured by the figure of the Missioner gazing out at the lantern spire of his new church. There was a tap at the door, and Mrs. Lidderdale snatched up the volume that Mark had let fall upon the floor when he emerged from the curtains, so that when Dora came in to light the gas and say that tea was ready, nothing of the stress of the last few minutes was visible. The Missioner was looking out of the window at his new church; his wife and son were contemplating the picture of an impervious Chinaman suspended in a cage where he could neither stand nor sit nor lie.

CHAPTER V
PALM SUNDAY

Mark's dream from which he woke to wonder if the end of the world was at hand had been a shadow cast by coming events. So far as the world of Lima Street was concerned, it was the end of it. The night after that scene in his father's study, which made a deeper impression on him than anything before that date in his short life, his mother came to sleep in the nursery with him, to keep him company so that he should not be frightened any more, she offered as the explanation of her arrival. But Mark, although of course he never said so to her, was sure that she had come to him to be protected against his father.

Mark did not overhear any more discussions between his parents, and he was taken by surprise when one day a week after his mother had come to sleep in his room, she asked him how he should like to go and live in the country. To Mark the country was as remote as Paradise, and at first he was inclined to regard the question as rhetorical to which a conventional reply was expected. If anybody had asked him how he should like to go to Heaven, he would have answered that he should like to go to Heaven very much. Cows, sheep, saints, angels, they were all equally unreal outside a picture book.

"I would like to go to the country very much," he said. "And I would like to go to the Zoological Gardens very much. Perhaps we can go there soon, can we, mother?"

"We can't go there if we're in the country."

Mark stared at her.

"But really go in the country?"

"Yes, darling, really go."

"Oh, mother," and immediately he checked his enthusiasm with a sceptical "when?"

"Next Monday."

"And shall I see cows?"

"Yes."

"And donkeys? And horses? And pigs? And goats?"

To every question she nodded.

"Oh, mother, I will be good," he promised of his own accord. "And can I take my grenadiers?"

"You can take everything you have, darling."

"Will Dora come?" He did not inquire about his father.

"No."

"Just you and me?"

She nodded, and Mark flung his arms round her neck to press upon her lips a long fragrant kiss, such a kiss as only a child can give.

On Sunday morning, the last Sunday morning he would worship in the little tin mission church, the last Sunday morning indeed that any of the children of Lima Street would worship there, Mark sat close beside his mother at the children's Mass. His father looking as he always looked, took off his chasuble, and in his alb walked up and down the aisle preaching his short sermon interspersed with questions.

"What is this Sunday called?"

There was a silence until a well-informed little girl breathed through her nose that it was called Passion Sunday.

"Quite right. And next Sunday?"

"Palm Sunday," all the children shouted with alacrity, for they looked forward to it almost more than to any Sunday in the year.

"Next Sunday, dear children, I had hoped to give you the blessed palms in our beautiful new church, but God has willed otherwise, and another priest will come in my place. I hope you will listen to him as attentively as you have listened to me, and I hope you will try to encourage him by your behaviour both in and out of the church, by your punctuality and regular attendance at Mass, and by your example to other children who have not had the advantage of learning all about our glorious Catholic faith. I shall think about you all when I am gone and I shall never cease to ask our Blessed Lord Jesus Christ to guard you and keep you safe for Him. And I want you to pray to Our Blessed Lady and to our great patron Saint Wilfred that they will intercede for you and me. Will you all do this?"

There was a unanimous and sibilant "Yes, father," from the assembled children, and then one little girl after being prodded by her companions on either side of her spoke up and asked the Missioner why he was going.

"Ah, that is a very difficult question to answer; but I will try to explain it to you by a parable. What is a parable?"

"Something that isn't true," sang out a too ready boy from the back of the church.

"No, no, Arthur Williams. Surely some other boy or girl can correct Arthur Williams? How many times have we had that word explained to us! A parable is a story with a hidden meaning. Now please, every boy and girl, repeat that answer after me. A parable is a story with a hidden meaning."

And all the children baa'd in unison:

"A parable is a story with a hidden meaning."

"That's better," said the Missioner. "And now I will tell you my parable. Once upon a time there was a little boy or a little girl, it doesn't matter which, whose father put him in charge of a baby. He was told not to let anybody take it away from him and he was told to look after it and wheel it about in the perambulator, which was a very old one, and not only very old but very small for the baby, who was growing bigger and bigger every day. Well, a lot of kind people clubbed together and bought a new perambulator, bigger than the other and more comfortable. They told him to take this perambulator home to his father and show him what a beautiful present they had made. Well, the boy wheeled it home and his father was very pleased with it. But when the boy took the baby out again, the nursemaid told him that the

169

baby had too many clothes on and said that he must either take some of the clothes off or else she must take away the new perambulator. Well, the little boy had promised his father, who had gone far away on a journey, that nobody should touch the baby, and so he said he would not take off any of the clothes. And when the nurse took away the perambulator the little boy wrote to his father to ask what he should do and his father wrote to him that he would put one of his brothers in charge who would know how to do what the nurse wanted." The Missioner paused to see the effect of his story. "Now, children, let us see if you can understand my parable. Who is the little boy?"

A concordance of opinion cried "God."

"No. Now think. The father surely was God. And now once more, who was the little boy?"

Several children said "Jesus Christ," and one little boy who evidently thought that any connexion between babies and religion must have something to do with the Holy Innocents confidently called out "Herod."

"No, no, no," said the Missioner. "Surely the little boy is myself. And what is the baby?"

Without hesitation the boys and girls all together shouted "Jesus Christ."

"No, no. The baby is our Holy Catholic Faith. For which we are ready if necessary to—?"

There was no answer.

"To do what?"

"To be baptized," one boy hazarded.

"To die," said the Missioner reproachfully.

"To die," the class complacently echoed.

"And now what is the perambulator?"

This was a puzzle, but at last somebody tried:

"The Body and Blood of Our Lord, Jesus Christ."

"No, no. The perambulator is our Mission here in Lima Street. The old perambulator is the Church where we are sitting at Mass and the new perambulator is—"

"The new church," two children answered simultaneously.

"Quite right. And now, who is the nursemaid? The nursemaid is the Bishop of London. You remember that last Sunday we talked about bishops. What is a bishop?"

"A high-priest."

"Well, that is not a bad answer, but don't you remember we said that bishop meant 'overseer,' and you all know what an overseer is. Any of your fathers who go out to work will tell you that. So the Bishop like the nursemaid in my parable thought he knew better what clothes the baby ought to wear in the new perambulator, that is to say what services we ought to have in the new St. Wilfred's. And as God is far away and we can only speak to Him by prayer, I have asked Him what I ought to do, and He has told me that I ought to go away and that He will put a brother in charge of the baby in the new perambulator. Who then is the brother?"

"Jesus Christ," said the class, convinced that this time it must be He.

"No, no. The brother is the priest who will come to take charge of the new St. Wilfred's. He will be called the Vicar, and St. Wilfred's, instead of being called the Lima Street Mission, will become a parish. And now, dear children, there is no time to say any more words to you. My heart is sore at leaving you, but in my sorrow I shall be comforted if I can have the certainty that you are growing up to be good and loyal Catholics, loving Our Blessed Lord and His dear Mother, honouring the Holy Saints and Martyrs, hating the Evil One and all his Spirits and obeying God with whose voice the Church speaks. Now, for the last time children, let me hear you sing *We are but little children weak*."

They all sang more loudly than usual to express a vague and troubled sympathy:

There's not a child so small and weak But has his little cross to take, His little work of love and praise That he may do for Jesus' sake.

And they bleated a most canorous *Amen*.

Mark noticed that his mother clutched his hand tightly while his father was speaking, and when once he looked up at her to show how loudly he too was singing, he saw that her eyes were full of tears.

The next morning was Monday.

"Good-bye, Mark, be a good boy and obedient to your mother," said his father on the platform at Paddington.

"Who is that man?" Mark whispered when the guard locked them in.

His mother explained, and Mark looked at him with as much awe as if he were St. Peter with the keys of Heaven at his girdle. He waved his handkerchief from the window while the train rushed on through tunnels and between gloomy banks until suddenly the world became green, and there was the sun in a great blue and white sky. Mark looked at his mother and saw that again there were tears in her eyes, but that they sparkled like diamonds.

CHAPTER VI
NANCEPEAN

The Rhos or, as it is popularly written and pronounced, the Rose is a tract of land in the south-west of the Duchy of Cornwall, ten miles long and six at its greatest breadth, which on account of its remoteness from the railway, its unusual geological formation, and its peninsular shape possesses both in the character of its inhabitants and in the peculiar aspects of the natural scene all the limitations and advantages of an island. The main road running south to Rose Head from Rosemarket cuts the peninsula into two unequal portions, the eastern and by far the larger of which consists of a flat tableland two or three hundred feet above the sea covered with a bushy heath, which flourishes in the magnesian soil and which when in bloom is of such a clear rosy pink, with nothing to break the level monochrome except scattered drifts of cotton grass, pools of silver water and a few stunted pines, that ignorant observers have often supposed that the colour gave its name to the whole peninsula. The ancient town of Rosemarket, which serves as the only channel of communication with the rest of Cornwall, lies in the extreme north-west of the peninsula between a wide creek of the Roseford river and the Rose Pool, an irregular heart-shaped water about four miles in circumference which on the west is only separated from the Atlantic by a bar of fine shingle fifty yards across.

The parish of Nancepean, of which Mark's grandfather the Reverend Charles Elphinstone Trehawke had been vicar for nearly thirty years, ran southward from the Rose Pool between the main road and the sea for three miles. It was a country of green valleys unfolding to the ocean, and of small farms fertile enough when they were sheltered from the prevailing wind; but on the southern confines of the parish the soil became shallow and stony, the arable fields degenerated into a rough open pasturage full of gorse and foxgloves and gradually widening patches of heather, until finally the level monochrome of the Rhos absorbed the last vestiges of cultivation, and the parish came to an end.

The actual village of Nancepean, set in a hollow about a quarter of a mile from the sea, consisted of a smithy, a grocer's shop, a parish hall and some two dozen white cottages with steep thatched roofs lying in their own gardens on either side of the unfrequented road that branched from the main road to follow the line of the coast. Where this road made the turn south a track strewn with grey shingle ran down between the cliffs, at this point not much more than grassy hummocks, to Nancepean beach which extended northward in a wide curve until it disappeared two miles away in the wooded heights above the Rose Pool. The metalled coast road continued past the Hanover Inn, an isolated house standing at the head of a small cove, to make the long ascent of Pendhu Cliff three hundred and fifty feet high, from the brow of which it descended between banks of fern past St. Tugdual's Church to the sands of Church Cove, whence it emerged to climb in a steep zigzag the next headland, beyond which it turned inland again to Lanyon and rejoined the main road to Rose Head. The church itself had no architectural distinction; but the solitary position, the churchyard walls sometimes washed by high spring tides, the squat tower built into the rounded grassy cliff that protected it from the direct attack of the sea, and its impressive antiquity combined to give it more than the finest architecture could give. Nowhere in the surrounding landscape was there a sign of human habitation, neither on the road down from Pendhu nor on the road up toward Lanyon, not on the bare towans sweeping from the beach to the sky in undulating waves of sandy grass, nor in the valley between the towans and Pendhu, a wide green valley watered by a small stream that flowed into the cove, where it formed a miniature estuary, the configuration of whose effluence changed with every tide.

The Vicarage was not so far from the church as the church was from the village, but it was some way from both. It was reached from Nancepean by a road or rather by a gated cart-track down one of the numerous valleys of the parish, and it was reached from the church by another cart-track along the valley between Pendhu and the towans. Probably it was an ancient farmhouse, and it must have been a desolate and austere place until, as at the date when Mark first came there, it was graced by the perfume and gold of acacias, by wistaria and jasmine and honeysuckle, by the ivory goblets of magnolias, by crimson fuchsias, and where formerly its grey walls grew mossy north and east by pink and white camelias and the waxen bells of lapagerias. The garden was a wilderness of scarlet rhododendrons from the thickets of which innumerable blackbirds and thrushes preyed upon the peas. The lawns were like meadows; the lily ponds were marbled with weeds; the stables were hardly to be reached on account of the tangle of roses and briers that filled the abandoned yard. The front drive was bordered by evergreen oaks, underneath the shade of which blue hydrangeas flowered sparsely with a profusion of pale-green foliage and lanky stems.

Mark when he looked out of his window on the morning after his arrival thought that he was in fairyland. He looked at the rhododendrons; he looked at the raindrops of the night sparkling in the morning sun; he looked at the birds, and the blue sky, and across the valley to a hillside yellow with gorse. He hardly knew how to restrain himself from waking his mother with news of the wonderful sights and sounds of this first vision of the country; but when he saw a clump of daffodils nodding in the grass below, it was no longer possible to be considerate. Creeping to his mother's door, he gently opened it and listened. He meant only to whisper "Mother," but in his excitement he shouted, and she suddenly roused from sleep by his voice sat up in alarm.

"Mother, there are seven daffodils growing wild under my window."

"My darling, you frightened me so. I thought you'd hurt yourself."

"I don't know how my voice came big like that," said Mark apologetically. "I only meant it to be a whisper. But you weren't dreadfully frightened? Or were you?"

His mother smiled.

"No, not dreadfully frightened."

"Well, do you think I might dress myself and go in the garden?"

"You mustn't disturb grandfather."

"Oh, mother, of course not."

"All right, darling. But it's only six o'clock. Very early. And you must remember that grandfather may be tired. He had to wait an hour for us at Rosemarket last night."

"He's very nice, isn't he?"

Mark did not ask this tentatively; he really did think that his grandfather was very nice, although he had been puzzled and not a little frightened by his bushy black eyebrows slanting up to a profusion of white hair. Mark had never seen such eyebrows, and he wondered whatever grandfather's moustache would be like if it were allowed to grow.

"He's a dear," said Mrs. Lidderdale fervidly. "And now, sweetheart, if you really intend to dress yourself run along, because Mother wants to sleep a little longer if she can."

The only difficulty Mark had was with his flannel front, because one of the tapes vanished like a worm into its hole, and nothing in his armoury was at once long enough and pointed enough to hook it out again. Finally he decided that at such an early hour of the morning it would not matter if he went out exposing his vest, and soon he was wandering in that enchanted shrubbery of rhododendrons, alternating between imagining it to be the cave of Aladdin or the beach where Sinbad found all the pebbles to be precious stones. He wandered down hill through the thicket, listening with a sense of satisfaction to the increasing squelchiness of the peaty soil and feeling when the blackbirds fled at his approach with shrill quack and flapping wings much more like a hunter than he ever felt in the nursery at Lima Street. He resolved to bring his gun with him next time. This was just the place to find a hippopotamus, or even a crocodile. Mark had reached the bottom of the slope and discovered a dark sluggish stream full of decayed vegetable matter which was slowly oozing on its course. Or even a crocodile, he thought again; and he looked carefully at a half-submerged log. Or even a crocodile . . . yes, but people had often thought before that logs were not crocodiles and had not discovered their mistake until they were half way down the crocodile's throat. It had been amusing to fancy the existence of crocodiles when he was still close to the Vicarage, but suppose after all that there really were crocodiles living down here? Feeling a little ashamed of his cowardice, but glossing it over with an assumption of filial piety, Mark turned to go back through the rhododendrons so as not to be late for breakfast. He would find out if any crocodiles had been seen about here lately, and if they had not, he would bring out his gun and . . . suddenly Mark was turned inside out by terror, for not twenty yards away there was without any possibility of self-deception a wild beast something between an ant-eater and a laughing hyena that with nose to the ground was evidently pursuing him, and what was worse was between him and home. There flashed through Mark's mind the memories of what other hunters had done in such situations, what ruses they had adopted if unarmed, what method of defence if armed; but in the very instant of the panoramic flash Mark did what countless uncelebrated hunters must have done, he ran in the opposition direction from his enemy. In this case it meant jumping over the stream, crocodile or not, and tearing his away through snowberries and brambles until he emerged on the moors at the bottom of the valley.

It was not until he had put half a dozen small streams between himself and the unknown beast that Mark paused to look round. Behind him the valley was lost in a green curve; before him another curve shut out the ultimate view. On his left the slope of the valley rose to the sky in tiers of blazing yellow gorse; to his right he could see the thickets through which he had emerged upon this verdant solitude. But beyond the thickets there was no sign of the Vicarage. There was not a living thing in sight; there was nothing except the song of larks high up and imperceptible against the steady morning sun that shed a benign warmth upon the world, and particularly upon the back of Mark's neck when he decided that his safest course was to walk in the direction of the valley's gradual widening and to put as many more streams as he could between him and the beast. Having once wetted himself to the knees, he began to take a pleasure in splashing through the vivid wet greenery. He wondered what he should behold at the next curve of the valley; without knowing it he began to walk more slowly, for the beauty of the day was drowsing his fears; the spell of earth was upon him. He walked more slowly, because he was passing through a bed of forget-me-nots, and he could not bear to blind one of those myriad blue eyes. He chose most carefully the destination of each step, and walking thus he did not notice that the valley would curve no more, but was opening at last. He looked up in a sudden consciousness of added space, and there serene as the sky above was spread the sea. Yesterday from the train Mark had had what was actually his first view of the sea; but the rain had taken all the colour out of it, and he had been thrilled rather by the word than by the fact. Now the word was nothing, the fact was everything. There it was within reach of him, blue as the pictures always made it. The streams of the valley had gathered into one, and Mark caring no more what happened to the forget-me-nots ran along the bank. This morning when the stream reached the shore it broke into twenty limpid rivulets, each one of which ploughed a separate silver furrow across the glistening sand until all were merged in ocean, mighty father of streams and men. Mark ran with the rivulets until he stood by the waves' edge. All was here of which he had read, shells and seaweed, rocks and cliffs and sand; he felt like Robinson Crusoe when he looked round him and saw nothing to break the solitude. Every point of the compass invited exploration and promised adventure. That white road running northward and rising with the cliffs, whither did it lead, what view was outspread where it dipped over the brow of the high table-land and disappeared into the naked sky beyond? The billowy towans sweeping up from the beach appeared to him like an illimitable prairie on which buffaloes and bison might roam. Whither led the sandy track, the summit of whose long diagonal was lost in the brightness of the morning sky? And surely that huddled grey building against an isolated green cliff must be grandfather's church of which his mother had often told him. Mark walked round the stone walls that held up the little churchyard and, entering by a gate on the farther side, he looked at the headstones and admired the feathery tamarisks that waved over the tombs. He was reading an inscription more legible than most on a headstone of highly polished granite, when he heard a voice behind him say:

"You mind what you're doing with that grave. That's my granfa's grave, that is, and if you touch it, I'll knock 'ee down."

Mark looked round and beheld a boy of about his own age and size in a pair of worn corduroy knickerbockers and a guernsey, who was regarding him from fierce blue eyes under a shock of curly yellow hair.

"I'm not touching it," Mark explained. Then something warned him that he must assert himself, if he wished to hold his own with this boy, and he added:

"But if I want to touch it, I will."

"Will 'ee? I say you won't do no such a thing then."

Mark seized the top of the headstone as firmly as his small hands would allow him and invited the boy to look what he was doing.

"Lev go," the boy commanded.

"I won't," said Mark.

"I'll make 'ee lev go."

"All right, make me."

The boy punched Mark's shoulder, and Mark punched blindly back, hitting his antagonist such a little way above the belt as to lay himself under the imputation of a foul blow. The boy responded by smacking Mark's face with his open palm; a moment later they were locked in a close struggle, heaving and panting and pushing until both of them tripped on the low railing of a grave and rolled over into a carefully tended bed of primroses, whence they were suddenly jerked to their feet, separated, and held at arm's length by an old man with a grey beard and a small round hole in the left temple.

"I'll learn you to scat up my tombs," said the old man shaking them violently. "'Tisn't the first time I've spoken to you, Cass Dale, and who's this? Who's this boy?"

"Oh, my gosh, look behind 'ee, Mr. Timbury. The bullocks is coming into the churchyard."

Mr. Timbury loosed his hold on the two boys as he turned, and Cass Dale catching hold of Mark's hand shouted:

"Come on, run, or he'll have us again."

They were too quick for the old man's wooden leg, and scrambling over the wall by the south porch of the church they were soon out of danger on the beach below.

"My gosh, I never heard him coming. If I hadn't have thought to sing out about the bullocks coming, he'd have laid that stick round us sure enough. He don't care where he hits anybody, old man Timbury don't. I belong to hear him tap-tapping along with his old wooden stump, but darn 'ee I never heard 'un coming this time."

The old man was leaning over the churchyard wall, shaking his stick and abusing them with violent words.

"That's fine language for a sexton," commented Cass Dale. "I'd be ashamed to swear like that, I would. You wouldn't hear my father swear like that. My father's a local preacher."

"So's mine," said Mark.

"Is he? Where to?"

"London."

"A minister, is he?"

"No, he's a priest."

"Does he kiss the Pope's toe? My gosh, if the Pope asked me to kiss his toe, I'd soon tell him to kiss something else, I would."

"My father doesn't kiss the Pope's toe," said Mark.

"I reckon he does then," Cass replied. "Passon Trehawke don't though. Passon Trehawke's some fine old chap. My father said he'd lev me go church of a morning sometimes if I'd a mind. My father belongs to come himself to the Harvest Home, but my granfa never came to church at all so long as he was alive. 'Time enough when I'm dead for that' he used to say. He was a big man down to the Chapel, my granfa was. Mostly when he did preach the maids would start screeching, so I've heard tell. But he were too old for preaching when I knawed 'un."

"My grandfather is the priest here," said Mark.

"There isn't no priest to Nancepean. Only Passon Trehawke."

"My grandfather's name is Trehawke."

"Is it, by gosh? Well, why for do 'ee call him a priest? He isn't a priest."

"Yes, he is."

"I say he isn't then. A parson isn't a priest. When I'm grown up I'm going to be a minister. What are you going to be?"

Mark had for some time past intended to be a keeper at the Zoological Gardens, but after his adventure with the wild beast in the thicket and this encounter with the self-confident Cass Dale he decided that he would not be a keeper but a parson. He informed Cass of his intention.

"Well, if you're a parson and I'm a minister," said Cass, "I'll bet everyone comes to listen to me preaching and none of 'em don't go to hear you."

"I wouldn't care if they didn't," Mark affirmed.

"You wouldn't care if you had to preach to a parcel of empty chairs and benches?" exclaimed Cass.

"St. Francis preached to the trees," said Mark. "And St. Anthony preached to the fishes."

"They must have been a couple of loonies."

"They were saints," Mark insisted.

"Saints, were they? Well, my father doesn't think much of saints. My father says he reckons saints is the same as other people, only a bit worse if anything. Are you saved?"

"What from?" Mark asked.

173

"Why, from Hell of course. What else would you be saved from?"

"You might be saved from a wild beast," Mark pointed out. "I saw a wild beast this morning. A wild beast with a long nose and a sort of grey colour."

"That wasn't a wild beast. That was an old badger."

"Well, isn't a badger a wild beast?"

Cass Dale laughed scornfully.

"My gosh, if that isn't a good one! I suppose you'd say a fox was a wild beast?"

"No, I shouldn't," said Mark, repressing an inclination to cry, so much mortified was he by Cass Dale's contemptuous tone.

"All the same," Cass went on. "It don't do to play around with badgers. There was a chap over to Lanbaddern who was chased right across the Rose one evening by seven badgers. He was in a muck of sweat when he got home. But one old badger isn't nothing."

Mark had been counting on his adventure with the wild beast to justify his long absence should he be reproached by his mother on his return to the Vicarage. The way it had been disposed of by Cass Dale as an old badger made him wonder if after all it would be accepted as such a good excuse.

"I ought to be going home," he said. "But I don't think I remember the way."

"To Passon Trehawke's?"

Mark nodded.

"I'll show 'ee," Cass volunteered, and he led the way past the mouth of the stream to the track half way up the slope of the valley.

"Ever eat furze flowers?" asked Cass, offering Mark some that he had pulled off in passing. "Kind of nutty taste they've got, I reckon. I belong to eat them most days."

Mark acquired the habit and agreed with Cass that the blossoms were delicious.

"Only you don't want to go eating everything you see," Cass warned him. "I reckon you'd better always ask me before you eat anything. But furze flowers is all right. I've eaten thousands. Next Friday's Good Friday."

"I know," said Mark reverently.

"We belong to get limpets every Good Friday. Are you coming with me?"

"Won't I be in church?" Mark inquired with memories of Good Friday in Lima Street.

"Yes, I suppose they'll have some sort of a meeting down Church," said Cass. "But you can come afterward. I'll wait for 'ee in Dollar Cove. That's the next cove to Church Cove on the other side of the Castle Cliff, and there's some handsome cave there. Years ago my granfa knawed a chap who saw a mermaid combing out her hair in Dollar Cove. But there's no mermaids been seen lately round these parts. My father says he reckons since they scat up the apple orchards and give over drinking cider they won't see no more mermaids to Nancepean. Have you signed the pledge?"

"What's that?" Mark asked.

"My gosh, don't you know what the pledge is? Why, that's when you put a blue ribbon in your buttonhole and swear you won't drink nothing all your days."

"But you'd die," Mark objected. "People must drink."

"Water, yes, but there's no call for any one to drink anything only water. My father says he reckons more folk have gone to hell from drink than anything. You ought to hear him preach about drink. Why, when it gets known in the village that Sam Dale's going to preach on drink there isn't a seat down Chapel. Well, I tell 'ee he frightened me last time I sat under him. That's why old man Timbury has it in for me whenever he gets the chance."

Mark looked puzzled.

"Old man Timbury keeps the Hanover Inn. And he reckons my pa's preaching spoils his trade for a week. That's why he's sexton to the church. 'Tis the only way he can get even with the chapel folk. He used to be in the Navy, and he lost his leg and got that hole in his head in a war with the Rooshians. You'll hear him talking big about the Rooshians sometimes. My father says anybody listening to old Steve Timbury would think he'd fought with the Devil, instead of a lot of poor leary Rooshians."

Mark was so much impressed by the older boy's confident chatter that when he arrived back at the Vicarage and found his mother at breakfast he tried the effect of an imitation of it upon her.

"Darling boy, you mustn't excite yourself too much," she warned him. "Do try to eat a little more and talk a little less."

"But I can go out again with Cass Dale, can't I, mother, as soon as I've finished my breakfast? He said he'd wait for me and he's going to show me where we might find some silver dollars. He says they're five times as big as a shilling and he's going to show me where there's a fox's hole on the cliffs and he's . . ."

"But, Mark dear, don't forget," interrupted his mother who was feeling faintly jealous of this absorbing new friend, "don't forget that I can show you lots of the interesting things to see round here. I was a little girl here myself and used to play with Cass Dale's father when he was a little boy no bigger than Cass."

Just then grandfather came into the room and Mark was instantly dumb; he had never been encouraged to talk much at breakfast in Lima Street. He did, however, eye his grandfather from over the top of his cup, and he found him less alarming in the morning than he had supposed him to be last night. Parson Trehawke kept reaching across the table for the various things he wanted until his daughter jumped up and putting her arms round his neck said:

"Dearest father, why don't you ask Mark or me to pass you what you want?"

"So long alone. So long alone," murmured Parson Trehawke with an embarrassed smile and Mark observed with a thrill that when he smiled he looked exactly like his mother, and had Mark but known it exactly like himself.

"And it's so wonderful to be back here," went on Mrs. Lidderdale, "with everything looking just the same. As for Mark, he's so happy that—Mark, do tell grandfather how much you're enjoying yourself."

Mark gulped several times, and finally managed to mutter a confirmation of his mother's statement.

"And he's already made friends with Cass Dale."

"He's intelligent but like his father he thinks he knows more than he does," commented Parson Trehawke. "However, he'll make quite a good companion for this young gentleman."

As soon as breakfast was over Mark rushed out to join Cass Dale, who sitting crosslegged under an ilex-tree was peeling a pithy twig for a whistle.

CHAPTER VII
LIFE AT NANCEPEAN

For six years Mark lived with his mother and his grandfather at Nancepean, hearing nothing of his father except that he had gone out as a missionary to the diocese of some place in Africa he could never remember, so little interested was he in his father. His education was shared between his two guardians, or rather his academic education; the real education came either from what he read for himself in his grandfather's ancient library of from what he learnt of Cass Dale, who was much more than merely informative in the manner of a sixpenny encyclopædia. The Vicar, who made himself responsible for the Latin and later on for the Greek, began with Horace, his own favourite author, from the rapid translation aloud of whose Odes and Epodes one after another he derived great pleasure, though it is doubtful if his grandson would have learnt much Latin if Mrs. Lidderdale had not supplemented Horace with the Primer and Henry's Exercises. However, if Mark did not acquire a vocabulary, he greatly enjoyed listening to his grandfather's melodious voice chanting forth that sonorous topography of Horace, while the green windows of the study winked every other minute from the flight past of birds in the garden. His grandfather would stop and ask what bird it was, because he loved birds even better than he loved Horace. And if Mark was tired of Latin he used to say that he wasn't sure, but that he thought it was a lesser-spotted woodpecker or a shrike or any one of the birds that experience taught him would always distract his grandfather's attention from anything that he was doing in order that he might confirm or contradict the rumour. People who are much interested in birds are less sociable than other naturalists. Their hobby demands a silent and solitary pursuit of knowledge, and the presence of human beings is prejudicial to their success. Parson Trehawke found that Mark's company was not so much of a handicap as he would have supposed; on the contrary he began to find it an advantage, because his grandson's eyes were sharp and his observation if he chose accurate: Parson Trehawke, who was growing old, began to rely upon his help. It was only when Mark was tired of listening to the translation of Horace that he called thrushes shrikes: when he was wandering over the cliffs or tramping beside his grandfather across the Rhos, he was severely sceptical of any rarity and used to make short work of the old gentleman's Dartford warblers and fire-crested wrens.

It was usually over birds if ever Parson Trehawke quarrelled with his parishioners. Few of them attended his services, but they spoke well of him personally, and they reckoned that he was a fine old boy was Parson. They would not however abandon their beastly habit of snaring wildfowl in winter with fish-hooks, and many a time had Mark seen his grandfather stand on the top of Pendhu Cliff, a favourite place to bait the hooks, cursing the scattered white houses of the village below as if it were one of the cities of the plain.

Although the people of Nancepean except for a very few never attended the services in their church they liked to be baptized and married within its walls, and not for anything would they have been buried outside the little churchyard by the sea. About three years after Mark's arrival his grandfather had a great fight over a burial. The blacksmith, a certain William Day, died, and although he had never been inside St. Tugdual's Church since he was married, his relations set great store by his being buried there and by Parson Trehawke's celebrating the last rites.

"Never," vowed the Parson. "Never while I live will I lay that blackguard in my churchyard."

The elders of the village remonstrated with him, pointing out that although the late Mr. Day was a pillar of the Chapel it had ever been the custom in Nancepean to let the bones of the most obstinate Wesleyan rest beside his forefathers.

"Wesleyan!" shouted the Parson. "Who cares if he was a Jew? I won't have my churchyard defiled by that blackguard's corpse. Only a week before he died, I saw him with my own eyes fling two or three pieces of white-hot metal to some ducks that were looking for worms in the ditch outside his smithy, and the wretched birds gobbled them down and died in agony. I cursed him where he stood, and the judgment of God has struck him low, and never shall he rest in holy ground if I can keep him out of it."

The elders of the village expressed their astonishment at Mr. Trehawke's unreasonableness. William Day had been a God-fearing and upright man all his life with no scandal upon his reputation unless it were the rumour that he had got with child a half lunatic servant in his house, and that was never proved. Was a man to be refused Christian burial because he had once played a joke on some ducks? And what would Parson Trehawke have said to Jesus Christ about the joke he played on the Gadarene swine?

There is nothing that irritates a Kelt so much as the least consideration for any animal, and there was not a man in the whole of the Rhos peninsula who did not sympathize with the corpse of William Day. In the end the dispute was settled by a neighbouring parson's coming over and reading the burial service over the blacksmith's grave. Mark apprehended that his grandfather resented bitterly the compromise as his fellow parson called it, the surrender as he himself called it. This was the second time that Mark had witnessed the defeat of a superior being whom he had been taught to regard as invincible, and it slightly clouded that perfect serenity of being grown up to which, like most children, he looked forward as the end of life's difficulties. He argued the justification of his grandfather's action with Cass Dale, and he found himself confronted by the workings of a mind naturally nonconformist with its rebellion against authority, its contempt of tradition, its blend of self-respect and self-importance. When Mark found himself in danger of being beaten in argument, he took to his fists, at which method of settling a dispute Cass Dale proved equally his match; and the end of it was that Mark found himself upside down in a furze bush with nothing to console him but an unalterable conviction that he was right and, although tears of pain and mortification were streaming down his cheeks, a fixed resolve to renew the argument as soon as he was the right way up again, and if necessary the struggle as well.

Luckily for the friendship between Mark and Cass, a friendship that was awarded a mystical significance by their two surnames, Lidderdale and Dale, Parson Trehawke, soon after the burial episode, came forward as the champion of the Nancepean Fishing Company in a quarrel with those pirates from Lanyon, the next village down the coast. Inasmuch as a pilchard catch worth £800 was in dispute, feeling ran high between the Nancepean Daws and the Lanyon Gulls. All the inhabitants of the Rhos parishes were called after various birds or animals that were supposed to indicate their character; and when Parson Trehawke's championship of his own won the day, his parishioners came to church in a body on the following Sunday and put one pound five shillings and tenpence halfpenny in the plate. The reconciliation between the two boys took place with solemn preliminary handshakes followed by linking of arms as of old after Cass reckoned audibly to Mark who was standing close by that Parson Trehawke was a grand old chap, the grandest old chap from Rosemarket to Rose Head. That afternoon Mark went back to tea with Cass Dale, and over honey with Cornish cream they were brothers again. Samuel Dale, the father of Cass, was a typical farmer of that part of the country with his fifty or sixty acres of land, the capital to work which had come from fish in the fat pilchard years. Cass was his only son, and he had an ambition to turn him into a full-fledged minister. He had lost his wife when Cass was a baby, and it pleased him to think that in planning such a position for the boy he was carrying out the wishes of the mother whom outwardly he so much resembled. For housekeeper Samuel Dale had an unmarried sister whom her neighbours accused of putting on too much gentility before her nephew's advancement warranted such airs. Mark liked Aunt Keran and accepted her hospitality as a tribute to himself rather than to his position as the grandson of the Vicar. Miss Dale had been a schoolmistress before she came to keep house for her brother, and she worked hard to supplement what learning Cass could get from the village school before, some three years after Mark came to Nancepean, he was sent to Rosemarket Grammar School.

Mark was anxious to attend the Grammar School with Cass; but Mrs. Lidderdale's dread nowadays was that her son would acquire a West country burr, and it was considered more prudent, economically and otherwise, to let him go on learning with his grandfather and herself. Mark missed Cass when he went to school in Rosemarket, because there was no such thing as playing truant there, and it was so far away that Cass did not come home for the midday meal. But in summertime, Mark used to wait for him outside the town, where a lane branched from the main road into the unfrequented country behind the Rose Pool and took them the longest way home along the banks on the Nancepean side, which were low and rushy unlike those on the Rosemarket side, which were steep and densely wooded. The great water, though usually described as heart-shaped, was really more like a pair of Gothic arches, the green cusp between which was crowned by a lonely farmhouse, El Dorado of Mark and his friend, and the base of which was the bar of shingle that kept out the sea. There was much to beguile the boys on the way home, whether it was the sight of strange wildfowl among the reeds, or the exploration of a ruined cottage set in an ancient cherry-orchard, or the sailing of paper boats, or even the mere delight of lying on the grass and listening above the murmur of insects to the water nagging at the sedge. So much indeed was there to beguile them that, if after sunset the Pool had not been a haunted place, they would have lingered there till nightfall. Sometimes indeed they did miscalculate the distance they had come and finding themselves likely to be caught by twilight they would hurry with eyes averted from the grey water lest the kelpie should rise out of the depths and drown them. There were men and women now alive in Nancepean who could tell of this happening to belated wayfarers, and it was Mark who discovered that such a beast was called a kelpie. Moreover, the bar where earlier in the evening it was pleasant to lie and pluck the yellow sea-poppies, listening to tales of wrecks and buried treasure and bygone smuggling, was no place at all in the chill of twilight; moreover, when the bar had been left behind and before the coastguards' cottages came into sight there was a two-mile stretch of lonely cliff that was a famous haunt of ghosts. Drowned light dragoons whose bodies were tossed ashore here a hundred years ago, wreckers revisiting the scene of their crimes, murdered excisemen . . . it was not surprising that the boys hurried along the narrow path, whistling to keep up their spirits and almost ready to cry for help if nothing more dangerous than a moth fanned their pale cheeks in passing. And after this Mark had to undo alone the nine gates between the Vicarage and Nancepean, though Cass would go with him as far along his road as the last light of the village could be seen, and what was more stay there whistling for as long as Mark could hear the heartening sound.

But if these adventures demanded the companionship of Cass, the inspiration of them was Mark's mother. Just as in the nursery games of Lima Street it had always been she who had made it worth while to play with his grenadiers, which by the way had perished in a troopship like their predecessors the light dragoons a century before, sinking one by one and leaving nothing behind except their cork-stands bobbing on the waves.

Mrs. Lidderdale knew every legend of the coast, so that it was thrilling to sit beside her and turn over the musty pages of the church registers, following from equinox to equinox in the entries of the burials the wrecks since the year 1702:

The bodies of fifteen seamen from the brigantine *Ann Pink* wrecked in Church Cove, on the afternoon of Dec. 19, 1757.

The body of a child washed into Pendhu Cove from the high seas during the night of Jan. 24, 1760.

The body of an unknown sailor, the breast tattooed with a heart and the initials M. V. found in Hanover Cove on the morning of March 3, 1801.

Such were the inscriptions below the wintry dates of two hundred years, and for each one Mark's mother had a moving legend of fortune's malice. She had tales too of treasure, from the golden doubloons of a Spanish galleon wrecked on the Rose Bar in the sixteenth century to the silver dollars of Portugal, a million of them, lost in the narrow cove on the other side of the Castle Cliff in the lee of which was built St. Tugdual's Church. At low spring tides it was possible to climb down and sift the wet sand through one's fingers on the chance of finding a dollar, and when the tide began to rise it was jolly to climb back to the top of the cliff and listen to tales of mermaids while a gentle wind blew the perfume of the sea-campion along the grassy slopes. It was here that Mark first heard the story of the two princesses who were wrecked in what was now called Church Cove and of how they were washed up on the cliff and vowed to build a church in gratitude to God and St. Tugdual on the very spot where they escaped from the sea, of how they quarrelled about the site because each sister wished to commemorate the exact spot where she was saved, and of how finally one built the tower on her spot and the other built the church on hers, which was the reason why the church and the tower were not joined to this day. When Mark went home that afternoon, he searched among his grandfather's books until he found the story of St. Tugdual who, it seemed, was a holy man in Brittany, so holy that he was summoned to be Pope of Rome. When he had been Pope for a few months, an angel appeared to him and said that he must come back at once to Brittany, because since he went to Rome all the women were become barren.

"But how am I to go back all the way from Rome to Brittany?" St. Tugdual asked.

"I have a white horse waiting for you," the angel replied.

And sure enough there was a beautiful white horse with wings, which carried St. Tugdual back to Brittany in a few minutes.

"What does it mean when a woman becomes barren?" Mark inquired of his mother.

"It means when she does not have any more children, darling," said Mrs. Lidderdale, who did not believe in telling lies about anything.

And because she answered her son simply, her son did not perplex himself with shameful speculations, but was glad that St. Tugdual went back home so that the women of Brittany were able to have children again.

Everything was simple at Nancepean except the parishioners; but Mark was still too young and too simple himself to apprehend their complicacy. The simplest thing of all was the Vicar's religion, and at an age when for most children religion means being dressed up to go into the drawing-room and say how d'you do to God, Mark was allowed to go to church in his ordinary clothes and after church to play at whatever he wanted to play, so that he learned to regard the assemblage of human beings to worship God as nothing more remarkable than the song of birds. He was too young to have experienced yet a personal need of religion; but he had already been touched by that grace of fellowship which is conferred upon a small congregation, the individual members of which are in church to please themselves rather than to impress others. This was always the case in the church of Nancepean, which had to contend not merely with the popularity of methodism, but also with the situation of the Chapel in the middle of the village. On the dark December evenings there would be perhaps not more than half a dozen worshippers, each one of whom would have brought his own candle and stuck it on the shelf of the pew. The organist would have two candles for the harmonium; the choir of three little boys and one little girl would have two between them; the altar would have two; the Vicar would have two. But when all the candle-light was put together, it left most of the church in shadow; indeed, it scarcely even illuminated the space between the worshippers, so that each one seemed wrapped in a golden aura of prayer, most of all when at Evensong the people knelt in silence for a minute while the sound of the sea without rose and fell and the noise of the wind scuttling through the ivy on the walls was audible. When the congregation had gone out and the Vicar was standing at the churchyard gate saying "good night," Mark used to think that they must all be feeling happy to go home together up the long hill to Pendhu and down into twinkling Nancepean. And it did not matter whether it was a night of clear or clouded moonshine or a night of windy stars or a night of darkness; for when it was dark he could always look back from the valley road and see a company of lanthorns moving homeward; and that more than anything shed upon his young spirit the grace of human fellowship and the love of mankind.

CHAPTER VIII
THE WRECK

One wild night in late October of the year before he would be thirteen, Mark was lying awake hoping, as on such nights he always hoped, to hear somebody shout "A wreck! A wreck!" A different Mark from that one who used to lie trembling in Lima Street lest he should hear a shout of "Fire! or Thieves!"

And then it happened! It happened as a hundred times he had imagined its happening, so exactly that he could hardly believe for a moment he was not dreaming. There was the flash of a lanthorn on the ceiling, a thunderous, knocking on the Vicarage door. Mark leapt out of bed; flinging open his window through which the wind rushed in like a flight of angry birds, he heard voices below in the garden shouting "Parson! Parson! Parson Trehawke! There's a brig driving in fast toward Church Cove." He did not wait to hear more, but dashed along the passage to rouse first his grandfather, then his mother, and then Emma, the Vicar's old cook.

"And you must get soup ready," he cried, standing over the old woman in his flannel pyjamas and waving his arms excitedly, while downstairs the cuckoo popped in and out of his door in the clock twelve times. Emma blinked at him in terror, and Mark pulled off all the bedclothes to convince the old woman that he was not playing a practical joke. Then he rushed back to his own room and began to dress for dear life.

"Mother," he shouted, while he was dressing, "the Captain can sleep in my bed, if he isn't drowned, can't he?"

"Darling, do you really want to go down to the sea on such a night?"

"Oh, mother," he gasped, "I'm practically dressed. And you will see that Emma has lots of hot soup ready, won't you? Because it'll be much better to bring all the crew back here. I don't think they'd want to walk all that way over Pendhu to Nancepean after they'd been wrecked, do you?"

"Well, you must ask grandfather first before you make arrangements for his house."

"Grandfather's simply tearing into his clothes; Ernie Hockin and Joe Dunstan have both got lanthorns, and I'll carry ours, so if one blows out we shall be all right. Oh, mother, the wind's simply shrieking through the trees. Can you hear it?"

"Yes, dearest, I certainly can. I think you'd better shut your windows. It's blowing everything about in your room most uncomfortably."

Mark's soul expanded in gratitude to God when he found himself neither in a dream nor in a story, but actually, and without any possibility of self-deception hurrying down the drive toward the sea beside Ernie and Joe, who had come from the village to warn the Vicar of the wreck and were wearing oilskins and sou'westers, thus striking the keynote as it were of the night's adventure. At first in the shelter of the holm-oaks the storm seemed far away overhead; but when they turned the corner and took the road along the valley, the wind caught them full in the face and Mark was blown back violently against the swinging gate of the drive. The light of the lanthorns shining on a rut in the road showed a field-mouse hurrying inland before the rushing gale. Mark bent double to force himself to keep up with the others, lest somebody should think, by his inability to maintain an equal pace that he ought to follow the field-mouse back home. After they had struggled on for a while a bend of the valley gave them a few minutes of easy progress and Mark listened while Ernie Hockin explained to the Vicar what had happened:

"Just before dark Eddowes the coastguard said he reckoned there was a brig making very heavy weather of it and he shouldn't be surprised if she come ashore tonight. Couldn't seem to beat out of the bay noways, he said. And afterwards about nine o'clock when me and Joe here and some of the chaps were in the bar to the Hanover, Eddowes come in again and said she was in a bad way by the looks of her last thing he saw, and he telephoned along to Lanyon to ask if they'd seen her down to the lifeboat house. They reckoned she was all right to the lifeboat, and old man Timbury who do always go against anything Eddowes do say shouted that of course she was all right because he'd taken a look at her through his glass before it grew dark. Of course she was all right. 'She's on a lee shore,' said Eddowes. 'It don't take a coastguard to tell that,' said old man Timbury. And then they got to talking one against the other the same as they belong, and they'd soon got back to the same old talk whether Jackie Fisher was the finest admiral who ever lived or no use at all. 'What's the good in your talking to me?' old man Timbury was saying. 'Why afore you was born I've seen' . . . and we all started in to shout 'ships o' the line, frigates, and cavattes,' because we belong to mock him like that, when somebody called 'Hark, listen, wasn't that a rocket?' That fetched us all outside into the road where we stood listening. The wind was blowing harder than ever, and there was a parcel of sea rising. You could hear it against Shag Rock over the wind. Eddowes, he were a bit upset to think he should have been talking and not a-heard the rocket. But there wasn't a light in the sky, and when we went home along about half past nine we saw Eddowes again and he said he'd been so far as Church Cove and should walk up along to the Bar. No mistake, Mr. Trehawke, he's a handy chap is Eddowes for the coastguard job. And then about eleven o'clock he saw two rockets close in to Church Cove and he come running back and telephoned to Lanyon, but they said no one couldn't launch a boat to-night, and Eddowes he come banging on the doors and windows shouting 'A Wreck' and some of us took ropes along with Eddowes, and me and Joe here come and fetched you along. Eddowes said he's afeard she'll strike in Dollar Cove unless she's lucky and come ashore in Church Cove."

"How's the tide?" asked the Vicar.

"About an hour of the ebb," said Ernie Hockin. "And the moon's been up this hour and more."

Just then the road turned the corner, and the world became a waste of wind and spindrift driving inland. The noise of the gale made it impossible for anybody to talk, and Mark was left wondering whether the ship had actually struck or not. The wind drummed in his ears, the flying grit and gravel and spray stung his face; but he struggled on hoping that this midnight walk would not come to an abrupt end by his grandfather's declining to go any farther. Above the drumming of the wind the roar of the sea became more audible every moment; the spume was thicker; the end of the valley, ordinarily the meeting-place of sand and grass and small streams with their yellow flags and forget-me-nots, was a desolation of white foam beyond which against the cliffs showing black in the nebulous moonlight the breakers leapt high with frothy tongues. Mark thought that they resembled immense ghosts clawing up to reach the summit of the cliff. It was incredible that this hell-broth was Church Cove.

"Hullo!" yelled Ernie Hockin. "Here's the bridge."

It was true. One wave at the moment of high tide had swept snarling over the stream and carried the bridge into the meadow beyond.

"We'll have to get round by the road," shouted the Vicar.

They turned to the right across a ploughed field and after scrambling through the hedge emerged in the comparative shelter of the road down from Pendhu.

"I hope the churchyard wall is all right," said the Vicar. "I never remember such a night since I came to Nancepean."

"Sure 'nough, 'tis blowing very fierce," Joe Dunstan agreed. "But don't you worry about the wall, Mr. Trehawke. The worst of the water is broken by the Castle and only comes in sideways, as you might say."

When they drew near the gate of the churchyard, the rain of sand and small pebbles was agonizing, as it swept across up the low sandstone cliffs on that side of the Castle. Two or three excited figures shouted for them to hurry because she was going to strike in Dollar Cove, and everybody began to scramble up the grassy slope, clutching at the tuffets of thrift to aid their progress. It was calm here in the lee; and Mark panting up the face thought of those two princesses who were wrecked here ages ago, and he understood now why one of them had insisted on planting the tower deep in the foundation of this green fortress against the wind and weather. While he was thinking this, his head came above the sky line, his breath left him at the assault of the wind, and he had to crawl on all fours toward the sea. He reached the edge of the cliff just as something like the wings of a gigantic bat flapped across the dim wet moonlight, and before he realized that this was the brig he heard the crashing of her spars. The watchers stood up against the wind, battling with it to fling lines in the vain hope of saving some sailor who was being churned to death in that dreadful creaming of the sea below. Yes, and there were forms of men visible on board; two had climbed the mainmast, which crashed before they could clutch at the ropes that were being flung to them from land, crashed and carried them down shrieking into the surge. Mark found it hard to believe that last summer he had spent many sunlit hours dabbling in the sand for silver dollars of Portugal lost perhaps on such a night as this a hundred years ago, exactly where these two poor mariners were lost. A few minutes after the mainmast the hull went also; but in the nebulous moonlight nothing could be seen of any bodies alive or dead, nothing except wreckage tossing upon the surge. The watchers on the cliff turned away from the wind to gather new breath and give their cheeks a rest from the stinging fragments of rock and earth. Away up over the towans they could see the bobbing lanthorns of men hurrying down from Chypie where news of the wreck had reached; and on the road from Lanyon they could see lanthorns on the other side of Church Cove waiting until the tide had ebbed far enough to let them cross the beach.

Suddenly the Vicar shouted:

"I can see a poor fellow hanging on to a ledge of rock. Bring a rope! Bring a rope!"

Eddowes the coastguard took charge of the operation, and Mark with beating pulses watched the end of the rope touch the huddled form below. But either from exhaustion or because he feared to let go of the slippery ledge for one moment the sailor made no attempt to grasp the rope. The men above shouted to him, begged him to make an effort; but he remained there inert.

"Somebody must go down with the rope and get a slip knot under his arms," the Vicar shouted.

Nobody seemed to pay attention to this proposal, and Mark wondered if he was the only one who had heard it. However, when the Vicar repeated his suggestion, Eddowes came forward, knelt down by the edge of the cliff, shook himself like a bather who is going to plunge into what he knows will be very cold water, and then vanished down the rope. Everybody crawled on hand and knees to see what would happen. Mark prayed that Eddowes, who was a great friend of his, would not come to any harm, but that he would rescue the sailor and be given the Albert medal for saving life. It was Eddowes who had made him medal wise. The coastguard struggled to slip the loop under the man's shoulders along his legs; but it must have been impossible, for presently he made a signal to be raised.

"I can't do it alone," he shouted. "He's got a hold like a limpet."

Nobody seemed anxious to suppose that the addition of another rescuer would be any more successful.

"If there was two of us," Eddowes went on, "we might do something."

The people on the cliff shook their heads doubtfully.

"Isn't anybody coming down along with me to have a try?" the coastguard demanded at the top of his voice.

Mark did not hear his grandfather's reply; he only saw him go over the cliff's edge at the end of one rope while Eddowes went down on another. A minute later the slipknot came untied (or that was how the accident was explained) and the Vicar went to join the drowned mariners, dislodging as he fell the man whom he had tried to save, so that of the crew of the brig *Happy Return* not one ever came to port.

It would be difficult to exaggerate the effect upon Mark Lidderdale of that night. He was twelve years old at the time; but the years in Cornwall had retarded that precocious development to which he seemed destined by the surroundings of his early childhood in Lima Street, and in many ways he was hardly any older than he was when he left London. In after years he looked back with gratitude upon the shock he received from what was as it were an experience of the material impact of death, because it made him think about death, not morbidly as so many children and young people will, but with the apprehension of something that really does come in a moment and for which it is necessary for every human being to prepare his soul. The platitudes of age may often be for youth divine revelations, and there is nothing so stimulating as the unaided apprehension of a great commonplace of existence. The awe with which Mark was filled that night was too vast to evaporate in sentiment, and when two days after this there came news from Africa that his father had died of black-water fever that awe was crystallized indeed. Mark looking round at his small world perceived that nobody was safe. To-morrow his mother might die; to-morrow he might die himself. In any case the death of his grandfather would have meant a profound change in the future of his mother's life and his own; the living of Nancepean would fall to some other priest and with it the house in which they lived. Parson Trehawke had left nothing of any value except Gould's *Birds of Great Britain* and a few other works of ornithology. The furniture of the Vicarage was rich neither in quality nor in quantity. Three or four hundred pounds was the most his daughter could inherit. She had spoken to Mark of their poverty, because in her dismay for the future of her son she had no heart to pretend that the dead man's money was of little importance.

"I must write and ask your father what we ought to do." . . . She stopped in painful awareness of the possessive pronoun. Mark was unresponsive, until there came the news from Africa, which made him throw his arms about his mother's neck while she was still alive. Mrs. Lidderdale, whatever bitterness she may once have felt for the ruin of her married life, shed fresh tears of sorrow for her husband, and supposing that Mark's embrace was the expression of his sympathy wept more, as people will when others are sorry for them, and then still more because the future for Mark seemed hopeless. How was she to educate him? How clothe him? How feed him even? At her age where and how could she earn money? She reproached herself with having been too ready out of sensitiveness to sacrifice Mark to her own pride. She had had no right to leave her husband and live in the country like this. She should have repressed her own emotion and thought only of the family life, to the maintenance of which by her marriage she had committed herself. At first it had seemed the best thing for Mark; but she should have remembered that her father could not live for ever and that one day she would have to face the problem of life without his help and his hospitality. She began to imagine that the disaster of that stormy night had been contrived by God to punish her, and she prayed to Him that her chastisement should not be increased, that at least her son might be spared to her.

Mrs. Lidderdale was able to stay on at the Vicarage for several weeks, because the new Vicar of Nancepean was not able to take over his charge immediately. This delay gave her time to hold a sale of her father's furniture, at which the desire of the neighbours to be generous fought with their native avarice, so that in the end the furniture fetched neither more nor less than had been expected, which was little enough. She kept back enough to establish herself and Mark in rooms, should she be successful in finding some unfurnished rooms sufficiently cheap to allow her to take them, although how she was going to live for more than two years on what she had was a riddle of which after a month of sleepless nights she had not found the solution.

In the end, and as Mrs. Lidderdale supposed in answer to her prayers, the solution was provided unexpectedly in the following letter:

Haverton House,
Elmhurst Road,
Slowbridge.
November 29th.
Dear Grace,

I have just received a letter from James written when he was at the point of death in Africa. It appears that in his zeal to convert the heathen to Popery he omitted to make any provision for his wife and child, so that in the event of his death, unless either your relatives or his relatives came forward to support you I was given to understand that you would be destitute. I recently read in the daily paper an account of the way in which your father Mr. Trehawke lost his life, and I caused inquiries to be made in Rosemarket about your prospects. These my informant tells me are not any too bright. You will, I am sure, pardon my having made these inquiries without reference to you, but I did not feel justified in offering you and my nephew a home with my sister Helen and myself unless I had first assured myself that some such offer was necessary. You are probably aware that for many years my brother James and myself have not been on the best of terms. I on my side found his religious teaching so eccentric as to repel me; he on his side was so bigoted that he could not tolerate my tacit disapproval. Not being a Ritualist but an Evangelical, I can perhaps bring myself more easily to forgive my brother's faults and at the same time indulge my theories of duty, as opposed to forms and ceremonies, theories that if carried out by everybody would soon transform our modern Christianity. You are no doubt a Ritualist, and your son has no doubt been educated in the same school. Let me hasten to give you my word that I shall not make the least attempt to interfere either with your religious practices or with his. The quarrel between myself and James was due almost entirely to James' inability to let me and my opinions alone.

I am far from being a rich man, in fact I may say at once that I am scarcely even "comfortably off" as the phrase goes. It would therefore be outside my capacity to undertake the expense of any elaborate education for your son; but my own school, which while it does not pretend to compete with some of the fashionable establishments of the time is I venture to assert a first class school and well able to send your son into the world at the age of sixteen as well equipped, and better equipped than he would be if he went to one of the famous public schools. I possess some influence with a firm of solicitors, and I have no doubt that when my nephew, who is I believe now twelve years old, has had the necessary schooling I shall be able to secure him a position as an articled clerk, from which if he is honest and industrious he may be able to rise to the position of a junior partner. If you have saved anything from the sale of your father's effects I should advise you to invest the sum. However small it is, you will find the extra money useful, for as I remarked before I shall not be able to afford to do more than lodge and feed you both, educate your son, find him in clothes, and start him in a career on the lines I have already indicated. My local informant tells me that you have kept back a certain amount of your father's furniture in order to take lodgings elsewhere. As this will now be unnecessary I hope that you will sell the rest. Haverton House is sufficiently furnished, and we should not be able to find room for any more furniture. I suggest your coming to us next Friday. It will be easiest for you to take the fast train up to Paddington when you will be able to catch the 6.45 to Slowbridge arriving at 7.15. We usually dine at 7.30, but on Friday dinner will be at 8 p.m. in order to give you plenty of time. Helen sends her love. She would have written also, but I assured her that one letter was enough, and that a very long one.

Your affectionate brother-in-law,

Henry Lidderdale.

Mrs. Lidderdale would no doubt have criticized this letter more sharply if she had not regarded it as inspired, almost actually written by the hand of God. Whatever in it was displeasing to her she accepted as the Divine decree, and if anybody had pointed out the inconsistency of some of the opinions therein expressed with its Divine authorship, she would have dismissed the objection as made by somebody who was incapable of comprehending the mysterious action of God.

"Mark," she called to her son. "What do you think has happened? Your Uncle Henry has offered us a home. I want you to write to him like a dear boy and thank him for his kindness." She explained in detail what Uncle Henry intended to do for them; but Mark would not be enthusiastic. He on his side had been praying to God to put it into the mind of Samuel Dale to offer him a job on his farm; Slowbridge was a poor substitute for that.

"Where is Slowbridge?" he asked in a gloomy voice.

"It's a fairly large place near London," his mother told him. "It's near Eton and Windsor and Stoke Poges where Gray wrote his Elegy, which we learned last summer. You remember, don't you?" she asked anxiously, for she wanted Mark to cut a figure with his uncle.

"Wolfe liked it," said Mark. "And I like it too," he added ungraciously. He wished that he could have said he hated it; but Mark always found it difficult to tell a lie about his personal feelings, or about any facts that involved him in a false position.

"And now before you go down to tea with Cass Dale, you will write to your uncle, won't you, and show me the letter?"

Mark groaned.

"It's so difficult to thank people. It makes me feel silly."

"Well, darling, mother wants you to. So sit down like a dear boy and get it done."

"I think my nib is crossed."

"Is it? You'll find another in my desk."

"But, mother, yours are so thick."

"Please, Mark, don't make any more excuses. Don't you want to do everything you can to help me just now?"

"Yes, of course," said Mark penitently, and sitting down in the window he stared out at the yellow November sky, and at the magpies flying busily from one side of the valley to the other.

The Vicarage,

Nancepean,

South Cornwall.

My dear Uncle Henry,

Thank you very much for your kind invitation to come and live with you. We should enjoy it very much. I am going to tea with a friend of mine called Cass Dale who lives in Nancepean, and so I must stop now. With love,

I remain,

Your loving nephew,

Mark.

And then the pen must needs go and drop a blot like a balloon right over his name, so that the whole letter had to be copied out again before his mother would say that she was satisfied, by which time the yellow sky was dun and the magpies were gone to rest.

Mark left the Dales about half past six, and was accompanied by Cass to the brow of Pendhu. At this point Cass declined to go any farther in spite of Mark's reminder that this would be one of the last walks they would take together, if it were not absolutely the very last.

"No," said Cass. "I wouldn't come up from Church Cove myself not for anything."

"But I'm going down by myself," Mark argued. "If I hadn't thought you'd come all the way with me, I'd have gone home by the fields. What are you afraid of?"

"I'm not afraid of nothing, but I don't want to walk so far by myself. I've come up the hill with 'ee. Now 'tis all down hill for both of us, and that's fair."

"Oh, all right," said Mark, turning away in resentment at his friend's desertion.

Both boys ran off in opposite directions, Cass past the splash of light thrown across the road by the windows of the Hanover Inn, and on toward the scattered lights of Nancepean, Mark into the gloom of the deep lane down to Church Cove. It was a warm and humid evening that brought out the smell of the ferns and earth in the high banks on either side, and presently at the bottom of the hill the smell of the seaweed heaped up in Church Cove by weeks of gales. The moon, about three days from the full, was already up, shedding her aqueous lustre over the towans of Chypie, which slowly penetrated the black gulfs of shadow in the countryside until Mark could perceive the ghost of a familiar landscape. There came over him, whose emotion had already been sprung by the insensibility of Cass, an overwhelming awareness of parting, and he gave to the landscape the expression of sentiment he had yearned to give his friend. His fear of seeing the spirits of the drowned sailors, or as he passed the churchyard gate of perceiving behind that tamarisk the tall spectre of his grandfather, which on the way down from Pendhu had seemed impossible to combat, had died away; and in his despair at losing this beloved scene he wandered on past the church until he stood at the edge of the tide. On this humid autumnal night the oily sea collapsed upon the beach as if it, like everything else in nature, was overcome by the prevailing heaviness. Mark sat down upon some tufts of samphire and watched the Stag Light occulting out across St. Levan's Bay, distant forty miles and more, and while he sat he perceived a glow-worm at his feet creeping along a sprig of samphire that marked the limit of the tide's advance. How did the samphire know that it was safe to grow where it did, and how did the glow-worm know that the samphire was safe?

Mark was suddenly conscious of the protection of God, for might not he expect as much as the glow-worm and the samphire? The ache of separation from Nancepean was assuaged. That dread of the future, with which the impact of death had filled him, was allayed.

"Good-night, sister glow-worm," he said aloud in imitation of St. Francis. "Good-night, brother samphire."

A drift of distant fog had obliterated the Stag Light; but of her samphire the glow-worm had made a moonlit forest, so brightly was she shining, yes, a green world of interlacing, lucid boughs.

Let your light so shine before men, that they may see your good works, and glorify your Father which is in heaven.

And Mark, aspiring to thank God Who had made manifest His protection, left Nancepean three days later with the determination to become a lighthouse-keeper, to polish well his lamp and tend it with care, so that men passing by in ships should rejoice at his good works and call him brother lighthouse-keeper, and glorify God their Father when they walked again upon the grass, harking to the pleasant song of birds and the hum of bees.

CHAPTER IX
SLOWBRIDGE

When Mark came to live with Uncle Henry Lidderdale at Slowbridge, he was large for his age, or at any rate he was so loosely jointed as to appear large; a swart complexion, prominent cheek-bones, and straight lank hair gave him a melancholic aspect, the impression of which remained with the observer until he heard the boy laugh in a paroxysm of merriment that left his dark blue eyes dancing long after the outrageous noise had died down. If Mark had occasion to relate some episode that appealed to him, his laughter would accompany the narrative like a pack of hounds in full cry, would as it were pursue the tale to its death, and communicate its zest to the listener, who would think what a sense of humour Mark had, whereas it was more truly the gusto of life.

Uncle Henry found this laughter boisterous and irritating; if his nephew had been a canary in a cage, he would have covered him with a table-cloth. Aunt Helen, if she was caught up in one of Mark's narratives, would twitch until it was finished, when she would rub her forehead with an acorn of menthol and wrap herself more closely in a shawl of soft Shetland wool. The antipathy that formerly existed between Mark and his father was much sharper between Mark and his uncle. It was born in the instant of their first meeting, when Uncle Henry bent over, his trunk at right angles to his legs, so that one could fancy the pelvic bones to be clicking like the wooden joints of a monkey on a stick, and offered his nephew an acrid whisker to be saluted.

"And what is Mark going to be?" Uncle Henry inquired.

"A lighthouse-keeper."

"Ah, we all have suchlike ambitions when we are young. I remember that for nearly a year I intended to be a muffin-man," said Uncle Henry severely.

Mark hated his uncle from that moment, and he fixed upon the throbbing pulse of his scraped-out temples as the feature upon which that dislike should henceforth be concentrated. Uncle Henry's pulse seemed to express all the vitality that was left to him; Mark thought that Our Lord must have felt about the barren fig-tree much as he felt about Uncle Henry.

Aunt Helen annoyed Mark in the way that one is annoyed by a cushion in an easy chair. It is soft and apparently comfortable, but after a minute or two one realizes that it is superfluous, and it is pushed over the arm to the floor. Unfortunately Aunt Helen could not be treated like a cushion; and there she was soft and comfortable in appearance, but forever in Mark's way. Aunt Helen was the incarnation of her own drawing-room. Her face was round and stupid like a clock's; she wore brocaded gowns and carpet slippers; her shawls resembled antimacassars; her hair was like the stuff that is put in grates during the summer; her caps were like lace curtains tied back with velvet ribbons; cameos leant against her bosom as if they were upon a mantelpiece. Mark never overcame his dislike of kissing Aunt Helen, for it gave him a sensation every time that a bit of her might stick to his lips. He lacked that solemn sense of relationship with which most children are imbued, and the compulsory intimacy offended him, particularly when his aunt referred to little boys generically as if they were beetles or mice. Her inability to appreciate that he was Mark outraged his young sense of personality which was further dishonoured by the manner in which she spoke of herself as Aunt Helen, thus seeming to imply that he was only human at all in so far as he was her nephew. She continually shocked his dignity by prescribing medicine for him without regard to the presence of servants or visitors; and nothing gave her more obvious pleasure than to get Mark into the drawing-room on afternoons when dreary mothers of pupils came to call, so that she might bully him under the appearance of teaching good manners, and impress the parents with the advantages of a Haverton House education.

As long as his mother remained alive, Mark tried to make her happy by pretending that he enjoyed living at Haverton House, that he enjoyed his uncle's Preparatory School for the Sons of Gentlemen, that he enjoyed Slowbridge with its fogs and laburnums, its perambulators and tradesmen's carts and noise of whistling trains; but a year after they left Nancepean Mrs. Lidderdale died of pneumonia, and Mark was left alone with his uncle and aunt.

"He doesn't realize what death means," said Aunt Helen, when Mark on the very afternoon of the funeral without even waiting to change out of his best clothes began to play with soldiers instead of occupying himself with the preparation of lessons that must begin again on the morrow.

"I wonder if you will play with soldiers when Aunt Helen dies?" she pressed.

"No," said Mark quickly, "I shall work at my lessons when you die."

His uncle and aunt looked at him suspiciously. They could find no fault with the answer; yet something in the boy's tone, some dreadful suppressed exultation made them feel that they ought to find severe fault with the answer.

"Wouldn't it be kinder to your poor mother's memory," Aunt Helen suggested, "wouldn't it be more becoming now to work harder at your lessons when your mother is watching you from above?"

Mark would not condescend to explain why he was playing with soldiers, nor with what passionate sorrow he was recalling every fleeting expression on his mother's face, every slight intonation of her voice when she was able to share in his game; he hated his uncle and aunt so profoundly that he revelled in their incapacity to understand him, and he would have accounted it a desecration of her memory to share his grief with them.

Haverton House School was a depressing establishment; in after years when Mark looked back at it he used to wonder how it had managed to survive so long, for when he came to live at Slowbridge it had actually been in existence for twenty years, and his uncle was beginning to look forward to the time when Old Havertonians, as he called them, would be bringing their sons to be educated at the old place. There were about fifty pupils, most of them the sons of local tradesmen, who left when they were about fourteen, though a certain number lingered on until they were as much as sixteen in what was called the Modern Class, where they were supposed to receive at least as practical an education as they would have received behind the counter, and certainly a more genteel one. Fine fellows those were in the Modern Class at Haverton House, stalwart heroes who made up the cricket and football teams and strode about the playing fields of Haverton House with as keen a sense of their own importance as Etonians of comparable status in their playing fields not more than two miles away. Mark when everything else in his school life should be obliterated by time would remember their names and prowess. . . . Borrow, Tull, Yarde, Corke, Vincent, Macdougal, Skinner, they would keep throughout his life some of that magic which clings to Diomed and Deiphobus, to Hector and Achilles.

Apart from these heroic names the atmosphere of Haverton House was not inspiring. It reduced the world to the size and quality of one of those scratched globes with which Uncle Henry demonstrated geography. Every subject at Haverton House, no matter how interesting it promised to be, was ruined from an educative point of view by its impedimenta of dates, imports, exports, capitals, capes, and Kings of Israel and Judah. Neither Uncle Henry nor his assistants Mr. Spaull and Mr. Palmer believed in departing from the book. Whatever books were chosen for the term's curriculum were regarded as something for which money had been paid and from which the last drop of information must be squeezed to justify in the eyes of parents the expenditure. The teachers considered the notes more important than the text; genealogical tables were exalted above anything on the same page. Some books of history were adorned with illustrations; but no use was made of them by the masters, and for the pupils they merely served as outlines to which, were they the outlines of human beings, inky beards and moustaches had to be affixed, or were they landscapes, flights of birds.

Mr. Spaull was a fat flabby young man with a heavy fair moustache, who was reading for Holy Orders; Mr. Palmer was a stocky bow-legged young man in knickerbockers, who was good at football and used to lament the gentle birth that prevented his becoming a professional. The boys called him Gentleman Joe; but they were careful not to let Mr. Palmer hear them, for he had a punch and did not believe in cuddling the young. He used to jeer openly at his colleague, Mr. Spaull, who never played football, never did anything in the way of exercise except wrestle flirtatiously with the boys, while Mr. Palmer was bellowing up and down the field of play and charging his pupils with additional vigour to counteract the feebleness of Mr. Spaull. Poor Mr. Spaull, he was ordained about three years after Mark came to Slowbridge, and a week later he was run over by a brewer's dray and killed.

CHAPTER X
WHIT-SUNDAY

Mark at the age of fifteen was a bitter, lonely, and unattractive boy. Three years of Haverton House, three years of Uncle Henry's desiccated religion, three years of Mr. Palmer's athletic education and Mr. Spaull's milksop morality, three years of wearing clothes that were too small for him, three years of Haverton House cooking, three years of warts and bad haircutting, of ink and Aunt Helen's confident purging had destroyed that gusto for life which when Mark first came to Slowbridge used to express itself in such loud laughter. Uncle Henry probably supposed that the cure of his nephew's irritating laugh was the foundation stone of that successful career, which it would soon be time to discuss in detail. The few months between now and Mark's sixteenth birthday would soon pass, however dreary the restrictions of Haverton House, and then it would be time to go and talk to Mr. Hitchcock about that articled clerkship toward the fees for which the small sum left by his mother would contribute. Mark was so anxious to be finished with Haverton House that he would have welcomed a prospect even less attractive than Mr. Hitchcock's office in Finsbury Square; it never occurred to him that the money left by his mother could be spent to greater advantage for himself. By now it was over £500, and Uncle Henry on Sunday evenings when he was feeling comfortably replete with the day's devotion would sometimes allude to his having left the interest to accumulate and would urge Mark to be up and doing in order to show his gratitude for all that he and Aunt Helen had conferred upon him. Mark felt no gratitude; in fact at this period he felt nothing except a kind of surly listlessness. He was like somebody who through the carelessness of his nurse or guardian has been crippled in youth, and who is preparing to enter the world with a suppressed resentment against everybody and everything.

"Not still hankering after a lighthouse?" Uncle Henry asked, and one seemed to hear his words snapping like dry twigs beneath the heavy tread of his mind.

"I'm not hankering after anything," Mark replied sullenly.

"But you're looking forward to Mr. Hitchcock's office?" his uncle proceeded.

Mark grunted an assent in order to be left alone, and the entrance of Mr. Palmer who always had supper with his headmaster and employer on Sunday evening, brought the conversation to a close.

At supper Mr. Palmer asked suddenly if the headmaster wanted Mark to go into the Confirmation Class this term.

"No thanks," said Mark.

Uncle Henry raised his eyebrows.

"I fancy that is for me to decide."

"Neither my father nor my mother nor my grandfather would have wanted me to be confirmed against my will," Mark declared. He was angry without knowing his reasons, angry in response to some impulse of the existence of which he had been unaware until he began to speak. He only knew that if he surrendered on this point he should never be able to act for himself again.

"Are you suggesting that you should never be confirmed?" his uncle required.

"I'm not suggesting anything," said Mark. "But I can remember my father's saying once that boys ought to be confirmed before they are thirteen. My mother just before she died wanted me to be confirmed, but it couldn't be arranged, and now I don't intend to be confirmed till I feel I want to be confirmed. I don't want to be prepared for confirmation as if it was a football match. If you force me to go to the confirmation I'll refuse to answer the Bishop's questions. You can't make me answer against my will."

"Mark dear," said Aunt Helen, "I think you'd better take some Eno's Fruit Salts to-morrow morning." In her nephew's present mood she did not dare to prescribe anything stronger.

"I'm not going to take anything to-morrow morning," said Mark angrily.

"Do you want me to thrash you?" Uncle Henry demanded.

Mr. Palmer's eyes glittered with the zeal of muscular Christianity.

"You'll be sorry for it if you do," said Mark. "You can of course, if you get Mr. Palmer to help you, but you'll be sorry if you do."

Mr. Palmer looked at his chief as a terrier looks at his master when a rabbit is hiding in a bush. But the headmaster's vanity would not allow him to summon help to punish his own nephew, and he weakly contented himself with ordering Mark to be silent.

"It strikes me that Spaull is responsible for this sort of thing," said Mr. Palmer. "He always resented my having any hand in the religious teaching."

"That poor worm!" Mark scoffed.

"Mark, he's dead," Aunt Helen gasped. "You mustn't speak of him like that."

"Get out of the room and go to bed," Uncle Henry shouted.

Mark retired with offensive alacrity, and while he was undressing he wondered drearily why he had made himself so conspicuous on this Sunday evening out of so many Sunday evenings. What did it matter whether he were confirmed or not? What did anything matter except to get through the next year and be finished with Haverton House?

He was more sullen than ever during the week, but on Saturday he had the satisfaction of bowling Mr. Palmer in the first innings of a match and in the second innings of hitting him on the jaw with a rising ball.

The next day he rose at five o'clock on a glorious morning in early June and walked rapidly away from Slowbridge. By ten o'clock he had reached a country of rolling beech-woods, and turning aside from the high road he wandered over the bare nutbrown soil that gave the glossy leaves high above a green unparagoned, a green so lambent that the glimpses of the sky beyond seemed opaque as turquoises amongst it. In quick succession Mark saw a squirrel, a woodpecker, and a jay, creatures so perfectly expressive of the place, that they appeared to him more like visions than natural objects; and when they were gone he stood with beating heart in silence as if in a moment the trees should fly like woodpeckers, the sky flash and flutter its blue like a jay's wing, and the very earth leap like a squirrel for his amazement. Presently he came to an open space where the young bracken was springing round a pool. He flung himself down in the frondage, and the spice of it in his nostrils was as if he were feeding upon summer. He was happy until he caught sight of his own reflection in the pool, and then he could not bear to stay any longer in this wood, because unlike the squirrel and the woodpecker and the jay he was an ugly intruder here, a scarecrow in ill-fitting clothes, round the ribbon of whose hat like a chain ran the yellow zigzag of Haverton House. He became afraid of the wood, perceiving nothing round him now except an assemblage of menacing trunks, a slow gathering of angry and forbidding branches. The silence of the day was dreadful in this wood, and Mark fled from it until he emerged upon a brimming clover-ley full of drunken bees, a merry clover-ley dancing in the sun, across which the sound of church bells was being blown upon a honeyed wind. Mark welcomed the prospect of seeing ugly people again after the humiliation inflicted upon him by the wood; and he followed a footpath at the far end of the ley across several stiles, until he stood beneath the limes that overhung the churchyard gate and wondered if he should go inside to the service. The bells were clanging an agitated final appeal to the worshippers; and Mark, unable to resist, allowed himself to flow toward the cool dimness within. There with a thrill he recognized the visible signs of his childhood's religion, and now after so many years he perceived with new eyes an unfamiliar beauty in the crossings and genuflexions, in the pictures and images. The world which had lately seemed so jejune was crowded like a dream, a dream moreover that did not elude the recollection of it in the moment of waking, but that stayed with him for the rest of his life as the evidence of things not seen, which is Faith.

It was during the Gospel that Mark began to realize that what was being said and done at the Altar demanded not merely his attention but also his partaking. All the services he had attended since he came to Slowbridge had demanded nothing from him, and even when he was at Nancepean he had always been outside the sacred mysteries. But now on this Whit-sunday morning he heard in the Gospel:

Hereafter I will not talk much with you: for the prince of this world cometh and hath nothing in me.

And while he listened it seemed that Jesus Christ was departing from him, and that unless he were quick to offer himself he should be left to the prince of this world; so black was Mark's world in those days that the Prince of it meant most unmistakably the Prince of Darkness, and the prophecy made him shiver with affright. With conviction he said the Nicene Creed, and when the celebrating priest, a tall fair man, with a gentle voice and of a mild and benignant aspect, went up into the pulpit and announced that there would be a confirmation in his church on the Feast of the Visitation of the Blessed Virgin Mary Mark felt in this newly found assurance of being commanded by God to follow Him that somehow he must be confirmed in this church and prepared by this kindly priest. The sermon was about the coming of the Holy Ghost and of our bodies which are His temple. Any other Sunday Mark would have sat in a stupor, while his mind would occasionally have taken flights of activity, counting the lines of a prayer-book's page or following the tributaries in the grain of the pew in front; but on this Sunday he sat alert, finding every word of the discourse applicable to himself.

On other Sundays the first sentence of the Offertory would have passed unheeded in the familiarity of its repetition, but this morning it took him back to that night in Church Cove when he saw the glow-worm by the edge of the tide and made up his mind to be a lighthouse-keeper.

Let your light so shine before men, that they may see your good works, and glorify your Father which is in heaven.

"I will be a priest," Mark vowed to himself.

Give grace, O heavenly Father, to all Bishops and Curates that they may both by their life and doctrines set forth thy true and lively word, and rightly and duly administer thy holy Sacraments.

"I will, I will," he vowed.

Hear what comfortable words our Saviour Christ saith unto all that truly turn to him. Come unto me all that travail and are heavy laden, and I will refresh you.

Mark prayed that with such words he might when he was a priest bring consolation.

Through Jesus Christ our Lord; according to whose most true promise, the Holy Ghost came down as at this time from heaven with a sudden great sound, as it had been a mighty wind, in the likeness of fiery tongues, lighting upon the Apostles, to teach them and to lead them to all truth;

The red chasuble of the priest glowed with Pentecostal light.

giving them both the gift of divers languages, and also boldness with fervent seal constantly to preach the Gospel unto all nations; whereby we have been brought out of darkness and error into the clear light and true knowledge of thee, and of thy Son Jesus Christ.

And when after this proper preface of Whit-sunday, which seemed to Mark to be telling him what was expected of his priesthood by God, the quire sang the Sanctus, *Therefore with Angels and Archangels, and with all the company of heaven, we laud and magnify thy glorious Name; evermore praising thee, and saying, Holy, Holy, Holy, Lord God of Hosts, heaven and earth are full of thy glory: Glory be to thee, O Lord most High. Amen,* that sublime proclamation spoke the fullness of his aspiring heart.

Mark came out of church with the rest of the congregation, and walked down the road toward the roofs of the little village, on the outskirts of which he could not help stopping to admire a small garden full of pinks in front of two thatched cottages that had evidently been made into one house. While he was standing there looking over the trim quickset hedge, an old lady with silvery hair came slowly down the road, paused a moment by the gate before she went in, and then asked Mark if she had not seen him in church. Mark felt embarrassed at being discovered looking over a hedge into somebody's garden; but he managed to murmur an affirmative and turned to go away.

185

"Stop," said the old lady waving at him her ebony crook, "do not run away, young gentleman. I see that you admire my garden. Pray step inside and look more closely at it."

Mark thought at first by her manner of speech that she was laughing at him; but soon perceiving that she was in earnest he followed her inside, and walked behind her along the narrow winding paths, nodding with an appearance of profound interest when she poked at some starry clump and invited his admiration. As they drew nearer the house, the smell of the pinks was merged in the smell of hot roast beef, and Mark discovered that he was hungry, so hungry indeed that he felt he could not stay any longer to be tantalized by the odours of the Sunday dinner, but must go off and find an inn where he could obtain bread and cheese as quickly as possible. He was preparing an excuse to get away, when the garden wicket clicked, and looking up he saw the fair priest coming down the path toward them accompanied by two ladies, one of whom resembled him so closely that Mark was sure she was his sister. The other, who looked windblown in spite of the serene June weather, had a nervous energy that contrasted with the demeanour of the other two, whose deliberate pace seemed to worry her so that she was continually two yards ahead and turning round as if to urge them to walk more quickly.

The old lady must have guessed Mark's intention, for raising her stick she forbade him to move, and before he had time to mumble an apology and flee she was introducing the newcomers to him.

"This is my daughter Miriam," she said pointing to one who resembled her brother. "And this is my daughter Esther. And this is my son, the Vicar. What is your name?"

Mark told her, and he should have liked to ask what hers was, but he felt too shy.

"You're going to stay and have lunch with us, I hope?" asked the Vicar.

Mark had no idea how to reply. He was much afraid that if he accepted he should be seeming to have hung about by the Vicarage gate in order to be invited. On the other hand he did not know how to refuse. It would be absurd to say that he had to get home, because they would ask him where he lived, and at this hour of the morning he could scarcely pretend that he expected to be back in time for lunch twelve miles and more from where he was.

"Of course he's going to stay," said the old lady.

And of course Mark did stay; a delightful lunch it was too, on chairs covered with blue holland in a green shadowed room that smelt of dryness and ancientry. After lunch Mark sat for a while with the Vicar in his study, which was small and intimate with its two armchairs and bookshelves reaching to the ceiling all round. He had not yet managed to find out his name, and as it was obviously too late to ask as this stage of their acquaintanceship he supposed that he should have to wait until he left the Vicarage and could ask somebody in the village, of which by the way he also did not know the name.

"Lidderdale," the Vicar was saying meditatively, "Lidderdale. I wonder if you were a relative of the famous Lidderdale of St. Wilfred's?"

Mark flushed with a mixture of self-consciousness and pleasure to hear his father spoken of as famous, and when he explained who he was he flushed still more deeply to hear his father's work praised with such enthusiasm.

"And do you hope to be a priest yourself?"

"Why, yes I do rather," said Mark.

"Splendid! Capital!" cried the Vicar, his kindly blue eye beaming with approval of Mark's intention.

Presently Mark was talking to him as though he had known him for years.

"There's no reason why you shouldn't be confirmed here," the Vicar said. "No reason at all. I'll mention it to the Bishop, and if you like I'll write to your uncle. I shall feel justified in interfering on account of your father's opinions. We all look upon him as one of the great pioneers of the Movement. You must come over and lunch with us again next Sunday. My mother will be delighted to see you. She's a dear old thing, isn't she? I'm going to hand you over to her now and my youngest sister. My other sister and I have got Sunday schools to deal with. Have another cigarette? No. Quite right. You oughtn't to smoke too much at your age. Only just fifteen, eh? By Jove, I suppose you oughtn't to have smoked at all. But what rot. You'd only smoke all the more if it was absolutely forbidden. Wisdom! Wisdom! Wisdom with the young! You don't mind being called young? I've known boys who hated the epithet."

Mark was determined to show his new friend that he did not object to being called young, and he could think of no better way to do it than by asking him his name, thus proving that he did not mind if such a question did make him look ridiculous.

"Ogilvie—Stephen Ogilvie. My dear boy, it's we who ought to be ashamed of ourselves for not having had the gumption to enlighten you. How on earth were you to know without asking? Now, look here, I must run. I expect you'll be wanting to get home, or I'd suggest your staying until I get back, but I must lie low after tea and think out my sermon. Look here, come over to lunch on Saturday, haven't you a bicycle? You could get over from Slowbridge by one o'clock, and after lunch we'll have a good tramp in the woods. Splendid!"

Then chanting the *Dies Irae* in a cheerful tenor the Reverend Stephen Ogilvie hurried off to his Sunday School. Mark said good-bye to Mrs. Ogilvie with an assured politeness that was typical of his new found ease; and when he started on his long walk back to Slowbridge he felt inclined to leap in the air and wake with shouts the slumberous Sabbath afternoon, proclaiming the glory of life, the joy of living.

Mark had not expected his uncle to welcome his friendship with the Vicar of Meade Cantorum; but he had supposed that after a few familiar sneers he should be allowed to go his own way with nothing worse than silent disapproval brooding over his perverse choice. He was surprised by the vehemence of his uncle's opposition, and it must be added that he thoroughly enjoyed it. The experience of that Whit-sunday had been too rich not to be of enduring importance to his development in any case; but the behaviour of Uncle Henry made it more important, because all this criticism helped Mark to put his opinions into shape, consolidated the position he had taken up, sharpened his determination to advance along the path he had discovered for himself, and gave him an immediate target for arrows that might otherwise have been shot into the air until his quiver was empty.

"Mr. Ogilvie knew my father."

"That has nothing to do with the case," said Uncle Henry.

"I think it has."

"Do not be insolent, Mark. I've noticed lately a most unpleasant note in your voice, an objectionably defiant note which I simply will not tolerate."

"But do you really mean that I'm not to go and see Mr. Ogilvie?"

"It would have been more courteous if Mr. Ogilvie had given himself the trouble of writing to me, your guardian, before inviting you out to lunch and I don't know what not besides."

"He said he would write to you."

"I don't want to embark on a correspondence with him," Uncle Henry exclaimed petulantly. "I know the man by reputation. A bigoted Ritualist. A Romanizer of the worst type. He'll only fill your head with a lot of effeminate nonsense, and that at a time when it's particularly necessary for you to concentrate upon your work. Don't forget that this is your last year of school. I advise you to make the most of it."

"I've asked Mr. Ogilvie to prepare me for confirmation," said Mark, who was determined to goad his uncle into losing his temper.

"Then you deserve to be thrashed."

"Look here, Uncle Henry," Mark began; and while he was speaking he was aware that he was stronger than his uncle now and looking across at his aunt he perceived that she was just a ball of badly wound wool lying in a chair. "Look here, Uncle Henry, it's quite useless for you to try to stop my going to Meade Cantorum, because I'm going there whenever I'm asked and I'm going to be confirmed there, because you promised Mother you wouldn't interfere with my religion."

"Your religion!" broke in Mr. Lidderdale, scornful both of the pronoun and the substantive.

"It's no use your losing your temper or arguing with me or doing anything except letting me go my own way, because that's what I intend to do."

Aunt Helen half rose in her chair upon an impulse to protect her brother against Mark's violence.

"And you can't cure me with Gregory Powder," he said. "Nor with Senna nor with Licorice nor even with Cascara."

"Your behaviour, my boy, is revolting," said Mr. Lidderdale. "A young Mohawk would not talk to his guardians as you are talking to me."

"Well, I don't want you to think I'm going to obey you if you forbid me to go to Meade Cantorum," said Mark. "I'm sorry I was rude, Aunt Helen. I oughtn't to have spoken to you like that. And I'm sorry, Uncle Henry, to seem ungrateful after what you've done for me." And then lest his uncle should think that he was surrendering he quickly added: "But I'm going to Meade Cantorum on Saturday." And like most people who know their own minds Mark had his own way.

CHAPTER XI
MEADE CANTORUM

Mark did not suffer from "churchiness" during this period. His interest in religion, although it resembled the familiar conversions of adolescence, was a real resurrection of emotions which had been stifled by these years at Haverton House following upon the paralyzing grief of his mother's death. Had he been in contact during that time with an influence like the Vicar of Meade Cantorum, he would probably have escaped those ashen years, but as Mr. Ogilvie pointed out to him, he would also never have received such evidence of God's loving kindness as was shown to him upon that Whit-sunday morning.

"If in the future, my dear boy, you are ever tempted to doubt the wisdom of Almighty God, remember what was vouchsafed to you at a moment when you seemed to have no reason for any longer existing, so black was your world. Remember how you caught sight of yourself in that pool and shrank away in horror from the vision. I envy you, Mark. I have never been granted such a revelation of myself."

"You were never so ugly," said Mark.

"My dear boy, we are all as ugly as the demons of Hell if we are allowed to see ourselves as we really are. But God only grants that to a few brave spirits whom he consecrates to his service and whom he fortifies afterwards by proving to them that, no matter how great the horror of their self-recognition, the Holy Ghost is within them to comfort them. I don't suppose that many human beings are granted such an experience as yours. I myself tremble at the thought of it, knowing that God considers me too weak a subject for such a test."

"Oh, Mr. Ogilvie," Mark expostulated.

"I'm not talking to you as Mark Lidderdale, but as the recipient of the grace of God, to one who before my own unworthy eyes has been lightened by celestial fire. *Mine eyes have seen thy salvation, O Lord.* As for yourself, my dear boy, I pray always that you may sustain your part, that you will never allow the memory of this Whitsuntide to be obscured by the fogs of this world and that you will always bear in mind that having been given more talents by God a sharper account will be taken of the use you make of them. Don't think I'm doubting your steadfastness, old man, I believe in it. Do you hear? I believe in it absolutely. But Catholic doctrine, which is the sum of humanity's knowledge of God and than which nothing more can be known of God until we see Him face to face, insists upon good works, demanding as it were a practical demonstration to the rest of the world of the grace of God within you. You remember St. Paul? *Faith, Hope, and Love. But the greatest of these is Love.* The greatest because the least individual. Faith will move mountains, but so will Love. That's the trouble with so many godly Protestants. They are inclined to stay satisfied with their own godliness, although the best of them like the Quakers are examples that ought to make most of us Catholics ashamed of ourselves. And one thing more, old man, before we get off this subject, don't forget that your experience is a mercy accorded to you by the death of our Lord Jesus Christ. You owe to His infinite Love your new life. What was granted to you was the visible apprehension of the fact of Holy Baptism, and don't forget St. John the Baptist's words: *I indeed baptize you with water unto repentance, but he that cometh after me is mightier than I. He shall baptise you with the Holy Ghost, and with fire: whose fan is in his hand, and he will thoroughly purge his floor, and gather his wheat into the garner; but he will burn up the chaff with unquenchable fire.* Those are great words for you to think of now, and during this long Trinitytide which is symbolical of what one might call the humdrum of religious life, the day in day out sticking to it, make a resolution never to say mechanically *The grace of our Lord Jesus Christ, and the love of God and the fellowship of the Holy Ghost, be with us all evermore. Amen.* If you always remember to say those wonderful words from the heart and not merely with the lips, you will each time you say them marvel more and more at the great condescension of Almighty God in favouring you, as He has favoured you, by teaching you the meaning of these words Himself in a way that no poor mortal priest, however eloquent, could teach you it. On that night when you watched beside the glow-worm at the sea's edge the grace of our Lord gave you an apprehension, child as you were, of the love of God, and now once more the grace of our Lord gives you the realization of the fellowship of the Holy Ghost. I don't want to spoil your wonderful experience with my parsonic discoursing; but, Mark, don't look back from the plough."

Uncle Henry found it hard to dispose of words like these when he deplored his nephew's collapse into ritualism.

"You really needn't bother about the incense and the vestments," Mark assured him. "I like incense and vestments; but I don't think they're the most important things in religion. You couldn't find anybody more evangelical than Mr. Ogilvie, though he doesn't call himself evangelical, or his party the Evangelical party. It's no use your trying to argue me out of what I believe. I know I'm believing what it's right for me to believe. When I'm older I shall try to make everybody else believe in my way, because I should like everybody else to feel as happy as I do. Your religion doesn't make you feel happy, Uncle Henry!"

"Leave the room," was Mr. Lidderdale's reply. "I won't stand this kind of talk from a boy of your age."

Although Mark had only claimed from his uncle the right to believe what it was right for him to believe, the richness of his belief presently began to seem too much for one. His nature was generous in everything, and he felt that he must share this happiness with somebody else. He regretted the death of poor Mr. Spaull, for he was sure that he could have persuaded poor Mr. Spaull to cut off his yellow moustache and become a Catholic. Mr. Palmer was of course hopeless: Saint Augustine of Hippo, St. Paul himself even, would have found it hard to deal with Mr. Palmer; as for the new master, Mr. Blumey, with his long nose and long chin and long frock coat and long boots, he was obviously absorbed by the problems of mathematics and required nothing more.

Term came to an end, and during the holidays Mark was able to spend most of his time at Meade Cantorum. He had always been a favourite of Mrs. Ogilvie since that Whit-sunday nearly two months ago when she saw him looking at her garden and invited him in, and every time he revisited the Vicarage he had devoted some of his time to helping her weed or prune or do whatever she wanted to do in her garden. He was also on friendly terms with Miriam, the elder of Mr. Ogilvie's two sisters, who was very like her brother in appearance and who gave to the house the decorous loving care he gave to the church. And however enthralling her domestic ministrations, she had always time to attend every service; while, so well ordered was her manner of life, her religious duties never involved the household in discomfort. She never gave the impression that so many religious women give of going to church in a fever of self-gratification, to which everything and everybody around her must be subordinated. The practice of her religion was woven into her life like the strand of wool on which all the others depend, but which itself is no more conspicuous than any of the other strands. With so many women religion is a substitute for something else; with Miriam Ogilvie everything else was made as nearly and as beautifully as it could be made a substitute for religion. Mark was intensely aware of her holiness, but he was equally aware of her capable well-tended hands and of her chatelaine glittering in and out of a lawn apron. One tress of her abundant hair was grey, which stood out against the dark background of the rest and gave her a serene purity, an austere strength, but yet like a nun's coif seemed to make the face beneath more youthful, and like a cavalier's plume more debonair. She could not have been over thirty-five when Mark first knew her, perhaps not so much; but he thought of her as ageless in the way a child thinks of its mother, and if any woman should ever be able to be to him something of what his mother had been, Mark thought that Miss Ogilvie might.

Esther Ogilvie the other sister was twenty-five. She told Mark this when he imitated the villagers by addressing her as Miss Essie and she ordered him to call her Esther. He might have supposed from this that she intended to confer upon him a measure of friendliness, even of sisterly affection; but on the contrary she either ignored him altogether or gave him the impression that she considered his frequent visits to Meade Cantorum a nuisance. Mark was sorry that she felt like that toward him, because she seemed unhappy, and in his desire for everybody to be happy he would have liked to proclaim how suddenly and unexpectedly happiness may come. As a sister of the Vicar of the parish, she went to church regularly, but Mark did not think that she was there except in body. He once looked across at her open prayer book during the *Magnificat*, and noticed that she was reading the Tables of Kindred and Affinity. Now, Mark knew from personal experience that when one is reduced to reading the Tables of Kindred and Affinity it argues a mind untouched by the reality of worship. In his own case, when he sat beside his uncle and aunt in the dreary Slowbridge church of their choice, it had been nothing more than a sign of his own inward dreariness to read the Tables of Kindred and Affinity or speculate upon the Paschal full moons from the year 2200 to the year 2299 inclusive. But St. Margaret's, Meade Cantorum, was a different church from St. Jude's, Slowbridge, and for Esther Ogilvie to ignore the joyfulness of worshipping there in order to ponder idly the complexities of Golden Numbers and Dominical Letters could not be ascribed to inward dreariness. Besides, she wasn't dreary. Once Mark saw her coming down a woodland glade and almost turned aside to avoid meeting her, because she looked so fay with her wild blue eyes and her windblown hair, the colour of last year's bracken after rain. She seemed at once the pursued and the pursuer, and Mark felt that whichever she was he would be in the way.

"Taking a quick walk by myself," she called out to him as they passed.

No, she was certainly not dreary. But what was she?

Mark abandoned the problem of Esther in the pleasure of meeting the Reverend Oliver Dorward, who arrived one afternoon at the Vicarage with a large turbot for Mrs. Ogilvie, and six Flemish candlesticks for the Vicar, announcing that he wanted to stay a week before being inducted to the living of Green Lanes in the County of Southampton, to which he had recently been presented by Lord Chatsea. Mark liked him from the first moment he saw him pacing the Vicarage garden in a soutane, buckled shoes, and beaver hat, and he could not understand why Mr. Ogilvie, who had often laughed about Dorward's eccentricity, should now that he had an opportunity of enjoying it once more be so cross about his friend's arrival and so ready to hand him over to Mark to be entertained.

"Just like Ogilvie," said Dorward confidentially, when he and Mark went for a walk on the afternoon of his arrival. "He wants spiking up. They get very slack and selfish, these country clergy. Time he gave up Meade Cantorum. He's been here nearly ten years. Too long, nine years too long. Hasn't been to his duties since Easter. Scandalous, you know. I asked him, as soon as I'd explained to the cook about the turbot, when he went last, and he was bored. Nice old pussy cat, the mother. Hullo, is that the *Angelus*? Damn, I knelt on a thistle."

"It isn't the *Angelus*," said Mark quietly. "It's the bell on that cow."

But Mr. Dorward had finished his devotion before he answered.

"I was half way through before you told me. You should have spoken sooner."

"Well, I spoke as soon as I could."

"Very cunning of Satan," said Dorward meditatively. "Induced a cow to simulate the *Angelus*, and planted a thistle just where I was bound to kneel. Cunning. Cunning. Very cunning. I must go back now and confess to Ogilvie. Good example. Wait a minute, I'll confess to-morrow before Morning Prayer. Very good for Ogilvie's congregation. They're stuffy, very stuffy. It'll shake them. It'll shake Ogilvie too. Are you staying here to-night?"

"No, I shall bicycle back to Slowbridge and bicycle over to Mass to-morrow."

"Ridiculous. Stay the night. Didn't Ogilvie invite you?"

Mark shook his head.

"Scandalous lack of hospitality. They're all alike these country clergy. I'm tired of this walk. Let's go back and look after the turbot. Are you a good cook?"

"I can boil eggs and that sort of thing," said Mark.

"What sort of things? An egg is unique. There's nothing like an egg. Will you serve my Mass on Monday? Saying Mass for Napoleon on Monday."

"For whom?" Mark exclaimed.

"Napoleon, with a special intention for the conversion of the present government in France. Last Monday I said a Mass for Shakespeare, with a special intention for an improvement in contemporary verse."

Mark supposed that Mr. Dorward must be joking, and his expression must have told as much to the priest, who murmured:

"Nothing to laugh at. Nothing to laugh at."

"No, of course not," said Mark feeling abashed. "But I'm afraid I shouldn't be able to serve you. I've never had any practice."

"Perfectly easy. Perfectly easy. I'll give you a book when we get back."

Mark bicycled home that afternoon with a tall thin volume called *Ritual Notes*, so tall that when it was in his pocket he could feel it digging him in the ribs every time he was riding up the least slope. That night in his bedroom he practised with the help of the wash-stand and its accessories the technique of serving at Low Mass, and in his enthusiasm he bicycled over to Meade Cantorum in time to attend both the Low Mass at seven said by Mr. Dorward and the Low Mass at eight said by Mr. Ogilvie. He was able to detect mistakes that were made by the village boys who served that Sunday morning, and he vowed to himself that the Monday Mass for the Emperor Napoleon should not be disfigured by such inaccuracy or clumsiness. He declined the usual invitation to stay to supper after Evening Prayer that he might have time to make perfection more perfect in the seclusion of his own room, and when he set out about six o'clock of a sun-drowsed morning in early August, apart from a faint anxiety about the *Lavabo*, he felt secure of his accomplishment. It was only when he reached the church that he remembered he had made no arrangement about borrowing a cassock or a cotta, an omission that in the mood of grand seriousness in which he had undertaken his responsibility seemed nothing less than abominable. He did not like to go to the Vicarage and worry Mr. Ogilvie who could scarcely fail to be amused, even contemptuously amused at such an ineffective beginning. Besides, ever since Mr. Dorward's arrival the Vicar had been slightly irritable.

While Mark was wondering what was the best thing to do, Miss Hatchett, a pious old maid who spent her nights in patience and sleep, her days in worship and weeding, came hurrying down the churchyard path.

"I am not late, am I?" she exclaimed. "I never heard the bell. I was so engrossed in pulling out one of those dreadful sow-thistles that when my maid came running out and said 'Oh, Miss Hatchett, it's gone the five to, you'll be late,' I just ran, and now I've brought my trowel and left my prayer book on the path. . . ."

"I'm just going to ring the bell now," said Mark, in whom the horror of another omission had been rapidly succeeded by an almost unnatural composure.

"Oh, what a relief," Miss Hatchett sighed. "Are you sure I shall have time to get my breath, for I know Mr. Ogilvie would dislike to hear me panting in church?"

"Mr. Ogilvie isn't saying Mass this morning."

"Not saying Mass?" repeated the old maid in such a dejected tone of voice that, when a small cloud passed over the face of the sun, it seemed as if the natural scene desired to accord with the chill cast upon her spirit by Mark's announcement.

"Mr. Dorward is saying Mass," he told her, and poor Miss Hatchett must pretend with a forced smile that her blank look had been caused by the prospect of being deprived of Mass when really. . . .

But Mark was not paying any more attention to Miss Hatchett. He was standing under the bell, gazing up at the long rope and wondering what manner of sound he should evoke. He took a breath and pulled; the rope quivered with such an effect of life that he recoiled from the new force he had conjured into being, afraid of his handiwork, timid of the clamour that would resound. No louder noise ensued than might have been given forth by a can kicked into the gutter. Mark pulled again more strongly, and the bell began to chime, irregularly at first with alternations of sonorous and feeble note; at last, however, when the rhythm was established with such command and such insistence that the ringer, looking over his shoulder to the south door, half expected to see a stream of perturbed Christians hurrying to obey its summons. But there was only poor Miss Hatchett sitting in the porch and fanning herself with a handkerchief.

Mark went on ringing. . . .

Clang—clang—clang! All the holy Virgins were waving their palms. Clang—clang—clang! All the blessed Doctors and Confessors were twanging their harps to the clanging. Clang—clang—clang! All the holy Saints and Martyrs were tossing their haloes in the air as schoolboys toss their caps. Clang—clang—clang! Angels, Archangels, and Principalities with faces that shone like brass and with forms that quivered like flames thronged the noise. Clang—clang—clang! Virtues, Powers, and Dominations bade the morning stars sing to the ringing. Clang—clang—clang! The ringing reached up to the green-winged Thrones who sustain the seat of the Most High. Clang—clang—clang! The azure Cherubs heard the bells within their contemplation: the scarlet Seraphs felt them within their love. Clang—clang—clang! The lidless Eye of God looked down, and Miss Hatchett supposing it to be the sun crossed over to the other side of the porch.

Clang—clang—clang—clang—clang—clang—clang—clang. . . .

"Hasn't Dorward come in yet? It's five past eight already. Go on ringing for a little while. I'll go and see how long he'll be."

Mark in the absorption of ringing the bell had not noticed the Vicar's approach, and he was gone again before he remembered that he wanted to borrow a cassock and a cotta. Had he been rude? Would Mr. Ogilvie think it cheek to ring the bell without asking his permission first? But before these unanswered questions had had time to spoil the rhythm of his ringing, the Vicar came back with Mr. Dorward, and the congregation, that is to say Miss Hatchett and Miss Ogilvie, was already kneeling in its place.

Mark in a cassock that was much too long for him and in a cotta that was in the same ratio as much too short preceded Mr. Dorward from the sacristy to the altar. A fear seized him that in spite of all his practice he was kneeling on the wrong side of the priest; he forgot the first responses; he was sure the Sanctus-bell was too far away; he wished that Mr. Dorward would not mutter quite so inaudibly. Gradually, however, the meetness of the gestures prescribed for him by the ancient ritual cured his self-consciousness and included him in its pattern, so that now for the first time he was aware of the significance of the preface to the Sanctus: *It is very meet, right, and our bounden duty, that we should at all times, and in all places, give thanks unto thee, O Lord, Holy Father, Almighty Everlasting God.*

Twenty minutes ago when he was ringing the church bell Mark had experienced the rapture of creative noise, the sense of individual triumph over time and space; and the sound of his ringing came back to him from the vaulted roof of the church with such exultation as the missal thrush may know when he sits high above the fretted boughs of an oak and his music plunges forth upon the January wind. Now when Mark was ringing the Sanctus-bell, it was with a sense of his place in the scheme of worship. If one listens to the twitter of a single linnet in open country or to the buzz of a solitary fly upon a window pane, how incredible it is that myriads of them twittering and buzzing together should be the song of April, the murmur of June. And this Sanctus-bell that tinkled so inadequately, almost so frivolously when sounded by a server in Meade Cantorum church, was yet part of an unimaginable volume of worship that swelled in unison with Angels and Archangels lauding and magnifying the Holy Name. The importance of ceremony was as deeply impressed upon Mark that morning as if he had been formally initiated to great mysteries. His coming confirmation, which had been postponed from July 2nd to September 8th seemed much more momentous now than it seemed yesterday. It was no longer a step to Communion, but was apprehended as a Sacrament itself, and though Mr. Ogilvie was inclined to regret the ritualistic development of his catechumen, Mark derived much strength from what was really the awakening in him of a sense of form, which more than anything makes emotion durable. Perhaps Ogilvie may have been a little jealous of Dorward's influence; he also was really alarmed at the prospect, as he said, of so much fire being wasted upon poker-work. In the end what between Dorward's encouragement of Mark's ritualistic tendencies and the "spiking up" process to which he was himself being subjected, Ogilvie was glad when a fortnight later Dorward took himself off to his own living, and he expressed a hope that Mark would perceive Dorward in his true proportions as a dear good fellow, perfectly sincere, but just a little, well, not exactly mad, but so eccentric as sometimes to do more harm than good to the Movement. Mark was shrewd enough to notice that however much he grumbled about his friend's visit Mr. Ogilvie was sufficiently influenced by that visit to put into practice much of the advice to which he had taken exception. The influence of Dorward upon Mark did not stop with his begetting in him an appreciation of the value of form in worship. When Mark told Mr. Ogilvie that he intended to become a priest, Mr. Ogilvie was impressed by the manifestation of the Divine Grace, but he did not offer many practical suggestions for Mark's immediate future. Dorward on the contrary attached as much importance to the manner in which he was to become a priest.

"Oxford," Mr. Dorward pronounced. "And then Glastonbury."

"Glastonbury?"

"Glastonbury Theological College."

Now to Mark Oxford was a legendary place to which before he met Mr. Dorward he would never have aspired. Oxford at Haverton House was merely an abstraction to which a certain number of people offered an illogical allegiance in order to create an excuse for argument and strife. Sometimes Mark had gazed at Eton and wondered vaguely about existence there; sometimes he had gazed at the towers of Windsor and wondered what the Queen ate for breakfast. Oxford was far more remote than either of these, and yet when Mr. Dorward said that he must go there his heart leapt as if to some recognized ambition long ago buried and now abruptly resuscitated.

"I've always been Oxford," he admitted.

When Mr. Dorward had gone, Mark asked Mr. Ogilvie what he thought about Oxford.

"If you can afford to go there, my dear boy, of course you ought to go."

"Well, I'm pretty sure I can't afford to. I don't think I've got any money at all. My mother left some money, but my uncle says that that will come in useful when I'm articled to this solicitor, Mr. Hitchcock. Oh, but if I become a priest I can't become a solicitor, and perhaps I could have that money. I don't know how much it is . . . I think five hundred pounds. Would that be enough?"

"With care and economy," said Mr. Ogilvie. "And you might win a scholarship."

"But I'm leaving school at the end of this year."

Mr. Ogilvie thought that it would be wiser not to say anything to his uncle until after Mark had been confirmed. He advised him to work hard meanwhile and to keep in mind the possibility of having to win a scholarship.

The confirmation was held on the feast of the Nativity of the Blessed Virgin. Mark made his first Confession on the vigil, his first Communion on the following Sunday.

CHAPTER XII
THE POMEROY AFFAIR

Mark was so much elated to find himself a fully equipped member of the Church Militant that he looked about him again to find somebody whom he could make as happy as himself. He even considered the possibility of converting his uncle, and spent the Sunday evening before term began in framing inexpugnable arguments to be preceded by unanswerable questions; but always when he was on the point of speaking he was deterred by the lifelessness of his uncle. No eloquence could irrigate his arid creed and make that desert blossom now. And yet, Mark thought, he ought to remember that in the eyes of the world he owed his uncle everything. What did he owe him in the sight of God? Gratitude? Gratitude for what? Gratitude for spending a certain amount of money on him. Once more Mark opened his mouth to repay his debt by offering Uncle Henry Eternal Life. But Uncle Henry fancied himself already in possession of Eternal Life. He definitely labelled himself Evangelical. And again Mark prepared one of his unanswerable questions.

"Mark," said Mr. Lidderdale. "If you can't keep from yawning you'd better get off to bed. Don't forget school begins to-morrow, and you must make the most of your last term."

Mark abandoned for ever the task of converting Uncle Henry, and pondered his chance of doing something with Aunt Helen. There instead of exsiccation he was confronted by a dreadful humidity, an infertile ooze that seemed almost less susceptible to cultivation than the other.

"And I really don't owe *her* anything," he thought. "Besides, it isn't that I want to save people from damnation. I want people to be happy. And it isn't quite that even. I want them to understand how happy I am. I want people to feel fond of their pillows when they turn over to go to sleep, because next morning is going to be what? Well, sort of exciting."

Mark suddenly imagined how splendid it would be to give some of his happiness to Esther Ogilvie; but a moment later he decided that it would be rather cheek, and he abandoned the idea of converting Esther Ogilvie. He fell back on wishing again that Mr. Spaull had not died; in him he really would have had an ideal subject.

In the end Mark fixed upon a boy of his own age, one of the many sons of a Papuan missionary called Pomeroy who was glad to have found in Mr. Lidderdale a cheap and evangelical schoolmaster. Cyril Pomeroy was a blushful, girlish youth, clever at the routine of school work, but in other ways so much undeveloped as to give an impression of stupidity. The notion of pointing out to him the beauty and utility of the Catholic religion would probably never have occurred to Mark if the boy himself had not approached him with a direct complaint of the dreariness of home life. Mark had never had any intimate friends at Haverton House; there was something in its atmosphere that was hostile to intimacy. Cyril Pomeroy appealed to that idea of romantic protection which is the common appendage of adolescence, and is the cause of half the extravagant affection at which maturity is wont to laugh. In the company of Cyril, Mark felt ineffably old than which upon the threshold of sixteen there is no sensation more grateful; and while the intercourse flattered his own sense of superiority he did feel that he had much to offer his friend. Mark regarded Cyril's case as curable if the right treatment were followed, and every evening after school during the veiled summer of a fine October he paced the Slowbridge streets with his willing proselyte, debating the gravest issues of religious practice, the subtlest varieties of theological opinion. He also lent Cyril suitable books, and finally he demanded from him as a double tribute to piety and friendship that he should prove his metal by going to Confession. Cyril, who was incapable of refusing whatever Mark demanded, bicycled timorously behind him to Meade Cantorum one Saturday afternoon, where he gulped out the table of his sins to Mr. Ogilvie, whom Mark had fetched from the Vicarage with the urgency of one who fetches a midwife. Nor was he at all abashed when Mr. Ogilvie was angry for not having been told that Cyril's father would have disapproved of his son's confession. He argued that the priest was applying social standards to religious principles, and in the end he enjoyed the triumph of hearing Mr. Ogilvie admit that perhaps he was right.

"I know I'm right. Come on, Cyril. You'd better get back home now. Oh, and I say, Mr. Ogilvie, can I borrow for Cyril some of the books you lent me?"

The priest was amused that Mark did not ask him to lend the books to his friend, but to himself. However, when he found that the neophyte seemed to flourish under Mark's assiduous priming, and that the fundamental weakness of his character was likely to be strengthened by what, though it was at present nothing more than an interest in religion, might later on develop into a profound conviction of the truths of Christianity, Ogilvie overlooked his scruples about deceiving parents and encouraged the boy as much as he could.

"But I hope your manipulation of the plastic Cyril isn't going to turn *you* into too much of a ritualist," he said to Mark. "It's splendid of course that you should have an opportunity so young of proving your ability to get round people in the right way. But let it be the right way, old man. At the beginning you were full of the happiness, the secret of which you burnt to impart to others. That happiness was the revelation of the Holy Spirit dwelling in you as He dwells in all Christian souls. I am sure that the eloquent exposition I lately overheard of the propriety of fiddle-backed chasubles and the impropriety of Gothic ones doesn't mean that you are in any real danger of supposing chasubles to be anything more important relatively than, say, the uniform of a soldier compared with his valour and obedience and selflessness. Now don't overwhelm me for a minute or two. I haven't finished what I want to say. I wasn't speaking sarcastically when I said that, and I wasn't criticizing you. But you are not Cyril. By God's grace you have been kept from the temptations of the flesh. Yes, I know the subject is distasteful to you. But you are old enough to understand that your fastidiousness, if it isn't to be priggish, must be safeguarded by your humility. I didn't mean to sandwich a sermon to you between my remarks on Cyril, but your disdainful upper lip compelled that testimony. Let us leave you and your virtues alone. Cyril is weak. He's the weak pink type that may fall to women or drink or anything in fact where an opportunity is given him of being influenced by a stronger character than his own. At the moment he's being influenced by you to go to Confession, and say his rosary, and hear Mass, and enjoy all the other treats that our holy religion gives us. In addition to that he's enjoying them like the proverbial stolen fruit. You were very severe with me when I demurred at hearing his confession without authority from his father; but I don't like stolen fruit, and I'm not sure even now if I was right in yielding on that point. I shouldn't have yielded if I hadn't felt that Cyril might be hurt in the future by my scruples. Now look here, Mark, you've got to see that I don't regret my surrender. If that youth doesn't get from religion what I hope and pray he will get . . . but let that point alone. My scruples are my own affair. Your convictions are your own affair. But Cyril is our joint affair. He's your convert, but he's my penitent; and Mark, don't overdecorate your building until you're sure the foundations are well and truly laid."

Mark was never given an opportunity of proving the excellence of his methods by the excellence of Cyril's life, because on the morning after this conversation, which took place one wet Sunday evening in Advent he was sent for by his uncle, who demanded to know the meaning of This. This was a letter from the Reverend Eustace Pomeroy.

The Limes,
38, Cranborne Road,
Slowbridge.
December 9.
Dear Mr. Lidderdale,

My son Cyril will not attend school for the rest of this term. Yesterday evening, being confined to the house by fever, I went up to his bedroom to verify a reference in a book I had recently lent him to assist his divinity studies under you. When I took down the book from the shelf I noticed several books hidden away behind, and my curiosity being aroused I examined them, in case they should be works of an unpleasant nature. To my horror and disgust, I found that they were all works of an extremely Popish character, most of them belonging to a clergyman in this neighbourhood called Ogilvie, whose illegal practices have for several years been a scandal to this diocese. These I am sending to the Bishop that he may see with his own eyes the kind of propaganda that is going on. Two of the books, inscribed Mark Lidderdale, are evidently the property of your nephew to whom I suppose my son is indebted for this wholesale corruption. On questioning my son I found him already so sunk in the mire of the pernicious doctrines he has imbibed that he actually defied his own father. I thrashed him severely in spite of my fever, and he is now under lock and key in his bedroom where he will remain until he sails with me to Sydney next week whither I am summoned to the conference of Australasian missionaries. During the voyage I shall wrestle with the demon that has entered into my son and endeavour to persuade him that Jesus only is necessary for salvation. And when I have done so, I shall leave him in Australia to earn his own living remote from the scene of his corruption. In the circumstances I assume that you will deduct a proportion of his school fees for this term. I know that you will be as much horrified and disgusted as I was by your nephew's conduct, and I trust that you will be able to wrestle with him in the Lord and prove to him that Jesus only is necessary to salvation.

Yours very truly,

Eustace Pomeroy.

P.S. I suggest that instead of £6 6s. 0d. I should pay £5 5s. 0d. for this term, plus, of course, the usual extras.

The pulse in Mr. Lidderdale's temple had never throbbed so remarkably as while Mark was reading this letter.

"A fine thing," he ranted, "if this story gets about in Slowbridge. A fine reward for all my kindness if you ruin my school. As for this man Ogilvie, I'll sue him for damages. Don't look at me with that expression of bestial defiance. Do you hear? What prevents my thrashing you as you deserve? What prevents me, I say?"

But Mark was not paying any attention to his uncle's fury; he was thinking about the unfortunate martyr under lock and key in The Limes, Cranborne Road, Slowbridge. He was wondering what would be the effect of this violent removal to the Antipodes and how that fundamental weakness of character would fare if Cyril were left to himself at his age.

"I think Mr. Pomeroy is a ruffian," said Mark. "Don't you, Uncle Henry? If he writes to the Bishop about Mr. Ogilvie, I shall write to the Bishop about him. I hate Protestants. I hate them."

"There's your father to the life. You'd like to burn them, wouldn't you?"

"Yes, I would," Mark declared.

"You'd like to burn me, I suppose?"

"Not you in particular."

"Will you listen to him, Helen," he shouted to his sister. "Come here and listen to him. Listen to the boy we took in and educated and clothed and fed, listen to him saying he'd like to burn his uncle. Into Mr. Hitchcock's office you go at once. No more education if this is what it leads to. Read that letter, Helen, look at that book, Helen. *Catholic Prayers for Church of England People by the Reverend A.H. Stanton.* Look at this book, Helen. *The Catholic Religion by Vernon Staley.* No wonder you hate Protestants, you ungrateful boy. No wonder you're longing to burn your uncle and aunt. It'll be in the *Slowbridge Herald* to-morrow. Headlines! Ruin! They'll think I'm a Jesuit in disguise. I ought to have got a very handsome sum of money for the good-will. Go back to your class-room, and if you have a spark of affection in your nature, don't brag about this to the other boys."

Mark, pondering all the morning the best thing to do for Cyril, remembered that a boy called Hacking lived at The Laurels, 36, Cranborne Road. He did not like Hacking, but wishing to utilize his back garden for the purpose of communicating with the prisoner he made himself agreeable to him in the interval between first and second school.

"Hullo, Hacking," he began. "I say, do you want a cricket bat? I shan't be here next summer, so you may as well have mine."

Hacking looked at Mark suspicious of some hidden catch that would make him appear a fool.

"No, really I'm not ragging," said Mark. "I'll bring it round to you after dinner. I'll be at your place about a quarter to two. Wait for me, won't you?"

Hacking puzzled his brains to account for this generous whim, and at last decided that Mark must be "gone" on his sister Edith. He supposed that he ought to warn Edith to be about when Mark called; if the bat was not forthcoming he could easily prevent a meeting. The bat however turned out to be much better than he expected, and Hacking was on the point of presenting Cressida to Troilus when Troilus said:

"That's your garden at the back, isn't it?"

Hacking admitted that it was.

"It looks rather decent."

Hacking allowed modestly that it wasn't bad.

"My father's rather dead nuts on gardening. So's my kiddy sister," he added.

"I vote we go out there," Mark suggested.

"Shall I give a yell to my kiddy sister?" asked Pandarus.

"Good lord, no," Mark exclaimed. "Don't the Pomeroys live next door to you? Look here, Hacking, I want to speak to Cyril Pomeroy."

"He was absent this morning."

Mark considered Hacking as a possible adjutant to the enterprise he was plotting. That he finally decided to admit Hacking to his confidence was due less to the favourable result of the scrutiny than to the fact that unless he confided in Hacking he would find it difficult to communicate with Cyril and impossible to manage his escape. Mark aimed as high as this. His first impulse had been to approach the Vicar of Meade Cantorum, but on second thoughts he had rejected him in favour of Mr. Dorward, who was not so likely to suffer from respect for paternal authority.

"Look here, Hacking, will you swear not to say a word about what I'm going to tell you?"

"Of course," said Hacking, who scenting a scandal would have promised much more than this to obtain the details of it.

"What will you swear by?"

"Oh, anything," Hacking offered, without the least hesitation. "I don't mind what it is."

"Well, what do you consider the most sacred thing in the world?"

If Hacking had known himself, he would have said food; not knowing himself, he suggested the Bible.

"I suppose you know that if you swear something on the Bible and break your oath you can be put in prison?" Mark demanded sternly.

"Yes, of course."

The oath was administered, and Hacking waited goggle-eyed for the revelation.

"Is that all?" he asked when Mark stopped.

"Well, it's enough, isn't it? And now you've got to help him to escape."

"But I didn't swear I'd do that," argued Hacking.

"All right then. Don't. I thought you'd enjoy it."

"We should get into a row. There'd be an awful shine."

"Who's to know it's us? I've got a friend in the country. And I shall telegraph to him and ask if he'll hide Pomeroy."

Mark was not sufficiently sure of Hacking's discretion or loyalty to mention Dorward's name. After all this business wasn't just a rag.

"The first thing is for you to go out in the garden and attract Pomeroy's attention. He's locked in his bedroom."

"But I don't know which is his bedroom," Hacking objected.

"Well, you don't suppose the whole family are locked in their bedrooms, do you?" asked Mark scornfully.

"But how do you know his bedroom is on this side of the house?"

"I don't," said Mark. "That's what I want to find out. If it's in the front of the house, I shan't want your help, especially as you're so funky."

Hacking went out into the garden, and presently he came back with the news that Pomeroy was waiting outside to talk to Mark over the wall.

"Waiting outside?" Mark repeated. "What do you mean, waiting outside? How can he be waiting outside when he's locked in his bedroom?"

"But he's not," said Hacking.

Sure enough, when Mark went out he found Cyril astride the party wall between the two gardens waiting for him.

"You can't let your father drag you off to Australia like this," Mark argued. "You'll go all to pieces there. You'll lose your faith, and take to drink, and—you must refuse to go."

Cyril smiled weakly and explained to Mark that when once his father had made up his mind to do something it was impossible to stop him.

Thereupon Mark explained his scheme.

"I'll get an answer from Dorward to-night and you must escape to-morrow afternoon as soon as it's dark. Have you got a rope ladder?"

Cyril smiled more feebly than ever.

"No, I suppose you haven't. Then what you must do is tear up your sheets and let yourself down into the garden. Hacking will whistle three times if all's clear, and then you must climb over into his garden and run as hard as you can to the corner of the road where I'll be waiting for you in a cab. I'll go up to London with you and see you off from Waterloo, which is the station for Green Lanes where Father Dorward lives. You take a ticket to Galton, and I expect he'll meet you, or if he doesn't, it's only a seven mile walk. I don't know the way, but you can ask when you get to Galton. Only if you could find your way without asking it would be better, because if you're pursued and you're seen asking the way you'll be caught more easily. Now I must rush off and borrow some money from Mr. Ogilvie. No, perhaps it would rouse suspicions if I were absent from afternoon school. My uncle would be sure to guess, and—though I don't think he would—he might try to lock me up in my room. But I say," Mark suddenly exclaimed in indignation, "how on earth did you manage to come and talk to me out here?"

Cyril explained that he had only been locked in his bedroom last night when his father was so angry. He had freedom to move about in the house and garden, and, he added to Mark's annoyance, there would be no need for him to use rope ladders or sheets to escape. If Mark would tell him what time to be at the corner of the road and would wait for him a little while in case his father saw him going out and prevented him, he would easily be able to escape.

"Then I needn't have told Hacking," said Mark. "However, now I have told him, he must do something, or else he's sure to let out what he knows. I wish I knew where to get the money for the fare."

"I've got a pound in my money box."

"Have you?" said Mark, a little mortified, but at the same time relieved that he could keep Mr. Ogilvie from being involved. "Well, that ought to be enough. I've got enough to send a telegram to Dorward. As soon as I get his answer I'll send you word by Hacking. Now don't hang about in the garden all the afternoon or your people will begin to think something's up. If you could, it would be a good thing for you to be heard praying and groaning in your room."

Cyril smiled his feeble smile, and Mark felt inclined to abandon him to his fate; but he decided on reflection that the importance of vindicating the claims of the Church to a persecuted son was more important than the foolishness and the feebleness of the son.

"Do you want me to do anything more?" Hacking asked.

Mark suggested that Hacking's name and address should be given for Mr. Dorward's answer, but this Hacking refused.

"If a telegram came to our house, everybody would want to read it. Why can't it be sent to you?"

Mark sighed for his fellow-conspirator's stupidity. To this useless clod he had presented a valuable bat.

"All right," he said impatiently, "you needn't do anything more except tell Pomeroy what time he's to be at the corner of the road to-morrow."

"I'll do that, Lidderdale."

"I should think you jolly well would," Mark exclaimed scornfully.

Mark spent a long time over the telegram to Dorward; in the end he decided that it would be safer to assume that the priest would shelter and hide Cyril rather than take the risk of getting an answer. The final draft was as follows:—

Dorward Green Lanes Medworth Hants

Am sending persecuted Catholic boy by 7.30 from Waterloo Tuesday please send conveyance Mark Lidderdale.

Mark only had eightpence, and this message would cost tenpence. He took out the *am*, changed *by 7.30 from Waterloo* to *arriving 9.35* and *send conveyance* to *meet*. If he had only borrowed Cyril's sovereign, he could have been more explicit. However, he flattered himself that he was getting full value for his eightpence. He then worked out the cost of Cyril's escape.

rd Class single to Paddington

rd Class return to Paddington (fc

rd Class single Waterloo to Galt

from Paddington to Waterloo

from Waterloo to Paddington (

dwiches for Cyril and Self

ger-beer for Cyril and Self (4 bc

—

The cab of course might cost more, and he must take back the eightpence out of it for himself. But Cyril would have at least one and sixpence in his pocket when he arrived, which he could put in the offertory at the Mass of thanksgiving for his escape that he would attend on the following morning. Cyril would be useful to old Dorward, and he (Mark) would give him some tips on serving if they had an empty compartment from Slowbridge to Paddington. Mark's original intention had been to wait at the corner of Cranborne Road in a closed cab like the proverbial postchaise of elopements, but he discarded this idea for reasons of economy. He hoped that Cyril would not get frightened on the way to the station and turn back. Perhaps after all it would be wiser to order a cab and give up the ginger-beer, or pay for the ginger-beer with the money for the telegram. Once inside a cab Cyril was bound to go on. Hacking might be committed more completely to the enterprise by waiting inside until he arrived with Cyril. It was a pity that Cyril was not locked in his room, and yet when it came to it he would probably have funked letting himself down from the window by knotted sheets. Mark walked home with Hacking after school, to give his final instructions for the following day.

"I'm telling you now," he said, "because we oughtn't to be seen together at all to-morrow, in case of arousing suspicion. You must get hold of Pomeroy and tell him to run to the corner of the road at half-past-five, and jump straight into the fly that'll be waiting there with you inside."

"But where will you be?"

"I shall be waiting outside the ticket barrier with the tickets."

"Supposing he won't?"

"I'll risk seeing him once more. Go and ask if you can speak to him a minute, and tell him to come out in the garden presently. Say you've knocked a ball over or something and will Master Cyril throw it back. I say, we might really put a message inside a ball and throw it over. That was the way the Duc de Beaufort escaped in *Twenty Years After*."

Hacking looked blankly at Mark.

"But it's dark and wet," he objected. "I shouldn't knock a ball over on a wet evening like this."

"Well, the skivvy won't think of that, and Pomeroy will guess that we're trying to communicate with him."

Mark thought how odd it was that Hacking should be so utterly blind to the romance of the enterprise. After a few more objections which were disposed of by Mark, Hacking agreed to go next door and try to get the prisoner into the garden. He succeeded in this, and Mark rated Cyril for not having given him the sovereign yesterday.

"However, bunk in and get it now, because I shan't see you again till to-morrow at the station, and I must have some money to buy the tickets."

He explained the details of the escape and exacted from Cyril a promise not to back out at the last moment.

"You've got nothing to do. It's as simple as A B C. It's too simple, really, to be much of a rag. However, as it isn't a rag, but serious, I suppose we oughtn't to grumble. Now, you are coming, aren't you?"

Cyril promised that nothing but physical force should prevent him.

"If you funk, don't forget that you'll have betrayed your faith and . . ."

At this moment Mark in his enthusiasm slipped off the wall, and after uttering one more solemn injunction against backing out at the last minute he left Cyril to the protection of Angels for the next twenty-four hours.

Although he would never have admitted as much, Mark was rather astonished when Cyril actually did present himself at Slowbridge station in time to catch the 5.47 train up to town. Their compartment was not empty, so that Mark was unable to give Cyril that lesson in serving at the altar which he had intended to give him. Instead, as Cyril seemed in his reaction to the excitement of the escape likely to burst into tears at any moment, he drew for him a vivid picture of the enjoyable life to which the train was taking him.

"Father Dorward says that the country round Green Lanes is ripping. And his church is Norman. I expect he'll make you his ceremonarius. You're an awfully lucky chap, you know. He says that next Corpus Christi, he's going to have Mass on the village green. Nobody will know where you are, and I daresay later on you can become a hermit. You might become a saint. The last English saint to be canonized was St. Thomas Cantilupe of Hereford. But of course Charles the First ought to have been properly canonized. By the time you die I should think we should have got back canonization in the English Church, and if I'm alive then I'll propose your canonization. St. Cyril Pomeroy you'd be."

Such were the bright colours in which Mark painted Cyril's future; when he had watched him wave his farewells from the window of the departing train at Waterloo, he felt as if he were watching the bodily assumption of a saint.

"Where have you been all the evening?" asked Uncle Henry, when Mark came back about nine o'clock.

"In London," said Mark.

"Your insolence is becoming insupportable. Get away to your room."

It never struck Mr. Lidderdale that his nephew was telling the truth.

The hue and cry for Cyril Pomeroy began at once, and though Mark maintained at first that the discovery of Cyril's hiding-place was due to nothing else except the cowardice of Hacking, who when confronted by a detective burst into tears and revealed all he knew, he was bound to admit afterward that, if Mr. Ogilvie had been questioned much more, he would have had to reveal the secret himself. Mark was hurt that his efforts to help a son of Holy Church should not be better appreciated by Mr. Ogilvie; but he forgave his friend in view of the nuisance that it undoubtedly must have been to have Meade Cantorum beleaguered by half a dozen corpulent detectives. The only person in the Vicarage who seemed to approve of what he had done was Esther; she who had always seemed to ignore him, even sometimes in a sensitive mood to despise him, was full of congratulations.

"How did you manage it, Mark?"

"Oh, I took a cab," said Mark modestly. "One from the corner of Cranborne Road to Slowbridge, and another from Paddington to Waterloo. We had some sandwiches, and a good deal of ginger-beer at Paddington because we thought we mightn't be able to get any at Waterloo, but at Waterloo we had some more ginger-beer. I wish I hadn't told Hacking. If I hadn't, we should probably have pulled it off. Old Dorward was up to anything. But Hacking is a hopeless ass."

"What does your uncle say?"

"He's rather sick," Mark admitted. "He refused to let me go to school any more, which as you may imagine doesn't upset me very much, and I'm to go into Hitchcock's office after Christmas. As far as I can make out I shall be a kind of servant."

"Have you talked to Stephen about it?"

"Well, he's a bit annoyed with me about this kidnapping. I'm afraid I have rather let him in for it. He says he doesn't mind so much if it's kept out of the papers."

"Anyway, I think it was a sporting effort by you," said Esther. "I wasn't particularly keen on you until you brought this off. I hate pious boys. I wish you'd told me beforehand. I'd have loved to help."

"Would you? I say, I am sorry. I never thought of you," said Mark much disappointed at the lost opportunity. "You'd have been much better than that ass Hacking. If you and I had been the only people in it, I'll bet the detectives would never have found him."

"And what's going to happen to the youth now?"

"Oh, his father's going to take him to Australia as he arranged. They sail to-morrow. There's one thing," Mark added with a kind of gloomy relish. "He's bound to go to the bad, and perhaps that'll be a lesson to his father."

The hope of the Vicar of Meade Cantorum and equally it may be added the hope of Mr. Lidderdale that the affair would be kept out of the papers was not fulfilled. The day after Mr. Pomeroy and his son sailed from Tilbury the following communication appeared in *The Times*:

Sir,—The accompanying letter was handed to me by my friend the Reverend Eustace Pomeroy to be used as I thought fit and subject to only one stipulation—that it should not be published until he and his son were out of England. As President of the Society for the Protection of the English Church against Romish Aggression I feel that it is my duty to lay the facts before the country. I need scarcely add that I have been at pains to verify the surprising and alarming accusations made by a clergyman against two other clergymen, and I earnestly request the publicity of your columns for what I venture to believe is positive proof of the dangerous conspiracy existing in our very midst to romanize the Established Church of England. I shall be happy to produce for any of your readers who find Mr. Pomeroy's story incredible at the close of the nineteenth century the signed statements of witnesses and other documentary evidence.

I am, Sir,

Your obedient servant,

Danvers.

The Right Honble. the Lord Danvers, P.C.

President of the Society for the Protection of the English Church against Romish Aggression.

My Lord,

I have to bring to your notice as President of the S.P.E. C.R.A. what I venture to assert is one of the most daring plots to subvert home and family life in the interests of priestcraft that has ever been discovered. In taking this step I am fully conscious of its seriousness, and if I ask your lordship to delay taking any measures for publicity until the unhappy principal is upon the high seas in the guardianship of his even more unhappy father, I do so for the sake of the wretched boy whose future has been nearly blasted by the Jesuitical behaviour of two so-called Protestant clergymen.

Four years ago, my lord, I retired from a lifelong career as a missionary in New Guinea to give my children the advantages of English education and English climate, and it is surely hard that I should live to curse the day on which I did so. My third son Cyril was sent to school at Haverton House, Slowbridge, to an educational establishment kept by a Mr. Henry Lidderdale, reputed to be a strong Evangelical and I believe I am justified in saying rightly so reputed. At the same time I regret that Mr. Lidderdale, whose brother was a notorious Romanizer I have since discovered, should not have exercised more care in the supervision of his nephew, a fellow scholar with my own son at Haverton House. It appears that Mr. Lidderdale was so lax as to permit his nephew to frequent the services of the Reverend Stephen Ogilvie at Meade Cantorum, where every excess such as incense, lighted candles, mariolatry and creeping to the cross is openly practised. The Revd. S. Ogilvie I may add is a member of the S.S.C., that notorious secret society whose machinations have been so often exposed and the originators of that filthy book "The Priest in Absolution." He is also a member of the Guild of All Souls which has for its avowed object the restoration of the Romish doctrine of Purgatory with all its attendant horrors, and finally I need scarcely add he is a member of the Confraternity of the "Blessed Sacrament" which seeks openly to popularize the idolatrous and blasphemous cult of the Mass.

Young Lidderdale presumably under the influence of this disloyal Protestant clergyman sought to corrupt my son, and was actually so far successful as to lure him to attend the idolatrous services at Meade Cantorum church, which of course he was only able to do by inventing lies and excuses to his father to account for his absence from the simple worship to which all his life he had been accustomed. Not content with this my unhappy son was actually persuaded to confess his sins to this self-styled "priest"! I wonder if he confessed the sin of deceiving his own father to "Father" Ogilvie who supplied him with numerous Mass books, several of which I enclose for your lordship's inspection. You will be amused if you are not too much horrified by these puerile and degraded works, and in one of them, impudently entitled "Catholic Prayers for Church of England People" you will actually see in cold print a prayer for the "Pope of Rome." This work emanates from that hotbed of sacerdotal disloyalty, St. Alban's, Holborn.

These vile books I discovered by accident carefully hidden away in my son's bedroom. "Facilis descensus Averni!" You will easily imagine the humiliation of a parent who, having devoted his life to bring the Gospel of Jesus Christ to the heathen, finds that his own son has fallen as low as the lowest savage. As soon as I made my discovery, I removed him from Haverton House, and warned the proprietor of the risk he was running by not taking better care of his pupils. Having been summoned to a conference of missionaries in Sydney, N.S.W., I determined to take my son with me in the hope that a long voyage in the company of a loving parent, eager to help him back to the path of Truth and Salvation from which he had strayed, might cure him of his idolatrous fancies, and restore him to Jesus.

What followed is, as I write this, scarcely credible to myself; but however incredible, it is true. Young Lidderdale, acting no doubt at the instigation of "Father" Ogilvie (as my son actually called him to my face, not realizing the blasphemy of according to a mortal clergyman the title that belongs to God alone), entered into a conspiracy with another Romanizing clergyman, the Reverend Oliver Dorward, Vicar of Green Lanes, Hants, to abduct my son from his own father's house, with what ultimate intention I dare not think. Incredible as it must sound to modern ears, they were so far successful that for a whole week I was in ignorance of his whereabouts, while detectives were hunting for him up and down England. The abduction was carried out by young Lidderdale, with the assistance of a youth called Hacking, so coolly and skilfully as to indicate that the abettors behind the scenes are USED TO SUCH ABDUCTIONS. This, my lord, points to a very grave state of affairs in our midst. If the son of a Protestant clergyman like myself can be spirited away from a populous but nevertheless comparatively small town like Slowbridge, what must be going on in great cities like London? Moreover, everything is done to make it attractive for the unhappy youth who is thus lured away from his father's hearth. My own son is even now still impenitent, and I have the greatest fears for his moral and religious future, so rapid has been the corruption set up by evil companionship.

These, my lord, are the facts set out as shortly as possible and written on the eve of my departure in circumstances that militate against elegance of expression. I am, to tell the truth, still staggered by this affair, and if I make public my sorrow and my shame I do so in the hope that the Society of which your lordship is President, may see its way to take some kind of action that will make a repetition of such an outrage upon family life for ever impossible.

Believe me to be,

Your lordship's obedient servant,

Eustace Pomeroy.

The publication of this letter stirred England. *The Times* in a leading article demanded a full inquiry into the alleged circumstances. *The English Churchman* said that nothing like it had happened since the days of Bloody Mary. Questions were asked in the House of Commons, and finally when it became known that Lord Danvers would ask a question in the House of Lords, Mr. Ogilvie took Mark to see Lord Hull who wished to be in possession of the facts before he rose to correct some misapprehensions of Lord Danvers. Mark also had to interview two Bishops, an Archdeacon, and a Rural Dean. He did not realize that for a few weeks he was a central figure in what was called THE CHURCH CRISIS. He was indignant at Mr. Pomeroy's exaggeration and perversions of fact, and he was so evidently speaking the truth that everybody from Lord Hull to a reporter of *The Sun* was impressed by his account of the affair, so that in the end the Pomeroy Abduction was decided to be less revolutionary than the Gunpowder Plot.

Mr. Lidderdale, however, believed that his nephew had deliberately tried to ruin him out of malice, and when two parents seized the opportunity of such a scandal to remove their sons from Haverton House without paying the terminal fees, Mr. Lidderdale told Mark that he should recoup himself for the loss out of the money left by his mother.

"How much did she leave?" his nephew asked.

"Don't ask impertinent questions."

"But it's my money, isn't it?"

"It will be your money in another six years, if you behave yourself. Meanwhile half of it will be devoted to paying your premium at the office of my friend Mr. Hitchcock."

"But I don't want to be a solicitor. I want to be a priest," said Mark.

Uncle Henry produced a number of cogent reasons that would make his nephew's ambition unattainable.

"Very well, if I can't be a priest, I don't want the money, and you can keep it yourself," said Mark. "But I'm not going to be a solicitor."

"And what are you going to be, may I inquire?" asked Uncle Henry.

"In the end I probably *shall* be a priest," Mark prophesied. "But I haven't quite decided yet how. I warn you that I shall run away."

"Run away," his uncle echoed in amazement. "Good heavens, boy, haven't you had enough of running away over this deplorable Pomeroy affair? Where are you going to run to?"

"I couldn't tell you, could I, even if I knew?" Mark asked as tactfully as he was able. "But as a matter of fact, I don't know. I only know that I won't go into Mr. Hitchcock's office. If you try to force me, I shall write to *The Times* about it."

Such a threat would have sounded absurd in the mouth of a schoolboy before the Pomeroy business; but now Mr. Lidderdale took it seriously and began to wonder if Haverton House would survive any more of such publicity. When a few days later Mr. Ogilvie, whom Mark had consulted about his future, wrote to propose that Mark should live with him and work under his superintendence with the idea of winning a scholarship at Oxford, Mr. Lidderdale was inclined to treat his suggestion as a solution of the problem, and he replied encouragingly:

Haverton House,

Slowbridge.

Jan. 15.

Dear Sir,

Am I to understand from your letter that you are offering to make yourself responsible for my nephew's future, for I must warn you that I could not accept your suggestion unless such were the case? I do not approve of what I assume will be the trend of your education, and I should have to disclaim any further responsibility in the matter of my nephew's future. I may inform you that I hold in trust for him until he comes of age the sum of £522 8s. 7d. which was left by his mother. The annual interest upon this I have used until now as a slight contribution to the expense to which I have been put on his account; but I have not thought it right to use any of the capital sum. This I am proposing to transfer to you. His mother did not execute any legal document and I have nothing more binding than a moral obligation. If you undertake the responsibility of looking after him until such time as he is able to earn his own living, I consider that you are entitled to use this money in any way you think right. I hope that the boy will reward your confidence more amply than he has rewarded mine. I need not allude to the Pomeroy business to you, for notwithstanding your public denials I cannot but consider that you were as deeply implicated in that disgraceful affair as he was. I note what you say about the admiration you had for my brother. I wish I could honestly say that I shared that admiration. But my brother and I were not on good terms, for which state of affairs he was entirely responsible. I am more ready to surrender to you all my authority over Mark because I am only too well aware how during the last year you have consistently undermined that authority and encouraged my nephew's rebellious spirit. I have had a great experience of boys during thirty-five years of schoolmastering, and I can assure you that I have never had to deal with a boy so utterly insensible to kindness as my nephew. His conduct toward his aunt I can only characterize as callous. Of his conduct towards me I prefer to say no more. I came forward at a moment when he was likely to be sunk in the most abject poverty, and my reward has been ingratitude. I pray that his dark and stubborn temperament may not turn to vice and folly as he grows older, but I have little hope of its not doing so. I confess that to me his future seems dismally black. You may have acquired some kind of influence over his emotions, if he has any emotions, but I am not inclined to suppose that it will endure.

On hearing from you that you persist in your offer to assume complete responsibility for my nephew, I will hand him over to your care at once. I cannot pretend that I shall be sorry to see the last of him, for I am not a hypocrite. I may add that his clothes are in rather a sorry state. I had intended to equip him upon his entering the office of my old friend Mr. Hitchcock and with that intention I have been letting him wear out what he has. This, I may say, he has done most effectually.

I am, Sir,
Yours faithfully,
Henry Lidderdale.
To which Mr. Ogilvie replied:
The Vicarage,
Meade Cantorum,
Bucks.
Jan. 16.
Dear Mr. Lidderdale,
I accept full responsibility for Mark and for Mark's money. Send both of them along whenever you like. I'm not going to embark on another controversy about the "rights" of boys. I've exhausted every argument on this subject since Mark involved me in his drastic measures of a month ago. But please let me assure you that I will do my best for him and that I am convinced he will do his best for me.
Yours truly,
Stephen Ogilvie.

CHAPTER XIII

WYCH-ON-THE-WOLD

Mark rarely visited his uncle and aunt after he went to live at Meade Cantorum; and the break was made complete soon afterward when the living of Wych-on-the-Wold was accepted by Mr. Ogilvie, so complete indeed that he never saw his relations again. Uncle Henry died five years later; Aunt Helen went to live at St. Leonard's, where she took up palmistry and became indispensable to the success of charitable bazaars in East Sussex.

Wych, a large village on a spur of the Cotswold hills, was actually in Oxfordshire, although by so bare a margin that all the windows looked down into Gloucestershire, except those in the Rectory; they looked out across a flat country of elms and willow-bordered streams to a flashing spire in Northamptonshire reputed to be fifty miles away. It was a high windy place, seeming higher and windier on account of the numbers of pigeons that were always circling round the church tower. There was hardly a house in Wych that did not have its pigeon-cote, from the great round columbary in the Rectory garden to the few holes in a gable-end of some steep-roofed cottage. Wych was architecturally as perfect as most Cotswold villages, and if it lacked the variety of Wychford in the vale below, that was because the exposed position had kept its successive builders too intent on solidity to indulge their fancy. The result was an austere uniformity of design that accorded fittingly with a landscape whose beauty was all of line and whose colour like the lichen on an old wall did not flauntingly reveal its gradations of tint to the transient observer. The bleak upland airs had taught the builders to be sparing with their windows; the result of such solicitude for the comfort of the inmates was a succession of blank spaces of freestone that delighted the eye with an effect of strength and leisure, of cleanliness and tranquillity.

The Rectory, dating from the reign of Charles II, did not arrogate to itself the right to retire behind trees from the long line of the single village street; but being taller than the other houses it brought the street to a dignified conclusion, and it was not unworthy of the noble church which stood apart from the village, a landmark for miles, upon the brow of the rolling wold. There was little traffic on the road that climbed up from Wychford in the valley of the swift Greenrush five miles away, and there was less traffic on the road beyond, which for eight miles sent branch after branch to remote farms and hamlets until itself became no more than a sheep track and faded out upon a hilly pasturage. Yet even this unfrequented road only bisected the village at the end of its wide street, where in the morning when the children were at school and the labourers at work in the fields the silence was cloistral, where one could stand listening to the larks high overhead, and where the lightest footstep aroused curiosity, so that one turned the head to peep and peer for the cause of so strange a sound.

Mr. Ogilvie's parish had a large superficial area; but his parishioners were not many outside the village, and in that country of wide pastures the whole of his cure did not include half-a-dozen farms. There was no doctor and no squire, unless Will Starling of Rushbrooke Grange could be counted as the squire.

Halfway to Wychford and close to the boundary of the two parishes an infirm signpost managed with the aid of a stunted hawthorn to keep itself partially upright and direct the wayfarer to Wych Maries. Without the signpost nobody would have suspected that the grassgrown track thus indicated led anywhere except over the top of the wold.

"You must go and explore Wych Maries," the Rector had said to Mark soon after they arrived. "You'll find it rather attractive. There's a disused chapel dedicated to St. Mary the Virgin and St. Mary Magdalene. My predecessor took me there when we drove round the parish on my first visit; but I haven't yet had time to go again. And you ought to have a look at the gardens of Rushbrooke Grange. The present squire is away. In the South Seas, I believe. But the housekeeper, Mrs. Honeybone, will show you round."

It was in response to this advice that Mark and Esther set out on a golden May evening to explore Wych Maries. Esther had continued to be friendly with Mark after the Pomeroy affair; and when he came to live at Meade Cantorum she had expressed her pleasure at the prospect of having him for a brother.

"But you'll keep off religion, won't you?" she had demanded.

Mark promised that he would, wondering why she should suppose that he was incapable of perceiving who was and who was not interested in it.

"I suppose you've guessed my fear?" she had continued. "Haven't you? Haven't you guessed that I'm frightened to death of becoming religious?"

The reassuring contradiction that one naturally gives to anybody who voices a dread of being overtaken by some misfortune might perhaps have sounded inappropriate, and Mark had held his tongue.

"My father was very religious. My mother is more or less religious. Stephen is religious. Miriam is religious. Oh, Mark, and I sometimes feel that I too must fall on my knees and surrender. But I won't. Because it spoils life. I shall be beaten in the end of course, and I'll probably get religious mania when I am beaten. But until then—" She did not finish her sentence; only her blue eyes glittered at the challenge of life.

That was the last time religion was mentioned between Mark and Esther, and since both of them enjoyed the country they became friends. On this May evening they stood by the signpost and looked across the shimmering grass to where the sun hung in his web of golden haze above the edge of the wold.

"If we take the road to Wych Maries," said Mark, "we shall be walking right into the sun."

Esther did not reply, but Mark understood that she assented to his truism, and they walked on as silent as the long shadows that followed them. A quarter of a mile from the high road the path reached the edge of the wold and dipped over into a wood which was sparse just below the brow, but which grew denser down the slope with many dark evergreens interspersed, and in the valley below became a jungle. After the bare upland country this volume of May verdure seemed indescribably rich and the valley beyond, where the Greenrush flowed through kingcups toward the sun, indescribably alluring. Esther and Mark forgot that they were exploring Wych Maries and thinking only of reaching that wide valley they ran down through the wood, rejoicing in the airy green of the ash-trees above them and shouting as they ran. But presently cypresses and sombre yews rose on either side of the path, and the road to Wych Maries was soft and silent, and the serene sun was lost, and their whispering footsteps forbade them to shout any more. At the bottom of the hill the trees increased in number and variety; the sun shone through pale oak-leaves and the warm green of sycamores. Nevertheless a sadness haunted the wood, where the red campions made only a mist of colour with no reality of life and flowers behind.

"This wood's awfully jolly, isn't it?" said Mark, hoping to gain from Esther's agreement the dispersal of his gloom.

"I don't care for it much," she replied. "There doesn't seem to be any life in it."

"I heard a cuckoo just now," said Mark.

"Yes, out of tune already."

"Mm, rather out of tune. Mind those nettles," he warned her.

"I thought Stephen said he drove here."

"Perhaps we've come the wrong way. I believe the road forked by the ash wood above. Anyway if we go toward the sun we shall come out in the valley, and we can walk back along the banks of the river to Wychford."

"We can always go back through the wood," said Esther.

"Yes, if you don't mind going back the way you came."

"Come on," she snapped. She was not going to be laughed at by Mark, and she dared him to deny that he was not as much aware as herself of an eeriness in the atmosphere.

"Only because it seems dark in here after that dazzling sunlight on the wold. Hark! I hear the sound of water."

They struggled through the undergrowth toward the sound; soon from a steep wooded bank they were gazing down into a millpool, the surface of which reflected with a gloomy deepening of their hue the colour but not the form of the trees above. Water was flowing through a rotten sluice gate down from the level of the stream upon a slimy water-wheel that must have been out of action for many years.

"The dark tarn of Auber in the misty mid region of Weir!" Mark exclaimed. "Don't you love *Ulalume*? I think it's about my favourite poem."

"Never heard of it," Esther replied indifferently. He might have taken advantage of this confession to give her a lecture on poetry, if the millpool and the melancholy wood had not been so affecting as to make the least attempt at literary exposition impertinent.

"And there's the chapel," Mark exclaimed, pointing to a ruined edifice of stone, the walls of which were stained with the damp of years rising from the pool. "But how shall we reach it? We must have come the wrong way."

"Let's go back! Let's go back!" Esther exclaimed, surrendering to the command of an intuition that overcame her pride. "This place is unlucky."

Mark looking at her wild eyes, wilder in the dark that came so early in this overshadowed place, was half inclined to turn round at her behest; but at that moment he perceived a possible path through the nettles and briers at the farther end of the pool and unwilling to go back to the Rectory without having visited the ruined chapel of Wych Maries he called on her to follow him. This she did fearfully at first; but gradually regaining her composure she emerged on the other side as cool and scornful as the Esther with whom he was familiar.

"What frightened you?" he asked, when they were standing on a grassgrown road that wound through a rank pasturage browsed on by a solitary black cow and turned the corner by a clump of cedars toward a large building, the presence of which was felt rather than seen beyond the trees.

"I was bored by the brambles," Esther offered for explanation.

"This must be the driving road," Mark proclaimed. "I say, this chapel is rather ripping, isn't it?"

But Esther had wandered away across the rank meadow, where her meditative form made the solitary black cow look lonelier than ever. Mark turned aside to examine the chapel. He had been warned by the Rector to look at the images of St. Mary the Virgin and St. Mary Magdalene that had survived the ruin of the holy place of which they were tutelary and to which they had given their name. The history of the chapel was difficult to trace. It was so small as to suggest that it was a chantry; but there was no historical justification for linking its fortunes with the Starlings who owned Rushbrooke Grange, and there was no record of any lost hamlet here. That it was called Wych Maries might show a connexion either with Wychford or with Wych-on-the-Wold; it lay about midway between the two, and in days gone by there had been controversy on this point between the two parishes. The question had been settled by a squire of Rushbrooke's buying it in the eighteenth century, since when a legend had arisen that it was built and endowed by some crusading Starling of the thirteenth century. There was record neither of its glory nor of its decline, nor of what manner of folk worshipped there, nor of those who destroyed it. The roofless haunt of bats and owls, preserved from complete collapse by the ancient ivy that covered its walls, the mortar between its stones the prey of briers, its floor a nettle bed, the chapel remained a mystery. Yet over the arch of the west door the two Maries gazed heavenward as they had gazed for six hundred years. The curiosity of the few antiquarians who visited the place and speculated upon its past had kept the images clear of the ivy that covered the rest of the fabric. Mark did not put this to the credit of the antiquarians; but now perceiving for the first time these two austere shapes of divine women under conditions of atmosphere that enhanced their austerity and unearthliness he ascribed their freedom from decay to the interposition of God. To Mark's imagination, fixed upon the images while Esther wandered solitary in the field beyond the chapel, there was granted another of those moments of vision which marked like milestones his spiritual progress. He became suddenly assured that he would neither marry nor beget children. He was astonished to find himself in the grip of this thought, for his mind had never until this evening occupied itself with marriage or children, nor even with love. Yet here he was obsessed by the conviction of his finite purpose in the scheme of the world. He could not, he said to himself, be considered credulous if he sought for the explanation of his state of mind in the images of the two Maries. He looked at them resolved to illuminate with reason's eye the fluttering shadows of dusk that gave to the stone an illusion of life's bloom.

"Did their lips really move?" he asked aloud, and from the field beyond the black cow lowed a melancholy negative. Whether the stone had spoken or not, Mark accepted the revelation of his future as a Divine favour, and thenceforth he regarded the ruined chapel of Wych Maries as the place where the vow he made on that Whit-sunday was accepted by God.

"Aren't you ever coming?" the voice of Esther called across the field, and Mark hurried away to rejoin her on the grassgrown drive that led round the cedar grove to Rushbrooke Grange.

"It's too late now to go inside," he objected.

They were standing before the house.

"It's not too late at all," she contradicted eagerly. "Down here it seems later than it really is."

Rushbrooke Grange lacked the architectural perfection of the average Cotswold manor. Being a one-storied building it occupied a large superficial area, and its tumbling irregular roofs of freestone, the outlines of which were blurred by the encroaching mist of vegetation that overhung them, gave the effect of water, as if the atmosphere of this dank valley had wrought upon the substance of the building and as if the architects themselves had been confused by the rivalry of the trees by which it was surrounded. The owners of Rushbrooke Grange had never occupied a prominent position in

201

the county, and their estates had grown smaller with each succeeding generation. There was no conspicuous author of their decay, no outstanding gamester or libertine from whose ownership the family's ruin could be dated. There was indeed nothing of interest in their annals except an attack upon the Grange by a party of armed burglars in the disorderly times at the beginning of the nineteenth century, when the squire's wife and two little girls were murdered while the squire and his sons were drinking deep in the Stag Inn at Wychford four miles away. Mark did not feel much inclined to blunt his impression of the chapel by perambulating Rushbrooke Grange under the guidance of Mrs. Honeybone, the old housekeeper; but Esther perversely insisted upon seeing the garden at any rate, giving as her excuse that the Rector would like them to pay the visit. By now it was a pink and green May dusk; the air was plumy with moths' wings, heavy with the scent of apple blossom.

"Well, you must explain who we are," said Mark while the echoes of the bell died away on the silence within the house and they waited for the footsteps that should answer their summons. The answer came from a window above the porch where Mrs. Honeybone's face, wreathed in wistaria, looked down and demanded in accents that were harsh with alarm who was there.

"I am the Rector's sister, Mrs. Honeybone," Esther explained.

"I don't care who you are," said Mrs. Honeybone. "You have no business to go ringing the bell at this time of the evening. It frightened me to death."

"The Rector asked me to call on you," she pressed.

Mark had already been surprised by Esther's using her brother as an excuse to visit the house and he was still more surprised by hearing her speak so politely, so ingratiatingly, it seemed, to this grim woman embowered in wistaria.

"We lost our way," Esther explained, "and that's why we're so late. The Rector told me about the water-lily pool, and I should so much like to see it."

Mrs. Honeybone debated with herself for a moment, until at last with a grunt of disapproval she came downstairs and opened the front door. The lily pool, now a lily pool only in name, for it was covered with an integument of duckweed which in twilight took on the texture of velvet, was an attractive place set in an enclosure of grass between high grey walls.

"That's all there is to see," said Mrs. Honeybone.

"Mr. Starling is abroad?" Esther asked.

The housekeeper nodded.

"And when is he coming back?" she went on.

"That's for him to say," said the housekeeper disagreeably. "He might come back to-night for all I know."

Almost before the sentence was out of her mouth the hall bell jangled, and a distant voice shouted:

"Nanny, Nanny, hurry up and open the door!"

Mrs. Honeybone could not have looked more startled if the voice had been that of a ghost. Mark began to talk of going until Esther cut him short.

"I don't think Mr. Starling will mind our being here so much as that," she said.

Mrs. Honeybone had already hurried off to greet her master; and when she was gone Mark looked at Esther, saw that her face was strangely flushed, and in an instant of divination apprehended either that she had already met the squire of Rushbrooke Grange or that she expected to meet him here to-night; so that, when presently a tall man of about thirty-five with brick-dust cheeks came into the close, he was not taken aback when Esther greeted him by name with the assurance of old friendship. Nor was he astonished that even in the wan light those brick-dust cheeks should deepen to terra-cotta, those hard blue eyes glitter with recognition, and the small thin-lipped mouth lose for a moment its immobility and gape, yes, gape, in the amazement of meeting somebody whom he never could have expected to meet at such an hour in such a place.

"You," he exclaimed. "You here!"

By the way he quickly looked behind him as if to intercept a prying glance Mark knew that, whatever the relationship between Esther and the squire had been in the past, it had been a relationship in which secrecy had played a part. In that moment between him and Will Starling there was enmity.

"You couldn't have expected him to make a great fuss about a boy," said Esther brutally on their way back to the Rectory.

"I suppose you think that's the reason why I don't like him," said Mark. "I don't want him to take any notice of me, but I think it's very odd that you shouldn't have said a word about knowing him even to his housekeeper."

"It was a whim of mine," she murmured. "Besides, I don't know him very well. We met at Eastbourne once when I was staying there with Mother."

"Well, why didn't he say 'How do you do, Miss Ogilvie?' instead of breathing out 'you' like that?"

Esther turned furiously upon Mark.

"What has it got to do with you?"

"Nothing whatever to do with me," he said deliberately. "But if you think you're going to make a fool of me, you're not. Are you going to tell your brother you knew him?"

Esther would not answer, and separated by several yards they walked sullenly back to the Rectory.

CHAPTER XIV

ST. MARK'S DAY

Mark tried next day to make up his difference with Esther; but she repulsed his advances, and the friendship that had blossomed after the Pomeroy affair faded and died. There was no apparent dislike on either side, nothing more than a coolness as of people too well used to each other's company. In a way this was an advantage for Mark, who was having to apply himself earnestly to the amount of study necessary to win a scholarship at Oxford. Companionship with Esther would have meant considerable disturbance of his work, for she was a woman who depended on the inspiration of the moment for her pastimes and pleasures, who was impatient of any postponement and always avowedly contemptuous of Mark's serious side. His classical education at Haverton House had made little of the material bequeathed to him by his grandfather's tuition at Nancepean. None of his masters had been enough of a scholar or enough of a gentleman (and to teach Latin and Greek well one must be one or the other) to educate his taste. The result was an assortment of grammatical facts to which he was incapable of giving life. If the Rector of Wych-on-the-Wold was not a great scholar, he was at least able to repair the neglect of, more than the neglect of, the positive damage done to Mark's education by the meanness of Haverton House; moreover, after Mark had been reading with him six months he did find a really first-class scholar in Mr. Ford, the Vicar of Little Fairfield. Mark worked steadily, and existence in Oxfordshire went by without any great adventures of mind, body, or spirit. Life at the Rectory had a kind of graceful austerity like the well-proportioned Rectory itself. If Mark had bothered to analyze the cause of this graceful austerity, he might have found it in the personality of the Rector's elder sister Miriam. Even at Meade Cantorum, when he was younger, Mark had been fully conscious of her qualities; but here they found a background against which they could display themselves more perfectly. When they moved from Buckinghamshire and the new rector was seeing how much Miriam appreciated the new surroundings, he sold out some stock and presented her with enough ready money to express herself in the outward beauty of the Rectory's refurbishing. He was luckily not called upon to spend a great deal on the church, both his predecessors having maintained the fabric with care, and the fabric itself being sound enough and magnificent enough to want no more than that. Miriam, though shaking one of those capable and well-tended fingers at her beloved brother's extravagance, accepted the gift with an almost childish determination to give full value of beauty in return, so that there should not be a servant's bedroom nor a cupboard nor a corridor that did not display the evidence of her appreciation in loving care. The garden was handed over to Mrs. Ogilvie, who as soon as May warmed its high enclosures bloomed there like one of her own favourite peonies, rosy of face and fragrant, ample of girth, golden-hearted.

Outside the Rectory Mark spent most of his time with Richard Ford, the son of the Vicar of Little Fairfield, with whom he went to work in the autumn after his arrival in Oxfordshire. Here again Mark was lucky, for Richard, who was a year or two older than himself and a student at Cooper's Hill whence he would emerge as a civil engineer bound for India, was one of those entirely admirable young men who succeed in being saintly without any rapture or righteousness.

Mark said one day:

"Rector, you know, Richard Ford really is a saint; only for goodness' sake don't tell him I said so, because he'd be furious."

The Rector stopped humming a joyful *Miserere* to give Mark an assurance of his discretion. But Mark having said so much in praise of Richard could say no more, and indeed he would have found it hard to express in words what he felt about his friend.

Mark accompanied Richard on his visits to Wychford Rectory where in this fortunate corner of England existed a third perfect family. Richard was deeply in love with Margaret Grey, the second daughter, and if Mark had ever been intended to fall in love he would certainly have fallen in love with Pauline, the youngest daughter, who was fourteen.

"I could look at her for ever," he confided in Richard. "Walking down the road from Wych-on-the-Wold this morning I saw two blue butterflies on a wild rose, and they were like Pauline's eyes and the rose was like her cheek."

"She's a decent kid," Richard agreed fervently.

Mark had had such a limited experience of the world that the amenities of the society in which he found himself incorporated did not strike his imagination as remarkable. It was in truth one of those eclectic, somewhat exquisite, even slightly rarefied coteries which are produced partly by chance, partly by interests shared in common, but most of all, it would seem, by the very genius of the place. The genius of Cotswolds imparts to those who come beneath his influence the art of existing appropriately in the houses that were built at his inspiration. They do not boast of their privilege like the people of Sussex. They are not living up to a landscape so much as to an architecture, and their voices lowered harmoniously with the sigh of the wind through willows and aspens have not to compete with the sea-gales or the sea.

Mark accepted the manners of the society in which good fortune had set him as the natural expression of an inward orderliness, a traditional respect for beauty like the ritual of Christian worship. That the three daughters of the Rector of Wychford should be critical of those who failed to conform to their inherited refinement of life did not strike him as priggish, because it never struck him for a moment that any other standard than theirs existed. He felt the same about people who objected to Catholic ceremonies; their dislike of them did not present itself to him as arising out of a different religious experience from his own; but it appeared as a propensity toward unmannerly behaviour, as a kind of wanton disregard of decency and good taste. He was indeed still at the age when externals possess not so much an undue importance, but when they affect a boy as a mould through which the plastic experience of his youth is passed and whence it emerges to harden slowly to the ultimate form of the individual. In the case of Mark there was the revulsion from the arid ugliness of Haverton House and the ambition to make up for those years of beauty withheld, both of which urged him on to take the utmost advantage of this opportunity to expose the blank surface of those years to the fine etching of the present. Miriam at home, the Greys at Wychford, and in some ways most of all Richard Ford at Fairfield gave him in a few months the poise he would have received more gradually from a public school education.

So Mark read Greek with the Vicar of Little Fairfield and Latin with the Rector of Wych-on-the-Wold, who, amiable and holy man, had to work nearly twice as hard as his pupil to maintain his reserve of instruction. Mark took long walks with Richard Ford when Richard was home in his vacations, and long walks by himself when Richard was at Cooper's Hill. He often went to Wychford Rectory, where he learnt to enjoy Schumann and Beethoven and Bach and Brahms.

"You're like three Saint Cecilias," he told them. "Monica is by Luini and Margaret is by Perugino and Pauline. . . ."

"Oh, who am I by?" Pauline exclaimed, clapping her hands.

"I give it up. You're just Saint Cecilia herself at fourteen."

"Isn't Mark foolish?" Pauline laughed.

"It's my birthday to-morrow," said Mark, "so I'm allowed to be foolish."

"It's my birthday in a week," said Pauline. "And as I'm two years younger than you I can be two years more foolish."

Mark looked at her, and he was filled with wonder at the sanctity of her maidenhood. Thenceforth meditating upon the Annunciation he should always clothe Pauline in a robe of white samite and set her in his mind's eye for that other maid of Jewry, even as painters found holy maids in Florence or Perugia for their bright mysteries.

While Mark was walking back to Wych and when on the brow of the first rise of the road he stood looking down at Wychford in the valley below, a chill lisping wind from the east made him shiver and he thought of the lines in Keats' *Eve of St. Mark*:

The chilly sunset faintly told Of unmatured green vallies cold, Of the green thorny bloomless hedge, Of rivers new with spring-tide sedge, Of primroses by shelter'd rills, And daisies on the aguish hills.

The sky in the west was an unmatured green valley tonight, where Venus bloomed like a solitary primrose; and on the dark hills of Heaven the stars were like daisies. He turned his back on the little town and set off up the hill again, while the wind slipped through the hedge beside him in and out of the blackthorn boughs, lisping, whispering, snuffling, sniffing, like a small inquisitive animal. He thought of Monica, Margaret, and Pauline playing in their warm, candle-lit room behind him, and he thought of Miriam reading in her tall-back chair before dinner, for Evensong would be over by now. Yes, Evensong would be over, he remembered penitently, and he ought to have gone this evening, which was the vigil of St. Mark and of his birthday. At this moment he caught sight of the Wych Maries signpost black against that cold green sky. He gave a momentary start, because seen thus the signpost had a human look; and when his heart beat normally it was roused again, this time by the sight of a human form indeed, the form of Esther, the wind blowing her skirts before her, hurrying along the road to which the signpost so crookedly pointed. Mark who had been climbing higher and higher now felt the power of that wind full on his cheeks. It was as if it had found what it wanted, for it no longer whispered and lisped among the boughs of the blackthorn, but blew fiercely over the wide pastures, driving Esther before it, cutting through Mark like a sword. By the time he had reached the signpost she had disappeared in the wood.

Mark asked himself why she was going to Rushbrooke Grange.

"To Rushbrooke Grange," he said aloud. "Why should I think she is going to Rushbrooke Grange?"

Though even in this desolate place he would not say it aloud, the answer came back from this very afternoon when somebody had mentioned casually that the Squire was come home again. Mark half turned to follow Esther, but in the moment of turning he set his face resolutely in the direction of home. If Esther were really on her way to meet Will Starling, he would do more harm than good by appearing to pry.

Esther was the flaw in Mark's crystal clear world. When a year ago they had quarrelled over his avowed dislike of Will Starling, she had gone back to her solitary walks and he conscious, painfully conscious, that she regarded him as a young prig, had with that foolish pride of youth resolved to be so far as she was concerned what she supposed him to be. His admiration for the Greys and the Fords had driven her into jeering at them; throughout the year Mark and she had been scarcely polite to each other even in public. The Rector and Miriam probably excused Mark's rudeness whenever he let himself give way to it, because their sister did not spare either of them, and they were made aware with exasperating insistence of the dullness of the country and of the dreariness of everybody who lived in the neighbourhood. Yet, Mark could never achieve that indifference to her attitude either toward himself or toward other people that he wished to achieve. It was odd that this evening he should have beheld her in that relation to the wind, because in his thoughts about her she always appeared to him like the wind, restlessly sighing and fluttering round a comfortable house. However steady the candle-light, however bright the fire, however absorbing the book, however secure one may feel by the fireside, the wind is always there; and throughout these tranquil months Esther had always been most unmistakably there.

In the morning Mark went to Mass and made his Communion. It was a strangely calm morning; through the unstained windows of the clerestory the sun sloped quivering ladders of golden light. He looked round with half a hope that Esther was in the church; but she was absent, and throughout the service that brief vision of her dark transit across the cold green sky of yester eve kept recurring to his imagination, so that for all the rich peace of this interior he was troubled in spirit, and the intention to make this Mass upon his seventeenth birthday another spiritual experience was frustrated. In fact, he was worshipping mechanically, and it was only when Mass was over and he was kneeling to make an act of gratitude for his Communion that he began to apprehend how he was asking fresh favours from God without having moved a step forward to deserve them.

"I think I'm too pleased with myself," he decided, "I think I'm suffering from spiritual pride. I think. . . ."

He paused, wondering if it was blasphemous to have an intuition that God was about to play some horrible trick on him. Mark discussed with the Rector the theological aspects of this intuition.

"The only thing I feel," said Mr. Ogilvie, "is that perhaps you are leading too sheltered a life here and that the explanation of your intuition is your soul's perception of this. Indeed, once or twice lately I have been on the point of warning you that you must not get into the habit of supposing you will always find the onset of the world so gentle as here."

"But naturally I don't expect to," said Mark. "I was quite long enough at Haverton House to appreciate what it means to be here."

"Yes," the Rector went on, "but even at Haverton House it was a passive ugliness, just as here it is a passive beauty. After our Lord had fasted forty days in the desert, accumulating reserves of spiritual energy, just as we in our poor human fashion try to accumulate in Lent reserves of spiritual energy that will enable us to celebrate Easter worthily, He was assailed by the Tempter more fiercely than ever during His life on earth. The history of all the early Egyptian monks, the history indeed of any life lived without losing sight of the way of spiritual perfection displays the same phenomena. In the action and reaction of experience, in the rise and fall of the tides, in the very breathing of the human lungs, you may perceive analogies of the divine rhythm. No, I fancy your intuition of this morning is nothing more than one of those movements which warn us that the sleeper will soon wake."

Mark went away from this conversation with the Rector dissatisfied. He wanted something more than analogies taken from the experience of spiritual giants, Titans of holiness whose mighty conquests of the flesh seemed as remote from him as the achievements of Alexander might appear to a captain of the local volunteers. What he had gone to ask the Rector was whether it was blasphemous to suppose that God was going to play a horrible trick on him. He had not wanted a theological discussion, an academic question and reply. Anything could be answered like that, probably himself in another twenty years, when he had preached some hundreds of sermons, would talk like that. Moreover, when he was alone Mark understood that he had not really wanted to talk about his own troubles to the Rector at all, but that his real preoccupation had been and still was Esther. He wondered, oh, how much he wondered, if her brother had the least suspicion of her friendship with Will Starling, or if Miriam had had the least inkling that Esther had not come in till nine o'clock last night because she had been to Wych Maries? Mark, remembering those wild eyes and that windblown hair when she stood for a moment framed in the doorway of the Rector's library, could not believe that none of her family had guessed that something more than the whim to wander over the hills had taken her out on such a night. Did Mrs. Ogilvie, promenading so placidly along her garden borders, ever pause in perplexity at her daughter's behaviour? Calling them all to mind, their attitudes, the expressions of their faces, the words upon their lips, Mark was sure that none of them had any idea what Esther was doing. He debated now the notion of warning Miriam in veiled language about her sister; but such an idea would strike Miriam as monstrous, as a mad and horrible nightmare. Mark shivered at the mere fancy of the chill that would come over her and of the disdain in her eyes. Besides, what right had he on the little he knew to involve Esther with her family? Superficially he might count himself her younger brother; but if he presumed too far, with what a deadly retort might she not annihilate his claim. Most certainly he was not entitled to intervene unless he intervened bravely and directly. Mark shook his head at the prospect of doing that. He could not imagine anybody's tackling Esther directly on such a subject. Seventeen to-day! He looked out of the window and felt that he was bearing upon his shoulders the whole of that green world outspread before him.

The serene morning ripened to a splendid noontide, and Mark who had intended to celebrate his birthday by enjoying every moment of it had allowed the best of the hours to slip away in a stupor of indecision. More and more the vision of Esther last night haunted him, and he felt that he could not go and see the Greys as he had intended. He could not bear the contemplation of the three girls with the weight of Esther on his mind. He decided to walk over to Little Fairfield and persuade Richard to make a journey of exploration up the Greenrush in a canoe. He would ask Richard his opinion of Will Starling. What a foolish notion! He knew perfectly well Richard's opinion of the Squire, and to lure him into a restatement of it would be the merest self-indulgence.

"Well, I must go somewhere to-day," Mark shouted at himself. He secured a packet of sandwiches from the Rectory cook and set out to walk away his worries.

"Why shouldn't I go down to Wych Maries? I needn't meet that chap. And if I see him I needn't speak to him. He's always been only too jolly glad to be offensive to me."

Mark turned aside from the high road by the crooked signpost and took the same path down under the ash-trees as he had taken with Esther for the first time nearly a year ago. Spring was much more like Spring in these wooded hollows; the noise of bees in the blossom of the elms was murmurous as limes in June. Mark congratulated himself on the spot in which he had chosen to celebrate this fine birthday, a day robbed from time like the day of a dream. He ate his lunch by the old mill dam, feeding the roach with crumbs until an elderly pike came up from the deeps and frightened the smaller fish away. He searched for a bullfinch's nest; but he did not find one, though he saw several of the birds singing in the snowberry bushes; round and ruddy as October apples they looked. At last he went to the ruined chapel, where after speculating idly for a little while upon its former state he fell as he usually did when he visited Wych Maries into a contemplation of the two images of the Blessed Virgin and St. Mary Magdalene. While he sat on a hummock of grass before the old West doorway he received an impression that since he last visited these forms of stone they had ceased to be mere relics of ancient worship unaccountably preserved from ruin, but that they had somehow regained their importance. It was not that he discerned in them any miraculous quality of living, still less of winking or sweating as images are reputed to wink and sweat for the faithful. No, it was not that, he decided, although by regarding them thus entranced as he was he could easily have brought himself to the point of believing in a supernatural manifestation. He was too well aware of this tendency to surrender to it; so, rousing himself from the rapt contemplation of them and forsaking the hummock of grass, he climbed up into the branches of a yew-tree that stood beside the chapel, that there and from that elevation, viewing the images and yet unviewed by them directly, he could be immune from the magic of fancy and discover why they should give him this impression of having regained their utility, yes, that was the word, utility, not importance. They were revitalized not from within, but from without; and even as his mind leapt at this explanation he perceived in the sunlight, beyond the shadowy yew-tree in which he was perched, Esther sitting upon that hummock of grass where but a moment ago he had himself been sitting.

For a moment, as if to contradict a reasonable explanation of the strange impression the images had made upon him, Mark supposed that she was come there for a tryst. This vanished almost at once in the conviction that Esther's soul waited there either in question or appeal. He restrained an impulse to declare his presence, for although he felt that he was intruding upon a privacy of the soul, he feared to destroy the fruits of that privacy by breaking in. He knew that Esther's pride would be so deeply outraged at having been discovered in a moment of weakness thus upon her knees, for she had by now fallen upon her knees in prayer, that it might easily happen she would never in all her life pray more. There was no escape for Mark without disturbing her, and he sat breathless in the yew-tree, thinking that soon she must perceive his glittering eye in the depths of the dark foliage as in passing a hedgerow one may perceive the eye of a nested bird. From his position he could see the images, and out of the spiritual agony of Esther kneeling there, the force of which was communicated to himself, he watched them close, scarcely able to believe that they would not stoop from their pedestals and console the suppliant woman with benediction of those stone hands now clasped aspiringly to God, themselves for centuries suppliant like the woman at their feet. Mark could think of nothing better to do than to turn his face from Esther's face and to say for her many *Paternosters* and *Aves*. At first he thought that he was praying in a silence of nature; but presently the awkwardness of his position began to affect his concentration, and he found that he was saying the words mechanically, listening the while to the voices of birds. He compelled his attention to the prayers; but the birds were too loud. The *Paternosters* and the *Aves* were absorbed in their singing and chirping and twittering, so that Mark gave up to them and wished for a rosary to help his feeble attention. Yet could he have used a rosary without falling out of the yew-tree? He took his hands from the bough for a moment and nearly overbalanced. *Make not your rosary of yew berries*, he found himself saying. Who wrote that? *Make not your rosary of yew berries*. Why, of course, it was Keats. It was the first line of the *Ode to Melancholy*. Esther was still kneeling out there in the sunlight. And how did the poem continue? *Make not your rosary of yew berries*. What was the second line? It was ridiculous to sit astride a bough and say *Paternosters* and *Aves*. He could not sit there much longer. And then just as he was on the point of letting go he saw that Esther had risen from her knees and that Will Starling was standing in the doorway of the chapel looking at her, not speaking but waiting for her to speak, while he wound a strand of ivy round his fingers and unwound it again, and wound it round again until it broke and he was saying:

"I thought we agreed after your last display here that you'd give this cursed chapel the go by?"

"I can't escape from it," Esther cried. "You don't understand, Will, what it means. You never have understood."

"Dearest Essie, I understand only too well. I've paid pretty handsomely in having to listen to reproaches, in having to dry your tears and stop your sighs with kisses. Your damned religion is a joke. Can't you grasp that? It's not my fault we can't get married. If I were really the scoundrel you torment yourself into thinking I am, I would have married and taken the risk of my strumpet of a wife turning up. But I've treated you honestly, Essie. I can't help loving you. I went away once. I went away again. And a third time I went just to relieve your soul of the sin of loving me. But I'm sick of suffering for the sake of a myth, a superstition."

Esther had moved close to him, and now she put a hand upon his arm.

"To you, Will. Not to me."

"Look here, Essie," said her lover. "If you knew that you were liable to these dreadful attacks of remorse and penitence, why did you ever encourage me?"

"How dare you say I encouraged you?"

"Now don't let your religion make you dishonest," he stabbed. "No man seduces a woman of your character without as much goodwill as deserves to be called encouragement, and by God *is* encouragement," he went on furiously. "Let's cut away some of the cant before we begin arguing again about religion."

"You don't know what a hell you're making for me when you talk like that," she gasped. "If I did encourage you, then my sin is a thousand times blacker."

"Oh, don't exaggerate, my dear girl," he said wearily. "It isn't a sin for two people to love each other."

"I've tried my best to think as you do, but I can't. I've avoided going to church. I've tried to hate religion, I've mocked at God . . ." she broke off in despair of explaining the force of grace, against the gift of which she had contended in vain.

"I always thought you were brave, Essie. But you're a real coward. The reason for all this is your fear of being pitchforked into a big bonfire by a pantomime demon with horns and a long tail." He laughed bitterly. "To think that you, my adored Essie, should really have the soul of a Sunday school teacher. You, a Bacchante of passion, to be puling about your sins. You! You! Girl, you're mad! I tell you there is no such thing as damnation. It's a bogey invented by priests to enchain mankind. But if there is and if that muddle-headed old gentleman you call God really exists and if he's a just God, why then let him damn me and let him give you your harp and your halo while I burn for both. Essie, my mad foolish frightened Essie, can't you understand that if you give me up for this God of yours you'll drive me to murder. If I must marry you to hold you, why then I'll kill that cursed wife of mine. . . ."

It was his turn now to break off in despair of being able to express his will to keep Esther for his own, and because argument seemed so hopeless he tried to take her in his arms, whereupon Mark who was aching with the effort to maintain himself unobserved upon the bough of the yew-tree said his *Paternosters* and *Aves* faster than ever, that she might have the strength to resist that scoundrel of Rushbrooke Grange. He longed to have the eloquence to make some wonderful prayer to the Blessed Virgin and St. Mary Magdalene so that a miracle might happen and their images point accusing hands at the blasphemer below.

And then it seemed as if a miracle did happen, for out of the jangle of recriminations and appeals that now signified no more than the noise of trees in a storm he heard the voice of Esther gradually gain its right to be heard, gradually win from its rival silence until the tale was told.

"I know that I am overcome by the saving grace of God," she was saying. "And I know that I owe it to them." She pointed to the holy women above the door. The squire shook his fist; but he still kept silence. "I have run away from God since I knew you, Will. I have loved you as much as that. I have gone to church only when I had to go for my brother's sake, but I have actually stuffed my ears with cotton wool so that no word there spoken might shake my faith in my right to love you. But it was all to no purpose. You know that it was you who told me always to come to our meetings through the wood and past the chapel. And however fast I went and however tight I shut myself up in thoughts of you and your love and my love I have always felt that these images spoke to me reproachfully in passing. It's not mere imagination, Will. Why, before we came to Wych-on-the-Wold when you went away to the Pacific that I might have peace of mind, I used always to be haunted by the idea that God was calling me back to Him, and I would run, yes, actually run through the woods until my legs have been torn by brambles."

"Madness! Madness!" cried Starling.

"Let it be madness. If God chooses to pursue a human soul with madness, the pursuit is not less swift and relentless for that. And I shook Him off. I escaped from religion; I prayed to the Devil to keep me wicked, so utterly did I love you. Then when my brother was offered Wych-on-the-Wold I felt that the Devil had heard my prayer and had indeed made me his own. That frightened me for a moment. When I wrote to you and said we were coming here and you hurried back, I can't describe to you the fear that overcame me when I first entered this hollow where you lived. Several times I'd tried to come down before you arrived here, but I'd always been afraid, and that was why the first night I brought Mark with me."

"That long-legged prig and puppy," grunted the squire.

Mark could have shouted for joy when he heard this, shouted because he was helping with his *Paternosters* and his *Aves* to drive this ruffian out of Esther's life for ever, shouted because his long legs were strong enough to hold on to this yew-tree bough.

"He's neither a prig nor a puppy," Esther said. "I've treated him badly ever since he came to live with us, and I treated him badly on your account, because whenever I was with him I found it harder to resist the pursuit of God. Now let's leave Mark out of this. Everything was in your favour, I tell you. I was sure that the Devil. . . ."

"The Devil!" Starling interrupted. "Your Devil, dear Essie, is as ridiculous as your God. It's only your poor old God with his face painted black like the bogey man of childhood."

"I was sure that the Devil," Esther repeated without seeming to hear the blasphemy, "had taken me for his own and given us to each other. You to me. Me to you, my darling. I didn't care. I was ready to burn in Hell for you. So, don't call me coward, for mad though you think me I was ready to be damned for you, and *I* believe in damnation. You don't. Yet the first time I passed by this chapel on my way to meet you again after that endless horrible parting I had to run away from the holy influence. I remember that there was a black cow in the field near the gates of the Grange, and I waited there while Mark poked about in this chapel, waited in the twilight afraid to go back and tell him to hurry in case I should be recaptured by God and meet you only to meet you never more."

"I suppose you thought my old Kerry cow was the Devil, eh?" he sneered.

She paid no attention, but continued enthralled by the passion of her spiritual adventure.

"It was no use. I couldn't come by here every day and not go back. Why, once I opened the Bible at hazard just to show my defiance and I read *Her sins which are many are forgiven for she loved much.* This must be the end of our love, my lover, for I can't go on. Those two stone Maries have brought me back to God. No more with you, my own beloved. No more, my darling, no more. And yet if even now with one kiss you could give me strength to sin I should rejoice. But they have made my lips as cold as their own, and my arms that once knew how to clasp you to my heart they have lifted up to Heaven like their own. I am going into a convent at once, where until I die I shall pray for you, my own love."

The birds no longer sang nor twittered nor cheeped in the thickets around, but all passion throbbed in the voice of Esther when she spoke these words. She stood there with her hair in disarray transfigured like a tree in autumn on which the sunlight shines when the gale has died, but from which the leaves will soon fall because winter is at hand. Yet her lover was so little moved by her ordeal that he went back to mouthing his blasphemies.

"Go then," he shouted. "But these two stone dolls shall not have power to drive my next mistress into folly. Wasn't Mary Magdalene a sinner? Didn't she fall in love with Christ? Of course, she did! And I'll make an example of her just as Christians make an example of all women who love much."

The squire pulled himself up by the ivy and struck the image of St. Mary Magdalene on the face.

"When you pray for me, dear Essie, in your convent of greensick women, don't forget that your patron saint was kicked from her pedestal by your lover."

Starling was as good as his word; but the effort he made to overthrow the saint carried him with it; his foot catching in the ivy fell head downward and striking upon a stone was killed.

Mark hesitated before he jumped down from his bough, because he dreaded to add to Esther's despair the thought of his having overheard all that went before. But seeing her in the sunlight now filled again with the voices of birds, seeing her blue eyes staring in horror and the nervous twitching of her hands he felt that the shock of his irruption might save her reason and in a moment he was standing beside her looking down at the dead man.

"Let me die too," she cried.

Mark found himself answering in a kind of inspiration:

"No, Esther, you must live to pray for his soul."

"He was struck dead for his blasphemy. He is in Hell. Of what use to pray for his soul?"

"But Esther while he was falling, even in that second, he had time to repent. Live, Esther. Live to pray for him."

Mark was overcome with a desire to laugh at the stilted way in which he was talking, and, from the suppression of the desire, to laugh wildly at everything in the scene, and not least at the comic death of Will Starling, even at the corpse itself lying with a broken neck at his feet. By an effort of will he regained control of his muscles, and the tension of the last half hour finding no relief in bodily relaxation was stamped ineffaceably upon his mind to take its place with that afternoon in his father's study at the Lima Street Mission which first inspired him with dread of the sexual relation of man to woman, a dread that was now made permanent by what he had endured on the bough of that yew-tree.

Thanks to Mark's intervention the business was explained without scandal; nobody doubted that the squire of Rushbrooke Grange died a martyr to his dislike of ivy's encroaching upon ancient images. Esther's stormy soul took refuge in a convent, and there it seemed at peace.

CHAPTER XV
THE SCHOLARSHIP

The encounter between Esther and Will Starling had the effect of strengthening Mark's intention to be celibate. He never imagined himself as a possible protagonist in such a scene; but the impression of that earlier encounter between his mother and father which gave him a horror of human love was now renewed. It was renewed, moreover, with the light of a miracle to throw it into high relief. And this miracle could not be explained away as a coincidence, but was an old-fashioned miracle that required no psychical buttressing, a hard and fast miracle able to withstand any criticism. It was a pity that out of regard for Esther he could not publish it for the encouragement of the faithful and the confusion of the unbelievers.

The miracle of St. Mary Magdalene's intervention on his seventeenth birthday was the last violent impression of Mark's boyhood. Thenceforward life moved placidly through the changing weeks of a country calendar until the date of the scholarship examination held by the group of colleges that contained St. Mary's, the college he aspired to enter, but for which he failed to win even an exhibition. Mr. Ogilvie was rather glad, for he had been worried how Mark was going to support himself for three or four years at an expensive college like St. Mary's. But when Mark was no more successful with another group of colleges, his tutors began to be alarmed, wondering if their method of teaching Latin and Greek lacked the tradition of the public school necessary to success.

"Oh, no, it's obviously my fault," said Mark. "I expect I go to pieces in examinations, or perhaps I'm not intended to go to Oxford."

"I beg you, my dear boy," said the Rector a little irritably, "not to apply such a loose fatalism to your career. What will you do if you don't go to the University?"

"It's not absolutely essential for a priest to have been to the University," Mark argued.

"No, but in your case I think it's highly advisable. You haven't had a public school education, and inasmuch as I stand to you *in loco parentis* I should consider myself most culpable if I didn't do everything possible to give you a fair start. You haven't got a very large sum of money to launch yourself upon the world, and I want you to spend what you have to the best advantage. Of course, if you can't get a scholarship, you can't and that's the end of it. But, rather than that you should miss the University I will supplement from my own savings enough to carry you through three years as a commoner."

Tears stood in Mark's eyes.

"You've already been far too generous," he said. "You shan't spend any more on me. I'm sorry I talked in that foolish way. It was really only a kind of affectation of indifference. I'm feeling pretty sore with myself for being such a failure; but I'll have another shot and I hope I shall do better."

Mark as a last chance tried for a close scholarship at St. Osmund's Hall for the sons of clergymen.

"It's a tiny place of course," said the Rector. "But it's authentic Oxford, and in some ways perhaps you would be happier at a very small college. Certainly you'd find your money went much further."

The examination was held in the Easter vacation, and when Mark arrived at the college he found only one other candidate besides himself. St. Osmund's Hall with its miniature quadrangle, miniature hall, miniature chapel, empty of undergraduates and with only the Principal and a couple of tutors in residence, was more like an ancient almshouse than an Oxford college. Mark and his rival, a raw-boned youth called Emmett who was afflicted with paroxysms of stammering, moved about the precincts upon tiptoe like people trespassing from a high road.

On their first evening the two candidates were invited to dine with the Principal, who read second-hand book catalogues all through dinner, only pausing from their perusal to ask occasionally in a courtly tone if Mr. Lidderdale or Mr. Emmett would not take another glass of wine. After dinner they sat in his library where the Principal addressed himself to the evidently uncongenial task of estimating the comparative fitness of his two guests to receive Mr. Tweedle's bounty. The Reverend Thomas Tweedle was a benevolent parson of the eighteenth century who by his will had provided the money to educate the son of one indigent clergyman for four years. Mark was shy enough under the Principal's courtly inquisition, but poor Emmett had a paroxysm each time he was asked the simplest question about his tastes or his ambitions. His tongue appearing like a disturbed mollusc waved its tip slowly round in an agonized endeavour to give utterance to such familiar words as "yes" or "no." Several times Mark feared that he would never get it back at all and that Emmett would either have to spend the rest of his life with it protruding before him or submit it to amputation and become a mute. When the ordeal with the Principal was over and the two guests were strolling back across the quadrangle to their rooms, Emmett talked normally and without a single paroxysm about the effect his stammer must have had upon the Principal. Mark did his best to reassure poor Emmett.

"Really," he said, "it was scarcely noticeable to anybody else. You noticed it, because you felt your tongue getting wedged like that between your teeth; but other people would hardly have noticed it at all. When the Principal asked you if you were going to take Holy Orders yourself, I'm sure he only thought you hadn't quite made up your mind yet."

"But I'm sure he did notice something," poor Emmett bewailed. "Because he began to hum."

"Well, but he was always humming," said Mark. "He hummed all through dinner while he was reading those book catalogues."

"It's very kind of you, Lidderdale," said Emmett, "to make the best of it for me, but I'm not such a fool as I look, and the Principal certainly hummed six times as loud whenever he asked me a question as he did over those catalogues. I know what I look like when I get into one of those states. I once caught sight of myself in a glass by accident, and now whenever my tongue gets caught up like that I'm wondering all the time why everybody doesn't get up and run out of the room."

"But I assure you," Mark persisted, "that little things like that—"

"Little things like that!" Emmett interrupted furiously. "It's all very well for you, Lidderdale, to talk about little things like that. If you had a tongue like mine which seems to get bigger instead of smaller every year, you'd feel very differently."

"But people always grow out of stammering," Mark pointed out.

"Thanks very much," said Emmett bitterly, "but where shall I be by the time I've grown out of it? You don't suppose I shall win this scholarship, do you, after they've seen me gibbering and mouthing at them like that? But if only I could manage somehow to get to Oxford I should have a chance of being ordained, and—" he broke off, perhaps unwilling to embarrass his rival by any more lamentations.

"Do forget about this evening," Mark begged, "and come up to my room and have a talk before you turn in."

"No, thanks very much," said Emmett. "I must sit up and do some work. We've got that general knowledge paper to-morrow morning."

"But you won't be able to acquire much more general knowledge in one evening," Mark protested.

"I might," said Emmett darkly. "I noticed a Whitaker's almanack in the rooms I have. My only chance to get this scholarship is to do really well in my papers; and though I know it's no good and that this is my last chance, I'm not going to neglect anything that could possibly help. I've got a splendid memory for statistics, and if they'll only ask a few statistics in the general knowledge paper I may have some luck to-morrow. Good-night, Lidderdale, I'm sorry to have inflicted myself on you like this."

Emmett hurried away up the staircase leading to his room and left his rival standing on the moonlit grass of the quadrangle. Mark was turning toward his own staircase when he heard a window open above and Emmett's voice:

"I've found another Whitaker of the year before," it proclaimed. "I'll read that, and you'd better read this year's. If by any chance I did win this scholarship, I shouldn't like to think I'd taken an unfair advantage of you, Lidderdale."

"Thanks very much, Emmett," said Mark. "But I think I'll have a shot at getting to bed early."

"Ah, you're not worrying," said Emmett gloomily, retiring from the window.

When Mark was sitting by the fire in his room and thinking over the dinner with the Principal and poor Emmett's stammering and poor Emmett's words in the quad afterwards, he began to imagine what it would mean to poor Emmett if he failed to win the scholarship. Mark had not been so successful himself in these examinations as to justify a grand self-confidence; but he could not regard Emmett as a dangerous competitor. Had he the right in view of Emmett's handicap to accept this scholarship at his expense? To be sure, he might urge on his own behalf that without it he should himself be debarred from Oxford. What would the loss of it mean? It would mean, first of all, that Mr. Ogilvie would make the financial effort to maintain him for three years as a commoner, an effort which he could ill afford to make and which Mark had not the slightest intention of allowing him to make. It would mean, next, that he should have to occupy himself during the years before his ordination with some kind of work among people. He obviously could not go on reading theology at Wych-on-the-Wold until he went to Glastonbury. Such an existence, however attractive, was no preparation for the active life of a priest. It would mean, thirdly, a great disappointment to his friend and patron, and considering the social claims of the Church of England it would mean a handicap for himself. There was everything to be said for winning this scholarship, nothing to be said against it on the grounds of expediency. On the grounds of expediency, no, but on other grounds? Should he not be playing the better part if he allowed Emmett to win? No doubt all that was implied in the necessity for him to win a scholarship was equally implied in the necessity for Emmett to win one. It was obvious that Emmett was no better off than himself; it was obvious that Emmett was competing in a kind of despair. Mark remembered how a few minutes ago his rival had offered him this year's Whitaker, keeping for himself last year's almanack. Looked at from the point of view of Emmett who really believed that something might be gained at this eleventh hour from a study of the more recent volume, it had been a fine piece of self-denial. It showed that Emmett had Christian talents which surely ought not to be wasted because he was handicapped by a stammer.

The spell that Oxford had already cast on Mark, the glamour of the firelight on the walls and raftered ceiling of this room haunted by centuries of youthful hope, did not persuade him how foolish it was to surrender all this. On the contrary, this prospect of Oxford so beautiful in the firelight within, so fair in the moonlight without, impelled him to renounce it, and the very strength of his temptation to enjoy all this by winning the scholarship helped him to make up his mind to lose it. But how? The obvious course was to send in idiotic answers for the rest of his papers. Yet examinations were so mysterious that when he thought he was being most idiotic he might actually be gaining his best marks. Moreover, the examiners might ascribe his answers to ill health, to some sudden attack of nerves, especially if his papers to-day had been tolerably good. Looking back at the Principal's attitude after dinner that night, Mark could not help feeling that there had been something in his manner which had clearly shown a determination not to award the scholarship to poor Emmett if it could possibly be avoided. The safest way would be to escape to-morrow morning, put up at some country inn for the next two days, and go back to Wych-on-the-Wold; but if he did that, the college authorities might write to Mr. Ogilvie to demand the reason for such extraordinary behaviour. And how should he explain it? If he really intended to deny himself, he must take care that nobody knew he was doing so. It would give him an air of unbearable condescension, should it transpire that he had deliberately surrendered his scholarship to Emmett. Moreover, poor Emmett would be so dreadfully mortified if he found out. No, he must complete his papers, do them as badly as he possibly could, and leave the result to the wisdom of God. If God wished Emmett to stammer forth His praises and stutter His precepts from the pulpit, God would know how to manage that seemingly so intractable Principal. Or God might hear his prayers and cure poor Emmett of his impediment. Mark wondered to what saint was entrusted the patronage of stammerers; but he could not remember. The man in whose rooms he was lodging possessed very few books, and those few were mostly detective stories.

It amused Mark to make a fool of himself next morning in the general knowledge paper. He flattered himself that no candidate for a scholarship at St. Osmund's Hall had ever shown such black ignorance of the facts of every-day life. Had he been dropped from Mars two days before, he could scarcely have shown less knowledge of the Earth. Mark tried to convey an impression that he had been injudiciously crammed with Latin and Greek, and in the afternoon he produced a Latin prose that would have revolted the easy conscience of a fourth form boy. Finally, on the third day, in an unseen passage set from the Georgics he translated *tonsisque ferunt mantelia villis* by *having pulled down the villas (i. e. literally shaved) they carry off the mantelpieces* which he followed up with translating *Maeonii carchesia Bacchi* as the *lees of Maeonian wine (i.e. literally carcases of Maeonian Bacchus).*

"I say, Lidderdale," said Emmett, when they came out of the lecture room where the examination was being held. "I had a tremendous piece of luck this afternoon."

"Did you?"

"Yes, I've just been reading the fourth Georgics last term, and I don't think I made a single mistake in that unseen."

"Good work," said Mark.

"I wonder when they'll let us know who's got the scholarship," said Emmett. "But of course you've won," he added with a sigh.

"I did very badly both yesterday and to-day."

"Oh, you're only saying that to encourage me," Emmett sighed. "It sounds a dreadful thing to say and I ought not to say it because it'll make you uncomfortable, but if I don't succeed, I really think I shall kill myself."

"All right, that's a bargain," Mark laughed; and when his rival shook hands with him at parting he felt that poor Emmett was going home to Rutland convinced that Mark was just as hard-hearted as the rest of the world and just as ready to laugh at his misfortune.

It was Saturday when the examination was finished, and Mark wished he could be granted the privilege of staying over Sunday in college. He had no regrets for what he had done; he was content to let this experience be all that he should ever intimately gain of Oxford; but he should like to have the courage to accost one of the tutors and to tell him that being convinced he should never come to Oxford again he desired the privilege of remaining until Monday morning, so that he might crystallize in that short space of time an impression which, had he been successful in gaining the scholarship, would have been spread over four years. Mark was not indulging in sentiment; he really felt that by the intensity of the emotion with which he would live those twenty-four hours he should be able to achieve for himself as much as he should achieve in four years. So far as the world was concerned, this experience would be valueless; for himself it would be beyond price. So far as the world was concerned, he would never have been to Oxford; but could he be granted this privilege, Oxford would live for ever in his heart, a refuge and a meditation until the grave. Yet this coveted experience must be granted from without to make it a perfect experience. To ask and to be refused leave to stay till Monday would destroy for him the value of what he had already experienced in three days' residence; even to ask and to be granted the privilege would spoil it in retrospect. He went down the stairs from his room and stood in the little quadrangle, telling himself that at any rate he might postpone his departure until twilight and walk the seven miles from Shipcot to Wych-on-the-Wold. While he was on his way to notify the porter of the time of his departure he met the Principal, who stopped him and asked how he had got on with his papers. Mark wondered if the Principal had been told about his lamentable performance and was making inquiries on his own account to find out if the unsuccessful candidate really was a lunatic.

"Rather badly, I'm afraid, sir."

"Well, I shall see you at dinner to-night," said the Principal dismissing Mark with a gesture before he had time even to look surprised. This was a new perplexity, for Mark divined from the Principal's manner that he had entirely forgotten that the scholarship examination was over and that the candidates had already dined with him. He went into the lodge and asked the porter's advice.

"The Principal's a most absent-minded gentleman," said the porter. "Most absent-minded, he is. He's the talk of Oxford sometimes is the Principal. What do you think he went and did only last term. Why, he was having some of the senior men to tea and was going to put some coal on the fire with the tongs and some sugar in his cup. Bothered if he didn't put the sugar in the fire and a lump of coal in his cup. It didn't so much matter him putting sugar in the fire. That's all according, as they say. But fancy—well, I tell you we had a good laugh over it in the lodge when the gentlemen came out and told me."

"Ought I to explain that I've already dined with him?" Mark asked.

"Are you in any what you might call immediate hurry to get away?" the porter asked judicially.

"I'm in no hurry at all. I'd like to stay a bit longer."

"Then you'd better go to dinner with him again to-night and stay in college over the Sunday. I'll take it upon myself to explain to the Dean why you're still here. If it had been tea I should have said 'don't bother about it,' but dinner's another matter, isn't it? And he always has dinner laid for two or more in case he's asked anybody and forgotten."

Thus it came about that for the second time Mark dined with the Principal, who disconcerted him by saying when he arrived:

"I remember now that you dined with me the night before last. You should have told me. I forget these things. But never mind, you'd better stay now you're here."

The Principal read second-hand book catalogues all through dinner just as he had done two nights ago, and he only interrupted his perusal to inquire in courtly tones if Mark would take another glass of wine. The only difference between now and the former occasion was the absence of poor Emmett and his paroxysms. After dinner with some misgivings if he ought not to leave his host to himself Mark followed him upstairs to the library. The principal was one of those scholars who live in an atmosphere of their own given off by old calf-bound volumes and who apparently can only inhale the air of the world in which ordinary men move when they are smoking their battered old pipes. Mark sitting opposite to him by the fireside was tempted to pour out the history of himself and Emmett, to explain how he had come to make such a mess of the examination. Perhaps if the Principal had alluded to his papers Mark would have found the courage to talk about himself; but the Principal was apparently unaware that his guest had any ambitions to enter St. Osmund's Hall, and whatever questions he asked related to the ancient folios and quartos he took down in turn from his shelves. A clock struck ten in the moonlight without, and Mark rose to go. He felt a pang as he walked from the cloudy room and looked for the last time at that tall remote scholar, who had forgotten his guest's existence at the moment he ceased to shake his hand and who by the time he had reached the doorway was lost again in the deeps of the crabbed volume resting upon his knees. Mark sighed as he closed the library door behind him, for he knew that he was shutting out a world. But when he stood in the small silver quadrangle Mark was glad that he had not given way to the temptation of confiding in the Principal. It would have been a feeble end to his first denial of self. He was sure that he had done right in surrendering his place to Emmett, for was not the unexpected opportunity to spend these few more hours in Oxford a sign of God's approval? *Bright as the glimpses of eternity to saints accorded in their mortal hour.* Such was Oxford to-night.

Mark sat for a long while at the open window of his room until the moon had passed on her way and the quadrangle was in shadow; and while he sat there he was conscious of how many people had inhabited this small quadrangle and of how they too had passed on their way like the moon, leaving behind them no more than he should leave behind from this one hour of rapture, no more than the moon had left of her silver upon the dim grass below.

Mark was not given to gazing at himself in mirrors, but he looked at himself that night in the mirror of the tiny bedroom, into which the April air came up sweet and frore from the watermeadows of the Cherwell close at hand.

"What will you do now?" he asked his reflection. "Yet, you have such a dark ecclesiastical face that I'm sure you'll be a priest whether you go to Oxford or not."

Mark was right in supposing his countenance to be ecclesiastical. But it was something more than that: it was religious. Even already, when he was barely eighteen, the high cheekbones and deepset burning eyes gave him an ascetic look, while the habit of prayer and meditation had added to his expression a steadfast purpose that is rarely seen in people as young as him. What his face lacked were those contours that come from association with humanity; the ripeness that is bestowed by long tolerance of folly, the mellowness that has survived the icy winds of disillusion. It was the absence of these contours that made Mark think his face so ecclesiastical; however, if at eighteen he had possessed contours and soft curves, they would have been nothing but the contours and soft curves of that rose, youth; and this ecclesiastical bonyness would not fade and fall as swiftly as that.

Mark turned from the glass in sudden irritation at his selfishness in speculating about his appearance and his future, when in a short time he should have to break the news to his guardian that he had thrown away for a kindly impulse the fruit of so many months of diligence and care.

"What am I going to say to Ogilvie?" he exclaimed. "I can't go back to Wych and live there in pleasant idleness until it's time to go to Glastonbury. I must have some scheme for the immediate future."

In bed when the light was out and darkness made the most fantastic project appear practical, Mark had an inspiration to take the habit of a preaching friar. Why should he not persuade Dorward to join him? Together they would tramp the English country, compelling even the dullest yokels to hear the word of God . . . discalced . . . over hill, down dale . . . telling stories of the saints and martyrs in remote inns . . . deep lanes . . . the butterflies and the birds . . . Dorward should say Mass in the heart of great woods . . . over hill, down dale . . . discalced . . . preaching to men of Christ. . . .

Mark fell asleep.

In the morning Mark heard Mass at the church of the Cowley Fathers, a strengthening experience, because the Gregorian there so strictly and so austerely chanted without any consideration for sentimental humanity possessed that very effect of liberating and purifying spirit held in the bonds of flesh which is conveyed by the wind blowing through a grove of pines or by waves quiring below a rocky shore.

If Mark had had the least inclination to be sorry for himself and indulge in the flattery of regret, it vanished in this music. Rolling down through time on the billows of the mighty Gregorian it were as grotesque to pity oneself as it were for an Arctic explorer to build a snowman for company at the North Pole.

Mark came out of St. John's, Cowley, into the suburban prettiness of Iffley Road, where men and women in their Sunday best tripped along in the April sunlight, tripped along in their Sunday best like newly hatched butterflies and beetles. Mark went in and out of colleges all day long, forgetting about the problem of his immediate future just as he forgot that the people in the sunny streets were not really butterflies and beetles. At twilight he decided to attend Evensong at St. Barnabas'. Perhaps the folk in the sunny April streets had turned his thoughts unconsciously toward the simple aspirations of simple human nature. He felt when he came into the warm candle-lit church like one who has voyaged far and is glad to be at home again. How everybody sang together that night, and how pleasant Mark found this congregational outburst. It was all so jolly that if the organist had suddenly turned round like an Italian organ-grinder and kissed his fingers to the congregation, his action would have seemed perfectly appropriate. Even during the *Magnificat*, when the altar was being censed, the tinkling of the thurible reminded Mark of a tambourine; and the lighting and extinction of the candles was done with as much suppressed excitement as if the candles were going to shoot red and green stars or go leaping and cracking all round the chancel.

It happened this evening that the preacher was Father Rowley, that famous priest of the Silchester College Mission in the great naval port of Chatsea. Father Rowley was a very corpulent man with a voice of such compassion and with an eloquence so simple that when he ascended into the pulpit, closed his eyes, and began to speak, his listeners involuntarily closed their eyes and followed that voice whithersoever it led them. He neither changed the expression of his face nor made use of dramatic gestures; he scarcely varied his tone, yet he could keep a congregation breathlessly attentive for an hour. Although he seemed to be speaking in a kind of trance, it was evident that he was unusually conscious of his hearers, for if by chance some pious woman coughed or turned the pages of a prayer-book he would hold up the thread of his sermon and without any change of tone reprove her. It was strange to watch him at such a moment, his eyes still tightly shut and yet giving the impression of looking directly at the offending member of the congregation. This evening he was preaching about a naval disaster which had lately occurred, the sinking of a great battleship by another great battleship through a wrong signal. He was describing the scene when the news reached Chatsea, telling of the sweethearts and wives of the lost bluejackets who waited hoping against hope to hear that their loved ones had escaped death and hearing nearly always the worst news.

"So many of our own dear bluejackets and marines, some of whom only last Christmas had been eating their plum duff at our Christmas dinner, so many of my own dear boys whom I prepared for Confirmation, whose first Confession I had heard, and to whom I had given for the first time the Body and Blood of Our Lord Jesus Christ."

He spoke too of what it meant in the future of material suffering on top of their mental agony. He asked for money to help these women immediately, and he spoke fiercely of the Admiralty red tape and of the obstruction of the official commission appointed to administer the relief fund.

The preacher went on to tell stories from the lives of these boys, finding in each of them some illustration of a Christian virtue and conveying to his listeners a sense of the extraordinary preciousness of human life, so that there was no one who heard him but was fain to weep for those young bluejackets and marines taken in their prime. He inspired in Mark a sense of shame that he had ever thought of people in the aggregate, that he had ever walked along a crowded street without perceiving the importance of every single human being that helped to compose its variety. While he sat there listening to the Missioner and watching the large tears roll slowly down his cheeks from beneath the closed lids, Mark wondered how he could have dared to suppose last night that he was qualified to become a friar and preach the

Gospel to the poor. While Father Rowley was speaking, he began to apprehend that before he could aspire to do that he must himself first of all learn about Christ from those very poor whom he had planned to convert.

This sermon was another milestone in Mark's religious life. It discovered in him a hidden treasure of humility, and it taught him to build upon the rock of human nature. He divined the true meaning of Our Lord's words to St. Peter: *Thou art Peter and on this rock I will build my church and the gates of Hell shall not prevail against it.* John was the disciple whom Jesus loved, but he chose Peter with all his failings and all his follies, with his weakness and his cowardice and his vanity. He chose Peter, the bedrock of human nature, and to him he gave the keys of Heaven.

Mark knew that somehow he must pluck up courage to ask Father Rowley to let him come and work under him at Chatsea. He was sure that if he could only make him grasp the spirit in which he would offer himself, the spirit of complete humility devoid of any kind of thought that he was likely to be of the least use to the Mission, Father Rowley might accept his oblation. He would have liked to wait behind after Evensong and approach the Missioner directly, so that before speaking to Mr. Ogilvie he might know what chance the offer had of being accepted; but he decided against this course, because he felt that Father Rowley's compassion might be embarrassed if he had to refuse his request, a point of view that was characteristic of the mood roused in him by the sermon. He went back to sleep for the last time in an Oxford college, profoundly reassured of the rightness of his action in giving up the scholarship to Emmett, although, which was characteristic of his new mood, he had by this time begun to tell himself that he had really done nothing at all and that probably in any case Emmett would have been the chosen scholar.

If Mark had still any doubts of his behaviour, they would have vanished when on getting into the train for Shipcot he found himself in an otherwise empty third-class smoking carriage opposite Father Rowley himself, who with a small black bag beside him, so small that Mark wondered how it could possibly contain the night attire of so fat a man, was sitting back in the corner with a large pipe in his mouth. He was wearing one of those square felt hats sometimes seen on the heads of farmers, and if one had only seen his head and hat without the grubby clerical attire beneath one might have guessed him to be a farmer. Mark noticed now that his eyes of a limpid blue were like a child's, and he realized that in his voice while he was preaching there had been the same sweet gravity of childhood. Just at this moment Father Rowley caught sight of someone he knew on the platform and shouting from the window of the compartment he attracted the attention of a young man wearing an Old Siltonian tie.

"My dear man," he cried, "how are you? I've just made a most idiotic mistake. I got it into my head that I should be preaching here on the first Sunday in term and was looking forward to seeing so many Silchester men. I can't think how I came to make such a muddle."

Father Rowley's shoulders filled up all the space of the window, so that Mark only heard scattered fragments of the conversation, which was mostly about Silchester and the Siltonians he had hoped to see at Oxford.

"Good-bye, my dear man, good-bye," the Missioner shouted, as the train moved out of the station. "Come down and see us soon at Chatsea. The more of you men who come, the more we shall be pleased."

Mark's heart leapt at these words, which seemed of good omen to his own suit. When Father Rowley was ensconced in his corner and once more puffing away at his pipe, Mark thought how ridiculous it would sound to say that he had heard him preach last night at St. Barnabas' and that, having been much moved by the sermon, he was anxious to be taken on at St. Agnes' as a lay helper. He wished that Father Rowley would make some remark to him that would lead up to his request, but all that Father Rowley said was:

"This is a slow train to Birmingham, isn't it?"

This led to a long conversation about trains, and slow though this one might be it was going much too fast for Mark, who would be at Shipcot in another twenty minutes without having taken any advantage of his lucky encounter.

"Are you up at Oxford?" the priest at last inquired.

It was now or never; and Mark took the opportunity given him by that one question to tell Father Rowley twenty disjointed facts about his life, which ended with a request to be allowed to come and work at Chatsea.

"You can come and see us whenever you like," said the Missioner.

"But I don't want just to come and pay a visit," said Mark. "I really do want to be given something to do, and I shan't be any expense. I only want to keep enough money to go to Glastonbury in four years' time. If you'd only see how I got on for a month. I don't pretend I can be of any help to you. I don't suppose I can. But I do so tremendously want you to help me."

"Who did you say your father was?"

"Lidderdale, James Lidderdale. He was priest-in-charge of the Lima Street Mission, which belonged to St. Simon's, Notting Hill, in those days. St. Wilfred's, Notting Dale, it is now."

"Lidderdale," Father Rowley echoed. "I knew him. I knew him well. Lima Street. Viner's there now, a dear good fellow. So you're Lidderdale's son?"

"I say, here's my station," Mark exclaimed in despair, "and you haven't said whether I can come or not."

"Come down on Tuesday week," said Father Rowley. "Hurry up, or you'll get carried on to the next station."

Mark waved his farewell, and he knew, as he drove back on the omnibus over the rolling wold to Wych that he had this morning won something much better than a scholarship at St. Osmund's Hall.

CHAPTER XVI
CHATSEA

When Mark had been exactly a week at Chatsea he celebrated his eighteenth birthday by writing a long letter to the Rector of Wych:

St. Agnes' House,
Keppel Street,
Chatsea.
St. Mark's Day.
My dear Rector,

Thank you very much for sending me the money. I've handed it over to a splendid fellow called Gurney who keeps all the accounts (private or otherwise) in the Mission House. Poor chap, he's desperately ill with asthma, and nobody thinks he can live much longer. He suffers tortures, particularly at night, and as I sleep in the next room I can hear him.

You mustn't think me inconsiderate because I haven't written sooner, but I wanted to wait until I had seen a bit of this place before I wrote to you so that you might have some idea what I was doing and be able to realize that it is the one and only place where I ought to be at the moment.

But first of all before I say anything about Chatsea I want to try to express a little of what your kindness has meant to me during the last two years. I look back at myself just before my sixteenth birthday when I was feeling that I should have to run away to sea or do something mad in order to escape that solicitor's office, and I simply gasp! What and where should I be now if it hadn't been for you? You have always made light of the burden I must have been, and though I have tried to show you my gratitude I'm afraid it hasn't been very successful. I'm not being very successful now in putting it into words. I know my failure to gain a scholarship at Oxford has been a great disappointment to you, especially after you had worked so hard yourself to coach me. Please don't be anxious about my letting my books go to the wall here. I had a talk about this with Father Rowley, who insisted that anything I am allowed to do in the district must only be done when I have a good morning's work with my books behind me. I quite realize the importance of a priest's education. One of the assistant priests here, a man called Snaith, took a good degree at Cambridge both in classics and theology, so I shall have somebody to keep me on the lines. If I stay here three years and then have two years at Glastonbury I don't honestly think that I shall start off much handicapped by having missed both public school and university. I expect you're smiling to read after one week of my staying here three years! But I assure you that the moment I sat down to supper on the evening of my arrival I felt at home. I think at first they all thought I was an eager young Ritualist, but when they found that they didn't get any rises out of ragging me, they shut up.

This house is a most extraordinary place. It is an old Congregational chapel with a gallery all round which has been made into cubicles, scarcely one of which is ever empty or ever likely to be empty so far as I can see! I should think it must be rather like what the guest house of a monastery used to be like in the old days before the Reformation. The ground floor of the chapel has been turned into a gymnasium, and twice a week the apparatus is cleared away and we have a dance. Every other evening it's used furiously by Father Rowley's "boys." They're such a jolly lot, and most of them splendid gymnasts. Quite a few have become professional acrobats since they opened the gymnasium. The first morning after my arrival I asked Father Rowley if he'd got anything special for me to do and he told me to catalogue the books in his library. Everybody laughed at this, and I thought at first that some joke was intended, but when I got to his room I found it really was in utter confusion with masses of books lying about everywhere. So I set to work pretty hard and after about three days I got them catalogued and in good order. When I told him I had finished he looked very surprised, and a solemn visit of inspection was ordered. As the room was looking quite tidy at last, I didn't mind. I've realized since that Father Rowley always sets people the task of cataloguing and arranging his books when he doubts if they are really worth their salt, and he complains that I have spoilt one of his best ordeals for slackers. I said to him that he needn't be afraid because from what I could see of the way he treated books they would be just as untidy as ever in another week. Everybody laughed, though I was afraid at first they might consider it rather cheek my talking like this, but you've got to stand up for yourself here because there never was such a place for turning a man inside out. It's a real discipline, and I think if I manage to deserve to stay here three years I shall have the right to feel I've had the finest training for Holy Orders anybody could possibly have.

You know enough about Father Rowley yourself to understand how impossible it would be for me to give any impression of his personality in a letter. I have never felt so strongly the absolute goodness of anybody. I suppose that some of the great mediæval saints like St. Francis and St. Anthony of Padua must have been like that. One reads about them and what they did, but the facts one reads don't really tell anything. I always feel that what we really depend on is a kind of tradition of their absolute saintliness handed on from the people who experienced it. I suppose in a way the same applies to Our Lord. I always feel it wouldn't matter a bit to me if the four Gospels were proved to be forgeries to-morrow, because I should still be convinced that Our Lord was God. I know this is a platitude, but I don't think until I met Father Rowley that I ever realized the force and power that goes with exceptional goodness. There are so many people who are good because they were born good. Richard Ford, for example, he couldn't have ever been anything else but good, but I always feel that people like him remain practically out of reach of the ordinary person and that the goodness is all their own and dies with them just as it was born with them. What I feel about a man like Father Rowley is that he probably had a tremendous fight to be good. Of course, I may be perfectly wrong and he may have had no fight at all. I know one of the people at the Mission House told me that, though there is nobody who likes smoking

214

better than he or more enjoys a pint of beer with his dinner, he has given up both at St. Agnes merely to set an example to weak people. I feel that his goodness was with such energy fought for that it now exists as a kind of complete thing and will go on existing when Father Rowley himself is dead. I begin to understand the doctrine of the treasury of merit. I remember you once told me how grateful I ought to be to God because I had apparently escaped the temptations that attack most boys. I am grateful; but at the same time I can't claim any merit for it! The only time in my life when I might have acquired any merit was when I was at Haverton House. Instead of doing that, I just dried up, and if I hadn't had that wonderful experience at Whitsuntide in Meade Cantorum church nearly three years ago I should be spiritually dead by now.

This is a very long letter, and I don't seem to have left myself any time to tell you about St. Agnes' Church. It reminds me of my father's mission church in Lima Street, and oddly enough a new church is being built almost next door just as one was being built in Lima Street. I went to the children's Mass last Sunday, and I seemed to see him walking up and down the aisle in his alb, and I thought to myself that I had never once asked you to say Mass for his soul. Will you do so now next time you say a black Mass? This is a wretched letter, and it doesn't succeed in the least in expressing what I owe to you and what I already owe to Father Rowley. I used to think that the Sacred Heart was a rather material device for attracting the multitude, but I'm beginning to realize in the atmosphere of St. Agnes' that it is a gloriously simple devotion and that it is human nature's attempt to express the inexpressible. I'll write to you again next week. Please give my love to everybody at the Rectory.

Always your most affectionate

Mark.

Father Rowley had been at St. Agnes' seven or eight years when Mark found himself attached to the Mission, in which time he had transformed the district completely. It was a small parish (actually of course it was not a parish at all, although it was fast qualifying to become one) of something over a thousand small houses, few of which were less than a century old. The streets were narrow and crooked, mostly named after bygone admirals or forgotten sea-fights; the romantic and picturesque quarter of a great naval port to the casual glance of a passer-by, but heartbreaking to any except the most courageous resident on account of its overcrowded and tumbledown condition. Yet it lacked the dreariness of an East End slum, for the sea winds blew down the narrowest streets and alleys, sailors and soldiers were always in view, and the windows of the pawnbrokers were filled with the relics of long voyages, with idols and large shells, with savage weapons and the handiwork of remote islands.

When Mark came to live in Keppel Street, most of the brothels and many of the public houses had been eliminated from the district, and in their place flourished various clubs and guilds. The services in the church were crowded: there was a long roll of communicants; the civilization of the city of God was visible in this Chatsea slum. One or two of the lay helpers used to horrify Mark with stories of early days there, and when he seemed inclined to regret that he had arrived so late upon the scene, they used to tease him about his missionary spirit.

"If he can't reform the people," said Cartwright, one of the lay helpers, a tall thin young man with a long nose and a pleasant smile, "he still has us to reform."

"Come along, Mark Anthony," said Warrender, another lay helper, who after working for seven years among the poor had at last been charily accepted by the Bishop for ordination. "Come along. Why don't you try your hand on us?"

"You people seem to think," said Mark, "that I've got a mania for reforming. I don't mean that I should like to see St. Agnes' where it was merely for my own personal amusement. The only thing I'm sorry about is that I didn't actually see the work being done."

Father Rowley came in at this moment, and everybody shouted that Mark was going to preach a sermon.

"Splendid," said the Missioner whose voice when not moved by emotion was rich in a natural unction that encouraged everyone round to suppose he was being successfully humorous, such a savour did it add to the most innutritious chaff. Those who were privileged to share his ordinary life never ceased to wonder how in the pulpit or in the confessional or at prayer this unction was replaced by a remote beauty of tone, a plangent and thrilling compassion that played upon the hearts of all who heard him.

"Now really, Father Rowley," Mark protested. "Do I preach a great deal? I'm always being chaffed by Cartwright and Warrender about an alleged mania for reforming people, which only exists in their imagination."

Indeed Mark had long ago grown out of the desire to reform or to convert anybody, although had he wished to keep his hand in, he could have had plenty of practice among the guests of the Mission House. Nobody had ever succeeded in laying down the exact number of casual visitors that could be accommodated therein. However full it appeared, there was always room for one more. Taking an average, day in, day out through the year, one might fairly say that there were always eight or nine casual guests in addition to the eight or nine permanent residents, of whom Mark was soon glad to be able to count himself one. The company was sufficiently mixed to have been offered as a proof to the sceptical that there was something after all in simple Christianity. There would usually be a couple of prefects from Silchester, one or two 'Varsity men, two or three bluejackets or marines, an odd soldier or so, a naval officer perhaps, a stray priest sometimes, an earnest seeker after Christian example often, and often a drunkard who had been dumped down at the door of St. Agnes' Mission House in the hope that where everybody else had failed Father Rowley might succeed. Then there were the tramps, some who had heard of a comfortable night's lodging, some who came whining and cringing with a pretence of religion. This last class was discouraged as much as possible, for one of the first rules of the Mission House was to show no favour to any man who claimed to be religious, it being Father Rowley's chief dread to make anybody's religion a paying concern. Sometimes a jailbird just released from prison would find in the Mission House an opportunity to recover his self-respect. But whoever the guest was, soldier, sailor, tinker, tailor, apothecary, ploughboy, or thief, he was judged at the Mission House as a man. Some of the visitors repaid their host by theft or fraud; but when they did, nobody uttered proverbs or platitudes about mistaken kindness. If one lame dog bit the hand that was helping him over the stile, the next dog that came limping along was helped over just as freely.

"What right has one miserable mortal to be disillusioned by another miserable mortal?" Father Rowley demanded. "Our dear Lord when he was nailed to the cross said 'Father, forgive them, for they know not what they do.' He did not say, 'I am fed up with these people I have come down from Heaven to save. I've had enough of it. Send an angel with a pair of pincers to pull out these nails.'"

If the Missioner's patience ever failed, it was when he had to deal with High Church young men who made pilgrimages to St. Agnes' because they had heard that this or that service was conducted there with a finer relish of Romanism than anywhere else at the moment in England. On one occasion a pietistic young creature, who brought with him his own lace cotta but forgot to bring his nightshirt, begged to be allowed the joy of serving Father Rowley at early Mass next morning. When they came back and were sitting round the breakfast table, this young man simpered in a ladylike voice:

"Oh, Father, couldn't you keep your fingers closed when you give the *Dominus vobiscum*?"

"Et cum spiritu tuo," shouted Father Rowley. "I can keep my fingers closed when I box your ears."

And he proved it.

It was a real box on the ears, so hard a blow that the ladylike young man burst into tears to the great indignation of a Chief Petty Officer staying in the Mission House, who declared that he was half in a mind to catch the young swab such a snitch on the conk as really would give him something to blubber about. Father Rowley evidently had no remorse for his violence, and the young man went away that afternoon saying how sorry he was that the legend of the good work being done at St. Agnes' had been so much exaggerated.

Mark wrote an account of this incident, which had given him intense pleasure, to Mr. Ogilvie. Perhaps the Rector was afraid that Mark in his ambition to avoid "churchiness" was inclining toward the opposite extreme; or perhaps, charitable and saintly man though he was, he felt a pang of jealousy at Mark's unbounded admiration of his new friend; or perhaps it was merely that the east wind was blowing more sharply than usual that morning over the wold into the Rectory garden. Whatever the cause, his answering letter made Mark feel that the Rector did not appreciate Father Rowley as thoroughly as he ought.

The Rectory,
Wych-on-the-Wold.
Oxon.
Dec. 1.
My dear Mark,

I was glad to get your long and amusing letter of last week. I am delighted to think that as the months go by you are finding work among the poor more and more congenial. I would not for the world suggest your coming back here for Christmas after what you tell me of the amount of extra work it will entail for everybody in the Mission House; at the same time it would be useless to pretend that we shan't all be disappointed not to see you until the New Year.

On reading through your last letter again I feel just a little worried lest, in the pleasure you derive from Father Rowley's treatment of what was no doubt a very irritating young man, you may be inclined to go to the opposite extreme and be too ready to laugh at real piety when it is not accompanied by geniality and good fellowship, or by an obvious zeal for good works. I know you will acquit me of any desire to defend extreme "churchiness," and I have no doubt you will remember one or two occasions in the past when I was rather afraid that you were tending that way yourself. I am not in the least criticizing Father Rowley's method of dealing with it, but I am a trifle uneasy at the inordinate delight it seems to have afforded you. Of course, it is intolerable for any young man serving a priest at Mass to watch his fingers all the time, but I don't think you have any right to assume because on this occasion the young man showed himself so sensitive to mere externals that he is always aware only of externals. Unfortunately a very great deal of true and fervid piety exists under this apparent passion for externals. Remember that the ordinary criticism by the man in the street of Catholic ceremonies and of Catholic methods of worship involves us all in this condemnation. I suppose that you would consider yourself justified, should the circumstances permit (which in this case of course they do not), in protesting against a priest's not taking the Eastward Position when he said Mass. I was talking to Colonel Fraser the other day, and he was telling me how much he had enjoyed the ministrations of the Reverend Archibald Tait, the Leicestershire cricketer, who throughout the "second service" never once turned his back on the congregation, and, so far as I could gather from the Colonel's description, conducted this "second service" very much as a conjuror performs his tricks. When I ventured to argue with the Colonel, he said to me: "That is the worst of you High Churchmen, you make the ritual more important than the Communion itself." All human judgments, my dear Mark, are relative, and I have no doubt that this unpleasant young man (who, as I have already said, was no doubt justly punished by Father Rowley) may have felt the same kind of feeling in a different degree that I should feel if I assisted at the jugglery of the Reverend Archibald Tait. At any rate you, my dear boy, are bound to credit this young man with as much sincerity as yourself, otherwise you commit a sin against charity. You must acquire at least as much toleration for the Ritualist as I am glad to notice you are acquiring for the thief. When you are a priest yourself, and in a comparatively short time you will be a priest, I do hope you won't, without his experience, try to imitate Father Rowley too closely in his summary treatment of what I have already I hope made myself quite clear in believing to be in this case a most insufferable young man. Don't misunderstand this letter. I have such great hopes of you in the stormy days to come, and the stormy days are coming, that I should feel I was wrong if I didn't warn you of your attitude towards the merest trifles, for I shall always judge you and your conduct by standards that I should be very cautious of setting for most of my penitents.

Your ever affectionate,

Stephen Ogilvie.

My mother and Miriam send you much love. We miss you greatly at Wych. Esther seems happy in her convent and will soon be clothed as a novice.

When Mark read this letter, he was prompt to admit himself in the wrong; but he could not bear the least implied criticism of Father Rowley.

St. Agnes' House,

Keppel Street,

Chatsea.

Dec. 3.

My dear Mr. Ogilvie,

I'm afraid I must have expressed myself very badly in my last letter if I gave you the least idea that Father Rowley was not always charity personified. He had probably come to the conclusion that the young man was not much good and no doubt he deliberately made it impossible for him to stay on at the Mission House. We do get an awful lot of mere loafers here; I don't suppose that anybody who keeps open house can avoid getting them. After all, if the young man had been worth anything he would have realized that he had made a fool of himself and by the way he took his snubbing have re-established himself. What he actually did was to sulk and clear out with a sneer at the work done here. I'm sorry I gave you the impression that I was triumphing so tremendously over his discomfiture. By writing about it I probably made the incident appear much more important than it really was. I've no doubt I did triumph a little, and I'm afraid I shall never be able not to feel rather glad when a fellow like that is put in his place. I am not for a moment going to try to argue that you can carry Christian charity too far. The more one meditates on the words, and actions of Our Lord, the more one grasps how impossible it is to carry charity too far. All the same, one owes as much charity to Father Rowley as to the young man. This sounds now I have written it down as if I were getting in a hit at you, and that is the worst of writing letters to justify oneself. What I am trying to say is that if I were to have taken up arms for the young man and supposed him to be ill-used or misjudged I should be criticizing Father Rowley. I think that perhaps you don't quite realize what a saint he is in every way. This is my fault, no doubt, because in my letters to you I have always emphasized anything that would bring into relief his personality. I expect that I've been too much concerned to draw a picture of him as a man, in doing which I've perhaps been unsuccessful in giving you a picture of him as a priest. It's always difficult to talk or write about one's intimate religious feelings, and you've been the only person to whom I ever have been able to talk about them. However much I admire and revere Father Rowley I doubt if I could talk or write to him about myself as I do to you.

Until I came here I don't think I ever quite realized all that the Blessed Sacrament means. I had accepted the Sacrifice of the Mass as one accepts so much in our creed, without grasping its full implication. If anybody were to have put me through a catechism about the dogma I should have answered with theological exactitude, without any appearance of misapprehending the meaning of it; but it was not until I came here that its practical reality—I don't know if I'm expressing myself properly or not, I'm pretty sure I'm not; I don't mean practical application and I don't mean any kind of addition to my faith; perhaps what I mean is that I've learnt to grasp the mystery of the Mass outside myself, outside that is to say my own devotion, my own awe, as a practical fact alive to these people here. Sometimes when I go to Mass I feel as people who watched Our Lord with His disciples and followers must have felt. I feel like one of those people who ran after Him and asked Him what they could do to be saved. I feel when I look at what has been done here as if I must go to each of these poor people in turn and beg them to bring me to the feet of Christ, just as I suppose on the shores of the sea of Galilee people must have begged St. Peter or St. Andrew or St. James or St. John to introduce them, if one can use such a word for such an occasion. This seems to me the great work that Father Rowley has effected in this parish. I have only had one rather shy talk with him about religion, and in the course of it I said something in praise of what his personality had effected.

"My personality has effected nothing," he answered. "Everything here is effected by the Blessed Sacrament."

That is why he surely has the right without any consideration for the dignity of churchy young men to box their ears if they question his outward respect for the Blessed Sacrament. Even Our Lord found it necessary at least on one occasion to chase the buyers and sellers out of the Temple, and though it is not recorded that He boxed the ears of any Pharisee, it seems to me quite permissible to believe that He did! He lashed them with scorn anyway.

To come back to Father Rowley, you know the great cry of the so-called Evangelical party "Jesus only"? Well, Father Rowley has really managed to make out of what was becoming a sort of ecclesiastical party cry something that really is evangelical and at the same time Catholic. These people are taught to make the Blessed Sacrament the central fact of their lives in a way that I venture to say no Welsh revivalist or Salvation Army captain has ever made Our Lord the central fact in the lives of his converts, because with the Blessed Sacrament continually before them, Which is Our Lord Jesus Christ, their conversion endures. I could fill a book with stories of the wonderful behaviour of these poor souls. The temptation is to say of a man like Father Rowley that he has such a natural spring of human charity flowing from his heart that by offering to the world a Christlike example he converts his flock. Certainly he does give a Christlike example and undoubtedly that must have a great influence on his people; but he does not believe, and I don't believe, that a Christlike example is of any use without Christ, and he gives them Christ. Even the Bishop of Silchester had to admit the other day that Vespers of the Blessed Sacrament as held at St. Agnes' is a perfectly scriptural service.

Father Rowley makes of the Blessed Sacrament Christ Himself, so that the poor people may flock round Him. He does not go round arguing with them, persuading them, but in the crises of their lives, as the answer to every question, as the solution of every difficulty and doubt, as the consolation in every sorrow, he offers them the Blessed Sacrament. All his prayers (and he makes a great use of extempore prayer, much to the annoyance of the Bishop, who considers it ungrammatical), all his sermons, all his actions revolve round that one great fact. "Jesus Christ is what you need," he says, "and Jesus Christ is here in your church, here upon your altar."

You can't go into the little church without finding fifty people praying before the Blessed Sacrament. The other day when the "King Harry" was sunk by the "Trafalgar," the people here subscribed I forget how many pounds for the widows and children of the bluejackets and marines of the Mission who were drowned, and when it was finished and the subscription list was closed, they subscribed all over again to erect an altar at which to say Masses for the dead. And the old women living in Father Rowley's free houses that were once brothels gave up their summer outing so that the money spent on them might be added to the fund. When the Bishop of Silchester came here last week for Confirmation he asked Father Rowley what that altar was.

"That is the ugliest thing I've ever seen," he said. But when Father Rowley told him about the poor people and the old women who had no money of their own, he said: "That is the most beautiful thing I've ever heard."

I am beginning to write as if it was necessary to convince you of the necessity of making the Blessed Sacrament the central feature of the religious life to-day and for ever until the end of the world. But, I know you won't think I'm doing anything of the kind, for really I am only trying to show you how much my faith has been strengthened and how much my outlook has deepened and how much more than ever I long to be a priest to be able to give poor people Jesus Christ in the Blessed Sacrament.

Your ever affectionate
Mark.

CHAPTER XVII
THE DRUNKEN PRIEST

Gradually, Mark found to his pleasure and his pride that he was becoming, if not indispensable to Father Rowley (the Missioner found no human being indispensable) at any rate quite evidently useful. Perhaps Father Rowley though that in allowing himself to rely considerably upon Mark's secretarial talent he was indulging himself in a luxury to which he was not entitled. That was Father Rowley's way. The moment he discovered himself enjoying anything too much, whether it was a cigar or a secretary, he cut himself off from it, and this not in any spirit of mortification for mortification's sake, but because he dreaded the possibility of putting the slightest drag upon his freedom to criticize others. He had no doubt at all in his own mind that he was perfectly justified in making use of Mark's intelligence and energy. But in a place like the Mission House, where everybody from lay helper to casual guest was supposed to stand on his own feet, the Missioner himself felt that he must offer an example of independence.

"You're spoiling me, Mark Anthony," he said one day. "There's nothing for me to do this evening."

"I know," Mark agreed contentedly. "I want to give you a rest for once."

"Rest?" the priest echoed. "You don't seriously expect a fat man like me to sit down in an armchair and rest, do you? Besides, you've got your own reading to do, and you didn't come to Chatsea as my punkah walla."

Mark insisted that he was getting along in his own way quite fast enough, and that he had plenty of time on his hands to keep Father Rowley's correspondence in some kind of order.

"All these other people have any amount to do," said Mark. "Cartwright has his boys every evening and Warrender has his men."

"And Mark Anthony has nothing but a fat, poverty-stricken, slothful mission priest," Father Rowley gurgled.

"Yes, and you're more trouble than all the rest put together. Look here, I've written to the Bishop's chaplain about that confirmation; I explained why we wanted to hold a special confirmation for these two boys we are emigrating, and he has written back to say that the Bishop has no objection to a special confirmation's being held by the Bishop of Matabeleland when he comes to stay here next week. At the same time, he says the Bishop doesn't want it to become a precedent."

"No. I can quite understand that," Father Rowley chuckled. "Bishops are haunted by the creation of precedents. A precedent in the life of a bishop is like an illegitimate child in the life of a respectable churchwarden. No, the only thing I fear is that if I devour all your spare time you won't get quite what you wanted to get by coming to live with us."

He laid a fat hand on Mark's shoulder.

"Please don't bother about me," said Mark. "I get all I want and more than I expected if I can be of the least use to you. I know I'm rather disappointing you by not behaving like half the people who come down here and want to get up a concert on Monday, a dance on Tuesday, a conjuring entertainment on Wednesday, a street procession on Thursday, a day of intercession on Friday, and an amateur dramatic entertainment on Saturday, not to mention acting as ceremonarius on Sunday. I know you'd like me to propose all sorts of energetic diversions, so that you could have the pleasure of assuring me that I was only proposing them to gratify my own vanity, which of course would be perfectly true. Luckily I'm of a retiring disposition, and I don't want to do anything to help the ten thousand benighted parishioners of Saint Agnes', except indirectly by striving to help in my own feeble way the man who really is helping them. Now don't throw that inkpot at me, because the room's quite dirty enough already, and as I've made you sit still for five minutes I've achieved something this evening that mighty few people have achieved in Keppel Street. I believe the only time you really rest is in the confessional box."

"Mark Anthony, Mark Anthony," said the priest, "you talk a great deal too much. Come along now, it's bedtime."

One of the rules of the Mission House was that every inmate should be in bed by ten o'clock and all lights out by a quarter past. The day began with Mass at seven o'clock at which everybody was expected to be present; and from that time onward everybody was so fully occupied that it was essential to go to bed at a reasonable hour. Guests who came down for a night or two were often apt to forget how much the regular workers had to do and what a tax it put upon the willing servants to manage a house of which nobody could say ten minutes before a meal how many would sit down to it, nor even until lights out for how many people beds must be made. In case any guest should forget this rule by coming back after ten o'clock, Father Rowley made a point of having the front door bell to ring in his bedroom, so that he might get out of bed at any hour of the night and admit the loiterer. Guests were warned what would be the effect of their lack of consideration, and it was seldom that Father Rowley was disturbed.

Among the guests there was one class of which a representative was usually to be found at the Mission House. This was the drunken clergyman, which sounds as if there was at this date a high proportion of drunken clergymen in the Church of England; but which means that when one did come to St. Agnes' he usually stayed for a long time, because he would in most cases have been sent there when everybody else had despaired of him to see what Father Rowley could effect.

About the time when Mark was beginning to be recognized as Father Rowley's personal vassal, it happened that the Reverend George Edward Mousley who had been handed on from diocese to diocese during the last five years had lately reached the Mission House. For more than two months now he had spent his time inconspicuously reading in his own room, and so well had he behaved, so humbly had he presented himself to the notice of his fellow guests, that Father Rowley was moved one afternoon to dictate a letter about him to Mark, who felt that the Missioner by taking him so far into his confidence had surrendered to his pertinacity and that thenceforth he might consider himself established as his private secretary.

"The letter is to the Lord Bishop Suffragan of Warwick, St. Peter's Rectory, Warwick," Father Rowley began. "My dear Bishop of Warwick, I have now had poor Mousley here for two months. It is not a long time in which to effect a lasting reformation of one who has fallen so often and so grievously, but I think you know me well enough not to accuse me of being too sanguine about drunken priests. I have had too many of them here for that. In his case however I do feel justified in asking you to agree with me in letting him have an opportunity to regain the respect due to himself and the reverence due to his priesthood by being allowed once more to the altar. I should not dream of allowing him to officiate without your permission, because his sad history has been so much a personal burden to yourself. I'm afraid that after the many disappointments he has inflicted upon you, you will be doubtful of my judgment. Yet I do think that the critical moment has arrived when by surprising him thus we might clinch the matter of his future behaviour once and for all. His conduct here has been so humble and patient and in every way exemplary that my heart bleeds for him. Therefore, my dear Bishop of Warwick, I hope you will agree to what I firmly trust will be the completion of his spiritual cure. I am writing to you quite impersonally and informally, as you see, so that in replying to me you will not be involving yourself in the affairs of another diocese. You will, of course, put me down as much a Jesuit as ever in writing to you like this, but you will equally, I know, believe me to be, Yours ever affectionately in Our Blessed Lord.

"And I'll sign it as soon as you can type it out," Father Rowley wound up.

"Oh, I do hope he will agree," Mark exclaimed.

"He will," the Missioner prophesied. "He will because he is a wise and tender and godly man and therefore will never be more than a Bishop Suffragan as long as he lives. Mark!"

Mark looked up at the severity of the tone.

"Mark! Correct me when I fall into the habit of sneering at the episcopate."

That night Father Rowley was attending a large temperance demonstration in the Town Hall for the purpose of securing if possible a smaller proportion of public houses than one for every eighty of the population, which was the average for Chatsea. The meeting lasted until nearly ten o'clock; and it had already struck the hour when Father Rowley with Mark and two or three others got back to Keppel Street. There was nothing Father Rowley disliked so much as arriving home himself after ten, and he hurried up to his room without inquiring if everybody was in.

Mark's window looked out on Keppel Street; and the May night being warm and his head aching from the effects of the meeting, he sat for nearly an hour at the open window gazing down at the passers by. There was not much to see, nothing more indeed than couples wandering home, a bluejacket or two, an occasional cat, and a few women carrying jugs of beer. By eleven o'clock even this slight traffic had ceased, and there was nothing down the silent street except a salt wind from the harbour that roused a memory of the beach at Nancepean years ago when he had sat there watching the glow-worm and decided to be a lighthouse-keeper keeping his lamps bright for mariners homeward bound. It was of streets like Keppel Street that they would have dreamed, with the Stag Light winking to port, and the west wind blowing strong astern. What a lighthouse-keeper Father Rowley was! How except by the grace of God could one explain such goodness as his? Fashions in saintliness might change, but there was one kind of saint that always and for every creed spoke plainly of God's existence, such saints as St. Francis of Assisi or St. Anthony of Padua, who were manifestly the heirs of Christ. With what a tender cynicism Our Lord had called St. Peter to be the foundation stone of His Church, with what a sorrowful foreboding of the failure of Christianity. Such a choice appeared as the expression of God's will not to be let down again as He was let down by Adam. Jesus Christ, conscious at the moment of what He must shortly suffer at the hands of mankind, must have been equally conscious of the failure of Christianity two thousand years beyond His Agony and Bloody Sweat and Crucifixion. Why, within a short time after His life on earth it was necessary for that light from heaven to shine round about Saul on the Damascus road, because already scoffers, while the disciples were still alive, may have been talking about the failure of Christianity. It must have been another of God's self-imposed limitations that He did not give to St. John that capacity of St. Paul for organization which might have made practicable the Christianity of the master Who loved him. *Woman, behold thy son! Behold thy mother!* That dying charge showed that Our Lord considered John the most Christlike of His disciples, and he remained the most Christlike man until twelve hundred years later St. Francis was born at Assisi. St. Paul, St. Augustine, St. Dominic, if Christianity could only produce mighty individualists of Faith like them, it could scarcely have endured as it had endured. *And now abideth faith, hope, charity, these three; but the greatest of these is charity.* There was something almost wistful in those words coming from the mouth of St. Paul. It was scarcely conceivable that St. John or St. Francis could ever have said that; it would scarcely have struck either that the three virtues were separable.

Keppel Street was empty now. Mark's headache had been blown away by the night wind with his memories and the incoherent thoughts which had gathered round the contemplation of Father Rowley's character. He was just going to draw away from the window and undress when he caught sight of a figure tacking from one pavement to the other up Keppel Street. Mark watched its progress, amused at the extraordinary amount of trouble it was giving itself, until one tack was brought to a sharp conclusion by a lamp-post to which the figure clung long enough to be recognized as that of the Reverend George Edward Mousley, who had been tacking like this to make the harbour of the Mission House. Mark, remembering the letter which had been written to the Bishop of Warwick, wondered if he could not at any rate for to-night spare Father Rowley the disappointment of knowing that his plea for re-instatement was already answered by the drunken priest himself. He must make up his mind quickly, because even with the zigzag course Mousley was taking he would soon be ringing the bell of the Mission House, which meant that Father Rowley would be woken up and go down to let him in. Of course, he would have to know all about it in the morning, but to-night when he had gone to bed tired and full of hope for temperance in general and the reformation of Mousley in particular it was surely right to let him sleep in ignorance. Mark decided to take it upon himself to break the rules of the house, to open the door to Mousley, and if possible to get him upstairs to bed quietly. He went down with a lighted candle, crept across the gymnasium, and opened the door. Mousley was still tacking from pavement to pavement and making very little headway against a strong current of drink. Mark thought he had better go out and offer his services as pilot, because Mousley was beginning to sing an extraordinary song in which the tune and the words of *Good-bye, Dolly, I must leave you,* had got mixed up with *O happy band of pilgrims.*

"Look here, Mr. Mousley, you mustn't sing now," said Mark taking hold of the arm with which the drunkard was trying to beat time. "It's after eleven o'clock, and you're just outside the Mission House."

"I've been just outside the Mission House for an hour and three quarters, old chap," said Mr. Mousley solemnly. "Most incompatible thing I've ever known. I got back here at a quarter past nine, and I was just going to walk in when the house took two paces to the rear, and I've been walking after it the whole evening. Most incompatible thing I've ever known. Most incompatible thing that's ever happened to me in my life, Lidderdale. If I were a superstitious man, which I'm not, I should say the house was bewitched. If I had a moment to spare, I should sit down at once and write an account of my most incompatible experience to the Society of Psychical Research, if I were a superstitious man, which I'm not. Yes. . . ."

Mr. Mousley tried to focus his glassy eyes upon the arcana of spiritualism, rocking ambiguously the while upon the kerb. Mark murmured something more about the need for going in quietly.

"It's very kind of you to come out and talk to me like this," the drunken priest went on. "But what you ought to have done was to have kept hold of the house for a minute or two so as to give me time to get in quietly. Now we shall probably both be out here all night trying to get in quietly. It's impossible to keep warm by this lamp-post. Most inadequate heating arrangement. It is a lamp-post, isn't it? Yes, I thought it was. I had a fleeting impression that it was my bedroom candle, but I see now that I was mistaken, I see now perfectly clearly that it is a lamp-post, if not two. Of course, that may account for my not being able to get into the Mission House. I was trying to decide which front door I should go in by, and while I was waiting I think I must have gone in by the wrong one, for I hit my nose a most severe blow on the nose. One has to remember to be very careful with front doors. Of course, if it was my own house I should have used a latch-key instanter; for I inevitably, I mean invariably, carry a latch-key about with me and when it won't open my front door I use it to wind my watch. You know, it's one of those small keys you can wind up watches with, if you know the kind of key I mean. I'd draw you a picture of it if I had a pencil, but I haven't got a pencil."

"Now don't stay talking here," Mark urged. "Come along back, and do try to come quietly. I keep telling you it's after eleven o'clock, and you know Father Rowley likes everybody to be in by ten."

"That's what I've been saying to myself the whole evening," said Mr. Mousley. "Only what happened, you see, was that I met the son of a man who used to know my father, a very nice fellow indeed, a very intellectual fellow. I never remember spending a more intellectual evening in my life. A feast of reason and a flowing bowl, I mean soul, s-o-u-l, not b-o-u-l. Did I say bowl? Soul. . . . Soul. . . ."

"All right," said Mark. "But if you've had such a jolly evening, come in now and don't make a noise."

"I'll come in whenever you like," Mr. Mousley offered. "I'm at your disposition entirely. The only request I have to make is that you will guarantee that the house stays where it was built. It's all very fine for an ordinary house to behave like this, but when a mission house behaves like this I call it disgraceful. I don't know what I've done to the house that it should conceive such a dislike to me. I say, Lidderdale, have they been taking up the drains or something in this street? Because I distinctly had an impression just then that I put my foot into a hole."

"The street's perfectly all right," said Mark. "Nothing has been done to it."

"There's no reason why they shouldn't take up the drains if they want to, I'm not complaining. Drains have to be taken up and I should be the last man to complain; but I merely asked a question, and I'm convinced that they have been taking up the drains. Yes, I've had a very intellectual evening. My head's whirling with philosophy. We've talked about everything. My friend talked a good deal about Buddhism. And I made rather a good joke about Confucius being so confusing, at which I laughed inordinately. Inordinately, Lidderdale. I've had a very keen sense of humour ever since I was a baby. I say, Lidderdale, you certainly know your way about this street. I'm very much obliged to me for meeting you. I shall get to know the street in time. You see, my object was to get beyond the house, because I said to myself 'the house is in Keppel Street, it can dodge about *in* Keppel Street, but it can't be in any other street,' so I thought that if I could dodge it into the corner of Keppel Street—you follow what I mean? I may be talking a bit above your head, we've been talking philosophy all the evening, but if you concentrate you'll follow my meaning."

"Here we are," said Mark, for by this time he had persuaded Mr. Mousley to put his foot upon the step of the front door.

"You managed the house very well," said the clergyman. "It's extraordinary how a house will take to some people and not to others. Now I can do anything I like with dogs, and you can do anything you like with houses. But it's no good patting or stroking a house. You've got to manage a house quite differently to that. You've got to keep a house's accounts. You haven't got to keep a dog's accounts."

They were in the gymnasium by now, which by the light of Mark's small candle loomed as vast as a church.

"Don't talk as you go upstairs," Mark admonished.

"Isn't that a dog I see there?"

"No, no, no," said Mark. "It's the horse. Come along."

"A horse?" Mousley echoed. "Well, I can manage horses too. Come here, Dobbin. If I'd known we were going to meet a horse I should have brought back some sugar with me. I suppose it's too late to go back and buy some sugar now?"

"Yes, yes," said Mark impatiently. "Much too late. Come along."

"If I had a piece of sugar he'd follow us upstairs. You'll find a horse will go anywhere after a piece of sugar. It is a horse, isn't it? Not a donkey? Because if it was a donkey he would want a thistle, and I don't know where I can get a thistle at this time of night. I say, did you prod me in the stomach then with anything?" asked Mr. Mousley severely.

"No, no," said Mark. "Come along, it was the parallel bars."

"I've not been near any bars to-night, and if you are suggesting that I've been in bars you're making an insinuation which I very much resent, an insinuation which I resent most bitterly, an insinuation which I should not allow anybody to make without first pointing out that it was an insinuation."

"Do come down off that ladder," Mark said.

"I beg your pardon, Lidderdale. I was under the impression for the moment that I was going upstairs. I have really been so confused by Confucius and by the extraordinary behaviour of the house to-night, recoiling from me as it did, that for the moment I was under the impression that I was going upstairs."

At this moment Mr. Mousley fell from the ladder, luckily on one of the gymnasium mats.

"I do think it's a most ridiculous habit," he said, "not to place a doormat in what I might describe as a suitable cavity. The number of times in my life that I've fallen over doormats simply because people will not take the trouble to make the necessary depression in the floor with which to contain such a useful domestic receptacle you would scarcely believe. I must have fallen over thousands of doormats in my life," he shouted at the top of his voice.

"You'll wake everybody up in the house," Mark exclaimed in an agony. "For heaven's sake keep quiet."

"Oh, we are in the house, are we?" said Mr. Mousley. "I'm very much relieved to hear you say that, Lidderdale. For a brief moment, I don't know why, I was almost as confused as Confucius as to where we were."

At this moment, candle in hand, and in a white flannel nightgown looking larger than ever, Father Rowley appeared in the gallery above and leaning over demanded who was there.

"Is that Father Rowley?" Mr. Mousley inquired with intense courtesy. "Or do my eyes deceive me? You'll excuse me from replying to your apparently simple question, Father Rowley, but I have met such a number of people to-night including the son of a man who used to know my father that I really don't know who *is* there, although I'm inclined to think that *I* am here. But I've had a series of such a remarkable series of adventures to-night that I should like your advice about them. I've been spending a very intellectual evening, Father Rowley."

"Go to bed," said the mission priest severely. "I'll speak to you in the morning."

"Father Rowley isn't annoyed with me, is he?" Mr. Mousley asked.

"I think he's rather annoyed at your being so late," said Mark.

"Late for what?"

"Is that you, Mark, down there?" asked the Missioner.

"I'm lighting Mr. Mousley across the gymnasium," Mark explained. "I think I'd better take him up to his room."

221

"If your young friend is as clever at managing rooms as he is at managing houses we shall get on splendidly, Father Rowley. I have perfect confidence in his manner with rooms. He soothed this house in the most remarkable way. It was jumping about like a pea in a pod till he caught hold of the reins."

"Mark, go to bed. I will see Mr. Mousley to his room."

"Several years ago," said the drunken priest. "I went with an old friend to see Miss Ellen Terry as Lady Macbeth. The resemblance between Father Rowley and Miss Ellen Terry is very remarkable. Good-night, Lidderdale, I am perfectly comfortable on this mat. Good-night."

In the gallery above Mark, who had not dared to disobey Father Rowley's orders, asked him what was to be done to get Mr. Mousley to bed.

"Go and wake Cartwright and Warrender to help me to get him upstairs," the Missioner commanded.

"I can help you. . . ." Mark began.

"Do what I say," said the Missioner curtly.

In the morning Father Rowley sent for Mark to give his account of what had happened the night before, and when Mark had finished his tale, the priest sat for a while in silence.

"Are you going to send him away?" Mark asked.

"Send him away?" Father Rowley repeated. "Where would I send him? If he can't keep off drink in this house and in these surroundings where else will he keep off drink? No, I'm only amused at my optimism."

There was a knock on the door.

"I expect that is Mr. Mousley," said Mark. "I'll leave you with him."

"No, don't go away," said the Missioner. "If Mousley didn't mind your seeing him as he was last night, there's no reason why this morning he should mind your hearing my comments upon his behaviour."

The tap on the door was repeated.

"Come in, come in, Mousley, and take a seat."

Mr. Mousley walked timidly across the room and sat on the very edge of the chair offered him by Father Rowley. He was a quiet, rather drab little man, the kind of little man who always loses his seat in a railway carriage and who always gets pushed further up in an omnibus, one of life's pawns. The presence of Mark did not seem to affect him, for no sooner was he seated than he began to apologize with suspicious rapidity, as if by now his apologies had been reduced to a formula.

"I really must apologize, Father Rowley, for my lateness last night and for coming in, I fear, slightly the worse for liquor. The fact is I had a little headache and went to the chemist for a pick-me-up, on top of which I met an old college friend, and though I don't think I had more than two glasses of beer I may have had three. They didn't seem to go very well with the pick-me-up. I assure you—"

"Stop," said Father Rowley. "The only assurance of any value to me will be your behaviour in the future."

"Oh, then I'm not to leave this morning?" Mr. Mousley gasped with open mouth.

"Where would you go if you left here?"

"Well, to tell you the truth," Mr. Mousley admitted, "I have been rather worried over that little problem ever since I woke up this morning. I scarcely expected that you would tolerate my presence any longer in this house. You will excuse me, Father Rowley, but I am rather overwhelmed for the moment by your kindness. I scarcely know how to express what I feel. I have usually found people so very impatient of my weakness. Do you seriously mean I needn't go away this morning?"

"You have already been sufficiently punished, I hope," said the Missioner, "by the humiliations you have inflicted on yourself both outside and inside this house."

"My thoughts are always humiliating," said Mr. Mousley. "I think perhaps that nowadays these humiliating thoughts are my chief temptation to drink. Since I have been here and shared in your hospitality I have felt more sharply than ever my disgrace. I have several times been on the point of asking you to let me be given some kind of work, but I have always been too much ashamed when it came to the point to express my aspirations in words."

"Only yesterday afternoon," said Father Rowley, "I wrote to the Bishop of Warwick, who has continued to interest himself in you notwithstanding the many occasions you have disappointed him, yes, I wrote to the Bishop of Warwick to say that since you came to St. Agnes' your behaviour had justified my suggesting that you should once again be allowed to say Mass."

"You wrote that yesterday afternoon?" Mr. Mousley exclaimed. "And the instant afterwards I went out and got drunk?"

"You mean you took a pick-me-up and two glasses of beer," corrected Father Rowley.

"No, no, no, it wasn't a pick-me-up. I went out and got drunk on brandy quite deliberately."

Father Rowley looked quickly across at Mark, who hastily left the two priests together. He divined from the Missioner's quick glance that he was going to hear Mr. Mousley's confession. A week later Mr. Mousley asked Mark if he would serve at Mass the next morning.

"It may seem an odd request," he said, "but inasmuch as you have seen the depths to which I can sink, I want you equally to see the heights to which Father Rowley has raised me."

CHAPTER XVIII
SILCHESTER COLLEGE MISSION

It was never allowed to be forgotten at St. Agnes' that the Mission was the Silchester College Mission; and there were few days in the year on which it was possible to visit the Mission House without finding there some member of the College past or present. Every Sunday during term two or three prefects would sit down to dinner; masters turned up during the holidays; even the mighty Provost himself paid occasional visits, during which he put off most of his majesty and became as nearly human as a facetious judge. Nor did Father Rowley allow Silchester to forget that it had a Mission. He was not at all content with issuing a half yearly report of progress and expenses, and he had no intention of letting St. Agnes' exist as a subject for an occasional school sermon or a religious tax levied on parents. From the first moment he had put foot in Chatsea he had done everything he could to make St. Agnes' be what it was supposed to be—the Silchester College Mission. He was particularly anxious that the new church should be built and beautified with money from Silchester sources, even if he also accepted money for this purpose from outside. Soon after Mark had become recognized as Father Rowley's confidential secretary, he visited Silchester for the first time in his company.

It was the custom during the summer for the various guilds and clubs connected with the parish to be entertained in turn at the College. It had never happened that Mark had accompanied any of these outings, which in the early days of St. Agnes' had been regarded with dread by the College authorities, so many flowers were picked, so much fruit was stolen, but which now were as orderly and respectable excursions as you could wish to see. Mark's first visit to Silchester was on the occasion of Father Rowley's terminal sermon in the June after he was nineteen. He found the experience intimidating, because he was not yet old enough to have learnt self-confidence and he had never passed through the ordeal either of a first term at a public school or of a first term at the University. Boys are always critical, and at Silchester with the tradition of six hundred years to give them a corporate self-confidence, the judgment of outsiders is more severe than anywhere in the world, unless it might be in the New Hebrides. Added to their critical regard was a chilling politeness which would have made downright insolence appear cordial in comparison. Mark felt like Gulliver in the presence of the Houyhnms. These noble animals, so graceful, so clean, so condescending, appalled him. Yet he had found the Silchester men who came to visit the Mission easy enough to get on with. No doubt they, without their background were themselves a little shy, although their shyness never mastered them so far as to make them ill at ease. Here, however, they seemed as imperturbable and unbending as the stone saints, row upon row on the great West front of the Cathedral. Mark apprehended more clearly than ever the powerful personality of Father Rowley when he found that these noble young animals accorded to him the same quality of respect that they gave to a popular master or even to a popular athlete. The Missioner seemed able to understand their intimate and allusive conversation, so characteristic of a small and highly developed society; he seemed able to chaff them at the right moment; to take them seriously when they ought to be taken seriously; in a word to have grasped without being a Siltonian the secret of Silchester. He and Mark were staying at a house which possessed super-imposed upon the Silchester tradition a tradition of its own extending over the forty years during which the Reverend William Jex Monkton had been a house master. It was difficult for Mark, who had nothing but the traditions of Haverton House for a standard to understand how with perfect respect the boys could address their master by his second name without prejudice to discipline. Yet everybody in Jex's house called him Jex; and when you looked at that delightful old gentleman himself with his criss-cross white tie and curly white hair, you realized how impossible it was for him to be called anything else except Jex.

For the first time since Mark, brooding upon the moonlit quadrangle of St. Osmund's Hall, bade farewell to Oxford, he regretted for a while his surrender of the scholarship to Emmett. What was Emmett doing now? Had his stammer improved in the confidence that his success must surely have brought him? Mark made an excuse to forsake the company of the four or five men in whose charge he had been left. He was tired of being continually rescued from drowning in their conversation. Their intentional courtesy galled him. He felt like a negro chief being shown the sights of England by a tired equerry. It was a fine summer day, and he went down to the playing fields to watch the cricket match. He sat down in the shade of an oak tree on the unfrequented side, unable in the mood he was in to ask against whom the College was playing or which side was in. Players and spectators alike appeared unreal, a mirage of the sunlight; the very landscape ceased to be anything more substantial than a landscape perceived by dreamers in the clouds. The trees and towers of Silchester, the bald hills of Berkshire on the horizon, the cattle in the meadows, the birds in the air exasperated Mark with his inability to put himself in the picture. The grass beneath the oak was scattered with a treasury of small suns minted by the leaves above, trembling patens and silver disks that Mark set himself to count.

"Trying not to yearn and trying not to yawn," he muttered. "Forty-four, forty-five, forty-six."

"You're ten out," said a voice. "We want fifty-six to tie, fifty-seven to win."

Mark looked up and saw that a Silchester man whom he remembered seeing once at the Mission was preparing to sit down beside him. He was a tall youth, fair and freckled and clear cut, perfectly self-possessed, but lacking any hint of condescension in his manner.

"Didn't you come over with Rowley?" he inquired.

Mark was going to explain that he was working at the Mission when it struck him that a Silchester man might have the right to resent that, and he gave no more than a simple affirmative.

"I remember seeing you at the Mission," he went on. "My name's Hathorne. Oh, well hit, sir, well hit!"

Hathorne's approbation of the batsman made the match appear even more remote. It was like the comment of a passer-by upon a well-designed figure in a tapestry. It was an expression of his own æsthetic pleasure, and bore no relation to the player he applauded.

"I've only been down to the Mission once," he continued, turning to Mark. "I felt rather up against it there."

"Well, I feel much more up against it in Silchester," replied Mark.

"Yes, I can understand that," Hathorne nodded. "But you're only up against form: I was up against matter. It struck me when I was down there what awful cheek it was for me to be calmly going down to Chatsea and supposing that I had a right to go there, because I had contributed a certain amount of money belonging to my father, to help spiritually a lot of people who probably need spiritual help much less than I do myself. Of course, with anybody else except Rowley in charge the effect would be damnable. As it is, he manages to keep us from feeling as if we'd paid to go and look at the Zoo. You're a lucky chap to be working there without the uncomfortable feeling that you're just being tolerated because you're a Siltonian."

"I was thinking," said Mark, "that I was only being tolerated here because I happened to come with Rowley. It's impossible to visit a place like this and not regret that one must remain an outsider."

"It depends on what you want to do," said Hathorne. "I want to be a parson. I'm going up to the Varsity in October, and I am beginning to wonder what on earth good I shall be at the end of it all."

He gave Mark an opportunity to comment on this announcement; but Mark did not know what to say and remained silent.

"I see you're not in the mood to be communicative," Hathorne went on with a smile. "I don't blame you. It's impossible to be communicative in this place; but some time, when I'm down at the Mission again, I'd like to have what is called a heart-to-heart talk. That was a good boundary. We shall win quite comfortably. So long!"

The tall, fair youth passed on; and although Mark never had that heart-to-heart talk with him in the Mission, because he was killed in a mountaineering accident in Switzerland that August, the memory of him sitting there under the oak tree on that fine summer afternoon remained with Mark for ever; and after that brief conversation he lost most of his shyness, so that he came to enjoy his visits to Silchester as much as the Missioner himself did.

As the new church drew near its completion, Mark apprehended why Father Rowley attached so much importance to as much of the money for it as possible coming directly from Silchester. He apprehended how the Missioner felt that he was building Silchester in a Chatsea slum; and from that moment that landscape like a mirage of the sunlight, that landscape into which he had been unable to fit himself when he first beheld it became his own, for now beyond the chimneypots he could always see the bald hills of Berkshire and the trees and towers of Silchester, and at the end of all the meanest alleys there were cattle in the meadows and birds in the air above.

Silchester was not the only place that Mark visited with Father Rowley. It became a recognized custom for him to travel up to London whenever the Missioner was preaching, and in London he was once more struck by the variety of Father Rowley's worldly knowledge and secular friends. One week-end will serve as a specimen of many. They left Chatsea on a Saturday morning travelling up to town in a third class smoker full of bluejackets and soldiers on leave. None of them happened to know the Missioner, and for a time they talked surlily in undertones, evidently viewing with distaste the prospect of having a Holy Joe in their compartment all the way to London; but when Father Rowley pulled out his pipe, for always when he was away from St. Agnes' he allowed himself the privilege of smoking, and began to talk to them about their ships and their regiments with unquestionable knowledge, they unbent, so that long before Waterloo was reached it must have been the jolliest compartment in the whole train. It was all done so easily, and yet without any of that deliberate descent from a pedestal, which is the democratic manner of so many parsons; there was none of that Friar Tuck style of aggressive laymanhood, nor that subtler way of denying Christ (of course with the best intentions) which consists of salting the conversation with a few "damns" and peppering it with a couple of "bloodies" to show that a parson may be what is called human. Father Rowley was simply himself; and a month later two of the bluejackets in that compartment and one of the soldiers were regular visitors to the Mission House, and what is more regular visitors to the Blessed Sacrament.

They reached London soon after midday and went to lunch at a restaurant in Jermyn Street famous for a Russian salad that Father Rowley sometimes spoke of with affection in Chatsea. After lunch they went to a matinée of *Pelleas and Mélisande*, the Missioner having been given two stalls by an actor friend. Mark enjoyed the play and was being stirred by the imagination of old, unhappy, far off things until his companion began to laugh. Several clever women who looked as if they had been dragged through a hedge said "Hush!"; even Mark, compassionate of the players' feelings should they hear Father Rowley laugh at the poignant nonsense they were uttering on the stage, begged him to control himself.

"But this is most unending rubbish," he said. "I've never heard anything so ridiculous in my life. Terrible."

The curtain fell on the act at this moment, so that Father Rowley was able to give louder voice to his opinions.

"This is unspeakable bosh," he repeated. "I can't understand anything at all that is going on. People run on and run off again and make the most idiotic remarks. I really don't think I can stand any more of this."

The clever women rattled their beads and writhed their necks like angry snakes without effect upon the Missioner.

"I don't think I can stand any more of this," he repeated. "I shall have apoplexy if this goes on."

The clever women hissed angrily about the kind of people that came to theatres nowadays.

"This man Maeterlinck must have escaped from an asylum," Father Rowley went on. "I never heard such deplorable nonsense in my life."

"I shall ask an attendant if we can change our seats," snapped one of the clever women in front. "That's the worst of coming to a Saturday afternoon performance, such extraordinary people come up to town on Saturdays."

"There you are," exclaimed Father Rowley loudly, "even that poor woman in front thinks they're extraordinary."

"She's talking about you," said Mark, "not about the people in the play."

"My good woman," said Father Rowley, leaning over and tapping her on the shoulder. "You don't think that you really enjoy this rubbish, do you?"

One of her friends who was near the gangway called out to a programme seller:

"Attendant, attendant, is it possible for my friends and myself to move into another row? We are being pestered with a running commentary by that stout clergyman behind that lady in green."

"Don't disturb yourselves, you foolish geese," said Father Rowley rising. "I'm not going to sit through another act. Come along, Mark, come along, come along. I am not happy. I am not happy," he cried in an absurd falsetto.

Then roaring with laughter at his own imitation of Mélisande, he went rolling out of the theatre and sniffed contentedly the air of the Strand.

"I told Lady Pechell we shouldn't arrive till tea-time, so we'd better go and ride on the top of a bus as far as the city."

It was an exhilarating ride, although Mark found that Father Rowley occupied much more than half of the seat for two. About five o'clock they came to the shadowy house in Portman Square in which they were to stay till Monday. The Missioner was as much at home here as he was at Silchester College or in a railway compartment full of bluejackets. He knew as well how to greet the old butler as Lady Pechell and her sister Mrs. Mannakay, to all of whom equally his visit was an obvious delight. Not even Father Rowley's bulk could dwarf the proportions of that double drawing-room or of that heavy Victorian furniture. He took his place among the cases of stuffed humming birds and glass-topped tables of curios, among the brocade curtains with shaped vallances and golden tassels, among the chandeliers and lacquered cabinets and cages of avadavats, sitting there like a great Buddha while he chatted to the two old ladies of a society that seemed to Mark as remote as the people in *Pelleas and Mélisande*. From time to time one of the old ladies would try to draw Mark into the conversation; but he preferred listening and let them think that his monosyllabic answers signified a shyness that did not want to be conspicuous. Soon they appeared to forget his existence. Deep in the lap of an armchair covered with a glazed chintz of Sèvres roses and sable he was enthralled by that chronicle of phantoms, that frieze of ghosts passing before his eyes, while the present faded away upon the growing quiet of the London evening and became remote as the distant roar of the traffic, which itself was remote as the sound of the sea in a shell. Fox-hunting squires caracoled by with the air of paladins; and there was never a lady mentioned that did not take the fancy like a princess in an old tale.

"He's universal," Mark thought. "And that's one of the secrets of being a great priest. And that's why he can talk about Heaven and make you feel that he knows what he's talking about. And if I can discern what he is," Mark went on to himself, "I can be what he is. And I will be," he vowed in the rapture of a sudden revelation.

On Sunday morning Father Rowley preached in the fashionable church of St. Cyprian's, South Kensington, after which they lunched at the vicarage. The Reverend Drogo Mortemer was a dapper little bachelor (it would be inappropriate to call such a worldly little fellow a celibate) who considered himself the leader of the most advanced section of the Catholic Party in the Church of England. He certainly had a finger in the pie of every well-cooked intrigue, knew everybody worth knowing in London, and had the private ears of several bishops. No more skilful place-finder existed, and any member of the advanced section who wanted a place for himself or for a friend had recourse to Mortemer.

"But the little man is all right," Father Rowley had told Mark. "Many people would have used his talents to further himself. He has every qualification for the episcopate except one—he believes in the Sacraments."

Mr. Mortemer was the only son of James Mortimer of the famous firm of Hadley and Mortimer. His father had become rich before he married the youngest daughter of an ancient but impoverished house, and soon after his marriage he died. Mrs. Mortemer brought up her son to forget that his father had been a tradesman and to remember that he was rich. In order to dissociate herself from a partnership which now existed only in name above the plate glass of the enormous shop in Oxford Street Mrs. Mortemer took to spelling her name with an "e," which as she pointed out was the original spelling. She had already gratified her romantic fancy by calling her son Drogo. Harrow and Cambridge completed what Mrs. Mortemer began, and if Drogo had not developed what his mother spoke of as a "mania for religion" there is no reason to suppose that he would not one day have been a cabinet minister. However, as it was, Mrs. Mortemer died cherishing with her last breath a profound conviction that her son would soon be a bishop. That he was not likely to become a bishop was due to the fact that with all his worldliness, with all his wealth, with all his love of wire-pulling, with all his respect for rank he held definite opinions and was not afraid to belong to a minority unpopular in high places. He had too a simple piety that made his church a power in spite of fashionable weddings and exorbitant pew rents.

"The sort of thing we're trying to do here in a small way," he said to Father Rowley at lunch, "is what the Jesuits are doing at Farm Street. My two assistant priests are both rather brilliant young people, and I'm always on the look out to get more young men of the right type."

"You'd better offer Lidderdale a title when he's ready to be ordained."

"Why, of course I will," said the dapper little vicar with a courteous smile for Mark. "Do take some more claret, Father Rowley. It's rather a specialty of ours here. We have a friend in Bordeaux who buys for us."

It was typical of Mr. Mortemer to use the plural.

"There you are, Mark Anthony. I've secured you a title."

"Mr. Mortemer is only being polite," said Mark.

"No, no, my dear boy, on the contrary I meant absolutely what I said."

He seemed worried by Mark's distrust of his sincerity, and for the rest of lunch he laid himself out to entertain his less important guest, talking with a slight excess of charm about the lack of vitality, loss of influence, and oriental barbarism of the Orthodox Church.

"*Enfin*, Asiatic religion," he said. "Don't you agree with me, Mr. Lidderdale? And our Philorthodox brethren who would like to bring about reunion with such a Church . . . the result would be dreadful . . . Eurasian . . . yes, I must confess that sometimes I sympathize with the behaviour of the Venetians in the Fourth Crusade."

Father Rowley looked at his watch and announced that it was time to start for Poplar, where he was to address a large gathering of Socialists in the Town Hall. Mr. Mortemer made a *moue*.

"Nevertheless I'm bound to admit that you have a strong case. Perhaps I'm like the young man with large possessions," he burst out with a sudden intense gravity. "Perhaps after all the St. Cyprian's religion isn't Christianity at all. Just Catholicism. Nothing else."

"You'd better come down to Poplar with Mark and me," Father Rowley suggested.

But Mr. Mortemer shook his head with a smile.

The Poplar meeting was crowded. In an atmosphere of good fellowship one speaker after another got up and denounced the present order. It was difficult to follow the arguments of the speakers, because the audience cheered so many isolated statements. A number of people shook hands with Father Rowley when he had finished his speech and wished that there were more parsons like him. Father Rowley had not indulged in political attacks, but had contented himself with praise of the poor. He had spoken movingly, but Mark was not moved by his words. He had a vague feeling that Father Rowley was being exploited. He was dazed by the exuberance of the meeting and was glad when it was over and he was back in Portman Square talking to Lady Pechell and Mrs. Mannakay while Father Rowley rested for an hour before he walked round the corner to preach in old Jamaica Chapel, a galleried Georgian conventicle that was now the Church of the Visitation, but was still generally known as Jamaica Chapel. Evensong was half over when the preacher arrived, and the church being full Mark was given a chair by the sidesman in a dark corner, which presently became darker when Father Rowley went up into the pulpit, for all the lights were lowered except those above the preacher's head, and nothing was visible in the church except the luminous crucifix upon the High Altar. The warmth and darkness brought out the scent of the many women gathered together; the atmosphere was charged with human emotion so that Mark sitting in his corner could fancy that he was lost in the sensuous glooms behind some *Mater Addolorata* of the seventeenth century. He longed to be back in Chatsea. He was dismayed at the prospect of one day perhaps having to cope with this quality of devotion. He shuddered at the thought, and for the first time he wondered if he had not a vocation for the monastic life. But was it a vocation if one longed to escape the world? Must not a true vocation be a longing to draw nearer to God? Oh, this nauseating bouquet of feminine perfumes . . . it was impossible to pay attention to the sermon.

Mark went to bed early with a headache; but in the morning he woke refreshed with the knowledge that they were going back to Chatsea, although before they reached home the journey had to be broken at High Thorpe whither Father Rowley had been summoned to an interview by the Bishop of Silchester on account of refusing to communicate some people at the mid-day celebration. Dr. Crawshay was at that time so ill that he received the Chatsea Missioner in bed, and on hearing that he was accompanied by a young man who hoped to take Holy Orders the Bishop sent word for Mark to come up to his bedroom, where he gave him his blessing. Mark never forgot the picture of the Bishop lying there under a chequered coverlet looking like an old ivory chessman, a white bishop that had been taken in the game and put off the board.

"And now, Mr. Rowley," Dr. Crawshay began when he had motioned Mark to a chair. "To return to the subject under discussion between us. How can you justify by any rubric of the Book of Common Prayer non-communicating attendance?"

"I don't justify it by any rubric," the Missioner replied.

"Oh, you don't, don't you?"

"I justify it by the needs of human nature," the Missioner continued. "In order to provide the necessary three communicants for the mid-day Mass. . . ."

"One moment, Mr. Rowley," the Bishop interrupted. "I beg you most earnestly to avoid that word. You know my old-fashioned Protestant notions," he added, and his eyes so tired with pain twinkled for a moment. "To me there is always something distasteful about that word."

"What shall I substitute, my lord?" the Missioner asked. "Do you object to the word 'Eucharist'?"

"No, I don't object to that, though why you should want a Greek name when we have a beautiful English name like the Lord's Supper, why you should want to employ such a barbarism as 'Eucharist' I don't know. However, if you must use Eucharist, use Eucharist. And now, by wandering off into a discussion of terminology I forget where we were. Oh yes, you were on the point of justifying non-communicating attendance by the needs of human nature."

"I am afraid, my lord, that in a district like St. Agnes' it is impossible always to ensure communicants for sometimes as many as four early Lord's Suppers said by visiting priests."

The Bishop's eyes twinkled again.

"Yes, there you rather have me, Mr. Rowley. Four early Lord's Suppers does sound, I must admit, a little odd."

"Four early Eucharists followed by another for children at half-past nine, and the parochial sung Mass—sung Eucharist."

"Children?" Dr. Crawshay repeated. "You surely don't let children go to the Celebration?"

"*Suffer little children to come unto Me, and forbid them not, for of such is the Kingdom of Heaven*," Father Rowley reminded the Bishop.

"Yes, yes, I happen to have heard that text before. But the devil, Mr. Rowley, can cite Scripture to his purpose."

"In the last letter I wrote to your lordship about the services at St. Agnes' I particularly mentioned our children's Eucharist."

"Did you, Mr. Rowley, did you? I had quite forgotten that."

Father Rowley turned to Mark for verification.

"Oh, if Mr. Rowley remembers that he did write, there is no need to call witnesses. I have had to complain a good deal of him, but I have never had to complain of his frankness. It must be my fault, but I certainly hadn't understood that there was definitely a children's Eucharist. This then, I fancy, must be the service at which those three ladies complained of your treatment of them."

"What three ladies?" asked the priest.

"Dear me, I'm growing very unbusinesslike, I'm afraid. I thought I had enclosed you a copy of their letter to me when I wrote to invite an explanation of your high-handed action."

The Bishop sighed. The details of these ecclesiastical squabbles distracted him at a time when he should soon leave this fretful earth behind him. He continued wearily:

"These were the three ladies who were refused communion by you at, as I understood, the mid-day Celebration, which now turns out to be what you call the children's Eucharist."

"It is perfectly true, my lord," Father Rowley admitted, "that on Sunday week three women did present themselves from a neighbouring parish."

"Ah, they were not parishioners?"

"Certainly not, my lord."

"Which is a point in your favour."

"Throughout the service they sat looking through opera-glasses at Snaith who was officiating, and greatly scandalizing the children, who are not used to such behaviour in church."

"Such behaviour was certainly most objectionable," the Bishop agreed.

"I happened to be sitting at the back of the church, thinking out my sermon, and their behaviour annoyed me so much that I sent for the sacristan to go and order a cab. I then went up and whispered to them that inasmuch as they were strangers it would be better if they went and made their Communion in the next parish where the service would be more lenient to their theory of worship. I took one of them by the arm, led her gently down the aisle and out into the street, and handed her into the cab. Her two companions followed her; I paid the cabman; and that was the end of the matter."

The Bishop lay back on the pillows and thought for a moment or two in silence.

"Yes," he said finally, "I think that in this case you were justified. At the same time your justification by the Book of Common Prayer lay in the fact that these women did not give you notice beforehand of their intention to communicate. I think I must insist that in future you make some arrangement with your workers and helpers to secure the requisite minimum of communicants for every celebration. Personally, I think six on a Sunday and four on a week-day far too many. I think the repetition has a tendency to cheapen the Sacrament."

"*By Him therefore let us offer the sacrifice of praise to God continually*," Father Rowley quoted from the Epistle to the Hebrews.

"Yes, yes, I know," said the Bishop. "But I wish you wouldn't drag in these texts. They really have nothing whatever to do with the point in question. Please realize, Mr. Rowley, that I allow you a great deal of latitude at St. Agnes' because I am aware of what a great influence for good you have been among these poor people."

"Your lordship has always been consideration itself."

"If that be your opinion, I want you to obey my ruling in this small matter. I am continually being involved in correspondence on your account with Vigilance Societies of the type of the Protestant Alliance, and I shall give myself the pleasure of answering their complaints without at the same time not, as I hope, impeding your splendid work. I wish also, if God allows me to leave this bed again, to take the next Confirmation in St. Agnes' myself. My presence there will afford you a measure of official support which will not, I venture to believe, be a disadvantage to your work. I do not expect you to modify your method of conducting the service too much. That would savour of hypocrisy, both on your side and on mine. But there are one or two things which I should prefer not to see again. Last time you dressed a number of your choir-boys in red cassocks."

"The servers, you mean, my lord?"

"Whatever you call them, they wear red cassocks, red slippers, and red skull caps. That I really cannot stand. You must put them into black cassocks and leave their caps and slippers in the vestry cupboard. Further, I do not wish that most conspicuous processional crucifix to be carried about in front of me wherever I go."

"Would you like the crucifix to be taken down from the altar as well?" Father Rowley asked.

"No, that can stay: I shan't see that one."

"What date will suit your lordship for the Confirmation?"

"Ought not the question to have been rather what date will suit you, for I have never yet been fortunate enough, and I never hope to be fortunate enough, to fix upon a date straight off that will suit you, Mr. Rowley. Let me know that later.

In any case, my presence must depend, alas, upon the state of my health. Now, how are you getting on with your new church?"

"We shall be ready to open it in the spring of next year if all goes well. Do you think that a new licence will be required? The new St. Agnes' is joined to the present church by the sacristy."

The Bishop considered the question for a moment.

"No, I think that the old licence will serve. There is no prospect yet of making St. Agnes' into a parish, and I would rather take advantage of the technicality, all things being considered. Good-bye, Mr. Rowley. God bless you."

The Bishop raised his thin arm.

"God bless your lordship."

"You are always in my prayers, Mr. Rowley. I think much about you lying here on the threshold of Eternal Life."

The Bishop turned to Mark who knelt beside the bed.

"Young man, I would fain be spared long enough to ordain you to the service of Almighty God, but you are still young and I am very near to death. You could not have before you a better example of a Christian gentleman than your friend and my friend Mr. Rowley. I shall say nothing about his example as a clergyman of the Church of England. Remember me, both of you, in your prayers."

The Bishop sank back exhausted, and his visitors went quietly out of the room.

CHAPTER XIX
THE ALTAR FOR THE DEAD

All went as well with the new St. Agnes' as the Bishop had hoped. Columns of red brick were covered in marble and alabaster by the votive offerings of individuals or the subscriptions of different Silchester Houses; the baldacchino was given by one rich old lady, the pavement of the church by another; the Duke of Birmingham contributed a thurible; Oxford Old Siltonians decorated the Lady Chapel; Cambridge Old Siltonians found the gold mosaic for the dome of the apse. Father Rowley begged money for the fabric far and wide, and the architect, the contractors, and the workmen, all Chatsea men, gave of their best and asked as little as possible in return. The new church was to be opened on Easter morning. But early in Lent the Bishop of Silchester died in the bed from which he had never risen since the day Father Rowley and Mark received his blessing. The diocese mourned him, for he was a gentle scholar, wise in his knowledge of men, simple and pious in his own life.

Dr. Harvard Cheesman, the new Bishop, was translated from the see of Ipswich to which he had been preferred from the Chapel Royal in the Savoy. Bishop Cheesman possessed all the episcopal qualities. He had the hands of a physician and the brow of a scholar. He was filled with a sense of the importance of his position, and in that perhaps was included a sense of the importance of himself. He was eloquent in public, grandiloquent in private. To him Father Rowley wrote shortly after his enthronement.

St. Agnes' House,
Keppel Street,
Chatsea.
March 24.
My Lord Bishop,
I am unwilling to trouble you at a moment when you must be unusually busy; but I shall be glad to hear from you about the opening of the new church of the Silchester College Mission, which was fixed for Easter Sunday. Your predecessor, Bishop Crawshay, did not think that any new licence would be necessary, because the new St. Agnes' is joined by the sacristy to the old mission church. There is no idea at present of asking you to constitute St. Agnes' a parish and therefore the question of consecration does not arise. I regret to say that Bishop Crawshay thoroughly disapproved of our services and ritual, and I think he may have felt unwilling to commit himself to endorsing them by the formal grant of a new licence. May I hear from you at your convenience, and may I respectfully add that your lordship has the prayers of all my people?
I am your lordship's obedient servant,
John Rowley.
To which the Lord Bishop of Silchester replied as follows:
High Thorpe Castle.
March 26.
Dear Mr. Rowley,
As my predecessor Bishop Crawshay did not think a new licence would be necessary I have no doubt that you can go ahead with your plan of opening the new St. Agnes' on Easter Sunday. At the same time I cannot help feeling that a new licence would be desirable and I am asking Canon Whymper as Rural Dean to pay a visit and make the necessary report. I have heard much of your work, and I pray that it may be as blessed in my time as it was in the time of my predecessor. I am grateful to your people for their prayers and I am, my dear Mr. Rowley,

Yours very truly,

Harvard Silton.

Canon Whymper, the Rector of Chatsea and Rural Dean, visited the new church on the Monday of Passion week. On Saturday Father Rowley received the following letter from the Bishop:

High Thorpe Castle.

April 9.

Dear Mr. Rowley,

I have just received Canon Whymper's report upon the new church of the Silchester College Mission, and I think before you open the church on Easter Sunday I should like to talk over one or two comparatively unimportant details with you personally. Moreover, it would give me pleasure to make your acquaintance and hear something of your method of work at St. Agnes'. Perhaps you will come to High Thorpe on Monday. There is a train which arrives at High Thorpe at 2.36. So I shall expect you at the Castle at 2.42.

Yours very truly,

Harvard Silton.

Mark paid his second visit to High Thorpe Castle on one of those serene April mornings that sail like swans across the lake of time. The episcopal standard on the highest turret hung limp; the castle quivered in the sunlight; the lawns wearing their richest green seemed as far from being walked upon as the blue sky above them. Whether it was that Mark was nervous about the result of the coming interview or whether it was that his first visit to High Thorpe had been the climax of so many new experiences, he was certainly much more sharply aware on this occasion of what the Castle stood for. Looking back to the morning when he and Father Rowley sat with Bishop Crawshay in his bedroom, he realized how much the personality of the dead bishop had dominated his surroundings and how little all this dignity and splendour, which must have been as imposing then as it was now, had impressed his imagination. There came over Mark, when he and Father Rowley were walking silently along the drive, such a foreboding of the result of this visit that he almost asked the priest why they bothered to continue their journey, why they did not turn round immediately and take the next train back to Chatsea. But before he had time to say anything Father Rowley had pulled the chain of the door bell, the butler had opened the door, and they were waiting the Bishop's pleasure in a room that smelt of the best leather and the best furniture polish. It was a room that so long as Dr. Cheesman held the see of Silchester would be given over to the preliminary nervousness of the diocesan clergy, who would one after another look at that steel engraving of Jesus Christ preaching by the Sea of Galilee, and who when they had finished looking at that would look at those two oil paintings of still life, those rich and sombre accumulations of fish, fruit and game, that glowed upon the walls with a kind of sinister luxury. Waiting rooms are all much alike, the doctor's, the dentist's, the bishop's, the railway-station's; they may differ slightly in externals, but they all possess the same atmosphere of transitory discomfort. They have all occupied human beings with the perusal of books they would never otherwise have dreamed of opening, with the observation of pictures they would never otherwise have thought of regarding twice.

"Would you step this way," the butler requested. "His lordship is waiting for you in the library."

The two culprits, for by this time Mark was oblivious of every other emotion except one of profound guilt, guilt of what he could not say, but most unmistakably guilt, walked along toward the Bishop's library—Father Rowley like a fat and naughty child who knows he is going to be reproved for eating too many tarts.

There was a studied poise in the attitude of the Bishop when they entered. One shapely leg trailed negligently behind his chair ready at any moment to serve as the pivot upon which its owner could swing round again into the every-day world; the other leg firmly wedged against the desk supported the burden of his concentration. The Bishop swung round on the shapely leg in attendance, and in a single sweeping gesture blotted the last page of the letter he had been writing and shook Father Rowley by the hand.

"I am delighted to have an opportunity of meeting you, Mr. Rowley," he began, and then paused a moment with an inquiring look at Mark.

"I thought you wouldn't mind, my lord, if I brought with me young Lidderdale, who is reading for Holy Orders and working with us at St. Agnes'. I am apt to forget sometimes exactly to what I have and have not committed myself and I thought your lordship would not object. . . ."

"To a witness?" interposed the Bishop in a tone of courtly banter. "Come, come, Mr. Rowley, had I known you were going to be so suspicious of me I should have asked my domestic chaplain to be present on my side."

Mark, supposing that the Bishop was annoyed by his presence at the interview, made a movement to retire, whereupon the Bishop tapped him paternally upon the shoulder and said:

"Nonsense, non-sense, I was merely indulging in a mild pleasantry. Sit down, Mr. Rowley. Mr. Lidderdale I think you will find that chair quite comfortable. Well, Mr. Rowley," he began, "I have heard much of you and your work. Our friend Canon Whymper spoke of it with enthusiasm. Yes, yes, with enthusiasm. I often regret that in the course of my ministry I have never had the good fortune to be called to work among the poor, the real poor. You have been privileged, Mr. Rowley, if I may be allowed to say so, greatly, immensely privileged. You find a wilderness, and you make of it a garden. Wonderful. Wonderful."

Mark began to feel uncomfortable, and he thought by the way Father Rowley was puffing his cheeks that he too was beginning to feel uncomfortable. The Missioner looked as if he was blowing away the lather of the soap that the Bishop was using upon him so prodigally.

"Some other time, Mr. Rowley, when I have a little leisure . . . I perceive the need of making myself acquainted with every side of my new diocese—a little leisure, yes . . . sometime I should like to have a long talk with you about all the details of your work at Chatsea, of which as I said Canon Whymper has spoken to me most enthusiastically. The question, however, immediately before us this morning is the licence of your new church. Since writing to you first I have thought the matter over most earnestly. I have given the matter the gravest consideration. I have consulted Canon Whymper and I have come to the conclusion that bearing all the circumstances in mind it will be wiser for you to apply, and I hope be granted, a new licence. With this decision in my mind I asked Canon Whymper in his capacity as Rural Dean to report upon the new church. Mr. Rowley, his report is extremely favourable. He writes to me of the noble fabric, noble is the actual epithet he employs, yes, the very phrase. He expresses his conviction that you are to be congratulated, most warmly congratulated, Mr. Rowley, upon your vigorous work. I believe I am right in saying that all the money necessary to erect this noble edifice has been raised by yourself?"

"Not all of it," said Father Rowley. "I still owe £3,000."

"A mere trifle," said the Bishop, dismissing the sum with the airy gesture of a conjurer who palms a coin. "A mere trifle compared with what you have already raised. I know that at the moment there is no question of constituting as a parish what is at present merely a district; but such a contingency must be borne in mind by both of us, and inasmuch as that would imply consecration by myself I am unwilling to prejudice any decision I might have to take later, should the necessity for consecration arise, by allowing you at the moment a wider latitude than I might be prepared to allow you in the future. Yes, Canon Whymper writes most enthusiastically of the noble fabric." The Bishop paused, drummed with his fingers on the arm of his chair as if he were testing the pitch of his instrument, and then taking a deep breath boomed forth: "But Mr. Rowley, in his report he informs me that in the middle of the south aisle exists an altar or Holy Table expressly and exclusively designed for what he was told are known as masses for the dead."

"That is perfectly true," said Father Rowley.

"Ah," said the Bishop, shaking his head gravely. "I did not indeed imagine that Canon Whymper would be misinformed about such an important feature; but I did not think it right to act without ascertaining first from you that such is indeed the case. Mr. Rowley, it would be difficult for me to express how grievously it pains me to have to seem to interfere in the slightest degree with the successful prosecution of your work among the poor of Chatsea, especially to make such interference one of the first of my actions in a new diocese; but the responsibilities of a bishop are grave. He cannot lightly endorse a condition of affairs, a method of services which in his inmost heart after the deepest confederation he feels is repugnant to the spirit of the Church Of England. . . ."

"I question that opinion, my lord," said the Missioner.

"Mr. Rowley, pray allow me to finish. We have little time at our disposal for a theological argument which would in any case be fruitless, for as I told you I have already examined the question with the deepest consideration from every standpoint. Though I may respect your opinions in my private capacity, for I do not wish to impugn for one moment the sincerity of your beliefs, in my episcopal, or what I may call my public character, I can only condemn them utterly. Utterly, Mr. Rowley, and completely."

"But this altar, my lord," shouted Father Rowley, springing to his feet, to the alarm of Mark, who thought he was going to shake his fist in the Bishop's face, "this altar was subscribed for by the poor of St. Agnes', by all the poor of St. Agnes', as a memorial of the lives of sailors and marines of St. Agnes' lost in the sinking of the *King Harry*. Your predecessor, Bishop Crawshay, knew of its existence, actually saw it and commented on its ugliness; yet when I told him the circumstances in which it had been erected he was deeply moved by the beautiful idea. This altar has been in use for nearly three years. Masses for the dead have been said there time after time. This altar is surrounded by memorials of my dead people. It is one of the most vital factors in my work there. You ask me to remove it, before you have been in the diocese a month, before you have had time to see with your own eyes what an influence for good it has on the daily lives of the poor people who built it. My lord, I will not remove the altar."

While Father Rowley was speaking the Bishop of Silchester had been looking like a man on a railway platform who has been ambushed by a whistling engine.

"Mr. Rowley, Mr. Rowley," he said, "I pray you to control yourself. I beg you to understand that this is not a mere question of red tape, if I may use the expression, of one extra altar or Holy Table, but it is a question of the services said at that altar or Holy Table."

"That is precisely what I am trying to point out to your lordship," said Father Rowley angrily.

"You yourself told me when you wrote to me that Bishop Crawshay disapproved of much that was done at St. Agnes'. It was you who put it into my head at the beginning of our correspondence that you were not asking me formally to open the new church, because you were doubtful of the effect your method of worship might have upon me. I don't wish for a moment to suggest that you were trying to bundle on one side the question of the licence, before I had had a moment to look round me in my new diocese, I say I do *not* think this for a moment; but inasmuch as the question has come before me officially, as sooner or later it must have come before me officially, I cannot allow my future action to be prejudiced by giving you liberties now that I may not be prepared to allow you later on. Suppose that in three years' time the question of consecrating the new St. Agnes' arises and the legality of this third altar or Holy Table is questioned, how should I be able to turn round and forbid then what I have not forbidden now?"

"Your lordship prefers to force me to resign?"

"Force you to resign, Mr. Rowley?" the Bishop repeated in aggrieved accents. "What can I possibly have said that could lead you to suppose for one moment that I was desirous of forcing you to resign? I make allowance for your natural disappointment. I make every allowance. Otherwise Mr. Rowley I should be tempted to characterize such a statement as cruel. As cruel, Mr. Rowley."

"What other alternative have I?"

"I should have said, Mr. Rowley, that you have one other very obvious alternative, and that is to accept my ruling upon the subject of this third altar or Holy Table. When I shall receive an assurance that you will do so, I shall with pleasure, with great pleasure, give you a new licence."

"I could not possibly do that," said the Missioner. "I could not possibly go back to my people to-night and tell them this Holy Week that what I have been teaching them for ten years is a lie. I would rather resign a thousand times."

"That is a far more accurate statement than your previous assertion that I was forcing you to resign."

"When will you have found a priest to take my place temporarily?" the Missioner asked in a chill voice. "It is unlikely that the Silchester College authorities will find another missioner at once, and I think it rests with your lordship to find a locum tenens. I do not wish to disappoint my people about the date of the opening of their new church. They have been looking forward to this Easter for so long now. Poor dears!"

Father Rowley sighed out the last ejaculation to himself, and his sigh ran through the Bishop's opulent library like a dull wind. Mark had a mad impulse to tell the Bishop the story of his father and the Lima Street Mission. His father had resigned on Palm Sunday. Oh, this ghastly dream. . . . Father Rowley leave Chatsea! It was unimaginable. . . .

But the Bishop was overthrowing the work of ten years with apparently as little consciousness of the ruin he was creating as a boar that has rooted up an ant-heap with his snout.

"Quite so. Quite so, Mr. Rowley. I certainly see your point," the Bishop declared. "I will do my best to secure a priest, but meanwhile . . . let me see. I need scarcely say how painful your decision has been, what pain it has caused me. Let me see, yes, in the circumstances I agree with you that it would be inadvisable to postpone the opening. I think from every point of view it would be wisest to proceed according to schedule. Could not this altar or Holy Table be railed off temporarily, I do not say muffled up, but could not some indication be given of the fact that I do not sanction its use? In that case I should have no objection, indeed on the contrary I should be only too happy for you to carry on with your work either until I can find a temporary substitute or until the Silchester College authorities can appoint a new missioner. Dear me, this is dreadfully painful for me."

Father Rowley stared at the Bishop in astonishment.

"You want me to continue?" he asked. "Really, my lord, you will excuse my plain speaking if I tell you that I am amazed at your point of view. A moment ago you told me that I must either remove this altar or resign."

"Pardon me, Mr. Rowley. I did not mention the word 'resign.'"

"And now," the Missioner went on without paying any attention to the interruption. "You are ready to let me stay at St. Agnes' until a successor can conveniently be found. If my teaching is as pernicious as you think, I cannot understand your lordship's tolerating my officiating for another hour in your diocese."

"Mr. Rowley, you are introducing into this unhappy affair a great deal of extraneous feeling. I do not reproach you. I know that you are labouring under the stress of strong emotion. I overlook the manner which you have adopted towards me. I overlook it, Mr. Rowley. Before we close this interview, which I must once more assure you is as painful for me as for you, I want you to understand how deeply I regret having been forced to take the action I have. I ask your prayers, Mr. Rowley, and please be sure that you always have and always will have my prayers. Have you anything more you would like to say? Do not let me give you the impression from my alluding to the heavy work of entering upon the duties and responsibilities of a new diocese that I desire to hurry you in any way this afternoon. You will want to catch the 4.10 back to Chatsea I have no doubt. Too early perhaps for tea. Good-bye, Mr. Rowley. Good-bye, Mr. . . ." the Bishop paused and looked inquiringly at Mark. "Lidderdale, ah, yes," he said. "For the moment I forgot. Good-bye, Mr. Lidderdale. A simple railing will, I think be sufficient for the altar in question, Mr. Rowley. I perfectly appreciate your motive in asking the Bishop of Barbadoes to officiate at the opening. I quite see that you did not wish to commit me to an approval of a ritual which might be more advanced than I might consider proper in my diocese. . . . Good-bye, good-bye."

Father Rowley and Mark found themselves once more in the drive. The episcopal standard floated in the wind, which had sprung up while they were with the Bishop. They walked silently to the railway station under a fast clouding sky.

CHAPTER XX
FATHER ROWLEY

The first episcopal act of the Bishop of Silchester drove many poor souls away from God. It was a time of deep emotional stress for all the St. Agnes' workers, and Father Rowley could not show himself in Keppel Street without being surrounded by a crowd of supplicants who with tears and lamentations begged him to give up the new St. Agnes' and to remain in the old mission church rather than be lost to them for ever. There were some who even wished him to surrender the Third Altar; but in his last sermon preached on the Sunday night before he left Chatsea, he spoke to them and said:

"In the name of the Father and of the Son and of the Holy Ghost. Amen. The 15th verse of the 21st Chapter of the Holy Gospel according to Saint John: *Feed my lambs.*

"It is difficult for me, dear people, to preach to you this evening for the last time as your missioner, to preach, moreover, the last sermon that will ever be preached in this little mission church which has meant so much to you and so much to me. By the mercy of God man does not realize at the moment all that is implied by an occasion like this. He speaks with his mouth words of farewell; but his heart still beats to what was and what is, rather than to what will be.

"When I took as my text to-night those three words of Our Lord to St. Peter, *Feed my Lambs*, I took them as words that might be applied, first to the Lord Bishop of this diocese, secondly to the priest who will take my place in this Mission, and thirdly and perhaps most poignantly of all to myself. I cannot bring myself to suppose that in this moment of grief, in this moment of bitterness, almost of despair I am able to speak fairly of the Bishop of Silchester's action in compelling me to resign what has counted for all that is most precious in my life on earth. And already, in saying that the Bishop has compelled me to resign, I am not speaking with perfect accuracy, inasmuch as if I had been willing to surrender what I considered one of the essential articles of our belief, the Bishop would have been glad to licence the new St. Agnes' and to give his countenance and his support to me, the unworthy priest in charge of it.

"I want you therefore, dear people, to try to look at the matter from the standpoint of the Bishop. I want you to try to understand that in objecting to our little altar for the dead he is objecting not so much to the altar itself as to the services said at that altar. If it had merely been a question between us of a third altar, whether here or in the new St. Agnes', I should have found it possible, however unwillingly, to ask you—you, who out of your hard-earned savings built that altar—to allow it to be removed. Yes, I should have been selfish enough to ask you to make that great sacrifice on my account. But when the Bishop insisted that I and the priests who have borne with me and worked with me and preached with me and prayed with me all these years should abstain from saying those Masses which we believe and which you believe help our dear ones waiting for the Day of Judgment—why, then, I felt that my surrender would have been a denial of our dear Lord, such a denial as St. Peter himself uttered in the hall of the high-priest's house. But the Bishop does not believe that our prayers here below have any efficacy or can in any way help the blessed dead. He does not believe in such prayers, and he believes that those who do believe in such prayers are wrong, not merely according to the teaching of the Prayer Book, but also according to the revelation of Almighty God. I do not want you to say, as you will be tempted to say, that the Bishop of Silchester in condemning our method of services at St. Agnes' is condemning them with an eye to public opinion or to political advantage. Alas, I have myself been tempted to say bitter words about him, to think bitter thoughts; but at this moment, with that last *Nunc Dimittis* ringing in my ears, *Lord now lettest Thou Thy servant depart in peace*, I realize that the Bishop is acting honestly and sincerely, however much he may be acting wrongly and hastily. It is dreadful for me at this moment of parting to feel that some of you here to-night may be turned from the face of God because you are angered against one of God's ministers. If any poor words of mine have power to touch your hearts, I beg you to believe that in giving us this great trial of our faith God is acting with that mysterious justice and omniscience of which we speak idly without in the least apprehending what He means. I shall say no more in defence and explanation of the Bishop's action, and if he should consider my defence and explanation of it a piece of presumption I send him at this solemn moment of farewell a message that I shall never cease to pray that he may long guide you on the way that leads up to eternal happiness.

"I can speak more freely of what your attitude should be towards Father Hungerford, the priest who is coming to take my place and who is going with God's help to do far more for you here than ever I have been able to do. I want you all to put yourselves in his place; I want you all to think of him to-night wondering, fearing, doubting, hoping, and praying. I want you to imagine how difficult he must be feeling the situation is for him. He will come here to-morrow conscious that there is nobody in this district of ours who does not feel, whether he be a communicant or not, that the Bishop had no right to intervene so soon and without greater knowledge of his new diocese in a district like ours. I cannot help knowing how much I myself am to blame in this particular; but, my dear people, it has been very hard for me during these last two weeks always to be brave and hopeful. Often I have found those entreaties on my doorstep almost more than I could endure to hear, those letters on my desk almost more than I could bear to read. So, if you want to do the one thing that can comfort me in this bitter hour of mine I entreat you to show Father Hungerford that your faith and your hope and your love do not depend on your affection for an unworthy priest, but upon that deeper, greater, nobler affection for the word of God. There is only one way in which you can show Father Hungerford that Jesus Christ lives in your hearts, and that is by going to Confession and to Communion and by hearing Mass as you have done all this time. Show him by your behaviour in the street, by your kindness and consideration at home, by your devotion and reverence in church, that you appreciate the mercies of God, that you appreciate what it means to have Jesus Christ upon your altar, that you are, in a word, Christians.

"And now at last I must think of those words of our dear Lord as they apply to myself: *Feed my lambs*. And as I repeat them, I ask myself again if I have done right, for I am troubled in spirit, and I wonder if I ought to have given up that third altar and to have remained here. But even as I wonder this, even as at this moment I stand in this pulpit for the last time, a voice within me forbids me to doubt. No, my clear folk, I cannot surrender that altar. I cannot come to you and say that what I have been teaching for ten years was of so little value, of so little importance, of so little worth, that for the sake of policy it can be abandoned with a stroke of the pen or a nod of the head. I stand here looking out into the future, hearing like angelic trumpets those three words sounding and resounding upon the great void of time:*Feed my lambs!* I ask myself what work lies before me, what lambs I shall have to feed elsewhere; I ask myself in my misery whether God has found me unworthy of the trust He gave me. I feel that if I leave St. Agnes' to-morrow with the thought that you still cherish angry and resentful feelings I shall sink to a lower depth of humiliation and depression than I have yet reached. But if I can leave St. Agnes' with the assurance that my work here will go steadily forward to the glory of God from the point at which I renounced it, I shall know that God must have some other purpose for the remainder of my life, some other mission to which He intends to call me. To you, my dear people, to you who have borne with me patiently, to you who have tolerated so sweetly my infirmities, to you who have been kind to my failings, to you who have taught me so much more of our dear Lord Jesus Christ than I have been able to teach you, to you I say good-bye. I cannot harrow your feelings or my own by saying any more. In the name of the Father, and of the Son, and of the Holy Ghost. Amen."

Notwithstanding these words, the first episcopal act of the Bishop of Silchester drove many poor souls away from God.

The effect upon Mark, had his religion been merely a pastime of adolescence, would have been disastrous. Owing to human nature's respect for the conspicuous there is nothing so demoralizing to faith as the failure of a leader of religion to set forth in his own actions the word of God. Mark, however, looked at the whole business more from an ecclesiastical angle. He had reason to condemn the Bishop for unchristian behaviour; but he preferred to condemn him for uncatholic behaviour. Dr. Cheesman and the many other Dr. Cheesmans of whom the Anglican episcopate was at this period composed never succeeded in shaking his belief in Christ; they did succeed in shaking for a short time his belief in the Church of England. There are few Anglo-Catholics, whether priests or laymen, who have never doubted the right of their Church to proclaim herself a branch of the Holy Catholic Church. This phase of doubt is indeed so common that in ecclesiastical circles it has come to be regarded as a kind of mental chicken-pox, not very alarming if it catches the patient when young, but growing more dangerous in proportion to the lateness of its attack. Mark had his attack young. When Father Rowley left Chatsea, he was anxious to accompany him on what he knew would be an exhausting time of travelling round to preach and collect the necessary money to pay off what was actually a personal debt. It seemed that there must be something fundamentally wrong with a Church that allowed a man to perambulate England in an endeavour to pay off the debt upon a building from ministrating in which he had been debarred. This debt, moreover, was presumably going to be paid by people who fully subscribed to teaching which had been officially condemned.

When Mark commented on this, Father Rowley pointed out that as a matter of fact a great deal of money had been sent by people who admired the practical side, or what they would have called the practical side of his work among the poor, but who at the same time thoroughly disapproved of its ecclesiastical form.

"In justice to the poor old Church of England," he said to Mark, "it must be pointed out that a good deal of this money has been given by devout Anglicans under protest."

"Yes, but that doesn't seriously affect the argument," said Mark. "You collect I don't know how many thousands of pounds to put up a magnificent church from which the Bishop of Silchester sees fit to turn you out, but for the debt on which you are still personally responsible. It's fantastic!"

"Mark Anthony," the priest said with a laugh, "you lack the legal mind. The Bishop did not turn me out. The Bishop can perfectly well say I turned myself out."

"It is all too subtle for me," said Mark. "But I'm not going to worry you with any more arguments. You've had enough of them to last you for ever. I do wish you'd let me stick to you personally and help you in any way possible."

"No, Mark Anthony," the priest replied. "I've done my work at St. Agnes', and you've done yours. Your business now is to take advantage of what has happened and to get back to your books, which whatever you may say have been more and more neglected lately. You'll find it of enormous help to be a good theologian. I have never ceased to regret my own shortcomings in that respect. Besides, I think you ought to spend a certain amount of time with Ogilvie before you go to Glastonbury. There is quite a lot of work to do if you look for it in a country parish like—what's the name of the place? Wych. Oh, yes, quite a lot of work. Don't bother your head about Anglican Orders and Roman Claims and the Catholicity of the Church of England. Your business is to save souls, your own included. Go back and read and get to know the people in Ogilvie's parish. Anybody can tackle a district like St. Agnes'; anybody that is who has the suitable personality. How many people can tackle an English country parish? I hardly know one. I should like to have you with me. I'm fond of you, and you're useful; but at your age to travel round from town to town listening to my begging would be all wrong. I might even go to America. I've had most cordial invitations from several American bishops, and if I can't raise the money in England I shall have to go there. If God has any more work for me to do I shall be offered a cure some day somewhere. I want you to be one of my assistant priests, and if you're going to be useful to me as an assistant priest, you really must have some theology behind you. These bishops get more and more difficult to deal with every year. Now, it's no good arguing. My mind's made up. I won't take you with me."

So Mark went back to Wych-on-the-Wold and brooded upon the non-Catholic aspects of the Anglican Church.

CHAPTER XXI
POINTS OF VIEW

Mark did not find that his guardian was much disturbed by his doubts of the validity of Anglican Orders nor much alarmed by his suspicion that the Establishment had no right to be considered a branch of the Holy Catholic Church.

"The crucial point in the Roman position is their doctrine of intention," said Mr. Ogilvie. "It always seems to me that this doctrine is a particularly dangerous one for them to play with and one that may recoil at any moment upon their own heads. There has been a great deal of super-subtle dividing of intentions into actual, virtual, habitual, and interpretative; but if you are going to take your stand on logic you must be ready to face a logical conclusion. Let us agree for a moment that Barlow and the other bishops who consecrated Matthew Parker had no intention of consecrating him as a bishop for the purpose of ordaining priests in the sense in which Catholics understand the word priest. Do the Romans expect us to believe that all their prelates in the time of the Renaissance had a perfect intention when they were consecrating? Or leave on one side for a moment the sacrament of Orders; the validity of other sacraments is affected by their extension of the doctrine beyond the interpretation of St. Thomas Aquinas. However improbable it may be that at one moment all the priests of the Catholic Church should lack the intention let us say of absolution, it *is* a *logical* possibility, in which case all the faithful would logically speaking be damned. It was in order to guard against this kind of logical catastrophe that the first split between an actual intention and a virtual intention was made. The Roman Church teaches that the virtual intention is enough; but if we argue that a virtual intention might be ascribed to the bishops who consecrated Parker, the Roman controversialists present us with another subdivision—the habitual intention, which is one that formerly existed, but of the present continuance of which there is no trace. Now really, my dear Mark, you must admit that we've reached a point very near to nonsense if this kind of logical subtlety is to control Faith."

"As a matter of fact," said Mark, "I don't think I should ever want to 'vert over the question of the validity of Anglican Orders. I haven't any doubts now of their validity, and I think it's improbable that I shall have any doubts after I'm ordained. At the same time, there *is* something wrong with the Church of England if a situation like that in Chatsea can be created by the whim of a bishop. Our unhappy union between Church and State has created a class of bishops which has no parallel anywhere else in Christendom. In order to become a bishop in England, at any rate of the kind that has a seat in the House of Lords, it is necessary to be a gentleman, or rather to have the outward and visible signs of being a gentleman, to be a scholar, or to be a diplomat. Of course, there will be exceptions; but if you look at almost all our bishops, you will find they have reached their dignity by social attainments or by political utility or sometimes by intellectual distinction, but hardly ever by religious fervour, or spiritual honesty, or fearless opinion. I can sympathize with the dissenters of the seventeenth century in blaming the episcopate for all spiritual maladies. I expect there were a good many Dr. Cheesmans in the days of Defoe. Look back and see how the bishops have always voted in the House of Lords with enthusiastic unanimity against every proposal of reform that was ever put forward. I wonder what will happen when they are called upon to face a real national crisis."

"I'm perfectly ready to agree with everything you say about bishops," the Rector volunteered. "But more or less, I'm sorry to add, it is a criticism that can be applied to all the orders of the priesthood everywhere in Christendom. What can we, what dare we say in favour of priests when we remember Our Lord?"

"When a man does try to follow the Gospel a little more closely than the rest," Mark raged, "the bishops down him. They exist to maintain the safety of their class. They have reached their present position by knowing the right people, by condemning the wrong people, and by balancing their fat bottoms on fences. Sometimes when their political patrons quarrel over a pair of mediocrities, a saintly man who is either very old or very ill like Bishop Crawshay is appointed as a stop-gap."

"Yes," the Rector agreed. "But our present bishops are only one more aspect of Victorian materialism. The whole of contemporary society can be criticized in the same way. After all, we get the bishops we deserve, just as we get the politicians we deserve and the generals we deserve and the painters we deserve."

"I don't think that's any excuse for the bishops. I sometimes dream of worming myself up and stopping at nothing in order to be made a bishop, and then when I have the mitre at last of appearing in my true colours."

"Our Protestant brethren think that is what many of our right reverend fathers in God do now," the Rector laughed.

These discussions might have continued for ever without taking Mark any further. His failure to experience Oxford had deprived him of the opportunity to whet his opinions upon the grindstone of debate, and there had been no time for academic argument in the three years of Keppel Street. In Wych-on-the-Wold there never seemed much else to do but argue. It was one of the effects of leaving, or rather of seeing destroyed, a society that was obviously performing useful work and returning to a society that, so far as Mark could observe performed no kind of work whatever. He was loath to criticize the Rector; but he felt that he was moving along in a rut that might at any moment deepen to a chasm in which he would be spiritually lost. He seemed to be taking his priestly responsibilities too lightly, to be content with gratifying his own desire to worship Almighty God without troubling about his parishioners. Mark did not like to make any suggestions about parochial work, because he was afraid of the Rector's retorting with an implied criticism of St. Agnes'; and that would have involved him in a bitter argument for which he would afterward be sorry. Nor was it only in his missionary duties that he felt his old friend was allowing himself to rust. Three years ago the Rector had said a daily Mass. Now he was content with one on Thursdays except on festivals. Mark began to take walks far afield, which was a sign of irritation with the inaction of the life round him rather than the expression of an interest in the life beyond. On one of these walks he found himself at Wield in the diocese of Kidderminster thirty miles or more away from home. He had spent the night in a remote Cotswold village, and all the morning he had been travelling through the level vale of Wield which, beautiful at the time of blossom, was now at midsummer a landscape without line, monotonously green, prosperous and complacent. While he was eating his bread and cheese at the public bar of the principal inn, he picked up one of the local newspapers and reading it, as one so often reads in such surroundings, with much greater particularity than the journal of a metropolis, he came upon the following letter:

To the Editor of the WIELD OBSERVER AND SOUTH WORCESTERSHIRE COURANT,

SIR,—The leader in your issue of last Tuesday upon my sermon in St. Andrew's Church on the preceding Sunday calls for some corrections. The action of the Bishop of Kidderminster in inhibiting Father Rowley from accepting an invitation to preach in my church is due either to his ignorance of the facts of the case, to his stupidity in appreciating them, or, I must regretfully add, to his natural bias towards persecution. These are strong words for a parish priest to use about his diocesan; but the Bishop of Kidderminster's consistent support of latitudinarianism and his consistent hostility towards any of his clergy who practise the forms of worship which they feel they are bound to practise by the rubrics of the Book of Common Prayer call for strong words. The Bishop in correspondence with me declined to give any reason for his inhibition of Father Rowley beyond a general disapproval of his teaching. I am informed privately that the Bishop is suffering from a delusion that Father Rowley disobeyed the Bishop of Silchester, which is of course perfectly untrue and which is only one more sign of how completely out of accord our bishops are with what is going on either in their own diocese or in any other. My own inclination was frankly to defy his Lordship and insist upon Father Rowley's fulfilling his engagement. I am not sure that I do not now regret that I allowed my church-wardens to overpersuade me on this point. I take great exception to your statement that the offertories both in the morning and in the evening were sent by me to Father Rowley regardless of the wishes of my parishioners. That there are certain parishioners of St. Andrew's who objected I have no doubt. But when I send you the attached list of parishioners who subscribed no less than £18 to be added to the two collections, you will I am sure courteously admit that in this case the opinion of the parishioners of St. Andrew's was at one with the opinion of their Vicar.—I am, Sir, your obedient servant,

ADRIAN FORSHAW.

Mark was so much delighted by this letter that he went off at once to call on Mr. Forshaw, but did not find him at home; he was amused to hear from the housekeeper that his reverence had been summoned to an interview with the Bishop of Kidderminster. Mark fancied that it would be the prelate who would have the unpleasant quarter of an hour. Presently he began to ponder what it meant for such a letter to be written and published; his doubts about the Church of England returned; and in this condition of mind he found himself outside a small Roman Catholic church dedicated to St. Joseph, where hopeful of gaining the Divine guidance within he passed through the door. It may be that he was in a less receptive mood than he thought, for what impressed him most was the Anglican atmosphere of this Italian outpost. The stale perfume of incense on stone could not eclipse that authentic perfume of respectability which has been acquired by so many Roman Catholic churches in England. There were still hanging on the pillars the framed numbers of Sunday's hymns. Mark pictured the choir boy who must have slipped the cards in the frame with anxious and triumphant and immemorial Anglican zeal; and while he was contemplating this symbolical hymn-board, over his shoulder floated an authentic Anglican voice, a voice that sounded as if it was being choked out of the larynx by the clerical collar. It was the Rector, a stumpy little man with the purple stock of a monseigneur, who showed the stranger round his church and ended by inviting him to lunch. Mark, wondering if he had reached a crossroad in his progress, accepted the invitation, and prepared himself reverently to hear the will of God. Monseigneur Cripps lived in a little Gothic house next to St. Joseph's, a trim little Gothic house covered with the oiled curls of an ampelopsis still undyed by autumn's henna.

"You've chosen a bad day to come to lunch," said Monseigneur with a warning shake of the head. "It's Friday, you know. And it's hard to get decent fish away from the big towns."

While his host went off to consult the housekeeper about the extra place for lunch, a proceeding which induced him to make a joke about extra 'plaice' and extra 'place,' at which he laughed heartily, Mark considered the most tactful way of leading up to a discussion of the position of the Anglican Church in regard to Roman claims. It should not be difficult, he supposed, because Monseigneur at the first hint of his guest's desire to be converted would no doubt welcome the topic. But when Monseigneur led the way to his little Gothic dining-room full of Arundel prints, Mark soon apprehended that his host had evidently not had the slightest notion of offering an *ad hoc* hospitality. He paid no attention to Mark's tentative advances, and if he was willing to talk about Rome, it was only because he had just paid a visit there in connexion with a school of which he was a trustee and out of which he wanted to make one kind of school and the Roman Catholic Bishop of Dudley wanted to make another.

"I had to take the whole question to headquarters," Monseigneur explained impressively. "But I was disappointed by Rome, oh yes, I was very disappointed. When I was a young man I saw it *couleur de rose*. I did enjoy one thing though, and that was going round the Vatican. Yes, they looked remarkably smart, the Papal Guards; as soon as they saw I was *Monsignore*, they turned out and presented arms. I'm bound to admit that I *was* impressed by that. But on the way down I lost my pipe in the train. And do you think I could buy a decent pipe in Rome? I actually had to pay five *lire*— or was it six?—for this inadequate tube."

He produced from his pocket the pipe he had been compelled to buy, a curved briar all varnish and gold lettering.

"I've been badly treated in Wield. Certainly, they made me Monseigneur. But then they couldn't very well do less after I built this church. We've been successful here. And I venture to think popular. But the Bishop is in the hands of the Irish. He cannot grasp that the English people will not have Irish priests to rule them. They don't like it, and I don't blame them. You're not Irish, are you?"

Mark reassured him.

"This plaice isn't bad, eh? I ordered turbot, but you never get the fish you order in these Midland towns. It always ends in my having plaice, which is good for the soul! Ha-ha! I hate the Irish myself. This school of which I am the chief trustee was intended to be a Catholic reformatory. That idea fell through, and now my notion is to turn it into a decent school run by secular clergy. All the English Catholic schools are in the hands of the regular clergy, which is a mistake.

It puts too much power in the hands of the Benedictines and the Jesuits and the rest of them. After all, the great strength of the Catholic Church in England will always be the secular clergy. And what do we get now? A lot of objectionable Irishmen in Trilby hats. Last time I saw the Bishop I gave him my frank opinion of his policy. I told him my opinion to his face. He won't get me to kowtow to him. Yes, I said to him that, if he handed over this school to the Dominicans, he was going to spoil one of the finest opportunities ever presented of educating the sons of decent English gentlemen to be simple parish priests. But the Bishop of Dudley is an Irishman himself. He can't think of anything educationally better than Ushaw. And, as I was telling you, I saw there was nothing for it but to take the whole matter right up to headquarters, that is to Rome. Did I tell you that the Papal Guards turned out and presented arms? Ah, I remember now, I did mention it. I was extraordinarily impressed by them. A fine body. But generally speaking, Rome disappointed me after many years. Of course we English Catholics don't understand that way of worshipping. I'm not criticizing it. I realize that it suits the Italians. But suppose I started clearing my throat in the middle of Mass? My congregation would be disgusted, and rightly. It's an astonishing thing that I couldn't buy a good pipe in Rome, don't you think? I must have lost mine when I got out of the carriage to look at the leaning tower of Pisa, and my other one got clogged up with some candle grease. I couldn't get the beastly stuff out, so I had to give the pipe to a porter. They're keen on English pipes, those Italian porters. Poor devils, I'm not surprised. Of course, I need hardly say that in Rome they promised to do everything for me; but you can't trust them when your back is turned, and I need hardly add that the Bishop was pulling strings all the time. They showed me one of his letters, which was a tissue of mis-statements—a regular tissue. Now, suppose you had a son and you wanted him to be a priest? You don't necessarily want him to become a Jesuit or a Benedictine or a Dominican. Where can you send him now? Stonyhurst, Downside, Beaumont. There isn't a single decent school run by the secular clergy. You know what I mean? A school for the sons of gentlemen—a public school. We've got magnificent buildings, grounds, everything you could wish. I've been promised all the money necessary, and then the Bishop of Dudley steps in and says that these Dominicans ought to take it on."

"I'm afraid I've somehow given you a wrong impression," Mark interposed when Monseigneur Cripps at last filled his mouth with plaice. "I'm not a Roman Catholic."

"Oh, aren't you?" said Monseigneur indifferently. "Never mind, I expect you see my point about the necessity for the school to be run by secular clergy. Did I tell you how I got the land for my church here? That's rather an interesting story. It belonged to Lord Evesham who, as perhaps you may know, is very anti-Catholic, but a thorough good sportsman. We always get on capitally together. Well, one day I said to his agent, Captain Hart: 'What about this land, Hart? Don't you think you could get it out of his lordship?' 'It's no good, Father Cripps,' said Hart—I wasn't Monseigneur then of course—'It's no good,' he said, 'his lordship absolutely declines to let his land be used for a Catholic church.' 'Come along, Hart,' I said, 'let's have a round of golf.' Well, when we got to the eighteenth hole we were all square, and we'd both of us gone round three better than bogie and broken our own records. I was on the green with my second shot, and holed out in three. 'My game,' I shouted because Hart had foozled his drive and wasn't on the green. 'Not at all,' he said. 'You shouldn't be in such a hurry. I may hole out in one,' he laughed. 'If you do,' I said, 'you ought to get Lord Evesham to give me that land.' 'That's a bargain,' he said, and he took his mashie. Will you believe it? He did the hole in two, sir, won the game, and beat the record for the course! And that's how I got the land to build my church. I was delighted! I was delighted! I've told that story everywhere to show what sportsmen are. I told it to the Bishop, but of course he being an Irishman didn't see anything funny in it. If he could have stopped my being made Monseigneur, he'd have done so. But he couldn't."

"You seem to have as much trouble with your bishops as we do with ours in the Anglican Church," said Mark.

"We shouldn't, if we made the right men bishops," said Monseigneur. "But so long as they think at Westminster that we're going to convert England with a tagrag and bobtail mob of Irish priests, we never shall make the right men. You were looking round my church just now. Didn't it remind you of an English church?"

Mark agreed that it did very much.

"That's my secret: that's why I've been the most successful mission priest in this diocese. I realize as an Englishman that it is no use to give the English Irish Catholicism. When I was in Rome the other day I was disgusted, I really was. I was disgusted. I thoroughly sympathize with Protestants who go there and are disgusted. You cannot expect a decent English family to confess to an Irish peasant. It's not reasonable. We want to create an English tradition."

"What between the Roman party in the Anglican Church and the Anglican party in the Roman Church," said Mark, "It seems a pity that some kind of reunion cannot be effected."

"So it could," Monseigneur declared. "So it could, if it wasn't for the Irish. Look at the way we treat our English converts. The clergy, I mean. Why? Because the Irish do not want England to be converted."

Mark did not raise with Monseigneur Cripps the question of his doubts. Indeed, before the plaice had been taken away he had decided that they no longer existed. It became clear to him that the English Church was England; and although he knew in his heart that Monseigneur Cripps was suffering from a sense of grievance and that his criticism of Roman policy was too obviously biased, it pleased him to believe that it was a fair criticism.

Mark thanked Monseigneur Cripps for his hospitality and took a friendly leave of him. An hour later he was walking back through the pleasant vale of Wield toward the Cotswolds. As he went his way among the green orchards, he thought over his late impulse to change allegiance, marvelling at it now and considering it irrational, like one astonished at his own behaviour in a dream. There came into his mind a story of George Fox who drawing near to the city of Lichfield took off his shoes in a meadow and cried three times in a loud voice "Woe unto the bloody city of Lichfield," after which he put on his shoes again and proceeded into the town. Mark looked back in amazement at his lunch with

Monseigneur Cripps and his own meditated apostasy. To his present mood that intention to forsake his own Church appeared as remote from actuality as the malediction of George Fox upon the city of Lichfield.

Here among these green orchards in the heart of England Roman Catholicism presented itself to Mark's imagination as an exotic. The two words "Roman Catholicism" uttered aloud in the quiet June sunlight gave him the sensation of an allamanda or of a gardenia blossoming in an apple-tree. People who talked about bringing the English Church into line with the trend of Western Christianity lacked a sense of history. Apart from the question whether the English Church before the Reformation had accepted the pretensions of the Papacy, it was absurd to suppose that contemporary Romanism had anything in common with English Catholicism of the early sixteenth century. English Catholicism long before the Reformation had been a Protestant Catholicism, always in revolt against Roman claims, always preserving its insularity. It was idle to question the Catholic intentions of a priesthood that could produce within a century of the Reformation such prelates as Andrews and Ken. It was ridiculous at the prompting of the party in the ascendancy at Westminster to procure a Papal decision against English Orders when two hundred and fifty years ago there was a cardinal's hat waiting for Laud if he would leave the Church of England. And what about Paul IV and Elizabeth? Was he not willing to recognize English Orders if she would recognize his headship of Christendom?

But these were controversial arguments, and as Mark walked along through the pleasant vale of Wield with the Cotswold hills rising taller before him at every mile he apprehended that his adhesion to the English Church had been secured by the natural scene rather than by argument. Nevertheless, it was interesting to speculate why Romanism had not made more progress in England, why even now with a hierarchy and with such a distinguished line of converts beginning with Newman it remained so completely out of touch with the national life of the country. While the Romans converted one soul to Catholicism, the inheritors of the Oxford Movement were converting twenty. Catholicism must be accounted a disposition of mind, an attitude toward life that did not necessarily imply all that was implied by Roman Catholicism. What was the secret of the Roman failure? Everywhere else in the world Roman Catholicism had known how to adapt itself to national needs; only in England did it remain exotic. It was like an Anglo-Indian magnate who returns to find himself of no importance in his native land, and who but for the flavour of his curries and perhaps a black servant or two would be utterly inconspicuous. He tries to fit in with the new conditions of his readopted country, but he remains an exotic and is regarded by his neighbours as one to whom the lesson must be taught that he is no longer of importance. What had been the cause of this breach in the Roman Catholic tradition, this curious incompetency, this Anglo-Indian conservatism and pretentiousness? Perhaps it had begun when in the seventeenth century the propagation of Roman Catholicism in England was handed over to the Jesuits, who mismanaged the country hopelessly. By the time Rome had perceived that the conversion of England could not be left to the Jesuits the harm was done, so that when with greater toleration the time was ripe to expand her organization it was necessary to recruit her priests in Ireland. What the Jesuits had begun the Irish completed. It had been amusing to listen to the lamentations of Monseigneur Cripps; but Monseigneur Cripps had expressed, however ludicrous his egoism, the failure of his Church in England.

Mark's statement of the Anglican position with nobody to answer his arguments except the trees and the hedgerows seemed flawless. The level road, the gentle breeze in the orchards on either side, the scent of the grass, and the busy chirping of the birds coincided with the main point of his argument that England was most inexpressibly Anglican and that Roman Catholicism was most unmistakably not. His arguments were really hasty foot-notes to his convictions; if each one had separately been proved wrong, that would have had no influence on the point of view he had reached. He forgot that this very landscape that was seeming incomparable England herself had yesterday appeared complacent and monotonous. In fact he was as bad as George Fox, who after taking off his shoes to curse the bloody city of Lichfield should only have put them on again to walk away from it.

The grey road was by now beginning to climb the foothills of the Cotswolds; a yellow-hammer, keeping always a few paces ahead, twittered from quickset boughs nine encouraging notes that drowned the echoes of ancient controversies. In such a countryside no claims papal or episcopal possessed the least importance; and Mark dismissed the subject from his mind, abandoning himself to the pleasure of the slow ascent. Looking back after a while he could see the town of Wield riding like a ship in a sea of verdure, and when he surveyed thus England asleep in the sunlight, the old ambition to become a preaching friar was kindled again in his heart. He would re-establish the extinct and absolutely English Order of St. Gilbert so that there should be no question of Roman pretensions. Doubtless, St. Francis himself would understand a revival of his Order without reference to existing Franciscans; but nobody else would understand, and it would be foolish to insist upon being a Franciscan if the rest of the Order disowned him and his followers. If anybody had asked Mark at that moment why he wanted to restore the preaching friars, he might have found it difficult to answer. He was by no means imbued with the missionary spirit just then; his experience at Chatsea had made him pessimistic about missionary effort in the Church of England. If a man like Father Rowley had failed to win the support of his ecclesiastical superiors, Mark, who possessed more humility than is usual at twenty-one, did not fancy that he should be successful. The ambition to become a friar was revived by an incomprehensible, or if not incomprehensible, certainly by an inexplicable impulse to put himself in tune with the landscape, to proclaim as it were on behalf of that dumb heart of England beating down there in the flowery Vale of Wield: *God rest you merry gentlemen, let nothing you dismay!* There was revealed to him with the assurance of absolute faith that all the sorrows, all the ugliness, all the soullessness (no other word could be found) of England in the first year of the twentieth century was due to the Reformation; the desire to become a preaching friar was the dramatic expression of this inspired conviction. Before his journey through the Vale of Wield Mark in any discussion would have been ready to argue the mistake of the Reformation: but now there was no longer room for argument. What formerly he thought now he knew.

The song of the yellow-hammer was louder in the quickset hedge; the trees burned with a sharper green; the road urged his feet.

"If only everybody in England could move as I am moving now," he thought. "If only I could be granted the power to show a few people, so that they could show others, and those others show all the world. How confidently that yellow-hammer repeats his song! How well he knows that his song is right! How little he envies the linnet and how little the linnet envies him! The fools that talk of nature's cruelty, the blind fatuous sentimental coxcombs!"

Thus apostrophizing, Mark came to a wayside inn; discovering that he was hungry, he took his seat at a rustic table outside and called for bread and cheese and beer. While he was eating, a vehicle approached from the direction in which he would soon be travelling. He took it at first for a caravan of gipsies, but when it grew near he saw that it was painted over with minatory texts and was evidently the vehicle of itinerant gospellers. Two young men alighted from the caravan when it pulled up before the door of the inn. They were long-nosed sallow creatures with that expression of complacency which organized morality too often produces, and in this quiet countryside they gave an effect of being overgrown Sunday-school scholars upon their annual outing. Having cast a censorious glance in the direction of Mark's jug of ale, they sat down at the farther end of the bench and ordered food.

"The preaching friars of to-day," Mark thought gloomily.

"Excuse me," said one of the gospellers. "I notice you've been looking very hard at our van. Excuse me, but are you saved?"

"No, are you?" Mark countered with an angry blush.

"We are," the gospeller proclaimed. "Or I and Mr. Smillie here," he indicated his companion, "wouldn't be travelling round trying to save others. Here, read this tract, my friend. Don't hurry over it. We can wait all day and all night to bring one wandering soul to Jesus."

Mark looked at the young men curiously; perceiving that they were sincere, he accepted the tract and out of courtesy perused it. The tale therein enfolded reminded him of a narrative testifying to the efficacy of a patent medicine. The process of conversation followed a stereotyped formula.

For three and a half years I was unable to keep down any sins for more than five minutes after I had committed the last one. I had a dizzy feeling in the heart and a sharp pain in the small of the soul. A friend of mine recommended me to try the good minister in the slum. . . . After the first text I was able to keep down my sins for six minutes . . . after twenty-two bottles I am as good as I ever was. . . . I ascribe my salvation entirely to. . . . Mark handed back the tract with a smile.

"Do you convert many people with this literature?" he asked.

"We don't often convert a soul right off," said Mr. Smillie. "But we sow the good seed, if you follow my meaning; and we leave the rest to Jesus. Mr. Bullock and I have handed over seven hundred tracts in three weeks, and we know that they won't all fall on stony ground or be choked by tares and thistles."

"Do you mind my asking you a question?" Mark said.

The gospel bearers craned their necks like hungry fowls in their eagerness to peck at any problems Mark felt inclined to scatter before them. A ludicrous fancy passed through his mind that much of the good seed was pecked up by the scatterers.

"What are you trying to convert people to?" Mark solemnly inquired.

"What are we trying to convert people to?" echoed Mr. Bullock and Mr. Smillie in unison. Then the former became eloquent. "We're trying to wash ignorant people in the blood of the Lamb. We're converting them from the outer darkness, where there is weeping and wailing and gnashing of teeth, to be rocked safe for ever in the arms of Jesus. If you'd have read that tract I handed you a bit more slowly and a bit more carefully, you wouldn't have had any call to ask a question like that."

"Perhaps I framed my question rather badly," Mark admitted. "I understand that you want to bring people to believe in Our Lord; but when by a tract or by a personal exhortation or by an emotional appeal you've induced them to suppose that they are converted, or as you put it saved, what more do you give them?"

"What more do we give them?" Mr. Smillie shrilled. "What more can we give them after we've given them Christ Jesus? We're sitting here offering you Christ Jesus at this moment. You're sitting there mocking at us. But Mr. Bullock and me don't mind how much you mock. We're ready to stay here for hours if we can bring you safe to the bosom of Emmanuel."

"Yes, but suppose I told you that I believe in Our Lord Jesus Christ without any persuasion from you?" Mark inquired.

"Well, then you're saved," said Mr. Bullock decidedly. "And you can ask the landlord for our bill, Mr. Smillie."

"But is nothing more necessary?" Mark persisted.

"*By faith are ye justified*," Mr. Bullock and Mr. Smillie shouted simultaneously.

Mark paused for a moment to consider whether argument was worth while, and then he returned to the attack.

"I'm afraid I think that people like you do a great deal of damage to Christianity. You only flatter human conceit. You get hold of some emotional creature and work upon his feelings until in an access of self-absorption he feels that the universe is standing still while the necessary measures are taken to secure his personal salvation. You flatter this poor soul, and then you go away and leave him to work out his own salvation."

"If you're dwelling in Christ Jesus and Christ Jesus is dwelling in you, you haven't got to work out your own salvation. He worked out your salvation on the Cross," said Mr. Bullock contemptuously.

"And you think that nothing more is necessary from a man? It seems to me that the religion you preach is fatal to human character. I'm not trying to be offensive when I tell you that it's the religion of a tapeworm. It's a religion for parasites. It's a religion which ignores the Holy Ghost."

"Perhaps you'll explain your assertion a little more fully?" Mr. Bullock invited with a scowl.

"What I mean is that, if Our Lord's Atonement removed all responsibility from human nature, there doesn't seem much for the Holy Ghost to do, does there?"

"Well, as it happens," said Mr. Bullock sarcastically, "Mr. Smillie and I here do most of our work with the help of the Holy Ghost, so you've hit on a bad example to work off your sneers on."

"I'm not trying to sneer," Mark protested. "But strangely enough just before you came along I was thinking to myself how much I should like to travel over England preaching about Our Lord, because I think that England has need of Him. But I also think, now you've answered my question, that *you* are doing more harm than good by your interpretation of the Holy Ghost."

"Mr. Smillie," interrupted Mr. Bullock in an elaborately off-hand voice, "if you've counted the change and it's all correct, we'd better get a move on. Let's gird up our loins, Mr. Smillie, and not sit wrestling here with infidels."

"No, really, you must allow me," Mark persisted. "You've had it so much your own way with your tracts and your talks this last few weeks that by now you must be in need of a sermon yourselves. The gospel you preach is only going to add to the complacency of England, and England is too complacent already. All Northern nations are, which is why they are Protestant. They demand a religion which will truckle to them, a religion which will allow them to devote six days of the week to what is called business and on the seventh day to rest and praise God that they are not as other men."

"*Render unto Cæsar the things that are Cæsar's and unto God the things that are God's*," said Mr. Smillie, putting the change in his pocket and untying the nosebag from the horse.

"*Ye cannot serve God and mammon*," Mark retorted. "And I wish you'd let me finish my argument."

"Mr. Smillie and I aren't touring the Midlands trying to find grapes on thorns and figs on thistles," said Mr. Bullock scathingly. "We'd have given you a chance, if you'd have shown any fruits of the Spirit."

"You've just said you weren't looking for grapes or figs," Mark laughed. "I'm sorry I've made you so cross. But you began the argument by asking me if I was saved. Think how annoyed you would have been if I had begun a conversation by asking you if you were washed."

"My last words to you is," said Mr. Bullock solemnly, looking out of the caravan window, "my last words to you are," he corrected himself, "is to avoid beer. You can touch up the horse, Mr. Smillie."

"I'll come and touch you up, you big-mouthed Bible thumpers," a rich voice shouted from the inn door. "Yes, you sit outside my public-house and swill minerals when you're so full of gas already you could light a corporation gasworks. Avoid beer, you walking bellows? Step down out of that travelling menagerie, and I'll give you 'avoid beer.' You'll avoid more than beer before I've finished with you."

But the gospel bearers without paying any attention to the tirade went on their way; and Mark who did not wait to listen to the innkeeper's abuse of all religion and all religious people went on his way in the opposite direction.

Swinging homeward over the Cotswolds Mark flattered himself on a victory over heretics, and he imagined his adversaries entering Wield that afternoon, the prey of doubt and mortification. At the highest point of the road he even ventured to suppose that they might find themselves at Evensong outside St. Andrew's Church and led within by the grace of the Holy Spirit that they might renounce their errors before the altar. Indeed, it was not until he was back in the Rectory that the futility of his own bearing overwhelmed him with shame. Anxious to atone for his self-conceit, Mark gave the Rector an account of the incident.

"It seems to me that I behaved very feebly, don't you think?"

"That kind of fellow is a hard nut to crack," the Rector said consolingly. "And you can't expect just by quoting text against text to effect an instant conversion. Don't forget that your friends are in their way as great enthusiasts probably as yourself."

"Yes, but it's humiliating to be imagining oneself leading a revival of the preaching friars and then to behave like that. What strikes me now, when it's too late, is that I ought to have waited and taken the opportunity to tackle the innkeeper. He was just the ordinary man who supposes that religion is his natural enemy. You must admit that I missed a chance there."

"I don't want to check your missionary zeal," said the Rector. "But I really don't think you need worry yourself about an omission of that kind so long before you are ordained. If I didn't know you as well as I do, I might even be inclined to consider such a passion for souls at your age a little morbid. I wish with all my heart you'd gone to Oxford," he added with a sigh.

"Well, really, do you know," said Mark, "I don't regret that. Whatever may be the advantages of a public school and university, the education hampers one. One becomes identified with a class; and when one has finished with that education, the next two or three years have to be spent in discovering that public school and university men form a very small proportion of the world's population. Sometimes I almost regret that my mother did not let me acquire that Cockney accent. You can say a lot of things in a Cockney accent which said without any accent sound priggish. You must admit, Rector, that your inner comment on my tale of the gospellers and the innkeeper is 'Dear me! I am afraid Mark's turning into a prig.'"

"No, no. I laid particular stress on the point that if I didn't know you as well as I do I might perhaps have thought that," the Rector protested.

"I don't think I am a prig," Mark went on slowly. "I don't think I have enough confidence in myself to be a prig. I think the way I argued with Mr. Bullock and Mr. Smillie was a bit priggish, because at the back of my head all the time I was talking I felt in addition to the arrogance of faith a kind of confounded snobbishness; and this sense of superiority came not from my being a member of the Church, but from feeling myself more civilized than they were. Looking back now at the conversation, I can remember that actually at the very moment I was talking of the Holy Ghost I was noticing how Mr. Bullock's dicky would keep escaping from his waistcoat. I wonder if the great missionary saints of the middle ages had to contend with this accumulation of social conventions with which we are faced nowadays. It seems to me that in everything—in art, in religion, in mere ordinary everyday life and living—man is adding daily to the wall that separates him from God."

"H'm, yes," said the Rector, "all this only means that you are growing up. The child is nearer to God than the man. Wordsworth said it better than I can say it. Similarly, the human race must grow away from God as it takes upon itself the burden of knowledge. That surely is inherent in the fall of man. No philosopher has yet improved upon the first chapter of Genesis as a symbolical explanation of humanity's plight. When man was created—or if you like to put it evolved—there must have been an exact moment at which he had the chance of remaining where he was—in other words, in the Garden of Eden—or of developing further along his own lines with free will. Satan fell from pride. It is natural to assume that man, being tempted by Satan, would fall from the same sin, though the occasion, of his fall might be the less heroic sin of curiosity. Yes, I think that first chapter of Genesis, as an attempt to sum up the history of millions of years, is astoundingly complete. Have you ever thought how far by now the world would have grown away from God without the Incarnation?"

"Yes," said Mark, "and after nineteen hundred years how little nearer it has grown."

"My dear boy," said the Rector, "if man has not even yet got rid of rudimentary gills or useless paps he is not going to grow very visibly nearer to God in nineteen hundred years after growing away from God for ninety million. Yet such is the mercy of our Father in Heaven that, infinitely remote as we have grown from Him, we are still made in His image, and in childhood we are allowed a few years of blessed innocency. To some children—and you were one of them—God reveals Himself more directly. But don't, my dear fellow, grow up imagining that these visions you were accorded as a boy will be accorded to you all through your life. You may succeed in remaining pure in act, but you will find it hard to remain pure in heart. To me the most frightening beatitude is *Blessed are the pure in heart, for they shall see God.* What your present state of mind really amounts to is lack of hope, for as soon as you find yourself unable to be as miraculously eloquent as St. Anthony of Padua you become the prey of despair."

"I am not so foolish as that," Mark replied. "But surely, Rector, it behoves me during these years before my ordination to criticize myself severely."

"As severely as you like," the Rector agreed, "provided that you only criticize yourself, and don't criticize Almighty God."

"But surely," Mark went on, "I ought to be asking myself now that I am twenty-one how I shall best occupy the next three years?"

"Certainly," the Rector assented. "Think it over, and be sure that, when you have thought it over and have made your decision with the help of prayer, I shall be the first to support that decision in every way possible. Even if you decide to be a preaching friar," he added with a smile. "And now I have some news for you. Esther arrives here tomorrow to stay with us for a fortnight before she is professed."

CHAPTER XXII
SISTER ESTHER MAGDALENE

Esther's novitiate in the community of St. Mary Magdalene, Shoreditch, had lasted six months longer than was usual, because the Mother Superior while never doubting her vocation for the religious life had feared for her ability to stand the strain of that work among penitents to which the community was dedicated. In the end, her perseverance had been rewarded, and the day of her profession was at hand.

During the whole of her nearly four years' novitiate Esther had not been home once; although Mark and she had corresponded at long intervals, their letters had been nothing more than formal records of minor events, and on St. John's eve he drove with the dogcart to meet her, wondering all the way how much she would have changed. The first thing that struck him when he saw her alight from the train on Shipcot platform was her neatness. In old days with windblown hair and clothes flung on anyhow she had belonged so unmistakably to the open air. Now in her grey habit and white veil of the novice she was as tranquil as Miriam, and for the first time Mark perceived a resemblance between the sisters. Her complexion, which formerly was flushed and much freckled by the open air, was now like alabaster; and although her auburn hair was hidden beneath the veil Mark was aware of it like a hidden fire. He had in the very moment of welcoming her a swift vision of that auburn hair lying on the steps of the altar a fortnight hence, and he was filled with a wild desire to be present at her profession and gathering up the shorn locks to let them run through his fingers like flames. He had no time to be astonished at himself before they were shaking hands.

"Why, Esther," he laughed, "you're carrying an umbrella."

"It was raining in London," she said gravely.

He was on the point of exclaiming at such prudence in Esther when he blushed in the remembrance that she was a nun. During the drive back they talked shyly about the characters of the village and the Rectory animals.

"I feel as if you'd just come back from school for the holidays," he said.

"Yes, I feel as if I'd been at school," she agreed. "How sweet the country smells."

"Don't you miss the country sometimes in Shoreditch?" he asked.

She shook her head and looked at him with puzzled eyes.

"Why should I miss anything in Shoreditch?"

Mark was abashed and silent for the rest of the drive, because he fancied that Esther might have supposed that he was referring to the past, rather than give which impression he would have cut out his tongue. When they reached the Rectory, Mark was moved almost to tears by the greetings.

"Dear little sister," Miriam murmured. "How happy we are to have you with us again."

"Dear child," said Mrs. Ogilvie. "And really she does look like a nun."

"My dearest girl, we have missed you every moment of these four years," said the Rector, bending to kiss her. "How cold your cheek is."

"It was quite chilly driving," said Mark quickly, for there had come upon him a sudden dismay lest they should think she was a ghost. He was relieved when Miriam announced tea half an hour earlier than usual in honour of Esther's arrival; it seemed to prove that to her family she was still alive.

"After tea I'm going to Wych Maries to pick St. John's wort for the church. Would you like to walk as far?" Mark suggested, and then stood speechless, horrified at his want of tact. He had the presence of mind not to excuse himself, and he was grateful to Esther when she replied in a calm voice that she should like a walk after tea.

When the opportunity presented itself, Mark apologized for his suggestion.

"By why apologize?" she asked. "I assure you I'm not at all tired and I really should like to walk to Wych Maries."

He was amazed at her self-possession, and they walked along with unhastening conventual steps to where the St. John's wort grew amid a tangle of ground ivy in the open spaces of a cypress grove, appearing most vividly and richly golden like sunlight breaking from black clouds in the western sky.

"Gather some sprays quickly, Sister Esther Magdalene," Mark advised. "And you will be safe against the demons of this night when evil has such power."

"Are we ever safe against the demons of the night?" she asked solemnly. "And has not evil great power always?"

"Always," he assented in a voice that trembled to a sigh, like the uncertain wind that comes hesitating at dusk in the woods. "Always," he repeated.

As he spoke Mark fell upon his knees among the holy flowers, for there had come upon him temptation; and the sombre trees standing round watched him like fiends with folded wings.

"Go to the chapel," he cried in an agony.

"Mark, what is the matter?"

"Go to the chapel. For God's sake, Esther, don't wait."

In another moment he felt that he should tear the white veil from her forehead and set loose her auburn hair.

"Mark, are you ill?"

"Oh, do what I ask," he begged. "Once I prayed for you here. Pray for me now."

At that moment she understood, and putting her hands to her eyes she stumbled blindly toward the ruined church of the two Maries, heavily too, because she was encumbered by her holy garb. When she was gone and the last rustle of her footsteps had died away upon the mid-summer silence, Mark buried his body in the golden flowers.

"How can I ever look any of them in the face again?" he cried aloud. "Small wonder that yesterday I was so futile. Small wonder indeed! And of all women, to think that I should fall in love with Esther. If I had fallen in love with her four years ago . . . but now when she is going to be professed . . . suddenly without any warning . . . without any warning . . . yet perhaps I did love her in those days . . . and was jealous. . . ."

And even while Mark poured forth his horror of himself he held her image to his heart.

"I thought she was a ghost because she was dead to me, not because she was dead to them. She is not a ghost to them. And is she to me?"

He leapt to his feet, listening.

"Should she come back," he thought with beating heart. "Should she come back . . . I love her . . . she hasn't taken her final vows . . . might she not love me? No," he shouted at the top of his voice. "I will not do as my father did . . . I will not . . . I will not. . . ."

Mark felt sure of himself again: he felt as he used to feel as a little boy when his mother entered on a shaft of light to console his childish terrors. When he came to the ruined chapel and saw Esther standing with uplifted palms before the image of St. Mary Magdalene long since put back upon the pedestal from which it had been flung by the squire of Rushbrooke Grange, Mark was himself again.

"My dear," Esther cried, impulsively taking his hand. "You frightened me. What was the matter?"

He did not answer for a moment or two, because he wanted her to hold his hand a little while longer, so much time was to come when she would never hold it.

"Whenever I dip my hand in cold water," he said at last, "I shall think of you. Why did you say that about the demons of the night?"

She dropped his hand in comprehension.

"You're disgusted with me," he murmured. "I'm not surprised."

"No, no, you mustn't think of me like that. I'm still a very human Esther, so human that the Reverend Mother has made me wait an extra year to be professed. But, Mark dear, can't you understand, you who know what I endured in this place, that I am sometimes tempted by memories of him, that I sometimes sin by regrets for giving him up, my dead lover so near to me in this place. My dead love," she sighed to herself, "to whose memory in my pride of piety I thought I should be utterly indifferent."

A spasm of jealousy had shaken Mark while Esther was speaking, but by the time she had finished he had fought it down.

"I think I must have loved you all this time," he told her.

"Mark dear, I'm ten years older than you. I'm going to be a nun for what of my life remains. And I can never love anybody else. Don't make this visit of mine a misery to me. I've had to conquer so much and I need your prayers."

"I wish you needed my kisses."

"Mark!"

"What did I say? Oh, Esther, I'm a brute. Tell me one thing."

"I've already told you more than I've told anyone except my confessor."

"Have you found happiness in the religious life?"

"I have found myself. The Reverend Mother wanted me to leave the community and enter a contemplative order. She did not think I should be able to help poor girls."

"Esther, what a stupid woman! Why surely you would be wonderful with them?"

"I think she is a wise woman," said Esther. "I think since we came picking St. John's wort I understand how wise she is."

"Esther, dear dear Esther, you make me feel more than ever ashamed of myself. I entreat you not to believe what the Reverend Mother says."

"You have only a fortnight to convince me," said Esther.

"And I will convince you."

"Mark, do you remember when you made me pray for his soul telling me that in that brief second he had time to repent?"

Mark nodded grimly.

"You still do think that, don't you?"

"Of course I do. He must have repented."

She thanked him with her eyes; and Mark looking into their depths of hope unfathomable put away from him the thought that the damned soul of Will Starling was abroad to-night with power of evil. Yes, he put this thought behind him; but carrying an armful of St. John's wort to hang in sprays above the doors of the church he could not rid himself of the fancy that his arms were filled with Esther's auburn hair.

CHAPTER XXIII
MALFORD ABBEY

Mark left Wych-on-the-Wold next day; although he did not announce that he should be absent from home so long, he intended not to return until Esther had gone back to Shoreditch. He hoped that he was not being cowardly in thus running away; but after having assured Esther that she could count on his behaving normally for the rest of her visit, he found his sleep that night so profoundly disturbed by feverish visions that when morning came he dreaded his inability to behave as both he would wish himself and she would wish him to behave. Flight seemed the only way to find peace. He was shocked not so much by being in love with Esther, but by the suddenness with which his desires had overwhelmed him, desires which had never been roused since he was born. If in an instant he could be turned upside down like that, could he be sure that upon the next occasion, supposing that he fell in love with somebody more suitable, he should be able to escape so easily? His father must have married his mother out of some such violent impulse as had seized himself yesterday afternoon, and resentment about his weakness had spoilt his whole life. And those dreams! How significant now were the words of the Compline hymn, and how much it behoved a Christian soul to vanquish these ill dreams against beholding which the defence of the Creator was invoked. He had vowed celibacy; yet already, three months after his twenty-first birthday, after never once being troubled with the slightest hint that the vow he had taken might be hard to keep, his security had been threatened. How right the Rector had been about that frightening beatitude.

Mark had taken the direction of Wychford, and when he reached the bridge at the bottom of the road from Wych-on-the-Wold he thought he would turn aside and visit the Greys whom he had not seen for a long time. He was conscious of a curiosity to know if the feelings aroused by Esther could be aroused by Monica or Margaret or Pauline. He found the dear family unchanged and himself, so far as they were concerned, equally unchanged and as much at his ease as he had ever been.

"And what are you going to do now?" one of them asked.

"You mean immediately?"

Mark could not bring himself to say that he did not know, because such a reply would have seemed to link him with the state of mind in which he had been thrown yesterday afternoon.

"Well, really, I was thinking of going into a monastery," he announced.

Pauline clapped her hands.

"Now I think that is just what you ought to do," she said.

Then followed questions about which Order he proposed to join; and Mark ashamed to go back on what he had said lest they should think him flippant answered that he thought of joining the Order of St. George.

"You know—Father Burrowes, who works among soldiers."

When Mark was standing by the cross-roads above Wychford and was wondering which to take, he decided that really the best thing he could do at this moment was to try to enter the Order of St. George. He might succeed in being ordained without going to a theological college, or if the Bishop insisted upon a theological course and he found that he had a vocation for the religious life, he could go to Glastonbury and rejoin the Order when he was a priest. It was true that Father Rowley disapproved of Father Burrowes; but he had never expressed more than a general disapproval, and Mark was inclined to attribute his attitude to the prejudice of a man of strong personality and definite methods against another man of strong personality and definite methods working on similar lines among similar people. Mark remembered now that there had been a question at one time of Father Burrowes' opening a priory in the next parish to St. Agnes'. Probably that was the reason why Father Rowley disapproved of him. Mark had heard the monk preach on one occasion and had liked him. Outside the pulpit, however, he knew nothing more of him than what he had heard from soldiers staying in the Keppel Street Mission House, who from Aldershot had visited Malford Abbey, the mother house of the Order. The alternative to Malford was Clere Abbey on the Berkshire downs where Dom Cuthbert Manners ruled over a small community of strict Benedictines. Had Mark really been convinced that he was likely to remain a monk for the rest of his life, he would have chosen the Benedictines; but he did not feel justified in presenting himself for admission to Clere on what would seem impulse. He hoped that if he was accepted by the Order of St. George he should be given an opportunity to work at one of the priories in Aldershot or Sandgate, and that the experience he might expect to gain would help him later as a parish priest. He could not confide in the Rector his reason for wanting to subject himself to monastic discipline, and he expected a good deal of opposition. It might be better to write from whatever village he stayed in to-night and make the announcement without going back at all. And this is what in the end he decided to do.

The Sun Inn,
Ladingford.
June 24.
My dear Rector,

I expect you gathered from our talk the day before yesterday that I was feeling dissatisfied with myself, and you must know that the problem of occupying my time wisely before I am ordained has lately been on my mind. I don't feel that I could honestly take up a profession to which I had no intention of sticking, and though Father Rowley recommended me to stay at home and work with the village people I don't feel capable of doing that yet. If it was a question of helping you by taking off your shoulders work that I could do it would be another matter. But you've often said to me that you had more time on your hands than you cared for since you gave up coaching me for an Oxford scholarship, and so I don't think I'm wrong in supposing that you would find it hard to discover for me any parochial routine work. I'm not old enough yet to fish for souls, and I have no confidence in my ability to hook them. Besides, I think it would bore you if I started "missionizing" in Wych-on-the-Wold.

I've settled therefore to try to get into the Order of St. George. I don't think you know Father Burrowes personally, but I've always heard that he does a splendid work among soldiers, and I'm hoping that he will accept me as a novice.

Latterly, in fact since I left Chatsea, I've been feeling the need of a regular existence, and, though I cannot pretend that I have a vocation for the monastic life in the highest sense, I do feel that I have a vocation for the Order of St. George. You will wonder why I have not mentioned this to you, but the fact is—and I hope you'll appreciate my frankness—I did not think of the O.S.G. till this morning. Of course they may refuse to have me. But I shall present myself without a preliminary letter, and I hope to persuade Father Burrowes to have me on probation. If he once does that, I'm sure that I shall satisfy him. This sounds like the letter of a conceited clerk. It must be the fault of this horrible inn pen, which is like writing with a tooth-pick dipped in a puddle! I thought it was best not to stay at the Rectory, with Esther on the verge of her profession. It wouldn't be fair to her at a time like this to make my immediate future a matter of prime importance. So do forgive my going off in this fashion. I suppose it's just possible that some bishop will accept me for ordination from Malford, though no doubt it's improbable. This will be a matter to discuss with Father Burrowes later.

Do forgive what looks like a most erratic course of procedure. But I really should hate a long discussion, and if I make a mistake I shall have had a lesson. It really is essential for me to be tremendously occupied. I cannot say more than this, but I do beg you to believe that I'm not taking this apparently unpremeditated step without a very strong reason. It's a kind of compromise with my ambition to re-establish in the English Church an order of preaching friars. I haven't yet given up that idea, but I'm sure that I ought not to think about it seriously until I'm a priest.

I'm staying here to-night after a glorious day's tramp, and to-morrow morning I shall take the train and go by Reading and Basingstoke to Malford. I'll write to you as soon as I know if I'm accepted. My best love to everybody, and please tell Esther that I shall think about her on St. Mary Magdalene's Day.

Yours always affectionately,

Mark.

To Esther he wrote by the same post:

My dear Sister Esther Magdalene,

Do not be angry with me for running away, and do not despise me for trying to enter a monastery in such a mood. I'm as much the prey of religion as you are. And I am really horrified by the revelation of what I am capable of. I saw in your eyes yesterday the passion of your soul for Divine things. The memory of them awes me. Pray for me, dear sister, that all my passion may be turned to the service of God. Defend me to your brother, who will not understand my behaviour.

Mark.

Three days later Mark wrote again to the Rector:

The Abbey,

Malford,

Surrey.

June 27th.

My dear Rector,

I do hope that you're not so much annoyed with me that you don't want to hear anything about my monastic adventures. However, if you are you can send back this long letter unopened. I believe that is the proper way to show one's disapproval by correspondence.

I reached Malford yesterday afternoon, and after a jolly walk between high hazel hedges for about two miles I reached the Abbey. It doesn't quite fulfil one's preconceived ideas of what an abbey should look like, but I suppose it is the most practicable building that could be erected with the amount of money that the Order had to spare for what in a way is a luxury for a working order like this. What it most resembles is three tin tabernacles put together to form three sides of a square, the fourth and empty side of which is by far the most beautiful, because it consists of a glorious view over a foreground of woods, a middle-distance of park land, and on the horizon the Hampshire downs.

I am an authority on this view, because I had to gaze at it for about a quarter of an hour while I was waiting for somebody to open the Abbey door. At last the porter, Brother Lawrence, after taking a good look at me through the grill, demanded what I wanted. When I said that I wanted to be a monk, he looked very alarmed and hurried away, leaving me to gaze at that view for another ten minutes. He came back at last and let me in, informing me in a somewhat adenoidish voice that the Reverend Brother was busy in the garden and asking me to wait until he came in. Brother Lawrence has a large, pock-marked face, and while he is talking to anybody he stands with his right hand in his left sleeve and his left hand in his right sleeve like a Chinese mandarin or an old washer-woman with her arms folded under her apron. You must make the most of my descriptions in this letter, because if I am accepted as a probationer I shan't be able to indulge in any more personalities about my brethren.

The guest-room like everything else in the monastery is match-boarded; and while I was waiting in it the noise was terrific, because some corrugated iron was being nailed on the roof of a building just outside. I began to regret that Brother Lawrence had opened the door at all and that he had not left me in the cloisters, as by the way I discovered that the space enclosed by the three tin tabernacles is called! There was nothing to read in the guest-room except one sheet of a six months' old newspaper which had been spread on the table presumably for a guest to mend something with glue. At last the Reverend Brother, looking most beautiful in a white habit with a zucchetto of mauve velvet, came in and welcomed me with much friendliness. I was surprised to find somebody so young as Brother Dunstan in charge of a monastery, especially as he said he was only a novice as yet. It appears that all the bigwigs—or should I say big-cowls?—are away at the moment on business of the Order and that various changes are in the offing, the most important being the giving up of their branch in Malta and the consequent arrival of Brother George, of whom Brother Dunstan spoke in a hushed voice. Father Burrowes, or the Reverend Father as he is called, is preaching in the north of England at the moment, and Brother Dunstan tells me it is quite impossible for him to say anything, still less to do anything, about my admission. However, he urged me to stay on for the present as a guest, an invitation which I accepted without hesitation. He had only just time to show me my cell and the card of rules for guests when a bell rang and, drawing his cowl over his head, he hurried off.

After perusing the rules, I discovered that this was the bell which rings a quarter of an hour before Vespers for solemn silence. I hadn't the slightest idea where the chapel was, and when I asked Brother Lawrence he glared at me and put his finger to his mouth. I was not to be discouraged, however, and in the end he showed me into the ante-chapel which is curtained off from the quire. There was only one other person in the ante-chapel, a florid, well-dressed man with a rather mincing and fussy way of worshipping. The monks led by Brother Lawrence (who is not even a novice yet, but a postulant and wears a black habit, without a hood, tied round the waist with a rope) passed from the refectory through the ante-chapel into the quire, and Vespers began. They used an arrangement called "The Day Hours of the English Church," but beyond a few extra antiphons there was very little difference from ordinary Evening Prayer. After Vespers I had a simple and solemn meal by myself, and I was wondering how I should get hold of a book to pass away the evening, when Brother Dunstan came in and asked me if I'd like to sit with the brethren in the library until the bell rang for simple silence a quarter of an hour before Compline at 9.15, after which everybody—guests and monks—are expected to go to bed in solemn silence. The difference between simple silence and solemn silence is that you may ask necessary questions and get necessary replies during simple silence; but as far as I can make out, during solemn silence you wouldn't be allowed to tell anybody that you were dying, or if you did tell anybody, he wouldn't be able to do anything about it until solemn silence was over.

The other monks are Brother Jerome, the senior novice after Brother Dunstan, a pious but rather dull young man with fair hair and a squashed face, and Brother Raymond, attractive and bird-like, and considered a great Romanizer by the others. There is also Brother Walter, who is only a probationer and is not even allowed wide sleeves and a habit like Brother Lawrence, but has to wear a very moth-eaten cassock with a black band tied round it. Brother Walter had been marketing in High Thorpe (I wonder what the Bishop of Silchester thought if he saw him in the neighbourhood of the episcopal castle!) and having lost himself on the way home he had arrived back late for Vespers and was tremendously teased by the others in consequence. Brother Walter is a tall excitable awkward creature with black hair that sticks up on end and wide-open frightened eyes. His cassock is much too short for him both in the arms and in the legs; and as he has very large hands and very large feet, his hands and feet look still larger in consequence. They didn't talk about much that was interesting during recreation. Brother Dunstan and Brother Raymond were full of monkish jokes, at all of which Brother Walter laughed in a very high voice—so loudly once that Brother Jerome asked him if he would mind making less noise, as he was reading Montalembert's Monks of the West, at which Brother Walter fell into an abashed gloom.

I asked who the visitor in the ante-chapel was and was told that he was a Sir Charles Horner who owns the whole of Malford and who has presented the Order with the thirty acres on which the Abbey is built. Sir Charles is evidently an ecclesiastically-minded person and, I should imagine, rather pleased to be able to be the patron of a monastic order.

I will write you again when I have seen Father Burrowes. For the moment I'm inclined to think that Malford is rather playing at being monks; but as I said, the bigwigs are all away. Brother Dunstan is a delightful fellow, yet I shouldn't imagine that he would make a successful abbot for long.

I enjoyed Compline most of all my experiences during the day, after which I retired to my cell and slept without turning till the bell rang for Lauds and Prime, both said as one office at six o'clock, after which I should have liked a conventual Mass. But alas, there is no priest here and I have been spending the time till breakfast by writing you this endless letter.

Yours ever affectionately,

Mark.

P.S. They don't say Mattins, which I'm inclined to think rather slack. But I suppose I oughtn't to criticize so soon.

To those two letters of Mark's, the Rector replied as follows:

The Rectory,

Wych-on-the-Wold,

Oxon.

June 29th.

My dear Mark,

I cannot say frankly that I approve of your monastic scheme. I should have liked an opportunity to talk it over with you first of all, and I cannot congratulate you on your good manners in going off like that without any word. Although you are technically independent now, I think it would be a great mistake to sink your small capital of £500 in the Order of St. George, and you can't very well make use of them to pass the next two or three years without contributing anything.

The other objection to your scheme is that you may not get taken at Glastonbury. In any case the Glastonbury people will give the preference to Varsity men, and I'm not sure that they would be very keen on having an ex-monk. However, as I said, you are independent now and can choose yourself what you do. Meanwhile, I suppose it is possible that Burrowes may decide you have no vocation, in which case I hope you'll give up your monastic ambitions and come back here.

Yours affectionately,

Stephen Ogilvie.

Mark who had been growing bored in the guest-room of Malford Abbey nearly said farewell to it for ever when he received the Rector's letter. His old friend and guardian was evidently wounded by his behaviour, and Mark considering what he owed him felt that he ought to abandon his monastic ambitions if by doing so he could repay the Rector some of his kindness. His hand was on the bell that should summon the guest-brother (when the bell was working and the guest-brother was not) in order to tell him that he had been called away urgently and to ask if he might have the Abbey cart to take him to the station; but at that moment Sir Charles Horner came in and began to chat affably to Mark.

"I've been intending to come up and see you for the last three days. But I've been so confoundedly busy. They wonder what we country gentlemen do with ourselves. By gad, they ought to try our life for a change."

Mark supposed that the third person plural referred to the whole body of Radical critics.

"You're the son of Lidderdale, I hear," Sir Charles went on without giving Mark time to comment on the hardship of his existence. "I visited Lima Street twenty-five years ago, before you were born that was. Your father was a great pioneer. We owe him a lot. And you've been with Rowley lately? That confounded bishop. He's our bishop, you know. But he finds it difficult to get at Burrowes except by starving him for priests. The fellow's a time-server, a pusher . . ."

Mark began to like Sir Charles; he would have liked anybody who would abuse the Bishop of Silchester.

"So you're thinking of joining my Order," Sir Charles went on without giving Mark time to say a word. "I call it my Order because I set them up here with thirty acres of uncleared copse. It gives the Tommies something to do when they come over here on furlough from Aldershot. You've never met Burrowes, I hear."

Mark thought that Sir Charles for a busy man had managed to learn a great deal about an unimportant person like himself.

"Will Father Burrowes be here soon?" Mark inquired.

"'Pon my word, I don't know. Nobody knows when he'll be anywhere. He's preaching all over the place. He begs the deuce of a lot of money, you know. Aren't you a friend of Dorward's? You were asking Brother Dunstan about him. His parish isn't far from here. About fifteen miles, that's all. He's an amusing fellow, isn't he? Has tremendous rows with his squire, Philip Iredale. A pompous ass whose wife ran away from him a little time ago. Served him right, Dorward told me in confidence. You must come and have lunch with me. There's only Lady Landells. I can't afford to live in the big place. Huge affair with Doric portico and all that, don't you know. It's let to Lord Middlesborough, the shipping man. I live at Malford Lodge. Quite a jolly little place I've made of it. Suits me better than that great gaunt Georgian pile. You'd better walk down with me this morning and stop to lunch."

Mark, who was by now growing tired of his own company in the guest-room, accepted Sir Charles' invitation with alacrity; and they walked down from the Abbey to the village of Malford, which was situated at the confluence of the Mall and the Nodder, two diminutive tributaries of the Wey, which itself is not a mighty stream.

"A rather charming village, don't you think?" said Sir Charles, pointing with his tasselled cane to a particularly attractive rose-hung cottage. "It was lucky that the railway missed us by a couple of miles; we should have been festering with tin bungalows by now on any available land, which means on any land that doesn't belong to me. I don't offer to show you the church, because I never enter it."

Mark had paused as a matter of course by the lychgate, supposing that with a squire like Sir Charles the inside should be of unusual interest.

"My uncle most outrageously sold the advowson to the Simeon Trustees, it being the only part of my inheritance he could alienate from me, whom he loathed. He knew nothing would enrage me more than that, and the result is that I've got a fellow as vicar who preaches in a black gown and has evening communion twice a month. That is why I took such pleasure in planting a monastery in the parish; and if only that old time-server the Bishop of Silchester would licence a chaplain to the community, I should get my Sunday Mass in my own parish despite my uncle's simeony, as I call it. As it is with Burrowes away all the time raising funds, I don't get a Mass at the Abbey and I have to go to the next parish, which is four miles away and appears highly undignified for the squire."

"And you can't get him out?" said Mark.

"If I did get him out, I should be afflicted with another one just as bad. The Simeon Trustees only appoint people of the stamp of Mr. Choules, my present enemy. He's a horrid little man with a gaunt wife six feet high who beats her children and, if village gossip be true, her husband as well. Now you can see Malford Place, which is let to Middlesborough, as I told you."

Mark looked at the great Georgian house with its lawns and cedars and gateposts surmounted by stone wyverns. He had seen many of these great houses in the course of his tramping; but he had never thought of them before except as natural features in the landscape; the idea that people could consider a gigantic building like that as much a home as the small houses in which Mark had spent his life came over him now with a sense of novelty.

"Ghastly affair, isn't it?" said the owner contemptuously. "I'd let it stand empty rather than live in it myself. It reeks of my uncle's medicine and echoes with his gouty groans. Besides what is there in it that's really mine?"

Mark who had been thinking what an easy affair life must be for Sir Charles was struck by his tone of disillusionment. Perhaps all people who inherited old names and old estates were affected by their awareness of transitory possession. Sir Charles could not alienate even a piece of furniture. A middle-aged bachelor and a cosmopolitan, he would have moved about the corridors and halls of that huge house with less permanency than Lord Middlesborough who paid him so well to walk about in it in his stead, and who was no more restricted by the terms of his lease than was his landlord by the conditions of the entail. Mark began to feel sorry for him; but without cause, for when Sir Charles came in sight of Malford Lodge where he lived, he was full of enthusiasm. It was indeed a pretty little house of red brick, dating from the first quarter of the nineteenth century and like so many houses of that period built close to the road, surrounded too on three sides by a verandah of iron and copper in the pagoda style, thoroughly ugly, but by reason of the mellow peacock hues time had given its roof, full of personality and charm. They entered by a green door in the brick wall and crossed a lawn sloping down to the little river to reach the shade of a tulip tree in full bloom, where seated in one of those tall wicker garden chairs shaped like an alcove was an elderly lady as ugly as Priapus.

"There's Lady Landells, who's a poetess, you know," said Sir Charles gravely.

Mark accepted the information with equal gravity. He was still unsophisticated enough to be impressed at hearing a woman called a poetess.

"Mr. Lidderdale is going to have lunch with us, Lady Landells," Sir Charles announced.

"Oh, is he?" Lady Landells replied in a cracked murmur of complete indifference.

"He's a great admirer of your poems," added Sir Charles, hearing which Lady Landells looked at Mark with her cod's eyes and by way of greeting offered him two fingers of her left hand.

"I can't read him any of my poems to-day, Charles, so pray don't ask me to do so," the poetess groaned.

"I'm going to show Mr. Lidderdale some of our pictures before lunch," said Sir Charles.

Lady Landells paid no attention; Mark, supposing her to be on the verge of a poetic frenzy, was glad to leave her in that wicker alcove under the tulip tree and to follow Sir Charles into the house.

It was an astonishing house inside, with Gothic carving everywhere and with ancient leaded casements built inside the sashed windows of the exterior.

"I took an immense amount of trouble to get this place arranged to my taste," said Sir Charles; and Mark wondered why he had bothered to retain the outer shell, since that was all that was left of the original. In every room there were copies, excellently done of pictures by Botticelli and Mantegna and other pre-Raphaelite painters; the walls were rich with antique brocades and tapestries; the ceilings were gilded or elaborately moulded with fan traceries and groining; great candlesticks stood in every corner; the doors were all old with floriated hinges and huge locks—it was the sort of house in which Victor Hugo might have put on his slippers and said, "I am at home."

"I admit nothing after 1520," said Sir Charles proudly.

Mark wondered why so fastidious a medievalist allowed the Order of St. George to erect those three tin tabernacles and to matchboard the interior of the Abbey. But perhaps that was only another outer shell which would gradually be filled.

Lunch was a disappointment, because when Sir Charles began to talk about the monastery, which was what Mark had been wanting to talk about all the morning, Lady Landells broke in:

"I am sorry, Charles, but I'm afraid that I must beg for complete silence at lunch, as I'm in the middle of a sonnet."

The poetess sighed, took a large mouthful of food, and sighed again.

After lunch Sir Charles took Mark to see his library, which reminded him of a Rossetti interior and lacked only a beautiful long-necked creature, full-lipped and auburn-haired, to sit by the casement languishing over a cithern or gazing out through bottle-glass lights at a forlorn and foreshortened landscape of faerie land.

"Poor Lady Landells was a little tiresome at lunch," said Sir Charles half to himself. "She gets moods. Women seem never to grow out of getting moods. But she has always been most kind to me, and she insists on giving me anything I want for my house. Last year she was good enough to buy it from me as it stands, so it's really her house, although she has left it back to me in her will. She took rather a fancy to you by the way."

Mark, who had supposed that Lady Landells had regarded him with aversion and scorn, stared at this.

"Didn't she give you her hand when you said good-bye?" asked Sir Charles.

"Her left hand," said Mark.

"Oh, she never gives her right hand to anybody. She has some fad about spoiling the magnetic current of Apollo or something. Now, what about a walk?"

Mark said he should like to go for a walk very much, but wasn't Sir Charles too busy?

"Oh, no, I've nothing to do at all."

Yet only that morning he had held forth to Mark at great length on the amount of work demanded for the management of an estate.

"Now, why do you want to join Burrowes?" Sir Charles inquired presently.

"Well, I hope to be a priest, and I think I should like to spend the next two years out of the world."

"Yes, that is all very well," said Sir Charles, "but I don't know that I altogether recommend the O.S.G. I'm not satisfied with the way things are being run. However, they tell me that this fellow Brother George has a good deal of common-sense. He has been running their house in Malta, where he's done some good work. I gave them the land to build a mother house so that they could train people for active service, as it were; but Burrowes keeps chopping and changing and sending untrained novices to take charge of an important branch like Sandgate, and now since Rowley left he talks of opening a priory in Chatsea. That's all very well, and it's quite right of him to bear in mind that the main object of the Order is to work among soldiers; but at the same time he leaves this place to run itself, and whenever he does come down here he plans some hideous addition, to pay for which he has to go off preaching for another three months, so that the Abbey gets looked after by a young novice of twenty-five. It's ridiculous, you know. I was grumbling at the Bishop; but really I can understand his disinclination to countenance Burrowes. I have hopes of Brother George, and I shall take an early opportunity of talking to him."

Mark was discouraged by Sir Charles' criticism of the Order; and that it could be criticized like this through the conduct of its founder accentuated for him the gulf that lay between the English Church and the rest of Catholic Christendom.

It was not much solace to remember that every Benedictine community was an independent congregation. One could not imagine the most independent community's being placed in charge of a novice of twenty-five. It made Mark's proposed monastic life appear amateurish; and when he was back in the matchboarded guest-room the impulse to abandon his project was revised. Yet he felt it would be wrong to return to Wych-on-the-Wold. The impulse to come here, though sudden, had been very strong, and to give it up without trial might mean the loss of an experience that one day he should regret. The opinion of Sir Charles Horner might or might not be well founded; but it was bound to be a prejudiced opinion, because by constituting himself to the extent he had a patron of the Order he must involuntarily expect that it should be conducted according to his views. Sir Charles himself, seen in perspective, was a tolerably ridiculous figure, too much occupied with the paraphernalia of worship, too well pleased with himself, a man of rank and wealth who judged by severe standards was an old maid, and like all old maids critical, but not creative.

CHAPTER XXIV
THE ORDER OF ST. GEORGE

The Order of St. George was started by the Reverend Edward Burrowes six years before Sir Charles Horner's gift of land for a Mother House led him to suppose that he had made his foundation a permanent factor in the religious life of England.

Edward Burrowes was the only son of a band-master in the Royal Artillery who at an impressionable moment in the life of his son was stationed at Malta. The religious atmosphere of Malta combined with the romantic associations of chivalry and the influence of his mother determined the boy's future. The band-master was puzzled and irritated by his son's ecclesiastical bias. He thought that so much church-going argued an unhealthy preoccupation, and as for Edward's rhapsodies about the Auberge of Castile, which sheltered the Messes of the Royal Artillery and the Royal Engineers, they made him sick, to use his own expression.

"You make me sick, Ted," he used to declare. "The sooner I get quit of Malta and quartered at Woolwich again, the better I shall be pleased."

When at last the band-master was moved to Woolwich, he hoped that the effect of such prosaic surroundings would put an end to Ted's mooning, and that he would settle down to a career more likely to reward him in this world rather than in that ambiguous world beyond to which his dreams aspired. Edward, who was by this time seventeen and who had so far submitted to his father's wishes as to be working in a solicitor's office, found that the effect of being banished from Malta was to stimulate him into a practical attempt to express his dreams of religious devotion. He hired a small room over a stable in a back street and started a club for the sons of soldiers. The band-master would not have minded this so much, especially when he was congratulated on his son's enterprise by the wife of the Colonel. Unfortunately this was not enough for Edward, who having got the right side of an unscrupulously romantic curate persuaded him to receive his vows of a Benedictine oblate. The band-master, proud and fond though he might be of his own uniform, objected to his son's arriving home from business and walking about the house in a cassock. He objected equally to finding that his own musical gifts had with his son degenerated into a passion for playing Gregorian chants on a vile harmonium. It was only consideration for his delicate wife that kept the band-master from pitching both cassock and harmonium into the street. The amateur oblate regretted his father's hostility; but he persevered with the manner of life he had marked out for himself, finding much comfort and encouragement in reading the lives of the saintly founders of religious orders.

At last, after a long struggle against the difficulties that friends and father put in his way, Edward Burrowes managed at the age of twenty-seven to get ordained in Canada, whither, in despair of escaping otherwise from the solicitor's office, he had gone to seek his own fortune. He took with him the oblate's cassock; but he left behind the harmonium, which his father kicked to pieces in rage at not being able to kick his son. Burrowes worked as a curate in a dismal lakeside town in Ontario, consoling himself with dreams of monasticism and chivalry, and gaining a reputation as a preacher. His chief friend was a young farmer, called George Harvey, whom he succeeded in firing with his own enthusiasm and whom he managed to persuade—which shows that Burrowes must have had great powers of persuasion—to wear the habit of a Benedictine novice, when he came to spend Saturday night to Monday morning with his friend. By this time Burrowes had passed beyond the oblate stage, for having found a Canadian bishop willing to dispense him from that portion of the Benedictine rule which was incompatible with his work as a curate in Jonesville, Ontario, he got himself clothed as a novice. About this period a third man joined Burrowes and Harvey in their spare-time monasticism. This was John Holcombe, who had emigrated from Dorsetshire after an unfortunate love affair and who had been taken on by George Harvey as a carter. Holcombe was the son of a yeoman farmer that owned several hundred acres of land. He had been educated at Sherborne, and soon by his capacity and attractive personality he made himself so indispensable to his employer that George Harvey's farm was turned into a joint concern. No doubt Harvey's example was the immediate cause of Holcombe's associating himself with the little community: but it still says much for Burrowes' powers of persuasion that he should have been able to impress this young Dorset farmer with the serious possibility of leading the monastic life in Ontario.

When another year had passed, an opportunity arose of acquiring a better farm in Alberta. It was the Bishop of Alberta who had been so sympathetic with Burrowes' monastic aspirations; and, when Harvey and Holcombe decided to move to Moose Rib, Burrowes gave up his curacy to lead a regular monastic life, so far as one could lead a regular monastic life on a farm in the North-west.

Two more years had gone by when a letter arrived from England to tell George Harvey that he was the heir to £12,000. Burrowes had kept all his influence over the young farmer, and he was actually able to persuade Harvey to devote this fortune to founding the Order of St. George for mission work among soldiers. There was some debate whether Father Burrowes, Brother George, and Brother Birinus should take their final vows immediately; but in the end Father Burrowes had his way, and they were all three professed by the sympathetic Bishop of Alberta, who granted them a constitution subject to the ratification of the Archbishop of Canterbury. Father Burrowes was elected Father Superior, Brother George was made Assistant Superior, and Brother Birinus had to concentrate in his person various monastic offices just as on the Moose Rib Farm he had combined in his person the duties of the various hands.

The immediate objective of the new community was Malta, where it was proposed to open their first house and where, in despite of the outraged dignity of innumerable real monks already there, they made a successful beginning. A second house was opened at Gibraltar and put in charge of Brother Birinus. Neither Malta nor Gibraltar provided much of a field for reinforcing the Order, which, if it was to endure, required additional members. Father Burrowes proposed that he should go to England and open a house at Aldershot, and that, if he could obtain a hearing as a preacher, he should try to raise enough funds for a house at Sandgate as well. Brother George and Brother Birinus in a solemn chapter of three accepted the proposal; the house at Gibraltar was given up; the Father Superior went to seek the fortunes of the Order in England, while the other two remained at their work in Malta. Father Burrowes was even more successful as a preacher than he hoped; ascribing the steady flow of offertories to Divine favour, he instituted during the next four years, priories at Aldershot and Sandgate. He began to feel the need of a Mother House, having now more than enough candidates for the Order of Saint George, where the novices could be suitably trained to meet the stress of active mission work. One of his moving appeals for this object was heard by Sir Charles Horner who, for reasons he had already explained to Mark and because underneath all his ecclesiasticism there did exist a genuine desire for the glory of God, had presented the land at Malford to the Order. Father Burrowes preached harder than ever, addressed drawing-room meetings, and started a monthly magazine called *The Dragon* to raise the necessary money to build a mighty abbey. Meanwhile, he had to be contented with those three tin tabernacles. Brother George, who had remained all these years in Malta, suggested that it was time for somebody else to take his place out there, and the Father Superior, although somewhat unwillingly, had agreed to his coming to Malford. Not having heard of anybody whom at the moment he considered suitable to take charge of what was now a distant outpost of the Order, he told Brother George to close the house. It was at this stage in the history of the Order that Mark presented himself as a candidate for admission.

Father Burrowes arrived unexpectedly two days after the lunch at Malford Lodge; and presently Brother Dunstan came to tell Mark that the Reverend Father would see him in the Abbott's Parlour immediately after Nones. Mark thought that Sir Charles might have given a mediæval lining to this room at least, which with its roll-top desk looked like the office of the clerk of the works.

"So you want to be a monk?" said Father Burrowes contemptuously. "Want to dress up in a beautiful white habit, eh?"

"I really don't mind what I wear," said Mark, trying not to appear ruffled by the imputation of wrong motives. "But I do want to be a monk, yes."

"You can't come here to play at it," said the Superior, looking keenly at Mark from his bright blue eyes and lighting up a large pipe.

"Curiously enough," said Mark, who had forgotten the Benedictine injunction to discourage newcomers that seek to enter a community, "I wrote to my guardian a few days ago that my impression of Malford Abbey was rather that it was playing at being monks."

The Superior flushed to a vivid red. He was a burly man of fair complexion, inclined to plumpness, and with a large mobile mouth eloquent and sensual. His hands were definitely fat, the backs of them covered with golden hairs and freckles.

"So you're a critical young gentleman, are you? I suppose we're not Catholic enough for you. Well," he snapped, "I'm afraid you won't suit us. We don't want you. Sorry."

"I'm sorry too," said Mark. "But I thought you would prefer frankness. If you will spare me a few minutes, I'll explain why I want to join the Order of St. George. If when you've heard what I have to say you still think that I'm not suitable, I shall recognize your right to be of that opinion from your experience of many young men like myself who have been tried and found wanting."

"Did you learn that speech by heart?" the Superior inquired, raising his eyebrows mockingly.

"I see you're determined to find fault," Mark laughed. "But, Reverend Father, surely you will listen to my reasons before deciding against them or me?"

"My instinct tells me you'll be no good to us. But if you insist on wasting my time, fire ahead. Only please remember that, though I may be a monk, I'm a very busy man."

Mark gave a full account of himself until the present and wound up by saying:

"I don't think I have any sentimental reasons for wanting to enter a monastery. I like working among soldiers and sailors. I am ready to put down £200 and I hope to be of use. I wish to be a priest, and if you find or I find that when the time comes for me to be ordained I shall make a better secular priest, at any rate, I shall have had the advantage of a life of discipline and you, I promise, will have had a novice who will have regarded himself as such, but yet will have learnt somehow to have justified your confidence."

The Superior looked down at his desk pondering. Presently he opened a letter and threw a quick suspicious glance at Mark.

"Why didn't you tell me that you had an introduction from Sir Charles Horner?"

"I didn't know that I had," Mark answered in some astonishment. "I only met him here a few days ago for the first time. He invited me to lunch, and he was very pleasant; but I never asked him to write to you, nor did he suggest doing so."

"Have you any vices?" Father Burrowes asked abruptly.

"I don't think—what do you mean exactly?" Mark inquired.

"Drink?"

"No, certainly not."

"Women?"

Mark flushed.

"No." He wondered if he should speak of the episode of St. John's eve such a short time ago; but he could not bring himself to do so, and he repeated the denial.

"You seem doubtful," the Superior insisted.

"As a matter of fact," said Mark, "since you press this point I ought to tell you that I took a vow of celibacy when I was sixteen."

Father Burrowes looked at him sharply.

"Did you indeed? That sounds very morbid. Don't you like women?"

"I don't think a priest ought to marry. I was told by Sir Charles that you vowed yourself to the monastic life when you were not much more than seventeen. Was that morbid?"

The Superior laughed boisterously, and Mark glad to have put him in a good humour laughed with him. It was only after the interview was over that the echo of that laugh sounded unpleasantly in the caves of memory, that it rang false somehow like a denial of himself.

"Well, I suppose we must try you as a probationer at any rate," said the Superior. And suddenly his whole manner changed. He became affectionate and sentimental as he put his hand on Mark's shoulder.

"I hope, dear lad, that you will find a vocation to serve our dear Lord in the religious life. God bless you and give you endurance in the path you have chosen."

Mark reproached himself for his inclination to dislike the Reverend Father to whom he now owed filial affection, piety, and respect, apart from what he owed him as a Christian of Christian charity. He should gain but small spiritual benefit from his self-chosen experiment if this was the mood in which he was beginning his monastic life; and when Brother Jerome, who was acting novice-master, began to instruct him in his monastic duty, he made up his mind to drive out that demon of criticism or rather to tame it to his own service by criticizing himself. He wrote on markers for his favourite devotional books:

Observe at every moment of the day the good in others, the evil in thyself; and when thou liest awake in the night remember only what good thou hast found in others, what evil in thyself.

This was Mark's addition to Thomas a Kempis, to Mother Juliana of Norwich, to Jeremy Taylor and William Law; this was Mark's sprout of holy wisdom among the Little Flowers of Saint Francis.

The Rule of Malford was not a very austere adaptation of the Rule of Saint Benedict; and, with the Reverend Father departing after Mark had been admitted as a probationer and leaving the administration of the Abbey to the priority of Brother Dunstan, a good deal of what austerity had been retained was now relaxed.

The Night Office was not said at Malford, where the liturgical worship of the day began with Lauds and Prime at six. On Mark devolved the duty of waking the brethren in the morning, which was done by striking the door of each cell with a hammer and saying: *The Lord be with you*, whereupon the sleeping brother must rise from his couch and open the door of his cell to make the customary response. After Lauds and Prime, which lasted about half an hour, the brethren retired to their cells to put them in order for the day and to meditate until seven o'clock, unless they had been given tasks out of doors. At seven o'clock, if there was a priest in the monastery, Mass was said; otherwise meditation and study was prolonged until eight o'clock, when breakfast was eaten. Those who had work in the fields or about the house departed after breakfast to their tasks. At nine Terce was said, which was not attended by the brethren working out of doors; at twelve Sext was said attended by all the brethren, and at twelve-fifteen dinner was eaten. After dinner, the brethren retired to their cells and meditated until one o'clock, when their various duties were resumed, interrupted only in the case of those working indoors by the office of None at three o'clock. At a quarter to five the bell rang for tea. Simple silence was relaxed, and the brethren enjoyed their recreation until six-fifteen when the bell rang for a quarter of an hour's solemn silence before Vespers. Supper was eaten after Vespers, and after supper, which was finished about eight o'clock, there was reading and recreation until the bell rang for Compline at nine-fifteen. This office said, solemn silence was not broken until the response to the *dominus vobiscum* in the morning. The rule of simple silence was not kept very strictly at this period. Two brethren working in the garden in these hot July days found that permitted conversation about the immediate matter in hand, say the whereabouts of a trowel or a hoe, was easily extended into observations about the whereabouts of Brother So-and-So during Terce or the way Brother Somebody-else was late with the antiphon. From the little incidents of the Abbey's daily round the conversation was easily extended into a discussion of the policy of the Order in general. Speculations where the Reverend Father was preaching that evening or that morning and whether his offertories would be as large during the summer as they had been during the spring were easily amplified from discussions about the general policy of the Order into discussions about the general policy of Christendom, the pros and cons of the Roman position, the disgraceful latitudinarianism of bishops and deans; and still more widely amplified from remarks upon the general policy of Christendom into arguments about the universe and the great philosophies of humanity. Thus Mark, who was an ardent Platonist, would find himself at odds with Brother Jerome who was an equally ardent Aristotelian, while the weeds, taking advantage of the philosophic contest, grew faster than ever.

Whatever may have been Brother Dunstan's faults of indulgence, they sprang from a debonair and kindly personality which shone like a sun upon the little family and made everybody good-humoured, even Brother Lawrence, who was apt to be cross because he had been kept a postulant longer than he expected. But perhaps the happiest of all was Brother Walter, who though still a probationer was now the senior probationer, a status which afforded him the most profound satisfaction and gave him a kindly feeling toward Mark who was the cause of promotion.

"And the Reverend Father has promised me that I shall be clothed as a postulant on August 10th when Brother Lawrence is to be clothed as a novice. The thought makes me so excited that I hardly know what to do sometimes, and

I still don't know what saint's name I'm going to take. You see, there was some mystery about my birth, and I was called Walter because I was found by a policeman in Walter Street, and as ill-luck would have it there's no St. Walter. Of course, I know I have a very wide choice of names, but that is what makes it so difficult. I had rather a fancy to be Peter, but he's such a very conspicuous saint that it struck me as being a little presumptuous. Of course, I have no doubt whatever that St. Peter would take me under his protection, for if you remember he was a modest saint, a very modest saint indeed who asked to be crucified upside down, not liking to show the least sign of competition with our dear Lord. I should very much like to call myself Brother Paul, because at the school I was at we were taken twice a year to see St. Paul's Cathedral and had toffee when we came home. I look back to those days as some of the happiest of my life. There again it does seem to be putting yourself up rather to take the name of a great saint like St. Paul. Then I thought of taking William after the little St. William of Norwich who was murdered by the Jews. That seems going to the other extreme, doesn't it, for though I know that out of the mouths of babes and sucklings shall come forth praise, one would like to feel one had for a patron saint somebody a little more conspicuous than a baby. I wish you'd give me a word of advice. I think about this problem until sometimes my head's in a regular whirl, and I lose my place in the Office. Only yesterday at Sext, I found myself saying the antiphon proper to St. Peter a fortnight after St. Peter's day had passed and gone, which seems to show that my mind is really set upon being Brother Peter, doesn't it? And yet I don't know. He is so very conspicuous all through the Gospels, isn't he?"

"Then why don't you compromise," suggested Mark, "and call yourself Brother Simon?"

"Oh, what a splendid idea!" Brother Walter exclaimed, clapping his hands. "Oh, thank you, Brother Mark. That has solved all my difficulties. Oh, do let me pull up that thistle for you."

Brother Walter the probationer resumed his weeding with joyful ferocity of purpose, his mind at peace in the expectation of shortly becoming Brother Simon the postulant.

What Mark enjoyed most in his personal relations with the community were the walks on Sunday afternoons. Sir Charles Horner made a habit of joining these to obtain the Abbey gossip and also because he took pleasure in hearing himself hold forth on the management of his estate. Most of his property was woodland, and the walks round Malford possessed that rich intimacy of the English countryside at its best. Mark was not much interested in what Sir Charles had to ask or in what Sir Charles had to tell or in what Sir Charles had to show, but to find himself walking with his monastic brethren in their habits down glades of mighty oaks, or through sparse plantations of birches, beneath which grew brakes of wild raspberries that would redden with the yellowing corn, gave him as assurance of that old England before the Reformation to which he looked back as to a Golden Age. Years after, when much that was good and much that was bad in his monastic experience had been forgotten, he held in his memory one of these walks on a fine afternoon at July's end within the octave of St. Mary Magdalene. It happened that Sir Charles had not accompanied the monks that Sunday; but in his place was an old priest who had spent the week-end as a guest in the Abbey and who had said Mass for the brethren that morning. This had given Mark deep pleasure, because it was the Sunday after Esther's profession, and he had been able to make his intention her present joy and future happiness. He had been silent throughout the walk, seeming to listen in turn to Brother Dunstan's rhapsodies about the forthcoming arrival of Brother George and Brother Birinus with all that it meant to him of responsibility more than he could bear removed from his shoulders; or to Brother Raymond's doubts if it should not be made a rule that when no priest was in the Abbey the brethren ought to walk over to Wivelrod, the church Sir Charles attended four miles away, or to Brother Jerome's disclaimer of Roman sympathies in voicing his opinion that the Office should be said in Latin. Actually he paid little attention to any of them, his thoughts being far away with Esther. They had chosen Hollybush Down for their walk that Sunday, because they thought that the view over many miles of country would please the ancient priest. Seated on the short aromatic grass in the shade of a massive hawthorn full-berried with tawny fruit, the brethren looked down across a slope dotted with junipers to the view outspread before them. None spoke, for it had been warm work in their habits to climb the burnished grass. It would have been hard to explain the significance of that group, unless it were due to some haphazard achievement of perfect form; yet somehow for Mark that moment was taken from time and placed in eternity, so that whenever afterward in his life he read about the Middle Ages he was able to be what he read, merely by re-conjuring that monkish company in the shade of that hawthorn tree.

On their way back to the Abbey Mark found himself walking with Mr. Lamplugh, the ancient priest, who turned out to have known his father.

"Dear me, are you really the son of James Lidderdale? Why, I used to go and preach at Lima Street in old days long before your father married. And so you're Lidderdale's son. Now I wonder why you want to be a monk."

Mark gave an account of himself since he left school and tried to give some good reasons why he was at Malford.

"And so you were with Rowley? Well, really you ought to know something about missions by now. But perhaps you're tired of mission work already?" the old priest inquired with a quick glance at Mark as if he would see how much of the real stuff existed underneath that probationer's cassock.

"This is an active Order, isn't it?" Mark countered. "Of course, I'm not tired of mission work. But after being with Father Rowley and being kept busy all the time I found that being at home in the country made me idle. I told the Reverend Father that I hoped to be ordained as a secular priest and that I did not imagine I had any vocation for the contemplative life. I have as a matter of fact a great longing for it. But I don't think that twenty-one is a good age for being quite sure if that longing is not mere sentiment. I suppose you think I'm just indulging myself with the decorative side of religion, Father Lamplugh? I really am not. I can assure you that I'm far too much accustomed to the decorative side to be greatly influenced by it."

The old priest laid a thin hand on Mark's sleeve.

"To tell the truth, my dear boy, I was on the verge of violating the decencies of accepted hospitality by criticizing the Order of which you have become a probationer. I am just a little doubtful about the efficacy of its method of training young men. However, it really is not my business, and I hope that I am wrong. But I *am* a little doubtful if all these excellent young brethren are really desirous . . . no, I'll not say another word, I've already disgracefully exceeded the limitations to criticism that courtesy alone demands of me. I was carried away by my interest in you when I heard whose son you were. What a debt we owe to men like your father and Rowley! And here am I at seventy-six after a long and useless life presuming to criticize other people. God forgive me!" The old man crossed himself.

That afternoon and evening recreation was unusually noisy, and during Vespers one or two of the brethren were seized with an attack of giggles because Brother Lawrence, who was in a rapt condition of mind owing to the near approach of St. Lawrence's day when he was to be clothed as a novice, tripped while he was holding back the cope during the censing of the *Magnificat* and falling on his knees almost upset Father Lamplugh. There was no doubt that the way Brother Lawrence stuck out his lower jaw when he was self-conscious was very funny; but Mark wished that the giggling had not occurred in front of Father Lamplugh. He wished too that during recreation after supper Brother Raymond would be less skittish and Brother Dunstan less arch in the manner of reproving him.

"Holy simplicity is all very well," Mark thought. "But holy imbecility is a great bore, especially when there is a stranger present."

Luckily Father Burrowes came back the following week, and Mark's deepening impression of the monastery's futility was temporarily obliterated by the exciting news that the Bishop of Alberta whom the brethren were taught to reverence as a second founder would be the guest of the Order on St. Lawrence's day and attend the profession of Brother Anselm. Mark had not yet seen Brother Anselm, who was the brother in charge of the Aldershot priory, and he welcomed the opportunity of witnessing those solemn final vows. He felt that he should gain much from meeting Brother Anselm, whose work at Aldershot was considered after the Reverend Father's preaching to be the chief glory of the Order. Brother Lawrence was a little jealous that his name day, on which he was to be clothed in Chapter as a novice, should be chosen for the much more important ceremony, and he spoke sharply to poor Brother Walter when the latter rejoiced in the added lustre Brother Anselm's profession would shed upon his own promotion.

"You must remember, Brother," he said, "that you'll probably remain a postulant for a very long time."

"But not for ever," replied poor Brother Walter in a depressed tone of voice.

"There may not be time to attend to you," said Brother Lawrence spitefully. "You may have to wait until the Bishop has gone."

"Oh dear, oh dear," sighed Brother Walter looking woeful. "Brother Mark, do you hear what they say?"

"Never mind," said Mark, "we'll take our final vows together when Brother Lawrence is still a doddering old novice."

Brother Lawrence clicked his tongue and bit his under lip in disgust at such a flippant remark.

"What a thing to say," he muttered, and burying his hands in his sleeves he walked off disdainfully, his jaw thrust before him.

"Like a cow-catcher," Mark thought with a smile.

The Bishop of Alberta was a dear old gentleman with silvery hair and a complexion as fresh and pink as a boy's. With his laced rochet and purple biretta he lent the little matchboarded chapel an exotic splendour when he sat in a Glastonbury chair beside the altar during the Office. The more ritualistic of the brethren greatly enjoyed giving him reverent genuflexions and kissing his episcopal ring. Brother Raymond's behaviour towards him was like that of a child who has been presented with a large doll to play with, a large doll that can be dressed and undressed at the pleasure of its owner with nothing to deter him except a faint squeak of protest such as the Bishop himself occasionally emitted.

CHAPTER XXV
SUSCIPE ME, DOMINE

Brother Anselm was to arrive on the vigil of St. Lawrence. Normally Brother Walter would have been sent to meet him with the Abbey cart at the station three miles away. But Brother Walter was in a state of such excitement over his near promotion to postulant that it was not considered safe to entrust him with the pony. So Mark was sent in his place. It was a hot August evening with thunder clouds lying heavy on the Malford woods when Mark drove down the deep lanes to the junction, wondering what Brother Anselm would be like and awed by the imagination of Brother Anselm's thoughts in the train that was bringing him from Aldershot to this momentous date of his life's history. Almost before he knew what he was saying Mark was quoting from *Romeo and Juliet*:

My mind misgivesSome consequence, yet hanging in the stars,Shall bitterly begin his fearful dateWith this night's revels.

"Now why should I have thought that?" he asked himself, and he was just deciding that it was merely a verbal sequence of thought when the first far-off peal of thunder muttered a kind of menacing contradiction of so easy an explanation. It would be raining soon; Mark thumped the pony's angular haunches, and tried to feel cheerful in the oppressive air.

Brother Anselm did not appear as Mark had pictured him. Instead of the lithe enthusiast with flaming eyes he saw a heavily built man with blunted features, wearing powerful horn spectacles, his expression morose, his movements ungainly. He had, however, a mellow and strangely sympathetic voice, in which Mark fancied that he perceived the power he was reputed to wield over the soldiers for whose well-being he fought so hard. Mark would have liked to ask him about life in the Aldershot priory; perhaps if Brother Anselm had been less taciturn, he would have broken if not the letter at any rate the spirit of the Rule by begging the senior to ask for his services in the Priory. But no sooner were they jogging back to Malford than the rain came down in a deluge, and Brother Anselm, pulling the hood of his frock over his head, was more unapproachable than ever. Mark wished that he had a novice's frock and hood, for the rain was pouring down the back of his neck and the threadbare cassock he wore was already drenched.

"Thank you, Brother," said the new-comer when the Abbey was attained.

It was dark by now, and, with nothing visible of the speaker except his white habit in the gloom, the voice might have been the voice of a heavenly visitant, so rarely sweet, so gentle and harmonious were the tones. Mark was much moved by that brief recognition of himself.

The wind rose high during the night; listening to it roaring through the coppice in which the Abbey was built, Mark lay awake for a long time in mute prayer that Brother Anselm might find peace and felicity in his new state. And while he prayed for Brother Anselm he prayed for Esther in Shoreditch. In the morning when Mark went from cell to cell, rousing the brethren from sleep with his hammer and salutation, the sun was climbing a serene and windless sky. The familiar landscape was become a mountain top. Heaven was very near.

Mark was glad that the day was so fair for the profession of Brother Anselm, and at Lauds the antiphon, versicle, and response proper to St. Lawrence appealed to him by their fitness to the occasion,

Gold is tried in the fire: and acceptable men in the furnace of adversity.

V. The Righteous shall grow as a lily.R. He shall flourish for ever before the Lord.

Mark concerned himself less with his own reception as a postulant. The distinction between a probationer and a postulant was very slight, really an arbitrary one made by Father Burrowes for his own convenience, and until he had to decide whether he should petition to be clothed as a novice Mark did not feel that he was called upon to take himself too seriously as a monk. For that reason he did not change his name, but preferred to stay Brother Mark. The little ceremony of reception was carried through in Chapter before the brethren went into the Oratory to say Terce, and Brother Walter was so much excited when he heard himself addressed as Brother Simon that for a moment it seemed doubtful if he would be sufficiently calm to attend the profession of Brother Anselm at the conventual Mass. However, during the clothing of Brother Lawrence as a novice Brother Simon quieted down, and even gave over counting the three knots in the rope with which he had been girdled. Ordinarily, Brother Lawrence would have been clothed after Mass, but this morning it was felt that such a ceremony coming after the profession of Brother Anselm would be an anti-climax, and it was carried through in Chapter. It took Brother Lawrence all he had ever heard and read about humility and obedience not to protest at the way his clothing on his own saint's day, for which he had been made to wait nearly a year, was being carried through in such a hole in the corner fashion. But he fixed his mind upon the torments of the blessed archdeacon on the gridiron and succeeded in keeping his temper.

Mark felt that the profession of Brother Anselm lost some of its dignity by the absence of Brother George and Brother Birinus, the only other professed members of the Order apart from Father Burrowes himself. It struck him as slightly ludicrous that a few young novices and postulants should represent the venerable choir-monks whom one pictured at such a ceremony from one's reading of the Rule of St. Benedict. Moreover, Father Burrowes never presented himself to Mark's imagination as an authentic abbot. Nor indeed was he such. Malford Abbey was a courtesy title, and such monastic euphemisms as the Abbot's Parlour and the Abbot's Lodgings to describe the matchboarded apartments sacred to the Father Superior, while they might please such ecclesiastical enthusiasts as Brother Raymond, appealed to Mark as pretentious and somewhat silly. In fact, if it had not been for the presence of the Bishop of Alberta in cope and mitre Mark would have found it hard, when after Terce the brethren assembled in the Chapter-room to hear Brother Anselm make his final petition, to believe in the reality of what was happening, to believe, when Brother Anselm in reply to the Father Superior's exhortation chose the white cowl and scapular (which in the Order of St. George differentiated the professed monk from the novice) and rejected the suit of dittos belonging to his worldly condition, that he was passing through moments of greater spiritual importance than any since he was baptized or than any he would pass through before he stood upon the threshold of eternity.

But this was a transient scepticism, a fleeting discontent, which vanished when the brethren formed into procession and returned to the oratory singing the psalm: *In Convertendo.*

When the Lord turned again the captivity of Sion: then were we like unto them, that dream.
Then was our mouth filled with laughter: and our tongue with joy.
Then said they among the heathen: The Lord hath done great things for them.
Yea, the Lord hath done great things for us already: whereof we rejoice.
Turn our captivity, O Lord: as the rivers in the south.
They that sow in tears: shall reap in joy.

He that now goeth on his way weeping, and beareth forth good seed: shall doubtless come again with joy, and bring his sheaves with him.

The Father Superior of the Order sang the Mass, while the Bishop of Alberta seated in his Glastonbury chair suffered with an expression of childlike benignity the ritualistic ministrations of Brother Raymond, the ceremonial doffing and donning of his mitre. It was very still in the little Oratory, for it was the season when birds are hushed; and even Sir Charles Horner who was all by himself in the ante-chapel did not fidget or try to peep through the heavy brocaded curtains that shut out the quire. Mark dared not look up when at the offertory Brother Anselm stood before the Altar and answered the solemn interrogations of the Father Superior, question after question about his faith and endurance in the life he desired to enter. And to every question he answered clearly *I will*. The Father Superior took the parchment on which were written the vows and read aloud the document. Then it was placed upon the Altar, and there upon that sacrificial stone Brother Anselm signed his name to a contract with Almighty God. The holy calm that shed itself upon the scene was like a spell on every heart that was beating there in unison with the heart of him who was drawing nearer to Heaven. Prostrating himself, the professed monk prayed first to God the Father:

O receive me according to thy word that I may live; and let me not be disappointed of my hope.

The hearts that beat in unison with his took up the prayer, and the voices of his brethren repeated it word for word. And now the professed monk prayed to God the Son:

O receive me according to thy word that I may live; and let me not be disappointed of my hope.

Once more his brethren echoed the entreaty.

And lastly the professed monk prayed to God the Holy Ghost:

O receive me according to thy word that I may live; and let me not be disappointed of my hope.

For the third time his brethren echoed the entreaty, and then one and all in that Oratory cried:

Glory be to the Father and to the Son and to the Holy Ghost; as it was in the beginning, is now, and ever shall be, world without end. Amen.

There followed prayers that the peace of God might be granted to the professed monk to enable him worthily to perform the vows which he had made, and before the blessing and imposition of the scapular the Bishop rose to speak in tones of deep emotion:

"Brethren, I scarcely dared to hope, when, now nearly ten years ago, I received the vows of your Father Superior as a novice, that I should one day be privileged to be present at this inspiring ceremony. Nor even when five years ago in the far north-west of Canada I professed your Father Superior and those two devoted souls who will soon be with you, now that their work in Malta is for the time finished, did I expect to find myself in this beautiful Oratory which your Order owes to the generosity of a true son of the Church. My heart goes out to you, and I thank God humbly that He has vouchsafed to hear my prayers and bless the enterprise from which I had indeed expected much, but which Almighty God has allowed to prosper more, far more, than I ventured to hope. All my days I have longed to behold the restoration of the religious life to our country, and now when my eyes are dim with age I am granted the ineffable joy of beholding what for too long in my weakness and lack of faith I feared was never likely to come to pass.

"The profession of our dear brother this morning is, I pray, an earnest of many professions at Malford. May these first vows placed upon the Altar of this Oratory be blessed by Almighty God! May our brother be steadfast and happy in his choice! Brethren, I had meant to speak more and with greater eloquence, but my heart is too full. The Lord be with you."

Now Brother Anselm was clothed in the blessed habit while the brethren sang:

Come, Holy Ghost, our souls inspire, And lighten with celestial fire.

The Father Superior of the Order gave him the paternal kiss. He begged the prayers of his brethren there assembled, and drawing the hood of his cowl over his head prostrated himself again before the Altar. The Mass proceeded.

If the strict Benedictine usage had been followed at Malford, Brother Anselm would have remained apart from the others for three days after his profession, wrapped in his cowl, alone with God. But he was anxious to go back to Aldershot that very afternoon, excusing himself because Brother Chad, left behind in charge of the Priory, would be overwhelmed by his various responsibilities. Brother Dunstan, who had wept throughout the ceremony of the profession, was much upset by Brother Anselm's departure. He had hoped to achieve great exaltation of spirit by Brother Anselm's silent presence. He began to wonder if the newly professed monk appreciated his position. Had himself been granted what Brother Anselm had been granted, he should have liked to spend a week in contemplation of the wonder which had befallen him. Brother Dunstan asked himself if his thoughts were worthy of a senior novice, of one who had for a while acted as Prior and been accorded the address of Reverend Brother. He decided that they were not, and as a penance he begged for the nib with which Brother Anselm had signed his profession. This he wore round his neck as an amulet against unbrotherly thoughts and as a pledge of his own determination to vow himself eternally to the service of God.

Mark was glad that Brother Anselm was going back so soon to his active work. It was an assurance that the Order of St. George did have active work to do; and when he was called upon to drive Brother Anselm to the station he made up his mind to conquer his shyness and hint that he should be glad to serve the Order in the Priory at Aldershot.

This time, notwithstanding that he had a good excuse to draw his hood close, Brother Anselm showed himself more approachable.

"If the Reverend Father suggests your name," he promised Mark, "I shall be glad to have you with us. Brother Chad is simply splendid, and the Tommies are wonderful. It's quite right of course to have a Mother House, but. . . ." He broke off, disinclined to criticize the direction of the Order's policy to a member so junior as Mark.

"Oh, I'm not asking you to do anything yet awhile," Mark explained. "I quite realize that I have a great deal to learn before I should be any use at Aldershot or Sandgate. I hope you don't mind my talking like this. But until this morning I had not really intended to remain in the Order. My hope was to be ordained as soon as I was old enough. Now since this morning I feel that I do long for the spiritual support of a community for my own feeble aspirations. The Bishop's words moved me tremendously. It wasn't what he said so much, but I was filled with all his faith and I could have cried out to him a promise that I for one would help to carry on the restoration. At the same time, I know that I'm more fitted for active work, not by any good I expect to do, but for the good it will do me. I suppose you'd say that if I had a true vocation I shouldn't be thinking about what part I was going to play in the life of the Order, but that I should be content to do whatever I was told. I'm boring you?" Mark broke off to inquire, for Brother Anselm was staring in front of him through his big horn spectacles like an owl.

"No, no," said the senior. "But I'm not the novice-master. Who is, by the way?"

"Brother Jerome."

The other did not comment on this information, but Mark was sure that he was trying not to look contemptuous.

Soon the junction came in sight, and from down the line the white smoke of a train approaching.

"Hurry, Brother, I don't want to miss it."

Mark thumped the haunches of the pony and drove up just in time for Brother Anselm to escape.

"Thank you, Brother," said that same voice which yesterday, only yesterday night, had sounded so rarely sweet. Here on this mellow August afternoon it was the voice of the golden air itself, and the shriek of the engine did not drown its echoes in Mark's soul where all the way back to Malford it was chiming like a bell.

CHAPTER XXVI
ADDITION

Mark's ambition to go and work at Aldershot was gratified before the end of August, because Brother Chad fell ill, and it was considered advisable to let him spend a long convalescence at the Abbey.

The Priory,

17, Farnborough Villas,

Aldershot.

St. Michael and All Angels.

My dear Rector,

I don't think you'll be sorry to read from the above address that I've been transferred from Malford to one of the active branches of the Order. I don't accept your condemnation of the Abbey as pseudo-monasticism, though I can quite well understand that my account of it might lead you to make such a criticism. The trouble with me is that my emotions and judgment are always quarrelling. I suppose you might say that is true of most people. It's like the palmist who tells everybody that he is ruled by his head or his heart, as the case may be. But when one approaches the problem of religion (let alone what is called the religious life) one is terribly perplexed to know which is to be obeyed. I don't think that you can altogether rule out emotion as a touchstone of truth. The endless volumes of St. Thomas Aquinas, through which I've been wading, do not cope with the fact that the whole of his vast intellectual and severely logical structure is built up on the assumption of faith, which is the gift of emotion, not judgment. The whole system is a petitio principii really.

I did not mean to embark on a discussion of the question of the Ultimate Cause of religion, but to argue with you about the religious life! The Abbot Paphnutius told Cassian that there were three sorts of vocation—ex Deo, per hominem, and ex necessitate. Now suppose I have a vocation, mine is obviously per hominem. I inherit the missionary spirit from my father. That spirit was fostered by association with Rowley. My main object in entering the Order of St. George was to work among soldiers, not because I felt that soldiers needed "missionizing" more than any other class, but because the work at Chatsea brought me into contact with both sailors and soldiers, and turned my thoughts in their direction. I also felt the need of an organization behind my efforts. My first impulse was to be a preaching friar, but that would have laid too much on me as an individual, and from lack of self-confidence, youthfulness, want of faith perhaps, I was afraid. Well, to come back to the Abbot Paphnutius and his three vocations—it seems fairly clear that the first, direct from God, is a better vocation than the one which is inspired by human example, or the third, which arises from the failure of everything else. At the same time they ARE all three genuine vocations. What applies to the vocation seems to me to apply equally to the community. What you stigmatize as our pseudo-monasticism is still experimental, and I think I can see the Reverend Father's idea. He has had a great deal of experience with an Order which began so amateurishly, if I may use the word, that nobody could have imagined that it would grow to the size and strength it has reached in ten years. The Bishop of Alberta revealed much to us of our beginnings during his stay at the Abbey, and after I had listened to him I felt how presumptuous it was for me to criticize the central source of the religious life we are hoping to spread. You see, Rector, I must have criticized it implicitly in my letters to you, for your objections are simply the expression of what I did not like to say, but what I managed to convey through the medium of would-be humorous description. One hears of the saving grace of humour, but I'm not sure that humour is a saving grace. I rather wish that I had no sense of humour. It's a destructive quality. All the great sceptics have been humourists. Humour is really a device to secure human comfort. Take me. I am inspired to become a preaching friar. I instantly perceive the funny side of setting out to be a preaching friar. I tell myself that other people will perceive the funny side of it, and that consequently I shall do no good as a preaching friar. Yes, humour is a moisture which rusts everything except gold. As a nation the Jews have the greatest sense of humour, and they have been the greatest disintegrating force in the history of mankind. The Scotch are reputed to have no sense of humour, and they are morally the most impressive nation in the world. What humour is allowed them is known as dry humour. The corroding moisture has been eliminated. They are still capable of laughter, but never so as to interfere with their seriousness in the great things of life. I remember I once heard a tiresome woman, who was striving to be clever, say that Our Lord could not have had much sense of humour or He would not have hung so long on the Cross. At the time I was indignant with the silly blasphemy, but thinking it over since I believe that she was right, and that, while her only thought had been to make a remark that would create a sensation in the room, she had actually hit on the explanation of some of Our Lord's human actions. And his lack of humour is the more conspicuous because he was a Jew. I was reading the other day a book of essays by one of our leading young latitudinarian divines, in which he was most anxious to prove that Our Lord had all the graces of a well-bred young man about town, including a pretty wit. He actually claimed that the pun on Peter's name was an example of Our Lord's urbane and genial humour! It gives away the latitudinarian position completely. They're really ashamed of Christianity. They want to bring it into line with modern thought. They hope by throwing overboard the Incarnation, the Resurrection of the Body, and the Ascension, to lighten the ship so effectually that it will ride buoyantly over the billows of modern knowledge. But however lightly the ship rides, she will still be at sea, and it would be the better if she struck on the rock of Peter and perished than that she should ride buoyantly but aimlessly over the uneasy oceans of knowledge.

I've once more got a long way from the subject of my letter, but I've always taken advantage of your patience to air my theories, and when I begin to write to you my pen runs away with me. The point I want to make is that unless there is a mother house which is going to create a reserve of spiritual energy, the active work of the Order is going to suffer. The impulse to save souls might easily exhaust itself in the individual. A few disappointments, unceasing hard work, the interference of a bishop, the failure of financial support, a long period in which his work seems to have come to a standstill, all these are going to react on the individual missioner who depends on himself. Looking back now at the work done by my father, and by Rowley at Chatsea, I'm beginning to understand how dangerous it is for one man to make himself the pivot of an enterprise. I only really know about my father's work at second hand, but look at Chatsea. I hear now that already the work is falling to pieces. Although that may not justify the Bishop of Silchester, I'm beginning to see that he might argue that if Rowley had shown himself sufficiently humble to obey the forces of law and order in the Church, he would have had accumulated for him a fresh store of energy from which he might have drawn to consolidate his influence upon the people with whom he worked. Anyway, that's what I'm going to try to acquire from the pseudo-monasticism of Malford. I'm determined to dry up the critical and humorous side of myself. Half of it is nothing more than arrogance. I'm grateful for being sent to Aldershot, but I'm going to make my work here depend on the central source of energy and power. I'm going to say that my work is per hominem, but that the success of my work is ex Deo. You may tell me that any man with the least conception of Christian Grace would know that. Yes, he may know it intellectually, but does he know it emotionally? I confess I don't yet awhile. But I do know that if the Order of St. George proves itself a real force, it will not be per hominem, it will not be by the Reverend Father's eloquence in the pulpit, but by the vocation of the community ex Deo.

Meanwhile, here I am at Aldershot. Brother Chad, whose place I have taken, was a character of infinite sweetness and humility. All our Tommies speak of him in a sort of protective way, as if he were a little boy they had adopted. He had—has, for after all he's only gone to the Abbey to get over a bad attack of influenza on top of months of hard work—he has a strangely youthful look, although he's nearly thirty. He hails from Lichfield. I wonder what Dr. Johnson would have made of him. I've already told you about Brother Anselm. Well, now that I've seen him at home, as it were, I can't discover the secret of his influence with our men. He's every bit as taciturn with them as he was with me on that drive from the station, and yet there is not one of them that doesn't seem to regard him as an intimate friend. He's extraordinarily good at the practical side of the business. He makes the men comfortable. He always knows just what they're wanting for tea or for supper, and the games always go well when Brother Anselm presides, much better than they do when I'm in charge! I think perhaps that's because I play myself, and want to win. It infects the others. And yet we ought to want to win a game—otherwise it's not worth playing. Also, I must admit that there's usually a row in the billiard room on my nights on duty. Brother Anselm makes them talk better than I do, and I don't think he's a bit interested in their South African experiences. I am, and they won't say a word about them to me. I've been here a month now, so they ought to be used to me by this time.

We've just heard that the guest-house for soldiers at the Abbey will be finished by the middle of next month, so we're already discussing our Christmas party. The Priory, which sounds so grand and gothic, is really the corner house of a most depressing row of suburban villas, called Glenview and that sort of thing. The last tenant was a traveller in tea and had a stable instead of the usual back-garden. This we have converted into a billiard room. An officer in one of the regiments quartered here told us that it was the only thing in Aldershot we had converted. The authorities aren't very fond of us. They say we encourage the men to grumble and give them too great idea of their own importance. Brother Anselm asked a general once with whom we fell out if it was possible to give a man whose profession it was to defend his country too great an idea of his own importance. The general merely blew out his cheeks and looked choleric. He had no suspicion that he had been scored off. We don't push too much religion into the men at present. We've taught them to respect the Crucifix on the wall in the dining-room, and sometimes they attend Vespers. But they're still rather afraid of chaff, such as being called the Salvation Army by their comrades. Well, here's an end to this long letter, for I must write now to Brother Jerome, whose name-day it is to-morrow. Love to all at the Rectory.

Your ever affectionate

Mark.

Mark remained at Aldershot until the week before Christmas, when with a party of Tommies he went back to the Abbey. He found that Brother Chad's convalescence had been seriously impeded in its later stages by the prospect of having to remain at the Abbey as guest-master, and though Mark was sorry to leave Aldershot he saw by the way the Tommies greeted their old friend that he was dear to their hearts. When after Christmas Brother Chad took the party back, Mark made up his mind that the right person was going.

Mark found many changes at the Abbey during the four months he had been away. The greatest of all was the presence of Brother George as Prior. The legend of him had led Mark to expect someone out of the ordinary; but he had not been prepared for a personality as strong as this. Brother George was six feet three inches tall, with a presence of great dignity and much personal beauty. He had an aquiline nose, strong chin, dark curly hair and bright imperious eyes. His complexion, burnt by the Mediterranean sun, made him seem in his white habit darker than he really was. His manner was of one accustomed to be immediately obeyed. Mark could scarcely believe when he saw Brother Dunstan beside Brother George that only last June Brother Dunstan was acting as Prior. As for Brother Raymond, who had always been so voluble at recreation, one look from Brother George sent him into a silence that was as solemn as the disciplinary silence imposed by the rule. Brother Birinus, who was Brother George's right hand in the Abbey as much as he had been his right hand on the Moose Rib farm, was even taller than the Prior; but he was lanky and raw-boned, and had not the proportions of Brother George. He was of a swarthy complexion, not given to talking much, although when he did speak he always spoke to the point. He and Brother George were hard at work ploughing up some derelict fields which they had persuaded Sir Charles Horner to let to the Abbey rent free on condition that they were put back into cultivation. The patron himself had gone away for the winter to Rome and Florence, and Mark was glad that he had, for he was sure that otherwise his inquisitiveness would have been severely snubbed by the Prior. Father Burrowes went away as usual to preach after Christmas; but before he went Mark was clothed as a novice together with two other postulants who had been at Malford since September. Of these Brother Giles was a former school-master, a dried-up, tobacco-coloured little man of about fifty, with a quick and nervous, but always precise manner. Mark liked him, and his manual labour was done under the direction of Brother Giles, who had been made gardener, a post for which he was well suited. The other new novice was Brother Nicholas whom, had Mark not been the fellow-member of a community, he would have disliked immensely. Brother Nicholas was one of those people who are in a perpetual state of prurient concern about the sexual morality of the human race. He was impervious to snubs, of which he received many from Brother George, and he had somehow managed to become a favourite of the Reverend Father, so that he had been appointed guest-master, a post that was always coveted, and one for which nobody felt Brother Nicholas was suited.

Besides the increase of numbers there had been considerable additions made to the fabric of the Abbey, if such a word as fabric may be applied to matchboard, felt, and corrugated iron. Mention has already been made of the new Guest-house, which accommodated not only soldiers invited to spend their furloughs at the Abbey, but also tramps who sought a night's lodging. Mark, as Porter, found his time considerably taken up with these casuals, because as soon as the news spread of a comfortable lodging they came begging for shelter in greater numbers than had been anticipated. A rule was made that they should pay for their entertainment by doing a day's work, and it was one of Mark's duties to report on the qualifications of these casuals to Brother George, whose whole life was occupied with the farm that he was creating out of those derelict fields.

"There's a black man just arrived, Reverend Brother. He says he lost his ship at Southampton through a boiler explosion, and is tramping to Cardiff," Mark would report.

"Can he plough a straight furrow?" the Prior would demand.

"I doubt it," Mark would answer with a smile. "He can't walk straight across the dormitory."

"What's he been drinking?"

"Rum, I fancy."

"Why did you let him in?"

"It's such a stormy night."

"Well, send him along to me to-morrow after Lauds, and I'll put him to cleaning out the pigsties."

Mark only had to deal with these casuals. Regular guests like the soldiers, who were always welcome, and ecclesiastically minded inquirers were looked after by Brother Nicholas. One of the things for which Mark detested Brother Nicholas was the habit he had of showing off his poor casuals to the paying guests. It took Mark a stern reading of St. Benedict's Rule and the observations therein upon humility and obedience not to be rude to Brother Nicholas sometimes.

"Brother," he asked one day. "Have you ever read what our Holy Father says about gyrovagues and sarabaites?"

Brother Nicholas, who always thought that any long word with which he was unfamiliar referred to sexual perversion, asked what such people were.

"You evidently haven't," said Mark. "Our Holy Father disapproves of them."

"Oh, so should I, Brother Mark," said Brother Nicholas quickly. "I hate anything like that."

"It struck me," Mark went on, "that most of our paying guests are gyrovagues and sarabaites."

"What an accusation to make," said Brother Nicholas, flushing with expectant curiosity and looking down his long nose to give the impression that it was the blush of innocence and modesty.

When, an hour or so later, he had had leisure to discover the meaning of both terms, he came up to Mark and exclaimed:

"Oh, brother, how could you?"

"How could I what?" Mark asked.

"How could you let me think that it meant something much worse? Why, it's nothing really. Just wandering monks."

"They annoyed our Holy Father," said Mark.

"Yes, they did seem to make him a bit ratty. Perhaps the translation softened it down," surmised Brother Nicholas. "I'll get a dictionary to-morrow."

The bell for solemn silence clanged, and Brother Nicholas must have spent his quarter of an hour in most unprofitable meditation.

Another addition to the buildings was a wide, covered verandah, which had been built on in front of the central block, and which therefore extended the length of the Refectory, the Library, the Chapter Room, and the Abbot's Parlour. The last was now the Prior's Parlour, because lodgings for Father Burrowes were being built in the Gatehouse, the only building of stone that was being erected.

This Gatehouse was to be finished as an Easter offering to the Father Superior from devout ladies, who had been dismayed at the imagination of his discomfort. The verandah was granted the title of the Cloister, and the hours of recreation were now spent here instead of in the Library as formerly, which enabled studious brethren to read in peace.

The Prior made a rule that every Sunday afternoon all the brethren should assemble in the Cloister at tea, and spend the hour until Vespers in jovial intercourse. He did not actually specify that the intercourse was to be jovial, but he look care by judicious teazing to see that it was jovial. In his anxiety to bring his farm into cultivation, Brother George was apt to make any monastic duty give way to manual labour on those thistle-grown fields, and it was seldom that there were more than a couple of brethren to say the Office between Lauds and Vespers. The others had to be content with crossing themselves when they heard the bell for Terce or None, and even Sext was sparingly attended after the Prior instituted the eating of the mid-day meal in the fields on fine days. Hence the conversation in the Cloister on Sunday afternoons was chiefly agricultural.

"Are you going to help me drill the ten-acre field tomorrow, Brother Giles?" the Prior asked one grey Sunday afternoon in the middle of March.

"No, I'm certainly not, Reverend Brother, unless you put me under obedience to do so."

"Then I think I shall," the Prior laughed.

"If you do, Reverend Brother," the gardener retorted, "you'll have to put my peas under obedience to sow themselves."

"Peas!" the Prior scoffed. "Who cares about peas?"

"Oh, Reverend Brother!" cried Brother Simon, his hair standing up with excitement. "We couldn't do without peas."

Brother Simon was assistant cook nowadays, a post he filled tolerably well under the supervision of the one-legged soldier who was cook.

"We couldn't do without oats," said Brother Birinus severely.

He spoke so seldom at these gatherings that when he did few were found to disagree with him, because they felt his words must have been deeply pondered before they were allowed utterance.

"Have you any flowers in the garden for St. Joseph?" asked Brother Raymond, who was sacristan.

"A few daffodils, that's all," Brother Giles replied.

"Oh, I don't think that St. Joseph would like daffodils," exclaimed Brother Raymond. "He's so fond of white flowers, isn't he?"

"Good gracious!" the Prior thundered. "Are we a girls' school or a company of able-bodied men?"

"Well, St. Joseph is always painted with lilies, Reverend Brother," said the sacristan, rather sulkily.

He disapproved of the way the Prior treated what he called his pet saints.

"We're not an agricultural college either," he added in an undertone to Brother Dunstan, who shook his finger and whispered "hush."

"I doubt if we ought to keep St. Joseph's Day," said the Prior truculently. There was nothing he enjoyed better on these Sunday afternoons than showing his contempt for ecclesiasticism.

"Reverend Brother!" gasped Brother Dunstan. "Not keep St. Joseph's Day?"

"He's not in our calendar," Brother George argued. "If we're going to keep St. Joseph, why not keep St. Alo—what's his name and Philip Neri and Anthony of Padua and Bernardine of Sienna and half-a-dozen other Italian saints?"

"Why not?" asked Brother Raymond. "At any rate we have to keep my patron, who was a dear, even if he was a Spaniard."

The Prior looked as if he were wondering if there was a clause in the Rule that forbade a prior to throw anything within reach at an imbecile sacristan.

"I don't think you can put St. Joseph in the same class as the saints you have just mentioned," pompously interposed Brother Jerome, who was cellarer nowadays and fancied that the continued existence of the Abbey depended on himself.

"Until you can learn to harness a pair of horses to the plough," said the Prior, "your opinions on the relative importance of Roman saints will not be accepted."

"I've never been used to horses," said Brother Jerome.

"And you have been used to saints?" the Prior laughed, raising his eyebrows.

Brother Jerome was silent.

"Well, Brother Lawrence, what do you say?"

Brother Lawrence stuck out his lower jaw and assumed the expression of the good boy in a Sunday School class.

"St. Joseph was the foster-father of Our Blessed Lord, Reverend Brother," he said primly. "I think it would be most disrespectful both to Our Blessed Lord and to Our Blessed Lady if we didn't keep his feast-day, though I am sure St. Joseph would have no objection to daffodils. No objections at all. His whole life and character show him to have been a man of the greatest humility and forbearance."

The Prior rocked with laughter. This was the kind of speech that sometimes rewarded his teasing.

"We always kept St. Joseph's day at the Visitation, Hornsey," Brother Nicholas volunteered. "In fact we always made it a great feature. We found it came as such a relief in Lent."

The Prior nodded his head mockingly.

"These young folk can teach us a lot about the way to worship God, Brother Birinus," he commented.

Brother Birinus scowled.

"I broke three shares ploughing that bad bit of ground by the fir trees," he announced gloomily. "I think I'll drill in the oats to-morrow in the ten-acre. It's no good ploughing deep," he added reproachfully.

"Well, I believe in deep ploughing," the Prior argued.

Mark realized that Brother Birinus had deliberately brought back the conversation to where it started in order to put an end to the discussion about St. Joseph. He was glad, because he himself was the only one of the brethren who had not yet been called upon to face the Prior's contemptuous teasing. He wondered if he should have had the courage to speak up for St. Joseph's Day. He should have found it difficult to oppose Brother George, whom he liked and revered. But in this case he was wrong, and perhaps he was also wrong to make the observation of St. Joseph's Day a cudgel with which to belabour the brethren.

The following afternoon Mark had two casuals who he fancied might be useful to the Prior, and leaving the ward of the gate to Brother Nicholas he took them down with him through the coppice to where over the bleak March furrows Brother George was ploughing that rocky strip of bad land by the fir trees. The men were told to go and report themselves to Brother Birinus, who with Brother Dunstan to feed the drill was sowing oats a field or two away.

"I don't think Brother Birinus will be sorry to let Brother Dunstan go back to his domestic duties," the Prior commented sardonically.

Mark was turning to go back to *his* domestic duties when Brother George signed to him to stop.

"I suppose that like the rest of them you think I've no business to be a monk?" Brother George began.

Mark looked at him in surprise.

"I don't believe that anybody thinks that," he said; but even as he spoke he looked at the Prior and wondered why he had become a monk. He did not appear, standing there in breeches and gaiters, his shirt open at the neck, his hair tossing in the wind, his face and form of the soil like a figure in one of Fred Walker's pictures, no, he certainly did not appear the kind of man who could be led away by Father Burrowes' eloquence and persuasiveness into choosing the method of life he had chosen. Yes, now that the question had been put to him Mark wondered why Brother George was a monk.

"You too are astonished at me," said the Prior. "Well, in a way I don't blame you. You've only seen me on the land. This comes of letting myself be tempted by Horner's offer to give us this land rent free if I would take it in hand. And after all," he went on talking to the wide grey sky rather than to Mark, "the old monks were great tillers of the soil. It's right that we should maintain the tradition. Besides, all those years in Malta I've dreamed just this. Brother Birinus and I have stewed on those sun-baked heights above Valetta and dreamed of this. What made you join our Order?" he asked abruptly.

Mark told him about himself.

"I see, you want to keep your hand in, eh? Well, I suppose you might have done worse for a couple of years. Now, I've never wanted to be a priest. The Reverend Father would like me to be ordained, but I don't think I should make a good priest. I believe if I were to become a priest, I should lose my faith. That sounds a queer thing to say, and I'd rather you didn't repeat it to any of those young men up there."

The monastery bell sounded on the wind.

"Three o'clock already," exclaimed the Prior. And crossing himself he said the short prayer offered to God instead of the formal attendance at the Office.

"Well, I mustn't let the horses get chilled. You'd better get back to your casuals. By the way, I'm going to have Brother Nicholas to work out here awhile, and I want you to act as guest-master. Brother Raymond will be porter, and I'm going to send Brother Birinus off the farm to be sacristan. I shall miss him out here, of course."

The Prior put his hand once more to the plough, and Mark went slowly back to the Abbey. On the brow of the hill before he plunged into the coppice he turned to look down at the distant figure moving with slow paces across the field below.

"He's wrestling with himself," Mark thought, "more than he's wrestling with the soil."

CHAPTER XXVII
MULTIPLICATION

At Easter the Abbey Gatehouse was blessed by the Father Superior, who established himself in the rooms above and allowed himself to take a holiday from his labour of preaching. Mark expected to be made porter again, but the Reverend Father did not attempt to change the posts assigned to the brethren by the Prior, and Mark remained guest-master, a duty that was likely to give him plenty of occupation during the summer months now close at hand.

On Low Sunday the Father Superior convened a full Chapter of the Order, to which were summoned Brother Dominic, the head of the Sandgate house, and Brother Anselm. When the brethren, with the exception of Brother Simon, who was still a postulant, were gathered together, the Father Superior addressed them as follows:

"Brethren, I have called this Chapter of the Order of St. George to acquaint you with our financial position, and to ask you to make a grave decision. Before I say any more I ought to explain that our three professed brethren considered that a Chapter convened to make a decision such as I am going to ask you to make presently should not include the novices. I contended that in the present state of our Order where novices are called upon to fill the most responsible positions it would be unfair to exclude them; and our professed brethren, like true sons of St. Benedict, have accepted my ruling. You all know what great additions to our Mother House we have made during the past year, and you will all realize what a burden of debt this has laid upon the Order and on myself what a weight of responsibility. The closing of our Malta Priory, which was too far away to interest people in England, eased us a little. But if we are going to establish ourselves as a permanent force in modern religious life, we must establish our Mother House before anything. You may say that the Order of St. George is an Order devoted to active work among soldiers, and that we are not concerned with the establishment of a partially contemplative community. But all of you will recognize the advantage it has been to you to be asked to stay here and prepare yourselves for active work, to gather within yourselves a great store of spiritual energy, and hoard within your hearts a mighty treasure of spiritual strength. Brethren, if the Order of St. George is to be worthy of its name and of its claim we must not rest till we have a priory in every port and garrison, and in every great city where soldiers are stationed. Even if we had the necessary funds to endow these priories, have we enough brethren to take charge of them? We have not. I cannot help feeling that I was too hasty in establishing active houses both at Aldershot and at Sandgate, and I have convened you to-day to ask you to vote in Chapter that the house at Sandgate be temporarily given up, great spiritual influence though it has proved itself under our dear Brother Dominic with the men of Shorncliffe Camp, not only that we may concentrate our resources and pay our debts, but also that we may have the help of Brother Dominic himself, and of Brother Athanasius, who has remained behind in charge and is not here today."

The Father Superior then read a statement of the Order's financial liabilities, and invited any Brother who wished, to speak his mind. All waited for the Prior, who after a short silence rose:

"Reverend Father and Brethren, I don't think that there is much to say. Frankly, I am not convinced that we ought to have spent so much on the Abbey, but having done so, we must obviously try and put ourselves on a sound financial basis. I should like to hear what Brother Dominic has to say."

Brother Dominic was a slight man with black hair and a sallow complexion, whose most prominent feature was an, immense hooked nose with thin nostrils. Whether through the associations with his name saint, or merely by his personality, Mark considered that he looked a typical inquisitor. When he spoke, his lips seemed to curl in a sneer. The expression was probably quite accidental, perhaps caused by some difficulty in breathing, but the effect was sinister, and his smooth voice did nothing to counteract the unpleasant grimace. Mark wondered if he was really successful with the men at Shorncliffe.

"Reverend Father, Reverend Brother, and Brethren," said Brother Dominic, "you can imagine that it is no easy matter for me to destroy with a few words a house that in a small way I had a share in building up."

"The lion's share," interposed the Father Superior.

"You are too generous, Reverend Father," said Brother Dominic. "We could have done very little at Sandgate if you had not worked so hard for us throughout the length and breadth of England. And that is what personally I do feel, Brethren," he continued in more emphatic tones. "I do feel that the Reverend Father knows better than we what is the right policy for us to adopt. I will not pretend that I shall be anything but loath to leave Sandgate, but the future of the whole order depends on the ability of brethren like myself," Brother Dominic paused for the briefest instant to flash a quick glance at Brother Anselm, "to recognize that our usefulness to the soldiers among whom we are proud and happy to spend our lives is bounded by our usefulness to the Order of St. George. I give my vote without hesitation in favour of closing the Priory at Sandgate, and abandoning temporarily the work at Shorncliffe Camp."

260

Nobody else spoke when Brother Dominic sat down, and everybody voted in favour of the course of action proposed by the Father Superior.

Brother Dominic, in addition to his other work, had been editing *The Dragon*, the monthly magazine of the Order, and it was now decided to print this in future at the Abbey, some constant reader having presented a fount of type. The opening of a printing-press involved housing room, and it was decided to devote the old kitchens to this purpose, so that new kitchens could be built, a desirable addition in view of the increasing numbers in the Abbey and the likelihood of a further increase presently.

Mark had not been touched by the abandonment of the Sandgate priory until Brother Athanasius arrived. Brother Athanasius was a florid young man with bright blue eyes, and so much pent-up energy as sometimes to appear blustering. He lacked any kind of ability to hide his feelings, and he was loud in his denunciation of the Chapter that abolished his work. His criticisms were so loud, aggressive, and blatant, that he was nearly ordered to retire from the Order altogether. However, the Father Superior went away to address a series of drawing-room meetings in London, and Brother George, with whom Brother Athanasius, almost alone of the brethren, never hesitated to keep his end up, discovering that he was as ready to stick up to horses and cows, did not pay attention to the Father Superior's threat that, if Brother Athanasius could not keep his tongue quiet, he must be sent away. Mark made friends with him, and when he found that, in spite of all his blatancy and self-assertion, Brother Athanasius could not keep the tears from his bright blue eyes whenever he spoke of Shorncliffe, he was sorry for him and vexed with himself for accepting the surrender of Sandgate priory so much as a matter of course, because he had no personal experience of its work.

"But was Brother Dominic really good with the men?" Mark asked.

"Oh, Brother Dominic was all right. Don't you try and make me criticize Brother Dominic. He bought the gloves and I did the fighting. Good man of business was Brother D. I wish we could have some boxing here. Half the brethren want punching about in my opinion. Old Brother Jerome's face is squashed flat like a prize-fighter's, but I bet he's never had the gloves on in his life. I'm fond of old Brother J. But, my word, wouldn't I like to punch into him when he gives us that pea-soup more than four times a week. Chronic, I call it. Well, if he doesn't give us a jolly good blow out on my name-day next week I really will punch into him. Old Brother Flatface, as I called him the other day. And he wasn't half angry either. Didn't we have sport last second of May! I took a party of them all round Hythe and Folkestone. No end of a spree!"

Mark was soon too much occupied with his duties as guestmaster to lament with Brother Athanasius the end of the Sandgate priory. The Reverend Father's drawing-room addresses were sending fresh visitors down every week to see for themselves the size of the foundation that required money, and more money, and more money still to keep it going. In the old Chatsea days guests who visited the Mission House were expected to provide entertainment for their hosts. It mattered not who they were, millionaires or paupers, parsons or laymen, undergraduates or board-school boys, they had to share the common table, face the common teasing, and help the common task. Here at the Abbey, although the guests had much more opportunity of intercourse with the brethren than would have been permitted in a less novel monastic house, they were definitely guests, from whom nothing was expected beyond observance of the rules for guests. They were of all kinds, from the distinguished lay leaders of the Catholic party to young men who thought emotionally of joining the Order.

Mark tried to conduct himself as impersonally as possible, and in doing so he managed to impress all the visitors with being a young man intensely preoccupied with his vocation, and as such to be treated with gravity and a certain amount of deference. Mark himself was anxious not to take advantage of his position, and make friends with people that otherwise he might not have met. Had he been sure that he was going to remain in the Order of St. George, he would have allowed himself a greater liberty of intercourse, because he would not then have been afraid of one day seeing these people in the world. He desired to be forgotten when they left the Abbey, or if he was remembered to be remembered only as a guestmaster who tried to make the Monastery guests comfortable, who treated them with courtesy, but also with reserve.

None of the young men who came down to see if they would like to be monks got as far as being accepted as a probationer until the end of May, when a certain Mr. Arthur Yarrell, an undergraduate from Keble College, Oxford, whose mind was a dictionary of ecclesiastical terms, was accepted and a month later became a postulant as Brother Augustine, to the great pleasure of Brother Raymond, who said that he really thought he should have been compelled to leave the Order if somebody had not joined it with an appreciation of historic Catholicism. Early in June Sir Charles Horner introduced another young man called Aubrey Wyon, whom he had met at Venice in May.

"Take a little trouble over entertaining him," Sir Charles counselled. And then, looking round to see that no thieves or highwaymen were listening, he whispered to Mark that Wyon had money. "He would be an asset, I fancy. And he's seriously thinking of joining you," the baronet declared.

To tell the truth, Sir Charles who was beginning to be worried by the financial state of the Order of St. George, would at this crisis have tried to persuade the Devil to become a monk if the Devil would have provided a handsome dowry. He had met Aubrey Wyon at an expensive hotel, had noticed that he was expensively dressed and drank good wine, had found that he was interested in ecclesiastical religion, and, having bragged a bit about the land he had presented to the Order of St. George, had inspired Wyon to do some bragging of what he had done for various churches.

"If I could find happiness at Malford," Wyon had said, "I would give them all that I possess."

Sir Charles had warned the Father Superior that he would do well to accept Wyon as a probationer, should he propose himself; and the Father Superior, who was by now as anxious for money as a company-promoter, made himself as pleasant to Wyon as he knew how, flattering him carefully and giving voice to his dreams for the great stone Abbey to be built here in days to come.

Mark took an immediate and violent dislike to the newcomer, which, had he been questioned about it, he would have attributed to his elaborate choice of socks and tie, or to his habit of perpetually tightening the leather belt he wore instead of braces, as if he would compel that flabbiness of waist caused by soft living to vanish; but to himself he admitted that the antipathy was deeper seated.

"It's like the odour of corruption," he murmured, though actually it was the odour of hair washes and lotions and scents that filled the guest's cell.

However, Aubrey Wyon became for a week a probationer, ludicrously known as Brother Aubrey, after which he remained a postulant only a fortnight before he was clothed as a novice, having by then taken the name of Anthony, alleging that the inspiration to become a monk had been due to the direct intervention of St. Anthony of Padua on June 13th.

Whether Brother Anthony turned the Father Superior's head with his promises of what he intended to give the Order when he was professed, or whether having once started he was unable to stop, there was continuous building all that summer, culminating in a decision to begin the Abbey Church.

Mark wondered why Brother George did not protest against the expenditure, and he came to the conclusion that the Prior was as much bewitched by ambition for his farm as the head of the Order was by his hope of a mighty fane.

Thus things drifted during the summer, when, since the Father Superior was not away so much, his influence was exerted more strongly over the brethren, though at the same time he was not attracting as much money as was now always required in ever increasing amounts.

Such preaching as he did manage later on during the autumn was by no means so financially successful as his campaign of the preceding year at the same time. Perhaps the natural buoyancy of his spirit led Father Burrowes in his disappointment to place more trust than he might otherwise have done in Brother Anthony's plan for the benefit of the Order. The cloister became like Aladdin's Cave whenever there were enough brethren assembled to make an audience for his luscious projects and prefigurations. Sundays were the days when Brother Anthony was particularly eloquent, and one Sunday in mid-September—it was the Feast of the Exaltation of the Holy Cross—he surpassed himself.

"My notion would be to copy," he proclaimed, "with of course certain improvements, the buildings on Monte Cassino. We are not quite so high here; but then on the other hand that is an advantage, because it will enable us to allot less space to the superficial area. Yes, I have a very soft spot for the cloisters of Monte Cassino."

Brother Anthony gazed round for the approbation of the assembled brethren, none of whom had the least idea what the cloisters of Monte Cassino looked like.

"And I think some of our altar furniture is a little mean," Brother Anthony continued. "I'm not advocating undue ostentation; but there is room for improvement. They understood so well in the Middle Ages the importance of a rich equipment. If I'd only known when I was in Sienna this spring that I was coming here, I should certainly have bought a superb reredos that was offered to me comparatively cheap. The columns were of malachite and porphyry, and the panels of *rosso antico* with scrolls of *lumachella*. They only asked 15,000 lire. It was absurdly cheap. However, perhaps it would be wiser to wait till we finish the Abbey Church before we decide on the reredos. I'm very much in favour of beaten gold for the tabernacle. By the way, Reverend Father, have you decided to build an ambulatory round the clerestory? I must say I think it would be effective, and of course for meditation unique. I shall have to find if my money will run to it. Oh, and Brother Birinus, weren't you saying the other day that the green vestments were rather faded? Don't worry. I'm only waiting to make up my mind between velvet and brocade for the purple set to order a completely new lot, including a set in old rose damask for mid-Lent. It always seems to me such a mistake not to take advantage of that charming use."

Father Burrowes was transported to the days of his youth at Malta when his own imagination was filled with visions of precious metals, of rare fabrics and mighty architecture.

"A silver chalice of severe pattern encrusted round the stem with blue zircons," Brother Anthony was chanting in his melodious voice, his eyes bright with the reflection of celestial splendours. "And perhaps another in gold with the sacred monogram wrought on the cup in jacinths and orange tourmalines. Yes, I'll talk it over with Sir Charles and get him to approve the design."

The next morning two detectives came to Malford Abbey, and arrested Aubrey Wyon alias Brother Anthony for obtaining money under false pretences in various parts of the world. With them he departed to prison and a life more ascetic than any he had hitherto known. Brother Anthony departed indeed, but he was not discredited until it was too late. His grandiose projects and extravagant promises had already incited Father Burrowes to launch out on several new building operations that the Order could ill afford.

Perhaps the cloister had been less like the Cave of Aladdin than the Cave of the Forty Thieves.

After Christmas another Chapter was convened, to which Brother Anselm and Brother Chad were both bidden. The Father Superior addressed the brethren as he had addressed them a year ago, and finished up his speech by announcing that, deeply as he regretted it, he felt bound to propose that the Aldershot priory should be closed.

"What?" shouted Brother Anselm, leaping to his feet, his eyes blazing with wrath through his great horn spectacles.

The Prior quickly rose to say that he could not agree to the Reverend Father's suggestion. It was impossible for them any longer to claim that they were an active Order if they confined themselves entirely to the Abbey. He had not opposed the shutting down of the Sandgate priory, nor, he would remind the Reverend Father, had he offered any resistance to the abandonment of Malta. But he felt obliged to give his opinion strongly in favour of making any sacrifice to keep alive the Aldershot priory.

Brother George had spoken with force, but without eloquence; and Mark was afraid that his speech had not carried much weight.

The next to rise was Brother Birinus, who stood up as tall as a tree and said:

"I agree with Brother George."

And when he sat down it was as if a tree had been uprooted.

There was a pause after this, while every brother looked at his neighbour, waiting for him to rise at this crisis in the history of the Order. At last the Father Superior asked Brother Anselm if he did not intend to speak.

"What can I say?" asked Brother Anselm bitterly. "Last year I should have been true to myself and voted against the closing of the Sandgate house. I was silent then in my egoism. I am not fit to defend our house now."

"But I will," cried Brother Chad, rising. "Begging your pardon, Reverend Father and Brethren, if I am speaking too soon, but I cannot believe that you seriously consider closing us down. We're just beginning to get on well with the authorities, and we've a regular lot of communicants now. We began as just a Club, but we're something more than a Club now. We're bringing men to Our Lord, Brethren. You will do a great wrong if you let those poor souls think that for the sake of your own comfort you are ready to forsake them. Forgive me, Reverend Father. Forgive me, dear Brethren, if I have said too much and spoken uncharitably."

"He has not spoken uncharitably enough," Brother Athanasius shouted, rising to his feet, and as he did so unconsciously assuming the attitude of a boxer. "If I'd been here last year, I should have spoken much more uncharitably. I did not join this Order to sit about playing with vestments. I wanted to bring soldiers to God. If this Order is to be turned into a kind of male nunnery, I'm off to-morrow. I'm boiling over, that's what I am, boiling over. If we can't afford to do what we should be doing, we can't afford to build gatehouses, and lay out flower-beds, and sit giggling in tin cloisters. It's the limit, that's what it is, the limit."

Brother Athanasius stood there flushed with defiance, until the Father Superior told him to sit down and not make a fool of himself, a command which, notwithstanding that the feeling of the Chapter had been so far entirely against the head of the Order, such was the Father Superior's authority, Brother Athanasius immediately obeyed.

Brother Dominic now rose to try, as he said, to bring an atmosphere of reasonableness into the discussion.

"I do not think that I can be accused of inconsistency," he pointed out smoothly, "when we look back to our general Chapter of a year ago. Whatever my personal feelings were about closing the Sandgate priory, I recognized at once that the Reverend Father was right. There is really no doubt that we must be strong at the roots before we try to grow into a tall tree. However flourishing the branches, they will wither if the roots are not fed. The Reverend Father has no desire, as I understand him, to abandon the activity of the Order. He is merely anxious to establish us on a firm basis. The Reverend Brother said that we should make any sacrifice to maintain the Aldershot house. I have no desire to accuse the Reverend Brother of inconsistency, but I would ask him if he is willing to give up the farm, which, as you know, has cost so far a great deal more than we could afford. But of course the Reverend Brother would give up the farm. At the same time, we do not want him to give it up. We realize that under his capable guidance that farm will presently be a source of profit. Therefore, I beg the Reverend Brother to understand that I am making a purely rhetorical point when I ask him if he is prepared to give up the farm. I repeat, we do not want the farm given up.

"Another point which I feel has been missed. In giving up Aldershot, we are not giving up active work entirely. We have a good deal of active work here. We have our guest-house for casuals, and we are always ready to feed, clothe, and shelter any old soldiers who come to us. We are still young as an Order. We have only four professed monks, including the Reverend Father. We want to have more than that before we can consider ourselves established. I for one should hesitate to take my final vows until I had spent a long time in strict religious preparation, which in the hurry and scurry of active work is impossible. We have listened to a couple of violent speeches, or at any rate to one violent speech by a brother who was for a year in close touch with myself. I appeal to him not to drag the discussion down to the level of lay politics. We are free, we novices, to leave to-morrow. Let us remember that, and do not let us take advantage of our freedom to impart to this Mother House of ours the atmosphere of the world to which we may return when we will.

"And let us remember when we oppose the judgment of the Reverend Father that we are exalting ourselves without reason. Let us remember that it is he who by his eloquence and by his devotion and by his endurance and by his personality, has given us this wonderful house. Are we to turn round and say to him who has worked so hard for us that we do not want his gifts, that we are such wonderful fishers of men that we can be independent of him? Oh, my dear Brethren, let me beg you to vote in favour of abandoning all our dependencies until we are ourselves no longer dependent on the Reverend Father's eloquence and devotion and endurance and personality. God has blessed us infinitely. Are we to fling those blessings in His face?"

Brother Dominic sat down; after him in succession Brother Raymond, Brother Dunstan, Brother Lawrence, Brother Jerome, Brother Nicholas, and Brother Augustine spoke in support of the Father Superior. Brother Giles refused to speak, and though Mark's heart was thundering in his mouth with unuttered eloquence, at the moment he should rise he could not find a word, and he indicated with a sign that like Brother Giles, he had nothing to say.

"The voting will be by ballot," the Reverend Father announced. "It is proposed to give up the Priory at Aldershot. Let those brethren who agree write Yes on a strip of paper. Let those who disagree write No."

All knelt in silent prayer before they inscribed their will; after which they advanced one by one to the ballot-box, into which under the eyes of a large crucifix they dropped their papers. The Father Superior did not vote. Brother Simon, who was still a postulant, and not eligible to sit in Chapter, was fetched to count the votes. He was much excited at his task, and when he announced that seven papers were inscribed Yes, that six were inscribed No, and that one paper was blank, his teeth were chattering.

"One paper blank?" somebody repeated.

"Yes, really," said Brother Simon. "I looked everywhere, and there's not a mark on it."

All turned involuntarily toward Mark, whose paper in fact it was, although he gave no sign of being conscious of the ownership.

"*In a General Chapter of the Order of St. George, held upon the Vigil of the Epiphany of our Lord Jesus Christ, in the year of Grace, 1903, it was resolved to close the Priory of the Order in the town of Aldershot.*"

The Reverend Father, having invoked the Holy Trinity, declared the Chapter dissolved.

CHAPTER XXVIII
DIVISION

Mark was vexed with himself for evading the responsibility of recording his opinion. His vote would not have changed the direction of the policy; but if he had voted against giving up the house at Aldershot, the Father Superior would have had to record the casting vote in favour of his own proposal, and whatever praise or blame was ultimately awarded to the decision would have belonged to him alone, who as head of the Order was best able to bear it. Mark's whole sympathy had been on the side of Brother George, and as one who had known at first hand the work in Aldershot, he did feel that it ought not to be abandoned so easily. Then when Brother Athanasius was speaking, Mark, in his embarrassment at such violence of manner and tone, picked up a volume lying on the table by his elbow that by reading he might avoid the eyes of his brethren until Brother Athanasius had ceased to shout. It was the Rule of St. Benedict which, with a print of Fra Angelico's Crucifixion and an image of St. George, was all the decoration allowed to the bare Chapter Room, and the page at which Mark opened the leather-bound volume was headed: DE PRAEPOSITO MONASTERII.

"*It happens too often that through the appointment of the Prior grave scandals arise in monasteries, since some there be who, puffed up with a malignant spirit of pride, imagining themselves to be second Abbots, and assuming unto themselves a tyrannous authority, encourage scandals and create dissensions in the community. . . .*

"*Hence envy is excited, strife, evil-speaking, jealousy, discord, confusion; and while the Abbot and the Prior run counter to each other, by such dissension their souls must of necessity be imperilled; and those who are under them, when they take sides, are travelling on the road to perdition. . . .*

"*On this account we apprehend that it is expedient for the preservation of peace and good-will that the management of his monastery should be left to the discretion of the Abbot. . . .*

"*Let the Prior carry out with reverence whatever shall be enjoined upon him by his Abbot, doing nothing against the Abbot's will, nor against his orders. . . .*"

Mark could not be otherwise than impressed by what he read.

Ii qui sub ipsis sunt, dum adulantur partibus, eunt in perditionem. . . .

Nihil contra Abbatis voluntatem faciens. . . .

Mark looked up at the figure of St. Benedict standing in that holy group at the foot of the Cross.

Ideoque nos proevidemus expedire, propter pacis caritatisque custodiam, in Abbatis pendere arbitrio ordinationem monasterii sui. . . .

St. Benedict had more than apprehended; he had actually foreseen that the Abbot ought to manage his own monastery. It was as if centuries ago, in the cave at Subiaco, he had heard that strident voice of Brother Athanasius in this matchboarded Chapter-room, as if he had beheld Brother Dominic, while apparently he was striving to persuade his brethren to accept the Father Superior's advice, nevertheless taking sides, and thereby travelling along the road that leads toward destruction. This was the thought that paralyzed Mark's tongue when it was his turn to speak, and this was why he would not commit himself to an opinion. Afterward, his neutrality appeared to him a weak compromise, and he regretted that he had not definitely allied himself with one party or the other.

The announcement in *The Dragon* that the Order had been compelled to give up the Aldershot house produced a large sum of sympathetic contributions; and when the Father Superior came back just before Lent, he convened another Chapter, at which he told the Community that it was imperative to establish a priory in London before they tried to reopen any houses elsewhere. His argument was cogent, and once again there was the appearance of unanimity among the Brethren, who all approved of the proposal. It had always been the custom of Father Burrowes to preach his hardest during Lent, because during that season of self-denial he was able to raise more money than at any other time, but until now he had never failed to be at the Abbey at the beginning of Passion Week, nor to remain there until Easter was over.

The Feast of St. Benedict fell upon the Saturday before the fifth Sunday in Lent, and the Father Superior, who had travelled down from the North in order to be present, announced that he considered it would be prudent, so freely was the money flowing in, not to give up preaching this year during Passion Week and Holy Week. Naturally, he did not intend to leave the Community without a priest at such a season, and he had made arrangements with the Reverend Andrew Hett to act as chaplain until he could come back into residence himself.

Brother Raymond and Brother Augustine were particularly thrilled by the prospect of enjoying the ministrations of Andrew Hett, less perhaps because they would otherwise be debarred from their Easter duties than because they looked forward to services and ceremonies of which they felt they had been robbed by the austere Anglicanism of Brother George.

"Andrew Hett is famous," declared Brother Raymond at the pitch of exultation. "It was he who told the Bishop of Ipswich that if the Bishop made him give up Benediction he would give up singing Morning and Evening Prayer."

"That must have upset the Bishop," said Mark. "I suppose he resigned his bishopric."

"I should have thought that you, Brother Mark, would have been the last one to take the part of a bishop when he persecutes a Catholic priest!"

"I'm not taking the part of the Bishop," Mark replied. "But I think it was a silly remark for a curate to make. It merely put him in the wrong, and gave the Bishop an opportunity to score."

The Prior had questioned the policy of engaging Andrew Hett as Chaplain, even for so brief a period as a month. He argued that, inasmuch as the Bishop of Silchester had twice refused to licence him to parishes in the diocese, it would prejudice the Bishop against the Order of St. George, and might lead to his inhibiting the Father Superior later on, should an excuse present itself.

"Nonsense, my dear Brother George," said the Reverend Father. "He won't know anything about it officially, and in any case ours is a private oratory, where refusals to licence and episcopal inhibitions have no effect."

"That's not my point," argued Brother George. "My point is that any communication with a notorious ecclesiastical outlaw like this fellow Hett is liable to react unfavourably upon us. Why can't we get down somebody else? There must be a number of unemployed elderly priests who would be glad of the holiday."

"I'm afraid that I've offered Hett the job now, so let us make up our minds to be content."

Mark, who was doing secretarial work for the Reverend Father, happened to be present during this conversation, which distressed him, because it showed him that the Prior was still at variance with the Abbot, a state of affairs that was ultimately bound to be disastrous for the Community. He withdrew almost immediately on some excuse to the Superior's inner room, whence he intended to go downstairs to the Porter's Lodge until the Prior was gone. Unfortunately, the door of the inner room was locked, and before he could explain what had happened, a conversation had begun which he could not help overhearing, but which he dreaded to interrupt.

"I'm afraid, dear Brother George," the Reverend Father was saying, "I'm very much afraid that you are beginning to think I have outlived my usefulness as Superior of the Order."

"I've never suggested that," Brother George replied angrily.

"You may not have meant to give that impression, but certainly that is what you have succeeded in making me feel personally," said the Superior.

"I have been associated with you long enough to be entitled to express my opinion in private."

"In private, yes. But are you always careful only to do so in private? I'm not complaining. My only desire is the prosperity and health of the Order. Next Christmas I am ready to resign, and let the brethren elect another Superior-general."

"That's talking nonsense," said the Prior. "You know as well as I do that nobody else except you could possibly be Superior. But recently I happen to have had a better opportunity than you to criticize our Mother House, and frankly I'm not satisfied with the men we have. Few of them will be any use to us. Birinus, Anselm, Giles, Chad, Athanasius if properly suppressed, Mark, these in varying degrees, have something in them, but look at the others! Dominic, ambitious and sly, Jerome, a pompous prig, Dunstan, a nincompoop, Raymond, a milliner, Nicholas, a—well, you know what I think Nicholas is, Augustine, another nincompoop, Lawrence, still at Sunday School, and poor Simon, a clown. I've had a dozen probationers through my hands, and not one of them was as good as what we've got. I'm afraid I'm less hopeful of the future than I was in Canada."

"I notice, dear Brother George," said the Father Superior, "that you are prejudiced in favour of the brethren who follow your lead with a certain amount of enthusiasm. That is very natural. But I'm not so pessimistic about the others as you are. Perhaps you feel that I am forgetting how much the Order owes to your generosity in the past. Believe me, I have forgotten nothing. At the same time, you gave your money with your eyes open. You took your vows without being pressed. Don't you think you owe it to yourself, if not to the Order or to me personally, to go through with what you undertook? Your three vows were Chastity, Poverty, and Obedience."

There was no answer from the Prior; a moment later he shut the door behind him, and went downstairs alone. Mark came into the room at once.

"Reverend Father," he said. "I'm sorry to have to tell you that I overheard what you and the Reverend Brother were saying." He went on to explain how this had happened, and why he had not liked to make his presence known.

"You thought the Reverend Brother would not bear the mortification with as much fortitude as myself?" the Father Superior suggested with a faint smile.

It struck Mark how true this was, and he looked in astonishment at Father Burrowes, who had offered him the key to his action.

"Well, we must forget what we heard, my son," said the Father Superior. "Sit down, and let's finish off these letters."

An hour's work was done, at the end of which the Reverend Father asked Mark if his had been the blank paper when the votes were counted in Chapter, and when Mark admitted that it had been, he pressed him for the reason of his neutrality.

"I'm not sure that it oughtn't to be called indecision," said Mark. "I was personally interested in the keeping on of Aldershot, because I had worked there."

"Then why not have voted for doing so?" the Superior asked, in accents that were devoid of the least grudge against Mark for disagreeing with himself.

"I tried to get rid of my personal opinion," Mark explained. "I tried to look at the question strictly from the standpoint of the member of a community. As such I felt that the Reverend Brother was wrong to run counter to his Superior. At the same time, if you'll forgive me for saying so, I felt that you were wrong to give up Aldershot. I simply could not arrive at a decision between the two opinions."

"I do not blame you, my son, for your scrupulous cast of mind. Only beware of letting it chill your enthusiasm. Satan may avail himself of it one day, and attack your faith. Solomon was just. Our Blessed Lord, by our cowardly standards, was unjust. Remembering the Gadarene swine, the barren fig-tree, the parable of the wedding-guest without a garment, Martha and Mary. . . ."

"Martha and Mary!" interrupted Mark. "Why, that was really the point at issue. And the ointment that might have been sold for the benefit of the poor. Yes, Judas would have voted with the Reverend Brother."

"And Pontius Pilate would have remained neutral," added Father Burrowes, his blue eyes glittering with delight at the effect upon Mark of his words.

But when Mark was walking back to the Abbey down the winding drive among the hazels, he wished that he and not the Reverend Father had used that illustration. However, useless regrets for his indecision in the matter of the priory at Aldershot were soon obliterated by a new cause of division, which was the arrival of the Reverend Andrew Hett on the Vigil of the Annunciation, just in time to sing first Vespers.

It fell to Mark's lot to entertain the new chaplain that evening, because Brother Jerome who had become guest-master when Brother Anselm took his place as cellarer was in the infirmary. Mark was scarcely prepared for the kind of personality that Hett's proved to be. He had grown accustomed during his time at the Abbey to look down upon the protagonists of ecclesiastical battles, so little else did any of the guests who visited them want to discuss, so much awe was lavished upon them by Brother Raymond and Brother Augustine. It did not strike Mark that the fight at St. Agnes' might appear to the large majority of people as much a foolish squabble over trifles, a cherishing of the letter rather than the spirit of Christian worship, as the dispute between Mr. So-and-so and the Bishop of Somewhere-or-other in regard to his use of the Litany of the Saints in solemn procession on high days and holy days.

Andrew Hett revived in Mark his admiration of the bigot, which would have been a dangerous thing to lose in one's early twenties. The chaplain was a young man of perhaps thirty-five, tall, raw-boned, sandy-haired, with a complexion of extreme pallor. His light-blue eyes were very red round the rims, and what eyebrows he possessed slanted up at a diabolic angle. His voice was harsh, high, and rasping as a guinea fowl's. When Mark brought him his supper, Hett asked him several questions about the Abbey time-table, and then said abruptly:

"The ugliness of this place must be soul-destroying."

Mark looked at the Guest-chamber with new eyes. There was such a force of assertion in Hett's tone that he could not contradict him, and indeed it certainly was ugly.

"Nobody can live with matchboarded walls and ceilings and not suffer for it," Hett went on. "Why didn't you buy an old tithe barn and live in that? It's an insult to Almighty God to worship Him in such surroundings."

"This is only a beginning," Mark pointed out.

"A very bad beginning," Hett growled. "Such brutalizing ugliness would be inexcusable if you were leading an active life. But I gather that you claim to be contemplative here. I've been reading your ridiculous monthly paper *The Dragon*. Full of sentimental bosh about bringing back the glories of monasticism to England. Tintern was not built of tin. How can you contemplate Almighty God here? It's not possible. What Divine purpose is served by collecting men under hundreds of square feet of corrugated iron? I'm astonished at Charles Horner. I thought he knew better than to encourage this kind of abomination."

There was only one answer to make to Hett, which was that the religious life of the Community did not depend upon any externals, least of all upon its lodging; but when Mark tried to frame this answer, his lips would not utter the words. In that moment he knew that it was time for him to leave Malford and prepare himself to be a priest elsewhere, and otherwise than by what the Rector had stigmatized as the pseudo-monastic life.

Mark wondered when he had left the chaplain to his ferocious meditations what would have been the effect of that diatribe upon some of his brethren. He smiled to himself, as he sat over his solitary supper in the Refectory, to picture the various expressions he could imagine upon their faces when they came hotfoot from the Guest-chamber with the news of what manner of priest was in their midst. And while he was sipping his bowl of pea-soup, he looked up at the image of St. George and perceived that the dragon's expression bore a distinct resemblance to that of the Reverend Andrew Hett. That night it seemed to Mark, in one of those waking trances that occur like dreams between one disturbed sleep and another, that the presence of the chaplain was shaking the flimsy foundations of the Abbey with such ruthlessness that the whole structure must soon collapse.

"It's only the wind," he murmured, with that half of his mind which was awake. "March is going out like a dragon."

After Mass next day, when Mark was giving the chaplain his breakfast, the latter asked who kept the key of the tabernacle.

"Brother Birinus, I expect. He is the sacristan."

"It ought to have been given to me before Mass. Please go and ask for it," requested the chaplain.

Mark found Brother Birinus in the Sacristy, putting away the white vestments in the press. When Mark gave him the chaplain's message, Brother Birinus told him that the Reverend Brother had the key.

"What does he want the key for?" asked Brother George when Mark had repeated to him the chaplain's request.

"He probably wishes to change the Host," Mark suggested.

"There is no need to do that. And I don't believe that is the reason. I believe he wants to have Benediction. He's not going to have Benediction here."

Mark felt that it was not his place to argue with the Reverend Brother, and he merely asked him what reply he was to give to the chaplain.

"Tell him that the key of the Tabernacle is kept by me while the Reverend Father is away, and that I regret I cannot give it to him."

The priest's eyes blazed with anger when Mark returned without the key.

"Who is the Reverend Brother?" he rasped.

"Brother George."

"Yes, but what is he? Apothecary, tailor, ploughboy, what?"

"Brother George is the Prior."

"Well, please tell the Prior that I should like to speak to him instantly."

When Mark found Brother George he had already doffed his habit, and was dressed in his farmer's clothes to go working on the land.

"I'll speak to Mr. Hett before Sext. Meanwhile, you can assure him that the key of the Tabernacle is perfectly safe. I wear it round my neck."

Brother George pulled open his shirt, and showed Mark the golden key hanging from a cord.

On receiving the Prior's message, the chaplain asked for a railway time-table.

"I see there is a fast train at 10.30. Please order the trap."

"You're not going to leave us?" Mark exclaimed.

"Do you suppose, Brother Mark, that no bishop in the Establishment will receive me in his diocese because I am accustomed to give way? I should not have asked for the key of the Tabernacle unless I thought that it was my duty to ask for it. I cannot take it from the Reverend Brother's neck. I will not stay here without its being given up to me. Please order the trap in time to catch the 10.30 train."

"Surely you will see the Reverend Brother first," Mark urged. "I should have made it clear to you that he is out in the fields, and that all the work of the farm falls upon his shoulders. It cannot make any difference whether you have the key now or before Sext. And I'm sure the Reverend Brother will see your point of view when you put it to him."

"I am not going to argue about the custody of God," said the chaplain. "I should consider such an argument blasphemy, and I consider the Prior's action in refusing to give up the key sacrilege. Please order the trap."

"But if you sent a telegram to the Reverend Father . . . Brother Dominic will know where he is . . . I'm sure that the Reverend Father will put it right with Brother George, and that he will at once give you the key."

"I was summoned here as a priest," said the chaplain. "If the amateur monk left in charge of this monastery does not understand the prerogatives of my priesthood, I am not concerned to teach him except directly."

"Well, will you wait until I've found the Reverend Brother and told him that you intend to leave us unless he gives you the key?" Mark begged, in despair at the prospect of what the chaplain's departure would mean to a Community already too much divided against itself.

"It is not one of my prerogatives to threaten the prior of a monastery, even if he is an amateur," said the chaplain. "From the moment that Brother George refuses to recognize my position, I cease to hold that position. Please order the trap."

"You won't have to leave till half-past nine," said Mark, who had made up his mind to wrestle with Brother George on his own initiative, and if possible to persuade him to surrender the key to the chaplain of his own accord. With this object he hurried out, to find Brother George ploughing that stony ground by the fir-trees. He was looking ruefully at a broken share when Mark approached him.

"Two since I started," he commented.

But he was breaking more precious things than shares, thought Mark, if he could but understand.

"Let the fellow go," said Brother George coldly, when Mark had related his interview with the chaplain.

"But, Reverend Brother, if he goes we shall have no priest for Easter."

"We shall be better off with no priest than with a fellow like that."

"Reverend Brother," said Mark miserably, "I have no right to remonstrate with you, I know. But I must say something. You are making a mistake. You will break up the Community. I am not speaking on my own account now, because I have already made up my mind to leave, and get ordained. But the others! They're not all strong like you. They really are not. If they feel that they have been deprived of their Easter Communion by you . . . and have you the right to deprive them? After all, Father Hett has reason on his side. He is entitled to keep the key of the Tabernacle. If he wishes to hold Benediction, you can forbid him, or at least you can forbid the brethren to attend. But the key of the Tabernacle belongs to him, if he says Mass there. Please forgive me for speaking like this, but I love you and respect you, and I cannot bear to see you put yourself in the wrong."

The Prior patted Mark on the shoulder.

"Cheer up, Brother," he said. "You mustn't mind if I think that I know better than you what is good for the Community. I have had a longer time to learn, you must remember. And so you're going to leave us?"

"Yes, but I don't want to talk about that now," Mark said.

"Nor do I," said Brother George. "I want to get on with my ploughing."

Mark saw that it was as useless to argue with him as attempt to persuade the chaplain to stay. He turned sadly away, and walked back with heavy steps towards the Abbey. Overhead, the larks, rising and falling upon their fountains of song, seemed to mock the way men worshipped Almighty God.

CHAPTER XXIX
SUBTRACTION

Mark had not spent a more unhappy Easter since the days of Haverton House. He was oppressed by the sense of excommunication that brooded over the Abbey, and on the Saturday of Passion Week the versicles and responses of the proper Compline had a dreadful irony.

V. O King most Blessed, govern Thy servants in the right way. R. Among Thy Saints, O King most Blessed. V. By holy fasts to amend our sinful lives. R. O King most Blessed, govern Thy Saints in the right way. V. To duly keep Thy Paschal Feast. R. Among Thy Saints, O King most Blessed.

"Brother Mark," said Brother Augustine, on the morning of Palm Sunday, "*did* you notice that ghastly split infinitive in the last versicle at Compline? *To duly keep.* I can't think why we don't say the Office in Latin."

Mark felt inclined to tell Brother Augustine that if nothing more vital than an infinitive was split during this holy season, the Community might have cause to congratulate itself. Here now was Brother Birinus throwing away as useless the bundle of palms that lacked the blessing of a priest, throwing them away like dead flowers.

Sir Charles Horner, who had been in town, arrived at the Abbey on the Tuesday, and announced that he was going to spend Holy Week with the Community.

"We have no chaplain," Mark told him.

"No chaplain!" Sir Charles exclaimed. "But I understood that Andrew Hett had undertaken the job while Father Burrowes was away."

Mark did not think that it was his duty to enlighten Sir Charles upon the dispute between Brother George and the chaplain. However, it was not long before he found out what had occurred from the Prior's own lips and came fuming back to the Guest-chamber.

"I consider the whole state of affairs most unsatisfactory," he said. "I really thought that when Brother George took charge here the Abbey would be better managed."

"Please, Sir Charles," Mark begged, "you make it very uncomfortable for me when you talk like that about the Reverend Brother before me."

"Yes, but I must give my opinion. I have a right to criticize when I am the person who is responsible for the Abbey's existence here. It's all very fine for Brother George to ask me to notify Bazely at Wivelrod that the brethren wish to go to their Easter duties in his church. Bazely is a very timid man. I've already driven him into doing more than he really likes, and my presence in his church doesn't alarm the parishioners. In fact, they rather like it. But they won't like to see the church full of monks on Easter morning. They'll be more suspicious than ever of what they call poor Bazely's innovations. It's not fair to administer such a shock to a remote country parish like Wivelrod, especially when they're just beginning to get used to the vestments I gave them. It seems to me that you've deliberately driven Andrew Hett away from the Abbey, and I don't see why poor Bazely should be made to suffer. How many monks are you now? Fifteen? Why, fifteen bulls in Wivelrod church would create less dismay!"

Sir Charles's protest on behalf of the Vicar of Wivelrod was effective, for the Prior announced that after all he had decided that it was the duty of the Community to observe Easter within the Abbey gates. The Reverend Father would return on Easter Tuesday, and their Easter duties would be accomplished within the Octave. Withal, it was a gloomy Easter for the brethren, and when they began the first Vespers with the quadruple Alleluia, it seemed as if they were still chanting the sorrowful antiphons of Good Friday.

My spirit is vexed within Me: and My heart within Me is desolate.

Is it nothing to you, all ye that pass by: behold and see if there be any sorrow like unto My sorrow, which is done unto Me.

What are these wounds in Thy Hands: Those with which I was wounded in the house of My friends.

Nor was there rejoicing in the Community when at Lauds of Easter Day they chanted:

V. In Thy Resurrection, O Christ. R. Let Heaven and earth rejoice, Alleluia.

Nor when at Prime and Terce and Sext and None they chanted:

This is the day which the Lord hath made; we will rejoice and be glad in it.
And when at the second Vespers the Brethren declared:

V. Christ our Passover is sacrificed for us, therefore let us keep the Feast.
R. Not with the old leaven, nor with the leaven of malice and wickedness; but with the unleavened Bread of sincerity and truth. Alleluia.

scarcely could they who chanted the versicle challenge with their eyes those who hung down their heads when they gave the response.

The hour of recreation before Compline, which upon great Feasts was wont to be so glad, lay heavily upon the brethren that night, so that Mark could not bear to sit in the Cloister; there being no guests in the Abbey for his attention, he sat in the library and wrote to the Rector.

The Abbey,
Malford, Surrey.
Easter Sunday.
My dear Rector,

I should have written before to wish you all a happy Easter, but I've been making up my mind during the last fortnight to leave the Order, and I did not want to write until my mind was made up. That feat is now achieved. I shall stay here until St. George's Day, and then the next day, which will be St. Mark's Eve, I shall come home to spend my birthday with you. I do not regret the year and six months that I have spent at Malford and Aldershot, because during that time, if I have decided not to be a monk, I am none the less determined to be a priest. I shall be 23 this birthday, and I hope that I shall find a Bishop to ordain me next year and a Theological College to accept responsibility for my training and a beneficed priest to give me a title. I will give you a full account of myself when we meet at the end of the month; but in this letter, written in sad circumstances, I want to tell you that I have learnt with the soul what I have long spoken with the lips—the need of God. I expect you will tell me that I ought to have learnt that lesson long ago upon that Whit-Sunday morning in Meade Cantorum church. But I think I was granted then by God to desire Him with my heart. I was scarcely old enough to realize that I needed Him with my soul. "You're not so old now," I hear you say with a smile. But in a place like this one learns almost more than one would learn in the world in the time. One beholds human nature very intimately. I know more about my fellow-men from association with two or three dozen people here than I learnt at St. Agnes' from association with two or three hundred. This much at least my pseudo-monasticism has taught me.

We have passed through a sad time lately at the Abbey, and I feel that for the Community sorrows are in store. You know from my letters that there have been divisions, and you know how hard I have found it to decide which party I ought to follow. But of course the truth is that from the moment one feels the inclination to side with a party in a community it is time to leave that community. Owing to an unfortunate disagreement between Brother George and the Reverend Andrew Hett, who came down to act as chaplain during the absence of the Reverend Father, Andrew Hett felt obliged to leave us. The consequence is we have had no Mass this Easter, and thus I have learned with my soul to need God. I cannot describe to you the torment of deprivation which I personally feel, a torment that is made worse by the consciousness that all my brethren will go to their cells to-night needing God and not finding Him, because they like myself are involved in an earthly quarrel, so that we are incapable of opening our hearts to God this night. You may say that if we were in such a state we should have had no right to make our Easter Communion. But that surely is what Our Blessed Lord can do for us with His Body and Blood. I have been realizing that all this Holy Week. I have felt as I have never felt before the consciousness of sinning against Him. There has not been an antiphon, not a versicle nor a response, that has not stabbed me with a consciousness of my sin against His Divine Love.

"What are these wounds in Thy Hands: Those with which I was wounded in the house of My friends."

But if on Easter eve we could have confessed our sins against His Love, and if this morning we could have partaken of Him, He would have been with us, and our hearts would have been fit for the presence of God. We should have been freed from this spirit of strife, we should have come together in Jesus Christ. We should have seen how to live "with the unleavened Bread of sincerity and truth." God would have revealed His Will, and we, submitting our Order to His Will, should have ceased to think for ourselves, to judge our brethren, to criticize our seniors, to suspect that brother of personal ambition, this brother of toadyism. The Community is being devoured by the Dragon and, unless St. George comes to the rescue of his Order on Thursday week, it will perish. Perhaps I have not much faith in St. George. He has always seemed to me an unreal, fairy-tale sort of a saint. I have more faith in St. Benedict and his Holy Rule. But I have no vocation for the contemplative life. I don't feel that my prayers are good enough to save my own soul, let alone the souls of others. I *must* give Jesus Christ to my fellow-men in the Blessed Sacrament. I long to be a priest for that service. I don't feel that I want by my own efforts to make people better, or to relieve poverty, or to thunder against sin, or to preach them up to and through Heaven's gates. I want to give them the Blessed Sacrament, because I know that nothing else will be the slightest use to them. I know it more positively to-night than I have ever known it, because as I

269

sit here writing to you I am starved. God has given me the grace to understand why I am starved. It is my duty to bring Our Lord to souls who do not know why they are starved. And if after nearly two years of Malford this passion to bring the Sacraments to human beings consumes me like a fire, then I have not wasted my time, and I can look you in the face and ask for your blessing upon my determination to be a priest.

Your ever affectionate

Mark.

When Mark had written this letter, and thus put into words what had hitherto been a more or less nebulous intention, and when in addition to that he had affixed a date to the carrying out of his intention, he felt comparatively at ease. He wasted no time in letting the Father Superior know that he was going to leave; in fact he told him after he had confessed to him before making his Communion on Easter Thursday.

"I'm sorry to lose you, my dear boy," said Father Burrowes. "Very sorry. We are just going to open a priory in London, though that is a secret for the moment, please. I shall make the announcement at the Easter Chapter. Yes, some kind friends have given us a house in Soho. Splendidly central, which is important for our work. I had planned that you would be one of the brethren chosen to go there."

"It's very kind of you, Reverend Father," said Mark. "But I'm sure that you understand my anxiety not to lose any time, now that I feel perfectly convinced that I want to be a priest."

"I had my doubts about you when you first came to us. Let me see, it was nearly two years ago, wasn't it? How time flies! Yes, I had my doubts about you. But I was wrong. You seem to possess a real fixity of purpose. I remember that you told me then that you were not sure you wanted to be a monk. Rare candour! I could have professed a hundred monks, had I been willing to profess them within ten minutes of their first coming to see me."

The Father Superior gave Mark his blessing and dismissed him. Nothing had been said about the dispute between the Prior and the Chaplain, and Mark began to wonder if Father Burrowes thought the results of it would tell more surely in favour of his own influence if he did not allude to it nor make any attempt to adjudicate upon the point at issue. Now that he was leaving Malford in little more than a week, Mark felt that he was completely relieved of the necessity of assisting at any conventual legislation, and he would gladly have absented himself from the Easter Chapter, which was held on the Saturday within the Octave, had not Father Burrowes told him that so long as he wore the habit of a novice of the Order he was expected to share in every side of the Community's life.

"Brethren," said the Father Superior, "I have brought you back news that will gladden your hearts, news that will show I you how by the Grace of God your confidence in my judgment was not misplaced. Some kind friends have taken for us the long lease of a splendid house in Soho Square, so that we may have our priory in London, and resume the active work that was abandoned temporarily last Christmas. Not only have these kind friends taken for us this splendid house, but other kind friends have come forward to guarantee the working expenses up to £20 a week. God is indeed good to us, brethren, and when I remember that next Thursday is the Feast of our great Patron Saint, my heart is too full for words. During the last three or four months there have been unhappy differences of opinion in our beloved Order. Do let me entreat you to forget all these in gratitude for God's bountiful mercies. Do let us, with the arrival once more of our patronal festival, resolve to forget our doubts and our hesitations, our timidity and our rashness, our suspicions and our jealousies. I blame myself for much that has happened, because I have been far away from you, dear brethren, in moments of great spiritual distress. But this year I hope by God's mercy to be with you more. I hope that you will never again spend such an Easter as this. I have only one more announcement to make, which is that I have appointed Brother Dominic to be Prior of St. George's Priory, Soho Square, and Brother Chad and Brother Dunstan to work with him for God and our soldiers."

In the morning, Brother Simon, whose duty it was nowadays to knock with the hammer upon the doors of the cells and rouse the brethren from sleep with the customary salutation, went running from the dormitory to the Prior's cell, his hair standing even more on end than it usually did at such an hour.

"Reverend Brother, Reverend Brother," he cried. "I've knocked and knocked on Brother Anselm's door, and I've said 'The Lord be with you' nine times and shouted 'The Lord be with you' twice, but there's no answer, and at last I opened the door, though I know it's against the Rule to open the door of a brother's cell, but I thought he might be dead, and he isn't dead, but he isn't there. He isn't there, Reverend Brother, and he isn't anywhere. He's nowhere, Reverend Brother, and shall I go and ring the fire-alarm?"

Brother George sternly bade Brother Simon be quiet; but when the Brethren sat in choir to sing Lauds and Prime, they saw that Brother Anselm's stall was empty, and those who had heard Brother Simon's clamour feared that something terrible had happened.

After Mass the Community was summoned to the Chapter room to learn from the lips of the Father Superior that Brother Anselm had broken his vows and left the Order. Brother Dunstan, who wore round his neck the nib with which Brother Anselm signed his profession, burst into tears. Brother Dominic looked down his big nose to avoid the glances of his brethren. If Easter Sunday had been gloomy, Low Sunday was gloomier still, and as for the Feast of St. George nobody had the courage to think what that would be like with such a cloud hanging over the Community.

Mark felt that he could not stay even until the patronal festival. If Brother George or Brother Birinus had broken his vows, he could have borne it more easily, for he had not witnessed their profession; fond he might be of the Prior, but he had worked for human souls under the orders of Brother Anselm. He went to Father Burrowes and begged to leave on Monday.

"Brother Athanasius and Brother Chad are leaving tomorrow," said the Father Superior, "Yes, you may go."

Brother Simon drove them to the station. Strange figures they seemed to each other in their lay clothes.

"I've been meaning to go for a long time," said Brother Athanasius, who was now Percy Wade. "And it's my belief that Brother George and Brother Birinus won't stay long."

"I hoped never to go," said Brother Chad, who was now Cecil Masters.

"Then why are you going?" asked the late Brother Athanasius. "I never do anything I don't want to do."

"I think I shall be more help to Brother Anselm than to soldiers in London," said the late Brother Chad.

Mark beamed at him.

"That's just like you, Brother. I am so glad you're going to do that."

The train came in, and they all shook hands with Brother Simon, who had been cheerful throughout the drive, and even now found great difficulty in looking serious.

"You seem very happy, Brother Simon," said Mark.

"Oh, I am very happy, Brother Mark. I should say Mr. Mark. The Reverend Father has told me that I'm to be clothed as a novice on Wednesday. All last week when we sung, '*The Lord is risen indeed, and hath appeared unto Simon,*' I knew something wonderful was going to happen. That's what made me so anxious when Brother Anselm didn't answer my knock."

The train left the station, and the three ex-novices settled themselves to face the world. They were all glad that Brother Simon at least was happy amid so much unhappiness.

CHAPTER XXX
THE NEW BISHOP OF SILCHESTER

The Rector of Wych thought that Mark's wisest plan if he wished to be ordained was to write and ask the Bishop of Silchester for an interview.

"The Bishop of Silchester?" Mark exclaimed. "But he's the last bishop I should expect to help me."

"On the contrary," said the Rector, "you have lived in his diocese for more than five years, and if you repair to another bishop, he will certainly wonder why you didn't go first to the Bishop of Silchester."

"But I don't suppose that the Bishop of Silchester is likely to help me," Mark objected. "He wasn't so much enamoured of Rowley as all that, and I don't gather that he has much affection or admiration for Burrowes."

"That's not the point; the point is that you have devoted yourself to the religious life, both informally and formally, in his diocese. You have shown that you possess some capacity for sticking to it, and I fancy that you will find the Bishop less unsympathetic than you expect."

However, Mark was not given an opportunity to put the Bishop of Silchester's good-will to the test, for no sooner had he made up his mind to write to him than the news came that he was seriously ill, so seriously ill that he was not expected to live, which in fact turned out a true prognostication, for on the Feast of St. Philip and St. James the prelate died in his Castle of High Thorpe. He was succeeded by the Bishop of Warwick, much to Mark's pleasure and surprise, for the new Bishop was an old friend of Father Rowley and a High Churchman, one who might lend a kindly ear to Mark's ambition. Father Rowley had been in the United States for nearly two years, where he had been treated with much sympathy and where he had collected enough money to pay off the debt upon the new St. Agnes'. He had arrived home about a week before Mark left Malford, and in answer to Mark he wrote immediately to Dr. Oliphant, the new Bishop of Silchester, to enlist his interest. Early in June Mark received a cordial letter inviting him to visit the Bishop at High Thorpe.

The promotion of Dr. Aylmer Oliphant to the see of Silchester was considered at the time to be an indication that the political party then in power was going mad in preparation for its destruction by the gods. The Press in commenting upon the appointment did not attempt to cast a slur upon the sanctity and spiritual fervour of the new Bishop, but it felt bound to observe that the presence of such a man on the episcopal bench was an indication that the party in power was oblivious of the existence of an enraged electorate already eager to hurl them out of office. At a time when thinking men and women were beginning to turn to the leaders of the National Church for a social policy, a government worn out by eight years of office that included a costly war was so little alive to the signs of the times as to select for promotion a prelate conspicuously identified with the obscurantist tactics of that small but noisy group in the Church of England which arrogated to itself the presumptuous claim to be the Catholic party. Dr. Oliphant's learning was indisputable; his liturgical knowledge was profound; his eloquence in the pulpit was not to be gainsaid; his life, granted his sacerdotal eccentricities, was a noble example to his fellow clergy. But had he shown those qualities of statesmanship, that capacity for moderation, which were so marked a feature of his predecessor's reign? Was he not identified with what might almost be called an unchristian agitation to prosecute the holy, wise, and scholarly Dean of Leicester for appearing to countenance an opinion that the Virgin Birth was not vital to the belief of a Christian? Had he not denounced the Reverend Albert Blundell for heresy, and thereby exhibited himself in active opposition to his late diocesan, the sagacious Bishop of Kidderminster, who had been compelled to express disapproval of his Suffragan's bigotry by appointing the Reverend Albert Blundell to be one of his examining chaplains?

"We view with the gravest apprehension the appointment of Dr. Aylmer Oliphant to the historic see of Silchester," said one great journal. "Such reckless disregard, such contempt we might almost say, for the feelings of the English people demonstrates that the present government has ceased to enjoy the confidence of the electorate. We have for Dr. Oliphant personally nothing but the warmest admiration. We do not venture for one moment to impugn his sincerity. We do not hesitate to affirm most solemnly our disbelief that he is actuated by any but the highest motives in lending his name to persecutions that recall the spirit of the Star Chamber. But in these days when the rapid and relentless march of Scientific Knowledge is devastating the plain of Theological Speculation we owe it to our readers to observe that the appointment of Dr. Aylmer Oliphant to the Bishopric of Silchester must be regarded as an act of intellectual cowardice. Not merely is Dr. Oliphant a notorious extremist in religious matters, one who for the sake of outworn forms and ceremonies is inclined to keep alive the unhappy dissensions that tear asunder our National Church, but he is also what is called a Christian Socialist of the most advanced type, one who by his misreading of the Gospel spreads the unwholesome and perilous doctrine that all men are equal. This is not the time nor the place to break a controversial lance with Dr. Oliphant. We shall content ourselves with registering a solemn protest against the unparagoned cynicism of a Conservative government which thus gambles not merely with its own security, but what is far more unpardonable with the security of the Nation and the welfare of the State."

The subject of this ponderous censure received Mark in the same room where two and a half years ago the late Bishop had decided that the Third Altar in St. Agnes' Church was an intolerable excrescence. Nowadays the room was less imposing, not more imposing indeed than the room of a scholarly priest who had been able to collect a few books and buy such pieces of ancient furniture as consorted with his severe taste. Dr. Oliphant himself, a tall spare man, seeming the taller and more spare in his worn purple cassock, with clean-shaven hawk's face and black bushy eyebrows most conspicuous on account of his grey hair, stood before the empty summer grate, his long lean neck out-thrust, his arms crossed behind his back, like a gigantic and emaciated shadow of Napoleon. Mark felt no embarrassment in genuflecting to salute him; the action was spontaneous and was not dictated by any ritualistic indulgence. Dr. Oliphant, as he might have guessed from the anger with which his appointment had been received, was in outward semblance all that a prelate should be.

"Why do you want to be a priest?" the Bishop asked him abruptly.

"To administer the Sacraments," Mark replied without hesitation.

The Bishop's head and neck wagged up and down in grave approbation.

"Mr. Rowley, as no doubt he has told you, wrote to me about you. And so you've been with the Order of St. George lately? Is it any good?"

Mark was at a loss what to reply to this. His impulse was to say firmly and frankly that it was no good; but after not far short of two years at Malford it would be ungrateful and disloyal to criticize the Order, particularly to the Bishop of the diocese.

"I don't think it is much good yet," Mark said. He felt that he simply could not praise the Order without qualification. "But I expect that when they've learnt how to combine the contemplative with the active side of their religious life they will be splendid. At least, I hope they will."

"What's wrong at present?"

"I don't know that anything's exactly wrong."

Mark paused; but the Bishop was evidently waiting for him to continue, and feeling that this was perhaps the best way to present his own point of view about the life he had chosen for himself he plunged into an account of life at Malford.

"Capital," said the Bishop when the narrative was done. "You have given me a very clear picture of the present state of the Order and incidentally a fairly clear picture of yourself. Well, I'm going to recommend you to Canon Havelock, the Principal of the Theological College here, and if he reports well of you and you can pass the Cambridge Preliminary Theological Examination, I will ordain you at Advent next year, or at any rate, if not in Advent, at Whitsuntide."

"But isn't Silchester Theological College only for graduates?" Mark asked.

"Yes, but I'm going to suggest that Canon Havelock stretches a point in your favour. I can, if you like, write to the Glastonbury people, but in that case you would be out of my diocese where you have spent so much of your time and where I have no doubt you will easily find a beneficed priest to give you a title. Moreover, in the case of a young man like yourself who has been brought up from infancy upon Catholic teaching, I think it is advisable to give you an opportunity of mixing with the moderate man who wishes to take Holy Orders. You can lose nothing by such an association, and it may well happen that you will gain a great deal. Silchester Theological College is eminently moderate. The lecturers are men of real learning, and the Principal is a man whom it would be impertinent for me to praise for his devout and Christian life."

"I hardly know how to thank you, my lord," said Mark.

"Do you not, my son?" said the Bishop with a smile. Then his head and neck wagged up and down. "Thank me by the life you lead as a priest."

"I will try, my lord," Mark promised.

"Of that I am sure. By the way, didn't you come across a priest at St. Agnes' Mission House called Mousley?"

"Oh rather, I remember him well."

"You'll be glad to hear that he has never relapsed since I sent him to Rowley. In fact only last week I had the satisfaction of recommending him to a friend of mine who had a living in his gift."

272

Mark spent the three months before he went to Silchester at the Rectory where he worked hard at Latin and Greek and the history of the Church. At the end of August he entered Silchester Theological College.

CHAPTER XXXI
SILCHESTER THEOLOGICAL COLLEGE

The theological students of Silchester were housed in a red-brick alley of detached Georgian houses, both ends of which were closed to traffic by double gates of beautifully wrought iron. This alley known as Vicar's Walk had formerly been inhabited by the lay vicars of the Cathedral, whose music was now performed by minor canons.

There were four little houses on either side of the broad pavement, the crevices in which were gay with small rock plants, so infrequent were the footsteps that passed over them. Each house consisted of four rooms and each room held one student. Vicar's Walk led directly into the Close, a large green space surrounded by the houses of dignitaries, from a quiet road lined with elms, which skirted the wall of the Deanery garden and after several twists and turns among the shadows of great Gothic walls found its way downhill into the narrow streets of the small city. One of the houses in the Close had been handed over to the Theological College, the Principal of which usually occupied a Canon's stall in the Cathedral. Here were the lecture-rooms, and here lived Canon Havelock the Principal, Mr. Drakeford the Vice-Principal, Mr. Brewis the Chaplain, and Mr. Moore and Mr. Waters the Lecturers.

There did not seem to be many arduous rules. Probably the most ascetic was one that forbade gentlemen to smoke in the streets of Silchester. There was no early Mass except on Saints' days at eight; but gentlemen were expected, unless prevented by reasonable cause, to attend Matins in the Cathedral before breakfast and Evensong in the College Oratory at seven. A mutilated Compline was delivered at ten, after which gentlemen were requested to retire immediately to their rooms. Academic Dress was to be worn at lectures, and Mark wondered what costume would be designed for him. The lectures took place every morning between nine and one, and every afternoon between five and seven. The Principal lectured on Dogmatic Theology and Old Testament history; the Vice-Principal on the Old and New Testament set books; the Chaplain on Christian worship and Church history; Mr. Moore on Pastoralia and Old Testament Theology; and Mr. Waters on Latin, Greek, and Hebrew.

As against the prevailing Gothic of the mighty Cathedral Vicar's Walk stood out with a simple and fragrant charm of its own, so against the prevailing Gothic of Mark's religious experience life at the Theological College remained in his memory as an unvexed interlude during which flesh and spirit never sought to trouble each other. Perhaps if Mark had not been educated at Haverton House, had not experienced conversion, had not spent those years at Chatsea and Malford, but like his fellow students had gone decorously from public school to University and still more decorously from University to Theological College, he might with his temperament have wondered if this red-brick alley closed to traffic at either end by beautifully wrought iron gates was the best place to prepare a man for the professional service of Jesus Christ.

Sin appeared very remote in that sunny lecture-room where to the sound of cawing rooks the Principal held forth upon the strife between Pelagius and Augustine, when prevenient Grace, operating Grace, co-operating Grace and the *donum perseverantiae* all seemed to depend for their importance so much more upon a good memory than upon the inscrutable favours of Almighty God. Even the Confessions of St. Augustine, which might have shed their own fierce light of Africa upon the dark problem of sin, were scarcely touched upon. Here in this tranquil room St. Augustine lived in quotations from his controversial works, or in discussions whether he had not wrongly translated ἐφ᾽ ᾧ πάντες ἥμαρτον in the Epistle to the Romans by *in quo omnes peccaverunt* instead of like the Pelagians by *propter quod omnes peccaverunt*. The dim echoes of the strife between Semipelagian Marseilles and Augustinian Carthage resounded faintly in Mark's brain; but they only resounded at all, because he knew that without being able to display some ability to convey the impression that he understood the Thirty-Nine Articles he should never be ordained. Mark wondered what Canon Havelock would have done or said if a woman taken in adultery had been brought into the lecture-room by the beadle. Yet such a supposition was really beside the point, he thought penitently. After all, human beings would soon be degraded to wax-works if they could be lectured upon individually in this tranquil and sunny room to the sound of rooks cawing in the elms beyond the Deanery garden.

Mark made no intimate friendships among his fellows. Perhaps the moderation of their views chilled him into an exceptional reserve, or perhaps they were an unusually dull company that year. Of the thirty-one students, eighteen were from Oxford, twelve from Cambridge, and the thirty-first from Durham. Even he was looked at with a good deal of suspicion. As for Mark, nothing less than God's prevenient grace could explain his presence at Silchester. Naturally, inasmuch as they were going to be clergymen, the greatest charity, the sweetest toleration was shown to Mark's unfortunate lack of advantages; but he was never unaware that intercourse with him involved his companions in an effort, a distinct, a would-be Christlike effort to make the best of him. It was the same kind of effort they would soon be making when as Deacons they sought for the sick, poor, and impotent people of the Parish. Mark might have expected to find among them one or two of whom it might be prophesied that they would go far. But he was unlucky. All the brilliant young candidates for Ordination must have betaken themselves to Cuddesdon or Wells or Lichfield that year.

Of the eighteen graduates from Oxford, half took their religion as a hot bath, the other half as a cold one. Nine resembled the pale young curates of domestic legend, nine the muscular Christian that is for some reason attributed to the example of Charles Kingsley. Of the twelve graduates from Cambridge, six treated religion as a cricket match played before the man in the street with God as umpire, six regarded it as a respectable livelihood for young men with normal brains, social connexions, and weak digestions. The young man from Durham looked upon religion as a more than respectable livelihood for one who had plenty of brains, an excellent digestion, and no social connexions whatever.

Mark wondered if the Bishop of Silchester's design in placing him amid such surroundings was to cure him for ever of moderation. As was his custom when he was puzzled, he wrote to the Rector.

The Theological College,
Silchester.
All Souls, '03.
My dear Rector,

My first impressions have not undergone much change. The young men are as good as gold, but oh dear, the gold is the gold of Mediocritas. The only thing that kindles a mild phosphorescence, a dim luminousness as of a bedside match-tray in the dark, in their eyes is when they hear of somebody's what they call conspicuous moderation. I suppose every deacon carries a bishop's apron in his sponge-bag or an archbishop's crosier among his golf-clubs. But in this lot I simply cannot perceive even an embryonic archdeacon. I rather expected when I came here that I should be up against men of brains and culture. I was looking forward to being trampled on by ruthless logicians. I hoped that latitudinarian opinions were going to make my flesh creep and my hair stand on end. But nothing of the kind. I've always got rather angry when I've read caricatures of curates in books with jokes about goloshes and bath-buns. Yet honestly, half my fellows might easily serve as models to any literary cheapjack of the moment. I'm willing to admit that probably most of them will develop under the pressure of life, but a few are bound to remain what they are. I know we get some eccentrics and hotheads and a few sensual knaves among the Catholic clergy, but we do not get these anæmic creatures. I feel that before I came here I knew nothing about the Church of England. I've been thrown all my life with people who had rich ideas and violent beliefs and passionate sympathies and deplorable hatreds, so that when I come into contact with what I am bound to accept as the typical English parson in the making I am really appalled.

I've been wondering why the Bishop of Silchester told me to come here. Did he really think that the spectacle of moderation in the moulding was good for me? Did he fancy that I was a young zealot who required putting in his place? Or did he more subtly realize from the account I gave him of Malford that I was in danger of becoming moderate, even luke-warm, even tepid, perhaps even stone-cold? Did he grasp that I must owe something to party as well as mankind, if I was to give up anything worth giving to mankind? But perhaps in my egoism I am attributing much more to his lordship's paternal interest, a keener glance to his episcopal eye, than I have any right to attribute. Perhaps, after all, he merely saw in me a young man who had missed the advantages of Oxford, etc., and wished out of regard for my future to provide me with the best substitute.

Anyway, please don't think that I live in a constant state of criticism with a correspondingly dangerous increase of self-esteem. I really am working hard. I sometimes wonder if the preparation of a "good" theological college is the best preparation for the priesthood. But so long as bishops demand the knowledge they do, it is obvious that this form of preparation will continue. There again though, I daresay if I imagined myself an inspired pianist I should grumble at the amount of scales I was set to practice. I'm not, once I've written down or talked out some of my folly, so very foolish at bottom.

Beyond a slight inclination to flirt with the opinions of most of the great heresiarchs in turn, but only with each one until the next comes along, I'm not having any intellectual adventures. One of the excitements I had imagined beforehand was wrestling with Doubt. But I have no wrestles. Shall I always be spared?
Your ever affectionate,
Mark.

Gradually, as the months went by, either because the students became more mellow in such surroundings or because he himself was achieving a wider tolerance, Mark lost much of his capacity for criticism and learned to recognize in his fellows a simple goodness and sincerity of purpose that almost frightened him when he thought of that great world outside, in the confusion and complexity of which they had pledged themselves to lead souls up to God. He felt how much they missed by not relying rather upon the Sacraments than upon personal holiness and the upright conduct of the individual. They were obsessed with the need of setting a good example and of being able from the pulpit to direct the wandering lamb to the Good Shepherd. Mark scarcely ever argued about his point of view, because he was sure that perception of what the Sacraments could do for human nature must be given by the grace of God, and that the most exhaustive process of inductive logic would not avail in the least to convince somebody on whom the fact had not dawned in a swift and comprehensive inspiration of his inner life. Sometimes indeed Mark would defend himself from attack, as when it was suggested that his reliance upon the Sacraments was only another aspect of Justification by Faith Alone, in which the effect of a momentary conversion was prolonged by mechanical aids to worship.

"But I should prefer my idolatry of the outward form to your idolatry of the outward form," he would maintain.

"What possible idolatry can come from the effect upon a congregation of a good sermon?" they protested.

"I don't claim that a preacher might not bring the whole of his congregation to the feet of God," Mark allowed. "But I must have less faith in human nature than you have, for I cannot believe that any preacher could exercise a permanent effect without the Sacraments. You all know the person who says that the sound of an organ gives him holy thoughts, makes him feel good, as the cant phrase goes? I've no doubt that people who sit under famous preachers get the same kind of sensation Sunday after Sunday. But sooner or later they will be worshipping the outward form—that is to say the words that issue from the preacher's mouth and produce those internal moral rumblings in the pit of the soul which other listeners get from the diapason. Have your organs, have your sermons, have your matins and evensong; but don't put them on the same level as the Blessed Sacrament. The value of that is absolute, and I refuse to consider It from the point of view of pragmatic philosophy."

All would protest that Mark was putting a wrong interpretation upon their argument; what they desired to avoid was the substitution of the Blessed Sacrament for the Person of the Divine Saviour.

"But I believe," Mark argued, "I believe profoundly with the whole of my intellectual, moral, and emotional self that the Blessed Sacrament *is* our Divine Saviour. I maintain that only through the Blessed Sacrament can we hope to form within our own minds the slightest idea of the Person of the Divine Saviour. In the pulpit I would undertake to present fifty human characters as moving as our Lord; but when I am at the Altar I shall actually give Him to those who will take Him. I shall know that I am doing as much for the lowest savage as for the finest product of civilization. All are equal on the altar steps. Elsewhere man remains divided into classes. You may rent the best pew from which to see and hear the preacher; but you cannot rent a stone on which to kneel at your Communion."

Mark rarely indulged in these outbursts. On him too Silchester exerted a mellowing influence, and he gained from his sojourn there much of what he might have carried away from Oxford; he recaptured the charm of that June day when in the shade of the oak-tree he had watched a College cricket match, and conversed with Hathorne the Siltonian who wished to be a priest, but who was killed in the Alps soon after Mark met him.

The bells chimed from early morning until sombre eve; ancient clocks sounded the hour with strikes rusty from long service of time; rooks and white fantail-pigeons spoke with the slow voice of creatures that are lazily content with the slumbrous present and undismayed by the sleepy morrow. In Summer the black-robed dignitaries and white choristers, themselves not more than larger rooks and fantails, passed slowly across the green Close to their dutiful worship. In Winter they battled with the wind like the birds in the sky. In Autumn there was a sound of leaves along the alleys and in the Gothic entries. In Spring there were daisies in the Close, and daffodils nodding among the tombs, and on the grey wall of the Archdeacon's garden a flaming peacock's tail of Japanese quince.

Sometimes Mark was overwhelmed by the tyranny of the past in Silchester; sometimes it seemed that nothing was worth while except at the end of living to have one's effigy in stone upon the walls of the Cathedral, and to rest there for ever with viewless eyes and cold prayerful hands, oneself in harmony at last with all that had gone before.

"Yet this peace is the peace of God," he told himself. "And I who am privileged for a little time to share in it must carry away with me enough to make a treasure of peace in my own heart, so that I can give from that treasure to those who have never known peace."

The peace of God, which passeth all understanding, keep your hearts and minds in the knowledge and love of God, and of his Son Jesus Christ our Lord; and the blessing of God Almighty, the Father, the Son, and the Holy Ghost, be amongst you and remain with you always.

When Mark heard these words sound from the altar far away in the golden glooms of the Cathedral, it seemed to him that the building bowed like a mighty couchant beast and fell asleep in the security of God's presence.

After Mark had been a year at the Theological College he received a letter from the Bishop:

High Thorpe Castle.

Sept. 21, '04.

Dear Lidderdale,

I have heard from Canon Havelock that he considers you are ready to be ordained at Advent, having satisfactorily passed the Cambridge Preliminary Theological Examination. If therefore you succeed in passing my examination early in November, I am willing to ordain you on December 18. It will be necessary of course for you to obtain a title, and I have just heard from Mr. Shuter, the Vicar of St. Luke's, Galton, that he is anxious to make arrangements for a curate. You had better make an appointment, and if I hear favourably from him I will licence you for his church. It has always been the rule in this diocese that non-graduate candidates for Holy Orders should spend at least two years over their theological studies, but I am not disposed to enforce this rule in your case.

Yours very truly,

Aylmer Silton.

This expression of fatherly interest made Mark anxious to show his appreciation of it, and whatever he had thought of St. Luke's, Galton, or of its incumbent he would have done his best to secure the title merely to please the Bishop. Moreover, his money was coming to an end, and another year at the Theological College would have compelled him to borrow from Mr. Ogilvie, a step which he was most anxious to avoid. He found that Galton, which he remembered from the days when he had sent Cyril Pomeroy there to be met by Dorward, was a small county town of some eight or nine thousand inhabitants and that St. Luke's was a new church which had originally been a chapel of ease to the parish church, but which had acquired with the growth of a poor population on the outskirts of the town an independent parochial status of its own. The Reverend Arnold Shuter, who was the first vicar, was at first glance just a nervous bearded man, though Mark soon discovered that he possessed a great deal of spiritual force. He was a widower and lived in the care of a housekeeper who regarded religion as the curse of good cooking. Latterly he had suffered from acute neurasthenia, and three or four of his wealthier parishioners—they were only relatively wealthy—had clubbed together to guarantee the stipend of a curate. Mark was to live at the Vicarage, a detached villa, with pointed windows and a front door like a lychgate, which gave the impression of having been built with what material was left over from building the church.

"You may think that there is not much to do in Galton," said Mr. Shuter when he and Mark were sitting in his study after a round of the parish.

"I hope I didn't suggest that," Mark said quickly.

The Vicar tugged nervously at his beard and blinked at his prospective curate from pale blue eyes.

"You seem so full of life and energy," he went on, half to himself, as though he were wondering if the company of this tall, bright-eyed, hatchet-faced young man might not prove too bracing for his worn-out nerves.

"Indeed I'm glad I do strike you that way," Mark laughed. "After dreaming at Silchester I'd begun to wonder if I hadn't grown rather too much into a type of that sedate and sleepy city."

"But there is plenty of work," Mr. Shuter insisted. "We have the hop-pickers at the end of the summer, and I've tried to run a mission for them. Out in the hop-gardens, you know. And then there's Oaktown."

"Oaktown?" Mark echoed.

"Yes. A queer collection of people who have settled on a derelict farm that was bought up and sold in small plots by a land-speculator. They'll give plenty of scope for your activity. By the way, I hope you're not too extreme. We have to go very slowly here. I manage an early Eucharist every Sunday and Thursday, and of course on Saints' days; but the attendance is not good. We have vestments during the week, but not at the mid-day Celebration."

Mark had not intended to attach himself to what he considered a too indefinite Catholicism; but inasmuch as the Bishop had found him this job he made up his mind to give to it at any rate his deacon's year and his first year as a priest.

"I've been brought up in the vanguard of the Movement," he admitted. "But you can rely on me, sir, to be loyal to your point of view, even if I disagreed with it. I can't pretend to believe much in moderation; but I should always be your curate before anything else, and I hope very much indeed that you will offer me the title."

"You'll find me dull company," Mr. Shuter sighed. "My health has gone all to pieces this last year."

"I shall have a good deal of reading to do for my priest's examination," Mark reminded him. "I shall try not to bother you."

The result of Mark's visit to Galton was that amongst the various testimonials and papers he forwarded two months later to the Bishop's Registrar was the following:

To the Right Reverend Aylmer, Lord Bishop of Silchester.

I, Arnold Shuter, Vicar of St. Luke's, Galton, in the County of Southampton, and your Lordship's Diocese of Silchester, do hereby nominate Mark Lidderdale, to perform the office of Assistant Curate in my Church of St. Luke aforesaid; and do promise to allow him the yearly stipend of £120 to be paid by equal quarterly instalments; And I do hereby state to your Lordship that the said Mark Lidderdale intends to reside in the said Parish in my Vicarage; and that the said Mark Lidderdale does not intend to serve any other Parish as Incumbent or Curate.

Witness my hand this fourteenth day of November; in the year of our Lord, 1904.

Arnold Shuter,
St. Luke's Vicarage,
Galton,
Hants.

I, Arnold Shuter, Incumbent of St. Luke's, Galton, in the County of Southampton, bonâ fide undertake to pay Mark Lidderdale, of the Rectory, Wych-on-the-Wold, in the County of Oxford, the annual sum of one hundred and twenty pounds as a stipend for his services as Curate, and I, Mark Lidderdale, bonâ fide intend to receive the whole of the said stipend. And each of us, Arnold Shuter and Mark Lidderdale, declare that no abatement is to be made out of the said stipend in respect of rent or consideration for the use of the Glebe House; and that I, Arnold Shuter, undertake to pay the same, and I, Mark Lidderdale, intend to receive the same, without any deduction or abatement whatsoever.

Arnold Shuter,
Mark Lidderdale.

CHAPTER XXXII
EMBER DAYS

Mark, having been notified that he had been successful in passing the Bishop's examination for Deacons, was summoned to High Thorpe on Thursday. He travelled down with the other candidates from Silchester on an iron-grey afternoon that threatened snow from the louring North, and in the atmosphere of High Thorpe under the rule of Dr. Oliphant he found more of the spirit of preparation than he would have been likely to find in any other diocese at this date. So many of the preliminaries to Ordination had consisted of filling up forms, signing documents, and answering the questions of the Examining Chaplain that Mark, when he was now verily on the threshold of his new life, reproached himself with having allowed incidental details and petty arrangements to make him for a while oblivious of the overwhelming fact of his having been accepted for the service of God. Luckily at High Thorpe he was granted a day to confront his soul before being harassed again on Ember Saturday with further legal formalities and signing of documents. He was able to spend the whole of Ember Friday in prayer and meditation, in beseeching God to grant him grace to serve Him worthily, strength to fulfil his vows, and that great *donum perseverantiæ* to endure faithful unto death.

"Not everyone that saith unto me, Lord, Lord," Mark remembered in the damasked twilight of the Bishop's Chapel, where he was kneeling. "Let me keep those words in my heart. Not everyone," he repeated aloud. Then perversely as always come volatile and impertinent thoughts when the mind is concentrated on lofty aspirations Mark began to wonder if he had quoted the text correctly. He began to be almost sure that he had not, and on that to torment his brain in trying to recall what was the exact wording of the text he desired to impress upon his heart. "Not everyone that saith unto me, Lord, Lord," he repeated once more aloud.

At that moment the tall figure of the Bishop passed by.

"Do you want me, my son?" he asked kindly.

"I should like to make my confession, reverend father in God," said Mark.

The Bishop beckoned him into the little sacristy, and putting on rochet and purple stole he sat down to hear his penitent.

Mark had few sins of which to accuse himself since he last went to his duties a month ago. However, he did have upon his conscience what he felt was a breach of the Third Commandment in that he had allowed himself to obscure the mighty fact of his approaching ordination by attaching too much importance to and fussing too much about the preliminary formalities.

The Bishop did not seem to think that Mark's soul was in grave peril on that account, and he took the opportunity to warn Mark against an over-scrupulousness that might lead him in his confidence to allow sin to enter into his soul by some unguarded portal which he supposed firmly and for ever secure.

"That is always the danger of a temperament like yours?" he mused. "By all means keep your eyes on the high ground ahead of you; but do not forget that the more intently you look up, the more liable you are to slip on some unnoticed slippery stone in your path. If you abandoned yourself to the formalities that are a necessary preliminary to Ordination, you did wisely. Our Blessed Lord usually gave practical advice, and some of His miracles like the turning of water into wine at Cana were reproofs to carelessness in matters of detail. It was only when people worshipped utility unduly that He went to the other extreme as in His rebuke to Judas over the cruse of ointment."

The Bishop raised his head and gave Mark absolution. When they came out of the sacristy he invited him to come up to his library and have a talk.

"I'm glad that you are going to Galton," he said, wagging his long neck over a crumpet. "I think you'll find your experience in such a parish extraordinarily useful at the beginning of your career. So many young men have an idea that the only way to serve God is to go immediately to a slum. You'll be much more discouraged at Galton than you can imagine. You'll learn there more of the difficulties of a clergyman's life in a year than you could learn in London in a lifetime. Rowley, as no doubt you've heard, has just accepted a slum parish in Shoreditch. Well, he wrote to me the other day and suggested that you should go to him. But I dissented. You'll have an opportunity at Galton to rely upon yourself. You'll begin in the ruck. You'll be one of many who struggle year in year out with an ordinary parish. There won't be any paragraphs about St. Luke's in the Church papers. There won't be any enthusiastic pilgrims. There'll be nothing but the thought of our Blessed Lord to keep you struggling on, only that, only our Blessed Lord Jesus Christ."

The Bishop's head wagged slowly to and fro in the silence that succeeded his words, and Mark pondering them in that silence felt no longer that he was saying "Lord, Lord," but that he had been called to follow and that he was ready without hesitation to follow Him whithersoever He should lead.

The quiet Ember Friday came to an end, and on the Saturday there were more formalities, of which Mark dreaded most the taking of the oath before the Registrar. He had managed with the help of subtle High Church divines to persuade himself that he could swear he assented to the Thirty-nine Articles without perjury. Nevertheless he wished that he was not bound to take that oath, and he was glad that the sense in which the Thirty-nine Articles were to be accepted was left to the discretion of him who took the oath. Of one thing Mark was positive. He was assuredly not assenting to those Thirty-nine Articles that their compilers intended when they framed them. However, when it came to it, Mark affirmed:

"I, Mark Lidderdale, about to be admitted to the Holy Order of Deacons, do solemnly make the following declaration:—I assent to the Thirty-nine Articles of Religion, and to the Book of Common Prayer, and the ordering of Bishops, Priests, and Deacons. I believe the doctrine of the Church of England, as therein set forth, to be agreeable to the Word of God; and in Public Prayer and Administration of the Sacraments I will use the Form in the said Book prescribed, and none other, except so far as shall be ordered by lawful authority.

"I, Mark Lidderdale, about to be admitted to the Holy Order of Deacons, do swear that I will be faithful and bear true Allegiance to His Majesty King Edward, his heirs and successors according to law.

"So help me God."

"But the strange thing is," Mark said to one of his fellow candidates, "nobody asks us to take the oath of allegiance to God."

"We do that when we're baptized," said the other, a serious young man who feared that Mark was being flippant.

"Personally," Mark concluded, "I think the solemn profession of a monk speaks more directly to the soul."

And this was the feeling that Mark had throughout the Ordination of the Deacons notwithstanding that the Bishop of Silchester in cope and mitre was an awe-inspiring figure in his own Chapel. But when Mark heard him say:

Receive the Holy Ghost for the office and work of a Priest in the Church of God, he was caught up to the Seventh Heaven and prayed that, when a year hence he should be kneeling thus to hear those words uttered to him and to feel upon his head those hands imposed, he should receive the Holy Ghost more worthily than lately he had received authority to execute the office of a Deacon in the Church of God.

Suddenly at the back of the chapel Mark caught sight of Miriam, who must have travelled down from Oxfordshire last night to be present at his Ordination. His mind went back to that Whit-Sunday in Meade Cantorum nearly ten years ago. Miriam's plume of grey hair was no longer visible, for all her hair was grey nowadays; but her face had scarcely altered, and she sat there at this moment with that same expression of austere sweetness which had been shed like a benison upon Mark's dreary boyhood. How dear of Miriam to grace his Ordination, and if only Esther too could have been with him! He knelt down to thank God humbly for His mercies, and of those mercies not least for the Ogilvies' influence upon his life.

Mark could not find Miriam when they came out from the chapel. She must have hurried away to catch some slow Sunday train that would get her back to Wych-on-the-Wold to-night. She could not have known that he had seen her, and when he arrived at the Rectory to-morrow as glossy as a beetle in his new clerical attire, Miriam would listen to his account of the Ordination, and only when he had finished would she murmur how she had been present all the time.

And now there was still the oath of canonical obedience to take before lunch; but luckily that was short. Mark was hungry, since unlike most of the candidates he had not eaten an enormous breakfast that morning.

Snow was falling outside when the young priests and deacons in their new frock coats sat down to lunch; and when they put on their sleek silk hats and hurried away to catch the afternoon train back to Silchester, it was still falling.

"Even nature is putting on a surplice in our honour," Mark laughed to one of his companions, who not feeling quite sure whether Mark was being poetical or profane, decided that he was being flippant, and looked suitably grieved.

It was dusk of that short winter day when Mark reached Silchester, and wandered back in a dream toward Vicar's Walk. Usually on Sunday evenings the streets of the city pattered with numerous footsteps; but to-night the snow deadened every sound, and the peace of God had gone out from the Cathedral to shed itself upon the city.

"It will be Christmas Day in a week," Mark thought, listening to the Sabbath bells muffled by the soft snow-laden air. For the first time it occurred to him that he should probably have to preach next Sunday evening.

And the Word was made flesh, and dwelt among us.

That should be his text, Mark decided; and, passing from the snowy streets, he sat thinking in the golden glooms of the Cathedral about his sermon.

EXPLICIT PRÆLUDIUM

Rich Relatives
Chapter One

IT may have been that the porter at York railway station was irritated by Sunday duty, or it may have been that the outward signs of wealth in his client were not conspicuous; whatever the cause, he spoke rudely to her.

Yet Jasmine Grant was not a figure that ought to have aroused the insolence of a porter, even if he *was* on Sunday duty. To be sure, her black clothes were not fashionable; and a journey from the South of Italy to the North of England, having obliterated what slight pretensions to cut they might once have possessed, had left her definitely draggled. Although the news of having to wait nearly five hours for the train to Spaborough had brought tears of disappointment into her eyes, and although the appeal of tears had been spoilt by their being rubbed off with the back of a dusty glove, Jasmine's beauty was there all the time—a dark, Southern beauty of jetty lashes curling away from brown eyes starry-hearted; a slim Southern charm of sunburnt, boyish hands. Something she had of a young cypress in moonlight, something of a violoncello, with that voice as deep as her eyes. But for the porter she was only something of a nuisance, and when she began to lament again the long wait he broke in as rudely as before:

"Now it's not a bit of good you nagging at me, miss. If the 4.42 goes at 4.42, I can't make it go before 4.42, can I?"

Then perhaps the thought of his own daughters at home, or perhaps the comforting intuition that there would be shrimps for tea at the close of this weary day, stirred his better nature.

"Why don't you take a little mouch round the walls? That's what people mostly does who get stuck in York. They mouch round the walls if it's fine, like it is, and if it's raining they mouch round the Minster. And I've known people, I have, who've actually come to York to mouch round the walls, so you needn't be so aggravated at having to see them whether you like it or not, as you might say. And now," he concluded, "I suppose the next thing is you'll want to put your luggage in the cloak-room!"

He spoke with a sense of sacrilege, as if Jasmine had suggested laying her luggage on the high altar of the Minster.

"Well, that means me having to go and get a truck," he grumbled, "because the cloak-room's at the other end of the station from what we are here."

The poor girl was already well aware of the vastness of York railway station, a vastness that was accentuated by its emptiness on this fine Sunday afternoon. Fresh tears brimmed over her lids; and as in mighty limestone caverns stalagmites drop upon the explorer, so now from the remote roof of glass and iron a smutty drop descended upon Jasmine's nose.

"Come far, have you?" asked the porter, with this display of kindly interest apologizing as it were for the behaviour of the station's roof.

"Italy."

"Organland, eh?"

The thought of Italy turned his mind toward music, and he went whistling off to fetch a truck, leaving his client beside a heap of luggage that seemed an intrusion on the Sabbath peace of the railway station.

From anyone except porters or touring actors accustomed all their lives to the infinite variations of human luggage, Jasmine's collection, which alternately in the eyes of its owner appeared much too large and much too small, too pretentious and too insignificant, too defiant and too pathetic, might have won more than a passing regard. But since the sparse frequenters of the station were all either porters or actors, nobody looked twice at the leather portmanteau stamped SHOLTO GRANT, at the hold-all of carpet-bagging worked in a design of the Paschal Lamb, at the two narrow wooden crates labelled with permits to export modern works of art from Italy, or at a decrepit basket of fruit covered with vine leaves and tied up with bunches of tricoloured ribbon; and as for the owner, she was by this time so hopelessly bedraggled by the effort of bringing this luggage from the island of Sirene to the city of York only to find that there was no train on to Spaborough for five hours that nobody looked twice at her.

Somewhere outside in the sheepish sunlight of England an engine screamed with delight at having escaped from the station; somewhere deep in the dust-eclipsed station a retriever howled each time he managed to wind his chain round the pillar to which it was attached. Then a luggage train ran down a dulcimer scale of jolts until it finally rumbled away into silence like the inside of a hungry giant before he falls asleep; after which there was no sound of anything except the dripping of condensed steam from the roof to the platform. Jasmine began to wonder if there would ever be another train to anywhere this Sunday, and if the porter intended to leave her alone with her luggage on the platform until to-morrow morning. Everything in England was so different from what she had been accustomed to all her life; people behaved here with such rudeness and such evident dislike of being troubled that perhaps ... but her apprehensions were interrupted by the whining of the porter's truck, which he pushed before him like a truant child being thumped homeward by its mother. The luggage was put on the truck, and the porter, cheered by the noise he was making, broke into a vivacious narrative, of which Jasmine did not understand a single word until he stopped before the door of the cloak-room and was able to enunciate this last sentence without the accompaniment of unoiled wheels:

"...and which, of course, made it very uncomfortable for her through her being related to them."

At the moment the difficulty of persuading a surly cloak-room clerk, even more indignant than the porter at being made to work on Sunday afternoon, that the two crates were lawful luggage for passengers, prevented Jasmine's attempting to trace the origin of the porter's last remark; but when she was blinking in the sunlight outside the station preparatory to her promenade of the walls of York, it recurred to her, and its appropriateness to her own situation made her regret that she had not heard more about *Her* and *Them*. Was not she herself feeling so uncomfortable on account of her relationship to *Them*, so miserable rather that if another obstacle arose in her path she would turn back and ... yes, wicked though the thought undoubtedly was, and imperil though it might her soul should she die before it was absolved ... yes, indeed she really would turn back and drown herself in that *puzzo nero* they called the English Channel. Here she was searching for a wall in a city that looked as large as Naples. Well, if she did not find it, she would accept her failure as an omen that fate desired her withdrawal from life. But no sooner had Jasmine walked a short way from the station than she found that the wall was ubiquitous, and that she would apparently be unable to proceed anywhere in York without walking on it; so she turned aside down a narrow passage, climbed a short flight of steps, and without thinking any more of suicide she achieved that prospect of the city which had been so highly recommended by the porter.

It was the midday Sabbath hour, when the bells at last were silent; and since it was fine August weather, the sky had achieved a watery and pious blue like a nun's eyes. Before her and behind her the river of the wall flowed through a champaign of roofs from which towers and spires rose like trees; but more interesting to Jasmine's lonely mood were the small back gardens immediately below the parapet on either side, from which the faintly acrid perfume of late summer flowers came up mingled with beefy smells from the various windows of the small houses beyond, where the shadowy inmates were eating their Sunday dinners. She felt that if this were Italy a friendly hand would be beckoning to her from one of those windows an invitation to join the party, and it was with another grudge against England that she sat down alone on a municipal bench to eat from a triangular cardboard box six triangular ham sandwiches. The restless alchemy of nature had set to work to change the essences of the container and the contents, so that the sandwiches tasted more like cardboard and the cardboard felt more like sandwiches; no doubt it would even have tasted more like sandwiches if Jasmine had eaten the box, which she might easily have done, for her taste had been blunted by the long journey, and she would have chewed ambrosia as mechanically had ambrosia been offered to her. The sandwiches finished, she ate half a dozen plums, the stones of which dropped on the path and joined the stones of other plums eaten by other people on the same bench that morning. Jasmine's mind went swooping back over the journey, past the bright azure lakes of Savoy, past the stiff and splendid *carabinieri* at the frontier, pausing for a moment to play hide-and-seek with olives and sea through the tunnels of the *riviera di levante* ... and then swooped down, down more swiftly until it reached the island of Sirene, from which it had been torn not yet four full days ago; the while Jasmine's foot was arranging the plum stones and a few loose pebbles into first an S and then an I and then a decrepit R, until they exhausted themselves over an absurdly elongated E.

The weathercock of the nearest church steeple found enough wind on this hot afternoon to indicate waveringly that what wind there was blew from the South. Some lines of Christina Rossetti often quoted by her father expressed, as only remembered poetry and remembered scents can, the inexpressible:

To see no more the country half my own,
Nor hear the half-familiar speech,
Amen, I say; I turn to that bleak North
Whence I came forth—
The South lies out of reach.
But when our swallows fly back to the South,
To the sweet South, to the sweet South,
The tears may come again into my eyes,
On the old wise,
And the sweet name to my mouth.

She evoked the last occasion at which she had heard her father murmur these lines. They had been dining on the terrace until the last rays of a crimson sunset had faded into a deep starry dusk. Mr. Cazenove had been dining with them, and from the street below a mandolin had decorated with some simple tune memories of bygone years. The two old friends had talked of the lovely peasant girls that haunted the Sirene of their youth, a Sirene not yet spoiled by tourists; an island that in such reminiscence became fabulous like the island of Prospero.

"But the loveliest of them all was Gelsomina," Mr. Cazenove had declared. Jasmine was thrilled when she could listen to such tales about her mother's beauty, that mother who lived for herself only as a figure in one of her father's landscapes, whose image for herself was merged in a bunch of red roses, so that even to this day, by dwelling on that elusive recollection of childhood, the touch of a red rose was the touch of a human cheek, and she could never see one without a thought of kisses.

"Yes, indeed she was! The loveliest of them all," Mr. Cazenove had repeated.

Her father had responded with these lines of Christina Rossetti, and she knew that he was thinking of a fatal journey to England, when the unparagoned Gelsomina had caught cold and died in Paris of pneumonia on the way North to attend the death of Grandfather Grant.

And now her father was dead too.

In a flood of woeful recollections the incidents of that fatal day last month overwhelmed her. She felt her heart quicken again with terror; she saw again the countenance of the fisherman who came with Mr. Cazenove to tell her that a squall had capsized the little cutter in the Bay of Salerno, and that the only one drowned was her father. Everybody in Sirene had been sympathetic, and everybody had bewailed her being alone in the world until letters had arrived from uncles and aunts in England to assure her that she should be looked after by them; and then nearly everybody had insisted that she must leave the island as soon as possible and take advantage of their offers. Yet here she was, more utterly alone than ever in this remote city of the North, with only a few letters from people whom she had never seen and for whom she felt that she should never have the least affection. She was penitent as soon as this confession had been wrung from her soul, and penitently she felt in her bag for the letters from the various relatives who had written to assure her that she was not as much alone in the world as this Sunday in York was making her believe.

Among these envelopes there was one that by its size and stiffness and sharp edges always insisted on being read first. There was a crest on the flap and a crest above the address on the blue notepaper.

317 Harley Street, W.,
July 29th.

My dear Jasmine,

Your Uncle Hector and I have decided that it would be best for you to leave Italy at once. Even if your father's finances had left you independent, we should never have consented to your staying on by yourself in such a place as Sirene. Your uncle was astonished that you should even contemplate such a course of action, but as it is, without a penny, you yourself must surely see the impossibility of remaining there. Your plan of teaching English to the natives sounds to me ridiculous, and your plan of teaching Italian to English visitors equally ridiculous. I once had an Italian woman of excellent family to read Dante with Lettice and Pamela during some Easter holidays we once spent in Florence, and I distinctly remember that her bill after three weeks was something under a sovereign. At the time I remember it struck me as extremely moderate, but I did not then suppose that a niece of mine would one day seriously contemplate earning a living by such teaching. No, the proper course for you is to come to England at once. Your uncle has received a letter from the lawyer (written, by the way, in most excellent English, a proof that if the local residents wish to learn English they can do so already) to say that when the furniture, books, and clothes belonging to your father have been sold, there will probably be enough to pay his debts, and I know it will be a great satisfaction to you to feel that. The cost of your journey to England your Uncle Hector is anxious to pay himself, and the lawyer has been instructed to make the necessary arrangement about your ticket. You will travel second class as far as London, and from London to Spaborough, where we shall be spending August, you had better travel third. The lawyer will be sent enough money to telegraph what day we may expect you. Grant, Strathspey House, Spaborough, is sufficient address. We have had a great family council about your future, and I know you will be touched to hear how anxious all your uncles and aunts have been to help you. But your Uncle Hector has decided that for the present at any rate you had better remain with us. How lucky it is that you should be arriving just when we shall be in a bracing seaside place like Spaborough, for after all these years in the South you must be sadly in need of a little really good air. Besides, you will find us all in holiday mood, just what you require after the sad times through which you have passed. Later on, when we go back to town, I daresay I shall be able to find many little ways in which you can be useful to me, for naturally we do not wish you to feel that we are encouraging you to be lazy, merely because we do not happen to approve of your setting up for yourself as a teacher of languages. By the way, your uncle is not Dr. Grant any longer. Indeed he hasn't been Dr. Grant for a long time.Didn't your father tell you even when he was knighted? But he is now a baronet, and you should write to him as Sir Hector Grant, Bt. Not Bart. Your uncle dislikes the abbreviation Bart. And to me, of course, as Lady Grant, not Mrs. Grant.

Love from us all,
Your affectionate
Aunt May.

The few tears that Jasmine let fall upon the blue notepaper were swallowed up in the rivulets of the watermark. Although she was on her way to meet this uncle and aunt and to be received by them as one of the family, she felt more lonely than ever, and hurriedly laying the envelope beside her on the bench, she dipped into the bag for another letter.

The Cedars,
North End Road,
Hampstead,
July 22nd.

Dear Jasmine,

I had intended to write you before on the part of Uncle Eneas and myself to say how shocked we were at the thought of your being left all alone in the world. Your Aunt May writes to me that for the present at any rate you will be with her, which will be very nice for you, because the honour which has just been paid to the family by making your Uncle Hector a baronet will naturally entail a certain amount of extra entertaining. I am only afraid that after such a merry household The Cedars will seem very dull, but Uncle Eneas has a lot of interesting stories about the Near East, and if you are fond of cats you will have plenty to do. We are great cat people, and I shall be glad to have someone with me who is really fond of them, as I hope you are. It is quite the country where we live in Hampstead, and the air is most bracing, as no doubt you know. I wonder if you ever studied massage?

Love from us both,
Your affectionate
Aunt Cuckoo.

Jasmine tried to remember what her father had said at different times about his second brother, but she could only recall that once in the middle of a conversation about Persian rugs he had said to Mr. Cazenove, "I have a brother in the East, poor chap," and that when Mr. Cazenove had asked him where, he had replied, "Constantinople or Jerusalem—some well-known place. He's in the consular service. Or he was." He had not seemed to be much interested in his brother's whereabouts or career. And then he had added meditatively, "He married a woman with a ridiculous name, poor creature. She was the daughter of somebody or other somewhere in the East." But her father was always vague like that about everything, and he always said "poor chap" about every man and "poor creature" about every woman. He had a kind and generous disposition, and therefore he felt everybody was to be pitied. Jasmine wished now that she had asked more about Uncle Eneas and Aunt Cuckoo. Cuckoo! Yes, it was a ridiculous name. Such a ridiculous name that it sounded as remote from reality as Rumplestiltzkin. No girl, however large the quantity of flax she must spin into gold before sunrise, could have guessed Aunt Cuckoo.

To-day I brew, to-morrow I bake,
And to-morrow the King's daughter I shall take,
For no one from wheresoever she came
Could guess that Aunt Cuckoo was my name.

Jasmine was feeling that she ought not to be laughing at her father's relatives like this so soon after he had died, when suddenly she woke up to the fact that they were just as much, even more, her relatives too. It was like waking up on Monday morning during the year in which she was sent to school with the Sisters of the Seven Dolours in Naples and could only come back to Sirene for the week-ends. With a shudder she placed Aunt Cuckoo on the bench and picked up Aunt Mildred.

> 23 The Crescent,
> Curtain Wells,
> July 20th.

My dear Jasmine,
Uncle Alec and I were terribly shocked to hear of your father's accident. Only a few weeks before I was suggesting a little visit to Rome, a place which Uncle Alec knows very well indeed, for he was military attaché there for six months in 1904, and was rather surprised that your father never took the trouble to come and visit him. Unfortunately, however, His Serene Highness was not well enough to make the journey this spring. Of course you know that for some time now Prince Adalbert of Pomerania has been living with us. You will like him so much when you pay us your visit. He is as simple as a child. We thought at first that he might be difficult to manage, but he has been no trouble and when the Grand Duke graciously entrusted his son to our keeping without an A.D.C., it was quite easy, because it left us a spare room. Baron Miltzen, the Chamberlain, runs over occasionally to see how the Prince is getting on, but the Grand Duchess, who never forgets that she was an English princess, prefers to make her younger son as English as possible, and will not allow any German doctors to interfere with the treatment prescribed by your Uncle Hector. Of course the poor boy will never be well enough to take an active part in the affairs of his country, and as he is not the heir, there is not much opposition in Pomerania to his being educated abroad. Indeed Baron Miltzen said to me only the last time he ran over that he thought an English education was probably the best in the world for anyone as simple as the dear Prince. If we cannot get away to the Riviera this winter you will have to pay us a visit and help to keep the Prince amused. We have dispensed with ceremony almost entirely, because we found that it excited the Prince too much. In fact it was finally decided to entrust him to us, because after the first levee he attended the poor fellow always wanted to walk backwards, and it took us quite a little time to cure him of this habit.

> *Love from us both,*
> *Your affectionate*
> *Aunt Mildred.*

Indeed Jasmine had heard about the Prince, because her father always told everybody he met that one of his brothers had been fool enough to take charge of a royal lunatic. She remembered thinking that he seemed proud of the fact, and she could never understand why, particularly as he spoke so contemptuously of his brother's part in the association. "Here's pleasant news," her father used to say, "my brother the Colonel has turned himself into a court flunkey. That's a pretty position for a Grant! Yes, yes.... He's taken charge of Prince Adalbert of Pomerania, the second son of the Grand Duke of Pomerania. You remember, who married Princess Caroline, the Duke of Gloucester's third daughter? I'm ashamed of my brother. I suppose he had to accept, though; I know it's hard to get out of these things when you mix yourself up with royalty. I really believe that I'm the only independent member of the family—the only one who can call his life his own."

Jasmine quickly took out Aunt Ellen's letter, lest she should seem to be criticizing her dead father by thinking any more about Prince Adalbert.

> The Deanery,
> Silchester,
> *July 21st.*

My dear Jasmine,
When your Uncle Arnold, wrote to you about your father's sad death, he forgot to add an invitation to come and stay with us later on. Now your Aunt May writes to me that it is definitely decided that you should come to England, and your six boy cousins are most eager to make your acquaintance. I say "boy" cousins, but alas! some of them are very much young men these days. I fear we are all growing old, though your poor father might have expected to live many more years if he had not been so imprudent. But even as a boy he was always catching cold through standing about sailing boats in the Round Pond when your grandfather was Vicar of St. Mary's, Kensington. However, we must not repine. God's wisdom is often hidden from us, and we must trust in His fatherly love. I wonder if you have learnt any typewriting? Uncle Arnold so dislikes continuous changes in his secretaries, and his work seems to increase every year. He only intended to do a short history of England before the Norman Conquest, but the more he goes on, the further he goes back, and if you were at all interested in Saxon life I do think it would be worth your while to see if you liked

typewriting. Ethelred has been learning it in the morning instead of practising the piano, but he does not seem to want to make a great deal of progress. It's so difficult to understand what children want sometimes. I suppose our Heavenly Father feels the same about all of us. When I am tempted to blame Ethelred I remember this. Of course as a Roman Catholic you have not been taught a very great deal about God, but we are all His children, and you must not grieve too much over your loss. "Not lost but gone before," you must say to yourself. I remember you every night in my prayers.

Your loving
Aunt Ellen.

Jasmine was asking herself how to set about learning to typewrite, and making resolutions to check a faint inclination to regret that she had so many rich relatives anxious to help her, when the languid puffs of air from the South swelled suddenly into a real wind and blew all the paper on the bench up into the air and down again into one of the little back gardens below the parapet—all the paper, that is, except Lady Grant's blue envelope, which even a gale could scarcely have disturbed.

Jasmine, brought up in Sirene, was not accustomed to conceal her feelings in the way that a well-educated English girl would have known how to conceal them. The loss of the letters dismayed her, and she showed as much by climbing on the parapet of the wall and gazing down into the garden below.

At that moment a much freckled young man with what is called sandy hair came along, and without looking to see if he was observed immediately scrambled up beside her. Even a Sunday school teacher on his way to class might have been forgiven for doing as much; but this young man was evidently nothing of the kind. Indeed, with his grey flannel trousers and Norfolk jacket, he imparted to the atmosphere of Sunday a distinct whiff of the previous afternoon; standing up there beside Jasmine, he looked like a golfer who had lost his ball.

"What have you dropped? A hairpin?" he asked.

Jasmine could not help laughing at the notion of bothering about a hairpin, and she pointed to Mrs. Eneas Grant's letter nestling among the branches of a sunflower; to where Mrs. Alexander Grant's invitation to amuse Prince Adalbert of Pomerania twitched nervously on the neat gravel path; and to where Mrs. Lightbody's suggestions, ghostly and practical, clung for a moment to a drain-pipe, before they collapsed into what was left on a broken plate of the cat's dinner.

The twelve-foot drop into the garden below was nothing: the young man accomplished it with an enthusiastic absence of hesitation. To gather up the letters was the labour of a minute. But to get back again was impossible, because the owner of the house, disgusted by the untidiness of Roman and mediæval masonry, had repaired and pointed that portion of the wall which bounded his garden.

"There isn't one niche for your foot," murmured Jasmine, almost tenderly solicitous.

"I must ring the bell and borrow a ladder," said the stranger. After a moment's search he announced in an indignant voice that the house apparently did not possess a bell.

A man in shirt sleeves, interrupted at the second or third of his forty Sabbath winks, leaned out of an upper window and asked Jasmine what she thought she was doing jibbering and jabbering on his garden wall; before she had time to explain, he perceived the young man in the garden, and asked him what he thought he was doing havering and hovering about among his flowers.

"I was looking for the bell."

"Bell! You long-legged fool! What d'you think I should keep a bell in my back garden for, when the children won't let the bells in front have a moment's peace?" Then he made a noise like a dog shut in a door. "Ough! Take your great feet out of my petunias, can't you! If I want my flowers trampled on, I can get a steam-roller to do it. I don't want your help."

"This lady dropped something in your garden," the young man explained, and the owner smiled bitterly.

"Aye," he went on, "that's what they all say. Please, mister, our Amy's dropped her damned doll in your garden, can she come round and fetch it back? It's like living in a dustbin. A scandal, that's what I say it is. A public scandal."

Then began one of those long arguments in which people roused from sleep seem to delight, provided always that they have been sufficiently roused to feel that it is not worth while going to sleep again. What occurred to lead up to the trespass was swept away as having occurred while the owner was still asleep; no amount of explanation as to why the young man was in his back garden was of any avail; no suggestions as to how he was to get out of it had any effect; and the argument might have continued until the 4.42 train from York to Spaborough had left the station, if in some inner room a child's voice had not begun to sing to the accompaniment of a harmonium:

There is a green hill far away
Without a city wall

"Aye, you silly little fool, that's right! Sing that now! It's a pity your dad doesn't live on a green hill without a city wall, and not in York."

The young man, who by this time had been rendered as argumentative as the owner, remarked that 'without' meant 'outside.'

"What's it matter what it means, if there wasn't a city wall?" retorted the owner, and vanished from the window before the young man could reply. From inside one of the rooms there was a fresh murmur of argument, which lasted until a noise between a moan and a thud was followed by a silence faintly broken by sobs. The slamming down of the lid of the harmonium had evidently relieved the feelings of the man in shirt sleeves, for when presently he came out into the

283

garden and found himself at close quarters with the intruder, he became genial and talkative, and began to point out the superiority of his dahlias.

"I reckon they're grand, I do," he said. "Like cauliflowers. Only, of course, cauliflowers wouldn't have the colour, would they?"

"Not if they were fresh," the young man agreed.

And then he began flatteringly to smell one of the dahlias. He seemed to be attributing to the flower as much importance as he would have attributed to a baby; it was easier to deal with a dahlia, because the dahlia did not dribble, although had it really been a baby, its mother would have been much more annoyed at its being smelt like this than was the man in shirt sleeves, who laughed and said:

"I wouldn't bother about the smell if I was you. Dahlia's don't have any smell. Size is what a dahlia's for."

"No, I was thinking it was a rose," the young man explained apologetically. The incident which had begun so rudely was ended, and except for the unseen child practising its little hymn, was ended harmoniously. The young man was taken through the house and conducted along the street as far as the next ingress to the walls. When he met Jasmine coming towards him, he felt as if he had known her for a long time, and that they were meeting like this by appointment.

"Well, that's finished," said the young man, after Jasmine had put the letters safely back in her bag. He eyed for a moment her black clothes.

"I suppose you're going to Sunday-school and all that?" he ventured.

"No, I'm just walking round the walls."

"Curious coincidence! So was I."

"Waiting for a train," she went on.

"Still more curious! So am I."

"Waiting for the 4.42."

"The final touch!" he cried. "So am I. Let's wait in unison."

They moved across to a circular bench set in an embrasure of the walls, overgrown here with ivy from which the sun drew forth a faint dusty scent. On this bench they sat down to exchange more coincidences. To begin with, they discovered that they were both going to Spaborough; soon afterward that they were both going to stay with uncles; and, as if this were not enough, that both these uncles were baronets, which even with the abnormal increase of baronets lately was, as the young man said, the most remarkable coincidence of all.

"And what's your name?" Jasmine asked.

"Harry."

She felt like somebody who had been offered as a present an object in which nothing but politeness had led her to express an interest.

"I meant your other name," she said quickly, rejecting as it were the offer of the more intimate first name.

"Vibart. My uncle is Sir John Vibart."

"Of course, how stupid of me," Jasmine murmured with a blush. "My name's Grant, of course," she hastened to add.

"Sir Hector Grant," the young man went on musingly. "Isn't he some kind of a doctor?"

"A nerve specialist," said Jasmine.

"I know," said the young man in accents that combined wisdom with sympathy.

The discovery of the baronets had removed the last trace of awkwardness which, easy though his manners were, was more perceptible in Mr. Vibart than in Jasmine, who in Sirene had never had much impressed upon her the sacred character of the introduction.

"I shall come and call on you at Spaborough," he vowed.

"Of course," she agreed; people called with much less excuse than this in Sirene.

"We might do some sailing."

She clapped her hands with such spontaneous pleasure of anticipation that Mr. Vibart remarked how easy it was to see that she had lived abroad. But almost before the echo of her pleasure had died away her eyes had filled with tears, for she was thinking how heartless it was of her to rejoice at the prospect of sailing when it was sailing that had caused her father's death. Anxious not to hurt Mr. Vibart's feelings, Jasmine began to explain breathlessly why she was looking so sad. The young man was silent for a minute when she stopped; then, weighing his words in solemn deliberation, he said:

"And, of course, that's why you're wearing black."

Jasmine nodded.

"I've brought with me all that were left of father's pictures. For presents, you know." She sighed.

"I know," said the young man wisely. He had in his own valise a cigar-holder for Sir John Vibart, the expense of procuring which he hoped would be more than covered by a parting cheque.

"And I should like to show them to you," Jasmine went on. "Perhaps we could get one out and look at it in the train."

"Hadn't we better wait until I come and call?" he suggested. "It's not fair to look at things in the train. Trains wobble so, don't they?"

Conversation about Sholto Grant's pictures passed easily into conversation about Jasmine's mother, because nearly all the pictures had been of her.

"She was a beautiful *contadina*, you know," Jasmine shyly told him.

Mr. Vibart, who supposed that her shyness was due to an attempt to avoid giving an impression of snobbishness in thus announcing the nobility of her ancestry, asked of what she was *contadina*. Jasmine, delighted at his mistake, laughed gaily.

"*Contadina* means country girl. Her name was Gelsomina, and she was the most beautiful girl in the island. Everybody wanted to paint her."

Mr. Vibart, struggling in the gulf between a baronet's niece and an artist's model had nothing to say, but he made up his mind to ask his uncle something about Italy. It was always difficult to find anything to talk about with the old gentleman; Italy as a topic ought to last through the better part of two bottles of Burgundy.

"And what's your name?" he asked at last.

"I was called after my mother."

"Oh, you were? Well, would you mind telling me your mother's name again, because I lost the last dozen letters?"

"Gelsomina—only I was always called Jasmine, which is the English for it."

As she spoke, all the bells in York began to ring at once, from the mastiff booming in York Minster to the rusty little cur yapping in a Methodist chapel close to where they were sitting, and with such gathering insistence in their clamour as to destroy the pleasure of these sunlit reminiscences.

"I suppose we ought to have a look at the Minster," Mr. Vibart suggested in the tone of voice in which he would have announced that he must open the door to a pertinacious caller. "Of course I'm not exactly dressed for Sunday afternoon service, but you're all right. Black's always all right for Sunday."

Jasmine's conception of going to church had nothing to do with dressing up, but it did seem to her extraordinary to go to church at this hour of the day. However, the evidence of the bells was unmistakable, and without a qualm she followed her companion's lead.

The strangeness of the hour for service was only matched by the strangeness of the congregation assembled for worship and the astonishing secularity of the interior. She could remember nothing as solemn and gloomy since she and her father had made a mistake in the time of the performance at the San Carlo Opera House in Naples and had arrived an hour early. She did not recognize the smell of immemorial respectability, and it almost choked her after the frank odours in the Duomo of Sirene—those frank odours of candles, perspiration, garlic, incense, and that indescribable smell which the skin of the newly peeled potato shares with the skin of the newly washed peasant. She did not think that the mighty organ, booming like a tempestuous midnight in Sirene, was anything but a reminder of the terrors of hell, and as a means of turning the mind toward heavenly contemplation she compared it most unfavourably with the love scenes of Verdi's operas that in Sirene provided a tremulous comment upon the mysteries being enacted at the altar. If there had been a sound of sobbing, she could have thought that she was attending a requiem; but, however melancholy the appearance of the worshipping women around, they were evidently enjoying themselves, and, what was surely the most extraordinary of all, actually taking part in the distant business of the priests, bobbing and whispering and mumbling as if they were priests themselves.

"I think I can smell dead bodies," said Jasmine to her companion.

Mr. Vibart was probably not a religious young man himself, but he had already affronted the religious sense of his neighbours by presenting himself before Almighty God in grey flannel trousers and a Norfolk jacket, and he was not anxious positively to flout it by letting Jasmine talk in church. People in the pews close at hand turned round to see what irreverent voice had interrupted their devotion, and Mr. Vibart tried to pretend that her remark had a religious bearing by offering her a share of his Prayer Book. This was too much for Jasmine. To stand up in front of the world holding half a book seemed to her as much an offence against church etiquette as when once long ago at school she had quarrelled with another little girl over the ownership of a rosary and they had tugged against each other until the rosary broke in a shower of tinkling shells upon the floor of the convent chapel.

The best solution of the situation was to go out, and out she went, followed by Mr. Vibart, who looked as uncomfortable as a man would look in leaving a stall in the middle of the row during Madame Butterfly's last song.

"I say, you know, you oughtn't to have done that," he murmured reproachfully.

"Done what?"

"Well, talked loudly like that, and then gone out in the middle of the service. Everybody stared at us like anything."

"Well, why did you joke with that Prayer Book?"

"I wasn't joking with the Prayer Book," Mr. Vibart affirmed in horror.

An emotion akin to dismay invaded Jasmine's soul. If she could so completely misunderstand this not at all alarming, this freckled and benevolent young man, how was she ever to understand her English relatives? She had been sufficiently depressed by England throughout the journey, but it was only now that she grasped what a profound difference it was going to make to be herself only half English. She was evidently going to misunderstand everything and everybody. Serious things were going to seem jokes, and, what was worse, real jokes would seem serious. She should offend with and in her turn be offended by trifles.

"I'm sorry," she said to Mr. Vibart. "You see, it was quite different from everything to which I've been accustomed all my life. Oh, do let's go and have an ice."

"Rather, if we can find a sweet-shop open."

Incomprehensible country, where ices were found in sweet-shops, and where sweet-shops were closed on Sunday! Jasmine gave it up. However, they did find a sweet-shop open, where she ate what tasted like a pat of butter frozen in an old box of soap, cost fourpence, and was called a vanilla ice-cream. She criticized it all the time she was eating it, and then found to her mortification that Mr. Vibart supposed that he should pay for it.

285

"In Sirene," Jasmine protested, "we all go and have ices when we have money, but we always pay for ourselves. And if I'd thought that you were going to pay, I should have pretended I thought it was very good."

The argument lasted a long time with illustrations and comparisons taken from life at Sirene, which were so vividly related that Mr. Vibart announced his intention of going there as soon as possible. Jasmine was so much gratified by her conversion of an Englishman that she surrendered about the payment for the ice, and when they got back to the station she allowed him to manage everything. It was certainly much easier. The surly cloak-room clerk handled the picture crates as tenderly as a child, and even said "upsi-daisy" when he delivered them back into their owner's possession. As for the porter with one hand he trundled his barrow along like a jolly hoop.

"I say, let's travel First," Mr. Vibart proposed, apparently the prey to a sudden and irresistible temptation towards extravagance.

"My ticket is third class," Jasmine objected.

"I know, so's mine," he said mysteriously. "But they know me on this line."

And by the way the porter and the cloak-room clerk and the guard and a small boy selling chocolates all smiled at him, Jasmine felt sure that he was telling the truth.

The journey from York to Spaborough took about two hours and a half, and the bloom of dusk lay everywhere on the green landscape before they arrived. For the first half Jasmine had been contented and gay, but now toward the end she fell into a pensive twilight mood, so that when at last Mr. Vibart broke the long silence by announcing "Next station is Spaborough" she was very near to weeping. She did not suppose that she should ever see again this companion of a few hours. She realized that she had served to while away for a time the boredom of his Sunday afternoon; but, of course, he would forget about her. Already with what a ruthlessly cheerful air he was reaching up to the rack for his luggage.

"What are those funny tools in that bag?" she asked.

"Those?" he laughed. "Those are golf clubs."

Jasmine looked no wiser.

"Haven't you ever played golf?"

"Is it a game?"

He nodded, and she sighed. How could a man who carried about with him on his travels a game be expected to remember herself? But it would never do for her to let him think that she considered his remembering her of the least importance one way or the other. Jasmine's knowledge of human nature was based upon the aphorisms in circulation among the young women of Sirene, few of which did not insist on the fact that to men the least eagerness in the opposite sex was distasteful. Jasmine had all the Latin love of a generalization, all the Latin distrust of the exception that tried its accuracy.

"I'll be very cold with him," she decided. But her coldness was tempered by sweetness, and if Mr. Vibart had ever tasted a really good ice-cream, he might have compared Jasmine with one when she said good-bye to him on the Spaborough platform.

"But isn't there anybody to meet you?" he asked, looking round.

"It doesn't matter. Please don't bother any more about me. I'm sure I've been enough of a bother already."

At that moment she caught sight of a chaise driven by a postilion in an orange jacket.

"Oh, I should like to ride in that!"

"But your people have probably sent a carriage."

"No, no!" Jasmine cried. "Let me ride in that," and before Mr. Vibart could persuade her to wait one minute while he enquired if any of the waiting motor-cars or carriages were intended for Miss Jasmine Grant, she had packed herself in and was waiting open-armed for the porter to pack her trunk in opposite.

"I shall see you again," Mr. Vibart prophesied confidently.

"Perhaps," she murmured. "Thank you for helping me at York. Drive to Strathspey House, South Parade," she told the postilion.

Then she blushed because she fancied that Mr. Vibart might suppose that she had called out the address so loudly for his benefit. She did not look round again, therefore, but watched the orange postilion jogging up and down in front, and the street lamps coming out one by one as the lamp-lighters went by with their long poles.

Chapter Two

THE origin of the house of Grant, like that of many another Scots family, is lost in the Scotch mists of antiquity. The particularly thick mist that obscured the origin of that branch of the family to which Jasmine belonged did not disperse until early in the nineteenth century, when the figure of James Grant, who began life nebulously as an under-gardener in the establishment of the sixth Duke of Ayr, emerged well-defined as a florist and nursery gardener in the Royal Borough of Kensington. The rhetorical questioning of the claims of aristocracy implied in the couplet:

When Adam delved, and Eve span
Who was then the gentleman?

was peculiarly appropriate to this branch, for Jamie, besides being a gardener himself, married the daughter of a Lancashire weaver called Jukes, who later on invented a loom and, what is more, profited by his talent. Although Jamie Grant's rapid rise was helped by the success of old Mr. Jukes' invention, he had enough talent of his own to take full advantage of the capital that his wife brought him on the death of her father; in fact by the year 1837 Jamie was as reputable as any florist in the United Kingdom. A legend in the family said that on the fine June morning when Archbishop Howley and Lord Chamberlain Conyngham rode from the death-bed of William IV at Windsor to announce to the little Princess in Kensington Palace her accession, the Archbishop begged a bunch of sweet peas for his royal mistress from old Jamie whose garden was close to the highway. If legend lied, then so did Jamie's son Andrew, who always declared that he was an eye-witness of the incident, and indeed ascribed to it his own successful career. Inasmuch as Andrew Grant died in the dignity of Lord Bishop Suffragan of Clapham, there is no reason to suppose that he was not speaking the truth. According to him the incident did not stop with the impulse of the loyal Archbishop to stand well with his queen on that sunny morning in June, but a few days later was turned into an event by Jamie's sending his son with another bunch of sweet peas to Lambeth Palace and asking his Grace to stand godfather to a splendid purple variety he had just raised. In these days when sweet peas that do not resemble the underclothing of cocottes without the scent are despised, the robust and strong-scented magenta *Archbishop Howley* no longer figures in catalogues; but at this period it was the finest sweet pea on the market. The Archbishop, who was a snob of the first water, liked the compliment; yes, and, anti-papist though he was, he did not object to the suggestion of episcopal violet in the dedication. He also liked young Andrew, and on finding that young Andrew wished to cultivate the True Vine instead of the Virginia creeper, he promised him his help and his patronage. James, who all his life had been applying the principle of selection to flowers, realizing that what could be done with sweet peas could be done equally well with human beings, gave Andrew his blessing, dipped into his wife's stocking, and contributed what was necessary to supplement the sizarship that shortly after this his son won at Trinity College, Cambridge.

Andrew Grant, during his career as a clergyman, was called upon to select with even more discrimination and rigour than his father before him. He had first to make up his mind that the Puseyite party was not going to oust the Evangelical party to which he had attached himself. He had later on to decide whether he should anathematize Darwin or uphold Bishop Colenso, a dilemma which he dodged by doing neither. He had also to choose a wife. He chose Martha Rouncivell, who brought him £1000 a year from slum rents in Sheffield and presented him with five children. Apart from the continual assertions of scurrilous High Church papers that he had ceased to believe in his Saviour, Andrew Grant's earthly life was mercifully free from the bitterness, the envy, and the disillusionment that wait upon success. His greatest grief was when the spiritual power that he fancied was perceptible in his youngest son Sholto, a spiritual power that might carry him to Canterbury itself, turned out to be nothing but an early manifestation of the artistic temperament. But that disappointment was mitigated by his consecration in 1890 as Lord Bishop Suffragan of Clapham, in which exalted rank he guarded London against the southerly onslaughts of Satan even as his brothers of Hampstead, Chelsea, and Bow were vigilant North, West, and East. It was a powerful alliance, for if the Bishop of Hampstead was High, the Bishop of Bow was Low, and if the Bishop of Chelsea was Broad, the Bishop of Clapham was Deep; although he preferred to characterize himself as Square.

When Archdeacon Grant was consecrated, he had to find a suitable episcopal residence, and this was not at all easy to find in South London. At last, however, he secured the long lease of a retired merchant's Gothic mansion on Lavender Hill, which after three years of fervid Lenten courses was secured to Holy Church by three appeals to the faithful rich. As soon as the Bishop was firmly installed in Bishop's House, he who had observed with displeasure the number of empty shields in the roll of Suffragan Bishops in Crockford's clergy list, applied for a grant of arms. He came from an old Scots family, and he felt strongly on the subject of coat-armour. When he first went up to Cambridge he had interested himself in heraldry to such purpose that he had been convinced of old Jamie's right to the three antique crowns of the House of Grant. And though the old boy said he should think more of three new half-crowns, he offered to use them as his trade-mark if Andrew really hankered after them. Andrew discouraged the proposed sacrilege, but all the way up from curate to vicar, from vicar to rural dean, from rural dean to archdeacon, from archdeacon to suffragan bishop, he did hanker after them, for the shadows of mighty ancestors loomed immense upon that impenetrable Scotch mist. When his eldest son was born, instead of calling him Matthew after his wife's brother, a safe candidate for future wealth, he called him Hector, because Hector was a fine old Scottish name, and most unevangelically he christened the three sons who followed Eneas, Alexander, and Sholto. When he became a bishop, he was more Caledonian than ever; perhaps the apron reminded him of the kilt. With his empty shield in Crockford's staring at him he went right out for the three antique crowns and applied to Lyon Court for a confirmation of these arms. His mortification may be imagined when he was informed that he was actually not armigerous at all, and that the coat which he proposed to wear, of course with a difference, was not his to wear. It was useless for the Bishop to claim, like Joseph, that the coat had been given to him by his father. The Reubens, Dans, and Naphtalis of the house of Grant were not going to put up with it; the three antique crowns were disallowed. For a while the Bishop pretended to exult in his empty shield. After all, he might hope to become a real bishop and contemplate one day the arms of the see against his name; in any case he felt that his mind should be occupied with a heavenly crown. But the ancestral ghosts haunted him; he could not bear the thought of Crockford's coming out year by year with that empty shield, and at last he applied for arms that should be all his own. On his suggestion Lyon granted him *Or, three chaplets of peaseblossom purpure, slipped and leaved vert;* but when for crest the Bishop demanded *A Bible displayed proper*, even that was disallowed, because another branch of the Grants had actually appropriated the Bible in the days of Queen Anne. "Then I will have the Book of Common Prayer displayed proper," said the Bishop. And the Book of Common Prayer he got, together with the Gaelic motto *Suas ni bruach*, which neither he nor his descendants ever learnt to pronounce properly, though they always understood that it meant something like *Excelsior*.

With such a motto it was not surprising that Sholto Grant's refusal to climb should upset his relations. Old Jamie must have dealt with many throwbacks when he was selecting his sweet peas; but it is improbable that any of them refused to climb at all, and though there is now a variety inappropriately called "Cupid" with scarcely more ambition than moss, these dwarfs have a commercial value. Sholto Grant had no commercial value. Sholto indeed had so little sense of profit that he actually failed to arrive in time to see his father die, and if the old gentleman's paternal instinct had not been much developed by his episcopate, and if he had not imbibed every evangelical maxim on the subject of forgiveness, he would probably have cut Sholto off with a shilling. As it was, he divided his money equally between his five children, and it can be readily imagined how indignant Hector, Eneas, and Alexander, who had all married well, had all worked hard to justify the family motto, and not one of whom could count on less than £2000 a year, felt on finding that the £20,000; which was all that the Bishop of Clapham's devotion to the Gospel had allowed him to leave to his family, was to be robbed of £4000 for Sholto, who had married an Italian peasant girl and spent his whole life painting unsaleable pictures in the island of Sirene. "Besides," as they acutely said, "Sholto does not appreciate money. He will only go and spend it." And spend it Sholto did, much to the disgust of his brothers, Sir Hector Grant, Bart., K.C.V.O., C.B.; Eneas Grant, Esq., C.M.G.; Lieutenant-Colonel Alexander Grant, D.S.O.; and even of his sister, Mrs. Arnold Lightbody, the wife of the Very Reverend the Dean of Silchester. Thus far had they climbed in the ten years that succeeded the Bishop of Clapham's death. Perhaps if they had reached such altitudes ten years before they might have been more willing to share with Sholto; but Dr. Grant of Harley Street, Mr. Grant of the Levant Consular Service, Captain Grant of the Duke of Edinburgh's Own Strathspey Highlanders (Banffshire Buffs), and Mrs. Lightbody, the wife of Canon Lightbody, were not far enough up the pea-sticks to neglect such a stimulus to growth as gold. Mrs. Hector, Mrs. Eneas, and Mrs. Alexander had their own grievance, for, as they reasonably asked, what had Sholto's wife contributed to the family ascent? They, who had followed the example set by Miss Jukes and Miss Rouncivell before them, were surely entitled to reproach the unendowed Gelsomina. It seemed so extraordinary too that a bishop should have nothing better to occupy a mind on the brink of eternity than speculating whether his youngest son would arrive in time to see him die. They had never yet observed the death of a prelate, but they could imagine well enough what it ought to be to know that a continental Bradshaw was not the book to prepare for a heavenly journey. And when a double knock sounded on the studded door of Bishop's House, the Bishop had actually sat up in bed, because he thought that it was his youngest son, arrived in time after all. But it was not Sholto, and the old man had had no business to sit up in bed and grab at the telegram like that. *"Wife dying in Paris forgive delay,"* he read out, gasping. After which with a smile he murmured, "Perhaps I shall meet poor Sholto's wife above," and without another word died. It was all very well for the chaplain to fold his arms upon his breast, but the assembled family felt that a bishop ought to have died in the hope of meeting his Maker, not an Italian daughter-in-law of peasant extraction.

During the ten years that had elapsed since then, Sholto had behaved exactly as his family had foreseen that he would behave. He had lost his wife, his money, and then most carelessly his own life, leaving an orphan to be provided for by her relatives. Luckily Sir Hector Grant, because he was the head of the family and because he had climbed a little higher than the rest, was willing to see what could be done with and what could be made of poor Sholto's daughter. Not that the others were slow in coming forward with offers of hospitality. Their letters to Jasmine were a proof of that. But they all felt that Strathspey House was the obvious place for the experiment to begin.

Strathspey House occupied what is called a commanding position on the fashionable South Cliff of Spaborough, looking seaward over the shrubberies of the Spa gardens. Sir Hector Grant had bought it about fifteen years ago, to the relief of the many ladies whom in a professional capacity he had advised to recuperate their nerves at the famous old resort. That trip to Spaborough had become such a recognized formula in his consultations that it would hardly have been decent for Dr. Grant himself to seek anywhere else recreation from his practice. In his Harley Street consulting room a coloured print of the eighteenth century entitled *A Trip to Spaborough* hung above the green marble clock that had been presented to him by a ruling sovereign for keeping his oldest daughter moderately sane long enough to marry the son of another ruling sovereign, and, what is more, cheat an heir presumptive with an heir apparent. In the caricaturist's representation a line of monstrously behooped and bewigged ladies and of gentlemen with bulbous red noses stood upon a barren cliff gazing at the sea. "Even in those days," Dr. Grant used to murmur, "you see, my dear lady ... yes ... even in those days ... but of course it's not quite like that now. No, it's—not—quite—like—that—now." The neurasthenic lady would certainly have made the prescribed trip even if it had been; but before she could express her complete subservience Dr. Grant would go on: "Air ... yes, precisely ... that's what you require ... air!... plenty of good—fresh—air! Bathing? Perhaps. That we shall have to settle later on. Yes, a little—later—on." And Dr. Grant's patients were usually so much braced up by their visit that they would begin telegraphing to him at all hours of the day and night to find out the precise significance of various symptoms unnoticed before the cure began to work its wonders.

But the claims of exigent ladies were not the only reason that determined Dr. Grant to acquire a house at the seaside. As a prophylactic against his two daughters', Lettice and Pamela, ever reaching the condition in which the majority of his female patients found themselves, their mother, who had an even keener instinct than her husband for the mode, suggested that he should build a house in the country, choosing a design that could be added to year by year as his fame and fortune increased. But when Mrs. Grant suggested building, the doctor replied, "Fools, May, build houses for wise men to live in," and forthwith bought Strathspey House to conclude the discussion. In this case the fool was a Huddersfield manufacturer whose fortunes had collapsed in some industrial earthquake and left him saddled with a double-fronted, four-storied, porticoed house, in which he had planned to meditate for many years on a successful business career put behind him. Actually he spent his declining years in a small boarding-house on the unfashionable north side of Spaborough, where he existed in a miserable obscurity, except as often as he could persuade a fellow-pensioner to walk with him all the way up to South Parade for the purpose of admiring the exterior of the house that had once been his—a habit, by the way, that vexed the new owner extremely, but for which, under the laws of England, he could discover no satisfactory remedy.

It is scarcely necessary to add that the Huddersfield manufacturer never called it Strathspey House. That was Dr. Grant's way of saying "My heart's in the Highlands a-chasing the deer," for it was down the dim glens of Strathspey that the prehistoric Grants had hunted in the mists of antiquity.

Although Mrs. Grant had never tried to persuade her husband into anything like the baronial castle that would have so well become him, she had never ceased to protest against a country seat in a popular seaside resort; but she had to wait fifteen years before she was able to say "I told you so" with perfect assurance that her husband would have to bow his head in acknowledgment of her clearer foresight. The actual date of her triumph was the first of August in the year before Jasmine's arrival, when the very next house in South Parade, separated from Strathspey House by nothing but a yard of sky and a hedge of ragged aucubas, was turned into a boarding-house and actually called Holyrood. Sir Hector Grant, K.C.V.O., C.B., would have found the proximity of a boarding-house irritating enough as he was; but a few months later he was created a baronet, and what had been merely irritating became intolerable. How could he advertise himself in Debrett as Sir Hector Grant, of Strathspey House, Spaborough, when next door was a boarding establishment called Holyrood? And if he described himself as Sir Hector Grant, of Harley Street, Borough of Marylebone, all the flavour would be taken out of the fine old Highland name and title. There was only one course of action. He must change Strathspey House to Balmoral, sell it to another boarding establishment, remove *A Trip to Spaborough* from his consulting room, buy a small glen in Banff or Elgin with a good Gaelic sound to its name, and send his patients to Strathpeffer. Yet after all, why should he bother? He had no male heir. What did it matter if he was Sir Hector Grant, of Harley Street, Borough of Marylebone? Sir Hector Grant, Bt., was good enough for anybody; he need not waste his money on glens. If old Uncle Matthew Rouncivell died soon and left him his fortune, and the old miser owed as much to his nephew's title, he should be able to buy a castle and retire from practice. Meanwhile his business was to make the most of that title while he was alive to enjoy it.

"Yes, perhaps it was a mistake to settle so definitely in Spaborough," he admitted to his wife. "But it's too late to begin building now. You and the girls won't want to keep up an establishment when I'm gone. Extraordinary thing that Ellen"—Ellen was his only sister—"should have six boys. However," he went on hurriedly, "we mustn't grumble."

The result of having no heir was that Sir Hector had to make the most of his title in his own lifetime, and he used to carry it about with him everywhere as a miner carries his gold. Journeys which a long and successful life should have made arduous at fifty-eight were now sweetened by his being able to register himself in hotel books as *Hector Grant, Bart*. Once a malevolent wit added an *S* to the *Bart*, in allusion to the hospital that produced him, and Sir Hector, gloating over the hotel book next morning, was so much shocked that he insisted upon the abbreviation *Bt.* ever afterwards. It was the second time that verbal ingenuity had made free with his titles. For his voluntary services to his country during the Boer war as consulting physician—people used to say that he had been called in to pronounce upon the sanity of the British generals on active service—he was made a Companion of the Bath, and when soon after appeared *Traumatic Neuroses. By Hector Grant, C.B.*, one reviewer suggested that the initials should be put the other way round, so old and out of date were the distinguished doctor's theories.

In appearance Sir Hector was extremely tall, extremely thin, extremely fair, with prominent bright blue eyes and a nodulous complexion. His manner, except with his wife and daughters, was masterful. Old maids spoke of his magnetism: women confided to him their love affairs: girls disliked him. It would be unjust to dispose of his success as lightly as the frivolous and malicious critic mentioned just now. He was not old-fashioned; he did keep abreast of all the Teutonic excursions into the vast hinterland of insanity; even at this period he was clicking his tongue in disapproval of the first stammerings of Freud. He was sensitive to the popular myth that alienists end by going mad themselves, and with that suggestion in view he was on his guard against the least eccentricity in himself or his family. *Mens sana in corpore sano*, he boasted that he had never worn an overcoat in his life.

He was once approached by the proprietors of a famous whisky for permission to put his portrait if not on the bottle at least on the invoice. Although he felt bound to refuse, the compliment to his typically Caledonian appearance pleased him, and now on his holiday, in a suit of homespun with an old cap stuck over with flies, Sir Hector regretted that the necessity for keeping one hand in his patients' pockets prevented his setting more than one foot upon his native heath, and even that one foot only figuratively.

Lady Grant, who had been the only daughter of a retired paper-maker and had brought her husband some two thousand pounds a year, was at fifty a tall fair woman with cheeks that formerly might not unludicrously have been compared to carnations, but which now with their network of little crimson lines were more like picotees. She was one of those women whom it is impossible to imagine with nothing on. Inasmuch as she changed her clothes three times a day, went to bed at night, got up in the morning, and in fact behaved as a woman of flesh and blood does behave, it was obvious that she and her clothes were not really one and indivisible. Yet so solid and coherent were they that if one of her dresses had hurried downstairs after her to say that she had put on the wrong one, it might not have surprised an onlooker with any effect of strangeness. At fifty her best feature was her nose, which of all features is least able to call attention to itself. Women with pretty complexions, women with shapely ankles, women with beautiful hair, women with liquid or luminous eyes, women with exquisite ears, women with lovely mouths, women with good figures, women with snowy arms, women with slim hands, women with graceful necks, all these have a property that bears a steady interest in becoming gestures. Powder-puffs, petticoats, combs, ear-rings, and a hundred other excuses are not wanting; but the only way of calling attention to a nose, at any rate in civilized society, is by blowing it, which, however delicate the laced handkerchief, is never a gesture that adds to the pleasure of the company. Lady Grant could do nothing with her magnificent nose except bring it into profile, and this gave her face a haughty and inattentive expression that made people think that she was unsympathetic. Enthusiasm cannot display itself nasally except among rabbits, and of course elephants. Lady Grant, resembling neither a rabbit nor an elephant, became more impassive than ever at those critical moments which, had she been endowed with good eyes, might have changed her whole character. As it was, her nose just overweighted her face, not with the effect of caricature that a toucan's nose produces, but with the stolidity and complacency of a grosbeak's. She was, for instance, as much gratified to be the wife of a baronet as her husband was to be a baronet itself; that intractable feature of hers turned all the simple pleasure into pompousness. It is true that by calling attention to her daughters' noses she was sometimes able to extract a compliment to her own; but at best this was a vicarious satisfaction, and when one day a stupid woman responded by suggesting that Pamela and Lettice had noses like their father, Lady Grant had to deny herself even this demand on the flattery of her friends, because Sir Hector's nose was hideous, really hideous.

Lady Grant had grumbled a good deal about her niece's arrival; actually she was looking forward to it. Several people had told her how splendid it was of her, and how like her it was to be so ready, and what a wonderful thing it would be for the niece. In fact in the ever-widening circle of her aunt's acquaintance Jasmine had already reached the dimensions of a large charitable organization. For some time Lady Grant had been protecting a poor cousin of her own, a Miss Edith Crossfield, who was so obviously an object for charity that the glory of being kind to her was rather dimmed. Miss Crossfield was so poor and so humble and so worthy that her ladyship would have had to own a heart as impassive as her nose not to have protected her. At first it had been interesting to impress poor Edith; but as time went on poor Edith proved so willing to be impressed by the least action of dear May that it became no longer very interesting to impress her. Moreover, now that she was the wife of a baronet, Lady Grant was not sure that it reflected creditably upon her to have such a poor relation. There was no romance in Edith; to speak bluntly, even harshly, she gave the show away. No, Edith must find herself lodgings somewhere in a nice unfashionable seaside town and be content with a pension. Sholto's existence in Sirene, his romantic and unfortunate marriage, his career as a painter, his death in the Bay of Salerno, such a history added to the family past, and if poor Jasmine would be more expensive than poor Edith, she would be more useful to her aunt, and more useful to darling Lettice and Pamela.

Lady Grant's daughters were tall blondes in their mid-twenties who had always hated each other, and whose hatred had never been relieved by being able to disparage each other's appearance, owing to their both looking exactly alike. They too, perhaps, were fairly pleased at the notion of Jasmine's arrival, because Cousin Edith was no use at all as a contrast to themselves; she merely lay untidily about the house like a duster left behind by a careless maid. Pamela and Lettice wanted to get married well and quickly; but since either was afraid of the other's getting married first, it began to seem as if neither of them would get married at all. Their passion was golf, and it was a pity that the pre-matrimonial methods of savages were not in vogue on the Spaborough links; Lettice and Pamela would have willingly been hit on the head by a suitor's golf club if they could have found themselves married on returning to consciousness. Such was the family to whose bosom Jasmine was being jogged along through the lamp-lit dusk of Spaborough.

It may be easily imagined that Lady Grant, after taking the trouble to send Nuckett with the car to meet her niece's arrival at Spaborough, was not pleased to find that she had driven up to Strathspey House behind an orange postilion.

"Didn't you see Nuckett?" she asked of Jasmine, whose attempt to kiss her aunt had been rather like biting hard on a soft pink sweet and finding nougat or some such adamantine substance within. Jasmine, wondering who Nuckett might be, assured her aunt that she had not seen him.

"Which means that he will wait down there for the 9.38. Hector!" she called to her husband, who was at that moment bending down to salute his niece, "Nuckett will be waiting at the station for the 9.38. What can we do about it?"

Sir Hector recoiled from the kiss, blew out his cheeks, and looked at his niece with the expression he reserved for wantonly hysterical young girls. There ensued a long discussion of the methods of communication with Nuckett, during which Jasmine's spirits, temporarily exhilarated by the ride behind the orange postilion, sank lower than at any point on the journey. Nor were they raised by the entrance of her two cousins, who were looking at her as if one of the servants had upset a bottle of ink which had to be mopped up before they could advance another step. At last the problem of Nuckett's evening was solved by entrusting the postilion with authority to recall him.

"You mustn't bother to dress for dinner to-night," conceded Lady Grant, apparently swept by a sudden gust of benevolence. "Pamela dear, take Jasmine to her room, will you?"

"Do you get much golf in Sirene?" enquired Pamela on the way upstairs.

Jasmine stared at her, or rather she opened wide her eyes in alarm, which had the effect of a stare on her cousin.

"No, I've never played golf."

It was Pamela's turn to stare now in frank horror at this revelation.

"Never played golf?" she repeated. "What did you do at home then?"

"I played picquet sometimes with father."

This was too much for Pamela, who could think of nothing more to say than that this was a chest of drawers and that that was a wardrobe, after which, with a hope for the success of her ablutions, she left Jasmine to herself.

Presently a maid tapped at the door.

"Please, miss, her ladyship would like to know where you would prefer the packing-cases put."

"Oh, couldn't you bring them up here?" Jasmine asked eagerly. "That is, of course," she added, "if it isn't too much trouble."

The maid protested that it would be no trouble at all; but her looks belied her speech.

"And if you could bring them up at once," added Jasmine quickly, "I should be very much obliged."

She had a plan in her head for softening her relatives, the successful carrying out of which involved having the crates in her room. After a few minutes they arrived.

"I'm afraid I can't open them with my umbrella," she said. She was not being facetious, for in her impetuousness she had tried, and broken the umbrella. "I wonder if you could find me a screw-driver?"

"Oh yes, miss, I daresay I could find a screw-driver."

"And a hammer," shouted Jasmine, rushing out of her room to the landing and calling down the stairs to the housemaid.

"I think I shall change my frock all the same," she decided. "Or at any rate I shall unpack; because if I don't unpack now, I shall never unpack."

In order not to lose the inspiration, Jasmine began to unpack with such rapidity that presently the room looked like the inside of a clothes-basket. Then she undressed with equal rapidity, mixing up washed clothes with unwashed clothes in her efforts to find a clean chemise. She found several chemises, but by this time it was impossible to say which or if any of them were clean, and when the housemaid came back with the screw-driver and the hammer, she spoke to her with Southern politeness:

"I say, I wonder if you could lend me a chemise. And, I say, what is your name?"

The housemaid winced at the request; but the traditions of service were too strong for her, and with no more than the last vibrations of a tremor in her voice, she replied:

"Oh yes, miss, I daresay I could find you a chemise. And, please, I'm called Hopkins, miss."

"Yes, but what's your other name?"

"Amanda, miss."

"What a pretty name!"

"Yes, miss," the housemaid agreed after a moment's hesitation. "But it's not considered a suitable name for service, and her ladyship gave orders when I came that I was to be called Hopkins."

"Well, I shall call you Amanda," said Jasmine decidedly. No doubt Hopkins thought that a young lady who was capable of borrowing a chemise from a housemaid was capable of calling her by her Christian name, and since she did not wish to encourage her ladyship's niece to thwart her ladyship's express wishes, she hurried away without replying.

While Hopkins was out of the room Jasmine attacked the crates, tearing them to pieces with her slim, brown, boyish hands as a monkey sheds a coconut. Then she took out the pictures and set them up round the room in coigns of vantage, two or three on the bed, one leaning against the looking-glass, one supported between the jug and the basin, and several more on chairs. This happened in the days before the Germans bombarded Spaborough and destroyed its tonic reputation; but between that date and this no room in Spaborough could have conveyed so completely the illusion of having been bombarded. Yet, as often happens with really untidy people, it is only when they have reduced their surroundings to the extreme of disorder that they begin to know where they are, and as soon as the room was littered with pictures, packing-case wood, and clothes, all jumbled and confused together, Jasmine was able to find not only the clean chemise she required, but all the other requisite articles of attire, so that when Hopkins came back Jasmine was able to wave at her in triumph one of her own chemises.

"Never mind, Amanda; I've found one."

"Oh yes, miss, but please, miss, with your permission I'd prefer you called me Hopkins. I wouldn't like it to be said I was going against her ladyship's wishes in private."

"Well, I like Amanda," persisted Jasmine obstinately.

"Yes, miss, and it's very kind of you to say so, I'm sure, and it would have pleased my mother very much. But her ladyship particularly passed the remark that she had a norror of fancy names, so perhaps you'd be kind enough to call me Hopkins."

"All right," agreed Jasmine, who, having only just arrived at Strathspey House, found it hard to sympathize with such servility. "But look here, the washing-stand's all covered with chips and nails. What shall I do?"

A moral struggle took place in Hopkins' breast, a struggle between the consciousness that dinner must inevitably be ready in five minutes and the consciousness that she ought to show Miss Grant where the bathroom was. In the end cleanliness defeated godliness—for punctuality was the god of Strathspey House—and she proposed a bath.

"Oh, can I have a bath?" cried Jasmine. "How splendid! But you are sure that you can spare the water? Oh, of course, I forgot. This isn't Sirene, is it?"

"No, miss," the housemaid agreed doubtfully. After seeing Jasmine's room security of location had somehow come to mean less to Hopkins; in fact she said, when she got back to the kitchen: "I give you my word, cook, I didn't know where I was."

It was a wonderful bath, and while Sir Hector downstairs kept taking his watch out of his pocket—with every passing minute it slid out more easily—Jasmine spent a quarter of an hour in delicious oblivion. At the end of it, Pamela came tapping at the door to tell her that dinner was ready, if she was. Jasmine was so full of water-warmed feelings that she leaped out of the bath, flung open the door, and all dripping wet and naked as she was assured her cousin that she herself was just ready.

"Is the island of Sirene inhabited by savages?" asked Pamela superciliously when she brought back news to the anxious dining-room.

This was considered a witty remark. Even Lettice smiled, for she already despised her cousin more than she hated her sister.

"And now," said Jasmine to herself when another quarter of an hour had gone by and she was dressed, "and now which picture shall I give them?"

She pulled down the cord of the electric light to illuminate better her choice, pulled it down so far that it would not go up again, but stayed hovering above the billowy floor like a sea-bird about to alight upon a wave. It was easy, or difficult, to choose for presentation one of Sholto Grant's pictures, because in subject and treatment they were all much alike. In every foreground there was a peasant girl among olive trees, in every middle distance olive groves, and in every background the rocks and sea of Sirene. The choice resolved itself into whether you wanted a bunch of anemones, a bunch of poppies, an armful of broom, or a basket of cherries; it was really more like shopping at a greengrocer's than choosing a picture. In the end Jasmine, who by now was herself beginning to feel hungry, chose fruit rather than flowers, and went downstairs with a four-foot square canvas.

"I ought to have warned you that in the country we always dine at half-past seven. It was my fault," said Lady Grant.

Penitence is usually as unconvincing as gratitude, and certainly nobody in the room, from Jasmine to Hargreaves the parlourmaid waiting to announce dinner, supposed for a moment that her ladyship was really assuming responsibility for the long wait.

"I thought perhaps you might like one of father's pictures," Jasmine began.

"Oh dear me ... oh yes," hemmed Lady Grant, who, to do her justice, did not want to hurt her niece's feelings, but who felt that the lusciousness of the scene presented might be too much for her husband's appetite. Sir Hector, craning at the picture, asked what the principal figure was holding in her basket.

"Cherries, aren't they?" suggested Lettice.

"Ah, yes, so they are," her father agreed. "Cherries.... Precisely.... Come, come, we mustn't let the soup get cold. The dessert can wait."

On the wings of a dreary little titter they moved toward the dining-room; Sir Hector, leading the way like a turkey-cock in a farmyard, murmured, whether in pity for the dead brother who could no longer feel hungry or in compassion for his art:

"Poor old Sholto. We must get it framed."

Chapter Three

JASMINE woke up next morning to a vivid acceptance of the fact that from now onward her life would not be her own. She had been too weary the night before to grasp fully what this meant. Now, while she lay watching the sun streaming in through the blind, the value of the long fine day before her was suddenly depreciated. On an impulse to defeat misgiving she jumped out of bed, sent up the blind with a jerk that admitted Monday morning to her room like a jack-in-the-box, stared out over the wide expanse of pale blue winking sea, sniffed the English seaside odour, clambered up on her dressing-table to disentangle the blind, failed to do so, descended again, and began to wonder how she should occupy herself from six o'clock to nine. And after the long morning, what a day stretched before her! A little talk with Uncle Hector about her father, a little talk with Aunt May on the same subject, a lesson in golf from her cousins, and, worst of all, the heavy foundation stones of the threatened intimacy between her and Miss Crossfield to be placed in position.

"We must get to know each other very well," Miss Crossfield had murmured when she said good night. "We must pull together."

And this had been said with such a gloating anticipation of combined effort and with such a repressed malignity beneath it all that if Miss Crossfield had added "the teeth of these rich relatives," Jasmine would not have thought the phrase extravagant.

She opened her door gently and looked out into the passage. Not even the sound of snoring was audible; nothing indeed was audible except a bluebottle's buzz on a window of ground glass that seemed alive with sunlight. She wandered on tiptoe along the pale green Axminster pile, went into the bathroom, crossed herself, and turned on the tap. The running water sounded so torrential at this hour of the morning that she at once clapped her hand over the tap to throttle the stream until she could cut it off; during the guilty quiet that succeeded, she hurried back to her bedroom, which by now was extremely hot. Before Jasmine stretched years and years of silent sunlit vacancy, in which she would be walking about on tiptoe and throttling every gush of spontaneous feeling just as she had throttled that bath tap.

"And I can't stand it," she said, banging her dressing-table with the back of her hairbrush.

She stopped in dismay at the noise, half expecting to hear cries of "Murder!" from neighbouring rooms. The pale blue sea winked below; the sun climbed higher. Jasmine sat down before the looking-glass to brush her hair. A milk-cart clinked; rugs were being shaken below. Jasmine still sat brushing her hair. The voices of gossiping servants were heard above the steady chirp of sparrows. When Jasmine's hair was more thoroughly brushed than it ever had been, she took her bath, and when her hair was dry she brushed it all over again.

At a quarter to nine Sir Hector found her waiting in the dining-room, the first down. His pleasure at such unexpected punctuality almost compensated him for the fact that she had dared to open his paper and, like all women, even his own wife, that she had turned an ordinary sixteen-page newspaper into a complicated puzzle.

"Well," he said pompously, "you wouldn't find better weather than this in Italy, would you?"

He managed to suggest that the glorious morning was Uncle Hector's own little treat, a little treat, moreover, that nobody but Uncle Hector would have thought of providing, or at any rate been able to provide.

"Yes," he went on, "and what a crime that all this should be vulgarized." He included the firmament in an ample gesture. "I expect your aunt told you that this will be our last summer in Spaborough? We didn't come here to be pestered by trippers. That boarding-house next door is a disgrace to South Parade. They were playing a gramophone last night—laughing and talking out there on the steps until after one o'clock. How people expect to get any benefit from their holidays I don't know. We'd always been free from that sort of rowdiness until they opened that pernicious boarding-house next door, and now it's worse than Bank Holiday. Some people seem blind to the beauty round them. I suppose when the moon gets to the full we shall hear them jabbering out there till dawn. What *have* you been doing to my paper? It's utterly disorganized!"

Jasmine diverted her uncle's attention from the newspaper to the basket of prickly pears that she had brought from Sirene, and invited him to try one.

Sir Hector examined his niece's unnatural fruit as the night before he had examined his brother's unnatural fruit.

"Well, I don't know," he hemmed. "We're rather old-fashioned people here, you know."

"I think the prickles have all been taken out," said Jasmine encouragingly, "but you'd better be careful in case they haven't."

Sir Hector had been on the verge of prodding one of the pears, but at his niece's warning he drew back in alarm; and just then the clock on the mantelpiece struck nine. Before the last stroke died away the whole family was sitting down to breakfast. Jasmine's punctuality was evidently a great satisfaction to her relatives, and if she did look rather like a chocolate drop that had fallen into the tray reserved for fondants, she felt much more at home now than she had at dinner last night. Nothing occurred to mar the amity of the breakfast-table until Lady Grant's fat fox-terrier began to tear round the room as if possessed by a devil, clawing from time to time at his nose with both front paws and turning somersaults. Lady Grant, who ascribed all the ills of dogs to picking up unlicensed scraps, rang the bell and asked severely if Hargreaves, whose duty it was to supervise the dog's early morning promenade, had allowed him to eat anything in the road; but it was Jasmine who diagnosed his complaint correctly.

"I think he has been sniffing the prickly pears," she said.

"But what dangerous things to leave about!" exclaimed her aunt. "Hargreaves, take the basket out into the kitchen and tell cook to empty them carefully—carefully, mind, or she may hurt herself—into the pineapple dish. She had better wear gloves. And if she can't manage them," Lady Grant called after the parlourmaid, who was gingerly carrying out the basket at arm's length, "if she can't manage them, they must be burnt. On no account must they be thrown into the dustbin. I'm sorry that we don't appreciate your Italian fruit," she added, turning to her niece, "I'm afraid you'll find us very stay-at-home people, and you know English servants hate anything in the least unusual."

"How they must hate me!" Jasmine thought.

"And what is the programme for to-day?" asked Sir Hector suddenly, flinging down the paper with such a crackle that Jasmine would not have been more startled if like a clown he had jumped clean through it into the conversation.

"Well, we *were* going to play golf," said Lettice disagreeably.

"Oh then, please do," said Jasmine hurriedly, for she felt that a future had been mutilated into imperfection by the responsibility of entertaining herself.

"Jasmine and I have a little business to talk over after breakfast," Sir Hector announced. "So you girls had better be independent this morning, and give Jasmine her first lesson this afternoon."

The girls looked at their father coldly.

"We've got a foursome on with Dick Onslowe and Claude Whittaker this morning, and if George Huntingford turns up this afternoon," said Lettice, "I've got a match with him. But if Pamela isn't engaged, I daresay she will look after Jasmine, that is if she can find her way to the club-house."

"But Roy Medlicott said he might get to the links this afternoon," protested Pamela. "And if he does, I shan't be able to look after Jasmine."

"Well, we might get Tommy Waterall to give her a lesson," proposed Lettice. Something in her cousin's intonation made Jasmine realize that Tommy Waterall was the charitable institution of that golf club, and she vowed to herself that she at any rate would not be beholden to him, even if she were successful in finding her way to the club-house, which was unlikely.

Jasmine's little talk with her uncle was the smallest ever known. Sir Hector, as a consulting nerve specialist, was accustomed to ask more questions than he answered, and since the only positive information he had to impart to his niece was the fact that she had not a penny in the world, the theme did not lend itself to eloquence.

"Yes, that's how your affairs stand," said Sir Hector. "But you mustn't worry yourself." He was just going to dilate on the deleterious effects of worry, as though Jasmine were a rich patient, when he remembered that whether she worried or not it was of no importance to him. His observations on worry, therefore, those very observations which had won for him a fortune and a title, were not placed at his niece's disposal. The little talk was over, and Sir Hector strode from the study to proclaim the news.

"We've had our little talk," he bellowed. Lettice and Pamela, delightfully equipped for golf in shrimp-pink jerseys, passed coldly by. It was one of those moments which do give a nose an opportunity of showing off, and Sir Hector, afraid of being snubbed, drew back into his study. When he heard the front door slam, he emerged again, and shouted louder than ever: "We have had our little talk!"

Lady Grant appeared from another door further along the hall, her hand pressed painfully to her forehead.

"Couldn't you wait a little while, dear, until I have finished doing the books?"

"Sorry," said Sir Hector, retreating again. He was wishing that he had at Strathspey House his Harley Street waiting-room into which he could have pushed Jasmine to occupy herself there with illustrated papers a month old and not disturb him by her presence. "Perhaps you might care to go and wait for your aunt in the drawing-room," he suggested finally. "I know she's very anxious to say a few words to you about your father—your poor father." The epithet was intended to be sympathetic, not sarcastic, but Jasmine bolted from the room with her handkerchief to her eyes.

"A leetle overwrought," murmured Sir Hector, as if he were talking to a patient. But soon he lighted a cigar and forgot all about his niece.

There are few places in this world that cast a more profound gloom upon the human spirit than a sunny English drawing-room at 9.45 a.m. Its welcome is as frigid as a woman who fends off a kiss because she has just made up her lips.

"If I feel like this now," said Jasmine to herself, "*Dio mio*, what shall I feel like in a month's time?"

She put away the handkerchief almost at once, for even grief was frozen in this house, and memories that yesterday would have brought tears to her eyes were to-day so hardly imaginable that they had no power to affect her. "I'm really just as much dead as father," she sighed to the Japanese blinds that rustled faintly in a faint breeze from the sea. On an impulse she rushed upstairs to her bedroom, took off her black clothes, and came down again to the dining-room in a yellow silk jersey and a white skirt.

"My dear Jasmine!... Already?..." ejaculated her aunt, when the household accounts were finished and she found her niece waiting for her in the drawing-room. "I don't know that your uncle will quite approve, so very soon after his brother's death."

"I don't believe in mourning."

"My dear child, are you quite old enough to give such a decided opinion on a custom which is universally followed—even by savages?"

"Father would perfectly understand my feelings."

"I daresay your father would understand, but I don't think your uncle will understand."

And one felt that Sholto's comprehension in Paradise was a poor thing compared with his brother's lack of it on earth.

"Anyway, I'm not going to wear black any longer," said Jasmine curtly.

"As you will," her aunt replied with grave resignation. "Oh, and before I forget, I have told Hopkins to show you exactly how the blind is pulled up in your room. I'm afraid you didn't keep hold of the lower tassel this morning. They're still trying to get it down, and I am very much afraid we shall have to send for a carpenter to mend it. If you pull the string on the right without holding the lower tassel——"

"I know," Jasmine interrupted. "I'm rather like that blind myself."

Lady Grant hoped inwardly that her niece was not going to be difficult, and changed the subject. "You have no doubt gathered by now exactly how you stand," she went on. "I know you've been having a little talk with your uncle, and I know that there is nothing more galling than a sense of dependency. So I was going to suggest that when we went back to Harley Street in September you should take Edith Crossfield's place and help me with my numerous—well, really I suppose I *must* call them that—my numerous charities. At present Cousin Edith only answers all my letters for me; but I daresay you will find many ways of making yourself much more useful than that, because you are younger and more energetic than poor Edith. Though, of course, while we are at Spaborough I want you to consider yourself as much on a holiday as we all are. Do make up your mind to get plenty of good fresh air and exercise. The girls are quite horrified to hear that you have never played golf, especially as they're so good at it themselves. Lettice is only four at the Scottish Ladies'. Or is it five? Dear me, I've forgotten! How angry the dear child would be!"

"I'm D—E—A—D, dead," Jasmine was saying to herself all the time her aunt was speaking.

And perhaps it was because she looked so much like a corpse that her aunt recommended a course of iron to bring back her roses. Lady Grant was so much accustomed wherever she looked, even if it were in her own glass, to see roses that Jasmine's pallor was unpleasant to her. Besides, it might mean that she really was delicate, which would be a nuisance.

"It's almost a pity," she said, "that your uncle did not postpone his little talk, so that you could have gone with the girls to the links. They have such wonderful complexions, I always think."

"Please don't worry about me," said Jasmine quickly. "I can amuse myself perfectly well by myself."

"My dear," said Lady Grant, asserting the purity of her motives with such a gentle air of martyrdom as Saint Agnes may have used toward Symphronius, "you misunderstand me. You are not at all in the way; but as I have some private letters to write, I was going to suggest that you and Cousin Edith should take a little walk and see something of Spaborough."

"Little walks, little talks, little talks, little walks," spun the jingle in Jasmine's mind.

At this moment the companion proposed for Jasmine floated into the room. Miss Crossfield was so thin, her movements and gestures were so indeterminate, and her arms wandered so much upon the air, that indoors she suggested a daddy-longlegs on a window-pane, and out of doors a daddy-longlegs floating across an upland pasture in autumn. It was perhaps this extreme attenuation that gave her subservience a kind of spirituality; with so little flesh to clog her good will, she was almost literally a familiar spirit. She materialized like one of those obedient genies in the Arabian Nights whenever Lady Grant rang the bell, and she endowed that ring with as much magic as if it had been the golden ring of Abanazar.

"Edith," said Lady Grant magnanimously, "I am writing my own letters this morning to give you the opportunity of taking Jasmine for a little walk. You had better take Spot with you—on the lead, of course."

That at any rate would tie Cousin Edith to earth, Jasmine thought, for Spot was so fat and so porcine that he was unlikely to run away and carry Cousin Edith with him in a Gadarene rush down the face of the cliff. Yes, with Spot to detain her, not much could happen to Cousin Edith.

But Jasmine was wrong. Spot had a fetish: the sensation of twigs or leaves faintly tickling his back gave him such exquisite pleasure that to secure it he would use the cunning of a morphinomaniac in pursuit of his drug. He would put back his ears and creep very slowly under the lower branches of a shrub, so that Cousin Edith, who in her affection for the family felt bound to indulge the dog to the whole length of his lead and even further, was lured after him deep into the chosen bush, so that finally, immaterial as she was, she was herself entangled in the upper branches.

"I think I'm getting rather scratched," she would cry helplessly to Jasmine, who would have to come to the rescue with a sharp tug at Spot's lead. This used to give such a shock to the bloated fox-terrier that, torn from his sensation of being scratched by canine houris, he would choke, while Cousin Edith, dancing feebly on the still autumn air, would beg Jasmine never again to be so rough with him.

The music of the Spa band grew louder while they were descending the winding paths of the cliff, until at last it burst upon Jasmine with the full force of an operatic finale and gave a throb of life to her hitherto lifeless morning. The music stopped before they reached the last curve of the descent, where they paused a moment to watch the movement of the dædal throng, above which parasols floated like great butterflies. From the sands beyond, above the chattering, came up the sound of children's laughter, and beyond that the pale blue winking sea was fused with the sky in the silver haze of August so that the furthest ships were sailing in the clouds.

And then, just when it really was beginning to seem worth while to be alive again, Cousin Edith's hand alighted uncertainly like a daddy-longlegs on Jasmine's arm and jigged up and down as a prelude to whispering in what, were that insect vocal, would certainly have been the voice of a daddy-longlegs:

"Do you think we can communicate with the dead?"

"No, I don't," said Jasmine sharply. "And if we could, I shouldn't want to."

Cousin Edith opened wide her globular eyes, which, like those of an insect, were set apparently on her face rather than in it. But before she could combat the blasphemy she had been lured by Spot deep into a privet bush, so deep that the old rhyme came into Jasmine's head about the man of Thessaly who scratched out his eyes in bushes and at his own will scratched them in again in other bushes. He must have had eyes like Cousin Edith's—external and globular.

"Poor old Spot," she murmured, disengaging her lips from a cobweb as genteelly as possible. "He so enjoys his little walk. Up here now, dear," she added, seeing that Jasmine was preparing to go down to the promenade.

"But shan't we go and listen to the music?"

"We have Spot with us."

"Well?"

Cousin Edith came very close to her and whispered:

"Dogs are not allowed on the promenade."

"Then let's tie him up and leave him here," suggested Jasmine.

Cousin Edith laughed. At least Jasmine supposed it was a laugh, even if it did sound more like the squeaking of a slate pencil. Indeed she was pretty sure that it was a laugh, because when it was finished Cousin Edith's fingers danced along her arm and she said:

"How droll you are! We'll go out by the north gate. Unless," she added, "you would like to sit in this summer-house for a little while and listen to the band from here."

There was a summer-house close at hand which, with the appearance of a decayed beehive, smelt of dry-rot and was littered with paper bags.

"I often sit here," Cousin Edith explained. Jasmine was tempted to reply that she looked as if she did; but a sense of inability to struggle any longer against the withering influence of the Grants came over her, and she followed Cousin Edith into the summer-house. There on a semicircular rustic seat they sat in silence, staring out at the dim green world, while Spot seduced a few strands of the tangled creeper round the entrance to play upon his back paradisal symphonies. Then Cousin Edith began to talk again; and while she talked a myriad little noises of insect life in the summer-house, which had been temporarily disturbed, began again—little whispers, little scratches, little dry sounds that were indefinable.

"You have no idea how kind Cousin May is. But, of course, she isn't Cousin May to you, she's Aunt May, isn't she?" Again the desiccated titter of Cousin Edith's mirth sounded. The myriad noises stopped in alarm for a moment, but quickly went on again. "Already she has planned for you a delightful surprise."

Jasmine's impulsive heart leaped toward the good intention of her aunt, and with an eager question in her eyes she jumped round so energetically that she shook the fabric, bringing down a skeleton leaf of ivy, which fluttered over Spot's back and gave him the finest thrill of the morning.

"What can it be?" she cried, clapping her hands. This was too much for the summer-house. Skeleton leaves, twigs, dead flies, mummied earwigs began to drop down in all directions.

"It's quite dusty in here," said Cousin Edith in a perplexed tone. "I think perhaps we had better be moving along."

"But the surprise?" Jasmine persisted.

Cousin Edith trembled with self-importance, and her long forefinger waved like an antenna when she bade Jasmine follow her in the direction of the promised revelation. They strolled along the winding paths of the shrubberies above the promenade until they reached the main entrance of the Spa.

"Will you hold Spot for a tiny minute? I have a little business here," Cousin Edith pleaded. Having adjured Spot to be a good dog, and promised him that she would not be long, Cousin Edith engaged the ticket clerk in a conversation, and so much did she appear to be pecking at her purse and so nearly did she seem to be ruffling her feathers when she bobbed her hat up and down that if she had presently flown into the office through the pigeon-hole and perched beside her mate on the desk inside it would have appeared natural. Jasmine might have wondered what Cousin Edith was doing if she had not been too much occupied with Spot, who in default of a convenient bush was trying to extract his dorsal sensations from a little girl's frock. When he was jerked away by a heavier hand than Cousin Edith's he began to growl, whereupon Jasmine smacked him with her glove, which so surprised the fat dog that he collapsed in the path and breathed stertorously to attract the sympathy of the passers-by. Cousin Edith came back from her colloquy with the clerk, and in a rapture of esoteric benevolence she pressed into Jasmine's palm a round green cardboard disk.

"Your season ticket," she murmured. "Cousin May—I mean Aunt May—asked me to buy you one while we were out."

Jasmine felt that she ought to jump in the air and embrace the gate-keeper in the excess of her joy. As for Cousin Edith, she watched her as one watches a child that has been given a sweet too large for its mouth. She seemed afraid that Jasmine would choke if she swallowed such a benefaction whole.

"And now," she said, as if after such a display of generosity it were incredible that there might be more to come, "and now Aunt May—there, I said it right that time!—Aunt May suggested that we might have a cup of chocolate together at the Oriental Café afterwards."

"Hullo!" cried a cheerful voice, which brought Jasmine back to earth from the dazzling prospects being offered by Cousin Edith. "Why, we've met even sooner than I hoped we should."

Jasmine's sandy-haired railway companion, looking delightfully at ease, every freckle in his face twinkling with geniality and pleasure, shook hands. For the first time she regretted that it was Cousin Edith's duty to hold Spot. If Cousin Edith had not been detained by the fat fox-terrier, she might have floated away like a child's balloon, such evident dismay did Mr. Vibart's irruption create in one who was under the obsession that all the young men in the world fit to be known were already friends of Lettice and Pamela. Jasmine introduced Mr. Vibart without any explanation, and poor Cousin Edith, who was too genteel, and had been too long dependent to know how to escape from an acquaintanceship she did not wish to be forced on her, allowed Mr. Vibart to shake her hand. When, however, he calmly suggested that they should all turn back and listen to the band, she pulled herself together and declared that it was quite impossible.

"The dog...." she began.

"Oh, we'll leave the dog with the gate-keeper," said Mr. Vibart.

"I'm afraid, Jasmine, your friend doesn't understand that dear old Spot is quite one of the family." And turning with a bitter-sweet smile to the intrusive young man: "Spot is a great responsibility," she added.

"I should think so," Mr. Vibart agreed, regarding with unconcealed disgust the fox-terrier, who, having been rolling on his back in the dust, looked now more like a sheep than a pig. Jasmine understood at once what Mr. Vibart wanted, and as she wanted the same thing so much herself she nearly answered his unspoken invitation by saying, "Very well, Mr. Vibart and I will go and listen to the band for half an hour, and when you've finished your chocolate at the café, we'll meet you here." She felt, however, that such independence of action was too precipitate for Spaborough.

"I'm afraid that we were just going to the Oriental Café," Cousin Edith had begun, when Mr. Vibart interrupted her.

"Capital! Just what I should like to do myself!"

Before Cousin Edith could do anything about it they were all on their way to the town; but by the time the café was reached she had perfected her strategy.

"Thank you very much for escorting us," she murmured. "Miss Grant and I are much obliged to you. You, of course, will prefer the smoking-room. We always go into the ladies' room."

The Oriental Café included among its appropriate features a zenana, outside the door of which, marked *LADIES ONLY*, Mr. Vibart was left disconsolate, although before it closed Jasmine had managed to whisper, "Strathspey House, South Parade."

Within the zenana, to which Spot was admitted as little boys under six are admitted to ladies' bathing-machines, Cousin Edith warned a young girl against the wiles of men.

"I shan't say anything to Aunt May about this unpleasant little business," she promised Jasmine, who was convinced that she would take the first opportunity to tell her aunt everything. "No, I shan't tell Aunt May," Cousin Edith went on, "because I think it would pain her. She's so particular about Lettice and Pamela, and we always have such nice men at Strathspey House." But lest Jasmine should suppose that the presence of nice men there implied a chance for her in the near future, she made haste to add:

"Though, of course, we must always be careful, even with the nicest men. I must say that it seems to me a dreadful idea that a young girl like you should be able to meet a man in the train, travel with him unprotected, and actually be accosted by him the next day. Ugh! I'm so glad we had Spot with us! Brave old Spot!" And in her gratitude to Spot for the preservation of their modesty she gave him half of one of the free biscuits that the Oriental Café allowed to the purchaser of a cup of chocolate.

"Do you know," went on Cousin Edith, flushed by the thought of their narrow escape and by the deliciously hot chocolate, "do you know that once, nearly five years ago, a man winked at me in a bus? I was quite alone inside, and the conductor was taking the fares on the top."

"What did you do?" Jasmine asked with a smile.

"Why, of course I rang the bell, got out almost before the bus had fully stopped, and walked the rest of the way. But it made such an impression on me that when I reached my friend's house she had to give me several drops of valerian, my heart was in such a state, what with walking so fast and being so frightened. Perhaps I oughtn't to have told you such a horrid story. But I'm older than you, and I want you to feel that I'm your friend. Oh yes, the things men do! Well, I was brought up very strictly, but I have a very strong imagination, and sometimes when I'm alone I just sit and gasp at the wickedness of men. And now," Cousin Edith concluded with an uneasy glance round the zenana, "I think we ought to hurry back as fast as we can. Come, Spot! Good old Spot! I'll show you the Aquarium, dear, as we go home. You can see the roof quite well when we turn round the corner from Marine Crescent."

Perhaps Cousin Edith thought that Jasmine's indiscretion would be more valuable as a weapon for herself if it was unrevealed, for she did not say a word to Lady Grant about the meeting at the gates of the Spa; indeed all the way home she talked about nothing except the wonder of possessing a season ticket of one's own, ascribing to the round green cardboard disk a potency such as few talismans have possessed.

"You will be able to go and see the fireworks on gala nights," she explained, "and you'll be able to go and hear concerts—though, of course, if you want to sit down you have to pay extra—and you'll be able to go and drink the waters—though, of course, you have to pay a penny for the glass—and you'll be able to take a short cut from South Parade to the beach—though, of course, you won't care for the beach, because it's apt to be a little vulgar—and then the promenade is far the best place to hear the pierrots from—though I'm afraid that even they have been getting vulgar lately. I'm so glad that Cousin May thought of making you this present. It makes me so happy for you, dear."

While Cousin Edith was extolling its powers, the green cardboard disk, which was originally about the size of a florin, seemed to be growing larger and larger in Jasmine's glove, until by the time South Parade was reached it seemed the size of a saucer. In fact it was only after Jasmine had warmly thanked her aunt for the kind thought that it shrank back into being a small green cardboard disk again. At least she was no longer aware of its burning her palm; but when she came to take off her gloves she found that this was because the ticket was no longer there. The loss of the Koh-i-nur diamond could not have been treated more seriously. The house was turned upside down, and small parties were sent out into South Parade to examine carefully every paving stone and to peer down the gratings of the drains. Sir Hector, who had been in charge of the operations conducted inside the house, suddenly became overheated and announced that it was useless to search any longer, but that when he paid his own afternoon visit to the Spa he would go into the question with the authorities, and if necessary actually buy another ticket.

"And perhaps your uncle will take you with him," said Lady Grant.

Cousin Edith clasped her hands in envious amazement. "Jasmine!" she exclaimed. "Do you hear that? Perhaps Sir Hector will take you with him!"

Lettice and Pamela did not come back to lunch, and at four o'clock Sir Hector sent Hargreaves up to Jasmine's room to inform her that he was ready. Two minutes later he sent Hargreaves up to say that he was waiting. Four minutes later he sent Hargreaves up to say that he would walk slowly on. Six minutes later, Jasmine, not quite sure which way her hat was facing or whether her dress was properly fastened, found Sir Hector, watch in hand, at the nearest entrance of the gardens.

"If there is ever any doubt about the time," he told her, "we always follow the clock in my room. Let me see. You have lost your season ticket, so that at this entrance you will have to pay. Wait a minute, however; I will see if the gate-keeper will let you through for once."

The gate-keeper was perfectly willing to trust Sir Hector's account of the accident to the season ticket, and Sir Hector, carrying himself more upright even than usual, observed to Jasmine as they walked along towards the main entrance, "You see they know me here."

"Now where are you going to keep this ticket so that you don't lose it like the other one?" asked Sir Hector when he had presented Jasmine with the second small green disk, for which the management had regretfully but firmly exacted another payment.

Jasmine proposed to put it in her purse.

"Yes," said Sir Hector judicially, "that might be a good place. But be very careful that you don't drop it when you want to take out any money."

"There's only tenpence halfpenny to take out," said Jasmine. "But I can put the ticket in the inside compartment, which is meant for gold."

"Good Heavens! I hope you don't carry much gold about with you," exclaimed her uncle.

"No, not very much," she replied. "A broken locket, that's all."

On the way to the promenade Sir Hector was saluted respectfully by various people; and several ladies sitting on sunny benches quivered as he went by, with that indescribable tribute of the senses which they accord to a popular Lenten preacher who passes them on the way to the pulpit.

"Some of my patients," Sir Hector explained.

Jasmine wondered if it would be more tactful to say that they looked very well or that they looked very ill; not being able to decide, she smiled. At that moment Sir Hector stopped beside a bath-chair.

"Duchess," he proclaimed in a voice sufficiently loud to be heard by all the passers-by, most of whom turned round and stared, first at the Duchess, then at Sir Hector, then at Jasmine, and finally at the chairman, "you are looking definitely better."

"Ah, Sir Hector, I wish I felt better."

"You will.... You will...." Sir Hector prophesied, and, raising his hat, he passed on.

"That," he said to Jasmine, "is Georgina, Duchess of Shropshire. Yes ... yes ... it's odd.... They're all my patients.... The Duchess of Shropshire, ... Georgina, Duchess of Shropshire, ... Eleanor, Duchess of Shropshire."

Jasmine, who came from Sirene, where any summer Italian duchesses bathing are to be found as thick as limpets on the rocks, was less impressed than she ought to have been.

"What's the matter with her?" she enquired.

Sir Hector never encouraged his patients to ask what was the matter with themselves, and he certainly did not approve of his niece's enquiry.

"You would hardly understand," he said severely, and then relapsed into silence, to concentrate upon threading his way through the crowd of the Promenade.

Sir Hector, who wished to be the cynosure of the promenaders floating with the opposite current, kept on the extreme edge of the downward stream, so that Jasmine, with two feet less height than her uncle and no title, found it difficult to make headway, so difficult indeed that in trying to keep up with him she got too much to the left and was swept back by the contrary stream, in which, though she managed to keep her season ticket, she lost herself. Several times during this promenade eternal as the winds of hell, she caught sight of her uncle's neck lifted above the swirl like a cormorant's, and once she managed to get to the outside of the stream and actually to pluck at his sleeve as he went by in the opposite direction; but her voice was drowned by the music, and he did not notice her. She was beginning to feel tired of walking round and round like this, and at last, finding herself working across to the right of the current, she struggled ashore, or in other words went into the concert room.

The concert room of the Spa looked like a huge conservatory full of dead vegetation. The hundreds of chairs stacked one upon another in rows seemed a brake of withered canes; the music-stands on the platform resembled the dried-up stalks of small shrubs; while the few palms and foliage plants that preserved their greenery only served to enhance the deadness all round, and were themselves streaked with decay. Outside, the gay throng passing and repassing like fish added a final touch to the desolation of the interior. Two small boys, with backward uneasy glances, were creeping furtively through the maze of chairs. Jasmine thought that they like herself had been overcome by the mystery haunting this light and arid interior, until a dull boom from the direction of the platform, followed by the screech of hurriedly moved chairs and the clatter of frightened feet made her realize that their cautious advance had been the preliminary to a daring attempt to bang, if only once, the big drum muffled in baize. No sooner had the boys successfully escaped than Jasmine was seized with a strong desire to bang the drum for herself, to bang it, however, much more loudly than those boys had banged it, to raise the drumstick high above her and bring it down upon the drum as a smith brings his hammer down upon the anvil. The longer she sat here, the harder she found it to keep away from the platform. Finally the temptation became too strong to be resisted; she snatched the baize cover from the instrument, seized the drumstick, and brought it down with a crash.

"I wish I could do that at Strathspey House," she sighed; and then, hearing a voice at the back of the hall, she turned round to see an indignant man in a green baize apron looking at her over folded arms.

"Here! you mustn't do that," he was protesting.

"I'm sorry," said Jasmine. "I simply couldn't help it."

"It isn't as if I didn't have to spend half my time as it is chasing boys out of here, but I never reckoned to have to go chasing after young ladies."

"No; I'm sorry," said Jasmine. She hesitated for a moment what to do; then she thought of her talisman and fumbled in her purse. The attendant wiped his hands on the apron in preparation for the half-crown that he estimated was the least remuneration he could receive for the loudest bang on that drum he had ever heard, and when Jasmine produced nothing but a season ticket he was inclined to be nasty.

"You needn't think you can come in here and rattle all the windows and fetch me away from my work just because you're a season ticket holder, which only makes it worse in my opinion, and I'll have to take your name and number, miss, and complain to the management. That's all there is to it. I've been asking to have this place closed when not in use, and now perhaps they'll do it. Only this morning I barked my shins something cruel trying to catch hold of a boy who was playing the banjo on the double bass. I've got your number, miss, 17874, and you'll hear from the management about it; and that's all there is to it."

He wiped his other hand on the apron and waited a moment; when Jasmine did not seem to understand what he wanted, he invited her to leave the hall forthwith, and retired to formulate his complaint. As for Jasmine, she rejoined the throng; but by now, in whatever direction she looked, she could not even see Sir Hector's long red neck, much less meet him face to face. She began to be bewitched by the continuous circling round the bandstand. It was really delicious on this golden afternoon to be borne round upon these mingled perfumes of scent and asphalt. The asphalt, softened by the heat, was pleasant to walk on, like grass, and it was only after circling for about half an hour that she realized how tiring it was to the feet. At this moment the music stopped; the opening bars of *God Save the King* were played; a patriotic gentleman next to her planted his foot on her own in his desire to remind people that he was an old soldier. Two minutes later the Promenade was empty, and Jasmine, with any number of chairs to choose from now, sat down.

She had not been there more than five minutes when round the corner came Mr. Vibart, walking in the way people walk when they have an object.

"I hoped I should find you on the Spa," he said. "I've just called at your home. Don't be frightened," he went on at Jasmine's expression of alarm, "I didn't ask for you. I rang the bell and asked if they had a vacant apartment, and how much the board was a day. Luck was on my side. The maid was just coming to from her swoon when an old boy looking like a turkey that's nearly had its neck wrung came shouting through the garden that he had lost Jasmine on the Promenade. I didn't wait to hear any more, but hurried down as fast as I could. And here I am, full of schemes. But I decided not to put any of them into practice until I'd seen you again."

"Oh, but it's all turned out much worse than what I expected," said Jasmine hurriedly. "You mustn't come and call or do anything like that. Why, I'm almost frightened to ring the bell myself, and if I heard any of my friends ring a bell I don't know what I should do. I'm not a bit of a success. I heard my aunt say *sotto voce* that she distrusted dark people. I lost a season ticket this morning which cost I don't know how many shillings. I've lost my uncle now. If you come and call, *sarò perduta io*. And now I must say good-bye and go back."

"Well, don't break into Japanese like that. Let's sit down and talk over the situation."

"No, no, no! I must say good-bye and hurry back."

"I don't want to compromise you and all that," the young man protested, "but it seems a pity not to enjoy this weather."

"No, please go away," Jasmine begged. "It's all perfectly different to anything I ever imagined. Quite different. I'm sorry I gave you my address this morning."

Jasmine was getting more and more nervous. She had an idea that Cousin Edith would be sent to look for her; if Cousin Edith found her talking to Mr. Vibart by the deserted bandstand she would suppose that the assignation had been made that morning. All sorts of ideas swirled into Jasmine's mind, and she began to hurry towards the winding path up the cliff.

"At any rate you might let me walk back with you as far as the entrance," he suggested.

"No, please, really. You make me nervous. You don't in the least understand my position."

Mr. Vibart looked so sad that Jasmine hesitated.

"Don't you play a game called golf?" she asked.

"Yes, I do play a game called golf," he laughed.

"Well, I believe they're going to teach me, so perhaps we might meet on the golf grounds," said Jasmine. "My cousins went there this morning and didn't come back for lunch, and I think they go every day."

"I see the notion. I must get to know them, what?"

"Yes, I don't think it will be very difficult," Jasmine answered. She was speaking simply, not maliciously. "They seem to know lots of people who play this game. But if you do meet them, for goodness' sake don't say you know me. Turn round! Turn round!" she cried in agony. "Turn round straight away in the other direction without looking back! Do what I tell you! Do what I tell you!"

Round the next bend of the laurel-edged walk Jasmine met Cousin Edith, who, unencumbered by Spot, was floating towards her as a daddy-longlegs floats towards a lamp.

Jasmine found it difficult to make her uncle understand how she had been lost.

"I cannot think where you got to," he said. "I looked about everywhere. Most extraordinary!"

"I'm sure she didn't mean to get lost, Sir Hector," Cousin Edith put in with just enough accent on the intention to create a suspicion of Jasmine's sincerity.

"No, of course she didn't mean to get lost," Sir Hector gobbled. "Nobody means to get lost. But you'll have to learn to keep your head, young lady. However, all's well that ends well, so we'll say no more about it. Where are the girls?"

Just then the girls came in, and Jasmine hoped that she was going to be invited to partake of the mysterious game that occupied so much of their time. All indeed promised well, for several allusions were made in the course of dinner to the necessity of introducing her to the joys of golf. Next morning, however, Lettice and Pamela went off as usual, and as an intoxicating treat for Jasmine it was proposed that Cousin Edith should show her the Castle.

"It might be a little far for Spot," Cousin Edith humbly objected.

"Yes, I think you are right," Lady Grant agreed. "So Spot shall take a little walk with his mother."

It was supposed to be necessary for Cousin Edith to translate into baby language for Spot his mother's wishes, after which she turned to Lady Grant and proclaimed intensely:

"He knows."

Spot was standing on three legs and scratching himself with the fourth, which was presumably his method of acknowledging the success of Cousin Edith's interpretation.

The walk up to the Castle was long and hot; the Castle was a little more uninteresting than most ruins are. Cousin Edith poetized upon the romance of the past; Jasmine counted two hundred and nine paper bags.

When they got back to Strathspey House it was obvious that something unpleasant had occurred during their absence. Cousin Edith tried all through lunch to give her impression of the delight Jasmine had tasted in going to the Castle; but her account of the morning's entertainment was received so coldly by her patrons that in the end she was silent, shrinking into such insignificance and humility that the faint clicking of her false teeth was her only contribution to actuality. After lunch a few whispers were exchanged between her and Lady Grant, at the conclusion of which she danced on tiptoe out of the dining-room, and Lady Grant turned to her niece.

"Your uncle wishes to speak to you," she announced gravely.

Sir Hector, who during these preliminaries had been hiding behind the newspaper, jumped up and took a letter from his pocket.

"Can you explain this?" he demanded.

His wife had moved over to the window and was looking out at the sky in the way that ladies look at the East window when something in the preacher's sermon is particularly applicable to a neighbour. Jasmine read the letter, which was from the director of the Spa:

> Spa Gardens Company, Limited,
> Spaborough,
> *August 15th.*
>
> *Dear Sir Hector Grant,*
> *I am writing to you personally and confidentially to ask you whether season ticket 17874 is really held by one of your family party. The caretaker of the Concert Room has complained to me that a young lady holding season ticket 17874, which was traced to the name of Miss Jasmine Grant, Strathspey House, removed the green baize cover from the big drum yesterday afternoon the 14th inst. and struck it several times. We have not been able to trace any reason for her behaviour, and I should be much obliged if you would give the matter your kind attention. The Company has of course no wish to take any action in the matter, and is content to leave all the necessary steps in your hands. I may add that the drum has been examined carefully, and I am glad to be able to assure you that it is quite uninjured. At the same time we rely on our season ticket holders to set an example to the casual visitors, and I am sure you will appreciate the delicacy of my position.*
>
> *Believe me, my dear Sir Hector Grant,*
> *Yours very faithfully,*
> *John Pershore,*
> *Managing Director.*

"Yes, I did bang the drum," Jasmine confessed.

Now if Sir Hector Grant had been asked by one of his patients to cure an uncontrollable impulse to beat big drums he would have known how to prescribe for her, and within a week or two of her visit ladies would have been going round each asking the other if she had heard of Sir Hector Grant's latest and most wonderful cure. His niece, however, did not present herself to him as a clinical subject; he had no desire to analyse her psyche for her own benefit or for the elucidation of the Flatus Complex.

"No wonder you were lost," he said bitterly. "I don't suppose you expected me to look for you among the drums? I don't wish to make a great fuss about nothing, but I should like to point out that you cannot accuse me of being backward in coming forward to ... er ... show our ... er ... affection, and we look, not unreasonably, I hope, for a little ... er ... sympathy on your side. I shall write to Mr. Pershore and explain that you were brought up in Italy and did not appreciate the importance of what you were doing. That will, I hope, close the matter. I cannot think why you don't go and play golf with the girls," he added fretfully.

"I should love to go and play golf," Jasmine declared.

Lady Grant now came forward from the window: perhaps, during this painful scene she had made up her mind that her niece must be added to the list of her charities.

"You must try to realize, my dear child," she said, shaking her head, "that our only idea is for you to be happy. Have you already forgotten that you lost your first season ticket? Have you forgotten even that it was your Uncle Hector himself who immediately offered to buy you another one? He has not said very much about the drum; but his restraint does not mean that he has not felt it all dreadfully. And he has had other things to upset him this morning. Only yesterday one of his oldest patients jumped out of a fourth storey window and was dashed to pieces. So we must all be a little considerate. Don't you think that you're too old to play with drums? What would you think if I went about beating drums? However, enough has been said."

Sir Hector blew his nose very loudly, and Jasmine on her way up to her room thought that if she could trumpet like that with her nose, she should be content to let drums alone.

Chapter Four

IT seemed to be the general opinion of Strathspey House that Jasmine was reckless, and in order to counteract a propensity that might one day cause serious trouble to her protectors it was decided to sow the seeds of prudence by making her a quarterly allowance of £10, on which she was to dress and provide herself with pocket money. The announcement of the largesse was made in such a way that if the first ten golden sovereigns had lain within her reach Jasmine would have been tempted to pick them up and fling them back at the donors. In order, however, that the possession of wealth might bring with it a sense of wealth's responsibilities it had been decided to open an account for her at the Post Office Savings Bank, and without even so much as an account book to throw, Jasmine found that all her verbal protestations were interpreted as a becoming sign of gratitude.

To say that Jasmine longed for the freedom of Sirene is to express nothing of the fierce ache she suffered every moment of the day for that happy island. Adam and Eve when their sons first began to quarrel could not have looked back with a sharper bitterness of desire to their childless Eden. The possibility of ever being able to go back there did not present itself even in the most distant future, and the thought that with each year the sound of Sirenian mandolins, the scent of Sirenian roses, and the brilliance of Sirenian moonlight would grow fainter dabbled Jasmine's pillow with tears when she fell asleep in the sentimental night-time, and when she woke made of the sun a heavy brass dish that extinguished instead of illuminating the new day.

Jasmine's last hope was that her cousins would offer to take her to the links; but a fortnight passed, on every evening of which it was decided that she should accompany Lettice and Pamela the following morning, and on every morning of which it was decided at the last moment that she had better wait until to-morrow. Her time was spent partly in dreary walks with Cousin Edith, partly in what Lady Grant euphemistically called checking her accounts, a process that consisted in Jasmine's having to be at her elbow for whatever assistance she required in managing the household and several of her exacting charities. In a rash moment Jasmine alluded to Aunt Ellen's suggestion about learning to typewrite. Aunt May declared that this was a capital notion, and presently Cousin Edith, on one of what she called her little expeditions, discovered in an obscure part of the town a second-hand typewriter that was really very cheap. A long discussion ensued whether or not Lady Grant was justified in spending the £3 10s. asked by the shopman. Cousin Edith for three successive days wrestled with him penny by penny until for £3 7s. 6d. she secured that typewriter, of which she was as proud as she would have been proud of her eldest child, that is, of course, with marriage previously understood. Once she even described it as graceful; and she used to play upon it ghostly sonatas, occasionally by mistake pressing too hard upon one of the stops and uttering a rudimentary scream of affright when she beheld an ambiguous letter take shape upon the paper. Jasmine, who was seriously expected to become proficient upon this machine, was not so fond of it. She put forward a theory that, when it had ceased to be a typewriter, it had been used by children as a toy, which shocked Cousin Edith.

"Or perhaps it was saved from a wreck," Jasmine went on.

"Oh, hush!" Cousin Edith breathed. "How can you say such things?"

Gradually Jasmine mastered some of the whims of the instrument; she learnt, for instance, that if one wanted a capital A, the birth of a capital A had to be helped by pressing down S at the same time; she also learnt to control the self-assertiveness of the Z, which used to butt in at the least excuse as if for years it had resented the infrequency of its employment and, thriving on idleness, was able now when the more common stops rattled like old bones to dominate them all.

Jasmine's mastery of the instrument was fatal to her. Nobody else could use it; and Lady Grant was so pleased with the effect of typewritten correspondence upon the dignity of her charities that Cousin Edith, deposed from whatever secretarial state was left to her, found herself betrayed by her own purchase. Sir Hector, with what was impressed upon Jasmine as unusual magnanimity even for Sir Hector, had invited his niece to accompany him once more upon his afternoon walks; but the arrival of the typewriter kept her so busy that Lady Grant began to say 'To-morrow' to these walks as her daughters said 'To-morrow' to the links. Finally Jasmine, in a rage, decapitated the Z stop, thereby producing such a perfect specimen of correspondence that her aunt, much moved, announced that she really should go to the links on the very next day, and that she herself would go with her. What happened to the typewriter between five o'clock that evening and the following morning was never known; but that epistle was its swan-song. Perhaps the execution of the Z stop, on whom the others had come to rely so completely, put too great a strain on their old bones, or perhaps Cousin Edith in the silence of the night severed the machine's spinal cord. Anyway, next morning, when Lady Grant, having proposed for the fifteenth time that visit to the links, asked Jasmine if she would be so kind as to type out a schedule of the rules of her club for Tired Sandwichmen, Jasmine announced that the machine was no longer working. Her aunt seemed unable to believe her, and insisted that the schedule should be done. Jasmine showed her the first four lines, which looked like a Magyar proclamation, and Lady Grant exclaimed, "What a waste of £3 7s. 6d.!" Cousin Edith, whose *amour propre* was wounded by this imputation, observed with the bitter mildness of pale India ale:

"Not altogether wasted, May. Jasmine has learnt typewriting. I wish that when I was young I had had such an opportunity."

"Well, perhaps we can go to the links after all," Lady Grant sighed. "The girls always take the tram, but we'll drive in the car. I don't think that you had better come, Edith. The last time, don't you remember, you received that nasty blow with the ball. Hector," she called, "you wouldn't mind if Cousin Edith gave you your lunch?"

Sir Hector bowed gallantly, and vowed that he should be delighted to be given his lunch by Cousin Edith. He was in a good temper that morning, for he had just been reading the obituary of a rival baronet of medicine. Cousin Edith did her best to make Jasmine sensible of the gratitude she owed to her aunt for this wonderful treat, and herself came as far as the front gate, holding Spot by the collar and waving until the car was out of sight.

Jasmine did not much enjoy her drive, because every time they turned a corner or a child crossed the road a quarter of a mile ahead, or a dog barked, or a sparrow flew up in front, her aunt gasped and clutched her wrist. And even when the road was straight and clear as far as they could see the drive was tiresome, because her aunt could talk about nothing except Nuckett's carefulness.

"Nuckett is such a careful driver. But of course he knows that your uncle would not keep him for a moment otherwise. We hesitated for a long time before we bought the car, and in fact it wasn't until we had given Nuckett a month's trial.... Oh, now there's a flock of sheep! Thank goodness it's Nuckett, who's always particularly careful with sheep ... ah!..."

And so on, in a mixture of complacency and terror, until they reached the links and Jasmine was really there.

Travellers have often related the alarm they felt at first when some savage chief, wishing to pay his distinguished visitors a compliment, arranged for a war-dance by the young men of his tribe. It was that kind of alarm which Jasmine felt when she found herself for the first time on golf links. She knew that it was a game. She kept assuring herself that it was only a game. But the Italian strain in her was continually asserting itself and making her wonder whether people who behaved thus in jest might not at any moment be seized with an extension of their madness and take to behaving thus in earnest.

Lady Grant, however, made her way calmly toward the club-house and put her name down for lunch with one guest, explaining to Jasmine that no doubt the girls would have arranged a luncheon party on their own account. Then she went into the ladies' room, picked up a ladies' paper, advised Jasmine to do the same, and ensconced herself comfortably in a wicker chair on the verandah, where she seemed inclined to stay for the rest of the morning. Half an hour later she looked up from the fifth paper and asked Jasmine how she liked golf.

"I don't think I understand it very well yet."

"It's an interesting game," said her aunt. "Your uncle wanted me to take it up last year, and I did have two lessons; but I think it's really more a game for young people, and your uncle decided that it was bad for my rheumatism. Still, I was beginning to realize its fascination—the holes, you know, and all that—and I believe that when you actually do hit the ball each time it's much less tiring. I tried to persuade your uncle to take it up himself, but he felt it was too late to begin, although of course he's a member of the club and plays bridge here every Thursday afternoon."

Another half-hour went by.

"Really," Lady Grant declared, "I think the advertisements nowadays are wonderful. Dear me, how you'll enjoy your first visit to London. You mustn't spend your allowance too quickly, my dear. You mustn't believe everything you see in the advertisements."

While Lady Grant was speaking, the rich voice of Lettice close at hand was unmistakably heard.

"He stimied me on the ninth."

Jasmine looked up apprehensively on an impulse to warn Lettice of her mother's presence before she gave herself away any more; but at that moment Lettice saw them and exclaimed rather crossly:

"Hullo, mother! Are *you* here?"

"Yes, dear, I have paid our long-promised visit. Did you have a good game?"

Lettice made a gesture of indifference, and there was a short pause. "I suppose you'll be going home for lunch?" she enquired.

"No, I've ordered lunch for Jasmine and myself here. But don't let that disturb you, dear. We shall amuse each other if you and Pamela are already engaged. We shall understand, shan't we, Jasmine?"

"As a matter of fact," said Lettice, "we are lunching with Harry Vibart and Claude Whittaker. We've a foursome on afterwards."

"Delightful," said her mother genially. "Don't you bother about us. I don't think I've looked at this week's *Country Life* yet; have you finished with it?" she asked Jasmine, who, having for some time been listlessly turning over the pages had suddenly found *Country Life* to be of such absorbing interest that she had buried her face in its faint oily smell. Lady Grant never really enjoyed looking at a paper unless she had taken it away from somebody else, and when her niece surrendered it she smiled at her.

"My dear Jasmine, how pale you are!" she exclaimed, and bade her ring the bell for a glass of water.

Jasmine, with a reproach for her treacherous Southern heart, tried to appear composed.

"No, really please, Aunt May," she murmured.

"But I insist, Jasmine. If you won't look after yourself, I must look after you. Ring the bell at once, there's a good girl, and you shall have a glass of water."

Jasmine, to conceal her emotion, accepted the excuse that her aunt offered, and did as she had been told.

"A glass of water for my niece, please, Frank," said Lady Grant to the waiter, and she managed to convey in the tone of her command that a glass of water for her niece would be different somehow from ordinary water. Perhaps it was, for when Frank brought it, all the people round looked up to watch Jasmine drinking it; and everyone who has drunk water in similar circumstances will know that it does then have a peculiar taste of its own, rather like that positive nothingness which is the flavour of permanganate of potash and peroxide of hydrogen.

Soon after this Pamela came out on the verandah, and she, like her sister, had to be reassured of the sanctity of her lunch.

"But at least," Jasmine thought, "he'll be able to see me, and perhaps when he sees me he'll ask to be introduced to Aunt May."

At this moment Frank appeared again and asked Lady Grant in an awe-struck whisper if she had not ordered cold chicken.

"Yes, Frank. Cold chicken for two."

"The head steward asks me to say, my lady, that unfortunately there is no more cold chicken left."

"Dear me," Lady Grant exclaimed, "what a disappointment! Well, perhaps Jasmine and I had better go home to lunch after all."

Neither Lettice nor Pamela made any attempt to detain her; and Jasmine decided to forget all about Mr. Vibart, and all about everything indeed that could ever for one moment lighten her future.

But Frank protested:

"I beg pardon, my lady, only the head steward requested me to inform your ladyship that there is cold duck."

"Then in that case I think we may as well stay," said her ladyship.

"The ducks are very tough," Lettice snapped.

"I beg pardon, Miss Grant," Frank respectfully argued, "the head steward is now procuring our ducks for the club from another farm. Will you take apple sauce, my lady?"

Lady Grant nodded decidedly.

"Very good, my lady."

And Frank glided away, leaving in Jasmine's mind the thought of a powerful and sympathetic personality.

Ten minutes later they went into the dining-room of the club, where a quantity of women with bright woollen jerseys and bright harsh voices shouted across the room the tale of their prowess, or gobbled down their food in a hurry to get off before the links became crowded. The men too seemed much excited by what they had achieved so far that morning. For the first time since she had been in England Jasmine divined that underneath the stolid Anglo-Saxon exterior palpitated ambition and romance and the dark emotions of Southern passion. These rosy barbarians who vied with one another in making their legs ridiculous with fantastic knickerbockers, whose cheeks were rasped by east winds, who illustrated with knife and fork and salt-cellar the vicissitudes of their pastime, became intelligible to her as the leaders of civilization. In Sirene she had always been proud of being English; but hitherto in Spaborough she had congratulated herself on being far more Italian. Now with the consciousness that one of these paladins had turned aside from his purposeful sport to observe herself, she was eager to join in all this; and if to smite a ball farther than other women was to be accounted desirable in the eyes of men, or if to stand on a hillock looking like a scarecrow in a gale was an invitation to love, then so be it; she should not disdain such wiles.

Lady Grant had chosen a small table in the window, one of those small tables with such a large vase of flowers in the middle that the feeder is left with the impression that he is eating off the rim of a flower-pot. Moreover, with the excuse that she did not like so much light, she had placed herself in a recess of the window, with the result that Jasmine had her back to the room and the light full in her eyes.

"I'm afraid you've got the light in your eyes," said her aunt, and she made signs with her nose that her niece should move over to the left, where at the next table a fat man with a back like the nether part of a rhinoceros was taking up so much space that it was obviously impossible for Jasmine to squeeze her chair between his back and the side of their table. She hesitated for a moment, hoping that her aunt would indicate the other side of the table where she herself had been sitting; but she did not offer to move her bag, which took up what space was left by the vase of flowers, and Jasmine was too anxious to have a view of the room to take the risk by moving it herself of being advised to stay where she was.

Frank, the waiter, who had come to her rescue once already, was the instrument chosen by destiny to preserve her a second time from disappointment. For just as he was handing the duck to Lady Grant, the fat man at the next table, outraged by some piece of news in the paper he was reading, threw himself back in his chair so violently that he swept the dish out of Frank's hand. The noise made everybody look in their direction, and Lady Grant and Jasmine, who had jumped up in affright, were conspicuous to the world. It was thus that Mr. Vibart, lunching at the far end of the room, perceived Jasmine, learned who Lady Grant was, and without a moment's hesitation came across and insisted that they should all lunch at his table. Lettice and Pamela did not dare to look as disagreeable as they felt, for each knew from her sister's countenance how ugly ill-temper made her. The host was so boisterously cheerful that the luncheon party appeared to be going splendidly, and when about two o'clock Lettice glanced at her watch and asked if they ought not to be getting along with the foursome before the links filled up, Jasmine thought that she could have no idea how old such fussiness made her seem.

"I say, Claude, do you know," Mr. Vibart said gravely to his companion, a young man to find any other adjective for whom would be a waste of time, "I say, Claude, I believe I did strain my leg in the ravine before the eighth. Most extraordinary! It's gone quite stiff." He called to another friend who was passing out of the dining-room unaccompanied. "Ryder! Are you engaged this afternoon? I wish you'd take my place in a foursome, like a good chap. I've strained my leg."

"Oh, let's postpone it," Lettice begged, with a desperate attempt to hide with an expression of concern the chagrin she felt.

"Oh no, don't do that," said Vibart. "Ryder might think you were trying to snub him. He's an awful sensitive fellow."

Claude Whittaker, whom Vibart had been kicking under the table with his strained leg, urged the prosecution of the foursome, and the two sisters, with a reputation of jolly good-fellowship to maintain, had to yield. When they were gone, Vibart turned to Lady Grant and asked if he could come and sit with her on the verandah. He said that he thought he could manage to limp as far as that.

"But how are you going to get home?" she asked.

"Oh, I shall get a lift in a car from somebody."

Lady Grant hesitated. She was wondering if she should offer to drive him in hers, or rather she was wondering if she could not manage to get him and Lettice into the car.

"Didn't I see you at York railway station about a fortnight ago?" Mr. Vibart was saying to Jasmine. "On a Sunday afternoon it was."

"My niece did pass through York," Lady Grant admitted unwillingly.

"I thought I recognized her. Are you staying long at Spaborough?"

"My niece is staying with us indefinitely," said Lady Grant. "But how long we stay in Spaborough will depend rather upon the weather. Besides, my husband's patients are waiting for him."

"They will become impatients if he doesn't go back soon," the young man laughed.

Lady Grant had never heard anybody make a joke about Sir Hector's profession, and if Mr. Vibart had not been the heir of an older baronetcy than her husband's she might have resented it.

"How long will it be before my daughters get back?" she asked after a while, when she found that the conversation between Jasmine and Mr. Vibart was steadily leaving her behind.

"I should guess in about an hour and a half."

"Well, in that case I think my niece and I ought to be getting home now," said Lady Grant. "Perhaps if I sent back the car," she added, "you would let my daughters drive you home?"

"Thank you very much," said Mr. Vibart. "I really think I ought not to wait so long as that. My leg seems to be getting stiffer every second. But that's all right. I shall get a lift. May I come and call on you one afternoon, as soon as my leg's a little better?"

"But of course we shall be delighted," said Lady Grant graciously. "Perhaps you will arrange a day with my daughter Lettice so that we are sure to be in? Good-bye, Mr. Vibart. I do hope your leg will soon be all right."

"Oh yes, I think it will," said Mr. Vibart. Nor was his optimism unjustified, for the very next afternoon it was well enough for him to call at Strathspey House, where, having forgotten to make any arrangement with Lettice, he found that Sir Hector had just gone out, that Lady Grant was lying down, and that Jasmine was by herself in the drawing-room. He knew that Lettice and Pamela were safely engaged on the links, and before Cousin Edith divined that something was going on in the house, he had had five minutes alone with Jasmine.

Mr. Vibart spent most of that five minutes in telling Jasmine how much he disliked her cousins; he was just going to demonstrate how much he must like her in order to put up with the company of such cousins for a whole fortnight of foursomes when Cousin Edith came in. Naturally in what she called her intimate heart-to-heart talks with the dear girls, and what they called keeping Cousin Edith from feeling too keenly her position, she had been told a good deal about young Mr. Vibart, nephew and heir of Sir John Vibart; and in her anxiety to stand well with Lettice and Pamela she had committed a kind of vicarious bigamy, so earnestly had she encouraged both of the girls to believe that she was the chosen of Mr. Vibart. The moment she heard—and she heard these things by being as tactful with the servants as she was with the family—that Mr. Vibart was in the house and was shut up in the drawing-room with Miss Jasmine, she was alert to defend the honour of her patrons. She knew, of course, that such an insignificant girl as Jasmine had no chance of rivalling either dearest Lettice or darling Pamela; but at the same time Cousin Edith's profound distrust of all men disinclined her to run any risks. Besides, she saw no reason why Jasmine should be puffed up with an undue sense of her own importance by being allowed to suppose that she was capable of entertaining anybody like Mr. Vibart.

It may well be imagined, therefore, with what dismay Cousin Edith discovered that Mr. Vibart was identical with what had already been magnified by time's distorting hand into an agent of White Slavery, which was the only kind of appeal she could allow Jasmine to be capable of making.

She was now in a dilemma: if she revealed the secret of that meeting in the Spa, she would have implied that the impression made by Jasmine was capable of enduring, though it had been stamped and surcharged over and over again by the images of Lettice and Pamela; on the other hand, if she kept quiet, and if by any inconceivable chance—and men were men—this young man should really prefer Jasmine to her cousins, she would run the risk of being suspected as an accomplice. On the whole, Cousin Edith decided that it was far safer to betray both parties. She resolved, while assuring Jasmine of her intention to keep the secret of her previous acquaintance with Mr. Vibart, to do her best to prevent its ripening into anything more permanent, and at the first opportunity, by somehow involving Jasmine with her aunt, to procure her banishment from the family, and thus remove what seemed likely to be a rival to Lettice, Pamela, and herself. Thanks to Cousin Edith's discretion nobody suspected that the two young people were interested in one another. Indeed it would have needed a considerable display of affection to have convinced Lettice and Pamela Grant that anybody so foreign-looking as Jasmine was capable of attracting anybody so English-looking as Harry Vibart. So Lettice and Pamela supposed that his now daily visits were paid for them, and though they would have been better pleased to observe his admiration wax daily on the links, they were much too fond of him to let him play golf a moment before his leg was completely healed; moreover, since they did not want him to feel that he was depriving them of a pleasure, they protested that as a matter of fact they were growing tired of golf, and that one round in the morning was enough for anybody. There was a charming display of sisterly affection when Lettice entreated Pamela and Pamela implored Lettice not to give up golf on her account.

"Poor Claude Whittaker will feel quite deserted," Lettice declared spitefully.

"Yes," Pamela replied. "Only this morning he asked me why you always went home for lunch nowadays."

"I don't know why he should ask that," Lettice exclaimed.

"Don't you, dear?" her sister sweetly marvelled.

"For he can't be missing me," said Lettice, "because he's so devoted to you."

"Oh no, my dear, he's much more devoted to you," replied Pamela.

"They're such affectionate girls," Lady Grant whispered to Mr. Vibart. "They really do admire each other, and that's so rare in sisters nowadays." Lady Grant always implied by her disapproval of the present that she and all to do with her were survivals of the Golden Age. "And really," she went on in a low voice, "everybody likes them. I know that as a mother I ought not to talk so fondly, but I do believe that they are the most popular girls anywhere."

Mr. Vibart nodded in absent-minded sagacity.

"I never met your uncle, Mr. Vibart," Sir Hector said importantly.

"No, sir, he keeps very much to himself."

"Quite so. Quite so." Sir Hector wanted Vibart to realize that baronets had certain instincts and habits which he, as one of the species, emphasized in his own manner of life. "No, when I get away for a few weeks' rest," he went on, "I like to rest; and as I know that your uncle comes to Spaborough for the same reasons as myself, I haven't disturbed him with a card. A fine name, a fine name! Fourteenth in precedence, I believe? A Jacobean creation? Yes, to be sure." Sir Hector wished that he were a Jacobean creation himself, and he often thought when he saw himself in the glass that he looked like a Jacobean creation. So he did, just as Jacobean furniture in Tottenham Court Road looks very like the real thing.

"My title dies with me," he sighed, "and to me there's always something very sad in the thought of a title's becoming extinct. You, I believe, are the last representative?"

Vibart nodded.

"You ought to marry," said Sir Hector, and though the advice was given by the baronet, it sounded as though it were given by the doctor.

"I certainly must," Vibart agreed lightly. "By the way, you haven't forgotten that to-night's a gala night at the Spa?"

"Indeed no," said Lady Grant. "Aren't we expecting you to dinner, so that you can escort us afterwards to see the fireworks?"

Later, when the composition of the evening's party was being discussed, Jasmine perceived a suggestion hovering on her aunt's lips that she should stay at home and keep her uncle company. But Sir Hector on this occasion was somewhat obtuse for a man who had won rank, money, and reputation by his ability to indulge feminine whims, and he decided that contrary to his usual custom he would himself attend the gala.

"I like Vibart," he affirmed when the guest had gone home to dress. "A very decent fellow indeed. It must be a great consolation to Sir John to feel that the title will be in good hands. A very fine young fellow indeed! I shall quite enjoy going to the fireworks with him."

There was only the problem of Spot's loneliness to be considered, which it was decided that Cousin Edith should be called upon to solve.

"Poor old Spot," said Cousin Edith deprecatingly. "Spot shall stay with me. Yes, he shall, the good old dog! Poor Spot! Good old Spot! I shall be able to see the rockets beautifully from my window. And Spotticums will be able to see the rockets too. Yes, he will, the clever old Spot!"

It was a fine night; the gardens of the Spa were crowded with people, the sky with stars. Sir Hector, who was tall enough to be independent of his place in the largest crowd, kept ejaculating, "What a splendid view we have got! We really are remarkably lucky to have found such an excellent place! By Jove, that was a magnificent shower of gold! Upon my soul, I'd forgotten how good the Spa fireworks were."

Every time Sir Hector applauded a new pyrotechnic effect, the people in his immediate neighbourhood all stretched their necks and stood on tiptoe to see if they too could not catch a glimpse of what had aroused his enthusiasm. The result of this continual straining and struggling by the crowd was to separate one from another the various members of the Strathspey House party.

"Don't bother about the fireworks," said Vibart to Jasmine when one of Sir Hector's loud expressions of approval had been followed by a kind of panic of curiosity in his neighbourhood and Jasmine, in order not to be swept down over the slope of the cliff, had been compelled to catch hold of Mr. Vibart's arm. "Let's get out of this squash and take a breather."

It was only when they had pushed their way through to the outskirts of the crowd that they discovered the full enchantment of the night. A hump-backed moon, the colour of an old guinea, was lying large upon the horizon; fairy lamps bordered the paths that wound about the bosky cliffs; and from time to time bursting rockets were reflected in streaks of colour upon the tranquil and hueless sea. They strolled along until they found a deserted corner of the promenade, where, leaning over the parapet, they watched swarming on the sands below the people who were come to watch the fireworks as freely as they might watch the stars every night of their lives. Beyond the crowd stretched a wide expanse of wet sand, already glimmering faintly in response to the rising moon. From the beach below a shadow under the parapet breathed up to them in a hoarse voice:

"Lovely night for a sail, sir."

"Why, there's not a breath of wind," Vibart contradicted.

"Lovely breeze about half a mile out, sir. Better have a couple of hours' nice sail, sir."

"It would be rather jolly," Vibart suggested with a glance at Jasmine. She, her eyes brimming with memories of the South, could not gainsay him.

"The whiting's biting something lovely to-night, sir," tempted the hoarse voice again. "There's a party just come in, sir, took 'em by the dozen in half an hour."

A tempting exit to the sands was visible close to where they were standing, the tall iron turnstile of which was like a gate to the moon. Vibart hurried through.

"And now you must come," he pointed out, "because I can't get back."

"That's right, lady," breathed the voice. "He can't get back."

A maroon crashed overhead, and before the echoes had died away Jasmine was on the free side of the turnstile. The voice, which belonged to a burly longshoreman, led the way seaward, and when they were clear of the crowd on the beach shouted:

"*Mermaid*, ahoy! Jonas Pretty is my own name," he added.

Some of the crew flopped toward them like walruses and helped them along planks over the ribbed and rippling sands to the *Mermaid's* dinghy; and presently they were aboard with the crew grunting over the oars to catch the legendary breeze half a mile off shore.

In the last act of *The Merchant of Venice* Shakespeare has said all that there is to say about moonlight and its effect upon young people, and if Harry Vibart was less expressive than young Lorenzo, Jasmine Grant was at least as susceptible as pretty Jessica. She had a moment's sadness in the recollection of her father's death after such a night in the Bay of Salerno; but it was no more than a transient gloom, like a thin cloud that scarcely dims the face of the moon in its swift voyage past. Indeed, the sorrowful memory actually added something to her joy of the present; for fleeting though the emotion was, it endured long enough to stir the depths of her heart and to make her more grateful to her companion for the beauty of this night.

The skipper of the *Mermaid* had spoken the truth: the light breeze he had promised did arrive, and presently the grunt of oars gave place to the lisp and murmur of water and to airy melodies aloft.

"Magnificent, eh what?" Vibart asked.

"Glorious," Jasmine agreed.

Pointing to a small craft half a mile away to starboard, he quoted two lines of verse:

A silver sail on a silver sea
Under a silver moon.

"That really exactly expresses it, don't you think?"

"Perfectly," she agreed.

"Funny that those lines should come so pat. I don't usually spout poetry, you know. It really is awfully good, isn't it?—

A sil*ver sail on a* sil*ver sea*
Under a silver *moon!*"

He marked the beat more emphatically at the second time of quoting. "It's really awfully musical. You know, I admire a chap who can write poetry like that. Some people rather despise poets, but if you come to think what a lot of pleasure they give....

A silver *sail on a* silver *sea*
Under a silver moon!"

"Who wrote it?" asked Jasmine idly.

"Oh, great Scott, don't ask me. It's extraordinary enough that I should remember the lines. I must have learnt them at my dame's school. Years ago. Quite fifteen years ago. Terrific, isn't it? I'm twenty-four, you know. That's the worst of being an heir. I wanted to go out and try my hand at coffee in British East, but my old great-uncle kicked up a fuss. He's a funny old boy. Likes to have me around, and then grumbles all the time because I'm not doing anything. Says my conversation would cure a defaulting solicitor of insomnia. I bucked him up rather, though, by talking about Italy. Do you know, I think he'd rather like you.

A silver sail on a *silver* sea
Under *a silver moon.*

"Dash it, I can't get those lines out of my head. It's worse than a tune. Yes, I think he'd rather like you, Miss Grant. Miss Grant! That sounds absurd on a night like this. Now, I think Jasmine's a charming name. Jasmine! It seems to fit in so well with ... *a silver sail* ... look, here, do you mind stopping me if I begin again? Jasmine! Would you jump overboard if I called you Jasmine?"

"I'd rather you called me Jasmine."

"And of course you'll return the compliment? My name's Harry. It's a perfectly normal name, so you needn't blush."

Mr. Jonas Pretty interrupted any embarrassment with the news that the whiting were biting. Presently the boat was in a confusion of fish. As fast as they dropped the lines they had to tug them in again with half a dozen iridescent victims squirming and leaping and flapping on the hooks, and in half an hour the bottom of the boat was aglow with silver fire.

"Well, I think we've caught enough," said Harry Vibart. "And I mustn't keep you out late, Jasmine. Better sail back now, Skipper."

"Aye, aye, sir."

Mr. Pretty shouted a number of unintelligible and raucous commands, and the breeze immediately died away.

"Lost that nice little wind we had," he grumbled. "That means a bit of a pull back. You wouldn't like to stay out all night, sir, with the whiting biting so lovely? There's a lot of gentlemen likes to do that and come back with the sunrise."

"No, no, this lady has to get home."

Mr. Pretty shook his head reproachfully at such a lack of adventurous spirit.

"It'll be a long pull back, sir."

Indeed the lights of Spaborough did look very far away.

"Can't be helped. We must get back. How long will it take?"

"About a couple of hours, sir."

"What?"

"We'd better steer for the harbour."

Jasmine did not blame Harry—in the excitement of pulling up her line she had fallen easily into calling him by his Christian name—for the flight of the wind.

"I say, it's awfully sporting of you to be so decent about it," he said, turning her behaviour into an excuse to take her hand.

"It's not your fault."

During the long pull back to the harbour Harry Vibart quoted no more poetry; indeed he hardly seemed to notice the moonlight, so deeply was he engaged in telling Jasmine all about his early life and his present life, and what he should do when he inherited his uncle's title and estate.

"Of course I shall have to get married."

"Of course," she agreed.

They looked at each other for a brief instant; but almost simultaneously they looked away again and began to count the whiting. Soon afterward they reached the harbour.

The clocks of Spaborough were striking the apprehensive hour of one when Jasmine and Harry Vibart, each carrying a large bunch of fish, disembarked at the pier of the old harbour.

"I'm afraid that they really will be very cross," said Jasmine. "But never mind, I've had a glorious evening, and I've enjoyed myself, more than I ever have since I left Sirene."

"They might be cross if we hadn't got these whiting," Harry pointed out. "But you can't go against evidence like this. I don't see a carriage anywhere, do you?"

"Perhaps it's too late."

From the old fishing town to South Parade was at least an hour's walk uphill all the way. The whiting began to weigh rather heavily. It was obvious that Jasmine would not be able to carry her bunch, and Harry relieved her of it. After climbing for about five minutes he began to feel that the bunches were more than even he could manage, and pulling off four fish as he would have pulled off four bananas, he offered them to a policeman who was standing at the corner.

"Just caught," he explained cheerfully.

"Thank you, sir," said the constable. "I'll wrap them up and leave them on this window-sill."

"Don't lose them," said Vibart. "They're fresh."

"That's all right, sir. I'll wrap them up in the evening paper. I'm not off duty till six."

"They'll still be quite fresh then," said Vibart encouragingly.

He looked round to see if there was anybody else to whom he could make a present of fresh fish; as there was nobody else in sight, he advised the constable to have two more, and so make up the half-dozen. Another five minutes of slow ascent passed, during which the whiting seemed to have grown into cod. A wretched old woman asleep in an archway, her head bowed in her lap, offered a good opportunity for charity, and Harry was just going to lay a couple of whiting in her lap when Jasmine suggested that if the old woman put her head down any lower she would touch them with her face, which might startle her too much and spoil the pleasure of the surprise.

"Well, I'll lay them on the pavement beside her," said Harry. He also put a couple on her other side, so that she would be sure to see them and not miss her breakfast.

"It's jolly to think how happy she'll be when she wakes up."

"But if she hasn't got anywhere to sleep," Jasmine objected, "I don't suppose she's got anywhere to cook whiting."

"Oh yes," he assured her, "she'll get them cooked all right. Oh, rather! She'll find some workmen who are mending the road."

"But how will that help her to cook whiting?"

"Oh, they always have a fire. I don't know why, but they always do. Still not a carriage to be seen!"

The clocks struck a quarter-past one. The whiting had grown from cod to sharks. They toiled on without meeting a soul till the clocks struck the half-hour, and the whiting from sharks were become whales.

"It would be a pity to go back without these confounded fish," said Vibart, "because it really was a remarkable catch. Besides, fresh whiting's tremendously good for breakfast. It does seem a most extraordinary thing that there's not a carriage anywhere. I think I'll try another way of carrying them—one on each end of my stick, and then I'll put my stick over my shoulder like a milkmaid."

He was demonstrating how much easier it was to carry whiting in this way, and saying what an extraordinary thing it was that he had not thought of doing so before, when both bunches slipped forward, the front one falling into the road and the second one only being prevented from joining its companion by Vibart's shoulder.

"That's a pity," he said. "But I don't think we ought to pick them up, do you? They're rather dusty, and I really think we've got enough. There must be at least sixty left. Only it seems rather wasteful to leave a lot of whiting in a road."

"Come along," Jasmine urged. "For goodness' sake let's leave them and get back. Now, if you give me one end of the stick and take the other yourself we can easily carry the rest between us."

Just as the clock struck two they reached Strathspey House. It seemed as dead in the moonlight as a spent firework; and Jasmine's heart sank.

"It does look as if they were very angry indeed," she said.

"They'll soon cheer up when they see the whiting," Vibart prophesied. "I'll ring."

He rang repeatedly, but there was no answer.

"Perhaps I'd better knock."

He knocked repeatedly; several windows in Balmoral were opened, and dim heads stared down inquisitively; but Strathspey House remained mute.

"Why doesn't that beastly dog bark?" complained Vibart. "It barks all day long. Perhaps I'd better shout."

"Oh no, don't shout."

"Will you ring the bell while I knock again?"

The orchestral effect achieved what the solo had failed to achieve. Sir Hector put out his long neck and asked severely if that were his niece.

"We got slightly becalmed, sir," said Vibart. "But we had a splendid catch. You'll be delighted when you see all the whiting we've brought back for you. Between sixty and seventy. They're so fresh that you'll be able to have them for breakfast both to-morrow and the day after."

But Sir Hector did not reply, and for nearly ten minutes Strathspey House gave no further sign of recognition. Then the front door was opened by Hargreaves, so completely dressed that it was hard to believe that she had really been roused from bed by Sir Hector's method of internal communication.

From a landing above Lady Grant's voice was heard. "You'd better go up to bed at once, Jasmine, and we will talk about your escapade in the morning."

"I'm afraid there's not much I can do," said Harry, somewhat abashed by the discouraging reception. "But I'll get round as soon as I can in the morning and explain that it was all my fault. You mustn't be angry with Miss Grant, Lady Grant," he called up. "I'm the only person to blame. Can you see our haul of whiting? You ought to have a look at them before they're cooked."

The slamming of a distant door was Lady Grant's reply to this.

"Bit annoyed, I'm afraid," he said, shaking his head, and then, turning to the parlourmaid, he asked her where she would like to put the fish.

The question was answered by the fish, because the main string broke, and they went slithering all over the hall.

"I don't know, sir, I'm sure where they'd better be put," said Hargreaves, looking rather frightened.

"Can't you get a dish or something from the kitchen?"

"No, sir, I'm afraid I can't. Cook always has her ladyship's orders to take the key of the basement door up to bed with her, and she's rather funny about being woke up."

"But look here," Vibart protested, "we can't leave all these splendid fish to get trodden on. They're whiting! You know, those fish they usually serve like kittens running after their tails. They won't have any tails left if they're going to be walked over by everybody."

He looked round the hall, and his eye fell upon the card-tray.

"Here's the very thing," he cried, and emptying the cards into the umbrella stand, he began to heap as many whiting as he could on the tray. "Well, that's saved enough for breakfast. We'll put the rest in a corner. Lend me your apron."

The prim Hargreaves was as much taken aback by this suggestion as her colleague Hopkins had been taken aback by Jasmine's attempt to borrow a chemise on the evening of her arrival. But mechanically she divested herself, and the whiting were hung up in a bundle on the hat-rack.

"I'll be round very early," Harry promised Jasmine. "Sorry I've let you in for trouble. I enjoyed myself—well, tremendously."

"So did I," she said. "Tremendously."

Hargreaves without her apron seemed scarcely willing to open the door for him; but she managed to do it somehow, and Jasmine went slowly upstairs to the sound of bolts being driven home, of chains clanking, and latches clicking. It was like being taken back to prison.

Immediately after breakfast the next morning Lady Grant showed her sense of the gravity of the occasion by postponing her household duties until she had had what she called an explanation with her niece about her behaviour last night. As soon as they were closeted in the drawing-room, Jasmine, supposing that she really was anxious for an explanation, began to give a perfectly straightforward account of the misadventure. Lady Grant, however, cut her short before she had time even to explain the accident by which she and Vibart were separated from the rest of the party.

"I am sorry, my dear Jasmine, to find that your only object is to make excuses for your behaviour. There is nothing I dislike so much as excuses."

"But I haven't begun to excuse myself yet," Jasmine retorted.

Her aunt smiled patiently. "Perhaps you will allow me to say without interruptions what I was going to say. I am willing to make every allowance for you, remembering that you have been brought up in a wild island in the south of Italy, and remembering that your poor father had odd notions about the education of young girls. But you are old enough to realize that Spaborough is not Sirene, and that to come back at two o'clock in the morning after spending the whole night sailing about with a young man on the open sea is not a very kind way of showing your affection for your relations, who have been only too anxious to do everything on their side to help you. You cannot complain of the warmth of your welcome in England, and you must admit that your Uncle Hector and I showed ourselves ready to do all we could to rescue you from the condition in which you found yourself after your father's death. I do not wish to say too much about Mr. Vibart's conduct. I can only express my surprise that Sir John Vibart's nephew should so absolutely deceive us in this way. And I blame Cousin Edith greatly. Please do not think that I have not already spoken to her very severely for the part she played in what I can only call a vulgar intrigue. She should, of course, have let me know at once that you and this young man had made each other's acquaintance at a railway station. The idea of it! I should have thought that your natural nice-minded feelings, if not your conscience, would have told you that casual conversation with young men at railway stations is not the way in which young girls in your position behave."

"I don't see any difference between speaking to a young man at a railway station and speaking to a young man at a golf club," Jasmine argued.

"Please do not add to your faults by being rude," Lady Grant begged. "Your rudeness only shows that you are, as I suspected, insensible to kindness. I have had so much ingratitude in the course of my various charities from all sorts and conditions of people whom I have tried to help that I no longer expect gratitude. But if I do not expect gratitude I certainly do not expect rudeness. I do not wish to recapitulate what your uncle has done for you; but I hope that when you come to yourself and think over what he has done for you you will realize how much there has been. Who was it sent you your fare from Sirene to Spaborough? Your uncle. Who was it, when you lost your season ticket before you had even used it once, bought you another one? Your uncle. Who was it that was so glad to give you an opportunity of learning the typewriter? Your uncle. Who was it that did his utmost to get us the best view of the fireworks yesterday evening? Your uncle. Finally, who was it, when the servants had gone to bed and the house was locked up, rang the bell in Hargreaves' room? Your uncle. I shall not go on, Jasmine, because I see by your face that you are hardening your heart. Well, luckily you have other uncles and aunts who have come forward to help you. I have just telegraphed to your Aunt Cuckoo at Hampstead to find out if she will be ready to receive you to-morrow. And although I think that you deserve that she should be told of your behaviour here, I am not going to tell her anything about it. I am not going to say a single word to prejudice your Aunt Cuckoo against you. But I most earnestly beg you, my dear Jasmine, to behave a little differently in Hampstead. Your Uncle Hector and I, who have daughters of our own, will always understand girls better than your Uncle Eneas or your Aunt Cuckoo can. Frankly, I do not think you will enjoy yourself as much in Hampstead as you have enjoyed yourself here, or as you might have enjoyed yourself here, if you had not displayed such a wilful spirit. What puzzles me is your unwillingness to make friends with Lettice and Pamela. It cannot be *their* fault, because they are friends with everybody. Even Mr. Vibart, who must be almost without any decent feelings of any kind whatsoever, liked Lettice and Pamela. Well, I am glad we have had this little explanation. When next you come to stay with us—for although at present your uncle is so much annoyed at being woken up last night that he has said quite positively that he will never have you to stay with us again, I am sure, knowing his goodness as I do, that he will ask you—when next you come to stay with us, I say, perhaps in London, I hope you won't go sailing about with young men half through the night. Of course you would not be able to do any actual sailing in London, but I mean the equivalent of sailing, like riding about on the outside of omnibuses at all hours. I fear that in your present hardened mood nothing can touch you, but I think that at least you might express your sorrow at making poor Spot so ill."

"Is Spot ill?" asked Jasmine.

"He is not ill any longer," said her aunt. "But you know how careful I am about his diet. Apparently he found one of those fish which you left lying about in the hall and was sick seven times this morning."

The explanation was over. The next morning Jasmine left Strathspey House, and late that afternoon was met at King's Cross by her Aunt Cuckoo. Cousin Edith shook her head a great deal at Jasmine's disgrace, but she was so glad to see the last of her that she could not resist waving her handkerchief to the departing car. As for Mr. Vibart, he called five times during the day, and every time Hargreaves, thinking of her apron, was glad to be authorized to inform him with cold politeness that nobody was at home.

Chapter Five

JASMINE's first experience of being succoured by rich relatives might have discouraged her from expecting a happy result from the second. Yet, although the Eneas Grants would be as much her patrons as the Hector Grants, there was something in the sound of 'Aunt Cuckoo' that suggested to her mind the anticipation of a positively more congenial atmosphere. It showed considerable elasticity to feel even subconsciously cheerful on this journey, with the weather south of York becoming overcast and a hundred miles of London breaking into a drench of rain, which turned to dripping fog on the outskirts of the city and made King's Cross an inferno of sodden gloom. In the first confusion of alighting from the train, Jasmine felt like a twig precipitated toward the drain of a gutter. In this din, in this damp and dusky chill made more obscure by fog and engine smoke and human breath, it hardly seemed worth while to have an opinion of one's own upon destination. Swept along toward the exits, Jasmine would soon have found herself astray in the phantasmagoria of the great squalid streets outside had she not been rescued by a porter whose kindly interest and paternal manner persuaded her to consider with due attention the advantages and disadvantages of the various routes from King's Cross to Hampstead.

A complicated but economical itinerary had no sooner been settled than a woman glided up to Jasmine with what in the press of the traffic seemed an almost ghostly ease of movement and asked in an appropriately toneless voice if she were her niece.

Jasmine, without thinking that amid the incalculable permutations and combinations of city life it was at least as probable that she was not this woman's niece as that she was, replied without hesitation that she was.

"Then how do you do?" said Aunt Cuckoo, offering first her right hand, then her left hand, and finally a cheek, the touch of which was like menthol on Jasmine's warm lips.

"I'm very well, thank you," she assured her aunt, transforming the conventional greeting into an important question by the gravity with which she answered it.

"Yes, it's a pity you got a porter," Aunt Cuckoo continued. "A great pity. Because I've got a porter as well. And it doesn't seem worth while, does it, to have two porters?" Jasmine agreed helplessly. "Unless your luggage is very heavy indeed," Aunt Cuckoo added, "and if it *is* very heavy indeed, we can't take it back with us in the brougham, and then I don't know what to do. Yes, it's a pity really you got a porter so quickly. Aunt May wrote us that you were rather impulsive."

She sighed; the rival porters waiting for a decision sighed too. Finally Jasmine took a shilling from her bag, presented it to her porter, and said "Thank you very much."

"Thank *you* very much, miss," said the porter, respectfully touching his cap and retiring from the contest. Aunt Cuckoo without commenting upon Jasmine's action, asked wearily if her luggage was in the back or the front of the train. By good luck Jasmine did know this, because Sir Hector's last bellowed words at Spaborough had been: "Don't forget that your luggage will be in the back part of the train! You are in a through carriage!"

By this time Jasmine's luggage had been reduced to one trunk. The crates with her father's pictures had on her uncle's advice been left at Strathspey House to be brought to London with the rest of the furniture when the family moved. The carpet bag had been presented to Hopkins as a parting gift, because Hopkins had once said how much it would appeal to a little niece of hers in Battersea. The basket of prickly pears had long ago been burnt, because Aunt May had supposed it capable of introducing subtropical insects into Strathspey House. There was therefore nothing left but her trunk, which Aunt Cuckoo decided was neither too large nor too heavy for the brougham. In fact, as a piece of luggage she made light of it altogether, and only gave her porter twopence, at which he said: "I shan't argue about it, mum. It's not worth arguing about."

"Are you dissatisfied?" asked Aunt Cuckoo.

The porter called upon Heaven with upturned eyes to witness his treatment and invited Aunt Cuckoo to keep her twopence.

"You want it more than I do, mum," he said.

The drive from King's Cross to Hampstead took a long time. No doubt the horse and the coachman were both tired, for Aunt Cuckoo explained that she had been shopping in London all day and that really she ought to have gone home much earlier. The small brougham looked like one of those commercial broughams in which old-fashioned travellers drive round to exhibit their wares to old-fashioned firms. Nor did the coachman look like a proper coachman, because he had a moustache, which somehow made the cockade in his hat look like a moustache too. When he stood up to push the trunk into place, Jasmine noticed that he was wearing baggy trousers under his coat, and for a moment she wondered if it could possibly be Uncle Eneas himself who was driving them. Afterward she discovered that he was really the gardener who consented to drive the brougham occasionally, because the horse was useful to his horticulture.

The climb up to the summit of the Heath seemed endless; Jasmine was glad when they got on to level ground again and the cardboard boxes fell back into place. Every time the rays of a passing lamp splashed the brougham Jasmine felt that she ought to say something, but before she had time to think of anything to say it was dark again; and the next splash of light always came as a surprise, so that in the end she gave up trying to think of anything to say and counted the lamp-posts instead. Driving in a brougham with Aunt Cuckoo reminded her of playing hide-and-seek in a wardrobe, when, although one was delighted to have found a good place in which to hide, one hoped that the searchers would not be long in finding it out.

Half-way down the tree-shaded slope of North End Road on the far side of the Heath the brougham turned aside down a short drive and pulled up before an irregular and what appeared in the darkness a rather attractive house. When the door was opened by a sallow butler, Jasmine perceived that the reason for her aunt's prolonged silence during the drive back was a large black respirator, of which she unmuzzled herself before she asked the butler something in a language which Jasmine did not understand, but which she afterwards found was Greek. Then, turning to her niece, she divulged as if it was a family secret that Uncle Eneas had gone to dine at his club that night.

Jasmine was not sorry to be spared the anxiety of another introduction so soon, and she eagerly accepted her aunt's proposal to dine earlier than usual so that she could get a good night's rest after the tiring journey.

"I've ordered *pilau* for you," Aunt Cuckoo announced. Jasmine wondered what this was and hoped it would not be too rich a dish. The oriental hangings in the dining-room portended an exotic type of food, and she had been rather shaken by the train.

"But it's just like our own *risotto*," she exclaimed when the heap of well-greased rice sown with morsels of meat was put before her.

"Very likely," said Aunt Cuckoo, and the tone in which she accepted Jasmine's comparison was so remote and vague that if Jasmine had likened the *pilau* to anything in the scale of edibility between Chinese birds' nests and ordinary bread and butter, she would probably have assented with the same toneless equanimity.

Jasmine liked her bedroom at The Cedars much better than her bedroom at Strathspey House. Uncle Eneas' consular career had naturally set its mark on his possessions. Strathspey House had been furnished first with all the things that were not wanted in Harley Street and then with the new and inexpensive suites that were considered appropriate to a holiday house. Moreover, Strathspey House itself was a creation not much older than Sir Hector's baronetcy. The Cedars was a century and a half years old, a rambling irregular countrified house with a large garden leading directly to the Heath; it possessed externally a colour and character of its own which in combination with the oriental taste of Eneas Grant produced an effect that Jasmine much esteemed after the newness of Strathspey House. In this bedroom there were Turkish and Persian rugs, thread-bare, but rich in hues; photographs with cypresses and minarets along the sky-line; paintings on rice-paper of bashi-bazouks and many other elaborate old Eastern costumes; and hanging by the fireplace a horse's tail set in an ivory handle to whisk away the flies. The Cedars was not Italy, but at least it seemed to recognize that somewhere there was sunlight. Jasmine fell asleep almost happily, and coming down to breakfast next morning after a struggle with punctuality she found to her relief that breakfast at The Cedars consisted of the civilized coffee taken in bed and that she alone was expected to devour eggs and bacon at the unnatural hour of nine a.m. After this first breakfast she, like her uncle and aunt, kept to her room.

Eneas Grant was obviously the brother of Sir Hector; and when Jasmine found that there was a tendency among her relatives to insist upon the importance and value of this family likeness, so much so indeed that it was crystallized into a phrase: 'A Grant! Oh yes, he's obviously a Grant,' she realized that her father had probably alienated himself from the esteem of his family as much by his outward dissimilarity as by the divergence of his tastes. Eneas was tall and thin; but neither his tallness nor his thinness ever reached the impressive ungainliness of angularity that was Sir Hector's outstanding characteristic. Eneas, like his brother, was intensely proud of his good health, and in the contemptuous way he alluded to anybody who lacked good-health he suggested that the ill-health was due to a moral lapse. He was a non-smoker and a teetotaller, and to both abstentions he attributed the moral value that so many ascetics attribute to any abstention from life's minor comforts. He was good enough, however, to allow as much to human weakness as not to condemn any man for moderate indulgence in either nicotine or alcohol, although to any man who fell a prey to the major human failings, like women or cards, he was merciless.

"I see no reason why a man should run after women," Uncle Eneas used to declare; and there hung about Mrs. Grant after twenty years of married life such an aura of antique virginity that one felt quite sure he was speaking the truth. Like many men who boast of their immunity from all the fleshly attacks of the tempter, Eneas Grant was greedy; indeed he was more than greedy, he was a glutton. A dish of curried prawns roused the glow of concupiscence in his milky blue eyes. Jasmine found it embarrassing at first to watch her uncle's tongue rubescent with all that vaunted good-health titillate itself in anticipation along the sparse hairs of his grey moustache, just as Spot titillated his back upon the leaves of shrubberies. Uncle Hector had been greedy with the frank greed of a man who at the beginning of a meal sharpens his knife upon the steel with a preliminary bravura and gusto. This greed of Uncle Eneas was colubrine. It really did seem as if he actually were fascinating the new dish; as if the curried prawns would presently rise of their own accord and abjectly, one after another, jump into his mouth. Jasmine would look up apprehensively to see if Niko the butler were not observing contemptuously this display of greed. But Niko seemed to encourage his master; one felt that, if the curried prawns should presume to show the slightest hesitation at coming forward to be devoured, Niko would complete with his fingers what his master's snakish eyes had failed to effect.

Like most teetotallers and non-smokers Eneas was a ruthless talker. He had innumerable stories of his career which, to do him justice, were at a first hearing entertaining enough; but after one had wandered with him on his famous expedition to negotiate with the Mirdite clan in Albania, had watched the eagles soaring above the gorges of the Black Drin or the passes of the Brseshda, had noticed curiously the mediæval costumes of the inhabitants, had been regaled with gigantic feasts by hospitable chieftains, and had heard mass said by moustachioed priests whose rifles were leaning against the altar, one tired of Albania; at the third time of hearing one became as it were mentally saddle-sore and yearned to be back home. It was entertaining, for the first time, to hear him tell how once, in the old days, while walking like God in his garden at Salonika, inhaling the perfumed breeze of the Balkan dusk, there had suddenly fallen at his feet, flung over the garden wall, a matchbox which when opened was discovered to contain a human ear. That story, heard for the first time, provided a genuine shudder. But when one had heard it six or seven or eight or nine times one was stifled by the preliminary perfumes, dazzled by the preliminary sunset, and prayed for some change in the weather and some new bit of anatomy in the matchbox, a human eye or a human finger—anything rather than a human ear.

"A perfectly ordinary matchbox," Mr. Grant used to say. "I just stooped down to open it and found inside a human ear. You of course see the point of that?"

The first time Jasmine had not seen the point, and had been interested to be told that the ear belonged to some British subject under the protection of her uncle who had refused to pay his ransom to the brigands that held him captive on Mount Olympus. But once the point had been seized, and repetition gave the poor gentleman as many ears as the breasts of the Ephesian Diana, the story became grindingly, exasperatingly tiresome.

Even more tiresome were those stories that turned upon the listener's acquaintance with official etiquette. Uncle Eneas cherished the memories of former grandeur, and he was never tired of counting over for Jasmine the number of guns to which a consul was entitled when he paid a visit of ceremony to any warship that visited the port to which he was accredited. The echoes of their booming still rumbled among the files and dockets of his brain. He had preserved even more vividly the memory of one or two occasions on which these grandeurs had been denied him by mistake, for like most consuls of the Levant service, whether they be or be not teetotallers and non-smokers, Eneas Grant was an aggrieved and disappointed man who had retired with that disease of the mental outlook which is known as consulitis. Yet Eneas Grant had less to complain of than most of his colleagues. The bitterness of finding himself in a post where he must come into direct competition with embassies or legations had not often fallen to his lot. He had indeed spent two galling years as Chief Dragoman at Constantinople, where he was responsible for all the practical work of the Embassy and considered that he was treated with less respect than an honorary attaché. But he had had Salonika; he had taken an important part in the Aden demarkation; he had reported a massacre of Christians in Southern Asia Minor and had been commended by the Foreign Office for his diligence; his name had been blessed by the fig merchants of Smyrna. He had eaten rich food in quantity for a number of years, and he possessed a rich wife, who had never given him a moment of uneasiness, neither when the bulbuls were singing to the roses of Constantinople nor amid the murmurous gardens of Damascus.

Aunt Cuckoo was a daughter of the wealthy old Levantine family of Hewitson, who brought her husband such a handsome dowry that he was able ever afterward to claim by some obscure process of logic that he had really served his country for nothing.

"The point is," he used to argue, "the point is that I can give up my consular career when I choose." And the student-interpreters, vice-consuls, and consuls of the Levant service, some of whom had rashly married lovely but penniless Greeks, wondered why the deuce he didn't hurry up and do so and thus give them a lift all round.

Aunt Cuckoo, being without children, had devoted herself to cats—Angora cats, a breed to which she became attached during the time that her husband was consul in that city. Angora cats lack even as much humanity as Persian cats; compared with Siamese or Javanese cats they are not human at all- Indeed, as a substitute for the emotions and cravings of womanhood they are not much more effective than bundles of cotton-wool would be. In the eyes of the world Aunt Cuckoo's childlessness was atoned for by the purity and perfection of her Angora breed; but she herself had to satisfy her own maternal instincts more profoundly by coddling, almost by cuddling for twenty years a bad arm. And really what better substitute for a baby could a childless woman find than a bad arm? Sometimes, of course, it really does hurt; but then sometimes a baby cuts its teeth, has convulsions or croup, is prone to flatulence and breaks out into spots. An arm exhibits the phenomena of growth and decay, and if a baby becomes an inky little boy, and an inky little boy becomes an exigent young man, an arm gets older and becomes as exigent as its owner will allow it to be. A bad arm can be shown to people even by an elderly lady without blushing, whereas children after a certain age cannot be exhibited in their nudity. Aunt Cuckoo's bad arm was the chief consolation of her loneliness, and it was only natural that the morning after Jasmine's arrival she should take her niece aside and enquire in a whisper if she should like to see her bad arm. Jasmine welcomed the introduction with an unspoken hope that there was nothing nasty to see. Nor was there. It was apparently the perfectly normal arm that any woman over fifty might possess. Age had blunted the contours; twenty years of testing the efficiency of various lotions and liniments had gradually stained its pristine alabaster; but there was nothing whatever to see, no tumour malignant or benign, no ulcer indolent or irritable.

"I am going to try a new system of massage," Aunt Cuckoo confided. "And I can't help thinking how nice it would be if you could have a few lessons."

And as Uncle Eneas for his part was convinced that a more valuable lesson would be the art of jiu-jitsu, in whatever direction she looked Jasmine could see nothing before her but muscular development.

"The point about jiu-jitsu," Uncle Eneas explained, "is the independence it gives you. My own feeling is that women should be as far as possible independent."

Aunt Cuckoo looked up at this. It had never struck her before that such was her husband's opinion.

"Now don't *you* suggest learning jiu-jitsu," he said quickly.

"I don't think my arm would let me," his wife replied.

"And you ought to get plenty of walking," Uncle Eneas added, turning to Jasmine. "At your age I always walked for an hour and a half before breakfast. I remember once at Broussa...." and he was off on one of his entirely topographical stories, dragging his listeners through landscapes that for them were as shifting, as uncertain, as nebulous and confused as the landscapes of other people's dreams.

Perhaps Aunt Cuckoo yielded less to her husband than superficially she appeared. Certainly nothing more was said about jiu-jitsu, whereas the massage scheme made considerable progress. Two days later a gaunt blonde, with that look professional nurses sometimes have of being nuns who have succumbed to the temptations of the flesh, invested The Cedars. She advanced upon poor Aunt Cuckoo with such a grim air that Jasmine began to think that it was rather a pity that she had not learnt jiu-jitsu in order to defend herself against this barbarian.

"This is Miss Hellner," said Aunt Cuckoo, timorously offering the introduction in the manner of a propitiatory sacrifice. "Miss Hellner," she went on imploringly, "who has made such a wonderful improvement in my bad arm. I want my niece to get a few hints from you, Miss Hellner. She is anxious to take up massage professionally."

Miss Hellner's cold blue eye, as cold and blue as one of her Scandinavian fjords, was fixed upon the victim; no amount of talk about Jasmine's future was going to deter her from her duty.

"Will you please unbutton the sleeve?" she requested in a guttural voice, which Aunt Cuckoo prepared to obey.

"The arm has been rather better the last few days," the patient suggested. "So perhaps it won't be necessary to repeat last week's treatment."

"Three times that treatment is repeated," said Miss Hellner inexorably. "That is the rule."

"Oh dear," Aunt Cuckoo murmured with a dolorous little giggle. "I'm afraid I'm going to have rather a painful time. But don't go away, Jasmine. It's going to hurt me very much, but it will be very interesting for you to watch. Miss Hellner is so expert."

But flattery was impotent against Miss Hellner, who by now had seized the arm and was kneading it, pinching it, digging her knuckles into it—and bony knuckles they were too—trying to tear it in half apparently with her thumbs, burrowing and boring, while all the time Aunt Cuckoo ejaculated "Ouch!" or "Ah!" and to one viciously penetrating use of the forefinger as a gimlet "Yi! Yi!"

At last Miss Hellner stopped, and Aunt Cuckoo lay back on the sofa with a sigh, occasionally giving a glance of ineffable tenderness to where her bad arm, as red as a new-born baby, lay upon her breast.

"If your arm is not well after one more treatment...."

"One more treatment," echoed Aunt Cuckoo dutifully, "Yes?"

"You will have to take the oil cure."

"The oil cure?" asked the patient, pleasantly excited at the prospect of a new treatment. "What does that consist of?"

"First you take an ice bath."

"Yes," said Aunt Cuckoo, "our bathroom is *very* nice."

"Ice bath," repeated the nurse severely.

"Oh, I see," said Aunt Cuckoo with less enthusiasm. "You mean a cold bath."

"Ice bath," Miss Hellner almost shouted. "With lumps of ice to float. Then I rub you with oil of olives."

Aunt Cuckoo nodded gratefully; after the ice such a proceeding sounded luxurious.

"Then with nothing on you will do the gymnastic. Up and down the room. Backwards and forwards. So."

"Dear me, with nothing on? Absolutely nothing? Couldn't I keep a small towel?"

"Nothing on," repeated the masseuse obstinately. "Then you sit for ten minutes in the window with the fan."

"But surely not with nothing on except a fan?"

"With nothing on," the masseuse insisted. "Then——" She paused impressively, while Aunt Cuckoo looked excessively agitated, and Jasmine wondered what ultimate ordeal she was going to prescribe. Surely she could not intend to make the patient sit in the garden or drive in the brougham with nothing on?

"Then you will drink a large glass of lemonade and absorb the oil," Miss Hellner announced.

"Good gracious! Not a very large glass of oil?"

"It is the lemons who drink the oil. It was not you yourself," Miss Hellner explained scornfully.

"Jasmine," said Aunt Cuckoo with one finger lifted in solemn admonition, "don't let me forget to order the lemons in good time."

The lemonade was such a simple and peaceable climax that Aunt Cuckoo was evidently anxious to try it; she did not ask her niece to remind her about the ice, and in order to prevent Miss Hellner's reminding her she suggested that Jasmine should have a short lesson in the art of massage.

"Oh, but I think watching you has been enough lesson for to-day" objected Jasmine, who feared the example that is better than the precept. "I don't think I could take in any more at first."

"She must come to the school of Swedish culture," Miss Hellner decided.

Thus it was that Jasmine found herself engaged on Mondays, Wednesdays, and Fridays to travel from Hampstead to Baker Street, with every prospect, unless fate should intervene to save her, of becoming by profession a masseuse, the last profession she would ever have chosen for herself.

On the days when she did not go to Baker Street she had to comb the cats. To comb seven Angora cats was almost as tiring as massage.

"I suppose this is the way your arm got bad?" she once suggested to her aunt.

"Oh, no, dear," said Aunt Cuckoo. "When I was young I used to write a great deal. I wrote six novels about life in the Levant, and then I had writer's cramp."

That evening when she went up to her bedroom Jasmine found her aunt's novels waiting to be read—eighteen volumes published in the style of the early 'nineties and the late 'eighties, with titles like *The Sultan's Shadow* and *The Rose of Sharon*. She read bits of each one in turn, and then abruptly felt that she had had enough, just as one feels that one has had enough Turkish-delight. Unfortunately Aunt Cuckoo said there was nothing she liked better than really intelligent criticism. So between reading the novels, learning massage, and combing the cats there was not much leisure for Jasmine, and what leisure she had was more than filled by rapid walks with Uncle Eneas over the Heath. Sirene is not a place that predisposes people to walk fast, and Uncle Eneas was continually being amazed that a niece thirty-five years younger than himself should be unable to quicken her pace to suit his own. Sometimes he said this in such a severe tone that Jasmine was half afraid that he would buy a lead and compel her to keep up with him. Luckily she was not expected to talk, and she soon discovered that she was only expected to say once in every ten minutes 'What an extraordinary life you have had, Uncle Eneas,' to maintain him in a perfectly good temper.

Aunt May had written Jasmine a long letter from Spaborough expressing her delight at the news that she was treating Uncle Eneas and Aunt Cuckoo with more consideration than she had shown towards Uncle Hector and herself, announcing the imminent return of the family to Harley Street and magnanimously offering to give Jasmine lunch on her 'massage days,' inasmuch as Harley Street was, as no doubt she knew, quite close to Baker Street. Cousin Edith also wrote warmly and effusively; but the paleness of the ink, the thinness of the pen, and the flimsiness of the paper made the letter seem like an old letter found in a secret drawer and addressed to somebody who had been dead a century. She did not hear from Harry Vibart, and she wondered if he had written to her at Strathspey House and if her relatives there had kept back the letter. She supposed that she should never see him again, and she began to fear that she, like so many other girls, should drift into a profession to which she was not particularly attracted, or into a marriage for which she was not particularly anxious, or perhaps, worst of all, that she should merely shrink and shrink and shrink into a desiccated old maid like Cousin Edith. It was not an exhilarating prospect; Mustapha, the patriarch of the Angora cats, had his fur combed out less gently than usual that morning.

Life was seeming unutterably dreary when Aunt Cuckoo came into the room, her eyes flashing with anticipation, her being rejuvenated by excitement, to say that one of the maids had a stiff neck, and to ask if Jasmine would immediately go to her room and operate on it.

Jasmine followed her aunt upstairs, and expressed her sense of life's disillusionment by the vigour with which she manipulated, man-handled indeed, the neck and shoulders of the young woman, who after numerous vain protests burst into hysterical tears and gave a month's notice.

"Funny, isn't it," said Aunt Cuckoo when they left the room, "what little gratitude you find among the lower classes nowadays?"

"I think I did rather hurt her," said Jasmine, who was by now feeling rather penitent.

"*I* think you did it very well," said Aunt Cuckoo, "and *I* am very pleased with you. And of course her shoulders are so much harder than my poor arm."

Aunt Cuckoo, for all her folly, had for Jasmine a certain pathos, and during the late autumn and winter while she stayed at The Cedars she to some extent grew accustomed to the atmosphere of cold storage which prevailed there; she began to contemplate the slow freezing of herself during the years to come into an Aunt Cuckoo; she preferred the notion of a frozen self, which after all would always be liable to melt, to the notion of a withered self like Cousin Edith's, which would indubitably never bourgeon again. She did sometimes lunch with the Hector Grants at Harley Street, and she found them more insufferable every time she went there. Aunt Cuckoo could not help feeling gratified by this, because for many years now she had been jealous of Lady Grant.

"Of course I should not like to appear as if I was criticizing her," she would say to Jasmine. "But I understand what you mean about Lettice and Pamela, and I can't help feeling that they have been spoilt. It's the same with cats," she murmured, in a vague effort to elucidate the moral atmosphere.

When Aunt Cuckoo talked like this, Jasmine began to wonder if she could confide in her about Harry Vibart; but when she had to frame the words, her account of the affair began to seem so pretentious and exaggerated that she could not bring herself to the point, would blush in embarrassment, and hide her confusion by an energetic combing of Mustapha.

In the middle of the winter Aunt Cuckoo began to throw out hints of what Jasmine might expect from herself and Uncle Eneas in the future. She never went so far as a definite statement that they intended to make her their heiress; the prospect of future wealth was merely hinted at like the landscape under a false dawn. Yet even this glimmer over something beyond was enough to alarm Jasmine with the idea that her uncle and aunt would suppose that she was aiming at an inheritance. She tried by diligent combing of cats, by concentration upon the massage of Aunt Cuckoo's arm, and by the rapidity of her walking pace, to show that she appreciated what was being done for her in the present; but the moment Aunt Cuckoo began to talk of the future she was discouragingly rude. Nevertheless these hints, notwithstanding Jasmine's reception of them, would probably have taken a more definite shape if on the anniversary of the conversion of Saint Paul Aunt Cuckoo had not taken shelter from a sudden storm of rain in a small Catholic mission church at Golders Green. Here she felt vague aspirations at the sight of half a dozen poor people praying in the rich twilight of imitation glass windows; but she was more particularly and more deeply impressed by the behaviour of a woman in rusty mourning in bringing a pallid little boy to the feet of a saintly image that was attracting Aunt Cuckoo's attention and everybody's attention by lifting his habit and pointing to a sore on his leg. After praying to an accompaniment of maternal prods the child was bidden to deposit at the base of the image a bandage of lint, after which he stuck six candles on the pricket, lighted them, and followed his mother out of the church with many a backward glance to observe the effect of his illumination. Aunt Cuckoo was puzzled by all this, and overtaking the woman in the porch asked what it meant. She was told that the saint's name was Roch and that he had miraculously cured her little boy of an ulcerous leg. Aunt Cuckoo's arm immediately began to pain her acutely. On feeling this pain she went back into the church and prayed shyly, for she was not a Catholic and she had only heard the saint's name for the first time. The pain vanished as abruptly as it came, and Aunt Cuckoo, thrilled by the miracle, hurried home to tell Jasmine all about it. As soon as her mind had turned its attention to miracles Aunt Cuckoo began to fancy that she was being specially favoured by Heavenly manifestations.

"Of course one has said 'How miraculous!' before," she assured her niece. "But one employs terms so loosely. I learned that when I used to write." Aunt Cuckoo's voice, from many years of tonelessness, was, now that she was able to feel a genuine excitement, full of astonishing little squeaks and tremolos which had she been a clock would have led the listener to oil the works at once. "And the healing of my bad arm wasn't the only miracle," she hurried on. "Oh no, dear. I assure you it stopped raining the moment I came out of church, and you know how difficult it is to find a taxi when one requires one. Well, would you believe it, lo and behold, one pulled up just outside the church, and the moment I was inside it started to pour again. I'm so glad that you're a Catholic, dear. There, you see I'm already learning not to say Roman Catholic...."

It was at this point that Jasmine became discouraging. Her religion had always been such a matter-of-fact business in Sirene and the existence of Protestants so natural in a world divided into rich touring English folk and poor dear predatory Italians that her aunt's intentions shocked her.

"You're not thinking of becoming a Christian—I mean a Catholic," she gasped.

"Who knows?" said Aunt Cuckoo in the vague and awful tones of a Sibyl. "And I should have thought, Jasmine, that you would have been the first to rejoice."

Jasmine felt that her aunt was presenting her out of a profusion of miracles with one all for herself; but realizing what everybody would say she was so ungracious that Aunt Cuckoo went and offered it to the parish priest instead.

Father Maloney was at first inclined to resent Aunt Cuckoo's suggestion that St. Roch should have healed a Protestant; but when her ardour and humility had been sufficiently tried, he agreed to receive her into the Church, and though he did not encourage her to believe in any more miracles, he was privately inclined to hold the pious opinion that a well-to-do convert's arrival in the unfinished condition of the new sacristy was as nearly miraculous as anything in his career.

A month later, notwithstanding Uncle Eneas' severe indictment of the crimes of the papacy, Aunt Cuckoo became a Catholic. Miss Hellner was dismissed; Jasmine was bidden to consider massage an invention of the devil; the Angora cats were sold; Aunt Cuckoo was confirmed. Her husband who in the course of their married life had successfully cured her of singing after dinner, of writing novels, of spiritualism, of Christian science, of a dread of premature burial, of a belief in the immortality conferred by sour milk, and of eating nuts the last thing at night and the first thing in the morning, was defeated by this craze; her ability to resist her husband's disapproval convinced Aunt Cuckoo more firmly than ever that she was the recipient of a special dose of grace. Yet although Catholicism supplied most of Aunt Cuckoo's emotional needs, it could not entirely stifle her unsatisfied maternal instinct, so that sometimes, when St. Roch was busy with other patients, she looked back regretfully to the days when her arm really hurt, and her faith was exposed to the insinuations of the Evil One. She turned her attention to juvenile saints and became much wrapped up in St. Aloysius Gonzaga until she found that he objected to his mother's seeing him undress when he was eight years old and that he had fainted because a footman saw him with one sock off at the age of four. St. Aloysius evidently did not require her maternal love, and she lavished it on St. Stanislas Kostka instead; but even with him she felt awkward, until at last St. Teresa, most practical of women, came to her rescue in the middle of the Sursum Corda. Three months after her conversion Aunt Cuckoo arrived home from mass on Lady Day with an expression in her pale blue eyes that would have required the cobalt of Fra Angelico to represent.

"Eneas," she announced, "I have decided to adopt a baby."

To the consular mind of Mr. Grant such a procedure evoked endless complications in the future. His mind leaped forward twenty years to the time when this baby would require a passport, and he wondered if there were a special form for adopted babies. He seemed to fancy vaguely that there was, and he asked what the nationality of the baby would be.

"A Catholic baby," Aunt Cuckoo proclaimed.

Her husband explained to her that she must not confuse religion with nationality, and then suddenly with a grimace of real ferocity he said:

"I hope you don't intend to adopt an Irish baby?"

"A Catholic baby," Aunt Cuckoo repeated obstinately.

"This kipper is rather strong," said Eneas.

But it was not strong enough to divert Aunt Cuckoo from her own trail.

"I spoke to Father Maloney about it this morning after mass," she persisted.

"Damn Father Maloney!" said Eneas.

Jasmine was wondering to herself what part she would be called upon to play with regard to the baby. But whatever she had to do would be less tiring than combing Angora cats or trying to keep up with Uncle Eneas on the slopes of Hampstead Heath. Uncle Eneas protested all day for a week against the baby; Aunt Cuckoo appealed to St. Teresa, secured her support by a novena, and defeated him once more. Father Maloney discovered a Catholic bank-clerk, the victim of chronic alcoholism, who with the help of a tuberculous wife had brought into the world twelve children, the youngest of which, now ten months old, he secured for Aunt Cuckoo. At the formal conveyance of the baby Uncle Eneas asked whether it were a boy or a girl, and when Aunt Cuckoo replied that she did not know, he, apostrophizing heaven, wondered if ever since the world began a vaguer woman had walked the earth.

"It's a boy," said Father Maloney soothingly.

"What's his name?" asked Aunt Cuckoo.

"Michael Francis Joseph Mary Aloysius," said Father Maloney.

"Good God!" exclaimed Uncle Eneas.

"We'll call him Frank," Aunt Cuckoo decided, and her husband was almost appeased. He had not realized that anything so ordinary could be extracted from that highly coloured mosaic of names.

At first Aunt Cuckoo was glad of Jasmine's help, and of the advice of the very latest product in professional nurses. But when she found that the nurse had theories in the bringing up of babies that by no means accorded with her own sentimental views, and that Jasmine was inclined to support the nurse, she began to be a little resentful of her niece.

"You don't understand, my dear," she said. "You see you aren't a mother."

"Well, but nor are you," Jasmine pointed out. This retort so much annoyed Aunt Cuckoo that she began to hint, much more obviously than she had hinted at future prosperity, at the inconvenience of Jasmine's presence in The Cedars.

Possibly Aunt Cuckoo's desire to be relieved of any responsibility for her niece's future might not have matured so rapidly had not Uncle Eneas been converted if not to the baby's religion at any rate of its company by the obvious pleasure his entrance into the room caused the creature. No man is secure against flattery; the cult of the dog as a domestic animal proves that. No doubt if on its adopted father's entrance into a room the baby had shrieked, turned black in the face or vomited, he would have been tempted to take refuge in the society of his niece from such implied contempt. But the baby always demonstrated rapture at the approach of Uncle Eneas. Its toes curled over sensuously; its fingers clutched at strings of celestial music; it dribbled and made that odd noise which is called crowing. It said La-la-la-la-la very rapidly and tried to leap in the air. Probably it was fascinated by a prominent and brilliantly coloured red wen on Uncle Eneas' cheek, because if ever he bent over to pay his respects the baby would always make distinct efforts to grasp this wen with one hand, while with the other it would try to grasp his tie-pin, a moderately large single ruby not unlike the wen. Luckily for itself the baby could not express what exactly kindled its young enthusiasm, and Uncle Eneas naturally began to believe that the infant was exceptionally intelligent. His wife encouraged this opinion; all the servants encouraged this opinion; even the professional nurse encouraged this opinion. It was obvious that the baby would be henceforth ineradicable. Moreover by acquiring a baby already ten months old, what Uncle Eneas called the early stewed raspberry stage of babyhood had been passed elsewhere, and the exciting first attempts at conversation and locomotion were already in sight. As yet neither Uncle Eneas nor Aunt Cuckoo had gone beyond hints about the problem of Jasmine's future, but she began to feel sensitive about staying longer at The Cedars and to ask herself what she was going to do presently. At this point the baby, with what had it not been a baby might have been called cynical coquetry, roused the demons of jealousy by suddenly making shameless advances to Jasmine. Nothing would please the infant now but that Jasmine should play with it continually: Uncle Eneas and Aunt Cuckoo were greeted with yells of disapproval. With Spring rapidly coming to the prime it was felt that such an unnatural preference indicated the need for a change of air. Jasmine sensed an exchange of diplomatic notes among her relatives. She shrank within herself at the thought that none too much willingness was anywhere being displayed to receive her.

"I thought it would be rather nice for you to go down to Curtain Wells and stay with your Uncle Alexander for a while in this beautiful spring weather," said Aunt Cuckoo. "But it appears that the only spare room is in the hands of the decorators."

And on another day she said: "I am rather surprised that your Aunt May doesn't invite you to stay with her in Harley Street for the season. They have become so ultra-fashionable nowadays that one might have supposed that they would have invited you to Harley Street to share in the general atmosphere of gaiety. I do hope that dear little Frank is not going to grow up quite so self-absorbed as Lettice and Pamela."

"If you want me to go away," said Jasmine desperately, "why don't you say so? I never wanted to come to England. I'll go back to Sirene with what massage I know and earn my living there."

"But who has given you the least idea that you are unwelcome?" said Aunt Cuckoo. "It was of you I was thinking. I am afraid that dear baby's arrival has made us less able to amuse you than we were. And I don't like to suggest that you should take entire charge of him."

At this moment Uncle Eneas came blustering into the room.

"I've had a letter from Uncle Matthew," he proclaimed. "He's got an idea into his head that he wants to go down to the seaside. Some fool of a doctor's been stuffing him up with that notion. He says he thinks we ought to go to the seaside, and says it would be a good idea to share expenses, we paying two-thirds and he paying one-third. The mean old screw! How like him that is! And if we take baby he'll only want to pay a quarter."

"Oh, but I think Uncle Matthew would be too frightening for dear baby," said Aunt Cuckoo. "Why shouldn't Jasmine go and stay with him?" she suggested.

"That wouldn't suit his plan," said Uncle Eneas. "If Jasmine went he would have to pay for her as well as for himself."

"But don't you think that if Jasmine went to stay with him at Muswell Hill, she would do as well as a change of air?"

"By Jove, that's quite a notion," said Uncle Eneas, looking at his niece as people look at the sky to see if it is going to rain. Jasmine was trying to remember what she knew about Uncle Matthew. He existed in her mind as an incredibly old gentleman of boundless wealth who years ago had bought a picture of her father.

"I think you would like Uncle Matthew so much," Aunt Cuckoo was saying persuasively. "Of course he's very old and he's a little eccentric. I think old people often are eccentric, don't you? But he's very well off, and it really does seem a wonderful solution of the difficulty."

"You mean the difficulty of having me on your hands?" Jasmine bluntly demanded.

"Please don't say that," Aunt Cuckoo begged. "Surely you heard what your uncle said? Our difficulty is that we don't want to disturb Uncle Matthew with precious Baboose. I don't think he would quite understand how the little pet came to us."

So long as she was to be tossed about like a ball, Jasmine thought she might just as well be tossed into an old gentleman's lap as anywhere else, and soon after this, gathering from a fragment she overheard of a low colloquy between her uncle and aunt that her introduction to Uncle Matthew would intensely annoy the Hector Grants, she made up her mind not to oppose, but even to press forward the proposed visit.

"Where is Muswell Hill?" she asked.

"Oh, it's on a hill," said Aunt Cuckoo vaguely. "I don't know what bus you take. It's a large house, and as he has only one servant everything gets a little dusty. Whenever I go there I always take a duster with me, because Uncle Matthew so appreciates a little attention. At least I'm sure he does really appreciate it, though of course he's reached that age when people don't seem to appreciate anything. What do you think, dear?" she turned to ask her husband. "We might invite him to dinner."

It was extraordinary how much the baby's arrival had strengthened Aunt Cuckoo's position in the household. In the old days she would never have dreamed of asking anyone to dinner; but her vicarious maternity gave her as much importance as if she had really borne a child at the age of fifty-two. Eneas had correspondingly shrunk with regard to his wife, though with everybody else he was as pompous as ever.

"Now I'm going to give you a few hints," said Aunt Cuckoo to Jasmine. "Dear old Uncle Matthew is very fond of pictures."

"Yes, I remember he bought one of father's years and years ago."

"Oh, hush, hush!" Aunt Cuckoo breathed. "He's not at all fond of buying anything now. You must *give* him one of your father's pictures. In fact, if I might suggest it, you had better give him all that you have left. We shall send the brougham over to fetch him, and I don't see any reason why you should not drive back with him to Muswell Hill after dinner. We could put the pictures on the luggage rack, and your trunk could be sent over by Carter Paterson the next day. You could put what you wanted for the night in quite a small bag, which I will lend you."

Religion was making Aunt Cuckoo as practical as St. Teresa herself. Perhaps it was lucky for Uncle Eneas that she had adopted a baby; he would have found a new order of nuns much more expensive.

The invitation was sent to Uncle Matthew, and the next day the answer came back written on the back of the same sheet of paper. In a postscript he had added: "*I wish you wouldn't seal your envelopes to me, as I cannot turn them so easily. People nowadays seem to have no idea of economy. Every envelope should be used twice over.*"

"It's really not avarice," Aunt Cuckoo explained. "It's only eccentricity."

She was longing more than ever to get Jasmine out of the house. That afternoon darling baby had pulled Uncle Eneas' moustache with a suggestion of viciousness, and though Uncle Eneas had said in a fatuous voice, "Poor little man, he doesn't know that it hurts," Aunt Cuckoo was inclined to think that Baby did know it hurt, and that he had been prompted to the outrage by Jasmine's influence.

Uncle Matthew was apparently a difficult person to entertain at dinner because he liked to be well fed and at the same time he did not like to see anything wasted. If the least bit too much was given him, he would overeat himself rather than let anything be wasted, which often made him ill afterwards. Aunt Cuckoo's dinners in the past had usually been failures, because in those days her temperament was far too vague to calculate nicely the necessary quantity of food. The development of her practical qualities promised greater success now. Besides, now that Jasmine was here, she could not make a mistake, because if there was too much Jasmine could be given a larger helping than she wanted, and if there was too little Jasmine could be given less. It was debated whether it would be wise to warn Uncle Matthew in advance of Jasmine's existence, of which he was probably unaware, inasmuch as the Hector Grants had every interest in not telling him; and it was finally decided to say nothing about her until she was introduced to him. Aunt Cuckoo was anxious to explain that Jasmine had come all the way from Sirene to lay at his feet her father's dying wish in the shape of four pictures; but Uncle Eneas' more cautious consular nature did not approve of this plan. There was also some discussion whether anything should be said about Baby. Aunt Cuckoo in the pride of maternity had no doubts; but Uncle Eneas with the approach of Uncle Matthew's visit was feeling more and more like a nephew and less and less like a father.

"I don't think the old boy will understand our deliberately procuring a child in that way. I know he has always regarded children as unpleasant accidents."

"But suppose darling Baboose cries?"

"Well, he mustn't," the adopted father decided. "Or if he does, we must say that it's a baby in the street outside. It's impossible really to arrange a suitable reception in advance. That last tooth has been giving him a good deal of trouble, you know, and he may ... well, he may in fact take it out of the old gentleman. No, I feel sure that a meeting between them would be most inappropriate."

Aunt Cuckoo gave way. She was too anxious to palm off Jasmine on Uncle Matthew not for once to sacrifice Baby's dignity as the heir of The Cedars.

Chapter Six

UNCLE Matthew Rouncivell was not of course so old as his relatives boasted that he was, but he was old enough to be considered incapable of lasting much longer and old enough to justify any member of the family in adding a few years to the correct total, which was seventy-six. He had been fifteen years younger than the wife of the Bishop of Clapham, and though he had scoffed at his sister for marrying a parson, he had to admit in the end that Andrew had made the most of a poor profession. Uncle Matthew's mean and acquisitive boyhood had been the consolation of his father's declining years, and he started life with a comfortable fortune notwithstanding what had been robbed from him as a dowry to marry off his sister. Their father, Samuel Rouncivell, had invested largely in property that seemed likely to put difficulties in the way of far-off municipal improvements, or as he preferred to put it, lay along the lines of future urban development. He and his son after him had a remarkable flair for buying up decrepit slums that would afterward turn out to be the only possible site for a new town hall or public library. And then the keen eye old Samuel had for the arteries of traffic! Why, it was as keen as an anatomist's for the arteries of the human body. In whatever direction tramlines or railroads desired to flow, there stood Samuel ready to apply his tourniquet, which was sometimes nothing more than one tumbledown cottage plastered with signs of ancient lights. This sense of direction was transmitted to Matthew, who when one of the big London termini had to be enlarged trebled his fortune at a stroke. Now, at seventy-six, he could not be worth less than fifteen thousand a year, and as he did not spend five hundred, every year he lived was making him wealthier. Long ago he had married a beautiful young woman who a few months later was killed in a riding accident. Since then he had spent a solitary and misanthropic life, grinding his tenants, amassing a quantity of unusual walking-sticks and bad modern pictures, and collecting what he called antiques. His only amusement was the malicious delight he took in leading the various groups of his relations to suppose one after another that he was contemplating them as his beneficiaries. Thin-lipped and beaky, he had a fat flabby back and pale flabby cheeks, and the skin of his neck was mottled and scaly as a snake's slough. He usually wore a frock-coat that resembled the green slime on London railings in wet weather; but when he dined out he took with him a black velvet smoking cap worked in arabesques of yellow silk and a pair of slippers made of leopard's fur to which moth had given a mangy appearance. He liked to dine early, and it was six o'clock of a fine evening in early May when he arrived at The Cedars, his frock-coat reinforced by a grey muffler long enough and thick enough to have kept a Zulu moderately warm at the North Pole. He did not seem in a good temper, and when Niko helped him to disengage himself from the muffler, he asked with a growl if the fool thought he was spinning a top. However, when he entered the dining-room and saw poor Sholto Grant's pictures all aglow in the rich horizontal sunlight, he cheered up for a moment, until a suspicion that his nephew Eneas was proposing to sell him the pictures intervened and spoilt his pleasure. He at once began to criticize and cheapen the pictures so ruthlessly that Jasmine could hardly keep back her tears. In Crispano's Café at Sirene she had once heard a futurist painter criticizing her father's pictures, and she had been so angry that she had upset the coffee over him on her way out. To hear Uncle Matthew one might suppose that such bad pictures had never been painted since the world began; yet she could say nothing.

"I'm sorry you don't like them," said Aunt Cuckoo, "because Jasmine has brought them back for you all the way from Sirene."

"Eh? What's that?" demanded Uncle Matthew, twisting round on one of his sticks and thumping the floor with the other. "Who's Jasmine?"

"Jasmine is poor Sholto's daughter."

"What? Another?" the old gentleman growled.

"No, he only had one."

"I can't think why people want to have children at all," Uncle Matthew sniffed. Eneas congratulated his wife with a complacent glance on their reserve about Baby. "So you brought back these pictures for me, did you?" the old gentleman continued. "Humph! I did buy one of your father's pictures a long time ago, and I don't say it was bad, but he asked too much for it. And now if I accept these I shall have to buy frames for them," he concluded indignantly.

But the insistency of Sholto's pictures, the indubitable, the positive proclamation of their being what they were, the full value they gave of blue water, bright flowers, and rosy cheeks, softened the old gentleman's heart. They really did express for him his own taste in art, and inasmuch as they were a present he could not quite conceal his gratification.

"I hope you haven't gone and ordered a very extravagant dinner for me," he said gruffly to hide as far as possible the least amenity in his manner.

Aunt Cuckoo reassured him, and, the gong ringing at that moment, they moved toward the dining-room. Uncle Matthew disdained an arm, preferring to rely upon his two sticks.

"Wonderful how he bears himself for an old gentleman, isn't it?" whispered Uncle Eneas to Jasmine. "We're a long-lived family. There's no doubt about that." He was too anxious for the success of the evening to brag more particularly about his own athletic qualities.

The dinner consisted of various Eastern dishes, on all of which the old gentleman looked with an approving eye, because each dish gave the impression of being a hash of something unfinished the day before. The richness of their flavouring appealed to his palate, and the zest with which his nephew filled up his own plate had its effect upon his own appetite. Jasmine got into disgrace early in the meal by leaving half a plate of *pilau* untouched, but she was able to recover some of her lost ground by refusing wine.

"Good girl!" Uncle Matthew exclaimed, and turning to his nephew he asked why there was wine on the table when he knew that there was nothing of which he disapproved so much as wine. Eneas glared angrily at his wife. It was only since Father Maloney had been dining with them occasionally that wine had been seen at The Cedars. The offending decanter was removed, and everybody finished what water was left in his tumbler with an expression of critical enjoyment.

"Have you written about those rooms yet?" Uncle Matthew asked presently.

Eneas shook his head weightily. "The trouble is I shall have to stay in London until the end of July. I've been asked by the Foreign Office to do some work for them—expert work in Turkish which nobody else can do at present." Then he wavered. "But perhaps Cuckoo...."

His wife cut him short. "I shan't be able to get away until July," she said; but she went on roguishly: "So we thought that perhaps if you were very good, Uncle Matthew, we'd lend you Jasmine for a little while."

Eneas could not withhold a glance of admiration; he even resolved not to allude to the mistake over the wine when Uncle Matthew was gone. He admitted to himself that he should never have thought of suggesting that Jasmine was a loan, or of putting Uncle Matthew in the position of a little boy being given a treat.

"Lend me Jasmine?" the old gentleman repeated. "And what am I to do with Jasmine, pray?"

"She's invaluable," said Aunt Cuckoo, leaning across the dining-table and squeezing her niece's hand. "And I wouldn't lend her to anybody else but you. Everybody's clamouring for her."

Uncle Matthew looked at his great-niece with the expression that for many years he had been wont to accord to proffered bargains.

"You told us you wanted a change," Aunt Cuckoo persisted. "And as soon as you told us we made up our minds that whatever it cost us *you* should have Jasmine."

Throughout the evening Aunt Cuckoo made it appear that Jasmine really was indispensable, and by dint of never committing herself to anything without asking Jasmine if she agreed with her and of never formulating any plan without asking Jasmine first if she approved of it and of never wanting anything without asking Jasmine if she would fetch it for her, she really did manage to impress Uncle Matthew that by taking away Jasmine from The Cedars he would be robbing a nephew and niece. This was too keen a pleasure for the old gentleman to deny himself, and when he left that evening he went away with a solemn promise that Jasmine should be delivered to him at eleven o'clock the following morning.

"We don't usually let the carriage go out two days running," said Aunt Cuckoo in a final burst of abnegation, "but for dear Jasmine's sake we will."

"A very successful evening, my dear," Uncle Eneas observed when the visitor was gone.

"And that precious lamb upstairs never made a sound."

"The young rascal! He knew. *He* knew," the adoptive father idiotically chuckled.

Jasmine wondered what he was supposed to know—perhaps, she thought with a shade of malice, that he might one day inherit Uncle Matthew's fortune if Uncle Matthew died in ignorance of his existence. She could not bring herself to imagine that any money would be left to Lettice and Pamela. Ah, but there were others whom she had not yet seen, those six boy cousins at Silchester, and Uncle Alexander with his lunatic prince. Why had she ever consented to leave

Sirene? Whichever way she looked in England there was nothing to be seen except an endless vista of servitude. Girls in books always struck out for themselves, but perhaps they were the only girls who were written about. There must be hundreds of others like herself who remained slaves. Not at all, they finally got married; they worked hard and....

"It's really a ghastly prospect," she exclaimed aloud.

"*Uscirò pazza!* I'm like some cheap novel in a circulating library gradually getting more and more dog's-eared, more and more dirty and greasy, and all the time being passed on and on—oh! I can't stand it much longer...."

Jasmine did not set out to Muswell Hill with much hope in her heart. She felt as if she was being posted to Matthew Rouncivell, Esq., and the kisses of her uncle and aunt remained on her cheeks like postage stamps.

Rouncivell Lodge was a double-fronted, two-storied house which was built of brown brick in the first quarter of the nineteenth century, probably by some prosperous city merchant, as a country residence. It had remained what was practically a country residence until a few years ago, when old Matthew Rouncivell sacrificed the couple of acres of garden behind the house and built on the site large blocks of bright red flats, leaving no land to his own house except the shrubbery in front, which was divided into three segments by a semicircular drive; in the largest of these stood a Doric summer-house converted by Mr. Rouncivell into a smoking-room. The proximity of the flats and the amount of sky they cut off added to the gloom of the shrubbery, which was a mass of rank ivy and euonymus bushes, of American rhododendrons, lilacs that never flowered, privets, and Portuguese laurels. Moreover, although the flats were what the agent called high-class residential flats, the landlord, possibly with the vague notion of guarding what was left of the privacy he had himself destroyed, had had them planned to present to anybody entering the gates of Rouncivell Lodge their domestic windows, which, with dish-cloths drying on every sill, gave them the squalid appearance of tenement buildings.

The old gentleman himself, when, wearing his velvet smoking-jacket, his tasselled smoking-cap, and a pair of goloshes over his fur slippers, he visited the smoking-room to smoke his weekly cigar, found the flavour of the cigar was enhanced by calculating how much a year each window in sight brought him in. This meditation was so comforting that he used really to enjoy his smoke, although the cigars, which were of poor quality when he bought them, had not been improved by their storage in the damp Doric summer-house. However, he smoked them literally to the bitter end; this bitter end he used to stick upon a penknife, and even when each puff nearly blistered his tongue he still enjoyed it, because he had made a calculation that merely by the amount more of a cigar he smoked than anyone else he had gained on the whole year two complete cigars. He was always making calculations. He would even calculate how much each spine of the shark's backbone that was the only decoration of the walls of his smoking-room cost him. And as for the cost of Jasmine's food, he could have told you to a spoonful of soup.

The centre of Rouncivell Lodge was occupied by a very wide staircase lighted from above by a large skylight and bounded by walls the entire area of which was covered with a collection of astonishingly banal pictures. The visitor realized with a shock of knowledge that the pictures from the exhibition of the Royal Academy went every year to accommodation provided by staircases like this. The most rapid, the most inattentive glance at these pictures was enough to produce a sense of almost intolerable fatigue, because each picture was so obviously what it set out to be that the eye was not allowed a blink between a Sussex down, a Devonshire harbour, a Dorset pasture, and a London slum, and the amount of narrative compressed into the space was as if a dozen bad novelists had simultaneously read a dozen of their worst chapters. The massed effect was as confused and brilliant as a wall covered with varnished scraps. The brightness of the staircase and the gaudiness of the pictures were accentuated by the comparative gloom of the rooms on either side, particularly those at the back of the house, which from having been designed to look over a spacious garden were some of them now only six feet from the walls of the new flats. The still close atmosphere created by windows that were never opened from one year's end to the other was tainted by the odour of varnish and stale sunlight; the rooms on the ground floor smelt perpetually of half-past-two on Sunday afternoon, partly of clean linen, partly of gravy.

There were six bedrooms, all of them with large four-poster beds, and all of them haunted by that strange frigidity, that frigidity almost of death which is produced by the least superfluity of china. They were furnished in an eclectic style, but the china was kept strictly to its own kind; thus one bedroom would be red, blue, and gold with Crown Derby; another, and this the most attractive, rose and lavender with Lowestoft; and there was one nightmare of a room filled with black and rose Sèvres.

"I don't like the idea of your sleeping in any of these rooms," Mr. Rouncivell grumbled to Jasmine. She thought at first that he meant to suggest their discomfort, but he went on: "You'll have to be very careful not to break anything. Just because there are three toilet sets, it doesn't mean that you can break what you like. This china has taken me a long time to collect, and it has cost me a great deal of money, what's more. Look at that slop-pail. You dare use that slop-pail!"

"Couldn't I have a less valuable set in my room?" Jasmine suggested.

"Less valuable?" the old man echoed fiercely. "What do you mean by less valuable? Do you want me to provide you with china you can throw about the room?"

"Which bedroom do you use?" she asked to change the subject.

"Bedroom? Did you say bedroom? I don't sleep in a bedroom. I sleep in the bathroom."

He took her to the furthest door along the passage and showed her what she thought was the most depressing room she had ever seen in her life. It was such a small bathroom that having chosen it for a bedroom Uncle Matthew had actually to sleep in the bath itself, or rather on a box mattress which he had fixed on top of it. The window of the room, already sufficiently gloomy from looking out on the flats, was made still more gloomy by its panes being plastered with ferns and the faded plumage of tropical birds. A board was nailed to the sill on which was a brush with scarcely more bristles than Uncle Matthew had hairs, a comb with four teeth, and a safety razor. Safety razors had brought a peculiar pleasure into the old man's life, because since their introduction he had been able to calculate every morning how many less blades he used than anybody else would have used.

After seeing this room Jasmine began to be rather apprehensive where she should sleep; but with many admonitions she was finally awarded the Lowestoft room, which, if she had to live surrounded by china, was the ware she would have chosen. There was only one servant in the house, an elderly woman with a yellow face called Selina, to whom Uncle Matthew presented Jasmine with a solemnity that was accentuated by a din of multitudinous clocks striking noon all over the house with an accompaniment of cuckoos, chimes, and musical voluntaries.

"Twelve o'clock," Uncle Matthew announced.

"At least," said Jasmine. And then she blushed, because she had not meant to be anything more than anxious to please the old man by an assumption of cheerful interest. "I meant ... I was surprised to find it was so early."

"You'll be more surprised than that before you leave this house," said Selina bitterly. "You'll be more surprised than that. You'll have the surprise of your life. You'll be so surprised that you won't know whether you're on your head or your heels."

After this prophecy, the application of which Jasmine could not guess, Selina did not speak to the guest except in monosyllables, and she passed a dreary enough week in being shown Uncle Matthew's antiques and in trying to hold the balance between greediness and wastefulness at their sombre meals. At the end of the week he chose from his collection of walking-sticks a Jersey cabbage-stalk, which he offered to lend her for promenades about the shrubbery.

"You've taken his fancy," said Selina, grabbing her arm when Jasmine, cabbage-stalk in hand, was pretending to enjoy walking up and down the drive.

"I wish I could take yours," she replied.

"You have," said the housekeeper. "And you're going to have tea with me this blessed afternoon. It isn't the surprise I intended for you."

"But it's a very nice surprise," said Jasmine.

"It's a surprise to me. Which is God's way," she added more enigmatically than ever.

Selina belonged to one of those small religious sects which have done so much to solve, to their own satisfaction at any rate, the obscure problems of eschatology. Ceaseless meditation upon the fact that ninety-nine per cent of the human race were damned made Selina gloomy, for she was not naturally a misanthropist and took no pleasure in the thought. Sometimes, moreover, she had doubts even about her own salvation, and on such days the household suffered. Jasmine's arrival at Rouncivell Lodge induced her to proclaim her conviction that with no exception at all the whole of the human race was to be damned eternally. Gradually, however, she realized that in any case she could not hope to inherit the whole of Uncle Matthew's fortune, and she decided that the few years between Uncle Matthew's death and her own projection into eternal torment would be more pleasantly and more profitably passed with Jasmine than alone on what might be an inadequate pension. No sooner had she reached this conclusion than she heard a voice in the night telling her that she was saved; the following morning she cooked some cakes and invited Jasmine to tea with her in the kitchen, the character of which accounted, Jasmine felt, for the housekeeper's yellow complexion; the room was as warm and nearly as dark as the inside of an oven. A large American clock, which only had to be wound up annually, was ticking over the high black mantelpiece; crickets were clicking somewhere behind the range; a green Norwich canary was pecking at his seeds; the hostess was rustling the tea in a canister.

Selina came to the point at once, and postponing the discussion of Jasmine's chances in the eternal future asked her frankly how she proposed to provide for the temporal future.

"That's a question we're both entitled to ask, as you might say. Don't eat those cakes too fast, or you'll have indigestion. What I mean to say is Mr. Rouncivell's rich and you're not. You'll excuse the familiarity? As soon as I saw your box, I said to myself: 'She's not rich.' Well, that's nothing, is it? I'm not rich myself. But that doesn't say we shouldn't live in hope. And that doesn't mean that I'm not provided for in a manner of speaking. Well, I like your looks, and I don't mind telling you that a lady friend of mine in Catford has taken two rooms for my retirement when Mr. Rouncivell's earthly troubles are over; for I wouldn't have you think he's not going to have worse troubles in the next world. That's neither here nor there. He can't expect to keep me for ever, that's a sure thing. If I'm one of the elect, he must just lump it. Only as soon as I heard you was coming I said to myself: 'Now, don't take an instant dislike to her before you've seen her. Make friends and talk things over quietly in your own kitchen.' You're eating those cakes too fast. Oh yes, I know they're very light and eat theirselves in a manner of speaking, but you're eating them too fast. Wait a bit and you shall have a cup of tea before you eat another one. You help me and I'll help you. That's all there is to it. Yes, now you're choking, you see. Supposing Mr. Rouncivell was to leave you everything, you *would* take care, wouldn't you, that those two rooms of mine in Catford which my lady friend is occupying at present was nicely furnished with what you might call any little tit-bits I chose for myself? Now, there's the clock in the hall, for instance. I've been listening to that clock these twenty years, and I've a fancy I should like to go on listening to it until I die. The beds you can have. Well, I mean to say, I never really cared for sleeping in a four-post bed. Too human altogether, I'm bound to say. The posts, I mean."

Jasmine had made several attempts to interrupt this stream of conversation, and once she would have succeeded if Selina had not filled her mouth at the moment of speech with a small tart. At last, however, she managed to protest that she expected nothing from Uncle Matthew.

"And that's where you're quite right," said Selina. "Don't expect nothing, and you won't be disappointed. If I expected, I shouldn't be taking you into my confidence, as it were, like I am doing. But if you'll only do what I say and follow my advice, you can have it all. There's that Lettice and that Pamela coming down with their darling Uncle Matthew here and their darling Uncle Matthew there. But he sees through it. Oh yes, he sees through all of them, the same as anybody else might see through glass. He wants to leave his money to somebody who'll look after it and not go and spend it. All you've got to do is to scrimp and scrape and let him see as you're like himself. I suppose you think he paid for those cakes you're eating? Not at all. They're paid for out of my savings to show you I'm your friend. You help me and I'll help you; and you can't say that's going against the Gospel, can you? Do unto others as you would they should do unto you. So what you've got to do is keep on admiring the way I save money, and I won't let any chance go by of whispering in his ear that his money is safer with you than with any of them. All I ask for myself is a few tit-bits when the poor old gentleman's in the ground. He's got *no* religion; he hates dogs, he hates poor people, he hates hospitals, he hates public parks, he hates everything. So there you are. I've been very plain spoken with you, and you can't say the contrary; very plain spoken, I've been. I'm one of the elect, and I can afford to be plain spoken. It doesn't matter what I say or what I do, our loving heavenly Father's waiting for me at this very moment, because He told me so last night. So far as I can see at present, you're not one of the elect. I'm sorry for it, because I've taken a rare fancy to you. But if we don't meet, in the heavenly courts, we can be friends so long as we're on earth. Oh yes, it's all in the Gospel."

The housekeeper's frankness was not displeasing to Jasmine, although she was much amused at the idea of inheriting money from anybody. However, for the first month of her stay with Uncle Matthew she was, without realizing it, quite a success, because having no money to spend, she gave him the impression that she was of a saving disposition. It never entered his head that anybody could be actually without one halfpenny, and he applauded her disinclination to visit shops and theatres, her habit of walking to where she wanted to go rather than of riding on omnibuses, her transformation of a spring hat into a summer hat, as admirable economies.

"You're doing a treat," whispered Selina cunningly. "Last night I peeped through his keyhole, and he was reading his will."

It was a strange existence for a girl of nineteen, this life with Uncle Matthew, and there were moments when she really did have daydreams about inheriting a vast fortune and going back to Sirene. It was not so much the idea of the money as of the return to her beloved island which twined itself round her thoughts. There would be such delightful things to do. She would buy that villa her father had always talked about buying one day; she would buy up all the pictures of her father that she could find and have a permanent exhibition of them in a large studio; she would invite Lettice and Pamela to stay with her and make their visit much more pleasant than they had made hers; she would invite Aunt Cuckoo and Uncle Eneas to bring the baby to Sirene, and she would make *their* visit very pleasant; and, above all, she would always take care that no people ever had to leave Sirene just because they could not afford to go on living there. Oh yes, and then there was Cousin Edith. She would certainly make an allowance to her so that she need never again be snubbed by Aunt May. Poor Cousin Edith, how polite she would be if she did inherit all Uncle Matthew's money. She would be so sorry about the way she had behaved about Harry Vibart. Harry Vibart? What could she do for him? She would never be able to marry him if she were an heiress, because she would always be afraid that he only wanted to marry her for her money. What a pity he did not propose to her before she inherited. She would not accept him, of course, but if he did not marry anybody else, and if he asked her again when she was rich, why perhaps ... but what nonsense all this dreaming was! She ought to be ashamed of herself.

And then she would jump up from the chair in which she was sitting, jump up so abruptly that all the knick-knacks would rattle and clink, and taking her Jersey cabbage-stalk, she would wander up and down the drive and become interested by such dull little incidents. Far the most exciting thing that happened all that month was a white butterfly that went dancing past and seemed to be flying south; and once an errand boy tried to stand on his head in his empty basket just outside the gates of Rouncivell Lodge. But that was only moderately exciting. Sometimes Uncle Matthew would come and stump up and down beside her and tell her how much a square foot the wood of whatever walking-stick he was using that morning fetched. And then he would think that it was too cold to be out of doors, and she would have to go in with him and mount a crazy step-ladder to lift down some ornament that he wanted to move. Or else she would have to wind up all the twelve tunes in his musical box, an elaborate instrument with little drums, the parchment of which was illuminated with posies, as much unlike real drums as the tinkling music from old operas was unlike a real band. When all the tunes had been played, Uncle Matthew always told her to be careful how she closed the lid, because the case was worth a lot of money and the tunes had been favourites of his wife.

That young wife of Uncle Matthew who died so long ago! It was difficult to think of her as his wife. Her portrait, in a full-skirted riding habit and wearing a hat such as only undertakers and mutes wear nowadays, hung over the mantelpiece in the dining-room, and Uncle Matthew used to talk about her as Clara, which made it seem all the more absurd to think that were she alive now Lady Grant would be calling her Aunt Clara. Jasmine had never disliked Uncle Matthew, and his devotion to the memory of his dead wife kindled the beginnings in her of a genuine affection. She divined now why he slept in that bleak uncomfortable bathroom, divined that it was due to a sentimental horror of occupying any room that contained relics of her too intimate to be spoken of. Jasmine used to ponder the old trunks, locked and strapped and full no doubt of mouldering clothes, that stood in every bedroom except her own. And even in her own bedroom the chests of drawers had both of them two locked drawers, containing who should say now what souvenirs of girlhood? Jasmine asked the housekeeper about Clara; but Selina knew no more than herself.

"I've never caught so much as a tiny glimpse of anything," she said. "And of course she was dead almost before I was born, though not before I was thought of, because my Pa was set on having a little girl of his own a considerable number of years before he actually did. Yes, Mr. Rouncivell cherishes her memory very dearly, and if ever he unlocks any of her boxes or drawers, he always takes care to bolt himself in first. In the room that is, of course. She was well-born too. Oh yes, an undoubted lady—the only daughter of an esquire."

One day Uncle Matthew took from the middle of his walking-sticks a slim malacca cane, the silver handle of which was cut to represent a mailed hand grasping a pistol.

"Loaded with lead," he observed, "just like a real pistol. That was Clara's favourite stick, and it's stood in this stand ever since she had it first. If you like...."

But he thought better of his offer and recommended Jasmine to look well after her Jersey cabbage-stalk. Jasmine liked to think that the unpleasant side of Uncle Matthew had not been developed until Clara's death. She tried to get accustomed to his meanness, making all sorts of excuses for it, and sometimes she actually encouraged him in it, as one humours an invalid's petulance and selfishness. She never felt nearly so much of a poor relation with him as with the others, and it was a satisfaction to feel that he regarded all of them as every bit as much poor relations as herself. Well, time was passing: already people were writing less frequently from Sirene. The city sunlight glittered upon the dusty leaves of the shrubs; Selina was a perpetual diversion; Jasmine was as happy as a Java sparrow in a cage, and almost as happy as the sparrows on the roof of Rouncivell Lodge. As for Uncle Matthew, he became less grumpy every day.

"Which means you suit him," said Selina. "You suit him the same as I suit him. Yes, in a manner of speaking, I fit that man like a glove."

Uncle Matthew had other reasons for supposing that in Jasmine he had discovered a treasure, for no sooner had the information that she was staying with him gone the round of her relatives than she received pressing invitations to come and stay with them as soon as dear Uncle Matthew could spare her. Perhaps Aunt Cuckoo, who had always been considered the most foolish of the family, had proved herself the wisest. The more the others wrote to ask Jasmine to stay with them, the more Uncle Matthew expressed himself content with her company, and the more Selina, with knowing looks and headshakes, implied her success.

"You'll be his heir, you'll be his heir, you'll be his heir!" she breathed exultingly. "And I've written to Mrs. Vokins she can rent the kitchen an extra two days a week as from per now. What did he do yesterday? Sent me out for a bottle of indelible ink. Indelible ink is only used for two things—wills and washing. Oh, there's not a doubt about it."

The yellow-faced housekeeper was so confident of success that when Lady Grant visited Rouncivell Lodge a few days later she alarmed her by open references to Jasmine's good fortune. Lady Grant hurried home and told Lettice and Pamela that, whatever their engagements during the crowded end of June, they must be prepared to sacrifice themselves. Nothing could be allowed to interfere with the affection they owed Uncle Matthew. The poor old gentleman was in his dotage; he was on the edge of the grave; he was being got at by that odious housekeeper and Jasmine.

"After all our kindness," Lady Grant lamented. "It does seem a little hard that she should turn the poor old dear against us. It's a crime."

"It's worse than a crime," declared Cousin Edith fervidly, "it's a——" But she could not think of anything worse than a crime except the sin against the Holy Ghost, and fond though she was of Cousin May, she did not think that Jasmine's behaviour was that—no, not quite that ... but worse than a crime.... "it's an unnatural sin," she triumphantly concluded after a little longer reflection.

"Don't be ridiculous!" This was from Sir Hector.

"Lettice and Pamela must go and stay with him," their mother decided. "Now please, dear children, don't look so disagreeable."

Lady Grant sat down at once and wrote to propose the visit. Next morning Uncle Matthew tossed the letter across the breakfast table to Jasmine.

317 Harley Street, W.
June 20.

My dearest Uncle Matthew,

Poor Lettice and Pamela are both getting so tired of gaiety that ever since they went and had tea with you last they've been at me to ask you to invite them to stay with you at Rouncivell Lodge. If three are too many for you (or even two) Jasmine could come here and stay with either Lettice and Pamela, whichever you didn't have with you. If Lettice came now, Pamela could come in July, and I thought that you would like to come and spend the summer holidays with us wherever you liked. We thought of going to Littlehampton, but anywhere will suit us. Do send a p.c. to say you expect either or both. I'll send you all our news by the girls. Hector has been awarded an honorary degree by the University of Cambridge. He has just been trying on his robes. How expensive such things are! And of course his brother's affairs cost him more than he could well afford. But he never grumbles, though sometimes after a hard day he talks of giving up his cigars.

Ever your affectionate niece,
May Grant.

"Oh, I hope you won't send me away," Jasmine begged. She was not perhaps actually enjoying herself at Rouncivell Lodge, but she greatly preferred walking about the shrubbery with her Jersey cabbage-stalk to walking round the Chamber of Horrors with Cousin Edith, which had been the last dissipation provided for her at Harley Street.

Therefore, when Uncle Matthew told her to write and say he could not have either Lettice or Pamela, she was overjoyed to do so. It did not strike her that it was a good opportunity to score off the Hector Grants, and she wrote so simply that her letter gave the impression of a security that irritated her relations much more than an attempt on her side to be clever.

"She's perfectly sure of herself," Lady Grant gasped. "She's wormed herself in."

"I always thought she was deeper than she pretended," Cousin Edith said with a shake of her head. "Do you remember, May, I said to you once: 'Still waters run deep'? Only of course she wasn't still. She was never still really. She was always jumping up and...."

"Oh, for heaven's sake, Edith, don't babble on like that!" Sir Hector interrupted. "Eighty pounds for these robes, my dear. That's a nice sum to pay for a morning's masquerade."

"Little beast," said Pamela loudly. "I detested her from the first. By the way, I saw the Vibart youth at the Grave-Smiths' dance last night. I didn't say anything about it at the time, because I was afraid that Lettice might be upset."

"Me upset?" Lettice exclaimed angrily. "Why should I have been upset?"

"Now, please, darlings, don't quarrel," their mother begged. "This is not the moment to quarrel among ourselves."

"I say, I've got rather a notion," Pamela announced. "Why shouldn't we ask the Vibart youth here and tell him where dear Cousin Jasmine is to be found? *That* would annoy Uncle Matthew."

"What would annoy Uncle Matthew?" asked Lettice scornfully.

"Sorry you still can't bear the thought of your beloved's treachery," said Pamela with a malicious affectation of sympathy. "But if you could calm your beating heart for the sake of the family, you'd see what I meant."

"If Pamela thinks she can say what she likes to me just because...."

"Now hush, darling. Don't lose your temper, my pet. I see what Pamela means," interposed Lady Grant soothingly.

"You always take Pamela's side."

"Now, my darling, I must entreat you not to argue so absurdly."

"I should have thought it would have been obvious to the meanest intelligence," said Pamela with lofty sarcasm.

"Oh, would you, cleversticks?" her sister sneered.

"Obvious to anybody that if the Vibart youth hangs round Uncle Matthew's, Uncle Matthew will think twice of being so fond of our sweet cousin."

"Pamela, you're a genius," her mother declared proudly.

"Oh, she is, she is!" cried Cousin Edith, clapping her hands with excitement, for the scheme appealed to the innate procuress within her. "I should never have thought of anything half as clever. She's a...."

"Edith," her own rich cousin interposed, "I wish you wouldn't be quite so enthusiastic."

"I'm so sorry," Edith murmured humbly. "Shall I go and give Spottles his bath? Poor old boy, he's been rolling again, Cook says." And by the way in which she washed her own hands as she went out of the room Cousin Edith managed to suggest with suitable regret that she too had been rolling.

Within three days of this conversation Harry Vibart called on Jasmine at Rouncivell Lodge.

"Look here," he said reproachfully, "why didn't you ever write?"

"You never wrote to me." Jasmine tried to be cold and dignified, but she was so glad to see him again that it was not a successful attempt.

"I wrote you six letters."

"I never got them. I expect my aunt wouldn't allow them to be forwarded."

Vibart was sure that Jasmine was misjudging her. No one could have been more anxious to help him find Jasmine. Why, she had taken the trouble to write to Mrs. Grave-Smith for his address, had asked him to lunch and then volunteered Jasmine's address, and, what is more, advised him to go and call on her.

The Italian half of Jasmine was capable of being suspicious; it warned her that people like Aunt May did not so abruptly change their point of view. Why should she have sent him here? Why?... Why?... It must be that Lettice and Pamela had a chance of being married at last and that in a spasm of generosity she wished to help her niece ... or was it that she was afraid of having her on her hands, and hoped to palm her off on Harry Vibart? Such an idea froze her, and the young man, taken aback by her change of expression, asked what was the matter.

"I'm afraid you must have found it a very long way up to Muswell Hill," she said stiffly.

"Longish. Longish," he agreed. "But I took a taxi."

At this moment the window of the room in which they were sitting was darkened by a shadow, and there was Uncle Matthew with his face pressed against the pane and wearing an expression of malevolence, ferocity, and alarm. When they looked up, he waved his sticks above his head and snarled at them.

"It's a lunatic," exclaimed Harry Vibart.

"No, no, it's my uncle."

"I say, I'm awfully sorry. Perhaps he's ill."

Uncle Matthew was still waving his sticks so oddly and making such strange faces that Jasmine was alarmed and ran out to see what was upsetting him.

"Are you ill?" she asked.

"Ill? Ill? No. But I shall be ill in a moment. Listen!"

From the direction of the gates of Rouncivell Lodge the engine of a taxi throbbed upon the warm June air.

"He thinks it's an aeroplane," Vibart whispered. "Poor old chap, he's probably afraid it's going to fall on the house. Old people who haven't seen many of them do often get worried like that. It's all right, sir," he added in a louder voice, "it's only my taxi running up the twopences."

"Take it away," the old gentleman screamed. "Take it away, and take yourself away with it. Who are you? What do you mean by coming here and visiting my niece and keeping a taxi buzzing outside the gate? Do you realize that it's costing a penny a minute? Take it away!"

Harry looked at Jasmine, and she signed to him that it would be right to humour her uncle. She really was afraid that he was going to have a fit.

"Perhaps I may call another day?" the young man suggested in a despondent tone of voice.

"Certainly not. You'll be driving up next in a golden coach. If you want to squander your money, squander it some other way."

It was useless to argue with the infuriated old gentleman, and Vibart took himself off.

"That's the last I shall see of him," thought Jasmine, turning sadly to follow her uncle into the house. Later on, however, when Uncle Matthew had recovered from the shock to his parsimony, he enquired who her visitor was, and she thought that she was able to reassure him.

"Well," said the old gentleman, "perhaps I was a little hasty. Yes, I think I was. Does he smoke?"

"Not cigars," said Jasmine quickly. "At least I've never seen him smoking a cigar."

"He can come and see you twice a week. Once in the morning and once in the afternoon. And then perhaps later on we'll ask him to lunch. But don't count on that. And now come and sit with me in the smoking-room. Because I must smoke a cigar to calm my nerves after that shock."

They passed out into the hall, and on his way through Uncle Matthew cast a glance, as his custom was, at the numerous walking-sticks.

"Whose is this?" he asked, picking a malacca from the stand. "H. V." he read. "This is your friend's. You see, my dear, he's careless through and through. I never left a walking-stick in somebody else's house. Never in all my life."

"I think you made him rather nervous," Jasmine explained apologetically. But the old gentleman paid no attention: he was searching for something he missed.

"Where is it?"

"Where's what?"

"Clara's silver-handled cane."

"I don't see it," Jasmine stammered apprehensively.

"It's gone. That villain must have stolen it."

"If Mr. Vibart has taken one of your sticks, Uncle Matthew, he must have done so by mistake."

"The young scoundrel! The young blackguard!" He became incoherent with rage.

"But, Uncle Matthew, if he has taken one of your sticks he'll bring it back."

"Hers! Hers!" the old gentleman was gasping.

"Oh, dear Uncle Matthew, I'm so dreadfully sorry."

"My poor little wife's! He's taken my poor little wife's silver-handled cane. And she was so fond of it. Her favourite. The ruffian! The—the—tramp! He might have taken any other but that. Oh dear! Oh damn! Why do you bring these people here, you abominable girl?"

That afternoon Jasmine arrived in Harley Street, and had to explain that Uncle Matthew would not have her to stay with him any longer. The Hector Grants welcomed her with something like friendliness, but the next day, when Vibart brought back the missing stick, it was Pamela who claimed the privilege of returning it to Uncle Matthew, and a few days later it was thought advisable for Jasmine to pay her promised visit to Aunt Ellen and Uncle Arnold at Silchester.

Chapter Seven

JASMINE had protested against the visit to Silchester; and this protest was in the opinion of the Hector Grants conclusive evidence of a thwarted intention to corrupt poor old Uncle Matthew. Her resentment of the humiliating unconcern for her own dignity that was being displayed in thus sending her round from one group of relatives to another was brushed aside as no more than the expression of a natural chagrin at finding that her schemes had miscarried. They did not, of course, accuse her in so many words of being crafty; but Jasmine understood well enough at what they were hinting, and the consciousness that she had allowed Selina to discuss her prospects in the old gentleman's will, coupled with the memory of her own dreams of what she should do if he did leave his money to her, gave Jasmine a sufficiently acute sense of guilt to cut short any further opposition to the Silchester visit.

"I simply cannot understand your prejudice against the Deanery," Aunt May avowed. "There must be something else which you are trying to conceal." One of Aunt May's foibles was to regard as potential jackdaws everybody not situated so advantageously as herself. "It can't merely be that you don't want to greet your Aunt Ellen. There must be some other reason. I'm sorry your friend Mr. Vibart should have made such an unfortunate impression on poor old Uncle Matthew. But that is not our fault, is it?"

"I never said that anything was your fault, Aunt May," Jasmine responded. "I know perfectly well that everything is my fault, and that's why I don't want to upset any more of my relations by this behaviour of mine that they seem to find so dreadful."

"Nobody has found your behaviour dreadful," Aunt May gently contradicted. "Try not to exaggerate. I don't think I have ever called you anything worse than inconsiderate."

"Well, but you hate having me on your hands," Jasmine burst out. "You hate it. Why don't you let me go back to Sirene?"

"I've already explained to you," continued Aunt May more gently than ever, "I've already explained to you that your uncle could not accept such a responsibility. What would people say if a man in his position allowed his niece aged nineteen to set up an establishment on her own in a place like Italy?"

"People wouldn't say anything at all," Jasmine argued. "People are not so violently interested in me as all that."

"No, dear, that may be. But they are interested in your uncle, and we have to think of him, have we not? Besides, I should have supposed that you would have been glad to meet your poor father's only sister. She is the kindest of women, and Uncle Arnold is the kindest of men. I cannot say how painful it is for me to feel that *I* have not succeeded in rousing the least little bit of affection. I was ready to make all kinds of excuses for you last year when you first arrived. I realized that excuses had to be made then. But now you have been nearly a year in England, and it is surely not unreasonable to expect you to begin to show a little self-control. I'm afraid your visit to Uncle Matthew has done you no good. I was strongly opposed to it from the beginning and told Aunt Cuckoo as much quite plainly. But Aunt Cuckoo gets Ideas into her head. This turning Roman Catholic, this adopting a baby, this packing you off to poor old Uncle Matthew. Ideas! However, it is not our business to discuss Aunt Cuckoo.... You say you don't believe your relations in Silchester want you. I contend they have shown quite clearly that they do. And I should also like to point out that, if you decline to go, you will grievously wound your Aunt Ellen, who is not...."

"Very well, I'll go, I'll go! I'll do anything you want if you'll only stop lecturing me!" Jasmine could almost have flung herself on her knees before Aunt May if by doing so she could have stopped this conversation. There had been a sweet-shop on the way to the School of Swedish Culture, with an apparatus that went on winding endlessly round and round a skein of fondant that apparently always remained of the same size and consistency. Jasmine used to avert her head at last as she went by, so depressing became the sight of that sweet and sticky mess being wound round and round and round ... her aunt's little talks reminded her of it.

Aunt May confided in Cousin Edith after this outburst that she had wondered for a minute or two if Jasmine was really human. Cousin Edith tried to look as though she still wondered if Jasmine was really human, and all she got for her desire to be agreeable was to be asked if she had a stiff neck.

It was quarter day by now, and Jasmine was advised to spend her allowance on suitable summer frocks; she was also advised not to buy too many, because next quarter day she would be requiring suitable autumn frocks, and she was to bear in mind that clothes for autumn and winter were more expensive. Jasmine longed to refuse her allowance, but her vanity was too strong for her pride; unable to contemplate appearing before her six boy cousins in the dowdy remains of last year's wardrobe, she accepted the money, and despising herself for being so weak, she bought a flowered muslin frock and a white linen coat and skirt, the latter of which was condemned as an extravagance by Aunt May, who had no belief in the English climate. Jasmine might have spared herself the humiliation of accepting Uncle Hector's allowance, because a day or two later Aunt Cuckoo, in a rapture over some alleged conversational triumph of Baboose, sent her a present of five pounds, over which Cousin Edith sizzled but a little less appetizingly than if it had been a present from Aunt May herself.

"Well, I declare," she exhaled. "If you aren't a lucky girl!"

And as the lucky possessor of five pounds all her own, Jasmine set out next day to meet another set of rich relatives.

The journey to Silchester in glowing blue midsummer weather through the fat pasture lands of Berkshire and Hampshire gave Jasmine such a new and such a pleasurable aspect of England that she began to wonder if she had been suffering all this year from a jaundiced point of view, if indeed Aunt May's assumption of martyrdom had any justification from her own behaviour. This landscape through which the train was passing with such an effect of deliberate and conscious enjoyment, with such an air of luxuriousness really, soothed her mind, warmed her heart, put her soul to bed and tucked it comfortably and safely in for some time to come. She determined to meet her new uncle and aunt in the same spirit as the train's; they were to be the natural products of such a landscape, and whether they placidly accepted her arrival like those rotund sheep or whether they threw their legs in the air and swished their tails like those lean and spotted cows pretending to be frightened of the train, she would survey them as amiably and as philosophically. Jasmine was smiling at herself for using such a long word when they ran into a tunnel, one of those long smelly tunnels in which the train seems to bang itself from side to side in despair of ever getting out. Yes, thought Jasmine, even if Uncle Arnold and Aunt Ellen were as stiff as this window, as unreceptive and unsympathetic as this strap and as ungenerous as the blue electric bulb in the roof of the compartment, she would still be philosophical, oh yes, and very very amiable, she vowed as the train escaped from the tunnel, and the air odorous with sun and grass deliciously fanned her. As for Harry Vibart, it was absurd to go on thinking of him. She might as well fall in love with a jack-in-the-box. Fall in love? She detected a faster heart-beat, a suggestion of creeping gooseflesh. Fall in love? Jasmine would have liked to lecture her own self now; she felt as censorious of her involuntary self as Aunt May. But it was no fun to lecture one's involuntary self unless it were done *viva voce*, and if she did that the woman on the other side of the carriage, who ever since Waterloo had been fecklessly trying to separate the green gooseberries in her string bag from the cracknel biscuits and French beans, might be alarmed. But how could she have ... of course it wasn't really his fault about the stick; in fact, he probably considered himself badly treated in the matter. But he must not come down to Silchester and create another scene there. Besides, what right or reason had she to let him come down there? He had never given her the slightest justification for supposing that he was anything more than mildly interested in her. To be sure, he had insisted that he had written to her half a dozen times. But had he? The proper course of action for herself, the dignified and in the circumstances the easiest attitude for her to adopt, was one of kindly discouragement. Yes, she would write to him from the Deanery and tell him plainly that she hoped he would not think of coming down to visit her there. She had just reached this decision when the train steamed into Silchester station.

Jasmine was waiting on the platform in the expectation of being presently accosted by any one of the several dowdy women round her when both her arms were roughly grabbed and she found herself apparently in the custody of two boy scouts.

"I say, are you Cousin Jasmine?" asked the smaller of the two in a squeaky voice.

Simple and obvious though the question seemed, it had an extraordinary effect on the other boy, who instantly let go of her arm in order to engage in what to Jasmine's alarmed vision looked to be a life-and-death struggle with his companion, which did not end until the smaller boy had cried in his squeaky voice 'Pax, Edred,' several times. Edred, however, was for prolonging the agonies of the requested armistice by twisting his brother's arm—for the ferocity with which they had fought was surely a sign that they were as intimately related—and making numerous conditions before he agreed to grant a cessation of hostilities.

"Will you swear not to chisel again if I let go your arm?"

"Yes, I swear."

"Will you swear not to be a rotten little chiseller, and when I say 'bags I asking' next time not go and ask yourself straight off?"

"Yes, I swear. Oh, shut up, Edred. You're hurting my arm most frightfully. You are a dirty cad!"

"What did you call me?" Edred fiercely enquired with a repetition of the torture.

"I said you were a frightfully decent chap. Ouch! You devil! The decentest chap in all the world."

"Well, kneel down and lick my boot," Edred commanded loftily, "and you can have pax."

"No, I say, don't be an ass," protested the younger. "Ouch! Shut up! You'll break my wrist if you don't look out, you foul brute!"

And then, in despair at the severity of the armistice conditions, he wrenched himself free and returned with fury to the attack. The fresh struggle continued until an old gentleman was knocked backward over a luggage truck, after which Edred told his brother to shut up fighting, because people were beginning to stare at them.

"Sorry to keep you waiting, Cousin Jasmine," he said genially, "but I had to give young Ethelred a lamming for being such a beastly little cheat. He's too jolly fond of it."

"Speak for yourself," Ethelred retorted. "You know mother said I'd got to come with you this time." And then he turned in explanation to Jasmine. "The last time Edred bagged going to see Canon Donkin off from the station he stood on the step outside the carriage door all the way along the platform until the train was going too fast for him to jump off, the consequence of which was he got carried on to Basingstoke. Father was sick as muck about it."

"It was rather a wheeze," said Edred simply but proudly. "I very nearly fell off. I would have, if old Donkin hadn't got hold of my collar. And I had an ice at Basingstoke," he added tauntingly to his brother.

"Well, so could I have had an ice too if I'd done the same, greedy guts," replied the brother.

"No, you couldn't."

"Yes, I could."

And the fight would have begun all over again if Jasmine had not entreated them to find her luggage. As this process involved making a nuisance of themselves in every direction they accepted the job with alacrity. When the trunk was found, Edred suggested as rather a wheeze that Ethelred should have it put on his back like a porter, and Ethelred, in high approval of such a course, accepted the position with zest. He was swaying about on the platform to the exquisite enjoyment of his brother when an old lady, who was evidently a stranger to Silchester, asked Jasmine if she was not ashamed to let a little boy like that carry such a heavy trunk. At that moment Ethelred was carried forward by the impetus of the trunk, which slid over his shoulders, and cannoned into the stream of people passing through the ticket barrier. The odd thing was that none of the station officials seemed to interfere with the behaviour of her cousins until the ticket collector, from having had most of his tickets knocked out of his hand, lost his temper momentarily and aimed a blow at Ethelred with his clip.

"How are we going to the Deanery?" Jasmine enquired when at last to her relief she found herself on the edge of the kerb outside the station.

"Edwy's going to drive us in the governess-cart," they informed her. Jasmine had not the slightest idea what a governess-cart was; but it sounded a fairly safe kind of vehicle.

"Edwy's rather bucked at driving you," said Edred. "He's going to pretend it's a Roman chariot. You'll be awfully bucked too," he added confidently to his cousin. "It's rather hard cheese we've got your luggage, because it will make a squash. I say, why shouldn't we leave it here?"

"Oh no, please," Jasmine protested.

"Right-o," said Edred. "But it would be quite safe here on the kerb. You see, Ethel and I wanted to drive, and if you left your luggage here we could come back and fetch it."

Jasmine, however, was firm in her objection to this plan, and at that moment a fat boy of about fifteen, whose voice was at its breaking stage, was seen standing up in a governess-cart shouting what Jasmine recognized as the correct language of a Roman charioteer from *The Last Days of Pompeii*. She asked the other two which cousin this was.

"I say, don't you know?" Edred exclaimed in incredulous surprise. "That's old Edwy, only we call him Why, and we call me Because, and we call Ethelred Ethel."

"No we don't, so shut up," contradicted Ethelred.

"Well, he looks like a girl, doesn't he, Cousin Jasmine?"

Jasmine was spared the embarrassment of a reply by Edwy's pulling up with the governess-cart.

"Did you win?" both the younger brothers asked eagerly.

Edwy nodded absently; his whip had coiled itself round a lamp-post. Greetings between herself and this third cousin over, Jasmine was invited to get in and recommended to sit well forward and not get tangled up with the reins. Her box was placed opposite her, and the younger boys mounted.

"Good Gum," Edwy exclaimed with contempt. "We can't race anything with this load, can we?"

Jasmine, perceiving the narrow High Street of Silchester winding before her, was thankful for the news.

"I tell you what we could do," Edred suggested. "We could pretend that it was three chariots, and that we were all three driving one against the other."

Edwy considered this offer for a moment, then "Right-o" he agreed calmly, and off they went. It might have been less dangerous if Edwy had raced another cart as originally intended, because with the convention they were then following both his younger brothers had to have a hand on the reins. They also had to have a turn with the whip. The extraordinary thing to Jasmine was that this reeling progress down the High Street did not seem to attract a single glance. She commented on the public indifference, and the boys explained that the natives were used to them.

"Monday and Tuesday were much worse than we are," said Edred.

"Monday and Tuesday?"

"Edmund and Edgar. The pater was only a Canon Residentiary in those days. He's been Dean for six years now. He's the youngest Dean that ever lived. Or the youngest Dean alive; I forget which. Then he was Regius Professor of Anglo-Saxon at Oxford."

"The youngest Dean that ever lived in Silchester, you ass," interposed Edwy with a gruff squeak.

"Oh well, it's all the same, and ass yourself!"

Jasmine, who feared the effect of another fight in the cart, changed the subject with an enquiry about Oxford.

"I can't remember being there," said Ethelred proudly. And his elder brothers appeared quite jealous of what was evidently a family distinction.

"Last lap!" Edwy shouted. "Don't go on jabbering about Oxford."

They were driving along a quiet road of decorous Georgian houses, at the end of which was a castellated gateway.

"Here's the Close," Edred cried as they passed under the arch into a green and grey world. "Blue leads! Blue leads!"

"Shut up, you fool, I'm Blue!" yelled the youngest.

While the rival charioteers punched each other behind their brother's back, Purple in the personification of Edwy pulled up at the Deanery and claimed to be the victor. The serenity of the Close after that break-neck drive from the station was complete. The voices of the charioteers arguing about their race blended with the chatter of the jackdaws speckling the great west front of the Cathedral in a pleasant enough discordancy of sound that only accentuated the surrounding peacefulness. Upon the steps that led up to the west door the figures of tourists or worshippers appeared against the legended background no larger than birds. At no point did the world intrude, for the houses of the dignitaries round their quadrangle of grass had nothing to do with the world, and if a town of Silchester existed, it was hidden as completely by the massed elm trees that rose up behind the low houses of the Dean and Chapter as the ancient Roman city was hidden in the grass that now waved above its buried pavements and long lost porticoes.

"It really is glorious here, isn't it?" Jasmine exclaimed.

"Yes, it's rather decent," Edred allowed. "We've got a swannery at the back of our garden, and that's rather decent too. They get awfully waxy sometimes. The swans, I mean," he supplemented. And in such surroundings, Jasmine felt, even swans had no business to lose their tempers.

The Deanery itself was externally the gravest and most impressive of the many grave and impressive houses round the Close. Beheld thus it presented such an imperturbable perfection of appearance that before he knocked upon its door or rang its bright brass bell, the most self-satisfied visitor would always accord it the respect of a momentary pause. But when the door was opened—and it was opened by a butler with all the outward and visible signs of what a decanal butler ought to be—that air of prosperous comfort, of dignity and solid charm, vanished. It was not that the entrance-hall was ill-equipped. Everything was there that one could have expected to find in a Dean's hall; but everything had an indescribably battered look, the irreverent mark that an invading army passing through Silchester might have left upon the Deanery, had some of the soldiers been billeted there. It was haunted by a sense of everything's having served some other purpose from that for which it was originally intended, and the farther one penetrated into the house the more evident were the ravages of whatever ruinous influence had been at work. Even Jasmine with her slight experience of English houses was taken aback by the contradiction between the exterior and the interior of the Deanery. She was used to entering Italian palaces and finding interiors as bare and comfortless as a barrack; but in them the discomfort and bareness had always been due to the inadequate means of their owners. It was certainly not poverty that caused the contradiction at the Deanery. The solution of the puzzle burst upon her when with a simultaneous onrush her cousins, each shouting at the top of his voice 'Bags I telling the mater Jasmine is here,' stormed the staircase like troops. The butler, listening to their yells dying away along the landing above, paused for a moment from the gracious pomp of his ministrations and observed to Jasmine: "Very high-spirited young gentlemen."

"But is the pony quite safe?" she asked, looking back to where the governess-cart with her trunk still inside was waiting driverless outside the door.

"Yes, miss, she's not a very high-spirited animal, and she's usually very quiet after the young gentlemen have driven her."

Again the yells resounded, this time with increasing volume as the three boys drew nearer, leaping, sliding, rolling, and cannoning down the staircase abreast. Jasmine received a thump from Edred, who was the first to reach her, a thump that was evidently the sign of victory, because the other two immediately resigned her to his escort for the necessary presentation to her aunt, while they went out to attend to the pony.

Aunt Ellen's room had escaped the pillaged appearance which upstairs at the Deanery was even more conspicuous than below; it was crowded with religious pictures in religious Oxford frames, religious Gothic furniture, and religious books. Apart from the fruit of her own religious tastes, Aunt Ellen had directly inherited from the Bishop of Clapham his religious equipment (accoutrements would be too highly coloured a word for the relics of that broad-minded prelate); and perhaps because she was fond of her episcopal father she had hesitated to sacrifice his memory, together with her husband and the rest of the household, upon the common altar of those six household gods, her sons. At any rate, when she carefully explained to her niece that the room was a sanctuary not so much for her own use as for old time's sake, Jasmine accepted its survival as due to some sentimental reason. But if Aunt Ellen's room had escaped, Aunt Ellen herself had certainly not. The weather-beaten gauntness of Uncle Eneas and Uncle Hector was in Aunt Ellen much exaggerated, although an aquiline nose preserved her from being what she otherwise certainly would have been, a grotesque of English womanhood, or rather, what English people would like to consider a grotesque of English womanhood; Jasmine, however, with many years' experience of English tourists landing at Sirene after a rough voyage across the Bay of Naples, considered Aunt Ellen to be typically English. She had acquired that masculine look which falls to so many women who have produced a number of sons. When Jasmine knew her better she found that her religious views and emotions resembled the religious views and emotions that are so widely spread among men of action, such as sea captains and Indian colonels. Her ignorance of anything except the gentlemanly religion of the professional classes was unlimited; her prejudice was unbounded. Jasmine soon discovered that the main reason why she had not been invited to the Deanery before was her aunt's fear of introducing a papist into the household. It was this, apparently, that weighed much more with her than the accounts she had received from Lady Grant of their niece's behaviour. True, she informed Jasmine that she had been anxious to correct the looseness of her moral tone. But how could she compete with priest-craft? She actually asked her niece this! Her religious apprehensions were only overcome by the menace of waking up one morning to find Jasmine the sole heiress of Uncle Matthew's fortune, which, as she wrote to her sister-in-law, without presuming to impugn the disposition of God, would be entirely unjust. It was not that she dreaded a direct competition with her own boys, because, proud though she was of them and of herself for having produced them, she never deceived herself into supposing that a personal encounter between them and their uncle would be anything but fatal, not merely to their chances of ultimate wealth, but also to her own. On her own chances she did build. She could not believe that her uncle (painfully without belief in a future state as he was) would ignore the rights of a niece married to the Dean of Silchester. After all, a Dean was something more than a religious figure; he was a worldly figure. Aunt Ellen was sharply aware of the might of a Dean, because that might was mainly exercised by her, the Dean himself by now taking not the least interest in anything except the history of England before the Conquest. Jasmine had derived an entirely false impression of her aunt from her letters, which, filled as they were with religious sentimentality, suggested that Aunt Ellen was softer than the rest of the family, that perhaps she was even like her own beloved father. She found, however, that except where her sons were concerned Aunt Ellen was hard, fierce, martial, and domineering. All her affection she had kept for her sons, all her duty for God. Jasmine was not so much discouraged as she might have been by her aunt's personality, because she found at any rate her three youngest cousins a great improvement on Lettice and Pamela, and if the three eldest ones turned out to be only half as amusing, she felt that she should not dislike her visit to the Deanery. Besides, she had the satisfaction of knowing that this was quite definitely only a visit, and that there was no proposal pending to attach her permanently to the household as a poor relation.

Jasmine did not discover all this about her aunt at their first meeting; the conversation then was crammed with the commonplace of family news; and how Aunt Ellen would have resented the notion that any news about the Grants could be described as commonplace! She might have gone on talking until tea-time if Edred's continuous kicking of the leg of her father's favourite table had not suggested a diversion in the form of Jasmine's long-delayed introduction to the Dean. She had hesitated to interfere directly with her son's harmless if rather irritating little pleasure; but the varnish was beginning to show signs of Edred's boots, and she announced that, although Uncle Arnold was working, he would no doubt in the circumstances forgive them for disturbing him.

Jasmine smiled pleasantly at the implied compliment, not realizing that the circumstances were the table's, not hers.

"I say, need I go?" asked Edred. He dreaded these visits to the study, because they sometimes ended in his being detained to copy out notes for his father.

"No, dear, you need not go."

Edred dashed off with a whoop of delight, turning round in the doorway to shout to Jasmine that he would be in the garden with Why and Ethel should she wish presently to be shown the swans.

"Poor boy," sighed Aunt Ellen when he was gone, and upon Jasmine's asking what was the matter with him, she told her that he had just failed for Osborne.

"It's such a blow to him," she murmured in a plaintive voice that was ridiculously out of keeping with her rockbound appearance. "If he had passed, he had made up his mind to become an admiral, and now I suppose we must send him back to school in September. Poor little boy, he's quite heartbroken. I've had to be very gentle with him lately."

Jasmine supposed it might be tactless to observe that Edred showed no signs of heartbreak, and instead of commenting she enquired sympathetically what Ethelred was going to do.

"Ah, poor Ethelred's a great problem. He wants to be an engineer, and really he is very clever with his fingers; but his father is quite opposed to anything in the nature of technical education until he's had an ordinary education. I think myself it is a pity, but Uncle Arnold is quite firm on that point. Ethelred was at Mr. Arkwright's school until Easter, but the school doctor wrote and told us that he thought the air on the east coast was too bracing for him. In fact, he insisted on his leaving for the dear boy's own sake."

"And Edwy?"

"Ah, poor Edwy! His heart is weak, and we can only hope that with care he will become strong enough for the Army by the time he goes to Sandhurst."

"Is his heart very weak?" Jasmine asked.

"Oh, very weak," her aunt replied, "and he has set it—his heart, I mean—on being a soldier, and so he is working with Canon Bompas, one of the minor canons. A great enthusiast of the Boy Scout movement. A delightful man who was in the Army before he took Orders, and who, as he often says jokingly, though of course quite reverently, still belongs to the artillery. He is a bachelor, though of course," added Aunt Ellen, "not from conviction. As you perhaps know, the Church of England is opposed to celibacy of the clergy. Yes, poor Edwy! He had such a lovely voice. I wish it hadn't broken just before you arrived."

It was hard to believe that Edwy's voice, which now alternated between the high notes of a cockatoo and the low notes of a bear, had ever been beautiful, and Jasmine was inclined to ascribe its alleged beauty to maternal fondness.

"Edmund and Edgar won't be back from Marlborough until the end of the month; but Edward is coming in a fortnight. He delighted us all by winning a scholarship at Trinity. He's so happy at Cambridge, dear boy; though I think everybody is happy at Cambridge, don't you?"

Jasmine agreed, though she really had no opinion on the subject.

"Well, come along," said her aunt, "and we'll go and find your uncle. Quite a walk," she added, "for his study is at the far end of the top storey. His library is downstairs, of course, but he found that it didn't suit him for work, and though it's rather inconvenient having to carry books backwards and forwards up and downstairs, we all realize how important it is that he should be quiet, and nobody minds fetching any book he wants."

This was said with so much meaning that Jasmine immediately visualized herself carrying books up and down the Deanery stairs day in day out through the whole of the summer.

"I told you about the difficulty he had with his typewriting, and how anxious he was that Ethelred should learn, but the dear boy's mind was so bent on mechanics that he was always taking the machine to pieces. Very cleverly, I'm bound to say. But of course it occupied a good deal of his time. So now he practises the piano again instead. People tell me he's very musical."

While Aunt Ellen was talking, they were walking up and down short irregular flights of stairs and along narrow corridors, the floors of which were billowy with age, until at last they came to a corridor at the head of which was a large placard marked SILENCE.

"The boys are not allowed along here," said their mother with a sigh, as if by not being allowed along here they were being deprived of the main pleasure of their existence.

"Uncle Arnold does not like us to knock," she explained when they came to the door at the end of the corridor, on which was another label DO NOT KNOCK. She opened the door, and Jasmine was aware of a long, low, sunny room under a groined ceiling, the gabled windows of which were shaded with lucent green. The floor was littered with docketed papers and heaped high with books from which cardboard slips protruded. From the fact that the windows looked out on the Close instead of on the garden, Jasmine divined that the Cathedral Close was considerably quieter than the Deanery garden. Seated at a large table at the far end of the room was her uncle, or rather what she supposed to be her uncle, for her first impression was that somebody had left a large ostrich egg on the table.

"Jasmine," her aunt announced.

The ostrich egg remained motionless; but the scratching of a pen and the slow regular movement of a very plump white hand across a double sheet of foolscap indicated that the room contained human life. At the end of a minute the egg lifted itself from the table, and Jasmine found herself confronted by a very bright pair of eyes and offered that very plump white hand. After meeting so many tall, gaunt relatives, it was a great pleasure to meet one who was actually shorter than herself. It was not merely that the Dean was shorter than herself which attracted her. He was regarding her with an expression that, had she not been assured of his entire attention's being concentrated upon Anglo-Saxon history, she would have supposed to be friendly, even affectionate; at any rate it was an unusually pleasant expression for a relative. It was probably that first impression of the Dean's head as an ostrich egg which led her to compare him to a bird; but the longer she looked at him—and she had to look quite a long time because her uncle said nothing at all—the more she thought he resembled a bird. His eyes were like a bird's, small, bright, hard, and round; he put his head on one side like a bird; and his thin legs, encased in gaiters beneath that distinct paunch, completed the resemblance.

"Not finished yet, my dear?" his wife asked in the way in which one asks an invalid if he should like to sit up for an hour or two while the sun was shining.

"No, my dear, not quite," the Dean replied; and his voice had a trill at the back of it like a bird's. "About six more volumes."

Mrs. Lightbody sighed. "The way he works! But don't forget, my dear, that the Archdeacon is coming to dinner."

In some odd way Jasmine divined that the Dean thought 'Damn.' She felt like somebody in a fairy tale who is granted the gift of understanding the speech of animals and the tongues of birds. What he actually said was: "Delightful! Don't open the '58 port. Foljambe has no palate."

He had put his head more than ever on one side by now, so that with one eye he was able to read over what he had just been writing, looking at the foolscap as a thrush contemplates a snail before he attacks it.

"I'm afraid that we—I mean that I've disturbed your work," Jasmine murmured.

"Yes," agreed the Dean, and so rapidly did he sit down that his niece was scarcely conscious of the movement until she saw the ostrich egg lying on the table again.

"Now I must take Jasmine to her room," proceeded Aunt Ellen, and she managed to convey in her tone that it was the Dean who had interrupted her and not she the Dean. He did not reply vocally; but as his hand travelled along the paper, a short white forefinger raised itself for a moment in acknowledgement of her remark, and then quickly drooped down to the penholder again.

Jasmine did not suppose that she had made any impression on her uncle, and she felt rather sad about this, because she was sure that if he would only give her an opportunity of being her natural self he would find her sympathetic. She was surprised, therefore, when he and Archdeacon Foljambe arrived in the drawing-room that evening after dinner, to perceive her uncle making straight for herself, exactly like a water wagtail with his funny little strut and funny little way of putting his hands behind his coat and flirting his tail.

"Can you type?" he asked.

And the twinkle in his eyes seemed to endow his question with a suggestion of daring naughtiness, so that when Jasmine told him that she did type, she felt that she was admitting the presence of a lighter side to her nature.

"Come up to my study to-morrow morning about half-past nine. I'll have a chair cleared for you by then."

And thus it was that Jasmine found herself booked to help Uncle Arnold every morning of the week. Yet in helping him she was not in the least aware of being made use of; on the contrary the work had a delicious flavour of impropriety. The machine itself was a good one, so good that it had survived Ethelred's attempted dissection of it; and Uncle Arnold, who when a difficult Anglo-Saxon problem required solution used to tap upon the table with his fingers, did not seem to mind the noise the typewriter made any more than a nuthatch on one branch might object to the pecking of a yaffle at another. Jasmine, remembering that her aunt had alluded in her first letter to the Dean's dislike of constantly changing typists, asked him one day on their way down to lunch why he had had so much trouble with his secretaries.

"One used a particularly vicious kind of scent. Another was continually scratching at her garter. One used to breathe over my head when she came across to give me what she had been doing. Another thought she knew how to punctuate. And one who had studied history at Lady Margaret's quoted Freeman against me! My clerical position forbade me to swear at them. My brain in consequence became surcharged with blood. So I used to work them to death, and when one of them who refused to be worked to death and refused to give notice ... Jasmine! this must never go beyond you and me...."

"No, Uncle Arnold," she promised eagerly. "But do tell me how you got rid of her."

"I used to put drawing pins on her chair. Not a word to a soul! My wife would suspect me of being a papist like yourself if she found out, and the Bishop, who now thinks I'm mad, would then be sure of it. Never let a bishop be sure of anything. He thrives on ambiguity."

Apart from her work with the Dean, Jasmine enjoyed herself immensely in garden games with the three youngest boys. The Deanery garden was a wonderful place, and to Jasmine it afforded a complete explanation of the affection that English people had for England. She had been so unhappy all this past year that she had come to think of Italy as having the monopoly of earth's beauty. But this garden was as beautiful as anything in Italy, this garden with wide green lawns, bird-haunted when she looked out of her window in the lucid air of the morning, bird-haunted when at dusk she would gaze at them from the candle-lit dining-room. The shrubberies here were glossy and thick, not at all like the shrubbery at Rouncivell Lodge. A high wall bright with snapdragon bounded the garden on the side of the Cathedral, and beyond it loomed the south transept and a grove of mighty elms. There was a lake in which floated half a dozen swans that puffed themselves out with esteem of their own white grace, while in the water they regarded those mirrored images of themselves, the high-sailing clouds of summer, or perhaps more proudly their own splendid ghosts. There was an enclosed garden where fat vegetables were girdled with familiar flowers, blue and yellow and red, an aromatic garden loud with bees. Finally there was an ancient tower, the resort of owls and bats, which the Dean sometimes spoke of restoring. But he never did; and the mouldering traceries, the lattices long empty of glass, and the worm-eaten corbels of oak grey with age went on decaying all that fine July. It would have been a pity to restore the tower, Jasmine thought, and replace with sharp modern edges that dim and immaterial building in its glade of larches. The dead lower branches of the trees wove a mist for the paths, on the pallid grass of which grew clusters of orange and vermilion toadstools; it would be a pity to intrude on such a place with the tramp of restoring workmen.

Jasmine's zest in the middle ages, her absorption in pre-Norman days, her surrender to the essential England were at first faintly troubled by having to attend mass at a little Catholic mission chapel built of corrugated iron. But from being pestered by Aunt Ellen to compare the facilities for worship in Silchester Cathedral with those in the church of the Immaculate Conception, Bog Lane, she began to wonder if the externals of history could effect as much as she had supposed. If the Cathedral was spacious, the mind of Aunt Ellen was not; if the church of the Immaculate Conception was tawdry ... but why make comparisons? She had never noticed in Sirene how ugly sham flowers looked upon the altar; when she made this discovery in Silchester, she was instantly ashamed of herself; and when she looked again, it seemed as if the gilt daisies in their tarnished vases were alive, as if they were nosegays gathered in Italy. If the church of the Immaculate Conception, Bog Lane, was hideous, what about the English church at Sirene? That was a poky enough affair. But again, why make comparisons? There were rich relatives and poor relations in churches just as much as in everything else.

Jasmine was fighting loyally against her inclination to criticize, when one blazing day at the end of July the Dean proposed a visit to the remains of Roman Silchester, at which his three sons expressed horror and dismay.

"Why, what's the matter with Old Silchester?" she asked.

"Oh, it's a most stinking bore! A most frightful fag!" groaned Edred.

"Father makes us sweat ourselves to death digging in the sun," croaked Edwy.

"And last time when I chivied a Holly Blue, or it may have been only a Chalk Hill Blue, he cursed me like anything," lamented Ethelred.

The boys groaned again in unison.

"There's nothing to see."

"There's nothing to do."

"It's absolutely foul."

"Father jaws all the time about history, which I hate," said Edred. "I say, can't you put him off taking us?"

But Jasmine declared that they were horribly unappreciative, and declined to intervene.

"Well, anyway," said Ethelred hopefully, "Lord George Sanger's Circus is coming the second week in August."

The thought of that sustained the boys to face a long summer's day among the ruins of the ancient city.

In the end the day was delightful. The Dean preferred his niece as a listener to his sons, and as Mrs. Lightbody had been unable to come, he was not driven by her irritating crusade on behalf of the boys' amusement to insisting upon their attention. The result was that they vanished soon after lunch to hunt butterflies, while the Dean expounded his theory of Old Silchester. Jasmine sat back enjoying the perfume of hot grass, the murmurous air, the gentle fluting of a faint wind, while the Dean proved conclusively that the Saxon invasion utterly swept away every trace of Roman civilization in Britain. The Dean's shadow while he wandered backward and forward among the scanty remains grew longer, and beneath his exposition the Roman Empire, so far as its effect on England was concerned, went down like the sun. Jasmine had been asleep, and she woke up suddenly in the fresh airs of sunset. Half a mile away the boys were coming back over the expanse of grey-green grass to display their captures.

"And how pathetic it is," the Dean was saying, "to think of this outpost of a mighty empire succumbing so easily to those invaders from over the German ocean. The last time they excavated here at all systematically, they turned over some of the rubbish heaps of the camp. Curiously enough they actually found the skins of the nutty portion of the pine-cone from *Pinus Pinea*, which is eaten to this day in southern Italy."

"*Pinocchi!*" cried Jasmine, leaping to her feet in excitement.

"Yes, *pinocchi*," the Dean confirmed. "The soldiers must have had packets of them sent from Rome by their sweethearts and wives and mothers. And that is one more proof that they remained strangers, whereas the Saxons bred themselves into the soul of the country."

While they jogged back in the waggonette through the twilight, Jasmine dreamed of those dead Roman soldiers, and herself longed for freshly roasted *pinocchi*. The boys jabbered about butterflies. The Dean went to sleep.

"I'm enjoying myself here comparatively," said Jasmine to herself that night. "But only comparatively. I still love Italy best."

But she was enjoying herself, and she hoped that she should not have to leave Silchester yet awhile.

Chapter Eight

EDWARD had written from Cambridge at the end of the term to say that his friend Lord Gresham was urging him to explore Brittany in an extended walking tour, and he had wondered in postscript if it would seem very rude should he not arrive home until the beginning of August; in view of the fact that the walking tour was to be in the company of Lord Gresham, his mother had been positive that it would be much more rude if he did arrive home, and she had telegraphed to him accordingly. Edmund and Edgar came home from Marlborough at the end of July. It was Edmund's last term at school, and he was going up to Cambridge in October with an exhibition at Pembroke and a reputation as a good man in the scrimmage. Edgar, who was seventeen, had another year of school before him. Jasmine knew from the youngest boys that 'Monday' and 'Tuesday' in their day had terrorized the inhabitants of Silchester much more ruthlessly and extensively than their juniors. Golf, however, had of late attracted their superfluous energy, and they spent the first fortnight of their holidays in trying to make what they described as a 'sporting' four-hole course in the Deanery garden. From their point of view the epithet was a happy one, for during the first match they broke a window of the dining-room and several cucumber frames, while in searching for lost balls they spoiled the gardener's chance of a prize at the horticultural show that year. The younger boys, jealous of such competent destruction, filled a ginger-beer bottle with gunpowder and blew a hole in the bottom of the lake. Jasmine, who was still working with her uncle, only heard of these events as nuns hear a vague rumour of the outside world. The proofs of the fifth volume were absorbing the Dean's attention; and even when Edred shot a guinea-pig belonging to the Senior Canon's youngest daughter he declined to interfere, much to the satisfaction of his wife, who considered that the Senior Canon should be ashamed to own a daughter young enough to take an interest in guinea-pigs. In fact it was not until a model aeroplane, subscribed for unitedly by the three youngest boys and flown by Ethelred from the ancient oak in the middle of the Close, maintained a steady course in the direction of the Dean's window, and to his sons' pride and pleasure flew right in to land on his table, scatter his notes with the propeller, and upset the ink over his manuscript, that he was moved to direct action. He then banished them to work in an allotment garden attached to the Deanery, where on the outskirts of Silchester for six hours a day they gathered what their father called the fruits of a chastened spirit. The punishment was ingenious and severe, because their enemy the head gardener benefited directly by their labour, and because the allotment afforded no kind of diversion except futile attempts to hit with catapults the bending forms of labourers out of range in the surrounding allotments.

The Dean worked harder than ever when his youngest sons were removed; and Jasmine, finding that she was being useful enough to be able to shake off the thought that she was an infliction, and that there was no hint of a wish for her departure from the Deanery, was anxious to prevent anything's happening to upset what so far were the jolliest weeks she had passed since she left Sirene. Although she had thought a certain amount about Harry Vibart, she had not allowed herself to grow sentimental over him, and after this sojourn at the Deanery, she had quite convinced herself that it would be wiser not to see him again. She had, of course, no reason to suppose that he wanted to see her again; at the same time she had had no reason to suppose as much at Rouncivell Lodge before he suddenly turned up with such disastrous results. His interruption had not mattered so much there, because she was only negatively happy at the time. Here she was something like positively happy, and it seemed from every point of view prudent to write him a letter and as sympathetically as possible to ask him not to disturb the present situation. She wondered whether if she sent it to him in the care of his uncle at Spaborough it would ultimately reach him. By a series of roundabout questions she arrived at the discovery that by looking up Sir John Vibart in Burke she could ascertain his address. When she had found that Sir John Vibart lived at Whiteladies, near Long Escombe in the North Riding of Yorkshire, she devoted herself to the composition of the following letter:—

The Deanery,
Silchester,
August 6th.

Dear Harry,

She had been tempted to go back to *Mr. Vibart*, but inasmuch as she was writing to ask him not to see her again, the formal address seemed to lend a gratuitous and unnecessary coldness to her request, and even to give him the idea that she was offended with him.

I am staying down here with my uncle the Dean, who is very nice and is writing a history of England before the Norman Conquest. I went with him to see the remains of the Roman city of something or other, a very long name, but it is quite near here, and fancy, in the rubbish heaps of the old Roman camp, they have actually found the skins—husks, I mean—of pinocchi. In case you do not know what a pinocchio is, I must tell you that they are the nutty part of the pinecombs from the big umbrella pines that grow all round Naples and Rome. It made tears come into my eyes to think of those Roman soldiers having those boxes of pinocchi sent to them by their mothers and friends all the way to England.

She had written *sweethearts* at the first draft, but the word looked wrong somehow in a letter that was meant to be discouraging.

I work quite hard at typewriting, and this is a very good machine. The only thing is that it won't do dipthongs, which is a pity, because Uncle Arnold gets very angry if Saxon names are not spelt with dipthongs. There are six cousins here who are called after the six boy kings. Uncle Arnold calls them Eadward, Eadmund, Eadgar, Eadwig, Ædred and Æthelred; but other people call them Eddy, Monday, Tuesday, Why, Because, and Ethel. Edward, who is the eldest, I haven't seen yet. He is at Cambridge. I hope you are enjoying yourself wherever you are, and that you haven't been taking any more people's walking-sticks!

Kindest regards,
Yours sincerely,
Jasmine Grant.

P.S. I think it would be better if you didn't come down here and try to see me.

Jasmine was very proud of this postscript; it did not strike her that the bee's sting is in its tail. She would have been astonished if anybody had told her that it was unkind to end up with such an afterthought, did she seriously mean to forbid Harry Vibart to see her again. And she would have been still more astonished and a good deal horrified if anybody had suggested that the prohibition put like that might actually have the air of an invitation, should the recipient of the letter choose to regard it cynically.

However, she did not receive so much as a bare acknowledgment of her letter, and she convinced herself, perhaps a little regretfully, that Harry Vibart, offended by her request, had decided not to bother any more about her.

Meanwhile Edward had arrived. Edward was one of those young men of whom it can be postulated immediately that he could never have been called anything else except Edward. He was a tall and awkward, an extremely industrious, a clever and an immensely conceited young man, who hid the natural gloom established by years of nervous dyspepsia, or more bluntly by chronic indigestion, under a pretentious solemnity of manner. His arrival at Silchester coincided with a change of weather, and the rainy days that attended in his wake created in Jasmine's mind an impression that he was even more of a wet blanket than she might otherwise have thought. For the first few days he hung about the rooms like a low cloud, telling long stories about his tour in Brittany with Lord Gresham, stories that for the most part were about taking the wrong road and putting up at the wrong inn. When he had bored his family so successfully that every member of it had reached the point of regarding life from the standpoint of a nervous dyspeptic, he grew more cheerful and aired his latest discoveries in modern literature. Then he decided to keep a journal, with the intention, it was understood, of immortalizing his spleen. Like most people who keep journals, he was usually a day or two in arrears, and when people saw him pompously entering the room with a notebook under his arm, they used to hasten anywhere to escape being asked what he had done on Thursday morning between eleven and one. At last the sun appeared again, and Edward, looking at Jasmine—by the intensity of his regard it might have been the first time he had seen her—

divined, as if the sun had possessed the power of X-rays, that she lacked education. Edward, whose success in life had been the success of his education, considered that he owed it to his cousin to remedy her deficiencies; keeping in view his principle of never offering to give something for nothing, he suggested that, in exchange for his teaching her Latin, she should teach him Italian. Jasmine would have willingly taught him Italian without the advantage of learning Latin; but she did not wish to appear ungracious, and the bargain was made. Edward advanced much more rapidly in Italian than she advanced in Latin, partly because he was better accustomed to study than she was, and partly because of the four hours a day they devoted to mutual instruction, three and a half hours were devoted to Italian and only half an hour to Latin. The result of this was that by the end of September he was reading Petrarch with fluency, while she had only reached the first conjugation of verbs and the second declension of nouns.

"You're very slow," Edward reproved her. "I can't understand why. It ought to be just as easy for you to learn Latin as it is for me to learn Italian. It's absolutely useless to go on to the third declension until you remember the genitive plural of *dominus*. *Dominorum*, not *dominurum*."

"I said *dominorum*."

"Yes, but you mustn't pronounce it like Italian."

"I'm not," Jasmine argued. "I think the trouble is that I've got a slight Neapolitan accent, and you think I'm saying *urum* when I'm really saying *orum*. You forget that I've got to unlearn my pronunciation to suit yours."

"Well, that applies equally to me," Edward argued.

The result of these difficulties was that Edward gave up trying to teach Jasmine Latin and confined himself entirely to learning Italian from her. About this time he read somewhere that the only way to master a language was to fall in love with somebody who speaks it. Such an observation struck him as a useful tip, in the same way as when he was at school he would remember the useful tip:

Tolle me, mi, mu, mis,
Si declinare domus vis.

He therefore proceeded to fall in love with Jasmine in the same earnest acquisitive way in which he would have proceeded to buy a highly recommended new type of notebook. Edward's notion of falling in love was that he should be able to introduce into an ordinary conversation phrases that otherwise and outside his study of Petrarch would have sounded extravagant. He made up his mind that if Jasmine showed the least sign of taking him seriously—and he realized that he had to bear in mind that cousins are marriageable—he would explain that it was merely practice. At the same time he found her personable, even charming, and if without involving himself or committing himself too far he could for the rest of the summer establish between himself and her a mildly sentimental relationship, which at the same time would be of great benefit to his Italian, he should be able to go up to Cambridge next term with the satisfactory thought that during the Long Vacation he had improved his French, strengthened his friendship with Lord Gresham, effected an excellent beginning with Italian, amused himself incidentally, and made sufficient progress with his reading for the first part of the Classical Tripos not to feel that he had neglected the main current of his academic career.

Unfortunately for Edward's plans he found that Jasmine was inclined to laugh at him when in the middle of rehearsing a dialogue from the *Italian Traveller's Vade Mecum* between himself and a laundress he indulged in Petrarchan apostrophes. Now Edward was not inclined to laughter either at his own expense or at the expense of life in general, because his conception of the universe only allowed laughter to depend upon minor mistakes in behaviour or scansion. Therefore in order to cure Jasmine of her frivolity he was driven into being more serious and less academic than he had intended. In other words, Edward, even if he was already a perfectly formed prig, was not yet twenty-one, and to put the matter shortly, he really did fall in love with Jasmine; so much so indeed that he ceased to make love to her in Italian and began to make love to her in English. Jasmine, apprehensive of all the trouble such a state of affairs would stir up and knowing what an additional grievance it would create against her in the minds of her relatives, begged him not to be foolish. The more she begged him not to be foolish, the more foolish Edward became, so foolish indeed that he began to let his infatuation be suspected by his brothers, the result of which was that he lost the authority hitherto maintained for him by his attitude of discouraging gloom. In a weak moment he even allowed himself to bribe Ethelred to leave him alone with Jasmine in the dusky garden one evening after dinner, and Ethelred, realizing that Edwy and Edred would soon discover for themselves such a source of profit from their eldest brother, it might be to his own disadvantage, resolved to enter into a formal compact of blackmail with both of them.

Thenceforth Edward found himself being gradually deprived of various little possessions that however valueless in themselves had for him the sentimental importance he attached to everything connected with himself. In order to secure twilit walks with his cousin that she, poor girl, with one eye on a jealous mother, did her best to avoid, Edward parted with his choicest cricket bat, presented for the highest score in a junior match in the days before dyspepsia cramped his style; with a collection of birds' eggs made at the age of fourteen; in fact with everything that, should he die now, would have led anybody to suppose that he was once human. Finally he was reduced to forking out small sums of money to purchase the good will of his three youngest brothers. Their demands grew more exorbitant, and Edward, who had already decided to become a Government servant after that triumphant university career which was to crown his triumphant school career, tried to be firm. Indeed he smacked Edwy's head, and when he had done so felt that he had been firm. Unfortunately it was the worst moment he could have chosen to be firm—yes, he was certainly intended to be a Government servant—because the blackmailers had something up their sleeves, and of what that was Jasmine received the first intimation in the shape of a letter from Edwy.

Dear Jasmine,

If you will meet the undersigned by the blasted elm at the corner of the heath to-night at half-past eight, you will hear of something to your advantage. I mean the elm that was struck by lightening last spring at the corner of the paddock. But in future I shall not call it the paddock. The enclosed token will tell you what.

(signed)
A friend and well-wisher.

The enclosed token was a lock of hair tied up with the end of a bootlace. Jasmine supposed that the three youngest cousins had discovered a new kind of game in the pleasure and excitement of which they wished her to share; glad of an excuse to escape Edward's attentions after dinner, she presented herself at the blasted elm and tried to appear as mysterious as the requirements of the game demanded.

She had not been waiting more than a minute when three cloaked figures stealthily approached the trysting-place. They were all wearing what Jasmine hoped were only discarded hats of the Dean, and when they drew nearer she perceived that they were also wearing gaiters of the Dean. She wondered if the Dean had so many gaiters to spare for his sons' pranks, and she began to fear that some of his present wardrobe had been requisitioned. Edwy's voice, in trying to assume the appropriate bass of a conspirator, ran up to a high treble at the third word he uttered, which set his brothers off laughing so unrestrainedly that in order to conceal such an intrusion of their own modern personalities, they had to pommel each other until Edwy at last rescued his voice from the heights and called upon Jasmine to follow his lead. She, still supposing that some game of buried treasure or capture by brigands was afoot followed with appropriate caution along the winding paths of the shrubbery to that favourite haunt of mystery, the ruined tower.

"Fair maiden," the eldest conspirator growled, "your betrothed awaitest you within."

"You've surely never persuaded Edward to hide himself up there?" she laughed.

"Edward avaunt!" he hissed. "The doom of Edward is sealed."

"Sealed!" echoed Edred, more successfully hoarse than his brother.

Ethelred was unable to take up his cue, being choked by laughter.

"I say, do you think she ought to climb up by the rope-ladder?" Edred asked, falling back into his ordinary voice for the moment.

"Shut up, you ass," replied Edwy in the same commonplace accents. "Maiden," he continued in a bass that was now truly diabolic, "the ladder of knotted sheets for thy fell purpose awaitest thee."

"A terribly appropriate adjective," Jasmine observed with a smile. "I'm not really to climb up that, am I?"

"No," said Edwy reluctantly. "An thou wilt, thou cannest enter by the door."

"Poor Edward!" murmured Jasmine. "How he must be hating this!"

"Foolish maiden," Edwy reproached her. "It is not Edward who you seekest, but one more near, no, I mean more dear, but one more dear to thee. My trusty followers and me will watch without whilst thou speaketh with him."

The air of Bartelmytide was moist and chill, and Jasmine, with regretful thoughts of the Deanery fires which had just begun, hurried into the tower to finish off her part of the performance. She was not to be let off until she had mounted to the upper room, and though in the darkness the ladder felt more than usually wobbly and the stones on either side more than usually covered with cobwebs, she went boldly on, and had no sooner reached the upper room than she was aware that there was somebody there, somebody who did not greet her with the flash of a dark lantern, but with the flicker of a cigar-lighter.

"Well, this is a rum way to meet you again," Harry Vibart exclaimed genially.

"But...." Jasmine stammered, "I thought I told you not to come down here."

Vibart was too tactful to say that he had supposed the forbidding postscript was at least a suggestion if not an invitation that he should come down, and looking as suitably penitent as he could by the wavering beams of the cigar-lighter, he explained that he had only done so with great caution, and added a hope that she would forgive him.

"Yes, but supposing my uncle and aunt find out that you have arranged to meet me like this?"

"Oh, I didn't arrange to meet you like this," Vibart explained. "Those three young sportsmen downstairs arranged that. The only thing I did was to make enquiries beforehand where you were living, and somehow they got it into their heads—of course you'll think it ridiculous, I know—but ... well, to put it shortly, they imagined ... that I was ... rather keen on you."

"I suppose you realize that I am very angry indeed?" said Jasmine.

"Oh yes, I realize that," Vibart admitted. "I can see you're very angry. But don't you think that to-morrow I might call in the ordinary way? That's the main object of this interview. I've really rather enjoyed sitting up here thinking about you. I should have enjoyed it even more if something that was either a small bat or a large spider hadn't fallen on my head. But what about to-morrow?"

"Oh no, please," she expostulated. "No, no, no, you really mustn't. I'm quite enjoying myself here. I'm quite happy, and I know that if you arrive on the scene, something's bound to happen to make everything go wrong."

"That's very discouraging of you."

"I don't mean to be discouraging."

"You may not mean to be, but you certainly are. Look here, Jasmine, I've been thinking a tremendous lot lately about you, and if you'll risk it, I'll risk it."

"Risk what?"

"Well, you see ... confound this patent lighter; it's gone out."

The upper room of the tower was in complete darkness, and Jasmine was inclined to hope that it would remain in darkness; she felt that even the mild illumination of the cigar-lighter gave too intimate a revelation of her countenance for any promise to be made. Harry was gaining time for his reply by devoting himself to the cigar-lighter, and Jasmine felt that if this tension was continued, she should presently begin to emit white sparks herself.

"Risk what?" she repeated.

"Risk being cut off by my uncle and not having a penny to bless ourselves with, and getting married on what I made this August. I've had a topping August. I'm £84 10s. up on the bookies. And though of course it's not much for two, it would give us enough for an economical honeymoon, and I've got a friend who would give me a job in a teak forest in Burmah. It's a very useful wood, you know. They make boats of it and the better kind of packing-cases."

"Stop! Stop!" she exclaimed.

"What's the matter? Have you got a spider on you? Show me where it is and I'll brush it off. I'm frightfully afraid of spiders, but I'm so fond of you, you darling little girl, that I'll...."

"Oh, you mustn't call me that," Jasmine interrupted.

"Don't you like being called a darling little girl?" he asked with a sigh of relief. "Well, I promise you I won't ever call you that again. I assure you that it took a lot to work myself up to the scratch and get off that term of endearment. But, Jasmine, I love you. Look here, murmur something pleasant for goodness' sake. I'm feeling an awful ass now I've said it."

But Jasmine could not murmur anything at all. By what she had read of love and of the way people declared their love, she would have supposed that Harry Vibart was making fun of her. And yet something in the tone of his voice forbade her to think that. Moreover, the way her own heart was beating prevented her wanting to think that. So she stayed silent, while he occupied himself with the cigar-lighter in case her eyes should tell him what her tongue refused to speak. He managed at last to kindle the wick, and holding the little instrument of revelation above his head so that from the vastness of the gloom around he could conjure her beloved countenance, he stood waiting for the answer. In the few seconds that had fluttered past, Jasmine felt that she had grown up, and now when she looked at the freckled young man, so obviously fearful of having made a fool of himself, she felt several years older than he, so much older that she was able to speak to him with what it seemed was a weight of worldly knowledge behind her.

"I'm afraid you've been rather impetuous," she said austerely. "I could never dream of asking you to give up anything on my account." Jasmine gained eloquence from not meaning a word of what she said, and unaware that she was trying to persuade herself rather than Harry of the imprudence of his project, she grew more eloquent with every word she uttered. "You must remember that I have not a penny in the world, and that you cannot afford to marry a girl without a dowry. I know that in England men do marry even quite ordinary girls without a dowry, but I should never feel happy if I were married like that."

"What on earth have dowries got to do with being in love? Do you love me? Do you think you could get to love me?"

"You've no right to ask me that," said Jasmine, "unless you are able to marry me."

"Well, I told you I was £84 10s. up on the bookies this August. I should have proposed in July, but I had rather a rotten Goodwood, and...."

"Yes, but you can't afford a wife with only that. Why, even if my uncle went on allowing me £10 a quarter...."

"I told you there was a risk. I asked you if you would risk it," he interrupted in an aggrieved voice. "Anyway, the point I want to get at is this: do you or do you not care for me?"

"I like you very much," Jasmine admitted politely.

"Yes, well, that sounds rather as if I was a mutton chop. Look here, you know, you're driving me into making a scene. When I first saw you at York, I fell in love with you. I didn't mean to tell you that, because it sounds ridiculous. But I did. Then when you were such a little sport on that mackerel hunt, I loved you more than ever. And then you were whisked off. I felt desperate, and I tried to kill my love. Please don't laugh. I know it's almost impossible not to laugh if a chap talks like this, and I should have laughed myself a year ago. But do you realize that you've driven me into reading books? That's a pretty desperate state of affairs. I can't pass a railway book-stall now without buying armfuls of the most atrocious rot. And the worse it is, the more I enjoy it. About fifty darlings a page is my style now. Where was I? Oh yes, I tried to kill my love. You know, playing golf, and all that sort of thing. But as soon as I heard where you were, I came to see you. Well, it was bad luck to drop that brick over the old boy's malacca, and I felt desperate. And then when I got your letter on top of the worst Goodwood anybody ever had, I said to myself that, unless I was fifty pounds up by the end of August, I'd go out to the Colonies and work myself to death. Well, I made more than that fifty pounds, and here I am. I'd got a lot of jolly things all ready to say to you, but now I'm here I can't say anything. Jasmine, I'm as keen as mustard on you. There!"

He had spoken with such vehemence that the cigar-lighter had long ago been puffed out; in the darkness Jasmine felt her hand grasped.

"What a topping little hand," he murmured. "It's as soft as a puppy's paw. Topping!"

Jasmine had an impulse to let herself sigh out her happiness upon his shoulder; she knew somehow that his arms were open, and that the touch of his tweeds would be as refreshing to her tired spirit as if she were to fling herself into the sunburnt scented grass of a remote meadow; she could not summon to her aid a single argument against letting herself be folded in his embrace. Then, just as she was surrendering to the moment, a clod of earth was flung through the ruined oriel of the tower, and from down below came hoarse cries of "Cavé! Cavé! Edward's coming down the path! You'd better bunk!"

"What's up?" asked Vibart, making fresh efforts to kindle his cigar-lighter. "Who's Edward?"

"Oh, I knew this would happen! I knew this would happen!" Jasmine exclaimed distractedly. "I told you not to come down here."

"But who's Edward?" Vibart persisted.

"It's my cousin. He's dreadfully in earnest, and he thinks he's in love with me."

"Well, I'm not particularly afraid of Edward; but if it's the fashion here to be afraid of him, I'll pretend to be afraid of him too, and the best way of showing our terror is to sit here holding each other's hands until the dangerous fellow passes on. The closer we keep together, the less frightened we shall be."

"It's nothing to joke about," she said. "He's evidently suspicious about something, or he would never have come out into the garden to look for me in the tower."

Jasmine was sure that the conspirators, in their desire for a more dramatic climax than they might otherwise have secured, had conveyed a mysterious warning to Edward, who, when she was nowhere to be found in the house had, preserving his own dignity as far as possible, set out upon a voyage of discovery.

Whatever the conspirators had done in the way of precipitating this climax, they were now doing their best to deflect Edward from the path. The methods they chose, however, were not sufficiently subtle, and they only had the effect of putting their eldest brother in a very bad temper, as was evident from the threats that were audible outside.

"Look here, young Edred, I'll give you the biggest thrashing you ever had in your life if you fling any more of those toadstools at me. All right, Edwy, I can recognize you, and you'll find out when you go indoors again that you can't wear the pater's gaiters without trouble. Where's Jasmine?"

And then, like the croak of a night-bird, Edwy's response was heard.

"Recreant knight, the maiden whom thou seekest is safe from thy lustful arm. Beware of advancing another step."

"You young swine, I'll give you the biggest licking you ever had in your life!" retorted Edward, still advancing in the direction of the door.

"Look here," Vibart whispered to Jasmine, "I think I ought to go out and help those sportsmen."

At this moment Ethelred, who had retreated into the tower, came up the ladder and told them not to worry, because he had invented something that was going to put Edward out of action the moment he attempted to advance beyond the first rung.

"No, please, Ethelred," Jasmine begged. "Don't make matters worse than they are."

"No, really it's all right, I swear," Ethelred promised. "Don't get excited. And if you want to elope to-night, Edwy's made all the necessary arrangements. He's got the ladder hidden by the stable, and the pony's harnessed, and if you're pursued, he's going to put people off the scent by saying the house is on fire; or he may be trying to set it on fire really, I can't remember; and he's only told Wilson"—Wilson was one of the under-gardeners—"so you needn't be in a funk of being found out. And look here," he added to Vibart, "you won't forget that man-lifting kite, will you? Because Edwy's awfully keen to go up with it."

"That's all right," Vibart promised. "You stave off Edward, and I'll send you a kite that will lift an elephant."

"Don't encourage him," said Jasmine. "You don't understand how dreadful all this is going to be for me."

By this time Edward, undeterred by the missiles of Edwy or Edred, had reached the foot of the ladder, and was asking Jasmine in that academic voice she so much disliked if she was in the tower.

"If those young brutes have been playing practical jokes on you, *carissima*, just let me know and I'll give them a lesson they won't forget."

"Will you, you stinking pig?" muttered Ethelred, bending over and releasing a heavy weight on his brother's head.

"Heavens! What have you done?" Jasmine cried in apprehension.

"It's all right. It's only a bag of flour," Ethelred explained. "And I think it hit him absolutely plum."

However it hit Edward, it had the effect of rousing him to fury; without pausing to consider that the steps of the ladder were broken and that the floor of the tower contained several holes and that his sense of direction was considerably impeded by the flour in his eyes, he came charging up the ladder. Just as he reached the top there was a crack of giving wood, followed by a crash, a cry, a thud, and several groans.

"Great Scott! He's really damaged himself this time," said Vibart.

"I say, I didn't work that," Ethelred protested a little tremulously.

Edred and Edwy, who had followed in their brother's wake, were calling up that he had broken his leg. Vibart's cigar-lighter refused to shed even a momentary flicker on the scene, and there was nothing for it but to send one of the boys below back to the house for help. Jasmine begged Harry Vibart to escape if he could, but when he tried the floor with a view to letting himself down, the rotten planking began to break off, so that he had to draw back lest the whole floor of the room should collapse and precipitate himself and Jasmine upon the prostrate and groaning form of Edward underneath. He then attempted in response to Jasmine's entreaties to escape from the oriel window, but no sooner had he put himself into a position to make the drop than she begged him with equal urgency to come back.

"You might break your leg too, and it would be so dreadfully embarrassing to have you and Edward both in bed. My aunt would hate looking after you, and I should never be allowed to look after you."

"Are you sure of that?" he asked.

"Sure, sure. But why do you ask?"

"Because, if I thought there was a chance of getting you as my nurse, I'd break every bone in my body with the greatest pleasure."

The only one who escaped without damage moral or physical from that evening was Ethelred. When the Dean and Mrs. Lightbody with Edgar and Edmund, gardeners and lanterns and ladders, and an improvised stretcher, arrived at the tower, Ethelred managed somehow to get back to the house unperceived, and was able to claim, relying upon the loyalty of his fellow-conspirators, that he had gone to bed immediately after dinner with a bad headache. The rest of the family suffered in various degrees. Edwy suffered from being caught wearing his father's best gaiters, Edred from being caught wearing his father's best hat. The Dean suffered in his character as owner of the gaiters and the hat. Mrs. Lightbody suffered in her deepest feelings as a mother, as the wife of the Dean of Silchester, and as an aunt. Harry Vibart suffered from the ridiculous situation in which he found himself, and from the unpleasant situation in which his imprudence had placed Jasmine. Edward suffered from a broken leg, but derived some pleasure from the effort he had made to be noble. His nobility of behaviour consisted in abstaining from any comment on Vibart's presence in the tower, and the consciousness of his nobility was so sharp that the pain of his fractured limb was dull in comparison. Yet Jasmine was so unreasonable as to think him lacking in generosity because he did not explain away Vibart's presence, explain away his own accident, explain away the whole situation, in fact. She even blamed him for what had occurred, ascribing the disaster to his vanity in supposing that she would send him a message by the boys to meet her in the tower. But then Jasmine had suffered most of anybody; and it was she who was to discover that Aunt May at her worst was angelic beside Aunt Ellen.

"I'm bound to say, Jasmine, that I did not imagine the existence of such depravity. A servant would not behave like that. And what is so lamentable is that the boys knew that you were up in the tower with that young man. It seems to me almost criminal to put such ideas into their little heads. I've been so strict with them. I've even wondered sometimes if I could let them read the Bible to themselves. Your poor uncle has aged twenty years in the last twenty-four hours."

What really had happened to Uncle Arnold was a bad cold from going out in his slippers without a hat. But Aunt Ellen was enjoying herself too much for accuracy. She was in the raptures of a grand improvisation. Presently her fancy soared; she indulged in Gothic similes.

"It was like a witches' sabbath. And poor Edward! Not a word has he said in blame of you. He lies there as patient as a martyr. And then I suppose you'll go off this afternoon and confess to your priest down in Bog Lane, and come back under the impression that you're as white as driven snow. To me such a pretence of religion is disgusting."

"Perhaps you don't realize, Aunt Ellen," said Jasmine, "that Edward has been making love to me for weeks, and that I've had to laugh at him to prevent his doing something silly."

"What do you mean, doing something silly, you wicked and vulgar girl? I cannot think where you got such a mind. A servant would not get such disgusting ideas into her head. I suppose we must put it down to your mother."

"Stop!" said Jasmine, white with anger. "Stop, will you? Or I shall throw this inkpot at you." And when Aunt Ellen did stop, she was half sorry, because she was hating her so much that she was really wanting to throw the inkpot at her. However, she put it back on the table, rushed from her aunt's presence up to her own room, where, after weeping for an hour, she sat down and wrote to Harry Vibart.

Dear Mr. Vibart,

I hope you realize by now that you acted abominably in coming down here after what I said in my letter. I never want to see you again. Please understand that I mean it this time. However, I'm going back to Italy almost at once where people know how to behave themselves. I hate England. I've been miserable here, and you've made me more miserable than anybody.

Then she signed herself *Jasmine Grant* and fiercely blotted him out of her life.

Chapter Nine

AFTER the scene with her aunt, Jasmine longed to leave the Deanery at once, for she suffered torments of humiliation in having to stay on there in a disgrace that was being published all over Silchester. The Dean himself was kind, and perhaps it was because he understood the difficulty of her position that he asked her to come and work with him. But such an easy way out for Jasmine did not please his wife, who was continually coming up to the study and worrying him with her fears about the progress of Edward's fracture in order to impress both him and Jasmine with their heartless conduct in thus working away regardless of the martyr downstairs. The Dean was a kind-hearted man, but he considered his work on pre-Norman Britain the most important thing in life; finding it impossible to proceed under the stress of these continual interruptions, he presently announced that he must go to Oxford for a week or two and do some work in the Bodleian.

As soon as he had gone, Aunt Ellen's treatment of her niece became something like a persecution. She forbade the youngest boys to play with her; she took a delight in making the most cruel remarks to her before Edmund and Edgar; she was rude to her in front of the servants. Jasmine was on the verge of a nervous breakdown, and she was by now so passionately anxious to leave Silchester that she was actually on the verge of writing to Aunt May to ask if she could not come back to London. She did write to Aunt Cuckoo, who wrote back a pleasant little letter iced over with conventional expressions of affection like the pink mottoes on a white birthday cake. She was sorry to hear that Jasmine was unable to appreciate Aunt Ellen. She realized that the atmosphere in the higher circles of the Church of England was unsympathetic, *but* Baboose had shown symptoms of croup. She hoped that later in the autumn Jasmine could come and spend a week or two at The Cedars, *but* just now it was advisable to keep Baboose at Torquay. Uncle Eneas sent his love, *but* he was not very well, and Jasmine would understand how difficult it was to fit an extra person in seaside lodgings. She was sorry that Jasmine was unhappy, "*but* our wonderful religion will console you better than my poor self," she wound up.

"But! But!" Jasmine cried aloud. "Butter would be the right word."

Such was the state of affairs at the Deanery when one morning about a fortnight after Edward broke his leg, Cherrill the butler announced a visitor to see Jasmine. After what she had suffered from that ill-timed visit of Harry Vibart, her heart sank, particularly as Cherrill did not announce the visitor in a way that would have led anybody to suppose that his news would be welcome.

"For me?" Jasmine repeated. "Are you sure?"

"Yes, miss," said Cherrill firmly. "This, er...." he hesitated for a moment, "...elderly person wishes to speak with you for a moment on behalf of Miss Butt."

"Miss Butt?" Jasmine repeated. "Who's she?" For a moment she thought that her nervous condition was developing insanity and that the name was something to do with her outburst against the 'buts' of Aunt Cuckoo.

"Perhaps if you would come down, miss," suggested Cherrill, "to ascertain from the ... person more in full what exactly she does require, you could enquire from her who Miss Butt is."

Jasmine asked if the visitor had given her own name, and when Cherrill said that she had given the name of Mrs. Vokins she remembered that Mrs. Vokins was Selina's friend at Catford. It was all very odd, and without more ado she went downstairs.

In the dining-room a small thin woman with a long red nose came forward to shake hands with Jasmine in the serious way in which people who are not accustomed to shaking hands very often do.

"You've been sent here by Selina?" asked Jasmine impulsively. The question seemed to take Mrs. Vokins aback; she had evidently been primed with a good deal of formality to undertake her mission.

"I am Miss Butt's lady friend from Catford," she explained with an assumption of tremendous dignity.

"I remember her talking about you very often."

"Yes, miss," sighed Mrs. Vokins, taking out her handkerchief and dabbing the corners of her eyes. She evidently supposed that any reference to her in conversation must have included the sorrows of her past life, and she now put on the air of one to whom a response to sympathy is the most familiar emotion.

"And you have a message for me from Selina?"

"No, not a message, a letter. Miss Butt was unwilling to put it in the pillar-box for fear your aunt should look at it."

"My aunt?"

"That was how Miss Butt came to send me in place of the pillar-box. She wanted me to put the letter in my stocking for safety, but suffering as I do from vericlose veins, I asked Miss Butt to kindly permit of it being put in my handbag. You must excuse it smelling slightly of salts, but I'm very subject to headaches ever since my trouble."

Jasmine opened the letter, which was strongly perfumed with gin. The negotiations being conducted in such a ladylike polite spirit, Jasmine was not surprised to find Selina's letter couched in the same style.

Dear Miss Grant,

This is to inform you that poor old Mr. Rouncivell has been took very bad with inflammation of the bowls screaming and yelling himself hoarse fit to frighten anybody. I don't want to say more than I ought in a letter, but knowing what I know, I tell you you ought to come back with my lady friend Mrs. Vokins at once and not knowing if you have the money for your fare I take the liberty of enclosing a postal order for two pounds. Mrs. Vokins has a brother-in-law who is a fourwheeler and will drive you back to Muswell Hill as per arrangement.

"This is all very mysterious," Jasmine commented.

"Yes, miss, so it is, I'm sure," Mrs. Vokins agreed. "But then, as my friend Miss Butt says, life's very mysterious. And I said, answering her, 'Yes, Miss Butt, and death's very mysterious.' And she said, 'You're right, Mrs. Vokins, it is.' Miss Butt's very worried. Oh yes, I can tell you she's very worried, because she's given up the kitchen which I was using for her three times a week. If I might presume to give advice as a married woman, which I was before my poor husband died, I'd advise you to pack up your box and come along with me by the afternoon train, which my brother-in-law will meet with his cab. You need have no fear of familiarity, miss, because he was a coachman before he was a cabman, and was hounded out of his job by one of these motor-cars. Inventions of the Devil, as I call them."

"But does Selina want me to help her look after my poor uncle?"

"I'm sorry, miss, to appear stand-offish, and it's through no wish of mine, I'm sure, but Miss Butt's last words to me was: 'Keep your mouth shut, Mrs. Vokins.'"

Jasmine was too deeply moved by the thought of the poor old gentleman lying in pain at Rouncivell Lodge, and too much touched by Selina's kindly thought in enclosing her fare, to delay a moment in answering her request. In any case it was obvious that she would have to leave the Deanery almost at once, and it seemed an interposition of providence that she should have such a splendid excuse to escape from the ridiculous and humiliating position in which Edward's folly and Harry Vibart's thoughtlessness had placed her.

It was dark when the cab pulled up a hundred yards away from the gates of Rouncivell Lodge, and Jasmine hoped that the necessity for all this caution would soon be finished, because she was finding the gin-scented hushes of Mrs. Vokins that filled the interior of the dank old cab trying to her fatigued and hungry condition. However, there was not long to wait before Selina's voice, which always sounded to Jasmine as if the housekeeper had been eating a lot of stale biscuits without being able to obtain a drink of water after them, greeted her.

"Such goings on!" she snapped, and then turning to the cabman went on in her dry voice: "Perhaps, Mr. Vokins, you'll have the goodness to carry Miss Grant's trunk round to the back entrance without ringing."

"I suppose the horse will stand all right?" said the cabman doubtfully.

"Of course the horse will stand all right," said Selina. "My father was a coachman before you knew the difference between a horse and a donkey, Mr. Vokins."

"William," supplemented his sister-in-law, "remember what I told you on your doorstep first thing this morning."

Mr. Vokins without another word went off to leave Jasmine's trunk where he had been told to leave it. While he was gone, the conversation was kept strictly to the minor incidents of Mrs. Vokins' mission.

"You got off then quite comfortably, Mrs. Vokins?" Selina enquired.

"Yes, Miss Butt, thank you. I had no trouble. Or I should say none but what come from me being so silly as to break my smelling salts in my bag by not noticing I had put my bag *under* me on the seat instead of *beside* me as I had the intention of. Oh yes, when anyone makes up their mind to it, you can get about nowadays and no mistake."

"And you gave Miss Grant the postal order all right, Mrs. Vokins?" enquired Selina sharply.

"We haven't known each other all these years, Miss Butt," replied her friend with elaborate haughtiness, "for you to have any need to ask me *sech* a question *now*."

"It was so kind of you, Selina, to think of that," said Jasmine, putting out her hand to touch the yellow-faced housekeeper's arm. Selina blew her nose violently, and then observed that a little quietness from everybody would not come amiss.

It was not until the two Vokins had disappeared into the December night and Selina had conducted Jasmine with the most elaborate caution along the gloomy path known as the Tradesmen's Entrance and had seen her safely seated by the kitchen fire that she allowed herself the luxury of a complete explanation; and even then she broke off just when she had gathered her skirts together before sitting down to observe that Jasmine was looking very pale, and to ask if she was hungry.

"I haven't had any dinner," Jasmine explained.

"Well, there's nothing but muffins; but I suppose you wouldn't object to muffins. If a Frenchman who isn't hungry can eat frogs and snails, you can eat muffins when you are."

"I should love some muffins," said Jasmine, and she ate four while Selina sat back and stared hard at her all the time. As soon as she had finished, the narrative opened.

"Well, it's best to begin at the beginning, as they say, and when you got into trouble over Her walking-stick, that there Pamela planted herself down here. And now perhaps you'll understand why I said nothing in front of Mrs. Vokins?"

Jasmine looked bewildered.

"Well, of course, she poisoned him. Oh, undoubtedly she poisoned him. Well, I mean to say, people don't fall ill for nothing, do they?"

"Selina!" Jasmine gasped. "You're making the most dreadful accusation. You really ought to be careful."

"That's what I am being. Careful. If I wasn't careful, I should have gone and hollered it out in the streets, shouldn't I? But I know better. Before I'd hollered it out once or twice I should have been asked to eat my words, if you'll excuse the vulgar expression. And then where should I have been?"

"Yes, but I don't think you ought to say things like that even to me. After all...." Jasmine hesitated; she was debating indeed whether to say 'Miss Pamela' or 'Pamela.' If she used the former, she should seem to be dissociating herself too much from Selina, which in view of having accepted the loan of that money would be snobbish; and yet if she called her simply 'Pamela' she should seem to be associating herself too intimately with Selina, even perhaps to be endorsing the terrible accusation, which was only one of Selina's ridiculous exaggerations, on the level of her theory that the human race was without exception damned. "After all," she had found the way to put it, "my cousin, you see she *is* my cousin."

"Well," Selina granted unwillingly, "if she didn't poison him with arsenic, she poisoned his mind. The things she used to say at the dinner-table! Well, I give you my word, I was in two twos once or twice whether I wouldn't bang her on the head with the cover of the potato dish. I give you my word, it was itching in my hand. Nasty sneering way of talking! I don't know where people who calls theirselves ladies learn such manners. And no sooner had that there Pamela gone than that there Lettice appeared. Lettice, indeed! There's not much green about her. Anyone more cunning I've never seen. Nasty insinuendos, enough to make anyone sick! Small wonder the poor old gentleman had no appetite for his food! And of course she attempted to set him against me. Well, on one occasion he akcherly used language to me which I give you my word if he'd of been a day younger I wouldn't have stood it. Language I should be sorry to use to a convick myself. Well, there have been times when I've wondered if the Lord wasn't a little bit too particular. You know what I mean, a little too dictatorial and old-fashioned. But I give you my word since I've had two months of them I sympathize with Him. Yes, I sympathize with Him! And if I was Him, I'd do the same thing. Well, I never expected to enjoy looking down out of Heaven at a lot of poor souls burning; but if this goes on much longer, I shall begin to think that it's one of the glories of Paradise. I could watch the whole lot of them burning by the hour. And that's not the worst I've told you. Even if they didn't akcherly poison him, they're glad he's ill, and I wouldn't mind who heard me say that. I'd go and shout out that this very moment in Piccadilly Circus. And their mother! Nosey, nasty, stuck-up—well, it's no use sitting here and talking about what they are. What we've got to do is to spoil their little game. If I go up to see if he wants anything, I get ordered out of the room like the dirt beneath their feet. 'We've got to be very careful,' says that smarmy doctor they've got in to annoy me. 'Very careful.' says I, looking at him very meaning. 'Terrible to hear anyone suffer like that,' he says. 'Yes, it is terrible,' says I. 'And the terrible thing is,' he says, 'that however much one wants to alleviorate the pain, we daren't do it. And whyever won't he come out of that dreadful little room,' he says, 'when there's all those nice bedrooms lying empty?' 'You let him be where he is,' I said, 'it's his house, isn't it?' And then, before I could stop them, they started lifting the box mattress and trying to move him out of the bathroom. And the way he screamed and carried on, it was something shocking to hear him! And I know the reason perfectly well. Underneath the mattress *in* the bath he keeps his coffin. Many's the time he's congratulated himself to me on getting that coffin so cheap. 'It's oak, Selina,' he used to say, 'and I got it cheap for a misfit, and it fills up the bath a treat.' Well, it stands to reason, doesn't it, that now of all times he wants to keep it handy? 'No deal coffins for me, Selina,' he used to say. Besides, it's my belief he's got his will inside of that coffin. Depend upon it, he's got his own reasons for not wishing to be moved. So I stood in the doorway, and I said very fierce: 'If you want to move him, you'll have to move me first.' And then it came over me all of a sudden that if I got you back here to help we might be able to do something both together."

In spite of Selina's marvels and exaggerations and absurd misconstructions, her tale convinced Jasmine of Uncle Matthew's hatred of being taken charge of by the Hector Grants. Naturally she sympathized with his point of view on this matter. To be helpless in the hands of the Hector Grants struck her as a punishment far in excess of anything that the old gentleman deserved. She did not feel that it was her duty to interfere in the slightest degree with the normal process of his will, but she did feel that she had a right if he were not comfortable to protest her own anxiety to look after him, even more, to insist upon looking after him. She supposed that her Aunt May would attribute the lowest motives to this intention; Aunt May, however, always attributed low motives to everybody, and the lowest motives of all to her niece.

"Well?" asked Selina sharply when Jasmine did not offer any remarks upon her tale.

"I'm sorry," said Jasmine, pulling herself together. "I was wondering what excuse I should be able to give my aunt for seeming to interfere."

"Excuse?" Selina repeated angrily. "No excuse is needed, I assure you, for putting yourself forward on his behalf, as you might say. What he requires is looking after. What he's getting is nothing of the kind."

At that moment a scream rang through the house. Jasmine looked at Selina in horror.

"What did I tell you?" the housekeeper demanded triumphantly. "I told you he carried on something awful, and you wouldn't believe me. It's a wonder he hasn't started in screaming before. I've never known him quiet for so long at a stretch. Bloodcurdling, I call it. You often read of bloodcurdling screams. Now you can hear them for yourself. There he goes again."

And it really was bloodcurdling to hear from that old man's room what sounded like the shrieks of a passionate, frightened, tortured child. It had the effect of rousing Jasmine to an immediate encounter with her aunt, an encounter to brace herself up to which, until she had heard Uncle Matthew scream, had been growing more and more difficult with every moment of delay. Now she sprang out of her chair and hurried up the wide central staircase, past the countless figures in the pictures that stared at her when she passed like a frightened crowd. She ran too quickly for Selina to keep up with her, and when she turned down into the passage at the end of which was her uncle's little room, she beheld what, without the real agony and pain at the back of it, would have been a merely grotesque sight. The box-mattress on which Uncle Matthew was lying was half-way through the door of his bedroom, carried by two men of respectful and sober appearance whom she recognized as two male nurses that she had once seen on the steps of Sir Hector's house in Harley Street arming an old man with a shaven head into a brougham. The old man's eyes had been wild and tragic, and their wildness and tragedy had been rendered more conspicuous to Jasmine by the very respect with which the attendants treated him and the very sobriety of their manner and appearance; to such an extent indeed that the personalities of the two men, if two such colourless individuals could be allowed to possess personality, had been tinged, or rather not so much tinged as glazed over, with a sinister aura. So now when she saw them for the second time, struggling in the doorway while her uncle held fast to the frame and tried to prevent the bed's being carried out, she had a swift and sickening sensation of horror. She was hurrying down the passage to protest against the old gentleman's being moved against his will, when her aunt emerged from one of the nearer bedrooms and stood before her.

"What are you doing to Uncle Matthew?" demanded Jasmine furiously, not pausing to explain her own presence. She had a moment's satisfaction in perceiving that Lady Grant was obviously taken aback at seeing her there; but her aunt soon recovered herself sufficiently to reply with her wonted coldness:

"It scarcely seems to concern you, my dear; and may I enquire in my turn what *you* are doing *here*?"

"Oh, you needn't think you can put me off like that," Jasmine went on apace. "I've left Silchester, and I'm going to stay here until Uncle Matthew is better, and I'll answer no questions until he is better."

"Indeed? That will be for your uncle and me to decide."

"Oh no, it won't. You're not my guardians. You weren't appointed my guardians, and you've got no say in the matter at all. If Uncle Matthew doesn't want to be taken out of his own room, why should he be, when he's ill?"

Another person now appeared, a sleek, pale, old young man, whom Jasmine recognized from Selina's allusion as the 'smarmy' doctor. She took advantage of his presence to run past her aunt and speak to the old gentleman, who was so much occupied in holding on to the frame of the door that he was apparently unconscious of his niece's arrival.

"If you please, miss," said one of the nurses, "you'd better not excite the patient just now."

Jasmine paid no attention to this advice, but knelt down and with all the force she could achieve kept on calling out to know what Uncle Matthew wanted, until at last the old gentleman was induced to recognize her. He was evidently pleased at her arrival, so much pleased that he offered her his hand in greeting, a gesture which cost him his hold on the frame of the door. The male nurses were quick to take advantage of this, and while Jasmine was still on her knees, they hurried him along the passage and vanished through the door from which Lady Grant had just emerged. Jasmine realized that her interference had only succeeded in helping the other side, and in a mist of mortification and self-reproach she followed the bed into the room prepared to receive the sick man. She was bound to admit to herself that the room was well chosen and admirably prepared. Yet she knew that the more careful the preparations, the more acutely would they aggravate her uncle's discomfort. The fire burning lavishly in the grate, the flowers blooming wastefully on the table, the sick room's glittering equipment, they would seem to him detestable extravagances which in his feeble condition he was powerless to prevent. As soon as Uncle Matthew was safely out of his little bath-bedroom, Lady Grant locked the door and put the key in her bag; but Selina arrived on the scene in time for this action by her ladyship, to whom she proceeded to give, or rather at whom she proceeded to throw a piece of her mind. When the housekeeper paused for breath, her ladyship merely said coldly that if she did not behave herself, she would find herself and her boxes in the street.

"This kind of thing has been going on long enough," Lady Grant proclaimed to the world. "It was time for his relations to interfere."

Jasmine, when she made an effort to consider the situation calmly, could not help acknowledging that by that world to which she had appealed all the right and all the reason would be awarded to her aunt. An abusive housekeeper trying to interfere between doctor and patient would stand little chance of obtaining even a hearing for her point of view, especially when that doctor was Sir Hector Grant. Moreover, she began to ask herself, might not Selina have merely got a bee buzzing in her bonnet about interference for the sake of interference? Had not her own judgment been wrought up by Selina's mysterious way of summoning her to Rouncivell Lodge and by the stifling atmosphere that enwrapped it to imagining what was, after all, looked at sanely, a melodramatic and improbable situation? One thing she was determined to do, however, and that was to stay in the house herself, not for any purpose connected with wills concealed in coffins under beds, but simply in order to be able to devote herself to Uncle Matthew's comfort. If her aunt really was trying to manipulate the old gentleman's end—and of course the idea was absurd—but if she were, she would find her niece's presence an obstacle to the success of her schemes, and if her wicked intentions were nothing more than the creation of Selina's highflown fancy.... Jasmine broke off her thoughts and went back to her uncle's new room, where, pulling up a chair beside his bed, she took his hand and asked if he did not feel a little better. The effort he had made to resist removal had exhausted him, and he was lying on the box-mattress breathing so faintly and looking so pale that she rose again in alarm to call the doctor, who was talking to Lady Grant outside. She had not moved a step from the bed before Uncle Matthew called to her in a weak voice, a voice, however, that still retained the accent of command, and bade her sit down again. It was at least a satisfaction to feel that he had grasped the fact of her presence and that he was evidently anxious to keep her by his side. Presently, when the respectful and sober male nurses had respectfully and soberly left the house, like two plumbers who had accomplished their job, the doctor came back to ask softly if Mr. Rouncivell could not bring himself to change his bed as well as his room. The old gentleman made no further opposition, but allowed himself to be lifted down from the box-mattress and tucked up in the big four-poster, after which the box-mattress, upon which he had slept for so many years in his bath, was carried away. Jasmine was now alone with him, and he beckoned her to lean over to catch what she feared might be his last whisper.

She was unnecessarily nervous.

"They think I'm going to die," he chuckled. "But I'm not. Ha! Ha!"

Five minutes afterward he was peacefully sleeping.

Downstairs Jasmine was allowed the pleasure of thoroughly and extensively defying her aunt. Nothing that Lady Grant said could make her flinch from her avowed determination not to leave Rouncivell Lodge until her uncle was definitely better. Only when she was satisfied on this point would she agree to go wherever she was sent. She even took a delight in drawing such a heightened picture of the affair with Edward and Harry Vibart at the Deanery as to call down upon her the epithet 'shameless.' She announced that if after she had visited Uncle Alec and Aunt Mildred she found that she did not get on better with them than with the rest of her relations, she should somehow borrow the money to return to Sirene, whence nothing should induce her ever to return to England.

"It occurs to me," said Lady Grant, "that you are trying to be impertinent."

"I don't care what occurs to you," Jasmine retorted. "I am simply telling you what I intend to do. I've got a kind of fondness for Uncle Matthew—not a very deep fondness, but a kind of fondness—and although you think me so heartless, I really am anxious about him, and I really should like to stay here until he's better."

It must have been difficult for Lady Grant to refrain from giving expression to the implication that was on the tip of her tongue; but she did refrain, and Jasmine could not help admiring her for doing so. However, she was determined to provoke a discussion about that very implication, and of her own accord she assured her aunt that she need be under no apprehension over Uncle Matthew's money, because she had no intention of trying to influence him in any way whatever.

"Impudent little wretch!" Aunt May gasped. And Jasmine gloried in her ability to have wrung from that cold and well-mannered woman such a betrayal of her radical femininity.

Jasmine did not expect to have the house to herself; nevertheless, in spite of continual visits from Lettice and Pamela, from Aunt Cuckoo and Aunt Ellen—the last-named greeting Jasmine as an abbess might greet a runaway nun—most of Uncle Matthew's entertainment fell upon her shoulders. This was not that the others did not take their turn at the bedside, but when they did, the old gentleman always pretended to be asleep, whereas with Jasmine he was conversational, much more conversational, indeed, than he had ever been when he was well. One day she felt that she really was forgiven when he asked her to go down to the hall and bring up his collection of sticks, all of which in turn he looked at and stroked and fondled; after this he made Jasmine put down in pencil the cost of each one, add up the sum, divide it by the number of sticks, and establish the average cost of each. When he had established the average cost, all the sticks that had cost more he made her put on one side, and all the sticks that had cost less on the other. After the sticks were classified, she was told to fetch various pieces of bric-à-brac on which he was anxious to gloat, as a convalescent child gloats over his long-neglected toys; finally one afternoon the musical-box was brought up, and the whole of its twelve tunes played through twice over.

Next morning he announced that he should get up.

"Oh no, I'm not dead yet," he said. "And, after all, why should I be? I'm only seventy-six. I've got a lot more years to live before I die."

Since the old gentleman had been out of danger, Selina had ceased to worry; but she still insisted that his will was in the coffin, and that time would prove her words true one of these days.

"Depend upon it," she told Jasmine, "they meant him to die without leaving any will at all. They meant him to die untested. Oh yes, that's what they meant him to do, and her ladyship—though why she should call herself a ladyship any more than Mrs. Vokins is beyond me, and I've known many real ladyships in my time—oh yes, her ladyship had worked it all out. She knew she couldn't expect to get it all, the cunning Isaacs. So she thought she'd have it divided amongst the lot, thinking as half a loaf's better than no bread. You'd have been a loser and I'd have been a loser by that game. And depend upon it the old gentleman saw through her, and made up his mind he would not die. Oh dear, if he'd only make up his mind to get salvation, there's no reason why he should worry about anything at all. No reason whatever. Think how nice it would be if we could all meet in Heaven one day and talk over all this. Oh, wouldn't it be nice? Think of the lovely weather they must always get in Heaven. I suppose we should be sitting about out of doors half the time. Or that's my notion anyway. But you and he won't be there, so what's the use in making plans to meet?"

Chapter Ten

JASMINE was not even yet cynical enough to keep herself from feeling hurt when Uncle Matthew on his recovery did not press her to stay on with him at Rouncivell Lodge, and, what was even more pointed, did not suggest that she might accompany him to Bournemouth, where in accordance with the prescription of Sir Hector Grant he was to regain all the vigour possible for a man of his age to enjoy. The Hector Grants, in their eagerness to help the old gentleman's convalescence, had taken a furnished house among the pines, the superb situation of which, with a great show of deference and affection, he had been invited to enjoy. Perhaps the old gentleman, who had been for several weeks the unwilling host of so many anxious relations, wanted to get back some of the expenses of hospitality. Jasmine thought that he owed as much to her devotion as to insist on her company; Uncle Matthew, however, did not appear sensible of any obligation, and he accepted Lettice and Pamela as his companions for alternate weeks without a murmur on behalf of Jasmine. Lettice and Pamela themselves were furious. They would have much preferred to sacrifice any prospects in Uncle Matthew's will to the dances of the autumn season; nor were they appeased by their mother's suggestion that separation from each other for a time might lead to many offers of marriage from young men who had hitherto been perplexed by the difficulty of choosing between them.

"I suppose you want me to go and stay with Uncle Alec and Aunt Mildred?" Jasmine asked one day when Lady Grant was demanding from the world at large what was the wisest thing to do with Jasmine and when Cousin Edith was apparently sunk in too profound an abyss of incertitude to be able to reply for the world at large.

"Why should you suppose that?" Lady Grant enquired gently.

"Well, they're the only relatives left to whom I haven't been passed on," said Jasmine. She was still able to hold her own against Aunt May in the bandying of words; but the failure of Uncle Matthew to appreciate her services had been fatal to any advance toward a real independence, and she was already beginning to wonder if it was worth while being rude to Aunt May, and if she might not be more profitably occupied in ousting Cousin Edith and securing for herself Cousin Edith's humiliating but superficially comfortable position in the household at Harley Street.

"What curious expressions you do employ, Jasmine. When I was your age, I should never have dreamed of employing such expressions. But then in my young days we were taught manners."

"And deportment," Cousin Edith added. "Don't you remember, Cousin May, how strict about that the Miss Watneys used to be in the dear old days at school?"

But Lady Grant did not wish to remember that she was once at school with Cousin Edith, and in order to snub Cousin Edith she had to forgo the pleasure of lecturing Jasmine upon her curious use of verbs.

"It is quite a coincidence," she went on, "that you should mention Uncle Alec and Aunt Mildred, because only this morning I received an invitation for you to go and stay with them at Curtain Wells. The trouble is that since the unfortunate affair at your Aunt Ellen's I feel some responsibility for your behaviour. Uncle Alec and Aunt Mildred are very strict about the Prince. They have to be. And inasmuch as one of the reasons for entrusting him to them was the advantage of being given Uncle Hector's particular attention, really I don't know...."

At this moment Sir Hector himself came into the room, and his wife broke off to ask him what he thought.

"What do you think, my dear, about this proposed visit to Alec and Mildred? Could you recommend Jasmine in the circumstances? I know that in many ways she might make herself very useful. You must learn ludo, Jasmine, if we let you go. The Prince is very fond of ludo. But——" Lady Grant paused, and Jasmine, who did not at all want to entertain the royal lunatic, hurriedly suggested that she should go and live with Selina at Rouncivell Lodge while Uncle Matthew was recuperating at Bournemouth.

"What extraordinary notions you do get hold of," her aunt declared.

"Extraordinary!" Cousin Edith echoed.

Both ladies looked at Sir Hector as if they supposed that he would at once certify his niece insane after such a remark. He did not seem to find the notion so extraordinary, and his wife went on hurriedly, for she was realizing that Jasmine's suggestion of living with Selina attracted her husband.

"I'm inclined to think that Selina will not stay long at Rouncivell Lodge," she said. "After her behaviour during poor old Uncle Matthew's illness you may be sure that she will receive no help from me. Frankly, I shall do my best to persuade Uncle Matthew that she is an unsuitable person."

How glad Jasmine would have been to retort with a sarcastic remark about Aunt May's behaviour! But she could not; she was falling back into complete dependency; she would soon begin to wither, and she gazed at Cousin Edith as if she were a Memento Mori, a skeleton whose fingers pointed warningly at the future.

"Anyway," said Jasmine to herself when she took her seat in the train at Paddington, "this is the last lot. And if they're worse than the others it won't be so bad to come back to Harley Street."

Colonel Alexander Grant was and always had been outwardly the most distinguished of the Grants. He had escaped the excessive angularity of his elder brothers, and although he was much better looking than Sholto, Jasmine's father, there was between them a family likeness, by which Jasmine was less moved than she felt she ought to be. In fact, the amount she had lately had to endure of family duties, family influence, family sensibilities, had made her chary of seeming to ascribe any importance at all even to her own father so far as he was a relation. The Colonel, in addition to being an outwardly distinguished officer in a Highland regiment of repute, had married one of the daughters of old Sir Frederick Willoughby, who was Minister at the Court of the Grand Duke of Pomerania at the time when Captain Grant, as he then was, found himself in Pomerania on matters connected with his profession. He had not been married long when the Boer War broke out, his success in which as an intelligence officer put into his head the idea of becoming a military attaché, an ambition that with the help of his father-in-law, then Ambassador at Rome, he was able to achieve.

His wife may not have brought him as much money as the wives of Hector and Eneas, but she brought him quite enough to sustain without financial worries the semi-political, semi-military positions that he found so congenial, and through his success in which, coupled with his double relationship to Sir Frederick Willoughby and Sir Hector Grant, he was given the guardianship of the lunatic Prince Adalbert of Pomerania.

Enough pretence of state was kept up at 23, The Crescent, Curtain Wells, to make the Colonel and his wife feel their own importance. He had the Distinguished Service Order, could still reasonably turn the pages of the *London Gazette* two or three times a year with a good chance of finding himself with the C.M.G., and had not yet quite given up hope of the Bath. He had picked up in Rome the Crown of Italy, in Madrid the Order of Isabella the Catholic, while from Pomerania he had received the cordon of St. Wenceslaus, and the third class of the Order of the Black Griffin (with Claws). His responsibility for the younger son of a royal house gave him in Curtain Wells, after the Mayor, the Member, and the Master of Ceremonies at the Pump Room, the most conspicuous position among his fellow-townsmen, and when the barouche which by the terms of the guardianship had to be maintained for His Serene Highness made a splendid progress past the arcades and along the dignified streets of the old watering-place, Colonel Grant, observing the respectful glances of the citizens, felt that his career had been a success.

Aunt Mildred, even as a girl, had been considered eccentric for a Willoughby; her marriage with a soldier of fortune had done nothing to cure this reputation; association with Prince Adalbert had done a great deal to develop it. To this eccentricity was added a strong squint.

Military attachés are notorious for the cynical way in which they sacrifice everybody to their careers, and it might be argued in favour of Colonel Grant that he had sacrificed himself as cynically as any of his friends.

Jasmine's visit opened inauspiciously, because by mistake she travelled down to Curtain Wells by an earlier train than the one to which she had been recommended by her aunt; she therefore arrived at The Crescent about two o'clock without having been met at the station. When her aunt came to greet her in the drawing-room, Jasmine had an impression that she was still eating, and apologized for interrupting her lunch.

"Lunch?" repeated Aunt Mildred, still making these curious sounds of eating. "We finished lunch at twelve, and we dine at four." The sound of eating continued, and made Jasmine so shy that she was speechless until she suddenly realized that what she had mistaken for incomplete mastication was merely the automatic play of Aunt Mildred's muscles on a loosely fitting set of false teeth. Mrs. Alexander Grant, unaware that she was making this noise, did not pay any attention to her niece's want of tact; but Jasmine was so much embarrassed that she evidently did not make a favourable first impression.

The spacious Georgian proportions of the drawing-room at 23, The Crescent, were destroyed by a mass of marquetry furniture, antimacassars, and photographs in plush and silver frames of royal personages, the last of which gave the room an unreal and uninhabited appearance like the private parlour of a public-house where respectable groups of excursionists take tea on Sunday afternoon; for these people with ridiculous coiffures and costumes, signing themselves Albertina or Frederica or Adolphus, were as little credible as a publican's relatives.

However, Jasmine was too anxious about her presentation to His Serene Highness to notice anything very much, and if she had offended her aunt by arriving too soon or by not knowing the time for dinner, she made up for it by asking how she was to address the Prince. This was a topic on which her aunt obviously liked to expatiate, and she was delighted to be asked to instruct Jasmine how to curtsey, and to inform her that he was always addressed as 'Sir' in the English manner, because his mother, the Grand Duchess, had expressed a wish that the more formal German mode of salutation should be dispensed with in order to provide a suitable atmosphere of simplicity for the simple soul of her youngest son.

"Is he very mad?" asked Jasmine.

"Good heavens, child," her aunt gasped, "I beg you will not use that word here. Mad? He's not mad at all."

At that moment the door opened to admit a diminutive figure in livery. Jasmine was just going to curtsey under the impression that it was the Prince, when she heard her aunt say, "What is it now, Snelson?" in time to realize that it was the butler.

"His Serene Highness is being rather troublesome, madam," said Snelson.

"Oh? What is the matter?"

"Well, madam, when he got up this morning he would put on his evening dress, and now he wants to go for a drive in evening dress."

"Why, Snelson?"

"I think he wants to go to the theatre again. He enjoyed himself very much last night. Quite a pleasure to hear him chuckling when he got home. I told him if he was a good boy he should go again next week, but he went and lost his temper, and now he's gone and thrown all his lounge suits into the area. The maids are picking them up as fast as they can. Perhaps you could come up and speak to him, madam? He's got it into his head I'm trying to keep him from the theatre."

"Such a boy!" sighed Aunt Mildred, and her intense squint gave Jasmine a momentary illusion that she was referring to Snelson. "Such a boy! You see what a boy he is. He's as interested in life as a sparrow. *You're* going to be devoted to him, of course. You'll rave about him."

Jasmine was wondering why this was so certain, when one of the maids came in to say that it was not a bit of good her collecting His Serene Highness's clothes, because as fast as they were collected, he was throwing them out of the window again.

"And he's started screaming," added the maid.

"Snelson, you ought never to have left him," Aunt Mildred said severely. "You ought to have known he would start screaming. You should have sent for me to come up."

"I've locked him in his room, madam."

"Yes, and you know that always makes him scream. He hates being locked in his room."

Aunt Mildred went away with Snelson, and Jasmine was left to herself, until Uncle Alexander came in and got over the awkwardness of avuncular greetings by asking her what all the fuss was about. She told him about the Prince's throwing his clothes out of the window, which her uncle attributed to excitement over her visit.

"No, I don't think it's that," said Jasmine. "I think he wants to go to the theatre again."

"Oh no, he's excited about your visit. You must humour him. Very nice fellow really. Very nice chap. And as sane as you or me if you take him the right way. I think Snelson irritates him. If he wants to put on evening dress, why shouldn't he put on evening dress? So silly to thwart him about a little thing like that. I can always manage him perfectly well. I spoke to my brother Hector about it, and he agreed with me that there are only two ways to deal with lunatics ... with patients, I mean ... either to give way to them in everything or to give way to them in nothing."

Jasmine thought this sounded excellent if ambiguous advice.

"Now I humour him," said the Colonel. "The other day he heard some tactless people talking about electric shocks, and he got it into his head that he couldn't touch anything without getting an electric shock. Well, you can imagine what a nuisance that was to everybody. What did I do? I humoured him. I put a saucer on his head and told him he was insulated, and he went about carrying that saucer on his head for a week as happy as he could be. He's forgotten all about electricity now. Take my advice: humour him." At this point Snelson came down again.

"If you please, sir, Mrs. Grant says His Highness insists on wearing his evening dress."

"Well, let him wear his evening dress, damme, let him wear it," the Colonel shouted. "Let him wear it. Let him wear his pyjamas if he wants to wear his pyjamas."

"Very good, sir," said Snelson in an injured voice as he retired.

A few minutes later the subject of all this discussion appeared in the drawing-room.

Prince Adalbert Victor Augustus of Pomerania was a tall and very thin young man, though on account of his habit of walking with a furtive crouch he did not give an impression of height. He had a sparse beard, the hairs of which seemed to wave about upon his chin like weeds in the stream of a river. This beard did not add the least dignity to his countenance, but he was allowed to keep it because it was considered unsafe to trust him with a razor, and he would never allow Snelson to shave him. He walked round an ordinary room as if he were crossing a narrow and dangerous Alpine pass, and he would never let go his hold of any piece of furniture until he was able to grasp the next piece along the route of his progress. Owing to this way of moving about, Jasmine, when he first came into the room, thought he was going to attack her. She supposed that it would be discourteous to watch him all the way round the room, and she could not help feeling nervous when she heard him behind her. Mrs. Grant, perhaps because she was nearly as idiotic as the Prince himself, assumed the airs of a mother with him, and always addressed him as Bertie.

"Now, Bertie, be a good boy," she said, "and come and shake hands with my niece. You've heard all about her. This is little Miss Jasmine."

The Prince suddenly released the piece of furniture he was holding, and just as some child makes up its mind to venture upon a crucial dash in a game like Puss-in-the-corner, he rushed up to Jasmine, and after muttering "I like you very much, thank you, little Miss Jasmine," he at once rushed back to his piece of furniture so rapidly that Jasmine had no time to curtsey. She was not yet used to the direction of her aunt's eyes, and now observing that they were apparently fixed upon herself in disapproval, she began her obeisance. The Prince evidently liked her curtsey, for he began curtseying too, until the Colonel said in a sharp whisper: "For goodness' sake don't excite him. The one thing we try to avoid is exciting him with unnecessary ceremony." So evidently her aunt had not been looking at her, and this was presently obvious, because while she was telling Snelson to order the barouche, her eyes were still fixed on Jasmine.

"Are you coming for a drive, dear?" she asked her husband. "It was quite sunny this morning when I woke up."

The Colonel shook his head.

"And now, Bertie," she went on, "be a good boy and put on your other suit."

"I want to go to the theatre," the Prince argued.

"Well, you shall go to the theatre to-night."

"I want to go now," the Prince persisted.

"Now come along, your Serene Highness," said Snelson. "Try and not give so much trouble, there's a good chap. You can go to the theatre to-night."

However, the Prince did not go to the theatre that night, for after a stately drive through Curtain Wells, from which Jasmine on the grounds of untidiness after a journey excused herself, they sat down to play bridge after dinner. Jasmine did not know how to play bridge. Her uncle told her that her ignorance of the game did not matter, because she could always be dummy, the Prince also being perpetual dummy. Even as a dummy, the Prince wasted a good deal of time, because he had to be allowed to play the cards that were called for, and it took him a long time to distinguish between suits, let alone between court cards and common cards. He had a habit, too, of suddenly throwing all his cards up into the air, so that Snelson was kept in the room to spend much of his time in routing about on the floor for the cards that his royal master had flung down. The Prince had other obstructive habits, like suddenly getting up in order to shake hands with everybody in turn, which, asMrs. Grant said, expressed his delightful nature, although it rather interfered with the progress of the game.

When the Colonel, with Jasmine as his dummy partner, had beaten his wife and the Prince, he became jovial, and there being still half an hour before the Prince had to compose his excitement prior to going to bed, a game of ludo was suggested. This would have been a better game if Prince Adalbert had not wanted to change the colour of his counters all the time, which made it difficult to know who was winning, and impossible to say who had really won. The Colonel, after humouring him in the first game, grew interested in a big lead he had established with Red in the second game and objected to the Prince's desire to change him into Green. It was in vain that Jasmine and her aunt offered him Yellow or Blue: he was determined to have Red, and when the Colonel declined to surrender his lead, the Prince decided that the game was tiddly-winks, which caused it to break up in confusion.

Prince Adalbert was really too idiotic to be bearable for long. Living in the same house with him was like living on terms of equality with a spoilt monkey. There were times, of course, when his intelligence approximated to human intelligence, one expression of which was a passion for collecting. It began by his going down to the kitchen when the servants were occupied elsewhere and collecting the material and utensils for the preparation of dinner. Not much damage was done on this occasion, except that the unbaked portion of a Yorkshire pudding was concealed in the piano. On another occasion he collected all Jasmine's clothes and hid them under his bed. Aunt Mildred evinced a tendency to blame Jasmine for this, even going so far as to suggest that she had encouraged him to collect her clothes, though in what way this encouragement was deduced except from Jasmine's usual untidiness was not made clear. Snelson was ordered to keep a sharper look out on his master, as it was feared that from collecting inside the house, he might begin to collect outside the house, which, as the Colonel said, would be an intolerable bore. The passion for collecting was soon after this exchanged for a desire to cohabit with owls, the Prince having observed on one of his drives a tame owl in a wicker cage outside a small fruiterer's shop. The owner of the bird was persuaded to part with it at a price, and the Prince drove home in a state of perfect bliss with his pet on the opposite seat.

"It's really lovely to watch him," said Aunt Mildred.

"Never known him so mad about anything as His Serene Highness is now about owls," said Snelson. "He'll sit and talk to that owl by the hour together."

The Prince's devotion to the bird occupied his mind so completely that it was thought prudent to import two more owls in case anything should happen to the particular one upon which he was lavishing such love. The first owl remained his favourite, however, and it really did seem to return his affection, in a negative kind of way, by never actually biting the Prince, although it bit everybody else in the house. Jasmine had no hesitation about encouraging him in this passion, because it kept him so well occupied that bridge, ludo, and tiddly-winks were put on one side, and the Prince himself no longer screamed when he had to go to bed. In fact, he was only too anxious after dinner to get back to his room in order to pass the evening saying, 'Tu-whit, tu-whoo!' to his owls. Unfortunately there was begotten from this association an ambition in the Prince's mind to become an owl himself, and when one evening the Colonel found him with six feathers stuck in his hair, perched on the rail of the bed and trying to eat a mouse he had caught, the owls were banished. The Prince's desire to be an owl was not so easily disposed of. For some time after his pets had disappeared he replied to all questions with 'Tu-whit, tu-whoo!' and once when the Colonel impatiently told him to behave himself like a human being, he rushed at him and bit his finger.

"Who started him off in this ridiculous owl idea?" the Colonel demanded of his wife irritably. "Nice thing if the Baron comes over to find out how he's getting on, and finds that he believes himself to be an owl. You know perfectly well that they don't really approve of his being looked after in England, and I can't understand why Jasmine doesn't make herself more pleasant to him. We all thought before she came that she would be a recreation for him. It seems to me that he's much madder now than he's ever been yet."

"Oh, hush, dear!" Aunt Mildred begged her husband, having vainly tried with signs to fend off the threatened admission of the Prince's state of mind.

345

But the Colonel's finger was hurting him acutely, and he would not agree to keep up the pretence of the Prince's sanity.

"You can't expect me to go about pretending he's not mad. Why, the people come out of the shops now in order to hear him calling out 'Tu-whit, tu-whoo!' as he drives past. Supposing he starts biting people in the street? I really do think," he added, turning to Jasmine, "that you might put yourself out a little bit to entertain him. Of course, if he bites you, we shall have to do something about it, but I don't think he will bite you."

Luckily the Prince's memory was not a strong one, and a week after the owls had been banished, he had forgotten that such birds existed.

From envying the life and habits of an owl His Serene Highness passed on to imitating Mrs. Alexander Grant's squint. This was an embarrassing business, because evidently neither the Colonel nor Snelson liked to correct him too obviously for fear of hurting Mrs. Grant's feelings. As for her, either she did not notice that he was manipulating his eyes in an unusual manner, or she supposed that he was paying her a compliment. She was such a conceited and idiotic woman that she would have been flattered even by such imitation. When he first began to squint across the table at Jasmine, she supposed that it was an old habit of his temporarily revived; but in the passage the next day Snelson came up to her and asked if she had noticed anything wrong about His Serene Highness's eyes. Jasmine suggested that he was squinting a little bit, and Snelson replied: "It's those owls."

"I thought he had forgotten all about them."

"He's for ever now trying to make his eyes look like an owl's."

"Oh," said Jasmine doubtfully, "I hadn't realized that. I thought that perhaps...." and then she stopped, for it could not be her place to comment to the butler on his mistress's squint.

"You think he's trying to imitate the old lady?" asked Snelson in that hoarse whisper that clung to his ordinary method of speech from his manner of asking people at dinner what wine they would take. "Oh no, he wouldn't ever imitate her. He might imitate you, though!"

"In what way?" asked Jasmine, rather alarmed.

"Oh, you never can tell," said Snelson. "He's that ingenious, he'd imitate anybody. He started off imitating me once, and, of course, through me not being very tall, I didn't quite like it. The Colonel thought he was imitating a frog when he came into the room like me, and if I hadn't been here so long, I should have left. I wish you'd take him up a bit—you know, encourage him a bit, and all that. Time hangs very heavy on his hands, poor chap. I got the cook's little nephew once to come in and amuse him of an afternoon, but it was stopped. Etiquette you know, and all that. Of course, etiquette's all very well in its way, and I'm not going to say etiquette isn't necessary within bounds; but he wants amusing. If you can bring him in a toy now and again when you go out for a walk. I don't mean anything as looks as if it could be eaten, because he'll start in right off on anything as looks as if it could be eaten. But any little nice toy, not that small as he can get it right into his mouth, and not that big as he can hurt himself with it."

Jasmine supposed that Snelson knew what he was talking about, and next day she bought the Prince a small clockwork engine. He enjoyed this for about two minutes; then he got angry with it and stamped on it; and when Snelson told him to behave himself, he pulled Snelson's hair, upon which the Colonel intervened and reproved Jasmine for exciting His Serene Highness. The atmosphere at 23, The Crescent, began to get on Jasmine's nerves. It seemed to her pitiable that for the sake of the honour of being guardians of a royal imbecile her uncle and aunt should abandon themselves to a mode of life that in her eyes was degrading. The long dinners dragged themselves out in the November twilights, and though the Prince ate so fast that if only he had been concerned dinner would have been over in ten minutes, a pretence of ceremony was maintained, and the endless courses must have put a strain on the china of the establishment, for there used to be long waits, during which the Colonel had a theory that His Serene Highness's moral stability would be increased by twiddling his thumbs.

"You may have noticed," he used to say to Jasmine, "how much I insist on his using his thumbs. You no doubt realize that the main difference between men and monkeys is that we can use our thumbs. The Prince has a tendency always to carry his thumbs inside his fingers. I'm sure that if I could only get him to twiddle them long enough every day, it would be of great benefit to his development."

After dinner the old round of double dummy bridge followed by ludo had begun again, and though an attempt was made to vary the games by the introduction of halma, halma had to be given up, because once when the Colonel had succeeded in establishing an impregnable position, His Serene Highness without any warning popped into his mouth the four pieces that were holding that position.

Nor were the drives on fine mornings in the royal barouche much of a diversion. Jasmine could not help feeling ashamed to be sitting opposite His Serene Highness when he made one of his glibbering progresses through Curtain Wells. It seemed to her that by accepting a seat which marked her social inferiority she was endorsing the detestable servility of the tradesmen who came out and fawned upon what was after all no better than a royal ape. She felt that presently she should have to break out—exactly in what way she did not know, but somehow, she was sure. Otherwise she felt that the only alternative would be to become as mad as the Prince himself. Indeed, so much did he get on her nerves that she found herself imitating him once or twice in front of her glass, and she began to realize that the proverbial danger of associating with lunatics was not less great than it was reputed to be.

Then came the news that the mother of Prince Adalbert, the Grand Duchess herself, proposed to pay a visit to England shortly, and, what was more, intended to honour The Crescent, Curtain Wells, by staying in it one whole night. This news carried Aunt Mildred to the zenith of self-congratulation, at which height the prospect of the world at her feet was suddenly obscured by a profound pessimism about the behaviour of her household during the royal visit.

"She is travelling strictly incognito, and is not even to bring a lady-in-waiting," she lamented.

"Incognita, my dear," corrected the Colonel, who had once added an extra hundred pounds a year to his pay by proficiency in one European language.

"I have it," cried Aunt Mildred, and in the pleasure of her inspiration she squinted so hard that Jasmine for a moment thought she had something far more serious than an inspiration. "I have it: you shall act as parlourmaid when the Grand Duchess comes!"

"Me?" echoed the Colonel, who in the vigour of her declaration had forgotten to allow for the squint. However much he owed to his wife for advancement in his profession, he could not quite stand this.

"Not you, silly," she said, "Jasmine."

"What on earth is that going to effect?" he asked.

"Now don't be so hasty, Alec. You've always tried to snub my little ideas. I am much more sensible than you think. And more sensible than anybody thinks," she added. "Ada is an excellent parlourmaid, but she is a nervous, highly strung girl, and I'm quite sure that the mere prospect of entertaining the Grand Duchess...."

"But *she's* not going to entertain the Grand Duchess," interrupted the Colonel.

"Now please don't muddle me up with petty little distinctions between one word and another," said Aunt Mildred. "You know perfectly well what I mean. 'Look after' if you prefer it. Ada has never been trained to look after royalty."

"Nor have I," Jasmine put in. "Snelson's the only person in this house who has been trained to look after royalty."

"Jasmine, I'd rather you were not vulgar," said Aunt Mildred reprovingly. "It's extraordinary the way girls nowadays don't respect anything. If you and Uncle Alec would only wait a moment and not be so ready both of you to pounce on me before I have finished what I was going to say, you might have understood that the suggestion was made partly because I appreciate your manners, partly because I have travelled a great deal and don't find your little foreign ways so irritating as your other relations did.... Where was I? If you and your uncle *will* argue with me, I can't be expected to plan things out as I should like. Where was I, Alec?"

"I really don't know," said the Colonel almost bitterly. "All I know is that Ada's a perfectly good parlourmaid fit to wait on anybody. If the Grand Duchess comes without a lady-in-waiting, she comes without a lady-in-waiting to please herself. Really, my dear, you give the impression that you are unused to royalty."

To what state the hitherto tranquil married life of Colonel and Mrs. Alexander Grant might have been reduced if the discussion about the fitness of Jasmine to act as temporary parlourmaid during the Grand Duchess's visit had gone on much longer, it would be hard to say. The problem was solved, for Jasmine at any rate, by two telegrams arriving within half an hour of one another, one from Aunt May to say that Lettice and Pamela were both ill with scarlet fever, and another from Aunt Cuckoo to say that her little son was ill without specifying the complaint. Both telegrams concluded with the suggestion that Jasmine should pack up at once and come to the rescue. Jasmine would have preferred to go straight away to Aunt Cuckoo; but aware as she was of Aunt Cuckoo's fickleness and knowing that, if she did go to Aunt Cuckoo in preference to Aunt May, Aunt May would never forgive her, a prospect that a short time ago she would not have minded, but which now she rather dreaded, for since her visit to Curtain Wells she was feeling afraid of the future, she tried to avoid making a decision for herself by consulting Uncle Alec and Aunt Mildred. Both of them were sure that she should go to Aunt May, and Aunt Mildred pointed out with what for her was excellent logic: "Lettice and Pamela are both ill and they are both her daughters, whereas this infant is not Aunt Cuckoo's son, and if Aunt Cuckoo deliberately adopts sons she ought to be able to look after them herself."

"In fact," the Colonel said, "I should not be surprised to receive a telegram from Eneas asking *me* to look after Aunt Cuckoo. Well, we shall miss you here," he added; but Jasmine could see that he was really very glad that she was going. Aunt Mildred too was evidently not sorry to escape from the argument about the parlourmaid. Now she could go on believing for the rest of her life that if Jasmine had stayed she would have had her way and turned her into a temporary parlourmaid for the benefit of the Grand Duchess.

The Prince, whose capacity for differentiating the various human emotions was most indefinite, danced up and down with delight at hearing that Jasmine was going away. Aunt Mildred tried to explain that he was really dancing with sorrow; but it appeared presently that the Prince had an idea that he was going away with her, and that he really had been dancing with delight, his capacity for differentiating the human emotions not being quite so indefinite as it was thought to be. When he found that Jasmine was going away without him, he could not be pacified until Snelson had got into a large clothes-basket, and pretended to be something that Jasmine never knew. Whatever it was, the Prince was reconciled to her departure, and the last she saw of him he was sitting cross-legged in front of the clothes-basket with an expression on his face of divine content. She thought to herself with a laugh as she drove off that Snelson would probably spend many hours in the clothes-basket during the next two or three weeks. In fact, he would probably spend most of his time in that clothes-basket, until the Prince found another pet upon which to lavish his admiration, or until he grew envious of Snelson's lot and decided to occupy the clothes-basket himself.

Chapter Eleven

THERE is no doubt that if Lady Grant could have found the smallest pretext for blaming her niece, she would have held her responsible for the scarlet fever which had attacked her daughters. As it was, she had to be content with dwelling upon the inconvenience of Jasmine's succumbing to the malady.

"You so easily might catch it," she pointed out, "that I do hope you'll bear in mind what a nuisance it would be for us all if you did catch it. Of course, those who understand about these things may decide it would be more prudent if you did not expose yourself to any risk by going to visit the poor girls." Lady Grant could never miss an opportunity to emphasize the mysterious and sacerdotal omniscience that belonged to the profession of medicine. "Those who understand about these things will tell us what we must do. But meanwhile, although I am only speaking as an ignoramus in these matters, I should say that if you always remembered to disinfect your clothes and all that sort of thing and were very careful to follow the doctor's directions, there would be no danger of your catching scarlet fever yourself. I need not tell you what a terrible blow it was to me when I had to give my consent to their being taken away from Harley Street to a nursing home. A terrible blow! But your uncle felt that it would not be fair to his patients if they stayed in the house. That's the worst of being a doctor. He has to think of everybody. Poor dear children, and there's so little one can do! In fact there's really nothing one can do except take the darlings grapes every day."

The rules of the nursing home were more strict than Lady Grant had expected, and, much to her indignation, permission to visit the patients was denied to Jasmine, who thereupon suggested that, since she could not be of any use in nursing her cousins, she ought to go and help Aunt Cuckoo with the illness of her adopted son.

"And what about me?" demanded her aunt. "You seem to forget, my dear child, and your Aunt Cuckoo seems to forget, that I have a slight claim to consideration. As if the girls' illness was not enough, Cousin Edith must needs go and carelessly visit some friend of hers at Enfield and bring back with her a violent cold, so that what with her sniffling and sneezing and snuffling it's quite impossible to stay in the same room with her. So, at this moment of all others, I am left entirely at the mercy of the servants, who after all have quite enough work of their own to run the house properly, and really I'm afraid I cannot see why you should go to Aunt Cuckoo."

It was thus that Jasmine found herself after what Aunt May now called her adventures of the last eighteen months in that very position which Aunt May had no doubt arranged in her mind when she first wrote and insisted on her niece's leaving Sirene and coming to England. Cousin Edith's cold, which Jasmine had to admit was one of the most aggressive, the most persistent, the most maddening colds she had ever listened to, was ascribed by Aunt May to the London climate in winter, and as soon as Jasmine was fairly at work on her aunt's correspondence, Cousin Edith was sent away to recuperate in Bognor, where it was generally understood at 317, Harley Street she would remain for the rest of her life. If anything more than the cold had been needed to confirm Aunt May in her resolve to get rid of Cousin Edith, it was the death of Spot.

"So long as poor old Spot was alive," she said to Jasmine, "I never liked to send poor Edith away. The poor old dog was very devoted to her, and I'm bound to say that poor Edith with all her faults was very devoted to dear old Spot. But Spot has gone now, and I don't feel inclined to form fresh ties by getting a puppy. Puppies have to be trained, and I very much doubt if Cousin Edith is capable of training a puppy nowadays. She seems to have gone all to pieces since she caught this cold. I told her at the time that I could not understand why she wanted to make that long journey to Enfield. She came back on the outside of the tram, you know. It's all so unnecessary."

Spot had died when the famous cold was at its worst, and the grief Cousin Edith had tried to express was not more effective than a puddle in a deluge. The body was sent to the Dogs' Cemetery, and through having to represent Cousin Edith at the funeral Jasmine nearly caught a cold herself. She did sneeze once or twice when she got home; but Aunt May talked at such length about colds that Jasmine made up her mind that she simply would not have a cold, and she actually succeeded in driving it away, for which her aunt took all the credit.

The night before Cousin Edith left to recuperate at Bognor she invited Jasmine up to her room, when Jasmine realized that the poor relation was perfectly aware what a long convalescence hers was going to be, and perfectly aware that her visit to the seaside would only be terminated by her death.

"In many ways, of course," she said, "I shall enjoy Bognor, and in many ways I shall probably be happier at Bognor than I have ever been here. I quite understand that Cousin May requires somebody more active than myself. She is a woman of immense energy, and when I look at her nose I sometimes think that there may after all be something in character reading by the face. I often meant to take it up seriously. I once bought a book on physiognomy when I was a girl and gave readings at a bazaar. I made quite a lot of money, I remember—sixteen shillings. It was for a new set of bells for my uncle's church at Market Addleby. As his curate said to me, very beautifully and poetically, I thought, when I handed him the sixteen shillings: 'You will always be able to think, Miss Crossfield'—my uncle never encouraged him to call us by our Christian names on account of the parish—'always able to think every time the new bells ring out for one of our great Church festivals, that your little labour of love this afternoon and this evening has contributed a melodious note to one of the most joyful chimes.' I remember my uncle, who was a very jocular man for a clergyman, observed when this was repeated to him that if I had only made a little more money it might have been called Edith's five-pound note. I remember we all laughed very much at this at the time. But as I was saying to you, my dear ... let me see, what was I saying to you?... oh yes, I remember now, I wanted to give you this little brooch which contains some of my grandmother's hair when she was a baby. I've often noticed that you've very few little mementoes; I noticed it because I haven't very many myself. Now with regard to this room, which you will probably occupy when I've gone, it really is a delightful room, in fact the only little fault it has is that the bell doesn't ring. In some respects that is not a bad fault, because no doubt the servants do not like answering bells all the time, and I think I have been rather tactful in never once suggesting that it should be mended. I'm only telling you this so that you shall not go on ringing and ringing and ringing and ringing under the impression that the bell is making the least sound. I remember it was quite a long time before I found out that it was broken, and I derived an impression at first that the servants were deliberately not answering this particular bell. I shall miss poor old Spot very much, but Hargreaves has a married sister whose cat has a very nice kitten which she wants to give away, and her little boy is meeting me with it in a basket at Victoria to-morrow. If you are ever down at Bognor at any time, of course I shall be very glad to see you and give you a cup of tea. My address will be 88, Seaview Terrace. You can see the sea from the corner of the road, so you won't forget the name of the road. But how will you remember the number? Of course, it's eleven times eight, but you might forget that too."

"I'll write it down," said Jasmine brightly.

Cousin Edith looked dubious. "Of course, yes, to be sure you can do that. But supposing you mislay the address?"

"Well, I don't think I shall ever forget eighty-eight," Jasmine affirmed with conviction.

Cousin Edith had worn black ever since it was settled that she was to leave Harley Street, or perhaps it was a tribute to the late Spot. Jasmine, looking at her, thought that she resembled a daddy-longlegs less nowadays and more one of those wintry flies that survive the first frosts of autumn and spend their time walking up and down window panes in an attempt to suggest that if the window were open they would be out and about, delighting in the brisk wintry weather.

"Well, good-bye," Cousin Edith was saying. "I shall be in such confusion to-morrow morning that I may not have time then to say good-bye to you properly. I won't kiss you on the mouth because of my cold. I wonder if you will be as sorry to leave 317, Harley Street as I am, when *you* have been here fifteen years."

Jasmine thought for a moment that Cousin Edith was being malicious and sarcastic; but apparently she meant exactly what she had said.

The next day Jasmine moved into the vacant room, and if Cousin Edith's mourning brooch had contained a lock of her own hair instead of a grandmother's she would not have thought it inappropriate, for the departure of the poor relation had impressed her mind like a death more than a visit to the seaside.

It is hardly possible to picture anybody who lives between Baker Street and Portland Road, however happy he may be, however much in love with life he may feel, as able to maintain an attitude toward life more vital than the exhibition of waxworks in the galleries of Madame Tussaud. There were moments when Jasmine felt that the waxworks were the real population of this district, and sometimes when in the late dusk or at night she was walking down Harley Street or any of the neighbouring streets she would receive a strong impression that all the houses were serving like stage scenery to give nothing but an illusion of reality. This morbid fancy might be justified by the fact that so many of the houses actually were unoccupied at night, and that in the daytime they were haunted not inhabited by figures in the world of medicine who by the uniformity and convention of their gestures and observations had no more life than waxworks. Moreover, passers-by in Harley Street and the neighbourhood had among them such a large proportion of sick men and women that even if one ignored the successive brass plates of the doctors, their presence alone would be enough to cast a gloom on any observer that happened to come into daily contact with such a procession of afflicted individuals.

Jasmine's window, high up in the front of the house, never contributed anything to the gaiety of her private meditations, and she used to think that if a famous prisoner, he of Chillon or any other, had been invited to change his outlook with her own, he would soon have begged to be put back in his dungeon. Many human beings, ailing, miserable, poverty-stricken, victims of misfortune or suppliants of fate, have found in a window their salvation. Jasmine was not one of these. She never seemed able to look out of her window without seeing some hunched-up man or wrapped-up woman who was being helped up a flight of steps, at the head of which the conventionally neat parlourmaid would admit them to their doom; and she used to picture these patients when the sleek doors closed behind them being greeted by the various doctors in attitudes like those of the poisoners in the Chamber of Horrors. There was one figure, that of Neil Cream, a gigantic man with a ragged beard and glasses, who stood for her behind every door in Harley Street. In fact, Jasmine was suffering now when she was twenty the kind of nervous distortions of imagination and apprehension through which most London children pass at about eight. And really, considering her experiences in England since she arrived from Italy, so many of them had to do with disease and death and madness that her morbid condition was excusable. When she was staying with Uncle Alec and Aunt Mildred she had been amused by Prince Adalbert, but now, looking back at that experience, she began to feel frightened, just as when one sees a ghost, one is more frightened when the ghost has vanished than when it is actually present. Looking back now on Uncle Matthew's illness she was again seized by a fear and repulsion which at the time had been merged in indignation. Looking back on her visit to Aunt Cuckoo and Uncle Eneas, the whole of it was now shrouded in an atmosphere of unhealthiness; and looking back further still to her last memory of Sirene, even that was blackened by the sorrow of her father's sudden death. As for the house she was living in at the moment, her sensitive mind could not fail to be affected by the thought that so many of the people who passed along that spacious hall and waited round that sombre table littered with old *Punches* and *Tatlers* and odd numbers of unusual magazines were either mad or moving in the direction of madness. Sir Hector Grant's waiting-room was probably one of the most oppressive in Harley Street, because it had no window, but was lighted from above by a green dome of glass, to Jasmine curiously symbolical of the kind of imprisonment to which madness subjects the human soul. The absence of Lettice and Pamela at the nursing home, although Jasmine had not the slightest desire to see them or hear them ever again, added in its own way to the general air of depression. When Lettice and Pamela were in the house the sense of contact with the ordinary frivolities of the world was never absent; but without them the house became nothing but a cul-de-sac, a kind of condemned cell, so deep did it lie under the spell of dreadful verdicts.

In addition to these influences that spoilt her leisure time, Jasmine's work with her aunt did not encourage her to look upon the brighter side of life. Those numerous charities were no doubt a pleasure and a pride to their originator, but Jasmine, who lacked the sustenance of the egotism that inspired them, was only impressed by the continuous reminder they gave her of the world's misery. The Club for Tired Sandwichmen was for Aunt May something upon which to congratulate herself, an idea that had occurred to no other prominent philanthropist. It was Jasmine's duty to harrow subscribers' feelings with details of the private lives of sandwichmen in order to extract from them as much as would help to maintain the three bleak rooms in a small street off Leicester Square, where these wrecks and ruins of human endeavour could take refuge from the rain and cold outside. Upon Lady Grant herself the individual made not the least impression unless he came into the Club drunk and broke one of the chairs, in which case she interested herself sufficiently in his future to banish him from the paradise she had created.

When Jasmine first again took up secretarial work for her aunt, she wrote all the letters.

"But really I think I shall have to find you another typewriter," said Aunt May after a week of this. "I always understood that convent-educated girls were taught to write well; but your handwriting resembles the marks made by a fly that has fallen into the ink-pot."

"I think I feel rather like a fly that has fallen into the ink-pot," said Jasmine.

Her aunt did not pay any attention to this retort; but a few days later the new typewriter arrived, and it was conferred upon her as if it was a motor-car for her own use.

"I really do think that with this beautiful new machine you might do some of Sir Hector's work too," suggested Aunt May. "That is, if he can be persuaded to send a typewritten letter."

Luckily for Jasmine Sir Hector's ideas of the courtesy owing from a medical baronet did not allow him to do this. He continued to employ a clerk with a copper-plate hand to send in his bills, so Jasmine was not called upon to help him in any way.

"You will have a lot of time on your hands," Aunt May regretfully sighed after her husband had declined the use of the typewriter for himself. "Don't I remember your once saying that you sewed very well? That, surely, they must have taught you at the convent. Cousin Edith used sometimes to sew for me, and there is always her machine standing idle."

Perhaps Cousin Edith's ingratiating touch had spoilt that machine for another. When Jasmine tried her hand on it, it behaved like an angry dog, gathering up the piece of work, the hem of which it was being invited to stitch, worrying it and pleating it and tearing pieces off it and chewing up these pieces, until first the needle snapped and then some of the mechanism made a noise like a half empty box of bricks. It was plain that nothing more could be done with it.

"Ruined," declared Aunt May when she came upstairs to see how Jasmine was getting on. "Well, I hope you'll take a little more trouble over the flowers for the dinner-table to-night."

The only mechanical device that Jasmine could think of in connection with flowers was a lawn-mower, so she felt safe in promising that the dinner-table should present an appearance of a little more trouble having been taken with it than with the piece of work in the sewing-machine. These dinner parties were by no means the least irritating products of her cousins' illness, which had struck Lady Grant as an excellent opportunity for inviting all their most ineligible acquaintanceswhile her daughters were away; and Jasmine, who did not enjoy even the pleasure of being able to choose between more than two evening frocks, felt bored by these dreary men and women, for whose existence she could not imagine any possible reason, let alone discover a reason for asking them out to dinner. Two or three days before one of these occasions Aunt May's invariable formula was that Jasmine was going to be put next to a most interesting man, and always half an hour before the gong sounded she would decide that she must take Mrs. So-and-so's or Miss What's-her-name's place next to somebody who was not interesting at all. She was used, in fact, by her aunt very much as umbrellas are used to reserve seats in a train.

A month or five weeks passed thus, after which Lettice and Pamela emerged from hospital, unable to talk of anything for several days except the details of their peeling. It was now decided that they required change of air, and the question of Jasmine's ability to look after her uncle while his wife and daughters went to Mentone was debated at some length.

"It would be such an opportunity for you to learn housekeeping," said Aunt May. "And if you were a success, who knows, I might even let you take entire charge of the house when I come back. I wonder...." She hesitated, awe-struck by her vision of the future. "I don't want to move Cousin Edith from Bognor. Her cold is quite well now, and it would be such a pity to start her off with it again. And she's apt to irritate your uncle in little things. Of course, he likes people to be attentive to him; but he hates them to make a show of being attentive. And Cousin Edith was always rather apt to make a show of being attentive. You won't do that, will you, dear?"

Jasmine promised that she would not do that, and in the end she was left with her uncle in charge of the house. She decided at once that the only way to manage Hargreaves and Hopkins and the rest of the servants was to make friends of them and become as it were one of themselves. On the whole she rather liked this, and she found that down in the kitchen below the level of Harley Street even Cook became a human figure. As for Hopkins and Hargreaves, they were like butterflies emerging from those two pupæ that waited on the other side of the baize door separating the world below stairs from the world above.

Jasmine found that this communion with the servants was the only natural way in which she could still associate with humanity, and in consequence of it she found herself being more and more completely cut off every day from the family with which she was living. Lady Grant would unquestionably have condemned such society as degrading; but since nothing was offered her in its place, Jasmine continued to frequent the servants' company, and before many weeks had elapsed she had almost come to regard her cousins, her aunt, and her uncle from the point of view of the servants' hall, as eccentric beings living in a queer inaccessible world. She used to think that she might just as well have been left quietly in Sirene. Looking back on the motives for bringing her to England, it was now clear to Jasmine that no real consideration for her future had actuated any of her relatives. She did not mean to suggest to herself that they had consciously or deliberately thought out a plan by which she could be made useful to each in turn; but they all of them had tried to make her useful, and she supposed that such an attempt was like the instinct that leads a person to accept a useless ornament for a bad debt rather than be left with nothing. They had probably all been afraid that if she stayed in Sirene by herself, sooner or later some scandal would supervene which would necessitate more trouble in the future than they felt bound to exert in the present. Really, she thought to herself, she should be happier if she quite definitely ceased to be Miss Jasmine Grant, and became Jasmine, a parlourmaid. But, of course, Jasmine would be considered too flowery a name for service, and she should be known as Grant. Grant! A not unimpressive name for a parlourmaid. She once actually discussed the project with Hargreaves, Hopkins, and Cook; but they evidently thought she was mad to suggest such a thing; they evidently thought it would be better to go on serving in Heaven than begin to reign in Hell; not one of them had a trace of Lucifer in her temperament.

And so a dreary year passed away, a long dreary year during which Jasmine's most breathless and most daring ambition was to be a parlourmaid, her most poignant regret that she had not stayed long enough at Curtain Wells to have rehearsed the part.

"I cannot say how greatly I think you have improved, Jasmine," said Aunt May one day just a year after Jasmine had gone to Harley Street. "You were so wild at first, so heedless and impulsive. But I notice with pleasure that you are quite changed. I was speaking about it to your uncle to-day, and I suggested to him that as a token of our appreciation of the effort you have made to recognize what we have already done for you we should allow you an extra ten pounds a year. You are at present getting ten pounds a quarter, and we discussed for quite half an hour whether it would be better to allow you twelve pounds ten shillings a quarter or to present you with the extra ten pounds all at once, say on your birthday or at Christmas or on some such occasion. Of course, we did not want you to suppose that you are to regard this in any way as a substitute for a Christmas present. It is not. No, you are to regard it as an expression of our approval."

Ever since she had been in England, Jasmine had ceased to believe in the reality of anything talked about beforehand, so she thought no more about that extra ten pounds. But sure enough at Christmas she received it, and not only the ten pounds, but also a parrot-headed umbrella from Aunt May, a sachet of handkerchiefs from Lettice, the particular monstrosity in porcelain that was in vogue at the time from Pamela, and a kiss from Sir Hector.

Although Lettice and Pamela were not yet even engaged to be married, social life at 317, Harley Street was conducted on the principle that at any moment they might be. There could have been few young men about town who had escaped having tea there at least once. None of them interested Jasmine in the least, and it was perhaps just as well that she was not interested, because if she had been interested she would certainly have had no opportunity of displaying her interest owing to the fact that she always had to pour out tea. A woman pouring out tea for one man can make of the gesture a most alluring business; but a woman pouring out tea for twenty young men cannot escape disenchantment, however charming she may be at leisure. The fumes of the teapot, the steam from the kettle, the wrinkles provoked by her attempt to remember who said he did and who said he did not take sugar, all these combine to ravage the sweetest face. As for the dinner parties, although they belonged to another order of dinner parties compared with those given when Lettice and Pamela were away, there always seemed to be one person at least for whose presence of a dinner party, nay more, for whose very existence in the world no excuse could be found. This person invariably took in Jasmine. No doubt her relatives individually never intended to be positively unkind. Whatever unkindness came to the surface was inherent in her position as a poor relation. Besides, nowadays she seldom offered any occasion for people to be unkind to her. She sometimes would ask herself with a show of indignation how she had allowed herself to surrender to this extent; but she had to admit that from the moment she entered Strathspey House she had foreseen the possibility of such a life's being in store for herself, and looking back at her behaviour during the first eighteen months of her stay, she could not see that at any point she had made a really determined stand against this kind of life. To be sure, she had had a few quarrels and arguments; she had delivered a few retorts. But what ineffective self-assertion it had all been! She had had at any rate one opportunity of striking out for herself during Uncle Matthew's illness, and what a muddle she had made of it, because she had been too proud to force herself upon Uncle Matthew, and because with a foolish dignity that was in reality nothing but humility she had given way to his unwillingness to confess an obligation.

And another year passed; a year of writing letters for her aunt in the morning, of going downstairs to see Cook about this, and of going upstairs to talk to Hargreaves about that, of running round the corner to Debenham and Freebody's to see if they could match this for the girls, or of spending the whole morning at Marshall and Snelgrove's with her aunt to see if they could match that for her.

On Christmas morning Lady Grant took her niece aside and confided to her that, so heavy had been her own expenses and so heavy had been Sir Hector's expenses, she was sure Jasmine would understand if she did not receive the extra ten pounds as usual. To hear Aunt May, one might have supposed that the donation had been customary since her niece's birth.

"Our expenses are going to be even heavier this year," she announced. "There is so much entertaining to do nowadays."

When she first came to England Jasmine might have commented at this point on the fact that Lettice would be thirty next birthday and that Pamela was well in sight of being twenty-nine. But two complete years in Harley Street had taken away her desire to score visibly, and she was content nowadays with a faint smile to herself.

"What are you laughing at?" her aunt asked. "It is one of the few rather irritating little tricks you still have, that habit of smiling to yourself suddenly when I am talking to you. Some people might think you were laughing at me."

"Oh no, Aunt May," Jasmine protested.

"No, of course I know you are not laughing at me," her aunt allowed. "But I think it's a habit you should try to cure yourself of. It's apt to make you seem a little vapid sometimes."

"Yes, I often feel rather vapid," Jasmine admitted.

"Then all the more reason why you should not let other people notice it," said her aunt; and Jasmine did not argue the point further.

The loss of the ten pounds meant that Jasmine would not be able to have a new evening frock that winter. She was not yet sufficiently dulled by Harley Street not to feel disappointed at this. It has to be a very beautiful evening frock which does not look dowdy after being worn twice a week throughout the year, and the better of Jasmine's two evening frocks was nothing more than pretty and simple on the evening she put it on for the first time.

"Another long miserable year," she thought. "Nothing new till the twenty-fifth of March. All this quarter's allowance has gone in Christmas presents."

Jasmine's most conspicuous present that year was a sunshade that Aunt May had bought at the July sales.

"As if one wanted a sunshade in England," Jasmine said to herself.

Chapter Twelve

THE new year opened with such a blaze of entertaining that even Hargreaves, who was much more reticent than Hopkins, allowed herself to observe to Jasmine that it really seemed as if her ladyship was determined to find husbands for Miss Lettice and Miss Pamela at last. The atmosphere of the house was charged with that kind of accumulated energy which is the external characteristic of all great charitable efforts. If Lettice had been a new church tower that had to be paid for or if Pamela had been a new wing for a hospital, it would have been impossible to promote a fiercer intensity of desire to accomplish something at all costs no matter what or how. January twinkled like a Christmas tree with minor festivals; but on February 14th—the date was appropriate, although it was not chosen deliberately—Lady Grant was to give a large dance in the Empress Rooms.

"And if it's successful," she told Jasmine, "I daresay I shall give another dance in May."

Jasmine refrained from saying "If it's unsuccessful, you mean," and merely indulged in one of those irritating little smiles.

"Oh, and by the way," her aunt added, "did you see that your old friend Harry Vibart has succeeded to the title?"

She looked at her niece keenly when she made this announcement; but Jasmine was determined not to give her the gratification of a self-conscious blush. Nor was it very difficult to appear indifferent to the news, because, as she assured herself, Harry Vibart, by his readiness to acquiesce in her decree of banishment and by his complete silence for over two and a half years, was no longer of any emotional importance. At the same time, no girl who had been compelled to spend such an empty or rather such a drearily full two years as she had just spent could have helped letting her mind wander back for a moment, could have helped wondering whether if she had behaved differently, everything might not have been different.

"Of course, one does not want to say too much," said Lady Grant, "but one cannot help remembering what great friends he and the girls were some years ago, and really I think ... yes, really I think, Jasmine, it would be only polite if we sent him an invitation."

Jasmine's heart began to beat faster; not on account of the prospect of meeting Harry Vibart again, but with the effort of preventing herself from saying what she really thought of her aunt's impudent distortion of the true facts of the case.

The re-entry of one person from the past into her life was followed by the re-entry of another; for that very afternoon, a bleak January afternoon of brown fog, Hopkins came up to tell Jasmine that Miss Butt had called to see her and to ask where should she be shown? The only people who ever came to see Jasmine were dressmakers with whom she had been negotiating on behalf of her aunt and her cousins, and for whose misfits Jasmine was to be held responsible. These dressmakers were usually interviewed in the dining-room; but Hopkins informed Jasmine that Miss Butt had emphatically declined to be shown upstairs and had expressed a wish to interview her in the servants' hall. Such a request had affronted Hopkins' conception of etiquette, and she was anxious to know what Jasmine intended to do about it. Jasmine was on sufficiently intimate terms with the servants by now to explain at once that Miss Butt and her ladyship were never on any account to be allowed to meet face to face, and she asked Hopkins if she thought that Cook would mind if in the circumstances she made use of the servants' hall.

"No, Miss Jasmine, I don't think she would at all," said Hopkins. "In fact from what I could see of it when I come upstairs, they was getting on very well together. But I didn't think it right to say you'd come down and see her there, until I had found out from you whether you would."

"All right, Amanda, I'll come down at once." Nowadays Jasmine was allowed in her own room to call Hopkins Amanda.

Mrs. Curtis, the cook of 317, Harley Street, was a woman of some majesty, and when she was seated in her arm-chair on the right of the hearth in the servants' hall, she conveyed as much as anyone Jasmine had ever seen the aroma of a regal hospitality mingled with a regal condescension. When Jasmine beheld the scene in the servants' hall she could easily have imagined that she was watching a meeting between two queens. Selina, in a crimson blanket coat, wearing a ruby coloured hat much befurred, with a musquash stole thrown back from her shoulders, was evidently informing Mrs. Curtis of the state of her kingdom; Mrs. Curtis was nodding in august approval, and from time to time turning her head to invite a comment from Hargreaves, who like a lady-in-waiting, stood at the head of her chair, whispering from time to time: "Quite so, Mrs. Curtis." Grouped on the other side of the table and not venturing to sit down, the junior servants listened to the conversation like respectful and attentive courtiers.

As soon as Selina saw Jasmine, she jumped up from her chair and embraced her warmly.

"An old friend come to see you," said Cook with immense benignity.

"Dear Selina!" Jasmine exclaimed. "How nice to see you again!"

"The pleasure's on both sides," said Selina. "Mrs. Vokins is dead."

Jasmine looked at Selina in astonishment. Nothing in the style of her attire suggested such an announcement; in fact, she could not remember ever having seen Selina wear colours before, and that she should have chosen to break out into crimson on the occasion of her friend's death was incomprehensible.

"When did she die?"

"Six months ago," said Selina. "And I went into strict mourning for six months. Last night she appeared to me, as I've just been telling Mrs. Curtis here. She said she was very happy in heaven; told me to stop mourning for her, and pop round to see you."

"Wonderful, isn't it?" Mrs. Curtis demanded from her juniors, who murmured an unanimous and discreet echo of assent.

"Then Mrs. Vokins was saved after all?" said Jasmine. "I remember you used to think that she couldn't be saved."

"Some of us think wrong sometimes," said Selina.

"That's true, Miss Butt," put in Cook.

"Some of us think very wrong sometimes," Selina continued. "And it's perfectly clear Mrs. Vokins was sent down to me to say as I'd been thinking wrong."

"Wonderful, isn't it?" Cook demanded once more.

"'I'm very happy in heaven, Miss Butt,' was her words, and though I hadn't time to ask exackly which of my friends and relations was up there with her, I put it to myself it was unlikely Mrs. Vokins would call and tell me she was very happy unless she shortly expected me to join her. She was never a woman who cared to disappoint anybody. So I'm looking forward to seeing a lot of people I never expected to see again. In fact I've given up the Children of Zion and turned Church of England, which my poor mother always was, until a clergyman spoke to her in a way no clergyman ought to speak, telling her what to do and what not to do, until she turned round in his face and became a Primitive Methodist, where she always poured out the tea at the New Year's gathering. Yes, Mrs. Vokins has been a good friend to me, and she's been a good friend to you, because she put it into my head to come down here and ask you if you'd like to come and live in my rooms at Catford where she used to live, with the use of the kitchen three times a week as per arrangement."

"Dear Selina, it's very kind of you to invite me," said Jasmine, "but ..." she broke off with a sigh.

"Which means you won't come," said Selina. "That I expected; and if Mrs. Vokins hadn't of been in such a hurry, I should have told her as much before she went. She vanished in a moment before I even had time to say how well she was looking. 'Radiant as an angel,' they say; and Mrs. Vokins was looking radiant. 'You certainly are looking celestial,' was what I should like to have said."

"Why haven't you been to see me all these two years?" asked Jasmine.

At this point, Mrs. Curtis, realizing that Jasmine and her friend might have matters to discuss which it would be undignified for them to discuss before the servants, asked the scullery-maid sharply if she intended to get those greens ready, or if she expected herself, Mrs. Curtis, to get them ready. The reproof administered to the scullery-maid was accepted by her fellow-servants as a hint for them to leave Jasmine and her visitor together, and when they were gone Mrs. Curtis, rising from her arm-chair like Leviathan from the deep, supposed that after all she should have to go and look after that girl.

"For girls, Miss Butt, nowadays.... Well, I needn't tell you what girls are. You know."

"Yes, I know," said Selina. "A lot of rabbits."

"That's very true, Miss Butt; a lot of rabbits," echoed Cook solemnly as she sailed from the room.

"Well, why haven't you been to see me, Selina?" Jasmine persisted when they were alone.

"Why haven't you been to see *me*?"

"How could I? Uncle Matthew never invited me. Surely, Selina, you can understand I didn't want to force myself where I wasn't wanted. The last thing I wanted to do was to give him the impression that I wanted anything from him. He's had plenty of opportunities to ask for me if he wished to see me. My cousins have been over to see him lots of times."

"They have," agreed Selina, grimly.

"And they never brought me back any message."

"That doesn't say no message was sent," said Selina. "You know as well as I know Mr. Rouncivell never sends a letter of his own accord. He can't bring himself to it. I've seen him sit by the hour holding a stamp in his hand the same as I've seen boys holding butterflies between their fingers."

"Well, you could have written to me," Jasmine pointed out.

"I could have," Selina asserted. "And I ought to have; but I didn't. It's not a bit of good you going on talking about what people ought to have done. If we once get on that subject we shall go on talking here for ever. And it's no good being offended with me, even if you won't show a Christian spirit and go and live at Catford. I think you ought to have learnt to forgive by now. I've been forgiving people by the dozen these last two days. And although I don't think I shall, still you never know, and I may go so far as to forgive *her*," Selina declared pointing with her forefinger at the ceiling to indicate whom she meant.

Jasmine tried to explain that she no longer felt herself capable of taking such a drastic step as going to live in Catford. She found it hard to convince Selina how impossible it was to accept her charity, and she was quite sure that her relatives would not dream of continuing her allowance should she go to Catford.

"In fact, my dear Selina, I think you'd better let me alone. I think that some people in this world are meant to occupy the kind of position I occupy, and I've got hardened to it. I don't really care a bit any more. I have enjoyed seeing you very much, and I hope you will come and see me again. It really isn't worth while for me to make any effort to get away from this. It really isn't."

Selina lectured Jasmine for a while on her lack of Christian spirit—evidently Christian spirit to her mind conveyed something between willingness to forgive and courage to defy—and then rising abruptly she said she must be off. Jasmine heard nothing more from her for some time after this.

Ten days before the dance at the Empress Rooms Sir Hector, for what he insisted was the first time in his life, was taken ill. He was apparently not suffering from anything more serious than a slight bronchial cold, but he made such a fuss about it that Jasmine was ready to believe it really was the first time in his life he had ever been ill. In addition to his apprehensions about his own condition and the various maladies that might supervene, he seemed to think that his illness was something in the nature of a national disaster, like a coal strike or a great war.

"Dear me," said his wife. "I'm afraid it looks as if you won't be at the dance."

"Dance!" shouted Sir Hector as loudly as his cold would let him. "Of course I shan't be at the dance. Even if I'm well enough to be out of bed, which is very improbable, I certainly shan't be well enough to go out. And if I were well enough to go out, which is practically impossible, I certainly shouldn't be well enough to stand about in draughts. No, I shall stay at home. It's a fearful nuisance being ill like this. I can't think why I should get ill. I never *am* ill."

"It's dreadfully disappointing," said Aunt May soothingly. "We had such a particularly nice lot of young men coming. All dancing men, too, so you wouldn't have had to talk to them for more than a minute. I don't like to put it off. I never think things go so well after they've been put off."

"Oh, no, for goodness' sake don't put it off," said Sir Hector. "Quite enough things have been put off on account of my illness as it is. The Duchess of Shropshire is in despair because I can't go and see her. She can't stand Williamson." Dr. Williamson was Sir Hector's assistant. "Nothing serious, of course, but it creates such a bad impression if a man like me is ill. It shakes my confidence in myself. I can't think where I got this cold."

"People do get colds very often in January," said his wife.

"Other people get colds. I never do. Now what is that horrible mess that Jasmine is holding in her hand? It's no good just feeding me up on these messes and thinking that that is going to cure me: because it isn't."

Jasmine was expecting every minute to hear her aunt regretfully inform her that owing to Sir Hector's condition it would be impossible for her to go to the ball, because somebody would be required to stay at home and look after the invalid. To her surprise nothing was said about this, and she began to turn her attention to a new evening frock. This was a moment when the extra ten pounds she failed to get at Christmas would have been useful. Notwithstanding the surrender of her pride, Jasmine still had a little vanity; and when she took out of her wardrobe the two evening dresses that had served her during the last year, and saw how worn and faded they were, she began to wonder if after all she should not be glad if her aunt settled things over her head by telling her that she could not go.

She was vexed, when she opened her aunt's correspondence that morning and read that Sir Harry Vibart accepted with pleasure Lady Grant's kind invitation for Wednesday, February 14th, to detect herself the prey of a sudden impulse to go to this dance at all costs. She debated with herself whether she should not ask Miss Hemmings, the little dressmaker in Marylebone High Street who made most of her things, to make her an evening frock on the understanding that she should be paid for it next quarter. At first Jasmine was rather timid about embarking upon such an adventure into extravagance; but she decided to do so, and when she had a moment to herself she slipped out of the house and hurried round to Miss Hemmings' little shop. Alas, Miss Hemmings; like Sir Hector, was also in bed with a bronchial cold; she was dreadfully sorry, but quite unable to oblige Miss Grant by the 14th.

"Oh, well, it's evidently not to be," Jasmine decided.

She got home in time to meet Selina coming up the area steps, dressed this time in a brilliant peacock blue blanket coat and an emerald green hat.

"Selina!" exclaimed Jasmine. "You seem to go in for nothing but clothes nowadays."

"You must dress a bit if you belong to the Church of England," said Selina sharply. "It's as different from the chapel as the stalls are from the pit. Don't forget that."

"Well, I've just been trying to get a frock for a dance on Wednesday, but my dressmaker's ill and...." Jasmine broke off; she did not wish to make Selina think that she was in need of money, for she felt that if she did, Selina would immediately offer to lend her some. And if she accepted Selina's charity it would be more than ever difficult to refuse to occupy those three rooms at Catford.

"Well, that's awkward," said Selina. "But I'll lend you anything you want."

"Oh, thank you very much, but it's an evening frock."

"Ah! That I don't go in for, and never shall. Low necks I shall never come to. Do you want to go to this party very much?"

"I do rather," Jasmine admitted.

"There's my bus," said Selina suddenly; and without a word of farewell she vanished round the corner shouting and waving her umbrella.

The next morning, which was Tuesday and the day before the dance, Jasmine received a postcard on which was printed the current price of coal. She thought at first that it had been put in her place by mistake; but looking at it again she saw written in a fine small hand between the Wallsends and the Silkstones *Come to Rouncivell Lodge to-morrow at eleven o'clock*; and between the Silkstones and the Cobbles the initials M. R.

Aunt May failed to understand how Uncle Matthew could be so inconsiderate as to invite Jasmine to Muswell Hill on the very day before she was giving a dance, and particularly when it would have been advisable in any case that Jasmine should be at home that morning in case her uncle wanted something.

"You must write and tell him you will go later on in the week."

Jasmine agreed to do so, but she added that she should have to give Uncle Matthew a reason for refusing to go and see him, and Aunt May, realizing that such a reason would involve herself with the old gentleman, gave a grudging assent to Jasmine's going that day. Jasmine had difficulty in escaping from Harley Street early enough to be punctual to her appointment with Uncle Matthew, but she managed it somehow, although at one time it seemed as if Sir Hector was wanting so many things which only Jasmine could provide that she should never get away. In the end when Lady Grant was calling 'Jasmine!' from the first landing, Hopkins replied 'Yes, my lady,' and before Lady Grant had time to explain that she did not want Hopkins, her niece was hurrying on her way north.

Jasmine wondered in what gay colours she should find Selina when she reached Rouncivell Lodge; but Selina met her at the gate in her customary black, and advised her sharply to make no allusions to her clothes in front of the old gentleman.

"Why haven't you been to see me before?" Uncle Matthew demanded as the clocks all over the house chimed eleven o'clock.

"I never go anywhere unless I'm asked."

"Well, don't put on your hoity-toity manners with me, miss. Do you expect me, at my age, to come trotting after you? I told your aunt several times I should like to see you."

"She never gave me your message."

"No, I suppose she didn't," said the old gentleman with a grim chuckle. "Now what's all this about wanting a dress for a ball? Do you expect me to provide you with dresses for balls?"

"Of course I don't," said Jasmine, looking angrily round to where Selina had been standing a moment ago. But the yellow-faced housekeeper had gone.

"Well, I've borrowed Eneas' carriage for the day, and I'll take you for a drive. I don't know how that fellow can afford to keep a carriage. I can't. At least, I can't afford to keep a carriage for other people to use, and that's what always happens. Oh, yes, they'd like me to have a carriage, I've no doubt. But I'm not going to have one."

"It's at the door, Mr. Rouncivell," said Selina, putting her head into the room.

Uncle Matthew was so voluminously wrapped up for this expedition that it seemed at first as if he would never be able to squeeze through the door of the brougham; but by unwinding himself from a plaid shawl he managed it.

"Where am I to drive to?" asked Uncle Eneas' gardener in an injured voice. He evidently disapproved of being lent to other people.

"Drive to London," said the old gentleman.

"Where?" the coachman repeated.

"To London, you idiot! Don't you know where London is?"

"London's a large place," said the coachman.

"I don't need you to tell me that. Drive to Regent Street."

The drive was spent in trying to accommodate Uncle Matthew's wraps to the temperature of the inside of the brougham, and in an attempt to calculate how much it cost Eneas to keep a horse, carriage, and coachman. This was a complicated calculation, because it involved deducting from the cost per week not merely the amount saved in artificial manures, but also the amount saved by growing bigger vegetables than would otherwise have been grown.

"But whatever way you look at it," said Uncle Matthew finally, "it's a dead loss!"

When they reached Regent Street, Uncle Matthew told Jasmine to stop the carriage at the first shop where women's clothes were sold.

"Women's clothes?" repeated Jasmine.

"Yes, women's clothes. I'm told you want a gown for a ball to-morrow. Well, I'm going to buy you one."

Jasmine could scarcely believe that it was Uncle Matthew who was talking, and her expression of amazement roused the old gentleman to ask her what she was staring at.

"Think I've never bought gowns for women before?" he asked. "I used to come shopping every day with my poor wife, fifty years ago."

The brougham had stopped at a famous and fashionable dressmaker's, and Jasmine wonderingly followed the old gentleman into the shop.

"I want a gown," said the old gentleman fiercely to the first lady who wriggled up to him and asked what he required.

They were accommodated with chairs in the showroom, and presently a young woman emerged from a glass grated door and walked past them in an Anglo-Saxon attitude.

"You needn't be shy of me," said Uncle Matthew. "I'm old enough to be your grandfather." The show-woman tittered politely at what she supposed was Uncle Matthew's joke.

"Do you like that model?" she said.

"Model?" echoed the old gentleman.

"That gown?" the show-woman enquired.

"Gown?" echoed Uncle Matthew. "What gown?"

"Miss Abels," the show-woman called, "would you mind walking past once more?"

"You don't mean to tell me that what she's wearing is an evening gown you propose to sell me?" asked Uncle Matthew, on whom an explanation of the young woman's behaviour was beginning to dawn. "Why, I never thought she was dressed at all."

The show-woman again tittered politely.

"We consider that one of our most becoming gowns," she said. "So simple, isn't it? Don't you like the lines? And it's quite a new shade. Angel's blush."

"It's very pretty," said Jasmine.

"Well," said Uncle Matthew, "I suppose you know what you want, and I daresay you're right to choose something simple. It's no good wasting money on a lot of frills. How much is that?"

"That gown," said the show-woman. "Let me see. That's a Paris model. Quite exclusive. Thirty-five guineas."

"What?" the old gentleman yelled. "Come out of the shop, come out of the shop!" he commanded Jasmine.

"I never heard of anything so monstrous in my life," he said indignantly to Jasmine on the pavement outside. "Thirty-five guineas! For a piece of stuff the size of three pocket-handkerchiefs! No wonder you can't afford to go to parties! Well, I made a mistake."

"But, Uncle Matthew," Jasmine explained, "I didn't want to go to a fashionable shop like this. There are lots of other shops where evening frocks don't cost so much."

"You can't have a dress made of less than that," he said.

"It isn't a question of amount. It's a question of cut and material."

But the old gentleman could not bring himself to go to another shop. He had suffered a severe shock, and he wished to be alone.

"I'll drive home by myself," he said. "You can get back to Harley Street quite easily from here. Thirty-five guineas! Why, poor Clara's bridal dress didn't cost that."

They were all very curious at Harley Street to know why Uncle Matthew had sent for Jasmine. She did not feel inclined to tell them the real reason, and she merely said that he wanted to see her. Aunt May, however, was feeling bitterly on the subject, and she was suspicious of Jasmine's reticence.

"It's a pity he should have fetched you all that way for nothing," she said. "You had better have done as I suggested and gone the day after the dance. We have all been so busy this morning that poor Uncle Hector has been rather neglected, and I've had to leave a great deal undone which will have to be done this afternoon, and I'm afraid he'll still feel a little neglected, so really, Jasmine, I don't know.... I suppose you'd be very disappointed if you didn't come to the dance, but really I don't know but that it may be necessary for you to stay at home to-morrow and look after Uncle Hector."

"I'll stay at home with pleasure," said Jasmine.

Her aunt looked at her. "Oh, you don't object to staying at home?"

"Why should I? I haven't got a frock fit to wear."

"Not got a frock fit to wear? Really, my dear, how you do exaggerate sometimes! That's a very becoming little yellow frock you wear. A very becoming little frock. You must be very anxious to impress somebody if you are not content to wear that."

Jasmine turned away without answering. She would not give her aunt the pleasure of seeing that the malicious allusion had touched her.

The following afternoon it was definitely decided that Sir Hector was too ill to be left in the hands of servants, and, very regretfully as she assured her, Lady Grant told her niece that she must ask her to stay at home.

"You mustn't be too disappointed, because perhaps I shall give another dance in April or May, and perhaps out of my own little private savings bank I may be able to add something to your March allowance that will enable you to get a frock which you do consider good enough to wear."

Jasmine thought that it would probably annoy her aunt if she looked as if she did not mind staying at home; so she very cheerfully announced her complete indifference to the prospect of going to the dance, and her intention of reading Sir Hector to sleep. Dinner was eaten in the feverish way in which dinners before balls are always eaten. Before starting Pamela called Jasmine into her room to admire her frock, and Jasmine took a good deal of pleasure in telling her that she was not sure, but she thought she liked Lettice's frock better; and to Lettice, whom she presently visited, she said after a suitable pause that she was afraid Pamela's frock suited *her* better than her own did. Hargreaves and Hopkins, who were both indignant at Jasmine's being left behind, took the cue from her and they both praised so enthusiastically the other's dress to each sister, that the two girls went off to the dance feeling thoroughly ill-tempered.

"What would you like me to read you, Uncle Hector?" asked Jasmine when the house was silent.

"Well, really, I don't know," he said. "I don't think there's anything nowadays worth reading. I don't care about these modern writers. I don't understand them. But if they came to me as patients, I should know how to prescribe for them."

"Shall I read you some Dickens?" Jasmine suggested.

"It's hardly worth while beginning a long novel at this time of the evening."

"I might read you *The Christmas Carol*."

"Oh, I know that by heart," said Sir Hector.

"Well, what shall I read you? Shall I read you something from Thackeray's *Book of Snobs*?"

"No, I know that by heart, too," said Sir Hector.

"If you don't like modern writers, and you know all the other writers by heart...."

"Well, if you want to read something," said Sir Hector at last, as if he were gratifying a spoilt child, "you had better read me Mr. Balfour's speech in the House last night."

It was lucky for Mr. Balfour that Sir Hector had not been present when he made the speech, for at every other line he ejaculated: "Rot! Unmitigated rot! Rubbish! The man doesn't know what he's talking about! What an absurd statement! Read that again, will you, my dear? I never heard such piffle!"

In spite of Sir Hector's interruptions, Jasmine stumbled through Mr. Balfour's speech, and she was just going to begin Mr. Asquith's reply when the door of the bedroom opened and Uncle Matthew walked in.

Sir Hector's first instinct when this apparition presented itself was to grab the thermometer and take his temperature; but perceiving that Jasmine was as much surprised as himself and that it was certainly not a feverish delusion, he stammered out a greeting.

"I don't advise you to come into the room, though," he said. "I've got a dreadful cold."

"I thought you were never ill," said Uncle Matthew.

"Well, I'm not. It's a most extraordinary thing. Where I got this cold I cannot imagine," Sir Hector was declaiming when Uncle Matthew cut him short. Jasmine always felt like giggling when Sir Hector was talking to his uncle, because she could not get used to the idea that both Sir Hector and herself should address him as Uncle Matthew. She was still young enough to conceive all people over fifty merged in contemporary senility.

"I thought you were going to a dance," said Uncle Matthew to Jasmine.

"Oh, Jasmine very kindly offered to stay behind and look after me," Sir Hector explained.

"Well, I'll look after you," said Uncle Matthew.

His nephew stared at him.

"Yes, I'll look after you," the old gentleman repeated. "What time do you take your medicine? *You* had better get along to the dance," he said to Jasmine.

"But Jasmine can't go off to a dance by herself," Sir Hector protested.

"Can't she?" said Uncle Matthew. "Well, then I'll go with her, and Selina shall look after you."

He went to the door and called downstairs to his housekeeper.

"I never heard anything so ridiculous," Sir Hector objected.

"Didn't you?" said the old gentleman sardonically. "I'm surprised to hear that. You've been listening to the sound of your own voice for a good many years now, haven't you?"

Perhaps Sir Hector's cold was worse than one was inclined to think, from his grumbling, for if he had not been feeling very ill the prospect of being left in charge of Selina must have cured him instantly.

"When do you take your medicine?" asked Uncle Matthew.

The old gentleman was evidently determined that whatever else was left undone for his nephew's comfort, he should have his full dose of medicine at the hands of the housekeeper. Selina came into the room and settled herself down by the bed with an air of determination that plainly showed the patient what he was in for. Selina's new and more optimistic creed would probably not tend so far as to include Sir Hector Grant among the saved, and what between the patient's pessimism about his state in this world and Selina's pessimism about his state in the world to come, Jasmine felt that if she was ever going to be appreciated by Uncle Hector she should be appreciated by him that night. Meanwhile Uncle Matthew, after settling his nephew, was hurrying her downstairs.

"I have found you a gown after all," he announced, "and a much prettier gown than anything you could find in London nowadays. If that gown yesterday cost thirty-five guineas, the one I have got for you would have cost a hundred and thirty-five guineas."

"Where is it?"

"Where is it?" her uncle repeated. "Why waiting upstairs in your bedroom, of course, for you to put it on. Now be quick, because I don't want to be kept up all night by this ball. I have not been out as late as this for thirty-one years. I'll give you a quarter of an hour to get ready."

Jasmine ran upstairs to her room, where she found Hargreaves and Hopkins standing in astonishment before the dress which Uncle Matthew had brought her. The fragrance of rosemary and lavender pervaded the air, and Jasmine realized that it came from the frock. Uncle Matthew was right when he said that it was unlike any frock that could be found nowadays.

"Wherever did he get it?" wondered Hargreaves.

"It's beautiful material," said Hopkins.

Jasmine was not well enough versed in the history of feminine costume to know how exactly to describe the frock; but she saw at once that it belonged to a bygone generation, and she divined in the same instant that it was a frock belonging to Uncle Matthew's dead wife, one of the frocks that all these years had been kept embalmed in a trunk that was never opened except when he was alone. It was an affair of many flounces and furbelows, the colour nankeen and ivory, the material very fine silk with a profusion of Mechlin lace.

"Whoever saw the like of it?" demanded Hargreaves.

"Whoever did?" Hopkins echoed.

"It would be all right if it had been a fancy dress ball," said Hargreaves.

"Of course, it would have been lovely if it had been fancy dress," Hopkins agreed.

"Well, though it isn't a fancy dress ball," said Jasmine, "I am going to wear it."

The maids held up their hands in astonishment. But Jasmine knew that the crisis of her life had arrived. If she failed in this crisis she saw before her nothing but fifteen dreary years stretching in a vista that ended in the sea front at

Bognor. She realized that, if she rejected this dress and failed to recognize what was probably the first disinterested and kindly action of Uncle Matthew since his wife's death, she should forfeit all claims to consideration in the future. Along with her sharp sense of what her behaviour meant to her in the future, there was another reason for wearing the dress, a reason that was dictated only by motives of consideration for Uncle Matthew himself. It seemed to her that it would be wicked to reject what must have cost him so much emotion to provide. What embarrassment or self-consciousness was not worth while if it was going to repay the sympathy of an old man so long unaccustomed to show sympathy? What if everyone in the ballroom did turn round and stare at her? What if her aunt raged and her cousins decided that she had disgraced them by her eccentric attire? What if Harry Vibart muttered his thanks to Heaven for having escaped from a mad girl like herself? Nothing really mattered except that she should be brave, and that Uncle Matthew should be able to congratulate himself on his kindness.

While Jasmine was driving from Harley Street to the Empress Rooms, she felt like an actress before the first night that was to be the turning-point of her career. She was amused to find that Uncle Matthew had again borrowed the Eneas Grants' brougham, and she could almost have laughed aloud at the thought of Uncle Hector's being dosed by Selina; but presently the silent drive—Uncle Matthew was more voluminously muffled than ever—deprived her of any capacity for being amused, and the thought of her arrival at the dance now filled her with gloomy apprehension. The brougham was jogging along slowly enough, but to Jasmine it seemed to be moving like the fastest automobile, and the journey from Marylebone to Kensington seemed a hundred yards. When they pulled up outside the canopied entrance, Jasmine had a momentary impulse to run away; but the difficulty of extracting Uncle Matthew from the brougham and of unwrapping him sufficiently in the entrance hall to secure his admission as a human being occupied her attention; and almost before she knew what was happening, she had taken the old gentleman's arm and they were entering the ballroom, where the sound of music, the shuffle of dancing feet, the perfume and the heat, the brilliance and the motion, acted like a sedative drug.

And then the music stopped. The dancers turned from their dancing. A thousand eyes regarded her. Lady Grant's nose grew to monstrous size.

"Hullo!" cried a familiar voice. "I say, I've lost my programme, so you'll have to give me every dance to help me through the evening."

Jasmine had let go Uncle Matthew's arm and taken Harry Vibart's, and in a mist, while she was walking across the middle of the ballroom, she looked back a moment and saw Uncle Matthew, like some pachydermatous animal, moving slowly in the direction of her aunt's nose.

THE END

Poor Relations
CHAPTER I

THERE was nothing to distinguish the departure of the *Murmania* from that of any other big liner leaving New York in October for Liverpool or Southampton. At the crowded gangways there was the usual rain of ultimate kisses, from the quayside the usual gale of speeding handkerchiefs. Ladies in blanket-coats handed over to the arrangement of their table-stewards the expensive bouquets presented by friends who, as the case might be, had been glad or sorry to see them go. Middle-aged gentlemen, who were probably not at all conspicuous on shore, at once made their appearance in caps that they might have felt shy about wearing even during their university prime. Children in the first confusion of settling down ate more chocolates from the gift boxes lying about the cabins than they were likely to be given (or perhaps to want) for some time. Two young women with fresh complexions, short skirts, tam o' shanters, brightly colored jumpers, and big bows to their shoes were already on familiar terms with one of the junior ship's officers, and their laughter (which would soon become one of those unending oceanic accompaniments that make land so pleasant again) was already competing with the noise of the crew. Everybody boasted aloud that they fed you really well on the *Murmania*, and hoped silently that perhaps the sense of being imprisoned in a decaying hot-water bottle (or whatever more or less apt comparison was invented to suggest atmosphere below decks) would pass away in the fresh Atlantic breezes. Indeed it might be said, except in the case of a few ivory-faced ladies already lying back with the professional aloofness of those who are a prey to chronic headaches, that outwardly optimism was rampant.

It was not surprising, therefore, that John Touchwood, the successful romantic playwright and unsuccessful realistic novelist, should on finding himself hemmed in by such invincible cheerfulness surrender to his own pleasant fancies of home. This was one of those moments when he was able to feel that the accusation of sentimentality so persistently laid against his work by superior critics was rebutted out of the very mouth of real life. He looked round at his fellow passengers as though he would congratulate them on conforming to his later and more profitable theory of art; and if occasionally he could not help seeing a stewardess with a glance of discreet sympathy reveal to an inquirer the ship's provision for human weakness, he did not on this account feel better disposed toward morbid intrusions either upon art or life, partly because he was himself an excellent sailor and partly because after all as a realist he had unquestionably not been a success.

"Time for a shave before lunch, steward?" he inquired heartily.

"The first bugle will go in about twenty minutes, sir."

John paused for an instant at his own cabin to extract from his suitcase the particular outrage upon conventional headgear (it was a deerstalker of Lovat tweed) that he had evolved for this voyage; and presently he was sitting in the barber shop, wondering at first why anybody should be expected to buy any of the miscellaneous articles exposed for sale at such enhanced prices on every hook and in every nook of the little saloon, and soon afterward seriously considering the advantage of a pair of rope-soled shoes upon a heeling deck.

"Very natty things those, sir," said the barber. "I laid in a stock once at Gib., when we did the southern rowt. Shave you close, sir?"

"Once over, please."

"Skin tender?"

"Rather tender."

"Yes, sir. And the beard's a bit strong, sir. Shave yourself, sir?"

"Usually, but I was up rather early this morning."

"Safety razor, sir?"

"If you think such a description justifiable—yes—a safety."

"They're all the go now, and no mistake ... safety bicycles, safety matches, safety razors ... they've all come in our time ... yes, sir, just a little bit to the right—thank you, sir! Not your first crossing, I take it?"

"No, my third."

"Interesting place, America. But I am from Wandsworth myself. Hair's getting rather thin round the temples. Would you like something to brisken up the growth a bit? Another time? Yes, sir. Thank you, sir. Parting on the left's it, I think?"

"No grease," said John as fiercely as he ever spoke. The barber seemed to replace the pot of brilliantine with regret.

"What would you like then?" He might have been addressing a spoilt child. "Flowers-and-honey? Eau-de-quinine? Or perhaps a friction? I've got lavingder, carnation, wallflower, vilit, lilerk...."

"Bay rum," John declared, firmly.

The barber sighed for such an unadventurous soul; and John, who could not bear to hurt even the most superficial emotions of a barber, changed his mind and threw him into a smiling bustle of gratification.

"Rather strong," John said, half apologetically; for while the friction was being administered the barber had explained in jerks how every time he went ashore in New York or Liverpool he was in the habit of searching about for some novel wash or tonic or pomade, and John did not want to make him feel that his enterprise was unappreciated.

"Strong is it? Well, that's a good fault, sir."

"Yes, I suppose it is."

"What took my fancy was the natural way it smelled."

"Yes, indeed, painfully natural," John agreed.

He stood up and confronted himself in the barber's mirror; regarding the fair, almost florid man, rather under six feet in height, with sanguine blue eyes and full, but clearly cut, lips therein reflected, he came to the comforting conclusion that he did not look his forty-two years and nine months; indeed, while his muffled whistle was shaping rather than uttering the tune of *Nancy Lee*, he nearly asked the barber to guess his age. However, he decided not to risk it, pulled down the lapels of his smoke-colored tweed coat, put on his deerstalker, tipped the barber sufficiently well to secure a parting caress from the brush, promised to meditate the purchase of the rope-soled shoes, and stepped jauntily in the direction of the luncheon bugle. If John Touchwood had not been a successful romantic playwright and an unsuccessful realistic novelist, he might have found in the spectacle of the first lunch of an Atlantic voyage an illustration of human madness and the destructive will of the gods. As it was, his capacity for rapidly covering the domestic offices of the brain with the crimson-ramblers of a lush idealism made him forget the base fabric so prettily if obviously concealed. As it was, he found an exhilaration in all this berserker greed, in the cries of inquisitive children, in the rumpled appearance of women whom the bugle had torn from their unpacking with the urgency of the last trump, in the acrid smell of pickles, and in the persuasive gesture with which the glistening stewards handed the potatoes while they glared angrily at one another over their shoulders. If a cynical realist had in respect of this lunch observed to John that a sow's ear was poor material for a silk purse, he would have contested the universal truth of the proverb, for at this moment he was engaged in chinking the small change of sentimentality in just such a purse.

"How jolly everybody is," he thought, swinging round to his neighbor, a gaunt woman in a kind of draggled mantilla, with an effusion of good-will that expressed itself in a request to pass her the pickled walnuts. John fancied an impulse to move away her chair when she declined his offer; but of course the chair was fixed, and the only sign of her distaste for pickles or conversation was a faint quiver, which to any one less rosy than John might have suggested abhorrence, but which struck him as merely shyness. It was now that for the first time he became aware of a sickly fragrance that was permeating the atmosphere, a fragrance that other people, too, seemed to be noticing by the way in which they were looking suspiciously at the stewards.

"Rather oppressive, some of these flowers," said John to the gaunt lady.

"I don't see any flowers at our end of the table," she replied.

And then with an emotion that was very nearly horror John realized that, though the barber was responsible, he must pay the penalty in a vicarious mortification. His first impulse was to snatch a napkin and wipe his hair; then he decided to leave the table immediately, because after all nobody *could* suspect him, in these as yet unvexed waters, of anything but repletion; finally, hoping that the much powdered lady opposite swathed in mauve chiffons was getting the discredit for the fragrance, he stayed where he was. Nevertheless, the exhilaration had departed; his neighbors all seemed dull folk; and congratulating himself that after this first confused lunch he might reasonably expect to be put at the captain's table in recognition of the celebrity that he could fairly claim, John took from his pocket a bundle of letters which had arrived just before he had left his hotel and busied himself with them for the rest of the meal.

His success as a romantic playwright and his failure—or, as he would have preferred to think of it in the satisfaction of fixing the guilty fragrance upon the lady in mauve chiffons, his comparative failure—as a realistic novelist had not destroyed John's passion for what he called "being practical in small matters," and it was in pursuit of this that having arranged his letters in two heaps which he mentally labeled as "business" and "pleasure" he began with the former, as a child begins (or ought to begin) his tea with the bread and butter and ends it with the plumcake. In John's case, fresh from what really might be described as a triumphant production in New York, the butter was spread so thickly that "business" was too forbidding a name for such pleasantly nutritious communications. His agent had sent him the returns of the second week; and playing to capacity in one of the largest New York theaters is nearer to a material paradise than anything outside the Mohammedan religion. Then there was an offer from one of the chief film companies to produce his romantic drama of two years ago, that wonderful riot of color and Biblical phraseology, *The Fall of Babylon*. They ventured to think that the cinematographer would do his imagination more justice than the theater, particularly as upon their dramatic ranch in California they now had more than a hundred real camels and eight real elephants. John chuckled at the idea of a few animals compensating for the absence of his words, but nevertheless ... the entrance of Nebuchadnezzar, yes, it should be wonderfully effective ... and the great grass-eating scene, yes, that might positively be more impressive on the films ... with one or two audiences it had trembled for a moment between the sublime and the ridiculous. It was a pity that the offer had not arrived before he was leaving New York, but no doubt he should be able to talk it over with the London representatives of the firm. Hullo here was Janet Bond writing to him ... charming woman, charming actress.... He wandered for a few minutes rather vaguely in the maze of her immense handwriting, but disentangled his comprehension at last and deciphered:

THE PARTHENON THEATRE.
Sole Proprietress: Miss Janet Bond.
October 10, 1910.

DEAR MR. TOUCHWOOD,—I wonder if you have forgotten our talk at Sir Herbert's that night? I'm so hoping not. And your scheme for a real Joan of Arc? Do think of me this winter. Your picture of the scene with Gilles de Rais—you see I followed your advice and read him up—has *haunted* me ever since. I can hear the horses' hoofs coming nearer and nearer and the cries of the murdered children. I'm so glad you've had a success with *Lucrezia* in New York. I don't *think* it would suit me from what I read about it. You know how *particular* my public is. That's why I'm so anxious to play the Maid. When will *Lucrezia* be produced in London, and where? There are many rumours. Do come and see me when you get back to England, and I'll tell you who I've thought of to play Gilles. I *think* you'll find him very intelligent. But of course everything depends on your inclination, or should I say inspiration? And then that wonderful speech to the Bishop! How does it begin? "Bishop, thou hast betrayed thy holy trust." Do be a little flattered that I've remembered that line. It needn't *all* be in blank verse, and I think little Truscott would be so good as the Bishop. You see how *enthusiastic* I am and how I *believe* in the idea. All good wishes.

John certainly was a little flattered that Miss Bond should have remembered the Maid's great speech to the Bishop of Beauvais, and the actress's enthusiasm roused in him an answering flame, so that the cruet before him began to look like the castelated walls of Orleans, and while his gaze was fixed upon the bowl of salad he began to compose *Act II. Scene I—Open country. Enter Joan on horseback. From the summit of a grassy knoll she searches the horizon.* So fixedly was John regarding his heroine on top of the salad that the head steward came over and asked anxiously if there was anything the matter with it. And even when John assured him that there was nothing he took it away and told one of the under-stewards to remove the caterpillar and bring a fresh bowl. Meanwhile, John had picked up theother bundle of letters and begun to read his news from home.

65 HILL ROAD,
St. John's Wood, N.W.,
October 10.

DEAR JOHN,—We have just read in the *Telegraph* of your great success and we are both very glad. Edith writes me that she did have a letter from you. I dare say you thought she would send it on to us but she didn't, and of course I understand you're busy only I should have liked to have had a letter ourselves. James asks me to tell you that he is probably going to do a book on the Cymbalist movement in literature. He says that the time has come to take a final survey of it. He is also writing some articles for the *Fortnightly Review*. We shall all be so glad to welcome you home again.

Your affectionate sister-in-law,
BEATRICE TOUCHWOOD.

"Poor Beatrice," thought John, penitently. "I ought to have sent her a line. She's a good soul. And James ... what a plucky fellow he is! Always full of schemes for books and articles. Wonderful really, to go on writing for an audience of about twenty people. And I used to grumble because my novels hadn't world-wide circulations. Poor old James ... a good fellow."

He picked up the next letter; which he found was from his other sister-in-law.

HALMA HOUSE,
198 Earl's Court Square, S.W.,
October 9.

DEAR JOHN,—Well, you've had a hit with *Lucrezia*, lucky man! If you sent out an Australian company, don't you think I might play lead? I quite understand that you couldn't manage it for me either in London or America, but after all you *are* the author and you surely have *some* say in the cast. I've got an understudy at the Parthenon, but I can't stand Janet. Such a selfish actress. She literally doesn't think of any one but herself. There's a chance I may get a decent part on tour with Lambton this autumn. George isn't very well, and it's been rather miserable this wet summer in the boarding house as Bertram and Viola were ill and kept away from school. I would have suggested their going down to Ambles, but Hilda was so very unpleasant when I just hinted at the idea that I preferred to keep them with me in town. Both children ask every day when you're coming home. You're quite the favourite uncle. George was delighted with your success. Poor old boy, he's had another financial disappointment, and your success was quite a consolation.

ELEANOR.

"I wish Eleanor was anywhere but on the stage," John sighed. "But she's a plucky woman. I *must* write her a part in my next play. Now for Hilda."

He opened his sister's letter with the most genial anticipation, because it was written from his new country house in Hampshire, that county house which he had coveted for so long and to which the now faintly increasing motion of the *Murmania* reminded him that he was fast returning.

AMBLES,
Wrottesford, Hants,
October 11.

MY DEAR JOHN,—Just a line to congratulate you on your new success. Lots of money in it, I suppose. Dear Harold is quite well and happy at Ambles. Quite the young squire! I had a little coolness with Eleanor—entirely on her side of course, but Bertram is really such a *bad* influence for Harold and so I told her that I did not think you would like her to take possession of your new house before you'd had time to live in it yourself. Besides, so many children all at once would have disturbed poor Mama. Edith drove over with Frida the other day and tells me you wrote to her. I should have liked a letter, too, but you always spoil poor Edith. Poor little Frida looks very peaky. Much love from Harold who is always asking when you're coming home. Mama is very well, I'm glad to say.

Your affectionate sister,
HILDA CURTIS.

"She might have told me a little more about the house," John murmured to himself. And then he began to dream about Ambles and to plant old-fashioned flowers along its mellow red-brick garden walls. "I shall be in time to see the colouring of the woods," he thought. The *Murmania* answered his aspiration with a plunge, and several of the rumpled ladies rose hurriedly from table to prostrate themselves for the rest of the voyage. John opened a fourth letter from England.

THE VICARAGE,
Newton Candover, Hants,
October 7.

MY DEAREST JOHN,—I was so glad to get your letter, and so glad to hear of your success. Laurence says that if he were not a vicar he should like to be a dramatic author. In fact, he's writing a play now on a Biblical subject, but he fears he will have trouble with the Bishop, as it takes a very broad view of Christianity. You know that Laurence has recently become very broad? He thinks the village people like it, but unfortunately old Mrs. Paxton—you know who I mean—the patroness of the living—is so bigoted that Laurence has had a great deal of trouble with her. I'm sorry to say that dear little Frida is looking thin. We think it's the wet summer. Nothing but rain. Ambles was looking beautiful when we drove over last week, but Harold is a little bumptious and Hilda does not seem to see his faults. Dear Mama was looking *very* well—better than I've seen her for ages. Frida sends such a lot of love to dearest Uncle John. She never stops talking about you. I sometimes get quite jealous for Laurence. Not really, of course, because family affection is the foundation of civil life. Laurence is out in the garden speaking to a man whose pig got into our conservatory this morning. Much love.

Your loving sister,
EDITH.

John put the letter down with a faint sigh: Edith was his favorite sister, but he often wished that she had not married a parson. Then he took up the last letter of the family packet, which was from his housekeeper in Church Row.

39 CHURCH ROW,
Hampstead, N.W.

DEAR SIR,—This is to inform you with the present that everythink is very well at your house and that Maud and Elsa is very well as it leaves me at present. We as heard nothink from Emily since she as gone down to Hambles your other house, and we hope which is Maud, Elsa and myself you wont spend all your time out of London which is looking lovely at present with the leaves beginning to turn and all. With dutiful respects from Maud, Elsa and self, I am,

Your obedient servant,
MARY WORFOLK.

"Dear old Mrs. Worfolk. She's already quite jealous of Ambles ... charming trait really, for after all it means she appreciates Church Row. Upon my soul, I feel a bit jealous of Ambles myself."

John began to ponder the pleasant heights of Hampstead and to think of the pale blue October sky and of the yellow leaves shuffling and slipping along the quiet alleys in the autumn wind; to think, too, of his library window and of London spread out below in a refulgence of smoke and gold; to think of the chrysanthemums in his little garden and of the sparrows' chirping in the Virginia-creeper that would soon be all aglow like a well banked-up fire against his coming. Five delightful letters really, every one of them full of good wishes and cordial affection! The *Murmania* swooped forward, and there was a faint tingle of glass and cutlery. John gathered up his correspondence to go on deck and bless the Atlantic for being the pathway to home. As he rose from the table he heard a voice say:

"Yes, my dear thing, but I've never been a poor relation yet, and I don't intend to start now."

The saloon was empty except for himself and two women opposite, the climax of whose conversation had come with such a harsh fitness of comment upon the letters he had just been reading. John was angry with himself for the dint so easily made upon the romantic shield he upheld against life's onset; he felt that he had somehow been led into an ambush where all his noblest sentiments had been massacred; five bells sounded upon the empty saloon with an almost funereal gravity; and, when the two women passed out, John, notwithstanding the injured regard of his steward, sat down again and read right through the family letters from a fresh standpoint. The fact of it was that there had turned out to be very few currants in the cake, for the eating of which he had prepared himself with such well-buttered bread. Few currants? There was not a single one, unless Mrs. Worfolk's antagonism to the idea of Ambles might be considered a gritty shred of a currant. John rose at once when he had finished his letters, put them in his pocket, and followed the unconscious disturbers of his hearth on deck. He soon caught sight of them again where, arm in arm, they were pacing the sunlit starboard side and apparently enjoying the gusty southwest wind. John wondered how long it would be before he was given a suitable opportunity to make their acquaintance, and tried to regulate his promenade so that he should always meet them face to face either aft or forward, but never amidships where heavily muffled passengers reclined in critical contemplation of their fellow-travellers over the top of the last popular novel. "Some men, you know," he told himself, "would join their walk with a mere remark about the weather. They wouldn't stop to consider if their company was welcome. They'd be so serenely satisfied with themselves that they'd actually succeed ... yes, confound them ... they'd bring it off! Yet, after all, I suppose in a way that without vanity I might presume they *would* be rather interested to meet me. Because, of course, there's no doubt that people *are* interested in authors. But, it's no good ... I can't do that ... this is really one of those moments when I feel as if I was still seventeen years old ... shyness, I suppose ... yet the rest of my family aren't shy."

This took John's thoughts back to his relations, but to a much less complacent point of view of them than before that maliciously apposite remark overheard in the saloon had lighted up the group as abruptly and unbecomingly as a magnesium flash. However inconsistent he might appear, he was afraid that he should be more critical of them in future. He began to long to talk over his affairs with that girl and, looking up at this moment, he caught her eyes, which either because the weather was so gusty or because he was so ready to hang decorations round a simple fact seemed to him like calm moorland pools, deep violet-brown pools in heathery solitudes. Her complexion had the texture of a rose in November, the texture that gains a rare lucency from the grayness and moisture by which one might suppose it would be ruined. She was wearing a coat and skirt of Harris tweed of a shade of misty green, and with her slim figure and fine features she seemed at first glance not more than twenty. But John had not passed her another half-dozen times before he had decided that she was almost a woman of thirty. He looked to see if she was wearing a wedding ring and was already enough interested in her to be glad that she was not. This relief was, of course, not at all due to any vision of himself in a more intimate relationship; but merely because he was glad to find that her personality, of which he was by now more definitely aware than of her beauty (well, not beauty, but charm, and yet perhaps after all he was being too grudging in not awarding her positive beauty) would be her own. There was something distinctly romantic in this beautiful young woman of nearly thirty leading her own life unimpeded by a loud-voiced husband.

Of course, the husband might have had a gentle voice, but usually this type of woman seemed a prey to bluffness and bigness, as if to display her atmosphere charms she had need of a rugged landscape for a background. He found himself glibly thinking of her as a type; but with what type could she be classified? Surely she was attracting him by being exceptional rather than typical; and John soothed his alarmed celibacy by insisting that she appealed to him with a hint of virginal wisdom which promised a perfect intercourse, if only their acquaintanceship could be achieved naturally, that is to say, without the least suggestion of an ulterior object. *She had never been a poor relation yet, and she did not intend to start being one now.* Of course, such a woman was still unmarried. But how had she avoided being a poor relation? What was her work? Why was she coming home to England? And who was her companion? He looked at the other woman who walked beside her with a boyish slouch, wore gold pince-nez, and had a tight mouth, not naturally tight, but one that had been tightened by driving and riding. It was absurd to walk up and down forever like this; the acquaintance must be made immediately or not at all; it would never do to hang round them waiting for an opportunity of conversation. John decided to venture a simple remark the next time he met them face to face; but when he arrived at the after end of the promenade deck they had vanished, and the embarrassing thought occurred to him that perhaps having divined his intention they had thus deliberately snubbed him. He went to the rail and leaned over to watch the water undulating past; a sudden gust caught his cap and took it out to sea. He clapped his hand too late to his head; a fragrance of carnations breathed upon the salt windy sunlight; a voice behind him, softly tremulous with laughter, murmured:

"I say, bad luck."

John commended his deerstalker to the care of all the kindly Oceanides and turned round: it was quite easy after all, and he was glad that he had not thought of deliberately letting his cap blow into the sea.

"Look, it's actually floating like a boat," she exclaimed.

"Yes, it was shaped like a boat," John said; he was thinking how absurd it was now to fancy that swiftly vanishing, utterly inappropriate piece of concave tweed should only a few seconds ago have been worn the other way round on a human head.

"But you mustn't catch cold," she added. "Haven't you another cap?"

John did possess another cap, one that just before he left England he had bought about dusk in the Burlington Arcade, one which in the velvety bloom of a July evening had seemed worthy of summer skies and seas, but which in the glare of the following day had seemed more like the shreds of barbaric attire that are brought back by travelers from exotic lands to be taken out of a glass case and shown to visitors when the conversation is flagging on Sunday afternoons in the home counties. Now if John's plays were full of fierce hues, if his novels had been sepia studies of realism which the public considered painful and the critics described as painstaking, his private life had been of a mild uniform pink, a pinkishness that recalled the chaste hospitality of the best spare bedroom. Never yet in that pink life had he let himself go to the extent of wearing a cap, which, even if worn afloat by a colored prizefighter crossing the Atlantic to defend or challenge supremacy, would have created an amused consternation, but which on the head of a well-known romantic playwright must arouse at least dismay and possibly panic. Yet this John (he had reached the point of regarding himself with objective surprise), the pinkishness of whose life, though it might be a protest against cynicism and gloom, was eternally half-way to a blush, went off to his cabin with the intention of putting on that cap. With himself for a while he argued that something must be done to imprison the smell of carnations, that a bowler hat would look absurd, that he really must not catch cold; but all the time this John knew perfectly well that what he really wanted was to give a practical demonstration of his youth. This John did not care a damn about his success as a romantic playwright, but he did care a great deal that these two young women should vote him a suitable companion for the rest of the voyage.

"Why, it's really not so bad," he assured himself, when before the mirror he tried to judge the effect. "I rather think it's better than the other one. Of course, if I had seen when I bought it that the checks were purple and not black I dare say I shouldn't have bought it—but, by Jove, I'm rather glad I didn't notice them. After all, I have a right to be a little eccentric in my costume. What the deuce does it matter to me if people do stare? Let them stare! I shall be the last of the lot to feel seasick, anyway."

John walked defiantly back to the promenade deck, and several people who had not bothered to remark the well-groomed florid man before now asked who he was, and followed his progress along the deck with the easily interested gaze of the transatlantic passenger.

For the rest of the voyage John never knew whether the attention his entrance into the saloon always evoked was due to his being the man who wore the unusual cap or to his being the man who had written *The Fall of Babylon*; nor, indeed, did he bother to make sure, for he was fortified during the rest of the voyage by the company of Miss Doris Hamilton and Miss Ida Merritt and thoroughly enjoyed himself.

"Now am I attributing to Miss Hamilton more discretion than she's really got?" he asked himself on the last night of the passage, a stormy night off the Irish coast, while he swayed before the mirror in the creaking cabin. John was accustomed, like most men with clear-cut profiles, to take advice from his reflection, and perhaps it was his dramatic instinct that led him usually to talk aloud to this lifelong friend. "Have I in fact been too impulsive in this friendship? Have I? That's the question. I certainly told her a lot about myself, and I think she appreciated my confidence. Yet suppose that she's just an ordinary young woman and goes gossiping all over England about meeting me? I really must remember that I'm no longer a nonentity and that, though Miss Hamilton is not a journalist, her friend is, and, what is more, confessed that the sole object of her visit to America had been to interview distinguished men with the help of Miss Hamilton. The way she spoke about her victims reminded me of the way that fellow in the smoking-saloon talked about the tarpon fishing off Florida ... famous American statesmen, financiers, and architects existed quite impersonally for her to be caught just like tarpon. Really when I come to think of it I've been at the end of Miss Merritt's rod for five days, and as with all the others the bait was Miss Hamilton."

John's mistrust in the prudence of his behavior during the voyage had been suddenly roused by the prospect of reaching Liverpool next day. The word positively exuded disillusionment; it was as anti-romantic as a notebook of Herbert Spencer. He undressed and got into his bunk; the motion of the ship and the continual opening and shutting of cabin doors all the way along the corridor kept him from sleep, and for a long time he lay awake while the delicious freedom of the seas was gradually enslaved by the sullen, prosaic, puritanical, bilious word—Liverpool. He had come down to his cabin, full of the exhilaration of a last quick stroll up and down the spray-whipped deck; he had come down from a long and pleasant talk all about himself where he and Miss Hamilton had sat in the lee of some part of a ship's furniture the name of which he did not know and did not like to ask, a long and pleasant talk, cozily wrapped in two rugs glistening faintly in the starlight with salty rime; he had come down from a successful elimination of Miss Merritt, his whole personality marinated in freedom, he might say; and now the mere thought of Liverpool was enough to disenchant him and to make him feel rather like a man who was recovering from a brilliant, a too brilliant revelation of himself provoked by champagne. He began to piece together the conversation and search for indiscretions. To begin with, he had certainly talked a great deal too much about himself; it was not dignified for a man in his position to be so prodigally frank with a young woman he had only known for five days. Suppose she had been laughing at him all the time? Suppose that even now she was laughing at him with Miss Merritt? "Good heavens, what an amount I told her," John gasped aloud. "I even told her what my real circulation was when I used to write novels, and I very nearly told her how much I made out of *The Fall of Babylon*, though since that really was a good deal, it wouldn't have mattered so much. And what did I say about my family? Well, perhaps that isn't so important. But how much did I tell her of my scheme for *Joan of Arc*? Why, she might have been my confidential secretary by the way I talked. My confidential secretary? And why not? I am entitled to a secretary—in fact my position demands a secretary. But would she accept such a post? Now don't let me be impulsive."

John began to laugh at himself for a quality in which as a matter of fact he was, if anything, deficient. He often used to chaff himself, but, of course, always without the least hint of ill-nature, which is perhaps why he usually selected imaginary characteristics for genial reproof.

"Impulsive dog," he said to himself. "Go to sleep, and don't forget that confidential secretaries afloat and confidential secretaries ashore are very different propositions. Yes, you thought you were being very clever when you bought those rope-soled shoes to keep your balance on a slippery deck, but you ought to have bought a rope-soled cap to keep your head from slipping."

This seemed to John in the easy optimism that prevails upon the borders of sleep an excellent joke, and he passed with a chuckle through the ivory gate.

The next day John behaved helpfully and politely at the Customs, and indeed continued to be helpful and polite until his companions of the voyage were established in a taxi at Euston. He had carefully written down the Hamiltons' address with a view to calling on them one day, but even while he was writing the number of the square in Chelsea he was thinking about Ambles and trying to decide whether he should make a dash across London to Waterloo on the chance of catching the 9:05 P.M. or spend the night at his house in Church Row.

"I think perhaps I'd better stay in town to-night," he said. "Good-by. Most delightful trip across—see you both again soon, I hope. You don't advise me to try for the 9:05?" he asked once more, anxiously.

Miss Hamilton laughed from the depths of the taxi; when she laughed, for the briefest moment John felt an Atlantic breeze sweep through the railway station.

"*I* recommend a good night's rest," she said.

So John's last thought of her was of a nice practical young woman; but, as he once again told himself, the idea of a secretary was absurd. Besides, did she even know shorthand?

"Do you know shorthand?" he turned round to shout as the taxi buzzed away; he did not hear her answer, if answer there was.

"Of course I can always write," he decided, and without one sigh he busied himself with securing his own taxi for Hampstead.

CHAPTER II

"I'VE got too many caps, Mrs. Worfolk," John proclaimed next morning to his housekeeper. "You can give this one away."

"Yes, sir. Who would you like it given to?"

"Oh, anybody, anybody. Tramps very often ask for old boots, don't they? Some tramp might like it."

"Would you have any erbjections if I give it to my nephew, sir?"

"None whatever."

"It seems almost too perky for a tramp, sir; and my sister's boy—well, he's just at the age when they like to dress theirselves up a bit. He's doing very well, too. His employers is extremely satisfied with the way he's doing. Extremely satisfied, his employers are."

"I'm delighted to hear it."

"Yes, sir. Well, it's been some consolation to my poor sister, I mean to say, after the way her husband behaved hisself, and it's to be hoped Herbert'll take fair warning. Let me see, you *will* be having lunch at home I think you said?"

John winced: this was precisely what he would have avoided by catching the 9:05 at Waterloo last night.

"I shan't be in to lunch for a few days, Mrs. Worfolk, no—er—nor to dinner either as a matter of fact. No—in fact I'll be down in the country. I must see after things there, you know," he added with an attempt to suggest as jovially as possible a real anxiety about his new house.

"The country, oh yes," repeated Mrs. Worfolk grimly; John saw the beech-woods round Ambles blasted by his housekeeper's disapproval.

"You wouldn't care to—er—come down and give a look round yourself, Mrs. Worfolk? My sister, Mrs. Curtis—"

"Oh, I should prefer not to intrude in any way, sir. But if you insist, why, of course—"

"Oh no, I don't insist," John hurriedly interposed.

"No, sir. Well, we shall all have to get used to being left alone nowadays, and that's all there is to it."

"But I shall be back in a few days, Mrs. Worfolk. I'm a Cockney at heart, you know. Just at first—"

Mrs. Worfolk shook her head and waddled tragically to the door.

"There's nothing else you'll be wanting this morning, sir?" she turned to ask in accents that seemed to convey forgiveness of her master in spite of everything.

"No, thank you, Mrs. Worfolk. Please send Maud up to help me pack. Good heavens," he added to himself when his housekeeper had left the room, "why shouldn't I be allowed a country house? And I suppose the next thing is that James and Beatrice and George and Eleanor will all be offended because I didn't go tearing round to see them the moment I arrived. One's relations never understand that after the production of a play one requires a little rest. Besides, I must get on with my new play. I absolutely *must*."

John's tendency to abhor the vacuum of success was corrected by the arrival of Maud, the parlor-maid, whose statuesque anemia and impersonal neatness put something in it. Before leaving for America he had supplemented the rather hasty preliminary furnishing of his new house by ordering from his tailor a variety of country costumes. These Maud, with feminine intuition superimposed on what she would have called her "understanding of valeting," at once produced for his visit to Ambles; John in the prospect of half a dozen unworn peat-perfumed suits of tweed flung behind him any lingering doubt about there being something in success, and with the recapture of his enthusiasm for what he called "jolly things" was anxious that Maud should share in it.

"Do you think these new things are a success, Maud?" he asked, perhaps a little too boisterously. At any rate, the parlor-maid's comprehension of valeting had apparently never been so widely stretched, for a faint coralline blush tinted her waxen cheeks.

"They seem very nice, sir," she murmured, with a slight stress upon the verb.

John felt that he had trespassed too far upon the confines of Maud's humanity and retreated hurriedly. He would have liked to explain that his inquiry had merely been a venture into abstract esthetics and that he had not had the least intention of extracting her opinion about these suits *on him*; but he felt that an attempt at explanation would embarrass her, and he hummed instead over a selection of ties, as a bee hums from flower to flower in a garden, careless of the gardener who close at hand is potting up plants.

"I will take these ties," he announced on the last stave of *A Fine Old English Gentleman*.

Maud noted them gravely.

"And I shall have a few books. Perhaps there won't be room for them?"

"There won't be room for them, not in your dressing-case, sir."

"Oh, I know there won't be room in that," said John, bitterly.

His dressing-case might be considered the medal he had struck in honor of *The Fall of Babylon*: he had passed it every morning on his way to rehearsals and, dreaming of the triumph that might soon be his, had vowed he would buy it were such a triumph granted. It had cost £75, was heavy enough when empty to strain his wrist and when full to break his back, and it contained more parasites of the toilet table and the writing desk than one could have supposed imaginable. These parasites each possessed an abode of such individual shape that leaving them behind made no difference to the number of really useful articles, like pajamas, that could be carried in the cubic space lined with blue corded silk on which they looked down like the inconvenient houses of a fashionable square. Therefore wherever John went, the fittings went too, a glittering worthless mob of cut-glass, pigskin, tortoiseshell and ivory.

"But in my portmanteau," John persisted. "Won't there be room there?"

"I might squeeze them in," Maud admitted. "It depends what boots you're wanting to take with you, sir."

"Never mind," he sighed. "I can make a separate parcel of them."

"There's the basket what we were going to use for the cat, sir."

"No, I should prefer a brown paper parcel," he decided. It would be improper for the books out of which the historical trappings of his *Joan of Arc* were to be manufactured to travel in a lying-in hospital for cats.

John left Maud to finish the packing and went downstairs to his library. This double room of fine proportions was, as one might expect from the library of a popular writer, the core—the veritable omphalos of the house; with its fluted pilasters, cream-colored panels and cherub-haunted ceiling, the expanse of city and sky visible from three sedate windows at the south end and the glimpse of a busy Hampstead street caught from those facing north, not to speak of the prismatic rows of books, it was a room worthy of art's most remunerative triumphs, the nursery of inspiration, and, save for a slight suggestion that the Muses sometimes drank afternoon tea there, the room of an indomitable bachelor. When John stepped upon the wreaths, ribbons, and full-blown roses of the threadbare Aubusson rug that floated like gossamer upon a green carpet of Axminster pile as soft as some historic lawn, he was sure that success was not a vacuum. In his now optimistic mood he hoped ultimately to receive from Ambles the kind of congratulatory benediction that the library at Church Row always bestowed upon his footsteps. Indeed, if he had not had such an ambition for his country house, he could scarcely have endured to quit even for a week this library, where fires were burning in two grates and where the smoke of his Partaga was haunting, like a complacent ghost, the imperturbable air. John possessed another library at Ambles, but he had not yet had time to do more than hurriedly stock it with the standard works that he felt no country house should be without. His library in London was the outcome of historical research preparatory to writing his romantic plays; and since all works of popular historical interest are bound with a much more lavish profusion of color and ornament even than the works of fiction to which they most nearly approximate, John's shelves outwardly resembled rather a collection of armor than a collection of books. There were, of course, many books the insides of which were sufficiently valuable to excuse their dingy exterior; but none of these occupied the line, where romance after romance of exiled queens, confession after confession of morganatic wives, memoir after memoir from above and below stairs, together with catch-penny alliterative gatherings as of rude regents and libidinous landgraves flashed in a gorgeous superficiality of gilt and text. In order to amass the necessary material for a play about Joan of Arc John did not concern himself with original documents. He assumed, perhaps rightly, that a Camembert cheese is more palatable and certainly more portable than a herd of unmilked cows. To dramatize the life of Joan of Arc he took from his shelves *Saints and Sinners of the Fifteenth Century* ... but a catalogue is unnecessary: enough that when the heap of volumes chosen stood upon his desk it glittered like the Maid herself before the walls of Orleans.

"After all," as John had once pointed out in a moment of exasperation to his brother, James, the critic, "Shakespeare didn't sit all day in the reading-room of the British Museum."

An hour later the playwright, equipped alike for country rambles and poetic excursions, was sitting in a first-class compartment of a London and South-Western railway train; two hours after that he was sitting in the Wrottesford fly swishing along between high hazel hedges of golden-brown.

"I shall have to see about getting a dog-cart," he exclaimed, when after a five minutes' struggle to let down the window with the aid of a strap that looked like an Anglican stole he had succeeded in opening the door and nearly falling head-long into the lane.

"You have to let down the window *before* you get out," said the driver reproachfully, trying to hammer the frameless window back into place and making such a noise about it that John could not bear to accentuate by argument the outrage that he was offering to this morning of exquisite decline, on which earth seemed to be floating away into a windless infinity like one of her own dead leaves. No, on such a morning controversy was impossible, but he should certainly take immediate steps to acquire a dog-cart.

"For it's like being jolted in a badly made coffin," he thought, when he was once more encased in the fly and, having left the high road behind, was driving under an avenue of sycamores bordered by a small stream, the water of which was stained to the color of sherry by the sunlight glowing down through the arches of tawny leaves overhead. To John this avenue always seemed the entrance to a vast park surrounding his country house; it was indeed an almost unfrequented road, grass-grown in the center and lively with rabbits during most of the day, so that his imagination of ancestral approaches was easily stimulated and he felt like a figure in a painting by Marcus Stone. It was lucky that John's sanguine imagination could so often satisfy his ambition; prosperous playwright though he was, he had not yet made nearly enough money to buy a real park. However, in his present character of an eighteenth-century squire he determined, should the film version of *The Fall of Babylon* turn out successful, to buy a lawny meadow of twenty acres that would add much to the dignity and seclusion of Ambles, the boundaries of which at the back were now overlooked by a herd of fierce Kerry cows who occupied the meadow and during the summer had made John's practice shots with a brassy too much like big-game shooting to be pleasant or safe. After about a mile the avenue came to an end where a narrow curved bridge spanned the stream, which now flowed away to the left along the bottom of a densely wooded hillside. The fly crossed over with an impunity that was surprising in face of a printed warning that extraordinary vehicles should avoid this bridge, and began to climb the slope by a wide diagonal track between bushes of holly, the green of which seemed vivid and glossy against the prevailing brown. The noise of the wheels was deadened by the heavy drift of beech leaves, and the stillness of this russet world, except for the occasional scream of a jay or the flapping of disturbed pigeons, demanded from John's illustrative fancy something more remote and Gothic than the eighteenth century.

"Malory," he said to himself. "Absolute Malory. It's almost impossible not to believe that Sir Gawaine might not come galloping down through this wood."

Eager to put himself still more deeply in accord with the romantic atmosphere, John tried this time to open the door of the fly with the intention of walking meditatively up the hill in its wake; the door remained fast; but he managed to open the window, or rather he broke it.

"I've a jolly good mind to get a motor," he exclaimed, savagely.

Every knight errant's horse in the neighborhood bolted at the thought, and by the time John had reached the top of the hill and emerged upon a wide stretch of common land dotted with ancient hawthorns in full crimson berry he was very much in the present. For there on the other side of the common, flanked by shelving woods of oak and beech and backed by rising downs on which a milky sky ruffled its breast like a huge swan lazily floating, stood Ambles, a solitary, deep-hued, Elizabethan house with dreaming chimney-stacks and tumbled mossy roofs and garden walls rising from the heaped amethysts of innumerable Michaelmas daisies.

"My house," John murmured in a paroxysm of ownership.

The noise of the approaching fly had drawn expectant figures to the gate; John, who had gratified affection, curiosity and ostentation by sending a wireless message from the *Murmania*, a telegram from Liverpool yesterday, and another from Euston last night to announce his swift arrival, had therefore only himself to thank for perceiving in the group the black figure of his brother-in-law, the Reverend Laurence Armitage. He drove away the scarcely formed feeling of depression by supposing that Edith could not by herself have trundled the barrel-shaped vicarage pony all the way from Newton Candover to Ambles, and, finding that the left-hand door of the fly was unexpectedly susceptible to the prompting of its handle, he alighted with such rapidity that not one of his smiling relations could have had any impression but that he was bounding to greet them. The two sisters were so conscious of their rich unmarried brother's impulsive advance that each incited her own child to responsive bounds so that they might meet him half-way along the path to the front door, in the harborage of which Grandma (whose morning nap had been interrupted by a sudden immersion in two shawls, and a rapid swim with Emily, the maid from London, acting as lifebuoy down the billowy passages and stairs of the old house) rocked in breathless anticipation of the filial salute.

"Welcome back, my dear Johnnie," the old lady panted.

"How are you, mother? What, another new cap?"

Old Mrs. Touchwood patted her head complacently. "We bought it at Threadgale's in Galton. The ribbons are the new hollyhock red."

"Delightful!" John exclaimed. "And who helped you to choose it? Little Frida here?"

"Nobody *helped* me, Johnnie. Hilda accompanied me into Galton; but she wanted to buy a sardine-opener for the house."

John had not for a moment imagined that his mother had wanted any advice about a cap; but inasmuch as Frida, in what was intended to be a demonstrative welcome, prompted by her mother, was rubbing her head against his ribs like a calf against a fence, he had felt he ought to hook her to the conversation somehow. John's concern about Frida was solved by the others' gathering round him for greetings.

First Hilda offered her sallow cheek, patting while he kissed it her brother on the back with one hand, and with the other manipulating Harold in such a way as to give John the impression that his nephew was being forced into his waistcoat pocket.

"He feels you're his father now," whispered Hilda with a look that was meant to express the tender resignation of widowhood, but which only succeeded in suggesting a covetous maternity. John doubted if Harold felt anything but a desire to escape from being sandwiched between his mother's crape and his uncle's watch chain, and he turned to embrace Edith, whose cheeks, soft and pink as a toy balloon, were floating tremulously expectant upon the glinting autumn air.

"We've been so anxious about you," Edith murmured. "And Laurence has such a lot to talk over with you."

John, with a slight sinking that was not altogether due to its being past his usual luncheon hour, turned to be welcomed by his brother-in-law.

The vicar of Newton Candover's serenity if he had not been a tall and handsome man might have been mistaken for smugness; as it was, his personality enveloped the scene with a ceremonious dignity that was not less than archidiaconal, and except for his comparative youthfulness (he was the same age as John) might well have been considered archiepiscopal.

"Edith has been anxious about you. Indeed, we have all been anxious about you," he intoned, offering his hand to John, for whom the sweet damp odors of autumn became a whiff of pious women's veils, while the leaves fluttering gently down from the tulip tree in the middle of the lawn lisped like the India-paper of prayer-books.

"I've got an air-gun, Uncle John," ejaculated Harold, who having for some time been inhaling the necessary breath now expelled the sentence in a burst as if he had been an air-gun himself. John hailed the announcement almost effusively; it reached him with the kind of relief with which in childhood he had heard the number of the final hymn announced; and a robin piping his delicate tune from the garden wall was welcome as birdsong in a churchyard had been after service on Sundays handicapped by the litany.

"Would you like to see me shoot at something?" Harold went on, hastily cramming his mouth with slugs.

"Not now, dear," said Hilda, hastily. "Uncle John is tired. And don't eat sweets just before lunch."

"Well, it wouldn't tire him to see me shoot at something. And I'm not eating sweets. I'm getting ready to load."

"Let the poor child shoot if he wants to," Grandma put in.

Harold beamed ferociously through his spectacles, took a slug from his mouth, fitted it into the air-gun, and fired, bringing down two leaves from an espalier pear. Everybody applauded him, because everybody felt glad that it had not been a window or perhaps even himself; the robin cocked his tail contemptuously and flew away.

"And now I must go and get ready for lunch," said John, who thought a second shot might be less innocuous, and was moreover really hungry. His bedroom, dimity draped, had a pleasant rustic simplicity, but he decided that it wanted living in: the atmosphere at present was too much that of a well-recommended country inn.

"Yes, it wants living in," said John to himself. "I shall put in a good month here and break the back of Joan of Arc."

"What skin is this, Uncle John?" a serious voice at his elbow inquired. John started; he had not observed Harold's scout-like entrance.

"What skin is that, my boy?" he repeated in what he thought was the right tone of avuncular jocularity and looking down at Harold, who was examining with myopic intensity the dressing-case. "That is the skin of a white elephant."

"But it's brown," Harold objected.

John rashly decided to extend his facetiousness.

"Yes, well, white elephants turn brown when they're shot, just as lobsters turn red when they're boiled."

"Who shot it?"

"Oh, I don't know—probably some friend of the gentleman who keeps the shop where I bought it."

"When?"

"Well, I can't exactly say when—but probably about three years ago."

"Father used to shoot elephants, didn't he?"

"Yes, my boy, your father used to shoot elephants."

"Perhaps he shot this one."

"Perhaps he did."

"Was he a friend of the gentleman who keeps the shop where you bought it?"

"I shouldn't be surprised," said John.

"Wouldn't you?" said Harold, skeptically. "My father was an asplorer. When I'm big I'm going to be an asplorer, too; but I sha'n't be friends with shopkeepers."

"Confounded little snob," John thought, and began to look for his nailbrush, the address of whose palatial residence of pigskin only Maud knew.

"What are you looking for, Uncle John?" Harold asked.

"I'm looking for my nailbrush, Harold."

"Why?"

"To clean my nails."

"Are they dirty?"

"Well, they're just a little grubby after the railway journey."

"Mine aren't," Harold affirmed in a lofty tone. Then after a minute he added: "I thought perhaps you were looking for the present you brought me from America."

John turned pale and made up his mind to creep unobserved after lunch into the market town of Galton and visit the local toyshop. It would be an infernal nuisance, but it served him right for omitting to bring presents either for his nephew or his niece.

"You're too smart," he said nervously to Harold. "Present time will be after tea." The sentence sounded contradictory somehow, and he changed it to "the time for presents will be five o'clock."

"Why?" Harold asked.

John was saved from answering by a tap at the door, followed by the entrance of Mrs. Curtis.

"Oh, Harold's with you?" she exclaimed, as if it were the most surprising juxtaposition in the world.

"Yes, Harold's with me," John agreed.

"You mustn't let him bother you, but he's been so looking forward to your arrival. *When* is Uncle coming, he kept asking."

"Did he ask *why* I was coming?"

Hilda looked at her brother blankly, and John made up his mind to try that look on Harold some time.

"Have you got everything you want?" she asked, solicitously.

"He hasn't got his nailbrush," said Harold.

Hilda assumed an expression of exaggerated alarm.

"Oh dear, I hope it hasn't been lost."

"No, no, no, it'll turn up in one of the glass bottles. I was just telling Harold that I haven't really begun my unpacking yet."

"Uncle John's brought me a present from America," Harold proclaimed in accents of greedy pride.

Hilda seized her brother's hand affectionately.

"Now you oughtn't to have done that. It's spoiling him. It really is. Harold never expects presents."

"What a liar," thought John. "But not a bigger one than I am myself," he supplemented, and then he announced aloud that he must go into Galton after lunch and send off an important telegram to his agent.

"I wonder ..." Hilda began, but with an arch look she paused and seemed to thrust aside temptation.

"What?" John weakly asked.

"Why ... but no, he might bore you by walking too slowly. Harold," she added, seriously, "if Uncle John is kind enough to take you into Galton with him, will you be a good boy and leave your butterfly net at home?"

"If I may take my air-gun," Harold agreed.

John rapidly went over in his mind the various places where Harold might be successfully detained while he was in the toyshop, decided that the risk would be too great, pulled himself together, and declined the pleasure of his nephew's company on the ground that he must think over very carefully the phrasing of the telegram he had to send, a mental process, he explained, that Harold might distract.

"Another day, darling," said Hilda, consolingly.

"And then I'll be able to take my fishing-rod," said Harold.

"He is so like his poor father," Hilda murmured.

John was thinking sympathetically of the distant Amazonian tribe that had murdered Daniel Curtis, when there was another tap at the door, and Frida crackling loudly in a clean pinafore came in to say that the bell for lunch was just going to ring.

"Yes, dear," said her aunt. "Uncle John knows already. Don't bother him now. He's tired after his journey. Come along, Harold."

"He can have my nailbrush if he likes," Harold offered.

"Run, darling, and get it quickly then."

Harold rushed out of the room and could be heard hustling his cousin all down the corridor, evoking complaints of "Don't, Harold, you rough boy, you're crumpling my frock."

The bell for lunch sounded gratefully at this moment, and John, without even washing his hands, hurried downstairs trying to look like a hungry ogre, so anxious was he to avoid using Harold's nailbrush.

The dining-room at Ambles was a long low room with a large open fireplace and paneled walls; from the window-seats bundles of drying lavender competed pleasantly with the smell of hot kidney-beans upon the table, at the head of which John took his rightful place; opposite to him, placid as an untouched pudding, sat Grandmama. Laurence said grace without being invited after standing up for a moment with an expression of pained interrogation; Edith accompanied his words by making with her forefinger and thumb a minute cruciform incision between two of the bones of her stays, and inclined her head solemnly toward Frida in a mute exhortation to follow her mother's example. Harold flashed his spectacles upon every dish in turn; Emily's waiting was during this meal of reunion colored with human affection.

"Well, I'm glad to be back in England," said John, heartily.

An encouraging murmur rippled round the table from his relations.

"Are these French beans from our own garden?" John asked presently.

"Scarlet-runners," Hilda corrected. "Yes, of course. We never trouble the greengrocer. The frosts have been so light ..."

"I haven't got a bean left," said Laurence.

John nearly gave a visible jump; there was something terribly suggestive in that simple horticultural disclaimer.

"Our beans are quite over," added Edith in the astonished voice of one who has tumbled upon a secret of nature. She had a habit of echoing many of her husband's remarks like this; perhaps "echoing" is a bad description of her method, for she seldom repeated literally and often not immediately. Sometimes indeed she would wait as long as half an hour before she reissued in the garb of a personal philosophical discovery or of an exegitical gloss the most casual remark of Laurence, a habit which irritated him and embarrassed other people, who would look away from Edith and mutter a hurried agreement or ask for the salt to be passed.

"I remember," said old Mrs. Touchwood, "that beans were a favorite dish of poor Papa, though I myself always liked peas better."

"I like peas," Harold proclaimed.

"I like peas, too," cried Frida excitedly.

"Frida," said her father, pulling out with a click one of the graver tenor stops in his voice, "we do not talk at table about our likes and dislikes."

Edith indorsed this opinion with a grave nod at Frida, or rather with a solemn inclination of the head as if she were bowing to an altar.

"But I like new potatoes best of all," continued Harold. "My gosh, all buttery!"

Laurence screwed up his eye in a disgusted wince, looked down his nose at his plate, and drew a shocked cork from his throat.

"Hush," said Hilda. "Didn't you hear what Uncle Laurence said, darling?"

She spoke as one speaks to children in church when the organ begins; one felt that she was inspired by social tact rather than by any real reverence for the clergyman.

"Well, I do like new potatoes, and I like asparagus."

Frida was just going to declare for asparagus, too, when she caught her father's eye and choked.

"Evidently the vegetable that Frida likes best," said John, riding buoyantly upon the gale of Frida's convulsions, "is an artichoke."

It is perhaps lucky for professional comedians that rich uncles and judges rarely go on the stage; their occupation might be even more arduous if they had to face such competitors. Anyway, John had enough success with his joke to feel much more hopeful of being able to find suitable presents in Galton for Harold and Frida; and in the silence of exhaustion that succeeded the laughter he broke the news of his having to go into town and dispatch an urgent telegram that very afternoon, mentioning incidentally that he might see about a dog-cart, and, of course, at the same time a horse. Everybody applauded his resolve except his brother-in-law who looked distinctly put out.

"But you won't be gone before I get back?" John asked.

Laurence and Edith exchanged glances fraught with the unuttered solemnities of conjugal comprehension.

"Well, I _had_ wanted to have a talk over things with you after lunch," Laurence explained. "In fact, I have a good deal to talk over. I should suggest driving you in to Galton, but I find it impossible to talk freely while driving. Even our poor old pony has been known to shy. Yes, indeed, poor old Primrose often shies."

John mentally blessed the aged animal's youthful heart, and said, to cover his relief, that old maids were often more skittish than young ones.

"Why?" asked Harold.

Everybody felt that Harold's question was one that should not be answered.

"You wouldn't understand, darling," said his mother; and the dining-room became tense with mystery.

"Of course, if we could have dinner put forward half an hour," said Laurence, dragging the conversation out of the slough of sex, "we could avail ourselves of the moon."

"Yes, you see," Edith put in eagerly, "it wouldn't be so dark with the moon."

Laurence knitted his brow at this and his wife hastened to add that an earlier dinner would bring Frida's bed-time much nearer to its normal hour.

"The point is that I have a great deal to talk over with John," Laurence irritably explained, "and that," he looked as if he would have liked to add "Frida's bed-time can go to the devil," but he swallowed the impious dedication and crumbled his bread.

Finally, notwithstanding that everybody felt very full of roast beef and scarlet-runners, it was decided to dine at half-past six instead of half-past seven.

"Poor Papa, I remember," said old Mrs. Touchwood, "always liked to dine at half-past three. That gave him a nice long morning for his patients and time to smoke his cigar after dinner before he opened the dispensary in the evening. Supper was generally cold unless he anticipated a night call, in which case we had soup."

All were glad that the twentieth century had arrived, and they smiled sympathetically at the old lady, who, feeling that her anecdote had scored a hit, embarked upon another about being taken to the Great Exhibition when she was eleven years old, which lasted right through the pudding, perhaps because it was trifle, and Harold did not feel inclined to lose a mouthful by rash interruptions.

After lunch John was taken all over the house and all round the garden and congratulated time after time upon the wisdom he had shown in buying Ambles: he was made to feel that property set him apart from other men even more definitely than dramatic success.

"Of course, Daniel was famous in his way," Hilda said. "But what did he leave me?"

John, remembering the £120 a year in the bank and the collection of stuffed humming birds at the pantechnicon, the importation of which to Ambles he was always dreading, felt that Hilda was not being ungratefully rhetorical.

"And of course," Laurence contributed, "a vicar feels that his glebe—the value of which by the way has just gone down another £2 an acre—is not his own."

"Yes, you see," Edith put in, "if anything horrid happened to Laurence it would belong to the next vicar."

Again the glances of husband and wife played together in mid-air like butterflies.

"And so," Laurence went on, "when you tell us that you hope to buy this twenty-acre field we all realize that in doing so you would most emphatically be consolidating your property."

"Oh, I'm sure you're wise to buy," said Hilda, weightily.

"It would make Ambles so much larger, wouldn't it?" suggested Edith. "Twenty acres, you see ... well, really, I suppose twenty acres would be as big as from...."

"Come, Edith," said her husband. "Don't worry poor John with comparative acres—we are all looking at the twenty-acre field now."

The fierce little Kerry cows eyed the prospective owner peacefully, until Harold hit one of them with a slug from his air-gun, when they all began to career about the field, kicking up their heels and waving their tails.

"Don't do that, my boy," John said, crossly—for him very crossly.

A short cut to Galton lay across this field, which John, though even when they were quiet he never felt on really intimate terms with cows, had just decided to follow.

"Darling, that's such a cruel thing to do," Hilda expostulated. "The poor cow wasn't hurting you."

"It was looking at me," Harold protested.

"There is a legend about Francis of Assisi, Harold," his Uncle Laurence began, "which will interest you and at the same time...."

"Sorry to interrupt," John broke in, "but I must be getting along. This telegram.... I'll be back for tea."

He hurried off and when everybody called out to remind him of the short cut across the twenty-acre field he waved back cheerfully, as if he thought he was being wished a jolly walk; but he took the long way round.

It was a good five miles to Galton in the opposite direction from the road by which he had driven up that morning; but on this fine autumn afternoon, going down hill nearly all the way through a foreground of golden woods with prospects of blue distances beyond, John enjoyed the walk, and not less because even at the beginning of it he stopped once or twice to think how jolly it would be to see Miss Hamilton and Miss Merritt coming round the next bend in the road. Later on, he did not bother to include Miss Merritt, and finally he discovered his fancy so steadily fixed upon Miss Hamilton that he was forced to remind himself that Miss Hamilton in such a setting would demand a much higher standard of criticism than Miss Hamilton on the promenade deck of the *Murmania*. Nevertheless, John continued to think of her; and so pleasantly did her semblance walk beside him and so exceptionally mild was the afternoon for the season of the year that he must have strolled along the greater part of the way. At any rate, when he saw the tower of Galton church he was shocked to find that it was already four o'clock.

CHAPTER III

THE selection of presents for children is never easy, because in order to extract real pleasure from the purchase it is necessary to find something that excites the donor as much as it is likely to excite the recipient. In John's case this difficulty was quadrupled by having to find toys with an American air about them, and on top of that by the narrowly restricted choice in the Galton shops. He felt that it would be ridiculous, even insulting, to produce for Frida as typical of New York's luxurious catering for the young that doll, the roses of whose cheeks had withered in the sunlight of five Hampshire summers, and whose smile had failed to allure as little girls those who were now marriageable young women. Nor did he think that Harold would accept as worthy of American enterprise those more conspicuous portions of a diminutive Uhlan's uniform fastened to a dog's-eared sheet of cardboard, the sword belonging to which was rusting in the scabbard and the gilt lancehead of which no longer gave the least illusion of being metal. Finally, however, just as the clock was striking five he unearthed from a remote corner of the large ironmonger's shop, to which he had turned in despair from the toys offered him by the two stationers, a toboggan, and not merely a toboggan but a Canadian toboggan stamped with the image of a Red Indian.

"It was ordered for a customer in 1895," the ironmonger explained. "There was heavy snow that year, you may remember."

If it had been ordered by Methuselah when he was still in his 'teens John would not have hesitated.

"Well, would you—er—wrap it up," he said, putting down the money.

"Hadn't the carrier better bring it, sir?" suggested the ironmonger. "He'll be going Wrottesford way to-morrow morning."

Obviously John could not carry the toboggan five miles, but just as obviously he must get the toboggan back to Ambles that night: so he declined the carrier, and asked the ironmonger to order him a fly while he made a last desperate search for Frida's present. In the end, with twilight falling fast, he bought for his niece twenty-nine small china animals, which the stationer assured him would enchant any child between nine and eleven, though perhaps less likely to appeal to ages outside that period. A younger child, for instance, might be tempted to put them in its mouth, even to swallow them if not carefully watched, while an older child might tread on them. Another advantage was that when the young lady for whom they were intended grew out of them, they could be put away and revived to adorn her mantelpiece when she had reached an age to appreciate the possibilities of a mantelpiece. John did not feel as happy about these animals as he did about the toboggan: there was not a single buffalo among them, and not one looked in the least distinctively American, but the stationer was so reassuring and time was going by so rapidly that he decided to risk the purchase. And really when they were deposited in a cardboard box among cotton-wool they did not look so dull, and perhaps Frida would enjoy guessing how many there were before she unpacked them.

"Better than a Noah's Ark," said John, hopefully.

"Oh yes, much better, sir. A much more suitable present for a young lady. In fact Noah's Arks are considered all right for village treats, but they're in very little demand among the gentry nowadays."

When John was within a quarter of a mile from Ambles he told the driver of the fly to stop. Somehow he must creep into the house and up to his room with the toboggan and the china animals; it was after six, and the children would have been looking out for his return since five. Perhaps the cows would have gone home by now and he should not excite their nocturnal apprehensions by dragging the toboggan across the twenty-acre field. Meanwhile, he should tell the fly to wait five minutes before driving slowly up to the house, which would draw the scent and enable him with Emily's help to reach his room unperceived by the backstairs. A heavy mist hung upon the meadow, and the paper wrapped round the toboggan, which was just too wide to be carried under his arm like a portfolio, began to peel off in the dew with a swishing sound that would inevitably attract the curiosity of the cows were they still at large; moreover, several of the china animals were now chinking together and, John could not help feeling with some anxiety, probably chipping off their noses.

"I must look like a broken-down Santa Claus with this vehicle," he said to himself. "Where's the path got to now? I wonder why people wiggle so when they make a path? Hullo! What's that?"

The munching of cattle was audible close at hand, a munching that was sometimes interrupted by awful snorts.

"Perhaps it's only the mist that makes them do that," John tried to assure himself. "It seems very imprudent to leave valuable cows out of doors on a damp night like this."

There was a sound of heavy bodies moving suddenly in unison.

"They've heard me," thought John, hopelessly. "I wish to goodness I knew something about cows. I really must get the subject up. Of course, they *may* be frightened of *me*. Good heavens, they're all snorting now. Probably the best thing to do is to keep on calmly walking; most animals are susceptible to human indifference. What a little fool that nephew of mine was to shoot at them this afternoon. I'm hanged if he deserves his toboggan."

The lights of Ambles stained the mist in front; John ran the last fifty yards, threw himself over the iron railings, and stood panting upon his own lawn. In the distance could be heard the confused thudding of hoofs dying away toward the far end of the twenty-acre meadow.

"I evidently frightened them," John thought.

A few minutes later he was calling down from the landing outside his bedroom that it was time for presents. In the first brief moment of intoxication that had succeeded his defeat of the cattle John had seriously contemplated tobogganing downstairs himself in order to "surprise the kids" as he put it. But from his landing the staircase looked all wrong for such an experiment and he walked the toboggan down, which lamplight appeared to him a typical product of the bear-haunted mountains of Canada.

Everybody was waiting for him in the drawing-room; everybody was flatteringly enthusiastic about the toboggan and seemed anxious to make it at home in such strange surroundings; nobody failed to point out to the lucky boy the extreme kindness of his uncle in bringing back such a wonderful present all the way from America—indeed one almost had the impression that John must often have had to wake up and feed it in the night.

"The trouble you must have taken," Hilda exclaimed.

"Yes, I did take a good deal of trouble," John admitted. After all, so he had—a damned sight more trouble than any one there suspected.

"When will it snow?" Harold asked. "To-morrow?"

"I hope not—I mean, it might," said John. He must keep up Harold's spirits, if only to balance Frida's depression, about whose present he was beginning to feel very doubtful when he saw her eyes glittering with feverish anticipation while he was undoing the string. He hoped she would not faint or scream with disappointment when it was opened, and he took off the lid of the box with the kind of flourish to which waiters often treat dish-covers when they wish to promote an appetite among the guests.

"How sweet," Edith murmured.

John looked gratefully at his sister; if he had made his will that night she would have inherited Ambles.

"Ah, a collection of small china animals," said Laurence, choosing a cat to set delicately upon the table for general admiration. John wished he had not chosen the cat that seemed to suffer with a tumor in the region of the tail and disinclined in consequence to sit still.

"Yes, I was anxious to get her a Noah's Ark," John volunteered, seeming to suggest by his tone how appropriate such a gift would have been to the atmosphere of a vicarage. "But they've practically given up making Noah's Arks in America, and you see, these china animals will serve as toys now, and later on, when Frida is grown-up, they'll look jolly on the mantelpiece. Those that are not broken, of course."

The animals had all been taken out of their box by now, but a few paws and ears were still adhering to the cotton-wool.

"Frida is always very light on her toys," said Edith, proudly.

"Not likely to put them in her mouth," said John, heartily. "That was the only thing that made me hesitate when I first saw them in Fifth Avenue. But they don't look quite so edible here."

"Frida never puts anything in her mouth," Edith generalized, primly. "And she's given up biting her nails since Uncle John came home, haven't you, dear?"

"That's a good girl," John applauded; he did not believe in Frida's sudden conquest of autophagy, but he was anxious to encourage her in every way at the moment.

Yes, the gift-horses had shown off their paces better than he had expected, he decided. To be sure, Frida did not appear beside herself with joy, but at any rate she had not burst into tears—she had not thrust the present from her sight with loathing and begged to be taken home. And then Harold, who had been staring at the animals through his glasses, like the horrid little naturalist that he was, said:

"I've seen some animals like them in Mr. Goodman's shop."

John hoped a blizzard would blow to-morrow, that Harold would toboggan recklessly down the steepest slope of the downs behind Ambles, and that he would hit an oak tree at the bottom and break his glasses. However, none of these dark thoughts obscured the remote brightness with which he answered:

"Really, Harold. Very likely. There is a considerable exportation of china animals from America nowadays. In fact I was very lucky to find any left in America."

"Let's go into Gallon to-morrow and look at Mr. Goodman's animals," Harold suggested.

John had never suspected that one day he should feel grateful to his brother-in-law; but when the dinner-bell went at half-past six instead of half-past seven solely on his account, John felt inclined to shake him by the hand. Nor would he have ever supposed that he should one day welcome the prospect of one of Laurence's long confidential talks. Yet when the ladies departed after dessert and Laurence took the chair next to himself as solemnly as if it were a fald-stool, he encouraged him with a smile.

"We might have our little talk now," and when Laurence cleared his throat John felt that the conversation had been opened as successfully as a local bazaar. Not merely did John smile encouragingly, but he actually went so far as to invite him to go ahead.

Laurence sighed, and poured himself out a second glass of port.

"I find myself in a position of considerable difficulty," he announced, "and should like your advice."

John's mind went rapidly to the balance in his passbook instead of to the treasure of worldly experience from which he might have drawn.

"Perhaps before we begin our little talk," said Laurence, "it would be as well if I were to remind you of some of the outstanding events and influences in my life. You will then be in a better position to give me the advice and help—ah—the moral help, of which I stand in need—ah—in sore need."

"He keeps calling it a little talk," John thought, "but by Jove, it's lucky we did have dinner early. At this rate he won't get back to his vicarage before cock-crow."

John was not deceived by his brother-in-law's minification of their talk, and he exchanged the trim Henry Clay he had already clipped for a very large Upman that would smoke for a good hour.

"Won't you light up before you begin?" he asked, pushing a box of commonplace Murillos toward his brother-in-law, whose habit of biting off the end of a cigar, of letting it go out, of continually knocking off the ash, of forgetting to remove the band till it was smoldering, and of playing miserable little tunes with it on the rim of a coffee-cup, in fact of doing everything with it except smoke it appreciatively, made it impossible for John, so far as Laurence was concerned, to be generous with his cigars.

"I think you'll find these not bad."

This was true; the Murillos were not actually bad.

"Thanks, I will avail myself of your offer. But to come back to what I was saying," Laurence went on, lighting his cigar with as little expression of anticipated pleasure as might be discovered in the countenance of a lodging-house servant lighting a fire. "I do not propose to occupy your time by an account of my spiritual struggles at the University."

"You ought to write a novel," said John, cheerfully.

Laurence looked puzzled.

"I am now occupied with the writing of a play, but I shall come to that presently. Novels, however...."

"I was only joking," said John. "It would take too long to explain the joke. Sorry I interrupted you. Cigar gone out? Don't take another. It doesn't really matter how often those Murillos go out."

"Where am I?" Laurence asked in a bewildered voice.

"You'd just left Oxford," John answered, quickly.

"Ah, yes, I was at Oxford. Well, as I was saying, I shall not detain you with an account of my spiritual struggles there.... I think I may almost without presumption refer to them as my spiritual progress ... let it suffice that I found myself on the vigil of my ordination after a year at Cuddesdon Theological College a convinced High Churchman. This must not be taken to mean that I belonged to the more advanced or what I should prefer to call the Italian party in the Church of England. I did not."

Laurence here paused and looked at John earnestly; since John had not the remotest idea what the Italian party meant and was anxious to avoid being told, he said in accents that sought to convey relief at hearing his brother-in-law's personal contradiction of a charge that had for long been whispered against him:

"Oh, you didn't?"

"No, I did not. I was not prepared to go one jot or one tittle beyond the Five Points."

"Of the compass, you mean," said John, wisely. "Quite so."

Then seeing that Laurence seemed rather indignant, he added quickly, "Did I say the compass? How idiotic! Of course, I meant the law."

"'The Five Points are the Eastward Position....'"

"It was the compass after all," John thought. "What a fool I was to hedge."

"The Mixed Chalice, Lights, Wafer Bread, and Vestments, but *not* the ceremonial use of Incense."

"And those are the Five Points?"

Laurence inclined his head.

"Which you were not prepared to go beyond, I think you said?" John gravely continued, flattering himself that he was re-established as an intelligent listener.

"In adhering to these Five Points," Laurence proceeded, "I found that I was able to claim the support of a number of authoritative English divines. I need only mention Bishop Ken and Bishop Andrews for you to appreciate my position."

"Eastward, I think you said," John put in; for his brother-in-law had paused again, and he was evidently intended to say something.

"I perceive that you are not acquainted with the divergences of opinion that unhappily exist in our national Church."

"Well, to tell you the truth—and I know you'll excuse my frankness—I haven't been to church since I was a boy," John admitted. "But I know I used to dislike the litany very much, and of course I had my favorite hymns—we most of us have—and really I think that's as far as I got. However, I have to get up the subject of religion very shortly. My next play will deal with Joan of Arc, and, as you may imagine, religion plays an important part in such a theme—a very important part. In addition to the vision that Joan will have of St. Michael in the first act, one of my chief unsympathetic characters is a bishop. I hope I'm not hurting your feelings in telling you this, my dear fellow. Have another cigar, won't you? I think you've dipped the end of that one in the coffee-lees."

Laurence assured John bitterly that he had no reason to be particularly fond of bishops. "In fact," he went on, "I'm having a very painful discussion with the Bishop of Silchester at this moment, but I shall come to that presently. What I am anxious, however, to impress upon you at this stage in our little talk is the fact that on the vigil of my ordination I had arrived at a definite theory of what I could and could not accept. Well, I was ordained deacon by the Bishop of St. Albans and licensed to a curacy in Plaistow—one of the poorest districts in the East End of London. Here I worked for three years, and it was here that fourteen years ago I first met Edith."

"Yes, I seem to remember. Wasn't she working at a girls' club or something? I know I always thought that there must be a secondary attraction."

"At that time my financial position was not such as to warrant my embarking upon matrimony. Moreover, I had in a moment of what I should now call boyish exaltation registered a vow of perpetual celibacy. Edith, however, with that devotion which neither then nor at any crisis since has failed me expressed her willingness to consent to an indefinite engagement, and I remember with gratitude that it was just this consent of hers which was the means of widening the narrow—ah—the all too narrow path which at that time I was treading in religion. My vicar and I had a painful dispute upon some insignificant doctrinal point; I felt bound to resign my curacy, and take another under a man who could appreciate and allow for my speculative temperament. I became curate to St. Thomas's, Kensington, and had hopes of ultimately being preferred to a living. I realized in fact that the East End was a cul-de-sac for a young and—if I may so describe myself without being misunderstood—ambitious curate. For three years I remained at St. Thomas's and obtained a considerable reputation as a preacher. You may or may not remember that some Advent Addresses of mine were reprinted in one of the more tolerant religious weeklies and obtained what I do not hesitate to call the honor of being singled out for malicious abuse by the *Church Times*. Eleven years ago my dear father died and by leaving me an independence of £417 a year enabled me not merely to marry Edith, but very soon afterwards to accept the living of Newton Candover. I will not detain you with the history of my financial losses, which I hope I have always welcomed in the true spirit of resignation. Let it suffice that within a few years owing to my own misplaced charity and some bad advice from a relative of mine on the Stock Exchange my private income dwindled to £152, while at the same time the gross income of Newton Candover from £298 sank to the abominably low nett income of £102—a serious reflection, I think you will agree, upon the shocking financial system of our national Church. It may surprise you, my dear John, to learn that such blows from fate not only did not cast me down into a state of spiritual despair and intellectual atrophy, but that they actually had the effect of inciting me to still greater efforts."

John had been fumbling with his check book when Laurence began to talk about his income; but the unexpected turn of the narrative quietened him, and the Upman was going well.

"You may or may not come across a little series of devotional meditations for the Man in the Street entitled Lamp-posts. They have a certain vogue, and I may tell you in confidence that under the pseudonym of The Lamplighter I wrote them. The actual financial return they brought me was slight. Barabbas, you know, was a publisher. Ha-ha! No, although I made nothing, or rather practically nothing out of them for my own purse, by leading me to browse among many modern works of theology and philosophy I began to realize that there was a great deal of reason for modern indifference and skepticism. In other words, I discovered that, in order to keep the man in the street a Christian, Christianity must adapt itself to his needs. Filled with a reverent enthusiasm and perhaps half-consciously led along such a path by your conspicuous example of success, I have sought to embody my theories in a play, the protagonist of which is the apostle Thomas, whom when you read the play you will easily recognize as the prototype of the man in the street. And this brings me to the reason for which I have asked you for this little talk. The fact of the matter is that in pursuing my studies of the apostle Thomas I have actually gone beyond his simple rugged agnosticism, and I now at forty-two years of age after eighteen years as a minister of religion find myself unable longer to accept in any literal sense of the term whatever the Virgin Birth."

Laurence poured himself out a third glass of port and waited for John to recover from his stupefaction.

"But I don't think I'm a very good person to talk to about these abstruse divine obstetrics," John protested. "I really haven't considered the question. I know of course to what you refer, but I think this is essentially an occasion for professional advice."

"I do not ask for advice upon my beliefs," Laurence explained. "I recognize that nobody is able to do anything for them except myself. What I want you to do is to let Edith, myself, and little Frida stay with you at Ambles—of course we should be paying guests and you could use our pony and trap and any of the vicarage furniture that you thought suitable—until it has been decided whether I am likely or not to have any success as a dramatist. I do not ask you to undertake the Quixotic task of trying to obtain a public representation of my play about the apostle Thomas. I know that Biblical subjects are forbidden by the Lord Chamberlain, surely a monstrous piece of flunkeyism. But I have many other ideas for plays, and I'm convinced that you will sympathize with my anxiety to be able to work undisturbed and, if I may say so, in close propinquity to another playwright who is already famous."

"But why do you want to leave your own vicarage?" John gasped.

"My dear fellow, owing to what I can only call the poisonous behavior of Mrs. Paxton, my patron, to whom while still a curate at St. Thomas's, Kensington, I gave an abundance of spiritual consolation when she suffered the loss of her husband, owing as I say to her poisonous behavior following upon a trifling quarrel about some alterations I made in the fabric of *my* church without consulting her, I have been subject to ceaseless inquisition and persecution. There has been an outcry in the more bigoted religious press about my doctrine, and in short I have thought it best and most dignified to resign my living. I am therefore, to use a colloquialism,—ah—at a loose end."

"And Edith?" John asked.

"My poor wife still clings with feminine loyalty to those accretions to faith from which I have cut myself free. In most things she is at one with me, but I have steadily resisted the temptation to intrude upon the sanctity of her intimate beliefs. She sees my point of view. Of her sympathy I can only speak with gratitude. But she is still an old-fashioned believer. And indeed I am glad, for I should not like to think of her tossed upon the stormy seas of doubt and exposed to the—ah—hurricanes of speculation that surge through my own brains."

"And when do you want to move in to Ambles?"

"Well, if it would be convenient, we should like to begin gradually to-morrow. I have informed the Bishop that I will—ah—be out in a fortnight."

"But what about Hilda?" John asked, doubtfully. "She is really looking after Ambles for me, you know."

"While we have been having our little talk in the dining-room Edith has been having her little talk with Hilda in the drawing-room, and I think I hear them coming now."

John looked up quickly to see the effect of that other little talk, and determined to avoid for that night at least anything in the nature of little talks with anybody.

"Laurence dear," said Edith mildly, "isn't it time we were going?"

John knew that not Hilda herself could have phrased more aptly what she was feeling; he was sure that in her opinion it was indeed high time that Edith and Laurence were going.

Laurence went over to the window and pulled aside the curtains to examine the moon.

"Yes, my dear, I think we might have Primrose harnessed. Where is Frida?"

"She is watching Harold arrange the animals that John gave her. They are playing at visiting the Natural History Museum."

John was aware that he had not yet expressed his own willingness for the Armitage family to move into Ambles; he was equally aware that Hilda was trying to catch his eye with a questioning and indignant glance and that he had already referred the decision to her. At the same time he could not bring himself to exalt Hilda above Edith who was the younger and he was bound to admit the favorite of his two sisters; moreover, Hilda was the mother of Harold, and if Harold was to be considered tolerable in the same house as himself, he could not deny as much of his forbearance to Laurence.

"Well, I suppose you two girls have settled it between you?" he said.

Hilda, who did not seem either surprised or elated at being called a girl, observed coldly that naturally it was for John to decide, but that if the vicarage family was going to occupy Ambles extra furniture would be required immediately.

"My dear," said Laurence. "Didn't you make it clear to Hilda that as much of the vicarage furniture as is required can be sent here immediately? John and I had supposed that you were settling all these little domestic details during your little talk together."

"No, dear," Edith said, "we settled nothing. Hilda felt, and of course I can't help agreeing with her, that it is really asking too much of John. She reminded me that he has come down here to work."

The last icicle of opposition melted from John's heart; he could not bear to think of Edith's being lectured all the way home by her husband under the light of a setting moon. "I dare say we can manage," he said, "and really, you know Hilda, it will do the rooms good to be lived in. I noticed this afternoon a slight smell of damp coming from the unfurnished part of the house."

"Apples, not damp," Hilda snapped. "I had the apples stored in one of the disused rooms."

"All these problems will solve themselves," said Laurence, grandly. "And I'm sure that John cannot wish to attempt them to-night. Let us all remember that he may be tired. Come along, Edith. We have a long day before us to-morrow. Let us say good-night to Mama."

Edith started: it was the first time in eleven years of married life that her husband had adopted the Touchwood style of addressing or referring to their mother, and it seemed to set a seal upon his more intimate association with her family in the future. If any doubts still lingered about the forthcoming immigration of the vicarage party to Ambles they were presently disposed of once and for all by Laurence.

"What are you carrying?" he asked Frida, when they were gathered in the hall before starting.

"Uncle John's present," she replied.

"Do not bother. Uncle John has invited us to stay here, and you do not want to expose your little animals to the risk of being chipped. No doubt Harold will look after them for you in the interim—the short interim. Come, Edith, the moon is not going to wait for us, you know. I have the reins. Gee-up, Primrose!"

"Fond as I am of Edith," Hilda said, when the vicarage family was out of hearing. "Fond as I am of Edith," she repeated without any trace of affection in accent or expression, "I do think this invasion is an imposition upon your kindness. But clergymen are all alike; they all become dictatorial and obtuse; they're too fond of the sound of their own voices."

"Laurence is perhaps a little heavy," John agreed, "a little suave and heavy like a cornflour shape, but we ought to do what we can for Edith."

He tactfully offered Hilda a share in his own benevolence, in which she ensconced herself without hesitation.

"Well, I suppose we shall have to make the best of it. Indeed the only thing that *really* worries me is what we are to do with the apples."

"Oh, Harold will soon eat them up," said John; though he had not the slightest intention of being sarcastic, Hilda was so much annoyed by this that she abandoned all discussion of the vicarage and talked so long about Harold's inside and with such a passionate insistence upon what he required of sweet and sour to prevent him from dropping before her very eyes, that John was able fairly soon to plead that the hour was late and that he must go to bed.

In his bedroom, which was sharp-scented with autumnal airs and made him disinclined for sleep, John became sentimental over Edith and began to weave out of her troubles a fine robe for his own good-nature in which his sentimentality was able to show itself off. He assured himself of Edith's luck in having Ambles as a refuge in the difficult time through which she was passing and began to visualize her past life as nothing but a stormy prelude to a more tranquil present in which he should be her pilot. That Laurence would be included in his beneficence was certainly a flaw in the emerald of his bounty, a fly in the amber of his self-satisfaction; but, after all, so long as Edith was secure and happy such blemishes were hardly perceptible. He ought to think himself lucky that he was in a position to help his relations; the power of doing kind actions was surely the greatest privilege accorded to the successful man. And what right had Hilda to object? Good gracious, as if she herself were not dependent enough upon him! But there had always been visible in Hilda this wretched spirit of competition. It had been in just the same spirit that she had married Daniel Curtis; she had not been able to endure her younger sister's engagement to the tall handsome curate and had snatched at the middle-aged explorer in order to be married simultaneously and secure the best wedding presents for herself. But what had Daniel Curtis seen in Hilda? What had that myopic and taciturn man found in Hilda to gladden a short visit to England between his life on the Orinoco and his intended life at the back of the uncharted Amazons? And had his short experience of her made him so reckless that nothing but his spectacles were found by the rescuers? What mad impulse to perpetuate his name beyond the numerous beetles, flowers, monkeys, and butterflies to which it was already attached by many learned societies had led him to bequeath Harold to humanity? Was not his collection of humming birds enough?

"I'm really very glad that Edith is coming to Ambles," John murmured. "Very glad indeed. It will serve Hilda right." He began to wonder if he actually disliked Hilda and to realize that he had never really forgiven her for refusing to be interested in his first published story. How well he remembered that occasion—twenty years ago almost to a day. It had been a dreary November in the time when London really did have fogs, and when the sense of his father's approaching death had added to the general gloom. James had been acting as his father's partner for more than a year and had already nearly ruined the practice by his inexperience and want of affability. George and himself were both in the city offices—George in wool, himself in dog-biscuits. George did not seem to mind the soul-destroying existence and was full of financial ambition; but himself had loathed it and cared for nothing but literature. How he had pleaded with that dry old father, whose cynical tormented face on its pillow smeared with cigar ash even now vividly haunted his memory; but the fierce old man had refused him the least temporary help and had actually chuckled with delight amidst all his pain at the thought of how his family would have to work for a living when he should mercifully be dead. Was it surprising, when that morning he had found at the office a communication from a syndicate of provincial papers to inform him of his story's being accepted, that he should have arrived home in the fog, full of hope and enthusiasm? And then he had been met with whispering voices and the news of his father's death. Of course he had been shocked and grieved, even disappointed that it was too late to announce his success to the old man; but he had not been able to resist telling Hilda, a gawky, pale-faced girl of eighteen, that his story had been taken. He could recall her expression in that befogged gaslight even now, her expression of utter lack of interest, faintly colored with surprise at his own bad taste. Then he had gone upstairs to see his mother, who was bathed in tears, though she had been warned at least six months ago that her husband might die at any moment. He had ventured after a few formal words of sympathy to lighten the burden of her grief by taking the auspicious communication from his pocket, where it had been cracking nervously between his fingers, and reading it to her. He had been sure that she would be interested because she was a great reader of stories and must surely derive a grateful wonder from the contemplation of her own son as an author. But she was evidently too much overcome by the insistency of grief and by the prospect of monetary difficulties in the near future to grasp what he was telling her; it had struck him that she had actually never realized that the stories she enjoyed were written by men and women any more than it might have struck another person that advertisements were all written by human beings with their own histories of love and hate.

"You mustn't neglect your office work, Johnnie," was what she had said. "We shall want every halfpenny now that Papa is gone. James does his best, but the patients were more used to Papa."

After these two rebuffs John had not felt inclined to break his good news to James, who would be sure to sneer, or to George, who would only laugh; so he had wandered upstairs to the old schoolroom, where he had found Edith sitting by a dull fire and dissuading little Hugh from throwing coals at the cat. As soon as he had told Edith what had happened she had made a hero of him, and ever afterwards treated him with admiration as well as affection. Had she not prophesied even that he would be another Dickens? That was something like sisterly love, and he had volunteered to read her the original rough copy, which, notwithstanding Hugh's whining interruptions, she had enjoyed as much as he had enjoyed it himself. Certainly Edith must come to Ambles; twenty years were not enough to obliterate the memory of that warm-hearted girl of fifteen and of her welcome praise.

But Hugh? What malign spirit had brought Hugh to his mind at a moment when he was already just faintly disturbed by the prospect of his relations' increasing demands upon his attention? Hugh was only twenty-seven now and much too conspicuously for his own good the youngest of the family; like all children that arrive unexpectedly after a long interval, he had seemed the pledge of his parents' renewed youth on the very threshold of old age, and had been spoiled, even by his cross-grained old father, in consequence: as for his mother, though it was out of her power to spoil him extravagantly with money, she gave him all that she did not spend on caps for herself. John determined to make inquiries about Hugh to-morrow. Not another penny should he have from him, not another farthing. If he could not live on what he earned in the office of Stephen Crutchley, who had accepted the young spendthrift out of regard for their lifelong friendship, if he could not become a decent, well-behaved architect, why, he could starve. Not another penny ... and the rest of his relations agreed with John on this point, for if to him Hugh was a skeleton in the family cupboard, to them he was a skeleton at the family feast.

John expelled from his mind all misgivings about Hugh, hoped it would be a fine day to-morrow so that he could really look round the garden and see what plants wanted ordering, tried to remember the name of an ornamental shrub recommended by Miss Hamilton, turned over on his side, and went to sleep.

CHAPTER IV

EARLY next morning John dreamed that he was buying calico in an immense shop and that in a dreamlike inconsequence the people there, customers and shopmen alike, were abruptly seized with a frenzy of destruction so violent that they began to tear up all the material upon which they could lay their hands; indeed, so loud was the noise of rent cloth that John woke up with the sound of it still in his ears. Gradually it was borne in upon a brain wrestling with actuality that the noise might have emanated from the direction of a small casement in his bedroom looking eastward into the garden across a steep penthouse which ran down to within two feet of the ground. Although the noise had stopped some time before John had precisely located its whereabouts and really before he was perfectly convinced that he was awake, he jumped out of bed and hurried across the chilly boards to ascertain if after all it had only been a relic of his dream. No active cause was visible; but the moss, the stonecrop and the tiles upon the penthouse had been clawed from top to bottom as if by some mighty tropical cat, and John for a brief instant savored that elated perplexity which generally occurs to heroes in the opening paragraphs of a sensational novel.

"It's a very old house," he thought, hopefully, and began to grade his reason to a condition of sycophantic credulity. "And, of course, anything like a ghost at seven o'clock in the morning is rare—very rare. The evidence would be unassailable...."

After toadying to the marvelous for a while, he sought a natural explanation of the phenomenon and honestly tried not to want it to prove inexplicable. The noise began again overhead; a fleeting object darkened the casement like the swift passage of a bird and struck the penthouse below; there was a slow grinding shriek, a clatter of broken tiles and leaden piping; a small figure stuck all over with feathers emerged from the herbaceous border and smiled up at him.

"Good heavens, my boy, what in creation are you trying to do?" John shouted, sternly.

"I'm learning to toboggan, Uncle John."

"But didn't I explain to you that tobogganing can only be carried out after a heavy snowfall?"

"Well, it hasn't snowed yet," Harold pointed out in an offended voice.

"Listen to me. If it snows for a month without stopping, you're never to toboggan down a roof. What's the good of having all those jolly hills at the back of the house if you don't use them?"

John spoke as if he had brought back the hills from America at the same time as he was supposed to have brought back the toboggan.

"There's a river, too," Harold observed.

"You can't toboggan down a river—unless, of course, it gets frozen over."

"I don't want to toboggan down the river, but if I had a Canadian canoe for the river I could wait for the snow quite easily."

John, after a brief vision of a canoe being towed across the Atlantic by the *Murmania*, felt that he was being subjected to the lawless exactions of a brigand, but could think of nothing more novel in the way of defiance than:

"Go away now and be a good boy."

"Can't I ..." Harold began.

"No, you can't. If those chickens' feathers...."

"They're pigeons' feathers," his nephew corrected him.

"If those feathers stuck in your hair are intended to convey an impression that you're a Red Indian chief, go and sit in your wigwam till breakfast and smoke the pipe of peace."

"Mother said I wasn't to smoke till I was twenty-one."

"Not literally, you young ass. Why, good heavens, in my young days such an allusion to Mayne Reid would have been eagerly taken up by any boy."

Something was going wrong with this conversation, John felt, and he added, lamely:

"Anyway, go away now."

"But, Uncle John, I...."

"Don't Uncle John me. I don't feel like an uncle this morning. Suppose I'd been shaving when you started that fool's game. I might have cut my head off."

"But, Uncle John, I've left my spectacles on one of the chimneys. Mother said that whenever I was playing a rough game I was to take off my spectacles first."

"You'll have to do without your spectacles, that's all. The gardener will get them for you after breakfast. Anyway, a Red Indian chief in spectacles is unnatural."

"Well, I'm not a Red Indian any longer."

"You can't chop and change like that. You'll have to be a Red Indian now till after breakfast. Don't argue any more, because I'm standing here in bare feet. Go and do some weeding in the garden. You've pulled up all the plants on the roof."

"I can't read without my spectacles."

"Weed, not read!"

"Well, I can't weed, either. I can't do anything without my spectacles."

"Then go away and do nothing."

Harold shuffled off disconsolately, and John rang for his shaving water.

At breakfast Hilda asked anxiously after her son's whereabouts; and John, the last vestige of whose irritation had vanished in the smell of fried bacon and eggs, related the story of the morning's escapade as a good joke.

"But he can't see anything without his spectacles," Hilda exclaimed.

"Oh, he'll find his way to the breakfast table all right," John prophesied.

"These bachelors," murmured Hilda, turning to her mother with a wry little laugh. "Hark! isn't that Harold calling?"

"No, no, no, it's the pigeons," John laughed. "They're probably fretting for their feathers."

"It's to be hoped," said old Mrs. Touchwood, "that he's not fallen into the well by leaving off his spectacles like this. I never could abide wells. And I hate to think of people leaving things off suddenly. It's always a mistake. I remember little Hughie once left off his woollen vests in May and caught a most terrible cold that wouldn't go away—it simply wouldn't go."

"How is Hugh, by the way?" John asked.

"The same as ever," Hilda put in with cold disapproval. She was able to forget Harold's myopic wanderings in the pleasure of crabbing her youngest brother.

"Ah, you're all very hard on poor Hughie," sighed the old lady. "But he's always been very fond of his poor mother."

"He's very fond of what he can get out of you," Hilda sneered.

"And it's little enough he can, poor boy. Goodness knows I've little enough to spare for him. I wish you could have seen your way to do something for Hughie, Johnnie," the old lady went on.

"John has done quite enough for him," Hilda snapped, which was perfectly true.

"He's had to leave his rooms in Earl's Court," Mrs. Touchwood lamented.

"What for? Getting drunk, I suppose?" John inquired, sternly.

"No, it was the drains. He's staying with his friend, Aubrey Fenton, whom I cannot pretend to like. He seems to me a sad scapegrace. Poor little Hughie. I wish everything wasn't against him. It's to be hoped he won't go and get married, poor boy, for I'm sure his wife wouldn't understand him."

"Surely he's not thinking of getting married," exclaimed John in dismay.

"Why no, of course not," said the old lady. "How you do take anybody up, Johnnie. I said it's to be hoped he won't get married."

At this moment Emily came in to announce that Master Harold was up on the roof shouting for dear life. "Such a turn as it give Cook and I, mum," she said, "to hear that garshly voice coming down the chimney. Cook was nearly took with the convolsions, and if it had of been after dark, mum, she says she's shaw she doesn't know what she wouldn't of done, she wouldn't, she's that frightened of howls. That's the one thing she can't ever be really comfortable for in the country, she says, the howls and the hearwigs."

"I'm under the impression," John declared, solemnly, "that I forbade Harold to go near the roof. If he has disobeyed my express commands he must suffer for it by the loss of his breakfast. He has chosen to go back on the roof: on the roof he shall stay."

"But his breakfast?" Hilda almost whispered. She was so much awed by her brother's unusually pompous phraseology that he began to be impressed by it himself and to feel the first faint intimations of the pleasures of tyranny: he began to visualize himself as the unbending ruler of all his relations.

"His breakfast can be sent up to him, and I hope it will attract every wasp in the neighborhood."

This to John seemed the most savage aspiration he could have uttered: autumnal wasps disturbed him as much as dragons used to disturb princesses.

"Harold likes wasps," said Hilda. "He observes their habits."

This revelation of his nephew's tastes took away John's last belief in his humanity, and the only retort he could think of was a suggestion that he should go at once to a boarding-school.

"Likes wasps?" he repeated. "The child must be mad. You'll tell me next that he likes black beetles."

"He trained a black beetle once to eat something. I forget what it was now. But the poor boy was so happy about his little triumph. You ought to remember, John, that he takes after his father."

John made up his mind at this moment that Daniel Curtis must have married Hilda in a spirit of the purest empirical science.

"Well, he's not to go training insects in my house," John said, firmly. "And if I see any insects anywhere about Ambles that show the slightest sign of having been encouraged to suppose themselves on an equal with mankind I shall tread on them."

"I'm afraid the crossing must have upset you, Johnnie," said old Mrs. Touchwood, sympathetically. "You seem quite out of sorts this morning. And I don't like the idea of poor little Harold's balancing himself all alone on a chimney. It was never any pleasure to me to watch tight-rope dancers or acrobats. Indeed, except for the clowns, I never could abide circuses."

Hilda quickly took up the appeal and begged John to let the gardener rescue her son.

"Oh, very well," he assented. "But, once for all, it must be clearly understood that I've come down to Ambles to write a new play and that some arrangement must be concluded by which I have my mornings completely undisturbed."

"Of course," said Hilda, brightening at the prospect of Harold's release.

"Of course," John echoed, sardonically, within himself. He did not feel that the sight of Harold's ravening after his breakfast would induce in him the right mood for Joan of Arc. So he left the breakfast table and went upstairs to his library. Here he found that some "illiterate oaf," as he characterized the person responsible, had put in upside down upon the shelves the standard works he had hastily amassed. Instead of setting his ideas in order, he had to set his books in order: and after a hot and dusty morning with the rows of unreadable classics he came downstairs to find that the vicarage party had arrived just in time for lunch, bringing with them as the advance guard of their occupation a large clothes basket filled with what Laurence described as "necessary odds and ends that might be overlooked later."

"It's my theory of moving," he added. "The small things first."

He enunciated this theory so reverently that his action acquired from his tone a momentous gravity like the captain of a ship's when he orders the women and children into the boats first.

The moving of the vicarage party lasted over a fortnight, during which John found it impossible to settle down to Joan of Arc. No sooner would he have worked himself up to a suitable frame of mind in which he might express dramatically and poetically the maid's reception of her heavenly visitants than a very hot man wearing a green baize apron would appear in the doorway of the library and announce that a chest of drawers had hopelessly involved some vital knot in the domestic communications. It was no good for John to ask Hilda to do anything: his sister had taken up the attitude that it was all John's fault, that she had done her best to preserve his peace, that her advice had been ignored, and that for the rest of her life she intended to efface herself.

"I'm a mere cipher," she kept repeating.

On one occasion when a bureau of sham ebony that looked like a blind man's dream of Cologne Cathedral had managed to wedge all its pinnacles into the lintel of the front door, John observed to Laurence he had understood that only such furniture from the vicarage as was required to supplement the Ambles furniture would be brought there.

"I thought this bureau would appeal to you," Laurence replied. "It seemed to me in keeping with much of your work."

John looked up sharply to see if he was being chaffed; but his brother-in-law's expression was earnest, and the intended compliment struck more hardly at John's self-confidence than the most malicious review.

"Does my work really seem like gimcrack gothic?" he asked himself.

In a fit of exasperation he threw himself so vigorously into the business of forcing the bureau into the house that when it was inside it looked like a ruined abbey on the afternoon of a Bank Holiday.

"It had better be taken up into the garrets for the present," he said, grimly. "It can be mended later on."

The comparison of his work to that bureau haunted John at his own writing-table for the rest of the morning; thinking of the Bishop of Silchester's objection to Laurence, he found it hard to make the various bishops in his play as unsympathetic as they ought to be for dramatic contrast; then he remembered that after all it had been due to the Bishop of Silchester's strong action that Laurence had come to Ambles: the stream of insulting epithets for bishops flowed as strongly as ever, and he worked in a justifiable pun upon the name of Pierre Cauchon, his chief episcopal villain.

"I wonder, if I were allowed to, whether I would condemn Laurence to be burnt alive. Wasn't there a Saint Laurence who was grilled? I really believe I would almost grill him, I really do. There's something exceptionally irritating to me about that man's whole personality. And I'm not at all sure I approve of a clergyman's giving up his beliefs. One might get a line out of that, by the way—something about a weathercock and a church steeple. I don't think a clergyman ought to surrender so easily. It's his business not to be influenced by modern thought. This passion for realism is everywhere.... Thank goodness, I've been through it and got over it and put it behind me forever. It's a most unprofitable creed. What was my circulation as a realist? I once reached four thousand. What's four thousand? Why, it isn't half the population of Galton. And now Laurence Armitage takes up with it after being a vicar for ten years. Idiot! Religion isn't realistic: it never was realistic. Religion is the entertainment of man's spirituality just as the romantic drama is the entertainment of his mentality. I don't read Anatole France for my representation of Joan of Arc. What business has Laurence to muddle his head with—what's his name—Colonel Ingoldsby—Ingersoll—when he ought to be thinking about his Harvest Festival? And then he has the effrontery to compare my work with that bureau! If that's all his religion meant to him—that ridiculous piece of gimcrack gothic, no wonder it wouldn't hold together. Why, the green fumed oak of a sentimental rationalism would be better than that. Confound Laurence! I knew this would happen when he came. He's taken my mind completely off my own work. I can't write a word this morning."

John rushed away from his manuscript and weeded furiously down a secluded border until the gardener told him he had weeded away the autumn-sown sweet-peas that were coming along nicely and standing the early frosts a treat.

"I'm not even allowed to weed my own garden now," John thought, burking the point at issue; and his disillusionment became so profound that he actually invited Harold to go for a walk with him.

"Can I bring my blow-pipe?" asked the young naturalist, gleefully.

"You don't want to load yourself up with soap and water," said John. "Keep that till you come in."

"My South American blow-pipe, Uncle John. It's a real one which father sent home. It belonged to a little Indian boy, but the darts aren't poisoned, father told mother."

"Don't you be too sure," John advised him. "Explorers will say anything."

"Well, can I bring it?"

"No, we'll take a non-murderous walk for a change. I'm tired of being shunned by the common objects of the countryside."

"Well, shall I bring *Ants*, *Bees*, and *Wasps*?"

"Certainly not. We don't want to go trailing about Hampshire like two jam sandwiches."

"I mean the book."

"No, if you want to carry something, you can carry my cleek and six golf balls."

"Oh, yes, and then I'll practice bringing eggs down in my mouth from very high trees."

John liked this form of exercise, because at the trifling cost of making one ball intolerably sticky it kept Harold from asking questions; for about two hundred yards he enjoyed this walk more than any he had ever taken with his nephew.

"But birds' nesting time won't come till the spring," Harold sighed.

"No," said John, regretfully: there were many lofty trees round Ambles, and with his mouth full of eggs anything might happen to Harold.

The transference of the vicarage family was at last complete, and John was penitently astonished to find that Laurence really did intend to pay for their board; in fact, the ex-vicar presented him with a check for two months on account calculated at a guinea a week each. John was so much moved by this event—the manner in which Laurence offered the check gave it the character of a testimonial and thereby added to John's sense of obligation—that he was even embarrassed by the notion of accepting it. At the same time a faint echo of his own realistic beginnings tinkled in his ear a warning not to refuse it, both for his own sake and for the sake of his brother-in-law. He therefore escaped from the imputation of avarice by suggesting that the check should be handed to Hilda, who, as housekeeper, would know how to employ it best. John secretly hoped that Hilda, through being able to extract what he thought of as "a little pin money for herself" out of it, might discard the martyr's halo that was at present pinching her brains tightly enough, if one might judge by her constricted expression.

"There will undoubtedly be a small profit," he told himself, "for if Laurence has a rather monkish appetite, Edith and Frida eat very little."

Perhaps Hilda did manage to make a small profit; at any rate, she seemed reconciled to the presence of the Armitages and gave up declaring that she was a cipher. The fatigue of moving in had made Laurence's company, while he was suffering from the reaction, almost bearable. Frida, apart from a habit she had of whispering at great length in her mother's ear, was a nice uninquisitive child, and Edith, when she was not whispering back to Frida or echoing Laurence, was still able to rouse in her brother's heart feelings of warm affection. Old Mrs. Touchwood had acquired from some caller a new game of Patience, which kept her gently simmering in the lamplight every evening; Harold had discovered among the odds and ends of salvage from the move a sixpenny encyclopedia that, though it made him unpleasantly informative, at any rate kept him from being interrogative, which John found, on the whole, a slight advantage. Janet Bond had written again most seriously about Joan of Arc, and the film company had given excellent terms for *The Fall of Babylon*. Really, except for two huffy letters from his sisters-in-law in London, John was able to contemplate with much less misgivings a prospect of spending all the winter at Ambles. Beside, he had secured his dog-cart with a dashing chestnut mare, and was negotiating for the twenty-acre field.

Yes, everything was very jolly, and he might even aim at finishing the first draft of the second act before Christmas. It would be jolly to do that and jolly to invite James and Beatrice and George and Eleanor, but not Hugh—no, in no circumstances should Hugh be included in the yuletide armistice—down to Ambles for an uproarious jolly week. Then January should be devoted to the first draft of the third act—really it should be possible to write to Janet Bond presently and assure her of a production next autumn. John was feeling particularly optimistic. For three days in succession the feet of the first act had been moving as rhythmically and regularly toward the curtain as the feet of guardsmen move along the Buckingham Palace Road. It was a fine frosty morning, and even so early in the day John was tapping his second egg to the metrical apostrophes of Uncle Laxart's speech offering to take his niece, Joan, to interview Robert de Baudricourt. Suddenly he noticed that Laurence had not yet put in his appearance. This was strange behavior for one who still preserved from the habit of many early services an excited punctuality for his breakfast, and lightly he asked Edith what had become of her husband.

"He hopes to begin working again at his play this morning. Seeing you working so hard makes him feel lazy." Edith laughed faintly and fearfully, as if she would deprecate her own profanity in referring to so gross a quality as laziness in connection with Laurence, and perhaps for the first time in her life she proclaimed that her opinion was only an echo of Laurence's own by adding, "*he* says that it makes him feel lazy. So he's going to begin at once."

John, whose mind kept reverting iambically and trochaically to the curtain of his first act, merely replied, without any trace of awe, that he was glad Laurence felt in the vein.

"But he hasn't decided yet," Edith continued, "which room he's going to work in."

For the first time a puff of apprehension twitched the little straw that might be going to break the camel's back.

"I'm afraid I can't offer him the library," John said quickly. "*And you shall see the King of France to-day*," he went on composing in his head. "No—*And you shall see King Charles*—no—*and you shall see the King of France at once*—no—*and you shall see the King of France forthwith. Sensation among the villagers standing round. Forthwith is weak at the end of a line. I swear that you shall see the King of France. Sensation.* Yes, that's it."

The top of John's egg was by this time so completely cracked by his metronomic spoon that a good deal of the shell was driven down into the egg: it did not matter, however, because appetite and inspiration were both disposed of by the arrival of Laurence.

"I wish you could have managed to help me with some of these things," he was muttering reproachfully to his wife.

The things consisted of six or seven books, a quantity of foolscap, an inkpot dangerously brimming, a paper-knife made of olive wood from Gethsemane, several pens and pencils, and a roll of blotting paper as white as the snow upon the summit of Mont Blanc, and so fat that John thought at first it was a tablecloth and wondered what his brother-in-law meant to do with it. He was even chilled by a brief and horrible suspicion that he was going to hold a communion service. Edith rose hastily from the table to help her husband unload himself.

"I'm so sorry, dear, why didn't you ring?"

"My dear, how could I ring without letting my materials drop?" Laurence asked, patiently.

"Or call?"

"My chin was too much occupied for calling. But it doesn't matter, Edith. As you see, I've managed to bring everything down quite safely."

"I'm so sorry," Edith went on. "I'd no idea...."

"I told you that I was going to begin work this morning."

"Yes, how stupid of me ... I'm so sorry...."

"Going to work, are you?" interrupted John, who was anxious to stop Edith's conjugal amenity. "That's capital."

"Yes, I'm really only waiting now to choose my room."

"I'm sorry I can't offer you mine ... but I must be alone. I find...."

"Of course," Laurence agreed with a nod of sympathetic knowingness. "Of course, my dear fellow, I shouldn't dream of trespassing. I, though indeed I've no right to compare myself with you, also like to work alone. In fact I consider that a secure solitude provides the ideal setting for dramatic composition. I have a habit—perhaps it comes from preparing my sermons with my eye always upon the spoken rather than upon the written word—I have a habit of declaiming many of my pages aloud to myself. That necessitates my being alone—absolutely alone."

"Yes, you see," Edith said, "if you're alone you're not disturbed."

John who was still sensitive to Edith's truisms tried to cover her last by incorporating Hilda in the conversation with a "What room do you advise?"

"Why not the dining-room? I'll tell Emily to clear away the breakfast things at once."

"Clear away?" Laurence repeated.

"And they won't be laying for lunch till a quarter-to-one."

"Laying for lunch?" Laurence gasped. "My dear Hilda! I don't wish to attribute to my—ah—work an importance which perhaps as a hitherto unacted playwright I have no right to attribute, but I think John at any rate will appreciate my objection to working with—ah—the bread-knife suspended over my head like the proverbial sword of Damocles. No, I'm afraid I must rule out the dining-room as a practicable environment."

"And Mama likes to sit in the drawing-room," said Hilda.

"In any case," Laurence said, indulgently, "I shouldn't feel at ease in the drawing-room. So I shall not disturb Mama. I had thought of suggesting that the children should be given another room in which to play, but to tell the truth I'm tired of moving furniture about. The fact is I miss my vicarage study: it was my own."

"Yes, nobody at the vicarage ever thought of interrupting him, you see," Edith explained.

"Well," said John, roused by the necessity of getting Joan started upon her journey to interview Robert de Baudricourt, "there are several empty bedrooms upstairs. One of them could be transformed into a study for Laurence."

"That means more arranging of furniture," Laurence objected.

"Then there's the garret," said John. "You'd find your bureau up there."

Laurence smiled in order to show how well he understood that the suggestion was only playfulness on John's side and how little he minded the good-natured joke.

"There is one room which might be made—ah—conducive to good work, though at present it is occupied by a quantity of apples; they, however, could easily be moved."

"But I moved them in there from what is now your room," Hilda protested.

"It is good for apples to be frequently moved," said Laurence, kindly. "In fact, the oftener they are moved, the better. And this holds good equally for pippins, codlins, and russets. On the other hand it means I shall lose half a day's work, because even if I *could* make a temporary beginning anywhere else, I should have to superintend the arrangement of the furniture."

"But I thought you didn't want to have any more furniture arranging to do," Hilda contested, acrimoniously. "There are two quite empty rooms at the other end of the passage."

"Yes, but I like the room in which the apples are. John will appreciate my desire for a sympathetic milieu."

"Come, come, we will move the apples," John promised, hurriedly.

Better that the apples should roll from room to room eternally than that he should be driven into offering Laurence a corner of the library, for he suspected that notwithstanding the disclaimer this was his brother-in-law's real objective.

"It doesn't say anything about apples in the encyclopedia," muttered Harold in an aggrieved voice. *"Apoplexy treatment of, Apothecaries measure, Appetite loss of. This may be due to general debility, irregularity in meals, overwork, want of exercise, constipation, and many other...."*

"Goodness gracious me, whatever has the boy got hold of?" exclaimed his grandmother.

"Grandmama, if you mix Lanoline with an equal quantity of Sulphur you can cure Itch," Harold went on with his spectacles glued to the page. "And, oh, Grandmama, you know you told me not to make a noise the other day because your heart was weak. Well, you're suffering from flatulence. The encyclopedia says that many people who are suffering from flatulence think they have heart disease."

"Will no one stop the child?" Grandmama pleaded.

Laurence snatched away the book from his nephew and put it in his pocket.

"That book is mine, I believe, Harold," he said, firmly, and not even Hilda dared protest, so majestic was Laurence and so much fluttered was poor Grandmama.

John seized the opportunity to make his escape; but when he was at last seated before his table the feet of the first act limped pitiably; Laurence had trodden with all his might upon their toes; his work that morning was chiropody, not composition, and bungling chiropody at that. After lunch Laurence was solemnly inducted to his new study, and he may have been conscious of an ecclesiastical parallel in the manner of his taking possession, for he made a grave joke about it.

"Let us hope that I shall not be driven out of my new living by being too—ah—broad."

His wife did not realize that he was being droll and had drawn down her lips to an expression of pained sympathy, when she saw the others all laughing and Laurence smiling his acknowledgments; her desperate effort to change the contours of her face before Laurence noticed her failure to respond sensibly gave the impression that she had nearly swallowed a loose tooth.

"Perhaps you'd like me to bring up your tea, dear, so that you won't be disturbed?" she suggested.

"Ah, tea ..." murmured Laurence. "Let me see. It's now a quarter-past two. Tea is at half-past four. I will come down for half an hour. That will give me a clear two hours before dinner. If I allow a quarter of an hour for arranging my table, that will give me four hours in all. Perhaps considering my strenuous morning four hours will be enough for the first day. I don't like the notion of working after dinner," he added to John.

"No?" queried John, doubtfully. He had hoped that his brother-in-law would feel inspired by the port: it was easy enough to avoid him in the afternoon, especially since on the first occasion that he had been taken for a drive in the new dogcart he had evidently been imbued with a detestation of driving that would probably last for the remainder of his life; in fact he was talking already of wanting to sell Primrose and the vicarage chaise.

"Though of course on some evenings I may not be able to help it," added Laurence. "I may *have* to work."

"Of course you may," John assented, encouragingly. "I dare say there'll be evenings when the mere idea of waiting even for coffee will make you fidgety. You mustn't lose the mood, you know."

"No, of course, I appreciate that."

"There's nothing so easily lost as the creative gift, Balzac said."

"Did he?" Laurence murmured, anxiously. "But I promise you I shall let nothing interfere with me *if*—" the conjunction fizzed from his mouth like soda from a syphon, "*if* I'm in the—ah—mood. The mood—yes—ah—precisely." His brow began to lower; the mood was upon him; and everybody stole quietly from the room. They had scarcely reached the head of the stairs when the door opened again and Laurence called after Edith: "I should prefer that whoever brings me news of tea merely knocks without coming in. I shall assume that a knock upon my door means tea. But I don't wish anybody to come in."

Laurence disappeared. He seemed under the influence of a strong mental aphrodisiac and was evidently guaranteeing himself against being discovered in an embarrassing situation with his Muse.

"This is very good for me," thought John. "It has taught me how easily a man may make a confounded ass of himself without anybody's raising a finger to warn him. I hope I didn't give that sort of impression to those two women on board. I shall have to watch myself very carefully in future."

At this moment Emily announced that Lawyer Deacle was waiting to see Mr. Touchwood, which meant that the twenty-acre field was at last his. The legal formalities were complete; that very afternoon John had the pleasure of watching the fierce little Kerry cows munch the last grass they would ever munch in his field. But it was nearly dusk when they were driven home, and John lost five balls in celebrating his triumph with a brassy.

Laurence appeared at tea in a velveteen coat, which probably provided the topic for the longest whisper that even Frida had ever been known to utter.

"Come, come, Frida," said her father. "You won't disturb us by saying aloud what you want to say." He had leaned over majestically to emphasize his rebuke and in doing so brushed with his sleeve Grandmama's wrist.

"Goodness, it's a cat," the old lady cried, with a shudder. "I shall have to go away from here, Johnnie, if you have a cat in the house. I'd rather have mice all over me than one of those horrid cats. Ugh! the nasty thing!"

She was not at all convinced of her mistake even when persuaded to stroke her son-in-law's coat.

"I hope it's been properly shooed out. Harold, please look well under all the chairs, there's a good boy."

During the next few days John felt that he was being in some indefinable way ousted by Laurence from the spiritual mastery of his own house. John was averse from according to his brother-in-law a greater forcefulness of character than he could ascribe to himself; if he had to admit that he really was being supplanted somehow, he preferred to search for the explanation in the years of theocratic prestige that gave a background to the all-pervasiveness of that sacerdotal personality. Yet ultimately the impression of his own relegation to a secondary place remained elusive and incommunicable. He could not for instance grumble that the times of the meals were being altered nor complain that in the smallest detail the domestic mechanism was being geared up or down to suit Laurence; the whole sensation was essentially of a spiritual eviction, and the nearest he could get to formulating his resentment (though perhaps resentment was too definite a word for this vague uneasiness) was his own gradually growing opinion that of all those at present under the Ambles roof Laurence was the most important. This loss of importance was bad for John's work, upon which it soon began to exert a discouraging influence, because he became doubtful of his own position, hypercritical of his talent, and timid about his social ability. He began to meditate the long line of failures to dramatize the immortal tale of Joan of Arc immortally, to see himself dangling at the end of this long line of ineptitudes and to ask himself whether bearing in mind the vastness of even our own solar system it was really worth while writing at all. It could not be due to anything or anybody but Laurence, this sense of his own futility; not even when a few years ago he had reached the conclusion that as a realistic novelist he was a failure had he been so profoundly conscious of his own insignificance in time and space.

"I shall have to go away if I'm ever to get on with this play," he told himself.

Yet still so indefinite was his sense of subordinacy at Ambles that he accused his liver (an honest one that did not deserve the reproach) and bent over his table again with all the determination he could muster. The concrete fact was still missing; his capacity for self-deception was still robust enough to persuade him that it was all a passing fancy, and he might have gone plodding on at Ambles for the rest of the winter if one morning about a week after Laurence had begun to write, the door of his own library had not opened to the usurper, manuscript in hand.

"I don't like to interrupt you, my dear fellow.... I know you have your own work to consider ... but I'm anxious for your opinion—in fact I should like to read you my first act."

It was useless to resist: if it were not now, it would be later.

"With pleasure," said John. Then he made one effort. "Though I prefer reading to myself."

"That would involve waiting for the typewriter. Yes, my screed is—ah—difficult to make out. And I've indulged in a good many erasures and insertions. No, I think you'd better let me read it to you."

John indicated a chair and looked out of the window longingly at the birds, as patients in the hands of a dentist regard longingly the sparrows in the dingy evergreens of the dentist's back garden.

"When we had our little talk the other day," Laurence began, "you will remember that I spoke of a drama I had already written, of which the disciple Thomas was the protagonist. This drama notwithstanding the probably obstructive attitude of the Lord Chamberlain I have rewritten, or rather I have rewritten the first act. I call the play—ah—*Thomas.*"

"It sounds a little trivial for such a serious subject, don't you think?" John suggested. "I mean, Thomas has come to be associated in so many people's minds with footmen. Wouldn't *Saint Thomas* be better, and really rather more respectful? Many people still have a great feeling of reverence for apostles."

"No, no, *Thomas* it is: *Thomas* it must remain. You have forgotten perhaps that I told you he was the prototype of the man in the street. It is the simplicity, the unpretentiousness of the title that for me gives it a value. Well, to resume. *Thomas. A play in four acts. By Laurence Armytage.* By the way, I'm going to spell my name with a y in future. Poetic license. Ha-ha! I shall not advertise the change in the *Times.* But I think it looks more literary with a y. *Act the First. Scene the First. The shore of the Sea of Galilee.* I say nothing else. I don't attempt to describe it. That is what I have learnt from Shakespeare. This modern passion for description can only injure the greatness of the theme. *Enter from the left the Virgin Mary.*"

"Enter who?" asked John in amazement.

"The Virgin Mary. The mother ..."

"Yes, I know who she is, but ... well, I'm not a religious man, Laurence, in fact I've not been to church since I was a boy ... but ... no, no, you can't do that."

"Why not?"

"It will offend people."

"I want to offend people," Laurence intoned. "If thy eye offend thee, pluck it out."

"Well, you did," said John. "You put in a *y* instead."

"I'm not jesting, my dear fellow."

"Nor am I," said John. "What I want you to understand is that you can't bring the Virgin Mary on the stage. Why, I'm even doubtful about Joan of Arc's vision of the Archangel Michael. Some people may object, though I'm counting on his being generally taken for St. George."

"I know that you are writing a play about Joan of Arc, but—and I hope you'll not take unkindly what I'm going to say—but Joan of Arc can never be more than a pretty piece of medievalism, whereas Thomas ..."

John gave up, and the next morning he told the household that he was called back to London on business.

"Perhaps I shall have some peace here," he sighed, looking round at his dignified Church Row library.

"Mrs. James called earlier this morning, sir, and said not to disturb you, but she hoped you'd had a comfortable journey and left these flowers, and Mrs. George has telephoned from the theater to say she'll be here almost directly."

"Thank you, Mrs. Worfolk," John said. "Perhaps Mrs. George will be taking lunch."

"Yes, sir, I expect she will," said his housekeeper.

CHAPTER V

MRS. GEORGE TOUCHWOOD—or as she was known on the stage, Miss Eleanor Cartright—was big-boned, handsome, and hawklike, with the hungry look of the ambitious actress who is drawing near to forty—she was in fact thirty-seven—and realizes that the disappointed adventuresses of what are called strong plays are as near as she will ever get to the tragedy queens of youthful aspiration. Such an one accustomed to flash her dark eyes in defiance of a morally but not esthetically hostile gallery and to have the whole of a stage for the display of what well-disposed critics hailed as vitality and cavaliers condemned as lack of repose, such an one in John's tranquil library was, as Mrs. Worfolk put it, "rather too much of a good thing and no mistake"; and when Eleanor was there, John experienced as much malaise as he would have experienced from being shut up in a housemaid's closet with a large gramophone and the housemaid. This claustrophobia, however, was the smallest strain that his sister-in-law inflicted upon him; she affected his heart and his conscience more acutely, because he could never meet her without a sensation of guilt on account of his not yet having found a part for her in any of his plays, to which was added the fear he always felt in her presence that soon or late he should from sheer inability to hold out longer award her the leading part in his play. George had often seriously annoyed him by his unwillingness to help himself; but at the thought of being married for thirteen years to Eleanor he had always excused his brother's flaccid dependence.

"George is a bit of a sponge," James had once said, "but Eleanor! Eleanor is the roughest and toughest loofah that was ever known. She is irritant and absorbent at the same time, and by gad, she has the appearance of a loofah."

The prospect of Eleanor's company at lunch on the morning after his return to town gave John a sensation of having escaped the devil to fall into the deep sea, of having jumped from the frying-pan into the fire, in fact of illustrating every known proverbial attempt to express the distinction without the difference.

"It's a great pity that Eleanor didn't marry Laurence," he thought. "Each would have kept the other well under, and she could have played Mary Magdalene in that insane play of his. And, by Jove, if they *had* married, neither of them would have been a relation! Moreover, if Laurence had been caught by Eleanor, Edith might never have married at all and could have kept house for me. And if Edith hadn't married, Hilda mightn't have married, and then Harold would never have been born."

John's hard pruning of his family-tree was interrupted by a sense of the house's having been attacked by an angry mob—an illusion that he had learnt to connect with his sister-in-law's arrival. To make sure, however, he went out on the landing and called down to know if anything was the matter.

"Mrs. George is having some trouble with the taxi-man, sir," explained Maud, who was holding the front-door open and looking apprehensively at the pictures that were clattering on the walls in the wind.

"Why does she take taxis?" John muttered, irritably. "She can't afford them, and there's no excuse for such extravagance when the tube is so handy."

At this moment Eleanor reached the door, on the threshold of which she turned like Medea upon Jason to have the last word with the taxi-driver before the curtain fell.

"Did Mr. Touchwood get my message?" she was asking.

"Yes, yes," John called down. "I'm expecting you to lunch."

When he watched Eleanor all befurred coming upstairs, he felt not much less nervous than a hunter of big game face to face with his first tiger; the landing seemed to wobble like a howdah; now he had fired and missed, and she was embracing him as usual. How many times at how many meetings with Eleanor had he tried unsuccessfully to dodge that kiss—which always seemed improper whether because her lips were too red, or too full, he could never decide, though he always felt when he was released that he ought to beg her husband's pardon.

"You were an old beast not to come and see us when you got back from America; but never mind, I'm awfully glad to see you, all the same."

"Thank you very much, Eleanor. Why are you glad?"

"Oh, you sarcastic old bear!"

This perpetual suggestion of his senility was another trick of Eleanor's that he deplored; dash it, he was two years younger than George, whom she called Georgieboy.

"No, seriously," Eleanor went on. "I was just going to wire and ask if I could send the kiddies down to the country. Lambton wants me for a six weeks' tour before Xmas, and I can't leave them with Georgie. You see, if this piece catches on, it means a good shop for me in the new year."

"Yes, I quite understand your point of view," John said. "But what I don't understand is why Bertram and Viola can't stay with their father."

"But George is ill. Surely you got my letter?"

"I didn't realize that the presence of his children might prove fatal. However, send them down to Ambles by all means."

"Oh, but I'd much rather not after the way Hilda wrote to me, and now that you've come back there's no need."

"I don't quite understand."

"Well, you won't mind having them here for a short visit? Then they can go down to Ambles for the Christmas holidays."

"But the Christmas holidays won't begin for at least six weeks."

"I know."

"But you don't propose that Bertram and Viola should spend six weeks here?"

"They'll be no bother, you old crosspatch. Bertram will be at school all day, and I suppose that Maud or Elsa will always be available to take Viola to her dancing-lessons. You remember the dancing-lessons you arranged for?"

"I remember that I accepted the arrangement," said John.

"Well, she's getting on divinely, and it would be a shame to interrupt them just now, especially as she's in the middle of a Spanish series. Her *cachucha* is ..." Eleanor could only blow a kiss to express what Viola's *cachucha* was. "But then, of course, I had a Spanish grandmother."

When John regarded her barbaric personality he could have credited her with being the granddaughter of a cannibal queen.

"So I thought that her governess could come here every morning just as easily as to Earl's Court. In fact, it will be more convenient, or at any rate, equally convenient for her, because she lives at Kilburn."

"I dare say it will be equally convenient for the governess," said John, sardonically.

"And I thought," Eleanor continued, "that it would be a good opportunity for Viola to have French lessons every afternoon. You won't want to have her all the time with you, and the French governess can give the children their tea. That will be good for Bertram's accent."

"I don't doubt that it will be superb for Bertram's accent, but I absolutely decline to have a French governess bobbing in and out of my house. It's bound to make trouble with the servants who always think that French governesses are designing and licentious, and I don't want to create a false impression."

"Well, aren't you an old prude? Who would ever think that you had any sort of connection with the stage? By the way, you haven't told me if there'll be anything for me in your next."

"Well, at present the subject of my next play is a secret ... and as for the cast...."

383

John was so nearly on the verge of offering Eleanor the part of Mary of Anjou, for which she would be as suitable as a giraffe, that in order to effect an immediate diversion he asked her when the children were to arrive.

"Let me see, to-day's Saturday. To-morrow I go down to Bristol, where we open. They'd better come to-night, because to-morrow being Sunday they'll have no lessons, which will give them time to settle down. Georgie will be glad to know they're with you."

"I've no doubt he'll be enchanted," John agreed.

The bell sounded for lunch, and they went downstairs.

"I've got to be back at the theater by two," Eleanor announced, looking at the horridly distorted watch upon her wrist. "I wonder if we mightn't ask Maud to open half-a-bottle of champagne? I'm dreadfully tired."

John ordered a bottle to be opened; he felt rather tired himself.

"Let us be quite clear about this arrangement," he began, when after three glasses of wine he felt less appalled by the prospect, and had concluded that after all Bertram and Viola would not together be as bad as Laurence with his play, not to mention Harold with his spectacles and entomology, his interrogativeness and his greed. "The English governess will arrive every morning for Viola. What is her name?"

"Miss Coldwell."

"Miss Coldwell then will be responsible for Viola all the morning. The French governess is canceled, and I shall come to an arrangement with Miss Coldwell by which she will add to her salary by undertaking all responsibility for Viola until Viola is in bed. Bertram will go to school, and I shall rely upon Miss Coldwell to keep an eye on his behavior at home."

"And don't forget the dancing-lessons."

"No, I had Madame What's-her-name's account last week."

"I mean, don't forget to arrange for Viola to go."

"That pilgrimage will, I hope, form a part of what Miss Coldwell would probably call 'extras.' And after all perhaps George will soon be fit."

"The poor old boy has been awfully seedy all the summer."

"What's he suffering from? Infantile paralysis?"

"It's all very well for you to joke about it, but you don't live in a wretched boarding-house in Earl's Court. You mustn't let success spoil you, John. It's so easy when everything comes your way to forget the less fortunate people. Look at me. I'm thirty-four, you know."

"Are you really? I should never have thought it."

"I don't mind your laughing at me, you old crab. But I don't like you to laugh at Georgie."

"I never do," John said. "I don't suppose that there's anybody alive who takes George as seriously as I do."

Eleanor brushed away a tear and said she must get back to the rehearsal.

When she was gone John felt that he had been unkind, and he reproached himself for letting Laurence make him cynical.

"The fact is," he told himself, "that ever since I heard Doris Hamilton make that remark in the saloon of the *Murmania*, I've become suspicious of my family. She began it, and then by ill luck I was thrown too much with Laurence, who clinched it. Eleanor is right: I *am* letting myself be spoilt by success. After all, there's no reason why those two children shouldn't come here. *They* won't be writing plays about apostles. I'll send George a box of cigars to show that I didn't mean to sneer at him. And why didn't I offer to pay for Eleanor's taxi? Yes, I am getting spoilt. I must watch myself. And I ought not to have joked about Eleanor's age."

Luckily his sister-in-law had finished the champagne, for if John had drunk another glass he might have offered her the part of the Maid herself.

The actual arrival of Bertram and Viola passed off more successfully. They were both presentable, and John was almost flattered when Mrs. Worfolk commented on their likeness to him, remembering what a nightmare it had always seemed when Hilda used to excavate points of resemblance between him and Harold. Mrs. Worfolk herself was so much pleased to have him back from Ambles that she was in the best of good humours, and even the statuesque Maud flushed with life like some Galatea.

"I think Maud's a darling, don't you, Uncle John?" exclaimed Viola.

"We all appreciate Maud's—er—capabilities," John hemmed.

He felt that it was a silly answer, but inasmuch as Maud was present at the time he could not, either for his sake or for hers give an unconditional affirmative.

"I swopped four blood-allys for an Indian in the break," Bertram announced.

"With an Indian, my boy, I suppose you mean."

"No, I don't. I mean for an Indian—an Indian marble. And I swopped four Guatemalas for two Nicaraguas."

"You ought to be at the Foreign Office."

"But the ripping thing is, Uncle John, that two of the Guatemalas are fudges."

"Such a doubtful coup would not debar you from a diplomatic career."

"And I say, what is the Foreign Office? We've got a French chap in my class."

"You ask for an explanation of the Foreign Office. That, my boy, might puzzle the omniscience of the Creator."

"I say, I don't twig very well what you're talking about."

"The attributes of the Foreign Office, my boy, are rigidity where there should be suppleness, weakness where there should be firmness, and for intelligence the substitution of hair brushed back from the forehead."

"I say, you're ragging me, aren't you? No, really, what is the Foreign Office?"

"It is the ultimate preserve of a privileged imbecility."

Bertram surrendered, and John congratulated himself upon the possession of a nephew whose perseverance and curiosity had been sapped by a scholastic education.

"Harold would have tackled me word by word during one of our walks. I shall enter into negotiations with Hilda at Christmas to provide for his mental training on condition that I choose the school. Perhaps I shall hear of a good one in the Shetland Islands."

When Mrs. Worfolk visited John as usual at ten o'clock to wish him good-night, she was enthusiastic about Bertram and Viola.

"Well, really, sir, if yaul pardon the liberty, I must say I wouldn't never of believed that Mrs. George's children *could* be so quiet and nice-behaved. They haven't given a bit of trouble, and I've never heard Maud speak so highly of anyone as of Miss Viola. 'That child's a regular little angel, Mrs. Worfolk,' she said to me. Well, sir, I'm bound to say that children does brighten up a house. I'm sure I've done my best what with putting flowers in all the vawses and one thing and another, but really, well I'm quite taken with your little nephew and niece, and I've had some experience of them, I mean to say, what with my poor sister's Herbert and all. I *have* put the tantalus ready. Good-night, sir."

"The fact of the matter is," John assured himself, "that when I'm alone with them I can manage children perfectly. I only hope that Miss Coldwell will fall in with my ideas. If she does, I see no reason why we shouldn't spend an extremely pleasant time all together."

Unfortunately for John's hope of a satisfactory coalition with the governess he received a hurried note by messenger from his sister-in-law next morning to say that Miss Coldwell was laid up: the precise disease was illegible in Eleanor's communication, but it was serious enough to keep Miss Coldwell at home for three weeks. "*Meanwhile,*" Eleanor wrote, "*she is trying to get her sister to come down from*"—the abode of the sister was equally illegible. "*But the most important thing is,*" Eleanor went on, "*that little V. shouldn't miss her dancing-lessons. So will you arrange for Maud to take her every Tuesday and Friday? And, of course, if there's anything you want to know, there's always George.*"

Of George's eternal being John had no doubts; of his knowledge he was less sanguine: the only thing that George had ever known really well was the moment to lead trumps.

"However," said John, in consultation with his housekeeper, "I dare say we shall get along."

"Oh, certainly we shall, sir," Mrs. Worfolk confidently proclaimed, "well, I mean to say, I've been married myself."

John bowed his appreciation of this fact.

"And though I never had the happiness to have any little toddlers of my own, anyone being married gets used to the idea of having children. There's always the chance, as you might say. It isn't like as if I was an old maid, though, of course, my husband died in Jubilee year."

"Did he, Mrs. Worfolk, did he?"

"Yes, sir, he planed off his thumb when he was working on one of the benches for the stands through him looking round at a black fellow in a turban covered in jewelry who was driving to Buckingham Palace. One of the new arrivals, it was; and his arm got blood poisoning. That's how I remember it was Jubilee year, though usually I'm a terror for knowing when anything did occur. He wouldn't of minded so much, he said, only he was told it was the Char of Persia and that made him mad."

"Why? What had he got against the Shah?"

"He hadn't got nothing against the Char. But it wasn't the Char; and if he'd of known it wasn't the Char he never wouldn't of turned round so quick, and there's no saying he wouldn't of been alive to this day. No, sir, don't you worry about this governess. I dare say if she'd of come she'd only of caused a bit of unpleasantness all round."

At the same time, John thought, when he sent for the children in order to make the announcement of Miss Coldwell's desertion, notwithstanding Mrs. Worfolk's optimism it was a pity that the first day of their visit should be a Sunday.

"I'm sorry to say, Viola, and, of course, Bertram, this applies equally to you, that poor Miss Coldwell has been taken very ill."

That strange expression upon the children's faces might be an awkward attempt to express their youthful sympathy, but it more ominously resembled a kind of gloating ecstacy, as they stood like two cherubs outside the gates of paradise, or two children outside a bunshop.

"Very ill," John went on, "so ill indeed that it is feared she will not be able to come for a few days, and so...."

Whatever more John would have said was lost in the riotous acclamations with which Bertram and Viola greeted the sad news. After the first cries and leaps of joy had subsided to a chanted duet, which ran somehow like this:

"Oh, oh, Miss Coldwell,
She can't come to Hampstead,
Hurrah, hurrah, hurrah,
Miss Coldwell's not coming:"
John ventured to rebuke the singers for their insensibility to human suffering.

"For she may be dangerously ill," he protested.

"How *fizzing*," Bertram shouted.

"She might die."

The prospect that this opened before Bertram was apparently too beautiful for any verbal utterance, and he remained open-mouthed in a mute and exquisite anticipation of liberty.

"What and never come to us ever again?" Viola breathed, her blue eyes aglow with visions of a larger life.

John shook his head, gravely.

"Oh, Uncle John," she cried, "wouldn't that be glorious?"

Bertram's heart was too full for words: he simply turned head over heels.

"But you hard-hearted little beasts," their uncle expostulated.

"She's most frightfully strict," Viola explained.

"Yes, we shouldn't have been able to do anything decent if she'd come," Bertram added.

A poignant regret for that unknown governess suffering from her illegible complaint pierced John's mind. But perhaps she would recover, in which case she should spend her convalescence at Ambles with Harold; for if when in good health she was strict, after a severe illness she might be ferocious.

"Well, I'm not at all pleased with your attitude," John declared. "And you'll find me twice as strict as Miss Coldwell."

"Oh, no, we shan't," said Bertram with a smile of jovial incredulity.

John let this contradiction pass: it seemed an imprudent subject for debate. "And now, to-day being Sunday, you'd better get ready for church."

"Oh, but we always dress up on Sunday," Viola said.

"So does everybody," John replied. "Go and get ready."

The children left the room, and he rang for Mrs. Worfolk.

"Master Bertram and Miss Viola will shortly be going to church, and I want you to arrange for somebody to take them."

Mrs. Worfolk hesitated.

"Who was you thinking of, sir?"

"I wasn't thinking of anybody in particular, but I suppose Maud could go."

"Maud has her rooms to do."

"Well, Elsa."

"Elsa has her dinner to get."

"Well, then, perhaps you would ..."

"Yaul pardon the liberty, sir, but I never go to church except of an evening *some*times; I never could abide being stared at."

"Oh, very well," said John, fretfully, as Mrs. Worfolk retired. "Though I'm hanged if *I'm* going to take them," he added to himself, "at any rate without a rehearsal."

The two children soon came back in a condition of complete preparation and insisted so loudly upon their uncle's company that he yielded; though when he found himself with a child on either side of him in the sabbath calm of the Hampstead streets footfall-haunted, he was appalled at his rashness. There was a church close to his own house, but with an instinct to avoid anything like a domestic scandal he had told his nephew and niece that it was not a suitable church for children, and had led them further afield through the ghostly November sunlight.

"But look here," Bertram objected, "we can't go through any slums, you know, because the cads will bung things at my topper."

"Not if you're with me," John argued. "I am wearing a top-hat myself."

"Well, they did when I went for a walk with Father once on Sunday."

"The slums round Earl's Court are probably much fiercer than the slums round Hampstead," John suggested. "And anyway here we are."

He had caught a glimpse of an ecclesiastical building, which unfortunately turned out to be a Jewish tabernacle and not open: a few minutes later, however, an indubitably Anglican place of worship invited their attendance, and John trying not to look as bewildered as he felt let himself be conducted by a sidesman to the very front pew.

"I wonder if he thinks I'm a member of parliament. But I wish to goodness he'd put us in the second row. I shall be absolutely lost where I am."

John looked round to catch the sidesman's eye and plead for a less conspicuous position, but even as he turned his head a terrific crash from the organ proclaimed that it was too late and that the service had begun.

By relying upon the memories of youthful worship John might have been able to cope successfully with Morning Prayer, even with that florid variation of it which is generally known as Mattins. Unluckily the church he had chosen for the spiritual encouragement of his nephew and niece was to the church of his recollections as Mount Everest to a molehill. As a simple spectator without encumbrances he might have enjoyed the service and derived considerable inspiration from it for the decorative ecclesiasticism of his new play; as an uncle it alarmed and confused him. The lace-hung acolytes, the candles, the chrysanthemums, the purple vestments and the ticking of the thurible affected him neither with Protestant disgust nor with Catholic devoutness, but much more deeply as nothing but incentives to the unanswerable inquiries of Bertram and Viola.

"What are they doing?" whispered his nephew.

"Hush!" he whispered back in what he tried to feel was the right intonation of pious reproof.

"What's that little boy doing with a spoon?" whispered his niece.

"Hush!" John blew forth again. "Attend to the service."

"But it isn't a real service, is it?" she persisted.

Luckily the congregation knelt at this point, and John plunged down with a delighted sense of taking cover. Presently he began to be afraid that his attitude of devotional self-abasement might be seeming a little ostentatious, and he peered cautiously round over the top of the pew; to his dismay he perceived that Bertram and Viola were still standing up.

"Kneel down at once," he commanded in what he hoped would be an authoritative whisper, but which was in the result an agonized croak.

"I want to see what they're doing," both children protested.

Bertram's Etons appeared too much attentuated for a sharp tug, nor did John feel courageous enough in the front row to jerk Viola down upon her knees by pulling her petticoats, which might come off. He therefore covered his face with his hands in what was intended to look like a spasm of acute reverence and growled at them both to kneel down, unless they wanted to be sent back instantly to Earl's Court. Evidently impressed by this threat the children knelt down; but they were no sooner upon their knees than the perverse congregation rose to its feet, the concerted movement taking John so completely unawares that he was left below and felt when he did rise like a naughty boy who has been discovered hiding under a table. He was not put at ease by Viola's asking him to find her place in the prayer-book; it seemed to him terrible to discern the signs of a vindictive spirit in one so young.

"Hush," he whispered. "You must remember that we're in the front row and must be careful not to disturb the——" he hesitated at the word "performers" and decided to envelop whatever they were in a cough.

There were no more questions for a while, nothing indeed but tiptoe fidgetings until two acolytes advanced with lighted candles to a position on each side of the deacon who was preparing to read the gospel.

"Why can't he see to read?" Bertram asked. "It's not dark."

"Hush," John whispered. "This is the gospel"

He knew he was safe in affirming so much, because the announcement that he was about to read the gospel had been audibly given out by the deacon. At this point the congregation crossed its innumerable features three times, and Bertram began to giggle; immediately afterward fumes poured from the swung censer, and Viola began to choke. John felt that it was impossible to interrupt what was presumably considered the *pièce de resistance* of the service by leading the two children out along the whole length of the church; yet he was convinced that if he did not lead them out their gigglings and snortings would have a disastrous effect upon the soloist. Then he had a brilliant idea: Viola was obviously much upset by the incense and he would escort her out into fresh air with the solicitude that one gives to a sick person: Bertram he should leave behind to giggle alone. He watched his nephew bending lower and lower to contain his mirth; then with a quick propulsive gesture he hurried Viola into the aisle. Unfortunately when with a sigh of relief he stood upon the steps outside and put on his hat he found that in his confusion he had brought out Bertram's hat, which on his intellectual head felt like a precariously balanced inkpot; and though he longed to abandon Bertram to his well merited fate he could not bring himself to walk up Fitzjohn's Avenue in Bertram's hat, nor could he even contemplate with equanimity the notion of Bertram's walking up under his. Had it been a week-day either of them might have passed for an eccentric advertisement, but on a Sunday....

"And if I stand on the steps of a church holding this minute hat in my hand," he thought, "people will think I'm collecting for some charity. Confound that boy! And I can't pretend that I'm feeling too hot in the middle of November. Dash that boy! And I certainly can't wear it. A Japanese juggler wouldn't be able to wear it. Damn that boy!"

Yet John would rather have gone home in a baby's bonnet than enter the church again, and the best that could be hoped was that Bertram dismayed at finding himself alone would soon emerge. Bertram, however, did not emerge, and John had a sudden fear lest in his embarrassment he might have escaped by another door and was even now rushing blindly home. Blindly was the right adverb indeed, for he would certainly be unable to see anything from under his uncle's hat. Viola, having recovered from her choking fit, began to cry at this point, and an old lady who must have noted with tender approval John's exit came out with a bottle of smelling-salts, which she begged him to make use of. Before he could decline she had gone back inside the church leaving him with the bottle. If he could have forced the contents down Viola's throat without attracting more attention he would have done so, but by this time one or two passers-by had stopped to stare at the scene, and he heard one of them tell his companion that it was a street conjurer just going to perform.

"Will anything make you stop crying?" he asked his niece in despair.

"I want Bertram," she wailed.

And at that moment Bertram appeared, led out by two sidesmen.

"Your little boy doesn't know how to behave himself in church," one of them informed John, severely.

"I was only looking for my hat," Bertram explained. "I thought it had rolled into the next pew. Let go of my arm. I slipped off the hassock. I couldn't help making a little noise, Uncle John."

John was grateful to Bertram for thus exonerating him publicly from the responsibility of having begotten him, and he inquired almost kindly what had happened.

"The hassock slipped, and I fell into the next pew."

"I'm sorry my nephew made a noise," said John to the sidesman. "My niece was taken ill, and he was left behind by accident. Thank you for showing him the way out, yes. Come along, Bertram, I've got your hat. Where's mine?" Bertram looked blankly at his uncle.

"Do you mean to say——" John began, and then he saw a passing taxi to which he shouted.

"Those smelling-salts belong to an old lady," he explained hurriedly and quite inadequately to the bewildered sidesman into whose hands he had thrust the bottle. "Come along," he urged the children, and when they were scrambling into the taxi he called back to the sidesmen, "You can give to the jumble sale any hat that is swept up after the service."

Inside the taxi John turned to the children.

"One would think you'd never been inside a church before," he said, reproachfully.

"Bertram," said Viola, in bland oblivion of all that her uncle had endured, "when we dress up to-day shall we act going to church, or finish Robinson Crusoe?"

"Wait till we see what we can find for dressing up," Bertram advised.

John displayed a little anxiety.

"Dressing up?" he repeated.

"We always dress up every Sunday," the children burst forth in unison.

"Oh, I see—it's a kind of habit. Well, I dare say Mrs. Worfolk will be able to find you an old duster or something."

"Duster," echoed Viola, scornfully. "That's not enough for dressing up."

"I didn't suggest a duster as anything but a supplement to your ordinary costume. I didn't anticipate that you were going to rely entirely upon the duster."

"I say, V, can you twig what Uncle John says?"

Viola shook her head.

"Nor more can I," said Bertram, sympathetically.

Before the taxi reached Church Row, John found himself adopting a positively deferential manner towards his nephew and his niece, and when they were once again back in the quiet house, the hall of which was faintly savoury with the maturing lunch he asked them if they would mind amusing themselves for an hour while he wrote some letters.

"For I take it you won't want to dress up immediately," he added as an excuse for attending to his own business.

The children confirmed his supposition, but went on to inform him that the domenical régime at Earl's Court prescribed a walk after church.

"Owing to the accident to my hat I'm afraid I must ask you to let me off this morning."

"Right-o," Bertram agreed, cheerfully. "But I vote we come up and sit with you while you write your letters. I think letters are a beastly fag, don't you?"

John felt that the boy was proffering his own and his sister's company in a spirit of altruism, and he could not muster enough gracelessness to decline the proposal. So upstairs they all went.

"I think this is rather a ripping room, don't you, V?"

"The carpet's very old," said Viola.

"Have you got any decent books?" Bertram inquired, looking round at the shelves. "Any Henty's, I mean, or anything?"

"No, I'm afraid I haven't," said John, apologetically.

"Or bound up Boys Own Papers?"

John shook his head.

"But I'll tell you what I have got," he added with a sudden inspiration. "Kingsley's *Heroes*."

"Is that a pi book?" asked Bertram, suspiciously.

"Not at all. It's about Greek gods and goddesses, essentially broad-minded divinities."

"Right-o. I'll have a squint at it, if you like," Bertram volunteered. "Come on, V, don't start showing off your rotten dancing. Come and look at this book. It's got some spiffing pictures."

"Lunch won't be very long," John announced in order to propitiate any impatience at what they might consider the boring entertainment he was offering.

Presently the two children left their uncle alone, and he observed with pride that they took with them the book. He little thought that so mild a dose of romance as could be extracted from Kingsley's *Heroes* would before the twilight of that November day run through 36 Church Row like fire. But then John did not know that there was a calf's head for dinner that night; he had not realized the scenic capacity of the cistern cupboard at the top of the house; and most of all he had not associated with dressing up on Sunday afternoon the histrionic force that Bertram and Viola inherited from their mother.

"Is it Androméda or Andrómeda?" Bertram asked at lunch.

"Andrómeda, my boy," John answered. "Perseus and Andromeda."

"I think it would make a jolly good play, don't you?" Bertram went on.

Really, thought John, this nephew was a great improvement upon that spectacled inquisitor at Ambles.

"A capital play," he agreed, heartily. "Are you thinking of writing it?"

"V and I thought we'd do it instead of finishing Robinson Crusoe. Well, you see, you haven't got any decent fur rugs, and V's awfully stupid about having her face blacked."

"It's my turn not to be a savage," Viola pleaded in defense of her squeamishness.

"I said you could be Will Atkins as well. I know I'd jolly well like to be Will Atkins myself."

"All right," Viola offered. "You can, and I'll be Robinson."

"You can't change like that in the middle of a play," her brother argued.

John, who appreciated both Viola's dislike of burnt-cork and Bertram's esthetic objection to changing parts in the middle of a piece, strongly recommended Perseus and Andromeda.

"Of course, you got the idea from Kingsley? Bravo, Bertram," he said, beaming with cordial patronage.

"And I suppose," his nephew went on, "that you'd rather we played at the top of the house. I expect it would be quieter, if you're writing letters. Mother said you often liked to be quiet." He alluded to this desire rather shamefully, as if it were a secret vice of his uncle, who hurriedly approved the choice of the top landing for the scene of the classic drama.

"Then would you please tell Mrs. Worfolk that we can have the calf's head?"

"The what?"

"V found a calf's head in the larder, and it would make a fizzing Gorgon's head, but Mrs. Worfolk wouldn't let us have it."

John was so much delighted with the trend of Bertram's ingenuity that he sent for Mrs. Worfolk and told her that the calf's head might be borrowed for the play.

"I'll take no responsibility for your dinner," said his housekeeper, warningly.

"That's all right, Mrs. Worfolk. If anything happens to the head I shan't grumble. There'll always be the cold beef, won't there?"

Mrs. Worfolk turned up her eyes to heaven and left the room.

"Well, I think I've arranged that for you successfully."

"Thank you, Uncle John," said Bertram.

"Thank you, Uncle John," said Viola.

What nice quiet well-mannered children they were, after all; and he by no means ought to blame them for the fiasco of the churchgoing; the setting had of course been utterly unfamiliar; these ritualistic places of worship were a mistake in an unexcitable country like England. John retired to his library and lit a Corona with a sense that he thoroughly deserved a good cigar.

"Children are not difficult," he said to himself, "if one tries to put oneself in their place. That request for the calf's head undoubtedly showed a rare combination of adaptiveness with for a schoolboy what was almost a poetic fancy. Harold would have wanted to know how much the head weighed, and whether in life it preferred to browse on buttercups or daisies; but when finally it was cooked he would have eaten twice as much as anybody else. I prefer Bertram's attitude; though naturally I can appreciate a housekeeper's feelings. These cigars are in capital condition. Really, Bertram's example is infectious, and by gad, I feel quite like a couple of hours with Joan. Yes, it's a pity Laurence hasn't got Bertram's dramatic sense. A great pity."

The sabbath afternoon wore on, and though John did not accumulate enough energy to seat himself at his table, he dreamed a good deal of wonderful situations in the fourth act, puffing away at his cigar and hearing from time to time distant shouts and scamperings; these, however, did not keep him from falling into a gentle doze, from which he was abruptly wakened by the opening of the library door.

"Ah, is that tea?" he asked cheerfully in that tone with which the roused sleeper always implies his uninterrupted attention to time and space.

"No, sir, it's me," a grim voice replied. "And if you don't want us all to be drowned where we stand, it being a Sunday afternoon, and not a plumber to be got, and Maud in the hysterics, and those two young Tartars screaming like Bedlamites, and your dinner ruined and done for, and the feathers gone from Elsa's new hat, per-raps you could come upstairs, Mr. Touchwood. Gordon's head indeed, and the boy as naked as a stitch!"

John jumped to his feet and hurried out on the landing; at the same moment Bertram with nothing to cover him except a pudding-shape on his head, a tea-tray on his arm, a Turkish scimitar at his waist, and the pinions of a blue and green bird tied round his ankles leapt six stairs of the flight above and alighting at his uncle's feet, thrust the calf's head into his face.

"You're turned to stone, Phineus," he yelled. "You can't move. You've seen the Gorgon."

"There he goes again with his Gordon and his Gladstone," said Mrs. Worfolk. "How dare you be so daring?"

"The Gorgon's sister," cried Bertram lunging at her with the scimitar. "Beware, I am invisible."

Whereupon he enveloped the calf's head in a napkin, held the tea-tray before his face, and darted away upstairs.

"I'm afraid he's a little over-excited," said John, doubtfully.

At this moment a stream of water began to flow past his feet and pour down upon him from the landing above.

"Why, the house is full of water," he gasped.

"It's what I'm trying to tell you, sir," Mrs. Worfolk fumed. "He's done something with that there cistern and burst it. I can't stop the water."

John followed Perseus on his wild flight up the stairs down which every moment water was flowing more freely. When he reached the cistern cupboard he discovered Maud bound fast to the disordered cistern, while Viola holding in her mouth a large ivory paper-knife and wearing what looked like Mrs. Worfolk's sealskin jacket that John had given her last Christmas was splashing at full length in a puddle on the floor and clawing at Maud's skirts with ferocious growls and grunts.

"You dare try to undress me again, Master Bertram," the statuesque Maud was screaming.

"Well, Andromeda's got practically nothing on in the book, and you said you'd rather not be the sea-monster," Bertram was arguing. "Andromeda," he cried seeing by the manner of his uncle's advance that the curtain must now be rung down upon the play, "I have turned the monster to stone. Go on, V, you can't move from now on."

Viola stiffened and without a twitch let the stream of water pour down upon her, while Bertram planting his foot in the small of her back waved triumphantly the Gorgon's head, both of whose ears gave way under the strain, so that John's dinner was soon as wet as he was.

The cistern emptied itself at last; Maud was released; Bertram and Viola were led downstairs to be dried and on Mrs. Worfolk's recommendation sent instantly to bed.

"I told you," said Bertram, "that if Miss Coldwell had come, we couldn't have done anything decent."

What woman, John wondered, might serve as a comparable deterrent? The fantastic idea of appealing for aid to Doris Hamilton flashed through his mind, but on second thoughts he felt that there would be something undignified in asking her to come at such a moment. Then he remembered how often he had heard his sister-in-law Beatrice lament her childlessness. Why should he not visit James and Beatrice this very evening? He owed them a visit, and his domestics were all obviously too much agitated even to contemplate the preparation of dinner. Mrs. Worfolk would perhaps be in a better temper when he got back and he would explain to her that the seal was a marine animal, the skin of which would not be injured by water.

"I think I'll ask Mrs. James to give us a helping hand this week," John suggested. "I shall be rather busy myself."

"Yes, sir, and so shall I, trying to get the house straight again which it looks more like Shooting the Chutes at Earl's Court than a gentleman's house, I'm bound to say."

"Still it might have been worse, Mrs. Worfolk. They might have played with another element. Fire, for instance. That would have been much more awkward."

"And it's thanks to me the house isn't on fire as well," Mrs. Worfolk shrilled in her indignation. "For if that young Turk didn't come charging down into the kitchen and trying to tell me that the kitchen-fire was a serpent and start attacking it tooth and nail. And there was poor Elsa shut up in the coal-cellar and hollering fit to break anyone's heart. 'She's Daniel in a tower of brass,' he says as bold as a tower of brass himself."

"And what were you, Mrs. Worfolk?" John asked.

"Oh, his lordship had the nerve to say I was an atlas. 'Yes,' I said, 'my lord, you let me catch hold of you and I'll make your behind look like an atlas before I've done with it.'"

"Do you think that Mrs. James could control them?" John asked.

"I wouldn't say as the Lord Mayor himself could control them, but it's not for me to give advice when good food can be turned into Gordon's heads. And whatever give them the idea, I don't know, for I'm sure General Gordon was a very handsome man to look at. Yaul excuse me, sir, but if you don't want to catch your death, you'd better change your things."

John followed Mrs. Worfolk's advice, and an hour later he was walking through the misty November night in the direction of St. John's Wood.

CHAPTER VI

IF a taxi had lurked in any of the melancholy streets through which John was making his way to Hill Road he would have taken refuge in it gratefully, for there was no atmosphere that preyed upon his mind with such a sense of desolation as the hour of evening prayer in a respectable Northern suburb. The occasional footsteps of uninspired lovers dying away into by-streets; the occasional sounds of stuffy worship proceeding from church or chapel; the occasional bark of a dog trying to obtain admittance to an empty house; the occasional tread of a morose policeman; the occasional hoot of a distant motor-horn; the occasional whiff of privet-shrubberies and of damp rusty railings; the occasional effusions of chlorotic gaslight upon the raw air, half fog, half drizzle; the occasional shadows that quivered upon the dimly luminous blinds of upper windows; the occasional mutterings of housemaids in basements—not even John's buoyant spirit could rise above such a weight of depressing adjuncts to the influential Sabbath gloom. He began to accuse himself of having been too hasty in his treatment of Bertram and Viola; the scene at Church Row viewed in retrospect seemed to him cheerful and, if the water had not reached his Aubusson rug, perfectly harmless. No doubt, in the boarding-house at Earl's Court such behavior had been considered impossible. Had not the children talked of finishing Robinson Crusoe and alluded to his own lack of suitable fur rugs? Evidently last week the drama had been interrupted by the landlady because they had been spoiling her fur rugs. John was on the point of going back to Church Row and inviting the children to celebrate his return in a jolly impromptu supper, when he remembered that there were at least five more Sundays before Christmas. Next Sunday they would probably decide to revive the Argonauts, a story that, so far as he could recall the incidents, offered many opportunities for destructive ingenuity. Then, the Sunday after, there would be Theseus and the Minotaur; if there were another calf's head in the larder, Bertram might easily try to compel Mrs. Worfolk to be the Minotaur and wear it, which might mean Mrs. Worfolk's resignation from his service, a prospect that could not be faced with equanimity. But would the presence of Beatrice exercise an effective control upon this dressing up, and could he stand Beatrice for six weeks at a stretch? He might, of course, engage her to protect him and his property during the first few days, and after that to come for every week end. Suppose he did invite Doris Hamilton, but, of course, that was absurd—suppose he did invite Beatrice, would Doris Hamilton—would Beatrice come? Could it possibly be held to be one of the duties of a confidential secretary to assist her employer in checking the exuberance of his juvenile relations? Would not Miss Hamilton decide that her post approximated too nearly to that of a governess? Obviously such a woman had never contemplated the notion of becoming a governess. But had she ever contemplated the notion of becoming a confidential secretary? No, no, the plan was fantastic, unreal ... he must trust to Beatrice and hope that Miss Coldwell would presently recover, or that Eleanor's tour would come to a sudden end, or that George would have paid what he owed his landlady and feel better able to withstand her criticism of his children. If all these hopes proved unfounded, a schoolboy, like the rest of human nature, had his price—his noiselessness could be bought in youth like his silence later on. John was turning into Hill Road when he made this reflection; he was within the area of James' cynical operations.

John's eldest brother was at forty-six an outwardly rather improved, an inwardly much debased replica of their father. The old man had not possessed a winning personality, but his energy and genuine powers of accomplishment had made him a successful general practitioner, because people overlooked his rudeness in the confidence he gave them and forgave his lack of sympathy on account of his obvious devotion to their welfare. He with his skeptical and curious mind, his passion for mathematics and hatred of idealism, and his unaffected contempt for the human race could not conceive a worse hell in eternity than a general practice offered him in life; but having married a vain, beautiful, lazy and conventional woman, he could not bring himself to spoil his honesty by blaming for the foolish act anything more tangible than the scheme of creation; and having made himself a damned uncomfortable bed with a pretty quilt, as he used to say, he had decided that he must lie on it. No doubt, many general practitioners go through life with the conviction that they were intended to devote themselves to original research; but Dr. Robert Touchwood from what those who were qualified to judge used to say of him had reason to feel angry with his fate.

James, who as a boy had shown considerable talent, was chosen by his father to inherit the practice. It was typical of the old gentleman that he did not assume this succession as the right of the eldest son, but that he deliberately awarded it to James as the most apparently adequate of his offspring. Unfortunately James, who was dyspeptic even at school, chose to imitate his father's mannerisms while he was still a student at Guy's and helping at odd hours in the dispensary. Soon after he had taken his finals and had seen his name engraved upon the brass plate underneath his father's, old Dr. Touchwood fell ill of an incurable disease and James found himself in full charge of the practice, which he proceeded to ruin, so that not long after his father's death he was compelled to sell it for a much smaller sum than it would have fetched a few years before. For a time he played alternately with the plan of setting up as a specialist in Harley Street or of burying himself in the country to write a monograph on British dragon-flies—for some reason these fierce and brilliant insects touched a responsive chord in James. He finally decided upon the dragon-flies and went down to Ockham Common in Surrey to search for *Sympetrum Fonscolombii*, a rare migrant that was reported from that locality in 1892. He could not prove that it was any more indigenous than himself to the sophisticated county, but in the course of his observations he met Beatrice Pyrke, the daughter of a prosperous inn-keeper in a neighboring town, and married her. Notwithstanding such a catch—he used to vow that she was more resplendent than even *Anax Imperator*—he continued to take an interest in dragon-flies, until his monograph was unluckily forestalled a few years later. It was owing to an article of his in one of the entomological journals that he encountered Daniel Curtis—a meeting which led to Hilda's marriage. In those days—John had not yet made a financial success of literature—this result had seemed to the embittered odonatist a complete justification of the many hours he had wasted in preparing for his never-to-be written monograph, because his sister's future had for some time been presenting a disagreeable and insoluble problem. Besides observing dragon-flies, James spent one year in making a clock out of fishbones, and another year in perfecting a method of applying gold lacquer to poker-work.

A more important hobby, however, that finally displaced all the others was foreign literature, in the criticism of which he frequently occupied pages in the expensive reviews, pages that gradually grew numerous enough to make first one book and then another. James' articles on foreign literature were always signed; but he also wrote many criticisms of English literature that were not signed. This hack-work exasperated him so much that he gradually came to despising the whole of English literature after the eighteenth century with the exception of the novels of George Meredith. These he used to read aloud to his wife when he was feeling particularly bilious and derive from her nervous bewilderment a savage satisfaction. In her the critic possessed a perpetual incarnation of the British public that he so deeply scorned, and he treated his wife in the same way as he fancied he treated the larger entity: without either of them he would have been intellectually at a loose end. For all his admiration of French literature James spoke the language with a hideous British accent. Once on a joint holiday John, who for the whole of a channel-crossing had been listening to his brother's tirades against the rottenness of modern English literature and his pæans on behalf of modern French literature, had been much consoled when they reached Calais to find that James could not make himself intelligible even to a porter.

"But," as John had said with a chuckle, "perhaps Meredith couldn't have made himself intelligible to an English porter."

"It's the porter's fault," James had replied, sourly.

For some years now the critic with his wife and a fawn-coloured bulldog had lived in furnished apartments at 65 Hill Road, a creeper-matted house of the early 'seventies which James characterized as quiet and Beatrice as handy; in point of fact it was neither, being exposed to barrel-organs and remote from busses. A good deal of the original furniture still incommoded the rooms; but James had his own chair, Beatrice had her own footstool, and Henri Beyle the bulldog his own basket. The fire-place was crowned by an overmantel of six decorative panels, all that was left of James' method of applying gold lacquer to poker-work. There were also three or four family portraits, which John for some reason coveted for his own library, and a drawer-cabinet of faded and decrepit dragon-flies. Some bookshelves filled with yellow French novels gave an exotic look to the drab room, which, whenever James was not smoking his unusually foul pipes, smelt of gravy and malt vinegar except near the window, where the predominant perfume was of ferns and oilcloth. Between the living-room and the bedroom were double-doors hidden by brown plush curtains, which if opened quickly revealed nothing but a bleak expanse of bed and a gray window fringed with ragged creepers. When a visitor entered this room to wash his hands he used to look at James' fishbone clock under its bell-glass on a high chest of drawers and shiver in the dampness; the fireplace was covered by a large wardrobe, and one of Beatrice's hats was often on the bed, the counterpane of which was stenciled with Beyle's paws. John, who loathed this bedroom, always said he did not want to wash his hands, when he took a meal at Hill Road.

The depression of his Sunday evening walk had made John less critical than he usually was of James' rooms, and he heard the gate of the front-garden swing back behind him with a sense of pleasurable expectation.

"There will be cold mutton for supper," he said to himself, thinking rather guiltily of the calf's head that he might have eaten and to partake of which he had not invited his brother and Beatrice. "Cold mutton and a very wet salad, with either tinned pears or tinned pineapple to follow—or perhaps stewed figs."

When John entered, James was deep in his armchair with Beyle snoring on his lap, where he served as a rest for the large book that his master was reading.

"Hullo," the critic exclaimed without attempting to rise. "You are back in town then?"

"Yes, I came back on Friday."

"I thought you wouldn't be able to stand the country for long. Remember what Horry Walpole said about the country?"

"Yes," said John, quickly. He had not the least idea really, but he had long ago ceased to have any scruples about preventing James first of all from trying to remember a quotation, secondly from trying to find it, thirdly from asking Beatrice where she had hidden the book in which it was to be found, and finally from not only reading it when the book was found, but also from reading page after page of irrelevant matter in the context. "Though Ambles is really very jolly," he added. "I'm expecting you and Beatrice to spend Christmas with me, you know."

James grunted.

"Well, we'll see about that. I don't belong to the Dickens Fellowship and I shall be pretty busy. You popular authors soon forget what it means to be busy. So you've had another success? Who was it this time—Lucretia Borgia, eh?" he laughed, bitterly. "Good lord, it's incredible, isn't it? But the English drama's in a sick state—a very sick state."

"All contemporary art is in a sick state according to the critics," John observed. "Critics are like doctors; they are not prejudiced in favor of general good-health."

"Well, isn't it in a sick state?" James demanded, truculently.

"I don't know that I think it is. However, don't let's begin an argument before supper. Where's Beatrice?"

"She bought a new hat yesterday and has gone to demonstrate its becomingness to God and woman."

"I suppose you mean she's gone to church? I went to church myself this morning."

"What for? Copy?"

"No, no, no. I took George's children."

"You don't mean to say that you've got *them* with you?"

John nodded, and his brother exploded with an uproarious laugh.

"Well, I was fool enough to marry before I was thirty," he bellowed. "But at any rate I wasn't fool enough to have any children. So you're going to sup with us. I ought to warn you it's cold mutton to-night."

"Really? Capital! There's nothing I like better than cold mutton."

"Upon my soul, Johnnie, I'll say this for you. You may write stale romantic plays about the past, but you manage to keep plenty of romantic sauce for the present. Yes, you're a born optimist. Look at your skin—pink as a baby's. Look at mine—yellow as a horse's tooth. Have you heard my new name for your habit of mind? Rosification. Rather good, eh? And you can rosify anything from Lucretia Borgia to cold mutton. Now don't look angry with me, Johnnie; you must rosify my ill-humor. With so many roses you can't expect not to have a few thorns as well, and I'm one of them. No, seriously, I congratulate you on your success. And I always try to remember that you write with your tongue in your cheek."

"On the contrary I believe I write as well as I can," said John, earnestly. "I admit that I gave up writing realistic novels, but that was because they didn't suit my temperament."

"No, by gad, they didn't! And, anyway, no Englishman can write a realistic novel—or any other kind of a novel if it comes to that. My lord, the English novel!"

"Look here," John protested. "I do not want to argue about either plays or novels to-night. But if you must talk about books, talk about your own, not mine. Beatrice wrote to me that you had something coming along about the French Symbolists. I shouldn't have thought that they would have appealed to you."

"They don't. I hate them."

"Well, why write a book about them? Their day has been over a long time."

"To smash them. To prove that they were a pretentious set of epileptic humbugs."

"Sort of Max Nordau business?"

"Max Nordau! I hope you aren't going to compare me with that flat-footed bus-conductor. No, no, Johnnie, the rascals took themselves seriously and I'm going to smash them on their own estimate of their own importance. I'm going to prove that they were on the wrong track and led nowhere."

"It's consoling to learn that even French literature can go off the lines sometimes."

"Of course it can, because it runs on lines. English literature on the contrary never had any lines on which to run, though in the eighteenth century it followed a fairly decent coaching-road. Modern English literature, however, is like a rogue elephant trampling down the jungle that its predecessors made some attempt to cultivate."

"I never knew that even moral elephants had taken up agriculture seriously."

James blew all the ashes of his pipe over Beyle in a gust of contempt, and rose from his chair.

"The smirk!" he cried. "The traditional British smirk! The gerumky-gerum horse-laugh! British humor! Ha-ha! Begotten by Punch out of Mrs. Grundy with the Spectator for godfather. '*Go to, you have made me mad.*'"

"It's a pity you can't tell me about your new book without flying into a rage," John said, mildly. "You haven't told me yet when it's to appear."

"My fourteen readers aren't languishing. But to repay politeness by politeness, my book will come out in March."

"I'm looking forward to it," John declared. "Have you got good terms from Worrall?"

"As good terms as a consumptive bankrupt might expect from Shylock. What does the British public care for criticism? You should hear me reading the proofs to Beatrice. You should really have the pleasure of watching her face, and listening to her comments. Do you know why Beatrice goes to church? I'll tell you. She goes to indulge in a debauch of the accumulated yawns of the week."

"Hush, here she is," John warned him.

James laughed again.

"Johnnie, you're *impayable*. Your sensitiveness to Beatrice betrays the fount of your success. You treat the British public with just the same gentlemanly gurgle. And above all you're a good salesman. That's where George failed when he tried whisky on commission."

"I don't believe you're half the misanthropist you make yourself out."

"Of course, I'm not. I love human nature. Didn't I marry Beatrice, and didn't I spend a year in making a clock out of fishbones to amuse my landlady's children, and wasn't I a doctor of medicine without once using my knowledge of poisons? I love mankind—but dragon-flies were more complex and dogs are more admirable. Well, Beatrice, did you enjoy the sermon?"

His wife had come in and was greeting John broadly and effusively, for when she was excited her loud contralto voice recaptured many rustic inflections of her youth. She was a tall woman, gaudily handsome, conserving in clothes and coiffure the fashions of her prime as queens do and barmaids who become the wives of publicans. On Sundays she wore a lilac broadcloth with a floriated bodice cut close to the figure; but she was just as proud of her waist on weekdays and discreet about her legs, which she wrapped up in a number of petticoats. She was as real or as unreal as a cabinet-photograph of the last decade of the nineteenth century: it depended on the attitude of the observer. Although there was too much of her for the apartments, it could not be said that she appeared out of place in them; in fact she was rather like a daughter of the house who had come home for the holidays.

"Why, it's John," she expanded in a voice rich with welcome. "How are you, little stranger?"

"Thank you very much for the flowers, Beatrice. They were much appreciated."

"I wanted you to know that we were still in the land of the livin'. You're goin' to stay to supper, of course? But you'll have to be content with cold mutton, don't you know."

There was a tradition among novelists that well-bred people leave out their final "g's"; so Beatrice saved on these consonants what she squandered upon aspirates.

"And how do you think Jimmie's lookin'?" she went on. "I suppose he's told you about his new book. Comin' out in March, don't you know. I feel awfully up in French poitry since he read it out to me. Don't light another pipe now, dear. The girl's gettin' the supper at once. I think you're lookin' very well, Johnnie, I do indeed. Don't you think he's lookin' very well, Jimmie? Has Bill Bailey been out for his run?" This was Beatrice's affectionate diminutive for Henri Beyle, the dog.

"No, I won't bother about my hands," John put in hastily to forestall Beatrice's next suggestion.

"We had such a dull sermon," she sighed.

Her husband grunted a request to spare them the details.

"Well, don't you know, it's a dull time for sermons now before Christmas. But it didn't matter, as what I really wanted was a puff of fresh air. Yes, I'd begun to think you'd forgotten all about us," she rambled on, turning archly to John. "I know we must be dull company, but all work and no play, don't you know ... yours is all plays and no work. Jimmie, I made a joke," she laughed, twitching her husband's sleeve to secure his attention. "Did you hear?"

"Yes, I heard," he growled.

"I thought it was rather good, didn't you, Johnnie?"

"Very good indeed," he assented, warmly. "Though I do work occasionally."

"Oh, of course, you silly thing, I wasn't bein' serious. I told you it was a joke. I know you must work a bit. Here comes the girl with supper. You'll excuse me, Johnnie, while I go and titivate myself. I sha'n't be a minute."

Beatrice retired to the bedroom whence she could be heard humming over her beautification.

"You're not meditating marriage, are you?" James mocked.

The bachelor shook his head.

"At the same time," he protested, stoutly, "I don't think you're entitled to sneer at Beatrice. Considering—" he was about to say "everything," but feeling that this would include his brother too pointedly he substituted, "the weather, she's wonderfully cheerful. And you know I've always insisted that these rooms are cramped."

"Yes, well, when a popular success oils my palm, John, we'll move next door to you in Church Row."

John wished that James would not always harp upon their respective fortunes: it made him feel uncomfortable, especially when he was sitting down to cold mutton. Besides, it was unfair; had he not once advised James to abandon criticism and take up—he had been going to suggest "anything except literature," but he had noticed James' angry dismay and had substituted "creative work." What had been the result? An outburst of contemptuous abuse, a violent renunciation of anything that approximated to his own work. If James despised his romantic plays, why could he not be consistent and despise equally the wealth they brought him? He honored his brother's intellectual sincerity, why could not his brother do as much for his?

"What beats me," James had once exclaimed, "is how a man like you who professes to admire—no, I believe you're honest—who does admire Stendhal, Turgenev, Flaubert and Merimée, who recognizes the perfection of *Manon Lescaut* and *Adolphe*, who in a word has taste, can bring himself to eructate the *Fall of Babylon*."

"It's all a matter of knowing one's own limitations," John had replied. "I tried to write realistic novels. But my temperament is not realistic."

"No, if it were," James had murmured, "you wouldn't stand my affectation of superiority."

It was this way James had of once in a very long while putting himself in the wrong that used always to heal John's wounded generosity. But these occasional lapses—as he supposed his cynical brother would call them—were becoming less and less frequent, and John had no longer much excuse for clinging to his romantic reverence for the unlucky head of his family.

During the first half of supper Beatrice delivered a kind of lecture on housekeeping in London on two pounds twelve shillings and sixpence a week, including bones for the dog; by the time that the stewed figs were put on the table this monologue had reduced both brothers to such a state of gloom by striking at James' experience and John's imagination, that the sourness of the cream came as a natural corollary; anything but sour cream would have seemed an obtrusive reminder of housekeeping on more than two pounds twelve shillings and sixpence a week, including bones for the dog. John was convinced by his sister-in-law's mood that she would enjoy a short rest from speculating upon the comparative versatility of mutton and beef, and by James' reception of her remarks that he would appreciate her housekeeping all the more after being compelled to regard for a while the long procession of chops that his landlady would inevitably marshal for him while his wife was away. The moment seemed propitious to the unfolding of his plan.

"I want to ask you both a favor," he began. "No, no, Beatrice, I disagree with you. I don't think the cream is really sour. I find it delicious, but I daren't ever eat more than a few figs. The cream, however, is particularly delicious. In fact I was on the point of inquiring the name of your dairy."

"If we have cream on Sundays," Beatrice explained, "Jimmie has to put up with custard-powder on Wednesdays. But if we don't have cream on Sundays, I can spare enough eggs on Wednesdays for real custard."

"That's very ingenious of you," John declared. "But you didn't hear what I was saying when I broke off in defense of the cream, *which* is delicious. I said that I wanted to ask a favor of you both."

"King Cophetua and the Beggar Maid," James chuckled. "Or were you going to suggest to Beatrice that next time you have supper with us she should experiment not only with fresh cream, but also with some rare dish like nightingales' tongues—or even veal, for instance?"

"Now, Jimmie, you're always puttin' hits in at me about veal; but if I get veal, it throws me out for the whole week."

John made another effort to wrench the conversation free from the topic of food:

"No, no, James. I was going to ask you to let Beatrice come and give me a hand with our nephew and our niece." He slightly accentuated the pronoun of plural possession. "Of course, that is to say, if Beatrice would be so kind."

"What do you want her to do? Beat them?" James asked.

"No, no, no, James. I'm not joking. As I explained to you, I've got these two children—er—staying with me. It appears that George is too overstrained, too ill, that is, to manage them during the few weeks that Eleanor will be away on tour, and I thought that if Beatrice could be my guest for a week or two until the governess has re-created her nervous system, which I understand will take about a month, I should feel a great weight off my mind. A bachelor household, you know, is not primarily constructed to withstand an invasion by children. You'd find them very difficult here, James, if you hadn't got Beatrice."

"Oh, Johnnie, I should love it," his sister-in-law cried. "That is if Jimmie could spare me."

"Of course, I could. You'd better take her back with you to-night."

"No, really?" said John. "Why that would be splendid. I'm immensely obliged to you both."

"He's quite anxious to get rid of me," Beatrice laughed, happily. "I sha'n't be long packin'. Fancy lookin' after Eleanor's two youngsters. I've often thought I *would* rather like to see if I couldn't bring up children."

"Now's your chance," John jovially offered.

"Jimmie didn't ever care much for youngsters," Beatrice explained.

Her husband laughed bitterly.

"Quite enough people hate me, as it is," he sneered, "without deliberately creating a child of my own to add to the number."

"Oh, no, of course, dear, I know we're better off as we are," Beatrice said with a soothing pat for her husband's round shoulders. "Only the idea comes into my head now and again that I'd just like to see if I couldn't manage them, that's all, dear. I'm not complaining."

"I don't want to hurry you away," James muttered. "But I've got some work to do."

"We'd better send the servant out to look for a taxi at once," John suggested. "It's Sunday night, you know."

Twenty minutes later, Beatrice looking quite fashionable now in her excitement—so many years had it obliterated—was seated in the taxi; John was half-way along the garden path on his way to join her, when his brother called him back.

"Oh, by the way, Johnnie," he said in gruff embarrassment, "I've got an article on Alfred de Vigny coming out soon in *The Nineteenth Century*. It can't bring me in less than fifteen guineas, but it might not be published for another three months. I can show you the editor's letter, if you like. I wonder if you could advance me ten guineas? I'm a little bothered just at the moment. There was a vet's bill for the dog and...."

"Of course, of course, my dear fellow. I'll send you a check to-night. Thanks very much for—er—releasing Beatrice, I mean—helping me out of a difficulty with Beatrice. Very good of you. Good-night. I'll send the check at once."

"Don't cross it," said James.

On the way back to Hampstead in the dank murkiness of the cab, Beatrice became confidential.

"Jimmie always hated me to pass remarks about havin' children, don't you know, but it's my belief that he feels it as much as anyone. Look at the fuss he makes of poor old Bill Bailey. And bein' the eldest son and havin' the pictures of his grandfather and grandmother, I'm sure there are times when he'd give a lot to explain to a youngster of his own who they really were. It isn't so interestin' to explain to me, don't you know, because they aren't my relations, except, of course, by marriage. I always feel myself that Jimmie for an eldest son has been very unlucky. Well, there's you, for instance. I don't mean to say he's jealous, because he's not; but still I dare say he sometimes thinks that he ought to be where you are, though, of course, that doesn't mean to say that he'd like you to be where he is. But a person can't help feelin' that there's no reason why you shouldn't both have been where you are. The trouble with Jimmie was that he wasted a lot of time when he was young, and sometimes, though I wouldn't say this to anybody but you, sometimes I do wonder if he doesn't think he married too much in a hurry. Then there were his dragon-flies. There they all are falling to pieces from want of interest. I don't suppose anybody in England has taken so much trouble as Jimmie over dragon-flies, but what is a dragon-fly? They'll never be popular with the general public, because though they don't sting, people think they do. And then that fellow—who is it—it begins with an M—oh dear, my memory is something chronic! Well, anyway, he wrote a book about bees, and it's tremendously popular. Why? Because a bee is well-known. Certainly they sting too, but then they have honey and people keep them. If people kept dragon-flies, it would be different. No, my opinion is that for an eldest son Jimmie has been very unlucky."

The next day Bertram disappeared to school at an hour of the morning which John remembered did exist in his youth, but which he had for long regarded as a portion of the great backward and abysm of time. Beatrice tactfully removed his niece immediately after breakfast, not the auroral breakfast of Bertram, but the comfortable meal of ten o'clock; and except for a rehearsal of the *bolero* in the room over the library John was able to put in a morning of undisturbed diligence. Beatrice took Viola for a walk in the afternoon, and when Bertram arrived back from school about six o'clock she nearly spoilt her own dinner by the assistance she gave him with his tea. John had a couple of quiet hours with *Joan of Arc* before dinner, when he was only once interrupted by Beatrice's coming as her nephew's ambassador to ask what was the past participle of some Latin verb, which cost him five minutes' search for a dictionary. After dinner John played two sets of piquet with his sister-in-law and having won both began to feel that there was a good deal to be said for a woman's presence in the house.

But about eleven o'clock on the morning of the next day James arrived, and not only James but Beyle the bulldog, who had, if one might judge by his behavior, as profound a contempt as his master for John's library, and a much more unpleasant way of showing it.

"I wish you'd leave your dog in the hall," John protested. "Look at him now; he's upset the paper-basket. Get down off that chair! I say, do look at him!"

Beyle was coursing round the room, steering himself with the kinked blob that served him for a tail.

"He likes the soft carpet," his master explained. "He thinks it's grass."

"What an idiotic dog," John scoffed. "And I suppose he thinks my Aubusson is an herbaceous border. Drop it, you brute, will you. I say, do put him downstairs. He's going to worry it in a minute, and all agree that bulldogs can't be induced to let go of anything they've once fairly gripped. Lie down, will you!"

James roared with laughter at his brother's disgust, but finally he turned the dog out of the room, and John heard what he fancied was a panic-stricken descent of the stairs by Maud or....

"I say, I hope he isn't chasing Mrs. Worfolk up and down the house," he ejaculated as he hurried out on the landing. What ever Beyle had been doing, he was at rest now and smiling up at John from the front-door mat. "I hope it wasn't Mrs. Worfolk," he said, coming back. "She's in a very delicate state just at present."

"What?" James shouted, incredulously.

"Oh, not in that way, my dear fellow, not in that way. But she's not used to having so many visitors in the house."

"I'm going to take one of them away with me, if that'll be any consolation to her," James announced.

"Not Beatrice?" his brother stammered.

James nodded grimly.

"It's all very fine for you with a mob of servants to look after you: but I can't spare Beatrice any more easily than you could spare Mrs. Worfolk. I've been confoundedly uncomfortable for nearly two days, and my wife must come back."

"Oh, but look here," John protested. "She's been managing the children magnificently. I've hardly known they were in the house. You can't take Beatrice away."

"Sorry, Johnnie, but my existence is not so richly endowed with comforts as yours. You'd better get a wife for yourself. You can afford one."

"But can't we arrive at a compromise?" John pleaded. "Why don't you come and camp out with me, too?"

"Camp out, you hypocrite!" the critic jeered. "No, no, you can't bribe me with your luxuries. Do you think that I could work with two children careering all over the place? I dare say they don't disturb your plays. I dare say you can't hear them above the clash of swords and the rolling of thunder, but for critical work I want absolute quiet. Sorry, but I'm afraid I must carry off Beatrice."

"Well, of course, if you must...." John murmured, despondently. And it was very little consolation to think, while Viola practised the *fandango* in the library preparatory to dislocating the household by removing Maud from her work to escort her to the dancing-class, that Beatrice herself would have liked to stay.

"However," John sternly resolved, "the next time that James tries to scoff at married life I shall tell him pretty plainly what I think of his affectation."

He decided ultimately to keep the children at Church Row for a week, to give them some kind of treat on Saturday, and on Saturday evening, before dinner, to take them back to their father and insist upon his being responsible for them. If by chance George proved to be really ill, which he did not suppose for a moment that he would, he should take matters firmly into his hands and export the children to Ambles until their mother came home: Viola could practise every known variety of Spanish dance over Laurence's head, or even in Laurence's room; and as for Bertram he could corrupt Harold to his heart's content.

On the whole, the week passed off well. Although Viola had fallen like Lucifer from being an angel in Maud's mind, she won back her esteem by behaving like a human little girl when they went to the dancing-class together and did not try to assume diabolic attributes in exchange for the angelic position she had forfeited. John was allowed to gather that Viola's chief claim to Maud's forgiveness was founded upon her encouragement of the advances made to her escort by a handsome young sergeant of the Line whom they had encountered in the tube.

"Miss Viola behaved herself like a little lady," Maud had informed John when they came home.

"You enjoyed taking her?"

"Yes, indeed, sir, it's a pleasure to go about with anyone so lady-like. Several very nice people turned round to admire her."

"Did they, Maud, did they?"

Later, when Viola's account of the afternoon reached him he wondered if the sergeant was one of those nice people.

Mrs. Worfolk, too, was reconciled to Bertram by the profound respect he accorded to her tales and by his appreciation of an album of family photographs she brought out for him from the bottom of her trunk.

"The boy can be as quiet as a mouse," she assured John, "as long as he isn't encouraged to make a hullabaloo."

"You think I encourage him, Mrs. Worfolk?"

"Well, sir, it's not my place to offer an opinion about managing children, but giving them a calf's head is as good as telling them to misbehave theirselves. It's asking for trouble. There he is now, doing what he calls his home work with a little plate of toffee I made for him—as good as gold. But what I do ask is where's the use in filling up a child's head with Latin and Greece. Teach a child to be a heathen goddess and a heathen goddess he'll be. Teach him the story of the Infant Samuel and he'll behave like the Infant Samuel, though I must say that one child who I told about God's voice, in the family to which I was nursemaid, had a regular fit and woke up screaming in the middle of the night that he could hear God routing about for him under the bed. But then he was a child with very old-fashioned notions and took the whole story for gospel, and his mother said after that no one wasn't to read him nothing except stories about animals."

"What happened to him when he grew up?" John asked.

"Well, sir, I lost sight of the whole family, but I dare say he became a clergyman, for he never lost this habit of thinking God was dodging him all the time. It was God here, and God there, till I fairly got the jumps myself and might have taken up with the Wesleans if I hadn't gone as third housemaid to a family where the master kept race-horses which gave me something else to think about, and I never had anything more to do with children until my poor sister's Herbert."

"That must have been a great change, Mrs. Worfolk."

"Yes, sir, so it was; but life's only one long changing about, though they do say there's nothing new under the sun. But good gracious me, fellows who make up mottoes always exaggerate a bit: they've got to, so as to keep up with one another."

When Friday evening arrived John nearly emphasized Mrs. Worfolk's agreement with Heraclitus by keeping the children at Church Row. But by the last post there came a letter from Janet Bond to beg an earlier production of *Joan of Arc* if it was by any means possible, and John looking at the infinitesimal amount he had written during the week resolved that he must stick to his intention of taking the children back to their father on the following day.

"What would you like to do to-morrow?" he inquired. "I happen to have a free afternoon, and—er—I'm afraid your father wants you back in Earl's Court, so it will be your last opportunity of enjoying yourselves for some time—I mean of our enjoying ourselves for some time, in fact, until we all meet at Ambles for Christmas."

"Oh, I say," Bertram protested. "Have we got to go back to rotten old Earl's Court? What a sell!"

"I thought we were going to live here always," Viola exclaimed.

"But don't you want to go back to your father?" John demanded in what he hoped was a voice brimming with reproaches for their lack of filial piety, but which he could not help feeling was bubbling over with something very near elation.

"Oh, no," both children affirmed, "we like being with you much best."

John's gratification was suddenly darkened by the suspicion that perhaps Eleanor had told them to flatter him like this; he turned swiftly aside to hide the chagrin that such a thought gave him, and when he spoke again it was almost roughly, because in addition to being suspicious of their sincerity he was vexed with himself for displaying a spirit of competitive affection. It occurred to him that it was jealousy rather than love which made the world go round—a dangerous reflection for a romantic playwright.

"I'm afraid it can't be helped," he said. "To-morrow is definitely our last day. So choose your own method of celebrating it without dressing up."

"Oh, we only dress up on Sundays," Viola said, loftily.

"I vote we go to the Zoo," Bertram opinionated after a weighty pause.

Had his nephew Harold suggested a visit to the Zoo, John would have shunned the proposal with horror; but with Bertram and Viola the prospect of such an expedition was positively enticing.

"I must beware of favoritism," John warned himself. "Yes, and I must beware of being blarneyed." Then aloud he added:

"Very well, we will visit the Zoo immediately after lunch to-morrow."

"Oh, but we must go in the morning," Bertram cried. "There won't be nearly time to see everything in the afternoon."

"What about our food?"

"We can eat there."

"But, my dear boy," John said. "You are confusing us with the lions. I much doubt if a human being *can* eat at the Zoo, unless he has a passion for peanuts and stale buns, which I have not."

"I swear you can," Bertram maintained. "Anyhow, I know you can get ices there in the summer."

"We'll risk it," John declared, adventurously; and the children echoed his enthusiasm with joy.

"We must see the toucans this time," Bertram announced in a grave voice, "and last time we missed the zebu."

"I shouldn't have thought that possible," John demurred, "with all those stripes."

"Not the zebra," Bertram severely corrected him. "The zebu."

"Never heard of the beast," John said.

"I say, V," Bertram exclaimed, incredulously. "He's never heard of the zebu."

Viola was too much shocked by her uncle's ignorance to do more than smile sadly.

"We'll show it you to-morrow," Bertram promised.

"Thanks very much. I shall enjoy meeting the zebu," John admitted, humbly. "And any other friends of yours in the animal world whose names begin with Z."

"And we also missed the ichneumon," Viola reminded her brother.

"Your last visit seems to have been full of broken appointments. It's just as well you're going again to-morrow. You'll be able to explain that it wasn't your fault."

"No, it wasn't," said Bertram, bitterly. "It was Miss Coldwell's."

"Yes," said Viola. "She simply tore past everything. And when Bertram gave the chimpanzee a brown marble instead of a nut and he nearly broke one of his teeth, she said it was cruel."

"Yes, fancy thinking *that* was cruel," Bertram scoffed. "He was in an awful wax, though; he bunged it back at me like anything. But I swopped the marble on Monday with Higginbotham Minor for two green commonys: at least I said it was the marble; only really I dropped it while we were waiting for the bus."

"You're a kind of juvenile Lord Elgin," John declared.

"What did he do?"

"He did the Greek nation over marbles, just as you did the chimpanzee and Higginbotham Minor."

Next morning John made arrangements to send the children's luggage to Earl's Court so that he should be able when the Zoological Gardens were closed to take them directly home and not be tempted to swerve from his determination: then under the nearest approach to a blue sky that London can produce in November they set out for Regent's Park.

John with his nephew and niece for guides spent a pleasant if exhausting day. Remembering the criticism leveled against Miss Coldwell's rapidity of transit, he loitered earnestly by every cage, although he had really had no previous conception of how many animals the Zoo included and began to dread a long list of uninvited occupants at the day's end. He had a charming triumph in the discovery of two more animals beginning with Z, to wit, the zibet and the zoril, which was the sweeter for the fact that they were both new beasts to the children. There was an argument with the keeper of the snake's house, because Bertram nearly blinded a lethargic alligator with his sister's umbrella, and another with the keeper of the giraffes, because in despite of an earnest plea not to feed them, Viola succeeded in tempting one to sniff moistly a piece of raspberry noyau. If some animals were inevitably missed, there were several welcome surprises such as seeing much more of the hippopotamus than the tips of his nostrils floating like two bits of mud on the surface of the water; others included the alleged visibility of a beaver's tail, a conjugal scene between the polar-bears, a truly demoniac exhibition of rage by the Tasmanian-devil, some wonderful gymnastics by a baby snow-leopard, a successful attempt to touch a kangaroo's nose, an indisputable wriggle of vitality from the anaconda, and the sudden scratching of its ear by a somnolent fruit-eating bat.

About ten minutes before the Gardens closed John, who was tired out and had somehow got his cigar-case full of peanuts, declared it was time to go home.

"Oh, but we must just have a squint at the Small Cats' House," Bertram cried, and Viola clasped her hands in apprehension at the bare idea of not doing so.

"All right," John agreed. "I'll wait for you three minutes, and then I'm going slowly along towards the exit."

The three minutes passed, and since the children still lingered he walked on as he had promised. When they did not catch him up as soon as he expected, he waited for a while and then with an exclamation of annoyance turned back.

"What on earth can they find to enjoy in this awful smell?" he wondered, when he entered the Small Cats' House to drag them out. The house was empty except for a bored keeper thinking of his tea.

"Have you seen two children?" John asked, anxiously.

"No, sir, this is the Small Cats' House," replied the keeper.

"Children," repeated John, irritably.

"No, sir. Or, yes, I believe there *was* a little boy and a little girl in here, but they've been gone some minutes now. It's closing time," he added, significantly.

John rushed miserably along deserted paths through the dusk, looking everywhere for Bertram and Viola without success.

"All out," was being shouted from every direction.

"Two children," he panted to a keeper by the exit.

"All out"

"But two children are lost in the Gardens."

"Closing time, sir. They must have gone out by another gate."

He herded John through the turnstile into the street as he would have herded a recalcitrant gnu into its inclosure.

"But this is terrible," John lamented. "This is appalling. I've lost George's children."

He hailed a taxi, drove to the nearest police-station, left their descriptions, and directed the driver to Halma House, Earl's Court Square.

CHAPTER VII

JOHN came to the conclusion while he was driving to Earl's Court that the distinctive anxiety in losing two children was to be sought for in an acute consciousness of their mobility. He had often enough lost such articles as sovereigns, and matchboxes, and income-tax demands; but in the disappearance of these he had always been consoled by the knowledge that they were stationary in some place or another at any given moment, and that somebody or another must find them at some time or another, with profit or disappointment to himself. But Bertram and Viola might be anywhere; if at this moment they were somewhere, before the taxi had turned the next corner they might be somewhere else. The only kind of loss comparable to this was the loss of a train, in which case also the victim was dismayed by the thought of its mobility. Moreover, was it logically possible to find two children, any more than it was possible to find a lost train? They could be caught like a train by somebody else; but except among gipsies, who were practically extinct, the sport of catching children was nowadays unknown. The classic instance of two lost children—and by the way an uncle came into that—was *The Babes in the Wood*, in which story they were neither caught nor found, though certainly their bodies were found owing to the eccentric behavior of some birds in the vicinity. It would be distressing to read in the paper to-morrow of two children's having been found under a drift of paper-bags in the bear-pit at the Zoo, hugged to death not by each other, but by the bears. Or they might have hidden themselves in the Reptile House—Bertram had displayed a dreadful curiosity about the effect of standing upon one of the alligators—and their fate might remain for ever a matter of conjecture. Yet even supposing that they were not at this moment regarding with amazed absorption—absorption was too ominous a word—with amazed interest the nocturnal gambols of the great cats, were they on that account to be considered safe? If it was a question of being crunched up, it made little difference whether one was crunched up by the wheels of an omnibus or by the jaws of a panther. To be sure, Bertram was accustomed to go to school by tube every morning, and obviously he must know by this time how to ask the way to any given spot....

The driver of the taxi was taking no risks with the traffic, and John's tightly strung nerves were relaxed; he began to perceive that he was agitating himself foolishly. The wide smoothness of Cromwell Road was all that was needed to persuade him that the shock had deprived him for a short time of common sense. How absurd he had been! Of course the children would be all right; but he should take good care to administer no less sharp a shock to George than he had experienced himself. He did not approve of George's attitude, and if the temporary loss of Bertram and Viola could rouse him to a sense of his paternal responsibilities, this disturbing climax of a jolly day would not have been led up to in vain. No, George's moral, mental, and physical laziness must no longer be encouraged.

"I shall make the whole business out to be as bad as possible," he decided. "Though, now that I have had time to think the situation out, I realize that there is really not the least likelihood of anything's serious having happened to them."

For James even when he was most exasperating John always felt an involuntary deference that stood quite apart from the sentimental regard which he always tried to owe him as head of the family; for his second brother George he had nothing but contempt. James might be wrongheaded; but George was fatheaded. James kept something of their father's fallen day about him; George was a kind of gross caricature of his own self. Every feature in this brother's face reproduced the corresponding feature in his own with such compelling suggestiveness of a potentially similar degeneration that John could never escape from the reproach of George's insistent kinship. Many times he had been seized by a strong impulse to cut George ruthlessly out of his life; but as soon as he perceived that gibbous development of his own aquiline nose, that reduplication of his own rounded chin, that bull-like thickening of his own sanguine neck, and that saurian accentuation of the eloquent pouches beneath his own eyes, John surrendered to the claims of fraternity and lent George as much as he required at the moment. If Daniel Curtis's desire to marry Hilda had always puzzled him, Eleanor's willingness to be tied for life to George was even more incomprehensible. Still, it was lucky that she had been taken with such a whim, because she was all that stood between George and absolute dependence upon his family, in other words upon his younger brother. Whatever Eleanor's faults, however aggressive her personality, John recognized that she was a hard worker and that the incubus of a husband like George (to whom she seemed curiously and inexplicably devoted) entitled her to a great deal of indulgence.

It was strange to look back now to the time when he and George were both in the city, himself in dog-biscuits and George in wool, and to remember that except their father everybody in the family had foretold a prosperous commercial career for George. Beyond his skill at Solo Whist and a combination of luck with judgment in betting through July and August on weight for age selling-plates and avoiding the big autumn handicaps, John could not recall that George had ever shown a glimmer of financial intelligence. Once or twice when he had visited his brother in the wool-warehouse he had watched an interview between George and a bale of wool, and he had often chuckled at the reflection that the protagonists were well matched—there had always been something woolly about George in mind and body; and when one day he rolled stolidly forth from the warehouse for the last time in order to enter into partnership with a deluded friend to act as the British agents for a society of colonial housewives, John felt that the deluded friend would have been equally well served by a bale of wool. When George and his deluded friend had tried the patience of the colonial housewives for a year by never once succeeding in procuring for them what they required, the partnership was dissolved, and George processed from undertaking to undertaking till he became the business manager of a theatrical touring company. Although as a business manager he reached the nadir of his incompetence he emerged from the post with Eleanor for wife, which perhaps gave rise to a family legend that George had never been so successful as when he was a business manager. This legend he never dispelled by a second exhibition of himself in the part, although he often spoke regretfully of the long Sundays in the train, playing nap for penny points. After he married Eleanor he was commission-agent for a variety of gentlemanly commodities like whisky and cigars; but he drank and smoked much more than he sold, and when bridge was introduced and popularized, having decided that it was the best investment for his share of Eleanor's salary, he abandoned everything else. Moreover, John's increasing prosperity gave his play a fine stability and confidence; he used to feel that his wife's current account merely lapped the base of a solid cliff of capital. A bad week at Bridge came to be known as another financial disappointment; but he used to say cheerfully when he signed the I.O.U. that one must not expect everybody in the family to be always lucky, and that it was dear old John's turn this week. John himself sometimes became quite giddy in watching the swift revolutions of the wheel of fortune as spun by George. The effect of sitting up late at cards usually made George wake with a headache, which he called "feeling overworked"; he was at his best in the dusky hours before dinner, in fact just at the time when John was on his way to explode in his ear the news of the children's disappearance; it was then that among the attenuated spinsters of Halma House his grossness seemed nothing more than a ruddy well-being and that his utter indifference to any kind of responsibility acquired the characteristics of a ripe geniality.

Halma House, Earl's Court Square, was a very large boarding-house, so large that Miss Moxley, the most attenuated spinster who lived in it, once declared that it was more like a residential hotel than a boarding-house, a theory that was eagerly supported by all the other attenuated spinsters who clung to its overstuffed furniture or like dusty cobwebs floated about its garish saloons. Halma House was indeed two houses squeezed or knocked (or whatever other uncomfortable verb can be found to express the welding) into one. Above the front-door of number 198 were the large gilt letters that composed HALMA: above the front-door of what was once number 200 the equally large gilt letters that made up HOUSE. The division between the front-door steps had been removed so as to give an almost Medician grandeur to the entrance, at the top of which beneath a folded awning a curved garden-seat against the disused door of number 20 suggested that it was the resort for the intimate gayety of the boarders at the close of a fine summer day; as Miss Moxley used to vow, it was really quite an oasis, with the plane-trees of the square for contemplation not to mention the noising of the sparrows and the distant tinkling of milk-cans, quite an oasis in dingy old London. But then Miss Moxley had the early symptoms of exophthalmus, a malady that often accompanies the poetic temperament; Miss Moxley, fluttering out for five minutes' fresh air before dinner on a gentle eve in early June, was capable of idealizing to the semblance of a careless pastoral group the spectacle of a half-pay major, a portly widow or two up from the country, and George Touchwood, all brushing the smuts from their noses while they gossiped together on that seat: this was by no means too much for her exophthalmic vision.

John's arrival at Halma House in raw November was not greeted by such evidence of communal felicity; on the contrary, when he walked up the steps, the garden-seat looked most defiantly uninviting; nor did the entrance hall with its writhing gilt furniture symbolize anything more romantic than the competitive pretentiousness of life in a boarding-house that was almost a residential hotel. A blond waiter whose hair would have been dishevelled but for the uses of perspiration informed him that Mr. Tooshvood was in his sitting-room, and led him to a door at the end of the hall opposite another door that gave descent to the dungeons of supply, the inmates of which seemed to spend their time in throwing dishes at one another.

The possession of this sitting-room was the outstanding advantage that George always claimed for Halma House, whenever it was suggested that he should change his quarters: Adam discoursing to his youngest descendant upon the glories of Eden could hardly have outbragged George on the subject of that sitting-room. John on the other hand disliked it and took pleasure in pointing out the impossibility of knowing whether it was a conservatory half transformed into a box-room or a box-room nearly turned into a conservatory. He used to call it George's amphibious apartment, with justice indeed, for Bertram and Viola with true appreciation had once selected it as the appropriate setting in which to reproduce Jules Verne's *Twenty Thousand Leagues under the Sea*. The wallpaper of dark blue flock was smeared with the glistening pattern as of seaweed upon rocks at low tide; the window was of ground-glass tinted to the hue of water in a swimming-bath on Saturday afternoon, and was surrounded by an elaborate arrangement of cork that masked a number of flower pots filled with unexacting plants; while as if the atmosphere was not already sufficiently aqueous, a stage of disheartened aspidistras cast a deep-sea twilight upon the recesses of the room, in the middle of which was a jagged table of particolored marble, and upon the walls of which were hung cases of stuffed fish. Mrs. Easton, the proprietress of Halma House, only lent the room to George as a favor: it was not really his own, and while he lay in bed of a morning she used to quarrel there with all the servants in turn. Moreover, any of the boarders who had bicycles stabled them in this advantageous apartment, the fireplace of which smoked. Nevertheless, George liked it and used to knit there for an hour after lunch, sitting in an armchair that smelt like the cushions of a third-class smoker and looking with his knitting needles and opaque eyes like a large lobster preening his antennæ in the corner of a tank.

When John visited him now, he was reading an evening paper by the light of a rugged mantle of incandescent gas and calculating how much he would have won if he had backed the second favorite for every steeplechase of the day.

"Hullo, is that you, John?" he inquired with a yawn, and one hand swam vaguely in his brother's direction while the other kept its fingers spread out upon the second favorites like a stranded starfish.

"Yes, I'm afraid I've got very bad news for you, George."

George's opaque eyes rolled slowly away from the races and fixed his brother's in dull interrogation.

"Bertram and Viola are lost," John proclaimed.

"Oh, that's all right," George sighed with relief. "I thought you were serious for a minute. Crested Grebe at 4 to 1—yes, my theory that you ought to back second favorites works out right for the ninth time in succession. I should have been six pounds up to-day, betting with level sovereigns. Tut-tut-tut!"

John felt that his announcement had not made quite the splash it ought to have made in George's deep and stagnant pool.

"I don't think you heard what I said," he repeated. "Bertram and Viola—*your* children—are definitely lost."

"I don't expect they are really," said George, soothingly. "No, no, not really. The trouble is that not one single bookie will take on this second-favorite system. Ha-ha—they daren't, the cowards! Don't you bother about the kids; no, no, they'll be all right. They're probably hanging on behind a van—they often do that when I'm out with them, but they always turn up in the end. Yes, I should have made twenty-nine pounds this week."

"Look here," said John, severely, "I want you clearly to understand that this is not a simple question of losing them for a few minutes or so. They have been lost now since the Zoo was closed this afternoon, and I am not yet convinced that they are not shut up inside for the night."

"Ah, very likely," said George. "That's just the kind of place they might get to."

"The prospect of your children's passing the night in the Zoo leaves you unaffected?" John demanded in the tone of an examining counsel.

"Oh, they'll have been cleared out by now," said George. "You really mustn't bother yourself about them, old boy."

"You have no qualms, George, at the notion of their wandering for hours upon the outskirts of Regent's Park?"

"Now don't you worry, John. I'm not going to worry, and I don't want you to worry. Why worry? Depend upon it, you'll find them safe and sound in Church Row when you get back. By the way, is your taxi waiting?"

"No, I dismissed it."

"I was afraid it might be piling up the twopences. Though I dare say a pyramid of twopences wouldn't bother you, you old plutocrat. Yes, these second favorites...."

"Confound the second favorites," John exclaimed. "I want to discuss your children."

"You wouldn't, if you were their father. They involve me in far too many discussions. You see, you're not used to children. I am."

John's eyes flashed as much as the melancholy illumination permitted; this was the cue for which he had been waiting.

"Just so, my dear George. You are used to children: I am not. And that is why I have come to tell you that the police have been instructed to return them, when found, to *you* and not to me."

George blinked in a puzzled way.

"To me?" he echoed.

"Yes, to you. To their father. Hasn't their luggage arrived? I had it sent back here this morning."

"Ah, yes," George said. "Of course! I was rather late getting up this morning. I've been overworking a bit lately, and Karl did mutter something about luggage. Didn't it come in a taxi?"

John nodded.

"Yes, I remember now, in a prepaid taxi; but as I couldn't remember that I was expecting any luggage, I told Karl to send it back where it came from."

"Do you mean to say that you sent their luggage back after I'd taken the trouble to...."

"That's all right, old boy. I was feeling too tired to deal with any problems this morning. The morning is the only opportunity I get for a little peace. It never occurred to me whose luggage it was. It might have been a mistake; in fact I thought it was a mistake. But in any case it's very lucky I did send it back, because they'll want it to-night."

"I'm afraid I can't keep them with me any longer."

Though irony might be lost on George's cold blood, the plain fact might wake him up to the actuality of the situation and so it did.

"Oh, but look here, old boy," he expostulated, "Eleanor won't be home for another five weeks. She'll be at Cardiff next week."

"And Bertram and Viola will be at Earl's Court," said John, firmly.

"But the doctor strongly recommended me to rest. I've been very seedy while you were in America. Stomachic, old boy. Yes, that's the trouble. And then my nerves are not as strong as yours. I've had a lot of worry lately."

"I'm sorry," John insisted. "But I've been called away on urgent business, and I can't leave the children at Church Row. I'm sorry, George, but as soon as they are found, I must hand them over to you."

"I shall send them down to the country," George threatened.

"When they are once more safely in your keeping, you can do what you like with them."

"To your place, I mean."

Normally John would have given a ready assent to such a proposal; but George's attitude had by now aroused his bitter disapproval, and he was determined that Bertram and Viola should be planted upon their father without option.

"Ambles is impossible," he said, decidedly. "Besides, Eleanor is anxious that Viola shouldn't miss her series of Spanish dances. She attends the dancing-class every Tuesday and Friday. No doubt your landlady will lend you Karl to escort her."

"Children are very difficult in a boarding-house," George argued. "They're apt to disturb the other guests. In fact, there was a little trouble only last week over some game—"

"Robinson Crusoe," John put in.

"Ah, they told you?"

"No, no, go on. I'm curious to know exactly what we missed at Church Row."

"Well, they have a habit, which Eleanor most imprudently encourages, of dressing up on Sundays, and as I've had to make it an understood thing that *none* of *my* clothes are to be used, they are apt to borrow other people's. I must admit that generally people have been very kind about lending their clothes; but latterly this dressing up has taken a more ambitious form, and on Sunday week—I think it was—"

"Yes, it would have been a Sunday," John agreed.

"On Sunday week they borrowed Miss Moxley's parrot for Robinson Crusoe. You remember poor Miss Moxley, John?"

"Yes, she lent you five pounds once," said John, sternly.

"Precisely. Oh yes, she did. Yes, yes, that was why I was so vexed about her lending her parrot."

"Why shouldn't she lend her parrot?"

"No reason at all why she shouldn't lend it; but apparently parrots are very excitable birds, and this particular one went mad under the strain of the children's performance, bit Major Downman's finger, and escaped by an upper window. Poor Miss Moxley was extremely upset, and the bird has never been seen since. So you see, as I told you, children are apt to be rather a nuisance to the other guests."

"None of the guests at Halma House keeps a tame calf?"

George looked frightened.

"Oh no, I don't think so. There's certainly never been the least sign of mooing in the garden. Besides, I'm sure Mrs. Easton would object to a calf. She even objects to dogs, as I had to tell James the other day when he came to see me *very* early about signing some deed or other. But what made you ask about a calf? Do you want one?"

"No, I don't want one: I hate cows and calves. Bertram and Viola, however, are likely to want one next week."

"You've been spoiling them, old chap. They'd never dare ask me for a calf. Why, it's preposterous. Yes, you've been spoiling them. Ah, well, you can afford it; that's one thing."

"Yes, I dare say I have been spoiling them, George; but you'll be able to correct that when they're once again in your sole charge."

George looked doubtful.

"I'm very strict with them," he admitted. "I had to be after they lost the parrot and burned Mrs. Easton's rug. It was most annoying."

"Yes, luckily I hadn't got any suitable fur rugs," John chuckled. "So they actually burnt Mrs. Easton's?"

"Yes, and—er—she was so much upset," George went on, "that she's—well—the fact is, they *can't* come back, John, because she's let their room."

"How much do you owe her?" John demanded.

"Oh, very little. I think only from last September. Well, you see, Eleanor was out of an engagement all the summer and had a wretched salary at the Parthenon while she was understudying—these actress-managers are awful harpies—do you know Janet Bond?"

"Yes, I'm writing a tragedy for her now."

"Make her pay, old boy, make her pay. That's my advice. And I know the business side of the profession. But to come back to Mrs. Easton—I was really very angry with her, but you see, I've got my own room here and it's uncommonly difficult to find a private room in a boarding-house, so I thought we'd stay on here till Eleanor's tour was over. She intends to save three pounds a week, and if I have a little luck over the sticks this winter, we shall be quite straight with Mrs. Easton, and then the children will be able to come back in the New Year."

"How much do you owe her?" John demanded for the second time.

"Oh, I think it's about twenty pounds—it may be a little more."

John knew how much the little more always was in George's calculations, and rang the bell, which fetched his brother out of the armchair almost in a bound.

"Old boy, I never ring the bell here," he expostulated. "You see, I never consider that my private room is included in the attendance."

George moved nervously in the direction of the door to make his peace with whoever should answer the unwonted summons; but John firmly interposed himself and explained that he had rung for Mrs. Easton herself.

"Rung for Mrs. Easton?" George repeated in terrified amazement. "But she may come!"

"I hope she will," replied John, becoming more divinely calm every moment in the presence of his brother's agitation.

A tangled head flung itself round the door like one of the minor characters in a Punch and Judy show.

"Jew ring?" it asked, hoarsely.

"Please ask Mrs. Easton to come down to Mr. Touchwood's sitting-room," said John, seriously.

The head sniffed and vanished.

"I wish you could realize, old chap, that in a boarding-house far more tact is required than anywhere else in the world," George muttered in melancholy apprehension. "An embassy isn't in it with a boarding-house. For instance, if I hadn't got the most marvelous tact, I should never have kept this room. However," he added more cheerfully, "I don't suppose for a moment that she'll come—unless of course she thinks that the chimney is on fire. Dash it, John, I wish you could understand some of the difficulties of my life. That's why I took up knitting. My nerves are all to pieces. If I were a rich man I should go for a long sea-voyage."

George fell into a silent brooding upon his misfortunes and ill-health and frustrated ambitions; John examined the stuffed fish upon the walls, which made him think of wet days upon the river and waiting drearily in hotel smoking-rooms for the weather to clear up. Then suddenly Mrs. Easton filled the room. Positive details of this lady's past were lacking, although the gossip of a long line of attenuated spinsters had evolved a rich apocrypha. It was generally accepted, however, that Halma House was founded partly upon settlements made in her favor long ago by a generous stockbroker and partly upon an insurance-policy taken out by her late husband Dr. Easton, almost on the vigil of his death, the only successful operation he ever performed. The mixed derivation of her prosperity was significantly set forth in her personal appearance: she either wore widow's black and powdered her face with pink talcum or she wore bright satins with plumed hats and let her nose shine: so that although she never looked perfectly respectable, on the other hand she never looked really fast.

"Good evening, ma'am," John began at once, assuming an air of Grandisonian courtesy. "My brother is anxious to settle his account."

The clouds rolled away from Mrs. Easton's brow; the old Eve glimmered for a moment in her fierce eye; if he had been alone with her, John would have thought that she was about to wink at him.

"I hear my nephew and niece have been taking liberties with your rug," he went on, but feeling that he might have expressed the last sentence better, he hurriedly blotted the check and with a bow handed it to the proprietress. "No doubt," he added, "you will overlook it this time? I am having a new rug sent to you immediately. What—er—skin do you prefer? Bear? I mean to say, the rug."

He tried to think of any other animal whose personality survived in rugs, but could think of none except a rabbit, and condemning the ambiguity of the English language waited in some embarrassment for Mrs. Easton to reply. She was by this time so surely convinced of John's interest in her that she opened to him with a trilling flutter of complacency like a turkey's tail.

"It happened to be a bearskin," she murmured. "But children will be children. We oughtn't to forget that we were all children once, Mr. Touchwood."

"So no doubt," John nervously continued, "you will be glad to see them when they come back to-night. Their room...."

"I shall give orders at once, Mr. Touchwood."

He wished that she would not harp upon the Mr. Touchwood; he seemed to detect in it a kind of reproachful formality; but he thanked her and hoped nervously she would now leave him to George.

"Oh dear me, why the girl hasn't lit the fire," Mrs. Easton exclaimed, evidently searching for a gracious action.

George eying his brother with a glance between admiration and disquietude told his landlady that he thought the fire smoked a little.

"I shall have the chimney swept to-morrow," she answered as grandly as if she had conferred a dukedom upon John and an earldom upon George.

Then with a special smile that was directed not so much toward the successful author as toward the gallant male she tucked away the check in her bodice, where it looked as forlorn as a skiff upon the tumultuous billows of the Atlantic, and went off to put on her green satin for dinner.

"We shall all hope to see you at half-past seven," she paused in the doorway to assure John.

"You know, I'll tell you what it is, old chap," said George when they were alone again. "*You* ought to have taken up the commission business and *I* ought to have written plays. But thanks very much for tiding me over this difficult time."

"Yes," said John, a little sharply. "Your wife's current account wasn't flowing quite strongly enough, was it?"

"Wonderful woman, Mrs. Easton," George declared. "She has a keen eye for business."

"And for pleasure too, I should imagine," said John, austerely. "But get on your coat, George," he added, "because we must go out and inquire at all the police stations in turn for news of Bertram and Viola. We can't stop here discussing that woman."

"I tell you the kids will be all right. You mustn't get fussy, John. It's absurd to go out now," George protested. "In fact I daren't. I must think of my health. Dr. Burnham who's staying here for a congress of medical men has given me a lot of advice, and as he has refused to charge me a penny for it, the least I can do is to pay attention to what he says. Besides, what are we going to do?"

"Visit all the police stations in London."

"What shall we gain by doing that? Have you ever been to a police station? They're most uncomfortable places to hang about in before dinner."

"Get on your coat," John repeated.

George sighed.

"Well, if you insist, I suppose you have the right to insist; but in my opinion it's a waste of time. And if the kids are in a police station, I think it would teach them a dashed good lesson to keep them there for awhile. You don't want to encourage them to lose themselves every day. I wish *you* had half a dozen kids."

John, however, was inflexible; the sight of his brother sitting in that aqueous room and pondering the might-have-beens of the race course had kindled in his breast the fire of a reformer; George must be taught that he could not bring children into the world without being prepared to look after them. He must and should be taught.

"Why, you'd take more trouble," he declared, "if you'd lost a fox terrier."

"Of course I should," George agreed. "I should have to."

John reddened with indignation.

"Don't be angry, old chap. I didn't mean that I should think more of a fox terrier. But, don't you see, a dog is dependent upon its collar, whereas Bertram and Viola can explain where they come from. Is it very cold out?"

"You'd better wear your heavy coat."

"That means I shall have to go all the way upstairs," groaned George.

The two brothers walked along the hall, and John longed to prod George with a heavy, spiked pole.

"Going out, Touchwood?" inquired an elderly man of military appearance, who was practicing golf putts from one cabbage rose to another on the Brussels carpet.

"Yes, I'm going out, Major. You know my brother, don't you? You remember Major Downman, John?"

George left his brother with the major and toiled listlessly upstairs.

"I think I once saw a play of yours, Mr. Touchwood."

John smiled as mechanically as the major might have returned a salute.

"*The Fall of Nineveh*, wasn't it?"

The author bowed an affirmative: it was hardly worth while differentiating between Nineveh and Babylon when he was just going out.

"Yes," the major persisted. "Wasn't there a good deal of talk about the scantness of some of the ladies' dresses?"

"There may have been," John said. "We had to save on the dresses what we spent on the hanging gardens."

"Quite," agreed the major, wisely. "But I'm not a puritan myself."

John bowed again to show his appreciation of the admission.

"Oh, no. Rather the reverse, in fact. I play golf every Sunday, and if it's wet I play bridge."

John wished that George would be quick with his coat.

"But I don't go in much for the theater nowadays."

"Don't you?"

"No, though I used to when I was a subaltern. By gad, yes! But it was better, I think, in my young days. No offense to you, Mr. Touchwood."

"Distance does lend enchantment," John assented.

"Quite, quite. I suppose you don't remember a piece at the old Prince of Wales? What was it called? Upon my soul, I've forgotten. It was a capital piece, though. I remember there was a scene in which the uncle—or it may not have been the uncle—no, I'm wrong. It was at the Strand. Or was it? God bless my soul, I don't know which it was. You don't remember the piece? It was either at the Prince of Wales or the Strand, or, by Jove, was it Toole's?"

Was George never coming? Every moment would bring Major Downman nearer to the heart of his reminiscence, and unless he escaped soon he might have to submit to a narrative of the whole plot.

"Do you know what I'm doing?" the Major began again. "I'm confusing two pieces. That's what I'm doing. But I know an uncle arrived suddenly."

"Yes, uncles are often rather fidgety," John agreed. "Ah, excuse me, Major. I see my brother coming downstairs. Good-by, Major, good-by. I should like to have a chat with you one of these days about the mid-Victorian theater."

"Delighted," the Major said, fervently. "I shall think of that play before to-night. Don't you be afraid. Yes, it's on the tip of my tongue. On the very tip. But I'm confusing two theaters. I see where I've gone wrong."

At that moment there was the sound of a taxi's arrival at Halma House; the bell rang; when George opened the door for John and himself to pass out, they were met by Mrs. Worfolk holding Viola and Bertram tightly, one in each hand.

"I told you they'd turn up," George said, and immediately took off his overcoat with a sigh of relief. "Well, you've given us a nice hunt," he went on with an indignant scowl at the children. "Come along to my room and explain where you've been. Good evening, Mrs. Worfolk."

In their father's sitting-room Bertram and Viola stood up to take their trial.

"Yes," opened Mrs. Worfolk, on whom lay the burden of narrating the malefactors' behavior. "Yes, I've brought back the infant prodigals, and a nice job I've had to persuade them to come quiet. In fact, I never had such a job since I took my poor sister's Herbert hollering to the hospital with a penny as he'd nearly choked himself with, all through him sucking it to get at some sweet stuff which was stuck to the edge. He *didn't* choke, though, because I patted him all down the street the same as if I'd been bowling a hoop, and several people looked at me in a very inquisitive way. Not that I ever pay attention to how people looks, except in church. To begin with, the nerve they've got. Well, I mean to say, when any one packs up some luggage and sends it off in a taxi, whoever expects to see it come back again almost at once? It came bouncing back, I do declare, as if it had been India rubber. 'Well,' as I said to Maud, 'It just shows how deep they are, and Mr. Touchwood'll have trouble with them before the day's done. You mark my words.' And, sure enough, just as I'd made up my mind that you wouldn't be in to tea, rat-a-tat-tat on the front door, and up drives my lord and my lady as grand as you like in a taxi. Of course, it give me a bit of a turn, not seeing you, sir, and I was just going to ask if you'd had an accident or something, when my lord starts in to argue with the driver that he'd only got to pay half fare for himself and his sister, the same as his father does when they travel by train. Oh, yes; he was going to pay the man himself. Any one would of thought it was the Juke of Wellington, to hear him arguing with that driver. Well, anyway, in the end, of course I had to pay the difference out of my housekeeping money, which you'll find entered in the book. And then, without so much as a blink, my lord starts in to tell how they'd gone into the Small Rat's House—"

"Cats," interrupted Viola, solemnly.

"Well, rats or cats, what does it matter, you naughty girl? It wasn't of rats or cats you were thinking, but running away from your poor uncle, as you perfeckly well know. Yes, indeed, sir, they went into this small house and dodged you like two pickpockets and then went careering out of the Zoo in the opposite direction. The first taxi that came along they caught hold of and drove back to Church Row. 'But your uncle intended for you to go back to your father, Mr. George, in Earl's Court,' I remarked very severely. 'We know,' they says to me, laughing like two hyenas. 'But we don't want to go back to Earl's Court,' putting in a great deal of rudeness about Earl's Court, which, not wanting to get them into worse trouble than what they will get into as it is, I won't repeat. 'And we won't go back to Earl's Court,' they said, what's more. 'We *won't* go back.' Well, sir, when I've had my orders given me, I know where I am, and the policeman at the corner being a friend of Elsa's, he helped; for, believe me or not, they struggled like two convicks with Maud and I. Well, to cut a long story short, here they are, and just about fit to be put to bed on the instant."

John could not fancy that Eleanor had contrived such an elaborate display of preference for his company, and with every wish to support Mrs. Worfolk by an exhibition of avuncular sternness he could only smile at his nephew and niece. Indeed, it cost him a great effort not to take them back with him at once to Hampstead. He hardened himself, however, and tried to look shocked.

"We wanted to stay with you," said Bertram.

"We wanted to stay with you," echoed Viola.

"We didn't *want* to dodge you in the Small Cats' House. But we had to," said Bertram.

"Yes, we had to," echoed Viola.

"Their luggage *'as* come back with them," interrupted Mrs. Worfolk, grimly.

"Oh, of course, they must stay here," John agreed. "Oh, unquestionably! I wasn't thinking of anything else."

He beckoned to Bertram and Viola to follow him out of the room.

"Look here," he whispered to them in the passage, "be good children and stay quietly at home. We shall meet at Christmas." He pressed a sovereign into each hand.

"Good lummy," Bertram gasped. "I wish I'd had this on the fifth of November. I'd have made old Major Downman much more waxy than he was when I tied a squib to his coat."

"Did you, Bertram, did you? You oughtn't to have done that. Though I can understand the temptation. But don't waste this on fireworks."

"Oh no," said Bertram. "I'm going to buy Miss Moxley a parrot, because we lost hers."

"Are you, Bertram?" John exclaimed with some emotion. "That shows a fine spirit, my boy. I'm very pleased with you."

"Yes," said Bertram, "because then with what you gave V we'll buy a monkey at the same time."

"Good heavens," cried John, turning pale. "A monkey?"

"That will be nice, won't it, Uncle John?" Viola asked, tenderly.

But perhaps it would escape from an upper window like the parrot, John thought, before Christmas.

When the children had been sent upstairs and Mrs. Worfolk had gone back to Hampstead, John told his brother that he should not stop to dinner after all.

"Oh, all right," George said. "But I had something to talk over with you. Those confounded children put it clean out of my mind. I had a strange letter from Mama this week. It seems that Hugh has got into rather a nasty fix. She doesn't say what it is, and I don't know why she wrote to me of all people. But she's evidently frightened about Hugh and asks me to approach you on his behalf."

"What on earth has he been doing now?" asked John, gloomily.

"I should think it was probably money," said George. "Well, I told you I'd had a lot of worry lately, and I *have* been very worried about this news of Hugh. Very worried. I'm afraid it may be serious this time. But if I were you, old chap, I should refuse to do anything about it. Why should he come to you to get him out of a scrape? You've done enough for him, in my opinion. You mustn't let people take advantage of your good nature, even if they are relations. I'm sorry my kids have been a bit of a nuisance, but, after all, they are still only kids, and Hugh isn't. He's old enough to know better. Mama says something about the police, but that may only be Hugh's bluff. I shouldn't worry myself if I were you. It's no good for us all to worry."

"I shall go and see Hugh at once," John decided. "You're not keeping anything from me, George? He's not actually under arrest?"

"Oh, no, you won't have to visit any more police stations to-night," George promised. "Hugh is living with his friend, Aubrey Fenton, at 22 Carlington Road, West Kensington."

"I shall go there to-night," John declared.

He had almost reached the front door when George called him back.

"I've been trying to work out a riddle," he said, earnestly. "You know there's a medicine called Easton's Syrup? Well, I thought ... don't be in such a hurry; you'll muddle me up ... and I shall spoil it...."

"Try it on Major Downman," John advised, crossly, slamming the door of Halma House behind him. "Fatuous, that's what George is, utterly fatuous," he assured himself as he hurried down the steps.

CHAPTER VIII

JOHN decided to walk from Earl's Court to West Kensington. Being still in complete ignorance of what Hugh had done, he had a presentiment that this time it was something really grave, and he was now beginning to believe that George knew how grave it was. Perhaps his decision to go on foot was not altogether wise, for he was tired out by a convulsive day, and he had never experienced before such a fathomless sinking of the stomach on the verge of being mixed up in a disagreeable family complication, which was prolonged by the opportunity that the walk afforded him for dismal meditation. While he hurried with bowed head along one ill-lighted road after another a temptation assailed him to follow George's advice and abandon Hugh, and not merely Hugh, but all the rest of his relations, a temptation that elaborated itself into going back to Church Row, packing up, and escaping to Arizona or British East Africa or Samoa. In the first place, he had already several times vowed never more to have anything to do with his youngest brother; secondly, he was justified in resenting strongly the tortuous road by which he had been approached on his behalf; thirdly, it might benefit Hugh's morals to spend a week or two in fear of the ubiquitous police, instead of a few stay-at-home tradesmen; fourthly, if anything serious did happen to Hugh, it would serve as a warning to the rest of his relations, particularly to George; finally, it was his dinner hour, and if he waited to eat his dinner before tackling Hugh, he should undoubtedly tackle him afterward in much too generous a frame of mind. Yes, it would be wiser to go home at once, have a good dinner, and start for Arizona to-morrow morning. The longer he contemplated it, the less he liked the way he had been beguiled into visiting Hugh. If the—the young bounder—no, really bounder was not too strong a word—if the young bounder was in trouble, why could he not have come forward openly and courageously to the one relation who could help him? Why had he again relied upon his mother's fondness, and why had she, as always, chosen the indirect channel by writing to George rather than to himself? The fact of the matter was that his mother and George and Hugh possessed similar loose conceptions of integrity, and now that it was become a question of facing the music they had instinctively joined hands. Yet George had advised him to have nothing more to do with Hugh, which looked as if his latest game was a bit too strong even for George to relish, for John declined to believe that George possessed enough of the spirit of competitive sponging to bother about trying to poach in Hugh's waters; Hilda or Eleanor might, but George.... George was frightened, that was it; obviously he knew more than he had told, and he did not want to be exposed ... it would not astonish him to learn that George was in the business with Hugh and had invented that letter from Mama to invoke his intervention before it was too late to save himself. What could it all be about? Curiosity turned the scale against Arizona, and John pressed forward to West Kensington.

The houses in Carlington Road looked like an over-crowded row of tall, thin men watching a football match on a cold day; each red-faced house had a tree in front of it like an umbrella and trim, white steps like spats; in a fantastic mood the comparison might be prolonged indefinitely, even so far as to say that, however outwardly uncomfortable they might appear, like enthusiastic spectators, they were probably all aglow within. If John had been asked whether he liked an interior of pink lampshades and brass gongs, he would have replied emphatically in the negative; but on this chill November night he found the inside of number 22 rather pleasant after the street. The maid looked doubtful over admitting him, which was not surprising, because an odor of hot soup in the hall and the chink of plates behind a closed door on the right proclaimed that the family was at dinner.

"Will you wait in the drawing-room, sir?" she inquired. "I'll inform Mr. Touchwood that you're here."

John felt a grim satisfaction in thus breaking in upon Hugh's dinner; there was nothing so well calculated to disturb even a tranquil conscience as an unexpected visit at such an hour; but the effect upon guilt would be....

"Just say that a gentleman wishes to speak to him for a minute. No name," he replied.

The walk through the dim streets, coupled with speculations upon the various crimes that his brother might have committed, had perhaps invested John's rosy personality with an unusual portentousness, for the maid accepted his instructions fearfully and was so much flustered by them that she forgot to turn up the gas in the drawing-room, of which John was glad; he assured himself that the heavily draped room in the subdued light gave the final touch to the atmosphere of horror which he aimed at creating; and he could not resist opening the door to enjoy the consternation in the dining-room just beyond.

"What is it?"

A murmur from the maid.

"Well, you'd better finish your soup first. I wouldn't let my soup get cold for anybody."

There followed a general buzz from the midst of which Hugh emerged, his long, sallow face seeming longer than usual in his anxiety, his long, thin neck craning forward like an apprehensive bird's, and his bony fingers clutching a napkin with which he dusted his legs nervously.

"Like a flag of truce," John thought, and almost simultaneously felt a sharp twinge of resentment at Hugh's daring to sport a dinner jacket with as much effrontery as if his life had been as white as that expanse of shirt.

"Good Lord," Hugh exclaimed when he recognized his brother. "I thought you were a detective, at least. Come in and have some grub, won't you? Mrs. Fenton will be awfully glad to see you."

John demurred at the invitation. Judging by what he had been told about Mrs. Fenton's attitude toward Hugh, he did not think that Touchwood was a welcome name in 22 Carlington Road.

"Aubrey!" Hugh was shouting. "One of my brothers has just blown in."

John felt sure that the rapid feminine voice he could faintly hear had a distinct note of expostulation in it; but, however earnest the objection, it was at once drowned in the boisterous hospitality of Aubrey, who came beaming into the hall—a well set up young man of about twenty-five with a fresh complexion, glasses, an opal solitaire in his shirt, and a waxy white flower in his buttonhole.

"Do come in," he begged, with an encouraging wave of his napkin. "We've only just begun."

Although John felt that by dining in this house he was making himself an accessory after the still undivulged fact, he was really so hungry by now that he could not bring himself to refuse. He knew that he was displaying weakness, but he compounded with his austere self by arguing that he was more likely to arrive at the truth if he avoided anything in the nature of precipitate action.

Mrs. Fenton did not receive her guest as cordially as her son; in fact, she showed plainly that she resented extremely his having been invited to dinner. She was a well-preserved woman and reminded John of a pink crystallized pear; her frosted transformation glistened like encrusted sugar round the stalk, which was represented by a tubular head ornament on the apex of the carefully tended pyramid; her greeting was sticky.

"My son's friend has spoken of you," Mrs. Fenton was saying, coldly, in reply to John's apologies for intruding upon her like this. He for his part was envying her ability to refer to Hugh without admitting his individual existence, when somebody kicked him under the table, and, looking up, he saw that Hugh was frowning at him in a cautionary manner.

"I've already met your brother, the writer," his hostess continued.

"My brother, James?" asked John in amazement. He could not envisage James in these surroundings.

"No, I have not had the pleasure of meeting him *yet*. I was referring to the dramatist, who has dined with me several times."

"But," John began, when another kick under the table silenced him.

"Pass the salt, will you, George, old boy?" Hugh said loudly.

John's soup was cold, but in the heat of his suppressed indignation he did not notice it. So George had been masquerading in this house as himself; no wonder he had not encouraged the idea of an interview with Hugh. Evidently a dishonest outrage had been perpetrated in his name, and though Hugh might kick him under the table, he should soon obtain his revenge by having Hugh kicked out of the house. John took as much pleasure in his dinner that evening as a sandbag might have taken in being stuffed with sand. He felt full when it was over, but it was a soulless affair; and when Mrs. Fenton, who had done nothing except look down her nose all through the meal, left the table, he turned furiously upon Hugh.

"What does this gross impersonation mean?" he demanded.

Aubrey threw himself figuratively between the brothers, which only seemed to increase John's irritation.

"We wanted to jolly the mater along," he explained. "No harm was intended, but Hughie was keen to prove his respectability; so, as you and he weren't on the most cordial terms, we introduced your brother, George, as yourself. It was a compliment, really, to your public character; but old George rather enjoyed dining here, and I'm bound to say he sold the mater some very decent port. In fact, you're drinking it now."

"And I suppose," said John, angrily, "that between you all you've perpetrated some discreditable fraud, what? I suppose you've been ordering shirts in my name as well as selling port, eh? I'll disown the bill. You understand me? I won't have you masquerading as a gentleman, Hugh, when you can't behave like one. It's obtaining money under false pretenses, and you can write to your mother till you're as blue in the face as the ink in your bottle—it won't help you. I can put up with laziness; I can tolerate stupidity; I can endure dissipation; but I'm damned if I'll stand being introduced as George. Port, indeed! Don't try to argue with me. You must take the consequences. Mr. Fenton, I'm sorry I allowed myself to be inveigled like this into your mother's house. I shall write to her when I get home, and I hope she will take steps to clear that impostor out. No, I won't have a cigar—though I've no doubt I shall presently receive the bill for them, unless I've also been passed off as a tobacconist's agent by George. As for him, I've done with him, too. I shall advertise in the *Times* that neither he nor Hugh has any business to order things in my name. I came here to-night in response to an urgent appeal; I find that I've been made a fool of; I find myself in a most undignified position. No, I will not have another glass of port. I don't know how much George exacted for it, but let me tell you that it isn't even good port: it's turbid and fiery."

John rose from the table and was making for the door, when Hugh took hold of his arm.

"Look here, old chap," he began.

"Don't attempt to soften me with pothouse endearments," said John, fiercely. "I will not be called 'old chap.'"

"All right, old chap, I won't," said Hugh. "But before you go jumping into the street like a lighted cracker, please listen. Nobody has been ordering anything in your name. You're absolutely off the lines there. Why, I exhausted your credit years ago. And I don't see why you should grudge poor old George a few dinners."

"You rascal," John stammered. "You impudent rascal!"

"Don't annoy him, Hughie," Aubrey advised. "I can see his point."

"Oh, you can, sir, can you?" John snapped. "You can understand, can you, how it affects me to be saddled with brothers like these and port like this?"

John was so furious that he could not bring himself to mention George or Hugh by name: they merely represented maddening abstractions of relationship, and he longed for some phrase like "my son's friend" with which he might disown them forever.

"You mustn't blame your brother George, Mr. Touchwood," urged Aubrey. "He's not involved in this latest affair. I'm sorry we told the mater that he was you, but the mater required jollying along, as I explained. She can't appreciate Hugh. He's too modern for her."

"I sympathize with Mrs. Fenton."

"You must forgive a ruse. It's just the kind of ruse I should think a playwright would appreciate. You know. Charley's Aunt and all that."

John clenched his fist: "Don't you mutter to me about a sense of humor," he said to Hugh, wrathfully.

"I wasn't muttering," replied Hugh. "I merely observed that a little sense of humor wouldn't be a bad thing. I'm sorry that George has been dragged like a red herring across the business, because it's a much more serious matter than simply introducing George to Mrs. Fenton as you and selling her some port which personally I think is not at all bad, eh, Aubrey?"

He poured himself out another glass to prove his conviction.

"You may think all this a joke," John retorted. "But I don't. I consider it a gross exhibition of bad taste."

"All right. Granted. Let's leave it at that," sighed Hugh, wearily. "But you don't give a fellow much encouragement to own up when he really is in a tight corner. However, personally I've got past minding. If I'm sentenced to penal servitude, it'll be your fault for not listening. Only don't say I disgraced the family name."

"Hugh's right," Aubrey put in. "We really are in a deuce of a hole."

"Disgrace the family name?" John repeated. "Allow me to tell you that when you hawk George round London as your brother, the playwright, I consider *that* is disgracing the family name."

"So that if I'm arrested for forgery," Hugh asked, "you won't mind?"

"Forgery?" John gasped.

Hugh nodded.

"Yes, we had bad luck in the straight," he murmured, tossing off two more glasses of port. "Cleared every hurdle like a bird and ... however, it's no good grumbling. We just didn't pull it off."

"No," sighed Aubrey. "We were beaten by a short head."

John sat down unsteadily, filled up half a glass of Burgundy with sherry, and drank it straight off without realizing that George's port was even worse than he had supposed.

"Whose name have you forged?" he brought himself to ask at last.

"Stephen Crutchley's."

"Good heavens!" he groaned. "But this is horrible. And has he found out? Does he know who did it?"

It was characteristic of John that he did not ask for how much his friend's name had been forged.

"He has his suspicions," Hugh admitted. "And he's bound to know pretty soon. In fact, I think the only thing to do is for you to explain matters. After all, in a way it was a joke."

"Yes, a kind of experimental joke," Aubrey agreed.

"But it has proved to me how easy it is to cash a forged check," Hugh continued, hopefully. "And, of course, if you talk to Crutchley he'll be all right. He's not likely to be very severe on the brother of an old friend. That was one of the reasons we experimented on him—that, and also partly because I found an old check book of his. He's awfully careless, you know, is Stephen—very much the high-brow architect and all that, though he doesn't forget to charge. In fact, so many people have had to pay for his name that it serves him right to find himself doing the same for once."

"Does Mrs. Fenton know anything of this?" John asked.

"Why, no," Aubrey answered, quickly. "Well, women don't understand about money, do they? And the mater has less idea of the wicked world than most. My father was always a bit of a recluse, don't you see?"

"Was he?" John said, sarcastically. "I should think his son will be a bit of a recluse, too, before he's done. But forgery! No, it's incredible—incredible!"

"Don't worry, Johnnie," Hugh insisted. "Don't worry. I'm not worrying at all, now that you've come along. Nobody knows anything for certain yet. George doesn't know. Mama doesn't know. Mrs. Fenton doesn't know. And Stevie only guesses."

"How do you know that he guesses?" John demanded.

"Well, that's part of the story, eh, Aubrey?" said Hugh, turning to his accomplice, who nodded sagely.

"Which I suppose one ought to tell in full, eh, Aubrey?" he went on.

"I think it would interest your brother—I mean—quite apart from his being your brother, it would interest him as a playwright," Aubrey agreed.

"Glasses round, then," called Hugh, cheerfully.

"There's a vacant armchair by the fireplace," Aubrey pointed out to John.

"Thanks," said John, stiffly. "I don't suppose that the comfort of an armchair will alleviate my feelings. Begin, sir," he commanded Hugh. "Begin, and get it finished quickly, for heaven's sake, so that I can leave this house and think out my course of action in solitude."

"Do you know what it is, Johnnie?" Hugh said, craning his neck and examining his brother with an air of suddenly aroused curiosity. "You're beginning to dramatize yourself. I suppose it's inevitable, but I wish you wouldn't. It gives me the same kind of embarrassed feeling that I get when a woman starts reciting. You're not subjective. That's the curse of all romantic writers. You want to get an objective viewpoint. You're not the only person on in this scene. I'm on. Aubrey's on. Mrs. Fenton and Stevie Crutchley are waiting in the wings, as it were. And, for all I know, the police may be waiting there, too, by this time. Get an objective viewpoint, Johnnie. Subjectivity went out with Rousseau."

"Confound your impudence," John spluttered.

"Yes, that's much better than talking about thinking out a course of action in solitude," Hugh approved. "But don't run away with the idea that I'm trying to annoy you. I'm not. I've every reason to encourage the romantic side of you, because finally it will be the romantic side of you that will shudder to behold your youngest brother in the dock. In fact, I'm going the limit on your romance. At the same time I don't like to see you laying it on too thick. I'll give you your fine feelings and all that. I'll grant you your natural mortification, etcetera, etcetera. But try to see my point of view as well as your own. When you're thinking out a course of action in solitude, you'll light a cigar with a good old paunch on it, and you'll put your legs up on the mantelpiece, unless you've grown old-maidish and afraid of scratching the furniture, and you'll pat your passbook, which is probably suffering from fatty degeneration. That's a good phrase, Aubrey?"

"Devilish good," the accomplice allowed. "But, look here, Hugh, steady—the mater gets rather bored if we keep the servants out of the dining-room too long, and I think your brother is anxious to have the story. So fire ahead, there's a good fellow."

Hugh looked hurt at the lack of appreciation which greeted the subtler shades of his discourse, but, observing that John looked still more hurt at being kept waiting, he made haste to begin without further reference to style.

"Well, you see, Johnnie, I've always been unlucky."

John made a gesture of impatience; but Hugh raised a sedative hand.

"I know there's nothing that riles lucky people so much as when unlucky people claim the prerogatives of their bad luck. I'm perfectly willing to admit that I'm lazier than you. But remember that energy is a gift, not an attainment. And I was born tired. The first stunning blow I had was when the old man died. You remember he always regarded me as a bit of an infant prodigy? So I was from his point of view, for he was over sixty when he begot me, and he used to look at me just as some people look at the silver cups they've won for races. But when he died, all the advantages of being the youngest son died with him, and I realized that I was an encumbrance. I'm willing to grant that I was a nuisance, too, but ... however, it's no use raking up old scores.... I'm equally willing to admit that you've always treated me very decently and that I've always behaved very rottenly. I'll admit also that my taste in clothes was beyond my powers of gratification; that I liked wine and women—or to put a nicer point upon it—whisky and waitresses. I did. And what of it? You'll observe that I'm not going to try to justify myself. Have another glass of port? No? Right-o; well, I will. I repeat I'm not going to attempt to justify myself, even if I couldn't, which I can, but in vino veritas, which I think you'll admit is Latin. Latin, I said. Precisely. Where was I?"

"Hugh, old boy, buck up," his friend prompted, anxiously.

"Come, sir," John said, trembling visibly with indignation. "Get on with your story while you can. I don't want to waste my time listening to the meanderings of a drunkard."

Hugh's eyes were glazing over like a puddle in frost, but he knitted his brows and regarded his brother with intense concentration.

"Don't try to take any literary advantage of me, Johnnie. You can dig out the longest word in the dictionary, but I've got a longer. Metempsychosis! Hear that? I'm willing to admit that I don't like having to say it, but you find me another man who can say it at all after George's port. Metempsychosis! And it's not a disease. No, no, no, no, don't you run away with the idea that it's a disease. Not at all. It's a religion. And for three years I've been wasting valuable knowledge like that on an architect's office. Do you think Stevie wants to hear about metempsychosis—that's the third time I've cleared it—of course he doesn't. Stephen Crutchley is a Goth. What am I? I'm a Palladian. There you have it. Am I right, Aubrey?"

"Quite right, old boy, only come to the point."

"That's all right, Aubrey, don't you be afraid. I'm nursing her along by the rails. You can lay a hundred pounds to a box of George's cigars bar one. And that one's me. Where was I? Ah, yes. Well, I'm not going to say a word against Stephen, Johnnie. He's a friend of yours. He's my boss. He's one of England's leading ecclesiastical architects. But that doesn't help me when I find myself in a Somersetshire village seven miles from the nearest station arguing with a deaf parson about the restoration of his moldy church. Does it? Of course not. It doesn't help me when I find myself sleeping in damp sheets and woken up at seven o'clock by a cross between a gardener and a charwoman for early service. Does it? Of course not. Architecture like everything else is a good job when you're waving the flag on top of the tower; but when you're digging the foundations it's rotten. Stevie and I have had our little differences, but when he's sober—I mean when I'm sober—he'll tell you that there's not one of his juniors he thinks better of than me. I'm against Gothic. I consider Gothic the muddle-headed expression of a muddle-headed period. But I've been loyal to Stevie, only...."

Hugh paused solemnly, while his friend regarded him with nervous solicitude.

"Only," Hugh repeated in a loud voice. "Metempsychosis," he murmured, and drinking two more glasses of wine, he sat back in his chair and shook his head in mute despair of human speech.

Aubrey took John aside.

"I'm afraid Hugh's too far gone to explain all the details to-night," he whispered. "But it's really very serious. You see he found an old check book of Mr. Crutchley's, and more from a joke than anything else he tried to see if it was difficult to cash a check. It wasn't. He succeeded. But he's suspected. I helped him indirectly, but of course I don't come into the business except as an accessory. Only, if you take my advice, you'll call on Mr. Crutchley as soon as you can, and I'm sure you'll be able to square things up. You'll know how to manage him; but Hugh has a way of exasperating him."

All the bland, the almost infantine simplicity of Aubrey Fenton's demeanor did not avail to propitiate John's rage; and when the maid came in with a message from his hostess to ask if it would soon be convenient to allow the table to be cleared, he announced that he should not remain another minute in the house.

"But can Hugh count on your support?" Aubrey persisted. He spoke like an election agent who is growing rapidly doubtful of his candidate's prospects.

"He can count on nothing," said John, violently. "He can count on nothing at all. On absolutely nothing at all."

Anybody who had seen Hugh's condition at this moment would have agreed with John. His eyes had already lost even as much life as might have been discerned in the slow freezing of a puddle, and had now assumed the glassy fixity and perfect roundness of two bottle-stoppers.

"He can count on nothing," John asseverated.

"I see," said Aubrey, tactfully. "I'll try and get that across to him. Must you really be going?"

"Immediately."

"You'll trot in and say ta-ta to the mater?"

John had no wish ever again to meet this crystallized lady, but his politeness rose superior to his indignation, and he followed the son of the house into the drawing-room. His last glimpse of Hugh was of a mechanical figure, the only gesture of which was awkwardly to rescue every glass in turn that the maid endeavored to include in her clearance of the table.

"It's scandalous," muttered John. "It's—it's abominable! Mrs. Fenton," he said with a courtly bow for her hospitality, "I regret that your son has encouraged my brother to impose himself upon your good-nature. I shall take steps to insure that he shall do so no longer. I beg your pardon, Mrs. Fenton, I apologize. Good-night."

"I've always spoilt Aubrey," she said. "And he always had a mania for dangerous toys which he never could learn to work properly. Never!" she repeated, passionately.

For an instant the musty sugar in which she was inclosed cracked and allowed John a glimpse of the feminine humanity underneath; but in the same instant the crystallization was more complete than ever, and when John released her hand he nearly took out his handkerchief to wipe away the stickiness.

"I say, what steps *are* you going to take to-morrow?" Aubrey asked.

"Never mind," John growled. Inasmuch as he himself had no more idea of what he intended to do than Aubrey, the reply was a good one.

Where Carlington Road flows into Hammersmith Road John waited for a passing taxi, apostrophizing meanwhile the befogged stars in the London sky.

"I shall not forget to-night. No, I certainly sha'n't. I doubt if any dramatist ever spent such another. A glimpse at all the animals of the globe, a lunch that would have made a jackal vomit, a search for two lost children, an interview with a fatuous brother, a loan of over thirty pounds, a winking landlady, a narrow escape from being bored to death by a Major, a dinner that gave me the sensation of being slowly buried alive, a glass of George's port, and for climax the news that my brother has committed a forgery. How can I think about Joan of Arc? A few more days like this and I shall never be able to think or write again—however, please God, there'll always be the cinema."

Whirring home to Hampstead John fell asleep, and when he had supplemented that amount of repose in the taxi by eight hours in his own bed, he woke next morning with his mind made up to square matters with Stephen Crutchley, to withdraw Hugh from architecture, to intern him until Christmas at Ambles, and in the New Year to transport him to British Honduras as a mahogany-planter. He had met on board the *Murmania* a mahogany-planter who was visiting England for the first time in thirteen years: the profession must be an enthralling one.

It was only when John reached the offices of Stephen Crutchley in Staple Inn that he discovered it was Sunday, which meant another whole day's idleness and suspense, and he almost fell to wishing that he was in church again with Bertram and Viola. But there was a sweet sadness in this old paved court, where a few sparrows chirped their plaintive monotone from an overarching tree, the branches of which fretted a sky of pearly blue, and where several dreary men were sitting upon the benches regarding their frayed boots. John could not remain unsusceptible to the antique charm of the scene, and finding an unoccupied bench he rested there in the timid sunlight.

"What a place to choose for a forgery," he murmured, reproachfully, and tried to change the direction of his thoughts by remembering that Dr. Johnson had lived here for a time. He had no sooner concentrated upon fancies of that great man than he began to wonder if he was not mistaken in supposing that he had lived here, and he looked round for some one who could inform him. The dreary men with frayed boots were only counting the slow minutes of divine service before the public-houses could open: they knew nothing of the lexicographer. But the subject of forgery was not to be driven away by memories of Dr. Johnson, because his friend, Dr. Dodd, suddenly jumped into the train of thought, and it was impossible not to conjure up that poor and learned gentleman's last journey to Tyburn nor to reflect how the latticed dormers on the Holborn side of the Inn were the same now as then and had actually seen Dr. Dodd go jolting past. John had often thought how incomprehensible it was that scarcely a century ago people should have been hanged for such crimes as forgery; but not it seemed rather more comprehensible. Of course, he should not like to know that his brother was going to be hanged; but for the sake of his future it would be an excellent thing to revive capital punishment for minor crimes. He should like when all this dreadful business was settled to say to his brother, "Oh, by the way, Hugh, I hear they've just passed a bill making forgery a capital offense once more. I think you'll like mahogany-planting."

But would the fear of death act as a deterrent upon such an one as Hugh, who after committing so dishonorable a crime had lacked even the grace to make his confession of it soberly? It was doubtful: Hugh was without shame. From boyhood his career had been undistinguished by a single decent action; but on the contrary it had been steadily marred by vice and folly from the time when he had stolen an unused set of British North Borneo stamps from the locker of his best friend at school to this monstrous climax. Forgery! Great heavens, had he ever yet envisaged Hugh listening abjectly (or worse impudently) to the strictures of a scornful judge? Had he yet imagined the headlines in the press? *Brother of distinguished dramatist sent to penal servitude. Judge's scathing comments.* Mr. Touchwood breaks down in court. *Miss Janet Bond's production indefinitely postponed.* Surely Stephen would not proceed to extreme measures, but for the sake of their lifelong sympathy spare his old friend this humiliation; yet even as John reached this conclusion the chink-chink of the sparrows in the plane-tree sounded upon the air like the chink-chink of the picks on Dartmoor. Hugh a convict! It might well befall thus, if his jaunty demeanor hardened Stephen's heart. Suppose that Stephen should be seized with one of those moral crises that can only be relieved by making an example of somebody? Would it not be as well to go down at once to his place in the country and try to square matters, unembarrassed by Hugh's brazen impenitence? Or was it already too late? John could not bring himself to believe that his old friend would call in the police without warning him. Stephen had always had a generous disposition, and it might well be that rather than wound John's pride by the revelation of his brother's disgrace he had made up his mind to say nothing and to give Hugh another chance: that would be like Stephen. No, he should not intrude upon his week-end; though how he was going to pass the long Sunday unless he occupied himself with something more cheerful than his own thoughts he did not know. Should he visit James and Beatrice, and take them out to lunch with a Symphony Concert to follow? No, he should never be able to keep the secret of Hugh's crime, and James would inevitably wind up the discussion by making it seem as if it were entirely his own fault. Should he visit George and warn him that the less intercourse he had with Hugh the better, yes, and incidentally observe to George that he resented his impersonation of himself at Mrs. Fenton's? No, George's company would be as intolerable as his port. And the children? No, no, let them dress up with minds still untainted by their Uncle Hugh's shame; let them enact Robinson Crusoe and if they liked burn Halma House to the ground. What was unpremeditated arson compared with deliberate forgery? But if there was a genuine criminal streak in the Touchwoods, how was he ever again to feel secure of his relations' honor? To-morrow he might learn that James had murdered Beatrice because she had slept through the opening chapters of *Lord Ormont and his Aminta.* To-morrow he might learn that George was a defaulting bookmaker, that Hilda had embezzled the whole of Laurence's board, and that Harold was about to be prosecuted by the Society for Prevention of Cruelty to Animals. Why, even his mother might have taken to gin-drinking in the small hours of the morning!

"God forgive me," said John. "I am losing my faith in humanity and my respect for my mother. Yet some imbeciles prate about the romance of crime."

John felt that if he continued to sit here brooding upon his relations he should be in danger of taking some violent step such as joining the Salvation Army: he remembered how an actor in *The Fall of Babylon* had brooded upon his inability to say his lines with just the emphasis he as author had required, until on the night before the opening he had left the theater and become a Salvationist. One of the loafers in the court shuffled up to John and begged him for a match; when John complied he asked for something to use it on, and John was so much distressed by the faint likeness he bore to his eldest brother that he gave him a cigar.

"Without me that is what they would all be by now, every one of them, James, George, and Hugh," he thought "But if I hadn't been lucky, so might I," he added, reprovingly, to himself, "though at any rate I should have tried to join a workhouse and not wasted my time cadging for matches in Staple Inn."

John was not quite clear about workhouses; he had abandoned realistic writing before he dealt with workhouse life as it really is.

"However, I can't sit here depressing myself all day; besides, this bench is damp. What fools those sparrows are to stay chirping in that tree when they might be hopping about in Hampshire—out of reach of Harold's air-gun of course—and what a fool I am! But it's no use for me to go home and work at Joan of Arc. The English archers will only be shooting broad arrows all the time. I'll walk slowly to the Garrick, I think, and have an early lunch."

Perversely enough the club did not seem to contain one sympathetic acquaintance, let alone a friend, that Sunday; and after lunch John was reduced to looking at the portraits of famous dead players, who bored him nearly as much as one or two of the live ones who were lounging in the smoking-room.

"This is getting unendurable," he moaned, and there seemed nothing for it but to sally forth and walk the hollow-sounding city. From Long Acre he turned into St. Martin's Lane, shook off the temptation to bore himself still more hopelessly by a visit to the National Gallery, and reached Cockspur Street. Three or four Sabbath loiterers were staring at a window, and John saw that it was the office of the Cunard Line and that the attraction was a model of the *S.S. Murmania.*

"What a fool I am!" John murmured much more emphatically than in Staple Inn. He was just going to call a taxi to drive him to Chelsea, when he experienced from yesterday a revulsion against taxis. Yesterday had been a nightmare of taxis, between driving to the Zoo and driving to the police station and driving home after that interview with the forger—by this time John had discarded Hugh as a relation—not to mention Mrs. Worfolk in a taxi, and the children in a taxi, and their luggage buzzing backward and forward between Earl's Court and Hampstead in a taxi. No, he should walk to Chelsea: a brisk walk with an objective would do him good. 83 Camera Square. It was indeed rather a tribute to his memory, he flattered himself, that he could remember her address without referring to her card. He should walk along the Embankment; it was only half-past two now.

It was pleasant walking by the river on that fine afternoon, and John felt as he strode along Grosvenor Road, his spirit rising with the eager tide, that after all there was nothing like the sea, nothing!

"As soon as I've finished Joan of Arc, I shall take a sea-voyage. It's all very well for George to talk about sea-voyages, but let him do some work first. Even if I do send him for a sea-voyage, how will he spend his time? I know perfectly well. He'll feel seasick for the first week and play poker for the rest of the passage. No, no, after the Christmas holidays at Ambles he'll be as right as a trivet without a sea-voyage. What is a trivet by the way? Now if I had a secretary, I should make a note of a query like that. As it is, I shall probably never know what a trivet is; but if I had a secretary, I should ask her to look it up in the dictionary when we got home. I dare say I've lost thousands of ideas by not having a secretary at hand. I shall have to advertise—or find out in some way about a secretary. Thank heaven, neither Hilda nor Beatrice nor Eleanor nor Edith knows shorthand. But even if Edith did know shorthand, she'd be eternally occupied with the dactylography—as I suppose *he'd* call it—of Laurence's apostolic successes—there's another note I might make. Of course, it's nothing wonderful as a piece of wit, but I might get an epigram worth keeping, say three times a week, if I had a secretary at my elbow. I don't believe that Stephen will make any difficulties about Hugh. Oh no, I don't think so. I was tired this morning after yesterday. This walk is making me see events in their right proportion. Rosification indeed! James brings out these things as if he were a second Sydney Smith; but in my opinion wit without humor is like marmalade without butter. And even if I do rosify things, well, what is it that Lady Teazle says? *I wish it were spring all the year round and that roses grew under our feet.* And it takes something to rosify such moral anemia as Hugh's. By the way I wonder just exactly whereabouts in Chelsea Camera Square is."

Now if there was one thing that John hated, if there was one thing that dragged even his buoyant spirits into the dust, if there was one thing worse than having a forger for a blood-relation, it was to be compelled to ask his way anywhere in London within the four miles radius. He would not even now admit to himself more than that he did not know the *exact* whereabouts of Camera Square. Although he really had not the remotest idea beyond its location in the extensive borough of Chelsea where Camera Square was, he wasted half-an-hour in dancing a kind of Ladies' Chain with all the side-streets off King's Road and never catching a glimpse of his destination. It was at last borne in upon him that if he wanted to call on Mrs. Hamilton at a respectable hour for afternoon tea he should simply have to ask his way.

Now arose for John the problem of choosing the oracle. He walked on and on, half making up his mind every moment to accost somebody and when he was on the point of doing so perceiving in his expression a latent haughtiness that held him back until it was too late. Had it not been Sunday, he would have entered a shop and bought sufficiently expensive to bribe the shopman from looking astonished at his ignorance. Presently, however, he passed a tobacconist's, and having bought three of the best cigars he had, which were not very good, he asked casually as he was going out the direction of Camera Square. The shopman did not know. He came to another tobacconist's, bought three more cigars, and that shopman did not know either. Gradually with a sharp sense of impending disgrace John realized that he must ask a policeman. He turned aside from the many inviting policemen in the main road, where the contemptuous glances of wayfarers might presume his rusticity, and tried to find a policeman in a secluded by-street. This took another half-an-hour, and when John did accost this ponderous hermit of the force he accosted him in broken English.

"Ees thees ze vay to Cahmehra Squah?" he asked, shrugging his shoulders in what he conceived to be the gesture of a Frenchman who had landed that morning from Calais.

"Eh?"

"Cahmehra Squah?" John repeated.

The policeman put his hand in his pocket, and John thought he was going to whistle for help; but it was really to get out a handkerchief to blow his nose and give him time to guess what John wanted to know.

"Say it again, will yer?" the policeman requested.

John repeated his Gallic rendering of Camera.

"I ain't seen it round here. Where do you say you dropped it?"

"Eet ees a place I vants."

What slow-witted oafs the English were, thought John with a compassionate sigh for the poor foreigners who must be lost in London every day. However, this policeman was so loutish that he felt he could risk an almost perfect pronunciation.

"Oh, Kemmerer Squer," said the policeman with a huge smile of comprehension. "Why, you're looking at it." He pointed along the road.

"Damn," thought John. "I needn't have asked at all. Sank you. Good-evening," he said aloud.

"The same to you and many of them, Napoleon," the policeman nodded.

John hurried away, and soon he was walking along a narrow garden, very unlike a London garden, for it was full of frost-bitten herbaceous flowers and smelt of the country. Not a house on this side of the square resembled its neighbor; but Number 83 was the most charmingly odd of all, two stories high with a little Chinese balcony and jasmine over a queer pointed porch of wrought iron.

"Yes, sir, Mrs. Hamilton is at home," said the maid.

The last bars of something by Schumann or Chopin died away; in the comparative stillness that succeeded John could hear a canary singing, and the tinkle of tea-cups; there was also a smell of muffins and—mimosa, was it? Anyway it was very delicious, he thought, while he made his overcoat as small as possible, so as not to fill the tiny hall entirely.

"Mr. Touchwood was the name?" the maid asked.

"What an intelligent young woman," he thought. "How much more intelligent than that policeman. But women are more intelligent in small things."

John felt very large as he bowed his head to enter the drawing-room.

CHAPTER IX

ASUDDEN apprehension of his bulk (though he was only comparatively massive) overcame John when he stood inside the tiny drawing-room of 83 Camera Square; and it was not until the steam from the tea-pot had materialized into Miss Hamilton, who in a dress of filmy gray floated round him as a cloud swathes a mountain, that he felt at ease.

"Why, how charming of you to keep your word," her well-remembered voice, so soft and deep, was murmuring. "You don't know my mother, do you? Mother, this is Mr. Touchwood, who was so kind to Ida and me on the voyage back from America."

Mrs. Hamilton was one of those mothers that never destroy the prospects of their children by testifying outwardly to what their beauty may one day come: neither in face nor in expression nor in gesture nor in voice did she bear the least resemblance to her daughter. At first John was inclined to compare her to a diminutive clown; but presently he caught sight of some golden mandarins marching across a lacquer cupboard and decided that she resembled a mandarin; after which wherever he looked in the room he seemed to catch sight of her miniature—on the willow-pattern plates, on the mantelpiece in porcelain, and even on the red lacquer bridge that spanned the tea-caddy.

"We've all heard of Mr. Touchwood," she said, picking up a small silver weapon in the shape of a pea-shooter and puffing out her already plump cheeks in a vain effort to extinguish the flame of the spirit-lamp. "And I'm devoted to the drama. Pouf! I think this is a very dull instrument, dear. What would England be without Shakespeare? Pouf! Pouf! One blows and blows and blows and blows till really—well, it has taught me never to regret that I did not learn the flute when there was a question of my having lessons. Pouf! Pouf!"

John offered his services as extinguisher.

"You have to blow very hard," she warned him; and he being determined at all costs to impress Miss Hamilton blew like a knight-errant at the gate of an enchanted castle. It was almost too vigorous a blast: besides extinguishing the flame, it blew several currants from the cake into Mrs. Hamilton's lap, which John in an access of good-will tried to blow off again less successfully.

"Bravo," the old lady exclaimed, clapping her hands. "I'm glad to see that it can be done. But didn't you write *The Walls of Jericho*? Ah no, I'm thinking of Joshua and his trumpet."

"*The Fall of Babylon*, mother," Miss Hamilton put in with a smile, in the curves of which quivered a hint of scornfulness.

"Then I was not so far out. *The Fall of Babylon* to be sure. Oh, what a fall was there, my countrymen."

She beamed at the author encouragingly, who beamed responsively back at her; presently she began to chuckle to herself, and John, hoping that in his wish to be pleasant to Miss Hamilton's mother he was not appearing to be imitating a hen, chuckled back.

"I'm glad you have a sense of humor," she exclaimed, suddenly assuming an intensely serious expression and throwing up her eyebrows like two skipping-ropes.

John, who felt as if he was playing a game, copied her expression as well as he was able.

"I live on it," she pursued. "And thrive moreover. A small income and an ample sense of humor. Yes, for thus one avoids extravagance oneself, but enjoys it in other people."

"And how is Miss Merritt?" John inquired of Miss Hamilton, when he had bowed his appreciation of the witticism. But before she could reply, her mother rattled on: "Miss Merritt will not take Doris to America again. Miss Merritt has written a book called *The Aphorisms of Aphrodite*."

The old lady's remarkable eyebrows were darting about her forehead like forked lightning while she spoke.

"The Aphorisms of Aphrodite!" she repeated. "A collection of some of the most declassical observations that I have ever encountered." Like a diver's arms the eyebrows drew themselves together for a plunge into unfathomable moral depths.

"My dear mother, lots of people found it very amusing," her daughter protested.

"Miss Merritt," the old lady asserted, "was meant for bookkeeping by double-entry, instead of which she had taken to book-writing by double-entente. The profits may be treble, but the method is base. How did she affect you, Mr. Touchwood?"

"She frightened me," John confessed. "I thought her manner somewhat severe."

"You hear that, Doris? Her ethical exterior frightened him."

"You're both very unfair to Ida. I only wish I had half her talents."

"Wrapped in a napkin," said the old lady, "you have your shorthand."

John's heart leapt.

"Ah, you know shorthand," he could not help ejaculating with manifest pleasure.

"I studied for a time. I think I had vague ideas once of a commercial career," she replied, indifferently.

"The suggestion being," Mrs. Hamilton put in, "that I discouraged her. But how is one to encourage shorthand? If she had learnt the deaf and dumb alphabet I might have put aside half-an-hour every day for conversation. But it is as hard to encourage shorthand as to encourage a person who is talking in his sleep."

John fancied that beneath the indifference of the daughter and the self-conscious humor of the mother he could detect cross-currents of mutual disapproval; he could have sworn that the daughter was beginning to be perpetually aware of her mother's presence.

"Or is it due to my obsession that relations should never see too much of each other?" he asked himself. "Yet she knows shorthand—an extraordinary coincidence. What a delightful house you have," he said aloud with as much fervor as would excuse the momentary abstraction into which he had been cast.

"My husband was a sinologue," Mrs. Hamilton announced.

"Was he indeed?" said John, trying to focus the word.

"And the study of Chinese is nearly as exclusive as shorthand," the old lady went on. "But we traveled a great deal in China when I was first married and being upon our honeymoon had but slight need of general conversation."

No wonder she looked like a mandarin.

"And to me their furniture was always more expressive than their language. Hence this house." Her black eyebrows soared like a condor to disappear in the clouds of her snowy hair. "But do not let us talk of China," she continued. "Let us rather talk of the drama. Or will you have another muffin?"

"I think I should prefer the muffin," John admitted.

411

Presently he noticed that Miss Hamilton was looking surreptitiously at her watch and glancing anxiously at the deepening twilight; she evidently had an appointment elsewhere, and he rose to make his farewells.

"For I'm sure you're wanting to go out," he ventured.

"Doris never cares to stay at home for very long," said her mother; and John was aware once again, this time unmistakably, of the cross-currents of mutual discontent.

"I had promised to meet Ida in Sloane Square."

"On the holy mount of Ida," the old lady quoted; John laughed out of politeness, though he was unable to see the point of the allusion; he might have concluded that after all Mrs. Hamilton was really rather stupid, perhaps even vain and tiresome, had she not immediately afterward proposed that he should give Doris time to get ready and have the benefit of her company along King's Road.

"For I assume you are both going in the same direction," she said, evoking with her eyebrows the suggestion of a signpost.

"My dear mother, Mr. Touchwood doesn't want to be bored with escorting me," her daughter was protesting.

John laughed at the idea of being bored; then he fancied that in such a small room his laughter might have sounded hysterical, and he raised the pitch of his voice to give the impression that he always laughed like that. In the end, after a short argument, Miss Hamilton agreed somewhat ungraciously to let John wait for her. When she was gone to get ready, her mother leaned over and tapped John's arm with a fan.

"I'm getting extremely anxious about Doris," she confided; the eyebrows hovering in her forehead like a hawk about to strike gave her listener the impression that she was really going to say something this time.

"Her health?" he began, anxiously.

"Her health is perfect. It is her independence which worries me. Hence this house! Her father's brother is only too willing to do anything for her, but she declines to be a poor relation. Now such an attitude is ridiculous, because she is a poor relation. To each overture from her uncle she replies with defiance. At one moment she drowns his remarks in a typewriter; at another she flourishes her shorthand in his face; and this summer she fled to America before he had finished what he was saying. Mr. Touchwood, I rely on you!" she exclaimed, thumping him on the shoulder with the fan.

John felt himself to be a very infirm prop for the old lady's ambition, and wobbled in silence while she heaped upon him her aspirations.

"You are a man of the world. All the world's a stage! Prompt her, my dear Mr. Touchwood, prompt her. You must have had a great experience in prompting. I rely on you. Her uncle *must* be allowed to help her. For pray appreciate that Doris's independence merely benefits charitable institutions, and in my opinion there is a limit to anonymous benevolence. Perhaps you've heard of the Home for Epileptic Gentlewomen? They can have their fits in peace and comfort entirely because my daughter refuses to accept one penny from her uncle. To a mother, of course, such behavior is unaccountable. And what is so unjust is that she won't allow me to accept a penny either, but has even gone so far as to threaten to live with Miss Merritt if I do. Aphorisms of Aphrodite! I can assure you that there are times when I do not regret that I possess an ample sense of humor. If you were a mother, Mr. Touchwood...."

"I *am* an uncle," said John, quickly. He was not going to let Mrs. Hamilton monopolize all the privileges of kinship.

"Then who more able to advise a niece? She will listen to you. Friends, Romans, countrymen, lend me your ears. You must remember that she already admires you as a playwright. Insist that in future she must admire you from the stalls instead of from the pit—as now. At present she is pinched. Do not misunderstand me. I speak in metaphors. She is pinched by straitened circumstances just as the women of China are pinched by their shoes. She declines to wear a hobble-skirt; but decline or not, she hobbles through life. She cannot do otherwise, which is why we live here in Camera Square like two spoonfuls of tea in an old caddy!"

"But you know, personally," John protested while the old lady was fanning back her lost breath, "personally, and I am now speaking as an uncle, personally I must confess that independence charms me."

"Music hath charms," said Mrs. Hamilton. "Who will deny it? And independence with the indefinite article before it also hath charms; but independence with no article at all, independence, the abstract noun, though it may be a public virtue, is a private vice. Vesuvius lends variety to the Bay of Naples; but a tufted mole on a woman's cheek affects the observer with abhorrence, like a woolly caterpillar lurking in the heart of a rose. Let us distinguish between the state and the individual. Do, my dear Mr. Touchwood, let us always preserve a distinction between wild nature and human nature."

John was determined not to give way, and he once more firmly asserted his admiration for independence.

"All the world's a stage," said Mrs. Hamilton. "Yes, and all the men and women merely players; yet life, Mr. Touchwood, is not a play. I have realized that since my husband died. The widow of a sinologue has much to realize. At first I hoped that Doris would marry. But she has never wanted to marry. Men proposed in shoals. But as I always said to them, 'What is the use of proposing to my daughter? She will never marry.'"

For the first time John began to pay a deep and respectful attention to the conversation.

"Really I should have thought," he began; but he stopped himself abruptly, for he felt that it was not quite chivalrous for him to appraise Miss Hamilton's matrimonial chances. "No doubt Miss Hamilton is very critical," he substituted.

"She would criticize anybody," the old lady exclaimed. "From the Creator of us all in general to her own mother in particular she would criticize anybody. Anybody that is, except Miss Merritt. Do not suppose, for instance, that she will not criticize you."

"Oh, I have no hope of escaping," John said.

"But pay no attention and continue to advise her. Really, when I think that on account of her obstinacy a number of epileptic females are enjoying luxurious convulsions while I am compelled to alternate between muffins and scones every day of the week, though I never know which I like better, really I resent our unnecessary poverty. As I say to her, whether we accept her uncle's offer or not, we are always poor relations; so we may as well be comfortably off poor relations."

"Don't you suppose that perhaps her uncle is all the fonder of her because of this independence?" John suggested. "I think I should be."

"But what is the use of that?" Mrs. Hamilton demanded. "Nothing is so bad for people as stunted affection. My husband spent all his patrimony—he was a younger son—everything he had in fact upon his passion for Chinese—well, not quite everything, for he was able to leave me a small income, which I share with Doris. Pray remember that I have never denied her anything that I could afford. Although she has many times plotted with her friend Ida Merritt to earn her own living, I have never once encouraged her in such a step. The idea to me has always been painful. A sense of humor has carried *me* through life; but Doris, alas, is infected with gloom. Whether it is living in London or whether it is reading Nietzsche I don't know, but she is infested with gloom. Therefore when I heard of her meeting you I was glad; I was almost reconciled to the notion of that vulgar descent upon America. Pray do not imagine that I am trying to flatter: you should be used to public approbation by now. John Hamilton is her uncle's name, and he has a delightful estate near the Mull of Kintyre—Glencockie House—some of the rents of which provide carpets for the fits of epileptic gentlewomen and some the children of indigent tradesmen in Ayr with colonial opportunities. Yet his sister-in-law must choose every morning between muffins and scones."

John tried unsuccessfully to change the conversation; he even went so far as to ask the old lady questions about her adventures in China, although it was one of the rules of his conduct never to expose himself unnecessarily to the reminiscences of travelers.

"Yes, yes," she would reply, impatiently, "the bells in the temple gardens are delicious. Ding-dong! ding-dong! But, as I was saying, unless Doris sees her way to be at any rate outwardly gracious ..." and so it went on until Doris herself, dressed in that misty green Harris tweed of the *Murmania*, came in to say that she was ready.

"My dear child," her mother protested. "The streets of London are empty on Sunday evening, but they are not a Highland moor. What queer notions of dress you do have, to be sure."

"Ida and I are going out to supper with some friends of hers in Norwood, and I want to keep warm in the train."

"One of the aphorisms of Aphrodite, I suppose, to wear a Norfolk-jacket—or should I say a Norwood jacket?—on Sunday evening. You must excuse her, Mr. Touchwood."

John was by this time thoroughly bored by the old lady's witticisms and delighted to leave her to fan herself in the firelight, while he and her daughter walked along toward King's Road.

"No sign of a taxi," said John, whose mind was running on shorthand, though he was much too shy to raise the topic for a second time. "You don't mind going as far as Sloane Square by motor-bus?"

A moment later they were climbing to the outside of a motor-bus; when John pulled the waterproof rug over their knees and felt the wind in his face while they swayed together and apart in the rapid motion, he could easily have fancied that they were once again upon the Atlantic.

"I often think of our crossing," he said in what he hoped was an harmonious mixture of small talk and sentiment.

"So do I."

He tried to turn eagerly round, but was unable to do so on account of having fastened the strap of the rug.

"Well, in Camera Square, wouldn't you?" she murmured.

"You're not happy there?" In order to cover his embarrassment at finding he had asked what she might consider an impertinent question John turned away to fasten the rug more tightly, which nearly kept him from turning around again at all.

"Don't let's talk about me," she begged, dismissing the subject with a curt little laugh. "How fast they do drive on Sunday."

"Yes, the streets are empty," he agreed. Good heavens, at this rate they would be at Sloane Square in five minutes, and he might just as well never have called on her. What did it matter if the streets were empty? They were not half as empty as this conversation.

"I'm working hard," he began.

"Lucky you!"

"At least when I say I'm working hard," he corrected himself, "I mean that I have been working hard. Just at present I'm rather worried by family matters."

"Poor man, I sympathize with you."

She might sympathize with him; but on this motor-bus her manner was so detached that nobody could have guessed it, John thought, and he had looked at her every time a street-lamp illuminated her expression.

"I often think of our crossing," he repeated. "I'm sure it would be a great pity to let our friendship fade out into nothing. Won't you lunch with me one day?"

"With pleasure."

"Wednesday at Princes? Or no, better say the Carlton Grill."

"Thanks so much."

"It's not easy to talk on a motor-bus, is it?" John suggested.

"No, it's like trying to talk to somebody whom you're seeing off in a train."

"I hope you'll enjoy your evening. You'll remember me to Miss Merritt?"

"Of course."

Sloane Square opened ahead of them; but at any rate, John congratulated himself, he had managed to arrange a lunch for Wednesday and need no longer reproach himself for a complete deadlock.

"I must hurry," she warned him when they had descended to the pavement.

"Wednesday at one o'clock then."

He would have liked to detain her with elaborate instructions about the exact spot on the carpet where she would find him waiting for her on Wednesday; but she had shaken him lightly by the hand and crossed the road before he could decide between the entrance in Regent Street and the entrance in Pall Mall.

"It is becoming every day more evident, Mrs. Worfolk," John told his housekeeper after supper that evening, "that I must begin to look about for a secretary."

"Yes, sir," she agreed, cheerfully. "There's lots of deserving young fellows would be glad of the job, I'm shaw."

John left it at that, acknowledged Mrs. Worfolk's wishes for his night's repose, poured himself out a whisky and soda, and settled himself down to read a gilded work at fifteen shillings net entitled *Fifteen Famous Forgers*. When he had read three shillings' worth, he decided that the only crime which possessed a literary interest for anybody outside the principals was murder, and went to bed early in order to prepare for the painful interview at Staple Inn next morning.

Stephen Crutchley, the celebrated architect, was some years older than John, old enough in fact to have been severely affected by the esthetic movement in his early twenties; he had a secret belief that was nourished both by his pre-eminence in Gothic design and by his wife's lilies and languors that he formed a link with the Pre-Raphaelites. His legs were excessively short, but short though they were one of them had managed to remain an inch shorter than the other, which in conjunction with a ponderous body made his gait something between a limp and a shamble. He had a long ragged beard which looked as if he had dropped egg or cigarette-ash on it according to whether the person who was deciding its color thought it was more gray or more yellow. His appearance was usually referred to by paragraph writers as leonine, and he much regretted that his beard was turning gray so soon, when what the same writers called his "tawny mane of hair" was still unwithered. He affected the Bohemian costume of the 'eighties, that is to say the velvet jacket, the flowered silk waistcoat, and the unknotted tie of deep crimson or old gold kept in place by a prelate's ring; he lunched every day at the Arts Club, and since he was making at least £6000 a year, he did not bother to go back to his office in the afternoon. John had met him first soon after his father's death in 1890 somewhere in Northamptonshire where Crutchley was restoring a church—his first big job—and where John was editing temporarily a local paper. In those days John reacting from dog-biscuits was every bit as romantic as he was now; he and the young architect had often talked the sun up and spoken ecstatically of another medieval renaissance, of the nobility of handicrafts and of the glory of the guilds. Later on, when John in the reaction from journalism embarked upon realistic novels, Crutchley was inclined to quarrel with him as a renegade, and even went so far as to send him a volume of Browning's poems with *The Lost Leader* heavily marked in red pencil. Considering that Crutchley was making more money with his gargoyles than himself with his novels John resented the accusation of having deserted his friend for a handful of silver; and as for the ribbon which he was accused of putting in his coat, John thought that the architect was the last person to underline such an accusation, when himself for the advancement of his work had joined every ecclesiastical society from the English Church Union to the Alcuin Club. There was not a ritualistic parson in the land who wanted with or without a faculty to erect a rood or reredos but turned to Crutchley for his design, principally because his watch-chain jingled with religious labels; although to do him justice, even when he was making £6000 a year he continued to attend Choral Eucharists as regularly as ever. When John abandoned realistic novels and made a success as a romantic playwright his friend welcomed him back to the Gothic fold with emotion and enthusiasm.

"You and I, John, are almost the only ones left," the architect had said, feelingly.

"Come, come, Stephen, you mustn't talk as if I was William de Morgan. I'm not yet forty, and you're not yet forty-five," John had replied, slightly nettled by this ascription of them to a bygone period.

Yet with all his absurdities and affectations Stephen was a fine fellow and a fine architect, and when soon after this he had agreed to take Hugh into his office John would have forgiven him if he had chosen to perambulate Chelsea in doublet and hose.

Thinking of Stephen as he had known him for twenty years John had no qualms when on Monday morning he ascended the winding stone steps that led up to his office in the oldest portion of Staple Inn; nor apparently had Hugh, who came in as jauntily as ever and greeted his brother with genial self-possession.

"I thought you'd blow in this morning. I betted Aubrey half-a-dollar that you'd blow in. He tells me you went off in rather a bad temper on Saturday night. But you were quite right, Johnnie; that port of George's is not good. You were quite right. I shall always respect your verdict on wine in future."

"This is not the moment to talk about wine," said John, angrily.

"I'm afraid that owing to George and his confounded elderberry ink I didn't put my case quite as clearly as I ought to have done," Hugh went on, serenely. "But don't worry. As soon as you've settled with Stevie, I shall tell you all about it. I think you'll be thrilled. It's a pity you've moved into Wardour Street, or you might have made a good story out of it."

One of the clerks came back with an invitation for John to follow him into Mr. Crutchley's own room, and he was glad to escape from his brother's airy impenitence.

"Wonderful how Stevie acts up to the part, isn't it?" commented Hugh, when he saw John looking round him at the timbered rooms with their ancient furniture and medieval blazonries through which they were passing.

"I prefer to see Crutchley alone," said John, coldly. "No doubt he will send for you when your presence is required."

Hugh nodded amiably and went over to his desk in one of the latticed oriel windows, the noise of the Holborn traffic surging in through which reminded the listener that these perfectly medieval rooms were in the heart of modern London.

"I should rather like to live in chambers here myself," thought John. "I believe they would give me the very atmosphere I require for Joan of Arc; and I should be close to the theaters."

This project appealed to him more than ever when he entered the architect's inmost sanctum, which containing nothing that did not belong to the best period of whatever it was, wrought iron or carved wood or embroidered stuff, impressed John's eye for a scenic effect. Nor was there too much of it: the room was austere, not even so full as a Carpaccio interior. Modernity here wore a figleaf; wax candles were burned instead of gas or electric light; and even the telephone was enshrined in a Florentine casket. When the oaken door covered with huge nails and floriated hinges was closed, John sat down upon what is called a Glastonbury chair and gazed at his friend who was seated upon a gilt throne under a canopy of faded azure that was embroidered with golden unicorns, wyverns, and other fabulous monsters in a pasture of silver fleurs-de-lys.

"Have a cigar," said the Master, as he liked to be called, pushing across the refectory table that had come out of an old Flemish monastery a primitive box painted with scenes of saintly temptations, but lined with cedar wood and packed full of fat Corona Coronas.

"It seems hardly appropriate to smoke cigars in this room," John observed. "Even a churchwarden-pipe would be an anachronism here."

"Yes, yes," Stephen assented, tossing back his hair with the authentic Vikingly gesture. "But cigars are the chief consolation we have for being compelled to exist in this modern world. I haven't seen you, John, since you returned from America. How's work?"

"*Lucretia* went splendidly in New York. And I'm in the middle of *Joan of Arc* now."

"I'm glad, I'm glad," the architect growled as fiercely as one of the great Victorians. "But for Heaven's sake get the coats right. Theatrical heraldry is shocking. And get the ecclesiastical details right. Theatrical ritual is worse. But I'm glad you're giving 'em Joan of Arc. Keep it up, keep it up. The modern drama wants disinfecting."

"I suppose you wouldn't care to advise me about the costumes and processions and all that," John suggested, offering his friend a pinch of his romantic Sanitas.

"Yes, I will. Of course, I will. But I must have a free hand. An absolutely free hand, John. I won't have any confounded play-actor trying to tell me that it doesn't matter if a bishop in the fifteenth century does wear a sixteenth century miter, because it's more effective from the gallery. Eh? I know them. You know them. A free hand or you can burn Joan on an asbestos gasfire, and I won't help you."

"Your help would be so much appreciated," John assured him, "that I can promise you an absolutely short hand."

The architect stared at the dramatist.

"What did I say? I mean free hand—extraordinary slip," John laughed a little awkwardly. "Yes, your name, Stephen, is just what we shall require to persuade the skeptical that it is worth while making another attempt with Joan of Arc. I can promise you some fine opportunities. I've got a particularly effective tableau to show the miserable condition of France before the play begins. The curtain will rise upon the rearguard of an army marching out of a city, heavy snow will fall, and above the silence you will hear the howling of the wolves following in the track of the troops. This is an historical fact. I may even introduce several wolves upon the stage. But I rather doubt if trained wolves are procurable, although at a pinch we could use large dogs—but don't let me run away with my own work like this. I did not come here this morning to talk about Joan of Arc, but about my brother Hugh."

John rose from his chair and walked nervously up and down the room, while Stephen Crutchley managed to exaggerate a slight roughness at the back of his throat into a violent fit of coughing.

"I see you feel it as much as I do," John murmured, while the architect continued to express his overwrought feelings in bronchial spasms.

"I would have spared you this," the architect managed to gasp at last.

"I'm sure you would," said John, warmly. "But since in what I hope was a genuine impulse of contrition not entirely dictated by motives of self-interest Hugh has confessed his crime to me, I am come here this morning confident that you will allow me to—in other words—what was the exact sum? I shall of course remove him from your tutelage this morning."

John's eloquence was not spontaneous; he had rehearsed this speech on the way from Hampstead that morning, and he was agreeably surprised to find that he had been able owing to his friend's coughing-fit to reproduce nearly all of it. He had so often been robbed of a prepared oration by some unexpected turn of the conversation that he felt now much happier than he ought under the weight of a family scandal.

"Your generosity...." he continued.

"No, no," interrupted the architect, "it is you who are generous."

The two romantics gazed at one another with an expression of nobility that required no words to enhance it.

"We can afford to be generous," said John, which was perfectly true, though the reference was to worth of character rather than to worth of capital.

"Eighty-one pounds six and eightpence," Crutchley murmured. "But I blame myself. I should not have left an old check book lying about. It was careless—it was, I do not hesitate to say so, criminally careless. But you know my attitude towards money. I am radically incapable of dealing with money."

"Of course you are," John assented with conviction. "So am I. Money with me is merely a means to an end."

"Exactly what it is with me," the architect declared. "Money in itself conveys nothing to me. What I always say to my clients is that if they want the best work they must pay for it. It's the work that counts, not the money."

"Precisely my own attitude," John agreed. "What people will not understand is that an artist charges a high price when he does not want to do the work. If people insist on his doing it, they must expect to pay."

"And of course," the architect added, "we owe it to our fellows to sustain the dignity of our professions. Art in England has already been too much cheapened."

"You've kept all your old enthusiasms," John told his friend. "It's splendid to find a man who is not spoilt by success. Eighty-one pounds you said? I've brought my check book."

"Eighty-one pounds six and eightpence, yes. It was like you, John, to come forward in this way. But I wish you could have been spared. You understand, don't you, that I intended to say nothing about it and to blame myself in silence for my carelessness? On the other hand, I could not treat your brother with my former confidence. This terrible business disturbed our whole relationship."

"I am not going to enlarge on my feelings," said John as he handed the architect the stolen sum. "But you will understand them. I believe the shock has aged me. I seem to have lost some of my self-reliance. Only this morning I was thinking to myself that I must really get a private secretary."

"You certainly should have one," the architect agreed.

"Yes, I must. The only thing is that since this dreadful escapade of Hugh's I feel that an unbusinesslike creature such as I am ought not to put himself in the hands of a young man. What is your experience of women? From a business point of view, I mean."

"I think that a woman would do your work much better than a man," said the architect, decidedly.

"So do I. I'm very glad to have your advice though."

After this John felt no more reluctant at parting with eighty-one pounds six and eightpence than he would have felt in paying a specialist two guineas for advising him to take a long rest when he wanted to take a long rest. His friend's aloofness from money had raised to a higher level what might easily have been a most unpleasant transaction: not even one of his heroes could have extricated himself from an involved situation more poetically and more sympathetically. It now only remained to dispose of the villain.

"Shall we have Hugh in?" John asked.

"I wish I could keep him with me," the architect sighed. "But I don't think I have a right to consult my personal feelings. We must consider his behavior in itself."

"In any case," said John, quickly, "I have made arrangements about his future; he is going to be a mahogany-planter in British Honduras."

"Of course I don't use mahogany much in my work, but if ever ..." the architect was beginning, when John waved aside his kindly intentions.

"The impulse is generous, Stephen, but I should prefer that so far as you are concerned Hugh should always be as if he had never been. In fact, I'm bound to say frankly that I'm glad you do not use mahogany in your work. I'm glad that I've chosen a career for Hugh which will cut him completely off from what to me will always be the painful associations of architecture."

While they were waiting for the sinner to come in, John tried to remember the name of the mahogany-planter whom he had met in the *Murmania*; but he could get no nearer to it than a vague notion that it might have been Raikes, and he decided to leave out for the present any allusion to British Honduras.

Hugh entered his chief's room without a blush: he could not have bowed his head, however sincere his repentance, because his collars would not permit the least abasement; though at least, his brother thought, he might have had the decency not to sit down until he was invited, and when he did sit down not to pull up his trousers in that aggressive way and expose those very defiant socks.

Stephen Crutchley rose from his throne and shambled over to the fireplace, leaning against the stone hood of which he took up an attitude that would have abashed anybody but Hugh.

"Touchwood," he began, "no doubt you have already guessed why I have asked you to speak to me."

Hugh nodded encouragingly.

"I do not wish to enlarge upon the circumstances of your behavior, because your brother, my old friend, has come forward to shield you from the consequences. Nor do I propose to animadvert upon the forgery itself. However lightly you embarked upon it, I don't doubt that by now you have sufficiently realized its gravity. What tempted you to commit this crime I do not hope to guess; but I fear that such a device for obtaining money must have been inspired by debts, whether for cards or for horse-racing, or perhaps even for women I do not pretend to know."

"Add waistcoats and whisky and you've got the motive," Hugh chirped. "I say, I think your trousers are scorching," he added on a note of anxious consideration.

"I do not propose to enlarge on any of these topics," said the architect, moving away from the fire and sniffing irritably the faint odor of overheated homespun. "What I do wish to enlarge upon is your brother's generosity in coming forward like this. Naturally I who have known him for twenty years expected nothing else, because he is a man of ideals, a writer of whom we are all proud, from whom we all expect great things and—however I am not going to enlarge upon his obvious qualities. What I do wish to say is that he and I have decided that after this business you must leave me. I don't suppose that you expected to remain; nor, even if you could, do I suppose that you would wish to remain. Perhaps you are not enough in sympathy with my aspirations for the future of English architecture to regret our parting; but I hope that this lesson you have had will be the means of bringing you to an appreciation of what your brother has done for you and that in British Honduras you will behave in such a way as to justify his generosity. Touchwood, good-by! I did not expect when you came to me three years ago that our last farewell would be fraught—would be so unpleasant."

John was probably much more profoundly moved by Crutchley's sermon than Hugh; indeed he was so much moved that he rose to supplement it with one of his own in which he said the same things about the architect that the architect had said about him, after which the two romantics looked at each other admiringly, while they waited for Hugh to reply.

"I suppose I ought to say I'm very sorry and all that," Hugh managed to mutter at last. "Good-by, Mr. Crutchley, and jolly good luck. I'll just toddle through the office and say good-by to all the boys, John, and then I dare say you'll be ready for lunch."

He swaggered out of the room; when the two friends were left together they turned aside with mutual sympathy from the topic of Hugh to discuss Joan of Arc and a new transept that Crutchley was designing. When the culprit put his head round the door and called out to John that he was ready, the two old friends shook hands affectionately and parted with an increased regard for each other and themselves.

"Look here, what's all this about British Honduras?" Hugh asked indignantly when he and his brother had passed under the arched entry of Staple Inn and were walking along Holborn. "I see you're bent on gratifying your appetite for romance even in the choice of a colony. British Honduras! British humbug!"

"I prefer not do discuss anything except your immediate future," said John.

"It's such an extraordinary place to hit on," Hugh grunted in a tone of irritated perplexity."

"The immediate future," John repeated, sharply. "To-night you will go down to Hampshire and if you wish for any more help from me, you will remain there in the strictest seclusion until I have time to settle your ultimate future."

"Oh, I shan't at all mind a few weeks in Hampshire. What I'm grumbling at is British Honduras. I shall rather enjoy Hampshire in fact. Who's there at present?"

John told him, and Hugh made a grimace.

"I shall have to jolly them up a bit. However it's a good job that Laurence has lost his faith. I shall be spared his Chloral Eucharists, anyway. Where are we going to lunch?"

"Hugh!" exclaimed his outraged brother stopping short in the middle of the crowded pavement. "Have you no sense of shame at all? Are you utterly callous?"

"Look here, Johnnie, don't start in again on that. I know you had to take that line with Stevie, and you'll do me the justice of admitting that I backed you up; but when we're alone, do chuck all that. I'm very grateful to you for forking out—by the way, I hope you noticed the nice little touch in the sum? Eighty-one pounds six and eightpence. The six and eightpence was for my lawyer."

"Do you adopt this sickeningly cynical attitude," John besought. "Forgery is not a joke."

"Well, this forgery was," Hugh contradicted. "You see, I got hold of Stevie's old check book and found he had quite a decent little account in Croydon. So I faked his signature—you know how to do that?"

"I don't want to know."

"You copy the signature upside down. Yes, that's the way. Then old Aubrey disguised himself with blue glasses and presented the check at the bank, just allowing himself five minutes to catch the train back to town. I was waiting at the station in no end of a funk. But it was all right. The clerk blinked for a minute, but old Aubrey blinked back at him as cool as you please, and he shoveled out the gold. Aubrey came jingling on to the platform like a milk-can just as the train was starting."

"I wish to hear no more."

"And then I found that Stevie was cocking his eye at this check book and scratching his head and looking at me and—well, he suspected me. The fact of the matter is that Stevie's as keen on his cash as anybody. I suppose this is a side account for the benefit of some little lady or other."

"Silence," John commanded.

"And then I lost my nerve, so that when Stevie started questioning me about his check book I must have looked embarrassed."

"I'm surprised to hear that," John put in, bitterly.

"Yes, I dare say I could have bluffed it out, because I'd taken the precaution to cash the check through Aubrey whom Stevie knows nothing about. But I don't know. I lost my nerve. Well, thanks very much for stumping up, Johnnie; I'm only glad you got so much pleasure out of it yourself."

"What do you mean—pleasure?"

"Shut up—don't pretend you didn't enjoy yourself, you old Pharisee. Look here where *are* we going to lunch? I'm carrying a bag full of instruments, you know."

John told Hugh that he declined to lunch with him in his present mood of bravado, and at the corner of Chancery Lane they parted.

"Mind," John warned him, "if you wish for any help from me you are to remain for the present at Ambles."

"My dear chap, I don't want to remain anywhere else; but I wish you could appreciate the way in which the dark and bloody deed was done, as one of your characters would say. You haven't uttered a word of congratulation. After all, it took some pluck, you know, and the signature was an absolutely perfect fake—perfect. The only thing that failed was my nerve afterwards. But I suppose I should be steadier another time."

John hurried away in a rage and walked up the Strand muttering:

"What *was* the name of that mahogany-planter? *Was* it Raikes or wasn't it? I must find his card."

It was not until he had posted the following letter that he recovered some of his wonted serenity.

36 CHURCH ROW,
Hampstead, N.W.,
Nov. 28, 1910.

MY DEAR MISS HAMILTON,—In case I am too shy to broach the subject at lunch on Wednesday I am writing to ask you beforehand if in your wildest dreams you have ever dreamt that you could be a private secretary. I have for a long time been wanting a secretary, and as you often spoke with interest of my work I am in hopes that the idea will not be distasteful to you. I should not have dared to ask you if you had not mentioned shorthand yesterday and if Mrs. Hamilton had not said something about your typewriting. This seems to indicate that at any rate you have considered the question of secretarial work. The fact of the matter is that in addition to my plays I am much worried by family affairs, so much so that I am kept from my own work and really require not merely mechanical assistance, but also advice on many subjects on which a woman is competent to advise.

I gathered also from your mother's conversation that you yourself were sometimes harassed by family problems and I thought that perhaps you might welcome an excuse to get away from them for awhile.

My notions of the salary that one ought to offer a private secretary are extremely vague. Possibly our friend Miss Merritt would negotiate the business side, which to me as an author is always very unpleasant. I should of course accept whatever Miss Merritt proposed without hesitation. My idea was that you would work with me every morning at Hampstead. I have never yet attempted dictation myself, but I feel that I could do it after a little practice. Then I thought you could lunch with me, and that after lunch we could work on the materials—that is to say that I should give you a list of things I wanted to know, which you would search for either in my own library or at the British Museum. Does this strike you as too heavy a task? Perhaps Miss Merritt will advise you on this matter too.

If Mrs. Hamilton is opposed to the idea, possibly I might call upon her and explain personally my point of view. In the meantime I am looking forward to our lunch and hoping very much that you will set my mind at rest by accepting the post. I think I told you I was working on a play with Joan of Arc as the central figure. It is interesting, because I am determined not to fall into the temptation of introducing a factitious love-interest, which in my opinion spoilt Schiller's version.

Yours sincerely,
JOHN TOUCHWOOD.

CHAPTER X

WHEN after lunch on Wednesday afternoon John relinquished Miss Hamilton to the company of her friend Miss Merritt at Charing Cross Station, he was relinquishing a secretary from whom he had received an assurance that the very next morning she would be at his elbow, if he might so express himself. In his rosiest moments he had never expected so swift a fulfilment of his plan, and he felt duly grateful to Miss Merritt, to whose powers of persuasion he ascribed the acceptance in spite of Mrs. Hamilton's usually only too effective method of counteracting any kind of independent action on her daughter's part. On the promenade deck of the *Murmania* Miss Merritt had impressed John with her resolute character; now she seemed to him positively Napoleonic, and he was more in awe of her than ever, so much so indeed that he completely failed to convey his sense of obligation to her good offices and could only beam at her like a benevolent character in a Dickens novel. Finally he did manage to stammer out his desire that she would charge herself with the financial side of the agreement and was lost in silent wonder when she had no hesitation in suggesting terms based on the fact that Miss Hamilton had no previous experience as a secretary.

"Later on, if you're satisfied with her," she said, "you must increase her salary; but I will be no party to over-payment simply because she is personally sympathetic to you."

How well that was put, John thought. Personally sympathetic! How accurately it described his attitude toward Miss Hamilton. He took leave of the young women and walked up Villiers Street, cheered by the pleasant conviction that the flood of domestic worries which had threatened to destroy his peace of mind and overwhelm his productiveness was at last definitely stayed.

"She's exactly what I require," he kept saying to himself, exultantly. "And I think I may claim without unduly flattering myself that the post I have offered her is exactly what she requires. From what that very nice girl Miss Merritt said, it is evidently a question of asserting herself now or never. With what a charming lack of self-consciousness she agreed to the salary and even suggested the hours of work herself. Oh, she's undoubtedly practical—very practical; but at the same time she has not got that almost painfully practical exterior of Miss Merritt, who must have broken in a large number of difficult employers to acquire that tight set of her mouth. Probably I shall be easy to manage, so working for me won't spoil her unbusinesslike appearance. To-morrow we are to discuss the choice of a typewriter; and by the way, I must arrange which room she is to use for typing. The noise of a machine at high speed would be as prejudicial to composition as Viola's step-dancing. Yes, I must arrange with Mrs. Worfolk about a room."

John's faith in his good luck was confirmed by the amazing discovery that Mrs. Worfolk had known his intended secretary as a child.

"Her old nurse in fact!" he exclaimed joyfully, for such a melodramatic coincidence did not offend John's romantic palate.

"No, sir, not her nurse. I never was not what you might call a nurse proper. Well, I mean to say, though I was always fond of children I seemed to take more somehow to the house itself, and so I never got beyond being a nursemaid. After that I gave myself up to rising as high as a housemaid *can* rise until I married Mr. Worfolk. Perhaps you may remember me once passing the remark that I'd been in service with a racing family? Well, after I left them I took a situation as upper housemaid with a very nice family in the county of Unts, and who came up to London for the season to Grosvenor Gardens. Then I met Mr. Worfolk who was a carpenter and he made packing-cases for Mr. Hamilton who was your young lady's pa. Oh, I remember him well. There was a slight argument between Mr. Worfolk and I—well, not argument, because ours was a very happy marriage, but a slight conversation as to whether he was to make cases for Chi-ner or Chi-nese knick-knacks, and Mr. Worfolk was wrong."

"But were you in service with Mr. Hamilton? Did he live in Huntingdonshire?"

"No, no, sir. You're getting very confused, if you'll pardon the obsivation. Very confused, you're getting. This Mr. Hamilton was a customer of Mr. Worfolk and through him coming to superintend his Chi-nese valuables being packed I got to know his little girl—your secretary as is to be. Oh, I remember her perfickly. Why, I mended a hole in her stocking once. Right above the garter it was, and she was so fond of our Tom. Oh, but he *was* a beautiful mouser. I've heard many people say they never saw a finer cat nowhere."

"You have a splendid memory, Mrs. Worfolk."

"Yes, sir. I have got a good memory. Why, when I was a tiny tot I can remember my poor grandpa being took sudden with the colic and rolling about on the kitchen hearth-rug, groaning, as you might say, in a agony of pain. Well, he died the same year as the Juke of Wellington, but though I was taken to the Juke's funeral by my poor mother, I've forgotten that. Well, one can't remember everything, and that's a fact; one little thing will stick and another little thing won't. Well, I mean to say, it's a good job anybody can't remember everything. I'm shaw there's enough trouble in the world as it is."

Mrs. Worfolk startled the new secretary when she presented herself at 36 Church Row next day by embracing her affectionately in the hall before she had explained the reason for such a demonstration. It soon transpired, however, that Miss Hamilton's memory was as good as Mrs. Worfolk's and that she had not forgotten those jolly visits to the carpenter long ago, nor even the big yellow Tomcat. As for the master of the house, he raised his housekeeper's salary to show what importance he attached to a good memory.

For a day or two John felt shy of assigning much work to his secretary; but she soon protested that, if she was only going to type thirty to fifty lines of blank verse every other morning, she should resign her post on the ground that it was an undignified sinecure.

"What about dictating your letters? You made such a point of my knowing shorthand."

"Yes, I did, didn't I?" John agreed.

Dictation made him very nervous at first; but with a little practice he began to enjoy it, and ultimately it became something in the nature of a vice. He dictated immensely long letters to friends whose very existence he had forgotten for years, the result of which abrupt revivals of intercourse was a shower of appeals to lend money to these companions of his youth. Yet this result did not discourage him from the habit of dictating for dictation's sake, and every night before he turned over to go to sleep he used to poke about in the rubbish-heap of the past for more forgotten friends. As a set off to incommoding himself with a host of unnecessary correspondents he became meticulously businesslike, and after having neglected Miss Janet Bond for several weeks he began to write to her daily about the progress of the play, which notwithstanding his passion for dictation really was progressing at last. Indeed he worked up the manageress of the Parthenon to such a pitch of excitement that one morning she appeared suddenly at Church Row and made a dramatic entrance into the library when John, who had for the moment exhausted his list of friends, was dictating a letter to *The Times* about the condition of some trees on Hampstead Heath.

"I've broken in upon your inspiration," boomed Miss Bond in tones that she usually reserved for her most intensely tragic moments.

In vain did the author asseverate that he was delighted to see her; she rushed away without another word; but that evening she wrote him an ecstatic letter from her dressing-room about what it had meant to her and what it always would mean to her to think of his working like that for her.

"But we mustn't deride Janet Bond," said the author to his secretary, who was looking contemptuously at the actress's heavy caligraphy. "We must remember that she will create Joan of Arc."

"Yes, it's a pity, isn't it?" Miss Hamilton commented, dryly.

"Oh, but won't you allow that she's a great actress?"

"I will indeed," she murmured with an emphatic nod.

Carried along upon his flood of correspondence John nevertheless managed to steer clear of his relations, and in his present frame of mind he was inclined to attribute his successful course like everything else that was prospering just now to the advent of Miss Hamilton. However, it was too much to expect that with his newly discovered talent he should resist dictating at any rate one epistolary sermon to his youngest brother, of whose arrival at Ambles he had been sharply notified by Hilda. This weighty address took up nearly a whole morning, and when it was finished John was disconcerted by Miss Hamilton's saying:

"You don't really want me to type all this out?"

"Why not?"

"Oh, I don't know. But it seems to me that whatever he's done this won't make him repent. You don't mind my criticizing you?"

"I asked you to," he reminded her.

"Well, it seems to me a little false—a little, if I may say so, complacently wrathful. It's the sort of thing I seem to remember reading and laughing at in old-fashioned books. Of course, I'll type it out at once if you insist, but it's already after twelve o'clock, and we have to go over the material for the third act. I can't somehow fit in what you've just been dictating with what you were telling me yesterday about the scene between Gilles de Rais and Joan. I'm so afraid that you'll make Joan preach, and of course she mustn't preach, must she?"

"All right," conceded John, trying not to appear mortified. "If you think it isn't worth sending, I won't send it."

He fancied that she would be moved by his sensitiveness to her judgment; but, without a tremor, she tore the pages out of her shorthand book and threw them into the waste-paper basket. John stared at the ruthless young woman in dismay.

"Didn't you mean me to take you at your word?" she asked, severely.

He was not altogether sure that he had, but he lacked the courage to tell her so and checked an impulse to rescue his stillborn sermon from the grave.

"Though I don't quite like the idea of leaving my brother at Ambles with nothing to occupy his energies," John went on, meditatively, "I'm doubtful of the prudence of exposing him to the temptations of idleness."

"If you want to give him something to do, why don't you intrust him with getting ready the house for your Christmas party? You are always worrying about its emptiness."

"But isn't that putting in his way temptations of a more positive kind?" he suggested.

"Not if you set a limit to your expenditure. Can you trust his taste? He ought to be an adept at furnishings."

"Oh, I think he'd do the actual furnishing very well. But won't it seem as if I am overlooking his abominable behavior too easily?"

With a great effort John kept his eyes averted from the waste-paper basket.

"You must either do that or refuse to have anything more to do with him," Miss Hamilton declared. "You can't expect him to be the mirror of your moral superiority for the rest of his life."

"You seem to take quite an interest in him," said John, a little resentfully.

Miss Hamilton shrugged her shoulders.

"All right," he added, hurriedly. "I'll authorize him to prepare the house for Christmas. He must fight his own battles with my sister, Hilda. At any rate, it will annoy her."

Miss Hamilton shook her head in mock reproof.

"Act Three. Scene One," the dramatist announced in the voice of a mystic who has at last shaken himself free from earthly clogs and is about to achieve levitation. It was consoling to perceive that his secretary's expression changed in accord with his own, and John decided that she really was a most attractive young woman and not so unsympathetic as he had been upon the verge of thinking. Moreover, she was right. The important thing at present, the only thing, in fact, was the progress of the play, and it was for this very purpose that he had secured her collaboration—well, perhaps collaboration was too strong a word—but, indeed, so completely had she identified herself with his work that really he could almost call it collaboration. He ought not to tax his invention at this critical point with such a minor problem as the preparation of Ambles for a family reunion. Relations must go to the deuce in their own way, at any rate until the rough draft of the third act was finished, which, under present favorable conditions, might easily happen before Christmas. His secretary was always careful not to worry him with her own domestic bothers, though he knew by the way she had once or twice referred to her mother that she was having her own hard fight at home. He had once proposed calling upon the old lady; but Doris had quickly squashed the suggestion. John liked to think about Mrs. Hamilton, because through some obscure process of logic it gave him an excuse to think about her daughter as Doris. In other connections he thought of her formally as Miss Hamilton, and often told himself how lucky it was that so charming and accomplished a young woman should be so obviously indifferent to—well, not exactly to himself, but surely he might allege to anything except himself as a romantic playwright.

Meanwhile, the play itself marched on with apparent smoothness, until one morning John dictated the following letter to his star:

MY DEAR MISS BOND,—Much against my will, I have come to the conclusion that without a human love interest a play about Joan of Arc is impossible. You will be surprised by my abrupt change of front, and you will smile to yourself when you remember how earnestly I argued against your suggestion that I might ultimately be compelled to introduce a human love interest. The fact of the matter is that now I have arrived at the third act I find patriotism too abstract an emotion for the stage. As you know, my idea was to make Joan so much positively enamoured of her country that the ordinary love interest would be superseded. I shall continue to keep Joan herself heart free; but I do think that it would be effective to have at any rate two people in love with her. My notion is to introduce a devoted young peasant who will follow her from her native village, first to the court at Chinon, and so on right through the play until the last fatal scene in the market place at Rouen. I'm sure such a simple lover could be made very moving, and the contrast would be valuable; moreover, it strikes me as a perfectly natural situation. Further, I propose that Gilles de Rais should not only be in love with her, but that he should actually declare his love, and that she should for a brief moment be tempted to return it, finally spurning him as a temptation of the Devil, and thereby reducing him to such a state of despair that he is led into the horrible practices for which he was finally condemned to death. Let me know your opinion soon, because I am at this moment working on the third act.

Yours very sincerely,
JOHN TOUCHWOOD.

To which Miss Bond replied by telegram:

Complete confidence in you, and think suggestion magnificent, there should be exit speech of renunciation for Joan to bring down curtain of third act.

JANET BOND.

"You agree with these suggestions?" John asked his secretary.

"Like Miss Bond, I have complete confidence in you," she replied.

He looked at her earnestly to see if she was laughing at him, and put down his pen.

"Do you know that in some ways you yourself remind me of Joan?"

It was a habit of John's, who had a brain like a fly's eye, to perceive historical resemblances that were denied to an ordinary vision. Generally he discovered these reincarnations of the past in his own personality. While he was writing *The Fall of Babylon* he actually fretted himself for a time over a fancied similarity between his character and Nebuchadnezzar's, and sometimes used to wonder if he was putting too much of himself into his portrayal of that dim potentate; and during his composition of *Lucretia* he was so profoundly convinced that Cæsar Borgia was simply John Touchwood over again in a more passionate period and a more picturesque costume that, as the critics pointed out, he presented the world with an aspect of him that would never have been recognized by Machiavelli. Yet, even when Harold was being most unpleasant, or when

Viola and Bertram were deafening his household, John could not bring himself to believe that he and Gilles de Rais, who was proved to have tortured over three hundred children to death, had many similar traits; nor was he willing to admit more than a most superficial likeness to the feeble Dauphin Charles. In fact, at one time he was so much discouraged by his inability to adumbrate himself in any of his personages that he began to regret his choice of Joan of Arc and to wish that he had persevered in his intention to write a play about Sir Walter Raleigh, with whom, allowing for the sundering years, he felt he had more in common than with any other historical figure. Therefore he was relieved to discover this resemblance between his heroine and his secretary, in whom he was beginning to take nearly as much interest as in himself.

"Do you mean outwardly?" asked Miss Hamilton, looking at an engraving of the bust from the church of St. Maurice, Orleans. "If so, I hope her complexion wasn't really as scaly as that."

"No, I mean in character."

"I suppose a private secretary ought not to say 'what nonsense' to her employer, but really what else can I say? You might as well compare Ida Merritt to Joan of Arc; in fact, she really is rather like my conception of her."

"I'm sorry you find the comparison so far-fetched," John said, huffily. "It wasn't intended to be uncomplimentary."

"Have you decided to introduce those wolves in the first act, because I think I ought to begin making inquiries about suitable dogs?"

When Miss Hamilton rushed away from the personal like this, John used to regret that he had changed their relationship from one of friendship to one of business. Although he admired practicalness, he realized that it was possible to be too practical, and he sighed sometimes for the tone that his unknown admirers took when they wrote to him about his work. Only that morning he had received a letter from one of these, which he had tossed across the table for his secretary's perusal before he dictated a graceful reply.

HILLCREST,
Highfield Road,
Hornsey, N.,
Dec. 14, 1910.

DEAR SIR:—I have never written to an author before, but I cannot help writing to ask you *when* you are going to give us another play. I cannot tell you how much I enjoy your plays—they take me into another world. Please do not imagine that I am an enthusiastic schoolgirl. I am the mother of four dear little children, and my husband and I both act in a dramatic club at Hornsey. We are very anxious to perform one of your plays, but the committee is afraid of the expense. I suppose it would be asking too much of you to lend us some of the costumes of *The Fall of Babylon*. I think it is your greatest work up till now, and I simply live in all those wonderful old cities now and read everything I can find about them. I was brought up very strictly when I was young and grew to hate the Bible—please do not be shocked at this—but since I saw *The Fall of Babylon* I have taken to reading it again. I went nine times—twice in the gallery, three times in the pit, twice in the upper circle and twice in the dress circle, once in the fifth row at the side and once right in the middle of the front row! I cut out the enclosed photo of you from *The Tatler*, and, would it be asking too much to sign your name? Hoping for the pleasure of a reply, I remain,

Your sincere admirer,
(MRS.) ENID FOSTER.

"What extraordinary lunatics there are in this world," Miss Hamilton had commented. "Have you noticed the one constant factor in these letters? All the women begin by saying that it is the first time they have ever written to an author; of course, they would say the same thing to a man who kissed them. The men, however, try to convey that they're in the habit of writing to authors. I think there's a moral to be extracted from that observation."

Now, John had not yet attained—and perhaps it was improbable that he ever would attain—those cold summits of art out of reach alike of the still, sad music and the hurdy-gurdies of humanity, so that these letters from unknown men and women, were they never so foolish, titillated his vanity, which he called "appealing to his imagination."

"One must try to put oneself in the writer's place," he had urged, reproachfully.

"Um—yes, but I can't help thinking of Mrs. Enid Foster living in those wonderful old cities. Her household will crash like Babylon if she isn't careful, and her family will be reduced to eating grass like Nebuchadnezzar, if the green-grocer's book is neglected any longer."

"You won't allow the suburbs to be touched by poetry?"

John had tried to convey in his tone that Miss Hamilton in criticizing the enthusiasm of Mrs. Foster was depreciating his own work. But she had seemed quite unconscious of having rather offended him and had taken down his answer without excusing herself. Now when in a spirit that was truly forgiving he had actually compared her to his beloved heroine, she had scoffed at him as if he was a kind of Mrs. Foster himself.

"You're very matter-of-fact," he muttered.

"Isn't that a rather desirable quality in a secretary?"

"Yes, but I think you might have waited to hear why you reminded me of Joan of Arc before you began talking about those confounded wolves, which, by the way, I have decided to cut out."

"Don't cut out a good effect just because you're annoyed with me," she advised.

"Oh no, there are other reasons," said John, loftily. "It is possible that in an opening tableau the audience may not appreciate that they are wolves, and if they think they're only a lot of stray dogs, the effect will go for nothing. It was merely a passing idea, and I have discarded it."

Miss Hamilton left him to go and type out the morning's correspondence, and John settled down to a speech by the Maid on the subject of perpetual celibacy: he wrote a very good one.

"She may laugh at me," said the author to himself, "but she *is* like Joan—extraordinarily like. Why, I can hear her making this very speech."

Miss Hamilton might sometimes profane John's poetic sanctuaries and sometimes pull his leg when he was on tiptoe for a flight like Mr. Keats' sweetpeas, but she made existence much more pleasant for him, and he had already reached the stage of wondering how he had ever managed to get along without her. He even went so far in his passion for historical parallels as to compare his situation before she came to the realm of France before Joan of Arc took it in hand. He knew in his heart that these weeks before Christmas were unnaturally calm; he had no hope of prolonging this halcyon time much further; but while it lasted he would enjoy it to the full. Any one who had overheard John announcing to his reflection in the glass an unbridled hedonism for the immediate future might have been pardoned for supposing that he was about to amuse himself in a very desperate fashion. As a matter of fact, the averred intention was due to nothing more exciting than the prospect of a long walk over the Heath with Miss Hamilton to discuss an outline of the fourth act, which John knew would gradually be filled in with his plans for writing other plays and finally be colored by a conversation, or, anyhow, a monologue about himself as a human being without reference to himself as an author.

"What is so delightful about Miss Hamilton," he assured that credulous and complaisant reflection, "is the way one can talk to her without there being the least danger of her supposing that one has any ulterior object in view. Notwithstanding all the rich externals of the past, I'm bound to confess that the relations between men and women are far more natural nowadays. I suppose it was the bicycle that began female emancipation; had bicycles been invented in the time of Joan of Arc she would scarcely have had to face so much ecclesiastical criticism of her behavior."

The walk was a success; amongst other things, John discovered that if he had had a sister like Miss Hamilton, most of his family troubles would never have arisen. He shook his head sadly at the thought that once upon a time he had tried to imagine a Miss Hamilton in Edith, and in a burst of self-revelation, like the brief appearance of two or three acres of definitely blue sky overhead, he assured his secretary that her coming had made a difference to his whole life.

"Well, of course you get through much more in the day now," she agreed.

John would have liked a less practical response, but he made the best of it.

"I've got so much wrapped up in the play," he said, "that I'm wondering now if I shall be able to tear myself away from London for Christmas. I dread the idea of a complete break—especially with the most interesting portion just coming along. I think I must ask you to take your holiday later in the year, if you don't mind."

He had got it out, and if he could have patted himself on the back without appearing ridiculous in a public thoroughfare he would have done so. His manner might have sounded brusque, but John was sure that the least suggestion of any other attitude except that of an employer compelled against his will to seem inconsiderate would have been fatal.

"That would mean leaving my mother alone," said Miss Hamilton, doubtfully.

John looked sympathetic, but firm, when he agreed with her.

"She would understand that literary work takes no account of the church calendar," he pointed out. "After all, what is Christmas?"

"Unfortunately, my mother is already very much offended with me for working with you at all. Oh, well, bother relations!" she exclaimed, vehemently. "I'm going to be selfish in future. All right, if you insist, I must obey—or lose my job, eh?"

"I might have to engage a locum tenens. You see, now that I've got into the habit of dictating my letters and relying upon somebody else to keep my references in order and—"

"Yes, yes," she interrupted. "I quite see that it would put you to great inconvenience if I cried off. All the same, I can't help being worried by the notion of leaving mother alone on Christmas Day itself. Why shouldn't I join you on the day after?"

"The very thing," John decided. "I will leave London on Christmas Eve, and you shall come down on Boxing Day. But I should travel in the morning, if I were you. It's apt to be unpleasant, traveling in the evening on a Bank Holiday. Hullo, here we are! This walk has given me a tremendous appetite, and I do feel that we've made a splendid start with the fourth act, don't you?"

"The fourth act?" repeated his secretary. "It seems to me that most of the time you were talking about the position of women in modern life."

John laughed gayly.

"Ah, I see you haven't even yet absolutely grasped my method of work. I was thinking all the while of Joan's speech to her accusers. I can assure you that all my remarks were entirely relevant to what I had in my head. That's the way I get my atmosphere. I told you that you reminded me of her, but you wouldn't believe me. In doublet and hose you would be Joan."

"Should I? I think I should look more like Dick Whittington in a touring pantomime. My legs are too thin for tights."

"By the way, I wonder if Janet Bond has good legs?" said John, pensively.

It was charming to be able to talk about women's legs like this without there being the slightest suggestion that they had any; yet, somehow the least promising topics were rehabilitated by the company of Miss Hamilton, and most of them, even the oldest, acquired a new and absorbing interest. John had registered a vow on the first day his secretary came that he would watch carefully for the least signs of rosifying her and he had renewed this vow every morning before his glass; but it was sometimes difficult not to attribute to her all sorts of mysterious fascinations, as on those occasions when he would have kept her working later than usual in the afternoon and when she would have been persuaded to stay for tea, for which she made a point of getting home to please her mother, who gave it a grand importance. John was convinced that even James would forgive him for thinking that in all England there was not a more competent, a more charming, a more—he used to pull himself up guiltily at about the third comparative and stifle his fancies in the particularly delicious cake that Mrs. Worfolk always seemed to provide on the days when his secretary stayed to tea.

It was on one of these rosified afternoons, full of candlelight and firelight and the warmed scent of hyacinths that Miss Hamilton rallied John about his exaggerated dread of his relations.

"For I've been working with you now for nearly three weeks, and you've not been bothered by them once," she declared.

"My name! My name!" he cried. "Touchwood?"

"I begin to think it's nothing but an affectation," she persisted. "*You're* not pestered by charitable uncles who want to boast of what they've done for their poor brother's only daughter. *You're* not made to feel that you've wrecked your mother's old age by earning your own living."

"Yes, they have been quiet recently," he admitted. "But there was such a terrible outbreak of Family Influenza just before you came that some sort of prostration for a time was inevitable. I hope you don't expect my brother, Hugh, to commit a forgery every week. Besides, that excellent suggestion of yours about preparing Ambles for Christmas has kept him busy, and probably all the rest of them down there too. But it's odd you should raise the subject, because I was going to propose your having supper here some Sunday soon and inviting my eldest brother and his wife to meet you."

"To-morrow is the last Sunday before Christmas. The Sunday after is Christmas Day."

"Is it really? Then I must dictate an invitation for to-morrow, and I must begin to see about presents on Monday. By Jove, how time has flown!"

"After all, what is Christmas?" she laughed.

"Oh, you must expect children to be excited about it," John murmured. "I don't like to disappoint *them*. But I'd no idea Christmas was on top of us like this. You'll help me with my shopping next week? I hope to goodness Eleanor won't come and bother me. She'll be getting back to town to-morrow. It's really extraordinary, the way the time has passed."

John dictated an urgent invitation to James and Beatrice to sup with them the following evening, and since it was too late to let them know by post, he decided to see Miss Hamilton as far as the tube and leave the note in person at Hill Road.

James arrived for supper in a most truculent mood, and this being aggravated by his brother's burgundy, of which he drank a good deal, referring to it all the while as poison, much to John's annoyance, embroiled him half way through supper in an argument with Miss Hamilton on the subject of feminine intelligence.

"Women are not intelligent," he shouted. "The glimmering intelligence they sometimes appear to exhibit is only one of their numerous sexual allurements. A woman thinks with her nerves, reasons with her emotions, and speculates with her sensations."

"Rubbish," said Miss Hamilton, emphatically.

"Now, Jimmie dear," his wife put in, "you'll only have indigestion if you get excited while you're eatin'."

"I shall have indigestion anyway," growled her husband. "My liver will be like dough to-morrow after this burgundy. I ought to drink a light moselle."

"Well, you can have moselle," John began.

"I loathe moselle. I'd as soon drink syrup of squills," James bellowed.

"All right, you shall have syrup of squills next time."

"Oh, Johnnie," Beatrice interposed with a wide reproachful smile. "Jimmie's only joking. He doesn't really like syrup of squills."

"For heaven's sake, don't try to analyze my tastes," said James to his wife.

John threw a glance at Miss Hamilton, which was meant to express "What did I tell you?" But she was blind to his signal and only intent upon attacking James on behalf of her sex.

"Women have not the same kind of intelligence as men," she began, "because it is denied to them by their physical constitution. But they have, I insist, a supplementary intelligence without which the great masculine minds would be as ineffective as convulsions of nature. Women work like the coral polyps...."

"Bravo!" John cried. "A capital comparison!"

"An absurd comparison!" James contradicted. "A ludicrous comparison! Woman is purely individualistic. The moment she begins to take up with communal effort, she tends to become sterile."

"Do get on with your supper, dear," urged Beatrice, who had only understood the last word and was anxious not "to be made to feel small," as she would have put it, in front of an unmarried woman.

John perceived her mortification and jumped through the argument as a clown through a paper hoop.

"Remember I'm expecting you both at Ambles on Christmas Eve," he said, boisterously. "We're going to have a real old-fashioned Christmas party."

James forgot all about women in his indignation; but before he could express his opinion Beatrice held up another paper hoop for the distraction of the audience.

"I'm simply longin' for the country," she declared. "Christmas with a lot of children is the nicest thing I know."

John went through the hoop with aplomb and refused to be unseated by his brother.

"James will enjoy it more than any of us," he chuckled.

"What!" shouted the critic. "I'd sooner be wrecked on a desert island with nothing to read but a sixpenny edition of the Christmas Carol. Ugh!"

John looked at Miss Hamilton again, and this time his appeal was not unheeded; she said no more about women and let James rail on at sentimental festivities, which, by the time he had finished with them, looked as irreparable as the remains of the tipsy-cake. There seemed no reason amid the universal collapse of tradition to conserve the habit of letting the ladies retire after dinner. As there was no drawing-room in his bachelor household, it would have been more comfortable to smoke upstairs in the library; but James returned to Fielding after demolishing Dickens and protested against being made to hurry over his port; so his host had to watch Beatrice escort Miss Hamilton from the dining-room with considerable resentment at what he thought was her unjustifiably protective manner.

"As my secretary," he felt, "Miss Hamilton is more at home in my house than Beatrice is. I suppose, though, that like everything else I have my relations are going to take possession of her now."

"Where did you pick up your lady-help?" James asked, when he and his brother were left alone with the wine.

"If you're alluding to Miss Hamilton," John said, sharply, "I met her on board the *Murmania*, crossing the Atlantic."

"I never heard any good come of traveling acquaintances. She has a good complexion; I suppose she took your eye by not being seasick. Beware of women with good complexions who aren't seasick, Johnnie. They always flirt."

"Are you supposed to be warning me against my secretary?"

"Any woman who finds herself at a man's elbow is dangerous. Nurses, of course, are the most notoriously dangerous—but a secretary who isn't seasick is nearly as bad."

"Thanks very much for your brotherly concern," said John, sarcastically. "You will be relieved to hear that the relationship between Miss Hamilton and myself is a purely practical one, and likely to remain so."

"Platonism was never practical," James answered with a snort. "It was the most impractical system ever imagined."

"Fortunately Miss Hamilton is sufficiently interested in her work and in mine not to bother her head about the philosophy of the affections."

James was irritating when he was criticizing contemporary literature; but his views of modern life were infuriating.

"I'm not accusing your young woman—how old is she, by the way? About twenty-nine, I should guess. A damned dangerous age, Johnnie. However, as I say, I'm not accusing her of designs upon you. But a man who writes the kind of plays that you do is capable of any extravagance, and you're much too old by now to be thinking about marriage."

"I don't happen to be thinking about marriage," John retorted. "But I refuse to accept your dictum about my age. I consider that the effects of age have been very much exaggerated by the young. You cannot call a man of forty-two old."

"You look much more than forty-two. However, one can't write plays like yours without exposing oneself to a good deal of emotional wear and tear. No, no, you're making a great mistake in introducing a woman into the house. Believe me, Johnnie, I'm speaking for your good. If I hadn't married, I might have preserved my illusions about women and compounded just as profitable a dose of dramatic nux vomica as yourself."

"What do you mean by a dose of dramatic nux vomica?"

"That's my name for the sort of plays you write, which unduly accelerate the action of the heart and make a sane person retch. However, don't take my remarks in ill part. I was simply commenting on the danger of letting a good-looking young woman make herself indispensable."

"I'm glad you allow her good looks," John said, witheringly. "Any one who was listening to our conversation would get the impression that she was as ugly and voracious as a harpy."

"Yes, yes. She's quite good-looking. Very nice ankles."

"I haven't noticed her ankles," John said, austerely.

"You will, though," his brother replied with an encouraging laugh. "By the way, what's that rascal, Hugh, been doing? I hear you've replanted him in the bosom of the family. Isn't Hugh rather too real for one of your Christmas parties?"

John, after some hesitation, had decided not to tell any of the others the details of Hugh's misdemeanor; he had even denied himself the pleasure of holding him up to George as a warning; hence the renewal of his interest in Hugh had struck the family as a mere piece of sentimentality.

"Crutchley didn't seem to believe he'd ever make much of architecture," he explained to James. "And I'm thinking of helping him to establish himself in British Honduras."

"Bah! For less than he'll cost you in British Honduras you could establish me as the editor of a new critical weekly," James grunted.

"There is still time for Hugh to make something of his life," John replied. He had not had the slightest intention of trying to score off his eldest brother by this remark, and he was shocked to see what a spasm of ill will twisted up his face.

"I suppose your young woman is responsible for this sudden solicitude for Hugh's career? I suppose it's she who has persuaded you that he has possibilities? You take care, Johnnie. You can't manipulate the villain in life as you can on the stage."

Now, Miss Hamilton, though she had not met him, had shown just enough interest in Hugh to give these remarks a sting; and John must have been obviously taken aback, for the critic at once recovered his good humor and proposed joining the ladies upstairs. Beatrice was sitting by the fire; her husband's absence had allowed her to begin the digestion of an unusually good dinner in peace, and the smoothness of her countenance made her look more than ever like a cabinet photograph of the early 'nineties. Miss Hamilton, on the other hand, seemed bored, and very soon she declared that she must go home lest her mother should be anxious.

"Oh, you have a mother?" James observed in such a tone that John thought it was the most offensive remark of the many he had heard him make that evening. He hoped that Miss Hamilton would not abandon him after this first encounter with his relations, and he tried to ascertain her impressions while she was putting on her things in the hall.

"I'm afraid you've had a very dull evening," he murmured, apologetically. "I hope my sister-in-law wasn't more tiresome than usual. What did she talk about?"

"She was warning me—no, I won't be malicious—she was explaining to me the difficulties of an author's wife."

"Yes, poor thing; I'm afraid my brother must be very trying to live with. I hope you were sympathetic?"

"So sympathetic," Miss Hamilton replied, with a mocking glance, "that I told her I was never likely to make the experiment. Good night, Mr. Touchwood. To-morrow as usual."

She hurried down the steps and was gone before he could utter a word.

"I don't think she need have said that," he murmured to himself on his way back to the library. "I've no doubt Beatrice was very trying; but I really don't think she need have said that to me. It wasn't worth repeating such a stupid remark. That's the way things acquire an undue importance."

With John's entrance the conversation returned to Miss Hamilton; but, though it was nearly all implied criticism of his new secretary, he had no desire to change the topic. She was much more interesting than the weekly bills at Hill Road, and he listened without contradiction to his brother's qualms about her experience and his sister-in-law's regrets for her lack of it.

"However," said John to his reflection when he was undressing, "they've got to make the best of her, even if they all think the worse. And the beauty of it is that they can't occupy her as they can occupy a house. I must see about getting Hugh off to the Colonies soon. If I don't find out about British Honduras, he can always go to Canada or Australia. It isn't good for him to hang about in England."

CHAPTER XI

WHETHER it was due to the Christmas card look of his new house or merely to a desire to flaunt a romantic hospitality in the face of his eldest brother, it is certain that John had never before in his life gone so benevolently mad as during the week that preceded Christmas in the year 1910. Mindful of that afternoon in the town of Galton when he had tried to procure for Harold and Frida gifts of such American appearance as would excuse his negligence, he was determined not to expose himself for a second time to juvenile criticism, and in the selection of toys he pandered to every idiosyncrasy he had so far observed in his nephews and nieces. Thus, for Bertram he bought a large stamp album, several sheets of tropical stamps, a toy theater, representatives of every species in the great genus marbles, a set of expensive and realistic masks, and a model fireman's outfit. For Viola he filled a trunk with remnants of embroideries and all kinds of stuffs, placing on top two pairs of ebony castanets and the most professional tambourine he could find; and, in order that nature might not be utterly subordinated to art, he bought her a very large doll, rather older in appearance than Viola herself; in fact, almost marriageable. In the hope of obliterating the disappointment of those china animals, he chose for Frida a completely furnished dolls' house with garage and stables attached, so grand a house, indeed, that by knocking all the rooms into one, she could with slight inconvenience have lived in it herself; this residence he populated with gentleman-dolls, lady-dolls, servant-dolls, nurse-dolls, baby-dolls, horses, carriages, and motors; nor did he omit to provide a fishmonger's shop for the vicinity. For Harold he bought a butterfly collector's equipment, a vacuum pistol, a set of climbing-irons, a microscope, and at the last moment a juvenile diver's equipment with air pumps and all accessories, which was warranted perfectly safe, though the wicked uncle wondered if it really was.

"I don't want a mere toy for the bathroom," he explained.

"Quite so, sir," the shopman assented, with a bow. "This is guaranteed for any ordinary village pond or small stream."

For his grown-up relations John bought the kind of presents that one always does buy for grown-up relations, the kind of presents that look very ornamental on the counter, seem very useful when the shopman explains what they are for, puzzle the recipient and the donor when the shopman is no longer there, and lie about the house on small tables for the rest of the year. In the general odor of Russia leather that clung to his benefactions John hoped that Miss Hamilton would not consider too remarkable the attaché case that he intended to give her, nor amid the universal dazzle of silver object to the few little luxuries of the writing-desk with which he had enhanced it. Then there were the presents for the servants to choose, and he counted much on Miss Hamilton's enabling him to introduce into these an utilitarian note that for two or three seasons had been missing from his donations, which to an outsider might have seemed more like lures of the flesh than sober testimonials to service. He also counted upon her to persuade Mrs. Worfolk to accompany Maud down to Ambles: Elsa was to be left in Church Row with permission to invite to dinner the policeman to whom she was betrothed and various friends and relations of the two families.

When the presents were settled John proceeded to lay in a store of eatables and drinkables, in the course of which enterprise he was continually saying:

"I've forgotten for the moment what I want next, but meanwhile you'd better give me another box of Elvas plums."

"Another drum? Yes, sir," the shopman would reply, licking his pencil in a way that was at once obsequious and pedantic, though it was not intended to suggest more than perfect efficiency.

When the hall and the adjacent rooms at 36 Church Row had been turned into rolling dunes of brown paper, John rushed about London in a last frenzy of unbridled acquisitiveness to secure plenty of amusement for the children. To this end he obtained a few well-known and well-tried favorites like the kinetoscope and the magic lantern, and a number of experimental diversions which would have required a trained engineer or renowned scientist to demonstrate successfully. Finally he bargained for the wardrobe of a Santa Claus whose dignified perambulations round the Christmas Bazaar of a noted emporium had attracted his fancy on account of the number of children who followed him everywhere, laughing and screaming with delight. It was not until he had completed the purchase that he discovered it was not the exterior of the Santa Claus which had charmed his little satellites, but the free distribution of bags of coagulated jujubes.

"I expect I'd better get the Christmas tree in the country," said John, waist-deep in the still rising drift of parcels. "I dare say the Galton shops keep those silver and magenta globes you hang on Christmas trees, and I ought to patronize the local tradesmen."

"If you have any local shopping to do, I'm sure you would be wise to go down to-day," Miss Hamilton suggested, firmly. "Besides, Mrs. Worfolk won't want to arrive at the last minute."

"No, indeed, I shan't, Miss," said the housekeeper. "Well, I mean to say, I don't think we ever shall arrive, not if we wait much longer. We shall require a performing elephant to carry all these parcels, as it is."

"My idea was to go down in the last train on Christmas Eve," John argued. "I like the old-fashioned style, don't you know?"

"Yes, old-fashioned's the word," Mrs. Worfolk exclaimed. "Why, who's to get the house ready if we all go trooping down on Christmas Eve? And if I go, sir, you must come with me. You know how quick Mrs. Curtis always is to snap any one up. If I had my own way, I wouldn't go within a thousand miles of the country; that's a sure thing."

John began to be afraid that his housekeeper was going back on her word, and he surrendered to the notion of leaving town that afternoon.

"I say, what is this parcel like a long drain-pipe?" he asked in a final effort to detain Miss Hamilton, who was preparing to make her farewells and leave him to his packing.

"Ah, it would take some finding out," Mrs. Worfolk interposed. "I've never seen so many shapes and sizes of parcels in all my life."

"They must have made a mistake," said John. "I don't remember buying anything so tubular as this."

He pulled away some of the paper wrapping to see what was inside.

"Ah, of course! They're two or three boxes of Elvas plums I ordered. But please don't go, Miss Hamilton," he protested. "I am relying upon you to get the tickets to Waterloo."

In spite of a strenuous scene at the station, in the course of which John's attempts to propitiate Mrs. Worfolk led to one of the porters referring to her as his mother, they managed to catch the five o'clock train to Wrottesford. After earnestly assuring his secretary that he should be perfectly ready to begin work again on Joan of Arc the day after her arrival and begging her on no account to let herself be deterred from traveling on the morning of Boxing Day, John sank back into the pleasant dreams that haunt a warm first-class smoking compartment when it's raining hard outside in the darkness of a December night.

"We shall have a green Christmas this year," observed one of his fellow travelers.

"Very green," John assented with enthusiasm, only realizing as he spoke that the superlative must sound absurd to any one who was unaware of his thoughts and hiding his embarrassment in the *Westminster Gazette*, which in the circumstances was the best newspaper he could have chosen.

John was surprised and depressed when the train arrived at Wrottesford to find that the member of the Ambles party who had elected to meet him was Hilda; and there was a long argument on the platform who should drive in the dogcart and who should drive in the fly. John did not want to ride on the back seat of the dogcart, which he would have to do unless he drove himself, a prospect that did not attract him when he saw how impatiently the mare was dancing about through the extreme lateness of the train. Hilda objected to driving with his housekeeper in the fly, and in the end John was compelled to let Maud and Mrs. Worfolk occupy the dogcart, while he and Hilda toiled along the wet lanes in the fly. It was decided to leave the greater portion of the luggage to be fetched in the morning, but even so it was after eight o'clock before they got away from the station, and John, when he found himself immured with Hilda in the musty interior of the hired vehicle was inclined to prophesy a blue Christmas this year. To begin with, Hilda would try to explain the system she had pursued in allotting the various bedrooms to accommodate the large party that was expected at Ambles. It was bad enough so long as she confined herself to a verbal exposition, but when she produced a map of the house, evidently made by Hugh on an idle evening, and to illuminate her dispositions struck away most of John's matches, it became exasperating. His brain was already fatigued by the puzzle of fitting into two vehicles four pieces, one of which might not move to the square next two of the remaining pieces, and another of which could not move backward.

"I leave it entirely to you," he declared, introducing at last into the intellectual torment of chess some of the happy irresponsibleness of bridge. "You mustn't set me these chess problems in a jolting fly before dinner."

"Chess!" Hilda sniffed with a shiver. "Draughts would be a better name."

She did not often make jokes, and before John had recovered sufficiently from his surprise to congratulate her with a hearty laugh, she was off again upon her querulous and rambling narration of the family news.

"If everything *had* been left to me, I might have managed, but Hugh's interference, apparently authorized by you, upset all my poor little arrangements. I need hardly say that Mama was so delighted to have her favorite at home with her that she has done everything since his arrival to encourage his self-importance. It's Hughie this and Hughie that, until I get quite sick of the sound of his name. And he's very unkind to poor little Harold. Apart from being very coarse and sarcastic in front of him, he is sometimes quite brutal. Only this morning he shot him in the upper part of the leg with a pellet from the poor little man's own air-gun."

John did laugh this time, and shouted "Merry Christmas!" to a passing wagon.

"I dare say it sounds very funny to you. But it made Harold cry."

"Come, come, Hilda, it's just as well he should learn the potentialities of his own instrument. He'll sympathize with the birds now."

"Birds," she scoffed. "Fancy comparing Harold with a bird!"

"It is rather unfair," John agreed.

"However, you won't be so ready to take Hugh's part when you see what he's been doing at Ambles."

"Why, what has he been doing?"

"Oh, never mind. I'd rather you judged for yourself," said Hilda, darkly. "Of course, I don't know what Hugh has been up to in London that you've had to send him down to Hampshire. I always used to hear you vow that you would have nothing more to do with him. But I know that successful people are allowed to change their minds more often than the rest of us. I know success justifies everything. And it isn't as if Hugh was grateful for your kindness. I can assure you that he criticizes everything you do. Any stranger who heard him talking about your plays would think that they were a kind of disgrace to the family. As for Laurence, he encourages him, not because he likes him, but because Hugh fills him up with stories about the stage. Though I think that a clergyman who has got into such a muddle with his bishops would do better not to make himself so conspicuous. The whole neighborhood is talking about him."

"What is Laurence's latest?"

"Why, stalking about in a black cloak, with his hair hanging down over his collar, stopping people in quiet lanes and reciting Shakespeare to them. It's not surprising that half the county is talking about his behavior and saying that he was turned out of Newton Candover for being drunk when the bishop took a confirmation, and *some* even say that he kept a ballet girl at the vicarage. But do you think that Edith objects? Oh, no! All that Laurence does must be right, because it's Laurence. She prays for him to get back his belief in the Church of England, though who's going to offer him another living I'm sure I don't know, so she might just as well spare her knees. And when she's not praying for him, she's spoiling him. She actually came out of her room the other morning with her finger up to her lips, because Laurence wasn't to be disturbed at that moment. I need hardly tell you I paid no attention and went on saying what I had to say to Huggins about the disgraceful way he's let the pears get so sleepy."

"It's a pity you didn't succeed in waking them up instead of Laurence," John chuckled.

"It's all very well for you to laugh, John, but if you could see the way that Edith is bringing up Frida! She's turning her into a regular little molly-coddle. I'm sure poor Harold does his best to put some life into the child, but she shrinks and twitches whenever he comes near her. I told Edith that it wasn't to be wondered at if Harold did tease her sometimes. She encourages him to tease her by her affectations. I used to think that Frida was quite a nice little girl when I only saw her occasionally, but she doesn't improve on acquaintance. However, I blame her mother more than I do her. Why, Edith doesn't even make the child take her cod-liver oil regularly, whereas Harold drinks his up like a little Trojan."

"Never mind," said John, soothingly. "I'm sure we shall all feel more cheerful after Christmas. And now, if you don't mind, I'm afraid I must keep quiet for the rest of the drive. I've got a scene to think about."

The author turned up the collar of his coat and retired into the further corner while Hilda chewed her veil in ruminative indignation until the mellow voice of Laurence, who had taken up a statuesque pose of welcome by the gate, broke the dank silence of the fly.

"Ah, John, my dear fellow, we are delighted to see you. The rain has stopped."

If Laurence had still been on good terms with his Creator, John might have thought from his manner that he had personally arranged this break in the weather.

"Is Harold there?" asked Hilda, sharply.

"Here I am, mother; I've just caught a Buff-tip, and it won't go into my poison-bottle."

"And what is a Buff-tip?" inquired Laurence in a tone of patronizing ignorance.

"Oh, it's a pretty common moth."

"Harold, darling, don't bother about moths or butterflies to-night. Come and say how d'ye do to dear Uncle John."

"I've dropped the cork of my poison-bottle. Look out, Frida, bother you, I say, you'll tread on it."

The combined scents of cyanide of potassium and hot metal from Harold's bull's-eye lantern were heavy upon the moist air; when the cork was found, Harold lost control over the lantern which he flashed into everybody's face in turn, so that John, rendered as helpless as a Buff-tip, walked head foremost into a sopping bush by the side of the path. However, the various accidents of arrival all escaped being serious, and the thought of dinner shortened the affectionate greetings. Remembering how Hugh had paid out Harold with his own air-gun, John greeted his youngest brother more cordially than he could ever have supposed it was possible to greet him again.

By general consent, the owner of the house was allowed to be tired that evening, and all discussion of the Christmas preparations was postponed until the next day. Harold made a surreptitious attempt to break into the most promising parcel he could find, but he was ill rewarded by the inside, which happened to be a patent carpet sweeper.

Before old Mrs. Touchwood went to bed, she took John aside and whispered:

"They're all against Hughie. But I've tried to make the poor boy feel that he's at home, and dear Georgie will be coming very soon, which will make it pleasanter for Hugh, and I've thought of a nice way to manage Jimmie."

"I think you worry yourself needlessly over Hugh, Mama; I can assure you he's perfectly capable of looking after himself."

"I hope so," the old lady sighed. "All my patience came out beautifully this evening. So I hope Hughie will be all right. He seemed to think you were a little annoyed with him."

"Did he tell you why?"

"Not exactly, but I understand it was something to do with money. You mustn't be too strict with Hugh about money, John. You must always remember that he hasn't got all the money he wants, and you must make allowances accordingly. Ah, dear, peace on earth, good-will towards men! But I don't complain. I'm very happy here with my patience, and I dare say something can be done to get rid of the bees that have made a nest in the wall just under my bedroom window. They're asleep now, but when they begin to buzz with the warm weather Huggins must try and induce them to move somewhere else. Good-night, my dear boy."

Next morning when John leaned out of his window to inhale the Hampshire air and contemplate his domain he was shocked to perceive upon the lawn below a large quadrangular excavation in which two workmen were actually digging.

"Hi! What are you doing?" he shouted.

The workmen stared at John, stared at one another, stared at their spades, and went on with their digging.

"Hi! What the devil are you doing?"

The workmen paid no attention; but the voice of Harold came trickling round the corner of the house with a gurgle of self-satisfaction.

"*I* didn't do it, Uncle John. I began geology last week, but I haven't dug up *anything*. Mother wouldn't let me. It was Uncle Hugh and Uncle Laurence. Mother knew you'd be angry when you saw what a mess the garden was in. It does look untidy, doesn't it? Huggins said he should complain to you, first thing. He says he'd just as soon put brown sugar on the paths as *that* gravel. Did you know that Ambles is built on a gravel subsoil, Uncle John? Aren't you glad, because my geology book says that a gravel subsoil is the healthiest...."

John removed himself abruptly out of earshot.

"What is that pernicious mess on the front lawn?" he demanded of Hugh half-an-hour later at breakfast.

"Ah, you noticed it, did you?"

"Noticed it? I should think I did notice it. I understand that you're responsible."

"Not entirely," Laurence interposed, gently. "Hugh and I must accept a joint responsibility. The truth is that for some time now I've felt that my work has been terribly at the mercy of little household noises, and Hugh recommended me to build myself an outside study. He has made a very clever design, and has kindly undertaken to supervise its erection. As you have seen, they are already well on with the foundations. The design which I shall show you after breakfast is in keeping with the house, and of course you will have the advantage of what I call my little Gazebo when I leave Ambles. Have I told you that I'm considering a brief experience of the realities of the stage? After all, why not? Shakespeare was an actor."

If John had been eating anything more solid than a lightly boiled egg at the moment he must have choked.

"You can call it your little Gazebo as much as you like, but it's nothing but a confounded summerhouse," he shouted.

"Look here, Johnnie," said Hugh, soothingly. "You'll like it when it's finished. This isn't one of Stevie's Gothic contortions. I admit that to get the full architectural effect there should be a couple of them. You see, I've followed the design of the famous dovecotes at...."

"Dovecoats be damned," John exploded. "I instructed you to prepare the house for Christmas; I didn't ask you to build me a new one."

"Laurence felt that he was in the way indoors," Edith explained, timidly.

"The impression was rather forced upon me," said Laurence with a glance at Hilda, who throughout the dispute had been sitting virtuously silent; nor did she open her thin lips now.

"He was going to pay for his hermitage out of the money he ought to have made from writing *Lamp-posts*," Edith went on in a muddled exposition of her husband's motives. "He wasn't thinking of himself at all. But of course if you object to his building this Gas—oh, I am so bad at proper names—he'll understand. Won't you, dear?"

"Oh, I shall understand," Laurence admitted with an expression of painfully achieved comprehension. "Though I may fail to see the necessity for such strong language."

Frida wiggled in the coils of an endless whisper from which her mother extricated her at last by murmuring:

"Hush, darling, Uncle John is a little vexed about something."

Hilda and her son still sat in mute self-righteousness; and Grandmama, who always had her breakfast in bed, was not present to defend Hugh.

"If it had been anywhere except on the lawn right in front of my room," John began more mildly.

"We tried to combine suitability of site with facility of access," Laurence condescended to explain. "But pray do not say another word," he added, waving his fingers like magic wands to induce John's silence. "The idea of my little Gazebo does not appeal to you. That is enough. I do not grudge the money already spent upon the foundations. Further discussion will irritate us all, and I for one have no wish to disturb the harmony of the season." Then exchanging his tone of polite martyrdom for the suave jocularity of a vicar, he continued: "And when are we to expect our Yuletide guests? I hear that the greater portion of your luggage is still in the care of the station-master at Wrottesford. If I can do anything to aid in the transport of what rumor says is our Christmas commissariat, do not hesitate to call upon my services. I am giving the Muse a holiday and am ready for anything. Harold, pass the marmalade, please."

John felt incapable of further argument with Laurence and Hugh in combination, and having gained his point, he let the subject of the Gazebo drop. He was glad that Miss Hamilton was not here; he felt that she might have been rather contemptuous of what he tried to believe was "good-nature," but recognized in his heart as "meekness," even "feebleness."

"When are Cousin Bertram and Cousin Viola coming?" Harold asked.

"Wow-wow-wow!" Hugh imitated, and he was probably expressing the general opinion of Harold's re-entry into the breakfast-table conversation.

"For goodness' sake, boy, don't talk about them as if they were elderly colonial connections," John commanded with the resurgent valor that Harold always inspired. "Bertram and Viola are coming to-morrow. By the way, Hilda, is there any accommodation for a monkey? I don't know for certain, but Bertram talked vaguely of bringing a monkey down. Possibly a small annex could be attached to the chickenhouse."

"A monkey?" Edith exclaimed in alarm. "Oh, I hope it won't attack dear Frida."

"I shall shoot him, if he does," Harold boasted. "I shot a mole last week."

"No, you didn't, you young liar," Hugh contradicted. "It was killed by the trap."

"Harold is always a very truthful little boy," said his mother, glaring.

"Is he? I hadn't noticed it," Hugh retorted.

"Far be it from me to indulge in odious comparisons," Laurence interposed, grandly. "But I cannot help being a trifle— ah—tickled by so much consideration's being exhibited on account of the temporary lodging of a monkey and so much animus—however, don't let us rake up a disagreeable topic."

John thought it was a pity that his brother-in-law had not felt the same about raking up the lawn when after breakfast he was telling Huggins to fill in the hole and hearing that it was unlikely to lose the scar for a long time.

"You could have knocked me down with a feather, sir, when they started in hacking away at a lovely piece of turf like that."

"I'm sure I could," John agreed, warmly.

"But what's done can't be undone, and the best way to mend a bad job would be to make a bed for ornamental annuals. Yes, sir, a nice bed in the shape of a star—or a shell."

"No thanks, Huggins, I should prefer grass again, even if for a year or two the lawn does look as if it had been recently vaccinated."

John's Christmas enthusiasm had been thoroughly damped by the atmosphere of Ambles and he regretted that he had let himself be persuaded into coming down two days earlier than he had intended. It had been Mrs. Worfolk's fault, and when his housekeeper approached him with a complaint about the way things were being managed in the kitchen John told her rather sharply that she must make the best of the present arrangements, exercise as much tact as possible, and remember that Christmas was a season when discontent was out of fashion. Then he retreated to the twenty-acre field to lose a few golf-balls. Alas, he had forgotten that Laurence had proclaimed himself to be in a holiday humor and was bored to find that this was so expansive as to include an ambition to see if golf was as difficult as people said.

"You can try a stroke if you really want to," John offered, grudgingly.

"I understand that the theory of striking involves the correct application of the hands to the club," said the novice. "I set much store by the old adage that well begun is half done."

"The main thing is to hit the ball."

"I've no doubt whatever about being able to hit the ball; but if I decide to adopt golf as a recreation from my dramatic work I wish to acquire a good style at the outset," Laurence intoned, picking up the club as solemnly as if he was going to baptize it. "What is your advice about the forefinger of my left hand? It feels to me somewhat ubiquitous. I assume that there is some inhibition upon excessive fidgeting."

"Keep your eye on the ball," John gruffly advised him. "And don't shift your position."

"One, two, three," murmured Laurence, raising the club above his shoulder.

"Fore!" John shouted to a rash member of the household who was crossing the line of fire.

A lump of turf was propelled a few feet in the direction of the admonished figure, and the ball was hammered down into the soft earth.

"You distracted me by counting four," Laurence protested. "My intention was to strike at three. However, if at first you don't succeed...."

But John could stand no more of it and escaped to Galton, where he bought a bushel of lustrous ornaments for the Christmas tree that was even now being felled by Huggins in a coppice remote from Harold's myopic explorations. Then for two days the household worked feverishly and unitedly in a prevalent odor of allspice; the children were decoyed from the house while the presents were mysteriously conveyed to the drawing-room, which had been consecrated to the forthcoming revelry; Harold, after nearly involving himself in a scandal by hiding himself under the kitchen-table during one of the servant's meals in order to verify the cubic contents of their several stockings, was finally successful in contracting with Mrs. Worfolk for the loan of one of hers; Frida whispered as ceaselessly as a grove of poplars; everybody's fingers were tattooed by holly-pricks; and the introduction of so much decorative vegetation into the house brought with it a train of somnambulant insects.

On Saturday afternoon the remaining guests arrived, and when John heard Bertram and Viola shouting merrily up and down the corridors he recognized the authentic note of Christmas gayety at last. James was much less disagreeable than he had expected, and did not even freeze Beatrice when she gushed about the loveliness of the holly and reminded everybody that she was countrified herself; Hilda and Eleanor were brought together by their common dread of Hugh's apparent return to favor; George exuded a gross reproduction of the host's good-will and wandered about the room reading jokes from the Christmas numbers to those who would listen to him; Laurence kissed all the ladies under the mistletoe, bending down to them from his majesty as patronizingly as in the days of his faith he used to communicate the poor of the parish; Edith clapped her hands every time that Laurence brought off a kiss and talked in a heart-felt tremolo about the Christmas-tides of her girlhood; Frida conceived an adoration for Viola; Hugh egged on Bertram to tease, threaten, and contradict Harold on every occasion; Grandmama in a new butter-colored gown glowed in the lamplight, and purred over her fertility, as if on the day she had accepted Robert Touchwood's hand nearly half a century ago she had foreseen this gathering and had never grumbled when she found she was going to have another baby.

"Snapdragon will be ready at ten," John proclaimed, "and then to bed, so that we're all fit for Christmas Day."

He was anxious to get the household out of the way, because he had formed a project to dress himself up that night as Santa Claus and, as he put it to himself, stimulate the children's fancy in case they should be awake when their stockings were being filled.

The clock struck ten; Mrs. Worfolk gave portentous utterance to the information that the snapdragon was burning beautiful; there was a rush for the pantry where the ceremony was to take place. Laurence picked out his raisins as triumphantly as if he were snatching souls from a discredited Romish purgatory. Harold notwithstanding his bad sight seemed to be doing well until Bertram temporarily disabled him by snatching a glowing raisin from the fiercest flame and ramming it down his neck. But the one who ate most of all, more even than Harold, was George, whose fat fingers would scoop up half-a-dozen raisins at a go, were they never so hot, until gradually the blue flames flickered less alertly and finally went out altogether in a pungency of burnt brandy.

"Half-past ten," John, who was longing to dress himself up, cried impatiently.

429

His efforts to urge the family up to bed were rather interfered with by Laurence, who detained Eleanor with numerous questions about going on the stage with a view to correcting a few technical deficiencies in his dramatic craftsmanship.

"I'm anxious to establish by personal experience the exact length of the interval required to change one's costume, and also the distance from one's green-room to the—ah—wings. I do not aim high. I should be perfectly satisfied with such minor parts as Rosencrantz or Metellus Cimber. Perhaps, Eleanor, you will introduce me to some of your theatrical friends after the holidays? There is a reduced day return up to town every Thursday. We might lunch together at one of those little Bohemian restaurants where rumor says that an excellent lunch is to be had for one and sixpence."

Eleanor promised she would do all she could, because John evidently wanted her to go to bed, and he was the uncle of her children.

"Thank you, Eleanor. I hope that as a catechumen I shall do honor to you. By the way, you will be interested in the part of Pontius Pilate's wife in my play. In fact I'm hoping that you will—ah—interpret it ultimately."

"Did you ever think of writing a play about Polonius's wife?" James growled on his way upstairs. "Good-night."

When the grown-ups were safely in their rooms, John could not understand why the children were allowed to linger in the passage, gossiping and bragging; they would never go to sleep at this rate.

"I've got two cocoons of a Crimson-underwing," Harold was saying.

"Poof!" Viola scoffed. "What are they. Bertram touched the nose of a kangaroo last time we went to the Zoo."

"Yes, and I prodded a crocodile with V's umbrella," added Bertram, acknowledging her testimonial by awarding his sister a kind of share in the exploit.

"Well, I was bitten by a squirrel once," related Harold in an attempt to keep his end up. "And that was in its nest, not in a cage."

"A squirrel!" Viola sneered. "Why, the tallest giraffe licked Bertram's fingers with his tongue, and they stayed wet for hours afterwards."

"Well, so could I, if I went to the Zoo," Harold maintained with a sob at the back of his throat.

"No, you couldn't," Bertram contradicted. "Because your fingers are too smelly."

"Much too smelly!" Viola corroborated.

Various mothers emerged at this point and put a stop to the contest; the hallowed and gracious silence of Christmas night descended upon Ambles, and John went on tiptoe up to his bedroom.

"The beard, I suppose, is the most important item," he said to himself, when he had unpacked his costume.

It was a noble beard, and when John had fixed it to his cheeks with a profusion of spirit-gum, he made up his mind that it became him so well that he would grow one of his own, which whitening with the flight of time would in another thirty years make him look what he hoped to be—the doyen of romantic playwrights. The scarlet robe of Santa Claus with its trimming of bells, icicles, and holly and its ruching of snow had been made in a single piece without buttons, so that when John put it over his head the beard caught in the folds and part of it was thinned out by an icicle. In trying to disentangle himself John managed to get one sleeve stuck to his cheek much more firmly than the beard had ever been. Nor were his struggles to free himself made easier by the bells, which tinkled with every movement and made him afraid that somebody would knock at the door soon and ask if he had rung. Finally he got the robe in place, plucked several bits of sleeve from his cheek, renovated the beard, gathered together the apples, oranges, sweets, and small toys he had collected for the stockings, looked at his watch, decided that it was at least an hour too early to begin, and lay down upon his bed, where notwithstanding the ticking of his beard he fell asleep. When he woke, it was after one o'clock; the house was absolutely still. He walked cautiously to the little room occupied by Frida, turned the handle, and felt his way breathlessly along the bed to where the stocking should be hung. Unfortunately, the bed had somehow got twisted round or else his beard had destroyed his sense of direction, for while he was groping for the stocking he dropped an orange on Frida's face, who woke with a loud scream.

"Hush, my little dear," John growled in what he supposed to be the correct depth for the character. "It's only Santa Claus."

"Go away, go away," shrieked the horrified child.

John tried to strike a match to reassure her, and at the cost of a shower of apples on the floor, which sounded like bombs in the tense darkness, he managed to illuminate his appearance for an instant. The effect on Frida was appalling; she screamed a thousand times louder than before and fled from the room. John ran after her to stop her before she woke up everybody else and spoilt his fantasy; but he was hampered by the costume and Frida gained the sanctuary of her parents' bedroom.

"I only hope the little idiot will frighten them more than I frightened her," muttered John, hurrying as fast as he could back to his own room.

Suddenly from the hall below he heard a sound of sleigh-bells that put to shame the miserable little tinkle that attended his own progress; above the bells rose peals of hearty laughter, and above the laughter Hugh's voice could be heard shouting:

"Wake up! Wake up! Good people all! Here's Santa Claus! Santa Claus! Wake up!"

Just as John reached his own room, Hugh appeared at the head of the stairs brandishing a lighted torch, while close behind him dragging Harold's toboggan loaded with toys was a really superb Santa Claus.

John locked his door and undressed himself savagely, tearing off his beard in handfuls and flinging all the properties into a corner.

"Anyway, whoever it is," he said, "he'll get the credit of driving Frida mad. That's one thing. But who is it? I suppose it's Laurence showing us how well he can act."

But it was Aubrey Fenton whom Hugh had invited down to Ambles for Christmas and smuggled into the house like this to sweeten the unpleasant surprise. What annoyed John most was that he himself had never thought of using the toboggan; but the new Santa Claus was an undoubted success with the children, and Frida's sanity was soon restored by chocolates. The mystery of the apples and oranges strewn about her bedroom remained a mystery, though Hilda tried to hint that her niece had abstracted them from the sideboard.

John was able to obtain as much sympathy as he wanted from the rest of the family over Hugh's importation of his friend. In fact they were so eager to express their disapproval of such calm self-assurance, not to mention the objectionable way in which he had woken everybody up in the middle of the night, that John's own indignation gradually melted away in the heat of their malice. As for Grandmama, she shut herself up in her bedroom on Christmas morning and threatened not to appear all day, so deep was her hatred of that young Fenton who was the author of all Hugh's little weaknesses—not even when she could shift the blame could she bring herself to call her son's vices and crimes by any stronger name. Aubrey, who lacked Hugh's serene insolence, wanted to go back to London and was so much abashed in his host's presence and so appreciative of what he had done in the affair of the check that John's compassion was aroused and he made the intruder welcome. His hospitality was rewarded, because it turned out that Aubrey's lifelong passion for mechanical toys saved the situation for many of John's purchases, nearly all of which he managed to set in motion; nor could it be laid to his account that one of the drawing-room fireworks behaved like an out-of-door firework, because while Aubrey was lighting it at the right end Harold was lighting it simultaneously at the other.

On the whole, the presentation of the Christmas gifts passed off satisfactorily. The only definite display of jealousy occurred over the diver's equipment given to Harold, which was more than Bertram notwithstanding his own fireman's outfit could suppress.

"I'll swop with you, if you like," he began mildly enough.

But Harold clutched the diver's mask to his breast and shrank from the proposal.

"I think you'd rather be a fireman," Bertram persisted. "Anybody can be a diver, can't they, V?"

Viola left her doll in a state of semi-nudity and advanced to her brother's support.

"You'd look much nicer as a fireman, Harold," she said, coaxingly. "I wish I could be a fireman."

"Well, you can if you like," he answered, sullenly, looking round with a hunted expression for his mother, who unluckily for her son was in another part of the house arguing with Mrs. Worfolk about the sauce for the plum-pudding.

"But wouldn't you rather wear a pretty brass helmet?" Viola went on.

"No, I wouldn't," said Harold, desperately wrapping himself in the rubber tubes that was so temptingly conspicuous a portion of his equipment.

"Oh, you little idiot," Viola burst out, impatiently. "What's the good of your dressing up as a diver? In those goggles you always look like a diver."

"I don't, do I, Frida?" Harold implored.

Now Frida was happy with her dolls'-house; she had no reason to be loyal to Harold, who had always treated her shamefully; but the spirit of the squaw rose in her breast and she felt bound to defend the wigwam against outside criticism. Therefore she assured Harold that in ordinary life he did not look in the least like a diver.

"Well," Bertram announced, throwing aside the last pretense of respecting property, "V and I want that diver's dress, because we often act *Twenty Thousand Leagues Under the Sea*."

"Well, I can act *Twenty Thousand Leagues Under the Sea* too."

"No you can't because you haven't read it."

"Yes, I have."

"What a bung!" exclaimed Bertram. "You've only read *A Journey to the Center of the Earth* and *Round the World in Eighty Days*."

Then he remembered Frida's attitude. "Look here, if you take the fireman's uniform you can set fire to Frida's house."

Frida yelled her refusal.

"And put it out, you little idiot," Bertram added.

"And put it out," Viola echoed.

Frida rushed to her mother.

"Mother, mother, don't let them burn my dolls'-house! Mother, you won't, will you? Bertram wants to burn it."

"Naughty Bertram!" said Edith. "But he's only teasing you, darling."

"Good lummy, what a sneak," Bertram commented, bitterly, to his sister.

Viola eyed her cousin with the scorn of an Antigon.

"Beastly," she murmured. "Come on, Bertram, you don't want the diver's dress!"

"Rather not. And anyway it won't work."

"It will. It will," cried Harold, passionately. "I'm going to practice in a water-butt the first fine day we have."

It happened that John was unable to feel himself happily above these childish jealousies, because at that moment he was himself smarting with resentment at his mother's handing over to James all that she still retained of family heirlooms. His eldest brother already had the portraits, and now he was to have what was left of the silver, which would look utterly out of place in Hill Road. If John had been as young as Bertram, he would have spoken his mind pretty freely on the subject of giving James the silver and himself a checkered woolen kettle-holder. It was really too disproportionate, and he did mildly protest to the old lady that she might have left a few things at Ambles.

"But Jimmie is the eldest, and I expect him to take poor Hugh's part. The poor boy will want somebody when I'm gone, and Jimmie is the eldest."

"He may be the eldest, but I'm the one who has to look after Hugh—and very often James for that matter."

"Ah well, you're the lucky one, but Jimmie is the eldest and Hugh is the baby."

"But James hasn't any children."

"Nor have you, my dear boy."

"But I might have," said John.

If this sort of thing went on much longer, he would, too—dozens of children.

"Bertram," John called out. "Come here, my boy, and listen to me. When I go back to London, you shall have a diving-suit too if I can find another."

Eleanor tossed her head back like a victorious game-cock; she would have crowed, if she could.

"Dinner is ready," announced Hilda fresh from a triumph over Mrs. Worfolk about the sauce and happily ignorant of the dreadful relegation of her son. After an unusually large meal even for Christmas the company lay about the drawing-room like exhausted Roman debauchees, while the pink and green paper caps out of the crackers one by one fluttered from their brows to the carpet. Snores and the occasional violent whizz of an overwound toy were all that broke the stillness. At tea-time everybody woke up, and Bertram was allowed to put on his fireman's uniform in order to extinguish a bonfire that Huggins had hoped would burn slowly over the holidays. After a comparatively light supper games were played; drawing-room fireworks were let off; Laurence blacked his nose in the magic lantern; and George walking ponderously across the room to fetch himself a cigar was struck on the ear by a projectile from the vacuum pistol, the red mark of which was visible for some time even on his florid countenance. Then, when the children became too quarrelsome to be any longer tolerated out of bed, a bowl of punch was brought in and Auld Lang Syne was sung. After which everybody agreed that it had been a very merry Christmas, and Grandmama was led weeping up to bed.

The next morning about midday John announced that he was driving to Wrottesford for the purpose of meeting Miss Hamilton.

"For though it is holiday time, I must do a certain amount of work," he explained.

"Miss Hamilton?" said Grandmama. "And who may Miss Hamilton be?"

Hilda, Edith, Eleanor, and Beatrice all looked very solemn and mysterious; James chuckled; Hugh brightened visibly.

"Well, I suppose we mustn't mind a stranger's coming to spoil our happy party," Hilda sighed.

"Ah, this will be your new secretary of whom rumor has already spoken," said Laurence. "Possibly she will give me some advice on the subject of the typing of manuscripts."

"Miss Hamilton will be very busy while she is staying here," said John, curtly.

Everybody looked at everybody else, and there was an awkward pause, which was relieved by Harold's saying that he would show her where he thought a goldfinch would make a nest in spring.

"Dear little man," murmured his mother with a sigh for his childish confidence.

"Shall *I* drive in to meet her?" Hugh suggested.

"No, thank you," said John, quickly.

"That's right, Johnnie," James guffawed. "You stick to the reins yourself."

CHAPTER XII

JOHN did not consider himself a first-class whip: if he had been offered the choice between swimming to meet his love like Leander, climbing into her father's orchard like Romeo, and driving to meet her with a dog-cart, he would certainly, had the engagement shown signs of being a long one, have chosen any mode of trysting except the last. This morning, however, he was not as usual oppressed by a sense of imperfect sympathy between himself and the mare; he did not think she was going to have hysterics when she blew her nose, nor fancy that she was on the verge of bolting when she tossed her chestnut mane; the absence of William the groom seemed a matter for congratulation rather than for regret; he felt as reckless as Phaeton, as urgent as Jehu, and the mare knew it. Generally, when her master held the reins, she would try to walk up steep banks or emulate in her capricious greed the lofty browsings of the giraffe; this morning at a steady swinging trot she kept to the middle of the road, passed two motor-cars without trying to box the landscape, and did not even shy at the new hat of the vicar's wife.

Later on, however, when John was safe in the station-yard and saw the familiar way in which Miss Hamilton patted the mare he decided not to take any risk on the return journey and in spite of his brother's parting gibe to hand over the reins to his secretary; nor was the symbolism of the action distasteful. How charming she looked in that mauve frieze! How well the color was harmonizing with the purple hedgerows! How naturally she seemed to haunt the woodland scene!

"Oh, this exquisite country," she sighed. "Fancy staying in London when you can write here!"

"It does seem absurd," the lucky author agreed. "But the house is very full at present. We shall be rather exposed to interruptions until the party breaks up."

He gave her an account of the Christmas festival, to which she seemed able to listen comfortably and appreciatively in spite of the fact that she was driving. This impressed John very much.

"I hope your mother wasn't angry at your leaving town," he said, tentatively. "I thought of telegraphing an invitation to her; but there really isn't room for another person."

"I'm afraid I can't say that she was gracious about my desertion of her. Indeed, she's beginning to put pressure on me to give up my post. Quite indirectly, of course, but one feels the effect just the same. Who knows? I may succumb."

John nearly fell out of the dog-cart.

"Give up your post?" he gasped. "But, my dear Miss Hamilton, the dog-roses won't be in bloom for some months."

"What have dog-roses got to do with my post?"

He laughed a little foolishly.

"I mean the play won't be finished for some months. Did I say dog-roses? I must have been thinking of the dog-cart. You drive with such admirable unconcern. Still, you ought to see these hedgerows in summer. Now the time I like for a walk is

432

about eight o'clock on a June evening. The honeysuckle smells so delicious about eight o'clock. There's no doubt it is ridiculous to live in London. I hope you made it quite clear to your mother you had no intention of leaving me?"

"Ida Merritt did most of the arguing."

"Did she? What a very intelligent girl she is, by the way. I confess I took a great fancy to her."

"You told mother once that she frightencd you."

"Ah, but I'm always frightened by people when I meet them first. Though curiously enough I was never frightened of you. Some people have told me that *I* am frightening at first. You didn't find that did you?"

"No, I certainly did not. And I can't imagine anybody else's doing so either."

Although John rather plumed himself upon the alarm he was credited with inspiring at first sight, he did not argue the point, because he really never had had the least desire to frighten his secretary.

"And your relations don't seem to find you very frightening," she murmured. "Good gracious, what an assemblage!"

The dog-cart had just drawn clear of the beechwood, and the whole of the Ambles party could be seen vigilantly grouped by the gate to receive them, which John thought was a lapse of taste on the part of his guests. Nor was he mollified by the way in which after the introductions were made Hugh took it upon himself to conduct Miss Hamilton indoors, while he was left shouting for William the groom. If it was anybody's business except his own to escort her into the house, it was Hilda's.

"What a very extraordinary thing," said John, fretfully, "that the *only* person who's wanted is not here. Where is that confounded boy?"

"I'm here," cried Bertram, responding to the epithet instinctively.

"Not you. Not you. I wanted William to take the mare."

When lunch was over John found that notwithstanding his secretary's arrival he was less eager to begin work again upon his play than he had supposed.

"I think I must be feeling rather worn out by Christmas," he told her. "I wonder if a walk wouldn't do you good after the journey."

"Now that's a capital notion," exclaimed Hugh, who was standing close by and overheard the suggestion. "We might tramp up to the top of Shalstead Down."

"Oh yes," Harold chimed in. "I've never been there yet. Mother said it was too far for me; but it isn't, is it, Uncle John?"

"Your mother was right. It's at least three miles too far," said John, firmly. "Oh, by the way, Hugh, I've been thinking over your scheme for that summerhouse or whatever you call it, and I'm not sure that I don't rather like the idea after all. You might put it in hand this afternoon. You'd better keep Laurence with you. I want him to have it in the way he likes it, although of course I shall undertake the expense. Where's Bertram? Ah, there you are. Bertram, why don't you and Viola take Harold down to the river and practice diving? I dare say Mr. Fenton will superintend the necessary supply of air and reduce the chances of a fatal accident."

"But the water's much too cold," Hilda protested in dismay.

"Oh well, there's always something to amuse one by a river without actually going into the water," John said. "You like rivers, don't you, Fenton? I'm afraid we can't offer you a very large one, but it wiggles most picturesquely."

Aubrey Fenton, who was still feeling twinges of embarrassment on account of his uninvited stay at Ambles, was prepared to like anything his host put forward for his appreciation, and he spoke with as much enthusiasm of a promenade along the banks of the small Hampshire stream as if he were going to view the Ganges for the first time. John, having disposed of him, looked around for other possible candidates for a walk.

"You look like hard work, James," he said, approvingly.

"I've a bundle of trash here for review," the critic growled.

"I'm sorry. I was going to propose a stroll up Shalstead Down. Never mind. You'll have to walk into your victims instead." And, by gad, he would walk into them too, John thought, after that dinner yesterday.

Beatrice and Eleanor were not about; old Mrs. Touchwood was unlikely at her age to venture up the third highest elevation in Hampshire; Hilda was occupied with household duties; Edith had a headache. Only George now remained unoccupied, and John was sure he might safely risk an invitation to him; he looked incapable of walking two yards.

"I suppose you wouldn't care for a constitutional, George?" he inquired, heartily.

"A constitutional?" George repeated, gaping like a chub at a large cherry. "No, no, no, no. I always knit after lunch. Besides I never walk in the country. It ruins one's boots."

George always used to polish his own boots with as much passionate care as he would have devoted to the coloring of a meerschaum pipe.

"Well, if nobody wants to climb Shalstead Down," said John beaming happily, "what do you say, Miss Hamilton?"

A few minutes later they had crossed the twenty-acre field and were among the chalk-flecked billows of the rising downs.

"You're a terrible fraud," she laughed. "You've always led me to believe that you were completely at the mercy of your relations. Instead of which, you order them about and arrange their afternoon and really bully them into doing all sorts of things they never had any intention of doing, or any wish to do, what's more."

"Yes, I seemed to be rather successful with my strategy to-day," John admitted. "But they were stupefied by their Christmas dinner. None of them was really anxious for a walk, and I didn't want to drag them out unwillingly."

"Ah, it's all very well to explain it away like that, but don't ever ask me to sympathize with you again. I believe you're a replica of my poor mother. Her tyranny is deeply rooted in consideration for others. Why do you suppose she is always trying to make me give up working for you? For her sake? Oh, dear no! For mine."

"But *you* don't forge my name and expect her to pay me back. *You* don't arrive suddenly and deposit children upon her doorstep."

"I dare say I don't, but for my mother Ida Merritt represents all the excesses of your relations combined in one person. I'm convinced that if you and she were to compare notes you would find that you were both suffering from acute ingratitude and thoroughly enjoying it. But come, come, this is not a serious conversation. What about the fourth act?"

"The fourth act of what?" he asked, vaguely.

"The fourth act of Joan of Arc."

"Oh, Joan of Arc. I think I must give her a rest. I don't seem at all in the mood for writing at present. The truth is that I find Joan rather lacking in humanity and I'm beginning to think I made a mistake in choosing such an abnormal creature for the central figure of a play."

"Then what have I come down to Hampshire for?" she demanded.

"Well, it's very jolly down here, isn't it?" John retorted in an offended voice. "And anyway you can't expect me to burst into blank verse the moment you arrive, like a canary that's been uncovered by the housemaid. It would be an affectation to pretend I feel poetical this afternoon. I feel like a jolly good tramp before tea. I can't stand writers who always want to be literary. I have the temperament of a country squire, and if I had more money and fewer relations I should hardly write at all."

"Which would be a great pity," said his secretary.

"Would it?" John replied in the voice of one who has found an unexpected grievance and is determined to make the most of it. "I doubt if it would. What is my work, after all? I don't deceive myself. There was more in my six novels than in anything I've written since. I'm a failure to myself. In the eyes of the public I may be a success, but in the depths of my own heart—" he finished the sentence in a long sigh, all the longer because he was a little out of breath with climbing.

"But you were so cheerful a few minutes ago. I'm sure that country squires are not the prey to such swift changes of mood. I think you must be a poet really."

"A poet!" he exclaimed, bitterly, with what he fancied was the kind of laugh that is called hollow. "Do I look like a poet?"

"If you're going to talk in that childish way I sha'n't say any more," she warned him, severely. "Oh, there goes a hare!"

"Two hares," said John, trying to create an impression that in spite of the weight of his despondency he would for her sake affect a light-hearted interest in the common incidents of a country walk.

"And look at the peewits," she said. "What a fuss they make about nothing, don't they?"

"I suppose you are comparing me to a peewit now?" John reproachfully suggested.

"Well, a moment ago you compared yourself to an uncovered canary; so if I've exceeded the bounds of free speech marked out for a secretary, you must forgive me."

"My dear Miss Hamilton," he assured her, "I beg you to believe that you are at liberty to compare me to anything you like."

Having surrendered his personality for the exercise of her wit John felt more cheerful. The rest of the walk seemed to offer with its wide prospects of country asleep in the winter sunlight a wider prospect of life itself; even Joan of Arc became once again a human figure.

It was to be feared that John's manipulation of his guests after lunch might have had the effect of uniting them against the new favorite; and so it had. When he and Miss Hamilton got back to the house for tea the family was obviously upon the defensive, so obviously indeed that it gave the impression of a sculptor's group in which each figure was contributing his posture to the whole. There was not as yet the least hint of attack, but John would almost have preferred an offensive action to this martyred withdrawal from the world in which it was suggested that he and Miss Hamilton were living by themselves. It happened that a neighbor, a colorless man with a disobedient and bushy dog, called upon the Touchwoods that afternoon, and John could not help being aware that to the eyes of his relations he and his secretary appeared equally intrusive and disturbing; the manner in which Hilda offered Miss Hamilton tea scarcely differed from the manner in which she propitiated the dog with a bun; and it would have been rash to assert that she was more afraid of the dog's biting Harold than of the secretary's doing so.

"Don't worry Miss Hamilton, darling. She's tired after her long walk. Besides, she isn't used to little boys. And don't make Mr. Wenlow's dog eat sugar if it doesn't want to."

Eleanor would ordinarily have urged Bertram to prove that he could achieve what was denied to his cousin. Yet now in the face of a common enemy she made overtures to Hilda by simultaneously calling off her children from the intruders.

"If I'd known that animals were so welcomed down here," James grumbled, "I should have brought Beyle with us."

It was not a polite remark; but the disobedient dog in an effusion of cordiality had just licked the back of James' neck, and he was not nearly so rude as he would have been about a human being who had surprised him, speaking figuratively, in the same way.

"Lie down, Rover," whispered the colorless neighbor with so rich a blush that until it subsided the epithet ceased to be appropriate.

Rover unexpectedly paid attention to the command, but chose Grandmama's lap for his resting place, which made Viola laugh so ecstatically that Frida felt bound to imitate her, with the result that a geyser of tea spurted from her mouth and descended upon her father's leg. Laurence rose and led his daughter from the room, saying:

"Little girls who choke in drawing-rooms must learn to choke outside."

"I'm afraid she has adenoids, poor child," said Eleanor, kindly.

"I know what that word means," Harold bragged with gloating knowledge.

"Shut up!" cried Bertram. "You know everything, glass-eyes. But you don't know there are two worms in your tea-cup."

"There aren't," Harold contradicted.

"All right, drink it up and see. I put them there myself."

"Eleanor!" expostulated the horrified mother. "*Do* you allow Bertram to behave like this?"

She hurriedly poured away the contents of Harold's cup, which proved that the worms were only an invention of his cousin. Yet the joke was successful in its way, because there was no more tea, and therefore Harold had to go without a third cup. Edith, whose agitation had been intense while her husband was brooding in the passage over Frida's chokes, could stay still no longer, but went out to assist with tugs and taps of consolation. The colorless visitor departed with his disobedient dog, and soon a thin pipe was heard in vain whistles upon the twilight like the lisp of reeds along the dreary margin of a December stream.

John welcomed this recrudescence of maternal competition, which seemed likely to imperil the alliance, and he was grateful to Bertram and Viola for their provocation of it. But he had scarcely congratulated himself, when Hugh came in and at once laid himself out to be agreeable to Miss Hamilton.

"You've put the summerhouse in hand?" John asked, fussily, in order to make it perfectly clear to his brother that he was not the owner of Ambles.

Hugh shook his head.

"My dear man, it's Boxing Day. Besides, I know you only wanted to get rid of me this afternoon. By the way, Aubrey's going back to town to-night. Can he have the dog-cart?"

John looked round at the unbidden guest with a protest on his lips; he had planned to keep Aubrey as a diversion for Hugh, and had taken quite a fancy to him. Aubrey however, had to be at the office next day, and John was distressed to lose the cheerful young man's company, although it had been embarrassing when Grandmama had shuddered every time he opened his mouth. Another disadvantage of his departure was the direction of the old lady's imagination toward an imminent marriage between Hugh and Miss Hamilton, which was extremely galling to John, especially as the rest of the family was united in suggesting a similar conjunction between her and himself.

"I don't want to say a word against her, Johnnie," Grandmama began to mutter one evening about a week later when every game of patience had failed in turn through congestion of the hearts. "I'm not going to say she isn't a lady, and perhaps she doesn't mean to make eyes at Hughie."

John would have liked to tell his mother that she was on the verge of senile decay; but the dim old fetish of parental respect blinked at him from the jungle of the past, and in a vain search for a way of stopping her without being rude he let her ramble on.

"Of course, she has very nice eyes, and I can quite understand Hughie's taking an interest in her. I don't grudge the dear boy his youth. We all get old in time, and its natural that with us old fogies round him he *should* be a little interested in Miss Hamilton. All the same, it wouldn't be a prudent match. I dare say she thinks I shall have something to leave Hugh, but I told her only yesterday that I should leave little or nothing."

"My dear Mama, I can assure you that my secretary—my secretary," John repeated with as much pomposity as might impress the old lady, "is not at all dazzled by the glamour of your wealth or James' wealth or George's wealth or anybody's wealth for that matter."

He might have said that the donkey's ears were the only recognizable feature of Midas in the Touchwood family had there been the least chance of his mother's understanding the classical allusion.

"I don't mean to hint that she's *only* after Hugh's money. I've no doubt at all that she's excessively in love with him."

"Really?" John exclaimed with such a scornfully ironical intonation that his mother asked anxiously if he had a sore throat.

"You might take a little honey and borax, my dear boy," she advised, and immediately continued her estimate of the emotional situation. "Yes, as I say, excessively in love! But there can't be many young women who resist Hugh. Why, even as a boy he had his little love affairs. Dear me, how poor papa used to laugh about them. 'He's going to break a lot of hearts,' poor papa used to say."

"I don't know about hearts," John commented, gruffly. "But he's broken everything else, including himself. However, I can assure you, Mama, that Miss Hamilton's heart is not made of pie-crust, and that she is more than capable of looking after herself."

"Then you agree with me that she has a selfish disposition. I *am* glad you agree with me. I didn't trust her from the beginning; but I thought you seemed so wrapped up in her cleverness—though when I was young women didn't think it necessary to be clever—that you were quite blind to her selfishness. But I *am* glad you agree with me. There's nobody who has more sympathy for true love than I have. But though I always said that love makes the world go round, I've never been partial to vulgar flirtations. Indeed, if it had to be, I'd rather they got engaged properly, even if it did mean a long engagement—but leading poor Hughie on like this—well, I must speak plainly, Johnnie, for, after all, I am your mother, though I know it's the fashion now to think that children know more than their parents, and, in my opinion, you ought to put your foot down. There! I've said what I've been wanting to say for a week, and if you jump down my throat, well, then you must, and that's all there is to it."

Now, although John thought his mother fondly stupid and was perfectly convinced when he asked himself the question that Miss Hamilton was as remote from admiring Hugh as he was himself, he was nevertheless unable to resist observing Hugh henceforth with a little of the jealousy that most men of forty-two feel for juniors of twenty-seven. He was not prepared to acknowledge that his opinion of Miss Hamilton was colored by any personal emotion beyond the unqualified respect he gave to her practical qualities, and he was sure that the only reason for anxiety about possible developments between her and Hugh was the loss to himself of her valuable services.

"I've reached an age," he told his reflection, whose crow's-feet were seeming more conspicuous than usual in the clear wintry weather, "when a man becomes selfish in small matters. Let me be frank with myself. Let me admit that I do dislike the idea of an entanglement with Hugh, because I *have* found in Miss Hamilton a perfect secretary whom I should be extremely sorry to lose. Is that surprising? No, it is quite natural. Curious! I noticed to-day that Hugh's hair is getting very thin on top. Mine, however, shows no sign of baldness, though fair men nearly always go bald before dark men. But I'm inclined to fancy that few observers would give me fifteen years more than Hugh."

If John had really been conscious of a rival in his youngest brother, he might have derived much encouragement from the attitude of all the other members of the family, none of whom seemed to think that Hugh had a look in. But, since he firmly declined to admit his secretary's potentiality for anything except efficient clerical work, he was only irritated by it.

"Are you going to marry Miss Hamilton?" Harold actually wanted to know one evening. He had recently been snubbed for asking the company what was the difference between gestation and digestion, and was determined to produce a conundrum that could not be evaded by telling him that he would not understand the answer. John's solution was to look at his watch and say it was time for him and Bertram to be in bed, hoping that Bertram would take it out of his cousin for calling attention to their existence. One of Bertram's first measures at Ambles had been to muffle, impede, disorganize and finally destroy the striking of the drawing-room clock. When this had been accomplished he could count every night on a few precious minutes snatched from the annihilation of bed during which he sat mute as a mummy in a kind of cataleptic ecstasy. The betrayer of this profound peace sullenly gathered up the rubbish with which he was wont to litter the room every night, and John saw Bertram's eye flash like a Corsican sharpening the knife of revenge. But whatever was in store for Harold lacked savor when John heard from the group of mothers, aunts, sisters, and sisters-in-law the two words "Children know" dying away in a sibilance of affirmative sighs.

After that it was small consolation to hear a scuffle outside in the hall followed by the crash of Harold's dispersed collections and a wail of protest. For the sake of a childish quarrel Hilda and Eleanor were not going to break up the alliance to which they were now definitely committed.

"It's so nice for poor Harold to have Bertram to play with him," volunteered one mother.

"Yes, and it's nice for Bertram too, because Harold's such a little worker," the other agreed.

Even George's opaque eyes glimmered with an illusion of life when he heard his wife praise her nephew; she had not surprised him so completely since on a wet afternoon, thirteen years ago, she accepted his hand. It was even obvious to Edith that she must begin to think about taking sides; and, having exhausted her intelligence by this discovery, she had not enough wit left to see that now was her opportunity to trade upon John's sentimental affection for herself, but proceeded to sacrifice her own daughter to the success of the hostile alliance.

"I think perhaps it's good for Frida to be teased sometimes," she ventured.

As for Beatrice, she was not going to draw attention to her childlessness by giving one more woman the chance of feeling superior to herself, and her thwarted maternity was placed at the disposal of the three mothers. Indeed it was she who led the first foray, in which she was herself severely wounded, as will be seen.

Among the unnecessary vexations and unsatisfactory pleasures which the human side of John inflicted upon the well-known dramatist, John Touchwood, was the collection of press-cuttings about himself and his work; one of Miss Hamilton's least congenial tasks was to preserve in a scrap-book these tributes to egoism.

"You don't really want me to stick in this paragraph from *High Life*?" she would protest.

"Which one is that?"

"Why, this ridiculous announcement that you've decided to live on the upper slopes of the Andes for the next few months in order to gather material for a tragedy about the Incas."

"Oh, I don't know. It's rather amusing, I think," John would insist, apologetically. Then, rather lamely, he would add, "You see, I subscribe."

Miss Hamilton, with a sigh, would dip her brush in the paste.

"I can understand your keeping the notices of your productions, which I suppose have a certain value, but this sort of childish gossip...."

"Gossip keeps my name before the public."

Then he would fancy that he caught a faint murmur about "lack of dignity," and once even he thought she whispered something about "lack of humor."

Therefore, in view of the importance he seemed to attach to the most irrelevant paragraph, Miss Hamilton could not be blamed for drawing his attention to a long article in one of those critical quarterlies or monthlies that are read in club smoking-rooms in the same spirit of desperation in which at railway stations belated travelers read time-tables. This article was entitled *What Is Wrong With Our Drama?* and was signed with some obscurely allusive pseudonym.

"I suppose I am involved in the general condemnation?" said John, with an attempt at a debonair indifference.

Had he been alone he might have refrained from a descent into particulars, but having laid so much stress upon the salvage of worthless flotsam, he could not in Miss Hamilton's presence ignore this large wreck.

"*Let us pause now to contemplate the roundest and the rosiest of our romantic cherubs.* Ha-ha! I suppose the fellow thinks that will irritate me. As a matter of fact, I think it's rather funny, don't you? Rather clever, I mean. Eh? *But, after all, should we take Mr. Touchwood seriously? He is only an exuberant schoolboy prancing about with a pudding-dish on his head and shouting 'Let's pretend I'm a Knight-at-Arms' to a large and susceptible public. Let us say to Mr. Touchwood in the words of an earlier romantic who was the fount and origin of all this Gothic stucco:*

hat can ail thee, Knight-

taggered by the critics' to

pit and gallery are full,

the play has gone.'

"I don't mind what he says about *me*," John assured his secretary. "But I do resent his parodying Keats. Yes, I do strongly resent that. I wonder who wrote it. I call it rather personal for anonymous criticism."

"Shall I stick it in the book?"

"Certainly," the wounded lion uttered with a roar of disdain. At least that was the way John fancied he said "certainly."

"Do you really want to know who wrote this article?" she asked, seriously, a minute or two later.

"It wasn't James?" the victim exclaimed in a flash of comprehension.

"Well, all I can tell you is that two or three days ago your brother received a copy of the review and a letter from the editorial offices. I was sorting out your letters and noticed the address on the outside. Afterwards at breakfast he opened it and took out a check."

"James would call me a rosy cherub," John muttered. "Moreover, I did tell him about Bertram and the pudding-dish when he was playing at Perseus. And—no, James doesn't admire Keats."

"Poor man," said Miss Hamilton, charitably.

"Yes, I suppose one ought to be sorry for him rather than angry," John agreed, snatching at the implied consolation. "All the same, I think I ought to speak to him about his behavior. Of course, he's quite at liberty to despise my work, but I don't think he should take advantage of our relationship to introduce a note of personal—well, really, I don't think he has any right to call me a round and rosy cherub in print. After all, the public doesn't know what a damned failure James himself is. I shouldn't so mind if it really was a big pot calling the kettle black. I could retaliate then. But as it is I can do nothing."

"Except stick it in your press-cutting book," suggested Miss Hamilton, with a smile.

"And then my mother goes and presents him with all the silver! No, I will not overlook this lapse of taste; I shall speak to him about it this morning. But suppose he asks me how I found out?"

"You must tell him."

"You don't mind?"

"I'm your secretary, aren't I?"

"By Jove, Miss Hamilton, you know, you really are...."

John stopped. He wanted to tell her what a balm her generosity was to his wound; but he felt that she would prefer him to be practical.

It was like the critic to welcome with composure the accusation of what John called his duplicity, or rather of what he called duplicity in the privacy of his own thoughts: to James he began by referring to it as exaggerated frankness.

"I said nothing more than I've said a hundred times to your face," his brother pointed out.

"That may be, but you didn't borrow money from me on the strength of what you said. You told me you had an article on Alfred de Vigny appearing shortly. You didn't tell me that you were raising the money as a post obit on my reputation."

"My dear Johnnie, if you're going to abuse me in metaphors, be just at any rate. Your reputation was a corpse before I dissected it."

"Very well, then," cried John, hotly, "have it your own way and admit that you're a body-snatcher."

"However," James continued, with a laugh that was for him almost apologetic, "though I hate excuses, I must point out that the money I borrowed from you was genuinely on account of Alfred de Vigny and that this was an unexpected windfall. And to show I bear you no ill will, which is more than can be said for most borrowers, here's the check I received. I'm bound to say you deserve it."

"I don't want the money."

"Yet in a way you earned it yourself," the critic chuckled. "But let me be quite clear. Is this a family quarrel? I don't want to quarrel with you personally. I hate your work. I think it false, pretentious and demoralizing. But I like you very much. Do, my dear fellow, let us contract my good taste in literature and bad taste in manners with your bad taste in literature and good taste in manners. Like two pugilists, let's shake hands and walk out of the ring arm-in-arm. Even if I hit you below the belt, you must blame your curves, Johnnie. You're so plump and rosy that...."

"That word is becoming an obsession with you. You seem to think it annoys me, but it doesn't annoy me at all."

"Then it is a family quarrel. Come, your young lady has opened her campaign well. I congratulate her. By the way, when am I to congratulate you?"

"This," said John, rising with grave dignity, "is going too far."

He left his brother, armed himself with a brassey, proceeded to the twenty-acre field, and made the longest drive of his experience. At lunch James announced that he and Beatrice must be getting back to town that afternoon, a resolution in which his host acquiesced without even a conventional murmur of protest. Perhaps it was this attitude of John's that stung Beatrice into a challenge, or perhaps she had been egged on by the mothers who, with their children's future to consider, were not anxious to declare open war upon the rich uncle. At any rate, in her commonest voice she said:

"It's plain that Jimmie and I are not wanted here any longer."

The mothers looked down at their plates with what they hoped was a strictly neutral expression. Yet it was impossible not to feel that they were triumphantly digging one another in the ribs with ghostly fingers, such an atmosphere of suppressed elation was discernible above the modest attention they paid to the food before them. Nobody made an effort to cover the awkwardness created by the remark, and John was faced with the alternative of contradicting it or acknowledging its truth; he was certainly not going to be allowed to ignore it in a burst of general conversation.

"I think that is rather a foolish remark, Beatrice," was his comment.

She shrugged her shoulders so emphatically that her stays creaked in the horrid silence that enveloped the table.

"Well, we can't all be as clever as Miss Hamilton, and most of us wouldn't like to be, what's more."

"The dog-cart will be round at three," John replied, coldly.

His sister-in-law, bursting into tears, rushed from the room. James guffawed and helped himself to potatoes. The various mothers reproved their children for breaches of table manners. George looked nervously at his wife as if she was on the point of following the example of Beatrice. Grandmama, who was daily receding further and further into the past, put on her spectacles and told John, reproachfully, that he ought not to tease little Beatrice. Hugh engaged Miss Hamilton in a conversation about Bernard Shaw. John, forgetting he had already dipped twice in mustard the morsel of beef upon his fork, dipped it again, so that his eyes presently filled with tears, to which the observant Harold called everybody's attention.

"Don't make personal remarks, darling," his mother whispered.

"That's what Johnnie said to me this morning," James chuckled.

When the dog-cart drove off with James and Beatrice at three o'clock to catch the 3:45 train up to town, John retired to his study in full expectation that when the mare came back she would at once turn round for the purpose of driving Miss Hamilton to catch the 5:30 train up to town: no young woman in her position would forgive that vulgar scene at lunch. But when he reached his desk he found his secretary hard at work upon the collection of material for the play as if nothing had happened. In the presence of such well-bred indifference the recollection of Beatrice's behavior abashed him more than ever, and, feeling that any kind of even indirect apology from him would be distasteful to Miss Hamilton, he tried to concentrate upon the grouping of the trial scene with an equal show of indifference to the mean events of family life. He was so far successful that the afternoon passed away without any allusion to Beatrice, and when the gong sounded for tea his equanimity was in order again.

After tea, however, Eleanor managed to get hold of John for what she called a little chat about the future, but which he detected with the mind's nose as an unpleasant rehash of the morning's pasticcio. He always dreaded this sister-in-law when she opened with zoological endearments, and his spirits sank to hear her exclaim boisterously:

"Now, look here, you poor wounded old lion, I'm going to talk to you seriously about Beatrice."

"There's nothing more to be said," John assured her.

"Now don't be an old bear. You've already made one poor aunt cry; don't upset me too."

Anybody less likely to be prostrated by grief than Eleanor at that moment John could not have imagined. She seemed to him the incarnation of a sinister self-assurance.

"Rubbish," he snapped. "In any case, yours would only be stage tears, you old crocodile—if I may copy your manner of speech."

"Isn't he in a nasty, horrid, cross mood?" she demanded, with an affected glance at an imaginary audience. "No, but seriously, John! I do want to give you a little advice. I suppose it's tactless of me to talk about advising the great man, but don't bite my head off."

"In what capacity?" the great man asked. "You've forgotten to specify the precise carnivore that will perform the operation."

"Oh dear, aren't we sarcastic this afternoon?" she asked, opening wide her eyes. "However, you're not going to frighten me, because I'm determined to have it out with you, even if you order the dog-cart before dinner. Johnnie, is it fair to let a complete stranger make mischief among relations?"

John played the break in Eleanor's voice with beautiful ease.

"I will not have Miss Hamilton's name dragged into these sordid family squabbles," he asseverated.

"I'm not going to say a word against Miss Hamilton. I think she's a charming young woman—a little too charming perhaps for you, you susceptible old goose."

"For goodness sake," John begged, "stick to the jungle and leave the farmyard alone."

"Now you're not going to rag me out of what I'm going to say. You know that I'm a real Bohemian who doesn't pay attention to the stupid little conventionalities that, for instance, Hilda or Edith might consider. Therefore I'm sure you won't misunderstand me when I warn you about people talking. Of course, you and I are accustomed to the freedom of the profession, and as far as I'm concerned you might engage half a dozen handsome lady secretaries without my even noticing it. But the others don't understand. They think it's funny."

"Good heavens, what are you trying to suggest?" John demanded.

He could manage the break, but this full pitch made him slog wildly.

"*I'm* not trying to suggest anything. I'm simply telling you what other people may think. You see, after all, Hilda and Edith couldn't help noticing that you did allow Miss Hamilton to make mischief between you and your brother. I dare say James was in the wrong; but is it a part of a secretary's duties to manage her employer? And James *is* your brother. The natural deduction for conventional people like Hilda and Edith was that—now, don't be annoyed at what I'm going to say, but I always speak out—I'm famous for my frankness. Well, to put it frankly, they think that Miss Hamilton can twist you round her little finger. Then, of course, they ask themselves why, and for conventional people like Hilda and Edith there's only one explanation. Of course, I told them it was all nonsense and that you were as innocent as an old lamb. I dare say you don't mind people talking. That's your business, but I shouldn't have been a good pal if I hadn't warned you that people will talk, if they aren't talking already."

"You've got the mind of an usher," said John. "I can't say worse than that of anybody. Wasn't it you who suggested a French governess should be given the freedom of Church Row and who laughed at me for being an old beaver or some other prudish animal because I objected? If I can be trusted with a French governess, I can surely be trusted with a confidential secretary. Besides, we're surrounded by an absolute *chevaux de frise* of chaperons, for I suppose that Hilda and Edith may fairly be considered efficient chaperons, even if you are still too youthfully Bohemian for the post."

Eleanor's age was the only vulnerable spot in her self-confidence, and John took advantage of it to bring her little chat to a bitter end.

"My dear Johnnie," she said, tartly, "I'm not talking about the present. I'm warning you about the future. However, you're evidently not in the mood to listen to anybody."

"No, I'm not," he assented, warmly. "I'm as deaf as an old adder."

The next day John, together with Mrs. Worfolk and Maud, left for Hampstead, and his secretary traveled with him up to town.

"Yes," his housekeeper was overheard observing to Elsa in the hall of 36 Church Row, "dog-cart is a good name for an unnatural conveyance, but give me a good old London cab for human beings. Turn again, Whittington, they say, and they're right. They may call London noisy if they like, but it's as quiet as a mouse when you put it alongside of all that baaring and mooing and cockadoodledoing in the country. Well, I mean to say, Elsa, I'm getting too old for the country. And the master's getting too old for the country, in my opinion. I'm in hopes he'll settle down now, and not go wearing himself out any more with the country. Believe me or not as you will, Elsa, when I tell you that the pore fellow had to play at ball like any little kid to keep himself amused."

"Fancy that, Mrs. Worfolk," Elsa murmured with a gentle intake of astonished breath.

"Yes, it used to make me feel all over melancholy to see him. All by himself in a great field. Pore fellow. He's lonely, that's what it is, however...."

At this point the conversation born upon whispers and tut-tut passed out of John's hearing toward the basement.

"I suppose my own servants will start gossiping next," he grumbled to himself. "Luckily I've learnt to despise gossip. Hullo, here's another bundle of press-cuttings.

"*It is rumored that John Touchwood's version of Joan of Arc which he is writing for that noble tragedienne, Miss Janet Bond, will exhibit the Maid of Orleans in a new and piquant light. The distinguished dramatist has just returned from France where he has been obtaining some startling scenic effects for what is confidently expected will be the playwright's most successful production. We are sorry to hear that Miss Bond has been suffering from a sharp attack of 'flu, but a visit to Dr. Brighton has—*"

These and many similar paragraphs were all pasted into the album by his secretary the next morning, and John was quite annoyed when she referred to them as worthless gossip.

"You don't know what gossip is," he said, thinking of Eleanor. "I ignore real gossip."

Miss Hamilton smiled to herself.

CHAPTER XIII

AFTER the Christmas party at Ambles John managed to secure a tranquillity that, however brief and deceptive he felt it was like to be, nevertheless encouraged him sufficiently to make considerable progress with the play while it lasted. Perhaps Eleanor's warning had sunk deeper than she might have supposed from the apparent result of that little chat with her brother-in-law about his future; at any rate, he was so firmly determined not to give the most evil mind the least opportunity for malicious exaggeration that in self-defense he devoted to Joan of Arc a more exclusive attention than he had hitherto devoted to any of his dramatic personages. Moreover, in his anxiety to prove how abominably unjust the insinuations of his family were, he imparted to his heroine some of his own temporary remoteness from the ordinary follies and failings of humanity.

"We are too much obsessed by sex nowadays," he announced at the club one afternoon, and was tempted to expatiate upon his romantic shibboleth to several worn out old gentlemen who had assented to this proposition. "After all," he argued, "life is not all sex. I've lately been enormously struck by that in the course of my work. Take Joan of Arc for instance. Do we find any sex obsession in her? None. But is she less psychologically interesting on that account? No. Sex is the particular bane of modern writers. Frankly, I cannot read a novel nowadays. I suppose I'm old-fashioned, but I'd rather be called old-fashioned than asked to appreciate one of these young modern writers. I suppose there's no man more willing than myself to march with the times, but I like the high roads of literature, not the muddy lanes...."

"The John Longs and John Lanes that have no turnings," a club wag put in.

"Look at Stevenson," the dramatist continued, without paying any attention to the stupid interruption. "When Stevenson wrote a love scene he used to blush."

"So would any one who had written love scenes as bad as his," sniggered a young man, who seemed oblivious of his very recent election to the club.

The old members looked at him severely, not because he had sneered at Stevenson, but because, without being spoken to, he had volunteered a remark in the club smoking-room at least five years too soon.

"I've got a young brother who thinks like you," said John, with friendly condescension.

"Yes, I know him," the young man casually replied.

John was taken aback; it struck him as monstrous that a friend of Hugh's should have secured election to *his* club. The sanctity of the retreat had been violated, and he could not understand what the world was coming to.

"How is Hugh?" the young man went on, without apparently being the least conscious of any difference between the two brothers. "Down at your place in Hampshire, isn't he? Lucky chap; though they tell me you haven't got many pheasants."

"I beg your pardon?"

"You don't preserve?"

"No, I do not preserve." John would have liked to add "except the decencies of intercourse between old and young in a club smoking-room"; but he refrained.

"Perhaps you're right," said the young man. "These are tough times for landed proprietors. Well, give my love to Hugh when you see him," he added, and turning on his heel disappeared into the haze of a more remote portion of the smoking-room.

"Who is that youth?" John demanded.

The old members shook their heads helplessly, and one of the waiters was called up to be interrogated.

"Mr. Winnington-Carr, I believe, sir," he informed them.

"How long has he been a member?"

"About a week, I believe, sir."

John looked daggers of exclamation at the other members.

"We shall have perambulators waiting in the lobby before we know where we are," he said, bitterly.

Everybody agreed that these ill-considered elections were a scandal to a famous club, and John, relinquishing the obsession of sex as a topic, took up the obsession of youth, which he most convincingly proved to be the curse of modern life.

It was probably Mr. Winnington-Carr's election that brought home to John the necessity of occupying himself immediately with his brother's future; at this rate he should find Hugh himself a member of his club before he knew where he was.

"I'm worrying about my young brother," he told Miss Hamilton next day, and looked at her sharply to watch the effect of this remark.

"Why, has he been misbehaving himself again?"

"No, not exactly misbehaving; but a friend of his has just been elected to my club, and I don't think it's good for Hugh to be hanging about in idleness. I do wish I could find the address of that man Raikes from British Honduras."

"Where is it likely to be?"

"It was a visiting-card. It might be anywhere."

"If it was a visiting-card, the most likely place to find it is in one of your waistcoat-pockets."

John regarded his secretary with the admiration that such a practical suggestion justified, and rang the bell.

"Maud, please bring down all my waistcoats," he told his valeting parlor-maid, who presently appeared in the library bowed down by a heap of clothes as a laborer is bowed down by a truss of hay.

In the twenty-seventh waistcoat that was examined the card was found:

Mr. Sydney Ricketts.
14 Lyonesse Road, Belize,
Balam, S.W., British Honduras.

"I thought his name was Raikes," John muttered, indignantly.

"Never mind. A rose by any other name...." Miss Hamilton began.

John might almost have been said to interrupt what she was going to say with an angry glare; but she only laughed merrily at his fierce expression.

"Oh, I beg your pardon—I'd forgotten your objection to roses."

Mr. Ricketts, who was fortunately still in London, accepted John's invitation to come and see him at Church Row on business. He was a lantern-jawed man with a tremendous capacity for cocktails, a sinewy neck, and a sentimental affection for his native suburb. At the same time, he would not hear a word against British Honduras.

"I reckon our regatta at Belize is the prettiest little regatta in the world."

"But the future of logwood and mahogany?" John insisted.

"Great," the visitor assured him. "Why don't *you* come out to us? You'd lose a lot of weight if you worked for a few months up the Zucara river. Here's a photograph of some of our boys loading logwood."

"They look very hot," said John, politely.

"They are very hot," said Mr. Ricketts. "You can't expect to grow logwood in Iceland."

"No, of course not. I understand that."

In the end it was decided that John should invest £2000 in the logwood and mahogany business and that sometime in February Hugh should be ready to sail with Mr. Ricketts to Central America.

"Of course he'll want to learn something about the conditions of the trade at first. Yes, I reckon your brother will stay in Belize at first," said the planter, scratching his throat so significantly that John made haste to fill up his glass, thinking to himself that, if the cocktails at the Belize Yacht Club were as good as Mr. Ricketts boasted, Hugh would be unlikely ever to see much more of mahogany than he saw of it at present cut and rounded and polished to the shape of a solid dining-room table. However, the more attractive Belize, the less attractive England.

"I think you told me this was your first visit home in fifteen years?" he asked.

"That's right. Fifteen years in B.H."

"B.H.?" repeated the new speculator, nervously.

"British Honduras."

"Oh, I beg your pardon. The initials associated themselves in my mind for the moment with another place. B.H. you call it. Very appropriate I should think. I suppose you found many changes in Balham on your return?"

"Wouldn't have known it again," said Mr. Ricketts. "For one thing they'd changed all the lamp-posts along our road. That's the kind of thing to teach a man he's growing old."

Perhaps Hugh wouldn't recognize Hampstead after fifteen years, John thought, gleefully; he might even pass his nearest relations in the street without a salute when like a Rip van Winkle of the tropics he returned to his native country after fifteen years.

"I suppose the usual outfit for hot climates will be necessary?"

Mr. Ricketts nodded; and John began to envisage himself equipping Hugh from the Army and Navy Stores.

"I always think there is something extraordinarily romantic about a tropical outfit," he ventured.

"It's extraordinarily expensive," said Mr. Ricketts. "But everything's going up. And mahogany's going up when I get back to B.H., or my name isn't Sydney Ricketts."

"There's nothing you particularly recommend?"

"No, they'll tell you everything you want at the Stores and a bit over, except—oh, yes, by the way, don't let him forget his shaker."

"Is that some special kind of porous overcoat?"

Mr. Ricketts laughed delightedly.

"Well, if that isn't the best thing I've heard since I was home. Porous overcoat! No, no, a shaker is for mixing drinks."

"Humph!" John grunted. "From what I know of my brother, he won't require any special instrument for doing that. Good-by, Mr. Ricketts; my solicitor will write to you about the business side. Good-by."

When John went back to his work he was humming.

"Satisfactory?" his secretary inquired.

"Extremely satisfactory. I think Hugh is very lucky. Ricketts assures me that in another fifteen years—that is about the time Hugh will be wanting to visit England again—there is no reason why he shouldn't be making at least £500 a year. Besides, he won't be lonely, because I shall send Harold out to British Honduras in another five years. It must be a fascinating place if you're fond of natural history, B.H.—as the denizens apparently call it among themselves," he added, pensively.

It could not be claimed that Hugh was enraptured by the prospect of leaving England in February, and John who was really looking forward to the job of getting together his outfit was disappointed by his brother's lack of enthusiasm. He simply could not understand anybody's failure to be thrilled by snake-proof blankets and fever-proof filters, by medicine-chests and pith helmets and double-fly tents and all the paraphernalia of adventure in foreign parts. Finally he delivered an ultimatum to Hugh, which was accepted albeit with ill grace, and hardening his heart against the crossed letters of protest that arrived daily from his mother and burying himself in an Army and Navy Stores' catalogue, he was able to intrench himself in the opinion that he was doing the best that could be done for the scapegrace. The worst of putting Hugh on his feet again was the resentment such a brotherly action aroused among his other relations. After the quarrel with James he had hardly expected to hear from him for a long time; but no sooner had the news about British Honduras gone the round of the family than his eldest brother wrote to ask him for a loan of £1000 to invest in a projected critical weekly of which he was to be the editor. James added that John could hardly grudge him as much as that for log-rolling at home when he was prepared to spend double that amount on Hugh to roll logs abroad.

"I can't say I feel inclined to help James after that article about my work," John observed to Miss Hamilton. "Besides, I hate critical weeklies."

It happened that the post next morning brought a large check from his agent for royalties on various dramas that in various theaters all over the world were playing to big business; confronted by that bright-hued token of prosperity he could not bring himself to sit down and pen a flat refusal to his brother's demand. Instead of doing that he merely delayed for a few hours the birth of a new critical weekly by making an appointment to talk the matter over, and it was only a fleeting pleasure that he obtained from adding a postscript begging James not to bring his dog with him when he called at Church Row.

"For if that wretched animal goes snorting round the room all the time we're talking," he assured his secretary, "I shall agree to anything in order to get rid of it. I shall find all my available capital invested in critical weeklies just to save the carpet from being eaten."

James seemed to have entirely forgotten that his brother had any reason to feel sore with him; he also seemed entirely unconscious of there being the least likelihood of his refusing to finance the new venture. John remembering how angry James had been when on a former occasion he had reminded him that Hugh's career was still before him, was careful to avoid the least suggestion of throwing cold water upon the scheme. Therefore in the circumstances James' unusual optimism, which lent his sallow cheeks some of the playwright's roses, was not surprising, and before the conversation had lasted many minutes John had half promised a thousand pounds. Having done this, he did try to retrieve the situation by advising James to invest it in railway-stock and argued strongly against the necessity of another journal.

"What are you going to call this further unnecessary burden upon our powers of assimilation?"

"*I* thought *The New Broom* would be a good title."

"Yes, I was positive you'd call it The New-Something-or-other. Why not The New Way to pay Old Scores? I'll back you to do that, even if you can't pay your old debts. However, listen to me. I'll lend the money to you personally. But I will not invest it in the paper. For security—or perhaps compensation would be a better word—you shall hand over to me the family portraits and the family silver."

"I'd rather it was a business proposition," James objected.

"My dear fellow, a new critical weekly can never be a business proposition. How many people read your books?"

"About a dozen," James calculated.

"Well, why should more people read your paper? No, you can have the money, but it must be regarded as a personal loan, and I must have the portraits and the silver."

"I don't see why you should have them."

"I don't see why you should start a new critical weekly."

John could not help enjoying the power that his brother's ambition had put in his hands and he insisted firmly upon the surrender of the heritage.

"All right, Jacob, I suppose I must sell my birthright for a mess of pottage."

"A printer's pie would describe it better," said John.

"Though why you want a few bad pictures and a dozen or so forks and spoons, I can't conceive."

"Why do you want them?" John countered.

"Because they're mine."

"And the money is mine."

James went away with a check for a thousand pounds in his pocket; but he went away less cheerful than he arrived. John, on the other hand, was much impressed by the manner in which he had dealt with his eldest brother; it was worth while losing a thousand pounds to have been able to demonstrate clearly to James once for all that his taste in literature was at the mercy of the romanticism he so utterly despised. And while he felt that he had displayed a nice dignity in forcing James to surrender the portraits and the silver, he was also pleasantly aware of an equally nice magnanimity in being willing to overlook that insulting article. But Miss Hamilton was at his elbow to correct the slightest tendency to be too well pleased with himself.

"After all I couldn't disappoint poor old James," he said, fishing for an encomium and dangling his own good heart as the bait. His secretary, however, ignored the tempting morsel and swam away into the deeps of romantic drama where his munificence seemed less showy somehow.

"You know best what you *want* to do," she said, curtly. "And now, have you decided upon this soliloquy for Joan in her dungeon?"

"What do you feel about it?"

She held forth upon the advantages of a quiet front scene before the trial, and the author took her advice. He wished that she were as willing to discant upon his treatment of James, but he consoled himself for her lack of interest by supposing that she was diffident about giving the least color to any suggestion that she might be influencing him to her own advantage.

Hugh came up to town in order to go more fully into the question of his future, and John regarding Miss Hamilton's attitude towards him tried to feel perfectly sure that she was going out of her way to be pleasant to Hugh solely with an idea of accentuating the strictly professional side of her association with himself. If this were not the case, he should be justified in thinking that she did really like Hugh very much, which would be an uncomfortable state of affairs. Still, explain it away as he might, John did feel a little uneasy, and once when he heard of a visit to the theater preceded by dinner he was upon the verge of pointing out to Hugh that until he was definitely established in mahogany and logwood he must be extremely careful about raising false hopes. He managed to refrain from approaching Hugh on the subject, because he knew that if he betrayed the least anxiety in that direction Hugh was capable of making it a matter of public jest. He decided instead to sound Miss Hamilton upon her views.

"You've never had any longing for the tropics?" he asked, as casually as he was able.

"Not particularly, though of course I should enjoy any fresh experience."

"I was noticing the other day that you seemed to dislike spiders; and, of course, the spiders in hot countries are terrible. I remember reading of some that snare birds, and I'm not sure that in parts of South America they don't even attack human beings. Many people of course do not mind them. For instance, my brother-in-law Daniel Curtis wrote a very moving account of a spider as large as a bat, with whom he fraternized on the banks of the Orinoco. It's quite a little classic in its way."

John noted with the warmest satisfaction that Miss Hamilton shuddered.

"Your poor brother," she murmured.

"Oh, he'll be all right," said John, hurriedly. "I'm equipping him with every kind of protection against insects. Only yesterday I discovered a most ingenious box which is guaranteed to keep one's tobacco from being devoured by cockroaches, and I thought Hugh looked very well in his pith helmet, didn't you?"

"I'm afraid I really didn't notice," Miss Hamilton replied, indifferently.

Soon after this conversation James' birthright was formally surrendered and John gave up contemplating himself upon a peak in Darien in order to contemplate himself as the head of an ancient and distinguished family. While the portraits were being hung in the library he discoursed upon the romance of lineage so volubly that he had a sudden dread of Miss Hamilton taking him for a snob, which he tried to counteract by putting into the mouth of Joan of Arc sentiments of the purest demophilism.

"I shall aim at getting all the material for the play complete by April 1st—my birthday, by the way. Yes, I shall be forty-three. And then I thought we might go into retreat and aim at finishing entirely by the end of June. That would enable Miss Bond to produce in September without hurrying the rehearsals. *Lucretia* will be produced over here in April. I think it would be rather jolly to finish off the play in France. Domrèmy, Bourges, Chinon, Orleans, Compiègne, Rouen—a delightful tour. You could have an aluminum typewriter...."

John's dreams of literature and life in France were interrupted by Mrs. Worfolk, who entered the room with a mystery upon her lips.

"There's the Reverend Armitage waiting to see you in the hall, sir. But he was looking so queer that I was in two minds if I ought to admit him or not. It was Elsa who happened to open the door. Well, I mean to say, Maud's upstairs doing her rooms, and Elsa was a bit frightened when she saw him, through her being engaged to a policeman and so her mind running on murders and such like. Of course as soon as I saw it was the Reverend Armitage I quieted her down. But he really does look most peculiar, if you'll pardon the obsivation on Mrs. Armitage's husband. I don't think he's actually barmy *yet*; but you know, he gives any one the idea he will be soon, and I thought you ought to be told before he started to rave up and down the house. He's got a funny look in his eye, the same as what a man once had who sat opposite me in a bus and five minutes afterwards jumped off on Hammersmith Bridge and threw himself into the river. Quite a sensation it created, I remember, and we all had to alight, so as the conductor could give what information he had to a policeman who'd only heard the splash."

Mrs. Worfolk had been too garrulous; before she had time to ascertain her master's views on the subject of admitting Laurence there was a tap at the door, and Laurence himself stalked into the room. Unquestionably, even to one who had not known him as a clergyman, he did present an odd appearance with his fur-lined cloak of voluminous black, his long hair, his bundle of manuscript and theatrical newspapers, and his tragic eye; the only article of attire that had survived his loss of faith was the clergyman's hat; but even that had lost its former meekness and now gave the effect of a farouche sombrero.

"Well met," he intoned, advancing solemnly into the room and gripping his brother-in-law's hand with dramatic effect. "I would converse with you, John."

"That's a blank verse line," said John. There really was not much else that he could have said to such an affected greeting.

"Probably, probably," Laurence muttered, shaking his head. "It's difficult for me to talk in prose nowadays. But I have news for you, John, good news. *Thomas* is finished."

"You needn't wait, Mrs. Worfolk," said John.

His housekeeper was standing by the door with a face wreathed in notes of interrogation and seemed unwilling to retire.

"You needn't wait, Mrs. Worfolk," he repeated, irritably.

"I thought you might have been wanting somebody fetched, sir."

John made an impatient gesture and Mrs. Worfolk vanished.

"You know Miss Hamilton, Laurence," said John, severely.

"Ah, Miss Hamilton! Forgive my abstraction. How d'ye do? But—ah—I was anxious to have a few words in private."

"Miss Hamilton is my confidential secretary."

"I bow to your domestic arrangements," said Laurence. "But—ah—my business is of an extremely private nature. It bears in fact directly upon my future."

John was determined to keep his secretary in the room. He had a feeling that money was going to be asked for, and he hoped that her presence would encourage him to hold out against agreeing to lend it.

"If you have anything to say to me, Laurence, you must say it in front of my secretary. I cannot be continually shooing her from the room like a troublesome cat."

The ex-vicar looked awkward for a moment; but his natural conceit reasserted itself and flinging back his cloak he laid upon the table a manuscript.

"Fresh from Miss Quirk's typewriting office here is *Thomas*," he announced. "And now, my dear fellow, I require a little good advice." There was flowing into his voice the professional unction of the clergyman with a north transept to restore. "Who was it that first said 'Charity begins at home'? Yes, a little good advice about my play. In deference to the Lord Chamberlain while reserving to my conscience the right to execrate his despotism I have expunged from my scenes the *central* figures of the gospel story, and I venture to think that there is now no reason why *Thomas* should not be—ah—produced."

"I'm afraid I can't invite you to read it to me just at present, Laurence," said John, hurriedly. "No, not just at present, I'm afraid. When I'm working myself I'm always chary of being exposed to outside influences. *You* wouldn't like and *I* shouldn't like to find in *Joan of Arc* echoes of *Thomas*. Miss Hamilton, however, who is thoroughly conversant with my point of view, would perhaps...."

"I confess," Laurence interrupted, loftily, "that I do not set much store by its being read. No, no. You will acquit me of undue self-esteem, my dear fellow, if I say at once in all modesty that I am satisfied with my labors, though you may be a little alarmed when I confide in you my opinion that it is probably a classic. Still, such is my deliberate conviction. Moreover, I have already allowed our little party at Ambles to hear it. Yes, we spent a memorable evening before the manuscript was dispatched to Miss Quirk. Some of the scenes, indeed, proved almost too dramatic. Edith was quite exhausted by her emotion and scarcely slept all night. As for Hilda, I've never seen her so overcome by anything. She couldn't say anything when I finished. No, no, I sha'n't read it to you. In fact, to be—ah—blunt, I could scarcely endure the strain a second time. No, what I want you to do, my dear fellow, is to—ah—back it. The phrase is Hugh's. We have all been thrilled down at Ambles by rumors of your generosity, and I know you'll be glad of another medium for exercising it. Am I unduly proud of my work if I say that it seems to me a more worthy medium than British Honduras or weekly papers?"

John had been gazing at Miss Hamilton with a mute appeal to save him while his brother-in-law was talking; she, however, bending lower every moment to hide her mirth made no attempt to show him a way of escape and John had to rely upon his own efforts.

"Wouldn't it be better," he suggested, mildly, "to submit your play to a manager before we—before you try to put it on yourself? I have never invested any money in my own plays, and really I...."

"My dear John, far be it from me to appear to cast the least slur—to speak in the faintest way at all slightingly of your plays, but I do not quite see the point of the comparison. Your plays—excellent as they are, most excellent—are essentially commercial transactions. My play is not a commercial transaction."

"Then why should I be invited to lose my money over it?"

Laurence smiled compassionately.

"I thought you would be glad of the opportunity to show a disinterested appreciation of art. In years to come you will be proud to think that you were one of the first to give practical evidence of your belief in *Thomas*."

"But perhaps I'm just as skeptical as your hero was. I may not believe in your play's immortality."

Laurence frowned.

"Come, my dear fellow, this is being petty. We are all counting on you. You wouldn't like to hear it said that out of jealousy you had tried to suppress a rival dramatist. But I must not let my indignation run away with me, and you must forgive my heat. I am overstrained. The magnitude of the subject has almost been too much for me. Besides, I should have explained at once that I intended to invest in *Thomas* all that is left of my own little capital. Yes, I am even ready to do that. Then I shall spend a year as an actor, after which I shall indulge my more worldly self by writing a few frankly commercial plays before I begin my next great tragedy entitled *Paul*."

John decided that his brother-in-law had gone mad; unable to think of any action more effective at such a crisis, he rang the bell. But when Maud came to inquire his need he could not devise anything to tell her except that Mr. Armitage was staying to lunch.

It was a most uncomfortable meal, because Miss Hamilton in order to keep herself from laughing aloud had to be preternaturally grave, and John himself was in a continuous state of nervous irritation at Laurence, who would let everything on his plate grow cold while he droned on without a pause about the simplicity of the best art. It was more than tantalizing to watch him gradually build up a mouthful upon his fork, still talking; slowly raise it to his lips, still talking; and wave the overloaded fork to and fro before him, still talking. But it was an agony to watch the carefully accumulated mouthful drop back bit by bit upon his plate, until at last very slowly and still talking he would insert one cold and tiny morsel into his patient mouth, so tiny a morsel that the mastication of it did not prevent him from still talking.

"I'm afraid you're not enjoying your lunch," his host said.

"Don't wait for me, my dear fellow; when I am interested in something else I cannot gobble my food. Though in any case," he added in a resigned voice, "I shall have indigestion. One cannot write plays like *Thomas* without exposing oneself to the ills that flesh is heir to."

After lunch, much to John's relief, his brother-in-law announced that he had an appointment with Eleanor and would therefore be unable to stay even long enough to smoke a cigar.

"Yes," he said. "Eleanor and I are going to interview one or two of her theatrical friends. No doubt I shall soon be able to proclaim myself a rogue and a vagabond. Yes, yes, poor Edith was quite distressed this morning when I told her that jestingly. However, she will be happy to hear to-night when I get back that her brother has been so large."

"Eh?"

"Not that Edith expected him to be otherwise. No, no, my dear fellow, Edith has a most exalted opinion of you, which indeed I share, if I may be permitted so to do. Good-by, John, and many thanks. Who knows? Our little lunch may become a red-letter day in the calendar of English dramatic art. Let me see, the tube-station is on the left as I go out? Good-by, John; I wish I could stay the night with you, but I have a cheap day-ticket which forbids any extension of my plans."

When John got back to the library he turned in bewilderment to his secretary.

"Look here. I surely never gave him the least idea that I was going to back his confounded play, did I?"

"On the contrary, you made it perfectly clear that you were not."

"I'm glad to hear you say so, because he has gone away from here apparently under the delusion that I am. He'll brag about it to Eleanor this afternoon, and before I know where I am she will be asking me to set George up with a racing-stable."

Eleanor did not go as far as that, but she did write to John and point out that the present seemed a suitable moment to deal with the question of George's health by sending him on a voyage round the world. She added that for herself she asked nothing; but John had an uneasy impression that it was only in the belief that he who asks not to him shall it be given.

"Take down two letters, please, Miss Hamilton," he said, grimly.

DEAR LAURENCE,—I am afraid that you went away yesterday afternoon under a misapprehension. I do *not* see my way to offer any financial contribution toward the production of your play. I myself passed a long apprenticeship before I was able to get one of my plays acted, and I do not think that you can expect to do otherwise. Do not imagine that I am casting any doubts upon the excellence of *Thomas*. If it is as good as you claim, you will have your reward without any help from me. Your idea of getting acquainted with the practical side of the stage is a good one. If you are not already engaged in the autumn, I think I can offer you one of the minor bishops in *Joan of Arc*.

Your affectionate brother-in-law,
JOHN TOUCHWOOD.

DEAR ELEANOR,—I must say decidedly that I do not perceive any likelihood of George's health deriving much benefit from a voyage round the world. If he is threatened with sleeping sickness, it would be rash to expose him to a tropical climate. If he is suffering from a sluggish liver, he will get no benefit from lolling about in smoking-saloons, whatever the latitude and longitude. I have repeatedly helped George with his schemes to earn a living for himself and he has never failed to squander my money upon capricious race-horses. You know that I am always willing to come forward on behalf of Bertram and Viola; but their father must show signs of helping himself before I do anything more for him. I am sorry that I cannot offer you a good part in *Joan of Arc*; there is really nothing to suit you for I presume you would not care to accept the part of Joan's mother. However, it has now been decided to produce *Lucretia* in April and I shall do my best to persuade Grohmann to offer you a part in that.

Your affectionate brother-in-law,
JOHN TOUCHWOOD.

John did not receive an answer to either of these letters, and out of an atmosphere of pained silence he managed to conjure optimistically an idea that Laurence and Eleanor had realized the justice of his point of view.

"You do agree with me that they were going too far?" he asked Miss Hamilton; but she declined to express an opinion.

"What's the good of having a confidential secretary, if I can't ask her advice about confidential matters?" he grumbled.

"Are you dissatisfied with me?"

"No, no, no. I'm not dissatisfied. What an exaggeration of my remark! I'm simply a little puzzled by your attitude. It seems to me—I may be wrong—that instead of ... well, at first you were always perfectly ready to talk about my relations and about me, whereas now you won't talk about anything except Joan of Arc. I'm really getting quite bored with Joan of Arc."

"I was only an amateur when I began," she laughed. "Now I'm beginning to be professional."

"I think it's a great mistake," said John, decidedly. "Suppose I insist upon having your advice?"

"You'd find that dictation bears two meanings in English, to only one of which are you entitled under the terms of our contract."

"Look here, have I done anything to offend you?" he asked, pathetically.

But she would not be moved and held her pencil so conspicuously ready that the author was impaled upon it before he could escape and was soon hard at work dictating his first arrangement of the final scene in a kind of indignant absent-mindedness.

Soon after this John received a note from Sir Percy Mortimer, asking if he could spare time to visit the great actor-manager some evening in the course of the current week. Between nine-thirty and ten was indicated as a suitable time, inasmuch as Sir Percy would then be in his dressing-room gathering the necessary momentum to knock down all the emotional fabric carefully built up in the first two acts by the most cunning of contemporary dramatists. Sir Percy Mortimer, whose name was once Albert Snell, could command anybody, so it ought not to have been remarkable that John rather flustered by the invitation made haste to obey. Yet, he must have been aware of an implied criticism in Miss Hamilton's smile, which flashed across her still deep eyes like a sunny wind, for he murmured, apologetically:

"We poor writers of plays must always wait upon our masters."

He tried to convey that Sir Percy was only a mortal like himself, but he failed somehow to eliminate the deep-rooted respect, almost it might be called awe of the actor that was perceptible under the assumed carelessness of the author.

"You see, it may be that he is anxious to hear some of my plans for the near future," he added.

If Sir Percy Mortimer was impressive in the smoking-room of the Garrick Club as himself, he was dumbfounding in his dressing-room as Lord Claridge, the ambassador, about to enter Princess Thingumabobski's salon and with diplomatic wiles and smiles to settle the future of several couples, incidentally secure for himself the heart and hand of a young heiress. His evening-dress had achieved an immaculation that even Ouida never dreamed of; he wore the Grand Cross of the Victorian Order with as easy an assurance as his father had worn the insignia of a local friendly society in Birmingham; he was the quintessential diplomat of girlish dreams, and it was not surprising that women were ready to remove even their hats to see him perform at matinees.

"Ah, it's very good of you to look me up, my dear fellow. I have just a quarter-of-an-hour. Godfrey!" He turned to address his valet, who might have been a cardinal driven by an ecclesiastical crisis like the spread of Modernism into attendance upon an actor.

"Sir Percy?"

"I do not wish to be disturbed until I am called for the third act."

"Very good, Sir Percy."

"And Godfrey!"

"Sir Percy?"

"The whisky and soda for Mr. Touchwood. Oh, and Godfrey!"

"Sir Percy?"

"If the Duke of Shropshire comes behind, tell His Grace that I am unavoidably prevented from seeing him until after the third act. I will *not* be interrupted."

"No, Sir Percy. I quite understand, Sir Percy."

The valet set the decanter at John's elbow and vanished like the ghost of a king.

"It's just this, my dear fellow," the actor-manager began, when John who had been trying to decide whether he should suggest Peter the Great or Augustus the Strong as the next part for his host was inclining towards Augustus. "It's just this. I believe that Miss Cartright, a former member of my company, is *also* a relation of yours."

"She is my sister-in-law," admitted John, swallowing both Peter and Augustus in a disappointed gulp.

"In fact, I believe that in private life she is Mrs. George Touchwood. Correct me if I am wrong in my names."

Sir Percy waited, but John did not avail himself of the offer, and he went on.

"Well, my dear fellow, she has approached me upon a matter which I confess I have found somewhat embarrassing, referring as it does to another man's private affairs; but as one of the—as—how shall I describe myself?—" He fingered the ribbon of the Victorian Order for inspiration. "As an actor-manager of some standing, I felt that you would prefer me to hear what she had to say in order that I might thereby adjudicate—yes, I think that is the word—without any—no, forgive me—

445

adjudicate is *not* the word. Adjudicate is too strong. What is the word for outsiders of standing who are called in to assist at the settlement of a trade dispute? Whatever the word is, that is the word I want. I understand from Miss Cartright—Mrs. George Touchwood in private life—that her husband is in a very grave state of health and entirely without means." Sir Percy looked at himself in the glass and dabbed his face with the powder-puff. "Miss Cartright asked me to use my influence with you to take some steps to mitigate this unpleasant situation upon which, it appears, people are beginning to comment rather unfavorably. Now, you and I, my dear fellow, are members of the same club. You and I have high positions in our respective professions. Is it wise? There may of course be a thousand reasons for leaving your brother to starve with an incurable disease. But is it wise? As a man of the world, I think not." He touched his cheeks with the hare's-foot and gave them a richer bloom. "Don't allow me to make any suggestion that even borders upon the impertinent, but if you care to accept my mediation—*that* is the word I couldn't remember." In his enthusiasm Sir Percy smacked his leg, which caused him a momentary anxiety for the perfection of his trousers. "Mediation! Of course, that's it—if you care, as I say, to accept my mediation I am willing to mediate."

John stared at the actor-manager in angry amazement. Then he let himself go:

"My brother is not starving—he eats more than any human being I know. Nor is he suffering from anything incurable except laziness. I do not wish to discuss with you or anybody else the affairs of my relations, which I regret to say are in most cases only too much my own affairs."

"Then there is nothing for me to do," Sir Percy sighed, deriving what consolation he could from being unable to find a single detail of his dress that could be improved.

"Nothing whatever," John agreed, emphatically.

"But what shall I say to Miss Cartright, who you *must* remember is a former member of my company, as well as your sister-in-law?"

"I leave that to you."

"It's very awkward," Sir Percy murmured. "I thought you would be sure to see that it is always better to settle these unpleasant matters—out of court, if I may use the expression. I'm so afraid that Miss Cartright will air her grievance."

"She can wash as much dirty linen as she likes and air it every day in your theater," said John, fiercely. "But my brother George shall *not* go on a voyage round the world. You've nothing else to ask me? Nothing about my plans for the near future?"

"No, no. I've a success, as you know, and I don't expect I shall want another play for months. You've seen my performance, of course?"

"No," said John, curtly, "I've not."

And when he left the actor-manager's dressing-room he knew that he had wounded him more deeply by that simple negative than by all the mighty insults imaginable.

However, notwithstanding his successful revenge John left the theater in a rage and went off to his club with the hope of finding a sympathetic listener into whose ears he could pour the tale of Sir Percy's megalomania; but by ill luck there was nobody suitable in the smoking-room that night. To be sure, Sir Philip Cranbourne was snoring in an armchair, and Sir Philip Cranbourne was perhaps a bigger man in the profession than Sir Percy Mortimer. Yet, he was not so much bigger but that he would have welcomed a tale against the younger theatrical knight whose promotion to equal rank with himself he had resented very much. Sir Philip, however, was fast asleep, and John doubted if he hated Sir Percy sufficiently to welcome being woken up to hear a story against him—particularly a story by a playwright, one of that miserable class for which Sir Philip as an actor had naturally a very profound contempt. Moreover, thinking the matter over, John came to the conclusion that the story, while it would tell against Sir Percy would also tell against himself, and he decided to say nothing about it. When he was leaving the club he ran into Mr. Winnington-Carr, who greeted him airily.

"Evening, Touchwood!"

"Good evening."

"What's this I hear about Hugh going to Sierra Leone? Bit tough, isn't it, sending him over to a plague spot like that? You saw that paragraph in *The Penguin*? Things we should like to know, don't you know? Why John Touchwood's brother is taking up a post in the tropics and whether John himself is really sorry to see him go."

"No, I did not see that paragraph," said John, icily.

Next morning a bundle of press-cuttings arrived.

"There is nothing here but stupid gossip," said John to his secretary, flinging the packet into the fire. "Nothing that is worth preserving in the album, I mean to say."

Miss Hamilton smiled to herself.

CHAPTER XIV

THE buzz of gossip, the sting of scandalous paragraph, even the blundering impertinence of the actor-knight were all forgotten the following afternoon when a telegram arrived from Hampshire to say that old Mrs. Touchwood was dying. John left London immediately; but when he reached Ambles he found that his mother was already dead.

"She passed away at five o'clock," Edith sobbed.

Perhaps it was to stop his wife's crying that Laurence abandoned at any rate temporarily his unbelief and proclaimed as solemnly as if he were still Vicar of Newton Candover that the old lady was waiting for them all above. Hilda seemed chiefly worried by the fact that she had never warned James of their mother's grave condition.

"I did telegraph Eleanor, who hasn't come; and how I came to overlook James and Beatrice I can't think. They'll be so hurt. But Mama didn't fret for anybody in particular. No, Hugh sat beside the bed and held her hand, which seemed to give her a little pleasure, and I was kept occupied with changing the hot-water bottles."

In the dining-room George was knitting lugubriously.

"You mustn't worry yourself, old chap," he said to John with his usual partiality for seductive advice. "You can't do anything now. None of us can do anything till the funeral, though I've written to Eleanor to bring my top-hat with her when she comes."

The embarrassment of death's presence hung heavily over the household. The various members sat down to supper with apologetic glances at one another, and nobody took a second helping of any dish. The children were only corrected in whispers for their manners, but they were given to understand by reproachful head-shakes that for a child to put his elbows on the table or crumble his bread or drink with his mouth full was at such a time a cruel exhibition of levity. John could not help contrasting the treatment of children at a death with their treatment at a birth. Had a baby arrived upstairs, they would have been hustled out of sight and sound of the unclean event; but over death they were expected to gloat, and their curiosity was encouraged as the fit expression of filial piety.

"Yes, Frida, darling, dear Grandmama will have lots and lots of lovely white flowers. Don't kick the table, sweetheart. Think of dear Grandmama looking down at you from Heaven, and don't kick the table-leg, my precious," said Edith in tremulous accents, gently smoothing back her daughter's indefinite hair.

"Can people only see from Heaven or can they hear?" asked Harold.

"Hush, my boy," his Uncle Laurence interposed. "These are mysteries into which God does not permit us to inquire too deeply. Let it suffice that our lightest actions are known. We cannot escape the omniscient eye."

"I wasn't speaking about God," Harold objected. "I was asking about Grandmama. Does she hear Frida kicking the table, or does she only see her?"

"At this solemn moment, Harold, when we should all of us be dumb with grief, you should not persist. Your poor grandmother would be pained to hear you being persistent like this."

Harold seemed to think he had tricked his uncle into answering the question, for he relapsed into a satisfied silence; Edith's eyes flashed gladly through her tears to welcome the return of her husband's truant orthodoxy. All managed to abstain while they were eating from any more conspicuous intrusion of the flesh than was inevitable; but there was a painful scene after supper, because Frida insisted that she was frightened to sleep alone, and refused to be comforted by the offer of Viola for company. The terrible increase of Grandmama's powers of hearing and seeing might extend to new powers of locomotion in the middle of the night, in which case Viola would be no protection.

"But Grandmama is in Heaven, darling," her mother urged.

"I want to sleep with you. I'm frightened. I want to sleep with you," she wailed.

"Laurence!" murmured Edith, appealingly.

"Death is a great leveler," he intoned. Grateful to the chance of being able to make this observation, he agreed to occupy his daughter's room and thereby allow her to sleep with her mother.

"You're looking sad, Bertram," John observed, kindly, to his favorite nephew. "You mustn't take this too much to heart."

"No, Uncle John, I'm not. Only I keep wishing Grandmama had lived a little longer."

"We all wish that, old man."

"Yes, but I only meant a very little longer, so that I needn't have gone back for the first week of term."

John nervously hurried his nephew up to bed beyond the scorching of Laurence's rekindled flames of belief. Downstairs, he tried to extract from the attitude of the grown-up members of the family the attitude he would have liked to detect in himself. If a few months ago John had been told that his mother's death would affect him so little he would have been horrified by the suggestion; even now he was seriously shocked at himself. Yet, try as he might, he could not achieve the apotheosis of the old lady that he would have been so content to achieve. Undoubtedly a few months ago he would have been able without being conscious of self-deception to pretend that he believed not only in the reality of his own grief, but also in that of the others. He would have taken his part in the utterance of platitudes about life and death, separation and reunion. His own platitudes would have been disguised with poetic tropes, and he might have thought to himself how well such and such a phrase was put; but he would quickly have assured himself that it was well put because it was the just expression of a deep emotion. Now he could not make a single contribution to the woeful reflections of those round him. He believed neither in himself nor in them. He knew that George was faintly anxious about his top-hat, that Hilda was agitated at the prospect of having to explain to James and Beatrice her unintentional slight, that Laurence was unable to resist the opportunity of taking the lead at this sorrowful time by reverting to his priestly office. And Hugh, for whom the old lady had always possessed a fond unreasoning affection, did his countenance express more than a hardly concealed relief that it was all over? Did he not give the impression that he was stretching his legs after sitting still in one position for too long? Edith, to be sure, was feeling some kind of emotion that required an endless flow of tears, but it seemed to John that she was weeping more for the coming of death than for the going of her mother. And the children, how could they be expected to feel the loss of the old lady? There under the lamp like a cenotaph recording the slow hours of age stood her patience-cards in their red morocco case; there they would be allowed to stand for a while to satisfy the brief craving for reverence, and then one of the children realizing that Grandmama had no more need of playing would take possession of them; they would become grubby and dog-eared in younger hands; they would disappear one by one, and the memory of that placid presence would hardly outlive them.

"It's so nice to think that her little annuity died with her," sighed Edith. She spoke of the annuity as if it were a favorite pug that had died out of sympathy with its mistress. "I should hate to feel I was benefiting from the death of somebody I loved," she explained presently.

447

John shivered; that remark of his sister's was like a ghostly footstep upon his own grave, and from a few years hence, perhaps much less, he seemed to hear the family lawyer cough before he settled himself down to read the last will and testament of John Touchwood.

"Of course, poor Mama had been dreadfully worried these last weeks," Hilda said. "She felt very much the prospect of Hugh's going abroad—and other things."

John regarded his elder sister, and was on the point of asking what she meant to insinuate by other things, when a lament from upstairs startled the assembled family.

"Come to bed, mother, come to bed, I want you," Frida was shrieking over the balustrade. "The door of Grandmama's room made a noise just now."

"You had better go," said Laurence in answer to his wife's unvoiced appeal; and Edith went off gratefully.

"It will always be a consolation to me," said Laurence, "that Mama was able to hear *Thomas* read to her. Yes, yes, she was so well upon that memorable evening. So very well. By the way, John, I shall arrange with the Vicar to read the burial service myself. It will add the last touch to the intimacy of our common grief."

In his own room that night John tried hard not to criticize anybody except himself. It was he who was cynical, he who was hard, he who was unnatural, not they. He tried to evoke from the past early memories of his mother, but he could not recall one that might bring a tear to his eye. He remembered that once she had smacked him for something George had done, that she had never realized what a success he had made of his life's work, that she was—but he tore the unfilial thoughts from his brain and reminded himself how much of her personality endured in his own. George, Edith, and himself resembled her: James, Hilda, and Hugh resembled their father. John's brothers and sisters haunted the darkness; and he knew that deep down in himself he blamed his father and mother for bringing them all into the world; he could not help feeling that he ought to have been an only child.

"I do resent their existence," John thought. "I'm a heartless egotist. And Miss Hamilton thinks I'm an egotist. Her manner towards me lately has been distant, even contemptuous. Could that suggestion of Hilda's have had any truth in it? Was Mama worried to death by Hugh's going abroad? Did James complain to her about my taking the portraits and the silver? Is it from any standpoint conceivable that my own behavior did hasten her end?"

John's self-reproaches were magnified in the darkness, and he spent a restless and unhappy night, trying to think that the family was more important than the individual.

"You feel it terribly, don't you, dear Johnnie?" Edith asked him next morning with an affectionate pressure upon his arm. "You're looking quite worn out."

"We all feel it terribly," he sighed.

During the three days before the funeral John managed to work himself up into a condition of sentimentality which he flattered himself was outwardly at any rate affecting. Continuous reminders of his mother's existence culminating in the arrival of a new cap she had ordered just before her last swift illness seemed to induce in him the illusion of sorrow; and without the least idea of what he intended to do with them afterwards he collected a quantity of small relics like spectacle-cases and caps and mittens, which he arranged upon his dressing-table and brooded over with brimming eyes. He indulged Harold's theories about the psychical state of his grandmother; he practiced swinging a golf club, but he never once took out a ball; he treated everybody to magnificent wreaths, and presented the servants as well as his nephews and nieces with mourning; he ordered black-edged note-paper; he composed an epitaph in the manner of Sir Thomas Browne with cadences and subtle alliterations. Then came the funeral, which ruined the last few romantic notions of grief that he had been able to preserve.

To begin with, Beatrice arrived in what could only be described as a towering rage: no less commonplace epithet would have done justice to the vulgarity of her indignation. That James the eldest son and she his wife should not have been notified of the dangerous condition of Mama, but should have been summoned to the obsequies like mere friends of the family had outraged her soul, or, as Beatrice herself put it, had knocked her down like a feather. Oh yes, she had always been considered beneath the Touchwood standard of gentility, but poor Mama had not thought the worse of her for that; poor Mama had many times gone out of her way to be specially gracious towards her; poor Mama must have "laid" there wondering why her eldest daughter-in-law did not come to give her the last and longest farewell. She had not been lucky enough to be blessed with children, but poor Mama had sometimes congratulated her upon that fact; poor Mama had realized only too well that children were not always a source of happiness. She knew that the undeserved poverty which had always dogged poor old Jimmie's footsteps had lately caused to be exacted from him the family portraits and the family silver pressed upon him by poor Mama herself; but was that a reason for excluding him from his mother's death-bed? She would not say whom she blamed, but she had her own ideas, and though Hilda might protest it was her fault, she knew better; Hilda was incapable of such barbarity. No, she would *not* walk beside James as wife of the chief mourner; she would follow in the rear of the funeral procession and hope that at any rate she was not grudged that humble place. If some people resented her having bought the largest wreath from a very expensive flower-shop, she was not too proud to carry the wreath herself; she had carried it all the way from town first-class to avoid its being crushed by heedless third-class passengers.

"And when I die," sobbed Beatrice, "I hope that James will remember we weren't allowed to see poor Mama before she went to Heaven, and will let me die quite alone. I'm sure I don't want my death to interfere with other people's amusements."

The funeral party gathered round the open grave; Laurence read the service so slowly and the wind was so raw that grief was depicted upon every countenance; the sniffing of many noses, above which rose Beatrice's sobs of mortification and rage, mingled with the sighing of the yews and the sexton's asthma in a suitably lachrymose symphony.

"Now that poor Mama has gone," said Hilda to her brother that afternoon, "I dare say you're anxious for me to be gone too."

448

"I really don't think you are entitled to ascribe to me such unnatural sentiments," John expostulated. "Why should I want you to die?"

He could indeed ask this, for such an event would inevitably connote his adoption of Harold.

"I didn't mean you wanted me to die," said Hilda, crossly. "I meant you would like me to leave Ambles."

"Not at all. I'm delighted for you to stay here so long as it suits your convenience. And that applies equally to Edith. Also I may say to George," he added with a glance at Eleanor, who had taken the opportunity of mourning to equip herself with a new set of black bearskin furs. Eleanor shook herself like a large animal emerging from the stream.

"And to me?" she asked with a challenge in her eyes.

"You must judge for yourself, Eleanor, how far my hospitality is likely to be extended willingly to you after last week," replied John, coldly. He had not yet spoken to his sister-in-law about the interference of Sir Percy Mortimer with his private affairs, and he now awaited her excuses of reproaches with a curiosity that was very faintly tinged with apprehension.

"Oh, I'm not at all ashamed of what I did," she declared. "George can't speak up for himself, and it was my duty to do all I could to help him in a matter of life and death."

John's cheeks flushed with stormy rose like a menacing down, and he was about to break over his sister-in-law in thunder and lightning when Laurence, entering the room at the moment and only hearing imperfectly her last speech, nodded and sighed:

"Yes, yes. Eleanor is indeed right. Yes, yes. In the midst of life...."

Everybody hurried to take advantage of the diversion; a hum of platitudes rose and fell upon the funereal air. John in a convulsion of irritability ordered the dog-cart to drive him to the station. He was determined to travel back to town alone; he feared that if he stayed any longer at Ambles his brother-in-law would revive the discussion about his play; he was afraid of Hugh's taking advantage of his mother's death to dodge British Honduras and of James' trading upon his filial piety to recover the silver and the family portraits.

When John got back to Church Row he found a note from Miss Hamilton to say she had influenza and was unlikely to be back at work for at least a week—if indeed, she added, she was able to come back at all. This unpleasant prospect filled him with genuine gloom, and it was with great difficulty that he refrained from driving immediately to Camera Square in order to remonstrate with her in person. His despondency was not lightened by Mrs. Worfolk's graveside manner and her assumption of a black satin dress hung with jet bugles that was usually reserved to mark the more cheerful festivals of the calendar. Worn thus out of season hung it about the rooms like a fog, and its numerous rustlings coupled with the housekeeper's sighs of commiseration added to the lugubrious atmosphere a sensation of damp which gave the final touch to John's depression. Next morning the weather was really abominable; the view over London from his library window showed nothing but great cobwebs of rain that seemed to be actually attached to a sky as gray and solid as a dusty ceiling. Action offered the only hope of alleviating life upon such a day, and John made up his mind to drive over to Chelsea and inquire about his secretary's health. He found that she was better, though still in bed; being anxious to learn more about her threatened desertion he accepted the maid's invitation to come in and speak to Mrs. Hamilton. The old lady looked more like a clown than ever in the forenoon while the rice-powder was still fresh upon her cheeks, and John found her humor as irritating as he would have found the humor of a real clown in similar circumstances. Her manner towards him was that of a person who is aware of, but on certain terms is willing to overlook a grave indiscretion, and she managed most successfully to make him feel that he was on his defense.

"Yes, poor Doris has been very seedy. And her illness has unluckily coincided with mine."

"Oh, I'm sorry ..." he began.

"Thank you. I'm used to being ill. I am always ill. At least, as luck will have it, I usually feel ill when Doris has anything the matter with her."

This John was ready to believe, but he tried to look at once shocked and sympathetic.

"Do not let us discuss my health," Mrs. Hamilton went on scorching her eyebrows in the aureole of martyrdom she wore. "Of what importance is my health? Poor Doris has had a very sharp attack, a very sharp attack indeed."

"I'm afraid that the weather...."

"It's not the weather, Mr. Touchwood. It is overwork." And before John could say a word she was off. "You must remember that Doris is not used to hard work. She has spent all her life with me, and you can easily imagine that with a mother always at hand she has been spared the least hardship. I would have done anything for her. Ever since my husband died, my life has been one long buffer between Doris and the world. You know how obstinately she has refused to let me do all I wanted. I refer to my brother-in-law, Mr. Hamilton of Glencockie. And this is the result. Nervous prostration, influenza, a high temperature—and sharp pains, which between ourselves I'm inclined to think are perhaps not so bad as she imagines. People who are not accustomed to pains," said the old lady, jealously, "are always apt to be unduly alarmed and to attribute to them a severity that is a leetle exaggerated. I suffer so much myself that I cannot take these pains quite as seriously as Doris does. However, the poor child really has a good deal to put up with, and of course I've insisted that she must never attempt such hard work again. I don't suppose you meant to be inconsiderate, Mr. Touchwood. I don't accuse you of deliberate callousness. Please do not suppose that I am suggesting that the least cruelty in your behavior; but you *have* overworked her. Moreover, she has been worried. One or two of our friends have suggested more in joke than in earnest that she might be compromised by her association with you. No doubt this was said in joke, but Doris lacks her mother's sense of humor, and I'm afraid she has fretted over this. Still, a stitch in time saves nine, and her illness must serve as an excuse for what with a curiously youthful self-importance she calls 'leaving you in the lurch.' As I said to her, 'Do not, my dear child, worry about Mr. Touchwood. He can find as many secretaries as he wants. Probably he thought he was doing you a good turn, and you've overstrained yourself in trying to cope with duties to which you have not been accustomed. You cannot expect to fly before you can walk.'"

The old lady paused to fan back her breath, and John seized the conversation.

"Does Miss Hamilton herself wish to leave me like this, or is it only you who think that she ought to leave me?"

"I will be frank with you," the old lady panted. "Doris has not yet made up her mind."

"As long as she is allowed to make up her own mind," said John, "I have nothing to say. But I hope you are not going to overpersuade her. After all she is old enough to know what she wants to do."

"She is not as old as her mother."

He shook his head impatiently.

"Could I see her?"

"See her?" the old lady answered in amazement. "See her, Mr. Touchwood? Didn't I explain that she was in bed?"

"I beg your pardon. I'd forgotten."

"Men are apt to forget somewhat easily. Come, come, do not let us get bitter. I took a great fancy to you when I met you first, and though I have been a little disappointed by the way in which you have taken advantage of Doris's eagerness for new experiences I don't really bear you any deep grudge. I don't believe you meant to be selfish. It is only a mother who can pierce a daughter's motives. You with your recent loss should be able to appreciate that particularly now. Poor Doris! I wish she were more like me."

"If you really think I have overworked her," said John, "I'm extremely sorry. I dare say her enthusiasm carried me away. But I cannot relinquish her services without a struggle. She has been, and she *is* invaluable," he added, warmly.

"Yes, but we must think of her health. I'm sorry to seem so *intransigente*, but I am only thinking of her."

John was not at all taken in by the old lady's altruism, but he was entirely at a loss how to argue in favor of her daughter's continuing to work for him. His perplexity was increased by the fact that she herself had written to express her doubtfulness about returning; it might conceivably be that she did not want to return and that he was misjudging Mrs. Hamilton's sincerity. Yet when he looked at the old lady he could not discover anything but a cold egotism in every fold of those flabby cheeks where the powder lay like drifted snow in the ruts of a sunless lane. It was surely impossible that Doris should willingly have surrendered the liberty she enjoyed with him; she must have written under the depressing effects of influenza.

While John was pondering his line of action Mrs. Hamilton had fanned herself into a renewed volubility; finding that it was impossible to cross the torrent of words that she was now pouring forth, he sat down by the edge of it, confused and deafened, and sometimes gasping a faint protest when he was splashed by some particularly outrageous argument.

"Well, I'll write to her," he said at last.

"I beg you will do nothing of the kind. In the present feeble state of her health a letter will only agitate her. I hope to persuade her to come with me to Glencockie where her uncle will, I know, once more suggest adopting her as his heiress...."

The old lady flowed on with schemes for the future of Doris in which there was so much talk of Scotland that in the end his secretary appeared to John like an advertisement for whisky. He saw her rosy-cheeked and tam-o-shantered, smiling beneath a fir-tree while mockingly she quaffed a glass to the health of her late employer. He saw her as a kind of cross between Flora Macdonald and Highland Mary by the banks of Loch Lomond. He saw her in every guise except that in which he desired to see her—bending with that elusive and ironical smile over the typewriter they had purchased together. Damn!

John made hurried adieus and fled to his taxi from the little house in Camera Square. The interview with Mrs. Hamilton had cost him half-a-crown and his peace of mind: it had cost the driver one halfpenny for the early edition of the *Star*. How much happier was the life of a taxi-driver than the life of a playwright!

"I wouldn't say as how Benedictine mightn't win at Kempton this afternoon," the driver observed to John when he alighted. "I reckon I'll have half-a-dollar on, any old way. It's Bolmondeley's horse and bound to run straight."

Benedictine did win that afternoon at six to one: indubitably the life of a taxi-driver was superior to his own, John thought as he turned with a shudder from the virgin foolscap upon his writing-desk and with a late edition of the *Star* sank into a deep armchair.

"A bachelor's life is a very lonely one," he sighed. For some reason Maud had neglected to draw the curtains after tea, and the black yawning window where the rain glistened drearily weighed upon his heart with a sense of utter abandonment. Ordinarily he would have rung the bell and pointed reproachfully to the omission; but this afternoon, he felt incapable of stirring from his chair to ring a bell. He could not even muster enough energy to poke the fire, which would soon show as little life as himself. He listened vainly for the footsteps of Maud or Mrs. Worfolk that he might call out and be rescued from this lethargy of despair; but not a sound was audible except the dripping rain outside and the consumptive coughs of the moribund fire.

"Perhaps I'm feeling my mother's death," said John, hopefully.

He made an effort to concentrate his mind upon an affectionate retrospect of family life. He tried to convince himself that the death of his mother would involve a change in the attitude of his relations. Technically he might not be the eldest son, and while his mother had been alive he had never assumed too definitely the rights of an eldest son. Practically, however, that was his status, and his acquisition of the family portraits and family silver could well be taken as the visible sign of that status; with his mother's death he might surely consider himself in the eyes of the world the head of the family. Did he want such an honor? It would be an expensive, troublesome, and ungrateful post like the Lord-Lieutenancy of Ireland. Why didn't Maud come and draw those curtains? A thankless job, and it would be more congenial to have a family of his own. That meant marriage. And why shouldn't he get married? Several palmists had assured him he would be married one day: most of them indeed had assured him he was married already.

"If I get married I can no longer be expected to bother about my relations. Of course in that case I should give back the portraits and the silver. My son would be junior to Bertram. My son would occupy an altogether inconspicuous position in the family, though he would always take precedence of Harold. But if my son had a child, Harold would become an uncle. No, he wouldn't. Harold would be a first cousin once removed. Harold cannot become an uncle unless Hilda marries again and has another child who has another child. Luckily, it's all very improbable. I'm glad Harold is never likely to be an uncle: he would bring the relationship into an even greater disrepute. Still, even now an uncle is disreputable enough. The wicked uncle! It's proverbial, of course. We never hear of the wicked cousin or the nefarious aunt. No, uncles share with stepmothers the opprobrium and with mothers-in-law the ridicule of the mob. Unquestionably, if I do marry, I shall still be an uncle, but the status may perhaps be merged in paternity. Suppose I marry and never have any children? My wife will be pitied by Hilda, Edith, and Eleanor and condoled with by Beatrice. She would find her position intolerable. My wife? I wish to goodness Maud would come in and draw those curtains. My wife? That's the question. At this stage the problem of her personality is more important than theoretical speculation about future children. Should I enjoy a woman's bobbing in and out of my room all the time? Suppose I were married at this moment, it would be my wife's duty to correct Maud for not having drawn those curtains. If I were married at this moment I should say, 'My dear, Maud does not seem to have drawn the curtains. I wonder why.' And my wife would of course ring the bell and remonstrate with Maud. But suppose my wife were upstairs? She might be trying on a new hat. Apparently wives spend a great deal of time with hats. In that case I should be no better off than I am at present. I should still have to get out of this chair and ring for Maud. And I should have to complain twice over. Once to Maud herself and afterwards all over again to my wife about Maud. Then my wife would have to rebuke Maud. Oh, it would be a terribly complicated business. Perhaps I'm better off as a bachelor. It's an odd thing that with my pictorial temperament I should never yet have visualized myself as a husband. My imagination is quite untrammeled in most directions. Were I to decide to-morrow that I would write a play about Adam and Eve, I should see myself as Adam and Eve and the Serpent and almost as the Forbidden Fruit itself without any difficulty. Why can't I see myself as a husband? When I think of the number of people and things I've been in imagination it really does seem extraordinary I should never have thought of being a husband. Apparently Maud has completely forgotten about the curtains. It looks as if I should have to give up all hope now of her coming in to draw them of her own accord. Poor Miss Hamilton! I do trust that horrible old clown of a mother isn't turning somersaults round her room at this moment and sending up her temperature to three figures. Of course, she must come back to me. She is indispensable. I miss her very much. I've accustomed myself to a secretary's assistance, and naturally I'm lost without her. These morbid thoughts about matrimony are due to my not having done a stroke of work all day. I will count seventeen and rise from this chair."

John counted seventeen, but when he came to the fatal number he found that his will to move was still paralyzed, and he went on to forty-nine—the next fatal number in his private cabbala. When he reached it he tightened every nerve in his body and leapt to his feet. Inertia was succeeded by the bustle of activity: he rang for Maud; he poked the fire; he brushed the tobacco-ash from his waistcoat; he blew his nose; he sat down at his desk.

My dear Miss Hamilton, [he wrote,] I cannot say how distressed I was to hear the news of your illness and still more to learn from your mother that you were seriously thinking of resigning your post. I'm also extremely distressed to hear from her that there are symptoms of overwork. If I've been inconsiderate I must beg your forgiveness and ask you to attribute it to your own good-will. The fact is your example has inspired me. With your encouragement I undoubtedly do work much harder than formerly. Today, without you, I have not written a single word, and I feel dreadfully depressed at the prospect of your desertion. Do let me plead for your services when you are well again, at any rate until I've finished Joan of Arc, for I really don't think I shall ever finish that play without them. I have felt the death of my poor mother very much, but I do not ascribe my present disinclination for work to that. No, on the contrary, I came back from the funeral with a determination to bury myself—that might be expressed better—to plunge myself into hard work. Your note telling me of your illness was a great shock, and your mother's uncompromising attitude this morning has added to my dejection. I feel that I am growing old and view with horror the approach of age. I've been sitting by the fire indulging myself in very morbid thoughts. You will laugh when I tell you that amongst them was the idea—I might call it the chimera of marriage. Do please get well soon and rescue me from myself.

Yours very sincerely,
JOHN TOUCHWOOD.

I do not, of course, wish to disturb the relationship between yourself and your mother, but my own recent loss has reminded me that mothers do not live forever.

CHAPTER XV

JOHN waited in considerable anxiety for Miss Hamilton's reply to his letter, and when a few days later she answered his appeal in person by presenting herself for work as usual he could not express in words the intensity of his satisfaction, but could only prance round her as if he had been a dumb domestic animal instead of a celebrated romantic playwright.

"And what have you done since I've been away?" she asked, without alluding to her illness or to her mother or to her threat of being obliged to leave him.

John looked abashed.

"Not very much, I'm afraid."

"How much?"

"Well, to be quite honest, nothing at all"

She referred sympathetically to the death of Mrs. Touchwood, and, without the ghost of a blush, he availed himself of that excuse for idleness.

"But now you're back," he added, "I'm going to work harder than ever. Oh, but I forgot. I mustn't overwork you."

"Nonsense," said Miss Hamilton, sharply. "I don't think the amount you write every day will ever do me much harm."

John busied himself with paper, pens, ink, and notebooks, and was soon as deep in the fourth act as if there had never been an intermission. For a month he worked in perfect tranquillity, and went so far as to calculate that if Miss Hamilton was willing to remain forever in his employ there was no reason why he should not produce three plays a year until he was seventy. Then one morning in mid-February Mr. Ricketts arrived in a state of perturbation to say that he had been unable to obtain any reply to several letters and telegrams informing Hugh when their steamer would leave. Now here they were with only a day before departure, and he was still without news of the young man. John looked guilty. The fact was that he had decided not to open any letters from his relations throughout this month, alleging to himself the interruption they caused to his work and trusting to the old superstition that if left unanswered long enough all letters, even the most disagreeable, answered themselves.

"I was wondering why your correspondence had dwindled so," said Miss Hamilton, severely.

"But that is no excuse for my brother," John declared. "Because I don't write to him, that is no reason why he shouldn't write to Mr. Ricketts."

"Well, we're off to-morrow," said the mahogany-planter.

An indignant telegram was sent to Hugh; but the prepaid answer came back from Hilda to say that he had gone off with a friend a fortnight ago without leaving any address. Mr. Ricketts, who had been telephoned for in the morning, arrived about noon in a taxi loaded with exotic luggage.

"I can't wait," he assured John. "The lad must come on by the next boat. I shan't go up country for a week or so. Good-by, Mr. Touchwood; I'm sorry not to have your brother's company. I was going to put him wise to the job on the trip across."

"But look here, can't you...." John began, despairingly.

"Can't wait. I shall miss the boat. West India Docks," he shouted to the driver, "and stop at the last decent pub in the city on the way through."

The taxi buzzed off.

Two days later Hugh appeared at Church Row, mentioned casually that he was sorry he had missed the boat, but that he had been doing a little architectural job for a friend of his.

"Very good bridge," he commented, approvingly.

"Over what?" John demanded.

"Over very good whisky," said Hugh. "It was up in the North. Capital fun. I was designing a smoking-room for a man I know who's just come into money. I've had a ripping time. Good hands every evening and a very decent fee. In fact, I don't see why I shouldn't start an office of my own."

"And what about mahogany?"

"Look here, I never liked that idea of yours, Johnnie. Everybody agrees that British Honduras is a rotten climate, and if you want to help me, you can help me much more effectively by setting me up on my own as an architect."

"I do not want to help you. I've invested £2,000 in mahogany and logwood, and I insist on getting as much interest on my money as your absence from England will bring me in."

"Yes, that's all very well, old chap. But why do you want me to leave England?"

John embarked upon a justification of his attitude, in the course of which he pointed out the dangers of idleness, reminded Hugh of the forgery, tried to inspire him with hopes of independence, hinted at moral obligations, and rhapsodized about colonial enterprise. As a mountain of forensic art the speech was wonderful: clothed on the lower slopes with a rich and varied vegetation of example and precept, it gradually ascended to the hard rocks of necessity, honor, and duty until it culminated in a peak of snow where John's singleness of motive glittered immaculately and inviolably to heaven. It was therefore discouraging for the orator when he paused and walked slowly up stage to give the culprit an opportunity to make a suitably penitent reply, after which the curtain was to come down upon a final outburst of magnanimous eloquence from himself, that Hugh should merely growl the contemptuous monosyllable "rot."

"Rot?" repeated John in amazement.

"Yes. Rot. I'm not going to reason with you...."

"Ah, indeed?" John interrupted, sarcastically.

"Because reason would be lost on you. I simply repeat 'Rot!' If I don't want to go to British Honduras, I won't go. Why, to hear you talk anybody would suppose that I hadn't had the same opportunities as yourself. If you chose to blur your intelligence by writing romantic tushery, you must remember that by doing so you yielded to temptation just as much as I did when I forged Stevie's name. Do you think I would write plays like yours? Never!" he proclaimed, proudly.

"It seems to me that the conversation is indeed going outside the limits of reason," said John, trying hard to restrain himself.

"My dear old chap, it has never been inside the limits. No, no, you collared me when I was down over that check. Well, here's what you paid to get me out of the mess." He threw a bundle of notes on the table. "So long, Johnnie, and don't be too resentful of my having demonstrated that when I *am* left for a while on my own I can earn money as well as you. I'm going to stay in town for a bit before I go North again, so I shall see you from time to time. By the way, you might send me the receipt to Carlington Road. I'm staying with Aubrey as usual."

When his brother had gone, John counted the notes in a stupor. It would be too much to say that he was annoyed at being paid back; but he was not sufficiently pleased to mention the fact to Miss Hamilton for two days.

"Oh, I am so glad," she exclaimed when at last he did bring himself to tell her.

"Yes, it's very encouraging," John agreed, doubtfully. "I'm still suffering slightly from the shock, which has been a very novel sensation. To be perfectly honest, I never realized before how much less satisfactory it is to be paid back than one thinks beforehand it is going to be."

In spite of the disturbing effect of Hugh's honesty, John soon settled down again to the play, and became so much wrapped up in its daily progress that one afternoon he was able without a tremor to deny admittance to Laurence, who having written to warn him that he was taking advantage of a further reduction in the price on day-tickets, had paid another visit to London. Laurence took with ill grace his brother-in-law's message that he was too busy on his own work to talk about anybody's else at present.

"I confess I was pained," he wrote from Ambles on John's own note-paper, "by the harsh reception of my friendly little visit. I confess that Edith and I had hoped you would welcome the accession of a relative to the ranks of contemporary playwrights. We feel that in the circumstances we cannot stay any longer in your house. Indeed, Edith is even as I pen these lines packing Frida's little trunk. She is being very brave, but her tear-stained face tells its own tale, and I confess that I myself am writing with a heavy heart. Eleanor has been most kind, and in addition to giving me several more introductions to her thespian friends has arranged with the proprietress of Halma House for a large double room with dressing-room attached on terms which I can only describe as absurdly moderate. Do not think we are angry. We are only pained, bitterly pained that our happy family life should suddenly collapse like this. However, excelsior, as the poet said, or as another poet even greater said, 'sic itur ad astra.' You will perhaps be able to spare a moment from the absorption of your own affairs to read with a fleeting interest that Sir Percy Mortimer has offered me the part of the butler in a comedy of modern manners which he hopes to stage—you see I am already up to the hilt in the jargon of the profession—next autumn. Eleanor considers this to be an excellent opening, as indeed so do I. Edith and little Frida laugh heartily when they are not too sad for such simple fun when I enter the room and assume the characteristic mannerisms of a butler. All agree I have a natural propensity for droll impersonation. Who knows? I may make a great hit, although Sir Percy warns me that the part is but a slight one. Eleanor, however, reminds me that deportment is always an asset for an actor. Have I not read somewhere that the great Edmund Kean did not disdain to play the tail end of a dragon erstwhile? I wish you all good luck in your own work, my dear John. People are interested when they hear you are my brother-in-law, and I have told them many tales of the way you are wont to consult me over the little technical details of religion in which I as a former clergyman have been able to afford you my humble assistance."

"What a pompous ass the man is," said John to his secretary. He had read her the letter, which made her laugh.

"I believe you're really quite annoyed that *he's* showing an independent spirit now."

"Not at all. I'm delighted to be rid of him," John contradicted. "I suppose he'll share George's aquarium at Halma House."

"You don't mind my laughing? Because it is very funny, you know."

"Yes, it's funny in a way," John admitted. "But even if it weren't, I shouldn't mind your laughing. You have, if I may say so, a peculiarly musical laugh."

"Are you going to have Joan's scaffold right center or left center?" she asked, quickly.

"Eh? What? Oh, put it where you like. By the way, has your mother been girding at you lately?"

Miss Hamilton shrugged her shoulders.

"She isn't yet reconciled to my being a secretary, if that's what you mean."

"I'm sorry," John murmured. "Confound all relations!" he burst out. "I suppose she'd object to your going to France with me to finish off the play?"

"She would object violently. But you mustn't forget that I've a will of my own."

"Of course you have," said John, admiringly. "And you will go, eh?"

"I'll see—I won't promise. Look here, Mr. Touchwood, I don't want to seem—what shall I call it—timid, but if I did go to France with you, I suppose you realize my mother would make such a fuss about it that people would end by really talking? Forgive my putting such an unpleasant idea into your innocent head; being your confidential secretary, I feel I oughtn't to let you run any risks. I don't suppose you care a bit how much people talk, and I'm sure I don't; at the same time I shouldn't like you to turn round on me and say I ought to have warned you."

"Talk!" John exclaimed. "The idea is preposterous. Talk! Good gracious me, can't I take my secretary abroad without bring accused of ulterior motives?"

"Now, don't work yourself into a state of wrath, or you won't be able to think of this terribly important last scene. Anyway, we sha'n't be going to France yet, and we can discuss the project more fully when the time comes."

John thought vaguely how well Miss Hamilton knew how to keep him unruffled, and with a grateful look—or what was meant to be a grateful look, though she blushed unaccountably when he gave it—he concentrated upon the site of his heroine's scaffold.

During March the weather was so bright and exhilarating that John and his secretary took many walks together on Hampstead Heath; they also often went to town, and John derived much pleasure from discussing various business affairs with her clerical support; he found that it helped considerably when dealing with the manager of a film company to be able to say "Will you make a note of that, please, Miss Hamilton?" The only place, in fact, to which John did not take her was his club, and that was only because he was not allowed to introduce ladies there.

"A rather mediæval restriction," he observed one day to a group assembled in the smoking-room.

"There was a time, Touchwood, when you used to take refuge here from your leading ladies," a bachelor member chuckled.

"But nowadays Touchwood has followed Adam with the rest of us," put in another.

"What's that?" said John, sharply.

There was a general burst of merriment and headshaking and wagging of fingers, from which and a succession of almost ribald comment John began to wonder if his private life was beginning to be a subject for club gossip. He managed to prevent himself from saying that he thought such chaff in bad taste, because he did not wish to give point to it by taking it too much in earnest. Nevertheless, he was seriously annoyed and avoided the smoking-room for a week.

One night, after the first performance of a friend's play, he turned in to the club for supper, and, being disinclined for sleep, because although it was a friend's play it had been a tremendous success, which always made him feel anxious about his own future he lingered on until the smoking-room was nearly deserted. Towards three o'clock he was sitting pensively in a quiet corner when he heard his name mentioned by two members, who had taken seats close by without perceiving his presence. They were both strangers to him, and he was about to rise from his chair and walk severely out of the room, when he heard one one say to the other:

"Yes, they tell me his brother-in-law writes his plays for him."

John found this so delightfully diverting an idea that he could not resist keeping quiet to hear more.

"Oh, I don't believe that," said the second unknown member.

"Fact, I assure you. I was told so by a man who knows Eleanor Cartright."

"The actress?"

"Yes, she's a sister-in-law of his."

"Really, I never knew that."

"Oh yes. Well, this man met her with a fellow called Armitage, an ex-monk who broke his vows in order to marry Touchwood's sister."

John pressed himself deeper into his armchair.

"Really? But I never knew monks could marry," objected number two.

"I tell you, he broke his vows."

"Oh, I see," murmured number two, who was evidently no wiser, but was anxious to appear so.

"Well, it seems that this fellow Armitage is a thundering fine poet, but without much experience of the stage. Of course, he wouldn't have had much as a monk."

"Of course not," agreed number two, decidedly.

"So, what does Johnnie Touchwood do—"

"Damned impudence calling me Johnnie," thought the subject of the duologue.

"But make a contract with his brother-in-law to stay out of the way down in Devonshire or Dorsetshire—I forget which—but, anyway, down in the depths of the country somewhere, and write all the best speeches in old Johnnie's plays. Now, it seems there's been a family row, and they tell me that Armitage is going to sue Johnnie."

"What was the row about?"

"Well, apparently Johnnie is a bit close. Most of these successful writers are, of course," said number one with the nod of an expert.

"Of course," agreed his companion, with an air of equally profound comprehension.

"And took advantage of his position as the fellow with money to lord it over the rest of his family. There's another brother—an awful clever beggar—James, I think his name is—a real first-class scientist, original research man and all that, who's spent the whole of his fortune on some great discovery or other. Well, will you believe it, but the other day when he was absolutely starving, Johnnie Touchwood offered to lend him some trifling sum if he would break the entail."

"I didn't know the Touchwoods were landed proprietors. I always understood the father was a dentist," said number two.

"Oh, no, no. Very old family. Wonderful old house down in Devonshire or Dorset—I wish I could remember just where it is. Anyway, it seems that the eldest brother clung on to this like anything. Of course, he would."

"Of course," number two agreed.

"But Johnnie, who's hard as flint, insisted on breaking the entail in his own favor, and now I hear he's practically turned the whole family into the street, including James' boy, who in the ordinary course of events would have inherited."

"Did Eleanor Cartright tell your friend this?" asked number two.

"Oh no, I've heard that from lots of people. It seems that old Mrs. Touchwood died of grief over the way Johnnie carried on. It's really a very grim story when you hear the details; unfortunately, I can't remember all of them. My memory's getting awfully bad nowadays."

Number two muttered an expression of sympathy, and the other continued:

"But one detail I do remember is that another brother—"

"It's a large family, then?"

"Oh, very large. As I was saying, the old lady was terribly upset not only about breaking the entail, but also over her youngest son, who had some incurable disease. It seems that he was forced by Johnnie to go out to the Gold Coast—I think it was—in order to see about some money that Johnnie had invested in rubber or something. As I say, I can't remember the exact details. However, cherchez la femme, I needn't add the reasons for all this."

"A woman?"

"Exactly," said number one. "Some people say it's a married woman, and others say it's a young girl of sixteen. Anyway, Johnnie's completely lost his head over her, and they tell me...."

The two members put their heads together so that John could not hear what was said: but it must have been pretty bad, because when they put them apart again number two was clicking his tongue in shocked amazement.

"By Jove, that will cause a terrific scandal, eh?"

John decided he had heard enough. Assuming an expression of intense superiority, the sort of expression a man might assume who was standing on the top of Mount Everest, he rose from his chair, eyed the two gossips with disdain, and strode out of the smoking-room. Just as he reached the door, he heard number one exclaim:

"Hulloa, see who that was? That was old Percy Mortimer."

"Oh, of course," said number two, as sapiently as ever, "I didn't recognize him for a moment. He's beginning to show his age, eh?"

On the way back to Hampstead John tried to assure himself that the conversation he had just overheard did not represent anything more important than the vaporings of an exceptionally idiotic pair of men about town; but the more he meditated upon the tales about himself evidently now in general circulation, the more he was appalled at the recklessness of calumny.

"One has joked about it. One has laughed at Sheridan's *School for Scandal*. One has admitted that human beings are capable of almost incredible exaggeration. But—no, really this is too much. I've gossiped sometimes myself about my friends, but never like that about a stranger—a man in the public eye."

John nearly stopped the taxi to ask the driver if *he* had heard any stories about John Touchwood; but he decided it would not be wise to run risk of discovery that he enjoyed less publicity than he was beginning to imagine, and he kept his indignation to himself.

"After all, it is a sign of—well, yes, I think it might fairly be called fame—a sign of fame to be talked about like that by a couple of ignorant chatterboxes. It is, I suppose, a tribute to my position. But Laurence! That's what annoyed me most. Laurence to be the author of my plays! I begin to understand this ridiculous Bacon and Shakespeare legend now. The rest of the gossip was malicious, but that was—really, I think it was actionable. I shall take it up with the committee. The idea of that pompous nincompoop writing Lucretia's soliloquy before she poisons her lips! Laurence! Good heavens! And fancy Laurence writing Nebuchadnezzar's meditation upon grass! By Jove, an audience would have some cause to titter then! And Laurence writing Joan's defense to the Bishop of Beauvais! Why, the bombastic pedant couldn't even write a satisfactory letter to the Bishop of Silchester to keep himself from being ignominiously chucked out of his living."

The infuriated author bounced up and down on the cushions of the taxi in his rage.

"Shall I give you an arm up the steps, sir?" the driver offered, genially, when John, having alighted at his front door, had excessively overpaid him under the impression from which he was still smarting of being called a skinflint.

"No, thank you."

"Beg pardon, sir. I thought you was a little bit tiddly. You seemed a bit lively inside on the way up."

"I suppose the next thing is that I shall get the reputation of being a dipsomaniac," said John to himself, as he flung open his door and marched immediately, with a slightly accentuated rigidity of bearing, upstairs to bed.

But he could not sleep. The legend of his behavior that was obviously common gossip in London oppressed him with its injustice. Every accusation took on a new and fantastic form, while he turned over and over in an attempt to reach oblivion. He began to worry now more about what had been implied in his association with Miss Hamilton than about the other stories. He felt that it would only be a very short time before she would hear of the tale in some monstrous shape and leave him forever in righteous disgust. Ought he, indeed, to make her aware to-morrow morning of what was being suggested? And even if he did not say anything about the past, ought he to compromise her more deeply in the future?

It was six o'clock before John fell asleep, and it was with a violent headache that he faced his secretary after breakfast. Luckily there was a letter from Janet Bond asking him to come and see her that morning upon a matter of importance. He seized the excuse to postpone any discussion of last night's revelation, and, telling Miss Hamilton he should be back for lunch, he decided to walk down to the Parthenon Theater in the hope of arriving there with a clearer and saner view of life. He nearly told her to go home; but, reflecting that he might come back in quite a different mood, he asked her instead to occupy herself with the collation of some scattered notes upon Joan of Arc that were not yet incorporated into the scheme of the play. He remembered, too, that it would be his birthday in three days' time, and he asked her to send out notes of invitation to his family for the annual celebration, at which the various members liked to delude themselves with the idea that by presenting him with a number of useless accessories to the smoking-table they were repaying him in full for all his kindness. He determined that his birthday speech on this occasion should be made the vehicle for administering a stern rebuke to malicious gossip. He would dam once for all this muddy stream of scandal, and he would make Laurence write a letter to the press disclaiming the authorship of his plays. Burning with reformative zeal and fast losing his headache, John swung down Fitzjohn's Avenue in the spangled March sunlight to the wicked city below.

The Parthenon Theater had for its acropolis the heights of the Adelphi, where, viewed from the embankment gardens below, it seemed to be looking condescendingly down upon the efforts of the London County Council to intellectualize the musical taste of the generation. In the lobby—it had been called the propylæum until it was found that such a long name had discouraged the public from booking seats beforehand through fear of mispronunciation—a bust of Janet Bond represented the famous statue Pallas Athene on the original acropolis, and the programme-girls, dressed as caryatides, supplied another charming touch of antiquity. The proprietress herself was the outstanding instance in modern times of the exploitation of virginity—it must have been a very profitable exploitation, because the Parthenon Theater itself had been built and paid for by her unsuccessful admirers. Each year made Janet Bond's position as virgin and actress more secure, and at the rate her reputation was growing it was probable that she would soon be at liberty to produce the most immodest plays. At present, however, she still applied the same standard of her conduct to her plays as to herself. Nor did she confine herself to that. She was also very strict about the private lives of her performers, and many a young actress had been seen to leave the stage door in tears because Miss Bond had observed her in unsuitable company at supper. Mothers wrote from all over England to beg Miss Bond to charge herself with the care of their stage-struck daughters; the result was a conventional tone among the supernumeraries slightly flavored with militant suffragism and the higher mathematics. Nor was art neglected; indeed some critics hinted that in the Parthenon Theater art was cultivated at the expense of life, though none of them attempted to gainsay that Miss Bond had learned how to make virtue pay without selling it.

In appearance the great tragedienne was somewhat rounder in outline than might have been expected, and more matronly than virginal, perhaps because she was in her own words a mother to all her girls. Her voice was rich and deep with as much variety as a cunningly sounded gong. She never made up for the stage, and she wore hygienic corsets: this intimate fact was allowed to escape through the indiscretion of a widespread advertisement, but its publication helped her reputation for decorum, and clergymen who read their wives' *Queen* or *Lady* commented favorably on the contrast between Miss Bond and the numerous open-mouthed actresses who preferred to advertise toothpaste. England was proud of Miss Bond, feeling that America had no longer any right to vaunt a monopoly of virtuous actresses; and John, when he rang the bell of Miss Bond's flat that existed cleverly in the roof of the theater, was proud of his association with her. He did not have to wait long in her austere study; indeed he had barely time to admire the fluted calyx of a white trumpet daffodil that in chaste symbolism was the only occupant of a blue china bowl before Miss Bond herself came in.

"I'm so hating what I'm going to have to say to you," she boomed.

This was a jolly way to begin an interview, John thought, especially in his present mood. He tried to look attentive, faintly surprised, dignified, and withal deferential; but, not being a great actor, he failed to express all these states of mind at a go, and only succeeded in dropping his gloves.

"Hating it," the actress cried. "Oh, hating it!"

"Well, if you'd rather postpone it," John began.

"No, no. It must be said now. It's just this!" She paused and fixed the author more intensely than a snake fixes a rabbit or a woman in a bus tries to see if the woman opposite has blacked her eyelashes. "Can I produce *Joan of Arc*?"

"I think that question is answered by our contract," replied John, who was used to leading ladies, and when they started like this always fell back at once in good order on business.

"Yes, but what about my unwritten contract with the public?" she demanded.

"I don't know anything about that," said the author. Moreover, I don't see how an unwritten contract can interfere with our written contract."

"John Touchwood, I'm going to be frank with you, fiercely frank. I can't afford to produce a play by you about a heroine like Joan of Arc unless you take steps to put things right."

"If you want me to cut that scene...."

"Oh, I'm not talking about scenes, John Touchwood. I'm talking about these terrible stories that everybody is whispering about you. I don't mind myself what you do. Good gracious me, I'm a broad-minded modern woman; but my public looks for something special at the Parthenon. The knowledge that I am going to play the Maid of Orleans has moved them indescribably; I was fully prepared to give you the success of your career, but ... these stories! This girl! You know what people are saying? You must have heard. How can I put your name on my programme as the author of *Joan of Arc*? How can I, John Touchwood?"

If John had not overheard that conversation at his club the night before, he would have supposed that Miss Bond had gone mad.

"May I inquire exactly what you have heard about me and my private life?" he inquired, as judicially as he could.

"Please spare me from repeating the stories. I can honestly assure you that I don't believe them. But you as a man of the world know very well how unimportant it is whether a story is true or not. If you were a writer of realistic drama, these stories, however bad they were, wouldn't matter. If your next play was going to be produced at the Court Theater, these stories would, if anything, be in favor of success ... but at the Parthenon...."

"You are talking nonsense, Miss Bond," interrupted John, angrily. "You are more in a condition to play Ophelia than Joan of Arc. Moreover, you shan't play Joan of Arc now. I've really been regretting for some weeks now that you were going to play her, and I'm delighted to have this opportunity of preventing you from playing her. I don't know to what tittle-tattle you've been listening. I don't care. Your opinion of your own virtue may be completely justified, but your judgment of other people's is vulgar and—however, let me recommend you to produce a play by my brother-in-law, the Reverend Laurence Armitage. Even your insatiable ambition may be gratified by the part of the Virgin Mary, who is one of the chief characters. Good morning, Miss Bond. I shall communicate with you more precisely through my agent."

John marched out of the theater, and on the pavement outside ran into Miss Ida Merritt.

"Ah, you're a sensible woman," he spluttered, much to her astonishment. "For goodness' sake, come and have lunch with me, and let's talk over everything."

John, in his relief at meeting Miss Merritt, had taken her arm in a cordial fashion, and steered her across the Strand to Romano's without waiting to choose a less conspicuously theatrical restaurant. Indeed in his anxiety to clear his reputation he forgot everything, and it was only when he saw various people at the little tables nudging one another and bobbing their heads together that he realized he was holding Miss Merritt's arm. He dropped it like a hot coal, and plunged down at a table marked "reserved." The head waiter hurried across to apprise him of the mistake, and John, who was by now horribly self-conscious, fancied that the slight incident had created a stir throughout the restaurant. No doubt it would be all over town by evening that he and his companion in guilt had been refused service at every restaurant in London.

"Look here," said John, when at last they were accommodated at a table painfully near the grill, the spitting and hissing from which seemed to symbolize the attitude of a hostile society. "Look here, what stories have you heard about me? You're a journalist. You write chatty paragraphs. For heaven's sake, tell me the worst."

"Oh, I haven't heard anything that's printable," Miss Merritt assured him, with a laugh.

John put his head between his hands and groaned; the waiter thought he was going to dip his hair into the hors d'œuvres and hurriedly removed the dishes.

"No, seriously, I beg you to tell me if you've heard my name connected in any unpleasant way with Miss Hamilton."

"No, the only thing I've heard about Doris is that your brother, Hugh, is always pestering her with his attentions."

"What?" John shouted.

"Coming, sir," cried the waiter, skipping round the table like a monkey.

John waved him away, and begged Miss Merritt to be more explicit.

"Why didn't she complain to me?" he asked when he had heard her story.

"She probably thought she could look after herself. Besides, wasn't he going to British Guiana?"

"He was," replied John. "At least he was going to some tropical colony. I've heard so many mentioned that I'm beginning myself to forget which it was now. So that's why he didn't go. But he shall go. If I have to have him kidnaped and spend all my savings on chartering a private yacht for the purpose, by Heaven, he shall go. If he shrivels up like a burnt sausage the moment he puts his foot on the beach he shall be left there to shrivel. The rascal! When does he pester her? Where?"

"Don't get so excited. Doris is perfectly capable of looking after herself. Besides, I think she rather likes him in a way."

"Never," John cried.

"Liver is finished, sair," said the officious waiter, dancing in again between John and Miss Merritt.

John shook his fist at him and leant earnestly over the table with one elbow in the butter.

"You don't seriously suggest that she is in love with him?" he asked.

"No, I don't think so. But I met him myself once and took rather a fancy to him. No, she just likes him as a friend. It's he who's in love with her."

"Under my very eyes," John ejaculated. "Why, it's overwhelming."

A sudden thought struck him that even at this moment while he was calmly eating lunch with Miss Merritt, as he somewhat loosely qualified the verb, Hugh might be making love to Miss Hamilton in his own house.

"Look here," he cried, "have you nearly finished? Because I've suddenly remembered an important appointment at Hampstead."

"I don't want any more," said Miss Merritt, obligingly.

"Waiter, the bill! Quick! You don't mind if I rush off and leave you to finish your cheese alone?"

His guest shook her head and John hurried out of the restaurant.

No taxi he had traveled in had ever seemed so slow, and he kept putting his head out of the window to urge the driver to greater speed, until the man goaded to rudeness by John's exhortations and the trams in Tottenham Court Road asked if his fare thought he was a blinking bullet.

"I'm not bullying you. I'm only asking you to drive a little faster," John shouted back.

The driver threw his eyes heavenward in a gesture of despair for John's sanity but he was pacified at Church Row by half-a-sovereign and even went so far as to explain that he had not accused John of bullying him, but merely of confusing his capacity for speed with that of a bullet's. John thought he was asking for more money, gave him half-a-crown and waving his arm, half in benediction, half in protest, he hurried into the hall.

"They've nearly finished lunch, sir," murmured Maud who was just coming from the dining-room. "Would you like Elsa to hot you up something?"

John without a word pounced into the dining-room, where he caught Hugh with a stick of celery half-way to his mouth and Miss Hamilton with a glass of water half-way down from hers in the other direction.

"Oh, I'm so sorry we began without you," said the culprits simultaneously.

John murmured something about a trying interview with Janet Bond, lit a cigar, realized it was rude to light cigars when people were still eating, threw the cigar away, and sat down with an appearance of exhaustion in one of those dining-room armchairs that stand and wait all their lives to serve a moment like this.

"I'm sorry, but I must ask you to go off as soon as you've finished your lunch, Hugh. I've a lot of important business to transact with Miss Hamilton."

"Oh, but I've finished already," she exclaimed, jumping up from the table.

It was the first pleasant moment in John's day, and he smiled, gratefully. He felt he could even afford to be generous to this intrusive brother, and before he left the room with Miss Hamilton he invited him to have some more celery.

"And you'll find a cigar in the sideboard," he added. "But Maud will look after you. Maud, look after Mr. Hugh, please, and if anybody calls this afternoon, I'm not at home."

CHAPTER XVI

JOHN'S first impulse had been to pour out in Miss Hamilton's ears the tale of his wrongs, and afterward, when he had sufficiently impressed her with the danger of the position in which the world was trying to place them, to ask her to marry him as the only way to escape from it. On second thoughts, he decided that she might be offended by the suggestion of having been compromised by him and that she might resent the notion of their marriage's being no more than a sop to public opinion. He therefore abandoned the idea of enlarging upon the scandal their association had apparently created and proposed to substitute the trite but always popular scene of the prosperous middle-aged man's renunciation of love and happiness in favor of a young and penurious rival. He recalled how many last acts in how many sentimental comedies had owed their success to this situation, which never failed with an audience. But then the average audience was middle-aged. Thinking of the many audiences on which from private boxes he had looked down, John was sure that bald heads always predominated in the auditorium; and naturally those bald heads had been only too ready to nod approval of a heroine who rejected the dashing jeune premier to fling herself into the arms of the elderly actor-manager. It was impossible to think of any infirmity severe enough to thwart an actor-manager. Yet a play was make-believe: in real life events would probably turn out quite differently. It would be very depressing, if he offered to make Doris and Hugh happy together by settling upon them a handsome income, to find Doris jumping at the prospect. Perhaps it would be more prudent not to suggest any possibility of a marriage between them. It might even be more prudent not to mention the subject of marriage at all. John looked at his secretary with what surely must have been a very eloquent glance indeed, because she dropped her pencil, blushed, and took his hand.

"How much simpler life is than art," John murmured. He would never have dared to allow one of his heroes in a moment of supreme emotion like this to crane his neck across a wide table in order to kiss the heroine. Any audience would have laughed at such an awkward gesture; yet, though he only managed to reach her lips with half an inch to spare, the kiss was not at all funny somehow. No, it ranked with Paolo's or Anthony's or any other famous lover's kiss.

"And now of course I can't be your secretary any longer," she sighed.

"Why? Do you disapprove of wives' helping their husbands?"

"I don't think you really want to get married, do you?"

"My dear, I'm absolutely dying to get married."

"Truly?"

"Doris, look at me."

And surely she looked at him with more admiration than he had ever looked at himself in a glass.

"What a time I shall have with mother," she gasped with the gurgling triumphant laugh of a child who has unexpectedly found the way to open the store-cupboard.

"Oh, no, you won't," John prophesied, confidently. "I'm not going to have such an excellent last scene spoilt by unnecessary talk. We'll get married first and tell everybody afterwards. I've lately discovered what an amazing capacity ordinary human nature has for invention. It really frightens me for the future of novelists, who I cannot believe will be wanted much longer. Oh no, Doris, I'm not going to run the risk of hearing any preliminary gossip about our marriage. Neither your mother nor my relations nor the general public are going to have any share in it before or after. In fact to be brief I propose to elope. Notwithstanding my romantic plays I have spent a private life of utter dullness. This is my last opportunity to do anything unusual. Please, my dearest girl, let me experience the joys of an actual elopement before I relapse into eternal humdrummery."

"A horrid description of marriage!" she protested.

"Comparative humdrummery, I should have said, comparative, that is to say, with the excesses attributed to me by rumor. I've often wanted to write a play about Tiberius, and I feel well equipped to do so now. But I'm serious about the elopement. I really do want to avoid my relations' tongues."

"I believe you're afraid of them."

"I am. I'm not ashamed to admit that I'm in terror of them," he said.

"But where are we going to elope to?"

John picked up the *Times*.

"If only the *Murmania*," he began. "And by Jove, she will too," he cried. "Yes, she's due to sail from Liverpool on April 1st."

"But that's your birthday," she objected.

"Exactly."

"And I've already sent out those invitations."

"Exactly. For some years my relations have made an April fool of me by dining at my expense on that day. I have two corner-cupboards overflowing with their gifts—the most remarkable exhibition of cheapness and ingenuity ever known. This year I am going to make April fools of them."

"By marrying me?" she laughed.

"Well, of course it's no use pretending that they'll be delighted by that joke, though I intend to play another still more elaborately unpleasant. At the back of all their minds exists one anxiety—the dispositions of my last will and testament. Very well. I am going to cure that worry forever by leaving them Ambles. I can't imagine anything more irritating than to be left a house in common with a number of people whom you hate. Oh, it's an exquisite revenge. Darling secretary, take down for dictation as your last task the following:

"'I, John Touchwood, playwright, of 36 Church Row, Hampstead, N.W., and Ambles, Wrottesford, Hants, do hereby will and bequeathe.'"

"I don't understand," she said. "Are you really making a will? or are you only playing a joke?"

"Both."

"But is this really to take effect when you're dead? Oh dear, I wish you wouldn't talk about death when I've just said I'll marry you."

John paused thoughtfully:

"It does seem rather a challenge to fate," he agreed. "I know what I'll do. I'll make over Ambles to them at once. After all, I am dead to them, for I'll never have anything more to do with any of them. Cross out what you took down. I'll alter the form. Begin as for a letter:

"'My dear relations,

"'When you read this I shall be far away.' ... I think that's the correct formula?" he asked.

"It sounds familiar from many books," she assured him.

"'Far away on my honeymoon with Miss Doris Hamilton.' Perhaps that sounds a little ambiguous. Cross out the maiden name and substitute 'with Mrs. John Touchwood, my former secretary. Since you have attributed to us every link except that of matrimony you will no doubt be glad of this opportunity to contradict the outrageous tales you have most of you' ... I say most of you," John explained, "because I don't really think the children started any scandal ... 'you have most of you been at such pains to invent and circulate. Realizing that this announcement will come as a sad blow, I am going to soften it as far as I can by making you a present of my country house in Hampshire, and I am instructing my solicitors to effect the conveyance in due form. From now onwards therefore one fifth of Ambles will belong to James and Beatrice, one fifth to George, Eleanor, Bertram, and Viola, and one fifth to Hilda and Harold, one fifth to Edith, Laurence, and Frida, and one fifth to Hugh.' ... I feel that Hugh is entitled to a proportionately larger share," he said with his eyes on the ceiling, "because I understand that I've robbed him of you."

"Who on earth told you that?" she demanded, putting down her pencil.

"Never mind," said John, humming gayly his exultation. "Continue please, Miss Hamilton! 'I shall make no attempt to say which fifth of the house shall belong to whom. Possibly Laurence and Hilda will argue that out between them, and if any structural alterations are required no doubt Hugh will charge himself with them. The twenty-acre field is included in the gift, so that there will be plenty of ground for any alterations or extensions deemed necessary by the future owners.'"

"How ridiculous you are ... John," she laughed. "It all sounds so absurdly practical—as if you really meant it."

"My dear girl, I do mean it. Continue please, Miss Hamilton! 'I have long felt that the collection of humming-birds made by Daniel Curtis in the Brazils should be suitably housed, and I propose that a portion of the stables should be put in order for their reception together with what is left of the collection of British dragon-flies made by James. My solicitors will supply a sum of £50 for this purpose and Harold can act as curator of what will be known as the Touchwood Museum. With regard to Harold's future, the family knows that I have invested £2000 in the mahogany plantations of Mr. Sydney Ricketts in British Honduras, and if Hugh does not take up his post within three months I shall ask Mr. Ricketts to accept Harold as a pupil in five years' time. He had better begin to study Hondurasian or whatever the language is called at once. Until Harold is called upon to make his decision I shall instruct Mr. Ricketts to put the interest with the capital. While on the subject of nephews and nieces, I may as well say that the family pictures and family silver will be sent back to Ambles to be held in trust for Bertram upon his coming of age. Furthermore, I am prepared to pay for the education of Bertram, Harold, Frida, and Viola at good boarding-schools. Viola can practice her dancing in the holidays. Bertram's future I will provide for when the time comes. I do not wish George to have any excuse for remaining at Halma House—and I have no doubt that a private sitting-room will be awarded to him at Ambles. In the event of undue congestion his knitting would not disturb Laurence's poetic composition, and his system of backing second favorites in imagination can be carried on as easily at Ambles as in London. If he still hankers for a sea voyage, the river with Harold and himself in a Canadian canoe will give him all the nautical adventure he requires. My solicitors have been instructed to place a canoe at his disposal. To James who has so often reproved me for my optimism I would say-once more "Beware of new critical weeklies" and remind him that a bird in the hand is worth two in the bush. In other words, he has got a thousand pounds out of me, and he won't get another penny. Eleanor has shown herself so well able to look after herself that I am not going to insult her by offering to look after her. Hilda with her fifth of the house and her small private income will have nothing to do but fuss about the proportionate expenses of the various members of the family who choose to inhabit Ambles. I am affording her an unique opportunity for being disagreeable, of which I'm sure she will take the fullest advantage. I may say that no financial allowance will be made to those who prefer to live elsewhere. As for Laurence, his theatrical future under the patronage of Sir Percy Mortimer is no doubt secure. However, if he grows tired of playing butlers, I hope that his muse will welcome him back to Ambles as affectionately as his wife.

"'I don't think I have anything more to say, my dear relations, except that I hope the presents you are bringing me for my birthday will come in useful as knick-knacks for your delightful house. You can now circulate as many stories about me as you like. You can even say that I have founded a lunatic asylum at Ambles. I am so happy in the prospect of my marriage that I cannot feel very hardly towards you all, and so I wish you good luck.

"'Your affectionate brother, brother-in-law, and uncle,

"'JOHN TOUCHWOOD.'

"Type that out, please, Miss Hamilton, while I drive down to Doctors Commons to see about the license and book our passage in the *Murmania*."

John had never tasted any success so sweet as the success of these two days before his forty-third birthday; and he was glad to find that Doris having once made up her mind about getting married showed no signs of imperilling the adventure by confiding her intention to her mother.

"Dear John," she said, "I bolted to America with Ida Merritt last year without a word to Mother until I sent her a wireless from on board. Surely I may elope with you ... and explain afterwards."

"You don't think it will kill her," suggested John a little anxiously. "People are apparently quite ready to accuse one of breaking a maternal heart as lightly as they would accuse one of breaking an appointment."

"Dear John, when we're married she'll be delighted."

"Not too delighted, eh, darling? I mean not so delighted that she'll want to come and gloat over us all day. You see, when the honeymoon's over, I shall have to get to work again on that last act, and your mother does talk a good deal. I know it's very intelligent talk, but it would be rather an interruption."

The only person they took into their confidence about the wedding, except the clergyman, the verger, and a crossing-sweeper brought in to witness the signing of the register was Mrs. Worfolk.

"Well, that's highly satisfactory! You couldn't have chosen a nicer young lady. Well, I mean to say, I've known her so long and all. And you expect to be back in June? Oh well, I shall have everything nice and tidy you may be sure. And this letter you want handed to Mr. James to be read to the family on your birthday? And I'm to give them their dinners the same as if you were here yourself? I see. And how many bottles of champagne shall I open? Oh, not to stint them? No, I quite understand. Of course, they would want to drink your healths. Certainly. And so they ought! Well, I'm bound to say I wish Mr. Worfolk could have been alive. It makes me quite aggravated to think he shouldn't be here. Well, I mean to say, he being a family carpenter had helped at so many weddings."

The scene on the *Murmania* did not differ much from the scene on board the same ship six months ago. John had insisted that Doris should wear her misty green suit of Harris tweed; but he himself had bought at the Burlington Arcade a traveling cap that showed plainly the sobering effects of matrimony. In the barber's saloon he invested in a pair of rope-soled shoes; he wanted to be sure of being able to support his wife even upon a heeling deck. Before dinner they went forward to watch the stars come out in the twilight—stars that were scarcely as yet more luminous in the green April sky than daisies in a meadow. They stood silent listening to the splash of the dusky sea against the bows, until the shore lamps began to wink astern.

"How savage the night looks coming after us," said John. "It's jolly to think that in the middle of all that blackness James is reading my birthday welcome to the family."

"Poor dears!"

"Oh, they deserve all they've got," he said, fiercely. "And to think that only six months ago I was fool enough to read their letters of congratulation quite seriously in this very ship. It was you with your remark about poor relations that put your foot through my picture."

"You're very much married already, aren't you, John?"

"Am I?"

"Yes, for you're already blaming me for everything."

"I suppose this is what James would call one of my confounded sentimental endings," John murmured.

"Whatever he called it, he couldn't invent a better ending himself," she murmured back. "You know, critics are very like disappointed old maids."

The great ship trembled faintly in the deeper motion, and John holding Doris to him felt that she too trembled faintly in unison. They stood like this in renewed silence until the stars shone clearly, and the shore lamps were turning to a gold blur. John may be excused for thinking that the bugle for dinner sounded like a flourish from *Lohengrin*. He had reason to feel romantic now.

THE END

The Vanity Girl
CHAPTER I
I

WEST KENSINGTON relies for romance more upon the eccentricities of individual residents than upon any variety or suggestiveness in the scenery of its streets, which indeed are mostly mere lines of uniform gray or red houses drearily elongated by constriction. Yet the suburb is too near to London for some relics of a former rusticity not to have survived; and it is refreshing for the casual observer of a city's growth to find here and there a row of old cottages, here and there a Georgian house rising from sooty flower-gardens and shadowed by rusty cedars, occasionally even an open space of building land, among the weeds of which ragged hedgerows and patches of degenerate oats still endure.

How Lonsdale Road, where the Caffyns lived, should have come to obtrude itself upon the flimsy architecture of the neighborhood is not so obvious. Situated near what used to be the western terminus of the old brown-and-blue horse-omnibuses, it is a comparatively wide road of detached, double-fronted, three-storied, square houses (so square that after the rows of emaciated residences close by they seem positively squat), built at least thirty years before anybody thought of following the District Railway out here. Each front door is overhung by a heavy portico, the stout pillars of which, painted over and over again according to the purse and fancy of the owner, vary in color from shades of glossy blue and green to drabs and buffs and dingy ivories. The steps, set some ten yards back from the pavement, are flanked by well-grown shrubs; the ground floor is partially below the level of the street, but there are no areas, and only a side entrance marked "Tradesmen" seems to acknowledge the existence of a more humble world.

There are thirty-six houses in Lonsdale Road, not one of which makes any sharper claim for distinction than is conferred by the number plainly marked upon the gas-lamp suspended from the ceiling of its portico. Here are no "Bellevues" or "Ben Lomonds" to set the neighborhood off upon the follies of competitive nomenclature; and although at the back of each house a large oblong garden contains a much better selection of trees and flowering shrubs than the average suburban garden, not even the mild pretentiousness of an appropriate arboreal name is tolerated. Away from the traffic of the main street with its toy dairies and dolls' shops, its omnibuses and helter-skelter of insignificant pedestrians, Lonsdale Road comes to an abrupt end before a tumble-down tarred fence that guards some allotments beside the railway, on the other side of which a high rampart with the outline of cumulus marks the reverse of the panoramic boundary of Earl's Court Exhibition. The road is a thoroughfare for hawkers, policemen, and lovers, because a narrow lane follows the line of the tumble-down fence, leading on one side to the hinterland of West Kensington railway station and on the other gradually widening into a terrace of small red-brick houses, the outworks of similar terraces beyond. Why anybody at least fifty years ago should have built in what must then have been open country or nursery gardens along the North End Road these thirty-six porticoed houses remains inexplicable. Whoever it was may fairly be honored as one of the founders of West Kensington, perhaps second only to the one who divined that by getting it called West Kensington instead of East Fulham or South Hammersmith, and so maintaining in the minds of the professional classes a consciousness of their gentility, he was doing as much for the British Empire as if he had exploited their physique in a new colony.

With whatever romance one might be tempted to embellish the origin of Lonsdale Road on account of an architectural superiority to the streets around, it would be fanciful merely for that to endow it with any influence upon the character of the people who live there. Apart from a house where the drains are bad, that has achieved the reputation of being haunted, because the landlord prefers to let it stay empty rather than spend money on putting the drains in order, Lonsdale Road possesses as unromantic a lot of residences as the most banal of West Kensington streets. The nearest approach to a scandal is the way human beings and cats go courting in the lane at the end; but since the former do not live in Lonsdale Road and the latter are not amenable to any ethical code administered by the police, the residents do not feel the burden of a moral responsibility for their behavior.

Such a dignified road within seven minutes of the railway station had in the year 1881 made a strong appeal to Mr. Gilbert Caffyn, who, having just been appointed assistant secretary to the Church of England Purity Society at the early age of twenty-six, with a salary of £150 a year, was emboldened by his father's death and the inheritance of another £200 a year in brewery shares to persuade Miss Charlotte Doyle that their marriage was immediately feasible. Mr. Caffyn had been all the more anxious to press for a happy conclusion of a two years' engagement because Mrs. Doyle was showing every sign of imminent decease, an event which would eliminate a traditionally unsatisfactory relationship and enrich her daughter with £300 a year of her own. Mr. Caffyn therefore sold a quarter of his shares, purchased a ninety-nine years' lease of 17 Lonsdale Road, the last house on the right-hand side away from the growing traffic of West Kensington, and got married. If No. 17 was nearest the railway, it was also rather larger than the other houses, an important consideration for the assistant secretary of the Church of England Purity Society, who was bound to expect at least as many children as a clergyman. Still, for all its extra windows, it was not a very large house; and when in the year 1902 Mr. Caffyn, now secretary of the Church of England Purity Society, with a salary of £400 a year, looked at his wife, his nine children, his two servants, and himself, he wondered how they all managed to squeeze in. He hoped that his wife, who had been mercifully fallow for seven years, would not have any more children, though it might almost be easier to have more children than to provide for the rapid growing up of those he had already. Why, his eldest son Roland was twenty. The question of his moving into cheap rooms to suit his position as the earner of a guinea a week at a branch bank had been mooted several times already, and Mr. Caffyn had been compelled to turn his study (which he never used) into a bedroom for him and his brother Cecil, now a lanky schoolboy of fifteen, rather than expose himself to the likelihood of having to supplement the bank clerk's salary from his own. Then there was Norah, who was eighteen ... but at this moment Mr. Caffyn realized that he had only eight minutes to catch his train up to Blackfriars, and the problem of Norah was put aside. It was a hot morning in late September, and he had long ceased to enjoy running to catch a train.

The departure of the head of the house shortly after his eldest son was followed by Cecil's hulking off to St. James's with half a dozen books under his arm, then by Agnes's and Edna's chattering down the road like a pair of wagtails to their school, and last of all by Vincent's apprehensive scamper to his school. In comparison with the noise during breakfast, the house was quiet; but Dorothy, the second girl, was fussing in the pantry, and Mrs. Caffyn was fussing in the dining-room, while Gladys and Marjorie, two very pretty children of eight and seven, were reiterating appeals to be allowed to play in the front garden. All these noises, added to the noises made by the servants about their household duties, seemed an indication to Norah Caffyn that she ought to take advantage of such glorious weather to wash her hair. She withdrew to the room shared with Dorothy and, having promised her mother to keep an eye on the children, devoted all her attention to herself. She set about the business of washing her hair with the efficiency she applied to everything personal; it used to annoy her second sister that, while she showed herself so practical in self-adornment, she would always be so wantonly obtuse about household affairs.

"I believe you make muddles on purpose," her sister used to declare.

"I don't want to be domestic, if that's what you mean," Norah would reply.

"Wasting your time always in front of a glass!"

"Sour grapes, my dear! If your hair waved like mine you'd look at yourself often enough."

But this morning Dorothy was making a cake, and Norah was able to linger affectionately over the shampoo, safe from her jealous sneers. When she had dried away with a towel enough of the unbecoming lankness she went over to the open window to recapture from the rich September sun the gold that should flash among her fawn-soft hair. Down below among the laurels and privets of the front garden her two youngest sisters were engaged upon some grubby and laborious task which, though they looked like two fat white rabbits, did not involve, so far as Norah could see, without leaning out of the window, any actual burrowing; and she was much too pleasantly occupied with her own thoughts to take the risk of having to interfere. She had propped against the frame of the wide-open window a looking-glass in which she was admiring herself; but the mirror was not enough, and she often glanced over with a toss of her head to the houses opposite, whence the retired colonel in No. 18 or the young heir of No. 16 might perhaps be able to admire her, too. But Norah was not only occupied in contemplating the beauty of her light-brown hair; she was equally engaged with her heart's desire. For the ninth time in two years she was deep in love, this time so deep indeed that she was trying to bring her mind to bear seriously upon the future and the problem of convincing her father that the affection she had for Wilfred Curlew was something far beyond the capacity of a schoolgirl presented itself anew for urgent solution. Yesterday, when her suitor had joined the family in the dining-room after supper, her father had looked at him with an expression of most discouraging surprise; if he should visit them again to-night, as he probably would, her father might pass from discouraging glances to disagreeable remarks, and might even attempt, when Wilfred was gone, to declare positively that he visited Lonsdale Road too often. Intolerable though it was that she at eighteen should still be exposed to the caprice of paternal taboos, it was obvious that until she made the effort to cut herself free from these antiquated leading-strings she should remain in subjection.

Norah regarded the not very costly engagement-ring of intertwined pansies bedewed with diminutive diamonds. In her own room this ring always adorned the third finger of her left hand, and while she was about the house during the day the third finger of her right hand; but when her father came back from the city it had to be concealed, with old letters and dance programs and moldering flowers, in a basket of girlish keepsakes, the key of which was continually being left on her dressing-table and causing her moments of acute anxiety in the middle of supper. If it was not a valuable ring, it was much the prettiest she had ever possessed, and it seemed to Norah monstrous that a father should have the power to banish such a token of seniority from the admiration of the world. What would happen if after supper to-night she announced her engagement? Some time or other in the future of family events one of the daughters would have to announce her engagement, and who more suitable than herself, the eldest daughter? Was there, after all, so much to be afraid of in her father? Was not this tradition of his fierceness sedulously maintained by her mother for her own protection? When she looked back at the past, Norah could see plainly enough how all these years the mother had hoodwinked her children into respecting the head of the family. He might not be conspicuously less worthy of reverence than the fathers of many other families she knew, but he was certainly not conspicuously more worthy of it. The romantic devotion their mother exacted for him might have been accorded to a parent who resembled George Alexander or Lewis Waller! But as he was—rather short than tall (he was the same height as herself), fussy (the daily paper must remain folded all day while he was at the office, so that he could be helped first to the news as he was helped first to everything else), mean (how could she possibly dress herself on an allowance of £6 5s. a quarter?)—such a parent was not entitled to dispose of his daughter; a daughter was not a newspaper to be kept folded up for his gratification.

"For I am beautiful," she assured her reflection. "It's not conceit on my part. Even my girl friends admit that I'm beautiful—yes, beautiful, not just pretty. Father ought to be jolly grateful to have such a beautiful daughter. I'm sure *he* has no right to expect beautiful children."

A figure moved like a shadow in the depths of one of the rooms in the house opposite, and Norah leaned a little farther out of the window to catch more sunbeams for her hair; but when the figure came into full view she was disgusted to find it was only the servant, who flapped a duster and withdrew without a glance at herself. "If father persists in keeping me hidden away in West Kensington," she grumbled, "he can't expect me to marry a duke. No, I'm eighteen, and I'll marry Wilfred—at least I'll marry him when he can afford to be married, but meanwhile I *will* be engaged. I'm tired of all this deception." Norah was pondering the virtue of frankness, when she heard a step behind her and, turning round, saw her mother's wonted expression of anxiety and mild disapproval.

"Oh well," said Norah, quickly, to anticipate the reproach on her lips, "this is the only place I can dry my hair. And, mother, I can't wait any longer to be engaged to Wilfred. I'm going to have it out with father to-night."

Mrs. Caffyn looked frightened, which was what Norah intended, for she felt in no mood to argue the propriety of sitting at an open window with her hair down, and had deliberately introduced the larger issue.

"My dear child, I hope you will do nothing of the kind. Father has been very worried during the last month by that horrid theater advertisement which upset Canon Wilbraham so much, and he won't be at all in the right mood."

Norah sighed patiently, avoided pouting, because she had been warned by a girl friend whose opinion she valued against spoiling the shape of her mouth, and with a shrug of her shoulders turned away and went on brushing her hair.

"My dear child," Mrs. Caffyn began, deprecatingly.

"Oh well, I can't sit in any other room! Besides, the kids are playing down below, and I can't keep an eye on them from anywhere else as well as I can from here."

"Playing in the front garden?" repeated Mrs. Caffyn, anxiously. Anything positive done by any of her children always made her anxious, and she hurried across to the window to call down to them. The two little girls had managed to smear themselves from head to foot with grimy garden-mold, and most unreasonably Mrs. Caffyn could not see that their grubbiness was of no importance compared with the question of whether Norah's hair was not always exactly the color of mignonette buds. She began to admonish them from the window, and they defended themselves against her reproaches by calling upon their eldest sister to testify that what they had done they had done with her acquiescence, since she had not uttered a word against their behavior. Norah declared that she could not possibly go down-stairs without undoing all the good of her shampoo, and in the end Mrs. Caffyn, after ringing ineffectually for her second daughter or one of the servants, had to go down herself and rescue Gladys and Marjorie from the temptations of the front garden.

"Thank Heaven for a little peace," sighed Norah to herself. She sat there in a delicious paradise of self-esteem and, looking at herself in the glass, was so much thrilled in the contemplation of her own beauty that she forgot all about her engagement, all about the lack of spectators, all about everything except the way her features conformed to what in women she most admired. She thought compassionately of her mother's faded fairness, and wondered with a frown of esthetic concern why her mother's face was so downy. If her own chin began to show signs of fluffing over like that, she would spend her last halfpenny on removing hairs that actually in some lights glistened like a smear of honey; luckily there was nothing in her own face that she wanted to change. Her mother must have been pretty once, but never more than pretty, because she had blue eyes. How glad she was that with her light hair went deep brown eyes instead of commonplace blue eyes, and that her mouth instead of being rather full and indefinite was a firm bow the beauty of which did not depend upon the freshness of youth. Not that she need fear even the far-off formidable thirties with such a complexion and such teeth. Apart from superfluous hairs her mother's complexion was still good, and even her father had white teeth. Her own nose, straight and small, was neither so straight nor so small as to be insipid, and her chin, tapering exquisitely, was cleft, not dimpled. Dimples seemed to Norah vulgar, and she could not imagine why they were ever considered worthy of admiration. No, with all her perfection of color and form she was mercifully free from the least suggestion of "dolliness"; she was too tall, and had much too good a figure ever to run any risk of that.

"I'm really more beautiful even than I thought, now that I'm looking at myself very critically. And, of course, I shall get more beautiful, especially when I've found out what way my hair suits me best. I shall make all sorts of experiments with it. There's bound to be one way that suits me better than others, if only it isn't too unfashionable. I suppose father hopes secretly that I shall make a brilliant marriage, because even he must realize that I am exceptionally beautiful."

She played condescendingly with the notion of being able to announce that she was engaged to a viscount, and imagined with what awe the family would receive the news.

"However, that's my affair," she decided. "It's not likely father will bring back a viscount to supper. Besides, I'm not mercenary, and if I choose to love a poor man I will. My looks were given to me, not to father, and if he thinks he's going to get the benefit of them he's made a great mistake."

Norah's meditations were suddenly interrupted by the entrance of her sister Dorothy, a dark, pleasant, practical girl of sixteen, who was already so much interested in household affairs that Norah feared her indifference to dress was due to something more than immaturity, was indeed the outcome of an ineradicable propensity toward dowdiness.

"I wish you wouldn't burst into rooms like that," she protested, crossly.

But Dorothy only hummed round the room in search of what she was looking for, and paid no more attention to her elder sister than a bee would have done.

"And if you've got to come up-stairs to our room when you're in the middle of cooking," Norah went on, "you might at least wipe your hands and your arms first. You're covering everything with flour," she grumbled.

"That's better than covering it with powder," retorted Dorothy.

"What a silly remark!"

"Is it, my dear? Sorry the cap fits so well."

Norah turned away from this obtrusive sister in disdain, asking herself for perhaps the thousandth time what purpose in life she was possibly intended to serve. Apart from the fact that she was dark and distinctly not even good-looking, there seemed no excuse for Dorothy's existence, and Norah made up her mind that she would not bother any more about trying to make her dress with good taste; it simply was not worth while.

"Eureka!" cried Dorothy, triumphantly waving an egg-beater.

"What a disgusting thing to leave in a bedroom!" Norah exclaimed.

Her sister courtesied exasperatingly in the doorway for answer, and before Norah could say another word was charging down the stairs three at a time in a series of diminishing thuds.

Norah turned back, with a shudder for her sister's savagery, to the contemplation of her own hair. In a revulsion against the indecency of family life she resolved firmly that, whatever the fuss, she would be engaged to Wilfred Curlew immediately, and that Wilfred himself must at all costs quickly accumulate enough money to enable her to marry him and escape from this den of sisters and brothers and parents.

"If father had only one child, or perhaps two, he might be entitled to interference with our private lives; but when he's got nine, he must expect us to look after ourselves. It's bad enough now when Cecil, Agnes, Edna, and Vincent are all at school and out of the way, at any rate for some of the time, but what will it be like in a few years?"

Norah shrank from the prospect of that overpopulated future for which the temporary emptiness of Lonsdale Road was no consolation, and, removing the mirror from the window-sill, she sat down at her dressing-table and devoted herself to the adjustment of the arcuated pad of mock hair that was an indispensable adjunct to the pompadour style then in vogue.

Norah had just succeeded in achieving what was hitherto her most successful effort with the pompadour when she heard somebody whistling for her from the pavement; going to the window, she saw that it was her friend, Lily Haden, whom she had known and hated at school two years ago, but whom now, by one of those unaccountably abrupt changes of feminine predilection, she liked very much. The new intimacy had only lately been begotten out of a chance rencounter, and perhaps it would never have been born if Roland, her eldest brother, had not condemned Lily from the altitude of his twenty-year-old priggishness and found in Dorothy a supporter of his point of view. That the brother and sister on either side of her should be hostile to a friend of hers was enough to make Norah fond of Lily, who belonged to a type of ethereal blonde that she hoped did not compete too successfully with herself. Occasionally, at the beginning of the new friendship, Norah was assailed by doubts about this, which intensified her prejudice against blue eyes, not to mention excessive slimness and immoderate length of neck. However, though Lily was not really at all interesting, it was impossible to deny that she was something more than pretty, and when, after a few carefully observed walks, Norah discovered that the percentage of people who looked twice at herself exceeded the percentage of those who looked twice at Lily, she was almost inclined to admit that Lily was beautiful. Quite sincerely, therefore, she was able to call down that she was awfully glad to see her friend; quite honestly, too, she was able to admire her standing there on the sunny pavement below.

The fine autumn weather had allowed the young women of West Kensington to prolong their summery charms with brightly tinted dresses, and in all the dull decades of their existence the houses of Lonsdale Road, even in their first lilac-scented May, had perhaps never beheld a truer picture of spring than this autumnal picture now before them of that tall, slim girl in her linen dress of powder-blue swaying gently as a fountain is swayed by the wind, and above her, framed by dingy bricks that intensified the brilliance of the subject, that other girl in a kimono tea-rose hued from many washings, herself like a tea-rose of exquisite color and form. Yet Mrs. Caffyn, when she hurried into Norah's room, could deduce no more from this rebirth of spring in autumn than a cause for the critical stares of neighbors, and begged her either to invite her friend indoors or to come away from the window.

"I wanted to ask Lily to lunch," said Norah, fretfully.

Mrs. Caffyn was in despair at the notion.

"You have plenty of time to talk to her. It's not yet twelve o'clock," she urged, "and with the children coming home from school and having to be got off again it *is* so difficult to manage with extra people at meals."

"Everything seems difficult to manage in this house."

"I'm sorry to disappoint you, but you must try to think of other people a little."

"It would be difficult to think of anything else in Lonsdale Road, mother dear. Lily," she called out from the window, "come up and talk to me before the animals come roaring home to be fed."

"Norah dear, I'd rather you didn't refer to your brothers and sisters like that," Mrs. Caffyn rebuked, with an attempt at authority that only made her daughter laugh. It may not have been a pleasant laugh to hear, and Mrs. Caffyn may have been right to leave the room with a shake of the head; but Norah's teeth were so white and regular that it was a delightful laugh to look at, and Norah was so intent on watching its effect in the glass that she did not notice her mother had gone away in vexation. Presently she and Lily were deep in the discussion of pompadour pads, so enthralling a subject that when Norah wanted to talk about her engagement it was nearly dinner-time, and she felt more than ever the injustice of not being able to invite her friend to the family meal.

"I must talk to you about Wilfred," she said. "We must have a long talk, because I'm determined to have it settled."

At that moment, with swinging of satchels and banging of doors and much noisy laughter, Agnes and Edna, getting on, respectively, for thirteen and fourteen, arrived back from the school that not so long ago Norah and Lily had themselves attended.

"But it's impossible to talk now," grumbled Norah; and as if to accentuate the truth of this remark her brother Vincent, aged ten, came tearing down the road, dribbling a tin can before him and intoxicated with the news of having been chosen to play half-back for his class. In another two years, he boasted, he would be in the Eleven.

"Why don't you come round to Shelley Mansions this evening?" Lily suggested. "We've invited some friends in."

One of the stipulations made about Norah's friendship with Lily had been that she should never visit the home of her friend, about whose mother all sorts of queer stories were current in West Kensington. To challenge family opinion on this point seemed to her an excellent preliminary to challenging it more severely by insisting on being openly engaged to Wilfred Curlew. She hesitated for a moment, and then announced that she would come.

"To supper?" Lily asked.

After another moment's hesitation Norah promised firmly that she would, and her friend hurried away just as Cecil, a loutish boy with sleeves and trousers much too short for him, slouched back from St. James's. The house which a little while ago had been gently murmurous with that absorbing conversation about pompadour pads now reverberated with the discordant cries of a large family; an overpowering smell of boiled mutton and caper sauce ousted the perfumes from Norah's room; her eyes flashed with resentment, and she went down-stairs to take her place at table.

II

If Norah had been a journalist like her suitor, Wilfred Curlew, she would have described the resolution she made on that September morning as an epoch-making resolution, for since the effect of it was rapidly and firmly to set her on the path of independence it certainly deserved one of the great antediluvian epithets.

Some months ago the Hadens had moved from their house in Trelawney Road because the landlord was so disobliging—as a matter of fact, he was unwilling to wait any longer for the arrears of rent—and they were now inhabiting Shelley Mansions, a gaunt block of flats built on the frontier of West Kensington to withstand the vulgar hordes of Fulham, and as such considered the ultimate outpost of gentility. Most of the tenants, indeed, like the Foreign Legion, were recruited from people who found that their native land was barred to them for various reasons; but if Shelley Mansions lacked the conveniences of civilized flat-life, such as lifts and hall-porters, they possessed one great convenience that was peculiar in West Kensington—nobody bothered about his neighbor's business. Mrs. Haden's elder daughter, Doris, was no longer at home, having recently gone on the stage and almost immediately afterward married; and the small flat, with two empty spare rooms so useful for boxes, was comparatively much larger than the Caffyns' house in Lonsdale Road, the respectability and solid charms of which were spoiled by overcrowding.

Mr. Haden was supposed to be in Burma; but people in the secure heart of West Kensington used to say that Mr. Haden had never existed, a topic that Norah remembered being debated at school, to the great perplexity of the younger girls, who could not imagine how, if there was no Mr. Haden, there could possibly be a Doris and Lily Haden. Nowadays, with years of added knowledge, Norah would have liked to ask her friend more particularly about her absent father; but she was of a cautious temperament, and decided it was easier to accept the Oriental interior of the Shelley Mansions drawing-room as evidence of the truth of the Burmese legend. Her instinct was always against too much intimacy with anybody, and she rather dreaded the responsibility of a secret that might interfere with the freedom of her relations with Lily. Whatever the origins of the household, she decided it was a much more amusing household than the one in Lonsdale Road, and if No. 17 could have achieved the same atmosphere by banishing Mr. Caffyn to Burma, Norah would willingly have packed him off by the next boat.

Mrs. Haden had a loud voice, an effusive manner, and a complexion like a field of clover seen from the window of a passing train. Her coiffure resembled in shape and texture a tinned pineapple; it was, too, almost the same color, probably on account of experimenting with henna on top of peroxide. Norah's inclination to be shocked at her hostess's appearance was mitigated by the pleasure it gave her in demonstrating that Lily's really golden hair was not more likely to prove permanent. Mrs. Haden earned her living by teaching elocution and by reciting. These recitations were mostly interruptions to the conversation of afternoon parties in private houses; but once a year at the Bijou Theater, Notting Hill, she gave a grand performance advertised in the press, when her own recitations were supplemented by a couple of one-act plays never acted before or since, for the production of which some moderately well-known professional friends used to give their services free in order to help Mrs. Haden and the authors. Notwithstanding her energy, she found it very hard to make both ends meet. Norah distinctly remembered that Doris and Lily Haden had left school on account of unpaid fees, and some of the objections raised now to her friendship with Lily were due to Mrs. Caffyn's knowledge that the tradesmen of West Kensington would not allow even a week's credit to the residents of Shelley Mansions. If Mrs. Haden could have overcome their prejudice, her hospitality would doubtless have been illimitable; with all the difficulties they made, it was extensive enough, and she need not have bothered to consecrate a special day to it. But perhaps it pleased her to think that she owned one of the days of the week, for she used to refer to the fame of her Thursdays with as much pride as if they were family jewels.

It was to one of these enslaved Thursdays that Lily had invited Norah, who at first sat shyly back in a wicker chair within the shade of a palm, afraid, so fiercely did Mrs. Haden fix her during a recitation of "Jack Barrett Went to Quetta," that the creakings of her chair were irritating the reciter. Gradually the general atmosphere of freedom and jollity communicated itself to the strange guest, and when the room was so full of tobacco smoke that it was impossible for anybody to recite or to sing or to dance without being almost asphyxiated, she had no qualms about obeying Mrs. Haden's deafening proclamation that everybody must stay to supper. A young man with a long nose, a long neck, an extravagantly V-shaped waistcoat like a medieval doublet, and a skin like a Blue Dorset cheese attached himself to Norah and advised her to sit close to him because he knew his way about the flat. Presumably the advantage of knowing your way about the flat was that you sat still while other people waited on you, and that you obtained second helpings from dishes that did not go round once. Norah seldom resisted an invitation that enabled her to keep quiet while others worked, not because she was lazy, but because rushing about was inclined to heighten her complexion unbecomingly; moreover, since the young man in the V-shaped waistcoat was enough like her notion of a distinguished actor to rouse a mild interest in him, and not sufficiently unlike a gentleman to destroy that interest, she was ready to listen to the advice he was anxious to give her about all sorts of things, but chiefly about the stage.

"Are you studying with Mrs. Haden?" he asked; and when Norah shook her head he turned to her gravely and said: "Oh, but you ought, you know. They may tell you she's a bit old-fashioned, but don't you believe them. Pearl Haden knows her job in and out, and if you've got any talent she'll produce it. Look at me. I was going out with Ma Huntley this autumn as her second walking gentleman, but she wouldn't offer more than two ten, and, as I told her, I really didn't feel called upon to accept less than three. After all, I can always get seven by waiting, and I didn't see why Ma should have me for two ten, especially as she expected me to find my own wigs and ruffles. No, you take my advice and study with Pearl Haden."

"You really recommend her, do you?" asked Norah, condescendingly.

She had never until that moment thought of going on the stage or of taking lessons in elocution from anybody, but the idea of being able to patronize the mother of a friend appealed to her, and, though she was a little doubtful of the way her brothers and sisters would accept her rendering of "Jack Barrett Went to Quetta," she supposed that Wilfred would admire it. One of the charms of being engaged was the security of admiration it provided.

"Though, of course," continued the gentleman in the V-shaped waistcoat, "with your appearance you oughtn't to have to bother much about anything else."

This was very gratifying to Norah; even if there should be trouble when she got home, the evening would have been worth while for this assurance that her looks were capable of making an impression upon artistic society.

"You really think I ought to go on the stage?" she asked, assuming the manner of a person who for a long while has been trying to make up her mind on this very point.

"Everybody ought to go on the stage," the gentleman in the V-shaped waistcoat enthusiastically announced; "at least, of course, not everybody, but certainly everybody who is obviously cut out for the profession like you. But don't be in a hurry to make up your mind," he added. "You're very young." He must have been nearly twenty-five himself. "There's no need to hurry. I was driven to it."

Norah appeared interested and sympathetic. She really was rather interested, because the idea had passed through her mind that Wilfred might go on the stage. If this young man could earn seven pounds a week, surely Wilfred, who was much better looking, could earn ten pounds a week, in which case they might be married at once.

"What drove you to it?" she asked, and then blushed in confusion; being driven to anything was associated in Norah's mind with drink, and she thought the young man might be embarrassed by her question.

"Oh, a woman!" he replied, in a lofty tone. "But don't let's talk about things that are past and over. Let's eat and drink to-day, for to-morrow—Did you ever read Omar Khayyam? A man in our crowd introduced me to him last year. I tell you, after Omar Khayyam Kipling isn't in it. I suppose you read a good deal of poetry?"

"A good deal," Norah admitted. "At least, I used to read a good deal."

This was true; she had read several volumes at school under the menaces of the literature mistress.

"Well, if I may offer you some advice," said the young man, "go on reading poetry. I may as well confess right out that poetry has been my salvation. Have some more of this shape? It's a little soft, but the flavor's excellent." After supper Norah took Lily aside and told her she must go home at once.

"But, Norah," protested the daughter of the flat, without being able to conceal a slight inflection of scorn, "the evening's only just beginning. Lots of people come in after supper always."

Norah resented Lily's tone of superiority; but inasmuch as this was her first experiment in open defiance, she decided not to go too far this time, especially as she was not quite sure how far her father's unreasonableness might not extend.

"Cyril Vavasour will see you home," said Lily. "He's awfully gone on you. He told me you were one of the most beautiful girls he'd ever met."

Norah could not help feeling flattered by such a testimonial from one whose experience among women had evidently been immense, and though she might have expected a superlative without qualification from somebody who met her in a West Kensington drawing-room, she realized that she must expect a slight qualification from a world-wanderer like Mr. Vavasour. A few minutes later Norah and her appreciative new acquaintance descended the echoing steps of Shelley Mansions and were soon safe from any suggestion of Fulham in the landscape and walking slowly through the familiar streets of West Kensington, which in the autumnal mistiness looked grave and imposing. The sky was clear above them, and a fat, yellow moon was rolling along behind a battlement of chimney-tops.

"O moon of my delight who know'st no wane!" quoted Mr. Vavasour, in a devout apostrophe.

Perhaps it was because he imagined himself in a Persian garden much farther away from West Kensington than even Fulham was that he allowed himself to take Norah's arm; nor did she make any objection. After all, he considered her one of the most beautiful girls he had ever met, and, being engaged to be married, she could allow her arm to be taken without danger or loss of dignity.

"And so you really advise me to go on the stage?" she asked, as if she would insinuate that the taking of her arm was only a gesture of interrogation.

"Absolutely," Mr. Vavasour replied.

"Yes, but of course my father's awfully old-fashioned, and he may think I oughtn't to go on the stage."

"Too much exposed to temptation and all that, I suppose?" suggested Mr. Vavasour.

"Oh no," said Norah, irritably, withdrawing her arm. "I didn't mean that. I meant he might think the family wouldn't like it."

She had intended to give the impression of belonging to a poor but noble family without giving the impression of being snobbish, and she was rather annoyed with Mr. Vavasour for not understanding at once what she meant.

"Oh, but people from the best families go on the stage nowadays," he assured her.

"Yes, I suppose they do," Norah agreed.

"And of course you could always change your name," he added.

"Yes, of course I could do that," she admitted.

"I changed mine, for instance," he told her.

"I like the name Vavasour."

"Yes, I rather liked it myself," he said; but he did not volunteer his own name, and she did not ask him to reveal what Howards or Montagus had plucked him forever from their family tree. In any case this was not the moment to embark on fresh confidences, for they were approaching the main street and Norah was almost sure that the figure standing at the corner of Lonsdale Road on the other side was her eldest brother, Roland.

"Don't come any farther," she said. "Perhaps we'll meet again at Lily's some day."

"We shall," Mr. Vavasour announced, with conviction. "Good night." He swept his hat from his head with a flourish and Norah shook hands with him. She had been rather afraid all the way back that he would try to kiss her good night, but gentle blood and the bright arc-lamp under which they were standing combined to deter him, and they parted as ceremoniously as if his V-shaped waistcoat was really a medieval doublet.

"Oh, it *was* you," said Roland.

"How do you mean it *was* me? Who did you think it was?"

"Do you know what the time is? Half past ten!"

"Thanks very much," said Norah, sarcastically. "The wrist-watch you gave me at Christmas is not yet broken."

"Don't be silly, Norah," he protested. "Father's in an awful wax. I've been hanging about here for the last half-hour, because I couldn't stand it."

They were walking quickly down Lonsdale Road, and Norah was thinking how clumsily he walked compared with Mr. Vavasour and yet how much better looking he was.

"Did Wilfred come?" she asked.

Her brother nodded. "Yes, but I told him you weren't in, and he went off in a bit of a gloom."

They had reached the gate of No. 17 by now, and the house seemed to Norah unreasonably hushed for this hour of the evening. Beyond the railway line the sky was lit up with the glare of the Exhibition, and the music that the military band was playing—it was a selection from "The Earl and the Girl"—was distinctly audible.

"Why should father object to my going out in the evening?" she asked, turning to her brother sharply. "He used to object to your smoking."

Roland removed from his mouth the large pipe and thought ponderously for a minute. It was quite true that only two years ago his father had objected to his smoking, and that with great difficulty he had been able to persuade him that bank clerks always smoked. Since that struggle his father had yielded him a grudging admission that he was grown up. The long years before he should be a bank manager rose like a huge array of black clouds before his vision, and though he disapproved of sisters acting on their own initiative, something in this autumnal night—perhaps it was only the sound of the distant band—created in him a sudden sympathy with any aspirations to freedom. Perhaps, if Norah had encouraged him at that moment, he would have stood up for her independence; but he felt that his company only irritated her and without a word he led the way up the steps, dimly aware that he and she had already set foot upon the diverging paths of their lives.

The dining-room had been cleared for action. Ordinarily at this hour the room was full of young people playing billiards on the convertible dining-table; but to-night the table had not been uncovered, the children had all gone to bed, and Mr. Caffyn was reading the *Daily Telegraph*, not as one might have supposed with enjoyment of the unusual peace, but, on the contrary, in a vague annoyance that his perusal of the leading article was not being interrupted by the butt-end of a cue or the chronicle of London Day by Day being punctuated by billiard-balls leaping into his lap. His patriarchal feelings had, in fact, been deeply wounded by his daughter's behavior, and though for the first time in months he had been able to put on his slippers without having to hold up a noisy game while they were being looked for, he was not at all grateful.

"I've had my supper," Norah informed him, brightly.

This really annoyed Mr. Caffyn extremely, for he had been looking forward to telling his daughter that her supper had been kept waiting until ten o'clock, when it had finally been removed in order to allow the servants to go to bed. At this moment Mrs. Caffyn, who had hurried down-stairs to the kitchen as soon as she heard Norah coming, arrived in the dining-room with a tray.

"She's had her supper," said Mr. Caffyn, indignantly.

"Oh, I was afraid—" his wife began.

"Oh no, she's had her supper," said Mr. Caffyn. "Good Heavens! I don't know what the world's coming to!"

Since her father was making a cosmic affair of her behavior in going out to supper without leave, Norah decided to give him something to worry about in earnest, and, seating herself in the arm-chair on the other side of the fireplace, she prepared to argue with him. Mrs. Caffyn began to murmur about going to bed and talking things over when father came back from the office to-morrow, but Norah waved aside all procrastination.

"I want to talk about my engagement," she began.

Roland, who had just reached the door, stopped. Wilfred Curlew was a friend of his; in fact, it was he who had first brought him to the house, and though he knew that anything in the nature of an engagement between him and one of his sisters was ridiculous, he hoped that a soothing testimony from him would prevent Wilfred's final exclusion from the family circle.

"Norah, dear child, it isn't nice to begin playing jokes upon your father at this hour, especially when he isn't very pleased with you," Mrs. Caffyn said, waving her eyes in the direction of the door.

"I'm not at all sleepy," said Norah, coldly. "And I'm not joking. I want to know if father is going to let Wilfred and me be openly engaged?" she persisted, holding up her left hand so that the gaslight illuminated the ring upon the third finger.

"And who may Wilfred be?" demanded Mr. Caffyn.

This seemed to Roland a suitable moment for his intervention, and, though he had for some time been aware that his father was growing impatient of their habitual visitor, he pretended to accept this attitude of Olympian ignorance and reminded him that Wilfred was a friend who sometimes came in during the evening.

"You said once, if you remember, that he was rather a clever fellow. As a matter of fact he's doing well, you know, considering that he's not long gone in for journalism. He's just been taken on the staff of the *Evening Herald*. He's been doing that murder in Kentish Town."

Mr. Caffyn rose from his chair and with an elaborate assumption of irony inquired if his daughter proposed to engage herself on the strength of a murder in Kentish Town. Norah had got up when her father did and was listening with a contemptuous expression while he dilated on the folly of long engagements.

"Yes, but I don't intend it to be a long engagement," Norah proclaimed, when he paused for a moment to chew his heavy mustache. "I intend to get married."

Mr. Caffyn swung round upon his heels and faced his daughter.

"This, I suppose, is the result of the education I've given you. Insolence and defiance! Don't say another word or you'll make me lose my temper. Not anotherword. Norah, I insist on silence. Do you hear me? You have grievously disappointed my fondest hopes. I have not been a strict father. Indeed, I have been too indulgent. But I never imagined *my* daughter capable of a folly like this. If I'd thought, twenty-one years ago, when I bought this house with the idea of creating a happy home for you all, that I should be repaid like this I would have.... I would have...."

But Mr. Caffyn's apodosis was never divulged, because, seized with an access of rage, he turned out the gas and hurried from the room. In the hall he shouted back to know if his wife was going to sit up all night. Mrs. Caffyn hurried after her husband as fast as she was able across the darkened room.

"I'm coming, dear, now. Yes, dear, I'm coming now. Ouch! My knee!... I'm sure Norah will be more sensible in the morning," she was heard murmuring on her way up-stairs.

"I suppose he thinks I shall go on living with him forever," exclaimed Norah, savagely throwing herself down into her father's arm-chair. "In my opinion most parents are fit to be only children. Light the gas again, Roland; I want to write a note to Wilfred."

III

By the time morning was come Norah had decided that she would rather go on the stage than be engaged to Wilfred Curlew. The extraordinary thing was that she should never have realized, before her conversation with Mr. Vavasour, how obviously the stage was indicated as the right career for her. It was true that she had never until now seriously contemplated a career, and the mild way she had accepted herself merely as the most important member of a large family was sufficient answer to the silly accusations made by her father last night. Perhaps he would begin to appreciate her now when he was on the point of losing her; perhaps he would regret that he had ever suggested she was indifferent to the claims of family life; in future she should take care to be indifferent to everybody's feelings except her own; she would teach her father a lesson. It never entered Norah's head that there would be any difficulty about going on the stage apart from paternal opposition, and she wondered how many famous people had owed their careers to a fortuitous event like her meeting with Mr. Vavasour. At any rate, it would not be more difficult to obtain her father's permission to embark on this suddenly conceived adventure than it would be to obtain his permission to wear on the third finger of her left hand the rather cheap ring that was the outward sign of her intention to marry Wilfred. Confronted by the two alternatives—success in the theater and matrimony with Wilfred—she felt that success was much the less remote of the two; in fact, the more she thought about it the farther away receded matrimony and the more clearly defined became success. "I don't want to be a great actress," she explained to herself; "I want to be a successful actress." She half made up her mind to go out and talk to Lily about the new project, but on second thoughts she decided not to alarm her parents by any prospect so definite as would be implied in availing herself of the practical assistance that Lily and her mother could afford her in carrying out her plan. It would be more tactful to present as alternatives the definite fact of being engaged to Wilfred or the indefinite idea of being able some time or other in the future to adopt the stage as a profession. The more Norah thought about Wilfred the less in love with him she felt, and the less in love with him she felt the easier would be her task to-night. In her note she had told him to come in after supper, as usual, but she had not said a word about her intention to precipitate their affair. Would it impress her father if she and Wilfred were to meet him at the station and approach the subject before supper? No, on the whole, she decided, it would be more prudent to provoke the final scene otherwise, and her heart quickened slightly at the thought of the surprise she was going to spring upon the family that evening.

Norah was unusually pleasant to everybody all day: she gave Vincent some sweets that she did not like herself; she offered to take Gladys and Marjorie for a walk in Kensington Gardens, because a rumor had reached her of a wonderful display of hats in one of the big shops in Kensington High Street. She noticed that when her father came back from the office he seemed to have forgotten about the scene of last night, and she saw her mother's spirits rising at the prospect of an undisturbed evening. After supper Mr. Caffyn sat down as usual in his arm-chair; Gladys and Marjorie, tired after their long walk and exhausted with the contemplation of shop-windows in which they had perceived nothing to interest themselves, went off to bed without trying for a moment's grace. The upper leaves of the dining-table were removed, and a party of billiards was made up with Norah and Cecil matched against Roland and Dorothy; Vincent was allowed to chalk the tips of the cues, Agnes and Edna to quarrel over the marking. Mrs. Caffyn, with a sigh of relief for the comfortable wheels on which the evening was running, took the arm-chair opposite her husband and read with unusual concentration what she imagined was yesterday's morning paper, but which, as a matter of fact, was the morning paper of a month ago. Soon the front-door bell rang, and a friend of Roland's, called Arthur Drake, with whom Norah had been in love for a week about a year ago and of whom Dorothy was slightly enamoured at the present, came in full of a new round game for the billiard-table that he had just learned in another house. Cecil went off to his home-work and left Arthur to explain the new game—a complicated invention in which five small skittles, a cork, and a bell suspended from the gas-bracket each played a part. Mr. Caffyn fended off the butt-ends of the cues that were continually bumping into him amid a great deal of shouting and laughter; Agnes trod on her mother's corn; Vincent grazed his knuckles in fielding a billiard-ball that was bound for his father's head.

"And where's old Wilfred?" Arthur Drake suddenly inquired.

Another ring at the front door answered his question and Norah's suitor came in. He was a loose-jointed young man of about twenty-two, with tumbled wavy hair, bright gray eyes, and a trick, when he was feeling shy, of supporting with one arm the small of his back. His long, dogmatic chin was balanced by an irregular and humorous mouth; his personality was attractive, and if he had earned five times as much as he earned as reporter on the staff of the *Evening Herald*, or even if he had been paid for the fierce and satirical articles he wrote on the condition of modern society for a socialist weekly called *The Red Lamp*, he might not have been considered an unsuitable mate for Norah. As it was, Mr. Caffyn looked up at him with as much abhorrence as he would have betrayed at the entrance into his dining-room of the dog that his children were always threatening to procure and the purchase of which he was constantly forbidding. Wilfred tried hard to lose himself in the round game, and whenever he was called upon to make a shot from the corner where Mr. Caffyn was sitting he did so with such unwillingness to disturb Mr. Caffyn that he always missed it. Every time he found an opportunity to pass Norah in the narrow gangway between the wall and the table he tried to squeeze her hand; and he did his best by bribing Vincent with some horse-chestnuts he had collected that morning at Kew, where his work had taken him to investigate an alleged outrage in the Temperate House, to inspire Vincent with an unquenchable desire to play Up Jenkins. Norah, however, had a plan of her own that made the notion of occasionally clasping Wilfred's hand under the table during Up Jenkins seem colorless, and Wilfred, who in his most optimistic prevision of the evening had not counted upon more than two or three kisses snatched by ruse, suddenly found himself invited by her to abandon the game and come into the drawing-room next door.

The drawing-room of No. 17 was invested every Wednesday afternoon by a quantity of punctilious ladies who came to call on Mrs. Caffyn. Owing to the number of its ornaments and the flimsiness of its furniture, it was not considered a suitable room for general use; moreover, as secretary of the Church of England Purity Society, it occasionally fell to Mr. Caffyn's lot to interview various clergymen there on confidential matters, and in a house like 17 Lonsdale Road, worn and torn by children, it was essential to preserve one room in a condition of gelid perfection. So rarely was the room used that the over-worked servants had not bothered to draw the curtains at dusk, and when Wilfred and Norah retired into its seclusion the chilly gloom was accentuated by the street-lamps gleaming through the bare lime-trees at the end of the garden. Norah told her lover to light the gas, and not even the sickly green incandescence availed to make her appear less beautiful to him in this desert of ugly knickknacks.

"No, don't pull the curtains," she said, quickly, "and don't kiss me here, because people might see you from the street. I didn't ask you to come in here to make love."

Perhaps a sense of the theater had always been dormant in Norah, for she went on as if she were making a set speech; but Wilfred was much too deep in love to let the cynicism upon which he plumed himself apply to her, and he listened humbly.

"We can't go on like this forever," she wound up. "We must be engaged openly. I told father that last night, but he won't hear of it, so what are we to do?"

"Darling, I'm ready to do anything."

"Oh, anything!" she repeated, petulantly. "What is anything? He'll be here in a minute, and you've got to tell him that unless he consents to our being engaged you'll persuade me to elope."

"Do you think he'd give way then?" Wilfred asked, doubtfully. He was very much in love with Norah, but he could not help remembering that he, too, had a father who, after an argument every Sunday evening, still allowed him ten shillings a week for pocket-money. If he were to elope, he should not only be certain to lose that supplement to his own earnings, but he should also involve in deeper discredit the profession he had adopted instead of the law, which Mr. Curlew, senior, had designed him to enter by way of the office of an old friend who was a solicitor.

Norah wished that her father would come in and interrupt what should have been a passionate scene, but which was in reality as cold as the room where it was being played. She watched herself and Wilfred, whom the incandescent gas did not set off to advantage, in the large mirror that formed the over-mantel of the fireplace, and she realized now, as she had never realized before in her life, how amazingly she stood out from her surroundings.

"You haven't kissed me once this evening," Wilfred began; but she shook herself free from his tentative embrace, and with one eye on the door for her father's entrance and the other on the mirror, or rather with both eyes at one moment on the door and immediately afterward on the mirror—a movement which displayed their brilliancy and depth—she went on enumerating to her suitor the material difficulties that made their engagement so hopeless.

"But I'm getting on," he insisted. "The editor was very pleased with the way I handled that Kentish Town murder. They don't consider me at all a dud in Fleet Street. I'm sure I give everybody in this house quite a wrong impression of myself because I feel nervous and awkward when I'm here; but I don't think there's really much doubt that in another couple of years I shall be in quite a different position financially. Besides, I hope to do original work, and if a friend of mine can raise the money to start this new weekly—"

"Oh, if, if, if!" interrupted Norah, impatiently.

"Norah, don't you love me any more?"

"Of course I love you," she said. "Don't be so stupid."

"You seem different to-night."

"You wouldn't like me to be always the same, would you?"

"No, but—" He broke off, and turned away with a sigh to regard the melancholy street-lamps twinkling through the lime-trees at the end of the garden.

"I think it's I who ought to be angry, not you," said Norah. "I offered to marry you at once, and you instantly began to make excuses."

"Norah!" protested the young man.

"Oh, how I hate everything!" she burst out, looking round her with a sharper consciousness than she had ever experienced before of the drawing-room's ugliness and life's banality. At this moment Mrs. Caffyn put her head timidly round the door.

"You'd better come back to the dining-room, dear," she advised. "I think father's just noticed you're not there."

"That's exactly what I meant him to do."

"Norah!" exclaimed her mother, in a shocked voice. "What has come over you these last two days?"

Wilfred was supporting the small of his back in an unsuccessful effort to look at ease, and Norah was wondering more than ever how she could ever have fancied herself in love with him. How awkward he appeared standing there, almost—she hesitated a moment before she allowed herself to think the worst it was possible to think of anybody—almost common! She looked half apprehensively at Wilfred to see if he had divined her unspoken thought. She would not like him to know that she was thinking him—almost common; he might never get over it. She was sure he was particularly sensitive on that point because in *The Red Lamp* he was always declaiming against snobbery.

Suddenly they heard the dining-room door open, and Mrs. Caffyn had barely time to breathe an agonized, "Oh, dear, what did I tell you would happen?" before the head of the house came in. Upon the dining-room an appalled silence must have fallen when Mr. Caffyn rose from his chair, and one could fancy the frightened players, cues in hands, huddled against the wall in dread of the imminent catastrophe. The whole house was electric as before an impending storm, and above the stillness the mutter of a passing omnibus sounded like remote thunder. With so much atmospheric help Mr. Caffyn ought to have been able to achieve something more impressive than his, "Oh, you're in here, are you? I wish you wouldn't light the gas in the drawing-room when there's no need for it."

"I thought you wouldn't like us to sit in the dark," Norah murmured, primly.

"Don't deliberately misunderstand me. You know perfectly well what I mean. Moreover, I don't think it's nice for the children; it may put all sorts of ideas into their young heads."

Inasmuch as Mr. Caffyn was secretary of the Church of England Purity Society with private means of his own, while his daughter's suitor was an agnostic journalist who had never yet earned more than thirty-five shillings in one week, it is perhaps not astonishing that the young man should have begun to apologize for lighting the gas needlessly. To Norah, however, these apologies sounded infinitely pusillanimous; from having been very much in love yesterday morning she had already reached indifference, and this final exhibition of cowardice brought her to the point of positively disliking Wilfred. Nevertheless, she managed somehow to impress her father with her intention to die rather than give him up, and after an argument of about ten minutes, in the course of which Norah did all the talking, her father all the shouting, and her mother and suitor all the fidgeting, Mr. Caffyn was at last sufficiently exasperated and ordered Wilfred Curlew to leave the house immediately. In spite of Mrs. Caffyn's entreaties the pitch of her husband's voice had been so piercing that he had probably managed not merely to put ideas into the heads of the children still in the dining-room, but even to corrupt the dreams of the sleeping innocents up-stairs.

"Gilbert dear," his wife besought. "The servants!"

"I pay my servants to attend to me, not to my affairs," said Mr. Caffyn, majestically. His wife might have replied that under the terms of their marriage contract it was she who paid the servants out of her own money; but having been married twenty-one years she had long ceased to derive any satisfaction from putting herself in the right. Poor Wilfred, finding that he must either say something to break the silence which had succeeded Mr. Caffyn's denunciation of his behavior or retire, preferred to retire, and with one arm firmly wedged into the small of his back he stumbled awkwardly down the hall to the front door. Norah made no attempt to alleviate the discomfiture of his exit; but Arthur Drake, with a chivalry, or, to put it at its lowest valuation, with a social tact that amazed her, covered Wilfred's retreat by such a display of farewell courtesies as made even the practical Dorothy pause and consider if there might not be something in love, after all.

"Bolt the door," Mr. Caffyn commanded. "And be sure that the chain is properly fastened."

Then rather at a loss how to maintain the level of his majesty and wrath, he luckily discovered that Vincent had not yet gone to bed, and exhorted the assembled family to tell him if he paid £8 a term to Mr. Randell for Vincent to grow up into a pot-boy or a billiard-marker. Cecil, the recent winner of a senior scholarship at St. James's, had been grinding at his homework in the bedroom, and he came out into the hall at this moment to plead pathetically for a few doors to be shut. His father improved the occasion by holding up Cecil as a moral example to the rest of the family, who were made to feel that if Gilbert Caffyn had not produced Cecil Caffyn, Gilbert Caffyn's life would have been wasted. The more he descanted upon Cecil's diligence and dutifulness the more sheepish Cecil himself became, so that with every fresh encomium his sleeves revealed another inch of ink-stained cuff. The only way to stop Mr. Caffyn and restore Cecil to the algebraical problem from which he had been raped by the noise outside his room seemed to be for everybody to go to bed. Agnes and Edna, their heads stuffed full of new ideas, went giggling up-stairs, whither Dorothy, yawning very elaborately, followed them. Roland decided that Cecil groaning over an algebra problem would be more endurable than having to listen to a renewal of the argument between Norah and his father, and he, too, retired. The gradual melting away of the audience quieted Mr. Caffyn, who, when he had lowered or extinguished all the gas-jets except those in the dining-room, felt that he had shown himself master of his own house, and returned to his arm-chair with the intention of nodding over the minor news in the paper until he was ready for bed himself. Norah, however, in spite of her mother's prods and whispered protests, brought him sharply back to the matter in dispute.

"Suppose I insist on being engaged to Wilfred?" she began.

"Good Heavens!" cried Mr. Caffyn. "Am I never to be allowed a little bit of peace? Here am I working all day to keep you clothed and fed, and every night of my life is made a burden to me. You don't appreciate what it is to have a father like me." His wife patted him soothingly and flatteringly upon the shoulder as if she would assure him that they all really appreciated the quality of his fatherhood very much. "Why, I know fathers," went on Mr. Caffyn, indignantly, "who spend every evening at their clubs, and upon my soul, I don't blame them. I was talking to the Bishop of Chelsea to-day. He came into the office to consult me about the scandalous language used at the whelk-stalls in Walham Road on Saturday nights—we're taking up the question with the municipal authorities. He told me I looked tired out. 'You look tired out, Mr. Caffyn,' he said. 'I am tired out, my lord,' I answered. And *he* was very sympathetic."

"You hear that, Norah dear?" said Mrs. Caffyn, twitching her fingers with nervousness. "Now don't worry your father any more."

"As soon as he answers my question I sha'n't worry him any more. Suppose I insist on being engaged to Wilfred Curlew? Suppose I run away and get married to him?"

"Have you any conception what marriage means?" demanded Mr. Caffyn. "Do you realize that I waited two years to marry your mother, and that I didn't propose to her until it was quite evident that my poor father must soon die? I suppose you don't want me to die, do you? Don't imagine that my death will make any difference, please."

"Gilbert, Gilbert!" begged his wife.

"Well, really, nowadays children behave in such an extraordinary fashion that it wouldn't surprise me at all to hear Norah was counting on my death."

"Gilbert, Gilbert!" she repeated, and looked in agony at the gas, as if she expected it to turn blue at such a horrible suggestion.

"If I don't marry Wilfred," Norah went on, "I must earn my own living."

"How?" inquired her father, with an assumption of blustering incredulity.

"By going on the stage."

"On the stage?" he repeated. "Do you realize that only yesterday I had to deal with the question of our attitude toward the posters of several theaters?"

"That wouldn't have anything to do with me," said Norah.

"But how are you going on the stage?" her father continued.

"I should try to get an engagement."

"Oh, would you, indeed? Ha-ha! Your mind seems to be running on engagements, my child. However, this engagement is even more visionary and improbable than the other one," said Mr. Caffyn, with a laugh. "I'm afraid you think it's easier than it is, my dear girl. I have a little experience of the stage—I regret to say chiefly of its worst side—and I can assure you that it's not at all easy, really."

"But if I can get an engagement?" persisted Norah.

"Why, in that case we'll talk about it," said her father. "Yes, yes, there'll be plenty of time to talk about that later on. And now if you have no objection I should like to read what Mr. Balfour is saying about Protection. It's a pity you don't try to take some interest in the affairs of your country instead of— However, I suppose that's *too* much to expect from the younger generation."

"I must have your promise," Norah insisted. "If I write to Wilfred to-night and tell him he mustn't come to the house any more, will you let me go on the stage?"

"We'll see about it," parried Mr. Caffyn.

"No, I must have a definite promise."

"Must, Norah? Do, dear child, remember that you're speaking to your father," murmured her mother.

"Oh, that's the modern way we bring up our children," said Mr. Caffyn. "Before I know where I am I shall have Vincent ordering me up to bed."

His wife laughed with such conjugal enthusiasm at his joke that the last vestige of Mr. Caffyn's ill humor disappeared, and, being suddenly struck with the extreme beauty of his eldest daughter as she waited there bright-eyed in expectation of his answer, he promised her that if she would break off all communication with that confounded young Curlew and could obtain an engagement for herself, he would probably not create any difficulties. Her face lit up with satisfaction and, bending over, she kissed her father on the forehead with as much good will as a young woman kisses an elderly lover who has promised her some diamonds she has long desired.

IV

Norah kept her word and wrote a letter to Wilfred Curlew in which she pointed out the impossibility of embarking on a prolonged and quite indefinite engagement, wished him good luck for the future, and made it clear that she did not intend to have anything more to do with him. The portion of the letter on which she most prided herself was the postscript: "*Don't think that I bear you any ill will. I don't.*" The peace that had lately fallen over South Africa left Wilfred no opportunity of putting his despair at the service of his country; but Norah's behavior benefited the young journalist in the long run by teaching him to mistrust human nature as much as God, a useful lesson for a democrat. Norah, having disembarrassed herself of her suitor, set out in earnest to get on the stage and confided her ambition to Lily. Mrs. Haden's advice was asked, and Norah as a friend of her daughter was given lessons in elocution and deportment without being charged a penny. Mrs. Haden demonstrated to her that she stood very little chance of getting on the stage until she could recite "Jack Barrett Went to Quetta" or "Soldier, Soldier, Come from the Wars" with what she called as much intention as herself; in other words, until the story of Jack Barrett was awarded as much pomp of utterance as the Messenger's speech in Hippolytus and the demobilized soldier greeted with Ophelia's driveling whine. Mrs. Haden would not allow that her pupil's looks were nearly as important as her ability to mouth Rudyard Kipling—perhaps, the pupil thought, because her mistress had a pretty daughter of her own. September deepened to October, October dimmed to November while Norah was wrestling with her dread of seeming ridiculous and was acquiring the unnatural diction that was to be of such value to her first appearance. The lessons came to an abrupt end soon after Mrs. Haden had begun upon her deportment, which to Norah seemed to consist of holding her hands as if she were waiting to rinse them after eating bread and treacle, and of sitting down on a chair as if she had burst one suspender and expected the other to go every minute. One morning when she arrived at Shelley Mansions for her lesson Lily came to the door of the flat and with fearful backward glances cried out that her mother was lying dead in bed.

"Dead?" echoed Norah, irritably. She was always irritated by a sudden alarm. "I wish you wouldn't—" She was going to say "play jokes," but she saw that Lily was speaking the truth, and, having been taught by Mrs. Haden how to suit the action to the word, the expression to the emotion, she contrived to look sympathetic.

"She must have died of heart, the doctor says. I went to see why she didn't ring for her tea and she didn't answer, and when I thought she was asleep she was really dead."

Norah shuddered.

"I'm awfully sorry I've disturbed you in the middle of all this," she murmured.

"But I'm glad you've come," said Lily.

"It's awfully sweet of you, my dear, to be glad; but I wouldn't dream of worrying you at such a moment. And don't stand there shivering in your nightgown. Take my advice and dress yourself. It will distract your mind from other things. You must come round and see me this afternoon, and I'll try to cheer you up. I shall stay in for you. Don't forget."

Norah hurried away from Shelley Mansions, thinking while she walked home how easily this untoward event in the Haden household might hasten the achievement of her own ambition. Lily would obviously have to do something at once, and it would be nice for her to have a companion with whom she could start her career upon the stage. Norah had not intended to take any definite steps until her nineteenth birthday in March, but she was anxious to show her sympathy with Lily, and it was much kinder, really, to make useful plans for the future than to hang about the stricken flat, getting in everybody's light. If Lily came this afternoon they would be able to discuss ways and means; it would be splendid for Lily to be taken right out of herself; it would be nice to invite her after the funeral to come and stay in Lonsdale Road, so that they could talk over things comfortably without always having to go out in this wet weather; yet such an excellent suggestion would be opposed by the family on the ground that there was no room for a stranger. How intolerable that the existence of so many brothers and sisters should interfere with the claims of friendship! Perhaps she could persuade Dorothy to sleep with Gladys and Marjorie for a week or two. She and Lily should have so much to talk over, and if Dorothy were in the room with them it would be an awful bore. Full of schemes for Lily's benefit, she approached her sister on the subject of giving up her bed.

"Anything more you'd like?" asked Dorothy, indignantly.

"I think," said Norah, "that you are without exception the most selfish girl I ever met in all my life."

Dorothy grunted at this accusation, but she refused to surrender her bed, and Norah soon gave up talking in general terms about people who were afraid to expose themselves to a little inconvenience for the sake of doing a kind action, because Lily arrived next day with the news that her sister had obtained leave to be "off" for a week and was advising her to do everything she could to get an engagement as soon as possible. There were problems of arrears of rent and unpaid bills from the solution of which it would be advantageous for Lily to escape by going on tour. The few personal possessions of their mother the sisters would divide between them, and the undertaker was to be satisfied at the expense of a fishmonger who, being new to West Kensington, had let Mrs. Haden run an account.

"And your father?" Norah could not help asking; but Lily avoided a reply, and Norah, who had been too well brought up to ask twice, formed her own conclusions.

"Anyway, my dear," she assured her friend, "you can count on me. I hadn't intended to do anything definite until I was nineteen, but of course I'm not going to desert you. So we'll go and interview managers together."

"Doris advises me to try Walter Keal," said Lily. "Dick—her husband—has given me a letter for him which may be useful, he says."

"Who's Walter Keal?"

"Don't you know?" exclaimed Lily. "He sends out all the Vanity shows."

Norah bit her lips in mortification. She hated not to know things and decided to avoid meeting Doris, who as a professional actress of at least a year's standing would be likely to patronize her.

"You see," Lily went on, "he'll be sending out 'Miss Elsie of Chelsea' at the end of December, and if we could get in the chorus we should be all right till June."

"The chorus?" echoed Norah, disdainfully. "I never thought of joining the chorus of a musical comedy."

"It might only be for a few months, and when you're with Walter Keal there's always the chance of getting to the Vanity."

"A Vanity girl!" repeated Norah, scornfully. "For everybody to look at!"

Lily told her friend that it was better to be looked at as a Vanity girl than to spend her life looking at other people from a window in West Kensington.

"But I can't sing," Norah objected.

"Sing! Who ever heard of a chorus-girl that could sing?"

The lowly position of a Vanity girl was not proof against the alchemy of Norah's self-esteem; she made up her mind to renounce Pinero and all his works and go into musical comedy.

When the two friends reached the small street off Leicester Square and saw extending up the steps of the building in which the offices of Mr. Walter Keal were situated an endless queue of girls waiting to interview the manager, Norah was discouraged.

"Oh, he has lots of companies," Lily explained. Then she addressed herself to a dirty-faced man with a collar much too large for him who was in charge of the entrance.

"You give me your letter, and it'll be all right."

"But it's for Mr. Keal himself," Lily protested.

"That's all right, my dear; your turn'll come."

The women immediately in front looked round indignantly at Lily, and Norah, who was beginning to feel self-conscious, begged her not to make a fuss. This was advice Lily always found easy to take, and, the introduction from her brother-in-law stowed away in the dirty-faced man's pocket, she and Norah took their places in the queue. Every ten minutes or so a good-looking girl, obviously well pleased with herself, would descend briskly from the glooms above; but mostly at intervals of about thirty seconds depressed women, powdering their noses as nonchalantly as possible, came down more slowly. Foot by foot Norah and Lily, who by now had a trail of women behind them, struggled higher up the steps. There was a continuous murmur of sibilant talk punctuated by shrill laughter, and the atmosphere, thickly flavored with cheap scent, perspiration, damp, clothes, and cigarette smoke, grew more oppressive with each step of the ascent. At last they turned the corner of the first landing and saw ahead of them a shorter flight; half-way up this, another landing crowded with girls came into view, the three doors opening on which were inscribed "Walter Keal's Touring Companies" in white paint; a muffled sound of typewriting seemed auspiciously business-like amid this babbling, bedraggled, powdered mass of anxious women. By the central door another dirty-faced man was ushering in the aspirants one at a time.

"We ought to have given my letter to him," said Lily.

"Well, don't go back for it now," Norah begged, looking in dismay at the throng behind.

They must have been waiting over two hours when at last they found themselves face to face with the janitor. A bell tinkled as a bright figure emerged from the door on the left and hurried away down the steps without regarding the envious glances of the unadmitted; immediately afterward the door in front of them opened, and they passed through to the office.

"One at a time," the janitor called; but Norah quickly shut the door behind them, and she and Lily were simultaneously presented for the inspection of Mr. Walter Keal.

The office was furnished with a large roll-top desk, three chairs, and a table littered with papers which a dowdy woman in pince-nez was trying to put in some kind of order. The walls were hung with playbills; the room was heavy with cigar smoke. Mr. Walter Keal, a florid, clean-shaven man with a diamond pin in his cravat, a Malmaison carnation in his buttonhole, and a silk hat on the back of his head, was bending over the desk without paying the least attention to the new-comers. Standing behind him in an attitude that combined deference toward Mr. Keal with insolence toward the rest of the world was a young man of Jewish appearance who stared critically at the two girls.

"You don't remember me, Mr. Keal," began Lily, timidly. "I was introduced to you once in the Strand by my brother-in-law, Richard Granville."

"I'm sure you were," interrupted Mr. Keal, curtly; but when he looked up and saw that Lily was pretty he changed his tone. "That's all right; don't be frightened. I've met so many girls in my time. Well, what can I do for you?"

"I had a letter of introduction from my brother-in-law, Mr. Granville," Lily began again.

"Never heard of the gentleman," said Mr. Keal.

Norah, feeling that she and Lily stood once more on an equality, came forward with assurance.

"We thought you were choosing girls for the chorus in 'Miss Elsie of Chelsea.'"

"Full up," the manager snapped.

The Jewish young man bent over and whispered something to his master, who took a long look at the girls.

"However, I might find you two extra places. What experience have you had? None, eh? Can you sing? You think so. Um—yes—all girls think they can sing. Well, I'll give you a chance, but I can't offer more than a guinea a week of seven performances. If you don't like to take that, there are plenty who will and be grateful. It's my Number One company."

Norah did not wait for Lily, but accepted for both of them.

"Are they going to let us have the club in Lisle Street, Fitzmaurice?" the manager turned to inquire of his assistant.

"Yes, Mr. Keal. The club has arranged to lend their concert-room every morning and afternoon this week, but if you want any evening calls we shall have to make other arrangements."

"But —— it all," Mr. Keal exclaimed, "when are we going to get the stage?"

"They won't be able to let us have it till the week before Christmas."

"That's a nice ruddy job," grumbled Mr. Keal. "All right, dears," he said, "go in there and get your contracts." He pointed to the room adjoining, where, amid an infernal rattle of typewriters, Lily and Norah sold their untried talents to Mr. Keal for a guinea a week of seven performances, extra matinées to be paid for at half rate, and a fortnight's salary in lieu of notice to be considered just. When she took up the pen to sign the contract Norah paused.

"You've put your own name, Lily," she said, doubtfully.

"Oh, I can't be bothered to think of a new name. Besides, my own is quite a good one for the stage."

"Yes, but I ought to change mine. I think I shall call myself Dorothy Lonsdale. Do you like that?"

"You've got a sister called Dorothy. Won't she be rather annoyed?"

Norah tried to think of another name, but she was confused by the noise of the typewriters, and at last she ejaculated, impatiently:

"Oh, bother, I must be Dorothy! I've always known it would suit me much better than her. I shouldn't mind if she called herself Norah. Besides, I sha'n't be Dorothy Caffyn, so what does it matter?"

They were told that their contracts would be handed to them at the rehearsal called for to-morrow morning at the Hungarian Artistes' Club, Lisle Street, Leicester Square.

"How easy it is, really," said Norah, when she and Lily were going down-stairs again, past the line of tired women still waiting to be admitted. "Though I thought his language was rather disgusting. Didn't you?"

"I didn't notice it," said Lily. "But you'll have to get used to bad language on the stage."

473

"I shall never get used to it," Norah vowed, with a disdainful glance at a particularly common-looking girl who, tossing the feathers in her hat like a defiant savage, called out:

"God! Flo, look at Mrs. Walter Keal coming down-stairs."

The girls round her laughed, and Norah hurried past angrily. She had been intending to patronize Lily; after that remark it was not so easy.

Just as they reached the foot of the first flight of steps the dirty-faced janitor bawled over the balustrade, "Mr. Keal can't see any more ladies to-day."

Sighs of disappointment and murmurs of indignation rose from the actresses; then they turned wearily round and prepared to encounter the December rain.

"You'd better come and call for me to-morrow," said Norah, "so that we can go to the rehearsal together. Think of me to-night when I'm trying to explain to father what I've done."

"Will he be very angry?"

"Yes, I expect he will, and though I know how to manage him it's always a nuisance having to argue," said Norah. "You're lucky not to have a father."

Lily looked at her friend quickly and suspiciously.

"I mean you're lucky to be quite on your own," she explained.

The moment Mr. Caffyn came home from the city that evening Norah revealed to him that she had got an engagement in a touring company and reminded him of his promise. As she had expected, he tried to go back on his word, and even brought up the old objection to a daughter of his going on the stage.

"Nobody will know that I'm your daughter," she said. "I shall change my name, of course."

"But people are sure to hear about it," Mr. Caffyn argued.

Norah pulled him up suddenly.

"It's no good going on about it, father. I've got an engagement and I'm going to accept it. If you try to prevent me I shall do something much worse."

Mr. Caffyn's dislike of the stage may not have been as deep as he pretended, or he may have thought that his daughter really intended to do something desperate and that he might be called upon to support her in married life, which would be more expensive than supporting her on the stage. Moreover, she seemed so confident that perhaps he might never have to support her on the stage, and what a delightful solution of her future that would be! After all, she was the eldest of six girls, and six girls rapidly growing up might become too much even for the secretary of the Church of England Purity Society to control successfully.

Mrs. Caffyn melted into tears at the idea of her eldest daughter's earning her own living, and Norah decided to profit by maternal weakness.

"The only thing, mother dear, is that I shall be very poor."

"Darling child!"

"You see, I don't like to ask father to make me a larger allowance than he makes at present."

"Oh no," agreed Mrs. Caffyn, apprehensively. "I beg you won't ask him to do that."

"So my idea was—" Norah began. She paused for a moment to think how she could express herself most tactfully. "Mother, you have a certain amount of money of your own, haven't you?"

"Yes, dear."

"And I suppose it's really you who makes me my allowance of twenty-five pounds a year? What I thought was that perhaps you'd rather give me a lump sum now when it would be more useful than go on paying me an allowance. Another thing is that I should hate to feel I was coming into money when you died, and, of course, if you gave me my money now I shouldn't feel that."

"My dear child, how am I to find any large sum of money now? It's very sweet of you to put it in that way, but you don't understand how difficult these matters are."

"How much money have you got of your own?" asked Norah.

Mrs. Caffyn thought this was rather an improper question; but Norah was looking so very grown up that she did not like to elude the answer as she had been wont to elude many answers of many childish questions through all these years of married life.

"Well, dear," she said, with the air of one who was revealing a dangerous family secret, "I suppose you're old enough to hear these things now. I have three hundred pounds a year of my own—at least, when I say of my own, you mustn't think that means three hundred a year to spend on myself. Your father is very just, and though he helps me as much as he is able, all the money is taken up in household expenses."

"Well, twenty-five pounds a year," said Norah, "at five per cent. is the interest on five hundred pounds."

"Is it, dear?" asked her mother, in a frightened voice.

"If you give me five hundred pounds now you wouldn't have to pay me twenty-five pounds a year. And if you lived for another twenty-five years you'd save one hundred and twenty-five pounds that way."

Mrs. Caffyn looked as if she would soon faint at these rapid calculations.

"How am I to get five hundred pounds?" she asked, hopelessly.

"You must go and see the manager of your bank."

"But Roland is a clerk in my bank," Mrs. Caffyn objected. "And what would *he* say?"

"Roland!" repeated Norah, with scorn. "You don't suppose Roland knows everything that goes on in the bank?"

"No, I suppose he doesn't," agreed Mrs. Caffyn, wonderingly.

"If you like *I'll* go and see the bank manager," Norah offered. "He took rather a fancy to me, I remember, when he came to supper with us once."

"Norah, how recklessly you talk!" protested Mrs. Caffyn. But Norah was firm and she did not rest until she had persuaded her mother to ask for an interview with the manager, to whom she made herself so charming and with whom she argued so convincingly that in the end she succeeded in obtaining the £500.

"Though what your father will say I don't like to think, dear," said Mrs. Caffyn, as she tremblingly mounted an omnibus to go home.

"I don't see why father should know anything about it, and if he does he can't say anything. It's your money."

"Let's hope he'll never find out," Mrs. Caffyn sighed, though she had little hope really of escaping from detection in what she felt was something perilously like a clever bank robbery—the sort of thing one read about in illustrated magazines.

Norah determined to be very cautious at rehearsals and she advised Lily to be the same.

"Of course, we shall gradually make friends with the other girls, but don't let's be in too much of a hurry, especially as we've got each other. And if you take my advice you'll be very reserved with the men."

Since Norah had found how easy it was to get on the stage her opinion of Mr. Vavasour had sunk, and since she had found how easy it was to get out of love her opinion of men in general had sunk. On the other hand, her opinion of herself as an actress and as a woman had risen proportionately. Meanwhile the rehearsals proceeded as rehearsals do, and the No. I company of "Miss Elsie of Chelsea" was harried from club-room to club-room, from suburban theater to metropolitan theater, until it was ready to charm the city of Manchester on Boxing Night.

On Christmas Eve, the last evening that Norah would spend at home for some time, she decided in an access of honesty to tell Dorothy that she had taken her name for purposes of the stage. Most unreasonably, Dorothy protested loudly against this, and it transpired in the course of the dispute that she had all her life resented being the only one of the family who had not been given two names. Norah's own second name, Charlotte, which was also her mother's, had never struck her before as anything in the nature of an asset, but now with much generosity she offered to lend it to Dorothy, who refused it as scornfully as she could without hurting her mother's feelings.

"Why couldn't you have taken Lina or Florence or Amy or Maud?" Dorothy demanded. These were the second names of the other sisters. "And, anyway, what's the matter with your own name?"

"I don't know," said Norah. "Dorothy Lonsdale struck me as a good combination, and the more I think of it the better I like it."

"Lonsdale," everybody repeated. "Are you going to call yourself Lonsdale?"

"It's the family name," Norah reminded them.

This was quite true; Lonsdale had been the maiden name of Mrs. Caffyn's mother, who, according to a family legend, had been a distant kinswoman of Lord Cleveden. Indeed, before Mr. Caffyn was married he had often used this connection to overcome his father's opposition to a long engagement. When he had bought the house in Lonsdale Road he had liked to think for a while that in a way he was doing something to restore the prestige of a distant collateral branch; the transaction had possessed a flavor of winning back an old estate. Naturally, as he grew older, he ceased to attach the same importance to mere birth, especially when he found that he did not require any self-assertion to get on perfectly well with the bishops who came to consult him about diocesan scandals. Therefore he was inclined to take his eldest daughter's part and applaud her choice of a stage name.

"But suppose I wanted to go on the stage myself?" Dorothy insisted. "I might want to use my own name."

"Well, so you could," Norah urged. "You could be Miss Dorothy Caffyn. But you won't go on the stage, so what's the good of arguing like that? Anyway, I've signed the contract as Dorothy Lonsdale, so there's nothing to be done. *I* can't change."

"I do think it's mean of you," expostulated the real Dorothy, bursting into tears.

Norah would not allow anybody to come and see her off at Euston on Christmas morning, and Mr. Caffyn, who did not at all like the idea of a four-wheeler's waiting outside his house on such a day, helped his daughter's plans by marshaling the whole family for church half an hour earlier than usual, so that the farewells were said indoors. Lily had left the flat a fortnight ago and, having been staying in some Bloomsbury lodgings recommended by her sister, was to meet her friend at the station. At a quarter to eleven, amid the clangor of church bells, the cab of Norah Caffyn turned out of Lonsdale Road into the main street of West Kensington, and at noon on the platform at Euston Miss Lily Haden wished a Merry Christmas to Miss Dorothy Lonsdale.

CHAPTER II

I

THE ostriches of northern Patagonia are said to indulge in co-operative nesting: half a dozen hens one after another proceed to lay in a shallow cavity numerous eggs, the incubation of which is left to a male bird. Similarly, for the consummation of a musical comedy half a dozen lyrists, librettists, and composers lay their heads together in a shallow cavity and leave the result of their labor to be given life by a producer. "Miss Elsie of Chelsea," not being an exceptional musical comedy, will not repay a more thorough analysis. The first act developed in a painter's studio; in the second act everybody from the models in the chorus to the millionaire and his daughter whom the painter wanted to marry were transported to Honolulu. It was produced at the Vanity Theater under Mr. John Richards's management in the early autumn of the year 1902, and for many seasons it attracted large audiences all over the civilized world.

During the first fortnight of the tour, a fortnight of unending rain in Manchester, Dorothy, as she must be called henceforth, was inclined to think that life on the stage was not much more exciting than life in West Kensington, and certainly twice as tiring. It was holiday time, with two performances a day for eight days, and only in the second week—or more strictly in the third week, for Boxing Day fell upon a Friday that year—was she able to look about her in the small world where she must spend the next six months of her existence. She soon came to the conclusion that such an environment would not be tolerable for longer, and she made up her mind to escape from touring as soon as possible into a London engagement.

While she was still rehearsing in town she had paid one or two visits to the Vanity Theater, partly because it pleased her to hand in a card inscribed, "Miss Dorothy Lonsdale. Mr. Walter Keal's Miss Elsie of Chelsea Co.," but chiefly with the object of studying the demeanor, dress, appearance, and talents of the various members of the Vanity chorus, especially of the show-girls. The result of her observations was a strong belief that she was as graceful, as well able to set off clothes, as beautiful, and as good an actress as any of them. At the same time, she had begun to hear girls in the company talk about "getting across the footlights" and had realized that her own personality's powers of projection were still untested. If at the end of the tour it was brought home to her that with all her qualities "off" she lacked the most important one of all "on," she should immediately retire from the stage forever. The life itself did not attract her, and to spend years growing older and older in the environment of a provincial company seemed to Dorothy wilful self-deception; liberty at such a price would be worse than a comfortable servitude to suburban convention.

When on that wet Christmas morning at Euston she had seen the companions to close contact with whom she was bound for six months—a polychromatic group of crude pink complexions, mauve veils, electric seal, and exaggerated boots, looking in the mass like a shop-window in a second-rate thoroughfare, the sort of shop-window that has bundles of overcoats hanging outside the doorway, which indeed the men resembled—she had felt a sudden revulsion from them all, which those days in Manchester had done nothing to cure.

The first fortnight's bills for board and lodging had already shown Dorothy that existence on a guinea a week was not going to be easy; if she were ever engaged for London, she should require money to dress herself well at the beginning of her career, and it was imperative to save every penny she possibly could now in order to preserve intact the £500 she had obtained from her mother. An immediate economy would be effected in their weekly expenses if she and Lily could persuade another girl to share lodgings with them, and Dorothy began to study the ranks of the chorus for a suitable partner. Of course, from a social point of view she would have preferred to live with one of the principals, but the principals had not yet paid any attention to her, and she would not risk making advances first; besides, their standard of living might be too high for one who did not intend to waste money on the provinces. But when she considered her companions of the chorus, the dreadful language many of them used, the outrageous stories they told at the top of their voices, and, worst of all, their cockney accents, Dorothy shrank from extending the enforced intimacy of the dressing-room to her weekly home. This problem had not been solved when on the third Sunday after Christmas the company left Manchester for Birmingham, and by the newly arranged order of traveling Miss Dorothy Lonsdale found herself allotted to share a compartment with Miss Lily Haden, Miss Fay Onslow, and Miss Sylvia Scarlett.

Miss Onslow was unmistakably the senior member of the chorus and had reached the happy period of an actress's life when she has no more need to bother about keeping her reminiscences too nicely in focus. She was, in fact, as even she herself admitted, not far off forty; in a railway train on a wet January afternoon the kindest observer would have assumed that her next landmark was fifty. A month ago Dorothy would have shuddered to find herself on an equality with such a person; but asperous is the astral road, and she had to make the best of Miss Onslow by treating her with at least as much cordiality as she would have shown to a small dressmaker from whom she wanted a dress by the end of the week. Gradually, as her new surroundings became familiar, Dorothy had brought herself to call Miss Onslow "Onzie," and though the abbreviation made her gorge rebel as from cod-liver oil, she bravely persevered. Instinctively she knew that this was the only woman in the chorus whose counsel she could trust, the only one who would honestly tell her if she looked better with or without an artificial teardrop. The sum of Onzie's experience was hers for the asking; the middle-aged actress was an academician of grease-paint, serving alike as a warning and an example to the student; while her knowledge of the various towns in which the company had dates was evidently profound. Already she had provided Dorothy with an address for Birmingham; but these rooms to be enjoyed without the prickings of extravagance required a third partner. Dorothy, anxious to profit still further by Onzie's experience, suggested that she should join Lily and herself; but that very experience for which the novice was greedy made the old professional shake her head:

"No, thank you, ducky," she said. "I always live alone nowadays. You see, I've got my own little peculiarities. Besides, when my best boy comes down to see me he likes to see me alone. When I was with the 'Geisha' crowd last year I obliged one of the girls by sharing rooms with her in Middlesbrough, and as luck would have it George selected Middlesbrough to pay me a little visit. He was really very aggravated indeed, and he said to me, 'Fay,' he said, 'whatever's the use of me coming all the way up to Middlesbrough if I can't ever see you?' So I had to tell the other girl—Lexie Sharp her name was—that the arrangement didn't work, and what do you think she did? Well, if you'll believe me, she went about telling everybody that I was jealous of her over George! Luckily for me she was a girl who was very well known for her tongue and nobody paid any attention to her; still, it was uncomfortable for me, though I deserved it for breaking one of my rules. Who knows? George may come up to Birmingham. It's just the sort of place he would select for a visit, because, being a London fellow, he feels out of it in too small a town. Of course, he has nothing to do with the stage himself. Oh dear me, no, nothing whatever! He lives at Tulse Hill with two aunts, one of which has a growth in the throat and may go off at any moment, which prevents George working, as she's so particular about having him always close at hand. Well, any one ought to understand an aunt's feelings—I'm sure I can—but some of the girls last year used to criticize him something dreadful behind my back, until really I was glad to say good-by to them all. But this seems a much nicer crowd we're in now."

"We've only been in it a fortnight," said Miss Scarlett from the other corner of the carriage.

Dorothy looked at the speaker curiously. She was a girl who had joined the company for the last three rehearsals and during this first fortnight in Manchester had kept herself apart. Lily had spoken to her once or twice, but Dorothy, who was afraid there might be an unpleasant reason for such deliberate seclusion, had begged Lily not to be in too great a hurry to make friends with her. During Onzie's monologue Miss Scarlett had apparently been unconscious of what was happening in the compartment, and from the corner opposite Lily she had been staring out at the landscape, that was scarred and grimed and misshapen by industry like the hands of the toilers who lived in it. She was different from all the other girls, Dorothy was thinking—rather foreign-looking with her deep, brown, slanted eyes and mass of untidy brown hair, her wide nose, high cheek-bones, and distinctly ugly mouth, the underlip of which only just escaped protruding. She was dressed, too, in a style that was quite unlike that of anybody else and without any regard for the prevailing fashion. Dorothy remembered with a flickering smile that when she had first seen her at rehearsals she had thought she was one of the Hungarian artistes who had come to see why her club-room was being used by a theatrical company. Now when in a deep voice she suddenly turned round and commented on Fay Onslow's last remark Dorothy was astonished to hear that she spoke the same kind of English as herself; she indeed, in her surprise, almost gave utterance aloud to her thought that this gipsy creature was a lady.

"Hell! I've left my cigarettes behind," the lady ejaculated.

"There now, what a nuisance for you!" said the good-natured Onzie. "Have one of mine, dear."

"Which are they? Turks or Virgins?" asked Miss Scarlett, leaning over and screwing up her eyes to see what Onzie was offering.

Dorothy corrected her opinion and decided that Miss Scarlett had been a lady once upon a time; yet even while she was condemning her vulgarity she was thinking that her ladyhood was not so far away in the past. Her speech and manner had the assurance of age, but she could not be much more than twenty-two or twenty-three, perhaps not even so much as that.

Presently the train stopped for a dreary Sunday wait, and while some of the gentlemen of the company, with a view to future favors, were scuttling about the platform in search of tea for the ladies from whom they would demand them, Dorothy took this opportunity of asking Lily what she thought about inviting Sylvia Scarlett to share their rooms at Birmingham.

"She seems quite different from the other girls," Dorothy explained. "I mean, she talked as if she was a lady. Don't you think so? And really, you know, we can't afford these rooms unless we do get a third person."

Lily was quite ready to accept Miss Scarlett's company, though, as Dorothy thought impatiently, she would have been equally willing to accept the dresser's, if Dorothy had thought of inviting the dresser to share rooms with them.

"Do you want a cup of tea, Lil?" a young man came along and asked at this moment. When Lily declared that she should love a cup of tea, he hurried off toward the buffet.

"Do you know him?" asked Dorothy, in surprise.

"Only since we joined the company."

"But he's one of the chorus-boys, isn't he?"

"Yes."

"And you let him call you Lily already?" Dorothy hoped it was no worse than Lily; it had sounded dreadfully like Lil.

"Why shouldn't I?"

"Of course, it's your own business," said Dorothy, turning coldly away to eye Sylvia Scarlett, who was striding up and down the platform with both hands in the pockets of a frieze overcoat and looking so independent of everybody in the world that she felt shy of interrupting her. At that moment Lily was carried off by the chorus-boy for a cup of tea, which, had it been arsenic, Dorothy could not have declined more indignantly, and she found herself alone upon the platform and exposed to the glances of the comedian, a debased sport from the famous Vanity comedian whose mannerisms he had reproduced in the provinces as well as he was able for fifteen years, and would probably continue to reproduce for as many more. A small and ugly man, Joe Wiltshire had become so hardened to women's snubs that by sheer recklessness and indiscrimination he managed to fill his bag. If he was weak with rocketing pheasants he never hesitated to pot a sitting rabbit; in other words, he made love to every woman he met and found 5 per cent. of them amenable. Now with a view to impressing the prettiest girl in the chorus he was being funny with two bottles of stout and a corkscrew; but though he managed to cheer up the porter on duty, he failed to amuse Dorothy, who seized an opportunity of escaping from the performance by attaching herself to Sylvia Scarlett on her return promenade.

"I say," she began, in her best West Kensington manner. "I hope you won't think it awful cheek on my part, but my friend and I—you know, that pretty, fair girl who was in our carriage—would be awfully glad if you'd join us this week in our digs. Awfully nice rooms, but rather expensive for two, though we ought to be able to manage quite reasonably with three. Of course, if you're already fixed—"

"I've never been fixed in my life," said Miss Scarlett, sharply, "and I certainly don't intend to be fixed in Birmingham."

"No, I say, shut up; don't laugh. Have you been on the stage long?"

"Two weeks and two days."

"Oh, I say, really, then this is your first shop?"

Dorothy felt more at ease now that she knew she had not got to deal with a veteran of the profession; this new girl was obviously not one to be patronized, but there was now no reason to anticipate patronage on her side. With the removal of this danger Dorothy became more natural in her manner, and by the time the line was cleared for the theatrical special to proceed the bargain had been struck by which Sylvia Scarlett would share rooms with herself and Lily.

"I say, I hope you don't mind my making personal remarks," said Dorothy, "but you're looking most awfully tired."

She had intended this remark to effect a breach in the other girl's reserve, but it apparently had the contrary effect of raising the barrier still higher. She drew back slightly huffed, and Sylvia, leaning over, with a quick expansive gesture put a hand on her arm and told her not to be offended if she was not being confidential, but that she was enjoying the luxury of complete privacy after a period of disagreeable publicity. Dorothy would have preferred more exact information; even in childhood she had always felt inclined to cry when people had asked her riddles, and Roland's favorite way of teasing her had been to invent riddles without answers; however, she comforted herself with the reflection that Sylvia really was a lady, which at any rate ought to be a guaranty that the answer to that conundrum was not vulgar like the dreadful answers to dressing-room conundrums.

The train dragged on through the wet January dusk and into the dripping night of blurred lamps and distant furnaces, of ghostly Sunday travelers and long platforms like stagnant streams. Conversation in the compartment hung heavily upon the air like the moist breath of the tired women in the four corners of it. Dorothy, whose touchstone of behavior was self-respect, asked herself why Fay Onslow should mind living with other girls, such intimate revelations of her private habits was she making in the course of this journey. If a woman as fat as she was did not feel the loss of her dignity in searching for a flea like that, why should she want to live alone? And that was by no means the least dignified thing she had done. This ostentatious disregard of life's little decencies was certainly a regrettable side of theatrical life. However, the fact that she herself had gone on the stage prevented Dorothy from betraying her disapproval of such behavior. It would have been contrary to her method of dealing with life to admit that she could even expose herself to anything unseemly, still less that she might succumb to it. From the moment that Dorothy went on the stage the profession became above criticism, and the sense of collective propriety that she inherited as her father's daughter was no longer capable of being shocked. She crucified her fastidiousness; she was persecutor and martyr at the same time and derived an equal consciousness of superiority from either aspect of herself; in fact, the only thing in life that seriously troubled Dorothy was a minute bleb of skin on her left eyelid, and even that could be removed by a beauty doctor.

It was raining harder than ever when the train reached Birmingham, and the girls decided to indulge in the luxury of a cab. The rooms looked as if they really would be very comfortable, and the landlady insisted proudly that managers had been known to stay in them, not mere business managers whose only aim in life seemed to be making fusses about the starching of their white shirts, but acting managers, one of whom had even brought his children, which, as she pointed out, proved that the lodgings were homely.

Sylvia was some time getting ready for supper, and Dorothy, thinking it would not be nice to begin without her, made Lily wait quite half an hour. When Sylvia did come down at last, Dorothy was nearly sure that she had been crying, and the mystery of her origin once more obtruded itself. Dorothy wished now that she had arranged for Sylvia and herself to share the second room instead of Lily and herself. This strange new girl perplexed her self-assurance, and she proposed that if the new association prospered—they drank to its success in the pale India ale which the landlady provided—they should take it week about to sleep in the single room. Dorothy tried to extract confidences from Sylvia by confiding in her the history of Lily as far as she knew it; when that did not elicit anything she offered a gilded version of her own prior circumstances. The following week at Derby she shared the bedroom with Sylvia and went so far as to give her an almost truthful account of the Wilfred Curlew business, but nothing could she get from Sylvia in return. Moreover, there was nothing in her belongings that afforded a clue to her history; there was not a single photograph or initialed ornament; all her possessions were left lying about the room, and her trunk was never locked; and when every morning the girls called at the stage door for their correspondence she only in the company never received a letter, nor even bothered to look if there was one waiting for her in the rack. But if Sylvia was mute about the past she was not at all reserved about the present. There was nobody like her for seizing upon the eccentricities of the various members of the company to make merry with, and if sometimes Dorothy felt that she went too far in laughing at herself, she could not be angry because she used to laugh as much, indeed more, at Lily. She was a match, too, for any landlady; and gradually, as the association begun at Birmingham hardened into permanency, Dorothy and Lily left the entire management of their weekly home to Sylvia: who had a delightful capacity for keeping the weekly bills reasonable without ever seeming to be economical.

Dorothy was too firmly convinced of the reality of her own beauty to be an idealist, but if in after life any portion of her early experience on the stage seemed to her worthy of idealization these first weeks with Sylvia and Lily seemed so. Partly this was due to her discovery that touring was not so unpleasant when she did not have to bother about anything except her own appearance; but chiefly it was due to her growing conviction of ultimate success. There was beginning to be no doubt that even from the chorus of a musical comedy company on tour her personality was getting across the footlights. Even Sylvia, the mercilessly critical Sylvia, had prophesied success for her, and Dorothy's dreams went past to the music of approaching triumphs. Her mind was all a pageant, and the commonplace of touring existence—the aroma of the theater, the flight from the great manufacturing towns on still Sabbath mornings of black frost, the kaleidoscopic mustering of the company at railway stations, the emptiness of new rooms untouched as yet by the transience of the three girls, the garish mirrors hung with velvet that held her beauty, the undulating horsehair sofas, the sea-shells on the mantelpiece, the fire glowing in the grate, the dim gas when they came home from the performance, the smell of Cheddar cheese in the little room, the bright gas shining on the three places laid for supper, the petticoats hanging over the bed up-stairs, the oil-cloth in the passages, the noise of the landlady's family in the stuffy kitchen—all these and a hundred more externals of touring existence were in the years to come regarded affectionately as winter is beheld from the radiance of a summer afternoon.

So from Derby "Miss Elsie of Chelsea" went to Leeds, from Leeds to Bradford, from Bradford to Liverpool, from Liverpool to Newcastle. Then from Newcastle the company ascended into Scotland, where genial landladies and cakes and enthusiastic audiences compensated for east winds.

Gradually, under the pressure of Sylvia's teasing, Dorothy allowed herself to make friends with the other girls and to be superficially polite with the men. She was never popular in the company in the way that for different reasons Sylvia and Lily were popular; but perhaps her disdain and conceit were pardoned as tokens of future success, because she was not ostracized as she certainly would have been ostracized without the fascination that favorites of fortune always exert upon the rest of mankind. Besides, people said such spiteful things behind her back that they had to be fairly pleasant to her face. The men in the chorus one after another tried in vain to attract her attention whenever the requirements of the scene gave them an excuse for talking to her. But Dorothy used to respond as if the dialogue could really be heard by the audience, which may have been artistic, but did not allow her admirers much opportunity of cultivating a friendship. Off the stage she would have nothing to do with any of them. The comedian made one or two more attempts to charm her with buffoonery, but she told him that he was even less funny off the stage than on, upon which he lost his temper and swore she was a stuck-up cow; an alleged lack of humor in Scotland had recently deprived Mr. Wiltshire of some of his best laughs, and he was in no mood to be criticized by a chorus-girl.

"If you speak to me again like that," said Dorothy, primly, "I shall complain to Mr. Warren."

"Wow-wow-wow!" the comedian mimicked.

"Never mind, Joe," said Sylvia, who was standing close by in the wings. "If you manage to break your leg with your next entrance you'll get a laugh, all right."

"You think yourself very funny, don't you?" growled Mr. Wiltshire.

"Yes, but I haven't got to convince a Scotch audience that I am," said Sylvia.

The comedian's cue came before he could retort, and, falling over his feet in a way that would have made a more southerly audience rock with mirth, he took the stage.

"Vulgar little beast!" said Dorothy.

Mr. Wiltshire never relaxed his efforts to charm the people of Edinburgh, Glasgow, Dundee, and Aberdeen to laughter, but he gave up trying to amuse Dorothy, and thenceforth devoted himself to girls with a keener sense of humor.

Once when Dorothy had refused to go for a long walk in the country round Aberdeen, the glittering of the granite buildings on a fine March morning tempted her out too late, and she wandered by herself along the sea-shore toward the mouth of the Don until she was able, so windless was the day, so warm the sun against the low sandy cliffs, to sit down on the beach. It happened that Mr. David Bligh, the tenor in "Miss Elsie of Chelsea," passed that way, and, seeing Dorothy, took a seat beside her. She had never intended her reserve with the other men in the company to include David Bligh, and from having felt rather sad at being left behind by Sylvia and Lily she now congratulated herself on her good fortune.

"All alone?" asked the tenor, fluting with his voice, as he always did when he was speaking to a woman.

"All alone," said Dorothy. "Isn't it too bad?"

They discussed loneliness with poetic similes harvested from the sea, upon the horizon of which nothing but a solitary tramp, hull down, was visible. So long as Mr. David Bligh's attention had been devoted to Miss May Seymour, the leading lady, Dorothy had been inclined to think that he was not very good-looking, that he did not possess a very good voice, and that probably he was not quite a gentleman. Now that he was beside her on this lonely beach she was inclined to modify all these judgments in his favor, and when suddenly he burst forth into "*Che gelido manino*," suiting the action to the word by simultaneously taking hold of her hand, she decided that not merely was his voice rather good, but that it was lovely.

"You really have a lovely voice," she told him.

He shrugged his shoulders, sighed, and with his stick drew some notes of music in the sand.

"I wonder why you never took up opera," she inquired, in tender astonishment.

"What's the good? The British public doesn't want British singers. Oh no," he said, with a glance full of reproach for the indifference of the sky, "I'm not fat enough for opera."

He went up the tonic scale to "la," frightening away some small sea-birds that had just alighted on the gleaming sand by the tide's edge.

"Let me hear your voice," he asked, abruptly.

Dorothy was gratified by this request. She had taken for granted the tenor's interest in her appearance, but that this should extend to her voice seemed to indicate something more profound than a casual attraction. She assured him that she was too shy, but he continued to persuade her, and at last she sang a part of one of the leading lady's songs.

"Yes, it would be worth while taking some trouble with it," he judged. "If you like I'll give you lessons. Have you got a piano in your rooms?"

"We have got a piano this week, as it happens," said Dorothy, "though I should doubt if it had ever been played on. Come to tea this afternoon, and we'll try it."

"You live with that Haden girl, don't you?"

"Do you think she's pretty?" Dorothy asked.

The tenor shrugged his shoulders.

"Oh yes, so-so. I really haven't noticed her much. She dyes her hair, I suppose."

"No, it's natural," said Dorothy, resisting the temptation to insert a qualifying, "I believe."

They discussed the varieties of feminine beauty; when the tenor had managed to convey without direct compliments that Dorothy had every feature a woman ought to have, she was convinced by his good taste that her voice must be out of the ordinary.

"Good gracious! It's past two o'clock," she exclaimed, at last, when her appetite began to assert itself in spite of ozone and flattery. "How time flies!"

"*I* dine at half past two. We'd better be strolling back."

It was after that hour when they reached Aberdeen, because David Bligh was continually stopping on the desolate roads that led across the low-lying lands between the city and the sea to illustrate with snatches of song many episodes of his adventurous life as an actor in musical comedy. Dorothy might have been bored by all this talk about himself if he had not made it so clear that he really did admire her; as it was, she assented warmly when he murmured, outside her lodgings:

"How quickly one can make friends sometimes!"

How quickly, indeed, when a man will show his admiration with his eyes and a woman with her ears.

The others had not returned from their expedition along Deeside when tea was finished, so Dorothy and the tenor took down the photographs and china ornaments from the top of the piano, and presently an unfamiliar sound brought in Mrs. Maclachlan, the landlady, to say that the piano had not been used since her eldest daughter died ten years ago, and that she would prefer that it was not used now. This was the kind of occasion on which Dorothy missed Sylvia, who would have known how to deal with the old woman; but David Bligh, without heeding her protests, continued to strum. Mrs. Maclachlan at once put the bass clef out of action by sitting down upon the notes, where, with arms akimbo, she maintained her position and poured forth a torrent of unintelligible Scots labials. Dorothy, horrified at the idea of a brawl with a woman who, even if she did let rooms, obviously belonged to the servant class, begged the actor not to play any more. In the end he agreed to resign from the contest with Mrs. Maclachlan on condition that Dorothy would try her voice on the piano in his rooms, where he was so encouraging about its quality that she gave herself up to serious study, one result of which was that henceforth she always had the second bedroom to herself, because her voice seemed to require most exercise when Sylvia and Lily required most sleep. The other girls in the company showed no inclination to believe that Dorothy's friendship with David Bligh was founded upon his skill in voice-production and they used to declare with conscious virtue that such singing-lessons were merely an excuse for making love.

"Be careful, dear, with Bligh," Fay Onslow warned Dorothy. "He's known all over the road for the way he treats girls. Look at May Seymour! Really, I'm quite sorry for the poor thing. I'm sure she's beginning to look her age."

This was good news about May Seymour, who had ignored her when she joined the company; but though in other respects the leading lady's fate might serve as a warning, Dorothy was much too secure of herself to need any advice about David Bligh. To be sure, he had several times seized the opportunity of examining his pupil's throat to kiss her, but she had accepted the kisses with no more sense of their reality than if they had been a doctor's bill, which in a way they were. However, Dorothy was not accustomed to let herself be over-charged, and these kisses were the only honorarium Mr. Bligh ever got. He was so much piqued by her indifference that he mistook for a grand passion the mortification set up by his failure to get her hopelessly in love with him, and he made such a complete fool of himself over Dorothy that the girls of the company were more annoyed than ever, and from having at first been charitably anxious about her virtue they now became equally severe upon her cruelty.

"The poor boy's getting quite thin," Fay Onslow declared. "You really oughtn't to treat him like that. It's beginning to show in his acting."

Dorothy consulted Sylvia about David Bligh's decline, not because she cared whether he was declining or not, but because it was an excuse to talk about herself.

"Serve him right," said Sylvia.

"But I shouldn't like to think that he was really suffering on my account."

"Lily and I are the only people who really suffer," said Sylvia.

"What do you mean?"

"My dear Dorothy, *we* have to listen to the practising."

"You don't really mind my practising, do you?"

"I get rather bored with it sometimes."

"Yes, I suppose it is rather boring sometimes."

Dorothy decided that it was also rather boring of Sylvia to switch the topic from her effect on David Bligh to the slight annoyance her practising might sometimes cause her friends. However, she forgave her by remembering that Sylvia had not the same inducement as herself to study singing.

Meanwhile, Dorothy's occupation of the leading man left Lily free to develop her deplorable taste for chorus-boys, and Dorothy found that her own habit of practising scales in the morning and going out for walks with David Bligh in the afternoon had resulted in continuous tea-parties at their rooms, to which, whenever she wanted to stay at home in the afternoon, she was most unfairly exposed. She might have put up with Lily's behavior for the rest of the tour if at last a moment had not come when it inconvenienced her personally. At Nottingham, which the company reached in mid-April, the weather was so fine that Dorothy accepted an invitation from an admirer in the front of the house to go for a picnic on the river Trent. Until now she had discouraged all introductions effected by the footlights, and she often marveled to Sylvia at the way other girls accepted invitations to private houses without knowing anything about their hosts. Perhaps she was already beginning to feel that David Bligh had taught her all he knew about voice-production, or perhaps the exceptionally smart automobile grumbling outside the stage-door struck her as a proper credential, or perhaps these April airs were irresistible.

"Really, you know, Sylvia," she said, "I think it would be rather fun to go. But I'm shocked at myself for suddenly breaking my rules like this. I wonder why I am breaking them. It must be the spring."

"The what?" repeated Sylvia.

"The spring," said Dorothy, hoping she did not look as affected as she felt.

"If you had said the springs," said Sylvia, "I would have agreed with you."

The owner of the car was the spoiled son of a rich lace manufacturer, and, according to the stage-door keeper, famous in Nottingham for his entertainment of actresses. What seemed more important to Dorothy was that he had just arrived from Cambridge for the Easter vacation, which decided her to accept his hospitality.

"You'll bring two friends?" suggested the young man.

"I'll bring the two girls with whom I share rooms."

"Topping!" he ejaculated, and with a sympathetic tootle of satisfaction the champing car leaped forward into the night.

"You can't come to-morrow?" gasped Dorothy, when with much graciousness she had advised Lily of the treat in store for her.

"No; I've promised to go with Tom to Sherwood Forest."

"Never mind, Maid Marian," said Sylvia. "We shall get along without you. If you see the ghost of my namesake Will in the greenwood, give him my love."

Dorothy was too angry to speak, and her resentment against Lily was increased next morning when the big car arrived with three young men, one of whom would have to spend an acrobatic day balancing himself on tête-à-têtes. Nor was the picnic a great success; early in the afternoon it came on to rain, and anything more dreary than the appearance of the river Trent was unimaginable.

"Never mind," said the host, "you'll have to come up to Cambridge; we'll entertain you properly there."

Apart from the rain which spoiled her hat, and the absence of Lily which ruined any intimate conversation about herself, Dorothy was chiefly upset by the contemptuous way in which these young Cambridge men referred to the leading man.

"Why on earth do managers dress actors up in yachting costume?" asked one of them. "I never saw such an ass as that man looked—David Blighter or whatever he calls himself."

Dorothy could see Sylvia checking an impulse not to accentuate her discomfiture by announcing her friendship with the despised tenor; but she felt sufficiently humiliated without that, and when they got back to their rooms she implored Sylvia to speak to Lily on the subject of being too friendly with the men in the company.

"It makes us all so cheap," Dorothy pointed out. "Of course, we're on tour and not likely to meet many friends who know us in London. Still, it is unpleasant. You heard the way those boys talked about David? What would they have said to Tom Hewitt? Besides, I get worried about Lily. She *is* very weak and she has been badly brought up. I'm awfully fond of her, as you know, and I'd do anything for her; but really I cannot stand that Hewitt creature, and I don't see why Lily should force him upon us."

"I think it's rather foolish of her myself," agreed Sylvia. "At the same time, I'm afraid that with Lily it's inevitable."

"Yes, but she lets him make love to her," protested Dorothy. "She doesn't care a bit about him, really, but she's too lazy to say 'no'. I came down the other day to find her sitting on his lap! Well, I think that's disgusting. *You* don't sit on people's laps; *I* don't sit on people's laps. Why should she? I know perfectly well what it is to be in love; I've been in love lots of times. I don't want you to think I'm setting out to make myself seem better than I am. As I told you, the only reason I went on the stage was because I couldn't marry the man I loved. So who more likely to have sympathy with people in love than myself? What I object to is playing about with boys of the company. Look at them! The most awful set of bounders imaginable. It's so bad for you and me to have them coming in and out of our rooms at all hours. That Hewitt creature actually proposed to come back to supper the other night. However, I told Lily that if he did I should go to a hotel. After all, we are a little different from the other girls of the company."

"I wonder if we are?" Sylvia queried.

"Of course we are," said Dorothy. "You surely don't consider yourself on a level with Fay Onslow? Or with Sadie Moore and Clarice Beauchamp? Those awful girls!"

"I think we're all about the same," said Sylvia. "Some of us drop our aitches, some of us our p's and q's, some of us sing flat and the others sing sharp; but alas! my dear Dorothy, we all look very much alike when we're waiting for the train on Sunday morning."

"I sing perfectly in tune," said Dorothy, coldly.

"Please don't snub, me, Dorothy," Sylvia begged. "I can hardly bear it."

"There's no need for you to be sarcastic; you must admit I'm right about Lily."

Sylvia suddenly produced an eye-glass and, fixing it in her eye, stared mockingly at Dorothy.

"What about David?" she asked.

"You can't compare me with Lily."

"No, but I might compare David with Tom," she said, letting the eye-glass drop in a way that Dorothy found extremely irritating.

After their host's remarks about the tenor Dorothy felt she could not argue the point farther, and now in addition to her anger against Lily she began to hate her singing-master. However, Sylvia must have felt that she was right and have spoken to Lily, because the following week at Leicester Lily, with most unwonted energy, attacked her on the subject:

"I don't know why you should grumble to Sylvia about me. I don't grumble to her about you. When have I ever grumbled about your practising? You say the only reason you let yourself get talked about with David Bligh is because he's useful to you. You say he's helping you with your voice. Well, Tom helps me with my bag. What's the difference? It's only since you were asked out by those men who had a car that you suddenly discovered how impossible Tom was and began laughing at his waistcoats. I didn't laugh at Cyril Vavasour's waistcoat, which was more extraordinary than Tom's."

"I've never grumbled about Tom's carrying your bag," Dorothy explained, patiently. "What I said to Sylvia was that I didn't think you ought to let him kiss you. I don't think it's dignified."

"Well, as long as he doesn't want to kiss you, I don't see what you've got to complain about."

The bare notion of Tom's wanting to kiss her was so unpleasant to Dorothy that she had to withdraw from the conversation. Thenceforth the breach between her and Lily began to widen; in fact, if it had not been for Sylvia she would have told Lily that she could not share rooms with her any longer. She was afraid, however, that Sylvia might be so sorry for Lily that she would find herself left alone, which would put her in an undignified position, because the other girls might say that it was because she wanted to carry on, as they would vulgarly express it, with Bligh; besides, living alone was too expensive.

Since Nottingham, Dorothy had been criticizing the tenor almost as sharply as she criticized Tom Hewitt, and she was in no mood to encourage the idea that there was anything between him and her; all her lessons now were merely repetitions of what he had taught her already, and it became obvious to Dorothy that he was what he was in the profession simply because he was not good enough to be anything better. He had so often bragged to her about his success with other girls that he deserved to suffer on her account, and she felt quite like Nemesis when soon after this, while they were walking in the town of Leicester, she told him that this was to be their last walk together.

"Don't stand still in that theatrical way," she commanded. "Everybody's looking at you."

The kidney-stones of the Leicester streets had been hurting her feet, and she was in no mood for mercy.

"So this is the end," fluted David Bligh, with such emotion that the top note narrowly escaped being falsetto. "After all these weeks you're going to throw me away like an old chocolate-box."

He swished his cane with such demonstrative violence that, without seeing what he was doing, he cut a passer-by hard on the knuckle and thereby provoked a scene of humble apologies that made Dorothy more furious than ever.

"At least you might not make me look a fool in a public thoroughfare," she told him.

"I'm awfully sorry, Dolly. I didn't know what I was doing for the moment."

"Don't call me Dolly," she said. "You know how I hate abbreviations."

"I don't seem to be able to do anything right this morning."

"Look at the ridiculous walk you've brought me! Nothing but cobble-stones, and passers-by bumping into one, and now we're getting down among the factories. You know how I hate being stared at."

"You didn't mind being stared at in Nottingham the week before last."

"Oh God! aren't you impossible!" cried Dorothy, herself now dramatically turning right round and leaving him undecided whether to follow her or retire in the opposite direction.

Half a dozen factory-girls, arm in arm, who, with the horrible quickness of their class for anything that causes discomfort to other people, had noticed the quarrel, began to shout after Dorothy that her little boy was crying for his mother; while she, in torments of rage and humiliation, and of hatred for the man who was the cause of them, hurried uphill toward a more civilized quarter of the town. Five minutes later the tenor overtook Dorothy and begged pardon for losing her like that; he explained that, having got involved in a crowd of factory-girls, he could not hurry without making himself more ridiculous.

"You don't mind making me ridiculous," she said, bitterly.

"My dear girl, it was you that turned away, not me."

"Oh, go to the devil!" she burst out. "I'll have nothing more to do with you. You can console yourself with May Seymour."

The people who turned to stare after the lovely girl that seemed an incarnation of this blue-and-white April day might have been as shocked as Dorothy was at herself to think that she had just descended to the level of an actor by telling him to go to the devil.

III

The month of May found the "Miss Elsie of Chelsea" company billed to appear in the suburban theaters, and Dorothy was called upon to make up her mind whether she should take rooms with Sylvia and Lily in the center of London or economize for a few weeks by staying at home. Four months of separation from her family had not made her particularly anxious to return to them. At the same time, since she was not yet a London actress, it might be more prudent to wait a little while before she cut herself off too completely from Lonsdale Road. The only thing that worried her about staying at home was the thought that all the members of her family would inevitably insist on going to see her act during the week that they were to play at the Grand Theater, Fulham. Even if her father should be shy of patronizing a musical comedy so near the Bishop of London's palace, she saw no way of preventing at any rate Roland and her sister Dolly from going; since she had stolen her sister's name, Dorothy, notwithstanding her dislike of abbreviations, had always managed to think of her as Dolly. Yes; it was obvious that whether she stayed up in town or stayed in West Kensington, she should be unable to prevent some of the family from going to see her, and, as they would not appreciate the fact that not even the greatest actresses begin by playing Lady Macbeth, she must make the best of their inspection.

So, one Sunday afternoon when the laburnum buds were yellowing in Lonsdale Road, Dorothy drove back to No. 17. Everything was much the same except that Dolly—Dorothy was firm from the moment she entered the house about refusing to answer any more to Norah—had, presumably in revenge for the loss of her name, taken her sister's bed. Mr. Caffyn was glad to hear that the difficulties and dangers of stage life had been exaggerated, and promised that he would warn the Bishop of Hampstead, who was billed to preside at a forthcoming meeting of the Church and Stage Society, not to make too much of them in his anxiety about theatrical souls. Dorothy succeeded in deterring her relations from going to the theater the first week at Camberwell; but the following week, when the playbills of "Miss Elsie of Chelsea" flaunted themselves in every shop-window of West Kensington, a large party, not merely of the immediate family, but of uncles and aunts and cousins raked together from every obscure suburb in London, swarmed for the Thursday matinée, and, what was worse, insisted on buzzing round Dorothy outside the stage-door in order to take her out to tea between the performances. They alluded with some disappointment to the inconspicuousness of the part she played, and they all agreed that the outstanding feature of the performance was the comedian. They thought it must be very nice for Dorothy to have such a splendid humorist perpetually at hand.

"But he's not funny off the stage," explained Dorothy, crossly.

This seemed greatly to surprise the aunts and uncles, who evidently did not believe her. In the middle of tea the party was joined by Roland, Cecil, and Vincent; not having been able to get away for the matinée, they had arrived to swell the family reunion before going to the evening performance, for which they had booked stalls in the very front row, where, later on, to Dorothy's intense disgust, she saw Wilfred Curlew sitting with them'. However, he did have the decency not to wait after the play to accompany herself and her brothers back to West Kensington.

The next morning, before she was dressed, Dorothy was informed that a young gentleman was waiting to see her in the drawing-room, and discovered, when she got down, that a representative of a monthly magazine called *The Boudoir* had come to ask for an interview. The young man, talking rather as if the magazine was a draper's shop, told her that his paper was making a special feature of beautiful actresses. He cannonaded Dorothy with all sorts of questions, and forced her to surrender the information that her favorite parts were Lady Teazle, Viola, Portia, and Beatrice.

"Comedy, in fact?" said the young man.

"Oh yes, comedy," Dorothy agreed, after a moment's hesitation to decide whether Portia, whose speech about the quality of mercy she had once declaimed at a school breaking-up, ought to be considered a comic figure.

"You have no ambitions for tragedy?"

"No," she told him. "I think there's enough tragedy in ordinary life."

"Would you recommend the stage as a profession?" he inquired.

"Rather a difficult question. It depends so much on the girl."

"Quite," agreed the young man, wisely. "But have you any advice for beginners?"

"My advice is to be natural," said Dorothy.

"Quite," agreed the young man again.

"Natural both on the stage and off," she added.

The young man, with an air of devout concentration, wrote down this valuable maxim, while Dorothy, looking at herself in the mirror, allowed various expressions of delicious naturalness to stand the test of her own critical observation.

"With whom did you study?" the interviewer inquired next.

"Principally with the late Mrs. Haden," said Dorothy, feeling very generous in mentioning Lily's mother after the way the daughter had behaved with Tom Hewitt. "A delightful teacher of the old school, now, alas! no longer with us."

The young man shook his head sadly.

"But my real lessons," Dorothy added, brightly, lest the loss of Mrs. Haden to art might be too much for the interviewer's emotions—"my real lessons were derived from watching famous actresses. No famous actress, continental or English, ever came to London whom I did not go to see. I often went without"—she paused to think what she could have gone without, for it might sound absurd to say that she went without clothes—"I often walked," she corrected herself, "in order to have the necessary money to buy a seat."

"That'll interest our readers very much," said the young man. "Yes, that's the personal note which always appeals to our readers." He sucked his pencil with relish. "And who is your favorite actress?"

"In England or abroad?"

"Oh, in England," the young man hurriedly explained; probably he was jibbing at the prospect of having to write a foreign name.

"In England, Ellen Terry, decidedly," Dorothy replied.

"Quite"; the young man sighed with relief. "Perhaps you would care to give me a photograph of yourself," he suggested.

"With pleasure," she said, taking from the mantelpiece one that she had sent her mother about a month ago.

"Of course," the interviewer hemmed, nervously, "that will be twelve and sixpence for the cost of reproduction."

"Twelve and six?" repeated Dorothy.

"The block will cost twelve and sixpence, that is to say."

"Twelve and six?" she repeated once more.

But she gave him the money; controlling her annoyance at the idea that this young man might be making a profit out of her innocence, she conducted him cheerfully to the door and presented him with a tulip from one of Dolly's flower-pots.

"You're fond of gardening?" he asked, with half-open note-book.

"I adore flowers," said Dorothy. "Good-by."

To her mother she explained the sad necessity she had been under of having to give away her favorite photograph.

"But, mother, I'll write for another one," she promised.

"Oh, Norah dear, I hope you will," said Mrs. Caffyn, much distressed.

"Only, as they're rather expensive, you won't mind giving me a guinea, will you?" Dorothy murmured, with a frown for the old "Norah."

"No, darling Norah—darling child, I mean, of course not. I'd no idea you were spending your salary like that," said Mrs. Caffyn, searching in her purse for the money.

That evening, during the first act a note was sent round to Dorothy from Wilfred Curlew to say that he had been to see her every night this week, and that he had persuaded a friend of his to give her some publicity in a magazine with which he was connected.

"At a cost of twelve and six," Dorothy scoffed to herself.

She did not send a word of thanks to Wilfred, and being unable from the stage to perceive his presence anywhere in the theater, she supposed that, having been there every night this week, he must by now have reached the gallery.

When the interview appeared the other girls were very jealous, and all of them vowed that they had never heard of *The Boudoir*.

"With a blush Miss Lonsdale handed our interviewer an exquisite bunch of flowers culled by the beautiful young actress from her garden, a 'thing of beauty' in the dreary desert of London streets," read out one of the girls.

"Good God, have mercy on us!" exclaimed Clarice Beauchamp, holding a hairpin dipped in eye-black over the gas. "It's a wonder the editor hasn't written before now to ask if he can't keep you."

The irritation in the dressing-room caused by the interview was allayed by a rumor that John Richards would visit the Alexandra Theater, Stoke Newington, where they were playing their last week in the suburbs, with a view to choosing girls for the Vanity production in the autumn. No confirmation could be obtained of this; but the chorus put on extra make-up and acted with all its eyes and all its legs for a shadowy figure at the back of one of the private boxes. After the first act the business manager, who had come behind for some purpose, was surrounded by all the girls, each of whom in turn begged him to tell her confidentially what Mr. Richards had said about the show and if he had had any criticisms to make about herself.

"Mr. Richards?" repeated the manager.

"Now, don't pretend you know nothing about it," they expostulated. "*We* know he's in front."

"Well, you know more than I do," said the manager.

"Then who is it at the back of the box on the prompt side?"

"You silly girls! That's the late mayor of Hackney."

"Then why do they make such a fuss of him?" persisted the girl who had started the rumor. "There was a carriage outside the box-office half an hour before the overture, and people were all round it, staring as if it was the king."

"It's a very sad story," the manager explained. "He's blind, poor fellow, and now, whenever he goes to the theater, they watch him being helped out of his brougham."

During the second act not an eye nor a leg was thrown in the direction of the mysterious stranger, whose identity was a great disappointment to the girls; they had counted on Mr. Richards visiting them in the course of the tour, and here it was coming to an end without a sign of him.

However, they were consoled by being told at the last minute that they were going to play three nights at Oxford before the tour came to a definite conclusion. Everybody agreed that it would be a delightful way to wind up, and when the company assembled at Paddington on a brilliant morning in earliest June, they seemed, in the new clothes they had been able to buy during the last month in London, more like a large picnic-party going up to Maidenhead than a touring company.

Dorothy had decided that the visit to Oxford was an occasion to justify breaking into the £500 she had got out of her mother, which was still practically intact, owing to the economy exerted all these weeks. Her new dresses and new hats, combined with that interview in *The Boudoir*, gave the rest of the chorus an impression that there was somebody behind Dorothy, and they regarded her with a jealous curiosity that was most encouraging.

IV

The three girls had only just finished dinner at their lodgings in Eden Square when Sylvia proposed a walk round Oxford. Dorothy agreed to go out if she were allowed time to change her things; but Lily declared that she was tired after the journey, and preferred to look at illustrated papers in deshabille. Many undergraduates turned their heads to stare at Dorothy's beauty or Sylvia's eye-glass when the two girls were walking down the High toward St. Mary's College, through the gates of which Sylvia calmly suggested that they should pass in order to explore the gardens.

"But suppose they tell us that girls aren't allowed to go in," Dorothy demanded, in a panic.

"We'll go out again."

"But we should look so foolish."

"We always look foolish," said Sylvia. "Anything more foolish than you look at the present moment I can't imagine, except myself."

Before Dorothy could prevent her, Sylvia had asked a tall and haughty undergraduate if there was any reason why they should not take a walk in the college grounds. The young man blushed painfully, and Dorothy, who could see that his embarrassment at being spoken to by an actress was causing intense delight to a group of idlers in the college lodge, was angry with Sylvia for exposing the two of them to a share in the ridicule.

"All right, Dorothy," said Sylvia, cheerfully. "He says we can."

The tall and haughty undergraduate strode away up the High to escape from his friends' chaff, and the two girls wandered about the college until they found themselves in the famous St. Mary's Walks, where upon a seat embowered in foliage they listened to the bells that were ringing down the golden day and ringing in the unhastening Sabbath eve. Close at hand, but hidden from view by leafy banks, the pleasurable traffic of the Cherwell sounded continuously in a low murmur of talk that, blending with the swish of paddles and comfortable sound of jostling punts, seemed the very voice of indolent June. Dorothy supposed that she, like nature, must be looking most beautiful in this bewitching light, and regretted that the only passers-by should be ecclesiastical figures bent in grave intercourse, or a few young men arguing in throaty voices about topics she did not recognize.

"I don't think we've chosen a very good place," she complained, with a discontented pout.

"We've chosen the place," said Sylvia, "where nearly four years ago, on a Sunday afternoon in August, I agreed to get married."

"Married?" repeated Dorothy, in amazement. "Are you married?"

"Yes, I believe I'm married for the present; but I sha'n't be soon."

"Oh, Sylvia, do tell me about it! I won't say a word to anybody else."

But Sylvia, having said so much, would say no more; jumping up and insisting that she was thirsty, she reminded Dorothy that they had promised to help Charlie Clinton entertain his brother and some undergraduate friends. Charlie Clinton was an obscure member of the company who had suddenly sprung into considerable prominence by revealing that he had a brother at Oxford and was himself the black sheep of a respectable family. Dorothy, realizing that the blackest sheep is better form than the whitest goat, had accepted the invitation, but she was not much impressed by the collection of undergraduates gathered in his rooms, and was vexed that she had wasted her most becoming hat on young men who wanted to talk about nothing but music. She was vexed, too, at finding that David Bligh had been invited, and that he was talking affectedly about good music and sounding with his fluty voice rather like an undergraduate himself. Lily came and danced a classical dance which seemed to please everybody else, though Dorothy could not see anything in it. Bligh sang German songs, and was so much applauded that he condescendingly proposed that his pupil should sing, who refused so angrily that none of the undergraduates dared approach her. It was indeed a thoroughly boring evening, and she wondered if Oxford was going to produce nothing better than this.

The theater on Monday night, notwithstanding the fine weather, was packed; but the audience was noisy, and the men in the chorus who had not been invited toCharlie Clinton's party severely condemned the bad manners of undergraduates.

"They're a rowdy lot of bounders, that's what they are," Tom Hewitt proclaimed, loosening the collar around his aggressive neck.

Dorothy, who had been looking forward to astonishing some of the girls in the dressing-room with her news about Sylvia, forgot everything in a delightful triumph she was able to enjoy at the expense of Clarice Beauchamp. A note was brought round after the first act addressed:

To the fair artist's model in pink.   Front row.   O. P. side.

Clarice Beauchamp had the impudence to contest Dorothy's right to open this note, and while some of the artist's models were rapidly transforming themselves into Polynesian beauties and others as rapidly assuming the aristocratic costumes of a millionaire's yachting-party, Clarice and Dorothy, who belonged to the latter division, argued heatedly. At last Fay Onslow, to whom the note could not possibly refer, was allowed to open it and give her verdict:

Fair lady, my name is Lonsdale. On the Grampian hills my father feeds his flock! In other words, will you and the lady with the monocle who yesterday afternoon picked out quite the most unattractive man in St. Mary's as your guide come and picnic with me on the upper river to-morrow? A friend of mine at the House is dying to meet you, but he is much too shy to write himself. If you can come, just send back your address by bearer and I'll send my tame cab to fetch you to-morrow at twelve o'clock.

Yours sincerely,
ARTHUR LONSDALE.

"I knew it was for me," said Dorothy. "Sylvia and I were in St. Mary's College yesterday afternoon."

Clarice Beauchamp, much mortified, had to surrender her claim to the note.

"But what a strange coincidence that he should be called Lonsdale!" Onzie exclaimed. "Most extraordinary, I call it. Who knows? He might be a relation."

"He might be," said Dorothy, calmly.

Lily looked up from her place as if she were going to speak, but, though she said nothing, Dorothy was glad that the terms of the note gave her no excuse for asking her to-morrow, even if Sylvia did maliciously propose that Lily should go instead of herself.

"Oh, but they particularly want you," Dorothy protested.

"Anyway, I can't go," Lily said; "I've promised to go round some of the colleges with Tom."

Dorothy winced at the threatened sacrilege.

Next morning a cab jingled up to the girls' lodgings, and they were driven to the nearest point of embarkation for a picnic on the upper river. Their host, a short young man with very fair hair and a round pink face, introduced himself and led the way to the Rollers, over which punts and canoes were dragged from the lower level of the Cherwell to the wider sweeps of the Isis. A tall young man who was standing by a couple of canoes moored to the bank came forward to greet them. His most immediately conspicuous feature was a pair of white flannel trousers down the seams of which ran stripes of vivid blue ribbon; but when he was introduced to Dorothy as Lord Clarehaven she forgot about his trousers in the more vivid blue of his name. All sorts of ideas rushed through her mind—a sudden dread that he might think Sylvia more attractive than herself, a sudden contempt for the party of the evening before, a sudden rapture in which blue sky, blue blood, and the blue stripes of the trousers merged exquisitely, and a sudden apprehension created by her pleated reflection in the water that she was not looking her best. After Lord Clarehaven she should not have been surprised if the first young man had also had a title; but he was apparently only Mr. Lonsdale, and, though entitled to respect as a friend of Lord Clarehaven, would probably interest Sylvia more than herself.

Dorothy's dread that she and Lord Clarehaven might not find themselves in the same canoe was soon dispelled, because Lord Clarehaven was evidently as eager for her company as she was for his, and they were soon leaving the others behind.

There is no form of conveyance which makes for so much intimacy of regard as a canoe, and Dorothy, when she had once been able to reassure herself by means of a pocket-mirror that she had not been ruffled by the cab-drive or by the nervous business of getting gracefully into a wabbling canoe, settled herself down to be admired at a distance of about four feet. Moreover, she indulged for the first time in her life in the pleasure of admiring somebody else, a state of mind which doubled her charm by taking away much of her self-consciousness. If Lord Clarehaven was below the standard of aristocracy set by our full-blooded lady novelists, he was equally far removed from the chinless convention of banal caricature. He had the long legs, the narrow hips and head, and the big teeth of the Norman; but his fair hair was already thinning upon a high, retreating forehead, his nose was small, and if the protuberant eyes that one sees in Pekinese spaniels and other well-bred mammals were a faint intimation of approaching degeneracy in the stock, Dorothy was not sufficiently versed in physiognomy to recognize such symptoms; already fascinated by his title and his trousers, she was quite ready to be fascinated by his eyes.

"I was lunching in St. Mary's yesterday with Arthur Lonsdale," he was explaining, "and I noticed you from the lodge. I should have come up and spoken to you myself, but I was rather frightened by your friend's eye-glass. In fact, I'm still not at all at ease with her. She looks deuced clever, I mean, don't you think?"

"She is awfully clever."

"Poor girl, but I suppose it's not such a bore for a girl as it would be for a man. I'm an awful ass myself, you know. I mean, I'm absolutely incapable of doing anything."

"How did you know we belonged to the company?" asked Dorothy, implying that with all his modesty he must possess acute powers of judgment hidden away somewhere.

"Well, to tell you the truth, we didn't know. Somebody said your friend was a medical student, only I wasn't going to have that, and some man said he'd noticed you at the station, so Lonnie and I went to the theater on the off-chance and tried to spot you."

"Which you did?"

"Oh, rather. Only, then we couldn't spot your name. I was all for Clarice Beauchamp."

"She's an awfully horrid girl," said Dorothy, quickly.

"Is she? I'm sorry to hear that. And Lonnie betted you were Fay Onslow. So we were quits. Funny thing you should have the same name as Lonnie. No relation, I suppose?"

He was evidently so sure of this that Dorothy was rather piqued and asked, loftily, which Lonsdale he was.

"Cleveden's son."

"Oh, then I am a relation," said Dorothy. "Though of course a very, very distant one."

"By Jove! that's great!" said Clarehaven.

He seemed enthusiastic, but Dorothy could not make out whether he believed her or not, and she rather wished she had kept the relationship for the dressing-room. She hoped that Sylvia would not give Lonsdale an impression that she claimed to be his first cousin; this abrupt plunge into the whirlpool of society might make her act extravagantly. What a pity that she had not known who he was before they met, and "Oh!" she cried, aloud.

"What's the matter?" Clarehaven asked.

"Nothing. At least I think I touched a fish," said Dorothy.

But her exclamation was caused by dismay at recalling that she had addressed him as "Arthur Lonsdale, Esquire," when for the first time in her life she might have written "The Honorable Arthur Lonsdale," for everybody to see. What must he have thought of her ignorance? And now here in a canoe with her was Lord Clarehaven, but, owing to the foolish modesty that English titles affect, she did not know if he was a marquis, an earl, a viscount, or a mere baron. The prospect of the green river was leaden with the thought of her stupidity.

"You're looking very sad," said Clarehaven. "What's the matter?"

"I was thinking how beautiful it was here," she sighed.

"Topping, isn't it?"

"Topping," she echoed, awarding to the utterance of the epithet as much emotion as if it were robbed from Shakespeare's magic store. Amid a sweet smell of grass and to the accompaniment of lapping water and a small sibilant wind they lunched on the salmon and mayonnaise, the prawns in aspic, the galantine and cold chicken, the meringues and strawberries of how many Oxford picnics. Above them dreamed a huge sky; elm-trees guarded the near horizon; wasps had not begun, nor did Sylvia tease Dorothy about being related to Lonsdale when Clarehaven presented them as long-lost cousins.

By the end of the afternoon Dorothy had sufficiently confirmed her admirer's first impression to be invited to lunch with him at Christ Church the following day, in which invitation Sylvia was of course included. Then slowly they drifted back down the river, on the dimples and eddies of which the overhanging trees cast a patina as upon the muscles of an ancient bronze.

"How unreal the theater seems!" sighed Dorothy when they drove up to the stage-door.

"Does it?" Sylvia laughed. "It seems to me much more real than our pretty behavior this afternoon."

V

Dorothy slept badly that night. Her regret for the mistake she had made in addressing Arthur Lonsdale as esquire magnified itself horribly in the mean little bedroom of the lodgings in Eden Square. All night long she was waking up to reproach herself for her stupidity in not taking the trouble to make sure who he was before she sent back the note. Her blunder was all the more unpardonable because she should have been sufficiently interested in receiving a letter from a namesake to take this trouble. And now suppose Lord Clarehaven were to put her under the necessity of addressing him on the outside of an envelope? How was she to know what to write? "Lord Clarehaven, Christ Church College"? It sounded rather empty. In any case, she should have to ask for him at the lodge to-morrow, and how the porter would sneer behind her back if she should make a mistake! In despair Dorothy wandered into the next room where Sylvia and Lily were sleeping tranquilly.

"Oh dear!" she lamented.

"What's the matter?" asked Sylvia, jumping up in bed.

"Sylvia, I can't sleep. I think there's a rat in my room. I suppose Arthur Lonsdale didn't say if Lord Clarehaven was a marquis, did he?"

"Damn your eyes, Dorothy, did you wake me up to ask that? Go and get hold of Debrett, if you want to know so badly."

Dorothy went back to her bedroom in peace of mind. Of course! How easy it was, really, and she fell into a delicious sleep, from which, notwithstanding her disturbed night, she was early awake to dress and be out of the house by ten o'clock in order to search the Oxford bookshops for a *Peerage*.

"We have a *Baronetage*" said one bookseller.

Dorothy shrugged her shoulders compassionately, and went from shop to shop until she found the big red volume of her desire. She paid without a moment's hesitation the price of it, called a cab, and drove back to Eden Square, that she might have plenty of time to devour the contents before going to Christ Church. Her breath came fast when she actually read Clarehaven and began to absorb the wonderful information below:

CLAREHAVEN, EARL OF. (Clare) [Earl U.K. 1816. Bt. E. 1660.]

ANTHONY GILBERT CLARE, 5th Earl, and 10th Baronet; *b.* Oct. 15, 1882; *s.* 1896; ed. at Eton and Christ Church; is 2d Lieut, in North Devon Dragoons, and patron of one living.

Arms—Purpure, two flanches ermine, on a chief sable a moon in her complement argent. *Crest*—A moon in her complement argent, arising from a cloud proper. *Supporters*—Two angels vested purpure, winged and crined or, each holding in the exterior hand a key or. *Motto*—*Claro non clango.*

Seat—Clare Court, Devonshire. *Town residence*—129 Curzon Street, W. *Club*—Bachelors'.

SISTERS LIVING

Lady Arabella. b. 1885.
Lady Constantia. b. 1887.

WIDOW LIVING OF FOURTH EARL

Augusta (Countess of Clarehaven) 2d dau. of 9th Earl of Chatfield: *m.* 1880 the 4th Earl who *d.* 1896. *Residence*—Clare Court, Devonshire.

PREDECESSORS—[1] Anthony Clare, *M.P.* for Devon (a descendant of Richard Fitzgilbert, Baron of Clare, a companion of the Conqueror, son of Gilbert Crispin, Earl of Brione in Normandy, who was son of Geoffrey, a natural son of Richard I. Duke of Normandy), was cr. a Bt. 1660; *d.* 1674; *s.* by his son [2] *Sir* Gilbert, 2d Bt.; *d.* 1710; *s.* by his son [3] *Sir* Anthony, 3d Bt.; *d.* 1747; *s.* by his nephew [4] *Sir* William, 4th Bt.; *d.* 1764; *s.* by his cousin [5] *Sir* Anthony, 5th Bt.; cr. *Baron Clarehaven* (peerage of Great Britain) 1796; *d.* 1802; *s.* by his son [6] Gilbert, 2d Baron; cr. *Viscount Clare* and *Earl of Clarehaven* (peerage of United Kingdom) 1816; *d.* 1826; *s.* by his son [7] Richard Crispin, 2d Earl. *b.* 1788. *m.* 1818 Lady Caroline Lacey who *d.* 1859, 2d dau. of 3d Marquess of Longlan; *d.* 1864; *s.* by his son [8] Geoffrey William, *P.C.*, 3d Earl. *b.* 1820; sometime Lord Lieut. of Devon; M.P. for S. Devon (C); Vice-Chamberlain of H. M. Queen Victoria's Household. *m.* 1845 the Hon. Louisa Travers, who *d.* 1890, dau. of the 26th Baron Travers; *d.* 1867; *s.* by his son [9] Gilbert Crispin, 4th Earl, *b.* 1845; Lieut. Royal Horse Guards, 1866-67: *m.* 1880 Lady Augusta Fanhope, 2d dau. of 9th Earl of Chatfield; *d.* 1896; *s.* by his son [10] Anthony Gilbert, 5th Earl and present peer; also Viscount Clare and Baron Clarehaven.

Half a dozen times word for word she read through these magic pages, until she felt that she simply could not make a mistake at lunch. Then a page or two farther on, past Clarendon and Clarina, she came to:

CLEVEDEN, BARON. (Lonsdale) [Baron G.B. 1762.]

CHARLES ARTHUR BRABAZON LONSDALE. *G.C.M.G., G.C.I.E.* 5th Baron; *b.* Oct. 10, 1858; *s.* 1888; ed. at Eton and at Ch. Ch. Oxford. (B.A. 1880); is a J.P. and D.L. for Warwickshire and Verderer of the Forest of Arden; Hon. Col. of Yeo.; sat as M.P. for West Warwick—(C) 1880-1884; was Assist. Private Sec. to the Premier—(M. Salisbury) 1885-6; Gov. and Com. in Ch. of E. Australia. 1893-99; and Gov. of Central India. 1899-1901; *K.C.M.G.* 1893; *G.C.M.G.* 1898; *G.C.I.E.* 1899: *m.* 1882 Lady Helen Druce (an Extra Woman of the Bed-chamber to H.M. Queen Victoria), dau. of 10th Earl of Monteith and has issue.

Arms—Argent, an oak tree englanté vert. *Crest*—A bugle horn or, enguiché and stringed vert. *Supporters*—On either side a forester sounding a horn proper. *Motto*—J'y serai.

Seat—Cressingham Hall, Warwick. *Clubs*—Carlton. Travellers'.

SON LIVING

Hon. ARTHUR GEORGE MORNINGTON. *b.* Feb. 24, 1883.

DAUGHTER LIVING

Hon. Sylvia May. *b.* 1885.

"Sylvia?" Dorothy said to herself. But she decided to stick to the name Dorothy, and went on reading about her family.

BROTHER LIVING

Rev. the Hon. George, *b.* 1860; ed. at Eton, and at St. Mary's Coll. Oxford. (B.A. 1883. M.A. 1886); is R. of Bingham-cum-Bingham Monachorum; *m.* 1894 Mary Alice, dau. of the late Rev. Francis Greville, V. of St. Wilfred's, Tilchester, and Hon. Canon of Tilchester, and has issue living, Arthur Brabazon—*b.* 1896. Mary—*b.* 1898. Georgina Maud—*b.* 1900. *Residence*—Bingham Rectory, Hants.

SISTERS LIVING

Hon. Frances Louisa, *b.* 1863. *m.* 1885 Sir William Honeywood-Greene, 6th Bt. *Residence*—Arden Towers, Warwick.

Hon. Caroline, *b.* 1865. *m.* 1886 Sir Stanley Pinkerton, K.C.V.O. Master of the King's Spaniels. *Residence*—210 Eaton Square, S.W.

Hon. Horatia. *b.* 1867.

There followed a couple of pages devoted to collateral branches of the Lonsdales. These were something new: the Clares apparently lacked collaterals. Presently it dawned on Dorothy that these collaterals treated of the more distant relations of the family, and in a fever she began to search for confirmation of the legend in Lonsdale Road that through their grandmother, Mrs. Doyle, the Caffyns were connected with Lord Cleveden. On and on she read through colonels and rectors with their numerous offspring, through consuls and captains and judges and doctors even; but there was no mention of Doyles, still less of Caffyns. The connection must indeed be very remote: perhaps it was hidden among the predecessors.

PREDECESSORS.—[1] George Lonsdale, Verderer of the Forest of Arden; M.P. for Warwickshire 1740-62; cr. *Baron Cleveden*, of Cressingham, co. Warwick (peerage of Great Britain) 1762; *d.* 1764; *s.* by his son [2] Arthur, 2d Baron; *d.* 1822; *s.* by his son [3] Charles, 3d Baron; *b.* 1790: *m.* 1830 the Hon. Horatia Brabazon, who *d.* 1851, dau. of 3d Viscount Brabazon; *d.* 1840; *s.* by his son [4] George Brabazon, 4th Baron; *b.* 1832; a Lord-in-Waiting to H. M. Queen Victoria 1858-64: *m.* 1856 Lady May Mornington, who *d.* 1895, 3d dau. of 11th Earl of Belgrove; *d.* 1888; *s.* by his son [5] Charles Arthur Brabazon, 5th Baron and present peer.

Dorothy sighed her disappointment, but resolved that she would adopt the family crest and motto as her own. *J'y serai* underneath a bugle-horn: how well it would look on her note-paper. Fired by its inspiration, she began to dress herself for lunch with the Earl of Clarehaven, and when, an hour later, she ushered Sylvia into the Christ Church lodge with a hardihood that contrasted strongly with the reluctance she had shown when Sylvia had dragged her into St. Mary's on Sunday, there was no need to inquire for Lord Clarehaven by his correct title, because the host was there himself to meet his guests and escort them across the spaciousness of Tom Quad to his rooms in Peckwater. It appeared that at the last minute an urgent summons to play cricket for the Eton Ramblers had prevented Lonsdale from coming. Dorothy, notwithstanding her knowledge of the Lonsdale collaterals, was not sorry, for she did not wish to discuss the relationship with one of the family, especially before Sylvia, to whom she now turned with a hint of patronage.

"My dear, you will be disappointed. Mr. Lonsdale is not coming to lunch."

Sylvia said she would try to put up with the disappointment and hoped that an equally entertaining substitute had been provided.

"I've asked a fellow called Tufton," said Clarehaven. "His father's a sleeping partner or something of jolly old John Richards at the Vanity, and I thought he might be useful. Besides, he's not at all a bad egg. We elected him to the Bullingdon this term."

Dorothy looked at her host gratefully and admiringly.

"How awfully sweet of you!" she murmured, with the lightest, briefest touch of her fingers on his wrist, and thinking how well the people who mattered knew how to do things.

They had reached Peckwater by now, the architecture of which, brightened by many window-boxes in full bloom, reminded Dorothy of streets in Mayfair. Her morning with Debrett had in fact turned her head so completely that she sought everywhere for illustrations of grandeur in the life around her; in this regard Clarehaven's rooms, by conforming perfectly to her notions of what they should be, made her want to kiss herself with satisfaction. To begin with, the door of his bedroom, slightly ajar, allowed a glimpse of numerous pairs of boots running up the scale from brogues to waders, which somehow spoke more eloquently of riches and leisure than if the luncheon-table had been laid with gold. Dorothy was contemplating the tints of these boots like a poet in an autumnal glade when Clarehaven presented Mr. Tufton, who, to do him justice, looked as well turned out as one of his host's hunting-tops and in a chestnut-colored suit with extravagantly rolled collar maintained his personality against the boots and the cigars and the brown sherry and the old paneling and the studies of grouse by Thorburn that gave this room its air of mellow opulence.

Dorothy told Mr. Tufton brightly that he had missed a wonderful afternoon yesterday.

"I was playing polo," he explained.

Dorothy, having an idea that polo was nearly as dangerous as bull-fighting, shuddered.

"I say, do you feel a draught?" inquired the host, anxiously.

"Oh no, it's delicious here."

A voice from the quad was shouting "Tony," and Dorothy, remembering Anthony from Debrett, could not resist telling Clarehaven that he was being called. Clarehaven was moving over to the window to discourage whoever was demanding his presence, when another voice came clearly up through the June air.

"Shut up, Ridgway! Tony's lunching some does, you silly ass!"

Dorothy could not help thinking that Sylvia ought to have pretended not to hear this allusion instead of bursting out into what was really a vulgar peal of laughter.

"I think there *is* a draught," said Mr. Tufton, closing the windows so gravely that one felt much of his inmost meditation was devoted to the tactful handling of moments like this.

"Are these your sisters?" Dorothy asked, picking up a photograph of two girls, each holding a foxhound.

"Yes, those are my sisters Bella and Connie," Clarehaven replied. "They're awful keen on puppy-walking."

Perhaps, after all, abbreviations were sometimes tolerable, and names like Arabella and Constantia were rather long.

"Isn't your second name Gilbert?" she asked.

"Yes. Dreadful infliction, isn't it?"

Dorothy decided not to say that her father's name was Gilbert, to which she had been leading up, and took her seat at table, noticing with pleasure that the full moon of the house of Clare adorned the silver. After lunch they looked at albums of snapshots, during the examination of which Mr. Tufton was most useful, because he was continually saying: "By Jove! Isn't that Lady Connie?" or: "By Gad! Isn't that the covert where Lady Bella got her left and right last October?" or: "Hello! I see Lady Clarehaven has followed my advice about the pergola." If Mr. Tufton could advise countesses as stately as the Countess of Clarehaven and refer to the daughters of an earl as Lady Bella and Lady Connie, what might not Dorothy do with patience and discretion? Meanwhile she took no risks, and if she had to mention the members of her host's family she alluded to them as "your mother" or "your elder sister" or "your younger sister."

"But what a glorious place Clare Court must be!" she exclaimed.

"Oh, I don't know," said the owner of it. "The train service is absolutely rotten."

"You'll have your new car this vac.," Mr. Tufton reminded him. "I wrote the firm a very strong letter yesterday." Then seeing that his friend was growing gloomy at the prospect of Devonshire even with a new car, he suggested a stroll round Meadows, and cleverly arranged to lag behind with Sylvia.

Clarehaven when he was alone with Dorothy did not find much more to say, but he was able to look at her with a more open admiration than when his glances had been disconcerted by Sylvia's monocle.

"You know I'm tremendously quelled by your friend," he avowed. "By Jove! you know, I feel she's always criticizing a fellow. Now with you I feel absolutely at my ease."

"I'm glad," Dorothy murmured. Then for two full moments she let her deep eyes flash into his.

"I say, when you look at me like that," said Clarehaven, solemnly, "you absolutely bring my heart into my mouth. By Gad! I feel it being hooked up like a trout."

"I'm afraid it's a very easy heart to hook," she laughed.

"Oh no, it's not! Oh no, really it's not! I can assure you that I'm not in the least susceptible."

"Ah, you'll forget all about me to-morrow."

"My dear Dorothy! You don't object to my calling you Dorothy? My dear Dorothy, if you knew how unlikely I am to forget all about you to-morrow...."

"Well?"

"Well, I'm not going to forget about you, that's all."

"We shall see."

"Yes, we shall," said Clarehaven, fiercely.

Dorothy was anxious to add still a small touch to his obvious appreciation, and she conceived the daring idea of inviting him back to tea in the lodgings. She felt that there in the dingy little room her grace and beauty would appear more desirable than ever, and if he should fancy from her invitation that she intended to make herself cheap he would soon perceive from her behavior how far removed she was from the average chorus-girl. Clarehaven applauded the suggestion, and though Sylvia looked rather bored by it, Tufton was enthusiastic; so they visited a pastry-cook's and bought lots of expensive cakes and chocolates, for which the guest of honor paid.

"How the poor live!" exclaimed Dorothy, pointing with a dramatic gesture at the drab little houses of Eden Square as if she would comment upon an aspect of Oxford that was hardly credible after Christ Church.

"Yes, this is our quad," chuckled Sylvia. "Old Tom!"

"I've never been here before," said Clarehaven, anxious to convince Dorothy that really he was not susceptible. "I've heard of Eden Square, of course, but this is my first visit. It's where all the theatrical people stay, isn't it, Tuffers?"

"It may be," replied Mr. Tufton, who, having paid for everything he possessed with money his father was making out of the theater, naturally did not wish to show himself too familiar with its domestic life.

"Number ten," said Dorothy, gaily. "Here we are!"

She opened the front door and led the way along a narrow passage to the sitting-room, and, flinging wide open the door, drew back for Clarehaven to enter first.

"You'll have to excuse the general untidiness," she warned him.

The sentence was out before she had time to realize that the general untidiness included a searing vision of Lily in an arm-chair, imparadised upon the lap of the impossible Tom Hewitt. Sylvia dashed forward to the rescue of Dorothy, who was standing speechless with mortification, and began introducing everybody to one another as fast as she could. Clarehaven's devotion to the stage did not seem impaired by this abrupt manifestation of low life behind the scenes, and Tufton, who in other company would probably have been as much outraged as Dorothy herself by such a reflection upon the source of his wealth, copied his friend's lead. Tom Hewitt with a mumbled excuse about having to see the manager retired as soon as possible. Lily, notwithstanding that her left cheek was flushed and that the hair on the left side of her head was more conspicuously a part of the general untidiness than the hair on the right, seemed utterly unconscious of having as good as torn up the Debrett in which Dorothy had invested this morning, and actually talked away in her languorous style to Clarehaven and Tufton as if Tom Hewitt's lap was the natural place on which to pass a lovely summer afternoon.

For Dorothy that tea-party was a martyrdom from which she began to think that she should never recover. Wherever she looked she saw that horrible picture of Lily and Tom. Once Clarehaven asked for another lump of sugar, and, tormented by the vision, she put two chocolates in his cup. Tufton passed his cup for a little more milk, and she emptied it away into the slop-bowl. Finally in an effort to restore her equanimity she took a chocolate that concealed a sticky caramel within, and when her mouth was all twisted and her teeth felt as if they were being pulled out by the roots Clarehaven asked if she could not spare him a photograph. He was being kind, thought Dorothy, miserably; the Fitzgilberts and Crispins and Clares of all those generations were gathering to help him hide the contempt he must feel for this tea-party; Lacy and Travers and Fanhope were behind him, pleading the obligations of nobility. And if he were not being kind she must suppose that he rather liked Lily, which would be worst of all. But what a lesson she had been given, what a lesson, indeed! If but once it might be granted to her that a folly should be expiated in the pain of the moment, she would never play tricks with fortune again.

When Clarehaven rose to make his farewells Dorothy did not attempt to detain him, but with a sorrowful grace shook his hand and would not even give him the photograph.

"No, no, I'd rather send you one from London."

"But you'll forget," he protested.

"No, I sha'n't. One hundred and twenty-nine Curzon Street. Or will you be at Clare Court?"

"I'll write to you."

"No, no," said Dorothy. It would never do for him to write to Lonsdale Road; besides, he might take it into his head to visit her there, which might be more disastrous than this tea-party. What would he think, for instance, of the misshapen boots that were usually waiting outside Roland's room like two large black-beetles? No, when she had thought out her campaign she would send him a photograph, and if, looking back on this afternoon, he decided that she was not worth while—well, she must put up with it. Dorothy was so sorry for herself that Clarehaven was flattered by her melancholy countenance into supposing that he had made a deep impression. In the narrow passage Tufton slipped behind and whispered to her that she must look her best to-night.

"Why?"

"Stable information," he said, and hurried after his friend, Lord Clarehaven.

When the three girls were alone together in the fatal sitting-room Dorothy's repressed rage with Lily broke out uncontrollably.

"I hope you don't think I'll ever live with you again after that disgusting exhibition. I suppose you think just because you went with me to Walter Keal that you can do as you like. I don't know what Sylvia thinks of you, but I can tell you what I think. You make me feel absolutely sick. That beastly chorus-boy! The idea of letting anybody like that even look at you! Thank Heaven, the tour's over. I'm going down to the theater. I can't stay in this room. It makes me blush to think of it. I'll take jolly good care who I live with in future."

Something in Lily's fragility, something in her still untidy hair and uncomprehending muteness, inflamed Dorothy beyond the bounds of toleration, and in despair of just words to humiliate her sufficiently she slapped her face.

"Hit her back, my lass," cried Sylvia, putting up her eye-glass to watch the fray; but Lily collapsed tearfully into the arm-chair, and Dorothy rushed out of the room.

The sight of Debrett's scarlet and gold upon her dressing-table was enough to reconjure all her mortification, and she was just going to weep her heart out upon the bed as, no doubt, below Lily was weeping hers out upon the shoulders of a ghostly Tom Hewitt, when Tufton's parting advice recurred to her. She had to look her best to-night. Why? He must have some reason to say that.

"*J'y serai*?" cried Dorothy, mustering all her family pride to keep back her tears.

VI

Although fortified by the motto, Dorothy was still suffering from the memory of that afternoon, and when she arrived at the theater to dress and saw Tom Hewitt standing by the stage-door she tried to pass him without acknowledging his salute.

"Mr. Richards will be in front to-night," he told her, portentously.

"Oh, we're always hearing that," said Dorothy. "I don't believe it."

"It's a fact. Warren told me so himself. And Mr. Keal's come down with him."

So this was why Tufton had advised her to look her best to-night; the visit could only mean that the great man wanted girls for the autumn production at the Vanity. Dorothy began to cheer up. Even if Lily's behavior had disgusted Lord Clarehaven irreparably, such behavior would not spoil her own chance of being engaged by John Richards, and at the Vanity there would be plenty of titled admirers. No doubt most of them would be younger sons or elder sons who had not yet succeeded, but ... "*j'y serai*," murmured Dorothy. "It's a good thing that I don't fall in love very easily. And it's lucky I didn't let myself cry," she added, congratulating her reflection in the dressing-room mirror.

Every girl was painting herself and powdering herself and pulling up her stockings and patting her hair and, regardless of the undergraduates she had met during the week, preparing to act as she had never acted before. Dorothy took neither more nor less trouble with her appearance than she took every night.

This time rumor was incarnate in fact, for the great Mr. Richards came and stood in the wings during a large portion of the play, and Dorothy, convinced that the one thing she ought not to do was to throw a single glance in his direction, devoted all her attention to the front of the house. There were lots of flowers; but nobody, neither principal nor chorus-girl, was handed such a magnificent basket of pink roses as herself, and nobody who had not suffered as she had suffered that afternoon in the depths could have been so gloriously thrilled on the heights as Dorothy was when the curtain fell at the close of the performance amid the shouts and cheers of youthful art-loving England, and she was stopped in the wings by Mr. Water Keal.

"Come here, dear," he said. "I want to introduce you to Mr. Richards."

The impresario was a large and melancholy man whose voice reverberated in the back of a cavernous throat with so high a palate that consonants were lost in its echoes and his speech seemed to consist entirely of vowels.

"Who sent you the prehy flowers, dear?" he asked, lugubriously.

"The Earl of Clarehaven," said Dorothy, with a brilliant smile.

"Ha—ha, vehy 'ice, vehy 'ice," he muttered, fondling the card attached. "Goo' gir'! Goo' gir'!"

The millionaire's yachting friends wore evening gowns for the latter part of the second act, and Dorothy in old rose, with her basket of flowers and exquisite neck and shoulders, was indeed looking her best.

"Goo' gir'!" Mr. Richards boomed once more; then as she passed from the royal presence he patted her shoulder in congratulation, dusted the powder from his fingers, lit an enormous cigar, and wandered away with Mr. Keal.

When Dorothy reached the dressing-room every girl was speculating on the depth of the impression she had made upon Mr. Richards, but not one of them could claim that the great man had patted her on the back or noticed her flowers. Presently the call-boy came with a message that Miss Lonsdale was to be at the theater to-morrow morning at eleven o'clock without fail, and it was obvious to the most jealous observer that Dorothy's chance had come. She was so much elated by her good fortune that she was reconciled to Lily, told everybody what a delightful lunch she had had with Lord Clarehaven and what a delightful picnic she had had with Lord Clarehaven and how she had met a cousin of hers, Arthur Lonsdale, who was the only son of Lord Cleveden.

"You know, he was governor of Central India," Dorothy reminded the dressing-room.

"India!" echoed Miss Onslow. "That sounds hot stuff, anyway."

Dorothy buried her face in the roses to get rid of the effluvium of such vulgarity. And then in the middle of her success, just when her true friends should have been most pleased, Sylvia, who had shared—well, not shared, but had been allowed to assist at her triumph—Sylvia it was who asked, in a voice audible to the whole dressing-room:

"On which side of the road are you related to young Lonsdale?"

Luckily the joke was too obscure to be generally understood; but Dorothy decided to banish Sylvia from the list of her friends that in Lily's company she might henceforth inhabit an outer darkness unlit by Debrett's scarlet and gold.

"I expect I shall soon forget what an awful life touring is," said Dorothy to herself that night, as she turned back the limp cotton sheets and looked distastefully at the hummocky mattress. There was a trenchant symbolism, too, in massacring a flea with Debrett; no other volume would have been heavy enough.

The next morning Mr. Richards seemed to be inviting her—so gentle were his accents, so soft his intonation—to join the Vanity company next September at three pounds a week. Mr. Keal and his Jewish assistant, Mr. Fitzmaurice, were present at her triumph; and when Dorothy was going down-stairs from the manager's office, Mr. Fitzmaurice hurried after her and begged her not to forget that it was he who had been the first to recognize her talents.

"Well, call me a cab, there's a good boy," said Dorothy, to reward him; and Mr. Fitzmaurice, who only six months ago had looked at her so critically on that wet December morning in Leicester Square, now ran hither and thither in the summer weather until he had found her a cab.

"What swank!" Dorothy heard Clarice Beauchamp say when, with a rattle and a dash, she drove up to the station, where the company were mustering for their last journey together. But she had only a gracious smile for poor Clarice; and at Paddington, although she parted with Sylvia and Lily cordially enough, she did not invite either of them to come and see her in Lonsdale Road.

CHAPTER III

I

NOT even the Irishman's passion for originality is strong enough to resist the common impulse of human nature to follow the course of the sun; he must migrate westward like the Saxon before him, and it is surely remarkable to find a theater holding out against a social tendency to which an Irishman succumbs. When a flood of new thoroughfares submerged old theatrical London in the last years of the nineteenth century and created a new theaterdom farther west; when the barbarous hoardings of the Strand Improvement obliterated so many resorts of leisure, and, like the people of Croton, the London County Council diverted a stream of traffic to flow where once was the Sybaris of Holywell Street and the Opéra Comique; when the Lyceum and the Adelphi changed the quality of their wares; when Terry's became a cinema palace and His Grace of Bedford sold Drury Lane overnight—the Vanity was almost the only theater that preserved its position and its character.

The peak of Ararat was not more welcome to the water-weary eyes of Noah than to patrons of a theater as old-fashioned as the Ark was the sight of that little island upon which the Vanity maintained itself amid the wrecks and ruins of the engulfed Strand. Close by, as if to commemorate the friendly rivalry of Church and Stage, upon another island St. Clement Dane's cleft the traffic of Fleet Street long after Temple Bar had been swept away; and it was agreeably appropriate that the church where Doctor Johnson, our greatest conservative, was wont to bow his head before the slow grinding of God's mills should have for company in a visible protest against the illusion of progress that monument of English conservatism, the Vanity Theater. More secure upon its island in the Strand than the Eddystone Lighthouse upon its rock in the Channel, the illuminated portico of the Vanity blazed away as brightly as it ever did before the destruction of the mean streets that used to obscure its glory. Not far off, the Savoy Hotel served as prologue and epilogue to its entertainments; and no alliance between one of the new theaters in Piccadilly and the Ritz or Carlton could yet claim to have superseded that time-honored alliance between the Vanity and the Savoy.

In the early 'seventies the sacred lamp of burlesque, as journalists moved to poesy by their theme have it, was lighted at the Vanity, and in the waning 'eighties the gas-lamp of burlesque, with nothing but an added brightness to mark the change, became the electric bulb of musical comedy. Time moved slowly at the Vanity; tenors grew hoarse and comedians grew stiff, but they were not easily superseded; many ladies grew stout, but the boards of the Vanity were strong, and even the places of those dearly loved by the gods who married young were only taken by others equally beloved and exactly like their predecessors; puns disappeared gradually from the librettos; the frocks of the chorus exaggerated the fashion of the hour; very seldom a melody was sufficiently novel to escape being whistled by the town; but in the opening years of the twentieth century the Vanity was intrinsically what the Vanity had been thirty years before and what no doubt it would be thirty years thence. The modish young men who applauded "Miss Elsie of Chelsea" sat in the stalls where their fathers and in some cases their grandfathers had applauded "Hamlet Up to Date." The fathers vowed that the Vanity had deteriorated since the days when mutton-chop whiskers were cultivated and the ladies of the chorus flirted bustles on the outside of a coach-and-four; but the sons were quite content with the present régime and considered jolly old John Richards as good as any impresario of the 'eighties. Unless the standard of beauty had universally declined at the dawn of the new century, that opinion of youth must be indorsed; it is doubtful if twenty more beautiful girls than the Vanity chorus contained in the autumn of 1903 could have been found in any other city or in any other country, and certainly not in any other theater. When a few years after this date John Richards was knighted for his services to human nature and applied to the College of Heralds for a grant of arms, a friend with a taste for Latin robbed Propertius for the motto and gave him *Tot milia formosarum*, which, though lending itself to a ribald translation of "The foremost harem of smiling Totties," was not less well deserved by John Richards than by Pluto, to whom the poet addressed the original observation.

Dorothy, by spending in complete seclusion the two months before rehearsals began, prepared herself to shimmer as clearly as she could in the shimmering galaxy that was to make "The River Girl" as big a hit as "Miss Elsie of Chelsea." She declined to accompany her family to the seaside in August, being sure that August at Eastbourne would be bad for her complexion; therefore she remained behind in Lonsdale Road with the cook, who by the time Dorothy had finished with her began to have ambitions to be a lady's maid. Nothing is more richly transfigured by unfamiliarity than the empty streets of a London suburb in mid-August, when their sun-dyed silence quivers upon the air like noon in Italy. At such a season the sorceress Calypso might not have disdained West Kensington for her spells; Dorothy, dream-haunted and with nothing more strenuous than singing-lessons and fashion papers to impinge upon the drowsy days, lived on self-enchantment. She never sent Lord Clarehaven the promised photograph, not did she even write him a letter; after deliberation she had decided that it would be more effective to appear upon his next horizon like a new planet rather than to wane slowly from his recollection like a summer moon. To write from an address at which it would be impossible to renew their acquaintance would be foolish. Besides, with such a future as hers at the Vanity was surely bound to be, did one Clarehaven more or less matter? He had served his purpose in demonstrating the ease with which she could reach beyond other girls; but, as Mary, the cook, had observed last night in recounting her rupture with the milkman, "plenty more mothers had sons," and if Clarehaven arrived impatiently at the same conclusion about the supply of daughters, that was better than exposing herself to the greater humiliation of being taken up in an idle moment and as readily dropped again. Dorothy's imagination had been touched by reading of three Vanity marriages that were now sharing the attention of the holiday press with giant gooseberries and vegetable marrows of mortal seeming. The younger son of a duke, the eldest son of a viscount, a Welsh baronet had, one after another, made those gaps in the Vanity chorus, to fill one of which Dorothy had been chosen by the provident Mr. Richards; she accepted the omen, and made up her mind that for her it should always be marriage or nothing.

It would be unfair at this stage in Dorothy's career to accuse her of formulating any definite plan to win a coronet, still less of casting her eye upon Lord Clarehaven's coronet in particular; but during these sun-drenched August days she did resolve to do nothing that might spoil the fulfilment of the augury. Left to herself, and free from the criticism of friends or relations, it would have been strange if Dorothy's estimate of her own powers had not been rather heightened by so much lazy self-contemplation. One day she had met an acquaintance marooned like herself upon this desert isle of holidays, and on being asked what she was doing in London at such a season, had replied truthfully enough that she was just looking round; but she did not add that she was looking round at herself in a mirror. This cloistral felicity lasted as long as the lime-trees in West Kensington kept their summer greenery; at the end of August the leaves began to wither, the rumble of returning cabs was heard more often every day, and the first rehearsal of "The River Girl" was called. Dorothy's seclusion was over; of the girls who passed through the Vanity stage-door that August morning there was none so fresh as she.

"How odd," she thought, "that only this time last year the notion of going on the stage had never even entered my head."

Dorothy had paused for a moment on the threshold of the theater, and was listening while the door swung to and fro behind her and syncopated the dull beat of the traffic in the Strand to a sort of ragtime tune. How different these rehearsals were going to be from those of last year in the Lisle Street club-room, and how right she had been to escape from the provinces so quickly.

From the first moment Dorothy felt more herself in the Vanity than she had felt all those six months of touring. She was, of course, stared at and criticized, but she was never acutely conscious of the jealousy that had glared from the eyes of her companions in the provinces. The beauty of her rivals in this metropolitan chorus only made her own beauty more remarkable; she, being the first to recognize this, accorded to her associates such a frank and such an obviously sincere admiration that she gained a reputation for simplicity, which the other girls ascribed to innocence. From innocence to mystery is but a short step in an ambient like the Vanity, and without a Lily or a Sylvia to tell the other girls too much about her, Dorothy developed the mysterious aspect of herself and left her innocence undefined. At the Vanity there was none of the destructive intimacy of touring life. Nobody ever saw the ladies of this chorus in polychrome on the wet platform of a Yorkshire railway station; nobody ever saw the ladies of this chorus tilting with a hatpin at pickled onions; nobody, in fact, had any excuse for being disillusioned by the ladies of the Vanity, because, being individually and collectively aware of their national importance, they were never really off the stage; indeed, except occasionally in their bedrooms, perhaps, they were never really behind the scenes. The fancy of a casual observer, who lingered for a moment at the stage-door to watch the ladies of the Vanity tripping out of their hansoms, was as much stimulated by the sight as the fancy of the regular patron who from the front of the house was privileged to observe them tripping on to the stage. They were brilliant butterflies by day and gorgeous moths by night; though nature forbids us to suppose that they never were caterpillars, their larval state is as unimaginable as the touch of time that worked the metamorphosis.

Dorothy did not allude to the chrysalis of West Kensington from which she had just emerged, nor did she mention more than she could help the caterpillar existence of touring. True to her native caution, she avoided committing herself to any sudden friendships that might afterward be regretted, but she fluttered round all the girls in turn, and with Miss Birdie Underhill and Miss Maisie Yorke, two members of the sextet sung from punts in the first act, she made a tolerably high excursion into the empyrean. Birdie and Maisie were tall blondes of the same type as herself, but, being some years older, they were beginning to think that, inasmuch as they had not been able to find even the younger son of a baron whose attentions conformed to his title, they ought to accept the hands of two devoted and moderately rich stock-brokers who had long and patiently admired them. Perhaps it was the first faint intimations of maternity demanding expression that led these two queens of the chorus to hint so graciously to Dorothy at the inheritance they designed for her. To pass from butterflies to bees for a metaphor, they fed her with queens' food (prepared by Romano's) and taught her that the drones must either be married or massacred—even both if necessary. Dorothy was too wise to think she knew everything, and, being acquisitive rather than mimetic, she gained from the two queens the cynicism of a wide experience without subjecting herself to the wear and tear of the process.

Lest a too exclusive attention to Miss Underhill and Miss Yorke should leave her stranded when they quitted the chorus, Dorothy frequented equally the company of a very lovely brunette called Olive Fanshawe, who was certainly the most popular girl in the dressing-room and of a sweet and gentle disposition, without either affectation or duplicity. Apart from the advantage of being friends with a girl so genuinely beloved, Dorothy was attracted to Olive Fanshawe's ivory skin and lustrous dark hair; that would set off her own roses and mignonette to perfection, and she was glad when Olive proposed that perhaps later on they might share a flat. She decided, however, to stay at home during the winter, or at any rate until she should have obtained a more prominent place in the chorus and be justified in launching out on her own with some prospect of practical homage in return.

Dorothy's early confidence in herself had been slightly shaken in the first six weeks of "The River Girl," because Clarehaven had not once been to see her, or, if he had, had never written to tell her how lovely she looked on the banks of a scene-painter's Thames. If he still took the least interest in her, he could easily have found out where she was, and it was significant that she had seen nothing of Tufton, either. Dorothy began to be afraid that those two days at Oxford had vanished from Clarehaven's memory; so, lacking as yet any great incentive to make the best of herself off the stage, she decided not to waste money either on a flat or on winter clothes. No address out of Mayfair would suit her, and no furs less expensive than sables would become her fair beauty. At nineteen she need not be in too much of a hurry, and she should certainly be wise to wait until the springtime would provide her with the prettiest frocks for much less outlay. As for taking a flat, why, anything might have happened by the spring.

Dorothy's plans, however, were precipitated by the behavior of her father. It appeared that a friendly archdeacon had warned Mr. Caffyn privately of the forthcoming sale of some church schools in the center of a large maritime town in the west of England in order that a cinema theater might be erected on their site to the glory of God, the profit of His Church, and the convenience of His little ones. The archdeacon drew Mr. Caffyn's attention to the clause in the contract by which the morality of every performance was secured, and strongly advised him to follow his own example and invest in the theater. Mr. Caffyn, who was not of a speculative temperament, felt that, though he should be unwise to risk brewery stock profitable enough at a date when the Liberal party had scarcely yet swelled the womb of politics, he was being offered an excellent opportunity to add to his wife's income, which was not yielding more than three and a half per cent. upon her capital. It was on top of this important decision that Dorothy came back from the theater one foggy November night to be met by her mother in the dim hall of No. 17.

"A most terrible thing has occurred," Mrs. Caffyn whispered. "Hush! Don't disturb Cecil. Tread quietly. The poor boy is tired out with working for his Christmas examinations, and father might hear us."

To Mrs. Caffyn the drawing-room seemed the only fit environment for an appalling problem the day had brought her, the only atmosphere that could brace her to confront its solution, but Dorothy, who was cold after her nerves by drinking the fresh tea brought in for a late arrival. Dorothy came down-stairs, rather cross at having been disturbed from her afternoon nap, and Mr. Caffyn, a Cenci of suburban prose, confronted his wife and daughter.

"I have seldom felt such a fool," he began upon a note of pompous reminiscence that whistled in his mustache like a wind through withered sedge on the margin of a December stream. "I have *never* felt such a fool," he corrected himself, "as I was made to feel this afternoon by my own wife and my own daughter. I go to your bank," he proclaimed, fixing his wife's wavering eye—"I go to your bank, and there, in the presence of my eldest son, I ask to see Mr. Jones, the manager, with a view to improving your financial position."

"How kind of you, dear," she murmured, in an attempt to propitiate him before it was too late.

"Yes," Mr. Caffyn went on, apparently not in the least softened by the compliment. "In your interest I abandon for a whole hour my own work—the work of the society I represent, although, mark you, I knew full well that by so doing I should be kept in the office another whole hour after my usual time."

Dorothy looked sarcastically at her wrist-watch, and her father bellowed like a bull on the banks of that stream in midsummer.

"Silence, Norah!"

"Are you speaking to me?" she inquired. "Because if you are, I'd rather, firstly, that you spoke to me without shouting; secondly, that you didn't call me Norah; and thirdly, that you didn't say I was talking when I was only looking at my watch."

Mr. Caffyn, throwing up his head in a mute appeal for Heaven to note his daughter's unnatural behavior, swallowed a crumb the wrong way, the noisy attempts to rescue which allowed his wife a moment's grace to dab her forehead with a handkerchief; her tears, like the crumb, had chosen another route, and the fresh tea was excessively hot.

"Where was I?" Mr. Caffyn demanded, indignantly, when he had disposed of the crumb.

"I think you'd just got to my bank, dear," his wife suggested, timidly.

"Ah yes! Well, Jones and I were going into the details of your investments, and I was just calculating what would be the amount of your extra income should I consent to your investing your capital in accordance with the advice of the Archdeacon of Brismouth, when Jones, who I may remark *en passant* has been a friend of mine for twenty years and should know better, calmly informs me that without consulting your husband you have withdrawn five hundred pounds from your capital in order to fling it away upon your daughter. I thought he was perpetrating a stupid joke; but he actually showed me a record of this abominable transaction, and I had no alternative but to accept his word. I need hardly say that any chance I might have had of finishing off my work at the society vanished as far as this afternoon was concerned, and so"—here Mr. Caffyn became bitterly ironical—"I ventured to permit myself the luxury of a hansom-cab from the offices of your bank to the corner of Carlington Road, where the four-mile circle of fares terminates, and now, if you please, I should like an explanation of this outrage."

"The explanation is perfectly simple," Dorothy began.

"I was speaking to your mother, not to you. The money is hers."

"Precisely," said his daughter, "and that is the explanation."

"Dearest child," Mrs. Caffyn implored her, "don't aggravate dear father. We must admit that we were both very much in the wrong, particularly myself."

"Not at all," said Dorothy, quickly cutting short her father's sigh of satisfaction at the admission. "Not at all. We were both absolutely in the right. The transaction was a purely business one. Mother has allowed me twenty-five pounds a year since my seventeenth birthday."

"Mother has allowed you?" echoed Mr. Caffyn. "Even if we grant that this sum was technically paid out of your mother's income, you must understand that it should be considered as coming from me—from me, your father."

"You and mother can settle that afterward. It doesn't invalidate my argument, which is that such a lump sum is likely to be more useful to me at the beginning of my career on the stage than an annual pittance—"

"Pittance?" repeated Mr. Caffyn, aghast. "Do you call twenty-five pounds a pittance?"

"Please don't go on interrupting me," said Dorothy, coldly. "I'm now doing a calculation in my head. Twenty-five pounds a year is five per cent.—"

"Five per cent.!" shouted Mr. Caffyn. "Your mother was only getting three and a half per cent."

"Oh, please don't interrupt," Dorothy begged, "because this is getting very complicated. In that case mother owes me, roughly, about another two hundred and fifty pounds. However, we'll let that pass. You are both released from all responsibility for me, and if you both live more than twenty years longer you will actually be making twenty-five pounds a year out of this arrangement. In twenty years you'll be sixty-eight, won't you? Well, there's no reason why you shouldn't live to seventy-two, and if you do you'll make one hundred pounds out of me. So I don't think you can grumble."

"Dear child," sobbed Mrs. Caffyn, "I don't think it's very polite, and it certainly isn't kind, to talk about poor father's age like that. Let's admit we both did wrong and ask him to forgive us."

"I am not going into the question of right and wrong," replied Dorothy, loftily. "It's quite obvious to me that you have a perfect right to do what you like with your own money and that I have a perfect right to avail myself of your kindness. Father's extraordinary behavior has made it equally clear to me that I can't possibly stay on in this house; in any case, the noise the children make in the morning will end by driving me away, and the sooner I go the better."

"I forbid you to speak to your parents like that," said Mr. Caffyn.

Dorothy could not help laughing at his authority, and he played his last card:

"Do you realize that you are not yet of age and that if I choose I can compel you to remain at home?"

"I don't think it would be worth your while," she told him, "for the sake of five hundred pounds, which in that case you'd certainly never see again. I don't want to break with my family completely, but if I find that your prehistoric way of behaving is liable to spoil my career, I sha'n't hesitate to do so."

Dorothy guessed that she had defeated her father; Mrs. Caffyn, too, must have guessed it, for she suddenly gasped:

"I think I must be going to faint."

And by summoning the memories of a mid-Victorian childhood she actually succeeded. Luckily her husband had eaten most of the cakes; so that when she was rescued from the wreck of the tea-table and helped up to her room only one sandwich was adhering to her best gown.

II

It is hardly necessary to say that Dorothy did not confide in the girls at the theater what had happened at home, but she let it be generally understood that she was now looking out for rooms, and she talked a good deal of where one could and where one could not live in a flat. About a week later Olive Fanshawe took her aside and asked if she was serious about moving into a flat at last; and, upon Dorothy's assuring her that she was, Olive divulged under the seal of great secrecy that a friend of hers, a man of high rank with much power and influence in the country, was anxious to do something for her.

"He's a strange man," she told Dorothy, "and though I know you'll think it's impossible for anybody to want to look after a girl in a flat without other things in return, he really doesn't make love to me at all. He gets tired of society and political dinners and the Palace."

"The Palace?" Dorothy repeated.

"Buckingham Palace. You didn't think I meant the Crystal Palace?" said Olive, with a laugh.

Dorothy, with Debrett for a footstool, when she chose to treat the volume thus, was offended by this raillery, and explained that she had only wished to know whether she meant St. James's Palace or Buckingham Palace.

"Darling, I was only teasing you.... Well, my friend wants to have a place where he can lunch quietly sometimes or have tea and forget about the cares of grandeur. You won't mind if I don't tell you his name, will you?"

Dorothy did mind extremely, but inasmuch as she had affected an air of mystery about herself and her origin, she felt she could not reasonably object to Olive's secrecy.

"He told me to find another girl to live with me," Olive continued, "and he said he would pay the rent of the flat and find all that's necessary in the way of decorations and furniture. I've been waiting such a long time for the right girl; I thought you didn't want to live up in town or I should have suggested it sooner. He's seen you from the front, and he admired you very much and couldn't understand why I didn't ask you at once."

Dorothy was struck by Olive's frankness and still more was she struck by her incapacity for jealousy. She could not think of any other girl who would have been so obviously pleased as Olive was to hear a friend admired by their own man. Three months at the Vanity had made Dorothy chary of believing the assertion that there was nothing more between her and the mysterious great one than good-fellowship, because she was quite sure by now that all men expected more, and her judgment of Olive's character led her to suppose that Olive would be too kind to refuse him more. However, that was her business, and since there was evidently going to be a simulation of complete innocence about the transaction, no offer could have suited her better.

"My dear Olive," she said, "nothing could be nicer for me, and of course I happen to be one of the few girls who would or could understand that there is nothing in it. What a pity the weather's so wet for house-hunting."

"That's what the great man said, and he told me to hire an electric brougham until I've found the place I want."

"Of course," said Dorothy, as if the idea of searching for a flat outside an electric brougham, a rare luxury in those days, was inconceivable.

For a fortnight she and Olive glided here and there along the dim, wintry streets, until at last they noticed that the stiff Georgian houses at the far end of Halfmoon Street bulged out into an efflorescence of bright new flats, which on inspection seemed to provide exactly the address and the comfort they required.

"It's an awfully good address," said Dorothy. "Clarges Street would have been a little nearer to Berkeley Square, but...." She forgave the extra block or two with a gesture.

"It's so quiet," added Olive.

"And really not far from Devonshire House, though from Stratton Street we should have overlooked the garden."

"But we can take San Toy for her walks in Green Park." San Toy was Olive's Pekinese spaniel.

"I shall have my bedroom in apple green," Dorothy announced. "Apple green with rose-du-barri curtains; and you'd better have cream with café-au-lait in yours, unless you have eau-de-nil and sage.... I think the fourth-story flat was the nicest."

"Yes, it's more romantic to be high up," Olive agreed.

"And the light is better for one's dressing-table," Dorothy added.

In dread of a maternal attempt to bring about a reconciliation between herself and her father, Dorothy had hoped to avoid spending Christmas at home. But the flat could not be ready until February; so, partly to keep her mother quiet, partly because she was a little apprehensive of the paternal prerogative with which Mr. Caffyn had threatened her minority, she consented on Christmas morning to be kissed by his mustache. Perhaps he was more willing to forgive her owing to his wife's conduct of her financial affairs having provided an excuse to transfer them into his own hands.

Dorothy's absence from the last Christmas gathering at home had not sharpened her appetite for this kind of celebration, and she did not at all like the sensation of being in the bosom of her family; Gulliver was scarcely more disgusted by the

Brobdingnagian maids of honor. Seizing the occasion to impress upon her younger brothers and sisters her disapproval of any inclination to boast about having a famously beautiful sister at the Vanity, she was mortified to learn that her career was regarded by the juniors as a slur upon their social standing. Cecil informed her bluntly that in his society—the society of industrious scholars at St. James's—actresses were regarded with horror, and that though an unpleasant rumor had pervaded the school of Caffyn's having a sister on the stage, he had managed to stifle such deleterious gossip. It seemed that the traditions of the preparatory school responsible for Vincent's budding social sense strictly forbade any allusion to family life in any form whatsoever; at Randell's *all* relatives were regarded as a disgrace, and only last term a boy had been called upon to apologize for the extraordinary appearance his mother had presented at the prize-giving. Another boy, whose father was reputed to belong to the Royal Academy, had been forced to allay with largess of tuck the hostile criticism leveled against a flowing cravat his parent had worn at the school sports. As for sisters, Vincent affirmed, their very existence was regarded as a shameful secret; but a sister on the stage ... he turned away in despair of words to express what a humiliation that would bring upon him were it known. Agnes and Edna assured Dorothy they had far too many enthralling topics of conversation already to bother about her; but when one or two of the mistresses had inquired how she was getting on and had regretted that she was not acting in Shakespeare, they had certainly not revealed that she was now called Dorothy Lonsdale, because the real Dorothy was also an old girl; so that even if one of the mistresses in an unbridled moment should visit the Vanity, she would search for Miss Norah Caffyn upon the program and come away no wiser than she went.

Meanwhile, the decoration and furnishing of the flat went on in strict accordance with Dorothy's ideas, since she had better taste than Olive, who, besides, was too much afraid of spending another person's money. Dorothy had not yet been introduced to the great man, but she was sure that he would like Olive to have all she wanted, or, in other words, all she herself wanted. They moved in during February, and it was arranged that the first Sunday evening should be dedicated to the entertainment of their benefactor, who had returned to town for the opening of Parliament. About six o'clock on the evening in question Dorothy rose from a deliciously deep and comfortable Chesterfield sofa, looked round her affectionately at her own drawing-room aglow with chintz and daffodils, and in her bedroom, when she sat down in front of a triple mirror to do her light-brown hair before dressing for dinner, apostrophized her good fortune aloud, and admired herself more than ever.

Dorothy acknowledged to herself that Olive's great man surpassed her preconception of him kindled by dressing-room legends; at first she had been inclined to criticize her friend's occasional ventures into political prophecy as self-importance or girlish credulity; but as soon as she saw the source of them she admitted that this time Olive's romanticism was justified. Their guest was a tall, grizzled man, more military to the outward eye than political, and he treated Olive with just the god-fatherly manner she had led Dorothy to expect. She made a good deal of fuss over him in the way of finding cushions for his head and mixing his cocktail with extra care; but nothing in her obviously sincere affection conveyed a hint of cloaking another kind of emotion. Although the great man preserved his own anonymity, he talked so freely about people of whom Dorothy had often read in the papers that his absorbing conversation soon made her forget the strain upon her curiosity to know who he was. He approved of the way the flat had been decorated and complimented the two girls on their good taste, all the credit of which Olive at once ascribed to her companion. About eleven o'clock the great man passed his hand over his eyes in a way that seemed to hint at a deep-seated, perhaps an incurable, fatigue, and announced that he must be going to bed.

"Though, unfortunately," he added, "I must write one or two letters first at my club. Happy children," he said, turning to them in the hall and holding a hand of each. "We must try to meet next Sunday evening; but I'm dreadfully busy, and I may not be able to get away."

Turning up the collar of his fur coat, he told Olive not to ring for the lift and walked very wearily, it seemed to Dorothy, down the stairs of the flats.

"I don't want to be inquisitive," she said, when they were back in the drawing-room still haunted by the ghost of an excellent cigar. "But I should like to know who he really is."

"Dorothy," her friend begged, "it's the only stipulation he's made, and I don't think it would be fair to break it."

"You don't trust me," Dorothy complained.

"My dear, it isn't that; but I certainly should have to tell him that I told you, and I'm sure he wouldn't like it. After all, we ought to be very grateful for this jolly flat where we're perfectly free and have nothing to bother about. Remember what happened to Psyche."

Dorothy was inclined to add "and also to Fatima"; but since she could not pretend that the great man did in any way remind her of Bluebeard and since the flat undoubtedly was delightful, she did her best to restrain her curiosity, even though sometimes it irritated her like prickly heat.

"It's a pity he had to go away to write his letters at a club," she said.

"But he couldn't write from this address."

"No, but we could keep some plain paper for him," said Dorothy. "And that reminds me, what is your crest?"

Olive looked alarmed.

"I don't think I've got a crest," she said. "My father's a solicitor in Warwickshire."

"Warwickshire?" repeated Dorothy. "That's an odd coincidence. I wonder if he knows Lord Cleveden."

Olive shook her head vaguely.

"He knows a good deal about Warwickshire; in fact, he's writing a book called *Warwickshire Worthies*. He's been writing it for years. Does Lord Cleveden come from Warwickshire?"

"Of course," said Dorothy, and then after a minute with a far-away look she added, "So do I."

"Oh, Dorothy, then there really is a mystery? I thought it was only dressing-room gossip."

"You have your secrets, Olive. Mayn't I be allowed mine? Though I suppose I haven't any legal right to it, I am going to put my crest on my note-paper, because I like the motto. It's a bugle-horn, and the motto is *J'y serai*. I needn't translate it for you, as you went to a convent in Belgium."

Olive laughed affectionately at her friend's little joke, and they decided to reap the full advantage of a quiet Sunday by going to bed early.

"He's a great dear, isn't he?" said Olive by the door of her room.

"Oh, a great dear. How horrid it is that a man like that would be so misjudged by the world that he has to keep his name a secret. But, of course, I understand his point of view. I've had some experience of family pride, and it's a tremendous thing to be up against. However, it will be all the same a hundred years hence. Good night, darling. Your great man is a great, great success."

"I'm so glad you like him, Dorothy dear."

"I like him immensely."

Just before Dorothy got into bed she called out to her friend, who in a dressing-gown of amber silk hurried to know what she wanted.

"I only wanted to tell you that you simply must get this new tooth-paste. I like it immensely."

"Oh, I'm glad it's a success," Olive exclaimed.

"It's a great, great success."

Dorothy wondered when she was fading into sleep how long it would be before she should be able to recommend a tooth-paste to the world at large, recommend it in glowing words with a photograph of herself smiling at the delicious tube.

III

Soon after Dorothy and Olive were established in Halfmoon Street Birdie Underhill and Maisie Yorke, by getting married on the same day at the same church to bridegrooms in the same profession, obtained as much publicity in the newspapers as was possible for two Vanity girls who had failed to acquire a title on abandoning the stage. The service in a double sense was fully choral, and the two queens had a train of bridesmaids from the Vanity, all looking as demure as Quakeresses in their dove-gray frocks, and certainly holding their own in the mere externals of maidenhood with the sisters of the bridegrooms, who were as fresh and rural as if Bayswater, their home, was in the Lake district and had been immortalized by Wordsworth in a sonnet. One reporter was so much impressed by the ceremony that his account of it was headed "Dignified Wedding of Two Vanity Girls."

"Yes," said Dorothy, when with Olive she was driving away from the reception, "it was charmingly done, of course; but, poor dears, it is rather a come-down."

"But I thought their men were awfully twee," said Olive.

"Twee" was society's attempt at this date to voice the ineffable, in which respect it was at least as successful as the terminology of most mystics and philosophers: yet although Plotinus might have been glad of it in the sunset-stained fog of neo-Platonism, the practical Dorothy considered that this was too transcendental for stock-brokers.

"After all," she said, poised serenely above the abyss of reality, "what is a stock-broker?"

"They'll be fairly well off, and they'll have nice houses, and children perhaps," Olive argued. "And I expect they're tired of the theater by now. I don't think either of them would ever have got anything better than the Punt Sextet; and Maisie told me when I was kissing her good-by and wishing her all happiness that she was twenty-seven. Isn't it terrible to think of?"

"Twenty-seven!" Dorothy echoed. She would have been less shocked if the sum had referred to Maisie's lovers rather than to her years. "Well, of course, she admitted once to me that she was twenty-four. I only hope that when I'm twenty-seven I sha'n't be singing with five other girls in punts."

"You won't be, darling. You'll either be a great star or you'll be brilliantly and happily married."

Olive was really a very easy girl to live with; and the former of these predictions seemed likely to come true when Dorothy was actually promoted to occupy one of the punts after the girl first selected had proved a failure in such a conspicuous position; the other vacant punt had been successfully filled by Queenie Molyneux. This girl, though she was not nearly so beautiful as Dorothy, had a good deal of talent, which gave even the two solo lines she was allowed in the sextet what any serious dramatic critic who had learned French at school would have called *espièglerie*. Miss Molyneux had reason to hope that such a phrase would one day be applied to her acting, because people whose judgment was to be trusted went about saying that she had a career before her, not merely in musical comedy, but perhaps even in real comedy, where she would be written about by critics who were not afraid to use foreign words at what they would call the "psychological moment." In view of the fact that Miss Molyneux might henceforth be considered a rival, Dorothy took care to be very friendly with her, and to be seen fairly often lunching with her at Romano's or supping at the Savoy, although she was a girl whose reputation even at the Vanity was whispered about, and whose private life far exceeded in *espièglerie* her two lines in the sextet. Notwithstanding this, it was Queenie Molyneux whom Dorothy chose to be her companion at a supper-party given by Lord Clarehaven soon after the beginning of the Easter holidays, seven months after the production of "The River Girl."

Clarehaven had reappeared without a word of warning, and in a note that he sent round to invite Dorothy and a friend to supper he seemed quite unconscious that there was anything in his behavior to be excused. He hoped that she had not forgotten him, as if his silence of nearly a year was perfectly natural; he mentioned that Lonsdale was with him, congratulated her upon her singing in the sextet, and begged for an answer to be sent down to the stage-door. Somehow it was not very difficult for Dorothy to forgive him, and she accepted the invitation. The obvious friend to have taken out with her would have been Olive Fanshawe, because Olive was a brunette and Queenie was not. However, if Clarehaven was capable of being even temporarily fascinated by another girl's outward charms, Dorothy felt that she might as well give him up at once; she did not intend her life to be spoiled by beauty competitions. Dorothy wanted to impress Clarehaven more deeply than with the skin-deep loveliness that belonged in her own style as much to Olive as to herself, and in order to impress him she felt that a moral contrast would be more effective than the hackneyed contrast between brunette and blonde. Of course, she did not mean the kind of moral contrast that Lily had provided on that dreadful afternoon in Oxford; that had been merely a painful exhibition of vulgarity. Olive was so sweet and good and well behaved that between them they might achieve the insipid, to obviate which Dorothy chose Queenie, who would set off, if not her complexion, at any rate her point of view.

At the end of the evening, when Clarehaven, hesitating for a barely perceptible moment, had said good-by to Dorothy outside Halfmoon Mansions and stepped reproachfully back into his hansom, she decided on her way up-stairs that the supper-party might be considered a success. To begin with, all the other people supping at the Savoy had stared at their table more than at any other. Then, Arthur Lonsdale had evidently taken a fancy to Queenie Molyneux, and if Dorothy was not mistaken Queenie had taken a fancy to him. His way of talking had been just the foil she required for her own, and when they drove away together to RidgemountMansions there was no doubt in Dorothy's mind that Lonsdale would tell the cab not to wait and end by missing that last train at Goodge Street. However, what happened to the cab or, for that matter, to Lonsdale and Queenie Molyneux was of slight importance beside the fact that Clarehaven had evidently lost nothing of his admiration for herself, or, if he had lost it, had regained it all and more this evening. When he and his friend compared notes to-morrow how sharply the difference between herself and some other Vanity girls would be brought home to him.

Yet, successful as the supper-party had been, it remained for the time another isolated event in the relations between herself and Clarehaven, from whom she had not heard another word during the vacation.

"He's frightened of you, that's what it is," said Miss Molyneux, whose friendship with Lonsdale, begun that night, was being hotly kept up, though she was running no risks by inviting Dorothy to be a spectator of it.

"Frightened of what?"

"Oh, he thinks you're too good to be amusing and not good enough for anything else. Arthur told me so. Not in so many words, but his lordship found the drive home rather lonely."

"Anything else?" repeated Dorothy. "What do you mean by anything else?"

"Why, to marry, of course," replied her friend.

It was strange that the first girl to express in words the thought that was haunting the undiscovered country at the back of Dorothy's mind should be the one girl at the Vanity to whom marriage probably meant less than to any other.

"But why not?" thought Dorothy, in bed that night. "He's independent. Nobody can stop him. Countess of Clarehaven," she murmured. The title took away her breath for a moment, and it seemed as if the very traffic of Piccadilly paused in the presence of a solemn mystery. "Countess of Clarehaven!"

The omnibuses rolled on their way again, and the idea took its place in the natural scheme of things. Queenie little thought that her scoffing allusion to the state of affairs between Clarehaven and herself would have such a contrary effect to what she intended. Queenie had meant to crow over her, but she had made a slip when she had let out that Clarehaven was frightened. It was not Clarehaven who was frightened; it was his friend Lonsdale. No doubt, Clarehaven had not yet whispered of marriage even to himself; no doubt he was merely thinking at present what a much luckier chap Lonsdale was than himself. But Lonsdale was frightened....

"And he has reason to be," said Dorothy, turning on the light and picking up Debrett.

It happened that the great man telephoned next morning to say that he was coming to lunch that day, and after lunch Dorothy alluded lightly to Lord Clarehaven.

"I believe I once met his mother," said the great man. "Wasn't she a daughter of Chatfield?"

Dorothy nodded.

"Yes, I remember the story now," he went on. "She had a good deal of trouble with her husband. But he's been dead some years, eh?"

"Eighteen ninety-six," said Dorothy.

"Yes, I thought so. I don't know anything about the son; he sounds, from your description, rather a young ass."

However deeply Dorothy would have resented such a comment from any one else, she accepted it from the great man as merited; she was even grateful to him for it; from the instant that Clarehaven presented himself to her vision as rather a young ass, it did not seem so impossible that she should one day marry him. These months at the Vanity had already considerably cheapened the peerage in Dorothy's estimation, and intercourse with the great man had imparted to her some of his own worldly contempt for inconspicuous young peers. Dorothy began to ponder the likelihood of being able to elevate Clarehaven from single "young assishness" to the dignity of the great man himself; a clever wife could do much, a beautiful wife more. She was so serenely confident of herself that when, a few days after this conversation, the subject of it telegraphed from Oxford to say he should call for her the following day to take her out to lunch, she was neither astonished nor at all unduly elated.

"You wouldn't mind his lunching here?" she asked Olive. "He's quite a nice boy. Rather young, of course, after the great man; but he'll improve."

Olive was delighted to welcome Clarehaven, and Dorothy was glad of an opportunity to display her independence and pleasant surroundings. She had warned Olive not to leave her alone with their guest after lunch, because she was anxious to avoid discouraging him too much by positively refusing to let him make love to her, although she wished him to go away with the impression that only luck had been against him.

"You seem very comfortable here," he commented, suspiciously, when, on his departure, Dorothy escorted him to the door of the flat.

"I am very comfortable," she admitted.

"Is it your flat or Miss Fanshawe's?"

"Both."

He looked round at the paneled hall and frowned.

"I can't make you out," he confessed.

"Isn't mystery woman's prerogative?" she asked, and then in case she had frightened him with such a long word she let him kiss her hand before he went away.

Certainly for a girl who was not much over twenty Dorothy could not be accused of clumsiness. Her admirer had gone away piqued by the richness of her surroundings, the correctness of her demeanor, most of all by the touch of her hand upon his lips. Yes, she might congratulate herself.

"Rather a dear!" said Olive.

"Yes," Dorothy agreed. "Rather—but dreadfully young. Though his title only dates back to the eighteenth century, the baronetcy is older, and his ancestors really did come over with the Conqueror."

And one felt that such antiquity compensated Dorothy for some of that youthfulness she deplored.

During the next fortnight Clarehaven paid several visits to town, but Dorothy was steadily unwilling to be much alone with him, and, finally, one hot afternoon in mid-May, exasperated by her indifference and caution, he went back to Oxford in a fit of petulance (temper would have been too strong a word to describe his behavior, which was like a spoiled child's) and relapsed into another spell of silence. A week or so after this Queenie Molyneux asked Dorothy one day how long it was since she had heard from Clarehaven, and when Dorothy countered the awkward question by asking, rather bitterly, how long it was since she had heard from Lonsdale, Queenie admitted that he, too, had been silent for some time.

"I'm afraid I'm too expensive for Lonnie," she laughed, lightly. "He's a nice boy, but love in a cottage would never suit me, and love anywhere else wouldn't suit him. So that's that."

"You don't know what it is to be in love," said Dorothy.

"Cut it out!" said Miss Molyneux. "I'd rather not learn."

Dorothy would have liked to cut her own tongue out for playing her false by uttering such a sentiment to a girl like Queenie. However, she had no wish to seem a whit less hard than her rival—Dorothy was beginning to achieve such a projection of her personality across the footlights that Queenie really had become a rival, though Queenie might have put it the other way round—and she consoled herself for Clarehaven's absence by giving a great deal of attention to the new frocks that the fine weather demanded; also in consequence of a suggestion by the great man she began to take riding-lessons, with which she made as rapid progress as with her dancing, to which she had already been devoting herself for some time.

Toward the end of the month Dorothy and Olive were criticizing the fashions in the windows of Bond Street when somebody slapped her on the back and, turning round with half a thought that she was being called upon to reply to a novel method of attack by Clarehaven, she perceived Sylvia Scarlett. It was typical of Sylvia to greet her like this on meeting her again for the first time after a year, but the old awe of Sylvia prevented her from expressing her dislike of such horseplay in Bond Street, and a sudden shyness drove her into self-assertion. She began to talk about lunching at Romano's and supping at the Savoy and of the success she had made in "The River Girl" sextet, to all of which Sylvia listened with a smile until she broke abruptly into her discourse with:

"Look here! A little less of the Queen of Sheba, if you don't mind. Don't forget I'm one of the blokes as is glad to smell the gratings outside a baker's."

Dorothy did not think this remark particularly amusing; there was quite enough genuine cockney to be endured on the stage without having to listen to an exaggerated imitation of it in Bond Street. Olive, however, was laughing, and Dorothy decided to take Sylvia down a peg by asking what she was doing now.

"Resting, Dolly, but always open to a good offer. Same old firm. Lily and Skinner. The original firm makes boots; we mar them. The trouble is that I can't find anything to skin; I tried Rabbit's, the rival boot-shop, but even they wanted cash. However, Lily's quite content to go on resting, so that's all right."

"My dear," exclaimed Dorothy, in affected dismay, "you're not still living with that dreadful girl?"

"Oh, go to hell!" said Sylvia, sharply, and strode off down Bond Street.

"What an attractive girl!" Olive exclaimed.

Dorothy stared at her in bewilderment.

"What do *you* see attractive in *her*?"

"She's just the sort of person who would amuse the great man," Olive declared.

"I'm sorry that I bore him so much."

Olive seized her hand.

"Dorothy," she murmured, reproachfully, "you know you don't bore him. He was only saying yesterday that he wished he could ride with you in the Row."

"You'd better get Sylvia Scarlett to share the flat with you," went on Dorothy.

"How can you say things like that? You know I love you better than anybody in the world. You know how beautiful I think you, how clever, Dorothy; it's really unkind to suggest that any other girl could take your place."

"If you're so anxious to know her," Dorothy continued, "I'll write and ask her to come and see us."

"Dorothy, you quite misunderstand me."

"I shouldn't like you to think I would stand in the way of your meeting anybody you took a fancy to, man or woman."

Olive protested again and again that Dorothy had utterly misjudged her and that she never wished to see Sylvia Scarlett again. The argument lasted so long and the whole question of whether or not Sylvia should be invited to Halfmoon Mansions assumed such importance that after lunch Dorothy wrote and invited Sylvia, and not merely Sylvia, but Lily as well, to come and have tea with them the next day. She told herself when she had posted the letter that she was probably committing a great folly by introducing to her friends two people who knew so much about her, and she asked herself in amazement what mad obstinacy had led her into such a course of action.

"Most girls would avoid her," she thought. "But if I avoid her, she'll despise me; and I *do* hate the way she can make people look idiotic."

Dorothy was not accustomed to analyze her emotions much; she was usually too fully occupied with the analysis of her features; but before she went to sleep that night she had admitted to herself that she was thoroughly frightened of Sylvia.

In the morning a messenger-boy brought the answer.

MULBERRY COTTAGE,
TINDERBOX LANE, W.

DEAR DOROTHY,—Rudeness evidently pays, and as Lily is bursting with curiosity to see you, we'll come to tea to-morrow. I'm tremendously impressed by your note-paper. Is the trumpet hanging in the corner a crest or a trade-mark? I thought when I first opened your letter that you had gone into the motor business. "*J'y serai*" is good, but I suggest "I blow my own trumpet" would be better, or, if you must have a French motto, you could change your crest to a whip and put underneath "*Je fais claquer mon fouet.*" But perhaps this would suit me better than you. Lily has buried at least half a dozen Tom Hewitts since last June, so we'll come unaccompanied by any skeletons to your feast. Don't mind my teasing you. I believe you wish me well. I much look forward to hearing your Abyssinian friend singing of Mount Abora. Forgive my allusions to literature and display of idiomatic French. They're the only things I can set off against Romano's and the Savoy.

Yours ever,
SYLVIA.

P.S.—It was decent of you to apologize for what you said about Lily, and perhaps you were right to be a little haughty with me after that remark of mine in the dressing-room at Oxford. I'll try to keep a check on myself in future if you'll be as charming as you know how to be when you choose.

"I'm afraid," said Dorothy, when she read this letter, "that Sylvia has grown rather affected. Poor girl, it will be good for her to meet some nice people again."

She did not read the postscript to Olive, but she was much relieved by it, and she showed her relief by praising Lily's beauty and telling Olive that in taking a fancy to Sylvia she had once more evinced her good taste.

"If one could only cure her of her affectations she would be a charming companion for the great man, but as it is.... We must get some people for this afternoon," she broke off, going to the telephone.

Dorothy took more trouble over Sylvia's party than over anything since she chose the decorations of the flat; difficult though it was, she managed to collect several men whom she supposed to be intelligent, chiefly because they had less money than her other friends. It was like looking for gold in an alms-bag to find in their circle enough men to whose intelligence even Dorothy could subscribe, and she asked herself doubtfully what the great man would have thought of the result. Well, well—Sylvia might be critical, but she had no right to be as critical as that, and perhaps one or two of them were more intelligent than she thought.

Among the men invited that afternoon was Harry Tufton, who had just been sent down from Oxford. Anxious to show himself worthy of his election to the Bullingdon, he had let himself be driven from his wonted gravity and discretion by some ambitious demon, and, after mixing his wine with this fiery spirit, had painted either the dean's nose or the dean's door red—the story varied with his listeners' credulity. Hence his arrival in London, where he had made haste to invite Dorothy out to supper and give her some news of his friend Lord Clarehaven. She had been engaged that evening, and now she bethought herself of asking him to tea. It was a daring move, but somehow she believed that Tufton would appreciate it, and perhaps be impressed by her ability to keep friends with girls like Sylvia and Lily. Nevertheless, it certainly was daring to invite the very person who had seen with his own eyes of what Lily was capable; it was also a temptation to Sylvia's tongue.

Dorothy considered that her party was a success, and she was pleased to observe that Sylvia was evidently struck by the intelligence of a young Liberal journalist called Vernon Townsend. This young man, lately down from Oxford, was delighting the select minority who read a brilliant weekly called *The Point of View* with his hebdomadal destructiveness as a critic of the drama. The Aristotelian way in which he used to prove in two thousand words winged with scorn that "The River Girl" was not so good a play as "John Gabriel Borkmann" was a great consolation to his readers, who were mostly unacted playwrights. After a column of Townsend's smoke they were sure that they were in the van of progress, riding, one might say, in the engine-driver's cab upon a mighty express that was thundering away from mediocrity. If sometimes in the course of their journey the coal-dust of realism made them look a little dirty, that was a small penalty to pay for riding in front of the common herd.

"It must be jolly to run the funicular up Parnassus," said Sylvia to this young man. "And jolly to drink of the Pierian spring or from the well of truth without either of them leaving a nasty taste in the mouth."

"Very good," he allowed, and laughed with the serious attention that critics give to jokes. "But you must take in *The Point of View*."

"I will. From your description it must have all the feverish brilliance of a young consumptive. I suppose the air on the top of Parnassus is good for this Keats of weekly reviews?"

"That's an extremely intelligent girl," said Mr. Townsend to his hostess. "Why haven't I ever noticed her on the stage?"

500

Mr. Townsend went often to the Vanity because he was searching for talent; he had a theory that all good actresses and all good plays were born to blush unseen.

"It's a good theory," said Sylvia, "and of course you'll add the audience. One might extract a moral from the fact that they're much more careless about turning down the lights during the performance of a play in Paris than they are in London. Dorothy, Mr. Townsend assures me that I ought to be a great actress."

Dorothy smiled encouragingly and passed on to see that her guests were well supplied with cakes. Yes, the party was going well. Sylvia was entertaining other people and herself being entertained. Lily was sitting languorously back in a deep chair, listening to a young candidate for Parliament whose father had so successfully imposed a patent medicine upon his contemporaries that there seemed no reason why his son should not as successfully cure the body politic. Dorothy frankly admitted Lily's beauty when Olive commented upon it.

"She's like a lovely spray of flowers," said Olive.

Dorothy thought that this was rather an exaggerated simile, and she could not help adding that she hoped Lily would not fade as quickly.

Presently Tufton came up to his hostess and begged her to do him the honor of a little talk.

"Everybody is very happy. Charming little party. Yes," he assured her. "But you mustn't tire yourself. Let me get you an ice."

Dorothy was flattered by this almost obsequious manner, and it flashed upon her that he was trying to get in with her, not, as the girls at the theater would have put it, "get off" like most men.

"Your two friends from Oxford are much improved," he began. "Do you remember our little scene after lunch? I felt for you tremendously. It's good of you to carry your old friends along with you on the path to success."

"You think I'm going to be successful?"

"You *are* successful. In confidence, you'll be encouraged to hear that Richards expects a lot from you. Yes, he told my father. You've not seen Clarehavenlately?" Dorothy shook her head, and Mr. Tufton nodded gravely; behind those solemn indications of cerebral activity two twin souls rubbed noses.

"Of course I haven't seen him just lately. You heard of my little joke? It had quite a 'varsity success. Yes, I painted the dean's door. Well, somebody had to pull the evening together, and I tossed up with Ulster—the Duke of Ulster—you haven't run across him? No? Awful good chap. Yes. 'Look here, Harry,' he said to me, 'something's got to be done. Which of us two is going to paint Dickie's door vermilion?' Dickie is the dean. 'Toss you,' said I. 'Right, said he. 'Woman,' said I, and lost. So I got a bucket of paint and splashed it around, don't you know. Everybody shouted, 'Jolly old Tuffers,' and the authorities handed me my passports. But, after all, what earthly use is a degree to me?"

Dorothy looked a wise negative and brought the conversation back to Clarehaven.

"I suppose you'll be seeing him again very soon now?"

Mr. Tufton nodded. "And I can prophesy that you'll be seeing him again very soon."

She shrugged her shoulders.

"You mustn't be cynical," he warned her.

"Can one help it?"

"You've no reason to be cynical. I suppose Clarehaven is almost my most intimate friend, and I can assure you that you have no reason to be cynical. Difficulties there have been, difficulties there will be, but always remember that I'm your friend whatever happens."

And most of all her friend, Dorothy thought, if she happened to become a countess.

After this tea-party Sylvia and Lily often came to Halfmoon Mansions; when in July Dorothy and Olive took a cottage at Sonning they were often invited down there for picnics on the Thames. The other girls at the theater could not understand why it was necessary to look beyond Maidenhead for repose and refreshment fromsinging in a punt every night; and although such of them as were invited to Sonning enjoyed themselves, they always went back to town more firmly convinced than ever that Dolly Lonsdale was a most mysterious girl. Yet it ought not to have been impossible to understand the pleasure of hurrying away from the Vanity to catch the eleven forty-five at Paddington, and of alighting from the hot train about a quarter to one of a warm summer night to be met by a scent of honeysuckle in the station road, to see the white flowers in their garden and the thatched roof of their cottage against the faintly luminous sky, and, while they paused for a moment to fumble in their bags among the powder-puffs and pocket-mirrors for the big key of their door, to listen to the train's murmur still audible far away in the stillness of the level country beyond.

"I ought always to live in the country," said Dorothy, gravely.

But in August rehearsals for "The Duke and the Dairymaid" began, and the cottage at Sonning had to be given up. The new production at the Vanity included a trio between the ducal tenor and two subsidiary dairymaids, to be one of whom Dorothy was chosen by the management. She might fairly consider that her new part was exactly three times as good as that she had played in the sextet; moreover, her salary was doubled, and by what could only be considered a stroke of genuine luck Queenie Molyneux, who would certainly have been chosen for the other dairymaid, was lured away to the rival production of "My Mistake" at the Frivolity Theater. Millie Cunliffe, who took her place, had a finer mouth than Queenie's, which was too large and expressive for anything except lines like those with which she led the Pink Quartet at the Frivolity; but Millie had not such a beautiful mouth as Dorothy, and it was not nearly so apt at singing or speaking; her ankles, too, were not so slim and shapely as Dorothy's, nor were they made for dancing like hers. So Dorothy enjoyed a vogue with gods and mortals, and was now plainly visible to the naked eye in the constellation of musical comedy.

The departure of Queenie Molyneux to the Frivolity had a more intimate bearing on Dorothy's future than the mere removal of a rival of the footlights to a safe distance: it gave her back Clarehaven.

That Savoy supper-party last Easter had not seemed likely at the time to lead to a situation even as much complicated as Dorothy's ambition to marry an earl. When Arthur Lonsdale escorted Queenie home afterward, he had probably counted upon such a climax to the entertainment; but he must have been astonished to hear from his friend next morning that Dorothy was not to be won lightly by a Savoy supper nor kept with the help even of the tolerably large income that friend enjoyed. From the moment that the immediate gratification of Clarehaven's passion was denied him, Lonsdale must have divined a danger of the affair's turning out serious, and he had obviously done all he could to discourage him from frequenting Dorothy's unresponsive company; she learned, indeed, from various sources that he was devoting his leisure to curing Clarehaven. Then suddenly the melody of Queenie's Pink Quartet enchained him, and he was always to be seen at the Frivolity. Long days cramming for the Foreign Office were followed by long evenings at the Frivolity and ... anyway, Queenie seemed to have decided she liked Lonsdale better than wealth. But if the melody of the Pink Quartet in "My Mistake" was an eternal joy, so, too, was the melody of the trio in "The Duke and the Dairymaid"; henceforth Clarehaven from his stall could nightly feed his passion for Dorothy without being subjected to the mockery and tutelage of his former companion. What between lunches at Verrey's and suppers at the Savoy it was not surprising that before the leaves had fallen from the London plane-trees he should have hung a necklace of pearls round her neck. Unfortunately, though Clarehaven showed his appreciation of Dorothy by figuratively robbing his coronet of its pearls, he did not go so far as to offer her the coronet itself; and when he suggested that she should leave Halfmoon Street for an equally pleasant flat round the corner, she was naturally very indignant and asked him what kind of a girl he thought she was.

"You don't care twopence about me," he said, woefully.

"How can I let myself care about you?" she countered. "You ought to know me well enough by this time to be sure that I would never accept such an offer as you've just made me. I know that you can't marry me. I know that you have your family to consider. In the circumstances, isn't it better, my dear Tony, that we should part? I'm dreadfully sorry that our parting should come after your proposal rather than before it. But horribly as you've misjudged me, somehow I can't bear you any ill will, and in token of my forgiveness I shall always wear these pearls. Pearls for tears, they say. I'm afraid that sometimes these old sayings come only too true."

"Yes, but I can't get along without you," protested Clarehaven.

She smiled sadly.

"I'm afraid you can get along without me in every way except one, only too easily."

"Why did you lead me on, if you weren't in earnest?"

"Lead you on?"

"You asked me back to the flat. You gave me every encouragement. Obviously somebody is paying for this flat, so why shouldn't I?"

"Lord Clarehaven!" exclaimed Dorothy, with the stern grandeur of an Atlantic cliff rebuffing a wave. "You have said enough."

She rang the bell and asked Effie, the maid whose attentions she shared with Olive, to show his lordship the door. His poor lordship left Halfmoon Mansions in such perturbation that he forgot to slip the usual sovereign into Effie's hand, and she cordially agreed with her mistress when he was gone that kind hearts are indeed more than coronets. Dorothy's simple faith in her own abilities had received such a shock that she began to cry; but it was restored by a sudden suspicion that she possessed a latent power for tragedy that might take her out of the squalid world of the Vanity into the ether of the legitimate drama. She had never suspected this inner fountain that grief had thus unsealed, and she let her tears go trickling down her cheeks with as much pleasure as a small boy who has found a watering-can on a secluded garden path.

"Don't carry on so, miss," Effie begged. "Men are brutes, and that's what all us poor women have to learn sooner or later. Don't take on about his lordship. A fine lordship, I'm sure. Give me plain Smith, if that's a lordship. Look at your poor eyes, miss, and don't cry any more."

Dorothy did look at her poor eyes, and immediately compromised with her emotions by going out and ordering a new dress. When she came back Olive, who had been given a heightened account of the scene by Effie, was exquisitely sympathetic; and the great man, when he was informed of Clarehaven's disgraceful offer, was full of good worldly advice and consolation.

"I think you can rely upon your powers of catalysis, Dorothy," he said.

She did not think her failure to understand such a strange word reflected upon her education, and asked him what it meant.

"In unchemical English, as unchemical as your own nice light-brown hair, *you* won't change; but if I'm not much mistaken you'll play the very deuce with Master Clarehaven's mental constitution."

This was encouraging; if Dorothy's faith in her beauty and abilities had been slightly shaken by Clarehaven's omission to marry her, the loss was more than made up for by an added belief in her own importance and in the beauty of her character.

Among the men who sometimes came to the flat was a certain Leopold Hausberg, a financier reputed to be already fabulously rich at the age of thirty-five, but endowed with an unfortunately simian countenance by the wicked fairy not invited to his circumcision. He possessed in addition to his wealth the superficial geniality and humor of his race, and was not accustomed to find that Englishwomen were better able than any others to resist Oriental domination. Hausberg had not concealed his partiality for Lily, and Dorothy, in her desire to accentuate her own virtue, told Sylvia, soon after Clarehaven's proposal, that it would be useful for Lily to have a rich friend like that. Sylvia flashed at her some objectionable word out of

Shakespeare and would not be mollified by Dorothy's exposition of the difference between her character and Lily's, although Dorothy took care to remind her of a remark she had once made when they were on tour together about the inevitableness of Lily's decline.

Dorothy had good reason, therefore, to feel annoyed with Sylvia when she found out presently that Sylvia was apparently working on Leopold Hausberg to do exactly what she herself had been so rudely scolded for suggesting. As much fuss was being made about Lily's behavior as if she had refused the dishonorable attentions of an earl; yet with all this ridiculous pretense Sylvia was taking care to do for Lily what she was either too stupid or too hypocritical to do for herself. If Lily's happiness lay in the devotion of vulgar young men, she might at least get the money she wanted for them out of Hausberg without letting a friend do her dirty work. When the continually cheated suitor approached Dorothy with complaints about the way Sylvia was managing the business she listened sympathetically to his hint that Sylvia was trying to keep Lily from him until she had made enough money for herself, and she took the first opportunity of being revenged upon Sylvia for the horrid Shakespearian epithet by telling her what Hausberg had said.

One Saturday night in November Olive and Dorothy came home immediately after the performance to rest themselves in preparation for a long drive in the country with the great man, who seldom had an opportunity for motoring and had made a great point of the enjoyment he was expecting to-morrow. They had not long finished supper when there was a furious ringing at the bell, and Hausberg, in a state of blind anger, was admitted to the flat by the frightened maid.

"By God!" he shouted to Dorothy. "Come with me!"

She naturally demurred to going out at this time of night, but Hausberg insisted that she was deeply involved in whatever it was that had put him in this rage, and in the end, partly from curiosity, partly from fear, she consented to accompany him. While they were driving along, Hausberg explained that he had at last persuaded Lily to abandon Sylvia and accept an establishment in Lauriston Mansions, St. John's Wood. He had furnished the flat regardless of expense, and this afternoon, when Lily was supposed to have been moving in, he had been sent the latch-key and bidden to present himself at midnight.

"Very well," said Hausberg between his teeth. "Wait until you see what.... You wait...." he became inarticulate with rage.

They had reached Lauriston Mansions and, though it was nearly one o'clock in the morning, a group of figures could be seen in silhouette against the lighted entrance, among which the helmets of a couple of policemen supplied the traditional touch of the sinister.

"Haven't you got it out yet?" Hausberg demanded of the porter, who replied in a humble negative.

"What *are* you talking about?" Dorothy asked, and then with authentic suddenness she felt the authentic nameless dread clutching authentically at her heart. Why, *it* must be a dead body; grasping Hausberg's arm and turning pale, she asked if Lily had killed herself.

"Killed herself?" echoed Hausberg. "Not she. I'm talking about this damned monkey that your confounded friends have left in my flat."

The porter came forward to say that there was a gentleman present who had a friend who he thought knew the address of one of the keepers of the monkey-house at the Zoo, and that if Mr. Hausberg would give orders for this gentleman to be driven in the car to his friend's address no doubt something could be done about expelling the monkey. The gentleman in question, a battered and crapulous cab-tout, presented himself for inspection, and one of the policemen offered to accompany him and impress the reported keeper with the urgency of the situation. While everybody was waiting for the car to return, the lobby of the flat became like the smoking-room of a great transatlantic steamer where travelers' tales are told, such horrible speculations were indulged in about the fierceness of the monkey.

"So long as it ain't a yourang-gatang," said one, "we haven't got nothing to be afraid of. But a yourang-gatang's something chronic if you can believe all they say."

"A griller's worse," said another.

"Is it? Who says so?"

"Why, any one knows there ain't nothing worse than a griller," declared the champion of that variety. "A griller 'll bite a baby's head off the same as any one else might look at you. A griller's worse than chronic; it's ferocious."

"Would it bite the head off of an yourang-gatang?" demanded the first theorist, truculently.

"Certainly it would; so when he's let out you'd better get behind George here so as to hide your ugly mug."

This caused a general laugh, and the upholder of the orang-utan seemed inclined to back his favorite with an appeal to force, until the porter interposed to prevent a squabble.

"Now, what's the good in arguing if it's a griller or a yourang-gatang?" he demanded, in a nasal whine. "All I know is it got my poor trouser leg into a rare old yourang-atangle when I was 'oppin it out of the front hall."

"Is there much damage done?" Hausberg asked.

"Damage?" repeated the porter. "Damage ain't the word. It looks as if there'd been a young volcano turned loose in the flat."

"But what I don't understand," Dorothy began, primly, "is why I have been brought into this."

Various ladies in light attire from the upper flats were beginning to peer over into the well of the staircase, and Dorothy was wondering if she were not being compromised by this midnight adventure.

"Let's get the monkey out first," said Hausberg, "and then I'll tell you why."

After listening for another three-quarters of an hour to disputes between the various supporters of the gorilla and the orang-utan, which extended to a heated argument about the comparative merits of Mr. Balfour and Mr. Chamberlain, the car came back, and the intruder, which was announced to be a chimpanzee, was ejected by the keeper, and, after an attempt to hand it over to the police, shut up till morning in a boot-hole.

The flat presented a desolate spectacle when Dorothy and Hausberg entered it; the chimpanzee had smashed the ornaments, ripped up the curtains, tore the paper from the walls, and wrenched off all the lamp-brackets; he had then apparently been seized with a revulsion against the bananas and nuts strewn about the passage for his supper and had gnawed the porter's hat.

"Now," said Hausberg, sternly, to the owner of the hat, who was tenderly nursing it, "just tell this lady exactly what has happened here."

"Well, sir, about twelve o'clock this morning a gentleman drove up to the mansions with a crate and said he was a friend of Mr. Hausberg's and had brought him a marble Venus for a present, and I was to put it in the hall of the flat. I particularly remember he said a Venus, because I thought he said a green'ouse, which surprised me for the moment, and I asked him if he didn't, mean a portable aquarium, which is what my wife's brother has in the window of his best parlor."

"Go on, you fool!" Hausberg commanded. "We don't want to hear about your wife's brother."

"Well, I accepted delivery of this Venus and between us we got this Venus—"

"Don't go on rhyming like that," said Hausberg. "Tell the story properly in plain prose."

"Between us—I mean to say me and the lift-boy together—we deposited in the hall this crate which had a tin lining for the chim-pansy to breathe with according to instructions duly received. When I turned up my nose at this Venus, which smelled very heavy, the gentleman, who didn't give his name, explained that you was intending to use it for a hat-stand, and told us not to wait, as he'd unpack the crate hisself. I looked at him a bit hard, but he give me something for me and the boy between us before we come down-stairs again, and I thought no more about it. The gentleman drove off about ten minutes afterward with a friendly nod, and I was just sitting down to my dinner in the domestic office on the ground floor when the people underneath—of course you'll understand I'm referring to the flat now—the people underneath came down and complained that something must have happened over their heads, as the noise was something shocking and bits of the ceiling was coming down, or they said it would be coming down in two two's if the noise wasn't stopped. Well, of course up I went to investigate, and when I opened the door and seed all the wall-paper hanging in strips I thought something funny must have occurred, and I felt a bit nervous and began swallering. Then all of a sudding, before I knew where I was, something had me by the trouser leg, and if I'd of been a religious man I'd of said right out it was the devil himself; but when I seed it was a great hairy animal I run for the front door and slammed it to behind me, it being on the jar for a piece of luck, because if it hadn't of been on the jar my calf was a goner."

"Why didn't you send for me at once?"

"Well, sir, how was I to know you hadn't put the chim-pansy there for the purpose?"

"Do you think I take flats for chimpanzees?" demanded Hausberg.

"No, sir, I don't, but if you'll pardon me, there's a lot of queer things goes on in these mansions, and I've learned not to interfere before I'm asked to, and sometimes not then. Only last week Number Fourteen got the D. T.'s on him and threw a sewing-machine at me when his young lady called me up to see what could be done about quieting him down. And now this here monkey has cost me a pair of trousers and a new hat with the name of the mansions worked on the front which I shall have to replace, and I only hope I sha'n't be the loser by it."

"Get out," snarled Hausberg.

He was in such a rage that he looked more like a large monkey than ever while he was striding in and out of every dismantled room; and Dorothy realized the extreme malice of the joke that had been played upon him.

"You know who did this?" he said to her, wrathfully.

She shook her head.

"Do you mean to tell me you don't know that it was your friend Lord Clarehaven?"

"Rubbish!" said Dorothy. "Why should he shut a chimpanzee in *your* flat?"

"Your friend Clarehaven," Hausberg went on, "and that little swine Lonsdale are responsible for this; but when I tell you that they drove down this afternoon to Brighton with Lily and that cursed friend of hers—"

"How do you know?" she interrupted, with some emotion.

"You don't suppose I set a girl up in a flat without having her watched first, do you? When I buy," said Hausberg, "I buy in the best market. Here's the detective's report."

He handed her a half-sheet of note-paper written in a copperplate hand with a record of Lily's day, ending up with the information that she and her friend Sylvia Scarlett, accompanied by the Earl of Clarehaven and the Honorable Arthur Lonsdale, had driven down to Brighton immediately after lunch and reached the Britannia Hotel at five o'clock, "as confirmed per telephone."

"Well," said Hausberg, grimly, "Lily has been paid out by losing my protection, but, by God! I'll get even with the rest of them soon or late."

"You don't really think that I had anything to do with this?" asked Dorothy. "Why, I haven't seen either Clarehaven or Lonsdale for a month! I didn't even know that they had met Sylvia and Lily. They didn't meet them in Halfmoon Street. Why do you drag me here at this hour of the night?"

Hausberg seemed convinced by her denials, and his manner changed abruptly.

"I'm sorry I suspected you as well. I might have known better. I see now that we've both been made to look foolish. What can I do to show you I'm sorry for behaving like this? We're old pals, Dorothy. I was off my head when I came round here and they told me the trick that had been played on me. Damn them! Damnthem! I'll—But what can I do to show you I'm sorry?"

"You'd better invest some money for me," said Dorothy, severely.

"How much do you want?"

"No, no," she said. "I've got two hundred and fifty pounds that I want to invest; only, of course, I must have a really good investment."

"That's all right," he promised. "I'll do a bit of gambling for you."

They had left the flat behind them and were walking slowly down-stairs when suddenly from one of the doors on the landing immediately below a man slipped out, paused for a moment when he heard their footsteps descending, thought better of his timidity, hurried on down, and was out of sight before they reached the landing.

"Good Heavens!" Dorothy ejaculated, seizing her companion's arm.

"I'm afraid I've made you jumpy," he said. "Poor old Dorothy, I shall have to find a jolly good investment to make up for it."

Hausberg was quite his old suave self again; it was Dorothy who was pale and agitated now.

"It was nothing," she murmured; but it was really a great deal, because the man she had seen was Mr. Gilbert Caffyn, the secretary of the Church of England Purity Society.

Dorothy did not enjoy her motor drive that Sunday. It was pale-blue November weather with the sun like a topaz hanging low in the haze above the Surrey hills, but the knowledge that Clarehaven all this month, perhaps even for longer, had been carrying on with Lily and Sylvia when she had taken such care to keep them apart tormented her beyond any capacity to enjoy the landscape or the weather. Heartless treachery, then, was the result of being kind to old friends—and oh, what an odious world it was! There would have to be a grand breaking of friendships presently—yes, and a grand dissolution of family ties as well, for, at any rate, in the midst of this miserable and humiliating affair she had at least been granted the consolation of catching out her father, which might be useful one day. Olive wondered, when the great man left them after supper, why Dorothy had been so gloomy on the drive. She had told the story of the chimpanzee so well, and the great man had laughed more heartily over it than over anything she could remember. Why was Dorothy so sad? Was there something she had left out? Surely on Hausberg's mere word she was not thinking anything horrid about Sylvia's going for a drive with Clarehaven? They had probably just driven down to Brighton for dinner to laugh over the chimpanzee.

"I shall see Sylvia once more," said Dorothy, "and that will be for the last time."

"But I'm sure you'll find Hausberg has made everything appear in the worst light," Olive protested. "I'm sure Sylvia would never snatch a man away from any girl."

"I don't understand how you can go on being friends with me and yet defend her," said Dorothy.

Olive begged her dearest Dorothy to wait for Sylvia's explanation before she got angry with herself, and on Monday afternoon Sylvia of her own accord came to the flat.

"I know everything," said Dorothy, frigidly.

"Then for Heaven's sake tell me what Hausberg said when he opened the door and saw the chimpanzee. Did he say, 'Are you there, Lily?' and did the chimpanzee answer with a cocoanut?"

"Chimpanzee," repeated Dorothy, wrathfully. "You who call yourself my friend deliberately set out to ruin my whole life, and when I reproach you with it you talk about chimpanzees!"

"Don't be silly, Dorothy," Sylvia scoffed. "Hausberg wanted a lesson for saying I was living on Lily, and with Arthur Lonsdale's help I gave him one."

"And what about Clarehaven?" asked Dorothy. "Did he help you?"

"Oh, that foolish fellow wanted a lesson, too. So I took him down to Brighton and gave him a jolly good one, though it wasn't so brutal as Hausberg's."

"Thanks very much," said Dorothy, sarcastically. "In future when my—my—"

"Your man. Say it out," Sylvia advised.

"When a friend of mine requires a lesson I prefer to give it him myself."

"My dear Dorothy," exclaimed Sylvia, with a laugh, "you're not upsetting yourself by getting any ridiculous ideas into your head about Clarehaven and myself? I assure you that—"

"I don't want your assurances," Dorothy interrupted. "It doesn't matter to me what you do with Clarehaven, except that as a friend of mine I think you might have been more loyal."

"Don't be foolish. I'm the last person to do anything in the least disloyal."

"Really?" sneered Dorothy.

"Clarehaven simply came down to Brighton to talk about you. He's suffering from the moth and star disease. Though you won't believe me, I was very fond of you, Dorothy dear; I am still, really," she added, with a little movement of affection that Dorothy refused to notice. "But I do think you're turning into a shocking little snob. That's the Vanity *galère*. No girl there could help being a snob unless she were as simple and sweet as Olive."

"Perhaps you'd like to steal Olive from me, too?" Dorothy asked, bitterly.

"I tell you," the other answered, "it's not a question of stealing anybody. I kept Clarehaven up all night drinking whiskies-and-sodas while I lectured him on his behavior to you. We sat in the sitting-room. If you want a witness, ask the waiter, who has varicose veins and didn't forget to remind us of the fact."

"I suppose Lonsdale and Lily were sitting up with you at this conference? Do you think I was born yesterday? Well, I warn you that I shall tell Queenie Molyneux what's happened."

"If you do," said Sylvia, "I've an idea that Lonsdale will be only too delighted. I fancy that's exactly what he wanted."

"This is all very sordid," said Dorothy, loftily. Then she told Sylvia that she never wished to see her again, and they parted.

Dorothy insisted that Olive ought also to quarrel with Sylvia, but, much to her annoyance, Olive dissented. She said that in any case the dispute had nothing to do with her, and actually added that in her opinion Sylvia had behaved rather well.

"I'm sure she's speaking the truth," she said.

Dorothy thought how false all friends were, and promised that henceforth she would think about no one except her own much-injured self.

"One starts with good resolutions not to be selfish," she told Olive, "and then one is driven into it by one's friends."

Sylvia's story seemed contradicted next day by the arrival of Clarehaven in a most complacent mood, for when Dorothy asked how he had enjoyed his week-end he did not seem at all taken aback and hoped that her Jew friend had enjoyed his.

"I wish I could make you understand just how little you mean to me," she raged. "How dare you come here and brag about your—your— Oh, I wish I'd never met you."

"If you don't care anything about me," he said, "I can't understand why you should be annoyed at my taking Sylvia Scarlett down to Brighton. I don't pretend to be in love with her. I'm in love with you."

Dorothy interrupted him with a contemptuous gesture.

"But it's true, Dorothy. I'm no good at explaining what I feel, don't you know; but ever since that day I first saw you in St. Mary's I've been terrifically keen on you. You drove me into taking up Sylvia. I don't care anything about Sylvia. Why, great Scot! she bores me to death. She talks forever until I don't know where I am. But I must do something. I can't just mope round London like an ass. You know, you're breaking my heart, that's what you're doing."

"You'd better go abroad," said Dorothy. "They mend hearts very well there."

"If you're not jolly careful I shall go abroad."

"Then go," she said, "but don't talk about it. I hate people who talk, just as much as you do."

Within a week Lord Clarehaven had equipped himself like the hero of a late nineteenth-century novel to shoot big game in Somaliland, and on the vigil of his departure Arthur Lonsdale came round to see Dorothy.

"Look here. You know," he began, "I'm the cause of all this. Hard-hearted little girls and all that who require a lesson."

"Yes, it's evident you've been spending a good deal of time lately with Sylvia," said Dorothy.

"Now don't start backfiring, Doodles. I've come here as a friend of the family and I don't want to sprain my tongue at the start. Poor old Tony came weeping round to me and asked what was to be done about it."

"It?" asked Dorothy, angrily. "What is *it*? The chimpanzee?"

"No, no, no. *It* is you and Tony. If you go on interrupting like this you'll puncture my whole speech. When Tony skidded over that rope of pearls and you froze him with a look, he came and asked my advice about what to do next. So I loosened my collar like Charles Wyndham and said: 'Make her jealous, old thing. There's only one way with women, which is to make them jealous. I'm going to make the Molyneux jealous. If you follow my advice, you'll do the same with the Lonsdale.'"

Dorothy nearly put her fingers in her ears to shut out any more horrible comparisons between herself and Queenie, but she assumed, instead, a martyred air and submitted to the gratification of her curiosity.

"Well, just about that fatal time," Lonsdale continued, "Tony and I went for a jolly little bump round at Covent Garden and bumped into Sylvia and Lily *en pierrette*, as they say at my crammer's, where they're teaching me enough French to administer the destinies of Europe for ten years to come. Where were we? Oh yes,*en pierrette*. 'Hello, hello' I said. 'Two jolly little girls *en pierrette*, and what about it? Well, we had two or three more bumps round, and Tony was getting more and more depressed about himself, and so I said, 'Why don't we go down to Brighton and cheer ourselves up?' 'That's all right,' said Sylvia, 'if you'll help me put a jolly old chimpanzee in a fellow's flat.' I said, I'll put a jolly old elephant, if you like.' You see, the notion was that when Hausberg opened the door of the flat he should say, 'Are you there, Lily?' It was all to be very amusing and jolly."

"And what has this to do with Clarehaven?" asked Dorothy.

"Wait a bit. Wait a bit. I'm changing gears at this moment, and if you interrupt I shall jam. You see, my notion was that Tony should buzz down to Brighton with us and ... well ... there's a nasty corner here.... I told you, didn't I, that the only way with hard-hearted little girls is to make them jealous? And the proof of the pudding, as they say, is in the eating, what? Anyway, no sooner did Queenie hear I'd eloped with an amorous blonde than we made it up. Look here, the road's clear now, so let's be serious. Tony's madly in love with you. It's no use telling me you're a good little girl, because look round you. Where's the evidence? I mean to say, your salary's six pounds a week. So, I repeat, where's the evidence? You may dream that you dwell in marble halls on six pounds a week, but you can't really do it."

"If Lord Clarehaven has sent you here to insult me," said Dorothy, "he might at least have had the courage to come and do it himself."

"You're taking this very unkindly. On my word of honor I assure you, Doodles, that Tony's trip to Brighton ended in talk. I know this, because I heard them. In fact, I summoned the night porter and asked him to stop the beehive next door."

"This conversation is not merely insulting," said Dorothy, "it's very coarse."

"I see you're prejudiced, Doodles. Now Queenie was also prejudiced; in fact, at one point she was so prejudiced that she jabbed me with a comb. But I calmed her down and she gradually began to appreciate the fact that not only is there a silver lining to every cloud, but that there is also a cloud to most silver linings. Bored with mere luxury, she realized that a good man's love—soft music, please—should not be lightly thrown away; and now, to be absolutely serious for one moment, what about commissioning me to buzz down to Devonshire and tell Tony that there's no need for him to go chasing the okapi through equatorial Africa?"

"All this levity may be very amusing to you, Mr. Lonsdale, but to me it is only painful."

"Well, of course, if you're going to take my friendly little run round the situation like that, there's nothing more to be said."

"Nothing whatever," Dorothy agreed.

Lonsdale retired with a shrug, and a day or two later Lord Clarehaven's departure for Mombasa was duly recorded in the *Morning Post*. Dorothy's self-importance had been so deeply wounded by the manner in which Lonsdale had commented upon her position in the world that for some time she could scarcely bear to meet people, and she even came near to relinquishing the publicity of the stage, because she began to feel that the nightly audience was sneering at her discomfiture. The gift of a set of Russian sables from Hausberg and the news that her investments were prospering failed to rouse her from the indifference with which she was regarding life. All that had seemed so rich in the flat now merely oppressed her with a sense of useless display. The continual assurances she received that only the melodious trio had saved "The Duke and the Dairymaid" from being something like a failure gave her no elation. Her silks and sables were no more to her than rags; her crystal flasks of perfumes, and those odorous bath-salts, in which the lemon and the violet blended so exquisitely the sharp with the sweet, had lost their savor; even her new manicure set of ivory-and-gold did not pass the unprofitable hours so pleasantly as that old ebony set of which she had been so proud in West Kensington, it seemed a century ago. Lonsdale by his attitude had made her feel that the luxury of her surroundings was not the natural expression of a personality predestined to find in rank its fit expression, but merely the stock-in-trade of a costly doll.

It was Tufton who provided Dorothy with a new elixir of life that was worth all the scent in Bond Street, and a restorative that made the most pungent toilet vinegar insipid as water.

"I don't think you ought to take it so badly," he said. "Shooting the rhino for the sake of a woman is better than throwing the other kind of rhino at her head. It shows that he's pretty badly hit."

"The rhino?" asked Dorothy, with a pale smile.

"No, no," protested Tufton, shocked at carrying a joke too far. "Clarehaven. Wait till he comes back. If he comes back as much in love as he went away you'll hear nothing more about flats round the corner. Curzon Street is also round the corner, don't forget, and my belief is that you'll move straight in from here."

"You're a good pal, Harry."

"Well, I don't think my worst enemy has ever accused me of not sticking to my friends."

This was true; but then Mr. Tufton did not make friends lightly. Old walls afford a better foothold to the climber than new ones.

When Dorothy pondered these words of encouragement she cheered up; and that night John Richards, who had watched her performance from the stage-box, told his sleeping partner that he intended to bring her along in the next Vanity production.

"She gets there," he boomed. "Goo' gir'! Goo' gir'!"

V

Dorothy indulged her own renewed *joie de vivre* by investigating the glimpse of her father's private *joie de vivre* vouchsafed to her that night in St. John's Wood, and without much difficulty she found out that for the last two years he had been maintaining there a second establishment, which at the very lowest calculation must be costing him £400 a year. It was not remarkable that he had wanted to obtain a higher rate of interest on his wife's capital. His daughter debated with herself how to play this unusual hand, and she decided not to lead these black trumps too soon, but to reserve them for the time when they might threaten her ace of hearts and that long suit of diamonds. At present she was not suffering the least inconvenience from her family, and since she went to live in Halfmoon Street it had not been her habit to visit Lonsdale Road more often than once a month. These visits, rare as winter sunshine in England, were not much warmer: the family basked for a while in the radiance of Dorothy's rich clothes, but they soon found that clothes only give heat to the person who wears them, and since Dorothy did not encourage them to follow the sun like visitors to the azure coast, they made the best of their own fireside and avoided any risk of taking cold by depending too much on her deceptive radiance.

Meanwhile, Hausberg had turned Dorothy's £250 into £500 by nothing more compromising than good advice; and by March, to celebrate her twenty-first birthday, the £500 had become £2,000. Not even then did Hausberg ask anything from her in return; occasionally a dim suspicion crossed her mind that a profound cause must lie underneath this display of good will, and she asked herself if he was patiently, very patiently, angling for her; but when time went by without his striking, the suspicions died away and did not recur. Moreover, her financial adviser was engaged in dazzling Queenie Molyneux with diamonds, to the manifest chagrin of Lonsdale, who had let the liaison between himself and Queenie come to mean much more to him than he had ever intended that evening at the Savoy. In the end his mistress was so much dazzled by the diamonds that she put on rose-colored spectacles to save her eyes and, looking through them at Hausberg, decided to accept his devotion. Lonsdale took the theft of his love hardly; whatever chance he might have had of entering the Foreign Office disappeared under an emotional strain that in so round and pink a young man was nearly grotesque. This seemed to Dorothy a suitable moment to repay evil with good, and when, shortly afterward, she saw the disconsolate lover gloomily contemplating a half-bottle of Pol Roger '98 on a solitary table at the Savoy she went over to him and offered to be reconciled.

He squeezed Dorothy's hand gratefully, sighed, and shook his head.

"I can't keep away from the old place. Every night we used to come here and—" The recollection was too much for him; he could do nothing but point mutely to the half-bottle.

"That makes you think," he said, at last. "After the dozens of bottles we've had together, to come down to that beastly little dwarf alone."

"And you've failed in your examination, too?" inquired Dorothy, tenderly rubbing it in.

"Just as well, Doodles, just as well. I should be afraid to attach myself even to an embassy at present."

The band struck up the music of the Pink Quartet.

"Good God!" he exclaimed. "This is too much. Here, Carlo, Ponto, Rover—What's your name?"

The waiter leaned over obsequiously.

"Here, take this fiver with my compliments to Herr Rumpelstiltzkin and ask him to cut out that tune and give us the 'Dead March' instead."

"Why not the 'Wedding March'?" asked Dorothy, maliciously.

"I give you my solemn word of honor," said Lonsdale, "that if only Queenie—well, I think I can get up this hill on the top speed—if I were the first, I *would* marry Queenie. You know, I'm beginning to think Tony made rather an ass of himself, buzzing off like that to Basutoland or wherever it is. By the way, has it ever struck you what an anomaly—that's a good word—I got that word out of a *précis* at my crammer's. It's a splendid word and can be used in summer and winter with impunity, what? Has it ever struck you what an anomaly it is that you can get a license to shoot big game and drive a car, but that you can't get a license to shoot Hausbergs? Well, well, if Queenie had your past and your own future and could cut out some of the presents, by Jove! I would marry her. I really would."

Dorothy said to herself that she had always liked Arthur Lonsdale in spite of everything, and when he asked her now if her friends were not waiting for her she told him that they could wait and gratified the forsaken one by sitting down at his table.

"Of course, when Queenie and I parted," he went on, "she made it absolutely clear to me that this fellow Hausberg meant nothing to her; in fact, between ourselves, she rather gave me to understand that things might go on as they were. But you know, hang it! I can't very well do that sort of thing. The funny thing is that the more I refuse, the more keen she gets. I mean to say it is ridiculous, really, because of course she can't be very much in love with *me*. To begin with, well, she's about twice my height, what? No, I think I shall have to go in for motor-cars. They used to be nearly as difficult to manage as women not so long ago, but they seem to be answering to civilization much more rapidly. It's a pity somebody can't blow along with some invention to improve women. Skidding all over the place, don't you know, as they do now ... but I cannot understand why Hausberg should have fixed on Queenie. I always thought he was after you, and I'm not sure he isn't. Did you turn him down?"

"He has only been helping me with some investments."

"I never heard of a Jew helping people with their investments just for the pleasure of helping."

"I had money of my own to invest," Dorothy explained. "Family money."

"Lonsdale money, in fact, eh?" laughed the heir of the house.

"Well, if you really want to know, it is Lonsdale money. Money left in trust for me by my grandmother, who was a Lonsdale. I know you laugh at this, but it's perfectly true."

"Oh no, I don't laugh at you," said Lonsdale. "I never thought you were a joke. In fact, I asked the governor if he could trace anything about your branch in the family history. But the trouble with him is that he's not very interested in anything except politics. Frightfully narrow-minded old boy. He's been abroad most of his life, poor devil. He's out of touch with things."

Dorothy thought that if her Lonsdale ancestry could appear sufficiently genuine to induce the heir of the family to consult his father about it there was not much doubt of its impressing the rest of the world. It happened that among the party with which she was supposed to be supping that night was a young Frenchman with some invention that was going to revolutionize the manufacture of motor-cars. She decided to introduce him to Lonsdale, and a month or two later she had the gratification of hearing that Lord Cleveden had been persuaded to allow his son the capital necessary to begin a motor business in which the Frenchman, with his invention, was to be one of the partners, and a well-known professional racing-motorist another. The firm expressed their gratitude to Dorothy not only by presenting her with a car, but also by paying her a percentage on orders that came through her discreet advertisement of their wares. If Clarehaven came back now and asked Lonsdale what she had been doing since he left England, surely he would no longer try to damn the course of their true love.

Just after Dorothy and Olive had left town for their holiday in July the great man died suddenly, and, naturally, Olive was very much upset by the shock.

"Never mind," said Dorothy. "Luckily I've made some money, so we needn't leave the flat."

"I wasn't thinking of that point of view," Olive sobbed. "I was thinking how good he'd always been to me and how much I shall miss him."

"Well, now you can tell me who he was," Dorothy suggested, consolingly.

"No, darling, oh no; this is the very time of all others when I wouldn't have anybody know who he was."

Dorothy, however, searched the papers, and she soon came to the conclusion that the great man was none other than the Duke of Ayr. Such a discovery thrilled her with the majesty of her retrospect, and she fancied that even Clarehaven would be a little impressed if he knew who Olive's friend was:

John Charles Chisholm-Urquhart, K.T., 9th and last Duke of Ayr; also Marquess and Earl of Ayr, Marquess and Earl of Dumbarton, Earl of Kilmaurs and Kilwinning, Viscount Dalry and Dalgarven, Viscount of Brackenbrae, Lord Urquhart, Inverew, and Troon, Baron Chisholm, Earl Chisholm, Baron Hurst, Baron Urquhart of Coylton, Lord Urquhart of Dumbarton, and Baron Dalgarven.

The last Duke of Ayr! Nobody in the world to inherit one of all those splendid titles! Not even a duchess to survive him!

The press commented just as ruefully as Dorothy upon the extinction of another noble house. Dukes and dodos, great families and great auks, one felt that they would soon all be extinct together.

"It's a great responsibility to marry a peer," Dorothy thought.

She gently and tactfully let Olive know that she had found out the identity of the great man, and they went together to stand for a minute or two outside Ayr House, where the hatchment, crape-hung, was all that was left of so much grandeur and of such high dignities and honors. Nor did Dorothy allude to the duke's omission to provide for Olive in his will, though, being a bachelor without an heir, he might easily have done so. No doubt death had found him unprepared; but the funeral must have been wonderful, with the pipers sounding "The Lament" for Chisholm when the coffin was lowered into the grave.

"I'm very glad they're closing 'The Duke and the Dairymaid' this week," said Dorothy. "I should hate to see that title now on every 'bus and every hoarding."

The Vanity's last production had not been such a success as either of its two predecessors, and many people about town began to say that if John Richards was not careful the Frivolity was going to cut out the Vanity. Therefore in the autumn of 1905 a tremendous effort was made to eclipse all previous productions with "The Beauty Shop." Early in August John Richards sent for Dorothy, gave her a song to study, and told her to come again in a week's time to let him hear what she made of it. To print baldly the words of this great song without the melody, without the six beauties supporting it from the background, without the entranced scene-shifters and the bewitched audience, without even a barrel-organ to recall it, is something like sacrilege, but here is one verse:

When your head is in a whirl.
And your hair won't curl,
And you feel such a very, very ill-used girl.
Chorus. Little girl!
    Then that is the time—
Chorus. Every time! Every time!
    To visit a Bond Street Beauty Shop.
Chorus. To visit our Bond Street Beauty Shop.
    And when you come out,
And you're seen about
In the places you formerly frequented—
Chorus. On the arm of her late-lamented.
    Why every one will cry,
Oh dear, oh lord, oh my!
There's Dolly with her collie!
All scented and contented!
Chorus. She's forgotten the late-lamented.
    For Dolly's out and about again,
She doesn't give a damn for a shower of rain.
Here's Dolly with her collie!
And London!   *Chorus.* Dear old London!
London is itself again!

"Goo' gir'" said Mr. Richards when Dorothy had finished and the dust in his little office in the cupola of the Vanity had subsided. "Goo' gir'. I thi' you'll ma' a 'ice 'ihel hit in that song."

The impresario was right: Dorothy did make a resounding hit; and a more welcome token of it than her picture among the letterpress and advertisements of every illustrated paper, the dedication of a new face-cream, and the christening of a brand of cigarettes in her honor, was the reappearance of Clarehaven with character and complexion much matured by the sun of Africa, so ripe, indeed, that he was ready to fall at her feet. She received him gently and kindly, but without encouragement; he was given to understand that his treatment had driven her to take refuge in art, the result of which he had just been witnessing from the front of the house. Besides, she told him, now that Olive's friend was dead, she must stay and look after her. People had misjudged Olive and herself so much in the past that she did not intend to let them misjudge her in future. She was making money at the Vanity now, and she begged Lord Clarehaven, if he had ever felt any affection for her, to go away again and shoot more wild animals. Cupid himself would have had to use dum-dum darts to make any impression on Dorothy in her present mood.

Such nobility of bearing, such wounded beauty, such weary grace, could only have one effect on a man who had spent so many months among hippos and black women, and without hesitation Clarehaven proposed marriage. Dorothy's heart leaped within her; but she preserved a calm exterior, and a sad smile expressed her disbelief in his seriousness. He protested; almost he declaimed. She merely shook her head, and the desperate suitor hurried down to Devonshire in order to convince his mother that he must marry Dorothy at once, and that she must demonstrate, either by visit or by letter, what a welcome his bride would receive from the family. Clarehaven lacked eloquence, and the dowager was appalled. Lonsdale was telegraphed for, and presently he came up to town to act as her emissary to beg Dorothy to refuse her son.

"It'll kill the poor lady," he prophesied. "I know you're not wildly keen on Tony, so let him go, there's a dear girl."

"I never had the slightest intention of doing anything else. You don't suppose that just when I've made my first success I'm going to throw myself away on marriage. You ought to know me better, Lonnie."

Lonsdale was frankly astonished at Dorothy's attitude; but he was glad to be excused from having to argue with her about the unsuitableness of the match, because he did sincerely admire her, and, moreover, had some reason to be grateful for her practical sympathy at the time of his break with Queenie Molyneux. He went away from Halfmoon Street with reassurances for the countess.

It was at this momentous stage in Dorothy's career that Mr. Caffyn, awed by the evidence of his daughter's fame he beheld on every side, chose to call for her one evening at the stage-door with a box of chocolates, in which was inclosed a short note of congratulation and an affectionately worded request that she would pay the visit to her family that was now long overdue.

Dorothy pondered for a minute her line of action before sending down word that she would soon be dressed and that the gentleman was to wait in her car. When she came out of the theater and told the chauffeur to drive her to West Kensington, Mr. Caffyn expressed his pleasure at her quick response to his appeal. They drove along, talking of matters trivial enough, until in the silence of the suburban night the car stopped before 17 Lonsdale Road.

"Good-by," said Dorothy.

"You'll come in for a bit?" asked her father, in surprise.

"Oh no; you'll be wanting to get to bed," she said.

"Well, it's very kind of you to drive me back," Mr. Caffyn told her, humbly. "Very kind indeed. You'll be interested to know that this is a much nicer motor than the Bishop of Chelsea's. He was kind enough to drive me back from the congress of Melanesian Missions the other day, and so I'm acquainted with his motor."

"He didn't drive you to Lauriston Mansions, did he?" Dorothy asked.

The sensitive springs of the car quivered for a moment in response to Mr. Caffyn's jump.

"What do you mean?" he stammered.

"Oh, I know all about it," his daughter began, with cold severity. "It's all very sordid, and I don't intend to go into details; but I want you quite clearly to understand once and for all that communication between you and me must henceforth cease until I wish to reopen it. It's extremely possible, in fact it's probable, in fact I may say it's certain that I'm shortly going to marry the Earl of Clarehaven, and inasmuch as one of the charms of my present position is the fact that I have no family, I want you all quite clearly to understand that after my marriage any recognition will have to come from me first."

Mr. Caffyn was too much crushed at being found out in his folly and hypocrisy to plead his own case, but he ventured to put in a word for his wife's feelings and begged Dorothy not to be too hard on her.

"You're the last person who has any right to talk about my mother. Come along, jump out, father. I must be getting back. I've a busy day to-morrow, with two performances."

The sound of Mr. Caffyn's pecking with his latch-key at the lock was drowned in the noise of the car's backing out of Lonsdale Road. Dorothy laughed lightly to herself when she compared this interview with the one she had had not so many months ago about the £500, which, by the way, she must send back to her mother if Hausberg advised her to sell out those shares. No doubt, such a sum would be most useful to her father with his numerous responsibilities.

"And now," she murmured to herself, "I see no reason why I shouldn't meet Tony's mother."

VI

Dorothy had not been entirely insincere with Lonsdale in comparing marriage with success to the detriment of marriage. Success is a wonderful experience for the young, in spite of the way those who obtain it too late condemn it as a delusion; few girls of twenty-one, luxuriously independent and universally flattered, within two years of going on the stage would have seen marriage even with an earl in quite such wonderful colors as formerly. Fame may have its degrees; but when Dorothy, traveling in her car, heard errand-boys upon the pavement whistling "Dolly and her Collie" she had at least as much right to feel proud of herself as some wretched novelist traveling by tube who sees a young woman reading a sixpenny edition of one of his works, or a mother whose dribbling baby is prodded by a lean spinster in a tram, or a hen who lays a perfectly ordinary egg and makes as much fuss over it as if it were oblong.

It was certain that if Dorothy chose she could have one of the two principal parts in the next Vanity production and be earning in another couple of years at least £60 a week. There was no reason why she should remain in musical comedy; there was no reason why she should not take to serious comedy with atmosphere and surreptitious curtains at the close of indefinite acts; there was no reason why some great dramatist should not fall in love with her and invert the usual method of sexual procedure by laying upon her desk the offspring of their spiritual union. The possibilities of the future in every direction were boundless.

At the same time even as a countess her starry beams would not necessarily be obscured. As Countess of Clarehaven she might have as many pictures of herself in the illustrated papers as now; she could not give her name to face-creams, but she might give it to girls' clubs: one countess had even founded a religious sect, and another countess had ... but when one examined the history of countesses there was as much variety as in the history of actresses. And yet as a Vanity countess would it not be most distinguished of all not to appear in the illustrated papers, not to found sects and dress extravagantly at Goodwood? Would it not be more distinguished to live quietly down in Devonshire and make no more startling public appearances than by sometimes opening a bazaar or judging a collection of vegetables? Would it not be more distinguished to be the mother of young Lord Clare and Lady Dorothy Clare, and Lady Cynthia Clare, and the Honorable Arthur Clare.... Dorothy paused; she was thinking how improper it was that the younger sons of an earl should be accorded no greater courtesy than those of a viscount or a baron, when his daughters were entitled to as much as the daughters of a duke or a marquess. And after all, why shouldn't Tony be created a marquess? That was another career for a countess she had omitted to consider—the political hostess, the inspiration and amanuensis of her husband's speeches to the House of Lords. Some infant now squalling in his perambulator would write his reminiscences of a great lady's *salon* in the early years of the twentieth century, when the famous Dorothy Lonsdale stepped out of the public eye, but kept her hold upon the public pulse as the wise and beautiful Marchioness of Clarehaven. The second Marquess of Clarehaven, she dreamed; and beneath this heading in a future Debrett she read below, "Wife Living of the First Marquess. Dorothy (Marchioness of Clarehaven)"; if Arthur Lonsdale married well, that marchioness might not object to one of her younger daughters marrying his eldest son. Dorothy started. How should she herself be recorded in Debrett? "Dorothy, daughter of Gilbert Caffyn"? Even that would involve a mild falsification of her birth certificate, and if her sister Dorothy married that budding young solicitor from Norbiton they might take action against her. She hurriedly looked up in Debrett and *Who's Who* all the other actresses who had married into the peerage. In Debrett their original names in their stark and brutal ugliness were immortally inscribed; but in *Who's Who* their stage names wereusually added between brackets. "The Earl of Clarehaven, *m.* 1905 Norah *d.* of G. Caffyn (known on the stage as Dorothy Lonsdale)." Ugh! At least she would not advertise the obvious horror of her own name so blatantly. She would not be more conspicuous than "Norah (Dorothy) *d.* of G. Caffyn." But how the girls at the theater would laugh! The girls at the theater? Why should the girls at the theater be allowed any opportunity of laughter—at any rate in her hearing? No, if she decided to accept Tony she should obliterate the theater. There should be no parade about her marriage; she would be married simply, quietly, and ruthlessly.

At the Vanity, Dorothy and her collie were a ravishing success; but she was a better actress off the stage than she was on, and she had soon persuaded herself that she really was still uncertain whether to accept Clarehaven's hand or not. The minor perplexities of stage name and real name, of town and country life, of publicity and privacy as a countess, magnified themselves into serious doubts about the prudence of marrying at all, and by the month of December Clarehaven was nearly distracted by her continuous refusals of him. The greater favorite she became with the public the more he desired her; and she would have found it hard to invent any condition, however flagrantly harsh, that would have deterred him from the match. Tufton almost went down on his knees to implore her to marry the lovesick young earl, his greatest friend; and even Lonsdale talked to Dorothy about her cruelty, and from having been equipped a month ago with invincible arguments against the match, now told her that in spite of everything, he thought she really ought to make the poor lad happy.

"He's as pale as a fellow I bumped in the back last Thursday, cutting round Woburn Square on the wrong side," he declared.

"No, he's not so sunburnt as he was," Dorothy agreed.

"Sunburnt? He's moonburnt—half-moonburnt—starburnt! But sunburnt! My dear Doodles, you're indulging in irony. That's what you're doing."

"I don't see why I should marry him when his mother hasn't even written me a letter. I don't want his family to feel that he's disgracing them by marrying me. If Lady Clarehaven will tell me with her own lips that she'll be proud for her son to marry me, why, then I'll think about it."

"No, really, dash it, my dear girl," Lonsdale expostulated. "You're being unreasonable. You're worse than a Surrey magistrate. Let the old lady alone until you're married and she has to make the best of a bad bargain."

"Thanks very much," Dorothy said. "That's precisely the attitude I wish to guard myself against."

Lonsdale's failure to soften Dorothy's heart made Clarehaven hopeless; he reached Devonshire to spend Christmas with his family in a mood so desperate that his mother began to be nervous. The head-keeper at Clare Court spoke with alarm of the way his lordship held his gun while getting over stiles.

"Maybe, my lady, that after lions our pheasants seem a bit tame to his lordship, though I disremember as I ever saw them wilder than what they be this year—but if you'll forgive the liberty, my lady, a gun do be as dangerous in Devonshire as in Africa, and 'tis my belief that his lordship has summat on his mind, as they say."

A shooting accident upon a neighboring estate the very day after this warning from the keeper determined Lady Clarehaven to put her pride in her pocket and write to Dorothy.

CLARE COURT, DEVON,
January 2, 1906.

DEAR MISS LONSDALE,—I fear you must have thought me most remiss in not writing to you before, but you will, perhaps, understand that down here in the country the notion of marrying an actress presents itself as a somewhat alarming contingency, and I was anxious to assure myself that my son's future happiness was so completely bound up in such a match that any further opposition on my part would be useless and unkind. Our friend Arthur Lonsdale spoke so highly of you and of the dignity of your attitude that I was much touched, and I must ask you to forgive my lack of generosity in not writing before to tell you how deeply I appreciated your refusal to marry my son. I understand now that his departure from England a year ago was due to this very cause, and I can only bow before the strength of such an affection and withdraw my opposition to the marriage. I am assuming, perhaps unjustifiably, that you love Tony as much as he loves you. Of course, if this is not so, it would be an impertinence on my part to interfere in your private affairs, and if you write and tell me that you cannot love Tony I must do my best as a mother to console him. But if you do love him, as I can't help feeling that you must, and if you will write to me and say that no barrier exists between you and him except the old-fashioned prejudice against what would no doubt be merely superficially an ill-assorted union, I shall welcome you as my daughter-in-law and pray for your happiness. I must, indeed, admit to being grievously worried about Tony. He has not even bothered to keep up the shooting-book, and such extraordinary indifference fills me with alarm.

Yours sincerely,
AUGUSTA CLAREHAVEN.

Dorothy debated many things before she answered this letter; but she debated longest of all the question of whether she should write back on crested note-paper or simple note-paper. Finally she chose the latter.

7 HALFMOON MANSIONS,
HALFMOON STREET, W
January 6, 1906.

511

DEAR LADY CLAREHAVEN,—Your letter came as a great joy to me. I don't think I have ever pretended that I did not love Tony with all my heart, and it was just because I did love him so much that I would not marry him without his mother's consent.

My own Puritan family disowned me when I went on the stage, and I said to myself then that I would never again do anything to bring unhappiness into a family. I should prefer that if I marry Tony the wedding should be strictly quiet. I cannot bear the way the papers advertise such sacred things nowadays. Having had no communication with my own family for more than two years, I do not want to reopen the painful memories of our quarrel. My only ambition is to lead a quiet, uneventful life in the depths of the country, and I hope you will do all you can to persuade Tony to remain in Devonshire. You will not think me rude if I do make one condition beforehand. I will marry him if you will promise to remain at Clare Court and help me through the difficult first years of my new position. Please write and let me have your promise to do this. You don't know how much it would help me to think that you and his sisters will be at my side. Perhaps you will think that I am assuming too much in asking this. I need not say that if you find me personally unsympathetic I shall not bear any resentment, and in that case Tony and I can always live in Curzon Street. But I do so deeply pray that you will like me and that his sisters will like me. Your letter has given me much joy, and I only wait for your answer to leave the stage (which I hate) forever.

Yours sincerely,
DOROTHY LONSDALE.

The dowager was won. By return of post she wrote:

MY DEAR DOROTHY,—Thank you extremely for your very nice letter. Please do exactly as you think best about the details of your wedding. You will receive a warm welcome from us all.

Yours affectionately,
AUGUSTA CLAREHAVEN.

During these negotiations Olive had been away at Brighton getting over influenza, and Dorothy decided to join her down there and be married out of town to avoid public curiosity. She had telegraphed to Clarehaven to leave Devonshire, and Mr. Tufton was enraptured by being called in to help with advice about the special license.

"My dear Dorothy," he assured her, enthusiastically, "you deserve the best—the very best."

"I don't want any one at the Vanity to know what's going to happen."

Tufton waved his hands to emphasize how right she was.

"It'll be a terrible blow to the public," he said, "and also to John Richards. You were his favorite, you know. Yes. And think of the beautiful women he has known! But you're right, you mustn't consider anybody except yourself."

"It's rather difficult for me to do that," Dorothy sighed.

"I know. I know. But you must do it. Clarehaven and I will come down with the license, and then ... my dear Dorothy, I really can't tell you how pleased I am. Do, do beg the dowager not to change that pergola. But I shall be down, I hope, some time in the spring."

"Of course."

"And what about Olive?" he asked.

"Poor Olive," she sighed. "And only last week she lost dear little San Toy. Yes, she'll miss me, I'm afraid, but she'll be glad I'm going to be so happy."

"All your friends will be glad."

"And now, Harry, please get me a really nice hansom, because I must simply tear round hard for frocks and frills."

Dorothy spent most of the money that Hausberg had made for her on old pieces of family jewelry; she also ordered numerous country tweeds; of frills she had enough.

A few days later Clarehaven, accompanied by Tufton and the special license, reached Brighton, where he and Dorothy were quietly married in the Church of the Ascension. Lady Clarehaven thought, when she drove back to the rooms to break the news to Olive, how few of the passers-by would think that she had just been married. She commented upon this to Tony, who replied with a laugh that Brighton was the last place in England where passers-by stopped to inquire if people were married.

"Tony," she said, with a pout, "I don't like that sort of joke, you know."

"Sorry, Doodles."

"And don't call me Doodles any more. Call me Dorothy."

Olive was, of course, tremendously surprised by her friend's announcement; but she tried not to show how much hurt she was by not having been taken into her confidence beforehand.

"I wanted it to be a complete secret," Dorothy explained. "And I didn't want all the papers in London to write a lot of rubbish about me."

"Darling, you can count on me as a pal to help you all I know. You've only got to tell me what you want."

Dorothy pulled herself together to do something of which she was rather ashamed, but for which she could perceive no alternative.

"Olive, I hate having to say what I'm going to say, and you must try to understand my point of view. I never intend to go near the stage-door of a theater again. I don't want to know any of my friends on the stage any more. If you want to help me, the best way you can help me is not to see me any more."

Clarehaven came into the room at this moment, and Dorothy rose to make her farewells.

"Good-by, Olive," she said. "We're going down to Clare Court to-morrow, and I don't expect we shall see each other again for a long time."

"I say," Clarehaven protested. "What rot, you know! Of course you'll meet again. Why, Olive must come down and recover from her next illness in Devonshire. We shall be pining for news of town by the spring, and—"

Lady Clarehaven looked at her husband, who was silent.

"Have you wired to your mother when we arrive to-morrow?" she asked.

"You're sure you won't drive down?"

"In January?" Dorothy exclaimed.

"Well, I've told the car to meet us at Exeter. That will only mean a seventy-mile drive—you won't mind that—and we'll get to Clare before dark."

"Forgive these family discussions in front of you," said Dorothy to her friend. Then shaking her hand formally, she went out of the room.

During the drive up to town, while Clarehaven was sitting back playing with his wife's wrist and looking fatuously content, he turned to her once and said:

"Dorothy, you *were* rather brutal with poor old Olive."

She withdrew her hand from his grasp, and not until he ceased condoling with Olive did she let him pick it up again.

"And oh dear, oh lord, oh my!" he exclaimed, "we must have the jolly old collie down at Clare."

"The collie?" she repeated. "What collie?"

"Your collie." He began to whistle the bewitching tune.

"Please don't. One hears it everywhere," she said, fretfully. "Olive will look after the dog. She's just lost her Pekinese."

CHAPTER IV

I

ABOUT the time that the fifth Earl of Clarehaven upset the lares and penates of his house by marrying a Vanity girl the people of Great Britain, having baited with red rags the golden calf of Victorianism until the poor beast had leaped from its pedestal and disappeared in the flowing tide, were now accepting from a lamasery of Liberal reformers the idol of silver speech, forgetting either that silver tarnishes more quickly than gold or that new brooms sweep clean, but soon wear out. However, the new era lasted for quite a month, and long enough for the Dowager Countess of Clarehaven to reach the conclusion that her son's marriage was a sign of the times. Poets extract consolation for their private woes and joys from observing that nature sympathizes with them. When they are fain to weep, the skies weep with them; April's weather follows the caprice of the girl next door; even great Ocean laughs when his little friend the rhymester gets two guineas for a sonnet. What is permitted to a poet will not be denied to a countess, and if the dowager considered her chagrin to be a feather in the mighty wing of revolution—to the widows of Conservative peers down in Devonshire the return of the Liberal party in 1906 seemed nothing less than revolution—she should not, therefore, be accused of exaggeration.

When in 1880 Lady Augusta Fanhope married the fourth Earl of Clarehaven she brought neither beauty nor wealth to that dissolute and extravagant man of thirty-five, who as a subaltern in the Blues had earned a kind of fame by the size of his debts and by the length of his whiskers. Soon after he succeeded to the title fashion made him cut short the whiskers; but his debts increased yearly, and if he had not died during his son's minority there would have been little left for that son to inherit. Nobody understood why he married Lady Augusta, herself least of all. Even when he was still alive she had taken refuge in the Anglican religion; when he died she presented a memorial window by Burne-Jones to Little Cherrington church. By now, when he had been dead ten years and his son was bringing an actress to rule over Clare Court, the dowager had come to regard her late husband as a saint. Fashion had trimmed his whiskers; time had softened his memory; the stained-glass window had done the rest.

"I'm glad your father never lived to see these dreadful Radicals sweeping the country," she said to her daughters on this January day that before it faded into darkness would bring such changes to Clare. What the dowager really meant to express was her relief that the last earl was not alive to meet his daughter-in-law; he ought not to have been easily shocked, but marriage with an actress would certainly have shocked him greatly, and his language when shocked was bad. The effect of Dorothy's letter had already worn a little thin; the dowager's pre-figuration of her approximated more closely every moment to an old standing opinion of actresses she had formed from a large collection of letters and photographs left behind by her husband, which she had lacked the courage to burn unread. Her daughters Arabella and Constantia argued that this Dorothy must be a "top-holer" to make their brother so desperate. Last month he had taken them for several long walks and waxed so eloquent over her beauty and charm and virtue that they had accepted his point of view; with less to lose than their mother and unaware of their father's weakness, they saw no reason why an actress should not make Tony as good a wife as anybody.

"But love is blind," said the dowager. None knew the truth of this better than she. "And in any case, dear children, beauty is only skin-deep."

"Luckily for us, mother," said Arabella.

"I think you exaggerate your plainness," the dowager observed. "You do not make the least attempt to bring out your good features. You, dearest Bella, have very nice ankles; but if you wear shoes like that and never pull up your stockings their slimness escapes the eye. And you, Connie, have really beautiful ears; but when you jam your cap down on your head like that you cause them to protrude in a way that cannot be considered becoming."

The girls laughed; they were too much interested in country life to bother about their appearance. Boots were made to keep out moisture and get a good grip of muddy slopes: caps were meant to stay on one's head, not to show off one's ears. Besides, they were ugly; they had decided as much when they were still children, and, now that they were twenty-one and nineteen, would be foolish to begin repining. Arabella's ankles might be slim, but her teeth were large and prominent; her eyes were pale as the wintry sky above them; her hands were knotted and raw; her nose stuck to her face like a piece of mud thrown at a fence; her hair resembled seaweed. As for Constantia, her nose was much too large; so was her tongue; so were her hands; her eyes were globular, like marbles of brown agate; everything protruded; she was like a person who has been struck on the back of the head in a crowd.

"The question is," said Arabella, "are we to drive over to Exeter to meet them? Because if we are I must tell Crowdy to see about putting us up some sandwiches."

"Well, unless you're very eager to go," the dowager pleaded, "I should appreciate your company. Were I left quite alone, I might get a headache, and I am so anxious to appear cheerful. I think we ought to assume that Dorothy will be as nervous as we are. I think it would be kind to assume that."

"I vote for letting Deacock take the car by himself," Constantia declared. "I always feel awkward at meeting even old friends at a station, and it'll be so awfully hard to talk with the wind humming in my ears."

When the noise of the car had died away among the knolls and hollows of the great park the dowager turned to her daughters:

"It's such a fine day for the season of the year that perhaps I might take a little drive in the chaise."

It was indeed a fine day of silver and faint celeste, such a one as in January only the West Country can give. The leafless woods and isolated clumps of trees breathed a dusky purple bloom like fruit; the grass was peacock green. The dowager, moved by the brilliance of the landscape and the weather to a complete apprehension of the fact that she was no longer mistress of Clare, had been seized with a desire to take a last sentimental survey of her dominion. Although her daughters had made other plans for the morning, they willingly put them aside to encourage such unwonted energy. While the pony was being harnessed, the dowager took Arabella's arm and walked up and down the pergola that ran like a battlement along a spur of the gardens and was the most conspicuous object to those approaching Clare Court through the park.

"It's too late to change it before Dorothy comes," she decided, mournfully. "But I do hope that there will be no more taking of Mr. Tufton's advice. I'm sure that curved seat he persuaded me to put at the end was a mistake. People deposit seats in gardens without thinking. Nobody will ever sit there. It simply means that one will always have to walk round it. So unnecessary! I do hope that Dorothy will give orders to remove it."

"Connie," Arabella exclaimed, with a joyful gurgle, "don't you love the way mother practises the idea of Dorothy? She used to be just the same when we were expecting a new governess."

Her sister, who was munching an apple, nodded her agreement without speaking.

The dowager was about to propose a descent by the terraces to visit her water-lily pool (which would have involved a tiresome climb up again for nothing, because the rose-hearted water-lilies of summer were nothing now but blobs of decayed vegetation) when the wheels of the chaise crackled on the drive and the girls insisted that if she were going to have enough time for an expedition before lunch she must start at once.

Clare Court viewed from the southeast appeared as a long, low house of gray stone with no particular indication of its age for the unprofessional observer, to whom, indeed, the chief feature might have seemed the four magnolias that covered it with their large glossy leaves, the rufous undersides of which, mingling with the stone, gave it a warmth of color that otherwise it would have lacked. The house was built on a moderate elevation, the levels of which were spacious enough to allow for ornamental gardens on the south side of the drive; these had been laid out in the Anglo-Italian manner with pergolas and statuary, yews instead of cypresses, and box-bordered terraces leading gradually down to the ornamental pool overhung on the far side by weeping willows. The kitchens and servants' quarters on either side of the house were masked by shrubberies and groves of tall pines, in the ulterior gloom of which the drive disappeared on the way to the stables and the home farm.

The dowager got into the chaise, and the pony, a dapple gray of some antiquity, proceeded at a pace that did not make it difficult for the two girls, who by now had summoned to heel half a dozen dogs of various breeds, to keep up with it on foot.

"Shall we turn aside and look at the farm?" Constantia suggested, where the road forked.

"No, I think I'd like to drive down to the sea first of all," said the dowager.

"Bravo, mother!" both her daughters applauded.

The dogs, understanding from their mistresses' accents that some delightful project was in the air, began to bark loudly while they scampered through the scraggy rhododendrons and put up shrilling blackbirds with as much gusto as if they were partridges. The drive kept in the shadow of the pines for about two hundred yards, until where the trees began to grow smaller and sparser it emerged upon a spacious sward that between bare uplands went rolling down to the sea a mile away. To one looking back Clare Court now appeared under a strangely altered aspect as a gray pile rising starkly from a wide lawn and unmellowed by anything except the salt northwest wind; even the dowager and her daughters, who had lived in it all these years, could never repress an exclamation of wonder each time they emerged from the dim pinewood and beheld it thus. On the other side of the house there had been sunlight and a rich prospect of parkland losing itself in trees and a carefully cultivated seclusion. Here was nothing except a line of gray-green downs undulating against space, in a dip of which was the shimmer of fusing sky and sea. Except at midsummer the pines were tall enough to cut off the low westering sun from the house, and on this January day from where they were standing in pale sunlight the gray pile seemed frozen. The sense of desolation was increased by a walled-up door in the center of the house, above which angelic supporters sustained the full moon of Clare on a stone escutcheon. The first baronet had failed to establish his right to the three chevronels originally borne by that great family and had been granted arms that accorded better with the rococo taste of his period.

"I've always wanted to plant a hedge of those hydrangeas with black stalks in front of the pines," said the dowager, pensively, "but unless they come blue they wouldn't look nice, and perhaps they wouldn't be able to stand the wind on this side. But the effect would be lovely in summer. Blue sky! Blue sea! Blue hydrangeas! Dark pine-trees and vivid grass! It really would be a wonderful effect. Of course, it may be that Tony's wife will be quite interested in flowers. One never can tell. Come along, Clement." Clement was the pony, so-called because he was such a saint.

The drive now skirted the edge of the downs in a gradual descent to Clarehaven, a small cove formed by green headlands as if earth had thrust out a pair of fists to scoop up some of the sea for herself. The ruins of two round towers were visible on both headlands; on the slopes of the westernmost stood a little church surrounded by tumble-down tombstones that, even as the bodies of those whom they recorded had become part of the earth on which they lived, were themselves growing yearly less distinguishable from the outcrops of stone that no mortal had set upon these cliffs. Two cottages marked the end of the drive, which lost itself beyond them in a rocky beach that was strewn with fragments of ancient masonry. At sight of the chaise several children had bolted into the cottages like disturbed rabbits, and presently a couple of women tying on clean aprons came out to greet the countess and offer the hospitality of their homes. Their husbands, one of whom was called Bitterplum, the other less picturesquely Smith, were mermen of toil, fishers in summer and for the rest of the year agricultural laborers.

"It's very kind of you, Mrs. Smith, and of you, too, Mrs. Bitterplum," said the dowager, "but I can only stay a few minutes. What a beautiful day, isn't it? You must get ready to welcome his lordship, you know. He'll be bringing her ladyship to see you very shortly. Are Bitterplum and Smith quite well?"

"Oh ess, ess, ess," murmured the wives, wiping their mouths with their aprons. Then Mrs. Smith volunteered:

"Parson Beadon's to the church."

At this moment a black figure appeared from the little building, and after experiencing some difficulty in locking the church door behind him hurried down the path to meet the important visitors. Mr. Beadon, the rector of Clarehaven-cum-Cherringtons, was a tall, lean man, the ascetic cast of whose countenance had been tempered by matrimony as the indigestible loaf of his dogma had been leavened by expediency. Although Lord Clarehaven was patron of the living that included Great Cherrington, its church warden was a fierce squire who owned most of the land round; here Mr. Beadon was nearly evangelical, with nothing more vicious than a surpliced choir to mark the corruption of nineteen hundred years of Christianity. At Little Cherrington, where the dowager worshiped and where she had her stained-glass window of the fourth earl, he indulged in linen vestments as a dipsomaniac might indulge in herb beer; but at Clarehaven, with none except Mrs. Bitterplum and Mrs. Smith to mark his goings on, he used to have private orgies of hagiolatry, from one of which he was now returning.

After Mr. Beadon had greeted the dowager and the two girls he asked, anxiously, if Tony had arrived, and confided with the air of a very naughty boy that he had been holding a little celebration of St. Anthony with special intention for the happiness of the marriage. St. Anthony was not on the dowager's visiting-list, having no address in the Book of Common Prayer; but she could hardly be cross with the rector for observing his festival, inasmuch as he had the same name as her son. Mr. Beadon was a good man whose services at Little Cherrington were exactly what she wanted and who had, moreover, written an excellent history of Clarehaven and the Devonshire branch of the Clare family. At the same time, the bishop was also a good man, and she devoutly hoped that the Bohemianism of Mr. Beadon's services at Clarehaven would not take away what was left to his episcopal appetite from the claims of diabetes.

"One of Mrs. Bitterplum's children has been serving me," said Mr. Beadon. "Yes, it was an impressive little—Eucharist." He had brought his lips together for Mass, and Eucharist came out with such a cough that the dowager begged him not to take cold. Mrs. Bitterplum brought him out a cup of chocolate, a supply of which he kept in her cottage to assuage the pangs of hunger after his long walk and arduous ritual on an empty stomach. He swallowed the chocolate quickly, not to lose the pleasure of company back to Little Cherrington; but with all the heat and hurry of his late breakfast he could not stop talking.

"Mrs. Bitterplum is always kind enough—yes—curious old West Country name...."

Arabella and Constantia had turned away to hide their smiles.

"I have failed hitherto to trace its origin. No.... Oh, indeed yes, when you're ready, Lady Clarehaven. Good day to you, Mrs. Smith. Good day, and thank you, Mrs. Bitterplum."

The pony's head had been turned inland, and Mr. Beadon talked earnestly to the dowager while the chaise was driving slowly back. The topic of the marriage led him along the by-paths of family lore in numerous allusions to the historical importance of the various spots where the dowager lingered during her last drive as mistress of Clare; but the rector's discourse was so much intruded upon by gossip of nothing more than parochial interest that it will be simpler to give a direct abstract of the family history.

In the middle of the thirteenth century a younger member of the great family of Clare whose demesnes stretched east and west from Suffolk to Wales fell in with one of those pirate Mariscos that from Lundy Island swept the Bristol Channel for ships laden with food and wine; in the course of his seafaring he had discovered a cove on the north coast of Devonshire that struck him as an excellent center for piracy on his own account, notwithstanding that his chief patron had recently been hanged, drawn, and quartered. He fortified his cove with round towers at either entrance and thus created Clarehaven, where his descendants for a hundred years or more levied toll on passing traffic and made an alliance with the gentleman pirates of Fowey, whom in the reign of Edward III they helped to drive back the discomfited men of Kent from the west. The baser sort of pirates that in time came to haunt Lundy made the less professional exploits of the Clares no longer worth while, and before the close of the fourteenth century they had for many years abandoned the sea and were reaping a more peaceful harvest from the land. During the great days of Elizabeth the old spirit was reincarnate in one or two members of the family, who fared farther than the Bristol Channel and rounded fiercer capes than Land's End; but when in the early years of the seventeenth century a great storm drove the sea to overwhelm Clarehaven, there was not more to destroy than a few cottages belonging to the fishermen that were now all that remained of the medieval pirates. Then came the Great Rebellion, when Anthony Clare, Esquire, mustered his grooms and fishermen to meet Sir Bevil Grenville marching from Cornwall for the king. Finding large Roundhead forces at Bideford between him and Sir Bevil, he retired again to the obscurity of North Devon until the glorious Restoration, when with a relative he appeared in Parliament as member for the borough of Clarehaven, and was created a baronet by Charles II for his loyalty. Sir Anthony, with a borough in his pocket and two thousand acres of land on which to develop agriculture and choose a site for a house, abandoned what was left of the old pirate's keep and began to build Clare Court. He chose an aspect facing the sea, but died before the house was finished; Sir Gilbert, his son, being more interested in digging for badgers than for foundations, suspended building and contented himself with half a house. Sir Anthony, the third baronet, took after his great-grandfather and dreamed of sailing north to help the Earl of Mar in 1715. He must often have stood in that now walled-up doorway under the escutcheon of his house and gazed northward between the uplands to the sea; luckily for his successors the days were long past when a Clare could go on board his own ship lying at anchor in Clarehaven as snug as a horse in his stable. Sheriffmuir was far from Devon, but the news of that ambiguous battle reached the baronet before he had taken a rash step forward for a lost cause. Every night for thirty years he was carried to bed drunk, and, though he was never too drunk to sip from a goblet which had not been previously passed across a finger-bowl to the king over the water, he was too drunk and gouty to come out in '45. The nephew who succeeded him two years later worked hard for the second George to atone for his uncle's disaffection, and the family came to be favorably regarded at court. Sir William was a bachelor and hated the sea. When not at St. James's he used to live in Clare Lodge, a trim, red-brick house he had built for himself about a mile eastward of the family mansion, overlooking the hamlet of Little Cherrington and many desirable acres of common land.

Mr. Beadon was discoursing of Sir William when the dowager paused to admire the view from Clare Lodge. An excellent tenant had lately vacated it, and she was wondering how long it would be before she and the girls should be living there. She turned her attention once more to the rector's mild criticism of Sir William, who had not attempted to make Clarehaven a real borough, but who had bought Little Cherrington, and inclosed all the acres he coveted. When he died in 1764, his cousin Anthony enjoyed a tolerably rich inheritance, to which he added by marrying a Miss Arabella Hopley with a dowry of £10,000. This lady, by the death of her brother in a hunting accident, some years later became heiress of Hopley Hall and three thousand acres of good land adjoining the Clare estate; Sir Anthony loyally sent the two members for his borough, which by now was reduced to three or four cottages moldering at the tide's edge, to vote for the government; and on being rewarded in the year 1796 with the barony of Clarehaven, he decided to finish Clare Court. Before his succession he had spent a good deal of time at the famous health resort of Curtain Wells, and he was not satisfied with the sea view that did not include sunshine; it was he who pulled down the kitchens and stables behind and built the present front of Clare Court. His son Gilbert was prominent during the Napoleonic wars for seeing that his tenantry kept a lookout for Bonaparte; and by putting down smuggling he performed a vicarious penance for the deeds of his ancestors. It was he who completed Clare Court; and in 1816, ten years before his death, he was created Earl of Clarehaven and Viscount Clare, a peer of that United Kingdom lately achieved by Pitt with such a mixture of glory and shame. To mark his appreciation of the divine favor the first earl built at Little Cherrington a chapel-of-ease to Clarehaven church, the congregation of which by that time was the three electors of the borough. He then bought the living of Great Cherrington, and presented this shamrock of a cure to his natural son, who became rector of Clarehaven-cum-Cherringtons. This gentleman paid a curate £40 a year to look after the three churches and was last seen in an intoxicated condition on the quay of Boulogne harbor.

The present incumbent, who was anxious that the dowager should not object to a step up he proposed to take next Easter by introducing colored vestments at Little Cherrington and linen vestments at Great Cherrington for those very early services that fierce Squire Kingdon would never get up to attend, perhaps alluded to the history of his predecessor in order to emphasize his own superiority. It was all very discreetly done, even to selecting the moment when the two girls were examining a shepherd's sick dog and therefore out of hearing.

"How different from the late lord," Mr. Beadon sighed. "Mrs. Beadon"—the rector paid tribute to his outraged celibacy by never referring to her as his wife—"Mrs. Beadon often wonders why I don't write a special memoir of him."

The dowager gazed affectionately at the chlorotic window by Burne-Jones.

"Perhaps his life was too quiet," she said. "I think the window is enough."

"*Claro non clango.* But when Mr. Kingdon dies," said the rector, tartly, "I understand that Mrs. Kingdon will erect an organ to *his* memory."

They passed out of the church and stood looking down into the lap of the fair landscape outspread before them, talking of other ancestors: of Richard, the second earl, who married the daughter of a marquis and saw Clarehaven disfranchised in 1832, by which time the borough was so rotten that there was nothing perceptible of it except a few seaweed-covered stones at low tide; it was he who destroyed a couple of good farms to provide himself with a park worthy of his rank, which he inclosed with a stone wall and planted trees, the confines of which his descendants now tried proudly to trace in the wintry haze. Lest any want of patriotism should be imputed to the second earl, Mr. Beadon reminded his listeners of how Geoffrey, the third earl, did his duty to his country, first as a member of Parliament for one of the divisions of Devonshire, when he showed the Whigs that the disfranchisement of his borough was not enough to keep a Clare out of Parliament, and afterward as Lord Lieutenant of the county; his duty to his sovereign by acting as Vice-Chamberlain to her Majesty's household. Of his son Gilbert, the fourth earl, enough has been said; though it may be added here that he sold Hopley Hall and many acres besides.

"On the whole, though, I think he was right," said Mr. Beadon. "These Radicals, you know."

"Come and have lunch with us," the dowager invited.

It would be the last independent hospitality she could offer at Clare Court.

II

While the dowager was presiding over lunch at Clare for the last time, while her daughters were getting more and more openly excited about the arrival of their sister-in-law, and while even Mr. Beadon partook of their excitement to such an extent that he ate much less than usual, Dorothy was sitting down to lunch in the restaurant-car of the Western express. Her old life was being left behind more rapidly and with less regret than the country through which the train was traveling. Happiness always widens the waist of an hour-glass. Dorothy was so happy in being a countess that on this railway journey time and space passed with equal speed; and she looked so happy that all those who recognized her or were informed by one of the waiters who she was commented upon her radiant air. They decided with that credulous sentimentality imported into Great Britain with Hengist and Horsa that she must be very deeply in love with her husband; no one suspected that she might be more deeply in love with herself. The head waiter, anxious to pay his own humble tribute to the happy pair, removed the vase of faded flowers from the table they occupied and put in its place another vase of equally faded flowers. If he could have changed the lunch as easily, no doubt he would have done so, but train lunches are as immemorial as elms, and it would have taken more than the marriage of a Vanity girl to a Devonshire nobleman to persuade the Great Western Railway Company that sauce tartare is not the only condiment, and that there are more fish in the sea than the anemic brill.

In days now mercifully forever fled Dorothy had often admired with a touch of envy the select minority of the human race that seemed able to obtain from the staff of a great railway station all the attention it wanted. Now she had entered that select minority, and perhaps nothing brought home more sharply the fact that she was a countess than the attitude of the station-master at Exeter.

"Welcome back to the West, my lord," he said to Clarehaven, who thanked him for his good wishes with the casual rudeness that minor officials of all countries find so attractive in their acknowledged patrons.

A perspiring woman with a little boy in her arms clutched the station-master's sleeve and begged to be informed if the express that was now lying along the platform like a great sleek snake was the slow train to whatever insignificant market-town she was bound. It was annoying for the station-master to have his little chat with Lord Clarehaven interrupted like this, especially by a woman who seemed under the impression that he was a porter. However, the official possessed a store of nobility from which to oblige an importunate inferior, and majestically he condescended to reveal that the slow train would leave in half an hour from the obscure platform it haunted. The station-master was forthwith invited to look after a much-dinted tin box while the perspiring and anxious creature's little boy was accommodated in the cloak-room; before he could protest she had darted off.

"Wonderful what they expect you to do for them, isn't it?" he laughed, with the lordly magnanimity that once inspired the English nation with confidence in the capacity of its chosen representatives to rule the world. At this moment a porter announced that his lordship's car was in the station-yard.

"Be under no apprehensions about your baggage, my lord," said the station-master. "I shall expedite it myself. Be under no apprehensions," he repeated; "it will certainly reach Cherrington Lanes to-night."

The porter, who was as eager as his chief to show his appreciation of being employed at a railway station patronized by Lord and Lady Clarehaven, overstepped the bounds of good will by picking up the perspiring woman's tin box in order to place it in the car. Luckily his chief perceived the horrible mistake in time and bellowed at him to take it out and leave it on the pavement outside the station. Then raising his cap, a gesture reserved for noblemen and irritation of the scalp, the station-master bowed Lord and Lady Clarehaven upon their way.

"Car going well, Deacock?"

"Not too well, my lord."

"Make the old thing hum, because I want her ladyship to reach Clarehaven before dark."

The chauffeur touched his cap, and the car answered generously to his efforts in spite of continual criticisms leveled against it by the owner.

"We must get a Lee-Lonsdale," he said to his wife.

"That would be very nice for Lonnie," she agreed. "Mine, of course, was more a car for town. So I sold it."

She did not add that her own Lee-Lonsdale had provided her with a bracelet of rubies.

"The setting is new," she had said to Tony when she showed him this heirloom. "But the stones are old."

And who should have contradicted her?

The green miles were rolled up like a length of silk; milestones fluttered like paper in the wake of the car; and by five o'clock they were driving through the lodge gates. Mrs. Crawley with nine little Crawleys, the fruit of Mr. Crawley's spare time from the peach-house at Clare, flung a few primroses into the car and cheered their new lady. Dorothy thought the primroses were very pretty and stood up to nod her thanks; she did not realize that even an earl's estate in Devonshire might find it hard to produce so many primroses in the month of January; but she looked so beautiful standing up in the car that Mrs. Crawley felt the exertions of her large and ubiquitous family were well rewarded. The car leaped forward again, followed by shrill cheers that lingered upon the evening air and echoed many times in Dorothy's heart. The spellbound hush of landed property held earth in thrall, and the countess wished to enjoy it.

"Not too fast through the park," she begged.

The car slowed down; at the top of the first incline from which the house was visible it stopped to give Dorothy a moment in which to admire her great possessions. The whole sky was plumed with multitudinous small clouds rosy as the ruffled throats of linnets in spring; on the summit of the last long incline before them Clare Court with its gardens and terraces and gleaming pergola dreamed in the enchantment of the wintry sunsets; in the dark groves on either side the trunks of the pines glowed like pillars of fire. Nothing broke the stillness except a mistlethrush singing very loud from an oak-tree close at hand, and when the bird was silent the lowing of a cow far away on some other earth, it seemed. Suddenly from woodland near the drive came a sound like pattering leaves; a line of fallow deer rippled forth and broke into startled groups that nosed the air now vibrant with the noise of dogs approaching.

"How lovely!" Dorothy exclaimed. "You never told me there were deer," she added, reproachfully, as if the absence of deer had been the one thing that all this time had kept her from accepting Clarehaven's hand. "And how divine it must be here in summer."

"Well, if you hadn't been such a timid little deer, we might have been here, anyway, last October."

Dorothy might have retorted that if Clarehaven had not been so bold a hart she might have been here the summer before last; but she did not remind him of that little flat round the corner, because the herd dashed off to a more remote corner of the park at sight of several dogs scampering down the drive with loud yaps of excitement, and Tony's sisters running behind. Dorothy jumped out of the car to meet her relations for the first time, glad to encounter them like this with dogs barking and so much of the conversation directed to keeping them in order, for she had half expected in that preludial hush to behold the dowager materializing from the misty dusk like a gigantic genie from an uncorked jar.

"Only two hours from Exeter. Pretty good for the old boneshaker, what?" said Tony. "Deacock drove her along like a thoroughbred."

The chauffeur touched his cap and, smiling complacently, leaned over to pat the tires of the car.

"Mother's waiting at the house," said Arabella. "She would have driven down in the chaise to meet Dorothy, but she didn't know exactly when you'd be here and was so afraid of catching cold just when she most wanted not to."

There followed a stream of gossip about the health of various animals, and about the way Marlow, the head-keeper, was looking forward to shooting Cherrington Long Covert, and how much afraid he had been that Tony would not be back before the end of the month, and how glad he was that he was back, in the middle of which Constantia informed Dorothy that there was a meet at Five Tree Farm two days hence and asked her if she was going to hunt for the rest of the season. Arabella kicked her sister so clumsily that Dorothy noticed the warning, and with a sudden impulse to risk all, even death, in the attempt, she replied that of course she intended to hunt for the rest of the season. Tony began to protest, but she cut him short.

"My dear boy, when I lived with my grandmother I always hunted. And I've kept up riding ever since."

"Well, that's topping," exclaimed Connie.

"Yes, that really is topping," echoed Arabella.

"But alas! I don't shoot," Dorothy confessed, "so if it won't bore you too much you'll have to give me lessons."

"Oh, rather," began Connie, immediately. "Well, you see, the most important thing is not to look across your barrels. I find that most people—Well, for instance, supposing you put up a woodcock...."

"I say, Connie, shut up, shut up," Tony exclaimed. "You can't begin at once. You'll put our eyes out in the car with that stick."

The shooting-lesson was postponed; and clambering into the car, in another five minutes they had all reached the house. Dorothy's first emotion at sight of the dowager was relief at finding that she was quite a head shorter than herself. In spite of Napoleon, height is, on the whole, an advantage to human beings in moments of stress. Dorothy had involuntarily imagined her mother-in-law as a tall, beaked woman with a cold and flashing eye, in fact with all the attributes the well-informed novelist usually awards to dowagers. This dowdy little woman, whose slight resemblance to a beaver was emphasized by wearing a cape made of that animal's fur, had to stand on tiptoe to greet her daughter-in-law, and it was unreasonable to be frightened of a woman who in an emotional crisis had to stand on tiptoe. Nevertheless, Dorothy was sincerely grateful for her kindly welcome, and took the first opportunity of whispering some of her hopes and fears for the future to her mother-in-law, who invited her, after tea, to come up-stairs to her den and have a little talk. When they entered the small square room in an angle of the house twilight was still sapphire upon the window-panes, one of which looked out over the park and the other mysteriously down into the grove of pines. Fussing about with matches, the dowager explained apologetically that she preferred always to trim and light her own lamp.

"One gets these little fads living in the depths of the country."

"Of course," Dorothy agreed, planning with herself some similar fad for the near future.

The lamp was lighted; the windows changed from sapphire to indigo as the jewel changes when it is no longer held against the light; in the golden glow the walls of the room broke into blossom, it seemed. Dorothy, reacting from Mr. and Mrs. Caffyn's taste in domestic decoration, had supposed that all well-bred and artistic people devoted themselves to plain color schemes such as she had elaborated in the Halfmoon Street flat; but here was a kind of decoration that, though she knew instinctively it could not be impeached on the ground of bad taste, did astonish her by its gaudiness. Such a prodigality of brilliant red-and-blue macaws, of claret-winged pompadouras and birds of paradise swooping from bough to bough of such brilliant foliage; such sprawling purple convolvuluses and cleft crimson pomegranates on the trellised screen; such quaint old china groups on the mantelpiece; such tumble-down chairs and faded holland covers; and everywhere, like fruit fallen from those tropic boughs, such vividly colored balls of wool.

"Oh," exclaimed Dorothy, divining in a flash of inspiration how to make the most of her totem, "it's exactly like my grandmother's room!"

"I am fond of my little den," said the dowager, "and as long as you so kindly want me to stay on at Clare I hope you won't turn me out of it."

Dorothy expostulated with a gesture; she would have liked to show her appreciation of the room in some perfect compliment, but she could think of nothing better than to suggest sharing it, a prospect that she did not suppose would attract her mother-in-law.

"I feel a dreadful intruder," she sighed.

"My dear child, please. I might have known that Tony would have chosen well for himself, and I do hope you understand—I tried to explain to you in my letter—how old-fashioned and out of the world we are down here. My husband was a very quiet man, and for the last ten years of his life a great invalid. The result was that I scarcely appreciated how things had changed in the world, and I foolishly fancied that Tony was just as much of a country cousin as myself. His sudden departure to Africa like that came as a great shock to me. One scarcely realizes down here that there is such a place as Africa." Heaven and her wall-paper were the only scenes of tropical luxuriance in the imagination of which the dowager indulged herself. "And, of course, my mother was very much upset at the idea of the marriage."

Dorothy started. Was there, then, a super-dowager to be encountered?

"I see that Tony has not told you about her. Chatfield Hall, where my brother lives, whom you will learn to know and love as Uncle Chat, is only fifteen miles from Clare."

Dorothy did not know how to prevent her mother-in-law's perceiving her mortification; to think that in her long study of Debrett she had omitted to make herself acquainted with what was therein recorded of the family of Fanhope! Really she did not deserve to be a countess!

"My mother," went on the dowager, "who as you've no doubt guessed is now an extremely old lady, was inclined to blame me for Tony's choice. She has always been accustomed to expect a good deal from her children. Even Uncle Chat has never yet ventured to introduce a motor-car to Chatfield. So you must not be disappointed if at first she's a little brusk. Poor old darling, she's almost blind, but her hearing is as acute as ever, and oh dear, I am so glad you have a pretty voice."

"Did you think I should have a cockney accent?" Dorothy asked.

"Well, to be frank, the contingency had presented itself," the dowager admitted. "And I am so glad you don't use too much scent. I know everybody uses scent nowadays, but my mother, whose sense of smell is even more acute than her hearing, abominates scent. It does seem so ironical that she should have kept her sense of smell and almost lost her sight. You mustn't be frightened by her; but if you are you must remember that we're all frightened by her, which ought to be a great consolation. I thought we would drive over and see her to-morrow. It would be nice to feel that the ice was broken."

"Even if I do get rather wet," Dorothy laughed.

The dowager smiled anxiously; she was not used to extensions of familiar phrases, and her daughter-in-law's remark made her sharply aware that a stranger was in the house.

"You think you'd rather wait a day or two before you go?" she suggested.

"Oh no, I think we ought to go and see Lady Chatfield as soon as possible," said Dorothy.

"I'm so glad you agree with me."

"I'm rather sensitive where mothers are concerned," said Dorothy.

She felt that now was her moment to win the dowager immovably to her side. There was something in the atmosphere of this gay little room, some intimacy as of a garden long tended by a gentle and lonely soul, that invited a contribution from one who was privileged to enter it like this. Dorothy felt that the room needed "playing up to." The medium that tempted her was the fairy-tale; a room like this was meant for fairy-tales.

"I told you, didn't I, that this room reminded me of my grandmother's room, and what you tell me about Lady Chatfield reminds me a little of her character. My grandmother was a Lonsdale, a descendant of a younger branch of the Cleveden Lonsdales. Her husband was an Irish landowner called Doyle who was involved somehow with political troubles. I don't quite know what happened, but he lost most of his money and died quite suddenly soon after my mother was born. My grandmother came back to England with her little daughter and settled down in Warwickshire, her native county. When my mother was quite young—about twenty—she fell in love with my father, who was reading for Holy Orders in the neighborhood. My grandmother opposed the match, but my mother ran away, and my father, instead of becoming a clergyman, took up rescue work in the slums."

"A fine thing to do," the dowager commented, approvingly.

"Yes, but unfortunately my grandmother was very proud and very unreasonable. She never forgave my mother, although she had me to live with her until I was eleven, when she died. I was brought up in the depths of the country and ever since I have always longed to get back to it. I used to ride with friends of my grandmother. One of them was the Duke of Ayr. Did you ever meet him? He died the other day, but of course I hadn't seen him for many years."

"I did meet him long ago," said the dowager. "He was a great influence for good in the country."

"Oh, a wonderful man," Dorothy agreed. "Well, the few family heirlooms my grandmother still possessed were left to me, together with a small sum of money, which I'm sorry to say my father spent. That was my excuse for going on the stage. I told him that it was his fault and his fault only that I had to earn my own living. But the rescue work had affected his common sense. He turned me out of the house. I lived for a whole year on fifty pounds. But I was determined to succeed, and when I met Tony and he asked me to marry him I refused, because I had grown proud. You can understand that, can't you? Tell me, dear Lady Clarehaven, that you can understand my anxiety to prove that I could be a success. Besides, when I was a child the estrangement between my mother and my grandmother had greatlyaffected my imagination. I didn't want to find myself the cause of estranging another mother from her son. Have you forgiven me? Do you think that you will ever love me?"

The dowager wept and declared that as soon as her own mother was pacified she should make it her business to reconcile Dorothy with hers.

"Oh no," cried Dorothy, "that's impossible. My father must learn a little humility first. When he has learned his lesson I will be reconciled with my family, but meanwhile haven't you a place in your heart for me?"

The dowager, so far as it was possible for a small woman to perform the action with one so much taller than herself, clasped Dorothy to her heart.

"How I wish my husband were alive to be with us this evening," she exclaimed.

It was probably as well that he was not; if he had been, neither age nor decency would have intervened to prevent the fourth earl from making love to his daughter-in-law. The fifth earl interrupted any further exchanges of confidences by bursting into the room to protest against his wife's desertion.

"Your mother has been so sweet to me, Tony," she said.

"Of course she has," he answered. "She knows what I've had to go through to bring off this coup."

"Indeed," the dowager confessed, "I never suspected he had such determination. Dear old boy, it only seems yesterday that he was such a little boy, and now—" She broke off with a sigh and patted him on the shoulder.

"Your mother and I have just decided that it would be best if I am presented to Lady Chatfield to-morrow," Dorothy announced.

"What?" cried Clarehaven. "No. Look here! Steady, mother! I'm absolutely against that. I'm sorry to appear the undutiful grandson and all that, but really, don't you know, I must discourage her a bit. I didn't bring Dorothy down to Clare to be buzzing over to Chatfield all the time. We'll get Uncle Chat over here to dinner one night, and that'll be quite enough."

The dowager looked appealingly at her daughter-in-law, who at once took matters into her own hands.

"Don't be absurd, Tony. Of course we shall go to-morrow."

He would have continued to protest, but his wife fixed him with those deep-brown eyes of hers.

"Now, don't go on arguing, there's a dear boy, or your mother will think we do nothing but quarrel."

Tony was silent, and the dowager regarded her daughter-in-law with open admiration. She had never seen one of the males of Clare or Fanhope quelled so completely since the days when she was a little girl and saw her own fierce old mother quell her husband.

That night in the bridal chamber of Clare the fifth earl chose a not altogether suitable costume of pink-silk pajamas in which to give utterance to his plans for the future. If Dorothy had been beautiful in the dowager's bower, she was much more fatally beautiful now in a dishabille of peach bloom and with her fawn-colored hair glinting in the candle-light against the dark panels of this ancient and somber room. When Clarehaven began to walk up and down in the excitement of his projects she went slowly across to a Caroline chair with high wicker back, sitting down in which she waited severely and serenely until he had finished. Tony might prance about in his pajamas, but he was no more free than a colt which a horse-breaker holds in tether to be jerked down upon his four legs when he has kicked his heels long enough.

"I didn't marry you," her husband was protesting, "to come and live down here and be ruled by Grandmother Chatfield. I don't give a damn for my grandmother; she's a meddlesome old woman who ought to have been dead ten years ago. As for Uncle Chat, he bores me to death. He can only talk about cigars and pigs. Look here, Doodles, we're going to stay here three or four more days, and then we're off to the Riviera. We'll make Lonnie come with us and drive down through France—topping roads—and I want to try the pigeons at Monte. After that I thought we'd go to Cairo, or perhaps we might go to Cairo first and take Monte on the way back. Anyway, Curzon Street will be ready by the beginning of May. I'm having it devilishly comfortably done up. I didn't tell you about that; it's going to be the most comfortable house in London. I tried every chair myself in Waring's. I'm sorry I had to bore you at all with my family, but I'm awfully fond of my mother, and I knew she wouldn't be happy till she'd seen you, and all that. Well, now it's done, and we can buzz on again as soon as possible."

"Any more plans?" asked Dorothy.

"No, I thought we'd go up to Scotland for August, and after that I don't see why we shouldn't have a good shoot here in September. But I haven't thought much about next autumn."

"That's where I'm cleverer than you," said his wife. "I've not only thought about next autumn, but about next week, and about next year, and the year after that, and the year after that, too. Listen, old thing. When you first met me you wanted to put me in a little flat round the corner, didn't you? Please don't interrupt me. You couldn't understand then why I wouldn't accept your offer; I don't think you really understand very much better even now. London for me doesn't exist any longer. How you can possibly expect me to go away from this glorious place, which I already love as if I'd lived here all my life, to tear about the Continent with you as if I wasn't your wife at all, I don't know. If you don't realize what you owe to your name, I realize it. I don't choose that people should say: 'There goes that ass Clarehaven who married a girl from the Vanity. Look at him!' I don't choose that people should point you out as my husband. I choose to be your wife, and I intend that all your family—and when I say your family I mean your mother's family, too—shall go down on their knees and thank God that you did marry a Vanity girl, and that a Vanity girl knew what she owed to her country in these dreadful days when common Radicals are trying to destroy all that we hold most sacred. I want you to take your place in the House of Lords, when you've lost that trick of talking to everybody as if they were waiters at the Savoy. Why, you don't deserve to be an earl!"

"My dear thing, you mustn't attach too much importance to a title. You must remember...."

"Are you trying to correct my tone?" she asked, coldly. "Because, let me tell you that all this false modesty about your position is only snobbery dressed out in a new disguise. Anyway, I didn't marry you to be criticized."

"Oh well, of course, if you insist on staying down here for the present I suppose I must," said Tony. "Anyway, I dare say we can have some jolly parties to cheer the place up a bit."

"No, we sha'n't have any jolly parties—at any rate yet awhile," said Dorothy. "I don't intend to begin by turning Clare gardens into bear gardens."

"Good Heavens! what is the matter with you?" he demanded. "What has my mother been saying?"

"Your mother hasn't been saying anything. I said all these things over to myself a thousand thousand times before I married you."

"Well, why didn't you tell me some of your ideas before you did marry me?" he muttered.

"Do you regret it?" she asked, standing up.

"Don't be a silly old thing, Doodles. Of course I don't regret it. But having married the loveliest girl in London, I should like to splash around a bit with you. My tastes are bonhomous. I'd always thought.... Dash it, I love you madly, you know that. I'm proud of you."

"Aren't you proud that the loveliest girl in London is willing to be loved by you only? God! my dear boy, you ought to be grateful that you've got me to yourself."

She held out her arms, and it was not remarkable that in those arms and with those lips Clarehaven forgot all about driving along the topping roads of France in a Lee-Lonsdale car. When his wife released him from the first real embrace she had ever given him he staggered like one who has been enchanted.

"Dash it...." he murmured, blinking his eyes to quench the fire that burned them. "I'm not very poetical, don't you know—but your kisses—well, really, do you know I think I shall take to reading poetry?"

III

The next morning Dorothy paced the picture-gallery of Clare that ran the whole length of the north side of the house. She had several ordeals to pass in the few days immediately ahead, and she derived much help from the contemplation of her predecessors at Clare. Gradually from the glances of those tranquil dames, some of whom for more than two centuries had gazed seaward through the panes of those high narrow windows mistily iridescent from a thousand salt gales, Dorothy caught an attitude toward life; from their no longer perturbable expressions, from their silent testimony to the insignificance of everything in the backward of time, she acquired confidence in herself. What was old Lady Chatfield except a picture, and how could she harm an interloper even more vulnerable than an actress? She should try this afternoon to think of the super-dowager as one of the long row of noble dames and console herself with the thought that in another hundred years the fifth Countess of Clarehaven would be accounted the loveliest of all the ladies in this gallery. Who was there to outmatch her? Even the first countess, with all Romney had yielded from his magic store of roses, would have to admit she was surpassed by her successor.

"But who shall paint my portrait?" Dorothy asked herself. "Romney should be alive now. There's no painter as good as he for my style of beauty. And how shall I be painted? If I manage to ride to hounds as triumphantly as I hope I shall, I might be painted in a riding-habit. The black would set off my hair and my complexion and my figure. I don't want everybody at the Academy to say that my dress is so wonderful, as if without a dress I should be nothing. Thirty years from now I will be painted again in some wonderful dress. But oh, if only I don't fail at the meet on Monday! If only—if only...."

At lunch Tony suggested that he should drive Dorothy to Chatfield in the car and that his mother and sisters should go in the barouche. The dowager reminded him how much his grandmother objected to motor-cars at Chatfield and urged that it was unfair on Dorothy to irritate the old lady wantonly.

"I never heard such nonsense," Tony exclaimed. "She'll soon be expecting us to row over to Chatfield in the Ark. Well, I sha'n't go at all. You and Dorothy had better drive over together in the victoria."

The dowager threw out a signal of distress to her daughter-in-law, who said firmly but kindly that they would all drive over together in the drag.

"We shall look like a village treat," muttered Tony, sulkily.

"But I'm anxious to see the country," said Dorothy. "And you drive much too fast in the car for me to see anything. I don't want to arrive blown to pieces."

Naturally in the end Dorothy had her way about going in the drag, and she wondered what Tony could have wished better than to swing through the gates of Chatfield Park and pull up with a clatter at the gates of Chatfield Hall. The very sound of the footman's feet alighting on the gravel drive was like a seal upon the dignity of their arrival. Uncle Chat came out to greet them, a round, red-faced man with short side-whiskers, dressed in a pepper-and-salt suit. He had been a widower for ten years, but his wife before she died—slowly frightened to death by her mother-in-law, as malicious story-tellers said—had left him two sons and two daughters. Paignton, the eldest boy, was a freshman at Trinity, Cambridge, and was at present away on a visit; Charles, the second boy, was still at home, with Eton looming in a day or so; Dorothy liked his fresh complexion and the schoolboy impudence that not even his grandmother had been able to squash. She told him that she was going to hunt on Monday for the first time for several years, and he promised to be her equerry and show her some gaps that might be welcome.

"But it's not difficult country," he assured her. "Not like Ireland."

"No. My great-grandfather was killed by an Irish wall," she said.

Tony looked up at this. Perhaps he was thinking that if she rode as recklessly as she talked she really would be killed out hunting. Of the other easy members of the family Mary and Maud were jolly girls still in the thrall of a governess, while Lady Jane, Tony's aunt, was milder even than his mother, and, having now been for over fifty years at the super-dowager's beck and call, had the look of one who is always listening for bells.

521

The super-dowager herself lived in a self-propelling invalid chair in which, though she was reputed to be blind, she propelled herself about the ground floor of Chatfield with as much agility as the mole, another animal whose blindness is probably exaggerated. Beyond occasionally knocking over a table, she did more damage with her tongue than with her chair and kept the kitchen in a state of continuous alarm. One of her favorite pastimes was to coast down the long corridor that divided them from the rest of the house, and, pulling up suddenly beside the cook, to accuse her of burning whatever dish she was preparing. The only servants at Chatfield who felt at all secure were those high-roosting birds, the housemaids.

"Who's making all this noise?" demanded the super-dowager, advancing rapidly into the hall soon after the Clarehaven party had arrived, and scattering the group right and left.

"Tony has brought his wife to see you," said her daughter. "They only reached Clare last night."

"Tony's wife?" repeated the old lady. "And who may she be? Chatfield, if Paignton marries an actress you understand that I leave here at once? I've made that quite clear, I hope?"

"If you have, Lady Chatfield," said Dorothy, "I'm sure that Paignton won't marry an actress."

"Who's that talking to me?"

At this moment Arabella and Constantia, who, because their noses were respectively too small and too large, easily caught cold, sneezed simultaneously.

"Augusta," said the super-dowager.

"Yes, mamma."

"Don't tell me that's not Bella and Connie, because I know it is. Can nothing be done about their taking cold like this? They never come here but they must go sneezing and sniffing about, until one might suppose Chatfield was draughty."

Considering that for her peregrinations the super-dowager insisted upon every door of the ground floor's being left open, one might have been justified in supposing so.

"Where's that girl?" demanded the old lady. "Why doesn't she come close? Has she got a cold, too?"

"No, no," laughed Dorothy, "I haven't got a cold."

"Your voice is pleasant, child," said the super-dowager. "Augusta, her voice is pleasant. Chatfield, her voice is pleasant. Clarehaven, come here. Your wife has a pleasant voice."

"Of course she has," said the grandson. "You ought to have heard her sing 'Dolly and her Collie.'"

If looks could have killed her husband, Dorothy would have been the third dowager present at that moment; but strange to say, the old lady seemed to like the idea of Dorothy's singing.

"She *shall* sing me 'Dolly and her Collie'; she shall sing it to me after tea. Come, let's have tea," and, giving a violent twirl to her wheel, the old lady shot forward in advance of the party toward the drawing-room, beating by a neck the footman at the door, who in order to avoid dropping the tray had to perform a pirouette like a comic juggler.

"Why did you make me look such a fool?" Dorothy muttered to Tony at the first opportunity.

"My dear girl, believe me, I'm the only person who knows how to manage the silly old thing."

Dorothy was miserable all through tea, wondering if the super-dowager was really in earnest about making her sing. She wondered what the servants would think, what her mother-in-law would think, what her uncle would think, what her new cousins would think, what the whole county of Devon would think, what all England would think of her humiliation. Perhaps the old lady was not in earnest. Perhaps it was merely a test of her dignity. Were ever sandwiches in the world so dry as these?

"What's that?" the super-dowager was exclaiming. "Certainly not! Nobody can hear this song except myself. I should never dream of allowing a public performance at Chatfield. This is not a performance. This is a contribution to my miserable old age."

The old lady swooped about the room like a hen driving intruding sparrows from her grain; when all were banished she swung rapidly backward and commanded Dorothy to begin. Poor Dorothy tried to explain how the effect of the song had depended upon the accessories. There had been the music, for instance.

"Never mind about the music," said the super-dowager.

"And there was a chorus of six."

"Never mind about the chorus."

"And then I haven't got my dog."

"Never mind about the dog."

Dorothy, who had thought that she had put "Dolly and her Collie" behind her forever, had to stand up and sing to Lady Chatfield as she had sung to Mr. Richards in the cupola of the Vanity not so many months ago.

"The words are rubbish," said the old lady. "The tune is catchy, but not so catchy as the tunes they used to write. Your voice is pleasant. Come nearer to me, child. They tell me you're handsome. Yes, well, I can almost see that you are. And I'm glad of it, for the Clares are an ugly race."

Considering that the super-dowager was directly responsible for Tony's mother, and therefore partially responsible for Arabella and Constantia, this opinion struck Dorothy as lacking proportion.

"Beauty is required in the family. You understand what I mean? Let's have none of these modern notions of waiting five or six years before you do your duty. Produce an heir."

The old lady said this so sharply that Dorothy felt as if she ought to put her hand in her pocket and produce one then and there.

"Call Tony in to me. Tony," she said, "you're an ass; but not such an ass as I thought you were."

"Good song, isn't it, grandmother?" he chuckled.

"Don't interrupt me. I said you were only not such an ass as I thought. You're still an ass. Your wife isn't. You understand what I mean? Produce an heir. Now I must go to bed." She swept out of the room like a swallow from under the eaves of a house.

On the way back to Clare, Bella and Connie could not contain their delight at the success Dorothy had made with their grandmother. Tompkins, the Chatfield butler, had confided in Connie just before she left that her ladyship had been heard to hum on entering her bedroom—an expression of superfluous good temper in which she had not indulged within his memory. The old lady was always cross at going to bed, probably because she could not wheel it about like her chair. Nor was grandmother the only victim to Dorothy's charm: Uncle Chat had been full of compliments; Charles and the girls had declared she was a stunner; Aunt Jane had corroborated Tompkins's story about humming.

The dowager, who always came away from Chatfield with a sense of renewed youth, though sometimes, indeed, feeling like a naughty little girl, was almost sprightly on the drive back to Clare. She had expected to be roundly scolded by her mother, and here she was going away with her pockets full of nuts, as it were; the little anxieties of daily life dropped from her shoulders, and when the drag met a very noisy motor in a narrow stretch of road she sat perfectly still and listened to the coachman's soothing clicks with profound trust in his ability to calm the horses.

"By the way, I hope you won't mind the suggestion, dear," she said to Dorothy, "but I think it would be nice to arrange a little dinner-party for Saturday night—just our particular neighbors, you know—Mr. and Mrs. Kingdon, Mr. and Mrs. Beadon, Mr. Hemming the curate, Doctor Lane, and Mr. Greenish of Cherrington Cottage."

Tony groaned.

"What could be nicer?" said Dorothy. "But...."

"You're going to say it sounds rather sudden. Yes—well, it will be sudden. But it struck me that it would be much nicer if we were a little sudden. You see, your wedding was rather sudden, and our neighbors will appreciate such a mark of intimacy. No doubt the Kingdons and the Beadons will have called this afternoon, and I thought that if you don't object I would send out the invitations myself and make it a sort of wedding breakfast. I know it all sounds very muddled, but my inspirations nearly always turn out well. I should like to feel on Sunday that we were all old friends. Besides, if you're really going to hunt on Monday, it will be nice for you to meet Mr. Kingdon, who is master of the Horley."

"I think it's a delightful idea," Dorothy exclaimed. "Thank you so much for suggesting it."

"This is going to be a terrible winter and spring," Clarehaven groaned.

"Tony, please don't be discouraging," said his mother. "I'm feeling so optimistic since our visit to Chatfield. Why, I'm even hoping to reconcile Mr. Kingdon and Mr. Beadon. Not, of course, that they're open enemies, but I should like the squire to appreciate the rector's beautiful character, and it seems such a pity that a few lighted candles should blind him to it. Mr. Kingdon will take in Dorothy; the rector will take me; you, Tony dear—please don't look so cross—ought to take in Mrs. Kingdon, who's a great admirer of yours—such a nice woman, Dorothy dear, with a most unfortunate inability to roll her r's—it's so sad, I think. Then the doctor will take in Mrs. Beadon; Mr. Greenish, Arabella; and Mr. Hemming, Connie."

"I like Tommy Hemming," said Connie. "He's a sport."

"I should call him a freak," Clarehaven muttered.

"We ought to do some riding to-morrow and Friday," his sister went on, quite unconcerned by his opinion of the curate. "I think Dorothy ought to ride Mignonette on Monday. She's a perfect ripper—a chestnut."

Dorothy liked the name, which reminded her of her own hair, and certainly had she chosen for herself she would have chosen a chestnut for the meet at Five Tree Farm. The dowager's forecast was right—both the Kingdons and the Beadons had called upon the new countess, and the dowager pattered up-stairs to her bird-bright room to send out invitations for Saturday.

"You see what you've let yourself in for," said Tony to his wife that night. "However, you'll be as fed up as I am when you've had one or two of these neighborly little dinners. And look here, Doodles, seriously I don't think you ought to hunt. I'm not saying you can't ride, but you ought to wait till next season, at any rate. You may have a nasty accident, and—well, yes, I'm the one to say it, after all—you may make a priceless fool of yourself."

"Do you think so?" Dorothy asked. "Do you think I made a priceless fool of myself when I sang to your grandmother this afternoon? If I can carry that off, I can certainly ride after a fox. Kiss me. You mean well, but you don't yet know what I can do."

A former Anthony kissed away kingdoms and provinces; this Anthony kissed away doubts and fears and scruples as easily.

Dorothy dressed herself very simply for the neighborly little dinner-party. She decided that white would be the best sedative for any tremors felt by the neighbors at the prospect of finding their society led by an actress; and she made up her mind to cast a special spell upon the M. F. H. and so guard herself from the consequences of any mistake she might make at the meet. There was nothing about Mr. Kingdon that diverged the least from the typical fox-hunting squire that for two hundred years has been familiar to the people of Great Britain. His neck was thick and red; his voice came in gusts; and he recounted as good stories of his own the jokes in *Punch* of the week before last. What deeper sense in Squire Kingdon was outraged by the rector's ritualism it would be hard to say, for his body did not appear to be the temple of anything except food and drink; perhaps, like the bull that he so much resembled, an imperfectly understood nervous system was wrought upon by certain colors. The congregation of Great Cherrington would scarcely have been stirred from their lethargic worship to see the squire with lowered head charge up the aisle, when Mr. Beadon began to play the picador with a colored stole, and toss Mr. Beadon over his shoulders into the font. Mrs. Kingdon was to her husband as a radish is to a beet-root. The weather is a bad lady's maid, and the weather had made of Mrs. Kingdon's complexion something that ought to have infuriated her husband as much as Mr. Beadon's colored stoles. In spite of her hard and highly colored appearance, she was a mild enough woman, given to deep sighs in pauses of the conversation, when she was probably thinking about the rolling of her r's and regretting that three of her children had inherited this impotency of palate or tongue.

"We must all pull together," she said to Dorothy, who expressed her anxiety to find herself lugging at the same rope as Mrs. Kingdon against whatever team opposed them.

"Very true, Mrs. Kingdon," the rector observed. "I wish the squire was always of your opinion."

"Mr. Beadon can never forget that he is a clergyman," whispered Mrs. Kingdon when the rector passed on.

Yet the monotone of Mr. Beadon's clericality had once been illuminated when he had broken that vow of celibacy to which he had attached such importance in order to marry Mrs. Beadon. In the confusion of the Sabine rape Mrs. Beadon might have found herself wedded, but that any man in cold blood and with many women to choose from should have deliberately chosen Mrs. Beadon passed normal comprehension. Her husband treated her in the same way as he treated the crucifix from Oberammergau that he kept in a triptych by his bed. He would admire her, respect her, almost worship her, and then abruptly he would shut her up with a little click. Mrs. Beadon was much thinner even than her husband; while she was eating, the upper part of her chest resembled a musical box, her throat a violin played pizzicato, the accumulated music of which expressed itself during digestion in remote trills and far-off scales. She was seldom vocal in conversation, but voluble in psalms and hymns; she performed many kind actions such as blowing little boys' noses on the way to school, and though she did not blow Dorothy's nose, she squeezed her hand and confided that the news of Lord Clarehaven's marriage had meant a great deal to her.

"Oh, so much!" she had time to repeat before her husband closed the doors of the triptych.

Mr. Hemming, the curate, was a muscular and, did not his clerical collar forbid one to suppose so, a completely fatuous young man. When he was pleased about anything he said, "Oh, cheers!" When he was displeased he shook his head in silence. Mr. Beadon told Dorothy that he was a loyal churchman, and certainly once in the course of the evening he came to the rescue of his rector, who had been pinned in a corner of the room, by asking the squire, why he wore a pink coat when he hunted. The squire replied that such was the custom for an M. F. H., and Mr. Hemming, with a guffaw, said that it was also the custom for a fisher of men to wear sporting colors. This irreverent attempt to put fishing on an equality with fox-hunting naturally upset the squire, and the dowager's hopes, of an early reconciliation between him and the rector were destroyed.

Of the other two guests, Doctor Lane was a pleasant, elderly gentleman whose chief pride was that he still read *The Lancet* every week. One felt in talking to him that a man who still read *The Lancet* after twenty-five years of Cherrington evinced a sensitiveness to medical progress that was laudable and peculiar. He was a widower without children and devoted what little leisure he had to the study of newts, salamanders, and olms; a pair of olms, which a friend had brought him back from Carniola, he kept in a subterranean tank in his garden, enhancing thereby in the eyes of the village his reputation as a physician. The last guest, Mr. Greenish, was a well-groomed bachelor of about forty, one of that class who suddenly appear for no obvious reason in remote country villages and devote themselves to gardening or other forms of outdoor life, who are useful about the parish, and who often play billiards well. They may be criminals hiding from justice; more probably they are people who have inherited money late in life from aunts, and who, having long dreamed of retiring into the country, do so at the first opportunity. Mr. Greenish did not hunt, but he was a good shot, and Clarehaven found him the least intolerable of his immediate neighbors.

It cannot be said that Dorothy found it difficult to shine at such a party; indeed, she was such a success that when the evening came to an end no doubt remained in the dowager's mind that to-morrow morning Little Cherrington church would have double its usual congregation to see the new countess. In fact, Mr. Kingdon was so much taken with her that he announced his own intention of worshiping at Little Cherrington, and the rector regretted that he had not known of this beforehand in order that he might have seized the opportunity, in the absence of the squire, to test the congregation of Great Cherrington with a linen chasuble. As a matter of fact, on the way home he plotted with Mr. Hemming to do this, and was successful in passing off the vestment on the congregation as a flaw in the curate's surplice.

Dorothy looked particularly attractive that Sunday in her coat and skirt of lavender box-cloth, for the fashion of the moment was one that well showed off a figure like hers. The rector's sermon on a text from the Song of Solomon alluded with voluptuous imagery to the romance of the married state, and, being entirely unintelligible to the congregation, was considered round the parishes to be one of the best sermons he had ever preached. If only to-morrow, thought Dorothy, when she walked out of the churchyard through a crowd of uncovered rustics, she could leave the hunting-field as triumphantly. Her rides on the preceding days with Clarehaven and the girls had been successful. They had all congratulated her, and any lingering anxiety in her husband's mind seemed to have passed away. As the moment drew near, however, Dorothy began to be nervous about breaches of hunting etiquette, and she spent Sunday afternoon in turning over the pages of bound volumes of *Punch* in order to extract from the weekly hunting joke hints what not to do. A succession of irate M. F. H.'s, purple in the face and shaking crops at presumptuous cockneys, haunted her dreams that night; when she woke to a moist gray morning, for the first time in her life she felt really nervous. It was in vain that she sought to reassure herself by recalling past triumphs on the stage or by telling herself how easily she had dealt with Lady Chatfield. Failure in either of those cases would not have been irremediable; but let her make no mistake, before to-day's dusk she should have settled the whole of her future life. If she made a fool of herself she should never escape from being pointed out as a Vanity girl; if she succeeded, the Vanity girl would be forgotten, and by sheer personal prowess she might lead the county. It was a tribute to Dorothy's complexion that not even on this rather shaky morning did she feel the need for rouge. Five Tree Farm was only three miles from Clare Court, and the meets there, being considered the best of the season, always had very large fields. She was disappointed that Tony was not in pink, but he told her he did not care enough about hunting to dress up for it.

"That's what I like about shooting," he said, "there isn't all this confounded putting it on."

The master cantered up and congratulated Dorothy on her first appearance with the Horley Hunt.

"We're going to draw Dedenham Copse first," he informed her, and cantered off again, shouting loudly to two unfortunate young men with bicycles who were doing no harm at all, but whom he persisted in abusing as "damned socialists." Suddenly, hounds gave tongue with changed, almost intolerable eager note; there was a thud of hoofs all round her; confused cries; the sound of a horn shrilling to the gray sky....

"Wonderful morning for scent," she heard somebody say, and flushed because she thought a personal remark had been passed about herself; but before she had time to worry who had said it and why it had been said Mignonette was nearly leading the field.

"Dorothy," shouted her husband, "for God's sake don't get too far in front. Hold your mare in a bit. And for God's sake don't ride over hounds."

But Dorothy paid no attention to him and was soon galloping with the first half-dozen. By her side appeared Charlie Fanhope.

"Topping run," he breathed. "I say, you're looking glorious. Awful to think I shall be on the way to Eton this time to-morrow."

She smiled at him; from out of the past came the memory of an old colored Christmas supplement on the walls of the nursery in Lonsdale Road. A girl and a boy on rocking-horses, brown and dapple-gray, the boy wearing a green-velvet cap and jacket, the girl befrilled and besashed, were both plunging forward with rosy smiles. Underneath it had been inscribed: "Yoicks! Tally-ho!" While her mare's heels thudded over the soft turf, Dorothy kept saying to herself, "Yoicks! Yoicks! Yoicks!" Charlie Fanhope, riding beside her, was as fresh and rosy as the boy in the picture.

"You can't take that gate, can you?" he was saying.

Before her like a ladder rose a five-barred gate. At the riding-school in Knightsbridge Dorothy had jumped obstacles quite as high; but those had been obstacles that collapsed conveniently when touched by the heels of her horse.

"I say I don't think you can take that gate," Charlie Fanhope repeated, anxiously. "I'll open it. I'll open it."

But Dorothy in a dream left all to Mignonette; remembering from real life to grip the pommel, to keep her wrists down, and to sit well back, she seemed to be uttering a prolonged gasp that was carried away by the wind as a diver's gasp is lost in the sound of the water. Where was her cousin? Left behind to crackle through one of those gaps he knew of. Yoicks! Yoicks! Yoicks! They were in a wide, down-sloping meadowland intensely green, and checkered with the black and red riders in groups; hounds were disappearing at the bottom of the slope in a thick coppice. Nursery pictures of Caldecott came back to Dorothy when she saw the squire with his horn and his mulberry-colored face and his huge bay horse go puffing past to investigate the check, which lasted long enough for Dorothy to receive many felicitations upon her horsewomanship.

"My word! Doodles," said her husband, cantering up to her side. "You really are a wonder, but for the Lord's sake be careful."

"I told you that you didn't yet really know me," she murmured; before he could reply, from the farthest corner of the coppice came the whip's "Viewhalloo." Hounds gave tongue again with high-pitched notes of excitement as of children playing. Forrard away! For-rard! They were off again with the fox gone away toward Maidens' Common, and before the merry huntsmen the prospect of the finest run in Devonshire. Thirty minutes at racing speed and never a check; wind singing; hoofs thudding; a view of the fox; Dorothy always among the first half-dozen riders.

They killed some twelve miles away from Clare in Tangley Bottom, and nobody would have accused the master, when he handed Dorothy the brush, of being influenced by the countess's charming company at dinner on Saturday night. Best of all in a day of superlatives, Clarehaven had taken a nasty toss; his wife had him in hand as securely as she had Mignonette.

"Glorious day," Connie sighed when at last they were walking through the gates of the park.

"Glorious," echoed Dorothy.

A faint flush low on the western sky symbolized her triumph. And though one or two malicious women said that it was a pity Lord Clarehaven should have married a circus girl, the legend never spread. Besides, they had not been introduced to the Diana of Clare, who soon had the county as securely in hand as her horse and her husband.

Dorothy, tired though she was, felt the need of confiding in somebody the tale of her triumph. She was even tempted to write to Olive. In the end she chose her mother; perhaps the kindness of the dowager had stirred a dormant piety.

She wrote:

MY DEAR MOTHER,—I am sorry I could not come and see you before I got married, but you can understand how delicate and difficult my position was, and how much everything depended on myself. No doubt, later on when I am thoroughly at home in my new surroundings, it will be easier for us to meet again. I don't know if father told you that I did explain to him my motives in treating you all rather abruptly. Or did he never refer to a little talk we once had? You will be glad to hear that I am very, very happy. My husband adores me, my mother-in-law has been more than kind, and my sisters-in-law equally so. On Thursday we drove over to Chatfield Hall to see my husband's grandmother, old Lady Chatfield, who is famous for speaking her mind, and of course not at all prejudiced in my favor by my having been on the stage. However, we had a jolly little talk together and everybody is delighted with the impression I made. On Saturday we had a small dinner-party. The rector, who is very High Church and would not, therefore, appeal to father, was there. Mr. Kingdon, the squire, would be more his style. There was also a Mr. Greenish, who promised to teach me gardening. Quite a jolly evening. Yesterday morning all the villagers cheered when I came out of church, and to-day I hunted with the Horley. I was rather a success. I hope you got the check for £500 I sent you, and that you will buy yourself something nice with it. It isn't exactly a present, but in a way it counts as one, doesn't it? You must try to be a little more firm with father in future. Don't forget that though I may seem heartless I am not really so. I hope you will write to me sometimes. You should address the envelope to The Countess of Clarehaven, but if you speak about me to your friends you should speak about me as Lady Clarehaven.

Your loving daughter,
DOROTHY CLAREHAVEN.

For two years Dorothy's life as a countess went quietly along, gathering in its train a number of pleasant little memories that in after years were to mean something more than pleasure. The major difficulties of her new position were all encountered and defeated in that first week; thenceforward nothing seriously disturbed her for long. In the autumn of the year in which Clarehaven married, the dowager, after consulting Dorothy, decided that his restlessness was finally cured and that the danger of his wanting to tear about the Continent in Lee-Lonsdale cars no longer threatened the family peace. In these circumstances the dowager thought it would be tactful to move into Clare Lodge with Arabella and Constantia.

She should not be too far away if her daughter-in-law had need of her, and by moving that little way off she should do much to prevent her son's chafing against the barriers of domesticity. It would be easier for Dorothy to act as hostess of the shooting-parties that were arranged for the autumn if she were apparent as the only hostess. In the administration of the village the two countesses shared equally—the dowager by superintending the making of soup and gruel for sick villagers, Dorothy by assisting at its distribution. The rector won Dorothy's heart by his readiness to discuss with her the history of the great family into which she had married, and by preparing a second edition of his *Clarehaven and the Clares* for when it should be wanted, affixing against the fifth earl's name an asterisk, like a second star of Bethlehem, that should direct the wise reader to this foot-note:

...The present Earl in January, 1906, delighted his many friends and well-wishers in the county by wedding the beautiful Miss Dorothy Lonsdale, a distant connection of that Lord Cleveden who is famous as a most capable administrator in the land of the golden wattle and upon "India's coral strand."

She for her part won Mr. Beadon's heart by often attending his services at Clarehaven, and not merely by attending herself, but by insisting upon Mrs. Bitterplum's and Mrs. Smith's attending, too. This arrangement suited everybody, because the dowager at Little Cherrington was able to worship her stained-glass window without a sense that, whatever she might be before God's throne, she was now of secondary importance in the church. The step up that the rector had promised himself for Easter was effected without an apoplexy from Mr. Kingdon, possibly because the white stole did not inflame his taurine eye. At Whitsuntide, however, when a red stole appeared, his face followed the liturgical sequence, and there was a painful scene in the churchyard on a hot morning in early June. Dorothy, on being appealed to by the rector, drove over to Cherrington Hall that afternoon and remonstrated with Mr. Kingdon on his inconsiderate behavior. She pointed out that Mrs. Beadon was in an interesting condition at the moment and that if Mr. Kingdon had his prejudices to consider, Mr. Beadon had his conscience; that it was not right for the squire to add fuel to the ancient rivalry between Great and Little Cherrington; and finally that inasmuch as the bishop was shortly coming to stay at Clare for a confirmation, it would be unkind to pain his sensitive diocesan spirit with these parochial disputes. Dorothy's arguments may not have convinced the squire, but her beauty and condescension penetrated where logic was powerless, and Mr. Beadon was allowed to preach for more than twenty bee-loud Sundays after Trinity wearing a grass-green stole round his neck and with never a word of protest from the squire. Nor were the Sundays within the octaves of St. Peter or St. James, of St. Lawrence or St. Bartholomew, profaned by the squire's objections to the tribute of red silk that Mr. Beadon paid to the blood of the martyrs. His wife celebrated her husband's victory by producing twins at Lammastide, and everybody in the neighborhood said that the religious tone of Cherrington was remarkably high.

In September Dorothy had her first shooting-party, to which, among others, Arthur Lonsdale and Harry Tufton were invited. Tony had been in camp with his yeomanry regiment during most of August; he seemed glad to be back at Clare; the shooting was good; the visits of his old friends from London did not apparently disturb him. Notwithstanding Connie's lessons, Dorothy never became a good shot; she really hated killing birds. However, she encouraged Clarehaven to go on with his favorite sport, and herself hunted hard all the season. She was much admired as a horsewoman, and the fact that she had not so long ago been a Vanity girl was already as dim as most old family curses are. In early spring Tony suggested that it would be a good idea to go up to town for the season.

"A very good idea," she agreed. "Bella and Connie ought to be presented." Dorothy spoke as calmly as if she had been presented herself. "It's a pity I can't present them," she added, "but I should not like to be presented myself. I don't think that actresses ought to be presented, even if they do retire from the stage when they marry. Sometimes an individual suffers unjustly; but it's better that one person should suffer than that all sorts of precedents should be started. Of course, your mother will present them."

"But look here, I thought we'd go up alone," Tony argued. "I told you I'd had the house done up very comfortably. I don't think the girls would enjoy London a bit."

"They may not enjoy it," said Dorothy, "but they ought to go."

May and June were spent in town in an unsuccessful attempt to induce many eligible bachelors even to dance with Arabella and Constantia, let alone to propose to them. Dorothy condoled with the dowager on Arthur Lonsdale's bad taste in not wanting to marry Arabella; Arthur himself was lectured severely on his obligations, and she could not understand why he would not stop laughing, particularly as Lady Cleveden herself had been in favor of the match. Dorothy went to the opera twice a week; but she refused to go near the Vanity. Once she drove over to West Kensington to see her mother, whose chin had more hairs than ever, but who otherwise was not much changed. The rest of the family alarmed her with the flight of time. Gladys and Marjorie were the Agnes and Edna of four years ago; Agnes and Edna themselves were getting perilously like the Norah and Dorothy of four years ago; Cecil was a medical student smoking bigger pipes than Roland, who himself had grown a very heavy black mustache. The countess managed to avoid seeing her father, and when her mother protested his disappointment she said that he would understand. Mrs. Caffyn was too much awed by having a countess for a daughter to insist, and she assured her that not only did she fully appreciate her reasons for withdrawing from open intercourse with her family, but that she approved of them. The countess gave her a sealskin coat for next winter, kissed her on both cheeks, and disappeared as abruptly from West Kensington as Enoch from the antediluvian landscape.

The responsibility of two plain sisters became too much for Clarehaven; after Ascot he admitted that he should be thoroughly glad to get back to Clare, which was exactly what his wife had hoped.

While Dorothy was studying with the rector the lives of obscure saints and the histories of prominent noblemen, she took lessons with the doctor in natural history and with Mr. Greenish in horticulture. Mr. Greenish enjoyed sending off on her account large orders to nursery gardeners all over England for rare shrubs that he had neither the money nor the space to buy for himself. Both at the Temple Show and at Holland House he had been continually at Lady Clarehaven's elbow with a note-book; and the glories of next summer in the Clare gardens made bright his wintry meditations. Mr. Greenish himself looked rather like a tuber, and it became a current joke that one day Dorothy would plant him in a secluded border. The dowager was delighted by her daughter-in-law's hobby, for which, though it ran to the extravagance of ordering the whole stock of a new orange tulip at a guinea a bulb, not to mention twenty roots of sunset-hued *Eremurus warer* at forty shillings apiece, and a hundred of topaz-hung *Eremurus bungei* at ten shillings, she had nothing but enthusiasm.

"My golden border will be lovely," Dorothy announced.

"It will be unique," Mr. Greenish added. "Lady Clarehaven is specializing in shades of gold, copper, and bronze," he explained to the dowager.

"These roots oddly resemble echinoderms," said Doctor Lane, looking at the roots of the *Eremurus*.

"I should have said starfish," Mr. Greenish put in.

"Starfish *are* echinoderms," said the doctor, severely.

"Wonderful!" the dowager exclaimed, with the eyes of a child looking upon the fairies. She herself never rose to the height of her daughter-in-law's Incalike ambitions; but her own Japanese tastes (expensive enough) were gratified. Those black-stemmed hydrangeas were ordered by the hundred to bloom by the edge of the pines, and Dorothy presented her with twenty-four of M. Latour-Marlias's newest and most expensive hybrid water-lilies. Nor did the hydrangeas come pink; they knew that they were being employed by a noble family and preserved the authentic blue of their patrons' blood. As the rector hoped before he died that popular clamor in the Cherringtons would compel him to flout his bishop by holding an open-air procession upon the feast of Corpus Christi, so Dorothy aspired to convert the two villages from vegetables to flowers. She knew, however, that it would be useless to attempt too much at first in this direction, and at Mr. Greenish's suggestion she decided to open her campaign by organizing a grand entertainment for the two Cherringtons, Clarehaven, and the several villages and hamlets in the neighborhood. Uncle Chat was called in to help with his advice, and while Tony was in camp she made her preparations. Marquees were hired from Exeter; the countryside pulsated with the spirit of competition. Dorothy drew up the bills herself with a nice compromise between the claims of age and strict precedence in her list of patrons.

CLAREHAVEN AND CHERRINGTON
AGRICULTURAL FÊTE AND
FLOWER SHOW

Saturday, August 31, 1907

UNDER THE PATRONAGE OF

The Earl of Chatfield; the Earl and Countess of Clarehaven; Lavinia, Countess of Chatfield; Augusta, Countess of Clarehaven; the Viscount Paignton; the Lady Jane Fanhope; the Lady Arabella Clare; the Lady Constantia Clare; the Lady Mary Fanhope; the Lady Maud Fanhope; George Kingdon, Esq., J.P., M.F.H., and Mrs. Kingdon; the Rev. Claude Conybeare Beadon, M.A., and Mrs. Beadon; Dr. Eustace Lane; Horatio Greenish, Esq.

Prizes for live stock, including poultry, pigeons, and rabbits.

Prizes for collections of mixed vegetables.

A special prize offered by the Earl of Chatfield for the best collection of runner-beans.

A special and very *valuable* prize offered by the Countess of Clarehaven for the best collection of *flowers* from a cottage garden.

A special prize offered by the Dowager Countess of Clarehaven for the best collection of wild flowers made by a village child within a four-mile radius of Clare Court.

A special prize offered by Doctor Lane for a collection of insect pests set and mounted by the scholars of Cherrington Church Schools and Horley Board Schools.

The Countess of Clarehaven has kindly consented to give away the prizes.

The band of the Loyal North Devon Dragoons (by kind permission of Colonel Budding-Robinson, M.V.O., and officers) will play during the afternoon.

Swings, roundabouts, cocoanut-shies, climbing greasy pole for a side of bacon offered by H. Greenish, Esq., sack-races, egg-and-spoon races, hat-trimming competition for agricultural laborers.

ILLUMINATIONS AND FIREWORKS

Entrance, one shilling. After five o'clock, sixpence. After eight, threepence. Children free.

REFRESHMENTS

It was a blazing day, one of those typical days when rustic England seems to consist entirely of large cactus dahlias and women perspiring in bombazine. Tony, to Dorothy's annoyance, had declined to open the proceedings with a speech, and with Uncle Chat also refusing, Mr. Kingdon had to be asked to address the competitors. He bellowed a number of platitudes about the true foundations of England's greatness, told everybody that he was a Conservative—a Tory of the old school. He might say amid all this floral wealth a Conservatory. Ha-ha! He had no use for new-fangled notions, and, by Jove! when he looked round at the magnificent display that owed so much to the energy and initiative of Lady Clarehaven, by Jove! he couldn't understand why anybody wanted to be anything else except a Conservative.

"No politics, squire," the village atheist cried from the back of the tent, and Mr. Kingdon, who had been badly heckled by that gentleman at a recent election meeting, descended from the rostrum.

When the time came to distribute the awards Dorothy sprang the little surprise of which only Mr. Greenish was in the secret, by making a speech herself. She spoke with complete self-assurance and, as the *North Devon Courant* said, "with a gracious comprehension of what life meant to her humbler neighbors."

"Fellow-villagers of the two Cherringtons and of Clarehaven," she began, evoking loud applause from Mr. and Mrs. Bitterplum and Mr. and Mrs. Smith, who between them had raised the largest marrow, for which they would shortly receive ten shillings as a token of England's gratitude, "in these days when so much is heard of rural depopulation I confess that looking round me at this crowded assembly I am not one of the alarmists. I confess that I see no signs of rural depopulation among the merry faces of the little children of our healthy North Devon breed. I regret that the committee did not include in its list of prizes another for the best collection of home-grown children." (Loud cheers from the audience, in the middle of which one of the little Smiths of Clarehaven had to be led out of the tent because there was some doubt whether in chewing one of the prize dahlias he had not swallowed an earwig.) "Meanwhile, I can only marvel at the enthusiasm and good will with which you have all worked to make our first agricultural fête the success it undoubtedly has been. I am told by people who understand these things that no finer runner-beans have ever appeared than the collection of runner-beans for which, after long deliberation by the judges, Mr. Isaac Hodge of Little Cherrington has been awarded the prize." (Cheers.) "I will not detain you with eulogies of the potatoes shown by our worthy neighbor, Mr. Blundell of Great Cherrington. Nor shall I detain you by singing the praises of the really noble beet-roots from the garden of Mr. Adam Crump of Horley Hill. But I should like to say here how much I regret that the collections of flowers fell so far below the standard set by the vegetables. We must remember that without beauty utility is of little use. This autumn I shall be happy to present flower seeds to all cottage gardens who apply for them. Mr. Greenish has kindly consented to act as my distributer. Next year I shall present five pounds and a silver cup for the best exhibit from these seeds. And now nothing remains for me except to congratulate once more the winners on their well-deserved success, and the losers on a failure that only the exceptional quality of the winning exhibits prevented being a success, too."

Amid loud cheers Dorothy pinned rosettes to the lapels of the perspiring competitors, shook hands with each one, to whom she handed his prize wrapped in tissue-paper, and, bowing graciously, descended from the dais.

"Now if I can make a speech like that at a flower-show," she said to her husband that evening, "why can't you speak in the House of Lords?"

The fact of the matter was that Dorothy was beginning to worry herself over Clarehaven's lack of interest in the affairs of his country. Since they had been married the only additional entry in Debrett under his title was the record of his being a J.P. for the county of Devon. Dorothy felt that this was not enough; he should be preparing himself by his demeanor in the House of Lords to be offered at least an under-secretaryship when the Radicals should be driven from power.

"All right," said Tony. "But I can't very well play the hereditary legislator and all that if you insist upon keeping me down in the country."

"When does Parliament reassemble?" she asked.

"Oh, I don't know. Some time in the autumn, I suppose."

"Very well, then, we'll go up to town on one condition, which is that you will make a speech. If you haven't spoken within a week of the opening I shall come back here."

Tony, in order to get away from Devonshire, was ready to promise anything, but at the end of October, on a day also memorable in the history of Clare for the largest battue ever held in those coverts, Dorothy told her husband that she was going to have a baby.

He flushed with the slaughter of hundreds of birds, she flushed with what all this meant to her and him and England, faced each other in the bridal chamber of Clare that itself was flushed with a crimson October sunset.

"Tony, aren't you wildly happy?"

"Why, yes ... of course I am ... only, Doodles, I suppose this means you won't go up to town? Oh well, never mind. Gad! you look glorious this evening." He put his arms round her and kissed her.

"Not that way," she murmured. "Not that way now."

V

The pride and joy that Dorothy felt were so complete that she would take no risk of spoiling them by allowing her husband to intrude upon her at such a time. This boy of hers—there was no fear in her sanguine and circumspect mind that she might produce a daughter—was the fruit of herself and the earldom. To this end had she let Clarehaven make love to her, and if now she should continue to allow him such liberty she should be cheapening herself like a woman of pleasure. If at first she had rejoiced in her own position as a countess, all that self-satisfaction was now incorporated in this unborn son to be magnified by him into nobility and all that was expressed by nobility in its fullest sense. The thrill that every woman, however much she may dread or resent it, feels at the first prospect of maternity was for Dorothy heightened beyond any comparison that would not be blasphemous. On this small green earth would walk a Viscount Clare that, having taken flesh from a Vanity girl, should be the savior of his country. It no longer mattered that her husband was blind to the duties of his rank when she held in her womb, not some political pawn-broker like Disraeli, but an incarnation of the benign genius of aristocracy, a being that would indeed ennoble herself. Yet the father of this prodigy regarded him merely as an unwelcome hindrance to his plan for spending the winter in London. If it were not for the duty she owed to a great house to produce other children, and so by every means in mortal power save the family from extinction, she should never again live with Tony as his wife. What had been all their kisses except the prelude to this event? Did he with his boots and his guns suppose that as a man he counted with this unborn son within her? Poor vain fool, not to have comprehended that every conjugal duty, every social obligation, every movement of her head, every flash of her eye, every offer of her hand since she came to Clare had been consecrated to this great issue. Yet his flimsy imagination, which, were it never so flimsy, might at such a moment have managed to spur his body to kneel in awe of the future, had thought of nothing except to make love as lightly as he had made incessant love to her ever since they were married. Love! What did she care for that kind of love? Only for this result, only because she had believed that perfect fruit comes from perfect blossom, had she yielded to him all of herself with passion, sometimes with ecstasy. And now her reward was at hand. The wild autumnal gales might sweep round the ancient house, but at last it was secure; she, Dorothy Lonsdale, had secured it.

There was no hunting, of course, for Dorothy this season, not even in so mild a form as cubbing, and, amorous of solitude, she often used to walk by herself to Clarehaven; there, on one of those green headlands that had withstood the sea when the fortifications of Clare had crumbled in the foaming tide, she would sit by the hour, drinking in from the salt blast strength and endurance for this son of hers dedicate from the womb to his country and to his order. On those wild days the little church, which belonged to the dim origins of the family and had been built by sea-rovers to abide in their hearts while they were seafaring, became a true shrine for her. She would take refuge there from the fury of the storm, and there sit in an ancient chair bleached and worm-eaten, her eyes fixed upon that east window stained by nothing save spindrift and scud from the sea. The wind would howl and shriek, would rattle at the hasps of the narrow windows like hands entreating shelter, would drum and whistle and moan by the old oaken doors, while Dorothy sat in a stillness of gray light, herself radiant with that first beauty of coming motherhood before the weary months of waiting have begun to drag the cheeks. There for hours she would sit, her eyes shining, her neck blue-veined with blood coursing to reinforce the second life that was in the making, her complexion not paragoned by the petal of any rose in all the roses that ever had or ever would bloom at Clare.

Everything in the little church had taken on a luminous gray from the open space of light by which it was surrounded. The altar was of granite; the candlesticks of pewter; the crucifix of silver. Wise with all his follies, the rector had chosen this church to express whatever, still untainted by expediency or snobbery, was left of his inmost aspirations, and here he had allowed nothing to affront the stark simplicity of such architecture. Here there were no chrysanthemums in brazen vases, only sprigs of sea-holly gathered by children on the salt edge of the downs, sea-holly from the fled summer that preserved the illusion of having been gathered yesterday. The benches had not been varnished; year by year they had slowly assumed that desiccated appearance of age which gives to wood thus mellowed a strangely immaterial look, a lightness and a grace, rough-hewn though it be, that varnished wood never acquires. In this building, wrought, it seemed, by labor of wind and cloud, of air and rain, Dorothy's coloring exceeded richness; when the yellow winter sun shone through the landward windows the effulgence mingled with the hue of her cheeks to incarnadine the very air around her and blush upon the stones beyond. How often had she sat thus in meditation upon nothing except the power and strength of her unborn son! Could her husband wait beside her in this church where his pirate ancestors, dripping with sea-water, had thanked God for their deliverance and for booty stacked upon the beach below? Not he! He would be trying to play with her wrist all the time, pecking at her with kisses like a canary at a lump of sugar.

Dorothy had no desire to make a secret of her condition; she was only too anxious that everybody who could appreciate its importance should be made aware of it. Yet there was nothing in her of the gross femininity that takes a pleasure in accentuating the outward signs of approaching motherhood and, as if it had done something unusual, rejoices in a physical condition that is attainable by all women. Dorothy's pride lay in giving an heir to a great family, not in adding another piece of carnality to the human race. Compared with most women, the grace and beauty with which she expressed her state was that of a budding daffodil beside a farrowing sow. So little indeed did Tony realize her condition that in January, on the anniversary of their wedding, he half jestingly rallied her on simulating it to keep him down in Clare. He added other reasons, which offended her so deeply that for the rest of these months she demanded a room to herself. Dorothy knew that by loosening the physical hold she had over him she was taking a risk, but she staked everything in the future upon the birth of this son, and she declined to imperil his perfection upon earth by unpleasant thoughts in these crucial months of his making. Perhaps, if she had been patient and taken a little trouble to explain her point of view more fully to Tony, he might have understood, but she was so intent upon aiding this other life within her that she could not spare a moment to educate her husband.

The super-dowager of Chatfield had kissed her grandson's wife on Christmas Eve, and when at Candlemas the old lady died Dorothy was sad to think she had not lived to kiss her son. The manner of her death was characteristic. February had come in with a spell of balmy weather, and Lady Chatfield, according to her habit on fine days, insisted upon going out to sun herself in front of the house. In this occupation she was often annoyed by hens invading the drive; to guard herself against their aggression she used always to be armed with several bundles of fagots, which she kept at her side to fling at the aggressive birds. Her son had often begged that she would allow the hens to be kept far enough away from the house to secure her against their trespassing; but the old lady really enjoyed the sport and passed many contented hours shooting at them like this with fagots. Unfortunately, that Candlemas morning, either she had come out insufficiently provided with ammunition or the birds were particularly venturesome. When the luncheon-bell rang there was not a fagot left, and a quantity of hens were clucking with impunity round her still form. At such a crisis her self-propelling chair must have refused to work for the first time; with ammunition exhausted, transport destroyed, communications cut, and the enemy advancing from every point, the old lady had died of exasperation. The dowager, grieved by what in her heart she felt was an unseemly way of dying and faintly puzzled how to picture her mother in the heavenly courts, spent a good deal of time in Little Cherrington church, praying that she would be humble in Paradise. The dowager's childlike and apprehensive fancy played round an apocalyptic vision of her mother criticizing the sit of a halo, or poking with a palm-branch just men in the eye. She confided some of these fears to Mr. Beadon, who tried to impress upon her his own conceptions of Eternal Life, gently and respectfully rebuking her for the materialism of which she was guilty. Dorothy found something most admirable in the super-dowager's death; she wished her own unborn son might inherit his great-grandmother's pertinacity and defiance for the time when, like intrusive poultry, democracy should invade the privileges of his order.

The dowager's loss of her mother was followed in March by a blow that upset her more profoundly. During a fierce gale a large elm-tree in Little Cherrington churchyard was blown down and in its fall broke the Burne-Jones window that commemorated the fourth earl. It was no great loss to art, but the effect upon the dowager was tremendous. The shock of seeing the irreverent winds of March blowing through that colored screen she had set up between herself and the reality of her husband destroyed the figment of him that her pampered imagination had elaborated, and she remembered him as he was—an ill-tempered gambler, a drunken spendthrift, always with that fixed leer of ataxy for a pretty woman ... she remembered how once she had overheard somebody say that Clarehaven was now a rake without a handle. Her conscience was pricked; she must warn Dorothy of what the Clare inheritance might include.

"Dorothy dear," she implored. "I don't like to seem interfering, but I do beg you not to leave Tony alone too much. I fear for him. I—" with whispers and head-shakes she poured out the true story of her married life.

But Dorothy, with her whole being concentrated upon that unborn son, had no vigilance to waste on Tony. If he should go to the bad, let him go. The sins of the fourth earl and the follies of the fifth should all be forgotten in that paragon the sixth. At the same time, the dowager's story left its mark on Dorothy; thenceforward, when she paced the long picture-gallery of Clare, she would often ask herself in affright what passions and vices, what weakness, shame, and folly, had been cloaked by those painted forms of ancestors. She would give him her flesh; but he must inherit from them also; from those unblinking eyes he must derive some of the gleams in his own. But it should be from his mother that he derived most ... then she caught her breath. If that were so he would have in him something of Gilbert Caffyn, of that hypocrite her father. When the dowager's window was broken air was let in upon Dorothy's painted screen as well. She was honest with herself on those mornings when she paced the long gallery; she made no more pretense of romantic origins; the Lonsdale bugle-horn was cracked and useless. By what she was should her son live, not by what she liked to think she might be. Some of the strength that she had summoned for him during those autumnal hours in the little church by the sea she begged now for herself; while she defied those frigid glances that ever watched her progress up and down, up and down that long gallery, she stripped herself of all sham glories and for the sake of him within her dedicated herself to truth. Lady Godiva, riding naked through the streets of Coventry, was not more heroic than Dorothy riding naked through her own mind for the sake of that Lucius-Clare-to-be called by courtesy Viscount Clare.

Dorothy had chosen Lucius for his name after that other viscount who was Secretary of State to Charles I, that Lucius Cary who was killed at Newbury and whose story she had happened upon while reading tales of the great dead. If Lucius, Viscount Clare, could be like Lucius, Viscount Falkland, what would West Kensington matter? What would the Vanity mean, or that flat round the corner? What would signify the plebeian soul of her father?

The only person at present to whom Dorothy confided the name she had chosen was Arabella. The two girls had been very sympathetic during those winter months, and had entirely devoted themselves to their sister-in-law. At first, when she had withdrawn herself every day to go and meditate in Clarehaven church, they had been shy of intruding upon her; but their interest in family affairs, from those of guinea-pigs to those of cottagers, had become so much a part of their ordinary life that they could not resist trying to obtain Dorothy's permission for them to be interested in hers. Connie, whose main object was to watch over Dorothy's physical well-being, was ready to give it as much devotion as she would have given to a favorite mare in foal or to a litter of blind retriever pups; Arabella, who had inherited some of the dowager's ability to dream, was content to sit for as long as Dorothy wanted her company and talk of nothing except the future greatness of her nephew. Connie brought pillows for Dorothy's back; Arabella brought her books, in one of which Dorothy read about that very noble gentleman, Lucius Cary.

In February Clarehaven went up to town, partly because shooting was over, partly because he did not want to attend his grandmother's funeral. His behavior was commented upon harshly by Fanhopes and Clares alike; barely two years after her marriage Dorothy found that she, who was supposed to have been going to bring the families to ruin and disgrace, was now regarded as their salvation. Whatever she said was listened to with respect, whatever she did was regarded with approval. Before her pregnancy, Dorothy's conceit would have been gratified by such deference; now it only possessed a value for her son's sake. She longed more than ever for general esteem; but she coveted it for him, that he might grow up with pride and confidence in his mother.

When primroses lightened the woods of Clare like an exquisite dawn between the dusk of violets and the deep noon of bluebells, Connie exercised her authority over her half of Dorothy, forbade so much reading indoors, and prescribed walks. Dorothy now haunted the recesses of the woodland; when Tony, who had received a number of reproachful letters for staying in town at such a time, came back, she was gentler with him than any of the others were.

Those days spent in watching the deer, already snow-flecked to match the dappled sunlight of the woods, had been so enriched by contemplation of the active grace and beauty of these wild things that Dorothy discovered in herself a new affection for Tony, an affection born of gratitude to him, because it was he who had given her all this. He came back on a murmurous afternoon of mid-May. Dorothy was sitting upon the summit of a knoll where a few tall beeches scarcely troubled the sunlight with their high fans of lucent green. Beneath her ran a meadow threaded with the gold of cowslips, and while she stared into cuckoo-haunted distances she heard above the buzzing of the bees the sound of his car. Starting up, she waved to him, so that he stopped the car and ran up the slope to greet her.

"Why, Doodles, what's the matter?" he exclaimed. "You've been crying."

He was embarrassed by her hot wet cheeks when she pressed them to his.

"No, they're happy tears," she said. "I was thinking of him and that one day all this will be his." She caught the landscape in a gesture. "All the autumn, Tony, I prayed for him to be great and strong, and all the winter that he might be great and good. Now I think I should be happy if he did nothing more remarkable than love this land—his land. Tony, don't you feel how wonderful it is that you and I should give somebody all this?"

Formerly, when Dorothy had talked about their son, the father had not been able to grasp that there would ever be such a person. Now in this month before the birth he experienced a sudden awe in regarding his wife. That embrace she had given him for welcome, her figure, the look in her eyes—they were strange to him; she was strange to him—a new mysterious creature that awed him as an abstraction of womanhood, not as a lovely girl that granted or refused him kisses.

"I say, Doodles, I feel an awful brute for going away like that."

She laughed lightly.

"You needn't. I was happier alone. Don't look so disconsolate. I'm glad you've come now."

"I didn't stay up for the Derby," he pleaded, in extenuation of his neglect.

She laughed again.

"Tony, you haven't yet heard his name. I've chosen Lucius."

"That's a rum name. Why Latin all of a sudden? Or if Latin, why not Marcus Antoninus, don't you know?"

"It's a name I like very much."

He looked at her suspiciously.

"Who did you know called Lucius?"

"Nobody. It's a name I like. That's all."

"You promise me you never knew anybody called Lucius?" He had caught her hand.

"Never."

"All right. You can have it."

But the nimbus round her motherhood was for the husband melted by the breath of jealousy. Let children come to interrupt their love, she would be his again soon; and what trumpery she made of those women with whom he had played in London as a lonely child plays with dolls.

Dorothy's confinement was expected about the middle of June. When the nurse arrived, for the first time in all these months she began to have fears. She never doubted that the baby would be a boy; but she had dark fancies of monstrosity and madness, and the nurse had all she could do to reassure her. The weather during the first week of the month was damp and gusty; after that gilded May-time it seemed worse than it really was. The rustling of the vexed foliage held a menace that the sharp whistle of the winter gales had lacked. However, by the middle of the month the weather had changed for the better, and the last day was perfect.

When Dorothy's travail began in the afternoon, the nurse asked for the mowing of the lawns to be stopped, because she thought the noise would irritate her patient. Dorothy, however, told her that she liked the noise; in the comparatively long intervals between the first pains the mower consoled her with its pretense of mowing away the minutes and thus of audibly bringing the time of her achievement nearer.

The car was sent off to Exeter for another doctor, notwithstanding Dorothy's wish that nobody except Doctor Lane should attend her. The old gentleman had much endeared himself by his lessons in natural history, and that he should crown his teaching by a practical demonstration of his knowledge struck her as singularly appropriate. Doctor Lane himself expressed great anxiety for assistance, because it looked as if the confinement was going to be long and difficult. So hard was her labor, indeed, that when the Exeter doctor arrived it was decided to give her chloroform.

"Nothing's the matter, is it?" she murmured, perceiving that preparations were going on round her. "Why doesn't he come? Nurse," she called, "if babies take a long time, it means usually that the head is very large, doesn't it?"

"Very often, my lady, yes. Oh yes, it does mean that very often. Try and lie a little bit easier, dear. That's right."

"I think I'm rather glad," said Dorothy, painfully. "Lord Salisbury had an enormous head."

"Fever?" whispered Doctor Lane, in apprehensively questioning tones. "Tut, tut!"

Dorothy tried to smile at the silly old thing; but the pain was too much for smiles.

There was another long consultation, and presently she heard Lord Clarehaven being sent for.

"What's the matter?" she asked, sharply. "I'm not going to die, am I? I won't. I won't. He mustn't be brought up by anybody else."

The nurse patted her hand. Outside some argument was going on, rising and falling like the lawn-mower.

"A pity it's so dark," Dorothy murmured. "The mower had stopped, and I liked the humming. All that talking in the corridor isn't so restful. What's the time?"

"About half past ten, my lady."

A mighty pain racked her, a rending pain that seemed to leave her with reluctance as if it had failed to hurt her enough. Her whole body shivered when the pain passed on, and she had a feeling that it was a personality, so complete was it, a personality that was only waiting in a corner of the room and gathering new strength to rend her again.

Delirium touched her with hot fingers. It seemed that her body was like the small triangle of uncut corn round which the reaper relentlessly hums. It was coming again; it would tear the fibers of her again; it was coming; the humming was nearer every moment. In an effort to check the incommunicable experiences of fever, she asked if it was not the lawn-mower that was humming.

"No, dear, it's the doctors talking to his lordship."

"What about?"

The humming ceased, for they gave her chloroform. When she came to herself she lay for a second or two with closed eyes; then slowly, luxuriously nearly, she opened them wide to look at her son. There was nobody.

"Where is he?" she gasped, sitting up, dizzy and sick with the drug, but with all her nerves strung to unnatural, uncanny perceptiveness.

The dowager was leaning over the bed and begging her to lie down.

"What's burning my face?" cried Dorothy.

"It must be my tears," her mother-in-law sobbed.

"Why are you crying? My boy, where is he? Where is he? Oh, tell me, tell me, please tell me!"

The dowager and the nurse were looking at each other pitifully.

"Dorothy, my poor child, he was born dead."

The mother shrieked, for a pain that cut her ten thousand times more sharply than all the pains of her travail united in a single spasm.

"It was a question, dear, of saving your life or losing the baby's."

"You're lying to me," Dorothy shrieked. "It was a monster! I know that. It was a monster, and it had to be strangled. Oh, Doctor Lane, Doctor Lane, why did you let them bring another doctor? You promised me you wouldn't."

"No, no," said the dowager. "It was a perfect little boy with such lovely little hands and toes. Everything perfect; but his head was too large, dear. It was a question of you or him, and of course Tony insisted that he should be sacrificed."

"Where is he? Tony!"

Her husband came in and knelt by the bed.

"Why did you do that? Why? Why didn't you let me die? He would have been so much better than me. Can't you understand? Can't you understand?"

Everybody had stolen from the room to leave them together; but when he leaned over to kiss her she struck him on the mouth.

"You only wanted me for one thing," she cried.

"Doodles, don't treat me like this. I can't express myself. I never imagined that anything could be so horrible. I was asked to decide. You don't suppose I could have lived with a cursed child who had killed you!"

"How dare you curse him?"

"Dorothy, we'll have another. Don't be so miserable."

Suddenly she felt that nothing mattered.

"Will we?" she asked, indifferently.

"And we'll go up to town this autumn."

"Yes, there's nothing to keep us here," she said, "now."

CHAPTER V

I

ONE HUNDRED AND TWENTY-NINE Curzon Street was the dowry that the third Marquess of Longlan provided for his daughter, Lady Caroline Lacey, on her marriage in 1818 with Viscount Clare, the only son of the second Earl of Clarehaven. It was a double-fronted Georgian house with a delicate fanlight over the door, from which a fan-shaped flight of steps guarded by a pair of tall iron flambeau-stands led down to the pavement. That famous old beau, the first marquess, had given an eye to the architecture, and, being himself a man of fine proportions, had seen to it that the rooms of his new house would set off his figure to advantage. Solid without being stolid, dignified but never pompous, graceful but nowhere flimsy, and for everybody except the servants, who lived like corpses in a crypt, convenient—the town residence of Lord Clarehaven was as desirable as those desirable young men of Assyria upon whom in their blue clothes Aholah doted not less promiscuously than house-agents have doted upon a good biblical word.

When the second earl took charge of his wife's dowry, the fashions of the Regency were in the meridian, and the house was decorated and furnished to suit the prevailing mode. Apart from the verse of the period, there have been few manifestations of art and craft more detestable either for beauty or for comfort than those of the Regency. Great bellying lumps of furniture as fat and foul as the First Gentleman himself, and with as much superfluity of ornament as the First Gentleman's own clothes, were introduced into 129 Curzon Street to spoil the fine severity of the Georgian structure. Ugly furniture was added by the third earl, whose taste—he was a vice-chamberlain of the royal household in the 'fifties—was affected by his position as a mind is affected by misfortune. The dowager during the esthetic ardors that glowed upon the first years of her married life hung a few green and yellow draperies in the drawing-room, and during the early 'nineties she stocked these with woolen spiders or with butterflies of silk and velvet; in fact, when the fifth earl took over the control of his town house it was filled from the cellars to the attics with the accumulated abominations of eighty-five barbarous years. No doubt he would never have noticed the ugliness of the furniture if the discomfort of it had not been so obtrusive; but when he was planning to live merrily with his bride in Curzon Street he invited Messrs. Waring & Gillow to bring the house up to date with its own period and the present, allowing them a free hand with everything except the chairs, beds, and sofas, of which it was stipulated that none was to rate form or style above comfort. On the whole the result was an improvement; and since there are always enough relays of new competitors in the race for originality, purchasers were soon found even for those triads of chairs that are still seen in mid-Victorian drawing-rooms like empty cruets upon the mantelpiece of a coffee-room, and Tony was able to get a good price for the furniture of Gillows, who were by now as thoroughly worm-eaten as their handicraft. The arrangement with the decorators being modified by Dorothy's unwillingness to live in London, he postponed the complete renovation of the house to that happy date in the future when he and she should agree that East West, town's best.

Now at Clare, when Dorothy was lying in bed, careless of everything, Tony invited her to choose patterns from the books of wall-papers and chintzes sent down by Messrs. Waring & Gillow. Finding his wife in no mood to choose anything, he decided to gratify as well as he was able the taste she had expressed five or six years ago in the Halfmoon Street flat. The result was a series of what are called "chaste color schemes," which after being debauched by numerous chairs upholstered in glossy scarlet leather became positively meretricious under the temptation of silver-cased blotters and almanacs; four months after Dorothy's confinement the transformation of 129 Curzon Street into the dream of a Vanity girl was complete. She was still in too listless a mood to do anything except give a tired assent to whatever her husband proposed; physically and emotionally she was worn out, and when a second agricultural fête and flower-show was billed for August 25, 1908, she scarcely had the heart to present in person the silver cup and five pounds for the best flowers grown from the seeds she had supplied with such enthusiasm. Every adjunct of the show accentuated her own failure; from the women with their new babies to the chickens and the parsnips, everything seemed a rebuke to her own sterility.

Dorothy's pride might often degenerate into mere self-confidence, but it had hitherto been her mainstay in life; her failure to produce that son had sapped the foundations of pride by destroying self-confidence; her dignity as Tony's wife had been assailed, and she began to fret about the shallowness of her feeling for her husband. She would have been able to support a blow that fell with equal heaviness upon both, because she would have rejoiced in proving to Tony that she was more courageous than he; but he, from want of imagination, had let her feel that she had made a fuss about nothing; his attitude had been such, indeed, that in resuming relations with him she could not dispel the morbid fancy that she was behaving like his kept mistress. Once, in her determination to define their respective views of marriage, she asked him how he could bear to make love to a woman who was apparently so cold; in his answer he implied that her coldness was rather attractive than otherwise.

"But if you thought I really hated you to come near me?" she pressed.

"You don't really," he replied, and she turned away with a sigh of exasperation at the astonishing lack of sensitiveness in the male.

"You're nervy and strung up just at present," he went on. "And perhaps it has been bad for you to have so much of me all the time. But when you go back to town and find that you're envied by other women...."

"Because I'm married to you?" she interrupted, sharply.

"No, no, Doodles, I'm not so conceited as all that. Envied because you will be the loveliest of them all. But other men will envy me because I've got you for a wife. I don't think you realize how lovely you are."

She did realize it perfectly; but she resented a compliment that was inspired by self-satisfaction.

"The pleasure in being married to me, then," she challenged, "is that you're keeping me from other men? You wouldn't mind if I told you that I hated you, that I only married you to have rank and money, that I hooked you in the way an angler hooks a fat trout?"

"I was quite content to be hooked," said Tony.

"If I were unfaithful to you?"

His eyes hardened for a moment, like those of a groom who is being defied by a jibbing horse.

"Try it, old thing," he advised, and the whistle that lisped gently between his set teeth made expressive the quick breaths of rage that such a question evoked.

It was the day after the flower-show; they were sitting on the curved seat at the end of the pergola. Dorothy's question had an effect upon the conversation as if a painter had begged them to sustain a certain attitude until he could perpetuate it by his art; the stillness of deep summer undisturbed by a bird's note or by a whisper of a falling leaf was like thick green paint from which their forms, hastily sketched in, faintly emerged. Tony's whistle had ceased and he was stroking his mustache as if the action could help him to realize that he was alive. There seemed no reason why they should not sit there forever, like the statues all round, or the ladies and lovers in a picture by Mr. Marcus Stone. It was Tony who broke the spell by getting up and announcing business with somebody somewhere.

Dorothy, left alone on the seat, watched his form recede along the pergola, and asked herself in perplexity what she wanted as a substitute for that well-groomed, easy, and assured piece of manhood. If she was trying to tell herself that she pined to love a man without thought of children or considerations of rank and fortune, she could always elope with the first philanderer that presented himself. But she could not imagine any man for whose sake she would sacrifice as much. To be sure, she was not yet twenty-five; there lay before her many long years, one of which a grand passion might shorten to an hour. But could she ever fall in love? It was not merely because she was hard and ambitious that she was not in love with

Tony and that she could not imagine herself in love with anybody else. In all her life no man had presented himself whom she could imagine in the occupation of anything like the half of one's personality that being in love would imply. Indeed, if she looked back upon the men she had known, she liked Tony best personally, apart from the material advantages that being married to him offered. Perhaps the mood she was in was nothing more than a morbid fastidiousness caused by physical exhaustion; perhaps by going up to town and leading another sort of life she should be able to view marriage more naturally. She had always criticized other women for the ease with which they fell into a habit of indulging themselves with the traditional prerogatives of their sex. Her own path had always lain so obviously in front of her nose that she had been impatient of the incommunicable aspirations expressed by other women with sighs and yearning glances; to her such women had always appeared like the tiresome people who are proud of not possessing what they would call "the bump of locality." Such dubious and apprehensive temperaments had always irritated her; madness itself was for Dorothy the result of a carefully cultivated hysteria; even illness had always seemed to her only a fraudulent method of securing attention. Was she now to array herself in the trappings of conventional femininity? She bent her mind—and it was not a pliable mind—as straight as she was able, and told herself that even if she failed ultimately to produce an heir no one could question her fitness and willingness to produce an heir. Anything that went wrong in the marriage would not be her fault. As a wife she had justified herself; and if motherhood was to be denied her—oh well, what did all this matter? She was too much exhausted to keep her mind straight, and at the first relaxation of her will it jumped away from her control like the mainspring of a watch, the quivering coils of which, though they were all of a piece, were impossible to trace consecutively to their beginning or end. The monotonous green of late summer depressed her wherever she looked; earth was hot and tired, as hot and tired as one of the women at the show yesterday. Life was not much more varied than a big turnip-field in which two or three coveys of birds were put up, some to be killed, some to be wounded, some to whir away into turnip-fields beyond.

"Which means that I'm still thoroughly exhausted," Dorothy murmured. "But I can't think of the past because he is there, and the future seems dreary because he will never be there."

When at the beginning of October the moment came to drive up to London, the problems of birth and death, of love and happiness, were overshadowed by the refusal of the car to go even as far as Exeter.

"We really must get a Lee-Lonsdale," said Tony. He made this announcement in the same tone, Dorothy reflected bitterly, as he had announced that they would have another baby.

When the butler opened the door of 129 Curzon Street, the house was full of birds' singing.

"Canaries, don't you know, and all that," Tony explained. "I thought you'd like to be reminded of the country."

Dorothy looked at him sharply to see if he was teasing her, but he was serious enough, and for the first time since that night in June when her son was born dead she was able to feel an affection for him so personal and so intimate that if they had been alone at the moment she might have flung herself into his arms. He had taken a box for the theater that night and was most eager for her to dine out with him, but she was much tired after the journey and excused herself. Since he was evidently dismayed by the prospect of an unemployed evening, she begged him to go without her, which after a short and not very stoutly contested argument he agreed to do.

Dorothy went up early to her bedroom, where for a long while she sat at the open window, listening to the traffic. How often she had sat thus at the window of her bedroom in Halfmoon Street and what promises of grandeur had then seemed implicit in the majestic sound. Only three years ago she had still been in Halfmoon Street; she could actually remember one October night like this, an October night when the still warm body of a dead summer was being pricked by wintry spears. On such a night as this Olive had called to her not to take cold, had warned her that it was bad for her voice to sit at an open window. She had been thinking about herself in Debrett and planning to be a marchioness; it was Olive's interruption which had brought home sharply to her the necessity of cutting herself off forever from the theater if she married Clarehaven. Yes, it had been a night just like this, and that other window was not five minutes away from where she was sitting now.

A taxi humming round a distant corner reminded Dorothy of an evening on the lawns at Clare when Doctor Lane had lectured her on the habits of night-jars.

"Country sights and country sounds," she exclaimed, and she shivered in a revulsion against them all, because, though she had proved her ability to share in that country life, the blind overseer Fate had withdrawn her to another environment and the overseer must always be propitiated.

The sound of the traffic was casting a spell upon Dorothy's tired nerves; she began to take pleasure in it, welcoming it as a sound familiar and cherished over many years. She looked back at herself a year ago sitting in Clarehaven church, with almost a blush for the affectation of it all, or rather for what must have seemed like affectation to other people. She had allowed herself to exaggerate everything, to dream sublimely and wake ridiculously, to be more than she was ever meant to be. Not music of wind and sea, but this dull music of London traffic was the fit accompaniment for her. She knew that now, when her own sighs absorbed in the countless sighs of the millions round her took their place in the great harmony of human sorrow. Above the castanets of hansoms and the horns of motors the omnibuses rolled like drums ... the hansoms were going back, back, the motors were going forward; but the omnibuses were going home, home, home. And was not her own journey through life like journeys she had taken as a child when the omnibus after a glittering evening went home, rumbling and rolling home?

Dorothy had nearly fallen asleep; waking to full consciousness with a start, she laughed at her fancies; quickly shutting the window, she drew the curtains and walked about the golden bedroom as if she would assure herself that the evening was not nearly spent yet, that not for her was some dim omnibus waiting to carry her home ... home. She checked the fresh impulse to dwell upon the monotonous rumble of the traffic and drove the sound from her mind. Of what could she complain, really? What other girl like herself would not envy her good fortune? What other girl would not laugh at her for thinking that life was dull because she had failed at the first attempt to produce a son? In this comfortable bedroom, amid flowers of chintz, was she not already more at home than she had ever been along the herbaceous borders of Clare? The fact was that her life at Clare had been a part sustained with infinite verve and accomplishment through many months, but always a part. Yes, it had been a part which she had sustained so brilliantly that she had nearly ruined the well-mounted but not very brilliant play in which she had been performing. The dowager had been right when she had expressed her fears for the effect upon Tony of his wife's behavior. She had considered her warning as kindly, but quite unnecessary; she had even pitied the poor little beaver-like dowager for likening her own position with that rake of a husband to that which Dorothy occupied in respect of the son. But the dowager had been right. Herself had risked the substance for the shadow, and in her lust for personal success she might abruptly have found that the play had stopped running. Luckily, it was not too late to remedy the mistake. Here was the scene set for a new act in which Tony must be allowed his chance. Poor old boy, he was not asking for much, and he was still so dependent upon her that it would be a pleasure to spoil him a little now. Should she not really be flattered that he loved her more than an heir to his name, his rank, and his fortune? What would it signify if the house of Clare became extinct? Would those ladies in the long gallery, those ladies simpering eternally at sea and sky, be a whit less immobile if children laughed on the lawns below? Would they blink their eyes or move a muscle of their rosy lips? Not they. And if strangers held their beauty in captivity, would they care? Not they. And if the earth fell into the sun so that nothing of poor mortality, not even Shakespeare, endured, would they simper less serenely in the moment before their painted lips blistered and were consumed? Not a whit less serenely. None of the people on other planets would care if the fifth Earl of Clarehaven was the last; even if the people of Mars had a telescope big enough to see what was happening on earth, they would only watch us with less compassion than we watch ants on a burning log.

"And if by chance they have got such a telescope," Dorothy murmured, "how absurd we must look."

Earth shrank to nothing even as she spoke, for on that thought she fell asleep where she was sitting and did not wake until Tony came back.

"Hullo, Doodles! Why do you go to sleep in your chair?" he asked.

"Did you enjoy the theater?"

"Well, as a matter of fact," he admitted, "I didn't use the box. I thought, as you wouldn't come, I'd drop in and have a look at the new show at the Vanity. Pretty good, really. Your friend Olive Fanshawe was in a quintet. She has a few lines to speak, too, and looks very jolly. I wish you'd come with me one night. I think you'd enjoy it."

"I will if you like," said Dorothy.

"No, really?" he exclaimed, his eyes lighting up. "Now, isn't that splendid! I'll tell you what we'll do. We'll have a party for my birthday next week. Dine at the Carlton. Two boxes at the Vanity, and supper afterward at the Savoy. I say I shall enjoy it, Doodles!"

"How old will you be?" she asked, with a smile.

"Twenty-six. Aging fast. Have to hurry up and enjoy ourselves while we can."

"I shall be twenty-five in March," she said.

Then suddenly she seemed able to throw off all her fatigue and to forget all her disappointment.

"Sorry I've been so dull these last few weeks," she murmured. "Tony, do you still love me?"

"You never need ask me that," he said. "But do you love me?"

She nodded.

"Couldn't you say it? You never have, you know. Couldn't you just whisper 'yes'?"

"Yes."

"Cleared it," he shouted, and while he was in his dressing-room she heard him singing:

"For Dolly's out and about again,
She doesn't give a damn for a shower of rain.
Here's Dolly with her collie!
And London, dear old London,
London is itself again."

This outburst was followed by a silence which was presently broken by a sound of torn paper.

"What are you tearing up, Tony?"

"Oh, nothing," he called back, in accents of elaborate indifference. "Only an old program."

In the morning Dorothy looked in the paper-basket, the bottom of which was lightly powdered by the fragments of a letter. She stooped to pick up the pieces; then she stopped.

"What does it matter who it was for? It was never sent. But I was only just in time."

On October 15th a party of eight visited "The Belle of Belgravia" at the Vanity. Besides Tony and Dorothy, there were Arthur Lonsdale, who had long forgotten all about Queenie Molyneux and could now watch a musical comedy as coldly as a dramatic critic whose paper did not depend on the theatrical advertisements. He brought his partner, Adrian Lee, whose pretty little wife, all cheeks and hair, looked much more like an actress than Dorothy, though she was really the daughter of a bishop. People used to wonder how a bishop came to have such a daughter; they forgot that while he was a vicar he had written a commentary on the Song of Solomon, with foot-notes as luscious as the plums that sink to the bottom of a cake. Harry Tufton came, and a Mrs. Foster-ffrench who went everywhere except where she most wanted to go and was always a little resentful that even with her two "f's" she could not hook herself up to some altitudes. However, that was Mrs. Foster-ffrench's private sorrow, and she did not let it mar a jolly evening. The other guests were Capt. Archibald Keith, late of the 16th Hussars, who had abandoned the cavalry in order to write the librettos of musical comedies, and a Mrs. Mainwaring, who kept a fashionable hat-shop in Bruton Street and was the widow of poor Dick Mainwaring, a brother of Lord

Hughenden. Everybody always spoke about him as poor Dick Mainwaring, but whether because he had been killed at Paardeburg or because he had married Rita Daubeny was uncertain; it probably varied with the point of view of the speaker. The friends of Mrs. Mainwaring put down any oddness in her behavior to French creole blood and a childhood in Martinique; to the former was also attributable her chic in hats; to the latter the dryness and pallor of her complexion; French blood or French brandy, Martinique or Martell, the Hon. Mrs. Richard Mainwaring certainly did stimulate conversation just as paprika stimulates the appetite. But however jocund her life, her hats were chaste, and however sharp her play, her name was honorable. Moreover, so many people owed her money that they had to be pleasant to her. Mrs. Foster-ffrench, in spite of her name, had no French blood to excuse her odd behavior; in fact, she had nothing except a hyphen and those two "f's." Mr. Foster-ffrench was a younger son who, having failed to grow sisal profitably in the Bahamas, was now experimenting in Mozambique with the jikungo or Inhambane nut, and liable at any moment to experiment with vanila in Tahiti or pearls on the Great Barrier Reef; the only experiment he was never likely to make was going back to Mrs. Foster-ffrench. Dorothy wondered what Tony found to attract him in such a gathering; yet he was in tremendous spirits, obviously delighted that Archie Keith should have met the Vanity comedian that afternoon and warned him who would be in front. He was proud that all the girls on the stage kept their eyes on Dorothy throughout the evening, proud that the comedian inserted two special gags for the benefit of the jolly party, which were rewarded by a loud burst of laughter; and when the alarmed audience trained their opera-glasses upon the boxes as a beleagured garrison might train their guns upon the wild yell of savages he was radiant. After the performance they sat round a large circular table in the Savoy, and when the orchestra played "Dolly and her Collie" there was so much applause from the tables all round that Dorothy could not help feeling rather proud of the pleasure her return to town had given and was touched to think that her memory was still green. The evening wound up at the Lees' flat in Berkeley Street, when Adrian Lee and Clarehaven hospitably lost a good deal of money to their guests in the course of three hours' baccarat.

Now that Dorothy had broken her rule and had visited the Vanity for the first time since she had left the boards, she felt that she could not maintain her policy of isolation any longer; she told Clarehaven as much when they were strolling back down Curzon Street and breathing in the air of night after those feverish rooms.

"Doodles, my dear thing, I'm delighted! I never wanted you to give up any of your old friends. It was you who insisted on cutting them out like that."

"And if," she went on, "we can sit in a box with Rita Mainwaring, I don't think I can keep up this pretense of not being able to meet Olive."

"I quite agree with you. I should love to meet Olive again."

"Then what about asking her to lunch?" Dorothy suggested.

"The sooner the better," he assented, enthusiastically.

A note was sent round to the Vanity, in which Dorothy, without making the least allusion to anything that had happened in the past, most cordially invited Olive to lunch with them two days later. Olive replied, thanking Dorothy for the invitation, but mentioned that she was now living with Sylvia Scarlett, and, since she did not like to go without her and since she knew Dorothy and Sylvia were no longer on good terms, was afraid she must decline lunch, though she promised to come and see her old friend some afternoon.

"Living with Sylvia Scarlett, eh?" commented Tony, with raised eyebrows.

They were sitting in the smoking-room, where in the silence that ensued the red arm-chairs seemed to be commenting upon this problem raised so suddenly, seemed, like wise and rubicund ministers of state, to be bringing their minds to bear silently upon things in general. "Sylvia Scarlett!" Dorothy kept saying to herself, while the scarlet leather answered her. She was perplexed. For one reason she should like to meet Sylvia again, because she felt that better, perhaps, than anybody Sylvia would appreciate her point of view. Could she but bring herself to be frank with Sylvia, she could think of no one who would respond with a more intelligent sympathy to the tale of her disappointment. Moreover, if she showed the least disinclination to exclude Sylvia she might give Tony the impression that she was still resenting that week-end at Brighton, a notion which her pride was not sufficiently subdued to contemplate with equanimity. Yet to make friends again with Sylvia openly would be to penetrate rather more deeply into the hinterland of the bohemian seacoast than she had intended, even after going to the Vanity with Mrs. Mainwaring and Mrs. Foster-ffrench.

"I suppose you wouldn't care to have Sylvia here," Tony said at last; "though of course...."

Dorothy interrupted him sharply. "Why not?" she asked. "Why should I object to have Sylvia here any more than I should object to being seen at the theater with Rita Mainwaring?"

"I thought that perhaps...." he began again.

She told him to ring for a messenger-boy and immediately wrote to invite Sylvia to lunch as well.

It was difficult, considering the circumstances in which Dorothy had parted from Sylvia and Olive, for any of the girls to avoid a feeling of constraint when they met again; Dorothy, for her part, had to make a great effort not to let her nervousness give an impression that she was being reserved with her old friends. Lonsdale, however, who had fortunately been invited, was very talkative, and Tony was in boisterous spirits, so boisterous, indeed, that once or twice Dorothy looked at him in surprise. When he returned her glance defiantly she wondered if she had not made a mistake in her policy; if before consenting to come down to her husband's level she had properly safeguarded herself. No doubt in spite of her disapproval he would have gambled and drunk and made an ass of himself with the Mainwarings and the Foster-ffrenches, but by withholding herself she would have retained, at any rate, as much power over him as would have kept him outwardly deferential to his wife. Now he was no longer afraid of her.

Dorothy was roused from her abstraction by hearing herself addressed as Cousin Dorothy by Lonsdale. He was in a corner with Sylvia, and they were amusing themselves, presumably at her expense; Dorothy darted an angry look at Sylvia, who shook her head with so mocking a disclaimer that Dorothy gave up the notion of confiding in her old friend. Sylvia evidently still regarded her with hostility and contempt, and was as ready to pour ridicule upon her now as she used to be in the dressing-room on tour. On tour! The days on tour crowded upon her memory. From the corner where Sylvia and Lonsdale were chatting she heard Lily's name mentioned. What was that? Lily had married a croupier in Rio de Janeiro? But how unimportant it was who married what in this world. After so short a time, life lost its tender hues of sunrise or sunset and became garish or dim. On tour! The funny old life trickled confusedly past her vision like a runaway film, and she took Olive's hand affectionately. Olive was as sympathetic as if she had never been treated so heartlessly that day in Brighton, as eager to hear that Dorothy was happy, as eager to accept her assurances that she was. Tears stood in her eyes when she was told about the baby; but somehow her sympathy was not enough for Dorothy, who only awarded her a half-hearted sort of confidence that was sentimentalized to suit the listener. If she could have confided in Sylvia she would have told the story without sparing herself, but Sylvia had snubbed her; and, anyway, the past was not to be recaptured by talking about it.

Notwithstanding Sylvia's indifference, Dorothy went out of her way to invite her often to Curzon Street that autumn and early winter. She was fascinated by her play at baccarat and *chemin de fer*; she wondered upon what mysterious capital she was drawing, for, though her name was not coupled with any man who would pay her debts, she was apparently able to lose as much money as she chose. It seemed impossible that it should be her own money; but so many things about Sylvia seemed impossible. In January Olive showed symptoms of a tendency to consumption; Sylvia, without waiting an instant to win back any of her losses, took her off to Italy for a long rest.

"*I* despise Tony, and *she* despises me," Dorothy thought. "But isn't she right?"

She looked round her at the drawing-room of 129 Curzon Street, where in a foliage of tobacco smoke the faces of the gamblers stared out like fruit, and upon the green tablecloth the cards lay like fallen petals. Was not Sylvia right to despise her for encouraging Mrs. Mainwaring and Captain Keith and Mrs. Foster-ffrench and half a dozen others like them? Was not Sylvia right to despise her for setting out as a countess so haughtily and coming down to this? How she must have laughed when Olive told her about the parting in Brighton, and how little she would believe her tales of rural triumphs like the meet at Five Tree Farm. Sylvia probably considered that she had found her true level in seeing that her gambling guests were kept well supplied with refreshments.

In March even Clarehaven grew tired of baccarat with Captain Keith and the rest of them, and one morning a big new six-cylinder Lee-Lonsdale was driven up to 129 Curzon Street by the junior member of the firm, who wanted to advertise his wares on the Continent. Clarehaven's man and Dorothy's maid took the heavy luggage by train; the car with Dorothy, Lonsdale, Clarehaven, and a chauffeur swept like an arpeggio the road from London to Dover, transhipped to Calais, and made a touring-car record from Paris to Monte Carlo, whence Lonsdale, after booking some orders, returned to England without it. Tony lost five thousand pounds at roulette, a small portion of which he recovered over pigeons. He would probably have lost much more had not Dorothy told him, on a rose-hung night of stars and lamplight, that she was going to have another baby and that she must go back to Clare.

The prospective father was so pleased with the news that he set out to beat the record established by Lonsdale on the way down, drove into a poplar-tree, and smashed the car. Dorothy had a miscarriage and lay ill for a month at a small village between Grenoble and Lyons. Tony was penitent; but he was obviously bored by having to spend this idle month in France, and as soon as Dorothy was well enough to travel and he had assured himself that she was not nervous after the accident, he drove northward faster than ever. They reached Clare at the end of May.

II

The bluebells were out when Dorothy came home, their pervasive sweetness sharpened by the pungency of young bracken; even as sometimes the heavenly clouds imitate the hills and valleys of earth or lie about at sunset like islands in a luminous and windless ocean, so now earth imitated heaven, and the bluebells lay along the woodland like drifts of sky. May was not gone when Dorothy came back; the cuckoo was not even yet much out of tune; the fallow deer did not yet display all their snowy summer freckles; the whitethroat still sang to his lady sitting close in the nettles by the orchard's edge; apple-blossom was still strewn upon the lengthening grass; the orange-tip still danced along the glades; the red and white candles upon the horse-chestnuts were not yet burned out. It was still May; but June like a grave young matron stood close at hand, and May like a girl grown tired of her flowers and of her finery would presently fall asleep in her arms. And like the merry month Dorothy pillowed her head upon the green lap of June. For several weeks she made no allusion to the accident on the way home from Monte Carlo; nor, beyond the perpetually manifest joy she took in the seasonable pageant, did she give any sign of her distaste for the way she and Tony had spent the past year. The problem of what was to happen next autumn was not yet ripe for discussion, and in order to enjoy fully the present peace Dorothy persuaded Clarehaven to accept an invitation to go fishing in Norway, after which he would camp with the yeomanry for three weeks; and then another year would have to be catered for so that not one minute of it should be wasted—in other words, that it should be squeezed as dry as an orange to extract from it the last drop of pleasure. Tony wanted her to come with him to Norway, but she made her health an excuse and sent him off alone.

In July the countess and the dowager were pacing the turf that ran by the edge of that famous golden border now in its prime. The rich light of the summer afternoon flattered the long line of massed hues which had been so artfully contrived. The unfamiliar beauty of the bronzed Himalayan asphodels, of citron kniphofias from Abyssinia and sulphur-lilies from the Caucasus, of ixias tawny as their own African lions, of canary-colored Mexican tigridias and primrose-hooded gladioli that bloom in the rain forest of the Victoria Falls, mingled with the familiar forms of lemon-pale hollyhocks and snapdragons, with violas apricot-stained, and with many common yellow flowers of cottage gardens to which the nurserymen had imparted a subtle and aristocratic shade.

"What a success your golden border has been," the dowager exclaimed.

Dorothy felt suddenly that she could not any longer tolerate such compliments. The life-blood of her marriage seemed to be running dry before her eyes while she was amusing herself with golden borders, and she wanted her mother-in-law to understand how critical the position was, and what disasters lurked in the future while the sun flattered the flowers, and she flattered her son's wife.

"I'm going to be very frank," Dorothy began. "I want to know more about Tony's father."

The dowager with a look of alarm leaned over the border to hide her embarrassment.

"My dear," she said, "how cleverly you've combined this little St.-John's-wort with these copper-colored rock-roses. They look delightful together."

"Why did you marry him?" Dorothy asked.

"Dorothy! Such a question, but really, I suppose—well, I don't know. I suppose really because he asked me."

"Your mother didn't insist upon it?"

"Well, of course, my mother didn't oppose it," the dowager admitted. "No, certainly not ... she didn't actually oppose it; in fact possibly ... yes ... well.... I think one might almost say that she.... Oh, aren't these trolliums gorgeous? They are trolliums, aren't they? I always get confused between trilliums and trolliums?"

"Troll*ius*. Persuaded you into it?" Dorothy supplemented. "Did you love him?"

This was altogether too intimate an inquiry, and the dowager, failing to bury her blushes in the opulent group of butter-colored flowers that she was bending over to admire, took refuge in her bringing-up.

"We were brought up differently in those days," she said. "I don't think that men depended upon their wives to quite the same extent they do now."

"I'm asking you all this," Dorothy explained, "because as far as the future is concerned Tony and I are standing now at crossroads. If I oppose or, even without opposing them, if I fail to share in his pleasures, my attitude won't have any sobering effect. But if I take part with him willingly and enjoy what he enjoys, it may be that I shall have enough influence to prevent his going too far. Frankly, he doesn't seem to have an idea that there may be something else in life besides self-indulgence, the instant and complete self-indulgence that he always allows himself. Money and rank only exist for him because they are useful to that end. The only thing he was ever denied for five minutes of his life was myself, and after a period of active sulking he got me. I suppose you spoiled him, really."

The dowager looked melancholy.

"I'm not reproaching you," said Dorothy. "I quite understand the temptation. That's why I asked if you ever loved your husband. I thought that perhaps you didn't and that you'd had to love Tony much more in consequence. I'm sorry about that son of mine, because I should have liked to prove that it is possible to devote oneself utterly to a son without spoiling him. Meanwhile, I'm afraid it's too late to do anything with Tony. You must forgive me for this attack upon illusions. I shall never make another. I only wanted you to know, because you were kind to me when I first came here, that I've done my best and that there's nothing more to be done."

"But you're so beautiful," said the dowager. "I was never beautiful."

"Oh, so far as keeping him more or less faithful is worth while, I don't suppose I shall have the least difficulty," Dorothy admitted. "But each time I tame him with a kiss I reduce my own self-respect a little bit, and I blunt his respect for me. If I were his mistress, my kisses would be bribes to make him spend money on me; as his wife my kisses are bribes to prevent his spending money on other women. Anyway, this is the last that you or any one else shall ever hear on this rather unpleasant subject. I think these tigridias that Mr. Greenish was so keen to combine with the ixias were a mistake. They are quite faded by the afternoon."

It was now Dorothy's turn to direct the conversation toward flowers, while the dowager endeavored to keep it personal.

"I've often thought," she began, "what a pity it was for you to cut yourself off so completely from your own family."

"I certainly shouldn't find them of any help to me now," said Dorothy.

"Well, I don't know. I think that a mother can always be helpful," the dowager argued. "I think it's a pity that you should have felt the necessity of eliminating your family like this. I dare say I was to blame in the first place, and I'm afraid that I gave you the impression that we were much more snobbish down here than wereally are. Your impulse was natural in the circumstances, but I had hoped that I had been able to prove to you that my opposition was only directed against your profession, and you who know what Tony is will surely appreciate my alarm at the idea of his marrying merely to gratify himself at the moment. My own dear old mother was perhaps a little more sensitive than I am to old-fashioned ideas of rank. She belonged to a period when such opinions were widely spread in the society she frequented. I confess that since she died I have found myself inclining more and more every day to what would once have been called Red Radicalism. You know, I really can't help admiring some of the things that this dreadful government is trying to do." The epithet was so persistently applied by the county that for the dowager it had lost any independent significance; it was like calling a tradesman "dear sir."

Dorothy was tempted to ask the dowager if she did believe the account she had given of her family, but she felt that if she suggested even the possibility of such skepticism she should be admitting its justification. And then suddenly she had a profound regret that her mother had never seen Clare, had never trodden this ancient turf nor sat beneath those cedar-trees. If the dowager had extended the courtesy of breeding to accept those legends her daughter-in-law had spread about herself, her courtesy would certainly not be withheld from accepting that daughter-in-law's mother. The idea took shape; it positively would be jolly to invite her mother to stay for a month at Clare. Tony would not be bored; he would be away all the time.

"And not merely your family," the dowager was saying. "Oh no, it's not merely cutting yourself from them, but also from your friends. I've heard somebody called Olive alluded to once or twice, and surely she would enjoy visiting here. Though please don't think me a foolish busybody. Perhaps Olive prefers London."

"Olive has just got married. She was married last week."

"Then I've heard you talk about a Sylvia, who possibly might care to stay down here. Dear child, don't misunderstand me, I beg. I'm only trying to suggest that you are conceivably making a mistake in dividing your life into two. After all, look at this border. See how the old-fashioned favorites of us all are improved by these rarer flowers. And do notice how well the simple flowers hold their own with those exotics that have been planted out from the greenhouse. You see what I'm trying to tell you? If Tony has certain tastes, if he likes people of whom you and I might even mildly disapprove, let him see them here in another setting. However, that you must decide later on. The only thing I should like to lay stress upon is your duty toward your family...."

"To my mother only," Dorothy interrupted. "I have no duty toward my father."

"Perhaps you will think differently when you have seen your mother. I like her so much already. How could I do otherwise when she has given me a daughter-in-law for whom I have such a great admiration?"

Dorothy took the dowager's hand and looked down earnestly and affectionately into her upturned gaze.

"Why are you always so sweet to me?" she asked.

"Whatever I am, my dear child, it is only the expression of what I feel."

That evening Dorothy wrote to her mother.

CLARE COURT, DEVON,
July 8, 1909.

MY DEAR MOTHER,—Such a long time since I saw you. Don't you think you could manage a visit to Clare next week? Come for at least a month. It will do you all the good in the world and I should so much enjoy seeing you. You will find my mother-in-law very sympathetic. I had thought of suggesting that you should bring Agnes and Edna with you, but I think that perhaps for the first time you'd rather be alone. The best train leaves Paddington at eleven-twenty. Book to Cherrington Lanes and change at Exeter. On second thoughts I'll meet you at Exeter on Wednesday next. So don't make any excuses.

Your loving daughter,
DOROTHY.

The prospect of her mother's visit was paradoxically a solace for Dorothy's disappointed maternity. The relation between them was turned upside down, and her mother became a little girl who must be looked after and kept from behaving badly, and who when she behaved well would be petted and spoiled.

Heaven knows what domestic convulsions and spiritual agitations braced Mrs. Caffyn to telegraph presently:

Am bringing three brats will they be enough.

For a moment Dorothy thought that she was coming with Vincent, Gladys, and Marjorie, so invariably did she picture her family as all of the same age as when seven years ago she first left Lonsdale Road to go to the stage. A little consideration led her to suppose that *hats* not *brats* were intended, and she telegraphed back:

You will want a nice shady hat for the garden.

Dorothy went to meet Mrs. Caffyn at Exeter in order that the three hours in the slow train between there and Cherrington Lanes might give her an opportunity of recovering herself from that agitation which had made her telegram so ambiguous. It was impossible to avoid a certain amount of pomp at the station, because the station-master, on hearing that her ladyship was expecting her ladyship's mother, led the way to the platform where the express would arrive and unrolled before her a red carpet of good intentions.

"Stand aside there," he said, severely, to a boy with a basket of newspapers.

"First stop Plymouth," shouted the porters when the express came thundering in.

"Stand aside," thundered the station-master, more loudly; perhaps he was addressing the train this time.

Mrs. Caffyn looked out of a second-class compartment and popped in again like some shy burrowing animal that fears the great world.

"What name, my lady, would be on the luggage?" asked the station-master when, notwithstanding her emersion from a second-class compartment, he had seen Mrs. Caffyn embraced by her ladyship.

"Caffyn! Caffyn!" he bellowed. "Stand aside there, will you? Both vans are being dealt with, my lady," he informed her.

The luggage was identified; a porter was bidden to carry it to No. 5 platform; and the station-master, taking from Mrs. Caffyn a string-bag in which nothing was left except a paper bag of greengages, led the way to the slow train for Cherrington.

"I traveled second-class," Mrs. Caffyn whispered, nervously, while the station-master was stamping about in a first-class compartment, dusting the leather seats and arranging the small luggage upon the rack. "I hesitated whether I ought not to travel third, but father was very nice about it."

"Please change this ticket to first-class as far as Cherrington Lanes, Mr. Thatcher," said Dorothy.

"Immediately, my lady," he announced; and as he hurried away down the platform Mrs. Caffyn regarded him as the Widow Twankay may have regarded the Genie of the Lamp.

"I've brought five hats with me," Mrs. Caffyn announced when the slow train was on its way and Mr. Thatcher was left standing upon the platform and apparently wondering if he could not give it a push from behind as a final compliment to her ladyship. "And now—oh dear, I must remember to call you Dorothy, mustn't I? By the way, you know that Dorothy is going to have a baby in November? Her husband is so pleased about it. He's doing very well, you know. Oh yes, the Norbiton

Urban District Council have intrusted him with—well, I'm afraid I've forgotten just what it is, but he's doing very well, and I thought you'd be interested to hear about Dorothy. But I really *must* remember not to call you Norah."

"It wouldn't very much matter, mother."

"Oh, wouldn't it?" Mrs. Caffyn exclaimed, brightening. "Well, now, I'm sure that's a great weight off my mind. All the way down I've been worrying about that. And now just tell me, because I don't want to do anything that will make you feel uncomfortable. What am I to call your sisters-in-law? I understand about your mother-in-law. She will be Lady Clarehaven. Is that right? But your sisters-in-law?"

"Bella and Connie."

"Bella and Connie?" repeated Mrs. Caffyn. "Nothing else? I see. Well, of course, in that case I don't think I shall feel at all shy."

Although Dorothy was no longer concerned whether her mother did or did not behave as if she were in the habit of visiting at great houses during the summer, she could not resist indulging her own knowledge a little, not with any idea of display, but because she enjoyed the feeling that somebody was dependent upon her superior wisdom in worldly matters. Mrs. Caffyn enjoyed her lessons, just as few women—or men, for that matter—can resist opening a book of etiquette that lies to hand. They would not buy one for themselves, because that would seem to advertise their ignorance; but if it can be read without too much publicity it will be read, for it makes the same appeal to human egoism that is made by a medical dictionary or a work on palmistry. One topic Dorothy did ask Mrs. Caffyn to avoid, which was the life of her own mother. After that conversation by the golden border she had little doubt that the dowager did not accept as genuine the tapestry she had woven of her life; but that was no reason for drawing attention to all the fabulous beasts in the background.

"Perhaps you'd better not say anything about Grandmother Doyle," Dorothy advised. "I had to give an impression that she was related to Lord Cleveden, and if you talk too much about her it would make me look rather foolish."

"But she did belong to the same family," said Mrs. Caffyn.

"Yes, but I'd rather you didn't mention it. You can talk about Roland and Cecil and Vincent, only please avoid the topic of Grandmother Doyle."

"Of course I'll avoid anything you like," Mrs. Caffyn offered. "And perhaps I'd better throw these greengages out of the window."

The dowager was much too tactful, as Dorothy had foreseen, to ask Mrs. Caffyn any questions; she, with a license to talk about her children, was never at a loss for conversation. There is no doubt that she thoroughly enjoyed herself at Clare, and with two garden hats worn alternately she sat in placid survey of her daughter's grandeur, drove with the dowager in the chaise, congratulated Mrs. Beadon and Mrs. Kingdon upon their children, patted every dog she met, and went home first-class surrounded by baskets of peaches.

Notwithstanding the dowager's advice, Dorothy sent her mother home before Tony came back, not because she was ashamed of her, but because she dreaded his geniality and cordial invitations to bring the whole family to Curzon Street. She could not bear the idea of her father's arriving at all hours, for since the revelation of his tastes that night in St. John's Wood she fancied that he would rather enjoy the excuse his son-in-law's house would offer him of forgetting that he was still secretary of the Church of England Purity Society. So long as Tony did not meet any of her family he would not bother about them; but if he did, the temptation to his uncritical hospitality would be too strong.

The partridges were very plentiful that autumn at Clare; the pheasants never gave better sport. Dorothy invited Olive and her husband, a pleasant young actor called Airdale, to visit Clare, but Olive had to decline, because she was going to have a baby. Sylvia Scarlett Dorothy did not invite; but Sylvia Lonsdale came with her brother, and late in the autumn the Clarehavens went to stay with the Clevedens in Warwickshire. Lord Cleveden talked to Tony about the need for a strong colonial policy, and Lady Cleveden talked to Dorothy about the imperative necessity of finding a wife for Arthur at once. The shooting was not so good as at Clare, and Tony decided that he required London as a tonic for the rural depopulation of his mind.

"These fellows who've been in administrative posts get too self-important," he confided to Dorothy. "Now I don't take any interest in the colonies. Except, of course, British East and the Straits. When a fellow talks to me about Queensland my mind becomes a blank. I feel as if I was being prepared for Confirmation, don't you know?"

They reached town toward the end of November, and within a week the old set was round them. Baccarat and *chemin de fer*, the Vanity and the Orient, smart little dances and rowdy little suppers, Mrs. Foster-ffrench and the Hon. Mrs. Richard Mainwaring, they were back in the middle of them all. Sylvia Scarlett turned up again, still apparently with plenty of money to waste on gambling. She and Dorothy drifted farther apart, if that were possible, and their coolness was added to by Sylvia's recommendation of a rising young painter called Walker for Dorothy's portrait, which Dorothy considered a failure, though when afterward she was painted by an artist who had already risen that was a failure, too. Sylvia seemed to misunderstand her wantonly; Dorothy armed herself against her old friend's contempt and tried to create an impression of complete self-sufficiency. Once in the spring an occasion presented itself for knocking down the barrier they had erected between themselves. Sylvia had just brought the sum of her losses at cards to over six hundred pounds, and Dorothy, on hearing of it, expressed her concern.

"I suppose you wonder where I find the money to lose?" Sylvia asked.

"Oh no, I wasn't thinking that. I'm not interested in your private affairs," said Dorothy, freezing at the other's aggressive tone.

"No?" said Sylvia. "You easily forget about your friends' private affairs, don't you? But I warned Olive that your chauffeur wouldn't be able to find the way to West Kensington."

"How can you...." the countess broke out. Then she stopped herself. If she tried to explain what had kept her from visiting Olive Airdale all these months, she should have to reveal her own intimate hopes, her own jealousy and disillusionment; she would prefer that Sylvia supposed it was nothing more than snobbery that kept her away from Olive. If once she began upon explanations she should have to explain why she so seldom visited or spoke of her family. She should have to admit that she could no longer answer for Tony, even so far as to be sure that he would not invite her father to sit down with him to baccarat. And even those explanations would not be enough; she should have to go back to the beginning of her married life and expose such rags and tatters of dreams. Her mind went back to that railway carriage on a wet January afternoon when "Miss Elsie of Chelsea" traveled from Manchester to Birmingham. She remembered the supper that was kept waiting for Sylvia and her cheeks all dabbled with tears and a joke she had made about trusting in God and keeping her powder dry. She had tried to win Sylvia's confidence then and she had been snubbed. Should she volunteer her own confidence now?

"I'm sorry you've lost so much money in my house," said the countess.

Then she blushed; the very pronoun seemed boastful.

"Never mind. I'm going down to Warwickshire to-morrow to help Olive bring an heir into the world."

"Does she want a girl or a boy?" Dorothy asked.

"My dear," said Sylvia, "she is so anxious not to show the least sign of favoritism even before birth that in order to achieve a perfect equipoise she'll either have to have twins or a hermaphrodite."

In April Dorothy heard that her friend actually had produced twins.

"It seems so easy," she sighed, "when one hears about other people."

"Cheer up, Doodles," said Tony. "I won four hundred last night. It's about time I got some of my own back from Archie Keith; he's been plucking us all for months, lucky devil. I shall chuck shimmy."

"I wish you would," said Dorothy.

"Solemn old Doodles," he laughed. "Harry Tufton wants me to take up racing. By Jove, I'm not sure I sha'n't. You'd like that better, wouldn't you?"

"I'd like anything better than these eternal cards," she declared, passionately.

At the same time she was a little nervous of the new project, and she took an early opportunity of speaking about it to Tufton, who addressed her with the accumulated wisdom of the several thousand hours he had spent in the Bachelors' Club.

"My dear Dorothy," he began, flashing her Christian name as his mother flashed her diamonds. "I'm very glad you've broached this subject. The fact is, Tony really must draw in a little bit. I don't know how much he's lost these last two years; but he has lost a good deal, and it certainly isn't worth while losing for the benefit of people like Archie Keith and Rita Mainwaring. Only the other day at the Bachelors' I was speaking to Hughenden, and he said to me, 'Harry, my boy, why don't you exercise your influence with Tony Clarehaven and get rid of that harpy who unfortunately has the right to call herself my sister-in-law?' Well, that was rather strong, don't you know? And your cousin Paignton spoke to me about him, told me his father was rather worried about Tony—the Chatfield push feel it's not dignified. As I said to him: 'My dear fellow, if you want to lose money, why don't you lose money in a gentlemanly way? There are always horses.'"

"But I don't want him to lose his money at all," Dorothy protested.

"Quite, quite," Mr. Tufton quacked. "But you'd prefer him to lose money over horses than present it free of income tax to Archie Keith and Rita Mainwaring? At this rate he'll soon lose all his old friends, as well as his money."

Dorothy looked at the speaker; she was wondering if this was the fidgeting of a more than usually apprehensive ship's rat.

III

The Clarehaven property outside the park itself did not now include more than three thousand acres; but some speculations in which the fourth earl indulged after selling the old Hopley estate had grown considerably in value during his son's minority; and when Tony came of age, in addition to his land, which, after the payment of the dowager's jointure and all taxes, brought him in a net income of about three thousand pounds a year, he had something like seventy thousand pounds invested in Malayan enterprises which paid 10 per cent, and brought up his net income to well over eight thousand pounds. He had already been forced to sell out a considerable sum for the benefit of Captain Keith, Mrs. Mainwaring, and the rest of them; but should he decide to start a racing-stable he would have plenty of capital left on which to draw. Dorothy protested that he ought not to look upon a racing-stable as a sound and safe investment for capital that was now producing a steady income and that, with rubber booming as it was, would probably be much augmented in the near future. Yet she was afraid to be too discouraging, for, whatever might be urged against horse-racing, it offered a more dignified activity to a gambler than baccarat.

Clarehaven began his career on the turf with a sobriety which contrasted with his extravagance at cards. He bought the stable of Mr. Tufton, senior, and, leaving it in the cautious hands of old William Cobbett at Newmarket, was content during his first season to compete in a few minor handicaps and selling-plates. Such betting as he did was, on the whole, lucky; he found himself toward the end of the season with a margin of profit; and triumphantly he announced to Dorothy that he was going to invest in some really first-class yearlings at Tattersall's and Doncaster. She did not dissuade him, because she had had a talk with honest old William Cobbett, who had assured her that his lordship was willing to listen to his advice, and that if he would be guided by him there was no reason why his lordship should not win some of the great classic races the year after next, fortune being favorable. He spoke of the black, white, and purple of Clarehaven as of colors once famous upon famous courses, and implied that Saturday afternoons at Windsor or Lingfield Park were hardly worthy of the time-honored combination. Dorothy could not help agreeing with the trainer; throughout this first season there had been a great deal too much of Captain Keith and Mrs. Foster-ffrench, too much of a theatrical garden-party about those Saturday afternoons, and although this year Tony had been lucky, another year he might be unlucky and fritter away his money and his reputation in the company of people who saw no difference between the green baize of a card-table and the green turf of a racecourse. Several people had talked of the fourth earl's great deeds upon the turf during the 'seventies; she, still susceptible to intimations of grandeur, viewed with dismay these degenerate week-ends and encouraged Tony to aim higher. If he would not speak in the House of Lords, he might at least win the Derby; and if he won the Derby, surely his lust for gambling would be satiated and he might retire to Clare to raise blood-stock. The idea of owning some mighty horse, the paragon of Ormonde or Eclipse or Flying Childers, obsessed her; she pictured ten years hence a small boy attired in Gainsborough blue, proudly mounted upon a race-horse that should be the sire and grandsire and great-grandsire of a hundred classic winners. She became poetical, so keen was her ambition, so vivid her hope; this mighty horse should be called Moonbeam, should be a ray from the full moon of Clare to illuminate them all—Anthony—herself, that son, who might almost be called Endymion. Why not? Disraeli had called one of his heroes Endymion. Affected? Yes, but Endymion Viscount Clare! Why should Endymion for a boy be more affected than Diana for a girl? And why not Diana, too? Lady Diana Clare! They might be twins. Why not? Mrs. Beadon had produced twins, Olive had produced twins. Moonshine suffused Dorothy's castle in Spain, and moonstruck she paced the battlements.

Tony bought a string of horses at Tattersall's, and at Doncaster paid £600 and £750, respectively, for two yearlings with which old William Cobbett expressed himself particularly well satisfied. It happened that year that a young Greek called Christides, who had lately come of age, won the Champagne Stakes and, in his elation, bought a yearling for three thousand guineas. It further happened that after a triumphal dinner he gave to several friends, among whom was Tony, he lost twice that sum at auction bridge. Though Mr. Christides was extremely rich, his native character asserted itself by an abrupt return to prudence. He had allowed himself a fixed sum to spend at Doncaster, and, having exceeded his calculations, he must sell the yearling—a black colt by Cyllene out of Maid of the Mist. There was no question that he was the pick of the yearlings; if old William Cobbett had not protested so firmly against the price, Clarehaven would have been tempted to buy him at the sale. Dorothy, with her mind still a tenant of Spanish castles, saw in the Maid of the Mist colt the horse of her dreams, and by letting her superstition play round the animal she became convinced that it held the fortunes of Clare. Was not the sire Cyllene, which easily became Selene—Dorothy was deep in moon-lore—and would not the offspring of Selene and Maid of the Mist be well called Moonbeam? Moreover, was not the colt black with one splash of white on the forehead? When, therefore, Mr. Christides offered the yearling to settle his losses with Tony, in other words for £2,722, Dorothy was anxious for him to accept. Old William Cobbett was frightened by the price, but he could urge nothing against the colt except, perhaps, the slightest tendency to a dipped back, so slight, however, that when Mr. Christides, still true to his native character, knocked off the odd £22, the small sum was enough to cure the slight depression.

Dorothy thoroughly enjoyed the winter that followed the purchase of the colt. As soon as Moonbeam—of course he was given the name at once—was safe in William Cobbett's stable the trainer admitted that there was not another yearling to touch him. In the two colts which he himself had advised his patron to buy he could hardly bring himself to take the least interest, and in fact both of them afterward did turn out disappointments, one bursting blood-vessels when called upon for the least effort, and the other a duck-hearted beast that for all his fine appearance never ran out a race. But Moonbeam was everything that a colt could be.

"The heart of a lion," said honest old William, "and as gentle as a dove with it all. Be gad! my lady, I believe you're a real judge of horseflesh, and damme—forgive the uncouth expression—but damme, if ever I go to another sale without you."

"But will he win the Derby?" Dorothy asked.

"Well now, come, come, come! This is early days to begin prophesying. But I wouldn't lay against him, no, begad! I wouldn't lay ten to one against him—not now I wouldn't. Dipped back? Not a bit. If ever I said his back was dipped I must have been dipped myself. You beauty! You love! You jewel!"

After which honest old William took out a bandana handkerchief as big and bright as the royal standard and blew his nose till the stable reverberated with the sound.

"See that? Not a blink," he chuckled. "Not a blink, begad! That colt, my lady, is the finest colt ever seen at Cobbett House. You bird! You gem!"

Tony himself was as enthusiastic as Dorothy or the trainer, and there was no talk of London for a long while. He rented a small hunting-lodge in the neighborhood to please Dorothy, and what between shooting over the Cambridgeshire turnips and hunting hard with two or three noted packs the winter went past quickly enough. Even better than the shooting and the hunting were the February days when Moonbeam was put into stronger work and, in the trainer's words, "ate it."

"He's a glutton for work," said honest old William.

Dorothy and he used to ride on the Heath and watch the horses at exercise, and if only Moonbeam was successful next season with his two-year-old engagements and if only he would win the Derby and if only next year she might have a son....

Moonbeam's first public appearance was at the Epsom Spring Meeting when he ran unplaced in the Westminster Plate, much to Dorothy's alarm.

"He wasn't intended to do anything," the trainer explained, soothingly. "This was just to see how he and Joe Flitten took to each other. Well, Joe, what do you think of him?"

"All right, Mr. Cobbett," said the young jockey, who was considered to be the most promising apprentice at headquarters.

The colt's next engagement was for the Woodcote Stakes at the Epsom Summer Meeting, when he was ridden by Harcourt, one of the leading jockeys of the day, and was backed to win a large sum. Something did go wrong this time, for, though he was running on strongly at the finish, he was again unplaced.

"Dash it!" Clarehaven exclaimed, ruefully. "I hope this isn't going to happen every time. You and her ladyship have made a mistake, I'm afraid, Cobbett. If you ask me, he pecked."

Honest old William looked very grave.

"If you ask *me*, my lord, it was his jockey. The colt was badly ridden. Still, it was a disappointment, there's no getting over it. But it's early days to begin fretting, and he was running on. No doubt about that. Tell you what, my lord, if you'll take my advice you'll give Joe Flitten the mount for Ascot, and if Joe doesn't bring out what there is in him, why then we'll have to put our heads together, that's all about it."

So Joe Flitten, the Cobbett Lodge apprentice, rode Moonbeam in the New Stakes, when the colt made most of his rivals at Epsom look like platers; although it was to be noted that Sir James Otway's unnamed colt by Desmond out of Diavola, which had won the Woodcote Stakes, did not run.

"Like common ordinary platers," honest old William avowed.

After this performance the racing-press began to pay attention to Moonbeam, and when in July he won the Hurst Park Foal Plate with ridiculous ease they admitted that his victory at Ascot was no fluke.

In August Tony rented a grouse-moor in Yorkshire. His other horses were not doing too well, but he was feeling prosperous, for Moonbeam had already repaid him several times over his losses at Epsom; and at the end of the month a jolly party drove over to York in a four-in-hand to see the colt canter away with the Gimcrack Stakes. At this meeting Dorothy really felt that Tony was what in another sense the press would have called "an ornament to the turf." There were no Mrs. Mainwarings and Captain Keiths with them at York, and she never felt less like a Vanity girl than when she heard the crowd cheering Moonbeam's victory—he was by now a popular horse—and looked round proudly at her party; at Uncle Chat with Paignton and Charlie Fanhope; at Bella and Connie, both bright red with joy; at Arthur and Sylvia Lonsdale, and at Miss Horatia Lonsdale, a delightful aunt who was helping Dorothy chaperon the girls, an easy enough task as regards Bella and Connie and not very difficult as regards her niece.

Finally in the autumn Moonbeam won the Middle Park Plate and was voted the finest two-year-old seen at Newmarket for several seasons.

"And now let him keep quiet till the Guineas," said William Cobbett, with a sigh of satisfaction.

"You wouldn't run him in the Dewhurst?"

"No, no, let him rest with what he's done."

"Cobbett is right," said Lord Stilton, one of the stewards of the Jockey Club, who came into the paddock at that moment. "You've got the Derby next year, Clarehaven, if you don't overwork him. That apprentice of yours is a treasure, Cobbett."

"A good boy, my lord."

"You don't know my wife," Tony was saying.

"My congratulations, Lady Clarehaven. I hear you picked out with my old friend William here."

Later on Dorothy was presented to Lady Stilton. She in turn presented her daughter, the beautiful and charming Lady Anne Varley, whose engagement to the young Duke of Ulster had just been announced.

"My dear Dorothy," said Harry Tufton that evening, "you must admit that my advice was good. How much better this sort of thing becomes you than ..." He waved his arms in a gesture of despair at finding any adjective sufficiently contemptuous for those evenings at Curzon Street before his lifelong friend, Tony Clarehaven, had followed his advice and sported the black, white, and purple colors so famous forty years ago.

The prospect of winning the Derby next year really did seem to have completed Tony's cure. He raised no objections when Dorothy insisted that his mother and his sisters should spend the autumn in town, and he actually went three times to the House of Lords to vote against some urgent measure of reform. He did not make a speech, but he coughed once in the middle of an oration by a newly created Radical peer, so significant and so nearly vocally expressive a cough that it deserved to be recorded in Hansard as a contribution to the debate.

Dorothy had been desirous of the dowager's help to consolidate a position in London society that now for the first time appeared tenable. Her meeting with Lady Stilton had given her a foothold on the really high cliffs, and if Tony did not spoil everything she saw no reason why she should not repeat on a larger scale in town her success in Devonshire. It was a pity that Bella and Connie were so ugly; if she could bring off brilliant matches for them, what a help that would be. Of course, it was not the season; most people were out of town notwithstanding that Parliament was sitting; but still surely somewhere in the crowded pages of Debrett could be found suitors for the hands of her sisters-in-law. The nearest approach to a match was when Lord Beccles, the lunatic heir of the Marquis of Norwich, became perfectly manageable if he was allowed to drive with Bella in Hyde Park, chaperoned by his nurse and watched by a footman who held a certificate from one of the largest private asylums in England. If Lord Beccles was a congenital idiot, there were three other sons of Lord Norwich who were sane enough, the eldest of whom, Lord Alistair Gay, agreed with Dorothy that, if Lady Arabella was willing, the marriage would be a kindness to his poor brother. Bella would not take the proposal seriously, and it was evident that she regarded her drives with the poor idiot in the light of a minor charity ranking with the care of a distempered dog or of a cottager's baby.

"You surely aren't serious, Dorothy," she laughed.

"Well, it would give you a splendid position. You would be a countess now and probably a marchioness very soon. Lady Norwich is dead. Lord Norwich is very old, and idiots often live a long time. I'm not suggesting that it would be anything more than a formal marriage, but you apparently don't mind his dribbling with excitement when he sees the Albert Memorial and.... However, I wouldn't persuade you into a match for anything. Only it doesn't seem to me that it would imply anything more than you do for him at present."

The dowager told Dorothy that she would rather dear Bella married somebody simpler than poor Lord Beccles, to which Dorothy retorted that it might be difficult to find even a commoner more simple. Moonbeam's victories as a two-year-old had restored that self-confidence which had been so shaken since her marriage; Dorothy, like most nations and most human beings, was more admirable in adversity than in triumph. The disposition she had shown to recognize her suburban family did not last; she knew that the integument with which she was so carefully wrapping up her reality could be stripped from it by her relations in a second. Only now, after she had been a countess for six years, had Dorothy discovered the narrow bridge that is swung over the center of the universe—the well-laid and lighted bridge so delicately adjusted to eternity that the least divergence from correctness by one of its frequenters might be enough to imperil its balance. That bridge Dorothy was now crossing with all her eyes for her feet, as it were, and she certainly could not afford to be distracted by a family. If Sylvia Scarlett had been in London to watch this new progress she would have made many unkind jokes about the countess; but Sylvia was away acting in America, and in any case she would have found the door of 129 Curzon Street closed against her.

The dowager worried over the way Dorothy was ignoring her mother, and, fortified with strong smelling-salts, she braved the Underground to pay a visit to West Kensington, an experience she so thoroughly enjoyed that she could not keep it a secret for long, but one day began to praise the beauty of Edna and Agnes.

"Frankly, my dear Dorothy," she told her daughter-in-law, "I must say I think that you would be likely to have much more success as a match-maker for your sisters than for dear Bella and dear Connie, who even in London seem unable to avoid that appearance of having just run up and down a very windy hill. Why not have Edna and Agnes to live with you until they're married? And when they are married invite the youngest two, who will also be very beautiful girls, I'm convinced. Really, I never saw such complexions as you and all your sisters have."

Dorothy thought the dowager's suggestion most impracticable.

"Yes, but my most impracticable suggestions nearly always turn out well."

Perhaps, so sure was she of the impression that Agnes and Edna would create in a London ballroom, the dowager would have had her way if she had remained in town for the spring, but in the month of February, anticipating St. Valentine's Day by a week, the Rev. Thomas Hemming wrote from Cherrington to say that Mrs. Paxton, his godmother, had just offered him the living of Newton Candover in Hampshire and would Lady Constantia Clare become Lady Constantia Hemming? Lady Constantia would. The trousseau was bought under the eyes of Dorothy, who, regardless of the fact that she was going to marry a parson, insisted that Connie should look beyond viyella for certain items. Soon after Easter Mr. Beadon had to find another curate and Connie's room at Clare Lodge was empty.

Tony was too much occupied with Moonbeam's chances of winning the two thousand guineas at the end of April to bother who married his sister; but he wrote her a generous check that compensated for the decline in value of the vicar's glebe at Newton Candover.

"And I suppose," said Dorothy, "that next January Connie will have a son."

"Never mind," said her husband. "Next June you and I shall have the Derby winner."

Honest William Cobbett had made no secret of his conviction that Moonbeam was going to canter away with the Guineas, and in the ring his patron's horse was favorite at five to two.

"It'll have to be something very hot and dark that can beat him," he told Clarehaven. "Has your lordship betted very plentiful?"

"I shall drop about ten thousand if the colt fails," said Clarehaven, airily. "But most of my big bets are for the Derby. I got sixes against him twice over to two thousand and fives twelve times in thousands. If he wins to-day I shall plunge a bit."

The trainer blinked his limpid blue eyes.

"Oh, then you don't consider you've done anything in the way of plunging so far?"

"Nothing," said Clarehaven, flicking his mount and calling to Dorothy to ride along with him to the Birdcage. They had taken a small house for the meeting, and they were just off to escort Moonbeam to the starting-post. Lonsdale and Tufton had also come down to Newmarket, the former mounted under protest on a hack which he rode as if he were driving a car.

"Well, so long, Cobbett," the owner cried. "Hope we shall all be feeling as happy in another half-hour as we are now."

"Never fear, my lord. As I told you, there's only the Diavola colt to be afraid of. There's not a bit of doubt he won the Dewhurst in rare fashion, and of course that made his win at Epsom in the Woodcote look good. And now Sir James has gone and sold him for seven thousand guineas with a contingency to this man Houston—somebody new to racing. Well, seven thousand guineas is a nice little price, and there's been a lot of money forthcoming from the Winsley crowd. Dick Starkey always tries to serve up something extra hot for Newmarket. There's nothing gives greater delight to a provincial stable like Starkey Lodge than to do us headquarter folk out of the Guineas, which, as you may say, is our specialty. Stupid name, though, to give such a nice-looking animal. Chimpanzee!"

Dorothy uttered an exclamation. She divined the owner's name at once, and when Lonsdale told her it was Leopold Hausberg who had been away in South Africa and returned more rich than ever with a license to call himself Lionel Houston in future, she was not at all surprised, but her heart began to beat faster.

"Come along, come along, you two. We sha'n't be in time to escort the horses from the Birdcage."

"I say, Tony," said Lonsdale, anxiously, "the bookies are shouting twenty to one bar two, and Moonbeam has gone out to eleven to four."

"Damn!" ejaculated his owner. "I wonder if there's time for me to get any more money on?"

"No, leave it alone," Lonsdale begged. "Good Heavens! It makes me feel absolutely sick when I think of having ten thousand pounds on the result of one race. Why, compared with that, flying is safer than walking."

Two Cambridge undergraduates riding by jostled his cob so roughly that for the next few moments his attention was bent on maintaining himself in the saddle.

"Flying would certainly be safer than riding for you," Clarehaven laughed.

"The horse's mechanism is primitive, that's what it is—it's primitive," said Lonsdale. "And to risk ten thousand pounds on a primitive mechanism like a horse—Shut up, you brute, *you're* not entered for the Guineas. I say, this steering-gear is very unreliable, you know."

Dorothy had wanted to ask Lonsdale more about the owner of Chimpanzee; but at this moment the sun burst forth from behind a great white April cloud full-rigged, the shadow of which floated over the glittering green of the Heath just as the horses emerged from the Birdcage, escorted on either side by horsemen and horsewomen of fame and beauty. It was a fair scene, to play a part in which Dorothy exultantly felt that it was worth while to lose even more than £10,000. The coats of the horses shimmered in the sunlight; the colors of the jockeys blended and shifted like flowers in the wind; no tournament of the Middle Ages with all its plumes and pennons could have offered a fairer scene.

Tufton joined his friends, and, turning their mounts, they rode back toward the winning-post.

"I say, Tony, Chimpanzee has shunted to three's—only a fraction's difference now between him and Moonbeam," he was murmuring.

"Tell me more about Houston," said Dorothy to Lonsdale. "I don't think I can bear to watch the race."

"Cheer-oh, Doodles! You can't feel more queasy than I do. And I've told you all I know about Houston."

"But why should he call his horse Chimpanzee?"

There was a roar from the crowd.

"They're off!"

They were off on that royal mile of Newmarket.

"Flitten was told to ride him out from the start. Damn him, why doesn't he do so?" said Tony.

"He is, old boy. He's all right. Don't get nervy," said Tufton.

"Which is Chimpanzee?"

"That bay on the outside."

"What colors?"

"Yellow. Harcourt up."

"Take him along! Take him along! Good God, he's not using the whip already, is he?"

"No, no! No, no!"

"Damnation!" cried Tony, "why didn't we keep to the inclosure? I believe my horse is beaten. Don't look round, you little blighter! It's not an egg-and-spoon race."

The spectators were roaring like the sea.

"Moonbeam! Chimpanzee! Moonbeam! Moonbeam!" was shouted in a crescendo of excitement.

There was a momentary lull.

"Moonbeam by a head," floated in a kind of unisonant sigh along the rails.

"O Lord!" Lonsdale gulped. "I'd sooner drive a six-cylinder Lee-Lonsdale at sixty miles an hour through a school treat."

The strain was over; the noble owner had led in the noble winner; the ceremonies of congratulation were done; there was a profitable settlement to expect on Monday; yet Dorothy was ill at ease. The resuscitation of Hausberg clouded her contentment. Coincidence would not explain his purchase of the Diavola colt, his naming of it Chimpanzee, and his running it to beat Moonbeam. To be sure, he had failed, but a man who had taken so much trouble to create an effect would bemore eager than ever after such a failure to ... "to do what?" she asked herself. Was he aiming at revenge? Such a fancy was melodramatic, absurd ... after all these years deliberately to aim at revenge for a practical joke. Besides, she had had nothing to do with the affair in St. John's Wood. Nor had Tony except as an accessory after the fact. Yet it was strange; it was even sinister. And how odd that Lonsdale should be present at this sinister resurrection.

"Lonnie," she said, "do you remember about the monkey?"

"What monkey? Did you have a monkey on Moonbeam?"

"Not money, you silly boy—the chimpanzee you put in Hausberg's rooms."

"Of course I remember it. So does he, apparently, as he's called his horse after it."

"I know. I feel nervous. I think he's going to bring us bad luck."

"Hello, Doodles, you're looking very gloomy for the wife of the man who is going to win the Derby," said Tony, coming up at that moment, all smiles. "I've just bet fifty pounds for you on one of Cobbett's fillies, which he says is a good thing for the Wilbraham. And the stable's in luck."

Dorothy won £250 in a flash, it seemed—the race was only four furlongs—and when in the last race of the day she backed the winner of the Bretby Handicap and won another £250 Tony told her cheerfully that she ought not to gamble because she was now a monkey to the good. Dorothy was depressed. The £500, outside the ill omen of its being called a monkey in slang, assumed a larger and more portentous significance by reminding her of the £500 she had borrowed from her mother when she first went on the stage and of the way she had invested some of it afterward with Leopold Hausberg. All her delight in Moonbeam's victory had been destroyed by a dread of the unknown, and she suddenly pulled Tony's sleeve, who was busily engaged in taking bets against his horse for the Derby. He turned round rather irritably.

"What is the matter with you?"

"Give it up," she begged. "Don't bet any more."

"Give up betting when I've just won twenty-five thousand pounds over the Guineas and am going to win one hundred and twenty-five thousand pounds over the Derby? Besides, I thought you were going to live happily ever afterward if Moonbeam won?"

545

He turned away again with a laugh, and Tufton's grave head-shake was not much consolation to Dorothy. She was walking away a few paces in order not to overhear Tony's jovial badinage with the bookmakers, when a suave voice addressed her over the shoulder and, looking round, she saw Leopold Hausberg.

"You've forgotten me, Lady Clarehaven," he was saying. "I must explain that I—"

"Yes, yes," Dorothy interrupted, quickly, "you're Mr. Houston. I've just been told so by Mr. Lonsdale, whom no doubt you also remember."

She mentioned Lonsdale's name deliberately to see if Houston would speak about the monkey or even show a hint of displeasure at the mention of Lonsdale's name, but there was no shadow on his countenance, and he only asked her if she would not introduce him to her husband.

"I should like to congratulate him," he said, "though his win hit me pretty hard."

At this moment Tony with a laugh closed his betting-book and joined them.

"By Jove! there's not a sportsman among you," he called back to the bookmakers. "What do you think, Doodles? There's not one of them who'll give me four thousand to a thousand against Moonbeam for the Derby.... I'm sorry, I didn't see you were talking to somebody."

Dorothy made the introduction.

"I'll give you four thousand to a thousand, Lord Clarehaven," the new-comer offered. "Or more if you wish to bet. I don't think my horse showed his true form to-day. He swerved badly at the start, and my jockey says he was kicked."

Clarehaven was delighted to find somebody who would lay against Moonbeam, and he entered in his book a bet of £20,000 to £5,000.

"I had the pleasure of meeting Lady Clarehaven before her marriage," Houston was explaining. "I should have called upon you long ago, but I've been away for some years in South Africa."

"Making money, eh?" said Tony, holding in his mouth like a cigarette the pencil that was going to make money for him.

"I've not done so badly," said the other, deprecatingly.

"Look here, you must dine with us to-night," Tony declared, cheerily. "We're having a little celebration at the Blue Boar."

"Delighted, I'm sure. That's what I always like about racing," said Houston, "it brings out all our best sporting qualities as a nation."

Dorothy thought her husband was going to say something rude, but she need not have been worried. He had no intention of being rude to a man who would lay so heavily against the horse he thought was bound to win. In fact, he went out of his way to be specially friendly to Houston, and during the month of May the financier was at Curzon Street almost every day. Moreover, he brought with him others like himself who were willing to bet heavily with Clarehaven, and Dorothy began to think that even Captain Keith and Mrs. Mainwaring and those Saturday afternoons of peroxide and pink powder at Windsor or Lingfield Park were better than this nightmare of hooked noses and splay mouths.

"Well," said Lonsdale, "if anybody ever talks to me again about the 'lost' tribes or the missing link, I shall ask him if he's looked in Curzon Street. He'll find both there."

"Tony's being a little bit promiscuous," said Henry Tufton. "But of course one *must* remember that the king was very fond of Jews. And then there was Disraeli, don't you know, and the late queen."

Just before the Derby, Houston, whom, in spite of the menace he seemed to hold out against the future of Tony's career on the turf, Dorothy could not help liking in the intervals when she forgot about her premonitions of misfortune, said to her in a tone that it would have been hard to accuse of insincerity:

"Look here, I want to show you I'm a true friend, and I warn you that my horse is going to win the Derby. Nothing can beat him. Tell Clarehaven to hedge. I wish I'd not laid that bet now, for I hate taking his money. I suppose he'd be insulted if I offered to cancel the bet? But I would, if he would."

Dorothy told Tony about Houston's offer; but he laughed at her and said that, like all Jews, Houston did not relish losing his money. Nevertheless, finding that his liabilities were alarmingly high and knowing that Houston, not content with laying against Moonbeam, was backing Chimpanzee wherever he could, Tony invested some money on the second favorite and declined to lay another halfpenny against him. As a matter of fact, the money he invested thus was in comparison with the thousands for which he had backed Moonbeam a trifle; but rumor exaggerated the sum, and when Chimpanzee won the Derby, with Moonbeam just shut out of a place, there were unpleasant rumors in the clubs.

Dorothy did not go to Epsom—her nerves could not have stood the strain—and when she heard of Moonbeam's defeat she was grateful to her impulse. Nowadays her self-confidence was very easily upset, and from the moment Houston had appeared upon the scene at Newmarket she had never in her heart expected that Moonbeam would win the great race.

It was Tony himself who brought her the bad news. In a gray tail-coat and with gray top-hat set askew upon his flushed face—flushed with more than temper and disappointment, she thought—he strode up and down the smoking-room at Curzon Street, swinging his field-glasses round and round by their straps, until she begged him not to break the chandelier.

"Break the chandelier," he laughed. "That's good, by Jove! What about breaking myself? You don't seem to understand what this means, my dear Doodles. I've lost sixty thousand pounds over that cursed animal. Sixty thousand pounds! Do you hear? And I've got four days to find the money. Do you realize I shall have to mortgage Clare in order to settle up on Monday?"

"Mortgage Clare?" Dorothy gasped; she turned white and swayed against the table. At that moment Tony let the straps escape from his hand and the glasses went crashing into a large mirror.

"Yes, mortgage Clare," he repeated, savagely.

It was only the noise of the broken glass that kept her from fainting; weakly she pointed at the mirror and with a wavering smile upon her usually firm lips she whispered something about seven years of bad luck.

"Well, it's nothing to laugh about," said Tony.

"I wasn't laughing. Oh, Tony, you can't lose Clare; you mustn't."

"Oh well, I mayn't lose it. I may have some luck late in the season. But my other horses have let me down badly so far."

"You won't go on betting?"

"How else am I to get back what I've lost? I can't make sixty thousand pounds by selling papers!"

"Oh, but you...." She put her hand up to her forehead and sank into one of those comfortable chairs upholstered in red leather. "How did Cobbett explain Moonbeam's defeat?" She felt that, however agonizing, she must have the tale of the race to give her an illusion of action, and to silence these bells that were ringing in her brain: "Clare! Clare! Clare!"

"Cobbett?" exclaimed Tony, viciously. "He's about fit to train a bus-horse to jog from Piccadilly to Sloane Street. 'The colt doesn't like the Epsom course, and that's about the size of it,' said Mr. Cobbett to me. 'Course be damned, you old plowboy!' I told him. 'If you hadn't insisted upon giving the mount to that cursed apprentice of yours my horse would have won.' 'I don't think it was the lad's fault, my lord,' said Cobbett, getting as red as a turkey-cock. 'Don't you dare to contradict me,' I said. By God! Doodles, I was in such a rage that it was all I could do not to take the obstinate old fool by the shoulders and shake the truth into him. 'I'd contradict the King of England, my lord, if I trained his horses and he told me I didn't know my business,' 'Well, I tell you that you don't know your business,' I answered. 'Why didn't you let me do as I wanted and get O'Hara over from France to ride him?' 'If you remember, my lord, in the Woodcote Stakes, we gave the mount to Harcourt, and he made a mess of the race.' I couldn't stand there shouting 'O'Hara! Not Harcourt!' It wouldn't have been dignified in the paddock, and so I just told him quietly that I should have to consider if after to-day's fiasco I could still intrust my horses to a man who wouldn't listen to reason; after that I pulled myself together with a couple of stiff brandies and drove the car home myself. By the way, I ran over a kid in Hammersmith and broke its leg or something. Altogether it's been my worst day from birth up."

Dorothy would have liked to reproach him for drinking, to have expressed her dismay at the accident to the child, to have whispered a word of hope for the future, to have taken his foolish flushed face between her hands and kissed it ... but the only speech and action she could trust herself to make or take was to ring for a footman to sweep up the broken glass from the floor of the smoking-room.

Two days later, while Tony was hard at work raising the money to pay his debts on Monday, a letter came from Newmarket:

COBBETT HOUSE., NEWMARKET,
June 7, 1912.

To the Earl of Clarehaven.

MY LORD,—After our conversation in the paddock at Epsom on Wednesday I must give your lordship notice that I must respectfully decline to train your horses any longer in my stables. I would be much obliged if your lordship will give instructions to who I must transfer them.

I am,

Yours respectfully,
W. COBBETT.

Houston, who happened to be with Tony when this letter arrived, asked him why he did not train with Richard Starkey at Winsley on the Berkshire Downs.

"Yes, that's all very well," said Clarehaven, "but what about the Leger?"

"I'm not going to run Chimpanzee for the Leger. In fact, I've sold him to an Australian syndicate for the stud. Your horse will be the only representative of the stable."

Finally Clarehaven's horses were transferred to Starkey Lodge, and Moonbeam, as the obvious choice of the stable, gave the public a good win at Doncaster. The victory did not do Clarehaven much good in narrower circles, where many people had backed Chimpanzee to win the Leger. The rumors that had gone round the clubs after the Derby sprang to life again, and with an added virulence circulated freely. Lord Stilton, as a friend of his father, warned Tony in confidence that he would not be elected to the Jockey Club and advised him to go slow for a while.

"If the Stewards wish for an explanation," said Tony, loftily, "they can have an explanation."

"It is not a question of your horse's running," said Lord Stilton. "Technically there are no grounds for criticism. But a certain amount of comment has beenaroused by your change of stables and by your friendship with this man Houston. Altogether, my dear fellow, I advise you to go slow—yes, to go slow."

Tony, with the amount of money he had won back by Moonbeam's victory in the Leger, did not feel at all inclined to go slow, and with Richard Starkey at his elbow he bought several highly priced yearlings at the Doncaster sales. He would show that pompous old bore Stilton that the Derby could be won without being a member of the Jockey Club.

IV

Moonbeam's victory in the St. Leger had apparently freed Clare from mortgages, and it enabled the owner to meet a large number of bills that fell due shortly afterward. Dorothy, who was continually hearing from Tony how decently Houston was behaving to him, began to wonder if her dread of the Jew had not been hysterical; and when in October he proposed a cruise round the Mediterranean in his new yacht she did not attribute to the proposal a new and subtle form of danger. She and Houston were talking together in the drawing-room at Curzon Street while Tony was occupied with somebody who had called on business. During the summer these colloquies down in the smoking-room had kept Dorothy's nerves strung up to expect the worst when she used to hear Tony accompany the visitor to the door and come so slowly up-stairs after he was gone. But since Doncaster the interviews had been much shorter, and Tony had often run up-stairs at the end of them, leaving the visitor to be shown out by a footman. Throughout that trying time Houston had been always at hand, suave and attentive, not in the least attentive beyond the limits of an old friendship, but rather in the manner of Tufton, though of course with greater age and experience at the back of it. His ugliness, which, when Dorothy had first beheld it again so abruptly that afternoon in the ring at Newmarket had appalled her, was by now so familiar again that she was no longer conscious of it, or if she was conscious of it she rather liked it. Such ugliness strengthened Houston's background, and when Tony's affairs seemed most desperate gave Dorothy a hope; the more rugged the cliff the more easily will the wrecked mariner scale its forbidding face. Yes, Houston had really been invaluable during an exhausting year, and when now he proposed this yachting trip she welcomed the project.

"I think it would be good for Clarehaven to get him away from England for a while—to give him a change of air and scene. We'll lure him with the promise of a few days at Monte Carlo, and something will happen to make it impossible to go near Monte Carlo, eh? A nice, quiet little party. I have cabins for eight guests. Three hundred ton gross. Nothing extravagant as a yacht goes."

"And what do you call her? *The Chimpanzee?*" asked Dorothy, with a smile.

"No, no, no," he replied. "*The Whirligig.* A good name for a small yacht, don't you think?"

"Tell me," said Dorothy, earnestly. "Why did you call your horse Chimpanzee? You know, when I first heard it, I felt you were still brooding over that stupid business in those flats. What were they called?"

"Lauriston Mansions."

"Ah, you haven't forgotten the name. I had. But what centuries ago all that seems."

"Does it?"

"To me, oh, centuries!" she exclaimed, vehemently.

Houston's eyes narrowed, as if he were seeking to bring that far-off scene into focus with the present.

"I oughtn't to have reminded you of it," said Dorothy, lightly. "It was tactless of me."

"Not at all," said Houston. "Besides, contemporary with that there are many pleasant hours to remember" ... he hesitated for a second and blew out the end of the sentence in a puff of cigarette smoke ... "with you."

"Yes, I have often wondered why you were so kind to me. I think I must have been very tiresome in those days."

"On the contrary, you were the loveliest girl in London."

"Girl," Dorothy half sighed.

"Come, my dear Lady Clarehaven." Was he mocking her with the title? "My dear Lady Clarehaven," he repeated, with the least trace of emphasis upon the conventional epithet. "You don't expect me to be so bold as to say what you are now?"

For one moment he opened wide his dark eyes, and in that moment Dorothy decided that the party on the yacht should include the dowager and Bella. Simultaneously with this decision she was saying, with a laugh of affected dismay, "Oh no, please, Mr. Houston."

Tony was not at first in favor of the proposed trip, and pleaded that he wanted to see how his yearlings wintered; but Houston insisted that Starkey would look after them better without being worried by the owner. Then Tony urged the claims of pheasants. He had neglected his pheasants of late, and it would be a pity to let the Clare coverts alone for another year.

"Besides, I ought to look after the property," he added.

Dorothy had heard this declaration of duty urged too often to be taken in by it any longer. A week in Devonshire would cure Tony of a landowner's anxiety whether about his pheasants or his peasants; after that he would discover in his bland way that London was more convenient than the country.

"You can get plenty of shooting in the Mediterranean," said Houston. "There's a desert island in the Ægean with mouflon that nobody ever succeeds in getting."

"What? I'll bet you two hundred to one in sovereigns that I bag a couple," Tony cried.

"I won't bet, because you'll lose your money. A friend of mine lay off for a week of fine weather—that's a rare occurrence in those waters—lost nearly a stone climbing the rocks, and at the end of it came away without hitting one."

"Ridiculous," Tony scoffed. "What gun did he use?"

"Don't ask me," laughed Houston. "All I know is he was a first-class shot, and if he couldn't succeed I don't believe anybody can."

"That's rot," Tony declared, angrily. "When are we going to start?"

"She's in commission and now lying at Plymouth, which will save your mother a long journey by train."

"My mother?" Tony echoed, in astonishment.

Dorothy revealed her plan for inviting the dowager and Bella, and Tony was so anxious to prove he was right about the mouflon that he made no objections.

"Then," Dorothy continued, "I thought Harry Tufton had better be asked. He'll be so good at buying souvenirs in port. Your mother is sure to want souvenirs, and you'd hate to scour round for them yourself."

"I suppose Lonnie couldn't come," Tony suggested.

Houston knitted his brows, but said hurriedly that Lonsdale would be an ideal passenger for a cruise. Dorothy did not like to oppose the suggestion; yet she was relieved when Lonsdale replied that, having luckily arrived on this earth many years after the Flood, he did not propose to slight dry land. "Sea-trips," he wrote, "beginning with the Ark's have always been crowded and unpleasant. Besides, I'm learning to fly."

"Silly ass!" said Tony, tearing up the note.

The dowager was rather fluttered by the notion of a cruise in a yacht. Her knowledge of the sea was chiefly derived from Lady Brassey's journal of a voyage in the *Sunbeam*, the continual references of which to seasickness were not encouraging. Bella, who since Connie's marriage had taken to writing short stories, was as eager for local color as a child for a box of paints, and her enthusiasm at the idea of visiting the classic sea was so loudly expressed that the dowager had not the heart to disappoint her. She did, however, make one stipulation that surprised her daughter-in-law.

"If I go," she said, "you must promise me to invite one of your sisters. Now please, Dorothy, listen to me. You owe it to them. Of course, I should like you to invite them all and your mother, who could talk to me while you were all climbing volcanoes and searching for the ruins of Carthage; but I dare say Mr. Houston won't have room. However, one of them you must invite."

And then suddenly the dowager's suggestion seemed to provide a perfect solution of a problem that had been vexing Dorothy. In thinking over Houston's attitude she had been forced to explain it by the existence of something like a tender feeling for herself. To speak of tenderness in connection with him seemed absurd; but she was beginning to fancy that perhaps in the old days he had in his heart all the time wanted her for himself. If that were so, he had certainly behaved very well both now and then. No doubt he had realized that so long as her marriage with Clarehaven was attainable he stood no chance; but if that should have definitely come to nothing, he must have intended to ask her to marry him. It was with that idea he had helped her with investments, had avoided the least hint of an ulterior motive, and had always treated her so irreproachably. If he had concealed his love so carefully in the past, it was not ridiculous to suppose that he might be in love with her now. The other day he had been on the verge of saying something much more intimate than anything in the most intimate conversation they had ever had together. Perhaps he fancied that she and Tony were nothing to each other now— alas! with gambling as his ruling passion Tony might have given Houston some reason to suppose that she no longer stood where she used to stand in his eyes—or perhaps with a real chivalry he had perceived the dangerous course that Tony was taking and wished to save her without obtruding himself too much. Poor ugly man, with all his wealth he was a pathetic figure. He would suffer when he saw how devoted she was to Tony; she had made up her mind to charm Tony back to his old adoration of herself; this cruise might be her last opportunity.

Then why not ask one of her sisters? Such a sister, reflecting if somewhat faintly her own glories, might console Houston for an eternal impossibility. In that case she must invite the eldest now at home, and with her roses and rich brown hair might serve as a substitute for herself.

"Of course she hasn't my personality," Dorothy admitted. "And she hasn't my brown eyes. But she is beautiful, and what an excellent thing it would be if Houston should marry her. Jews have such a sense of family duty."

With the inclusion of Agnes the party was complete, and in the middle of November *The Whirligig* left Plymouth for the Mediterranean. Tony's astonishment at the production of this beautiful sister-in-law was laughable; but if heavy weather in the Bay of Biscay had not blanched most of her roses, while Dorothy's own throve in the fierce Atlantic airs, that astonishment might have turned to something less laughable. Houston, indeed, did ask Dorothy once in an undertone if it was not rather imprudent of her deliberately to create a rival for herself; but by the time the yacht had rounded Cape St. Vincent and was lying at ease in the harbor of Cadiz Tony was nearly as much his wife's slave as he was in the first days of their marriage. Dorothy, who had felt a momentary qualm about the success of her project when she saw the effect of Agnes's fair form of England against this passionate beauty of the south, decided that, on the contrary, it would be this very effect that would impress Houston much more than Tony. So far as mortal women are concerned, she had never had to bother much about Tony except when she herself had been cold with him. The fickle goddess of fortune was her only rival; but on board *The Whirligig* he seemed out of reach of temptation by her. Yes, the party was well chosen. Tufton by this time had recovered sufficiently from the heavy seas to help the dowager obtain her souvenirs of the various ports at which they called, and she at last forgave him for his advice about the pergola; Bella, inspired by a visit to Fielding's tomb at Lisbon, which was the first assurance she had received that England even existed since the Lizard Light had dropped below the horizon, was much occupied with a diary of her impressions; Tony was occupied by herself; and what should Houston do except occupy himself with Agnes? At the same time Dorothy had her doubts. Whenever she was sitting quietly with Tony in some snug windless corner of the yacht their host would always find an excuse to intervene.

After Cadiz they called at Malaga, Cartagena, and Alicante, whence by Valencia and Barcelona they were to sail by the shores of France toward the lights of Monte Carlo, which Houston now wanted to visit, although in London he had said that nothing should induce him to take the yacht there. Tony unexpectedly argued against a visit to Monte Carlo, and was only eager to attack the mouflon on that inaccessible Ægean isle. So the yacht's course was set eastward from Alicante.

"Why did you change your mind about Monte Carlo?" Dorothy asked Houston.

"Isn't it fairly obvious?"

She thought he was going to seize her hand and plunge headlong into a declaration of passion; but he turned away quickly and called her attention to the view. They were passing the southern shores of Formentera, so close that upon the sandy beach flamingos preening their wings in the sunset were plainly visible. The yacht called at Cagliari and Palermo, visited the Ionian islands, and reached the Ægean by way of the Corinth canal. The bet about the mouflon had to be canceled in the end, because the sea was never sufficiently calm to allow a boat to be lowered off Antaphros, and was still less likely to remain calm long enough for a boat to leave the deserted island again. They made several attempts to land, sailing there from their headquarters at Aphros, the white houses of which, stained with the purple Bougainvillea and mirrored in the calm waters of the harbor, seemed eternally to promise fine weather. Luckily the island also offered sufficient entertainment to compensate Tony for the loss of the mouflon; there was a club of which many rich ship-owners were members, where high play at écarté was the rule, and Tony, with the good luck that often attends strangers, repaid his hosts by winning from them nearly twenty thousand drachmas. The war in the Balkans made it difficult for the yacht to visit Constantinople, which was her original destination; and it was decided to substitute Alexandria and allow the members of the party to spend a few days in Cairo; from Egypt they would cruise along the coast of Syria, turn westward again by Cyprus and Rhodes, and with luck land a boat at Antaphros on the journey home, for Tony still regretted those mouflon.

Agnes would probably have found her stay in Aphros romantic enough at any time; but now with the supreme romance of war added and with handsome young Aphriotes going north upon their country's business by every steamer, she wished no higher ecstasy from this wonderful voyage. Agnes had enjoyed a great success on the island, where she had taught the young men and maidens to dance whatever ragtime was then the mode in West Kensington; where with them, when the dancing was done, she had climbed to the ruined temple of Aphrodite on the heights above the town and sat beneath a waning semilune that emptied her silver upon the bare and rounded hills, upon the sea, and upon a necklace of sapphire islands, past which the troopship now winking in the harbor below would sail at dawn. Like father, like son, even love shoots more arrows than usual in time of war. Agnes did not think that Egypt or Palestine could offer better than this, and when the parents of her new friends Antonia and Ariadne Venieris invited her to stay with them in their ancient house until the yacht came back, she begged her sister to make it easy for her to accept this invitation. Dorothy saw no reason to refuse, and they sailed away without her.

Three weeks later, when the yacht reached Rhodes, Dorothy found a letter from Madame Venieris awaiting her arrival, in which she announced that Agnes had married a young lieutenant called Sommaripa; she did not know what Lady Clarehaven would think of her; she did not know how to make her excuses; but at least she could assure Lady Clarehaven that the bridegroom, who was now in Thrace, was an excellent young man, an orphan with plenty of money and well regarded at court. Meanwhile, the bride must be her guest until peace was signed and her husband was released from service.

Agnes herself wrote as follows:

APHROS,
January 19, 1913.

MY DEAR DOODLES,—I suppose you're awfully fed up with me; but he is such a perfect darling and so frightfully good-looking. He owns a lot of land and a castle in Aphros that belonged to the Venetians. His ancestors were Dukes of Aphros. He's an orphan and his name is—don't laugh—Phragkiskos (Francis!) Sommaripa. I shouldn't have married in such a tearing hurry if he hadn't been going to the front. I'm writing to mother and father, etc. I suppose they'll have fits; but I really don't believe there is such a place as Lonsdale Road any more. He told me I was another Aphrodite risen from the foam. Aphros is Greek for foam. I dare say it sounds rather exaggerated when written down, but when he said it with his foreign accent I collapsed in his arms. Oh, my dear, don't be cross when you come back with the yacht. Love to everybody on board.

Your loving sister,   AGNES SOMMARIPA.

The news of her sister's escapade—well, it was something more than an escapade—affected Dorothy with a jealousy that she recognized for what it was in time to prevent herself from betraying the emotion she felt; so eager, indeed, was she to hide it that she proclaimed her approval of what Agnes had done, and so emphatically that the dowager was much agitated lest Bella should follow her example; but Bella did nothing more alarming than to sit down forthwith in the saloon and begin a very passionate and romantic story founded upon fact and drenched in local color.

Meanwhile, the Italian governor of Rhodes was taking steps to assure himself that *The Whirligig* was not a Greek war-ship with evil designs upon the Turkish population, which he was petting as a nurse pets a child she has lately had the gratification of smacking. As soon as the police spies guaranteed the harmlessness of the yacht the governor was hospitable and invited the members of the party to shoot the red-legged partridges and woodcock upon the Rhodian uplands. Tony, Bella, and Tufton accepted the invitation; the dowager, fearful lest Bella should envy the repose of some fascinating Turk's harem in the interior, accompanied them in the motor-car as far as the road permitted, where she alighted and passed the time in picking the red and purple anemones that blew in myriads all around, until the sportsmen had killed enough birds and were ready for lunch.

Houston suggested to Dorothy that they should take a walk round the town while the others were away; she accepted, for she was anxious to shake off this brooding jealousy which had oppressed her since the news in Agnes's letter.

"I shouldn't worry myself about your sister," he was saying.

Dorothy frowned to think he should have read her thoughts so easily.

"I'm not worrying. I think she has done exactly right."

"Envying her, in fact," Houston added.

"Why should I envy her?"

He shrugged his shoulders.

"Don't we always rather envy the people who do things with such decision? Don't we sometimes feel that we're wasting time?"

He said this so meaningly that Dorothy pretended not to hear what he had said and looked up to admire the fortified gate of St. Catherine through which they were passing.

"It's like Oxford!" she exclaimed.

Her jealousy of Agnes was stimulated by this comparison, for when they came to the Street of the Knights she was reminded of that day when she walked down the High with Sylvia, that Sunday afternoon which had been the prelude of everything. How many years ago?

"O God!" she exclaimed, reverting in her manner, as she often used in Houston's company, to that hard Vanity manner. "O God! I shall be twenty-nine in March!"

"I'm over forty."

550

"But you're a man. What does your age matter?"

She was looking at him, and thinking while she spoke how ugly he was. Perhaps he realized her thought, for his face darkened with that blush of the very sallow complexion, that blush which seems more like a bruise.

"You mean I'm too hideous?"

"Don't be silly. Let's explore this gateway."

They passed under a Gothic arch and found themselves in a cloistered quadrangle, so much like a small Oxford college that only a tall palm against the blue sky above the roofs told how far they were from Oxford.

"It's uncanny," said Dorothy. "How stupid Tony was to go off shooting without first exploring the town. How stupid of him!"

Dorothy wanted her husband's presence as she had never wanted it; she wanted to help the illusion that she was back in Oxford with all the adventure of lifebefore her. She wanted to see him here in this familiar setting and revive ... what?

"I hope Agnes will be happy," she sighed.

Close by a couple of Jews in wasp-striped gabardines were arguing about something in a mixture of Spanish and Yiddish; without thinking and anxious only to get back to the present, Dorothy asked Houston if he could understand what they were talking about. Again that dark blush showed like a bruise.

"Why should I understand them?" he asked, savagely.

"No, of course. I really don't know," she stammered, in confusion, for she was thinking how much better a gabardine would suit Houston than his yachting-suit and how exactly his pendulous under lip resembled the under lips of the two disputants. An odd fancy came into her mind that she would rather like to be carried off by Houston, to be held in captivity by him in the swarming ghetto through which they had picked their way a few minutes ago, to sit peering mysteriously through the lattice of some crazy balcony ... to surrender to some one strong and Eastern and.... Oh, but this was absurd! The sun was hot in this quadrangle; she was in an odd state; it must be that the news about Agnes had upset her more than she had thought. At that moment her eyes rested upon the broken headpiece of a tomb that was leaning against the cloister, and she found herself reading in a dream: "Gilbert Clare of Clarehaven. With God. 1501." The palm still swayed against the blue sky; the Jews still chattered at one another. Dorothy looked round her with a dazed expression, and then impulsively knelt down among the rubble that surrounded the tombstone and read the words again: "Gilbert Clare of Clarehaven. With God. 1501." The Italian curator of the museum that was being formed in the old hospital drew near and explained to Dorothy in French that this was the tombstone of an English knight.

"An ancestor of mine," Dorothy told him.

The curator smiled politely; being a Latin, he certainly did not believe her.

"I've never seen you so much interested by anything," said Houston.

"I never have been so thrilled by anything," she declared. "Gilbert Clare of Clarehaven! Clarehaven! And when he left it he must have often thought of our little church on the headland; and when he died here, how he must have longed to be at home."

"Does Clare mean very much to you?" Houston asked.

"*You* could never imagine how much. For Clare I would do anything!"

"Anything? That's a rash statement."

"Anything," she repeated.

Houston tried to persuade the curator to let him have the tombstone for Dorothy to take away with her; but the curator was shocked at such a suggestion and explained that it was an unusual inscription—the earliest of the kind in English that he knew; he should have expected Latin at such a date.

The countess failed to rouse much enthusiasm in the earl about the tomb of his ancestor, but the dowager was glad he was with God; Bella had a subject for another story; and Tufton photographed it. The next day the wind seemed likely to shift round into the north, and *The Whirligig* left the exposed harbor, traveling past the mighty limestone cliffs of the Dorian promontory, past Cos and many other islands, until once more her anchor was dropped in the sheltered blue waters of Aphros.

There were interminable discussions at the house of Monsieur and Madame Venieris; but there was no doubt whatever that Agnes was married.

"And do you know, my dear Doodles," her sister added, when they were alone, "do you know I believe I'm already going to have a baby?"

Dorothy could stand no more; but when she begged that all speed should be made for England there came a series of breathless days during which Tony stalked the mouflon on the heights of Antaphros. In the end he actually did hit one, and though it fell at the foot of a difficult precipice he scrambled down somehow, raised the carcass with ropes, and rowed triumphantly away with it to the yacht. Houston tossed him double or quits for the sovereign he had won; Tony won five tosses in succession and thirty-two pounds.

"My luck's in," he shouted, gleefully. "Come on, Houston, full speed ahead. I want to see my horses again."

When the yacht reached Plymouth the whole party went ashore and traveled up to Clare.

"Yes," Houston admitted to Dorothy, "I can understand the appeal this sort of thing must have for anybody. It must be glorious here in summer. I suppose the deer look after themselves? Yes, it's a wonderful old place."

A week after their guests had left Tony and Dorothy followed them to London.

"Oh, by the way, Doodles," said Tony at Paddington, "I ought to have explained before, but I've got a little surprise for you. I had to sell one hundred and twenty-nine. I was offered a nailing good price."

"And where are we going to live?" she asked.

551

"Well, that's the surprise. You'll never guess. I've taken your old flat in Halfmoon Street."

Dorothy looked at Tony.

"You're not angry?" he asked.

"I think I'm past anger," she said, dully.

While they were driving to their new abode Dorothy decided that it would be easy to convince her family that such a romantic marriage was the right thing for Agnes, because her arguments would come from the depths of her heart.

"And *I* shall be twenty-nine in March," she kept thinking.

"Of course I kept all your favorite things," Tony was saying. "I sold the rest. The pictures fetched a deuced poor price. I hope that if the Clare pictures ever have to go I shall have more luck with them."

"I wonder you don't offer to sell me," said Dorothy, bitterly.

He squeezed her arm affectionately.

"Sha'n't have to do that just yet awhile. I'm going to have a lucky year. I felt that when I pipped that mouflon. Ever since I broke the glass at one hundred and twenty-nine I've been deuced uneasy. As soon as the house was sold I began winning at écarté, and then I pipped that mouflon."

V

The sale of the house in Curzon Street revived all Dorothy's worst fears. If Tony could successfully hide from her knowledge such a transaction he was capable of announcing one day that Clare itself was gone. Life had not offered much stability since that fatal June except for the brief period when Tony's career upon the turf had accorded with the traditions of his order and had seemed to possess the dignity that confers itself automatically upon those who put forth their hands to claim their due, her existence had been periodically shaken like a town in the shadow of a volcano. Was not his marriage judged from the outside a contribution to failure similar to the running of Moonbeam in the Derby? Was she herself much more than a disappointing race-horse? She had failed to keep her classic engagements at Clare; she had failed to carry her weight in the big handicap at Curzon Street. Was the flat in Halfmoon Street a selling-plate? Oh, this flat, how it was haunted with the ghosts of old ambitions! The color schemes and patterns of the chintz might be different, but how familiarly the bells rang, how familiar was the sound of the doors opening and shutting, and the light upon her dressing-table ... and the rumble of the traffic ... leading whither?

"Tony, what *do* you want?" she asked, passionately, one morning when the sparrows were maddening her with their monotonous chirping praise of the sunshine.

"I want to win the Derby," he said.

"And lose everything else, even me?" she asked.

"And lose nothing," he maintained, obstinately. "Starkey fears nothing."

Starkey feared nothing! Starkey with his long, thin nose and red hair!

By now two of Tony's yearlings stood out well above the rest. Of these a bay colt by Cyllene out of Midsummer Night and, therefore, a half-brother of Moonbeam, had run well in the Brocklesby Stakes at Lincoln, still better in the Westminster Plate at the Epsom Spring Meeting, and had cantered away with the Spring Two-year-old Stakes at Newmarket. He was considered to be a certainty for the Woodcote Stakes; but on Starkey's advice Tony ran instead a chestnut filly by Spearmint out of Blushrose, who won with considerable ease, beating horses that had shown up well in the previous races. Clarehaven was jubilant; Starkey feared nothing; they had next year's Derby in their hands. It had been just after this last victory that Tony had affirmed his only ambition in life to be the Derby. At Ascot, still running unnamed, the filly won the Coventry Stakes; half an hour afterward Moonbeam took the Ascot Stakes by five lengths, and two days later, starting as an odds on favorite, he won the Gold Cup without being extended; finally on the same day the Midsummer Night colt won the New Stakes and was named Full Moon, for certainly the fortunes of Clare seemed in their complement.

"There's never been such an Ascot," said Tony to his wife.

Houston had had to go to South Africa soon after he returned from the Mediterranean cruise; while he was still away, Tony's luck touched its zenith when Moonbeam won the Eclipse Stakes at Sandown Park.

"Though it's lucky Mr. Houston sold Chimpanzee to that Australian syndicate," said Starkey. "Because I give you my word, my lord, that Chimpanzee was a better horse than Moonbeam, just as the filly is better than the colt."

"I think you're wrong about Moonbeam," Tony argued, "though you may be right about the filly."

When Houston reached England in July he motored down to Winsley with the Clarehavens to discuss future plans with the trainer, and when the old argument about the respective merits of Chimpanzee and Moonbeam began, as usual, he laughed, saying that for him the discussion was a barren one, because after this Derby victory he did not intend to tempt fortune any more.

"I wish you could persuade Tony to follow your example," said Dorothy.

"Don't be silly, old thing. I haven't won the Derby yet," Tony proclaimed, in a hurt voice.

"Don't be afraid, my lord; you can't lose it next year, not if you tried. Of course I'm not going to say yet for certain whether it'll be with the colt or with the filly; but I think it'll be with the filly."

"Which reminds me," said Tony. "We haven't given the lady a name yet."

"Why not Vanity Girl?" Houston suggested.

"Of course," Tony shouted, gleefully. "Vanity Girl she is."

Dorothy protested that the name would bring bad luck and begged for Mignonette instead.

"Mignonette won a race at Liverpool only yesterday," said the trainer.

"But there must be plenty of other names that haven't been used," Dorothy insisted. "As we've got the Full Moon of Clare, why shouldn't we call the filly Supporting Angel?"

"Well," said Mr. Starkey, "with her ladyship's permission, I prefer Vanity Girl. It sounds like a winner."

Tony and Houston were emphatically in favor of Vanity Girl, and the filly was named accordingly. Dorothy stayed behind to contemplate the beautiful creature in her box, the fair, shimmering creature lately anonymous and now burdened with what was surely a title of ill omen.

"But you have no ambitions," said Dorothy. "If you fail you won't mind. What do you care about your purple clothing with its black border and its silver coronet?"

Dorothy left the dim, cool stable and emerged into the glare of the July noon. She felt sad about the filly's name, and, unwilling to meet the others until she had recovered from her depression, she walked away from Starkey Lodge, walked up the sloping single street of the little village of Winsley, the houses of which seemed to have drifted like leaves into this cranny of the bare downs. At the top of the street the village ended abruptly where a white road ran like a line of foam between a sea of grass that stretched skyward to right and left until the horizon faded into the summer haze.

"Thirty next March," said Dorothy, aloud. "And what have I done with my life?"

She envied the thistledown that floated by, envied its busy air and effect of traveling whither it would; compared with those winged seeds the blue butterflies seemed as irresolute and timorous of the future as herself ... herself.... A voice shouted that lunch was waiting, and there was Tony waving to her from the road. Lunch was waiting for herself; but for that thistledown what was waiting? Dorothy's clear-cut personality was becoming blurred; she never used to speculate about thistledown in cloud cuckoo land. Everybody noticed the change. Some had heard that there really was something between Dorothy Clarehaven and that fellow Houston; others knew for a positive fact that Tony Clarehaven neglected his wife; and all the women decided that she must be well over thirty by now.

Tony began to bet recklessly as soon as Houston returned, and by the autumn he was again in difficulties. Moonbeam failed to give two stone to a smart three-year-old in the Jockey Club Stakes, and he lost much more than Full Moon had made for him by winning the Boscawen Stakes the day before. But there had been no purchase at Tattersall's, no ambitious yearlings from Doncaster, for Tony had given his word to Dorothy that after next year's Derby he would retire from racing. In fact, to show that this time he was in earnest he sold all his horses except the two sons of Cyllene and Vanity Girl. The filly had just won a severe trial and on Starkey's advice was preferred to Full Moon for the Middle Park Plate. She was heavily backed, started a hot favorite, and was not placed. Tony declined to accept her running as true and backed her heavily to win the Dewhurst Plate. O'Hara was brought over from France to ride her, and she was again unplaced. Some people declared she was no stayer, some that her victories at Epsom and Ascot had been flukes; others spoke of coughing in the Starkey Lodge Stables; a few murmured that a coup for next year's Derby was being carefully engineered.

"I knew it would bring bad luck to call her Vanity Girl," Dorothy lamented. "Sell her. Get rid of her. Get rid of them all."

"Sell the Derby winner?" Tony ejaculated. "My dear Doodles, you surely must realize that her form at Newmarket was too bad to be true. If she can beat Full Moon at home, and if Full Moon can beat the winner of the Middle Park as he did in the Boscawen Stakes, one or other of them *must* win the Derby. We'll see how they winter. Meanwhile I've sold Moonbeam to Houston. He paid me twenty-six thousand pounds. He intends to start a stud; I'm bound to say he got my horse cheap; whatever Starkey says, Chimpanzee would never have beaten him again; but I wanted the money."

"I'm sorry you've had to sell Moonbeam, but do sell Vanity Girl, too. Don't bet any more on any of them. Run Full Moon for the Derby, and if he wins be content with that. Then we could start a stud at Clare ourselves. But do get rid of Vanity Girl."

She felt as the dowager must have felt when she was trying to dissuade Tony from marrying an actress; she instanced every disadvantage she could think of for the filly; but Tony was obstinate.

They were going out that afternoon to the Pierian Hall. Sylvia Scarlett, after over two years' absence in America, had returned to England and suddenly taken the fancy of the public with a new form of entertainment that was considered very futurist. Dorothy did not think that her performance deserved all the praise it had received, but she felt jealous of Sylvia's success and, turning to Tony in the interval, said, fiercely, that sometimes she wished she had never married him.

"I should have done better to stick to the stage," she vowed.

"If you're wishing you hadn't married me because you'd like to be doing this sort of thing," said Tony, "you can spare your regrets. This, my dear Doodles, is the rottenest show I ever saw in my life."

"But it's a success."

"Only because it's so devilish peculiar. If I walked down Bond Street in pajamas I should attract a certain amount of attention the first time I did it, but people would get used to it, and I should soon be forgotten. By the way, would you like to send round a card?"

"No, no," said Dorothy. "I've seen quite enough of her from where we are."

"Don't get bitter, Doodles. I don't know what's come over you lately. You seem to hate everything and everybody."

That winter was a miserable one, because Tony took to baccarat again, and, having been accustomed to bet on the turf in large sums, he carried his methods to the tables with such recklessness that Dorothy, unable to stand the strain, left him in London and went down to Clare. She had a notion to kill herself out hunting, but even in this she was unsuccessful, for in February all the hunters, including Mignonette, were sold. Moreover, at the end of the month a valuer arrived with an authorization from Tony to complete the details for a forthcoming auction of the whole property as it stood, pictures and all. Dorothy hastened up to London and demanded what was the matter.

"The matter is that I've got to sell Clare."

"Sell Clare?" she repeated. "I suppose you mean mortgage it?"

"Mortgage it? It's mortgaged already."

"But you paid that off."

"Yes, once. But you don't suppose that I've always got money handy?" he asked, petulantly. "Some damned firm has bought up all my bills; I'm being pressed all round; and the Jews won't lend me another farthing."

"Then you must sell the horses."

"The Derby winner? They're my only chance of keeping out of the bankruptcy court. They're all we have, Doodles."

"You have Clare."

"How can I pay the interest on the mortgages and live at Clare? Try to be a little reasonable. I've got a good offer, and the money will come in very handy for the final plunge."

"You're mad."

"All right. I'm mad."

"But your mother?"

"I've given Greenish notice to leave Cherrington Cottage and I'm reserving that from the sale."

"But what will your mother live on?"

"Oh, of course her jointure will be paid. Besides, I tell you that this season with Full Moon and Vanity Girl I simply can't go wrong. The mistake I made was playing baccarat with my ready cash."

"Won't Houston help you?"

"My dear Doodles, it's Houston who's going to buy Clare."

She was silent before the revelation of what for long she had surmised. The quadrangle of the hospital in Rhodes where she had admitted openly that for Clare she would do anything flashed upon her vision, and the thought of that Oriental patience practised for so long terrified her. His desire for her must have been kindled years ago, a desire that, once kindled, had been fed by the will to revenge himself for being what he was upon Clarehaven for being what *he* was. It was Houston who had subtly helped his rival along the road to ruin, taking him by the arm as it were to the edge of the precipice and toppling him over. Now it was her place to interview this enemy, plead with him, entreat him to be content with what he had done already ... but of what use would entreaties be? Of no use except to stimulate the lust of victory.

"You can't sell Clare to Houston," she was saying, mechanically, lest her silence should be noticed. "You can't sell Clare to Houston," she was repeating; and then she was off again, chasing the excited, restless ideas in her brain until she should have driven them like poultry into a corner and be able to pick the victim that should serve her best. Yes, yes, if Houston really did covet her, she still had a chance to preserve Clare. There was no weaker adversary for a woman whose heart was untouched than a man who was madly in love ... no weaker adversary.... Should she write to Houston and give him the idea that by pressing her hard he could win? In the past she had known how to cook a dozen geese in fierce ovens without cooking her own by mistake, without even burning her fingers. If Houston had waited years, he would surely be willing to risk a few more weeks.

"You can't sell Clare to Houston," she said, once more.

"For God's sake, don't go on repeating that like a parrot," said Tony. "I'm going round to settle the matter now."

A few moments later the door of the flat slammed behind him. Houston lived in Albany, not five minutes away, and Dorothy went across to the telephone.

"Yes? Who's speaking?"

"Dorothy Clarehaven. Listen," she said, hurriedly. "Once you lent me money, or at any rate you helped me make money, and you were always very decent about it. Won't you do the same thing again? You know that Tony is putting everything on the ability of one of our two horses to win the Derby. Tell me—there's every reason to suppose he will win the Derby—why shouldn't you lend him enough to prevent his selling Clare?"

"Why not, indeed?" said Mr. Houston. "But what's the security?"

"Aren't the horses a security?"

"Horses are very capricious, almost as capricious as women."

"Would you prefer a woman as security?" she asked, trying to rake up from nine years ago a coquetry that had once been so profitable. It was easier by telephone. "Supposing I offered myself as security?"

So much was she playing a part of long ago that instinctively she had used her old invincible gesture of lightly touching a man's sleeve. That also was easier by telephone.

"I could lend a good deal," twanged the voice of the buyer along the wires. "I could lend a good deal."

"Very well then," said Dorothy. "Lend *me* the money."

"By telephone? Not good enough. Come, come, let's be frank, let's be brutally frank. You know you're worth twenty Derby winners to me; but, as I said, women are more capricious than horses. I'm no longer a schoolboy. Are you in earnest or not?"

"Of course I'm in earnest," she said. "Why should you think I wasn't?"

"So much in earnest that you'll come to my rooms this afternoon and tell me so?"

"Yes, if you like," she replied, without hesitating. "But you must prove to me that you're in earnest too. Send me something on account."

"How much do you want?"

"Oh, I don't know," she said. "About fifty thousand pounds I suppose."

Dorothy's sense of proportion about large sums of money had been destroyed by her husband's extravagant betting. When one lives with a man who will win £50,000 at Ascot and lose it all and more the following week, it is difficult to preserve a table of comparative values. She supposed that £50,000 would represent about half the price of Clare, and the importance she attributed to Clare gave money such a relative unimportance that she saw nothing even faintly ridiculous in demanding a sum of this magnitude from Houston. Perhaps he was impressed by the size of her demand into believing that she really was in earnest about accepting his proposals; even a financier like himself might be excused for supposing that a woman, one of the most beautiful women in England and a countess to boot, does not ask for £50,000 without being in earnest. At the same time it appealed to his sense of humor that any woman, even England's most beautiful countess, should ask for £50,000 by telephone.

"Why, it's not even a note of hand," he chuckled, and his laugh, traveling from Albany to Halfmoon Street along the wires, lost its mirth on the way and reached Dorothy with the sound of a dropped banjo.

"Well, I must have something to prove you're in earnest," she argued, fiercely. "Tony is on his way to see you now. He'll be with you in another minute. Tell him that as a friend you can't let him sell Clare. Offer him enough to tide him over the Derby. I'm willing to risk everything on that."

"Are you trying to tell me that if Clarehaven pulls off the Derby our arrangement is canceled? Ring off. Nothing doing, dear lady."

Away in Albany she heard a bell shrill; it was like a prompter's warning of the play's ending.

"That's Tony now," she cried. "Do what I ask. Give him enough. He'll say how much is necessary for the moment. Lend it to him on the security of Clare. Buy up his mortgages. Do what you like, and if Tony comes back with Clare still his, at any rate until he has lost all or saved all on the Derby, I'll come to Albany this afternoon and thank you."

"Tangibly?" murmured Houston.

"Tangibly."

Her agitated breath had so bedewed the mouthpiece that when with trembling hands she replaced the holder it was like being released from a kiss.

VI

Tony came back from his visit to Houston in a temper of serene optimism.

"Well, Doodles," he cried, gaily, "I've saved Clare for you."

"Oh, you've saved Clare, have you?" She could not resist a slight accentuation of the pronoun, but he did not notice it.

"Yes, Houston was very decent. I told him how much I hated getting rid of the old place, and he was very decent. Of course he knows from Starkey that the Derby is a certainty and that in Full Moon and Vanity Girl I've got the two best three-year-olds in England."

"You're still infatuated with the filly?"

"Now wait a minute. Don't begin arguing till you hear what's been decided. Houston is going to lend me enough cash to pay off the present mortgages of Clare, and when that is done I'm going to mortgage the place to him on the understanding that if I don't settle up on the Monday after the Derby he takes immediate possession. I told him that I should want some ready money, and he offers to buy whichever horse I don't run in the Derby."

"Then sell him Vanity Girl," said Dorothy, quickly. She could hardly refrain from adding, "One of us he must have."

"Don't be in such a hurry. At present Full Moon has engagements in the Two Thousand Guineas and the Derby, also in the Grand Prix and the Leger. Vanity Girl is entered for the Thousand Guineas, the Derby, and the Oaks. I shall run Full Moon for the Guineas; if he wins he will be the Derby favorite. In that case I shall scratch Vanity Girl for the Thousand Guineas, and we'll have a secret trial at Winsley. Houston hasn't taken Moonbeam away yet, and Starkey is to put him into strong work for this trial. If Full Moon shows up best in the trial I shall sell Vanity Girl to Houston, who will run her in the Oaks; then I shall back Full Moon for the Derby till the cows come home. But if, as Starkey thinks and as I think, Vanity Girl is the goods, Houston is to have Full Moon for ten thousand pounds as soon as I've scratched him for the Derby. I don't want to scratch him until I've got my money out on the filly, but I shall get busy quickly, and the public will have plenty of time to know which horse I think is going to win. Then you and I, Doodles dear, will retire from the turf and live ever afterward at Clare."

"And if Full Moon doesn't win the Guineas?"

"Oh, I've thought of that. In that case I shall run Vanity Girl in the Thousand Guineas, declare to win with either in the Derby, and Houston is to have his pick after the race for ten thousand pounds."

"And you've thought out all this wonderful and complicated plan of campaign?"

"Not entirely," Tony admitted.

"Not at all," said Dorothy, sharply. "You know perfectly well that Houston thought out every detail of it."

She wondered if a man who could juggle like this with the future of horses might not be equally expert with women. But no, he wanted the woman; he did not want the horses. She sent a note round to Albany saying that a bad headache kept her at home that afternoon, but that she fully appreciated the good will he had just shown and that she hoped to see him at dinner to-morrow. She knew that she could not keep Houston at arm's-length indefinitely, but if she could keep him there until, at any rate, Clare was temporarily safe she should have a breathing-space until June. Then if Tony lost the Derby, she should have to offer herself to preserve Clare; but if he won, she and Clare would both be saved.

"God!" she cried to her soul, "with me it always seems that June is to decide everything."

When the following night Houston reproached her for breaking the appointment of yesterday she reminded him that he, too, had only made promises so far; but when Houston kept his word and freed Clare until the settling day after Epsom, she still held back.

"You'll appreciate me all the more for being kept waiting."

555

"I've waited years," he said.

"I'll go for a drive with you to-morrow."

So it went on until the week before the Guineas.

"You're trying to fool me. You think you can get something for nothing as easily now as you could when you were at the Vanity."

"Be reasonable, my dear man," she begged. "Your money is perfectly safe. What are you risking? If Tony loses the Derby you win me the moment you put in my hands the title-deeds of Clare. If Tony wins the Derby...." She let her deep-brown eyes gaze into his.

"Kiss me," said Houston. "Kiss me once and I'll believe you."

A good lady's maid is bound to enjoy a considerable amount of intimacy in her relationship with her mistress; no lover is allowed as much. Dorothy from youth had trained her kisses to be her servants; they had always served her well, and if a degree of intimacy was unavoidable it was always the intimacy of a servant, which does not count. One of these kisses she summoned to her aid now.

Tony proposed that Lonsdale should drive them down to Newmarket for the Guineas, but Lonsdale said he was booked to fly on that day.

"You never come near us now," said Dorothy, reproachfully.

"I can't stand that fellow Houston. I can't think how you can bear him around all the time."

"He's very amusing," said Dorothy.

"So's a bishop in a bathing-dress. If you want amusement you can get plenty of it," Lonsdale growled, "without having to depend on a fellow like that."

Tufton, who was as sensitive as a tress of seaweed to the atmosphere, had also neglected his old friends recently, and Dorothy knew by his manner that people must now be talking very hard about herself and Houston.

Tony kept his promise not to bet heavily on the result of the Guineas, and Full Moon's win did not do more than keep quiet a certain number of low-class creditors who had for some time been supplying Lord and Lady Clarehaven with such trifles as wine, food, and clothes. However, the win did seem to make the Derby a certainty for the stable; Full Moon and Vanity Girl, unlike Moonbeam, had both won at Epsom as two-year-olds, and if Vanity Girl could beat Full Moon, surely no horse in England could beat her on a course to which she had already shown her partiality. When the filly did not appear in the Thousand Guineas the quidnuncs, the how-nows, and the what-nots of the turf said she had wintered disappointingly and that she would never be seen in the Oaks. There was scarcely a sporting paper that did not assure its readers that they would soon hear of Vanity Girl's having been scratched for both the Derby and the Oaks. She was a flier, but a non-stayer, and the Stewards' Cup at Goodwood was her journey.

At the same time the quidnuncs, the how-nows, and the what-nots of the turf were puzzled to find that after Full Moon's victory in the Guineas no money from Starkey Lodge seemed to be going on the colt's chances for the Derby. All the touts set hard to work to solve what was called the Starkey Lodge Puzzle; Winsley and the hamlets round were frequented by inquisitive men whose pockets were bulging with sheaves of telegraph forms.

"They think we've got something up our sleeves," said the trainer to the owner. It was half past four o'clock of a morning early in May; Tony, Dorothy, Houston, and Starkey had just taken up their positions to watch the trial that was to decide which horse should carry the Clarehaven colors a month hence. They had motored down to Winsley the night before; and under a cold sky of turquoise scattered with pearls and amethysts they had ridden up here at dawn; but when their clothing had been taken off the horses, heads had popped up like rabbits from behind every hillock along the course.

"No good running it this morning," said the trainer, shouting some abuse at the touts and galloping his hack in the direction of the horses.

The sun was now well about the rounded edge of the downs; the air of the morning was lustrous and scented with young grass upon which the dew lay like golden wine.

"You can't get up too early for these touts," Starkey told them at breakfast, "and if we want to know where we are for the Derby a bit before any one else, we'll have to run the trial by moonlight. I'll keep 'em on the hop all the day before and tire some of these Nosey Parkers into staying at home for once in their lives."

Dorothy was never sorry of an excuse to spend a few days with the horses. They had caused her so much misery; but she had no ill will when she saw them.

"Yes," said the trainer. "A moonlight trial. That's the ticket. What with Full Moon and Moonbeam you can't say it isn't highly suitable. I'm not going to pretend that Moonbeam is up to his best form. Thinking Mr. Houston was going to take him to the stud, I only began putting him into strong work a month ago. So I thought we'd run them at weights for sex, and put in a couple of good handicappers belonging to Mr. Ginsberg to make a bit of a field."

At two o'clock there was the clank of a pail in the stable-yard, followed by a low murmur of voices and the grumble of the big yard gates being cautiously opened. Presently the team emerged and walked slowly up the village street, where half a dozen touts were fast asleep, because they must be up at dawn to haunt the entrance to the Starkey Lodge Stables. By the magic of the moon the horses in their clothing were turned into the caparisoned steeds of knights-at-arms setting forth upon a romantic quest. Dorothy, Houston, Tony, and the trainer followed on hacks; and even when far out of hearing of the most vigilant tout they continued to talk in half-tones. So breathless was the night that the thundering of the hoofs coming nearer and nearer over the turf seemed to vibrate the stars, and Dorothy had a fancy that presently all the people in the little villages below the rim of the downs would wake and run with lanterns up here to know if the moon had fallen down upon the great world.

Vanity Girl won the trial; Moonbeam was second; the winner of the Guineas was third.

"Well, I hope that's decisive enough," said Tony, gleefully. "Starkey, you were right!"

He and the trainer moved off in excited conversation. Houston took Dorothy's hand, and she did not try to withdraw it from his grasp; Vanity Girl was going to win the Derby; Clare would be safe in June; she should be safe in June. The benevolent moon, quite undisturbed by all this mad nocturnal galloping, gazed blandly at Dorothy's complaisance; she would not have put a cloud up to her face for much more than that, the unscrupulous old bawd.

A week later the following paragraph appeared in one of the sporting weeklies:

THE STARKEY LODGE PUZZLE

Rumor says that the young Earl of Clarehaven, who has recently had very heavy losses on the turf, positively intends to capture the Derby this year. It was only a few months ago that we had to condole with the gallant young nobleman on the sad necessity which forced him to sell that great horse Moonbeam last year to the well-known South African capitalist, Mr. Lionel Houston, who indorsed the public view that Moonbeam's defeat in the Derby by his own horse Chimpanzee was not true form when he sold Chimpanzee to an Australian syndicate of breeders and bought Moonbeam for the stud he is now forming, and which we have no doubt will give many famous new names to the history of English racing. But our readers' present concern is what is popularly known as the Starkey Lodge Puzzle. We have the highest authority for saying that this is no longer a puzzle. At an important trial held in great secrecy on the Starkey Lodge training-grounds it was conclusively established that Vanity Girl is more than likely to give the Blue Riband of the turf to Lord Clarehaven and console him for the failure of Moonbeam. It will interest our readers from the smallest punter upward to hear that Full Moon, the victor of the Two Thousand Guineas and the present Derby favorite, will not run at Epsom, having been sold like his half-brother to Mr. Lionel Houston, who no doubt intends to keep him for the St. Leger, a race which he is ambitious of winning. We need scarcely point out to our readers the obvious tip for this year's Derby, and we do not hesitate to plump right out for Vanity Girl as the winner. We were the only paper to advise our readers not to back Full Moon until the intentions of the stable were a little plainer, and to all those who failed to follow our advice we can only say, "I told you so." Lord Clarehaven has done well to scratch the winner of the Guineas, for there is no doubt that if both the colt and his stable companion had faced the starter at Epsom the public would have followed the son of Cyllene. As it is, we confidently expect to see Vanity Girl a raging favorite before the week is out, and we may remind our readers that Lord Clarehaven's beautiful chestnut has already shown that she likes the Epsom course by winning the Woodcote Stakes last year. Her running at Newmarket last autumn may be discounted. We happened to know that the stable was coughing; as we have hinted, the gallant young nobleman who sports the black, white, and purple was very hard hit by her defeats, and this expression of renewed confidence in the chestnut daughter of Spearmint cannot be disregarded.

The people who had hurried to put their money on Full Moon grumbled loudly; but the public appreciated the clear lead that Tony had given them. He had put his own money on Vanity Girl before the result of the trial leaked out, and though he had obtained tens against the first two thousand he wagered, the news ran round the clubs so quickly that even before the public was warned by the scratching of Full Moon that Vanity Girl was the hope of Clare, he was finding it hard to get fours against the filly; after that her price shortened to five to two; in the week before the race it was only six to four; in the ring on the day itself not a bookmaker was risking more than eleven to ten, and with money still pouring in faster than ever she seemed likely to start at odds on, an unprecedented price for a horse that had not been seen in public since two consecutive defeats in the autumn of the year before. The public could not be blamed for their eagerness to back the filly. It was generally known that Clarehaven either had to win the Derby or be ruined, and if he preferred Vanity Girl to the winner of the Guineas at such a crisis in his affair she must indeed be sure of her success. If the public had known that even his wife's honor was in pawn besides his house and his lands they could not have been more confident.

"If Vanity Girl fails," Dorothy asked, on the morning of the race, "you won't have a halfpenny left?"

"I might have an odd hundred pounds," Tony reckoned.

"And your mother—and Bella?"

He shrugged his shoulders.

"I suppose Uncle Chat will look after them."

"And us?"

"Oh, we'll emigrate or something. Rather fun, don't you know. I shall wangle something. The going will be hardish," he said, looking at the sky, "and that's always in her favor. She hated that Newmarket mud last autumn. Come on, Doodles, the car's waiting."

They walked down the steps of the flat, and the porter who had hurried out to shut the door of the car touched his cap.

"Good luck, my lady! Good luck, my lord! Shepherd's Market is on Vanity Girl to the last copper."

"Put on a sovereign for yourself, Galloway," said his lordship, grandly proffering the coin.

Several loafers who had sometimes run for his lordship's cabs shouted, "Hurrah for the Derby favorite!" and Tony flung them some silver to back his filly. The road to Epsom was thronged; Tony, who was obviously feeling nervous, had left the driving to the chauffeur, and was sitting back with Dorothy in the body of the car.

"I think Lonnie might have come with us," he said, fretfully.

"Does it bore you so much driving with me alone?" she asked.

"Don't be silly! Of course not. But I'm nervy and.... Oh, but what rot! Nothing can go wrong."

They were passing a four-in-hand with loud toots upon their Gabriel horn, which were being answered by the guard of the coach, when he suddenly recognized the occupants of the car. Standing up, he blew a dear "Viewhalloo!" and shouted: "Berkshire's on the filly, my lord, to the last baby! Hurrah for Vanity Girl!" There was a block in the traffic; the occupants of every vehicle in earshot, from the gray hats and laces of the four-in-hand to the pearlies and plumes of a coster's cart, applauded the earl and countess, each after his own fashion.

"Don't forget the Mile End Road, Mr. Hearl of Clarehaven," bawled one of the costers, "if that's who you are. Hoobeeluddiray!" he went on, and caught his moke an ecstatic thwack on the crupper.

In the ring friends and acquaintances crowded round them, eager to say how they had backed Vanity Girl and how fervently they hoped for her victory. There was no doubt that if the filly was beaten a groan of disappointment would resound through England.

"I think it's so sweet that Lord Clarehaven's horse should be called Vanity Girl," some foolish woman was babbling. "So sweet and romantic," she twittered on.

"Yes, what devotion," chirped another as foolish.

Tony wanted to go round to the paddock to have a few last words with Starkey and the jockey O'Hara, but Dorothy did not think she could bear to see the filly before the race.

"I'm so nervous," she said, "that I feel I should communicate my nerves to her. But don't you bother about me. I'll wait for you in the inclosure."

"Where's Houston?" said Tony, irritably. "I thought he was going to meet us."

At that moment a messenger-boy came up. "Are you the Earl of Clarehaven?" he asked, perkily, and handed Tony a note, which the latter read out:

"DEAR CLAREHAVEN,—To what will I'm sure be my lifelong regret, important business prevents me from being at Epsom to see your triumph. Believe me, my dear fellow, that there is no one who hopes more cordially than I do for your success to-day. My kindest regards to your wife and tell her from me that I'm looking forward to our Derby dinner at the Carlton to-night.

Yours ever sincerely,
LIONEL HOUSTON."

"Funny chap! But I believe he's sincere," Tony muttered, "though it would be all to his interest if I lost."

But how much to his interest, Dorothy thought, how little did Tony know.

She waited for him in the company of the twittering women until he returned from the paddock.

"They're going down now," he told her.

"Everything all right?" she asked.

"Yes, yes." He was biting his nails and cursing the focusing arrangements of his field-glasses.

"They're off!"

The roar of the crowd was like a mighty storm within which isolated remarks were heard like the spars of a ship going one by one.

"She isn't finding it so easy."

"He's taking her into the rails too soon."

"My God! I wouldn't lay sixpence there won't be an objection for crossing. Did you see that?"

"Go on, Vanity Girl! Go on!"

"Go on, you blasted favorite!"

"She's swishing her tail."

"No, she's not. That's ... yes, it's her. Vanity Girl! Vanity Girl!"

"Go on, Vanity Girl!"

The roaring died down to a suppressed murmur of agitation.

"What's the matter with the favorite?"

"O'Hara's flogging her along."

The horses flashed past the stand with the black, white and purple of Clarehaven twinkling in the ruck like a setting star.

"Tony!" Dorothy screamed. "She's beaten!"

"Oh well," said the owner, "don't make such a noise about it."

He was smiling a foolish, fixed smile, but he let his glasses drop from his hands on the toes of a lady close by.

"I'm very sorry, ma'am," said Tony, raising his hat. "I hope I didn't hurt you."

The injured lady glared at him; it was her first Derby, and perhaps she did not realize that it mattered who won or lost.

"Come on, Doodles," said Tony. "Home. For God's sake, let's get home."

He would not wait to hear any explanation of the filly's defeat, but pushed his way savagely through the crowd to find the car.

"Gorblime!" a ragged vender of unauthorized race-cards was ejaculating near the garage. "Gor strike me blurry well pink! She'd make a blurry tortoise crick his blurry neck looking round to see why she was dawdling behind. Race-horse? Why, I reckon a keb-horse could give her three stone and win in a blurry canter, I do. Vanity Girl? Vanity Bitch, that's what she ought to have been called."

VII

The news of the defeat had already reached Halfmoon Street, and Galloway inclined his head when they passed quickly from the car into the hall of the flats, as if his patrons were returning from a funeral.

"We must telephone round to the Carlton to say that the dinner is off," said Tony; even that small action he left to his wife, himself sitting for the rest of the evening mute of speech, but drumming upon the table with his fingers or sometimes tambourinating upon an ash-tray. His dinner consisted of anchovy sandwiches washed down by brandy. There was no word from Houston, and Dorothy supposed that he was waiting to hear from her. "Going! Going! Clare! Clare! Clare!" The auctioneer's hammer seemed to be striking her temples, and, passing her hand over her forehead, she realized that it was only Tony who was drumming upon the table or tambourinating upon the ash-tray. She went to bed before he did and, lying awake in the rosy light of the reading-lamp, she wondered if, perhaps, he would try to forget this day in her arms, half hoped he would, and picked up the hand-mirror beside her bed to see how she was looking. He must have sat up drinking till very late—she had fallen asleep and did not hear him come to bed—and in the morning his eyes were bloodshot, his razor tremulous.

The letter-box was choked with bills; but there were several letters of condolence, and a reminder of the Day of Judgment from an enthusiastic enemy of the turf who, with ill-concealed relish, advised his lordship to observe the hand of God in the retribution which had been meted out to him and to turn away from his wickedness. Finally there were letters from O'Hara, the jockey, and Houston.

EPSOM SUMMER MEETING 1914.
Wednesday evening.

MY LORD,—I had hoped to have a few words with your lordship after the race, but was told you already left the course. I was intending to say that I could not go through what I suffered to-day on Friday, and would be obliged if your lordship wouldn't insist I would ride Vanity Girl in the Oaks. My lord, the filly is tired, and I wouldn't say another race mightn't kill her dead. It's not for me to give advice to your lordship, but how you ever come to run her in the Derby I don't know. She never was a stayer. I saw that plainly enough last autumn at Newmarket. I'm going back to France as soon as I hear from your lordship you won't run her in the Oaks. I'm engaged to ride Full Moon in the Grand Prix by Mr. Houston, and I hope I won't have to suffer what I suffered this afternoon. It's enough to make a jockey chuck riding for good and all.

I am,

Your lordship's obedient servant,
PATRICK O'HARA.

Pardon me if I've written a bit unfeelingly. It wasn't the filly's fault. She was tired. She didn't seem to know where she was, somehow, and when I flogged her along it near broke my heart to do it. She couldn't seem to understand what she was wanted to do. Poor little lady, I was so savage I could have shot her. But afterward I went and had a look at her, and had a few words with Mr. Starkey when he was abusing her.

QZI ALBANY, W.
Wednesday.

DEAR CLAREHAVEN,—I'm not going to worry you with sympathy at such a moment. But I'm writing as soon as possible to let you know that last week, owing to circumstances which would not interest anybody except a business man, I was compelled to part with my Clare mortgages for ready money, and I'm afraid that without doubt Reinhardt and Co. will foreclose on Monday. I wish I could offer to lend you the money to put yourself straight again, but I have been speculating myself and for the moment am a little short. By the way, I think Full Moon is a good thing for the Grand Prix. Perhaps you might get a bit on. Kindest regards to Lady Clarehaven.

Sincerely,
LIONEL HOUSTON.

Tony telegraphed to scratch Vanity Girl for the Oaks and ordered that she should be sold outright for what she would fetch; £200 was the figure, a tenth of what she had cost as a yearling and an insignificant fraction of what she had cost in ruinous disappointment, to which, perhaps, dishonor was soon to be added.

Houston's letter showed plainly that nothing was to be hoped for in that quarter.

"Reinhardt and Co.," scoffed Tony. "In my opinion Reinhardt and Co. includes Houston."

Dorothy wondered if the communication was intended to bring her quickly to heel, to show her brutally that unless she kept her bargain Clare was lost. She supposed that somehow Houston would be ingenious enough to keep Tony from being suspicious when he found his house and lands restored to him, and she even wondered if under the demoralizing effect of gambling he would much mind if he did know. She looked at him with a feeling half compassionate, half contemptuous while he was calculating, with an optimism rapidly rising, every knickknack in the flat at four times its value in the sale-room. She persuaded him to go out and forget his troubles at the theater, and telephoned to the Albany that she was coming to see Mr. Houston after dinner.

Dorothy dressed herself in a frock of champagne silk and wore no jewelry except a drop pendant of black pearls, thinking ironically, when she fastened it round her neck, how premature Tony had been in estimating that it would fetch £500 at auction. She flung over her shoulders a diaphanous black opera-cloak stenciled in gold and, covering her face with a heavy veil of black Maltese lace, she passed out of Halfmoon Street and walked slowly up Piccadilly in the June starlight. On second thought she decided to enter Albany from Burlington Street instead of through the courtyard, and, turning into Bond Street, moved like a ghost along the pavements where on thronged mornings in old Vanity days her radiance and roses used to compete for the public regard with the luxurious shops on either side. Burlington Street at this hour was deserted, and the porter of Albany with his appearance of an antique coachman, and his manner between a butler's and a beadle's, dared not hesitate to admit such an empress, and perhaps marveled, when he watched her walk imperiously along the glass-roofed cloister that smelled of freshly watered geraniums toward QZI, with what honey the ugly tenant of it was able to attract this proud-pied moth.

Lady Clarehaven might have been excused for feeling a heroine, a Monna Vanna in the tent of the conqueror, when she found herself in the big square room which she now visited for the first time. She did not indulge herself with heroics, however; it seemed to her so natural for her to save Clare that the adventure was as commonplace as when once in early days on the stage she had pawned a piece of jewelry she did not like in order to save a set of furs to which she attached a great importance. She threw back the opera-cloak and sat down in an arm-chair to wait for Houston with as little perturbation as if she were waiting for a dinner guest in her own drawing-room.

Suddenly he appeared from an inner doorway and, turning on several more lights, looked at her. He was in evening dress, and the sudden glare gave the impression that he was going to perform; he looked more like an intelligent ape than ever when he was in evening dress.

"Well, here I am," she said.

Her coolness seemed to confuse him, and he began to ask her how she liked his rooms, to say that he had been lucky enough to take them on as they stood from a man called Prescott who had killed himself here. One had the impression that he had bought the furniture for a song on account of the unpleasant associations with a suicide.

"I'm rather tired of values," said Dorothy. "Clarehaven has been valuing the flat at Halfmoon Street."

"Will you have something to drink?"

"Do you think that I require stimulating? Thanks, I don't."

It was curious that this man, who in Rhodes had appeared so sinister and powerful and almost irresistible, should here in this decorous room with only a background of good-breeding appear fussy and ineffective.

"But let me recommend you to have a drink," Dorothy laughed. "For, now that you've got me, you're as awkward as a baboon with a porcelain teacup."

Her instinct told her that she must dispel this atmosphere of embarrassment unless she wanted to be bowed out of the chambers as from those of a money-lender who had been compelled most respectfully and without offense to refuse a loan to her ladyship. The allusion to the baboon was sufficient. The decorum of Albany was shattered and Houston held her in his arms.

At that moment the servant tapped at the door and announced that Lord Clarehaven was in the anteroom; before Houston could hustle his quaking servant outside and lock the door Tony appeared in the entrance, a riding-crop in his hands.

"My God! you rascal," he was saying, "I've just found out all about you. I've been fooled by you and that scoundrel of a trainer you recommended. I've been ... That trial.... I've seen.... I've understood ... you blackguard!" Without noticing Dorothy he had forced Houston across a chair and was thumping him with the crop. "Yes, I've heard all about you.... Of course people tell me afterward ... damned cowards.... You damned sneaking hound ... I.D.B.... hound.., you dog ... and there's nothing to be done because you were too clever ... curse you ... but I'll have you booted off every racecourse in England...."

By this time he had beaten Houston insensible, and, looking up, perceived his wife.

"Tony," she cried, "you really are rather an old darling."

"What are you doing here?" he panted.

"I was pleading for Clare."

"You oughtn't to have done that," he said, roughly. "You might get yourself talked about, don't you know. Come along. It's rather lucky I blew in. I met old Cobbett, who talked to me like a father. Too late, of course, and nothing can be done. Besides.... However, come along. As you're dressed we might see the last act."

"We've seen that already," said Dorothy. So brilliant and gay was she that Tony forgot about everything. So did she, and they walked home arm in arm along the deserted streets of Mayfair like lovers.

The scene in Albany was not made public property; Houston came to himself in time to prevent that. Dorothy accepted Tony's interruption as a sign that fortune did not intend her to preserve Clare, and she now watched almost with equanimity the fabric of a great family crumble daily to irreparable ruin. Then Full Moon, the winner of the Guineas, scratched ignominiously for the Derby, won the Grand Prix in a canter, and the following letter from the Earl of Stilton, K.G., appeared in the *Times*:

SIR,—In the interests of our national sport, which all Englishmen rightly regard as our most cherished possession, I call upon Lord Clarehaven to give a public explanation of his recent behavior. The facts are probably only too painfully known to many of your readers. In May Lord Clarehaven's horse, Full Moon, won the Two Thousand Guineas; two years ago his horse Moonbeam won the same race. Moonbeam ran fourth in the Derby and was transferred to the same stable as the winner, Chimpanzee. This horse, owned by Mr. Lionel Houston, was scratched for the St. Leger, and the race was won by Moonbeam. This was explicable; but when two years later another of Lord Clarehaven's horses wins the Two Thousand Guineas and finds his stable companion preferred to him to carry Lord Clarehaven's colors in the Derby, when, furthermore, the chosen filly runs like a plater, and when this morning we read that Full Moon, now in the ownership of Mr. Lionel Houston, has won the Grand Prix in a canter at a price which the totalizator puts at sixty-three to one, a proof that nobody in Paris considered the chances of this animal, the public may, perhaps, demand what it all means. They will ask still more when I inform them that I have absolute authority for saying that this horse was heavily backed in England, which proves that by some his chance was considered excellent. I have no wish to accuse his lordship of having deliberately deceived the public for his own advantage; but I do accuse him of folly that can only be characterized as criminal. Perhaps he has been the victim of his friend and of his trainer; at any rate, if his lordship was deceived about the chance of Vanity Girl, and if it is true that the defeat of Vanity Girl in the Derby represented to his lordship a loss of thousands of pounds in bets, he should make this clear. In that case I have no hesitation in accusing Mr. Lionel Houston, formerly known as Leopold Hausberg, of having deliberately conspired with the Starkey Lodge trainer to perpetrate a fraud not only upon their friend and patron, but also upon the public.

I have the honor to be, sir,

Your obedient servant,   STILTON.

Although Lord Stilton's letter hit the nail on the head, Tony was so furious at being called a fool in public that he sent the following letter to the paper:

SIR,—If Lord Stilton had not been my father's friend and a much older man than myself, I would pull his nose for the impudent letter he has written about me. The running of my filly in the Derby is an instance of the uncertainty of fortune, by which I am the greatest loser. I was convinced by a trial which I saw with my own eyes between Full Moon and Vanity Girl that the former did not stand a chance against the filly. It was I who insisted upon scratching him for the Derby so that the public might be spared the unpleasant doubt that always exists when an owner runs two horses in the same race. I sold the colt shortly after this trial to Mr. Houston, because I wished to put every halfpenny I could raise upon Vanity Girl. When I say that Mr. Houston is so little a friend of mine that I was unfortunately compelled to horsewhip him in his rooms on the day after the Derby, it will be understood even by Lord Stilton that there can be no possible suggestion of any collusion between myself and Mr. Houston. I do not know if Lord Stilton seriously means to insinuate that I have benefited by Full Moon's victory in the Grand Prix. If he does, the insinuation is cowardly and unjust. If Lord Stilton is so much concerned for the future of English sport, let him think twice before he hits a man who is down. Full Moon did not carry a halfpenny of my money.

I am, sir, etc.,   CLAREHAVEN.

This letter, with the reference to Lord Stilton's nose excised by a judicious editor, rehabilitated Tony in the eyes of the public and earned him a gracious apology from Lord Stilton, who also had to apologize much less graciously to Houston and Starkey, being threatened with legal proceedings unless he did so. Had there been the least chance of substantiating the ugly rumors, both earls might have gone to law; unfortunately legal advice said that neither of them stood a chance with the astute pair, and public opinion contented itself with compassion for the gallant young nobleman who had been thus victimized.

It may have been the victory of Full Moon in the Grand Prix with its suggestion of what might have been, or it may have been only the invincible optimism of the gambler, that started Tony off again upon his vice. When by the middle of July he and Dorothy found themselves with the rent of the flat paid up to Michaelmas, with enough furniture and enough clothes for present needs and with £250 in ready money, he told Dorothy that their only chance was for him to make money at cards. It was in vain that she argued with him; he seemed to have learned nothing from this disastrous summer, and with £100 in his pocket he went out one night, to return at six o'clock the next morning with £1,000.

"My luck's in again," he declared, "and I've got a thundering good system. You shall come with me every night, and I will give you two hundred pounds, which I must not exceed. Nothing that I say must induce you to give me another halfpenny. If I lose the two hundred pounds I must go away. It'll be all right, you'll see. I'm playing at Arrowsmith's place in Albemarle Street. Arrowsmith himself has promised not to advance me anything above two hundred pounds, so it'll be all right."

Dorothy begged him to be satisfied with the £1,000; but it was useless, and the following night she accompanied him. He won another £1,000, and when they had walked back under a primrose morning sky to Halfmoon Street Tony was so elated that he handed over all his winnings to Dorothy. The next night he lost the stipulated £200, but he came away still optimistic.

"I'm not going to touch that two thousand" he assured her. "I've got fifty left of my own, and one always wins when one's down to nothing; but on no account are you to offer me a halfpenny from your money. It's absolutely essential that you should bank everything I make."

The next evening Tony took the keeper of the hell aside and told him that he was to be sure not to let him exceed £50; if he should lose that, Arrowsmith was not to accept his I.O.U. and on no condition to allow him to go on. They were playing *chemin de fer* and Tony's luck had been poor; when his turn came to take the bank and he was stretching out his hand for the box of cards Arrowsmith told him he had already reached his limit.

"Oh, that's all right, Arrowsmith. I only meant that to count if I'd already had a bank."

"Excuse me, Lord Clarehaven, but I never go back on my word. The agreement we came to was...."

"That's all right," Tony interrupted, impatiently. "Dorothy, lend me some money."

"No, no. You made a promise, and really you must stick to it."

"Dash it! I haven't had a single bank this evening."

"You should have thought of that before."

"But, my dear girl, our agreement was that I shouldn't lose more than two hundred pounds at a sitting. I've only lost fifty pounds to-night."

"If I lend you any more," she said, "I must break into the two thousand pounds, which you told me I was not to do on any account."

The other players, with heavy, doll-like faces, sat round the table, waiting until the argument stopped and the game could be resumed. The keeper of the hell was firm; so was Dorothy; and Clarehaven had to yield his turn to his neighbor.

"I'll just stay and watch the play for a bit," he said. "It's only three o'clock." He took a banana from the sideboard and sat down behind the player who held the bank.

"No, no, come away," Dorothy begged him. "What is the good of tormenting yourself by watching other people play when you can't play yourself?"

"Damn it, Dorothy," he exclaimed, turning round angrily. "I wish to God I'd never brought you here. You always interfere with everything I want to do."

561

It happened that the bank which Tony had missed won steadily, and while the heavy-jowled man who held it raked in money from everybody, Tony watched him like a dog that watches his master eating. At last the bank was finished, and with a heavy sigh of satisfaction the owner of it passed on the box to his neighbor.

"How much did you make?" asked Tony, enviously.

"About two thousand five hundred. I'm not sure. I never count my winnings."

Tears of rage stood in Tony's eyes.

"God! Do you see what you've done for me by your confounded obstinacy?" he exclaimed to his wife.

All the way home he raged at her, and when they were in the flat he demanded that she should give him back all his £2,000.

"So you've reached the point," she said, bitterly, "when not even promises count?"

"If you don't give it back to me," Tony vowed, "I'll sell up the whole flat. Damn it, I'll even sell my boots," he swore, as he tripped over some outposts for which there was no place in the line that extended along the wall of his dressing-room.

Dorothy thought of that lunch-party in Christ Church and of the first time she had beheld those boots. She remembered that then she had beheld in them a symbol of boundless wealth. Now they represented a few shillings in a gambler's pocket. And actually next morning, in order to show that he had been serious the night before, Tony summoned two buyers of old clothes to make an offer for them.

"Don't be so childish," Dorothy exclaimed. "You can't sell your boots! Aren't you going down to camp this year?"

"To camp?" he echoed. "How the deuce do you think I'm going to camp without a halfpenny? No, my dear girl, a week ago I wrote to resign my commission in the N.D.D. You might make a slight effort to realize that we are paupers. And if you won't let me have any of that two thousand pounds we shall remain paupers."

At that moment a telegram was handed in:

> All officers of North Devon Dragoons to report at depot immediately.

"Hasn't that fool of an adjutant got my letter?" Tony exclaimed.

Another telegram arrived:

> Thought under circumstances you would want to cancel letter holding it till I see you.

"Circumstances? What circumstances?"

In the street outside a newspaper-boy was crying, "Austrian hultimatum! Austrian hultimatum!"

"My God!" Tony cried, a light coming into his eyes. "It can't really mean war? How perfectly glorious! Wonderful! Get out, you rascals!" and he hustled the old-clothes men out of the flat.

Three weeks later Dorothy received the following letter from Flanders:

DEAREST DOODLES,—You'd simply love this. I never enjoyed myself so much in all my life. Can't write you a decent letter because I'm just off chivvying Uhlans. It's got fox-hunting beat a thousand times. Sorry we had that row when I made such an ass of myself at Arrowsmith's that night. It's a lucky thing you were firm, because you've got just enough to go on with until I get back. Mustn't say too much in a letter; but I suppose we shall have chivvied these bounders back to Berlin in two or three months. Then I shall really have to settle down and do something in earnest. A man in ours says that Queensland isn't such a bad sort of hole. Old Cleveden put me against it by cracking it up so. It's suddenly struck me that Houston is probably a spy. If he is, you might make it rather unpleasant for him. I feel I haven't explained properly how sorry I am, but it's so deuced hard in a letter. By the way, Uncle Chat has just written rather a stupid letter about my mother's jointure. Perhaps you'd go down and talk to him about it. He ought to understand I'm too busy to bother about domestic finance at present. I had another notion—rather a bright one—that when I get back you and I could appear on the stage together. Rather a rag, eh? The captain of my troop was pipped last week. Awful good egg. I'm acting captain now. Paignton sends his love. Dear old thing, I wish you were out here with me.

Yours ever,
TONY.

A week later the fifth Earl of Clarehaven was killed in action.

CHAPTER VI

I

DOROTHY was at Little Cherrington when the news of Tony's death reached her. The dowager had already vacated Clare Lodge, and with a few of her dearest possessions was now established in Cherrington Cottage. Only extreme necessity could have driven her into that particular abode, because in order for her to go into it, Mr. Greenish had to go out of it, which upset Mr. Greenish so much that he went out of Cherrington altogether, out of Devonshire, even, and as far away as Hampshire. His choice of a county was the dowager's only consolation; Connie lived in Hampshire; the world was small; Mr. Greenish and Bella might even yet come together. Bella, absorbed in her short stories—one of which had been accepted, but not published, and another of which had been published but not paid for—found that the chief objection to being in Cherrington Cottage was the noise that the children made going to and from school. It was strange to find Bella, who in her youth had made as much noise even as Connie, so dependent now upon quiet; but in whatever divine hands mortals fall, their behavior usually changes radically afterward. We all know what love can do for anybody; we all know what the Salvation Army can do for anybody; and if Virgil's account of the Cumæan Sibyl may be trusted, the transforming influence of Apollo is second to none.

Tony's consideration in securing Cherrington Cottage to his mother could only have been bettered if he had made some provision for a sum of money to maintain it, or, for that matter, herself; delicious as the exterior of it undoubtedly was, the walls were not edible. The sudden stoppage in the payment of her jointure put the dowager in the humiliating position of having to ask her brother, Lord Chatfield, to pay the weekly bills, and it was with the intention of dealing with this matter that Dorothy had gone down much against her will to the scene that was consecrated to her greatest triumph and her greatest failure. Perhaps the nerves of the usually so genial Uncle Chat had been too much wrought upon by the outbreak of war. As deputy lieutenant of the county he had been harried by a series of telegrams from the War Office, each of which had contradicted its predecessor. He had had to lend not merely all his own horses to England, but to arrange to lend most of his neighbors', some of whom were not quite such willing lenders as his lordship. His eldest son, Paignton, was already at the front in the North Devon Dragoons, and his second son was assisting an elderly gentleman who had lived in obscurity since Tel-el-Kebir—where he had been jabbed in the liver by a dervish—to command, drill, and generally produce for their country's need the two hundred and ten rustics that at present constituted the Seventh Service Battalion of the King's Own Devon Light Infantry. His daughters, Lady Maud and Lady Mary, had given him no rest till they were allowed to do something or other; though before he understood what exactly this was the war had lasted many months longer than the greatest pessimist had believed possible. His sister, Lady Jane, in despair of finding anything else to do, was collecting mittens for the soldiers, a hobby which made the ground floor of Chatfield Hall look like a congested wool-warehouse in the city.

At such a moment the problem of his younger sister's financial future struck poor Uncle Chat as much more hopelessly insoluble than it would have seemed in those happy days when he had nothing to talk about except cigars and pigs. Bella immediately after the outbreak of war put down the pen and took up the sword, or in other words yearned to join the V.A.D., and it was the imperative need of finding money for Bella to gratify her patriotism in London that drove the dowager into discussing her finances with her brother. Dorothy, who could not bear the suggestion that Tony had heartlessly left for France without any heed of his family obligations, a suggestion that reflected upon herself, at once turned over to the dowager half of the £2,000 in the bank. Actually, she only left herself with something over £600, for extra money had had to be found for Tony's equipment and for the payment of bills he had overlooked. There was no reason to suppose that Uncle Chat was really criticizing her behavior in the least; but his air of general irritation gave her the impression that he was, which preyed upon her mind so much that she began to feel almost on a level with her unfortunate namesake who had lost the Derby. She fancied that everybody was ascribing Tony's mad career to his marriage, and thinking that if he had only married a nice girl in his own class none of these disasters would have happened. She fancied that the disapproval of the family which had been carefully concealed all these years out of deference to Tony's feelings was now making itself known, she was embittered by the imagined atmosphere of hostility, and she made up her mind that as soon as possible she would cut herself off from the Fanhopes and from what was left of the Clares.

Tony in his last letter had proposed that he and she should go on the stage when he came home, which of course would have been ridiculous; but, now that Tony was dead, there was surely nothing to prevent her return to the stage. When she got back to town she might go and ask Sir John Richards if he could not find a part in the autumn production at the Vanity Theater. Whatever was now lacking to her voice, whatever the years had added to her appearance, and notwithstanding the wear and tear that had added very little, would be counterbalanced in the eyes of the British public by the privilege of reading upon the program the name of the Countess of Clarehaven. Nothing was any longer owing to the family name; no, indeed, except Bella still bore it, and if third-rate stories were to appear in third-rate magazines under the signature of Arabella Clare, there was no reason why a bill of the play should not advertise the Countess of Clare. It happened that Harry Tufton had come down to Cherrington to assist at the memorial service which was to be held in Clarehaven church. Dorothy supposed that he was anxious to keep in with the Chatfields, and in speaking to him about her project she was not actuated by any desire for the sympathy of an old friend. She asked his advice in a practical spirit, because he was connected with the theater, and when he tried to discourage her by hinting at the fickleness of public affection, she discerned in his opposition to her plan nothing except the tired anxiety of one who was being importuned by an old friend to give the best advice compatible with the minimum of trouble to himself. Tufton's doubtfulness of her capacity still to attract the favor of an audience had the effect of strengthening her resolve to test his opinion; she asked him with that indifferent smile of hers, which had lost none of its magic of provocation, if he really thought that the British public was as fickle as himself. Tufton protested against the imputation, and excused himself for the evasion of friendship implicit in his attitude by pleading that the War Office kept him so very busy nowadays.

"Of course it was an awful blow when they wouldn't accept me for active service," he said, earnestly. "Heart, don't you know."

"Oh, your heart is weak," she inquired, with a mocking air of concern. "I suppose the very idea of war produced palpitations. Don't strain it going up-stairs in Whitehall."

"Somebody must do the work at home," he said, irritably.

"Yes, I feel so sorry for you poor Cinderellas," she murmured. "But never mind, you'll always be able to feel that if it wasn't for you the poor fellows at the front, don't you know, wouldn't be able to get along. I suppose you call yourselves the noble army of martyrs?"

It had been fun to twist the tail of that ship's rat, Dorothy thought, when she saw him hurry away from Cherrington to catch the first train back to town after the service.

The news of Tony's death had reached Cherrington on the morning of the day that Dorothy was going back to the flat. When she had made over half of her money to the dowager and was clear of the fancied atmosphere of hostility at Chatfield, she had begun to feel penitently that she had misjudged her mother-in-law and sister-in-law. It had seemed dreadful to leave them here in this cottage almost within sight and sound of the changes at Clare Court, and she had invited them to come and stay with her in Halfmoon Street until the flat was given up. The dowager had been unwilling to leave the country, and when the news of her son's death arrived was firm in her determination to remain in Cherrington.

"He was born here," she said, "and it is here that I shall always think of him best. I don't think I can afford to put up a window to his memory; he must just have a simple stone slab. I should like to copy that inscription at Rhodes. Do you remember it? 'Anthony, Fifth Earl of Clarehaven. With God. 1914.'"

Dorothy's grief at the death of Tony had for the moment been kept in control by the tremendous effort she had been called upon to make in facing the future; it was the future which had occupied her mind to the exclusion of any contemplation of the past. Now when her mother-in-law spoke these simple words she burst into tears. They linked Tony with so many generations of his house; and they brought home to her almost as a visible fact his death. She had spent so many years perpetually on the verge, as it were, of broken promises, of resolutions never carried out, of little optimisms and extenuations, that when the announcement of his death arrived it was more than usually true in her case that she did not at first realize it. The telegraphic form in which the news had been conveyed to her involuntarily merged itself with so many telegrams in the past which had turned out false, and only when the dowager stated his death like this in terms that admitted of no doubt did Dorothy suddenly confront the reality. She remembered that once a telegram had arrived almost on this very date to say that Tony could not get away from camp in time to be present at the annual show. There was no annual show this year—war had obliterated it—but on the afternoon of this day on which she had meant to return to town she walked, instead, about the field where the show had customarily been held, and so vivid was the familiar scene of hot women and blazing dahlias that she was transported back in imagination and found herself excusing on the ground of his military duties her husband's absence from this spectral exhibition. A farmer, one of her late tenants, passed her while she was wandering over the field, touched his cap, and begged to express his sorrow at the news.

"'Tis going to be a handsome year for partridges, too," he said. "But there, my lady, his lordship of late never seemed to care for partridges so much as he belonged. I remember when he was a youngster he'd regular walk me off my feet, as the saying is, after they birds. And he was uncommon fond of land-rails. Yes, it always seemed to give him a sort of extra pleasure, as you might say, when he could get a shot at a land-rail."

The reproach that was implied in the farmer's first words was mitigated by these reminiscences of Tony as a boy, and Dorothy thought that if her son had lived he would already be over six years old and within measurable distance of shooting his first land-rail in the company of the burly farmer beside her. Her son! Would it have made any difference to Tony if he had had an heir? Ought she to thank God or reproach Him for her childlessness?

Three days later Mr. Beadon sang for the late earl a requiem at Clarehaven church. Whoever should be the new owner of Clare—nobody had materialized from that mysterious firm of Reinhardt & Co.—he was not yet flaunting his proprietorship. The mourners passed slowly through the somber groves of pines and looked back at the empty house across the short herbage burnished by the drought of August, and the house empty and solemn, perhaps more solemn because it had not been dressed for grief, eyed with all its windows their progress seaward.

It would be cynical to say that at such a moment Mr. Beadon derived a positive pleasure from conducting a mass of requiem for the dead earl, and if for a moment he regarded with a kind of gloomy triumph Squire Kingdon's inevitable conformity to the majestic ritual of woe expressed by the catafalque from which depended the dead earl's hatchment, he made up by the grave eloquence of his funeral oration for any fleeting pettiness. The windows of the little church on the cliff were wide open to the serene air, and if ever the preacher fell mute for a space to recover from his emotion the plaint of the tide was heard in a monody above the mourners' tears; but above the preacher's voice, above all the sounds of nature in communion with human grief, there was continuously audible a gay chattering of birds among the tombs, of whinchats and stonechats that were mobilizing along these cliffs, unaware that there was anything very admirable or very adventurous about their impending migration. A cynic listening to those birds might have criticized the rector's sermon for its exaggeration of the spirit in which the young earl had set out to Flanders; a cynic might have given himself leave to doubt if the fifth Earl of Clarehaven was inspired by the same spirit as inspired Sir Gilbert Clare to defend Rhodes against the Moslem; but, whatever the spirit in which he had set forth, no cynic could impugn the spirit in which he had died; no living man, indeed, had any longer the right to sneer at his frailties and follies or to condemn his vices and his extravagance. Besides, a cynic contemporary with Sir Gilbert Clare may have questioned the spirit in which the Hospitaller had watched the cliffs of Devon fade out in the sunset. Who knows? There were stonechats and whinchats then as now.

On the morning after the requiem Dorothy was confronted with the possibility of an event that in its significance, should it come to fruition, would obliterate all that had happened in the past and would provide her in the future with a task so tremendous that she almost fell on her knees then and there to pray for strength and wisdom to sustain it. This was the possibility that she was going to have a child.

Such a prospect changed every plan for the future that she had been making and destroyed her freedom in the very moment it had been given back to her by the death of her husband. Her intention of proving to Harry Tufton that she could again be a favorite of the public must now be relinquished; her ambition to withdraw haughtily from the protection of Lord Chatfield must presumably be abandoned. Yet need they? She should not be too impulsive. Who now except herself had the right to say a word about her child's future? Who else could claim to be the guardian of its destiny? If she was right about her condition, she should rejoice that Tony was dead. If he had been alive and in that mood he was in before the outbreak of war solved his future so rapidly and so completely, this wonderful prospect would only have led to recriminations, even to open hatred. It would have been he who had robbed their child of its inheritance, and she could never have refrained from taunting him with his egotism. Nor was it likely that he would have been reformed by the prospect of being a father; he had not shown much inclination that way in the early years of their marriage; and even if for a while he had changed his habits, he would gradually have relapsed, and, moreover, with his genial and indulgent character he would have held out not merely a bad, but also an attractive, example, which would doubtless have been eagerly and assiduously imitated by any child of his. Yes, but now the future lay in her hands ... and meanwhile she must not be too sure that she was going to have a child at all, nor, even if it were established that she was, must she make too many plans in advance, because everything would be ruled by whether it was a boy or a girl. If it should be a girl, she might go back to the stage next year; she would only be thirty-one next March. It was odd how much younger thirty-one seemed than thirty. But if it should be a boy ... well, even if it should be a boy, why should she not go back to the stage and by her own exertions keep him, educate him, prepare him to be what he must be— landless, houseless, moneyless, but still the sixth Earl of Clarehaven? Stoic, indeed, should be his training, and his nobility should be won as well as conferred.

Several days of uncertainty went by, and finally Dorothy decided to ask Doctor Lane his opinion of her condition. He was a very old man now and no longer in practice, but at least he would know how to keep a secret, and a secret she intended his opinion to remain at present. Already plans were seething in her head for the immediate future, and when Doctor Lane assured her that she was going to have a baby, without saying a word even to the dowager she left next day for London.

Dorothy, who had been fancying that Tony's family wanted to be rid of her, soon found that, on the contrary, they would not let her alone, and when the lease expired at Michaelmas and while she was still wondering where she was going to live next, she received an invitation to join the dowager, Bella, and Lady Jane at the Chatfield town mansion in Grosvenor Square. It appeared that Lady Jane had by this time become so inextricably entangled in unknitted wool that the only way she could disentangle herself was by coming up to town to continue there with proper help the preparation of mittens against the winter cold.

"Not that it will be necessary," everybody said, "but it's as well to be prepared, and of course it *might* drag on till the spring."

The dowager, who had been worked up by her sister to feel that even though she had given a son to England she was still in debt, and Bella were among the twenty ladies collected by Lady Jane to make mittens, and the spinster was anxious to add Dorothy to her flock, for what between wool and ladies she was become very pastoral. So great pressure was put on Dorothy to make mittens, too. Uncle Chat was very penitent for his behavior over the jointure, and he now insisted that the money Dorothy had shared with her mother-in-law should be returned to her. Had it not been for her condition, she would have taken pleasure in refusing this; in the circumstances she accepted it, but she still did not say a word about her pregnancy, for reasons compounded of superstition and pride. Her experience of child-bearing had destroyed her self-confidence and she felt that she could not bear to have a great fuss made about her and to be installed in state at Chatfield Hall to wait there doing nothing through all this anxious winter of war. Nor did the manufacture of mittens in Grosvenor Square appeal to her. Moreover, it was possible that the news would not be welcome. She could not have borne to see Uncle Chat's face fall again at the prospect of having to support a grandnephew of the same rank as himself, and though she did not think that the dowager would attempt to interfere, or that she would be anything but delighted and tactful, there was the chance that after her son's death she might arrogate to herself a right to spoil her grandson. If Dorothy accepted for him the charity of his grandmother's family, she could not avoid admitting the dowager to the privilege of maternity; but if during the months of expectation she kept close her secret and if it were a boy, untrammeled by any obligations she should be at liberty to make her own decision about his up-bringing. More and more she was forming all her plans to fit the future of a boy, and one of her chief reasons for not relying upon the good will of the family was her desire to spare this son prenatal coddling by coddling herself.

Dorothy might have found it hard to analyze justly all the motives that inspired her to take the step she did; but whatever they were, a hot morning in late September found her sitting at the window of her old room in Lonsdale Road.

II

If outwardly Lonsdale Road presented the same appearance as it had presented on that September morning twelve years ago when Dorothy, after washing her hair, made up her mind to be engaged to Wilfred Curlew, the standpoint from which she now looked out of her window was so profoundly changed that the road itself was transmuted by the alchemy of her mind to achieve the significant and incommunicable landscape of a dream. It was as if in looking at Lonsdale Road she were looking at herself, and a much truer self than she ever used to see portrayed in that old mirror upon her dressing-table.

In an upper room of the house opposite a servant was dusting. Down below, amid that immemorial acrid smell of privet, two little girls were busily digging in the front garden. These were the daughters of her second sister, the rightful Dorothy, who was staying with her parents because her husband, Claude Savage, had left Norbiton for France with his regiment of territorials. Mrs. Savage, a dark, neat little woman, as capable a housewife as she had promised to become, and at twenty-eight not quite so annoying as formerly, came into the room from time to time and glanced out of the window to see that her little girls were not making themselves too dirty.

"Hope they're not disturbing you with their chattering."

"No, no," said the countess. "I like listening to them."

Ah, there was Edna down below, not as twelve years ago giggling back from school with Agnes, but wheeling a perambulator and from time to time bending cautiously over to arrange the coverlet over her sleeping baby. Edna was a dull edition of Agnes, and already at twenty-six much more like Mrs. Caffyn than any of her sisters. Her chin was rather furry; she was indefinite, not so indefinite as her mother because modern education had not permitted to her what was formerly considered a prerogative of woman. Edna had been married for about three years to Walter Hume, a young doctor in Golders Green, who was stationed at some northern camp with the R.A.M.C. She, too, was staying with her parents.

"Edna keeps on fussing with the coverlet," said Mrs. Savage, critically. "But she ought not to be walking along the sunny side of the pavement."

The countess did not pay much attention to the practical sister looking over her shoulders; she was thinking of Agnes and wondering what she was doing, and how her baby was getting on.

"Have you heard from Agnes lately?" she asked.

"Yes. Her husband has gone in for politics. But of course politics out there must be very different from what they are in England. You can't imagine Agnes as the wife of a politician. Tut-tut! Ridiculous!"

"What did she call her little boy?"

"Oh, gracious, don't ask me! Some perfectly absurd name. Could it be Xenophon? I know Claude laughed muchly when he heard it. Thank goodness, he wouldn't have let me choose such names for Mary and Ethel. I suppose Agnes is happy. She seems to be. I sometimes wonder where some of the members of our family get their taste for adventure."

"But you've no idea what a lovely place Aphros is ... it lies in the middle of a circle of islands and...."

"Yes, yes," Mrs. Savage interrupted, "but it's a long way from England, and the idea of living abroad doesn't appeal to me."

"Don't you ever want to travel?"

"Well, Claude and I had planned to go to Switzerland with a party this August, but of course the war put a stop to that."

"By the way, isn't the war rather an adventure for Claude?" the countess asked, with a smile.

"An adventure?" Mrs. Savage echoed. "It's a great inconvenience."

She bustled out of the room to look after her own daughters and give Edna some advice about hers; soon after she was gone Gladys and Marjorie, the prototypes of those little girls in the front garden, strolled in to gossip with their eldest sister. Although it was nearly noon, they were only just out of bed, because they had been up late at a dance on the night before. Gladys, a girl of twenty, was very like her eldest sister at the same age. She was not quite so tall and perhaps she lacked her air of having been born to grandeur, but she was sufficiently like to make Dorothy wonder if her career would at all resemble her own. On the whole, she thought that probably herself and Agnes had exhausted the right of the Caffyns to astonish their neighbors. Gladys and Marjorie, the latter a charming new edition of the original Dorothy, with flashing deep-blue eyes, dark hair, and an Irish complexion, were already, at twenty and nineteen, too free to be ambitious. Twelve years had made a great difference to the liberty of girls in West Kensington, and Mr. Caffyn no longer objected to the young men who came to his house, mostly in uniform nowadays, which provided one more excuse for emancipation. Gladys and Marjorie frequently arrived home unchaperoned from dances at three o'clock in the morning, and their father did not turn a hair; perhaps he was already so white that he was incapable of showing any more marks of life's fitful fever. No doubt he had long ago given up the ladies of Lauriston Mansions, and probably at no period in his career was he more qualified to be the secretary of the Church of England Purity Society than upon the eve of his retirement from the post. Dorothy had not seen her father since that night she drove him back in her car from the Vanity. Tacitly they had been friends at once when the countess came to live at home for a while; indeed, she fancied that she could grow quite fond of him, and she was even compelled to warn herself against a slight inclination to accept his flattery a little too complacently. Mrs. Caffyn, with a perversity that is often shown by blondes upon the verge of sixty, would not go white, and her hair was of so indefinite a shade as to be quite indescribably the very expression of her own indefinite personality.

Of the boys—it was odd to hear of the boys again—Roland had long been married and already had four children. At this rate he was likely to surpass his father, whom on a larger scale he was beginning to resemble. Roland was continually in a state of being expected to come and look the family up. He was so long in doing so that he became almost a myth to his eldest sister, and when at last, one afternoon, he did materialize with the largest mustache she had ever seen, his appearance gave her the same kind of thrill that she used to get at the Zoo, when at short intervals the sea-lion would emerge from the water and flap about among the rocks of his cage. It was obvious that Roland regarded her with a mixture of suspicion, jealousy, and disapproval, for he had not brought his wife with him, and when the countess asked him if he had also left his pipe at home, he growled out that he supposed she was far too grand for pipes. Dorothy remembered that sometimes when they were children he and she had seemed upon the path of mutual understanding, and, feeling penitent for her share in the way they had for twelve years been walking away from each other, she tried to be specially affectionate with Roland; but he was already out of earshot. He evidently was thinking that her abrupt re-entry into the family circle would probably mean a reduction in his share of any money left by their parents, because he was continually alluding to her financial state and his own. She tried to ascribe this to his position as the manager of a branch bank; but she knew in her heart that he was dividing £500 a year first by eight and then by nine and thinking what a difference to his holiday that extra £7 would make. Of Dorothy's other brothers, Cecil was in camp somewhere, and hoping to get to France soon with the R.A.M.C.; he had been married only a few months, and his wife was living in the nearest town to his quarters. Vincent, who had won a scholarship at Sydney Sussex College, Cambridge, had already enlisted and wrote home as confidently of promotion in the near future as twelve years ago he had boasted that he would soon be in the eleven of St. James's Preparatory School.

Perhaps the most striking result of the countess's return was the impetus it gave to Mrs. Caffyn's Wednesday afternoons. The punctilious ladies came as they had been coming steadily for twelve years; but a quantity of less punctilious ladies also came and were so much over-awed by meeting a countess in a West Kensington drawing-room that they had no appetite for cakes, which was just as well because otherwise the strain put upon the normal provision by so many extra visitors might have been too much for it. In addition to the Wednesday ladies, several friends of Dorothy's youth visited No. 17 in the evenings, and though by now the billiard-table was more like a neglected tennis-lawn, she played one or two games to remind her of old times, thinking how scornful she would have been twelve years ago if any one had prophesied to her such indulgence in sentiment. Among these friends of youth came Wilfred Curlew, who in outward appearance was the least changed of all. His career had been successful, if the editorship of a society paper can be considered success. Being a journalist, he rightly considered himself indispensable at home, and it is unlikely that his inaccurate and cheery paragraphs in *The Way of the World* did any more to make the war ridiculous than some of the inaccurate and cheery despatches sent home from the front by generals. A slight tendency which he had formerly had toward a cockney accent had been checked by an elocutionist who had imprisoned his voice in his throat, whence it was never allowed to stray. If Lady Clarehaven had once been a Vanity girl, Mr. Wilfred Curlew, the editor of *The Way of the World*, had once written fierce revolutionary articles about Society in *The Red Lamp*; and whereas Lady Clarehaven had long been indifferent to her past, Mr. Curlew was still sensitive about his, as sensitive as a man who oils the wheels of railway-coaches in termini would be if it were known that he had once been a train-wrecker.

After the first awkwardness of such a rencounter had worn off Dorothy found Wilfred entertaining. It was astonishing to learn how accurately the failings and follies of so many of her friends and acquaintances were known to the editor, who had never met one of them. At first he pretended that he had met them; but as gradually he saw more of the countess he gave up this pretense, and finally he revealed the existence in his mind of a perpetual and abominable dread that soon or late in one of his cheery paragraphs he should make a mistake, not, of course, a mistake of fact or even an unjust imputation—that would be nothing—but a mistake of form. He was really haunted day and night by such bogies as referring to a maid of honor after marriage without her prefix, though to have suggested that her behavior with somebody else's husband was less honorable than that would no more have troubled him than to state positively that her main hobby was breeding Sealyham terriers, when it was really communicating every Sunday at St. Paul's, Knightsbridge. If in Lonsdale Road Dorothy beheld her present self, in Wilfred Curlew she saw the reflection of what she was twelve years ago, enough of which old self still existed to make her feel proud that never in her most anxious moments had she revealed to another person her own dread of making a mistake.

One day after a long talk about well-known people in society, Curlew exclaimed from the depths of his inmost being, "If only I had you always!"

"Is this a proposal?" she laughed.

He rose and walked about the room in his agitated fashion; then supporting with one arm the small of his back as he used, and wrenching his voice back into his throat whence in his emotion it had nearly escaped, he paused to mutter:

"Presumptuous, I know, but sincere."

This phrase remained in Dorothy's mind for long afterward, and in her gloomiest hours she could always smile when she repeated gently to herself, "Presumptuous, I know, but sincere."

Naturally, she told Curlew as kindly as she could that his proposal was far outside the remotest bounds of possibility.

"Besides," she added, "you'd really be much better off without my help. Readers of your paper will always greatly prefer your view of society to my view. My view would pull your circulation down to nothing in less than no time."

"It's true," Curlew groaned. "How wise you are!"

Only that morning he had received a sharp reminder from the great brain of which *The Way of the World* was merely an inquisitive and insignificant tentacle, to say that the last three or four numbers of the paper had shown a marked falling off in their ability to provide what the public required.

"You have to admit that I am right," Dorothy pointed out kindly.

"Yes, but if you'd marry me, in a year or two I would give up journalism and write novels. I've got a theory about the form of the English novel which I should like to put into practice."

"I'm afraid," said Dorothy, "I have heard too many theories about the form of race-horses to believe much in theories of form about anything. Form is a capricious quality."

"It's an awful thing," poor Wilfred groaned, "for a man who knows he can write good stuff never to have an opportunity of doing so. I'm afraid I've sold my soul," he murmured, in a transport of remorse.

"We all of us do that sooner or later," she said. "And it's only when we don't get a good price for it that we repent."

Dorothy's faculty for aphorisms had no doubt been fostered by the respect which was accorded to her at Lonsdale Road, but she was far from talking merely for the sake of talking, and her inspiration was really the fruit of experience, not the mere flowering of words. She had, perhaps, been wiser than she had realized in coming home for a while. Notwithstanding those two younger sisters nearly as beautiful as herself, notwithstanding the knowledge generally diffused that she was without money, her beauty and rank were still sufficiently remarkable in West Kensington to preserve her dignity. Here she ran no risks of acquiring a deeper cynicism from the behavior of old friends like Tufton, and inasmuch as misfortune had made her more truly the equal of those around her she had no temptation now to lord it over her sisters, as no doubt they had expected she would; in the homage of West Kensington she let the pleasant side of herself develop and, by a strong effort resisting an inclination to worry about the future, she resigned herself to whatever fortune had in store for her.

Dorothy was not content with waiting for all her old friends to visit her; there was one whom she herself sought out soon after she reached West Kensington. She had not seen Olive Airdale since her marriage, and she was glad she was visiting her for the first time humbly and on foot, even if Olive should think that it was only in adversity that she cared to seek out the companions of her early days. What rubbish! As if Olive would think anything except that she was glad to see her old friend. It was an opalescent afternoon in mid-October when Dorothy rang the bell of the little red house in Gresley Road, and Olive's welcome of her was as if the mist over London had suddenly melted to reveal that very paradise which for the fanciful wayfarer existed somewhere behind these enchanting and transfigurative autumnal airs.

"My dearest Dorothy," she exclaimed. "But why do you reproach yourself? As if I hadn't always perfectly understood! I've been so worried about you. And I wish you could have met Jack—but of course he enlisted at once. You don't know him or you'd realize that of course he had to."

They talked away as if there had never been the smallest break in their association; Rose and Sylvius, those nice fat twins who would be five years old next April, interested the countess immensely now that she would soon be a mother herself.

"And Sylvia?" Dorothy asked.

"Oh, my dear, we don't know. Isn't it dreadful? None of us knows. She was engaged to be married to Arthur Madden—you remember him, perhaps at theFrivolity last year—and suddenly he married another girl and Sylvia vanished—utterly and completely. She went abroad, that's all we know."

So Sylvia with all her self-assurance had not been able to escape a fall. In Dorothy's present mood it would have been unfair to say that she was glad to find that Sylvia was vulnerable, but she did feel that if she ever met Sylvia again she should perhaps get back her old affection for her more easily. And while she was thinking this about Sylvia she suddenly realized that all these other people must be feeling the same about herself.

The revival of her intimacy with Olive made a great difference to Dorothy's stay in West Kensington, and she might even have stayed on at Lonsdale Road until her baby was born had not her two married sisters turned out to be going to have babies also. Though Dorothy had never possessed a very keen sense of humor, her sense of the ridiculous had been sufficiently developed to make her feel that the sight of three young women in an interesting condition round the dining-room table of No. 17 would be a little too much of a good thing. She therefore wrote to Doctor Lane to say that she wanted her child to be born in Devonshire, and asked for his advice. He suggested that she should go to a nursing-home he knew of in Ilfracombe. Thither she went in the month of January, taking with her from Lonsdale Road that old colored supplement inscribed "Yoicks! Tally-Ho"; and there, without any of those raptures that marked her first pregnancy, but with abundant health and serenity of purpose, she waited for her time to come, and at the end of April bore a posthumous son to Clarehaven.

III

Not until her son was actually born did Dorothy apprise the dowager of the event. It was lucky that spring was already warm over France and that the sudden famine of mittens did not inconvenience the troops at this season, because the instant withdrawal of the dowager, Lady Jane, and Lady Arabella from the house in Grosvenor Square left the twenty ladies they had gathered together with neither wool to continue their good work nor with addresses to which it could be sent. The dowager in a state of perfect happiness began to trace in the lineaments of the baby a strong likeness to her dead son, and, as Dorothy had expected, to lament loudly his disinheritance; Lady Jane insisted that he must be taken at once to Chatfield, where Uncle Chat would be more than delighted to look after him entirely; Bella, who had been working herself up into a state of great excitement over a baby that Connie expected to bring into the world at the end of May, ceased to take the least interest in Connie or her child and celebrated the advent of her nephew, the sixth earl, by abandoning prose for a pæan of rhapsodic verse. As for Dorothy, she who during the months of waiting had supposed that she had at last reached that high summit of complete indifference to the world, lost nearly all her superiority, and with her strength renewed and increasing every day was on fire to secure somehow or other to her son the material prosperity that his rank demanded. She was still averse to taking him to Chatfield, because even if at such an early age it was improbable that the externals of Chatfield would make the least impression upon his character, she did not like to surrender all her fine schemes of independence at once. She compromised by consenting to take the baby to Cherrington Cottage, where his arrival elicited from their former tenants a most moving demonstration of affection for the family.

Clare Court was still vacant, and during that summer Dorothy used to wheel the perambulator of her baby round and round the domains of which he had been robbed. For his name she had gone back to her old choice of Lucius, and she felt that by doing so she was conferring upon this posthumous son the greatest compliment in her capacity. The dowager was at first a little distressed that he was not christened Anthony, but when Dorothy read to her, out of a volume of Clarendon she borrowed from the rector, that this namesake was "'a person of such prodigious parts of learning and knowledge, of that inimitable sweetness and delight in conversation, of so flowing and obliging a humanity and goodness to mankind, and of that primitive simplicity and integrity of life, that if there were no other brand upon this odious and accursed civil war than that single loss, it must be most infamous and execrable to all posterity.' 'Thus,'" Dorothy read on, "'fell that incomparable young man, in the four-and-thirtieth year of his age, having so much despatched the true business of life that the eldest rarely attain to that immense knowledge, and the youngest enter not into the world with more innocency.'"

"Yes, yes," sighed the dowager. "Dear old Tony! He was in his thirty-second year. Dear old boy!"

Dorothy looked at her mother-in-law to see if she were serious; when she saw that indeed she was she had not the heart to say that the eulogy might as a description of Tony's life be considered somewhat elevated. After all, Tony had died for his king and his country; Lord Falkland had died for his king only.

On the anniversary of the fifth earl's death, when the wind at dusk was cooing round Cherrington Cottage like a mighty dove, Dorothy was seized with a sudden restlessness and a desire to encounter the mysterious and uneasy air of this gusty twilight of late summer. Her son was fast asleep, with both his grandmother and his aunt Arabella ready to minister to his most incomprehensible baby wish and serve him, were it possible, with the paradisal milk of which he dreamed. He had been restless all day, and now that he was sleeping so calmly Dorothy felt that she could allow herself to take air and exercise. Owing to the continued emptiness of the Court, she had grown into the habit of walking about the park whenever she felt inclined, and except for the solemnity and silence of the house itself she was hardly conscious that she was no longer the mistress of Clare, because the lodge-keepers and various servants of the estate were familiar to her and always showed how glad they were to see her among them.

The park that evening was haunted by strange noises; but Dorothy's mind never ran on the supernatural, and neither swooping owl, nor flitting bat, nor weasel swiftly jigging across her path, nor sudden scurry of deer startled at their drinking-pool alarmed her. She walked on until the dusk had deepened to a wind-blown starlight, and she found herself in the gardens, where on the curved seat of the pergola she sat until the moon rose and the statues shivered like ghosts in a light changing from silver to gray, from gray to silver, as the scud traveled over the moon's face. But Dorothy had no eyes that night for shadows. She was keeping the anniversary of the fifth earl's death by concentrating upon one supreme problem—the restoration of all these moonlit acres, of all these surging yews and cedars, of every stone and statue, to the rightful heir. If any ghost had walked in Clare that night she would have thought of nothing but the best way to retain him for her son's service. Each extravagant idea that came into her head seemed to stay there but for an instant before it was caught by the wind and blown out of reach forever. Restlessly she left the pergola and wandered round the empty house where the wind in the pines on either side was like a sea and the scent of the magnolias in bloom against the walls swirled upon the air with an extraordinary sweetness. She entered one of the groves and passed through to the lawn behind, where a wild notion came into her head, inspired by the wild night and this mad close of summer, to find an ax and deface the escutcheon of Clare, to mutilate the angelic supporters, to eclipse forever that stone moon in her complement, and so spoil for the intruding owner at least one of his trophies. The unheraldic moon was not yet above the pine-trees on the eastern side of the house, and such was the force of the wind blowing straight off the sea from the northwest—blowing here with redoubled force on account of the gap in the cliffs through which it had to travel—that when a cloud passed over the still invisible moon on the far side, Dorothy had the impression that the luminary was being blown out like a lamp, so dark did it then become here in the shadow of the house. She had an impulse to defy this wind, to walk down to the headland's edge and watch the waves leaping like angry, foaming dogs against the face of the cliff; but half-way to the sea she had to turn round, exhausted, and surrender to the will of the wind. Her hair blown all about her shoulders, spindrift and spume racing at her side, she let herself sail back along the lea toward the house, looking to any one who should see her like a mermaid cast up by the tempest upon a haunted island. Haunted it was, indeed, for just as the moon shining down a gorge of clouds rose above the pines she met the Caliban of this island.

"You!" she cried. "I knew it was you the whole time."

Houston was unable to speak for a minute, so frightened had he been by this apparition from the sea, so frightened was he to be wandering round this stolen house and in his wanderings to have provoked this spirit of the place, and in the end more frightened than ever, perhaps, to find who the spirit really was. Dorothy did not realize how strange she looked, how magical and debonair, how perilous, how wild; she whose brain was throbbing with one thought perceived in Houston's expression only the shame he should naturally feel for having robbed her son.

"You look tremendously blown about," he managed to say, finally. "Won't you come inside for a minute?"

Then suddenly as if the wind had got into his brain he said to her, "Dorothy, why don't you marry me and take all this back for yourself?"

"Could I?"

She had appealed to herself, not to him; but he, misunderstanding her question, began like a true Oriental to praise the gifts he would offer her.

"Stop," she commanded. "All these things that you want to give to me, will you give them to my son? Don't be so bewildered. You knew I had a son? I can't stop here to argue about myself and what I can give you or you can give me. If you will make over Clare as it stands with all its land—oh yes, and buy back the Hopley estate which Tony's father sold—to my son, I'll marry you."

"If you'll marry me I'll do anything," he vowed.

There was a momentary lull in the wind, and as if in the silence that followed he was able to grasp how much he had undertaken, he stammered, nervously:

"And you and I? Suppose you and I have children?"

"Well," said Dorothy, "they'll be half brothers and sisters of the sixth Earl of Clarehaven, which will be quite enough for *them*, won't it?"

And that night, while the wind still cooed round Cherrington Cottage, Dorothy, Countess of Clarehaven, wrote out for Debrett and read to Augusta, Countess of Clarehaven:

"Clarehaven, Earl of (Clare.) (Earl. U.K. 1816. Bt. 1660.) Lucius Clare; 6th Earl and 11th Baronet; *b.* April 25, 1915; *s.* 1915; is patron of one living.

"*Arms*—Purpure, two flanches ermine, on a chief sable a moon in her complement argent. *Crest*—A moon in her complement argent, arising from a cloud proper. *Supporters*—Two angels, vested purpure, winged and crined, or, each holding in the exterior hand a key or.

"*Seat*—Clare Court, Devonshire."

THE END

Made in the USA
Lexington, KY
01 September 2015